Glencoe
Communication
Applications

Teacher's Wraparound Edition

Virginia Hunter Myers

June Hubbell Smith

Marcia Myers Swanson

Maridell Fisher Fryar
Major Consultant

Glencoe McGraw-Hill

New York, New York   Columbus, Ohio   Woodland Hills, California   Peoria, Illinois

Glencoe/McGraw-Hill

A Division of The McGraw-Hill Companies

Printed in the United States of America

Send all inquiries to:
The McGraw-Hill Companies
8787 Orion Place
Columbus, Ohio 43240-4027

ISBN 0-02-817244-2
(Student Edition)

ISBN 0-02-817245-0
(Teacher's Wraparound Edition)

1 2 3 4 5 6 7 8 9 10 / 071 / 05 04 03 02 01 00

Practice for the Workplace

Promoting a Sense of Community How does it feel to move to a new city, attend a new school, join a new club, or begin a new job? It is normal to be concerned about how to meet new people and how they will respond to you.

BUSINESS PRACTICE *Activity*

Planning committees in the workplace are responsible for developing activities that promote a sense of community, commitment, and inclusion among employees. In groups of five or six, work as a planning committee. Make a list of activities that would result in cooperation and a sense of teamwork among students at your school. Present your ideas to the remainder of the class. As a class, discuss which activities offered at your ... available in the workplace.

Glencoe Communication Applications

What's the difference between successful communication and unproductive, muddled messages? Most often, it's the choices we make as communicators. With *Glencoe Communication Applications,* you help students learn to make appropriate and effective communication choices in a wide variety of professional and social contexts.

COMMUNICATION PRACTICE LAB

Classifying Norms

To learn how to distinguish prescribed norms from emergent norms, follow these steps:

Step 1 As a class, brainstorm a list of group norms. Then, write the list on the chalkboard.

Step 2 Copy the list of norms onto a sheet of paper.

Step 3 For each norm, ask yourself "Would this norm be taught to all new group members?" If so, write *Prescribed* beside that norm.

Step 4 For each remaining norm, ask "Is this norm a result of group members' interactions and personalities?" If so, write *Emergent* beside that norm.

Step 5 Compare your answers as a class and discuss any differences of opinion. Then discuss whether each norm might have a positive or negative effect on a group and why.

Organization

Glencoe Communication Applications is organized into four valuable units of study. Together these units help students progress from understanding the basics of communication to developing effective styles and techniques for different situations and finally to making expert presentations.

Each unit in the Student Edition is made up of three to six individual chapters which, in turn, are divided into smaller, easy-to-use sections. Each section in *Glencoe Communication Applications* comes complete with its own objectives, assessment, activities, and features to provide you with maximum flexibility in your instruction of the course.

*inter*NET ACTIVITY

Demographics Speakers must consider the demographics of their audiences. Use a reliable search engine or log on to www.census.gov to find information about the demographics of your community or state. How would demographics affect your giving a speech to community leaders in your community or state?

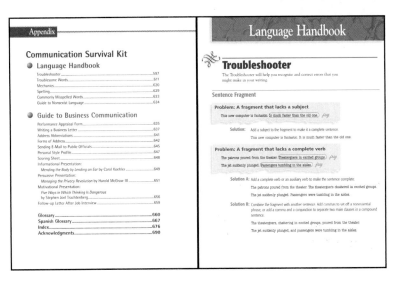

Communication Survival Kit

Appendix

Communication Survival Kit
- Language Handbook

Language Handbook

Troubleshooter

The Troubleshooter will help you recognize and correct errors that you might make in your writing.

Sentence Fragment

Problem: A fragment that lacks a subject

This new computer is fantastic. Is much faster than the old one. *frag*

Solution: Add a subject to the fragment to make it a complete sentence.

This new computer is fantastic. It is much faster than the old one.

Problem: A fragment that lacks a complete verb

The patrons poured from the theater. Theatergoers in excited groups. *frag*

The jet suddenly plunged. Passengers tumbling in the aisles. *frag*

Solution A: Add a complete verb or an auxiliary verb to make the sentence complete:

The patrons poured from the theater. The theatergoers shattered in excited groups.

The jet suddenly plunged. Passengers were tumbling in the aisles.

Solution B: Combine the fragment with another sentence. Add commas to set off a nonessential phrase, or add a comma and a conjunction to separate two main clauses in a compound sentence.

The theatergoers, chattering in excited groups, poured from the theater.

The jet suddenly plunged, and passengers were tumbling in the aisles.

In addition to its comprehensive instruction materials, the Student Edition also provides a handy Communication Survival Kit at the back of the book. An extensive collection of resources and reference materials, it includes a valuable and concise Language Handbook. This handbook helps students master troublesome and commonly misspelled words as well as problems in mechanics, spelling, and sexist language. In addition, the Survival Kit includes a useful Guide to Business Communication. The guide not only serves as a useful reference for everyday workplace communication but also provides students with a wealth of practical instruction for creating effective business letters, e-mail messages, and professional presentations. The Communication Survival Kit is just one of the many tools Glencoe provides to help you prepare students to become competent communicators in today's competitive marketplace.

Student Edition

Unit Opener

High-Interest Photo and **Unit Introduction** provide a starting point for discussion of the unit content.

Chapter Opener

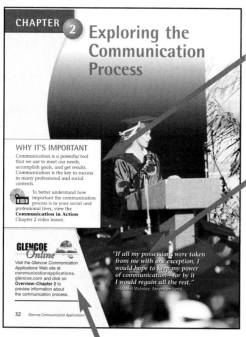

Why It's Important ties the quote to the chapter content.

Quote from contemporary or historical figure focuses on real-life communication.

Unit Contents conveniently lists the title of each chapter in the unit.

Unit Activity provides a step-by-step exploration of the unit topic. Students complete the activity as they progress through the unit.

Communication in Action **Video Lesson** and **Glencoe Online Chapter Overview** introduce or extend students' knowledge of the chapter's specific communication skills and concepts.

Section Opener

Terms to Learn introduces the section's new vocabulary in order of appearance.

Objectives provide measurable goals that students work toward as they progress through the section.

Attention Grabber helps build student interest in the section content.

Discussion Starter photo and caption provide a thought-provoking bridge to new communication concepts.

Communication Mini-Features

Practice for the Workplace applies a concept from the section to a realistic workplace scenario.

Internet Activity uses the Internet to help students research information and further their understanding of a communication concept.

Communication Strategies outlines or summarizes important concepts in a succinct bulleted list.

Global Communication ties some global or cultural aspect of communication to the section content.

Technology Activity provides students an opportunity to use current technology in communication.

Communication Practice Lab provides a step-by-step activity allowing students to practice a concept they have just learned.

Section Assessment

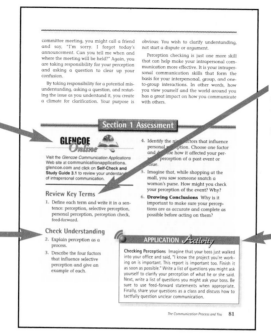

Glencoe Online Self-Check and Study Guide helps students review and assess what they have learned in the section.

Check Understanding items are tied directly to the section objectives, assessing what students have learned. The final item always applies critical thinking to section concepts.

Review Key Terms has students define the section's vocabulary terms and write each in a sentence.

Application Activity assesses students' understanding of the section's content and major objectives.

Chapter Assessment and Activities

Glencoe Online Chapter Activity gives students an additional opportunity to practice what they learned in the chapter.

Reading and Critical Thinking Skill has students apply various levels of critical thinking skills to the chapter content.

Skill Practice Activity reinforces the skill taught in one of the chapter's full-page special features, such as Critical Thinking Skill, Applying Reading Skill, Technology Skill, or Communication Through Writing.

Reviewing Key Terms assesses students' understanding of vocabulary terms from throughout the chapter.

Cooperative Learning Activity provides an opportunity for students to work with others to achieve one of the chapter's communication objectives.

Reviewing Key Concepts assesses students' understanding of the chapter's most important communication concepts.

Chapter Project is a cumulative, presentation-based assessment of the major skills and concepts taught in the chapter.

Full-Page Special Features

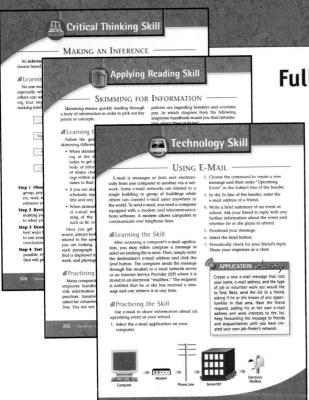

Critical Thinking Skill, Applying Reading Skill, and **Technology Skill** help students master a specific skill and apply it to communication. Each chapter features one of the three skill-builders, depending on which one ties best to the chapter content.

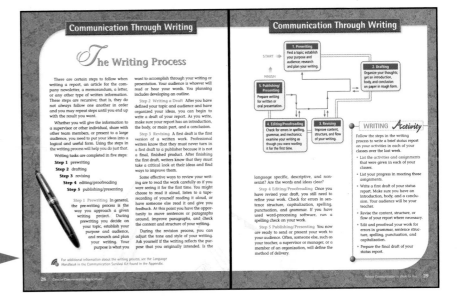

Communication Through Writing teaches students an important real-world writing concept and then applies it to communication.

Communication Self-Assessment gives students the opportunity to analyze their own communication skills and set goals according to their results.

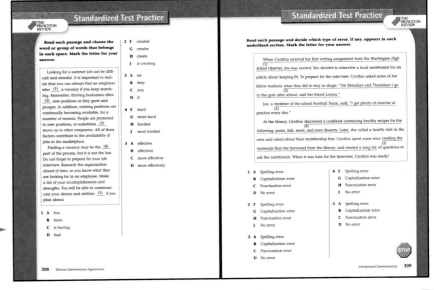

Standardized Test Practice uses communication-related content to familiarize students with standardized-test formats.

Teacher's Edition

TEACHER'S WRAPAROUND EDITION

Planning the Chapter

These four pages precede each chapter of the Student Edition, providing a clear overview of the organization of the chapter and a detailed look at the teaching, application, assessment, and technology materials available.

Focusing the Chapter and Section

Comprehensive point-of-use notes, strategies, and features provide effective, inclusive instructional support to help students learn the important concepts in *Glencoe Communication Applications.*

Glencoe Technology provides you with various resources to preview and engage students in the content of the chapter.

- **MindJogger Videoquiz** is a video quiz presented in a game-show format that allows students to preview, review, or reinforce chapter content.

- **Communication in Action** videodiscs and videotapes introduce or extend students' knowledge of the chapter's specific communication skills and concepts.

- **Glencoe Online** is an exclusive Web site for *Glencoe Communication Applications* that includes features such as appropriate Web site links, games, and activities.

Bellringer activities and **Graphic Organizer Transparencies** help you focus and introduce students to the important concepts of the section.

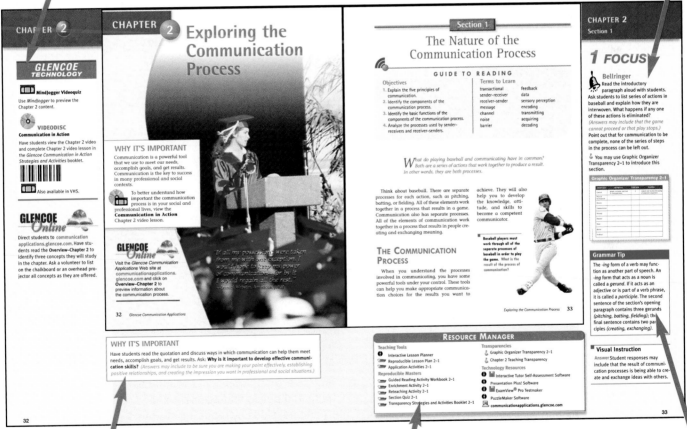

Why It's Important helps you preview the content of the chapter with students by springboarding from the quote in the Student Edition.

Resource Manager is a handy chart that gives a complete listing of teacher's classroom resources to use to teach, reinforce, extend, and assess the lesson. These print, transparency, and technology resources allow you to customize instruction to accommodate your own classroom needs and teaching style.

Grammar Tip gives you the opportunity to reinforce the importance of using good grammar in communication.

Teaching the Section

Core features and teaching options offer a wealth of interactive instructional support.

Core Features are point-of-use features and strategies that provide instructional aid targeted to specific areas of the Student Edition. Core features include

- *Visual Instruction*
- *Communication Tip*
- *Communication Strategies*
- *Communication Practice Lab*
- *Practice for the Workplace*
- *Did You Know?*
- *Business Brief*
- *Language Tip*
- *Global Communication*
- *Technology Activity*

CHAPTER 14
Section 3

Organizing Secondary Information
Students should realize that research does not stop with collecting information; thoughtful selection and editing is also involved. Large numbers of photocopied pages, for example, are not in a usable state until the material most relevant to the researcher has been highlighted for easy reference or transferred to cards or computer files.

Primary Sources
Point out that we are receiving primary source material all the time. It only becomes research, however, when it has been recorded and identified. Ask students to jot down three remarks that were made to them in the last twenty-four hours. For each quotation, have them record the speaker's name, the place, and the time the remark was made. Invite students to share their "research" with the class. L1

Visual Instruction
Answer Student responses may include that other primary sources are surveys, questionnaires, and personal experiences.

Communication Tip
No matter how well you have planned your presentation, it is advisable to collect more information than you think you need. Presentations sometimes change their direction in the writing stage. If you have done extra research, you can accommodate new ideas without going back to the library.

Interviews, such as this one in a mall, can be a form of primary research. Besides interviews, what other primary sources allow the researcher to gather information personally?

Organizing Secondary Information

As a researcher, it is important to develop a systematic method of organizing the information you find. Some researchers record their information on computer. Others use index cards or notebooks with different sections for the different types of information they find. Still others use file folders for each category of information. Regardless of which system you use, it is a good idea to follow these guidelines for accurately recording your information.

Following these guidelines will help you record your researched information so that it can be used in an ethical and responsible manner. It also will allow you to find the information again at a later date, if necessary.

462   *Glencoe Communication Applications*

---

topic, you may discover that you can't locate some of the information you need or want for your presentation. You may need to talk to experts on your topic or ask people firsthand how they feel about a specific issue. This type of information comes from a primary source. A primary source is someone, including yourself, who has firsthand knowledge or experience regarding a topic. A quote from one of your favorite musical performers is a primary source. So is information a person tells you directly. However, once you read the musician's words in a magazine or hear a news story about the performer's musical style, this becomes secondary-source information.

Obtaining information from primary sources is referred to as primary research. Primary research also includes any personal experiences and insights that you may have with a topic. Primary research can provide important information for many different types of presentations. If you have knowledge of a topic, your audience's perception of your credibility is likely to increase. Information in books and magazines can easily become outdated. However, primary research provides the most up-to-date information available.

Some primary sources can be found in libraries or on the Internet. Diaries, journals, autobiographies, and film and video footage of actual events as they occurred provide a firsthand perspective of an event. Other primary sources, such as interviews, allow the researcher to personally gather information.

Interviews Interviews are an excellent way to gather information on a topic. In addition, interviewing a primary source—such as an expert—can help you better understand the information and the people involved.

MULTIPLE LEARNING STYLES

Interpersonal Point out that there is nothing mysterious or difficult about primary research. We are in a position to research material and record our findings at any moment during the day. **Activity** Have students form pairs and interview each other on a subject they can both talk about without preparation: my favorite sport, family vacations, what I did last night, and so on. Direct them to take notes during the interview, including in their notes at least one direct quotation. After the interviews, have students write a paragraph or two summarizing their interviews, making sure that they include a passage directly quoting their subject. Invite volunteers to present their summaries to the class.

462

CAFETERIA QUESTIONNAIRE
In an effort to better meet your menu preferences, the cafeteria staff would like your responses to the following questions. Your input will be considered when next semester's menus are being planned. Please place your completed questionnaire in the box at the end of your serving line. Thank you!

1. How many times each week do you eat in the cafeteria?
   __0   __1   __2   __3   __4   __5

2. What type of meal do you usually purchase?
   __Full meal   __Sandwich   __A la carte

3. What is your favorite food served in the cafeteria?

4. What is your least favorite food served in the cafeteria?

5. What food would you like to have served that currently is not offered?

6. Would you prefer more fast food to be served in the cafeteria?
   __ Yes   __ No   __ No opinion

7. Would you be willing to pay more for fast food than for a standard cafeteria meal?
   __ Yes   __ No   __ No opinion

8. How would you rate the quality of the food served in the cafeteria?
   __ Excellent   __ Good   __ Average   __ Poor

9. What is your grade level?
   __ Freshman   __ Sophomore   __ Junior   __ Senior

So, when is an interview an appropriate source for your research? Consider your topic. Would direct statements or opinions from a primary source add clarity, interest, or credibility? If so, what information do you need, and who can provide it?

Once you have determined who is the best available resource, you can begin planning the actual interview. For information on conducting interviews for primary research, refer to Chapter 9, Communicating in Interviews.

Research Groups . . . organizations often conduct surveys to determine the public's understanding, opinion, or knowledge of an issue. They may survey individuals by asking them questions one-on-one, or they may administer a written survey, known as a questionnaire.

Oral surveys and written questionnaires are good tools for obtaining local and regional information that may not be available anywhere else. Careful planning can help you design a survey or questionnaire to obtain the exact information you need. Just as with interviews, first determine the purpose of the survey or questionnaire and the type of information you are seeking before you get to work. Do you want to know what presidential candidate people support? How your coworkers feel about your company's new vacation policy? What team most of your classmates want to win the Super Bowl? Each of these questions can be answered through a survey or questionnaire.

Survey Questions Once you have determined the purpose of your survey or questionnaire, ask yourself what types of questions will result in the information you need. Most questions used on surveys and questionnaires are formulated to generate a specific type of response. Look at the variety of questions in Figure 14–6. Some of the questions ask the respondents for a specific response, while others ask them to respond freely. Notice that respondents have been given the choice of answering "No opinion" when asked to indicate their feelings. It is important to offer a neutral response choice to keep results accurate.

Preparing for Professional Presentations   **463**

CHAPTER 14
Section 3

Interviews
Work with the class to list topics that would benefit from interviews as part of the research process. (*Examples might include sporting events, current news stories, or policy changes.*) Ask whom students would interview if researching a presentation on the football team, plans for the senior prom, or teenage drug abuse. Discuss the reasons for their choices. L1

Survey Questions
Have students review the Cafeteria Questionnaire shown in Figure 14–6. Point out that the information collected from a survey of this sort can be used for a number of purposes. To illustrate this, ask students to respond to the questions on a separate piece of paper, giving their opinions about their own cafeteria. On the chalkboard, compile a list of their answers, breaking these down into percentages where relevant. Ask students what conclusions they would draw from the results of individual questions and from the survey as a whole. If they were administering the cafeteria, what action would they consider taking as a result of this class's response? L2

Application Activities 14–3

COOPERATIVE LEARNING ACTIVITY

What makes a good questionnaire? What makes people fill one out? Remind students that many of us have thrown away lengthy, apparently irrelevant survey forms. Point out that creating questionnaires requires careful planning as to the purpose of the survey and the nature of the individual questions.

As a class, list four or five topics on which all students will have an opinion. Divide students into groups and assign each group a topic. Ask each group to create a questionnaire of no more than ten questions related to their topic. Have groups read their questionnaires to the class, explaining the purpose of their surveys and reasons for their choice of questions.

463

Meeting Individual Needs provides options to meet the needs of all your students, including
- English Language Learners
- Inclusion Strategies
- Students with Multiple Learning Styles
- Gifted and Talented

Cooperative Learning Activity reinforces learning and builds management and interpersonal skills by requiring students to work together to acquire, organize, and present information.

Connections relate the content to another discipline or to the students' lives.
- Interdisciplinary Connection
- Real-World Connection

Critical Thinking Activity allows students to think critically about communication strategies and concepts.

Extending the Content provides students with the opportunity to springboard from the content provided in the Student Edition.

Assessing the Section

Section assessment resources can help you evaluate students' mastery of the section content.

Assessment Resources provide thoughtful assessment of students' understanding of the section content.
- Interactive Tutor Self-Assessment
- Section Quizzes

Closing the Section

An end-of-the-section activity helps you wrap up the content of the section.

Reteaching and Enrichment Resources provide post-assessment tools for those students with special needs.
- Reteaching Activity
- Enrichment Activity

Extra-Credit Project provides students the opportunity to earn extra credit as they apply the communication applications concepts studied in the section.

Answers are provided for all questions in the Section Assessment section of the Student Edition.

PRINT RESOURCES

Glencoe Communication Applications includes numerous print resources that provide student activities, assess student performance, and offer time-saving materials for classroom management.

Communication Resources

- **Oral Presentation Activities** provides worksheets to help students prepare and present presentations based on real-life scenarios and then evaluate their own and others' presentations.

- **Application Activities** includes a variety of fun and creative activities that help students apply and extend the concepts presented in *Glencoe Communication Applications*.

- **Guided Reading Activity Workbook** provides strategies and activities to help students who have difficulty with reading comprehension.

- **Vocabulary Activities** offers various activities to help students learn the vocabulary presented in *Glencoe Communication Applications*.

- **Technology Application Activities** provides hands-on opportunities for students to apply technology skills used in professional contexts.

- **Reteaching Activities** offers alternative methods for students to learn chapter concepts and skills.

- **Enrichment Activities** encourages students to use critical-thinking skills to extend the chapter concepts and skills.

Assessment Resources

- Chapter and Unit Tests
- Section Quizzes
- Performance Assessment Activities

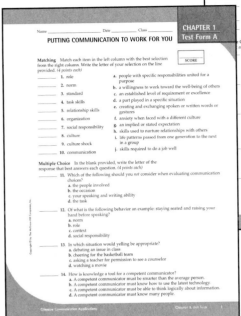

Spanish Resources

- Spanish Chapter and Unit Tests
- Spanish Section Quizzes
- Spanish Reteaching Activities
- Spanish Enrichment Activities
- Spanish Vocabulary Activities

Teacher Resources

- Reproducible Lesson Plans
- Guided Reading Activity Workbook
  Teacher Annotated Edition

 The Princeton Review

The Princeton Review, the nation's leading test preparation firm, has developed a series of practice booklets for Glencoe Language Arts. These resources can be used to help students prepare for the most commonly used standardized tests.

TECHNOLOGY RESOURCES

With *Glencoe Communication Applications,* you can draw upon a wealth of video, software, and Internet resources to engage students' interest and enhance their classroom experience.

Video Resources

- **Communication in Action** consists of a series of three videotapes or one videodisc. These videos can be used to extend students' knowledge of the chapter's specific communication skills and concepts. The videotapes are also available in Spanish.

- **MindJogger Videoquiz** offers video quizzes presented in a game-show format that allow students to preview, review, or reinforce chapter content. The quizzes are available on videodisc or VHS.

Transparencies

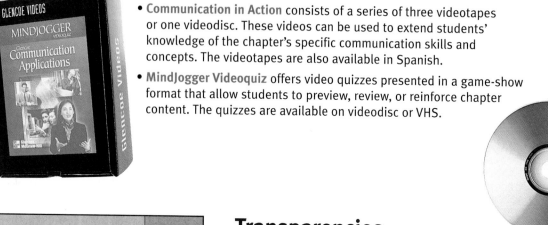

- **Teaching Transparencies** display a table, chart, or diagram shown in the Student Edition. They can be used to prompt class discussions or reinforce chapter content.

- **Graphic Organizer Transparencies** provide a graphic organizer for each section in the Student Edition to help students organize information. These transparencies are accompanied by a booklet containing strategies for using the graphic organizers.

Glencoe Communication Applications Web Site
communicationapplications.glencoe.com

Our Web site offers online resources for you as well as for students and parents.

Features include:
- appropriate Web site links
- additional activities, practice labs, and student self-checks
- teacher lesson plans for Web activities and practice labs
- teacher-to-teacher exchange
- and much more!

Software

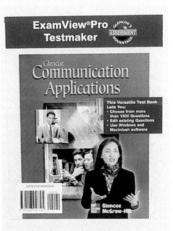

- **ExamView®Pro Testmaker** is an electronic database that allows you to customize tests to fit your students' special needs. This program allows you to edit, reorder, and add questions to create your own chapter and unit tests.

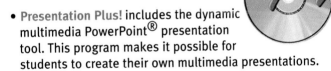

- **Presentation Plus!** includes the dynamic multimedia PowerPoint® presentation tool. This program makes it possible for students to create their own multimedia presentations.

- **PuzzleMaker** allows you to create your own crossword puzzles and word searches using chapter vocabulary.

- **Interactive Tutor Self-Assessment** is a highly motivational program that enables students to check their comprehension of a chapter by answering questions on the computer. The program allows students to pinpoint and correct their mistakes instantly.

- **Interactive Grammar Software** is a program that enables students to reinforce and review grammar skills.

- **Interactive Lesson Planner** helps you organize all the resources in *Glencoe Communication Applications* to create your own lesson plans on the computer.

Communication in Action Videos, Communication Strategies, and Communication Practice Labs **organize key communication skills and concepts for hands-on practice in and out of the classroom.**

Communication Self-Assessment, Communication Through Writing, and Skill Practice Activities **allow students to apply real-world interpersonal-communication strategies.**

TEACHING APPLIED COMMUNICATION

A cross the nation, business and industry leaders are cognizant of the link between employees' communication skills and organizational performance. Competent communicators are likely to be informed, articulate, and proactive participants, both at work and in their communities. Students lacking competence in specific communication skills diminish their own social and professional effectiveness; additionally, they weaken an organization's ability to accomplish its prescribed goals.

Addressing Communication Issues Facing Today's Workers

Working together, business leaders and educators have identified specific communication skills that, when mastered, enable today's youth to become productive members of America's workforce. Students enrolled in Applied Communication classes explore communication processes and related skills in conjunction with developing the reading, writing, and grammar skills needed to achieve life and workplace goals effectively. Students apply their developing skills to authentic social and professional contexts. Typical course objectives might include having students

- **apply the writing process** to produce fluent and organized documents. Students communicate purposeful information and ideas following accepted standards of grammar, spelling, vocabulary, and style.

- **implement reading strategies** to obtain and analyze information from a variety of workplace documents and selected literature. Sources of readings include written reports, professional journals, newsletters, fiction, and nonfiction.

- **demonstrate effective speaking, listening, and nonverbal skills.** Students identify, produce, and respond appropriately to oral and written messages, including text and graphics, for a variety of business contexts.

- **display characteristics of successful interpersonal relationships.** Students experience a variety of interpersonal and group business relationships including one-on-one, one-to-group, and team dynamics.

• **implement current technology.** Supported by technical readings and available multimedia tools, students use technology as a tool to complete workplace transactions.

• **use problem-solving and research skills** to obtain, analyze, and apply reliable data for a set purpose. Students select from a variety of informational, literary, mass media, or technical resources to research social and professional concepts.

Benefits of an Applied Communication Course

By applying effective communication skills and building upon the foundations of English-language instruction, students develop the skills and attitudes that enable them to function effectively at work. Students are able to obtain and keep gainful employment. They become more promotable in their jobs and learn the importance of forming productive on-the-job relationships with coworkers and team members. Integrated learning experiences allow students to participate meaningfully in decision-making processes in workplace environments and to make and evaluate all kinds of presentations to influence the decisions of others at work.

Working Together to Enhance Communication Skills

Through their association with groups and organizations in the workplace, individuals accomplish personal and professional goals. The organizations for which they work also enhance their ability to meet their objectives. Applied Communication courses provide high school students with a foundation in basic communication knowledge, functional literacy, and critical-thinking skills necessary to prepare a new generation to assume its responsibilities in the business world.

Global Communication, Practice for the Workplace, and Cooperative Learning features engage students in effective communication in groups in social and professional contexts.

Chapter Assessment and Activities, Communication Practice Labs, Technology and Internet Activities, the Student Edition, and the Technology Application Activities and Oral Presentation Activities ancillary booklets help students develop strong research and presentation skills.

Demographics Speakers must consider the demographics of their audiences. Use a reliable search engine or log on to **www.census.gov** to find information about the demographics of your community or state. How would demographics affect your giving a speech to community leaders in your community or state?

Literature Library

Glencoe Literature Library Correlation

As students learn about communication applications, you may want to have them observe the concepts in literature. The Glencoe Literature Library consists of fifty-five full-length novels or plays with related readings. This chart relates each Glencoe Literature Library book to three appropriate chapters in *Glencoe Communication Applications*.

Chapter	Books	Rationale
Chapter 1 Putting Communication to Work for You	*All Quiet on the Western Front,* Erich Maria Remarque	culture shock, social responsibility
	Island of the Blue Dolphins, Scott O'Dell	appropriate behavioral choices
	The Strange Case of Dr. Jekyll and Mr. Hyde, Robert Louis Stevenson	role of context in making appropriate behavioral choices
	Dragonwings, Laurence Yep	organizational culture, communication across diversity
	Jane Eyre, Charlotte Brontë	appropriate behavioral choices, individual and organizational culture
	Julie of the Wolves, Jean Craighead George	appropriate behavioral choices, communication across diversity
	A Separate Peace, John Knowles	role of context in making appropriate behavioral choices
	Shiloh, Phyllis Reynolds Naylor	role of context in making appropriate behavioral choices
	Tuck Everlasting, Natalie Babbit	culture shock, communication across diversity, social responsibility
	The Yearling, Marjorie Kinnan Rawlings	how roles and norms of context set standards for making appropriate choices
Chapter 2 Exploring the Communication Process	*...And the Earth Did Not Devour Him,* Tomás Rivera	self-talk, one-to-group communication
	The Brothers Karamazov, Fyodor Dostoevsky	levels of communication, principles of communication
	Frankenstein, Mary Shelley	components of the communication process
	Island of the Blue Dolphins, Scott O'Dell	self-talk, sensory perception
	Johnny Tremain, Esther Forbes	self-talk, one-to-group communication
	The Metamorphosis, Franz Kafka	sensory perception, self-talk
	One Day in the Life of Ivan Denisovich, Aleksandr Solzhenitsyn	data, feedback, noise, barriers, small-group communication
	The Scarlet Letter, Nathaniel Hawthorne	levels of communication
	The Slave Dancer, Paula Fox	sensory perception, channels, decoding
Chapter 3 The Communication Process and You	*A Wrinkle in Time,* Madeleine L'Engle	selective perception, perception checks, influences on self-concept
	Great Expectations, Charles Dickens	selective perception, perception checks, influences on self-concept
	A House for Mr. Biswas, V.S. Naipaul	use Johari window to evaluate personal interaction with others
	Missing May, Cynthia Rylant	selective perception, perception checks, influences on self-concept
	Nectar in a Sieve, Kamala Markandaya	influences on self-concept
	Night, Elie Wiesel	complete information as a basis for perception choices
	Picture Bride, Yoshiko Uchida	personal perception, personal interaction with others, self-concept
	The Glory Field, Walter Dean Myers	selective perception, influences on self-concept
	The Red Badge of Courage, Stephen Crane	self-concept, selective perception
	The Scarlet Letter, Nathaniel Hawthorne	relationship between self-concept and interpersonal communication
	A Separate Peace, John Knowles	influences on self-concept
	The Tempest, William Shakespeare	using the Johari window to evaluate personal interaction with others
Chapter 4 Discovering the Power of Oral Language	*The Adventures of Huckleberry Finn,* Mark Twain	oral language, dialect
	The Autobiography of Miss Jane Pittman, Ernest J. Gaines	dialect, power language
	A Midsummer Night's Dream, William Shakespeare	how oral language choices affect individuals personally and culturally
	Animal Farm, George Orwell	power language, social ritual, connotation
	Great Expectations, Charles Dickens	how oral language choices affect individuals personally and culturally

Chapter	Books	Rationale
	Dragonwings, Laurence Yep	how oral language choices affect individuals personally and culturally
	Wuthering Heights, Emily Brontë	how oral language choices affect individuals personally and culturally
Chapter 5 Understanding Nonverbal Communication	*The Call of the Wild*, Jack London	effective nonverbal strategies
	Frankenstein, Mary Shelley	characteristics of nonverbal communication
	I, Juan de Pareja, Elizabeth Borton de Treviño	types of nonverbal communication
	Island of the Blue Dolphins, Scott O'Dell	effective nonverbal strategies
	Johnny Tremain, Esther Forbes	how nonverbal skills convey confidence, poise, and assertiveness
	Julie of the Wolves, Jean Craighead George	characteristics and effects of nonverbal communication
	The Metamorphosis, Franz Kafka	types of nonverbal communication and their effects
	One Day in the Life of Ivan Denisovich, Aleksandr Solzhenitsyn	four characteristics of voice, nonverbal communication
	Shiloh, Phyllis Reynolds Naylor	characteristics of nonverbal communication
	The Slave Dancer, Paula Fox	nonverbal communication
	The Yearling, Marjorie Kinnan Rawlings	principles of nonverbal communication, kinesics
Chapter 6 Toward Effective Listening	*Nectar in a Sieve*, Kamala Markandaya	appropriate kinds of listening for a given situation
	Number the Stars, Lois Lowry	different kinds of listening
	Pride and Prejudice, Jane Austen	factors that can affect listening
	The Autobiography of Miss Jane Pittman, Ernest J. Gaines	interpreting, different kinds of listening
	The Autobiography of Benjamin Franklin, Benjamin Franklin	different kinds of listening, interpreting
	The Chosen, Chaim Potok	how to improve listening
	The Slave Dancer, Paula Fox	appropriate kinds of listening for a given situation
	The Tempest, William Shakespeare	appropriate kinds of listening for a given situation
	The Yearling, Marjorie Kinnan Rawlings	deliberative listening, listening in professional and social contexts
	Where the Red Fern Grows, Wilson Rawls	factors that affect listening, appropriate kinds of listening
Chapter 7 Building Effective Interpersonal Relationships	*...And the Earth Did Not Devour Him*, Tomás Rivera	teams, group goals, problem solving
	A Midsummer Night's Dream, William Shakespeare	personal styles, characteristics of productive interpersonal communication
	Animal Farm, George Orwell	four types of personal style, productive interpersonal communication
	Bridge to Terabithia, Katherine Paterson	four types of personal style, productive interpersonal communication
	Cyrano de Bergerac, Edmond Rostand	how differences in personal style affect interpersonal relationships
	Frankenstein, Mary Shelley	types of interpersonal relationships
	Hamlet, William Shakespeare	interpersonal relationships, personal style
	Jane Eyre, Charlotte Brontë	productive interpersonal communication, personal style
	Missing May, Cynthia Rylant	personal style, productive interpersonal communication
	Nectar in a Sieve, Kamala Markandaya	interpersonal relationships
Chapter 8 Developing Effective Interpersonal Skills	*A Tale of Two Cities*, Charles Dickens	strategies for dealing with differences, evaluative communication
	Bearstone, Will Hobbs	receiving criticism, evaluating effectiveness of communication
	Cyrano de Bergerac, Edmond Rostand	evaluate the effectiveness of your own and others' communication
	Jane Eyre, Charlotte Brontë	strategies for dealing with differences
	My Ántonia, Willa Cather	strategies for dealing with differences
	Pride and Prejudice, Jane Austen	etiquette and protocol
	So Far From the Bamboo Grove, Yoko Kawasima Watkins	strategies for dealing with differences
	The Chosen, Chaim Potok	strategies for dealing with differences
	The True Confessions of Charlotte Doyle, Avi	professional etiquette for offering and receiving criticism
	Witch of Blackbird Pond, Elizabeth George Speare	appropriate participation in conversations, strategies for dealing with differences in culture

Chapter	Books	Rationale
Chapter 9		
Exploring the Interview Process	*The Autobiography of Benjamin Franklin,* Benjamin Franklin	persuasive interview, kinds of questions
	I, Juan de Pareja, Elizabeth Borton de Treviño	types of interviews, types of questions
	One Day in the Life of Ivan Denisovich, Aleksandr Solzhenitsyn	information-gathering interview, investigative interview
	Picture Bride, Yoshiko Uchida	interview process, kinds of questions
	To Kill a Mockingbird, Harper Lee	roles in the interview process, kinds of questions
	The True Confessions of Charlotte Doyle, Avi	investigative interview, counseling interview
	Tuck Everlasting, Natalie Babbit	information-gathering interview, kinds of questions
	A Wrinkle in Time, Madeleine L'Engle	investigative interview, kinds of questions
Chapter 10		
Understanding the Nature of Groups	*And the Earth Did Not Devour Him,* Tomás Rivera	teams, group goal, problem solving
	Hatchet, Gary Paulsen	planning considerations, steps of the problem-solving process
	High Elk's Treasure, Virginia Driving Hawk Sneve	group goals, prescribed goals, emergent goals
	A House for Mr. Biswas, V.S. Naipaul	planning, problem-solving
	My Ántonia, Willa Cather	how groups are important to individuals, group goals
	Night, Elie Wiesel	group goals, prescribed goals, emergent goals
	Number the Stars, Lois Lowry	characteristics of a group
	The Adventures of Huckleberry Finn, Mark Twain	emergent goals, decision making
	The Call of the Wild, Jack London	how groups are important to individuals, effective group goals
	The Glory Field, Walter Dean Myers	how groups are important to individuals, problem solving
	The Scarlet Letter, Nathaniel Hawthorne	how groups are important to individuals
	Where the Red Fern Grows, Wilson Rawls	problem solving, brainstorming, decision making
Chapter 11		
Making Groups Work	*A Tale of Two Cities,* Charles Dickens	distinguishing between prescribed and emergent norms, groupthink
	...And the Earth Did Not Devour Him, Tomás Rivera	task needs, maintenance needs, group effectiveness
	Bearstone, Will Hobbs	prescribed norm, task need, maintenance need
	Missing May, Cynthia Rylant	three major roles group members play
	The Adventures of Huckleberry Finn, Mark Twain	group norms, groupthink, analyzing group dynamics
	The Autobiography of Benjamin Franklin, Benjamin Franklin	roles of group members, group dynamics
	The Clay Marble, Minfong Ho	effective and ineffective nonverbal behaviors in group meetings
	A Separate Peace, John Knowles	roles group members play, groupthink
	The True Confessions of Charlotte Doyle, Avi	prescribed and emergent norms, roles group members play
Chapter 12		
Managing Conflict	*A Tale of Two Cities,* Charles Dickens	conflict resolution, strategies for coping with unresolved conflict
	High Elk's Treasure, Virginia Driving Hawk Sneve	strategies for coping with unresolved conflict
	Picture Bride, Yoshiko Uchida	the three types of conflict, conflict-resolution strategies
	Shiloh, Phyllis Reynolds Naylor	negotiation, conflict-resolution strategies
	So Far From the Bamboo Grove, Yoko Kawasima Watkins	advantages and disadvantages of conflict, losses and gains in conflict resolution
	The Brothers Karamazov, Fyodor Dostoevsky	conflict diagnosing, conflict-resolution strategies
	The Clay Marble, Minfong Ho	analyze how relationships and interdependence impact conflicts
	The Metamorphosis, Franz Kafka	strategies for coping with unresolved conflict
	The Strange Case of Dr. Jekyll and Mr. Hyde, Robert Louis Stevenson	diagnosing conflict, strategies for coping with unresolved conflict
	Witch of Blackbird Pond, Elizabeth George Speare	conflict over values, conflict over policies
Chapter 13		
Functioning as a Leader	*Bridge to Terabithia,* Katherine Paterson	effective leadership styles, types of power
	Hamlet, William Shakespeare	leadership styles, types of power
	A House for Mr. Biswas, V.S. Naipaul	types of power, leadership styles
	I, Juan de Pareja, Elizabeth Borton de Treviño	preparation and communication skills for effective leadership
	Number the Stars, Lois Lowry	most effective leadership style in specific situations

Chapter	Books	Rationale
	The Clay Marble, Minfong Ho	three approaches for identifying potential leaders
	Where the Red Fern Grows, Wilson Rawls	effective leadership styles, types of power
	The Call of the Wild, Jack London	leadership styles, types of power
	The Adventures of Tom Sawyer, Mark Twain	effective leadership styles and communication methods
	To Kill a Mockingbird, Harper Lee	identifying leaders, communication skills for effective leadership
Chapter 14		
Preparing for Professional Presentations	*All Quiet on the Western Front*, Erich Maria Remarque	primary source, secondary source, persuasive presentation
	Great Expectations, Charles Dickens	analyze sources for qualifications, credibility, and accuracy
	Johnny Tremain, Esther Forbes	using accurate information to make communication decisions
	The Glory Field, Walter Dean Myers	ethos, how context affects the selection and limitation of a topic
	The House of Dies Drear, Virginia Hamilton	analyzing sources for qualifications, credibility, and accuracy
	Pride and Prejudice, Jane Austen	using accurate information to make communication decisions
	The Tempest, William Shakespeare	analyze the audience, occasion, and task, ethos
	To Kill a Mockingbird, Harper Lee	analyze the audience, occasion, and task
Chapter 15		
Organizing Presentations	*Animal Farm*, George Orwell	Monroe's Motivated Sequence, audience orientation
	Dragonwings, Laurence Yep	audience orientation, Monroe's Motivated Sequence
	Hamlet, William Shakespeare	attention device, Monroe's Motivated Sequence
	High Elk's Treasure, Virginia Driving Hawk Sneve	Monroe's Motivated Sequence
	Julie of the Wolves, Jean Craighead George	audience orientation, Monroe's Motivated Sequence
	So Far From the Bamboo Grove, Yoko Kawasima Watkins	Monroe's Motivated Sequence
	The Chosen, Chaim Potok	audience orientation, Monroe's Motivated Sequence
	Wuthering Heights, Emily Brontë	audience orientation, Monroe's Motivated Sequence
Chapter 16		
Supporting Presentations	*A Midsummer Night's Dream*, William Shakespeare	language devices that enhance presentations, parallelism, antithesis
	Hatchet, Gary Paulsen	three types of proofs, information to support and clarify main points
	My Ántonia, Willa Cather	oral style, visual images, figurative language
	The Red Badge of Courage, Stephen Crane	amplification device, figurative language
	The Adventures of Tom Sawyer, Mark Twain	logical, ethical, and pathetic proofs
	Witch of Blackbird Pond, Elizabeth George Speare	types of proof, supporting main points, testimony
	Wuthering Heights, Emily Brontë	pathetic proofs, amplification devices
Chapter 17		
Preparing for Presentations	*The Autobiography of Miss Jane Pittman*, Ernest J. Gaines	group presentation, internalization, visualization
	Hatchet, Gary Paulsen	choosing best delivery method for a given situation
	Night, Elie Wiesel	managing communication apprehension
	The House of Dies Drear, Virginia Hamilton	preparing, organizing, and participating in a group presentation
	The Strange Case of Dr. Jekyll and Mr. Hyde, Robert Louis Stevenson	strategies to manage communication apprehension, build self-confidence, and gain command of information
	Tuck Everlasting, Natalie Babbit	group presentations, impromptu delivery
	A Wrinkle in Time, Madeleine L'Engle	managing communication apprehension and building self-confidence
Chapter 18		
Making and Evaluating Group Presentations	*The Adventures of Tom Sawyer*, Mark Twain	effective verbal and nonverbal strategies in presentations
	All Quiet on the Western Front, Erich Maria Remarque	judgment by ethical standards, judgment by multiple standards
	Bearstone, Will Hobbs	evaluate effectiveness of one's own presentation
	Bridge to Terabithia, Katherine Paterson	critical listening, judgment by results
	The Brothers Karamazov, Fyodor Dostoevsky	judgment by multiple standards
	Cyrano de Bergerac, Edmond Rostand	effective verbal and nonverbal strategies in presentations
	The House of Dies Drear, Virginia Hamilton	achieving a positive stage presence
	The Red Badge of Courage, Stephen Crane	mastering performance anxiety, judgment by multiple standards

ASSESSMENT AND EVALUATION

Glencoe Communication Applications offers many opportunities for assessment and evaluation. Traditional assessment methods are provided to assess students' understanding of the chapter concepts and skills. Performance-based assessment is included to assess students' application of these concepts and skills. In addition, various media resources allow you to customize assessment materials to meet your students' needs.

Assessment Opportunities in the Student Edition

Three levels of assessment are included in the *Glencoe Communication Applications* Student Edition.

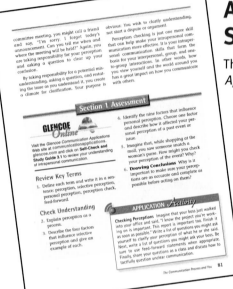

- **Section Assessment** provides evaluation of section objectives, vocabulary, and concepts. Students can review their understanding of concepts before moving on to the next section or chapter assessment.

- **Chapter Assessment and Activities** evaluates the main points of the chapter and provides various activities that allow students to apply chapter concepts. Students can use this feature to review key points in the chapter and check their understanding of the chapter concepts.

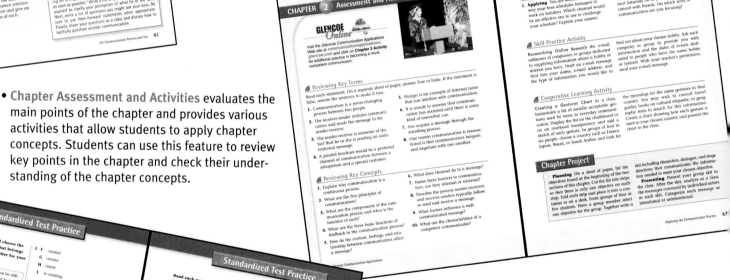

- **Standardized Test Practice** from The Princeton Review is provided at the end of each unit. Students answer questions similar to those found on most standardized tests.

Print and Media Assessment Materials

- **Section Quizzes** test key points in the section to check students' understanding.

- **Chapter and Unit Tests** assess students' knowledge of chapter content through the use of matching, multiple-choice, and short-answer questions.

- **Performance Assessment** includes activities that apply communication skills and require higher level thinking skills.

- **Oral Presentation Activities** provide performance-based assessment by supplying specific criteria on which students' oral presentations can be judged.

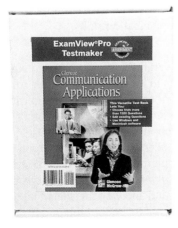

- **MindJogger Videoquiz** uses a game-show format to quiz students on chapter content. The video-quizzes are available on VHS or videodisc.

- **Interactive Tutor Self-Assessment** helps students test their own knowledge of chapter content. The computer provides immediate feedback so students can identify and correct their mistakes.

- **ExamView®Pro Testmaker** is a database of test questions that allows you to customize tests for your students' specific needs.

The Importance of Performance-Based Assessment

What is the best way to evaluate students' communication skills? Traditional assessment methods evaluate students' knowledge of communication concepts, but performance-based assessment can evaluate the application of students' communication skills. For this reason, performance-based assessment plays a large role in communication courses.

Performance-based activities allow students to practice the communication skills they have learned in each chapter. Students are able to apply their knowledge of communication concepts and refine their communication skills. As a method of assessment, these activities allow you to observe students'

demonstration of these skills and to evaluate their understanding of the concepts.

Glencoe Communication Applications provides many opportunities for performance-based assessment. Some activities and materials that utilize performance-based assessment include the Skill Practice Activity, Cooperative Learning Activity, and Chapter Project included in the **Chapter Assessment and Activities** in the Student Edition. Also, the **Performance Assessment Activities** and the worksheets that accompany the **Oral Presentation Activities** offer alternative performance-based assessment opportunities. By combining these resources, you can offer students multiple opportunities to practice and apply key communication skills.

Uses of Performance-Based Assessment

Student Self-Assessment

Performance-based assessment is one way to help students evaluate their own abilities. Students can judge their own products or performances based on a predetermined set of criteria. This process allows them to identify the areas where they are performing well and the areas where they need improvement. The performance-based assessment in *Glencoe Communication Applications* provides students with self-awareness and helps them monitor and adjust their own communication skills.

Peer Evaluation

Through the performance-based assessment available in *Glencoe Communication Applications,* students are able to reinforce their communication skills by observing and evaluating others. In order to evaluate others' presentations, students must have a clear understanding of the criteria on which they are being judged. This insight not only allows them to offer feedback to their peers but also helps them perform better themselves. In addition, performance-based assessment makes it possible for students to receive feedback from their peers as well as from you.

Portfolio Assessment

The performance-based assessment opportunities in *Glencoe Communication Applications* can be used for creating assessment portfolios. Students can select projects, evaluation worksheets, videotapes of their presentations, or other products to include in their portfolios. When assembling their portfolios, students should choose only those activities that they feel demonstrate their best work. In doing this, students receive another opportunity to evaluate their own communication skills.

Preparation for the Future

When students enter the workforce, they will be required to apply communication skills to their jobs. Among the communication tasks they might encounter are communicating with customers, writing letters or memos, and creating marketing materials. In order to complete these tasks successfully, students will need to demonstrate strong communication skills. The performance-based assessment opportunities in *Glencoe Communication Applications* allow students to practice using and applying the skills that they learn. As a result, students will be better prepared to work productively in a business environment.

Glencoe
Communication
Applications

Virginia Hunter Myers
June Hubbell Smith
Marcia Myers Swanson

Maridell Fisher Fryar
Major Consultant

**Glencoe
McGraw-Hill**

New York, New York   Columbus, Ohio   Woodland Hills, California   Peoria, Illinois

AUTHORS

Virginia Hunter Myers is an Associate Professor and Coordinator of Speech in the Division of Communication Arts at Wayland Baptist University in Plainview, Texas. Mrs. Myers has had a distinguished career teaching English, Speech, and Theatre in secondary and postsecondary schools in Texas. She has served as president of the Texas Speech Communication Association and vice president of the Texas Forensic Association. She has served on a variety of committees and task forces for state and national speech associations. She has authored two previous textbooks and presented numerous papers, programs, and seminars for professional communication associations as well as other organizations.

June Hubbell Smith is an Associate Professor of Communication at Angelo State University. Dr. Smith's research includes small group communication issues, communication methods, and organizational communication. She has presented at state and national communication conventions, is published in communication journals, and has served in various offices in the Texas Speech Communication Association.

Marcia Myers Swanson is an adjunct faculty member in the Career Education Division at Bryant and Stratton College in Virginia Beach, Virginia. Mrs. Swanson has taught professional communication courses at the secondary and postsecondary level in New York, Maryland, and Virginia. She has also served as a communication consultant for various corporations.

MAJOR CONSULTANT

Maridell Fisher Fryar taught speech communication and English and coached debate and competitive speech in both California and Texas at the middle, secondary, and postsecondary levels. She retired in 1993 from the Midland Independent School District, where she served as the Executive Director of Instruction, K–12. Ms. Fryar has served as president of the Texas Speech Communication Association, the West Texas Forensic Association, and the American Forensic Association. She has authored six textbooks, presented numerous workshops, and served in advisory capacities to the Texas Education Agency.

THE PRINCETON REVIEW

The Standardized Test Practice pages in this book were written by The Princeton Review, the nation's leader in test preparation. Through its association with McGraw-Hill, The Princeton Review offers the best way to help students excel on standardized assessments.

The Princeton Review is not affiliated with Princeton University or Educational Testing Service.

Glencoe/McGraw-Hill

A Division of The McGraw-Hill Companies

Send all inquiries to:

Glencoe/McGraw-Hill, 8787 Orion Place, Columbus, Ohio 43240

Printed in the United States of America.

ISBN 0-02-817244-2

1 2 3 4 5 6 7 8 9 10 071 06 05 04 03 02 01 00

Table of Contents

CHAPTER 4
Discovering the Power of Oral Language

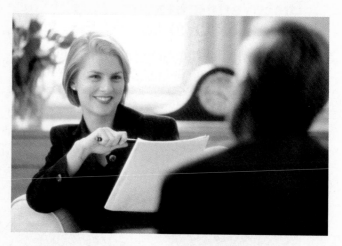

UNIT
② Interpersonal Communication

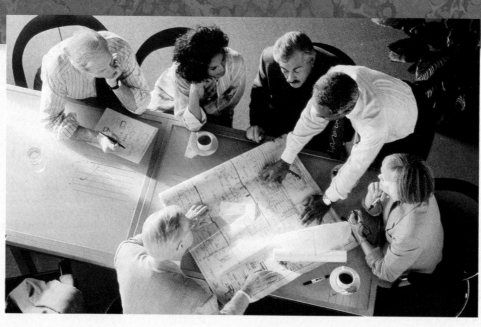

UNIT 3 Group Communication

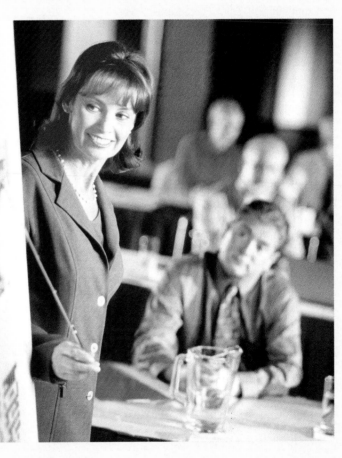

CHAPTER 18
Making and Evaluating Group Presentations

Appendix

Features

Unit Objective

Students will demonstrate knowledge of various communication processes in professional and social contexts.

Unit Overview

Unit 1 provides students with basic knowledge of various communication terms, processes, and concepts, allowing them to participate effectively in professional and social situations. They will apply these skills as they study the communication process, interpersonal communication, group communication, and how to make effective professional presentations.

Internet Address Book

Record useful Internet addresses in the space below for quick reference.

_____

_____

_____

_____

_____

_____

_____

_____

_____

_____

_____

_____

_____

_____

_____

_____

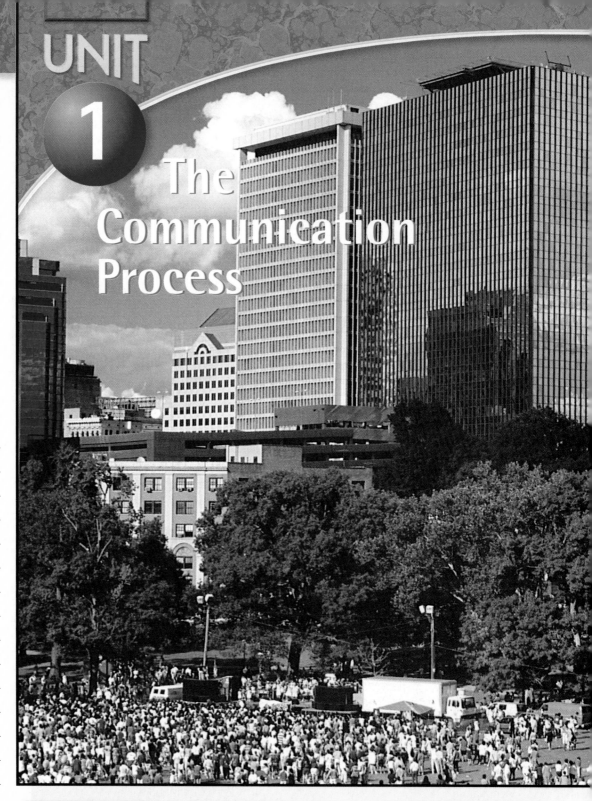

UNIT 1 The Communication Process

VISUAL INSTRUCTION ACTIVITY

Have a student volunteer describe what he or she sees in the photo on pp. xiv–1. Have other students add to the verbal description until they are satisfied that it is complete. Ask: **How, do you think, do people in the construction industry apply communication skills to do their job? What might be the results of ineffective communication?** *(Answers may include to work effectively as a team, to understand and give directions, and to enforce safety issues; negative effects may include insufficient or wrong materials, poor staffing, or accidents.)*

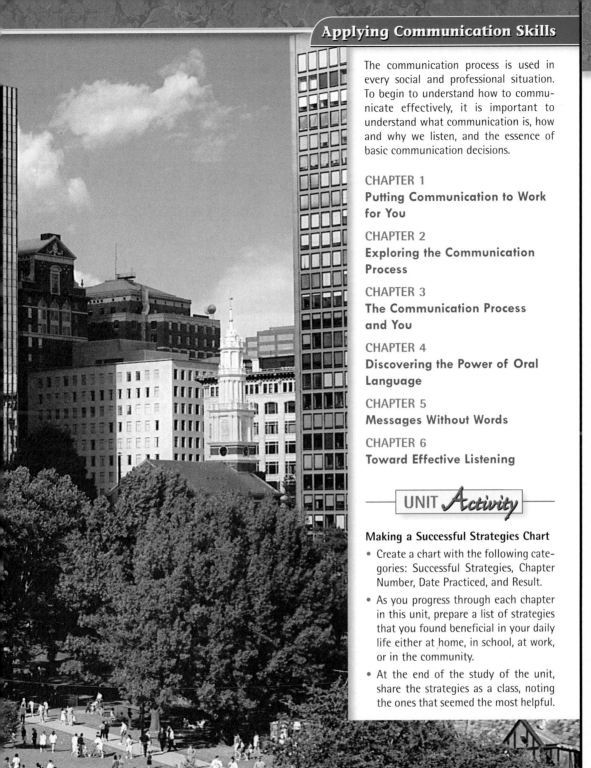

The communication process is used in every social and professional situation. To begin to understand how to communicate effectively, it is important to understand what communication is, how and why we listen, and the essence of basic communication decisions.

UNIT *Activity*

Making a Successful Strategies Chart

- Create a chart with the following categories: Successful Strategies, Chapter Number, Date Practiced, and Result.
- As you progress through each chapter in this unit, prepare a list of strategies that you found beneficial in your daily life either at home, in school, at work, or in the community.
- At the end of the study of the unit, share the strategies as a class, noting the ones that seemed the most helpful.

Introducing the Unit

Write the words *Communication Process* on the chalkboard. Point out that a process is a series of actions, changes, or functions that bring about an end result. Now ask students what they think a communication process is. Discuss students' concept the communication process; clarify misconceptions. Point out that Unit 1 examines what it means to communicate effectively in social and professional contexts.

Unit Assessment

After students have completed Unit 1, assign the Unit 1 Assessment in the *Glencoe Communication Applications Chapter and Unit Tests.*

Testmaker Use the *Glencoe Communication Applications ExamView® Pro Testmaker* software to create a customized Unit 1 test.

UNIT *Activity*

Point out to students that practical communication strategies are provided throughout the text. Assign the following strategies as needed:

Improving Attending Skills, p. 9
Improving Memory Skills, p. 15

For additional strategies, see the "Guide to Business Communication" in the Communication Survival Kit on pages 635–659.

COMMUNICATING IN THE COMMUNITY

To confirm to students the importance of communication in the workplace, invite a businessperson from your community to speak to the class. Prepare the speaker to describe the communication skills he or she uses in a typical workday. To make the point clear, you may wish to ask your guest to share examples of effective and ineffective listening practices and their effects on the speaker's business.

Chapter 1 Planning Guide

SECTION RESOURCES

Daily Objectives

Section 1

1. Use context as the basis to judge the appropriateness of a communication choice
2. Identify how context determines roles and norms
3. Explain the importance of making communication choices that are appropriate for self, listener, occasion, and task of a situation
4. Identify the tools needed to develop the mind-set of a competent communicator

Section 2

1. Explain the importance of organizations as contexts for communication
2. Describe three functions of organizations
3. Explain the concepts of personal and organizational culture
4. Analyze the seven elements of organizational culture
5. Identify appropriate strategies for communicating across diversity

Reproducible Resources

 Reproducible Lesson Plan 1-1
 Application Activities 1-1
 Guided Reading Workbook Activity 1-1
 Vocabulary Activity 1*
 Reteaching Activity 1-1*
 Enrichment Activity 1-1*
 Graphic Organizer Transparency Strategies and Activities 1-1

 Reproducible Lesson Plan 1-2
 Application Activities 1-2
 Guided Reading Workbook Activity 1-2
 Vocabulary Activity 1*
 Reteaching Activity 1-2*
 Enrichment Activity 1-2*
 Graphic Organizer Transparency Strategies and Activities 1-2

Multimedia Resources

 Graphic Organizer Transparency 1-1
 Chapter 1 Teaching Transparency
 Interactive Tutor Self-Assessment
 PuzzleMaker
 ExamView® Pro Testmaker
 Interactive Lesson Planner
 Communication in Action Video Chapter 1
 MindJogger
 communicationapplications.glencoe.com
 Presentation Plus!

 Graphic Organizer Transparency 1-2
 Chapter 1 Teaching Transparency
 Interactive Tutor Self-Assessment
 PuzzleMaker
 ExamView® Pro Testmaker
 Interactive Lesson Planner
 Communication in Action Video Chapter 1
 MindJogger
communicationapplications.glencoe.com
Presentation Plus!

Use Glencoe's *Presentation Plus!* multimedia teacher tool to easily present dynamic lessons that engage and motivate your students. Using Microsoft PowerPoint®, you can customize the presentations to create your own personalized lessons.

* Also available in Spanish

 Blackline Master   CD-ROM   Software

 Transparency   Videodisc   Videocassette   Web site

Chapter 1 Planning Guide

FOR THE TEACHER

Defining School Culture

Have students spend ten to fifteen minutes with a pencil and paper jotting down everything that comes to their minds about their school. What makes it unique? What are its traditions, values, systems, and rules? Is it a friendly place? Is it physically comfortable? Is it dark or bright, stuffy or airy? Who attends the school? How diverse are their backgrounds? They should write quickly, without thinking about their responses, until you tell them to stop.

Allow students to compare their lists with three or four classmates. After they read the lists carefully, have students compile one master list that team members agree describes the school in its many aspects. After all teams have created a sketch of the school's culture—the way life is conducted within the school—have them refine their cultural descriptions still further by sharing each group's list with those of other groups. As a class, decide which items to retain or discard and create a master list of your school's culture on the chalkboard.

Block Scheduling

Block scheduling differs from traditional class scheduling in the amount of time allotted to each period. The extended time frame provided by block scheduling affords you the opportunity to implement a greater number of research-oriented and activity-intense projects to motivate and involve your students. Activities that are particularly suited to use within the block-scheduling framework are identified throughout this chapter by the following designation:

CHAPTER RESOURCES

Resources for the Teacher

- **The Character of a Corporation: How Your Company's Culture Can Make or Break Your Business** by Rob Goffee and Gareth Jones, Harper Collins, 1998
- **Communicating at Work: Principles and Practices for Business and the Professions** by R.B. Adler and J. M. Elmhorst, McGraw-Hill, 1999
- **Corporate Communication** by Paul A. Argenti, Irwin, 1994

Resources for the Student

- **Manwatching: A Field Guide to Human Behavior** by Desmond Morris, H. N. Abrams, 1974
- **Rediscovering America's Values** by Frances Moore Lappe, Ballantine, 1989
- **Understanding a Company** by Jeffery B. Little, Chelsea House, 1988

KEY TO ABILITY LEVELS

Teaching Strategies have been coded for varying learning styles and abilities.

L1 **BASIC** activities for all students

L2 **AVERAGE** activities for average to above-average students

L3 **CHALLENGING** activities for above-average students

ELL **English Language Learner** activities

Chapter 1 Resource Manager

The following materials may be used when teaching the chapter. Materials for specific lessons are also shown at point-of-use in the margins of the Teacher's Wraparound Edition.

TEACHING TRANSPARENCIES

Chapter 1 Teaching Transparency

Graphic Organizer Transparency 1-1

Graphic Organizer Transparency 1-2

APPLICATION ACTIVITIES

Chapter 1, Section 1

Chapter 1, Section 2

Chapter 1, Cumulative

REINFORCEMENT AND REVIEW ACTIVITIES

Vocabulary Activity 1

Guided Reading Activity Workbook 1-1, 1-2

Reteaching Activities 1-1, 1-2

Chapter 1 Resource Manager

Glencoe's ASSESSMENT ADVANTAGE

ASSESSMENT AND EVALUATION

Section Quizzes 1–1, 1–2

Chapter 1 Test, Forms A & B

Performance Assessment Activity 1

ENRICHMENT AND EXTENSION

Technology Application Activity 1

Enrichment Activities 1–1, 1–2

ORAL PRESENTATION ACTIVITIES

Activities 1, 2

SPANISH RESOURCES

- 📁 Spanish Chapter and Unit Tests
- 📁 Spanish Vocabulary Activities
- 📁 Spanish Section Quizzes
- 📁 Spanish Reteaching Activities
- 📁 Spanish Enrichment Activities

MULTIMEDIA

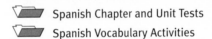

- Interactive Tutor Self-Assessment
- ExamView® Pro Testmaker
- PuzzleMaker
- Communication in Action Videodisc and Videocassette
- MindJogger
- Interactive Lesson Planner
- Presentation Plus!
- Writer's Assistant
- Glencoe Interactive Grammar
- **communicationapplications.glencoe.com**

TEACHER PLANNING AND SUPPORT

- 📁 Reproducible Lesson Plans
- Interactive Lesson Planner
- Presentation Plus!

Putting Communication to Work for You

WHY IT'S IMPORTANT

Choosing your words carefully can make a big difference in the messages you send. Making the appropriate choices in your actions and attitude, too, will help you be the most competent communicator you can be.

 To better understand the importance of making appropriate communication choices, view the **Communication in Action** Chapter 1 video lesson.

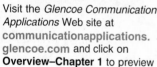

Visit the *Glencoe Communication Applications* Web site at **communicationapplications. glencoe.com** and click on **Overview–Chapter 1** to preview information about communication choices.

2 *Glencoe Communication Applications*

> *"The difference between the almost right word and the right word 'tis the difference between the lightning bug and the lightning."*
> —Mark Twain, American author and humorist

Communication Choices

GUIDE TO READING

Objectives

1. Use context as a basis to judge the appropriateness of a communication choice.
2. Identify how context determines roles and norms and sets standards for making appropriate choices.
3. Explain the importance of making communication choices that are appropriate for self, listener, occasion, and task of a situation.
4. Explain the importance of effective communication skills in professional and social contexts.
5. Identify the tools needed to develop the mind-set of a competent communicator.

Terms to Learn

communication
context
appropriateness
role
norm
standard
competent communicator
task skill
relationship skill

Look around you. You're just starting a new class on communication. How will it affect your school work? Your job? Your relationships? You may even be wondering, "Why should I study communication? I already know how to talk."

Communication involves much, much more than just the spoken word. The way you dress, the way you walk, and the way you act all speak volumes about who you are.

UNDERSTANDING COMMUNICATION CHOICES

Communication is the process of creating and exchanging meaning through symbolic interaction. These symbols may be verbal, which means in the form of spoken or written words, or nonverbal, perhaps in the form of gestures, eye contact, or tone of voice. In any interaction between people, the message is more than the actual words. It is the sum of all the parts of that interaction: words, gestures, attire, posture, and more.

> When researching possible careers, remember that in every career choice, verbal and nonverbal communication are necessary to doing an effective job. Identify several forms of nonverbal communication.

3

1 FOCUS

Bellringer

Have students choose partners they do not know well, and ask each pair to read the opening paragraph. Direct pairs to discuss the questions posed by the passage and to jot down answers. Using these answers as a springboard, discuss with the class the purpose of studying communication. *(Students' answers may include that the communication class will provide strategies for interacting with different groups and individuals in school and on the job.)*

You may use Graphic Organizer Transparency 1–1 to introduce this section.

Visual Instruction

Answer Nonverbal communication includes facial expression, gestures, posture and stance, and clothing.

RESOURCE MANAGER

Teaching Tools
- Interactive Lesson Planner
- Reproducible Lesson Plan 1–1
- Application Activities 1–1

Reproducible Masters
- Guided Reading Activity Workbook 1–1
- Enrichment Activity 1–1
- Reteaching Activity 1–1
- Section Quiz 1–1
- Transparency Strategies and Activities Booklet 1–1

Transparencies
- Graphic Organizer Transparency 1–1
- Chapter 1 Teaching Transparency

Technology Resources
- Interactive Tutor Self-Assessment Software
- Presentation Plus! Software
- ExamView® Pro Testmaker
- PuzzleMaker Software
- communicationapplications.glencoe.com

2 TEACH

Making Choices

Introduce the term *context* to the class (the situation in which an event occurs). Point out that the choices we make are often determined by the context; then, preview the opening pages of this section by writing the words *self, listener, occasion,* and *task* on the chalkboard. Ask: **How might a listener influence a speaker's behavior?** *(Answers may include that the speaker might speak louder or softer to draw the listener's attention if he or she did not appear to be listening carefully.)* Continue with the other terms, writing the students' ideas on the board. **L2**

Guided Reading Activity 1–1

Name _____ Date _____ Class _____	**GUIDED READING**
PUTTING COMMUNICATION TO WORK FOR YOU Communication Choices	**Activity 1–1**

As you read Section 1, answer the following items.

1. Give five examples of nonverbal communication. _____

2. What role does context play in making an appropriate communication choice? _____

3. List the four standards for judging whether a communication choice is an appropriate one. _____

4. A norm in a school or workplace can be stated in what two ways? _____

5. What is the appropriate dress for the first day of a new job? _____

6. What skill was ranked first in a survey of 500 managers? _____

7. List the five subjects that competent communicators know about. _____

8. What are the two types of attitudes, and which one is more effective? _____

9. How are our attitudes formed? _____

10. What are the two categories of skills necessary for making appropriate communication choices and using communication strategies effectively? _____

■ Visual Instruction

Answer Context provides the framework for communication. It enables one to identify what the appropriate communication choices for specific situations are.

■ Dressing in business attire like the attire in the photograph is appropriate for the context of an interview. What is the importance of context in communication?

Therefore, whether you are talking or not, you are constantly communicating messages to others about yourself.

Being aware of the messages you're sending will help you present an accurate picture of who you are and what you want to convey. For example, imagine that you have an opportunity to try for a summer internship at a local television station. In preparation for the job interview, you have researched the station's history, ratings, and broadcast market. However, you arrive at the interview wearing a swimsuit, a T-shirt, and sandals. Even if you impress the interviewer with your knowledge, you probably won't get the job. The message you've presented through your casual attire—you'd rather be at the beach than working—speaks much louder than your knowledge about the station.

4 *Glencoe Communication Applications*

MAKING CHOICES

When we have to make choices, our options usually aren't simply right or wrong. What may be acceptable for one occasion may be completely inappropriate for another. Dressing in a swimsuit, a T-shirt, and sandals isn't always a poor choice; that's what you'd expect to find at the beach. For the job interview, however, it was the wrong choice of attire.

Know the Context

What makes one communication choice better than another? As in the case of the swimsuit, it all depends upon the context. Context is the situation in which communication occurs. A beach is the perfect context for wearing a swimsuit.

Context includes the people present, the occasion, and the task. Context is important in communication because it provides a framework for communication and is the basis for making appropriate communication choices.

Appropriateness is what is suitable for a specific situation. The volume of your speaking voice, for example, varies according to what's appropriate in a given context. Shouting may be appropriate at a soccer game; however, it may get you into trouble during an exam. When you understand the specific contexts in which you are communicating, you can make the best choices for your behavior because you have a basis to decide if your communication choices are appropriate. In order to make these decisions, it is important to understand how roles and norms operate in a context.

Context Determines Roles and Norms

Each context has roles and norms. The communication behaviors appropriate to that context depend on both the roles you play

ENGLISH LANGUAGE LEARNERS

Context and Culture For learners of English, the problem of understanding context and appropriateness may be increased by their relative unfamiliarity with the culture in which they are living.

Activity Assign students to groups and ask them to create a list of typical social contexts, suggesting that they be as specific as possible: lunch in the cafeteria, a visit to the dentist, attending a funeral. Then, ask them to list choices for each of their contexts under the following categories: clothing, speech, behavior. Suggest that they identify choices that would be appropriate in their country of origin and in their adopted country. They can then examine similarities and differences. **ELL**

and the norms for communication behavior in that context. Understanding the roles and norms within professional and social contexts gives you a basis to decide if your communication choices are appropriate.

Context Determines Roles A role is a part played in a specific setting or situation. Your role will vary depending on the context you're in. Being aware of the roles you play and being flexible enough to change them as you change contexts will help you make the most appropriate communication choices possible.

For example, you often play the role of a student. However, carrying that role into your home or your circle of friends would be very awkward. Can you imagine raising your hand to get a friend's permission to speak? Or addressing your mom in the same way you do a teacher?

While those examples may make it seem simple enough to understand roles, in reality the line between roles can blur. Suppose your older sister is your boss at your after-school job. While she may tease you as your sibling at home, it would be inappropriate for her to do so as your boss. The context of the workplace determines the roles you will play.

When faced with complicated situations, it often is difficult to play the roles that have been set for you. Imagine that the grocery store where you and your sister work has to cut back on its number of employees. As a supervisor, your sister is forced to lay off an employee. Since you were the last to be hired, you may be the first to be released. Making choices expected of a boss probably will be difficult for your sister, since as a sister she may resist having to lay you off. However, if she can distinguish between her roles as boss and sister, she can make the appropriate choice to help ensure her success at her job.

Context Determines Norms Each context in which you find yourself brings with it its own norms too. A norm is a stated or implied expectation. In other words, a norm is a guideline of what's appropriate for a given context.

Dress code policies in a school or workplace can be considered norms. Many schools and offices have stated policies; they may be written in the school code of conduct or workplace employee manual. Your school's policies may state that certain types of clothing may not be worn during classes or some school activities. Having that norm written down leaves little room for interpretation or error.

■ **The role one plays as an employee in a fast food restaurant differs from the role one plays at home.** Identify two factors that will help you make the most appropriate choices in the roles you play.

Communication Tip

Although everyone's behavior and choices alter with the task and the occasion, most people have set certain standards for themselves. For example, you may use more slang terms when talking to friends than when talking with older people. Maintaining your standards is one part of your identity.

■ **Visual Instruction**

Answer Two factors that help you make appropriate role choices are context and the norms, or expectations, associated with the context.

BUSINESS BRIEF

In *Smart Moves*, a book of tips for the business person, Sam Deep and Lyle Sussman advise job applicants going for interviews to "dress well and to the other person's expectations." Ask students to reflect on this advice. Is it appropriate to dress for the situation when such dress does not reflect your usual choices?

CRITICAL THINKING ACTIVITY

Suggest to students that there are times when personal standards conflict with behavior that would normally be considered appropriate. Have students form groups and ask them to develop a scenario in which they might feel compelled to make a less appropriate choice for a particular context. For example, students might feel compelled to ignore a curfew when they are having a good time at a party. Encourage them to take note of disagreements within the group. Have groups present their scenarios to the class and invite other students to contribute to the discussion.

Identifying Contexts, Roles, and Norms

Ask students to divide a sheet of paper into three columns. In the first column, they should list different contexts in which they communicate (such as family, job, school, or sports). Ask them to list in the second column two roles (daughter, salesclerk, student, goalie on a soccer team) each context establishes. Direct them to describe briefly the norms associated with each. **L2**

Communication Tip

When roles overlap, which one should you assume? As a general rule, choose the more formal role until circumstances indicate that another one would be more appropriate. For example, if your father is also your math teacher, assume the role of student in school. It is probably unwise to address him as "Dad" during the first class!

COMMUNICATION
Strategies

MAKING APPROPRIATE COMMUNICATION CHOICES

✓ Understand the context.

✓ Define your role.

✓ Discover the communication norms.

✓ Set the standards based on self, listener, occasion, and task.

However, having a norm that is implied or understood is as binding as one that is written or stated. You can sometimes determine implied norms by observing others' behavior. Staying in tune with those implied norms is a key to being successful in both the social and professional worlds. For example, there are no written rules for dating. It's clear, though, that if you ask someone out for a dinner date, it's inappropriate to arrive late to meet him or her and ignore the person once you show up. Knowing what's expected of you on a date will make your time more enjoyable and increase the chances of a second invitation!

Imagine that you have just accepted a job as a sales clerk at your local pharmacy. During your interview, the supervisor didn't mention the store's dress code. You're due to arrive for your first day on the job in an hour. What should you wear? Would jeans and a T-shirt be appropriate? How do you know?

You can't err on the side of being overdressed. If you go to your job in slacks and a dress shirt and, once there, find out that khakis are acceptable, you've still made a positive first impression. Over time, you can relax your dress according to the norms of that workplace. On the other hand, if you had arrived the first day wearing

jeans, your supervisor might have questioned your judgment. Customers also might have had difficulty taking you seriously. You'd be faced with overcoming a negative first impression plus the other new job pressures.

Consider another example. Imagine that one of your main responsibilities at the pharmacy is taking telephone calls from customers and physicians. If no one tells you exactly what to say when you answer the phone, what should you do? Is the way you answer the phone at home appropriate for the context of the pharmacy? Until you have a chance to ask your boss, use the most professional and polite greeting you can. You should assume that the accepted norm is as high as any standard you can imagine; once you have confirmed the actual norm, you can adjust your behavior.

Context Sets the Standards

Part of making appropriate communication choices depends on the standards you've set. A standard is an established level of requirement or excellence. Your standards are important because they are the foundation on which you make your communication decisions. They also guide you to make the best communication choices for yourself.

There are no absolute rules in oral communication. You, as a communicator, have the responsibility to establish your own standards

■ **Figure 1–1 Context Sets the Standards**

Self
Listener
Occasion
Task

for the situations in which you find yourself. You want to be satisfied with each communication choice you make. As **Figure 1–1** shows, to get the most satisfaction, you should make your choices based on four standards—what is appropriate for yourself, your listener, the occasion, and the task.

Appropriate for Self
As you send and receive messages, your first standard for making a communication choice should be what is appropriate for you. This means knowing who you are, what you want to achieve, and how you want others to perceive you.

For example, if you want others to see you as serious about your job, you will want to make communication choices that give that impression. If you work a part-time job after school, you might want to make sure you arrive on time, wear the appropriate attire, and communicate courtesy to customers.

Appropriate for Your Listener
Part of choosing what is appropriate for a situation depends on the people involved. If you want others to respond to your messages, you consider their needs, desires, and limitations. This often requires you to be flexible and patient. It may mean making careful language choices, being aware of your own and others' nonverbal behaviors, and listening carefully to others.

Making appropriate communication choices that are true to yourself and your listeners can be difficult. It also may take courage to reach beyond your normal capabilities. For instance, the image you have of yourself may include being somewhat shy and serious. However, your pep squad coach might need you to communicate in a very animated and excited manner during a performance on the field. In order to be a successful pep squad member, you make a communication choice that meets the coach's needs in that context.

Practice for the Workplace

Appropriate Choices Communication situations in the workplace can be informal conversations or formal meetings; can be held in an office, on a factory floor, or in an auditorium; and can involve customers, coworkers, or supervisors. In any situation, your communication choice should be appropriate for the context.

BUSINESS PRACTICE *Activity*
In groups of four to six students, list the tasks that employees of a small retail clothing store would have to accomplish during a particular time period. Under each task, list appropriate communication choices for each. For example, one task might be to greet customers as they walk through the door. It would not be appropriate to ignore a customer, but it would be appropriate to ask if the customer needs any help. Once each group has completed its list, prepare a skit that acts out the appropriate communication choices. As a class, discuss the effects the choices would have on the success of the business.

Appropriate for the Occasion
Your coach may not need you to be completely full of energy at every practice—the occasion doesn't require it. The minute the half-time show begins, though, your enthusiastic self needs to shine through! The occasion, or time, place, and purpose, of an event makes specific demands on your communication.

The behavior you display during the half-time show won't be necessary for other occasions. Hanging out with friends after school, going to a student council meeting, and attending a tutoring session are occasions where you'll act differently than you would during the show. Each occasion brings with it different expectations of appropriate behavior.

Putting Communication to Work for You **7**

Practice for the Workplace

Appropriate Choices Bring the Business Practice Activity closer to home by asking students if they feel there is a generally accepted standard for appropriate choices in their school. Have groups of students create a chart similar to the one suggested in the text, but ask them to list examples of appropriate choices in typical school situations. Invite students to act out their examples for the class. Students' lists should consist of tasks along with appropriate choices. (*Answers may include such scenarios as helping customers find an item, listening to the customers' needs and wants, serving as a cashier, thanking customers for their purchases, and wishing them a good day*). **L2**

DID YOU KNOW?
The increasingly important medium of e-mail has its own set of norms—rules that people adhere to so as not to be misinterpreted when communicating electronically. Find out more about the conventions governing e-mail by keying in "netiquette" into a reliable Internet search engine.

MEETING INDIVIDUAL NEEDS
MULTIPLE LEARNING STYLES

Linguistic Point out that much of the time, people adjust their linguistic norms without thinking. Remind students that the language they use with friends in the cafeteria is probably not the same as the language they use when asking a teacher for a recommendation.

Activity Test students' ability to assess the norms of oral communication by providing a number of prompts that would each require a few sentences in response. (*Examples: explain why you were late, describe an accident, ask for a loan.*) Have students work in pairs to choose a prompt and prepare two responses: one for a friend and one for an employer or an adult in a position of authority.

GLOBAL COMMUNICATION

Norms During Negotiations

Encourage students to compare their findings on national differences in what is appropriate in a business setting. Ask students to suggest possible reasons for the differences. *(Students' findings will vary depending upon the country they chose to research. Their research should reflect a knowledge of norms with regard to discussing personal issues during business meetings with their chosen country.)* **L1**

Skills Most Looked for in Potential Employees

Ask students to close their books; then, write in random order on the board the eight skills listed in the table. Have students form pairs and decide the order in which they believe employers value these skills. Discuss their answers before referring to the actual table. **L2**

The Importance of Communication Skills

Encourage students to understand the role that verbal communication plays in their lives by having them keep a communication journal for one week. Ask them to make a chart for each day, broken down into one-hour columns for their normal waking hours. Direct them to fill in the chart at the end of each day, indicating the types of communication involved, their approximate duration, and the contexts in which they occurred. Have students share a typical day with their classmates. Ask them to calculate the number of waking hours they spent in verbal communication. **L2**

Appropriate for the Task Imagine that, in your attempt to better understand algebra through a tutoring session, you clap your hands, shout, and jump up and down. While your tutor may appreciate your enthusiasm, she'll probably give you a funny look. The task, or job, at hand didn't require the kind of behavior you displayed. Listening and taking notes would be more appropriate for the task of trying to make sense of algebra.

Getting your classmates pumped up about the big homecoming basketball game, on the other hand, calls for some shouting and jumping. The task you're trying to accomplish in that context is very different from that of the tutoring session. Being flexible enough to make the right choices, based on what's appropriate for the context, will prove to be important for your success.

Throughout your life, you will be faced with situations in which your idea about what's appropriate for a situation collides with the actual demands of the context. Others may expect more from you than you expect of yourself. The occasion or task of the situation may require certain behavior from you that is not your norm. The role you must play or

GLOBAL COMMUNICATION

Norms During Negotiations

The norm during business negotiations in Denmark is for business people to avoid making any personal comments to each other. Even complimenting someone on his or her attire can be considered inappropriate. Research the norms of other countries with respect to discussing personal issues during business meetings and share your findings with the remainder of the class.

Figure 1–2 Skills Most Looked for in Potential Employees

Rank	Skill
1	Oral communication
2	Self-motivation
3	Problem solving
4	Decision making
5	Leadership
6	Human relations
7	Teamwork
8	Work experience

norms you must obey might challenge you. In order to be successful, you'll need to put aside your preferences, wants, or needs and rise to that challenge!

A friend is one who chooses to help you, even when it is inconvenient for him or her. A granddaughter who chooses polite and respectful language in her grandfather's presence is a valued family member. A nurse who chooses soothing words and a pat on the arm when trying to calm a nervous patient will be a success. Being aware of the demands of certain contexts can help make appropriate choices seem obvious. Making these choices can help you become a more successful person in any context.

THE IMPORTANCE OF COMMUNICATION SKILLS

Every time that you interact with another human being you are communicating. As you just read, communicating includes the entire set of messages that you send, from the words you speak to the way you walk. In addition to the constant nonverbal communication you're involved in, you probably also spend a fair amount of time engaged in oral and written communication. While the skills needed to be effective in your oral and

MEETING INDIVIDUAL NEEDS   ENGLISH LANGUAGE LEARNERS

Family Norms Encourage English language learners to share some of their cultural traditions by pointing out that all families, like nationalities and businesses, have norms that often differ from those of their neighbors.

Activity Ask students to think of norms that their families observe that might be different from other families. *(Examples: taking off shoes at the door, eating certain foods, going camping on the Fourth of July)* Invite volunteers to describe their families' traditions to the class. Guide students to the understanding that there are a variety of norms even within a homogeneous society. A diverse society extends the horizons infinitely. **ELL**

written communication are already important in your school and social worlds, they will grow in importance as you develop relationships in your adult life and as you move into the professional world.

A business study based on responses from 1,000 employees shows staggering results. Those workers received an average of 178 messages each day via telephone, e-mail, fax, pager, and face-to-face communication. That's more than 22 messages every hour in a typical eight-hour work day. It also has been estimated that, on any given day, the average business executive spends about 45 minutes of each hour communicating!

Everyone communicates at work in a variety of ways. Depending upon your chosen field, specialized knowledge may play an important part in your job. When communicating with the maintenance crew, an airline pilot must be able to explain in detail any faults in the aircraft. Similarly, a legal assistant must be aware of the technical language used in legal briefs and rulings. More importantly, he or she must be able to communicate in that language. The assistant who can define thousands of legal terms but cannot speak clearly, put together complete thoughts, or write cohesive paragraphs will be of little use to any legal firm.

As **Figure 1–2** shows, oral and written communication skills are vital in any profession. A survey of 500 managers in retail, manufacturing, service, and finance industries revealed the priority they place on oral communication: They ranked it first in importance above other skills. In another study, 1,000 managers ranked the ability to communicate well higher than work-related experience and academic achievement. Communication skills even have an impact on other important employee qualities, such as problem solving, leadership, and teamwork.

COMMUNICATION *Strategies*

COMPETENT COMMUNICATORS KNOW ABOUT

- ✓ Communication
- ✓ Themselves
- ✓ Others (listeners, readers, and observers)
- ✓ The world around them
- ✓ Reason and logic

COMPETENT COMMUNICATOR

Once you've made the choice about what your actions say about you, you need to be sure your words also say what you mean. This helps you become a competent communicator. A competent communicator is someone who incorporates knowledge, attitude, and skills into his or her communication to communicate effectively and appropriately. This course will provide you with knowledge about effective and appropriate communication. Before you get into these vital details, though, it's important to get into the mind-set of a competent communicator. Being willing to acquire new knowledge and skills and having the right attitude will help you do just that!

Knowledge

Competent communicators recognize the need to be informed. It is important to have complete, accurate, and recent information in order to support ideas and to process messages from others. Knowledge also includes

The Skills of Competent Communicators

Brainstorm with the class the attributes of competent communicators. Have students read the paragraph under the heading Competent Communicator and ask them what they believe to be the importance of the three qualities specified: knowledge, attitude, and skills. Discuss these qualities briefly before continuing with the reading. **L2**

COMMUNICATION *Strategies*

COMPETENT COMMUNICATORS KNOW ABOUT

Invite students to assess their own strengths and weaknesses as communicators based on the five areas of knowledge listed. On a scale of 1–5 (with 1 indicating the least strength and 5 indicating the most), have students evaluate their own competencies in each of the five areas of knowledge. Invite volunteers to share their assessments with their classmates. Brainstorm with students how they might improve the areas in which they are weak. **L1**

MEETING INDIVIDUAL NEEDS

MULTIPLE LEARNING STYLES

Bodily-Kinesthetic Our reliance on sophisticated verbal communication is so great that many students may take its importance for granted. Point out that without a complex language structure, communication would be as imprecise as a game of charades.

Activity Ask for volunteers willing to pantomime a specific message in front of the class. Give them a written instruction to communicate wordlessly to their fellow students. (Provide any message that can be simply completed within the classroom: open your notebooks; number a page from one to five, skipping lines; write your name on the top, last name first) When the confusion subsides, discuss with the class the lessons learned about verbal communication.

Attitude Rating Scale

Have students copy across the middle of a piece of paper the rating scale illustrated on this page. Read to them a list of words and phrases representing common teenage experiences (watching television, ordering fast food, studying science, reading books, taking family vacations, working after school). Have each student write the item in a balloon attached to the point on the scale that best represents his or her attitude. Have students form pairs to compare attitudes. Create a master chart of the scale on the chalkboard and invite students to comment on the similarities and differences in attitudes. **L1**

Managing Attitudes

Point out that everyone has moods, but not everyone uses the same ways of controlling them. Remind students that some people go for a walk or play a favorite CD. Take a poll of what their strategies are and discuss the merits and practicalities of the methods students suggest. **L1**

GLENCOE
Online

For an additional Practice Lab for this section, have students visit the *Glencoe Communication Applications* Web site at **communicationapplications.glencoe.com.** Click on **Communication Practice Lab 1–1. L1**

Figure 1–3 Attitude Rating Scale

POSITIVE ⟨ enthusiastic   interested ⟨ neutral/disinterested ⟩ uninterested   apathetic   hostile ⟩ NEGATIVE

the ability to analyze and interpret information and to reason and think logically to reach decisions and make sound judgments. Knowledge also implies the ability to use information effectively. Finally, it includes having valid information and using "good common sense." For example, a knowledgeable voter tries to find out about candidates and issues before voting.

Attitudes

Attitudes influence the way you see yourself and other people. These views influence your choices, and in doing so, also impact your communication. As shown in **Figure 1–3**, attitudes generally are positive or negative. Your behavior in a situation tends to reflect the positive or negative tone of your attitude. As a result, your attitude greatly affects your communication choices. If you have a negative attitude in a class, you may not listen or participate effectively in that class, resulting in your being a less than competent communicator. On the other hand, if your attitude is positive and enthusiastic, you probably look forward to the class and exert extra effort to do well. Your positive attitude enhances your communication competence.

How Attitudes Impact Others

Have you ever heard the expression "One bad apple spoils the bunch"? This describes how attitudes impact others. Employees with negative attitudes about their jobs may criticize coworkers and complain about conditions in the workplace. Their negative thoughts, words, and behaviors can quickly impact other workers, who begin to respond and talk negatively as well. Employers generally appreciate employees who demonstrate positive attitudes and enthusiasm. This does not mean that employees with positive attitudes do not have concerns or issues at work. It only means that they have learned to deal with and reduce negative feelings so they—and others—aren't overwhelmed by them. They also have learned to communicate their concerns in a positive way. There is a strong link between employee attitudes, morale, productivity, communication, and positive human

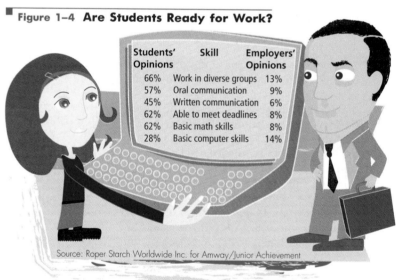

Figure 1–4 Are Students Ready for Work?

Students' Opinions	Skill	Employers' Opinions
66%	Work in diverse groups	13%
57%	Oral communication	9%
45%	Written communication	6%
62%	Able to meet deadlines	8%
62%	Basic math skills	8%
28%	Basic computer skills	14%

Source: Roper Starch Worldwide Inc. for Amway/Junior Achievement

10   *Glencoe Communication Applications*

EXTENDING THE CONTENT

Body Language In recent years, awareness has increased about the role of the body in communicating emotions and attitudes. Popular authors, such as zoologist Desmond Morris in *Man Watching*, have interpreted the messages implied in how we sit, walk, or listen. Point out that knowledge of body language is important to those interested in improving their people skills.
Activity Write on the board the following phrases: hands on hips; legs crossed, leaning back; arms folded across chest; standing slouched, eyes on ground; standing straight, eyes ahead. Ask a volunteer to model these poses and invite the class to interpret them. *(Suggested interpretations: angry; receptive/relaxed; defensive, inferior; confident.)*

interactions at work. Positive attitudes tend to reap positive results in professional and social contexts.

Managing Your Attitude Can you manage and control your attitudes? Yes, you can—and you probably should. The first step is to recognize how attitudes are formed. Your attitudes basically are the result of related experiences. For example, if you have had positive experiences in school, you probably have a positive attitude toward school. If you think of most of your experiences as negative, your attitude toward school may be negative.

Changing Your Attitude Can you change your attitudes from negative to positive? Yes. However, attitude adjustment may mean a change in your experiences. People sometimes change their environment, friends, interests, or perhaps even their jobs to "make a fresh start." This helps them bring about positive changes in attitudes that have gone sour. For example, to change a negative attitude to a positive one, you might choose to spend more time with positive people. You have the choice!

Skills

As **Figure 1–4** shows, the gap between students' and employers' views on students' workplace skill levels varies. Employers often are aware that competent communicators need a wide range and variety of communication skills. The skills necessary for making appropriate communication choices and for using communication strategies effectively can be divided into two categories: task skills and relationship skills.

Task Skills Task skills are the communication skills needed to do a job, complete a task, or reach a goal effectively. Task skills include logically thinking through problems at work or giving clear instructions for someone to complete a task. They might also include making the choice to listen in a particular situation so you can understand someone else's message. Task skills also include effectively using nonverbal behaviors such as gestures and eye contact to make your communication clear and meaningful to others.

Relationship Skills Relationship skills are the communication skills needed to nurture and maintain goodwill with people. They

COMMUNICATION PRACTICE LAB

Analyzing Your Task Skills

To analyze your task skills, follow these steps:

Step 1 As a class, brainstorm a list of communication tasks you perform in school or at home each day.

Step 2 Select one of the tasks that you think you do well.

Step 3 List all the communication skills you possess that help you perform that

task. For example, being a good listener and knowing teaching strategies can help you with the task of tutoring younger children.

Step 4 Which of these skills should you work on to make better? What other skills could you develop to help you perform the task?

COOPERATIVE LEARNING ACTIVITY

Point out to students that a positive attitude is essential to a well-run workplace, including their classrooms and school. In small groups, have students devise ten prompts to assess attitudes toward school. Each prompt should include a choice of three responses, representing negative, neutral, and positive attitudes. (Sample prompt: Most of my classes are (1) totally useless; (2) okay, I guess; (3) pretty interesting.) Have students complete their own assessment tests and give themselves a score from 10 (negative) to 30 (positive). Ask for a sampling of the best questions and compile a questionnaire that the class feels is a useful assessment of attitude.

COMMUNICATION PRACTICE LAB

Analyzing Your Task Skills

Have students carry out the analysis of communication tasks and skills as directed in the practice lab. Ask volunteers to present their analyses to the class. List on the chalkboard communication tasks and associated skills that students have chosen to analyze. Lead students to understand that the communication skills they possess are adapted to a variety of tasks.

(Students' lists will vary depending on the contexts and tasks they choose. The skills they need for effective communication to take place include focusing attention, synthesizing and summarizing information, and asking for clarification if needed.) **L2**

3 ASSESS

Assign Section 1 Assessment as a homework or in-class activity.

❶ Use *Interactive Tutor Self-Assessment Software* to review Section 1.

Section 1-1 Quiz

Name	Date	Class

SECTION QUIZ 1-1

PUTTING COMMUNICATION TO WORK FOR YOU
Communication Choices

Matching Match each item in the left column with the best selection from the right column. Write the letter of the item on the line provided. *(10 points each)*

SCORE

_____ 1. communication
_____ 2. appropriateness
_____ 3. standard
_____ 4. role
_____ 5. norm

a. an established level of requirement or excellence
b. a part played in a specific situation
c. the process of creating and exchanging spoken or written words or gestures
d. a stated or implied expectation
e. what is suitable for a specific situation

Multiple Choice In the blank provided, write the letter of the item that best answers each question. *(10 points each)*

_____ 6. What is a competent communicator?
a. someone who knows nonverbal signals
b. someone who talks a lot
c. someone who thinks, talks, and listens well
d. someone who listens very well

_____ 7. Which of the following is not a tool needed to be a competent communicator?
a. attitude
b. talkativeness
c. knowledge
d. skills

_____ 8. Which sentence best exemplifies the importance of making appropriate behavior choices?
a. It's my life, so I'll do what I want.
b. There is no I in team.
c. It's not my fault.
d. My behavior is affected by the person or people I'm with.

_____ 9. Which of the following is not a question to ask yourself in order to maintain high standards?
a. Would I want to be treated this way?
b. Would I want to explain myself on a national TV show?
c. How much money would I make?
d. What would my classmates think?

_____ 10. Why is context important in making communication choices?
a. It defines what is suitable for a situation.
b. It defines the norm.
c. It names all of the roles everyone will have.
d. It only gives you the occasion for the communication.

4 CLOSE

Have students turn back to the questions in the opening paragraph on page 3. Ask them how they would expand their answers in the light of what they have read in Section 1. As a class, try to come up with a good one-sentence answer to the question "Why should I study communication?"

Extra-Credit Project

Ask students to speak with an employer about communication skills that are important in his or her workplace. Help students develop a list of questions before they speak with the employer. Suggest that their questions touch on specific areas covered in this chapter, including norms, appropriateness, task and people skills, as well as verbal and nonverbal communication. Review all questions and help students revise them if necessary. Have students share their findings with the class.

include the ability to give and receive suggestions and praise. Tact, courtesy, and respect for others also are good relationship skills. They include listening carefully to others so you can understand the meanings and feelings they are attempting to convey. Relationship skills promote communication that allows you to interact successfully in any situation.

Realizing the importance of communication in the business world and understanding how your communication choices impact your social world can help you to develop the communication skills—verbal, nonverbal, and listening—that you need to be a competent communicator. Communication applications will help you to develop the professional and social identity you desire.

Section 1 Assessment

GLENCOE Online

Visit the *Glencoe Communication Applications* Web site at **communicationapplications. glencoe.com** and click on **Self-Check and Study Guide 1.1** to review your understanding of making communication choices.

Review Key Terms

1. Define each term and write it in a sentence: communication, context, appropriateness, role, norm, standard, competent communicator, task skill, relationship skill.

Check Understanding

2. Would yelling with an angry tone be appropriate at your school's awards banquet? Explain why or why not, based on your understanding of context.

3. What four standards are important for you to use when making communication choices?

4. How might poor communication skills affect whether or not a person gets hired for a job?

5. Identify and describe the three tools needed to begin to become a competent communicator.

6. **Apply** Imagine that you are a salesclerk at an electronics store. An angry customer confronts you about a faulty CD player. What specific task skills and relationship skills would you need to handle this situation?

APPLICATION Activity

Playing the Role of a Competent Communicator Imagine that you have been asked to coach tee ball for a team of first graders. In order to be an effective coach, there are some things you'll need to do to be prepared. Divide a piece of paper into three rows. Label them *Knowledge*, *Attitudes*, and *Skills*. Then divide each row into two columns, labeling them *Have* and *Need*. Think about the knowledge that you already possess to be a good tee ball coach. Fill in your charts. As a class, discuss your charts. Brainstorm ways to acquire the knowledge, attitudes, and skills you still need to be prepared to coach.

12   *Glencoe Communication Applications*

Section 1 Assessment Answers

1. Accept all reasonable sentences.
2. Answers may include that yelling would be inappropriate considering the nature of the event.
3. The standards are appropriateness for self, listener, occasion, and task.
4. Because employers value communication skills, a person with poor communication skills is less likely to be hired.
5. The three tools are knowledge, attitude, and skills.

6. Students may suggest that the salesclerk would need to demonstrate knowledge of the shop's policy about faulty equipment and any warranty that covered the product (task skills). An effective salesclerk might also defuse the situation by listening attentively and responding respectfully to the angry customer (relationship skills).

Application Activity Students' charts should have specific information in each of the six boxes under *Have* and *Need*.

Critical Thinking Skill

ANALYZING INFORMATION

To become a competent communicator, you must understand what is and what is not appropriate in a given context. Part of knowing what's appropriate is to analyze any information that is part of a communication exchange or part of preparing to communicate. Analyzing information involves breaking it into meaningful parts so that the speaker, reader, or listener can form an opinion about it.

Learning the Skill

To analyze information, use the steps that are listed below.

STEPS TO ANALYZE INFORMATION

Step 1	Identify the general topic of the information being relayed.
Step 2	Identify the main points of the piece of information.
Step 3	Summarize the information in your own words based on your understanding.

Practicing the Skill

Read the following passage and answer the questions that follow.

You probably won't be asked to write research papers on the job, but most likely you will have to research products and new ideas and write business letters, memos, and reports—all of which need to be organized and presented clearly. And though you might not have to give a formal speech before a large group, you may have to preside at a meeting or present ideas to a small group—and those ideas must be presented clearly, concisely, and with an effective style.

Writing papers and preparing speeches prepares you for on-the-job reports and correspondence. These assignments give you a chance to show initiative, use judgment, apply and interpret information, research resources, organize ideas, and polish your style. Public speaking skills also help you inform and persuade others at informal meetings and presentations. Good writers and speakers are not born, nor is there a secret to their success. Like any other skills, speaking and writing can be learned with practice and effort.

1. What is the main topic of the passage?
2. What are the main points of the passage?
3. Write a summary statement about the passage.

APPLICATION *Activity*

To help you analyze your interests with respect to a possible future career, do the following:

1. Find the description of a particular job you might want to pursue by researching jobs on the Internet, in newspapers, magazines, or books.
2. Analyze the job description by listing the main qualifications and responsibilities of the job.
3. Write a summary paragraph about your qualifications for the job in light of the tasks you have mastered and those you still need to learn to function effectively in that position.
4. Share your summary paragraph with other members of your class.

Analyzing Information

Point out that the word *analyze* does not hold any special mystery. It means to understand thoroughly, something that all students have the capacity of doing. To demystify the experience of analysis, suggest to students that after receiving information they ask themselves the following simple questions: What is this trying to say? and How would I put that into my own words? By this method, before attempting a formal summary, students will have established an informal understanding—a preliminary analysis. **L1**

Practicing the Skill

1. On the job, you will have to do research and to write business correspondence; you must learn to present your ideas clearly, concisely, and with an effective style; writing and speaking skills are learned skills; school is one place to practice these skills.
2. Answers may include that you need to practice writing and speaking skills in school because these skills will help you act as a competent communicator in your future workplace.
3. Summary statements may include that school-related research and speaking tasks help prepare students for writing and speaking applications in the workplace. They are means of developing effective written and oral communication skills through practice and effort.

Application Activity

Invite students to describe the means they used to research their jobs. After hearing the summary paragraphs, encourage students to reflect upon the process of analyzing information included in this activity.

MEETING INDIVIDUAL NEEDS
INCLUSION STRATEGIES

Less-Proficient Readers Students who have difficulty assimilating written material may find analyzing information easier to manage if they work in pairs and analyze as they read.

Activity Have students form pairs, assigning one to be reader and one to be recorder. Ask the reader to read aloud to his or her partner and to pause after each paragraph or other suitable point. At each pause, the reader should ask the recorder to describe in a sentence or two the main points of the passage. When the pair have agreed on a suitable summary, the recorder will write it down, and the reader will continue with the next section. After all pairs have completed this process, review the material with the class and invite students to share their summary sentences. Finally, have students write their own summary paragraphs.

1 FOCUS

Bellringer

Have students read the opening paragraph of this section, and ask them to consider specific ways in which a group would facilitate the task of building a house. *(Individuals would contribute different skills and experience; heavy work would be easier; more minds would speed up problem solving.)* Discuss their answers; then ask what problems working as a team might pose. *(Students may suggest personal differences, timekeeping, coordinating activities, etc.)* Finally, ask how effective communication could help reduce some of these problems.

You may use Graphic Organizer Transparency 1–2 to introduce this section.

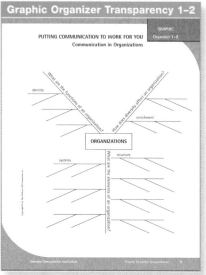

Graphic Organizer Transparency 1–2

Visual Instruction

Answer The benefits of membership in an organization include having the support of other members and being able to meet mutual needs and accomplish common goals with assistance.

Section 2

Communication in Organizations

GUIDE TO READING

Objectives

1. Explain the importance of organizations as contexts for communication.
2. Describe three functions of organizations.
3. Explain the concepts of personal and organizational culture.
4. Analyze the seven elements of organizational culture and their influence on members of the organization.
5. Identify appropriate strategies for communicating across diversity.

Terms to Learn

organization
culture
organizational culture
culture shock
social responsibility
conflict

Would you rather build a house by yourself or with a group of workers? Even with all the latest power tools, building it on your own would be a huge job.

Most people would agree that building a house with a team of people would be much more efficient than one person working alone. This also holds true for communication tasks. Every day, groups of people come together in professional and social situations to work, learn, and have fun. Communicating in these groups requires special skills. It's important to be prepared for the challenges that accompany being part of a diverse organization of people.

THE INFLUENCE OF ORGANIZATIONS

Given its importance to communication, being aware of context will be an essential part of your study in this course. You will focus mainly on acquiring knowledge and building skills to apply in two specific areas: professional and social organizations. In other words, your energy will focus on two worlds that have a great effect on your life—the world of work and the community in which you live.

Working alone on a task such as a large masonry job can be challenging. Identify some of the benefits of membership in an organization.

14   *Glencoe Communication Applications*

RESOURCE MANAGER

Teaching Tools

- Interactive Lesson Planner
- Reproducible Lesson Plan 1–2
- Application Activities 1–2

Reproducible Masters

- Guided Reading Activity Workbook 1–2
- Enrichment Activity 1–2
- Reteaching Activity 1–2
- Section Quiz 1–2
- Transparency Strategies and Activities Booklet 1–2

Transparencies

- Graphic Organizer Transparency 1–2
- Chapter 1 Teaching Transparency

Technology Resources

- Interactive Tutor Self-Assessment Software
- Presentation Plus! Software
- ExamView® Pro Testmaker
- PuzzleMaker Software
- communicationapplications.glencoe.com

In these two worlds, you'll be faced with many contexts. You may be a member of the ecology club at school or work part-time at a local construction company. In many contexts you'll find that you are not only a part of the group, club, team, or staff that seems most obvious but also a member of a larger organization. An organization is a number of people with specific responsibilities who are united for some purpose. Your school organization, for example, is composed of its teachers, students, and staff members, as well as the variety of groups they form. The organization's chief purpose is educating the youth of your community.

Organizations can be professional, relating directly to the workplace, or social, relating to a society's values, beliefs, interests, and the talents of its people. Professional organizations are set up to serve customers, clients, or stockholders. Social organizations are set up to complete the tasks of the society, community, and even the nation.

To be able to fully participate in the organizations that you're a part of requires understanding the context of each organization. Getting to know the people in your group, the setting for meetings, and the purpose of the organization are important. In addition, knowing your role within the organization as well as any written or implied norms will help you make choices that are appropriate to that organization. It also will help you become a valued organizational member.

FUNCTIONS OF ORGANIZATIONS

People develop interests, pursue various goals and ambitions, and meet many of their needs through their involvement in groups and organizations. Having a positive experience as a member of an organization will depend upon whether you receive benefits equal to or greater than the effort you must put into being a member. Membership can offer many benefits: a place to spend time with friends, a way to learn new skills, or an opportunity to earn academic credit, to name a few. In addition to specific benefits like these, the function of organizations is to fulfill three broader needs: identity, unity, and preservation.

COMMUNICATION

PRACTICE LAB

Evaluating Organizations

To evaluate the organization of your school, follow these steps:

Step 1 As a class, make a list of groups within the organization of your school.

Step 2 From the list, select one of the groups to which you do not belong.

Step 3 Identify the teachers or staff members involved in the group you chose. You may wish to use a school directory to help you.

Step 4 Talk with one of these individuals about the specific responsibilities the

group provides to the school or community. Ask the person about how the group contributes to the goal of the organization as a whole. Also ask him or her to share with you the kinds of communication skills that are most needed in that group.

Step 5 At your next class meeting, share your findings. Discuss the purposes groups provide in your school or community. Analyze how each of the chosen groups come together to form the organization of your school.

Putting Communication to Work for You **15**

2 TEACH

Functions of Organizations Point out that the three functions of organizations introduced on this page—identity, unity, and preservation—may not all be active to the same extent in every group. Brainstorm with the class a list of different organizations, including social, athletic, political, curriculum-related, and artistic ones. Then, have students form groups and ask each group to choose three of the organizations on the list and then make a chart indicating how each organization fulfills the needs of identity, unity, and preservation. Draw students' attention to the varied roles of organizations. **L2**

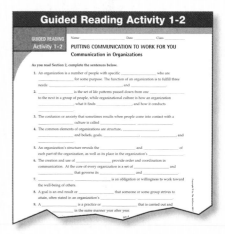

Guided Reading Activity 1-2

GUIDED READING Activity 1-2

PUTTING COMMUNICATION TO WORK FOR YOU
Communication in Organizations

As you read Section 2, complete the sentences below.

COMMUNICATION
PRACTICE LAB

Evaluating Organizations

Have students create information sheets for the school groups they researched. Design with the class a practical sheet format, including such facts as group meeting times, enrollment, purpose, goals, structure, and communication skills necessary. Arrange these sheets on the wall according to categories—sports, arts, academics, community service—in order to make a visual representation of the groups that function within the school. **L2**

MULTIPLE LEARNING STYLES

Interpersonal Teamwork makes tasks easier, but it takes skill and cooperation to organize an efficient team. Give students a taste of high-pressure teamwork with the following exercise.

Activity Divide students into groups of two or three. Give the groups a strictly timed period of twenty minutes (or a time of your choosing) in which to complete the following: (1) Identify a new group they feel the school needs, (2) write a letter to the principal requesting that such a group be formed, (3) send a written request to a teacher to serve as a faculty advisor, (4) produce a poster inviting new members to join, and (5) prepare an introductory speech for the first meeting. At the end of the timed period, have each group present the material they have completed, explaining how they organized their workload. Reflect with the class on the experience of teamwork.

Comparing Organizational Cultures

As an extra-credit assignment, invite students to learn more about organizational culture by researching the traditions and regulations of another high school. Point out that the culture of a school is more than just the rules contained in the student handbook. Encourage students to interview their peers at a neighboring school about activities, academics, and the general atmosphere. Have them present their findings to the class. **L3**

interNET ACTIVITY

Investigating Organizations Online After discussing the class's Internet research, have students form groups and direct them to organize the information they collected in charts or on posters. Charts or posters should indicate the type of information that is available about the organization. **L2**

Identity

The first reason why organizations are important is that they provide a chance for you to define who you are. If you were to list different ways to introduce yourself to others, you might say, "I am a student." You might also give more detail by saying, "I am a member of the junior class, an employee at the grocery store, a member of the National Honor Society, and the goalie for the Rockets hockey team." Regardless of the descriptions you choose, you probably identify yourself in relation to some group or organization to which you belong.

Unity

People throughout history have united to form colonies, governments, and corporations to meet mutual needs and to accomplish common goals. By joining together, people often can accomplish feats that no single individual can accomplish alone. In addition, working with others can build an individual's self-confidence, providing him or her with feelings of camaraderie and belonging. When people unite to achieve a common goal, individual differences are diminished and common ground can be established.

Preservation

Finally, organizations are important because they preserve the things we believe in and find important. Just as churches preserve religion, choirs, choruses, and orchestras preserve our musical heritage. Historical societies maintain our awareness of history and renew interest in historical issues, people, and events. Corporations and other professional organizations in our country help preserve our economic system. Some social organizations even contribute to our sense of charity and volunteerism.

interNET ACTIVITY

Investigating Organizations Online With classmates, generate a list of professional or social organizations that directly touch your lives. Limit your list to the five organizations in which you and your classmates are most interested. Log on to the Internet to find information about one of these five organizations. You might investigate the services it provides, benefits for individual members, and communication skills needed for successful participation. At your next class meeting, discuss your findings with the other students who investigated the same organization. As a group, organize your findings and then discuss them as a class.

CULTURE IN ORGANIZATIONS

An important aspect of every organization is its culture. Culture is the set of life patterns passed down from one generation to the next in a group of people. You may be most familiar with culture as a group's specific language, food, and dress. However, your family's holiday celebrations or its definitions of family roles are also examples of your family's culture. If family members say, "This is how we've done this since we were children," they have adopted a particular behavior as part of their culture.

Culture is learned behavior. You learn about your culture from members of your family, other students and teachers at school, and people in your community and nation.

INTERDISCIPLINARY CONNECTION

Social Studies Corporations and unions, though sometimes disagreeing with each other, have contributed to the economic drive that has made the United States so prosperous. Point out that many of these organizations have a rich and exciting history.

Activity Have students research the history and structure of a union or corporation of their choice. Ask them to establish what made this organization successful or notorious. How did it provide identity and unity for its members? What has been its impact upon society? Invite students to present their findings to their classmates. Discuss with the class the intersecting roles of organized labor and management.

Understanding Organizational Culture

You may gain a better understanding of organizational culture if you look at your personal culture. Your personal culture is a pattern of behaviors that includes the languages you speak, foods you eat, sports you play, activities you enjoy, clothes you wear, music you like, and holidays and traditions you observe. Your personal culture is the way you think and the way you do things.

Organizational culture follows the same principles. Organizational culture is how an organization thinks, what it finds important, and how it conducts business. Organizational culture is evident when a member talks about "the way we do things around here." Understanding the culture of an organization helps you know the role that you have in the organization. Understanding the culture of an organization also helps you determine the expected norms for your behavior.

Success in Organizations What does this mean to you? If you are to succeed in an organization, you need to be aware of as many aspects of that organization's culture as possible. Understanding an organization's culture can help you get a job when you prepare for and answer questions in an interview. It can help you keep a job because your attitudes and behavior support the beliefs and policies of the organization. It can help you make choices and build communication skills that can lead to promotion and recognition. Just as understanding your school's policies on dress codes, grading standards, and attendance can help you be a better student, understanding a professional organization's expectations about telephone etiquette, travel, and sick days can help you be a better employee.

Think about a time when you changed schools, tried out for a team, or joined a new club. Perhaps you have also had the experience of getting a job and entering the workplace. If you have done any or all of these things, you have encountered organizational culture. You may have made a smooth transition, adapting easily to the culture of the organization. On the other hand, you may have been overwhelmed by many of the different expectations you had to meet. People often refer to the type of reaction that you experienced as culture shock. Culture shock is the confusion or anxiety that sometimes results when people come into contact with a culture different from their own. Culture shock can happen in any organizational context.

"I don't know how it started, either. All I know is that it's part of our corporate culture."

© The New Yorker Collection 1994 Mick Stevens from cartoonbank.com. All Rights Reserved.

Putting Communication to Work for You **17**

Personal Culture
Ask students to construct a poster-board collage representing their personal cultures. Have them choose pictures illustrating their background, preferences, skills, style, and types of recreation. Invite students to present their collages to the class. **ELL**

Organizational Culture
Point out the differences among organizational cultures by having students perform a simple telephone survey. Have students contact two local employers and find out their policies on a single typical issue: dress code, timekeeping, holiday policy, or sick-leave. They might request an employee handbook of an organization and use it to identify an organization's personnel policies. Have students report their findings to class. Discuss the differences and similarities they have discovered. **L1**

Application Activities 1–2

ENGLISH LANGUAGE LEARNERS

Preserving Cultural Identity Cultural minorities, especially those speaking languages other than English, often work hard to maintain traditional skills and values. Point out that organizations serve an important purpose in preserving a culture's treasured traditions.

Activity Have students research an organization active within a minority community. Ask them to report on the structure of this organization and on its purpose and goals. How does it fulfill the functions of identity, unity, and preservation? Encourage English language learners to report on organizations to which they belong or that are active in their communities. Invite volunteers to present their findings to the class. **ELL**

Understanding Structure

Invite an administrator or member of the school board to your classroom to describe the structure of your school system, including staffing, areas of responsibility, and the organizational structure. **L1**

Systems Within the School

Brainstorm with students different ways their school communicates with them: assemblies, posters, homeroom announcements, phone calls, or hand-delivered notes. Why is there a need for such a variety of methods? Encourage students to consider means by which these systems could be improved. **L1**

BUSINESS BRIEF

Robert K. Cooper, a business consultant, claims that with effective communication skills, a company can turn customer complaints to its own advantage. The first step Cooper recommends is "a genuine acknowledgment of error." Have students respond to this idea. Ask if they feel it is good advice for personal, as well as corporate, behavior.

Figure 1–5 Elements of Organizational Culture

Elements of Culture

Even though all organizations are unique, they have several elements in common. As Figure 1–5 shows, they include structure, systems, values and beliefs, goals, environment, traditions, and heroes. How each organization approaches and implements these elements makes up the organization's culture.

It is wise to find out the specifics of these elements in each organization you want to join. Whether you're considering becoming a member of the staff at a large hospital or of the Habitat for Humanity team at your school, gathering information about the organization's culture can help you know what to expect from the organization. It also can help you understand what the organization expects from you.

Structure Professional and social organizations have a specific structure. Structure includes the parts of an organization as well as the relationship between those parts. The structure also reveals the functions and purposes of each part of the organization, as well as its place in the organization's hierarchy. This

hierarchy, or chain of command, shows the relationship between parts of the organization from the top down. Hierarchy answers questions about who is responsible to whom for what.

Your school district follows a specific structure and hierarchy. It probably has a board of education with officers and committees who have specific responsibilities. The school also has a superintendent who oversees a staff of assistant superintendents, directors, coordinators, principals, supervisors, teachers, staff members, and you, the student. The hierarchy of your school also defines the functions of each of its parts. Who makes what decisions? Which person or department is responsible for what areas?

Systems Communicating in an organization, no matter its size, requires order and coordination. This coordination can be achieved through systems, or networks of channels for orderly interaction. Otherwise, members would spend or waste all their time trying to communicate simple messages. Imagine that the 17 employees of a small

MEETING INDIVIDUAL NEEDS — MULTIPLE LEARNING STYLES

Musical Point out that music is more than just recreation. It is a powerful social force that can incite rebellion, unify diverse groups of people, stimulate thought, and create euphoria. Yet music itself promotes many subcultures.

Activity Have students choose a type of music—classical, jazz, country, ethnic/world, or one of the many types of rock/pop. How would you recognize an enthusiast? What is the atmosphere like at a concert? Remind them that since these are not formal organizations, there will be many exceptions to their generalizations. Have students present their research to the class, encouraging them to complement their presentations with classroom-appropriate musical examples.

company receive every communication of every person in the company. If you do the math for that 17-person company, can you imagine the communication conflicts that many messages might create?

While communication must be orderly, it also must be simple to achieve. Systems energize organizations by allowing information to flow easily within the structure. Systems also provide channels of communication to the community outside of the organization.

Again, your school can be used as an example of how systems operate within the structure of an organization. Think first of the methods that are used to inform students about events at your school. There may be morning announcements over the public address system, a school newspaper, or colorful posters in the hall to boost school spirit or to advertise upcoming plays, concerts, or athletic events.

Other Communication Systems in Organizations Some organizations also utilize other communication systems to keep the public informed. They may host open meetings to invite public participation and input on certain matters. Some organizations also hold hearings, town meetings, and focus groups to encourage members of the public to air their views, discuss issues, and solve problems.

Values and Beliefs At the core of every organization is a set of values and beliefs that governs its policies and actions. A value is a priority or an idea that is prized or cherished. It is what you or your organization considers important. A belief is an idea that someone holds to be true.

Personal Values Analyzing your own values and beliefs and how they provide a basis for your behavior can help you understand organizational values. As an individual, you may value good grades. You may believe that hard work in school will bring rewards in

the future in the form of scholarships or a good job. This set of values and beliefs probably influences your behavior. You may spend much of your free time studying and researching, working ahead on school projects, or organizing class notes. By influencing the behavior choices you make, your values help define the image other students have of you. The same is true of the values and beliefs of an organization.

Organizational Values Professional organizations such as companies usually value making a profit. Some businesses also place a high priority on the productivity and efficiency of employees. A company that recognizes the relationship between employee morale and productivity may provide a number of benefits for employees, such as insurance, profit sharing, or investment opportunities. It also may recognize and reward employees for loyalty,

These individuals work on a newspaper that helps inform and maintain open communication within their organization. Identify some of the ways your school informs students about events taking place within the school.

19

Changing Organizational Culture

Encourage students to discover how organizations change over time by having them research the evolving culture of their school. Suggest that they interview teachers or alumni to ask about dress codes, discipline, dances, academics, clubs, lunches, automobile privileges, and other aspects of school life in years past. Ask them to research not only how the school culture has changed but why those changes might have occurred. Students might invite volunteers to speak to the class. After their research is complete, have students discuss their findings with the class. **L2**

Values and Beliefs

Lead students to understand how values and beliefs influence organizational behavior by having them make a chart describing what motivates their own behavior. Ask them to list two or three activities that they often take part in. *(Examples: shooting baskets with friends, studying at the library)* Then, have them explain the values and beliefs that promote these activities. *(I want to be a star athlete; practice makes perfect. I enjoy the quiet atmosphere of the library when studying; studying helps me get good grades so that I can keep my grade point average up.)* Invite students to share their charts with the class. Point out that values can be negative as well as beneficial to society. **L2**

Visual Instruction

Answer Possible answers include PA announcements, bulletin board displays, flyers, school newspapers, newsletters sent home, school Internet, or local TV access.

COOPERATIVE LEARNING ACTIVITY

According to Andrew S. Grove, CEO of microchip giant Intel, the form of communication most useful to him is the brief conversation. However, he believes written reports are necessary because they often include more concrete information than conversation.

Divide the class into two groups: writers and talkers. Read to the students a brief item from a magazine or newspaper. Give them about five minutes to process this information. Ask the talkers to prepare to tell the story in their own words; have the writers summarize the story on paper. Have volunteers from both groups present their versions to the class. Discuss the differences in the two forms of communication. Ask students what they considered to be the strengths and the weaknesses of oral and written communication on the basis of this exercise.

Formulating a Mission Statement

Remind students that schools commonly include their goals in mission statements, which take the form of a paragraph or two stating the aims of the system. Brainstorm with the class a list of goals their school might achieve. Then have students form groups and ask them to compose a mission statement that they feel is appropriate for the school. Encourage groups to read and discuss their mission statements with the class. Finally, read to the class a copy of the school's actual mission statement and discuss its contents. **L3**

The School Environment

Ask students to describe the environmental qualities of an ideal classroom. Are there comfortable chairs? Are the desks in rows or groups? Are there pictures, poems, book shelves, reading areas? Make sure that they consider lighting, ventilation, and location. Finally, ask students which classrooms in their school come closest to their concept of an ideal educational environment. **L1**

■ Visual Instruction

Answer Answers may include that businesses promote social responsibility by contributing portions of their profits to causes, encouraging employees to volunteer, and allowing employees to volunteer on company time.

commitment, and leadership. Most companies strive to reach a balance between the profits needed to stay in business and the need to promote morale among employees.

Social Responsibility To reinforce this trend, many organizations are beginning to recognize the value of social responsibility. Social responsibility is an obligation or willingness to work toward the well-being of others. This may include placing a priority on environmental concerns and community issues. Many business executives believe that a healthy company cannot survive in an unhealthy society for long. That belief is echoed by others who consider it their social responsibility to support their workers, their workers' lives, and their communities.

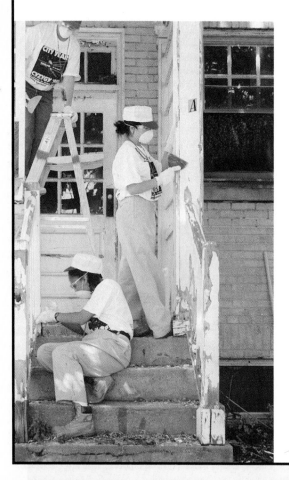

City Year is an organization that promotes social responsibility by encouraging young people to participate in community service projects such as restoring homes. **How do businesses promote social responsibility?**

Successful employees try to understand company values and beliefs in order to anticipate what their employer will look for in their performance. Employees then have a basis for making their own choices and can more accurately estimate the rewards and consequences of their behavior.

Goals Organizations set and try to achieve goals. A goal is an end result or outcome that someone strives to attain. Organizational goals stem from the organization's values and beliefs. Goals often are stated in mission statements. To be most effective, goals should be laid out in detail with specific plans within a set time.

A school district that values academic achievement may have a goal to raise test scores. A company that values diversity may set a goal of hiring more minorities. Service organizations often set goals for fund-raising. Employees are expected to share in efforts to reach company goals. Rewards and prizes often are offered as incentives to those who make outstanding contributions toward those goals.

Environment Environment refers to your physical surroundings. Your culture is reflected in your home, your school building, local architectural styles, and the condition of buildings or streets in your community. An organization's environment often reveals its values and culture. For example, a company with brightly colored walls and comfortable chairs may place importance on the energy level, comfort, and productivity of its employees. A school whose walls are covered with posters advertising an a cappella choir concert shows that its music program is a priority.

COOPERATIVE LEARNING ACTIVITY

The need to keep the public informed is a major concern of many large organizations. Point out that public relations officers—specialists in communication—have as part of their job maintaining the confidence and goodwill of the public.

Brainstorm with the class situations in which an organization would have to launch a vigorous communication campaign to inform and reassure the public *(examples: a product recall by a manufacturer; a meningitis outbreak at a hospital)*. Have students form groups and create a plan of action for the emergency. Ask them to come up with a variety of communication strategies: posters, letters, meetings, interviews. Ask each group to present its master plan to the class and to read or perform at least one of its strategies.

Environment can influence relationships, morale, and even productivity. What does the photo suggest about this school's environment?

Look around and evaluate the environment of your classroom. Is the room crowded or spacious? Colorful or drab? Does it present a bright, safe, and comfortable environment? Does it have a climate that invites participation, curiosity, and creativity? How do these conditions affect your feelings, your attitude, or your communication? Environment affects the quality of interaction. This, in turn, influences the relationships, morale, and productivity of individuals within that environment.

Traditions Organizations usually have traditions. A tradition is a practice or ceremony that is carried out and celebrated in the same manner year after year. Your school may have an annual homecoming celebration with traditional activities such as a pep rally, a football game, the crowning of the homecoming king and queen, and an after-game dance. Special ways of doing things set your school apart from other schools and provide an opportunity to celebrate your school.

Traditions in social and professional organizations usually are aimed at promoting higher morale and positive relations among members. Some businesses host holiday parties, awards banquets, and annual seminars. They

may recognize an employee of the month or sponsor employee sports teams. Such traditions provide a social dimension to organizations.

Heroes A hero is an individual who is respected and admired for the contributions he or she has made to an organization or to society as a whole. Heroes often serve as role models. Think for a moment about the heroes in your school. Perhaps a school hero is the star of the school play, the president of the National Honor Society, or a student with a physical challenge who has overcome overwhelming odds. Whether the school hero is a student body leader, an academic leader, a courageous student, an athlete, or simply a person who always smiles and offers encouragement to others, the hero represents the values of your school.

TECHNOLOGY *Activity*

Electronic Research and Reporting As a class, generate a list of heroes. Include people of different time periods to reflect a range of interests and organizations. Try to include people of different genders, ethnic groups, and ages. Do not neglect heroes from your own community or school. Divide the list so that each person in the class has one hero.

Use the Internet or an electronic encyclopedia to gather information about your hero. Analyze what characteristics and contributions might account for the hero's status. Using word-processing software, write a brief essay explaining whether or not you think your assigned hero would be a good role model. Share your essays as a class. Discuss whether each hero on your class list reflects the values or priorities of a group or organization.

TECHNOLOGY *Activity*

Electronic Research and Reporting Point out that the Internet is an important forum in which fan clubs and historical organizations exchange information about the heroes of today and yesterday. As an extension of their research on heroes, have students locate such a Web-based group and download information about its purposes and activities. Ask them to report on their findings and to consider whether they would want to be a part of this organization. *(Students' essays should examine a person who is considered a hero and indicate whether that person makes a good role model.)* **L2**

Evaluating Traditions
Compile with the class a list of traditions practiced at your school. Write them on the board and have students evaluate them using two criteria: purpose and effectiveness. Discuss what makes a tradition valuable and ask what the school would be like without traditions. Finally, have students suggest traditions that they would like to see established at the school, giving reasons for their suggestions. **L1**

Visual Instruction
Answer It suggests that the class follows the civic tradition of stating the pledge of allegience.

MEETING INDIVIDUAL NEEDS — MULTIPLE LEARNING STYLES

Visual-Spatial The public responds favorably to companies that are perceived to be working toward the welfare of the community and the natural environment. For this reason, most organizations promote themselves as socially responsible.

Activity Have students design an advertising poster featuring a product or a service of a real or fictitious company. Specify that the product must be promoted on the basis of its environmental- or community-friendly qualities. *(A good poster will be convincing, whether or not the message is accurate.)* Have students present their posters to the class and explain whether they believe the campaign indicates genuine social responsibility.

Remedying Negative Traditions

Tell students that some companies are being charged with violating laws when their practices discriminate against workers based on age, gender, race or ethnicity, religion, or disability. Invite students to do research that identifies examples of companies charged with discriminatory practices. Encourage them to explore the role that the government's Equal Employment Opportunity Commission (EEOC) and the court systems have had in remedying the discriminatory practices. Ask students to provide a synopsis of their research findings to the class. **L3**

Using Hero Status

Ask students to choose a hero recognized for his or her skill and accomplishments in a particular field. Then, have students consider how each individual has benefited self or others through his or her status. For example, students should consider whether the individual has used his or her status to promote causes that benefit society as a whole or community organizations, to endorse products and/or services, to promote his or her own image in another field, and so on. Ask students to express opinions about each hero and how each has used his or her hero status. Encourage students to save their evaluations for Chapter 2 when they will explore ethical choices. **L3**

▪ Visual Instruction

Answer A hero can provide inspiration and motivation within an organization, helping to create an organizational culture in which people take pride in and responsibility for work. Heroes may also encourage individuals to reach beyond the organization to provide services that benefit the entire community.

Professional and social organizations have heroes whose values and behaviors have won the respect of others. Mary Kay Ash, for example, is considered a hero by many business women because of her innovation, dedication, and hard work. Michael Jordan became a hero not only because of his skill in basketball but also because of his good nature and his positive attitude. John Glenn became a hero twice. He was acclaimed a hero as a young man with his first venture into space and became a hero again at age seventy-seven with his return to space after a long career in the United States Senate.

Not all heroes become famous, however, nor do they all serve as positive role models. A class clown may be a hero to unmotivated students because his or her disruptions provide comic relief. In the same manner, a dishonest or rebellious employee may become a hero to workers who feel victimized by management.

Whether positive or negative, heroes reflect the values of a segment of an organization's members. Heroes also influence the behavior of those individuals and ultimately affect the culture of the organization.

▪ Michael Jordan, Mary Kay Ash, and John Glenn became heroes because of their accomplishments within their respective organizations. **How can a hero affect the culture of an organization?**

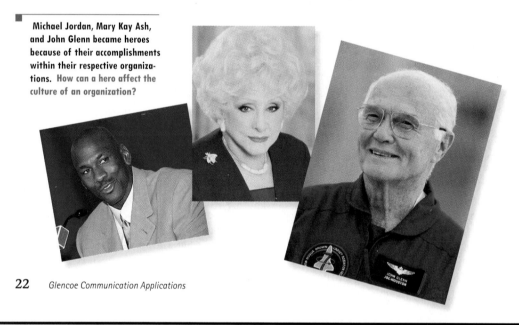

Just as heroes enrich our world, organizations enrich many aspects of your life. They provide you with outlets for your energy and creativity, teach you new skills, and help you help others. Additionally, as organizations add to your life, you also give something back. You provide fresh ideas, new solutions, and broader perspectives with the individual culture you bring to an organization.

DIVERSITY IN ORGANIZATIONS

As people join together to form companies, countries, churches, and communities, they form a rich mix of cultures. Today, many of the cultural barriers between people have been lowered—even erased in some cases. People of every race, gender, and any legal age work side by side. Segregation is becoming a trend of the past. Peace throughout much of the world has expanded markets and communication among nations, and technology allows us to instantly connect with almost anyone anywhere at any time. As shown in **Figure 1–6**, this trend toward a more diverse population will continue.

22   *Glencoe Communication Applications*

GIFTED AND TALENTED

Interior Space Many students take for granted the rooms in which they live and work. Point out that the design of space within a building is an art that has an important impact upon their lives. **Activity** Assign each student one of the following subjects as it relates to interior design: space, color, light, materials, or furnishings. Direct them to research and to write notes on their subject as homework; then, have them form subject-related groups and review one another's notes, adding to their own. Finally, have each group prepare a presentation on their element of interior design, explaining how it relates to the larger field and illustrating their talk with visual examples.

Figure 1-6 Projected Population Characteristics in the United States

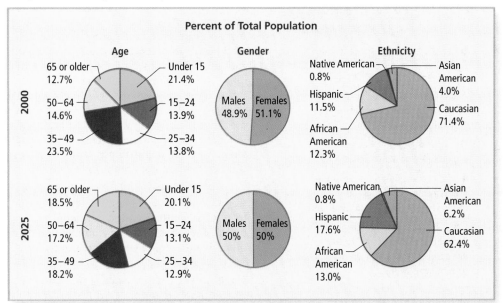

Percent of Total Population

It is important to remember, however, that this trend also may pose challenges. It is likely that in many of the organizations you join, you'll encounter people of different cultures, races, ages, religions, abilities, and genders. This is known as diversity, or variety, and it has become the norm in today's United States. Improved access for the physically challenged, increased immigration, longer life spans, and more opportunities for women all have added to diversity in organizations.

The United States and the organizations that are a part of it have become a sort of "salad bowl" of diversity. This salad bowl analogy, a term popular in multicultural studies today, suggests that each individual can retain and value his or her own personal culture while working cooperatively with others in an organization.

Because no two people are exactly alike, you encounter people of different ages and ethnic and religious backgrounds every day. Since you also are unique, you add to the diversity of

groups in which you participate. As a result, you may be aware of the demands on communication that result from people's differences. For instance, if a student from another state or country comes to your school, it may be a challenge for you to find a common interest that you can use as a basis for friendship. If you volunteer to visit residents of an assisted living facility, you probably will learn that you cannot use your school slang to communicate.

Effects of Diversity

The effects of diversity can be either positive or negative. Diversity can provide enrichment and interest and promote people's appreciation of cultural differences as they get to know one another. It can also cause conflict.

Enrichment Enrichment is a positive effect of diversity. Diversity can provide new interests, ideas, understandings, and appreciation for individuals. For example, sharing

Putting Communication to Work for You **23**

Diversity in Organizations
Point out that the United States used to be known as a melting pot; now it is more commonly referred to as a salad bowl. Ask students what these two metaphors imply about American society. Why do they think this change has occurred? Does one type of society have a particular advantage over the other? Encourage students to discuss the implications of a society that is increasingly becoming more diverse. *(Answers may include that as society becomes more diverse, groups will adopt other groups' traditions and practices as they continue to take pride in their own cultural traditions and practices.)* **L2**

Projected Population Characteristics in the United States
Have students study the chart and ask them to identify the major statistical differences in age and ethnicity between the years 2000 and 2025. *(The number of people aged 50 or older increases from around 27 percent to 36 percent of the total population. The Hispanic population increases from 11.5 percent to 17.6 percent, while the Caucasian percentage drops.)* How will these projected changes affect society in the United States? In a class discussion, lead students to understand some of the potential for both conflict and enrichment in these projections. **L2**

Grammar Tip

Many sentences begin with parenthetical expressions, such as *For example* and *In fact*. These words or phrases are set off by commas to indicate a slight pause in reading. Examples of parenthetical expressions used at the beginning of a sentence include "As a result," in the first line in column 2 and "For instance," in the next sentence. When a parenthetical expression appears in the middle of a sentence, commas are used before and after it.

ENGLISH LANGUAGE LEARNERS

Heroes of Other Cultures Remind students that the heroes they celebrate are not necessarily equally famous in other cultures. Point out that many societies have their own Babe Ruths, Abraham Lincolns, or Oprah Winfreys.

Activity Invite English language learners to list the heroes of their own cultures. Assign a name to each member of the class and have students research their subjects. (If not enough names are generated within the class, assign students a country and an area, such as India and film, Australia and sport, and Mexico and literature. Have them find their own heroes within these categories.) Ask students to present their findings to the class. **ELL** 🗂

Encountering Challenges

Ask students what challenges they have encountered on entering an organization. (If they have trouble recalling specific situations, remind them that the first day of school is a cultural challenge for most 6-year-olds.) Invite English language learners to share their experiences in adjusting to a new national culture. Ask whether any students would classify their experience as culture shock. Lead them to discuss why they found their experiences challenging. **ELL**

COMMUNICATION Strategies

DEALING WITH DIVERSITY

- Learn about other cultures.
- Avoid using language such as slang or dialect that is specific to your individual culture.
- See your differences as an opportunity to learn and grow.
- Avoid looking down on people who are different in age, gender, ethnicity, religion, or physical and mental abilities.
- Be willing to discuss cultural differences and adapt your behavior to minimize them.

experiences with a new student from another country might expand your knowledge about geography, history, or language. Talking with a parent or grandparent can help you to understand different times, different places, or different ways of life.

The expression "If two people think exactly alike, one of them is dispensable" can help explain the effect diversity can have on an organization. People from differing backgrounds often tend to view things differently, have different ideas about solving problems, and take different stands on issues. In organizations where people can express openly their ideas and where people listen to one another, both the organization and individuals can benefit, often leading to better ideas and better solutions to problems. In addition, diversity within an organization can help meet the needs of a diversity of customers and community members. As a result, the organization can anticipate many of the demands it will face in the world market.

Conflict Conflict is often a negative result of diversity. **Conflict** is the struggle between two or more parties who sense interference in achieving goals. It can disrupt work and distract people from reaching the goals of organizations. Different methods of problem solving, different work habits, and different communication styles may be viewed as threatening by some individuals. Any time these differences are judged "right" or "wrong," conflict is likely to follow. It is important to realize that the different ways of doing things don't create the conflict; the responses to the difference do.

Individuals who cooperate to share responsibilities and benefits can use their diversity to resolve conflicts. Using common goals to bridge the gaps between cultures can help them avoid judging each other's differences.

Most people today recognize that individuals of different ages, genders, and ethnicities can work together and learn from each other in professional and social organizations. As a result, they can increase the collective knowledge and experience of any organization.

Cultural Challenges

As you enter into organizations in the world around you, you often may encounter cultural challenges. As a result, real conflicts can occur. Think about the types of conflicts that might result in each of the following examples:

- A school strictly enforces its hair and dress codes. As a result, a young Native American student is required to cut his long hair before he may attend classes.

- A school club has a strict policy against students wearing jewelry that indicates religious preferences or cultural affiliation.

- A company's work schedule conflicts with the celebration of a particular culture's special holiday or observance.

INTERDISCIPLINARY CONNECTION

Social Studies Students probably know a little about the struggles that the United States has undergone in order to achieve basic civil rights for African Americans. They may not realize that the battle against discrimination has been fought by dispossessed populations on several fronts. Native Americans, Jews, women, the aging, the disabled, Latinos, and other ethnic groups have struggled to overcome prejudice in an often inflexible society.

Activity Have students select one of the groups listed above, or another of their choice, and research its struggle for equal opportunity. Ask them to design a poster illustrating the milestones of their group's campaign and to use this as a visual aid in a brief presentation to the class.

These students are required to wear school uniforms. Organizational policies, such as dress codes, sometimes conflict with personal beliefs. What choices do you have if your beliefs conflict with policy?

or procedures that present you with personal conflict, you have a more difficult choice. You may choose to leave the organization, try to change conflicting policies, or you may simply choose to make the best of your situation.

For example, if you enter a school that has dress and hair codes that are not to your liking, you may have no choice other than to conform. You might attempt to have these policies changed, but in the meantime you must be prepared to abide by the existing rules. In a work setting, your employer may not allow time off for a religious holiday that you observe. In this case, you might choose to negotiate for the time off—perhaps by working on a different holiday to make up the time. Basically, when you face a conflict with

- A factory's new uniforms are designed for safety and mobility, but they conflict with some employees' traditional cultural attire.

- An organizational policy appears to award promotions based on age, gender, or ethnic identity.

If you are faced with an organizational culture that threatens your personal culture, you have some important choices to make. Will you join the organization? If you already are a member, will you leave? One way to avoid getting involved in an incompatible organizational culture is to research it before you join. Although many areas of professional and social life may require some amount of compromise on your part, you may decide to keep looking for an organization that is a better cultural match for you.

Challenges of Policies and Procedures If, after becoming involved in an organization, you become aware of policies

© The New Yorker Collection 1981 Mischa Richter from cartoonbank.com.
All Rights Reserved.

Putting Communication to Work for You **25**

Many corporations have employee policy handbooks. These policies help employees know what a company's expectations are.

If possible, acquire the employee handbooks for several corporations. Have each group of students choose a handbook; examine its rules, benefits, and expectations; and analyze them for placement in categories. The groups could establish categories such as rules and expectations that foster positive employee relationships and rules that help prevent negative employee interactions. Allow time for each group to present its handbook categories.

Assessing Challenges

Have students review the five bulleted situations under the Cultural Challenges head. Ask them to rank each scenario according to how unjust they believe the organization's policies to be (with 1 representing the worst case and 5 the least serious). Let them compare and discuss their rankings with partners before sharing their views with the class. **L1**

Visual Instruction

Answer When personal beliefs conflict with organizational policies, you must make choices about whether to join the organization. If you are already a member, you must decide whether to leave the organization, make the best of the situation, or work to change policies.

3 ASSESS

Assign Section 2 Assessment as a homework or in-class activity.

Use *Interactive Tutor Self-Assessment Software* to review Section 2.

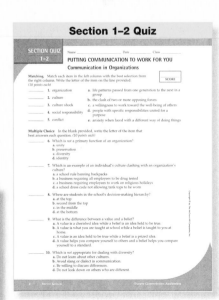

Reteaching Activity 1-2

RETEACHING
Activity 1-2 | PUTTING COMMUNICATION TO WORK FOR YOU
Communication in Organizations

Since you are a student, your school is an organization that you belong to. Within the school there are various situations and dynamics that are continuously evolving. Complete the outline below, giving examples for each subheading from your present school situation.

Organization: Your School
I. Functions
   A. Your identity:
   B. Unity of school population:
   C. Preservation:
II. Culture
   A. Organizational:
   B. Structure-hierarchy:
   C. Order and Coordination:
   D. Values and Beliefs:
   E. Goals:

Enrichment Activity 1-2

ENRICHMENT
Activity 1-2 | PUTTING COMMUNICATION TO WORK FOR YOU
Communication in Organizations

As you have read, diversity has become the norm in today's United States. Diversity involves different cultures, races, ages, religions, abilities, and genders. Lee Gardenswartz and Anita Rowe, in *Diverse Teams at Work: Capitalizing on the Power of Diversity*, explain that there are many myths about the realities of diverse teams. Read the excerpt below and answer the questions that follow.

Diverse teams have no corner on the market when it comes to conflict. We have been conducting team-building sessions for 18 years with groups in which people have been both similar and different in areas such as race, socioeconomic level, education, and lifestyle. These more obvious diversities have rarely been the source of conflict. Sometimes more subtle differences, such as those due to work experience on cross-functional teams, have produced friction. At other times, differences in values presented serious obstacles to cohesion. Any time human beings come together, the soil is fertile for conflict.

Having acknowledged this universal human tendency for conflict, it is also true that when teams experience dissimilarity based on culture, language, or a host of other factors, structure that increases awareness and understanding can go a long way toward mitigating conflict and misunderstanding.

—from *Diverse Teams at Work: Capitalizing on the Power of Diversity* by Lee Gardenswartz and Anita Rowe

1. What are some ways in which people differ from one another?
2. Besides the obvious differences, what can cause conflict in teams?
3. What can control conflict and misunderstanding in teams?
4. Does your school have a diversity program to teach students about their own similarities and differences? If so, describe the program. If not, explain how such a program might benefit your school.

4 CLOSE

Ask students to recall their responses to the question posed at the beginning of Section 2 on page 14. Would they modify their answers after having read the section? If so, in what ways? Have students jot down on a piece of paper the single most important thing they have learned about the structure and function of organizations.

Extra-Credit Project

Ask students to speak with three members of an organization of their choosing. Have them ask about the function, culture, and diversity of the organization, using the subheadings in this section as an outline for their interviews. Invite them to report on their findings to the class.

---

an organization's culture, your choices are to adapt, look elsewhere for an organization whose culture better matches your own, or negotiate and compromise.

Changing Organizational Culture

Can organizational culture change? Yes, but change in the business world usually is gradual. Fortunately, most successful corporations listen to their employees, clients, and customers and typically change their practices especially if this means an increase in profits and productivity. In the past, employee groups have been successful in persuading businesses to make changes such as more casual dress codes on Fridays, job sharing, and on-site child care at many companies.

As you move from the organization of your school into professional and social contexts, you'll want to be ready to be a competent communicator. Knowing the special challenges that communicating in organizations presents can only help you be prepared for the situations you'll face. Communication applications will get you ready for the wide world ahead of you!

Section 2 Assessment

GLENCOE Online

Visit the *Glencoe Communication Applications* Web site at **communicationapplications. glencoe.com** and click on **Self-Check and Study Guide 1.2** to review your understanding of the challenges to communicating in organizations.

Review Key Terms

1. Define each term and write it in a sentence: organization, culture, organizational culture, culture shock, social responsibility, conflict.

Check Understanding

2. Why is understanding the contexts of different organizations important?

3. Explain the three primary functions of organizations.

4. Why should you investigate the culture of a professional organization before you seek a job there?

5. How could information about an organization's goals, traditions, or heroes be used to predict the kind of skills needed by its members?

6. **Solve** Imagine that you work only with people of the opposite gender or who belong to a different age group or ethnic group. Explain your strategies to communicate effectively with them in the face of diversity.

APPLICATION *Activity*

Designing an Organization Think about the organizations of which you enjoy being a member or would like to become a member. What is it about their organizational cultures that appeals to you? How do they complement your personal culture? Using the seven elements of culture, design the organization of your ideal workplace. Make any changes to your organization's culture necessary for the profitability of your business.

26   *Glencoe Communication Applications*

Section 2 Assessment Answers

1. Accept all reasonable sentences.
2. It enables you to make appropriate choices and to participate fully.
3. to promote identity, unity, and preservation
4. to analyze whether there are conflicts between your individual culture and the organization's
5. Answers may include that these characteristics of an organization define an organization's personality and the type of workforce it values.

6. Answers may include learning more about your coworkers, avoiding slang and stereotypes, openly discussing your differences, and practicing tolerance.

Application Activity Students' designs should incorporate the seven elements of organizational culture discussed in this section.

Analyzing How You Communicate

How Do You Rate?

On a separate sheet of paper, answer the following questions. Put a check mark beside each skill you would like to improve.

KEY: A Always   **R** Rarely
       U Usually   **N** Never
       S Sometimes

1. I consider the context of a situation when I make communication choices.
2. I think about my listener when I choose language to explain something.
3. I think about what is appropriate or inappropriate to wear to a special occasion.
4. I stay informed on current events.
5. I generally have a positive attitude.
6. I participate in many organizations.
7. I benefit from my participation in organizations.
8. I have a firm grasp of the culture of my school.
9. I often experience a sense of community between my culture and the culture of the organization.
10. I change my behavior to meet the needs of a variety of populations.

How Do You Score?

Review your responses. Give yourself 5 points for every A, 4 for every U, 3 for every S, 2 for every R, and 1 for every N. Total your points and evaluate your score.

41–50 Excellent You may be surprised to find out how much you can improve your skills.

31–40 Good In this course, you can learn ways to make your skills better.

21–30 Fair Practice applying the skills taught in this course.

1–20 Needs Improvement Carefully monitor your improvement as you work through this course.

Setting Communication Goals

If you scored Excellent or Good, complete Part A. If your score was Fair or Needs Improvement, complete Part B.

Part A 1. I plan to put the following ideas into practice:
         2. I plan to share the following information about communication with the following people:

Part B 1. The behaviors I need to change most are:
         2. To bring about these changes I will take these steps:

Have students respond to the ten statements, using the key; then, have them evaluate their communication strengths as described below. Based on their scores, assign either Part A or Part B of the goal-setting activity. Invite students to share the results of their assessment with the class and to discuss strategies for improvement.

Communication Journal Activity

Encourage students to develop good reflective skills by keeping a regular record of their involvement in organizations to which they belong. Have them describe in their Communication Journals the context and culture of the group in question, including their interactions with fellow members.

Communication Tip

Point out that self-awareness is the first step to self-improvement. Students who achieved a low score on the assessment quiz have given honest thought to important questions and are in a position to set goals for improving their communication skills.

INTERDISCIPLINARY CONNECTION

Natural Science Remind students that organizations of cooperating, communicating individuals are not restricted to human society. Many species of living creatures, from apes to ants, rely upon mutual cooperation for defense, subsistence, and even recreation.

Activity Have students study and report upon a species of mammal, bird, or insect that lives in a cooperative organization. Make sure that students pay special attention in their research to the importance of communication within the organization. Ask them to include in their reports similarities and differences among human and animal societies and to point out any areas in which we could learn from our nonhuman neighbors.

Communication Through Writing

The Writing Process

The Writing Process

Objective: To learn the steps involved in creating a finished piece of written work.

Teaching Suggestions and Strategies

Connection to the Workplace

In the workplace, many employees prepare daily, weekly, and/or monthly status reports. They can use the writing process by jotting down notes as they accomplish tasks, incorporating the notes into a draft report, revising the report to include or exclude details, proofreading and editing the reports for accuracy, and preparing the final draft to be submitted. By following the steps of the process, they are able to ensure that their reports will provide the needed information in the required format.

Adapting the Writing Process

All good writers follow the steps involved in the writing process, but the sequence is not always as orderly as that described on these pages. It is important that students attempt to follow the process methodically. At the same time, point out that all the steps can be revisited. For example, during the process of editing, the writer may remember a better example or discover that a central idea is not clearly established. Saying "But I've already done that step" will not improve the paper. Explain that it is no disgrace to return to the prewriting stage. Ideas that seemed good at first may not come to life on the paper. It is far better to rethink concepts than to make do with mediocre material.

Finally, lead students to understand that all written work, at any stage, can be revised. It is a useful exercise to reassign a subject completed earlier in the year and to ask students to rewrite it from step one.

There are certain steps to follow when writing a report, an article for the company newsletter, a memorandum, a letter, or any other type of written information. These steps are recursive; that is, they do not always follow one another in order and you may repeat steps until you end up with the result you want.

Whether you will give the information to a supervisor or other individual, share with other team members, or present to a large audience, you need to put your ideas into a logical and useful form. Using the steps in the writing process will help you do just that.

Writing tasks are completed in five steps:

Step 1 prewriting
Step 2 drafting
Step 3 revising
Step 4 editing/proofreading
Step 5 publishing/presenting

Step 1 Prewriting In general, the pre-writing process is the way you approach a given writing project. During prewriting you decide on your topic, establish your purpose and audience, and research and plan your writing. Your purpose is what you want to accomplish through your writing or presentation. Your audience is whoever will read or hear your words. You planning includes developing an outline.

Step 2 Writing a Draft After you have defined your topic and audience and have organized your ideas, you can begin to write a draft of your report. As you write, make sure your report has an introduction, the body, or main part, and a conclusion.

Step 3 Revising A first draft is the first version of a written work. Professional writers know that they must never turn in a first draft to a publisher because it is not a final, finished product. After finishing the first draft, writers know that they must take a critical look at their ideas and find ways to improve them.

Some effective ways to review your writing are to read the work carefully as if you were seeing it for the first time. You might choose to read it aloud, listen to a tape-recording of yourself reading it aloud, or have someone else read it and give you feedback. At this point you have the opportunity to move sentences or paragraphs around, improve paragraphs, and check the content and structure of your writing.

During the revision process, you can adjust the tone and style of your writing. Ask yourself if the writing reflects the purpose that you originally intended. Is the

 For additional information about the writing process, see the *Language Handbook* in the Communication Survival Kit found in the Appendix.

COOPERATIVE LEARNING ACTIVITY

For many students, starting a writing task is a major hurdle. Point out that the prewriting step does not always require painstaking analysis. Sometimes, just filling a space with words is enough to get the writing process underway. Designate four or five areas of chalkboard as work stations for making lists. Label each station with the heading of a topic that will be accessible to all the students: pet care, advice for teens, a better school. Divide the class into groups and have them circulate from station to station, writing a new idea under each heading. When the lists are full, have students return to their desks and write for five minutes on any one of the subjects that interests them.

Communication Through Writing

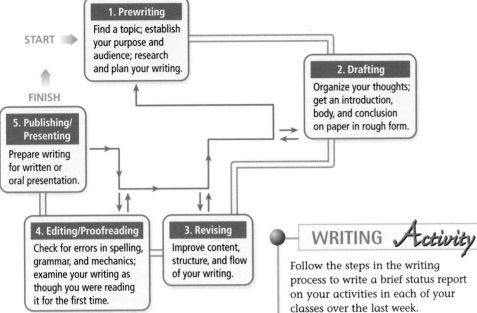

START ➡️

1. Prewriting
Find a topic; establish your purpose and audience; research and plan your writing.

FINISH

2. Drafting
Organize your thoughts; get an introduction, body, and conclusion on paper in rough form.

5. Publishing/ Presenting
Prepare writing for written or oral presentation.

4. Editing/Proofreading
Check for errors in spelling, grammar, and mechanics; examine your writing as though you were reading it for the first time.

3. Revising
Improve content, structure, and flow of your writing.

language specific, descriptive, and non-sexist? Are the words and ideas clear?

Step 4 Editing/Proofreading Once you have revised your draft, you still need to refine your work. Check for errors in sentence structure, capitalization, spelling, punctuation, and grammar. If you have used word-processing software, run a spelling check on your work.

Step 5 Publishing/Presenting You now are ready to send or present your work to your audience. Often, someone else, such as your teacher, a supervisor or manager, or a member of an organization, will define the method of delivery.

WRITING *Activity*

Follow the steps in the writing process to write a brief status report on your activities in each of your classes over the last week.

- List the activities and assignments that were given in each of your classes.
- List your progress in meeting those assignments.
- Write a first draft of your status report. Make sure you have an introduction, body, and a conclusion. Your audience will be your teacher.
- Revise the content, structure, or flow of your report where necessary.
- Edit and proofread your work for errors in grammar, sentence structure, spelling, punctuation, and capitalization.
- Prepare the final draft of your status report.

Teaching Activity

Encourage students to list more material than they think they may need in the prewriting stage. It is better to discard information than to run short.

One way to avoid writer's block in the drafting stage is for the writer to ask him- or herself questions and to record the answers. *(Example: How did the studying go for the biology quiz?)*

Reading a draft aloud is a useful way to hear problems that may have escaped the student visually in the editing stage.

Students who have difficulty spotting errors while editing and proofreading their work may find that reading the paper in reverse order, sentence by sentence, helps isolate problems.

Urge students to take pride in the appearance of their papers. If they have worked hard to write well, they should not neglect the finishing touches.

WRITING *Activity*

Encourage students to find a reader to assist in editing their work before completing the final draft. Remind them that even the most sophisticated word-processing software can misinterpret a writer's intentions in spelling and grammar.

Grammar Tip

A verb is in the active voice if the subject of the verb performs the action. (The player hit the ball.) If the subject has the action performed upon it, the verb is in the passive voice. (The ball was hit by the player.) For most purposes the active voice is stronger.

Additional Resources

Appendix, Language Handbook
Glencoe Writer's Assistant CD-ROM
Glencoe Interactive Grammar Software
Grade 9 Writer's Choice, Unit 2

GRAMMAR PRACTICE

Active and Passive Voice

Have students identify the verbs in the sentences below as active or passive voice and rewrite the sentences, changing the verb voice:

1. The cat was given a bowl of milk by Marco.
(passive) Marco gave the cat a bowl of milk.

2. All the presents will be opened by her.
(passive) She will open all the presents.

3. A unanimous vote elected Ms. Carson.
(active) Ms. Carson was elected by a unanimous vote.

4. The dog delighted the child. *(active)*
The child was delighted by the dog.

5. The note was ripped up angrily by the receiver. *(passive) The receiver angrily ripped up the note.*

CHAPTER 1 Assessment and Activities

GLENCOE Online

Visit the *Glencoe Communication Applications* Web site at **communicationapplications. glencoe.com** and click on **Chapter 1 Activity** for additional practice in putting communication to work for you.

Reviewing Key Terms

1. Communication
2. Context
3. Appropriateness
4. Standard
5. Organization
6. Organizational culture
7. Conflict
8. Culture shock
9. Competent communicator
10. Social responsibility

Reviewing Key Terms

On a separate sheet of paper, write the communication term defined in each item.

1. creating and exchanging meaning through symbolic interaction
2. specific situation in which communication occurs
3. what is suitable in a particular instance
4. guideline to use as a basis for making appropriate communication choices
5. people who have specific duties united for a particular purpose
6. "the way things are done around here"
7. difficulties resulting from individual or group differences
8. confusion resulting from the clash of two cultures
9. uses effective communication skills
10. willingness to help others

Reviewing Key Concepts

On a separate sheet of paper, answer the following questions in complete sentences.

1. Why is it critical to understand and analyze context when making communication choices?
2. Why is appropriateness an important consideration in communication?
3. What can be used as a guide to determine appropriateness?
4. What is the function of a standard in your communication choices?
5. What three criteria can be used to determine if someone is a competent communicator?
6. Name and describe the three needs fulfilled by membership in organizations.
7. Analyze and respond to the statement "Culture influences every aspect of an organization."
8. What are two possible effects of diversity within an organization?

Reviewing Key Concepts

1. You can make the best choices for your behavior when you understand context.
2. Appropriateness indicates what is suitable for a specific situation.
3. The people involved in communication help determine appropriateness.
4. A standard helps you behave in a way that you feel is correct.
5. A competent communicator has knowledge, a positive attitude, and good task and people skills.
6. Organizations fulfill three broad needs: identity, unity, and preservation.
7. Accept all reasonable responses.
8. Diversity can provide enrichment; it can also cause conflict.

Assessment and Activities

Reading and Critical Thinking Skill

1. **Making Predictions** Describe five communication tasks that you might be required to do as a worker in a business of your choice.

2. **Analysis** Why is the hierarchy of a corporation important to the organization's culture?

Skill Practice Activity

Analyzing Information Read the excerpt below and write a summary sentence of the passage.

> Whenever you make an important decision in your life, you first "weigh the consequences." A consequence is the result of an action or series of events. For example, if you were deciding whether to buy or rent a house, you might think about the advantages and disadvantages of both actions. In other words, you examine the various results of each action. By analyzing the possible outcomes or consequences, you arrive at a better understanding of the situation.

Cooperative Learning Activity

Communication Challenge Break up into groups of three to five students. One group of three will act as judges. The other groups will write a scenario of a communication situation they find challenging and make recommendations to remedy, solve, or avoid the situation. Each group will then act out its situation for the other class members and present its recommendations. After each presentation, other groups will list communication strategies they believe will remedy, solve, or avoid the situation. After all groups have presented, the three-judge panel will confer briefly to choose the group that generated the most appropriate list of suggestions. The panel will justify their choices to the class.

Chapter Project

Planning Choose a career or profession in which you are interested. Investigate your chosen profession. Consult a variety of sources for the information you need. Find the answers to these questions: What is the employment potential in this field? What kind of educational and vocational training is most needed for employment? Are there any special requirements for entering the field, such as qualifying exams, special fees, or licenses? What communication skills are especially helpful for getting a job, keeping a job, and getting promotions in this field? Record your findings and prioritize your ideas.

Presenting Use your findings to develop and give a three-minute presentation on your chosen career.

Reading and Critical Thinking Skill

1. **Making Predictions** Possible answers may include that students will be involved in such communication tasks as speaking on the telephone, listening to instructions, writing business reports, sending e-mail, participating in meetings, preparing written and visual materials for a presentation, and explaining benefits to a customer.

2. **Analysis** Hierarchy is important because it helps identify each individual's place within the organization and who is responsible for different tasks and the people who perform them.

Skill Practice Activity

Analyzing Information

Possible answer: By weighing the advantages and disadvantages of choices, an individual can make a more informed decision.

Cooperative Learning Activity

Communication Challenge

The Communication Challenge requires students to participate in written, verbal, and nonverbal communication. Suggest that within the groups, tasks should be divided according to students' strengths and interests. Students may wish to list a variety of challenging situations by identifying situations in brainstorming sessions or gathering ideas from news reports. Ask students to offer substantive suggestions for remedying, solving, or avoiding the challenging situation. Make sure they can also identify why the situation is challenging. You may wish to work with the panel of judges to establish rubrics for assessing each group's lists. These rubrics should be shared with the groups as they prepare their lists.

Chapter Project

Before students begin researching their chosen career, help them identify possible sources of information, such as career fairs, professional organizations, conversations with employers and employees in the field, educational organizations, and Internet sites that might offer career-related information. Establish rubrics for the presentation. For example, you may wish to offer points for addressing specific topics such as educational and special requirements needed, the communication skills needed to enter and succeed in the field, and the job-specific tasks. You may also wish to provide a rating system for the students' presentation skills, such as staying within the allotted time, remaining on topic, engaging the audience, and presentation style.

Chapter 2 Planning Guide

SECTION RESOURCES

Daily Objectives

Section 1

1. Explain the five principles of communication
2. Identify the components of the communication process
3. Identify the basic functions of the components of the communication process
4. Analyze the processes used by sender-receivers and receiver-senders

Section 2

1. Identify the five levels of communication
2. List the characteristics of a competent communicator
3. Analyze the behaviors of a competent communicator

Reproducible Resources

 Reproducible Lesson Plan 2-1
 Application Activities 2-1
 Guided Reading Workbook Activity 2-1
 Vocabulary Activity 2*
 Reteaching Activity 2-1*
 Enrichment Activity 2-1*
Graphic Organizer Transparency Strategies and Activities 2-1

 Reproducible Lesson Plan 2-2
 Application Activities 2-2
 Guided Reading Workbook Activity 2-2
 Vocabulary Activity 2*
 Reteaching Activity 2-2*
 Enrichment Activity 2-2*
Graphic Organizer Transparency Strategies and Activities 2-2

Multimedia Resources

 Graphic Organizer Transparency 2-1
 Chapter 2 Teaching Transparency
 Interactive Tutor Self-Assessment
 PuzzleMaker
 ExamView® Pro Testmaker
 Interactive Lesson Planner
Communication in Action Video Chapter 2
MindJogger
communicationapplications.glencoe.com
Presentation Plus!

 Graphic Organizer Transparency 2-2
 Chapter 2 Teaching Transparency
 Interactive Tutor Self-Assessment
 PuzzleMaker
 ExamView® Pro Testmaker
 Interactive Lesson Planner
 Communication in Action Video Chapter 2
MindJogger
communicationapplications.glencoe.com
Presentation Plus!

Use Glencoe's *Presentation Plus!* multimedia teacher tool to easily present dynamic lessons that engage and motivate your students. Using Microsoft PowerPoint®, you can customize the presentations to create your own personalized lessons.

* Also available in Spanish

 Blackline Master   CD-ROM   Software

 Transparency   Videodisc   Videocassette   Web site

Chapter 2 Planning Guide

Feedback and Messages

Practice giving feedback to a sender-receiver. With your class, brainstorm a chart of words students use often to respond to each other. Categorize each word as positive, negative, or neutral in connotation. Write each word in the appropriate column (headed Positive, Negative, or Neutral).

Divide students into teams of two. With their partners, have students role-play a conversation. One partner should talk about something or someone he or she enjoys a lot, such as a hobby, sport, or singer. The other person should listen attentively and give positive feedback. During the role play, have students switch to giving negative feedback. Reverse roles so that one does the talking and the other provides feedback. Discuss differences students noticed in the communication process.

Resources for the Teacher

- *Handbook of Rhetorical and Communication Theory* by Carroll C. Arnold and John W. Bowers, eds. Allyn & Bacon, 1984
- *Building Communication Theory* by Dominic Infante, Andrew Rancer, Deanna Womack, Waveland Press, 1996
- *Infosense: Turning Information into Knowledge* by Keith J. Devlin, W. H. Freeman & Co., 1999

Resources for the Student

- *The Communication Handbook* by Joseph Devito, Harper & Row, 1986
- *50 One-Minute Tips to Better Communication: A Wealth of Business Communication Ideas (Fifty-Minute Series Book)* by Phillip E. Bozek, Crisp Publications, 1997
- *How Come Every Time I Get Stabbed in the Back My Fingerprints Are on the Knife? And Other Meditations on Management* by Jerry B. Harvey, Jossey-Bass Publishers, 1999

Block Scheduling

Block scheduling differs from traditional class scheduling in the amount of time allotted to each period. The extended time frame provided by block scheduling affords you the opportunity to implement a greater number of research-oriented and activity-intense projects to motivate and involve your students. Activities that are particularly suited to use within the block-scheduling framework are identified throughout this chapter by the following designation:

Teaching Strategies have been coded for varying learning styles and abilities.

L1 **BASIC** activities for all students

L2 **AVERAGE** activities for average to above-average students

L3 **CHALLENGING** activities for above-average students

ELL **English Language Learner** activities

Chapter 2 Resource Manager

The following materials may be used when teaching the chapter. Materials for specific lessons are also shown at point-of-use in the margins of the Teacher's Wraparound Edition.

TEACHING TRANSPARENCIES

Chapter 2 Teaching Transparency

Graphic Organizer Transparency 2-1

Graphic Organizer Transparency 2-2

APPLICATION ACTIVITIES

Chapter 2, Section 1

Chapter 2, Section 2

Chapter 2, Cumulative

REINFORCEMENT AND REVIEW ACTIVITIES

Vocabulary Activity 2

Guided Reading Activity Workbook 2-1, 2-2

Reteaching Activities 2-1, 2-2

Chapter 2 Resource Manager

ASSESSMENT AND EVALUATION

Section Quizzes 2-1, 2-2

Chapter 2 Test, Forms A & B

Performance Assessment Activity 2

ENRICHMENT AND EXTENSION

Technology Application Activity 2

Enrichment Activities 2-1, 2-2

SPANISH RESOURCES

- Spanish Chapter and Unit Tests
- Spanish Vocabulary Activities
- Spanish Section Quizzes
- Spanish Reteaching Activities
- Spanish Enrichment Activities

MULTIMEDIA

- Interactive Tutor Self-Assessment
- ExamView® Pro Testmaker
- PuzzleMaker
- Communication in Action Videodisc and Videocassette
- MindJogger
- Interactive Lesson Planner
- Presentation Plus!
- Writer's Assistant
- Glencoe Interactive Grammar
- **communicationapplications.glencoe.com**

ORAL PRESENTATION ACTIVITIES

Activities 19, 20

TEACHER PLANNING AND SUPPORT

- Reproducible Lesson Plans
- Interactive Lesson Planner
- Presentation Plus!

CHAPTER 2

Exploring the Communication Process

WHY IT'S IMPORTANT

Communication is a powerful tool that we use to meet our needs, accomplish goals, and get results. Communication is the key to success in many professional and social contexts.

To better understand how important the communication process is in your social and professional lives, view the **Communication in Action** Chapter 2 video lesson.

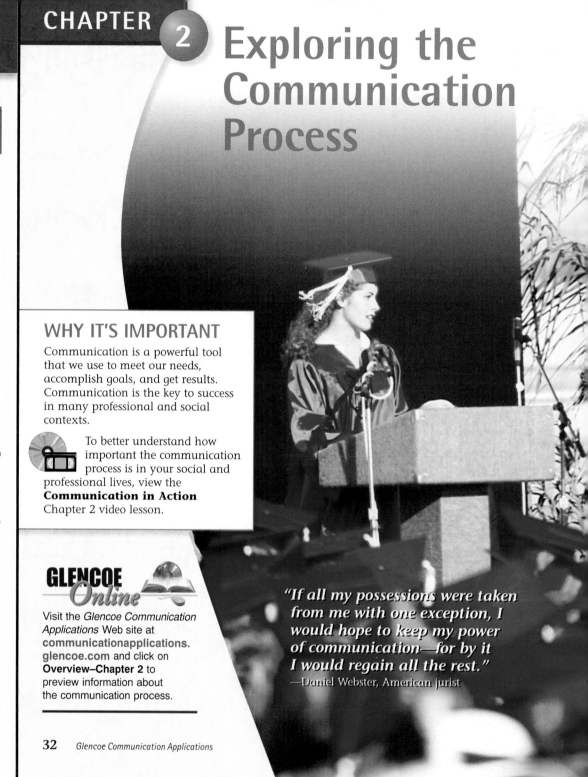

"If all my possessions were taken from me with one exception, I would hope to keep my power of communication—for by it I would regain all the rest."
—Daniel Webster, American jurist

WHY IT'S IMPORTANT

Have students read the quotation and discuss ways in which communication can help them meet needs, accomplish goals, and get results. Ask: **Why is it important to develop effective communication skills?** *(Answers may include to be sure you are making your point effectively, establishing positive relationships, and creating the impression you want in professional and social situations.)*

The Nature of the Communication Process

GUIDE TO READING

Objectives
1. Explain the five principles of communication.
2. Identify the components of the communication process.
3. Identify the basic functions of the components of the communication process.
4. Analyze the processes used by sender-receivers and receiver-senders.

Terms to Learn
transactional	feedback
sender-receiver	data
receiver-sender	sensory perception
message	encoding
channel	transmitting
noise	acquiring
barrier	decoding

What do playing baseball and communicating have in common? Both are a series of actions that work together to produce a result. In other words, they are both processes.

Think about baseball. There are separate processes for each action, such as pitching, batting, or fielding. All of these elements work together in a process that results in a game. Communication also has separate processes. All of the elements of communication work together in a process that results in people creating and exchanging meaning.

THE COMMUNICATION PROCESS

When you understand the processes involved in communicating, you have some powerful tools under your control. These tools can help you make appropriate communication choices for the results you want to achieve. They will also help you to develop the knowledge, attitude, and skills to become a competent communicator.

Baseball players must work through all of the separate processes of baseball in order to play the game. What is the result of the process of communication?

Exploring the Communication Process **33**

---

1 FOCUS

Bellringer
Read the introductory paragraph aloud with students. Ask students to list series of actions in baseball and explain how they are interwoven. What happens if any one of these actions is eliminated? *(Answers may include that the game cannot proceed or that play stops.)* Point out that for communication to be complete, none of the series of steps in the process can be left out.

You may use Graphic Organizer Transparency 2–1 to introduce this section.

Graphic Organizer Transparency 2–1

COMPONENT	DEFINITION	FUNCTION	EXAMPLE
Context	people, occasion, and task in communication	3	student and teacher discussing a homework assignment
Physical Environment			
Climate			
Communicator			
Message			
Channel			
Noise			
Barrier			
Feedback			

Grammar Tip

The *-ing* form of a verb may function as another part of speech. An *-ing* form that acts as a noun is called a *gerund*. If it acts as an adjective or is part of a verb phrase, it is called a *participle*. The second sentence of the section's opening paragraph contains three gerunds *(pitching, batting, fielding)*; the final sentence contains two participles *(creating, exchanging)*.

Visual Instruction

Answer Student responses may include that the result of communication processes is being able to create and exchange ideas with others.

RESOURCE MANAGER

Teaching Tools
- Interactive Lesson Planner
- Reproducible Lesson Plan 2–1
- Application Activities 2–1

Reproducible Masters
- Guided Reading Activity Workbook 2–1
- Enrichment Activity 2–1
- Reteaching Activity 2–1
- Section Quiz 2–1
- Transparency Strategies and Activities Booklet 2–1

Transparencies
- Graphic Organizer Transparency 2–1
- Chapter 2 Teaching Transparency

Technology Resources
- Interactive Tutor Self-Assessment Software
- Presentation Plus! Software
- ExamView® Pro Testmaker
- PuzzleMaker Software
- **communicationapplications.glencoe.com**

2 TEACH

The Flow of Action, Energy, and Results in the Communication Process

Ask students to explain why this process is considered to be circular. *(Students may say that a person sends out a message and waits for feedback to return to see if it has been understood.)* Why does it have continuity? *(Students may suggest that the process always occurs in the same sequence.)* Invite pairs of students to model conversations and have classmates point out where action, energy, and results occur. Also have them explain how the communication is circular and the process has continuity.
L2

Guided Reading Activity 2–1

Name _____ Date _____ Class _____ | GUIDED READING Activity 2-1

EXPLORING THE COMMUNICATION PROCESS
The Nature of the Communication Process

As you read Section 1, answer the following items.

1. List the three elements that define communication. _____
2. Name the five basic principles, or understandings, of what communication is. _____
3. List the seven reasons that explain why communication is complex. _____
4. What are the components of the communication process? _____
5. A positive physical environment can be described as what? _____
6. Explain the difference between a sender-receiver and a receiver-sender. _____
7. What is the function of a message, and what are the three kinds of messages? _____
8. Give at least four examples of a channel of communication. _____
9. Name the two forms of noise and explain how they differ. _____
10. List four barriers to communication. _____
11. Cite the three basic functions that feedback plays in the communication process. _____
12. What are the three processes used by sender-receivers? _____
13. Receiver-senders also go through three processes. List these. _____

Elements of Communication

In Chapter 1, communication is described as the process of human beings creating and exchanging meaning through symbolic interaction. You can break this definition down to further reveal that communication has three distinct elements: process, meaning, and symbols.

Communication as a Process As shown in Figure 2–1, communication is an interactive process—the parts and actions work together to achieve results. As individuals talk with one another, listen to one another, and use nonverbal behaviors to communicate their meanings and feelings, they are interacting. Energy and meaning are being exchanged between participants in the process.

Because it is a process, communication constantly moves, shifts, and changes; it does not stand still. The communication process is made up of individual components, and these components occur in a specific sequence: action, energy, and results. The components and actions involved in communication change from one situation to another, but the circular nature of communication and continuity of the process remain the same.

Just as any process involves energy, the communication process uses the mental and physical energy of people who speak, listen, use nonverbal behaviors, and interpret the verbal and nonverbal behaviors of others. As a result, communicators seek to use their energy wisely, as in building productive relationships and solving problems in groups.

Meaning in Communication

Meaning is an important part of the definition of communication. It includes the thoughts, ideas, and understandings that are created, exchanged, and shared by communicators. We

■ Figure 2–1 **Parts and Actions of a Process**

Components

Action

Process

Results

Energy

Sequence

constantly create meanings as our brains try to make sense of the world around us. We, as communicators, also seek to share those meanings and understandings with others. Each time we communicate with another person, we create new meanings and understandings.

For example, imagine that you are confused by an assignment for a history class. You decide to talk to your teacher. As a result of the conversation, both of you gain new understandings or new meanings. Later you discuss the project with another classmate. You communicate with one another to interpret information, talk about issues, solve problems, and make plans. Through the give-and-take of your interactions you develop still more understandings and ideas. In this way, exchanging and creating new meanings may result in a better project.

Symbols in Communication A symbol stands for an idea or a feeling. For example, a trophy is a symbol for a team's victory. We cannot communicate meanings and feelings by reading each other's minds. Symbolic interaction means that we rely on words (written and oral) and nonverbal behaviors such as gestures, eye contact, and facial expressions to communicate meanings and feelings.

34 *Glencoe Communication Applications*

ENGLISH LANGUAGE LEARNERS

MEETING INDIVIDUAL NEEDS

Aiding the Communication Process Students who are learning English have special barriers to overcome in communicating with English speakers. The words used to transmit messages are hard to decode if one does not know the language well. Adaptations of the way a message is delivered and specialized use of nonverbal cues help learners extract meaning from communication.
Activity Ask students to describe nonverbal cues they use to help them get meaning from communication. List several specific examples of communication (such as understanding directions or answering a question) on the board and have volunteers role-play them. Freeze frame the action to ask students to explain what message is being attempted, what is preventing the receiver from understanding it, and what would help the receiver get meaning from it. **ELL**

PRINCIPLES OF COMMUNICATION

As a communicator, it is important to understand what communication is before you can understand how to apply it to your life. To help you understand, consider the five basic principles, or understandings, of communication that are given below:

- transactional
- complex
- unavoidable
- continuous
- learned

Communication Is Transactional

Communication is a transactional process. A transactional process is one that involves an exchange. Communicators exchange messages, sending and receiving them at the same time. Each communicator is both a sender and a receiver of messages, often juggling several different messages at the same time.

In communication, participants also perform other transactions. They bargain and negotiate with one another to create and exchange meanings. Communicators involved in a conversation may be bargaining for acceptance as persons, for understanding of a particular behavior or action, for attention, or to persuade a listener to accept a particular point of view.

Another transactional characteristic of the action of communication is that all components and processes are interactive. In other words, each part and each action affect the others.

Communication Is Complex

Communication consists of a number of components and a series of interrelated processes. As shown in the chart below, communication is complex.

COMMUNICATION IS COMPLEX BECAUSE IT IS . . .

Interactive	Communication involves a series of complicated and interrelated processes. Each of these processes affects each of the others and becomes interactive as we communicate.
Symbolic	Meaning is communicated through the use of symbols. Because these symbols stand for meaning, they are always open to interpretation.
Personal and Cultural	Because words and gestures are symbols for meaning and feeling, they are very personal. A person's culture can also add a new or different meaning to a phrase or gesture.
Irreversible	Once you have sent a message, you cannot take it back. It is forever. You can only send additional messages to try to correct any mistakes or misunderstandings that may have been communicated along with your original message.
Impossible to Duplicate	Each interaction between a sender and a receiver is unique and happens only once in exactly the same way. The conditions of the communication will never again be exactly the same.
Circular	Communication involves original messages and feedback to those messages. Feedback is necessary to confirm that communication has occurred.
Purposeful	There is always a reason behind an intentional message. It has a stimulus and a purpose. Communication helps us meet needs such as the need to secure food and shelter, get and give information, belong, and be respected and valued as a person.

Exploring the Communication Process **35**

Principles of Communication

Use the chart on this page to recap the concepts introduced on pages 33–36. Have students cover the explanations with a sheet of paper and comment on how each trait in the first column applies to communication. As they uncover each explanation, ask a volunteer to read it aloud. **L1**

Communication Tip

Explain that transactions occurring during the communication process are reciprocal. Each party influences the other. This means that receivers as well as senders have an impact. As frequent listeners, students should recognize that they have this transactional power and learn to use it.

BUSINESS BRIEF

Business leaders agree that their ability to communicate effectively and create solid relationships is at the heart of their success. The ability to influence others with integrity has a profound influence on an organization's image, growth, and prosperity. At the same time, it is estimated that most people communicate at about 15 to 20 percent of their capability. Clearly, most organizations have a great margin for improvement.

EXTENDING THE CONTENT

Animal Talk Oral speech communication is a uniquely human activity. Philosopher Mortimer Adler observed that "there is communication among brute animals in a wide variety of ways, but no conversation." Being able to speak effectively is essential for full participation in our society, and this is a learned skill. People are born able to make noises, but they must learn speech through interaction with others.

Activity Ask students to work in pairs to investigate how an animal of their choice communicates with members of its species or with other species. Suggest that students identify the means of communication and the types of messages sent. They can extend the activity further by contrasting the animals' simple communication with the more sophisticated communication of humans.

Communicating by Refusing to Communicate

Students may doubt that this is a valid form of communication. Have a volunteer describe a scenario in which two people who are face-to-face attempt to avoid communicating. Ask the class to brainstorm a list of messages that were communicated in each instance. How does this activity enlarge their ideas about the symbols used to communicate? **L2**

Components of the Communication Process

Use the table on page 37 to summarize the pieces of the communication puzzle. Ask students to jot down questions the table brings to mind and read the next ten pages to find answers to their questions. **L1**

Communication Is Unavoidable

Even though most of us have heard someone say, "We're not communicating," the truth is that it is impossible not to communicate. Even a refusal to communicate is a type of communication.

Think about the last time you were alone on an elevator and then another person got on. You may have felt uncomfortable with a stranger in your personal space. To avoid communication, you might have looked straight ahead, stared at the floor, or casually examined the elevator's floor and ceiling. The stranger may have stood in the farthest corner of the elevator and stared straight ahead at the door. Were you communicating with one another? Believe it or not, the answer is yes. A great deal of energy was exchanged between the two of you even though you did not say a word to each other. You were telling each other "I'm uncomfortable communicating with you." Attempting to avoid communication is communication in itself.

Communication Is Continuous

Communication is ongoing. Once you have had an interaction with an individual, future communication with him or her is forever impacted by your initial communication and your memories of it. Even the business or social activity that was the context for the interaction is affected. For example, your communication with the salesperson at the music store will affect your feelings and behavior toward him or her, possibly the store, and perhaps even salespeople in general. Communication continues to influence future interactions and shape our relationships.

Skillful Communication Can Be Learned

Communication skills are mainly learned behaviors. Although you were taught how to read and write, you likely learned to speak and listen in your native language much more indirectly: by observing and mimicking the verbal and nonverbal behaviors of the people around you.

Fortunately, it is possible to improve your communication skills. No matter how effective you may believe them to be, listening, speaking, reading, and writing skills are all improved through practice.

COMPONENTS OF THE COMMUNICATION PROCESS

Communication has a specific set of interactive components. Each has a unique function in the process and affects the communication that takes place. The components of the communication process and their functions are shown in the chart on page 39.

Context

In Chapter 1, you learned that context includes people who are playing specific roles. It also includes the occasion and the task. The function of context in communication is found in that definition. It includes the place and time when the communication occurs and the relationship between the communicators. Context helps us make appropriate communication choices in a given situation. For example, it may not be considered appropriate for a student to get up and walk around during a class lecture. However, it is perfectly acceptable to do so while you are watching television at home.

MULTIPLE LEARNING STYLES

Linguistic How do oral and written communication processes differ? Both use words to send messages but require a somewhat different set of skills and qualities to be effective. Speakers use more familiar language, shorter and simpler sentences, and repeat key ideas more often. Speakers also tend to use more transitional words and adapt their language to the audience with more flexibility than writers.

Activity Assign topics to students in pairs, without having them discuss their assignments. One partner is to prepare a spoken response and the other a written one. Have students compare the results of each pair of responses, point out differences, and suggest reasons for the differences.

COMPONENTS OF THE COMMUNICATION PROCESS AND THEIR BASIC FUNCTIONS

Component	Basic Functions
Context	Provides the people, the occasion, and the task
Physical Environment	Influences the quality of interaction within the physical space
Climate	Influences the emotional, attitudinal, and intellectual tone of the communication
Communicator	Creates meaning, sends and receives messages, and exchanges meaning
Message	Conveys meaning, feeling, and various kinds of energy from sender-receiver to receiver-sender
Channel	Provides the space through which the message must pass; determines the method used to send the message
Noise	Interferes with or disrupts communication
Barrier	Blocks communication
Feedback	• Assures the sender-receiver that communication has occurred • Allows the receiver-sender to adjust or modify a message • Provides insight into the sender-receiver's communication

Physical Environment

The second component in the communication process is physical environment. The physical environment in communication functions to provide the surroundings or the space in which communication takes place. The physical environment affects the quality of interaction. A positive environment leads to better communication. Likewise, a negative environment can lead to communication problems. For example, think about how you feel and behave when your classroom is either too hot or too cold. The temperature of the room may become a distraction that affects your communication. If you are too hot, you may become irritable or sleepy. If you are too cold, you may become withdrawn, devoting all your energy to trying to stay warm.

Just as teachers understand the effects of physical environment on their students, business people recognize that environment can affect productivity. They understand that most people work best in environments that are safe, comfortable, clean, well lit, orderly, and cheerful.

Climate

A third component of the communication process is climate. You may ask what the function of climate is in communication. It is the emotional atmosphere—the tone in which interaction takes place. Emotions and attitudes create the climate. Also, the content of the communication and the history of the participants affect climate.

Negative Climate For example, upon entering a room full of people, you may sense an overall feeling of tension. The communicators' tones, facial expressions, and gestures may shout "We're stressed out!" whether the conversation communicates stress or not. In this case, the emotions and attitudes of the communicators are overriding the intellectual content of the conversation.

Exploring the Communication Process **37**

Influencing Environment and Climate of Communications

Over the next day, ask students to note differences in the way their various classrooms are set up. Have them point out which set-ups encourage listening and which enhance discussion and cooperative work. Guide students to explain how the arrangements encourage different styles of communication. Then, have students think of a person they know who is capable of creating a positive, warm climate of interaction. Have students list specific traits and behaviors of the person that affect his or her ability to create that climate. **L2**

INCLUSION STRATEGIES

Less-Proficient Readers Students who struggle with reading material need strategies for reading and for checking their comprehension. Help students establish a plan for reading longer sections such as the one on pages 36–47.

Activity Use the table on this page to preview the section. To establish a purpose for reading, have students treat each subheading in the section as a vocabulary term to be defined. They can then read each subsection to learn the role this component plays in communicating. Encourage students to generate symbols that could represent each component and help them remember its role. For example, a heart inside a sun shape could represent climate.

GLOBAL COMMUNICATION

Communication Climate

(Answers may include that an American might feel that the climate of the meeting was too restrictive while someone from Japan might feel that it was cooperative and productive.) **L1**

Ask students to observe interactions among their friends and note differences in conversation style and the way it affects communication climate. Students may note how their friends' use of tone, gesture, posture, and word choice affects their feelings about a communication.

This classroom is set up to encourage various types of student and teacher interaction. What kind of classroom arrangement might be set up for small group interaction?

Positive Climate Even just one or two people can affect the climate of an entire room. They can charge the climate with stress and tension, or they can provide a calming, soothing climate. Have you ever walked into a room where you sensed an overall relaxed feeling? People were smiling. The discussion was interesting and interactive. The climate in that room could be described as warm (emotions), positive (attitudes), and interesting (intellectual content).

Environment and Climate Architects often study the relationship between communication and climate when designing the spaces in which people live, learn, and work. A successful design considers the kind of interaction that is intended to take place within a particular environment. This, in

GLOBAL COMMUNICATION

Communication Climate

Americans are sometimes considered to be individualistic. This may become evident in meetings when individuals express their personal opinions openly and directly. In some cultures, such as Chinese, Korean, or Japanese, group goals and decisions often are valued more than individual efforts. The emphasis there is more on the group in workplace communication. Keeping this in mind, why might Americans and Japanese describe the climate of the same meeting differently?

MULTIPLE LEARNING STYLES

Visual-Spatial Recall of information and concepts is improved when they are presented in multiple modes. Students who learn best through visuals can benefit by manipulating spatial representations of ideas in the chapter.

Activity Provide magazines for students to scan. Have them locate and cut out photographs of spaces with different types of furniture arrangements. For each arrangement they clip, have students write a caption describing the communication climate it helps establish. Invite students to explain how specific climates encourage different moods and types of communication.

turn, helps create a desirable climate. For instance, teachers create an environment and influence the climate of a classroom when they design seating arrangements. For lectures, a teacher wants students to pay attention. He or she also will want to limit interaction between students. Therefore, students' desks or chairs may be arranged in rows facing the teacher. To invite a climate of active participation and discussion, the teacher may arrange chairs in small circles or seat students around tables so they can work together.

Communicator

The people involved in an interaction make up the fourth component in the communication process. The basic function of communicators is to create and exchange meaning. Because communicators send and receive messages at the same time, they are both sender-receivers and receiver-senders.

Sender-Receiver The sender-receiver is the person who sends a message to someone. At the same time the message is being sent, the sender-receiver is receiving and processing feedback from the receiver-sender.

Imagine that you have applied for a summer job at a local business. You approach the receptionist, give your name, and state that you have an appointment with the manager. Because you are the person beginning the give-and-take of the interaction, you assume the role of sender-receiver. As you send your message by speaking, you also are noting the receptionist's smile and listening to the suggestion that you sit in a nearby chair to wait for the manager. You have sent and received messages at the same time.

Receiver-Sender The receiver-sender is the person who receives, or believes he or she has received, a message. Like the sender-receiver, a receiver-sender obtains and provides feedback at the same time. The receptionist in this example is the receiver-sender. This person watches as

■ **Climate and physical environment affect the communication that takes place in a meeting.** How does the seating arrangement in the photograph encourage the audience to pay attention to the speaker?

Exploring the Communication Process **39**

The People Who Communicate (Sender-Receiver)

Ask the class to direct you in diagramming and numbering the stages in a communication between two people. Have them explain why the person who begins the process is called a sender-receiver, while the one who receives the message is called a receiver-sender. **L2**

■ **Visual Instruction**

Answer Students may respond that because the audience is facing the speaker, members of the audience are more likely to pay attention.

COOPERATIVE LEARNING ACTIVITY

By role-playing real-life situations, students can show how differing contexts and relationships among communicators transform a discussion of the same subject. Divide the class into groups of four or five. Have students write on 3" x 5" cards brief scenarios that include a topic of conversation as well as the *who, what, when, where,* and *why* of the communication. Each group draws a card and builds a skit based on its context. Audience members then suggest changes to the environment and the roles involved, and the group revises the skit appropriately. For example, a card might place four friends together at a restaurant after school making plans to attend a homecoming dance. If the scenario becomes a teen talking to parents in the living room about the same subject, communication changes. 🎁

Figure 2–2 Communication Process with Sender-Receiver and Receiver-Sender Added

Ask students to explain the two communicator roles, using the diagram in Figure 2–2. Have volunteers answer the following questions: Who initiates communication? *(sender-receiver)* Where do the individuals interact? *(At the point where messages are received and feedback sent.)* What role does feedback play in the communication process? *(It allows sender-receiver to assess success and adapt message.)*

The Communication Process—Context, Climate, Environment

Use Figure 2–2 to review the meaning of context, environment, and climate in terms of the communication process. Describe three specific scenarios: a telemarketing call, an introduction, and a lunch meeting of friends. Have volunteers describe the context, environment, and climate of each scenario. **L1**

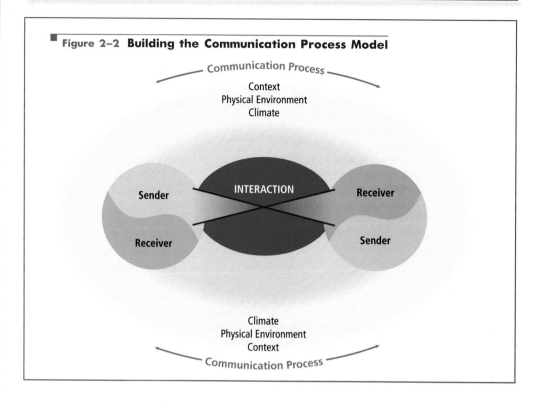

Figure 2–2 Building the Communication Process Model

Communication Process

Context
Physical Environment
Climate

Sender   INTERACTION   Receiver

Receiver   Sender

Climate
Physical Environment
Context

Communication Process

---

you—the sender-receiver—approach and listens to your explanation. The receptionist's feedback indicates that your message has been received. By smiling and initiating a new message, "If you'll wait over there for a moment, I'll try to find the manager," the receptionist has exchanged roles with you to become the sender-receiver. This person may make a mental note of your confident manner and think, "The manager probably will like this applicant." The receptionist also is receiving and sending messages at the same time.

You can see in **Figure 2–2** that communication requires lots of interaction—all at the same time—between communicators. In addition, the roles of these communicators change continually from sender-receiver to receiver-sender.

40   *Glencoe Communication Applications*

Message

Message probably is the most difficult component of the communication process to define. You might think that messages usually are clear and easy to understand. You also may assume that if a receiver-sender can hear your message, he or she can understand it. Finally, it is easy to believe that feedback is a sign that your message has been heard and understood.

Defining Message Interestingly, all of these assumptions can be false. A message is the information that is exchanged between communicators. What is the function of a message? Its purpose is to convey meanings and feelings between senders and receivers.

MEETING INDIVIDUAL NEEDS

INCLUSION STRATEGIES

Less-Proficient Readers Less-proficient readers may have difficulty remembering the content of what they have read. A systematic approach that requires them to monitor their comprehension as they read will help them increase their recall.

Activity Have students create an outline of each chapter section by using major and minor headings. They should leave a blank line after each item. As they read, students can review the paragraphs in that segment and note the most important idea.

Interpreting a Message Every message is open to interpretation—or misinterpretation. Just because someone sends a message doesn't mean that the exact message was understood by the receiver. In fact, messages can be misunderstood, or they might not be received at all. The Amelia Bedelia stories, by Peggy Parish, illustrate how messages can be misinterpreted. In the series, Amelia constantly misinterprets messages; for example, when asked to "dress," or stuff the turkey, she puts clothes on it.

Receiving a Message Receiver-senders at work also do not always receive a message as it was intended. Studies on the differences between male and female managers have uncovered differences in how men and women communicate, and these differences affect how messages are received by their staffs. For example, imagine that your manager says to you, "Would you do me a favor and back me up at tomorrow's meeting?" How might you, as the receiver-sender, interpret this request? Is the message a request you can refuse?

Does "back me up" mean take your boss's place? Be prepared to explain all the research behind your department's request for more technology funds? Or, does it mean that, if you're free, you should show up and sit quietly during the meeting?

Female managers tend to soften work-related directions with words like "do me a favor," "if you could," and "would you mind," while male managers, according to studies, are more direct in phrasing their requirements. Nevertheless, if messages are unclear to the receiver, misinterpretation and misunderstandings are bound to occur. Understanding more about messages can help you make your meanings clear.

■ **The receptionist and applicant are communicating; therefore, they are sending and receiving messages.** What is the function of message in the communication process?

Receiver–Sender   Sender–Receiver

Receiver–Sender   Sender–Receiver

Sender–Receiver   Receiver–Sender

Sender–Receiver   Receiver–Sender

Exploring the Communication Process **41**

Message
Explain that a message can be divided into three parts: (1) the ideas and feelings the sender-receiver wishes to communicate, (2) the symbols that express that meaning, accomplished by encoding, and (3) the form or organization of those symbols, for example, the syntax, grammar, and logical plan of a speech. Invite students to suggest strategies that help a receiver-sender get the message that is intended. What problems can arise to prevent the intended message from being received? *(Students may suggest cultural and gender differences, poor choices of symbols and forms, poor listening skills, and prejudices.)*

■ **Visual Instruction**

Answer The function of a message is to convey feelings and meanings between sender and receiver.

REAL-WORLD CONNECTION

Misinterpretation Receivers can interpret or receive messages in a way that differs from what the sender intended. The misunderstanding of a message could lead to conflict or the failure to respond properly. To avoid such results, the receiver could clarify the message by asking questions. **Activity** Have students ask a businessperson about communications that have been misinterpreted at the place of business. They should try to find out what the original message was, how it was interpreted, and what the results of the misinterpretation were. Students should record the information given and suggest ways the misinterpretation could have been avoided.

Figure 2–3 Communication Process Diagram with Message Components and Intention Added

Have students identify the new elements added to the diagram of the communication process. *(message content, feeling, relationships, and intent)*

Language Tip

Clear expression, logical organization, and accurate use of grammar and syntax are important to communicating the intended message to readers. Errors in spelling, punctuation, grammar, and logic may prevent a reader from understanding your meaning. They may also send a negative message about attitude and thought processes that speaks louder than your content or ideas. For example, a messy and error-filled essay for a college application sends the message that the writer is careless, lazy, and unable to think clearly.

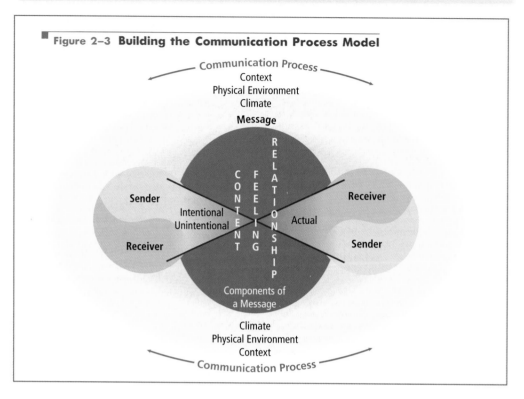

■ Figure 2–3 **Building the Communication Process Model**

Classifying a Message Messages can be classified by both the intentions of the person who sends the message and the interpretation of the person who receives it. There are three kinds of messages: intentional, unintentional, and actual. Notice how these have been added to the model in **Figure 2–3** above.

Intentional Message An intentional message is made up of the meanings and feelings one person wishes to send to another. When you open a conversation, you usually have a message you intend to send. You might say, "May I borrow your pencil?" "I'm here to apply for a job," or "Sorry I'm late for class."

Most of the time, you probably assume that your meaning is clear, whether or not it is. For example, when you ask "May I borrow your pencil?" your question appears to be a clearly worded message conveying your intent: You need a pencil. Typically, senders use their best language skills to send intentional messages that express specific meanings and feelings.

Unintentional Message An unintentional message is one that the sender-receiver either does not mean to send or is unaware of sending. An unintentional message can lead to communication problems if it contradicts or clouds a receiver-sender's interpretation of an intended message.

Unintentional messages can be tricky. In fact, the sender-receiver may be completely unaware of some meaning the receiver-sender has assigned to an intended message. For example, "May I borrow your pencil?" may unintentionally send the message as "I'm

INTERDISCIPLINARY CONNECTION

History In the Crimean War (1853–1856) allied forces of Europe fought Russian troops in what is now Ukraine. At the Battle of Balaklava, a brigade of British troops on horseback made a suicidal charge on entrenched Russian artillery; nearly half were killed. The tragedy occurred because of a misinterpretation of a message. The commander in chief specified that the cavalry should "advance rapidly to the front and try to prevent the enemy from carrying away the guns." He wanted the troops to proceed to Turkish posts the Russians had captured, but the messenger thought he meant they should attack the entrenched artillery.

Activity Have students research their history books, library books, encyclopedias, and the Internet to locate other examples of misinterpreted messages that have changed the course of history.

careless and can't keep track of my things" or "I'm never prepared for class." The receiver-sender may perceive you as making a habit of borrowing pencils in class.

Intentions stated in words may be contradicted altogether by your choice of language. For instance, you might not be aware of using poor grammar or of overusing some slang term. The same effect can be caused by nonverbal behaviors of which you are not even aware. Avoiding eye contact may send an unintended message that you are uninterested or have something to hide.

However, all these behaviors may unintentionally change the meaning of your intended message. Individuals constantly send unintentional messages that can cloud the meanings and feelings they intend to convey.

Actual Message An actual message is the message the receiver-sender receives. It is what he or she thinks the speaker is actually saying. What happens if the sender's intended message and the receiver's actual message differ? Misunderstandings occur when the meaning a receiver assigns to a sender's message does not relate to the meaning the sender attempted to convey.

Components of a Message Regardless of whether a message is intentional or unintentional, it is made up of three specific components: the content of the message, the communicators' feelings, and the relationship between the communicators.

Content When two or more people communicate, the main purpose of the interaction is to exchange information. At home, you may tell your parents what time you'll be home from practice. At school, your teacher may give you a formula to solve math problems. At work, you and your coworkers may discuss how to improve customer service to build up your client base. In all these examples, specific content, or information, is communicated between the sender-receivers and the receiver-senders.

Feeling When you talk, you not only send messages about what you are thinking but also how you feel about the topic. In addition, you convey how you feel about the situation in which you are involved. Sometimes, you may express your feelings in other ways besides simply stating them. For instance, you might not always state "I'm terribly bored with this meeting" or "I really enjoy your company." Instead, you may convey these messages through your attitudes or actions.

Relationship Another aspect of a message involves an equally important component: relationship. The relationship that exists between the communicators—from how much they like each other to the roles they

This student is saying one thing in words while communicating something entirely different through his body language. **What communication problems result from unintentional messages?**

Exploring the Communication Process **43**

Choosing Channels

Help students visualize the concept of channel by comparing the message to water and the channel to the way the water is moved. Channel is, in fact, both the route and the transportation by which the message travels. Invite students to list a number of different channels on the board. Then, have the class brainstorm examples of communications that commonly use those channels. For example, food advertisers may use television, radio, newspapers, placards on shopping carts, point-of-display ads, and coupons to stimulate sales. **L1**

■ Visual Instruction

Answer Channels of communication include face-to-face conversation, e-mail, letter, intercom, video, and radio.

---

play—affects the message. For example, you might speak casually with a friend about a pair of gym shoes you want to buy. However, the same conversation with a shoe store clerk might be more business-like. Relationship, therefore, is an important factor in both sending and receiving messages. At work, a suggestion from a well-liked coworker probably will be received more positively than a suggestion from a coworker you dislike or do not trust. Whether you are the sender-receiver or the receiver-sender, you can't always know for sure how the other person interprets your message. Because of these variables, messages can be misunderstood.

Channel

So far, you have learned that the context, physical environment, climate, communicator, and message all are components of the communication process. Another important component is the channel. Channel is the space in which the message is transmitted. In one sense channel is the method, or medium, by which the sender conveys the message. Examples of a channel of communication include face-to-face dialogue, a phone call, an e-mail, or a letter. Even voice-mail or answering-machine messages are channels. The basic function of the channel is to provide the means of transmitting a message.

Choosing the channel or medium of communication appropriate to the context is an important decision in professional and social situations. If you wish to communicate news of an upcoming sale to your preferred customers, you might want to consider making personal telephone calls or sending personal notes to these special customers. If you have less time to devote to the project, you might choose a less personal method such as a flyer. Each method conveys a different perception of the relationship between you and your customer. Different channels may yield different results.

Noise

Another component of the communication process is noise. Noise is anything that interferes with a message and is usually temporary. Noise has a negative function in communication. Both internal noise and external noise can be sources of communication difficulty.

Internal Noise Sometimes, communicators create their own noise. Interference that originates from and resides within a communicator is known as internal noise. For example, if you are sleepy, cold, or ill, you may find it difficult to concentrate on messages from others. Anger, preoccupation, and moodiness are other examples of internal noise. Internal noise—whether physical or emotional—can disrupt communication.

■ **The telephone represents a channel of communication.**
What are other channels of communication?

MULTIPLE LEARNING STYLES

Logical-Mathematical Students who apply reasoning skills to learn new concepts will enjoy analyzing the channels used to market specific products.

Activity Have students select a popular product and locate various channels used to advertise it. Ask students to collect data about the content, style, and components of ads in various channels. They can then design a table to organize their data comparatively. Finally, have students write an analysis of their findings. Why did the marketer choose these channels? How did the marketer make maximum use of the chosen channels to communicate?

External Noise External noise is a distraction in the channel or in the physical environment. The smell of rolls baking in the cafeteria may distract you as you try to take notes during class. The constant talking of a coworker may interfere with your ability to do your job efficiently. A speaker's sloppy appearance or unclear speech may create external noise in the communication channel that interferes with listeners' clear reception of the message.

Internal and external noise can exist in any part of the communication process. Trained communicators learn to overcome the obstacles noise presents. They work to develop concentration skills that help them neutralize noise, limit its effects, and improve their ability to focus on the task at hand. The following Communication Strategies can be used when trying to overcome noise.

Barrier

The eighth component of the communication process is barrier. The basic function of barrier is found in its definition. In communication, a barrier is any obstacle that blocks communication. Like noise, barriers can be internal or external. Unlike noise, they tend to be long-term problems.

Internal Barriers An internal barrier is a barrier that originates from or resides within a communicator. Some of the common barriers to communication are ignorance, prejudice, defensiveness, and competitiveness. These conditions may block a communicator's desire to communicate with others. They also can affect a communicator's interpretation of the messages of others.

If you and a coworker were to compete for the same promotion, competitiveness could destroy the trust needed for productive day-to-day communication. This lack of trust could negatively affect your job performance and even destroy the relationship between you and the coworker. This, in turn, could influence whether or not either of you is awarded the job.

Barriers can be extremely destructive in the communication process. They can cause communicators to tune out or seriously misinterpret the messages of others. Because barriers tend to run deep within communicators' thinking processes, they can be difficult to overcome.

COMMUNICATION *Strategies*

OVERCOMING NOISE

- Prepare, if possible, for the communication situation.
- Develop concentration skills.
- Neutralize internal distractions where possible.
- Focus on the task at hand.
- Speak clearly.
- Be aware of the listener's response.

Feedback

Have a volunteer define *feedback*. Point out that feedback must be observable. Ask students to recall one communication they had with another person today. Have them jot down a description of the feedback they gave and received. Suggest that they discuss the message with the person and determine whether their perceptions were accurate. **L2**

■ Visual Instruction

Answer Students might suggest such other external barriers as traffic noise, background music, sounds made by equipment being used in a business or classroom, and construction noise.

■ Airplane passengers sometimes have difficulty hearing messages relayed over the public address system due to external barriers within an airport. **Identify other external barriers to communication.**

External Barriers Like external noise, an external barrier exists in the channel or in other parts of the communication process. Two people who don't speak the same language may experience barriers to their communication. Unclear speech also can pose a barrier. Information mumbled unclearly over an airport's public address system may result in confused passengers who are put in danger of missing their flights.

Different interpretations of nonverbal signals often present barriers to communication. For example, the well-known thumbs-up gesture is open to many different interpretations around the world. In the United States, the gesture conveys a message of strong approval, such as "Well done," "You're doing great," or "Go for it." However, the same gesture can have very different meanings elsewhere. In Germany, for example, thumbs up means "one." So, you might use the thumbs-up sign

to order one glass of lemonade. However, if you used the same symbol in Japan, you probably would be surprised when your server returned with five full glasses. In Japan, thumbs up means "five." Interestingly, thumbs down seems to be bad news no matter in what country you are. It typically means something is wrong or bad.

Like spoken language, nonverbal language varies from country to country. Paying close attention to their own nonverbal cues can help travelers avoid barriers to communication.

In addition to nonverbal barriers, time and distance also may create barriers. Much of the technology of the twentieth century has been devoted to removing and neutralizing barriers created by time and distance. Telephones, fax machines, computer networks, e-mail, airplanes, subways, and freeways all help to minimize these common communication barriers.

Feedback

The final component of the communication process is feedback. Feedback is one person's observable response to another's message. When you acknowledge a friend's greeting with a smile and a wave, you send nonverbal feedback that says, "Thanks for that warm hello! Hello to you too!" Some feedback is oral, as when the taxi driver acknowledges the street address a rider asks to

46   *Glencoe Communication Applications*

MULTIPLE LEARNING STYLES

Interpersonal Discussion and generation of ideas by students working with their peers both improve comprehension of concepts and stimulate use of communication skills.

Activity Assign students to groups of two or three. Have each group discuss their experiences of competition for high grades in classes. How does competition for high grades affect communication among students? Between students and teachers? What barriers to learning might this competition cause? Invite groups to suggest ways in which classroom learning might be made more cooperative to enhance learning and communication.

be taken to. Finally, no response, too, is feed back. Even without words or gestures, this type of silent feedback is very powerful and can indicate how one person feels about another.

Feedback has three basic functions in the communication process:

- It assures the sender-receiver that communication has occurred.
- It allows the sender-receiver to adjust or modify a message for greater clarity and understanding by the receiver-sender.
- It provides insight into the communicator's message.

Assurance It is unsafe to assume that communication has occurred until there is feedback. If you do not return your friend's greeting, your friend may draw the wrong conclusion about your lack of an obvious response to the message. While it is possible that you saw and heard the greeting and just chose not to respond, your friend cannot even be sure you received the message until he or she receives some kind of feedback.

Adjustment Feedback completes the circular pattern of communication. It allows a sender-receiver to adjust a message when the feedback indicates that there is a lack of understanding by the receiver-sender. The sender-receiver may restate the idea, provide an example, or give a definition.

Insight Feedback from others can give communicators valuable insights into their own communication skills and styles. What kinds of results do you get when you communicate with others? How can you use feedback to adapt and build your verbal, nonverbal, and listening skills? Can feedback help you achieve better relationships or more effective results from your communication interactions? Learning to use feedback to adapt your communication can yield positive results.

Each of the nine components of the communication process has a powerful effect on understanding. By learning more about context, physical environment, climate, communicators, message, channel, noise, barriers, and feedback, you improve your ability to convey precise meanings and achieve results.

COMMUNICATION PRACTICE LAB

Identifying Components of the Communication Process

Follow these steps to identify components of a communication interaction.

Step 1 As a class, make a list of familiar places in your school or community where professional or social activities are carried out on a daily basis. For example, you might list the main office of your school, the local post office, or a local business.

Step 2 If possible, observe a communication interaction in a particular location. If

you cannot observe one, describe a situation that might take place in such a location.

Step 3 Identify each component of the communication process that was evident in the interaction.

Step 4 List the positive and negative effects of each component of the interaction.

Step 5 Present your communication situation to the class. Make sure you also give them your observations.

Exploring the Communication Process **47**

Using Feedback to Fine-Tune Communication

Have students select a person they will see several times one day and have them involve this person in several communication situations. They should make notes on the person's verbal and nonverbal feedback in each communication. Ask students to analyze the feedback to assess whether the message received was the intended message. If it was not, have them brainstorm other ways of communicating the messages, try again, and see if the results improve. **L1**

COMMUNICATION PRACTICE LAB

Identifying Components of the Communication Process

Have students follow the five steps in the Communication Practice Lab on this page to identify and evaluate the effects of components of the communication process in everyday situations. As a class, create charts listing the components (see page 37) with enough space for the students to write their observations. Reproduce the chart and instruct students to use one form for each communication they analyze. As you discuss students' observations in Step 3, ask them to explain which components are not directly observable. *(climate, internal noise, some barriers such as prejudice)* Have students brainstorm a list of positive behaviors they observed that enhanced the communication process. **L2**

INTERDISCIPLINARY CONNECTION

Language Arts High school students sometimes use flowery language, artificial phrasing, and inflated diction because of the mistaken impression that it shows their sophistication. Overwritten language interferes with effective communication. Explain that the most effective writing derives from saying exactly what you mean, in the most direct way possible, choosing words and figures of speech for their precision of meaning and feeling rather than their poetic sound.

Activity Ask students to locate famous quotations and rewrite them in the inflated language style discussed in the example above. They can read them aloud and have classmates identify and provide the original text of the quote. Write both versions on the board or overhead and have students analyze the differences.

GLENCOE Online

For additional Practice Labs for this section, have students visit the *Glencoe Communication Applications* Web site at **communicationapplications.glencoe.com**. Click on Communication Practice Lab 2–1. **L1**

Figures 2–4 and 2–5 Processes Used by Sender-Receivers and Receiver-Senders

Check comprehension of the section after students read by reproducing the forms from Figures 2–4 and 2–5 on the board, providing only the Sender-Receiver or Receiver-Sender labels. As volunteers complete the form, have them explain the processes in their own words. **L2**

ANALYZING THE ACTION

Picture a Hollywood movie set. The actors, sets, lights, and cameras are all in place. However, one element is still missing. The process of making a movie doesn't start until someone yells "Action!" As with movie making, communication needs action. The different parts of the communication process are all in place. Now it needs the energy of the participants to drive the process and make interaction possible.

At this point, the study of communication shifts to the action of the process. What purposes do each of the components of communication serve in the overall process? How does the function of each part affect the functions of other parts?

Processes Used by Sender-Receivers

In a car's engine, fuel provides the energy. What provides the energy in the communication process? As a sender-receiver, your ideas, feelings, needs, and goals fuel the process. In order to send message about them, you use a sequence of processes. As shown in **Figure 2–4**, sender-receivers use the following three processes:

■ **Figure 2–4 Processes Used by Sender-Receivers**

*inter*NET
A C T I V I T Y

- sensory perception
- encoding
- transmitting

Sensory Perception Think about all the data that your brain processes every day. Data is made up of those things that catch a communicator's attention, such as objects, people, sounds, thoughts, memories, and the messages sent by others. You take in this data through your senses. Sensory perception is the complex physical process of taking in data through the five senses. Seeing, hearing, smelling, tasting, and touching all are important sensory processes. How does a chef know something is burning on the stove? How does he or she know whether a pot of soup needs additional seasoning? The chef relies on the senses of smell and taste to acquire the information used in cooking.

Data by itself has no meaning until a person discovers it and assigns meaning to it.

INCLUSION STRATEGIES

MEETING INDIVIDUAL NEEDS

Special Needs Have students follow your example and summarize the three steps in several sender-receiver messages.

Activity Draw Figure 2–4 on the board. Review the three steps carefully with students and summarize an example sender-receiver message using the steps in the diagram.

Our knowledge of the world around us is driven by a variety of stimuli. Sometimes, a stimulus is external, driven by our senses. Other times, a fleeting memory, a thought, or other internal stimulus moves us to communicate. As the first step in the series of actions, sensory perception motivates the sender-receiver to communicate.

Encoding Once a stimulus from one of the senses is relayed to the brain, the brain immediately begins organizing the data and trying to assign meaning to it. This sorting and filtering process is called encoding. Encoding is the mental process of assigning meaning and language to data.

To encode a message, your brain performs two functions. First, it connects meaning to the data by filtering it through your previous knowledge and experience. Second, it filters the meaning through the brain's language center to assign a word symbol or language to the data.

What happens if there is no knowledge or experience to which your brain can relate the data? What happens if you have no specific word stored in your language memory to assign to the concept? In such instances, your brain will struggle through the encoding process. It will use what information it does have as best as it can to build upon similar or existing connections and relationships it stores away just for occasions like the one just described.

Transmitting Once you have encoded a message, you can transmit, or convey, it to someone else. Transmitting is the physical process of sending verbal and nonverbal messages. After encoding information, sender-receivers transmit it to receiver-senders. Together, verbal and nonverbal communication allow us to express what we mean and what we feel.

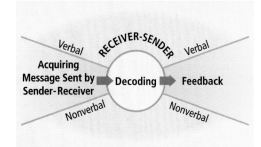

■ **Figure 2–5 Processes Used by Receiver-Senders**

Processes Used by Receiver-Senders

How do receiver-senders fit into the communication process? As shown in **Figure 2–5**, receiver-senders also go through three processes:

- acquiring the message
- decoding the message
- providing feedback to the message

Acquiring the Message The receiver-sender tunes in to the sender's message and acquires it through the senses. Acquiring is the physical process receiver-senders use to take in the sender's message. Acquiring can involve many senses all at once. You may smell the fragrance a friend is wearing, see the friend's smile, and shake hands. You also may hear the friend's voice and the words it conveys. Your senses are bombarded with verbal and nonverbal cues that you acquire at the same time and sort out as the sender's message.

Decoding the Message Once the acquired data is relayed to the receiver's brain, decoding begins. Decoding is the mental process receiver-senders use to create meaning from language. It is the opposite of

Exploring the Communication Process **49**

Sensory Input
Invite students to list some sounds, sights, smells, tastes, and touches that motivate them to initiate a communication in the following situations: being offered freshly baked cookies, standing in a crowded line, cheering in a grandstand, and hearing a joke. **L1**

Encoding
Elicit help from students in making a chart or figure that graphically represents the process of encoding information. Be sure students include the storehouse of memory that helps the brain assign meaning to new situations. **L3**

Acquiring Messages
Does bombarding the senses help or hurt communication? How much sensory input is too much? Invite students to describe examples from their experience. For example, students' study styles and environments vary widely. Have a group of student volunteers try a simple experiment controlling one or more sensory inputs and seeing how this affects the ability to decode. For example, they might see how the attempt to memorize a list given verbally is hampered by various kinds and amounts of noise. **L3**

Figure 2–6
Completed Figure of the Communication Process

Review the section using the figure as a transparency on an overhead projector. Ask students to define each term and provide examples. **L2**

3 ASSESS

Assign Section 1 Assessment as a homework or in-class activity.

🔵 Use Interactive *Tutor Self-Assessment Software* to review Section 1.

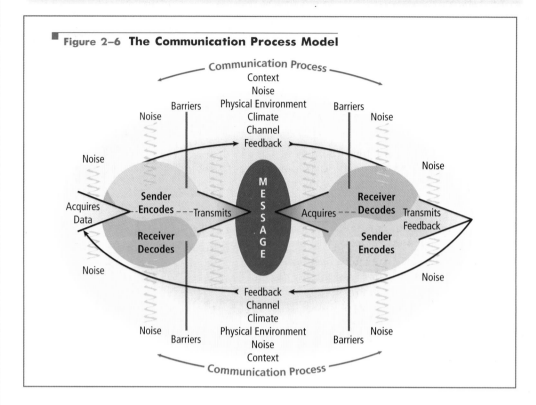

■ **Figure 2–6 The Communication Process Model**

encoding. The decoding process takes symbols such as words and gives them meaning. For example, a receiver hears a speaker's words and observes a variety of nonverbal cues. The receiver's brain goes to work, deciding what those words and other cues mean. The receiver's brain filters this information through its own bank of language skills and life experiences to determine what message the sender is trying to convey.

Providing Feedback When a receiver-sender takes in a sender-receiver's message, he or she responds by providing feedback. As you learned, feedback is the receiver-sender's observable response to what he or she has decoded as the message. Feedback includes both verbal and nonverbal

responses to a message. Even if a receiver-sender does not respond to a message, he or she still sends feedback to the sender-receiver.

By sending feedback to a message, the receiver-sender completes the cycle of action in the communication process. After acquiring the data of the original message, the receiver-sender decodes, or assigns meaning to, the words. He or she then creates feedback by encoding his or her own message and transmitting it to the original sender. This circular process requires sender-receivers and receiver-senders to continually switch roles and to do so, sometimes, at the same time. Together, the sender-receiver and the receiver-sender are jointly responsible for sending and receiving messages, and encoding and decoding meaning in the communication process.

CRITICAL THINKING ACTIVITY

Place students in groups of five. Ask each group to brainstorm ten reasons communication between two people who are face-to-face fails to take place as intended. *(For example, they may speak different languages, the receiver-sender may be distracted by activity or anxiety, the sender-receiver may send an unintended message through body language.)* Next, have groups analyze each reason to pinpoint which part of the communication process it affects; suggest that they refer to the completed communication process model on this page for help. Have groups present their analyses to the class. You may want to reproduce the communication process model on the board and have students add their reasons in the appropriate locations. Ask students to summarize any trends they observe.

How the Process Meets Needs

Once the processes used by sender-receivers and receiver-senders have been added to the model of the communication process, the model is complete, as shown in **Figure 2–6** on page 50. As the model indicates, communication is a complex process that you use to meet your goals and needs in social and professional contexts.

At some point in your day, you probably have used your communication skills to meet your own need to be respected and valued. Communication also helps you address your need to be included, interact with others, and form strong relationships. In addition, it helps you in practical ways when you need to get basic information about day-to-day living. Whether you are trying to make a good impression, win acceptance of an idea, understand others, or get others to understand you, you now have a chance to make the most appropriate and effective communication choices for yourself.

Section 1 Assessment

Visit the *Glencoe Communication Applications* Web site at **communicationapplications. glencoe.com** and click on **Self-Check and Study Guide 2.1** to review your understanding of the communication process.

Review Key Terms

1. Define each term and write it in a sentence: transactional, sender-receiver, receiver-sender, message, channel, noise, barrier, feedback, data, sensory perception, encoding, transmitting, acquiring, decoding.

Check Understanding

2. Define the five principles of communication.

3. What are the nine components of the communication process?

4. Describe the function of channel in the communication process.

5. What are the processes a sender-receiver follows to send a message and a receiver-sender follows once the original message has been sent? Explain each step.

6. **Hypothesize** Give one example of how a communicator's feedback might help you solve problems with a chosen channel of communication.

APPLICATION *Activity*

Creating a Model Think about what you have learned about communication. What does the word *communication* mean to you? Define it in your own words. Create a model of your concept of communication. Share your model with the class. Be prepared to answer questions about your definition and your model. Use feedback from your classmates to make any necessary improvements to your work. Display the completed model in your classroom.

Exploring the Communication Process **51**

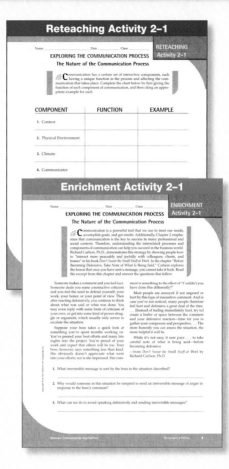

4 CLOSE

Have students reread the opening paragraph of the section on page 33 and their responses to the question. Based on what they have learned in the section, would they now respond differently to the question? What information changed their responses?

Extra-Credit Project

Ask students to investigate and analyze the communication process used by telemarketers to sell products and services. They should provide a written evaluation of the context, environment, climate, message, channel, noise, and barriers that exist in the telemarketing call.

Section 1 Assessment Answers

1. Accept all reasonable sentences.
2. Communication is transactional, complex, unavoidable, continuous, and learned.
3. Context, environment, climate, communicator, message, channel, noise, barrier, feedback
4. provides means of transmitting a message
5. Sender-receiver takes in data via sensory perception, encodes it, and transmits the encoded message verbally or nonverbally to the receiver. The receiver-sender acquires the message via the senses, decodes the information, assigns meaning to it, and provides observable feedback.
6. Accept all reasonable answers.

Application Activity Students should use symbols and labels creatively to create a clear visual representation of the communication process. Have students explain why the symbols are appropriate.

Technology Skill

Using E-Mail

Survey your class to tally the number of students who use e-mail regularly or often. Ask students to interview parents and other adults to find out the most common reasons for using e-mail: personal correspondence, business memos, etc. Invite a computer-literate member of the class to explain the process and give tips for communicating by e-mail. **L1**

Practicing the Skill

1. Survey students to learn the different ISPs used. Follow up the activity by noting differences in the way they provide e-mail service.

2. Model the parts of a generic e-mail format, if possible, on the overhead.

3. Stress the importance of entering the e-mail address exactly. Added spaces and misspellings mean the e-mail cannot be delivered.

4. Remind students that e-mail should be written with the same attention to Standard English as regular mail.

5. Demonstrate how to make corrections to an e-mail.

6. Point out that one cannot add to a message that has been sent. Additional information must be entered again using steps 1–6.

7. You may want to suggest that students ask their correspondent how long it took for them to receive the message.

Application Activity

Encourage students to share the results of their e-mail inquiries. Organize queries and responses by similar interests and have students create a "job-finders' clearinghouse" on a bulletin board.

USING E-MAIL

E-mail is messages or data sent electronically from one computer to another via a network. Some e-mail networks are limited to a single building or group of buildings while others can connect e-mail users anywhere in the world. To send e-mail, you need a computer equipped with a modem and telecommunications software. A modem allows computers to communicate over telephone lines.

Learning the Skill

After accessing a computer's e-mail application, you may either compose a message or select an existing file to send. Then, simply enter the destination's e-mail address and click the *Send* button. The computer sends the message through the modem to a local network server or an Internet Service Provider (ISP) where it is stored in an electronic "mailbox." The recipient is notified that he or she has received a message and can retrieve it at any time.

Practicing the Skill

Use e-mail to share information about an upcoming event at your school.

1. Select the e-mail application on your computer.

2. Choose the command to create a new message and then enter "Upcoming Event" in the Subject line of the header.

3. In the To line of the header, enter the e-mail address of a friend.

4. Write a brief summary of an event at school. Ask your friend to reply with any further information about the event and whether he or she plans to attend.

5. Proofread your message.

6. Select the Send button.

7. Periodically check for your friend's reply. Share your responses as a class.

APPLICATION *Activity*

Create a new e-mail message that lists your name, e-mail address, and the type of job or volunteer work you would like to find. Next, send the list to a friend, asking if he or she knows of any opportunities in that area. Have the friend respond, adding his or her own e-mail address and work interests to the list. Keep forwarding the message to friends and acquaintances until you have created your own job-finder's network.

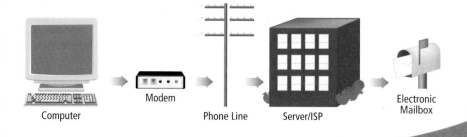

Computer — Modem — Phone Line — Server/ISP — Electronic Mailbox

---

EXTENDING THE CONTENT

E-Mail E-mail is also used to submit applications and forms, communicate with businesses, and contact individuals or organizations whose Web sites you have visited.

Activity Ask students to visit several Web sites related to a hobby or a subject matter that interests them. (To avoid student contact with undesirable sites, you may wish to provide a list of acceptable sites or to screen e-mail addresses if students are using school computers.) After scanning the site, they should note e-mail addresses listed and kinds of mail that the site requests. (Some, for example, request evaluations of the site or updates by viewers.)

Communicating for Success

GUIDE TO READING

Objectives
1. Identify the five levels of communication.
2. List the characteristics of a competent communicator.
3. Analyze the behaviors of a competent communicator.

Terms to Learn
intrapersonal communication
self-talk
interpersonal communication
small-group communication
one-to-group communication
mass communication
mass media

How would you complete the sentence "I spend most of my waking time . . ."? Would you answer that you spend most of your time with your family? Watching television? Going to class? Working at a part-time job?

Research shows that 75 percent of our waking time is spent communicating. Whether it is through oral language, written communication, or nonverbal cues, we are continually sending and receiving messages. For this process to occupy so much of our time, it must be fairly important. What makes communication such a vital part of our lives?

better you will be able to meet your communication goals and respond to those of others with whom you interact. Knowing the characteristics of oral communication will help you organize your own communication goals.

CHARACTERISTICS OF COMMUNICATION

You communicate for a reason, and that reason is to successfully achieve a goal. The stronger your communication skills, whether you are at home, at school, or at work, the

In order to succeed at a part-time job, such as at a garden center, you must develop effective communication skills. How much time during the day do we spend communicating?

Exploring the Communication Process **53**

---

1 FOCUS

Bellringer
Direct students to silently read the opening paragraph of the section and then write their responses to the sentence completion. Invite students to read their responses aloud. List the most common ones on the board and ask students how the activity involves communication.

✍ You may use Graphic Organizer Transparency 2–2 to introduce this section.

Graphic Organizer Transparency 2–2

Level of Communication										
Intrapersonal										
Interpersonal	✔									
Small Group	✔									
One-to-Group	✔									
Mass	✔									

Grammar Tip
A question mark is placed outside the ending quotation mark if the overall sentence in which the quote appears (and not the quoted matter) is a question. If the quoted matter itself is a question, the question mark is inside the quotation marks. The opening paragraph begins with a question that includes a quote that is a statement; the question mark is outside the quote marks.

Visual Instruction
Answer We spend about 75 percent of our waking time communicating.

RESOURCE MANAGER

Teaching Tools
- 📀 Interactive Lesson Planner
- 🗂 Reproducible Lesson Plan 2–2
- 🗂 Application Activities 2–2

Reproducible Masters
- 🗂 Guided Reading Activity Workbook 2–2
- 🗂 Enrichment Activity 2–2
- 🗂 Reteaching Activity 2–2
- 🗂 Section Quiz 2–2
- 🗂 Transparency Strategies and Activities Booklet 2–2

Transparencies
- ✍ Graphic Organizer Transparency 2–2
- ✍ Chapter 2 Teaching Transparency

Technology Resources
- 📀 💾 Interactive Tutor Self-Assessment Software
- 📀 Presentation Plus! Software
- 📀 💾 ExamView® Pro Testmaker
- 📀 PuzzleMaker Software
- 💻 communicationapplications.glencoe.com

2 TEACH

Levels of Communication

Introduce and explain the five levels of communication outlined on pages 54–56 (and summarized in the table on this page): intrapersonal, interpersonal, small group, one-to-group, and mass. Write each in a circle on the board. In smaller circles around the larger ones, write key words and examples you and the class generate. Students might copy this information into their notebooks for future reference. **L1**

Distinguishing *Intra-* and *Inter-*

Help students learn to differentiate between *intrapersonal* and *interpersonal* communication. Ask students to use a dictionary to find the meanings of the prefixes *intra-* ("within") and *inter-* ("between" or "among"). Then, students with limited English and students more proficient in English can work together to list words beginning with each prefix and state the meaning of each. (For example, *intramurals* are games scheduled within one school; *international* describes affairs between two or more nations.) **ELL**

Guided Reading Activity 2-2

FIVE LEVELS OF COMMUNICATION

Level of Communication	Business Example	Social Example
Intrapersonal	Should I tell my manager that her plan has a flaw?	Do I agree with the way this club plans to spend its money?
Interpersonal	Did you go to the meeting?	May I sit here?
Small Group	Who will volunteer to research the personnel needs for this project?	Who will make the signs for the fund-raiser?
One-to-Group	Over the next half hour, I intend to show our sales potential among 15- to 25-year-old consumers.	Remember, everyone needs to bring a dish for next week's potluck dinner.
Mass	The public is invited to attend a free financial workshop this weekend, sponsored by Fidelity Trust Enterprises, Inc.	As the weather gets warmer, remember to provide plenty of fresh water for your pets. For more tips on pet care, contact your local chapter of People for Pets.

Five Levels of Communication

Although many communication skills are important, oral communication skills are essential for success in all types of organizations. Whether you are interacting with your family, with your community, in your school, or at your place of work, communication occurs on five different levels. Each new level builds upon the previous, requiring specific skills in oral communication, nonverbal communication, and listening.

Five Levels of Communication

- intrapersonal
- interpersonal
- small group
- one-to-group
- mass

Intrapersonal Communication

The prefix *intra-* means *within*. Therefore, intrapersonal communication is the communication that occurs in your own mind. This sometimes is known as self-talk. Self-talk is the inner speech or mental conversations that we carry on with ourselves. You use this type of communication to think about something,

reason it out, and decide what it means. You also use it to interpret the world around you as you make choices and interpret messages from others. Your self-talk determines what you like or dislike and what you hold to be important. In this way, it becomes the basis for all your feelings, biases, prejudices, and beliefs.

All communication begins on the intrapersonal communication level. After all, it's what you tell yourself to do before you do it and what to say before you say it. Making wise communication decisions on the intrapersonal level is crucial to successful communication on other levels. You will learn more about intrapersonal communication in Chapter 3.

Interpersonal Communication

The prefix *inter-* means *between* or *among*. Therefore, interpersonal communication is communication between two people. The term interpersonal communication, however, is sometimes used for communication between three or more people in certain informal conversations. It can take the form of small talk, impromptu conversation, or planned conversation begun for a specific purpose.

54 *Glencoe Communication Applications*

COOPERATIVE LEARNING ACTIVITY

Self-Talk Many teenagers are in the habit of using negative self-talk, which leads to and worsens a negative self-image. What is more, negative self-talk prevents a person from realizing his or her real potential and may even impact health. Self-talk that dwells on problems, expectations of failure, exaggerations, and "should haves" is usually a mixture of half-truths, poor logic, and distortions of reality. It perpetuates anxiety, fear, guilt, even depression. On the other hand, training oneself to use positive self-talk helps reshape emotions, perceptions, and behaviors in a positive direction.

Activity Ask students to carefully "listen" to their self-talk and identify it as negative, positive, or neutral. Encourage them to suggest ways of making negative self-talk positive.

Next to intrapersonal communication, you probably use the interpersonal level of communication most often each day. When you say, "Hello, how are you?" "See you later," or anything in-between to another person, you are communicating on an interpersonal level. You also communicate interpersonally when you use technology to communicate, such as in a phone message or e-mail. Through interpersonal communication you maintain relationships with others. Your ability to cooperate with others, get others to cooperate, lead others, and help others solve problems relates directly to your skills in interpersonal communication.

Small-Group Communication

Small-group communication is communication within formal or informal groups or teams. This may include group interactions that result in decision making, problem solving, and discussions within an organization. In the organizational context, groups and teams have become increasingly important for making plans and recommendations, solving problems, and managing

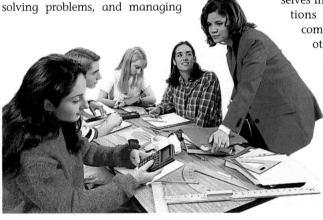

Working in small groups, like the students in the photograph, will help you to develop small-group communication skills. In what ways are small groups or teams utilized in many organizations?

conflicts. Because of this, practicing effective small-group communication skills can make you a valuable asset to any organization.

One-to-Group Communication

One-to-group communication involves a speaker who seeks to inform, persuade, or motivate an audience. It also includes the role of a listener as an evaluator of the presenter's message. Members of professional and social organizations often make formal and informal presentations for a variety of purposes.

One-to-group presentations often involve giving reports or speeches to groups or leading group discussions. If you give a report to your student council or make an introduction or announcement in a club meeting, you are using one-to-group communication. Similarly, people involved in professional and social organizations may find themselves giving fund-raising speeches, making informative reports to management, or giving pep talks and sales presentations. Individuals with strong presentation skills often find themselves in leadership or management positions because of their ability to communicate clearly and to influence others. They also tend to assume active roles in professional associations and social organizations.

The ability to listen to presentations and analyze and evaluate their content is equally important. Being able to follow a speaker's points, understand his or her claims and supporting information, and remember what has been said are vital communication skills. Responsible communicators recognize that listening skills are the basis for making wise choices and decisions.

Exploring the Communication Process **55**

Building Skills in Interpersonal Communication

Students will readily recognize that they communicate in a different style with a friend than they do in a class or with a group of peers. Point out to students that they will need to develop both interpersonal and small-group communication skills to succeed in a career. **L1**

■ Visual Instruction

Answer Many organizations make use of small-group dynamics in brainstorming, decision making, problem solving, and hands-on working sessions.

MEETING INDIVIDUAL NEEDS
INCLUSION STRATGIES

Learning Disabled Some students can assimilate large chunks of information best if the material is broken down into manageable segments.

Activity Read aloud the section on levels of communication or have students listen to it on tape as they read along. Check students' comprehension by pausing after each subsection to have them locate a definition for that type of communication. Create a large poster, including symbols or simple figures to demonstrate each level, and have students add examples on 3" x 5" cards around each type. As students discuss levels of communication, refer them to the chart and ask for volunteers to model each.

Leading Group Discussions
Point out to students that they often experience one-to-group communication situations in classes. Discuss the role played by the listener in such communications. Invite students who have given speeches to explain how they prepare. **L2**

Communication Tip

When you listen to a persuasive speech or sales presentation, watch for the types of appeals being made. Ask yourself whether the speaker is using sound logic to convince you to act or trying to pump up emotions using faulty logic.

Mass Media
Ask students to identify the media that have the greatest impact on them and explain why. Discuss concerns students have about the quality and content of the communications they receive over mass media. **L2**

Visual Instruction

Answer Radio, the Internet, movies, newspapers, magazines, newsletters, billboards, emergency sirens, broadcast devices, and weather alert systems are among the media students may mention.

Mass Communication

Mass communication is the electronic or print transmission of messages to the general public. Although mass communication is not conducted face to face, it still is considered a level of communication. In mass communication, individuals and groups use mass media to transmit messages. Mass media are outlets of communication, such as radio, television, film, and print, that are designed to reach large audiences.

Professional and social organizations often use mass media to disperse information on a broad scale. They also use various forms of mass media extensively for advertising purposes. In addition, some organizations such as police departments, health departments, and the National Weather Service use mass media to alert citizens to emergencies and disasters.

Recently, the wide use of mass communication has prompted citizens to analyze and evaluate the quality, content, and influence of media messages. We've learned that more information does not always mean better information. Users of mass media often compete for audiences by trying to be first with a breaking story. Other users may compete for your purchasing dollars by making sensational but unfounded claims. Often, sources and claims are not adequately confirmed, resulting in errors and, sometimes, outright falsehoods. Similarly, the lack of control over information posted on the Internet means that anyone can put information on the World Wide Web without taking personal responsibility for its truth. For these reasons, producers and consumers alike have a tremendous responsibility when they use the mass communication process.

BECOMING A COMPETENT COMMUNICATOR

As you learned in Chapter 1, if you are a competent communicator you are capable and well qualified to communicate. You build a base of knowledge and a positive attitude. You also work to acquire skills that allow you to deal with a variety of communication situations. Competent communicators use two specific sets of communication skills. They use certain skills to accomplish their goals and tasks, and other skills to build productive relationships. As **Figure 2–7** shows, learning to balance these different skills can be a challenge.

For example, suppose a friend stops you as you leave school to talk about a problem he or she is

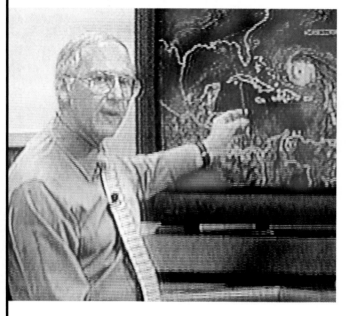

The National Weather Service uses television to alert citizens of disastrous weather situations. **Identify** other outlets of mass media communications.

INCLUSION STRATEGIES

Gifted Abler students will enjoy learning more about concepts they have studied and synthesizing them into an original presentation.

Activity Have students work with partners to research one of the channels of mass communication. Ask that they learn about its history, its present impact, and its growth potential. Have students analyze their information and create a "you-are-there" type skit that gives an inside look at the industry's beginnings and the ideas of its visionaries, past and present.

■ Figure 2-7 **Competent Communicator**

Task | Relationship

having. The friend is feeling a need to confide in you. You have an urgent practical need—you need to get to work on time. You also care about the relationship with your friend. At this point, you are caught in a dilemma.

Conflict between person and task is not unusual in professional and social contexts. Teachers sometimes have to explain failing grades to their students. Bosses sometimes have to lay off valued employees. Competent communicators strive to polish communication skills so they can deal with difficult situations to accomplish tasks and to preserve relationships.

Value of Good Business Communication

Some companies recognize that one way to improve customer service and increase business is to meet more of their clients' needs. To do so, they train employees to communicate with customers in a manner that makes the clients feel valued and important.

Businesses that specialize in meeting customers' needs value employees who treat clients with dignity, courtesy, and respect. They also recognize that, generally, everyone in a company has the responsibility of communicating with clients effectively and appropriately. This helps create a personal relationship between employees and customers. It also makes customers and employees alike feel important as individuals. By concentrating on individuals' communication needs as well as their need for a certain product or service, the company creates satisfied customers.

Characteristics of Competent Communicators

Competent communicators develop effective communication strategies and skills to achieve their goals. Sometimes we refer to

Practice for the Workplace

Evaluating Business Communication Meeting the needs of customers is a priority for many businesses. Without quality communication with customers, businesses can project a negative image and may even lose customers.

BUSINESS PRACTICE *Activity*

As a class, choose two students to act as a customer and a salesperson at a music store. Imagine that the customer needs help, but the store's only salesperson is on the phone and ringing up another customer's purchase. Act out the scenario by first having one student play the role of a distracted, uncooperative salesperson. Then have him or her portray a helpful salesperson. Make a list of appropriate communication choices for a salesperson and a customer in each situation. Make a second list of inappropriate communication choices for these types of business situations.

Exploring the Communication Process **57**

Practice for the Workplace

Evaluating Business Communication
Ask students to describe ways some businesses foster communication with customers. *(A starter example would be customer satisfaction surveys sent after a major purchase.)* Explore reasons businesspeople depend on these communications with customers. As customers, how do students want to be treated by salespeople? By clerks and checkout personnel? As businesspeople, how do they want to be treated by customers? Ask several students to interview businesspeople who meet the public daily to learn what their goals are and how they use communication to attain them. Have the students report their findings to the class. **L1**

Communication Tip

Active Listening

Effective listening is an invaluable skill for a communicator. When others feel you are really listening to them and attempting to understand not only what they say but why they say it, they will seek you out and also be more willing to listen to what you have to communicate. Active listening involves

1. Concentrating actively on what is said, not letting your thoughts wander to what you want to say or to other subjects.

2. Providing feedback; asking the speaker to repeat a point or give examples or repeating what you have heard and asking if this is correct.

3. Clarifying points you don't understand by asking questions or paraphrasing.

4. Being courteous; if you disagree, focus on the disagreement with the idea, not the person.

MEETING INDIVIDUAL NEEDS

MULTIPLE LEARNING STYLES

Musical Rhythm and melody are also powerful methods of communication, as the ongoing popularity of love songs and blues attest. Students with a feeling for music can enliven the study of communication with their contributions.

Activity Have one or more students write music and lyrics for a song about one of the mass media and its effect on people. Encourage originality, but explain that the song should express the nature of this form of communication and explore the types of relationships it creates. After practice, have the student(s) perform the song for the class.

Business-Client Relationships

What makes a client or customer feel valued and important? Discuss with students what types of messages make them feel this way. How can similar messages be ethically and honestly used by a businessperson who wishes to sell something to a customer? Ask students to carefully observe their next interaction with a salesclerk. Have them write a journal entry describing the communication and explaining how the clerk's messages affected them. Discuss students' experiences as a class. **L2**

DID YOU KNOW?

There is a crisis in organizational ethics. Employees steal from their own companies. Companies engage in illegal and unethical behavior toward their competitors and the public. From 1975–1985, two-thirds of Fortune Five Hundred firms were convicted of crimes such as fraud and illegal dumping of hazardous wastes. Yet, within most organizations, no code of principles exists for dealing with ethical situations.

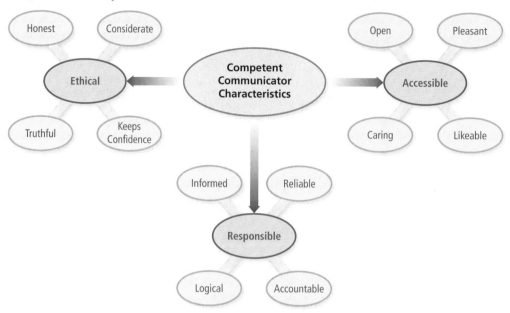

Figure 2–8 Competent Communicator Characteristics

a person as an effective, or competent, speaker or a competent, or effective, teacher. By this, we mean the person has shown the characteristics of the competent communicator and made appropriate communication choices.

Even though there is no one perfect way to communicate and there are no written rules to ensure success, competent communicators, including people successful in the business world, tend to share certain characteristics. As shown in **Figure 2–8** above, they are

- ethical
- responsible
- accessible

Ethical   Competent communicators are ethical. Ethics is the study of the general nature of morals, or a society's codes of conduct. Ethics also refers to the specific moral choices made by an individual in relationship to others. In communication, ethics has to do

with how we, personally, behave and how we treat others. In the world of work, ethics includes the standards governing the conduct of the members of a profession. In our personal lives, societies help establish standards for the actions and behaviors of its members.

According to some communication experts, there are five questions you can ask yourself to check whether you are acting ethically. You can find these questions on the Communication Strategies list.

Ethical communicators try to treat others as they, themselves, would like to be treated. They are honest and truthful. Ethical communicators also keep confidences and are cautious about spreading gossip or unfounded rumors. They consider the needs, rights, and feelings of other people.

Sacrificing ethics for other potential rewards can cause problems. A teen who lies to a parent to get his or her way may win a

58   *Glencoe Communication Applications*

MEETING INDIVIDUAL NEEDS
MULTIPLE LEARNING STYLES

Linguistic Improving their communication skills will aid students in many aspects of their lives. Before they can improve these skills, though, they must identify their own communication strengths and weaknesses.

Activity Have students assess their communication competencies informally, using Figure 2–8 and listing one characteristic of each area in which they would like to improve. Ask students to create a graphic organizer in which they state the communication traits to be improved and list at least three specific actions they can take to improve in each area.

COMMUNICATION Strategies

ACTING ETHICALLY

✓ **The Golden Rule:** Would I want to be treated this way by others?

✓ **The Professional Ethic:** How would a jury of my peers view this action?

✓ **The Global View:** Could our society continue to function if everyone acted like this?

✓ **The Utilitarian Rule:** Does this action do the most good for the most people over the longest period of time?

✓ **The TV Test:** Would I be comfortable explaining this action on a national TV show?

small battle but suffer greater consequences, such as a lack of trust and a loss of future privileges. A receptionist who doesn't forward a client's calls because of a personal vendetta may feel some sense of vengeance but lose his or her job if the unethical behavior is discovered.

For example, assume that a salesperson who fails to tell a customer that the used car he or she is considering buying is due for some expensive repairs. By not telling, the salesperson denies the customer the right to purchase the best car the customer can find for his or her money. Even though the salesperson may make a sale, he or she would be acting unethically and, possibly, illegally. An ethical communicator avoids

giving false information or withholding information that would deny others their right to make informed choices.

Responsible Competent communicators are responsible for their own communication choices and behavior. Responsible communicators are informed, make logical decisions on their own, account for their own actions, and are dependable.

Informed Responsible communicators are well informed and able to support what they say with facts or examples. They understand the need to be well versed on many topics in order to make sound communication choices. They act after first considering the most complete, accurate, reliable, and recent information available to them.

Imagine that you have been chosen to represent your school's views on a proposed teen center. You have been asked to attend your town's next community planning meeting.

In order to act as an ethical communicator, this salesperson should be honest about the product he is selling. **Describe an ethical communicator.**

Exploring the Communication Process **59**

Checking the Accuracy and Reliability of Information

From gossip to outdated data, irresponsible information fails to serve a constructive purpose and may cause active harm. Have students brainstorm a list of personal, public, and business sources that they depend on for timely, accurate, and reliable information. Ask several students to compile the information into a poster-size chart. Pair students and assign each pair one source. Have them decide what they would do if they could not depend on the reliability of that source's information. Ask students to add their suggestions to the chart and to explain their thinking to the class. **L2**

COMMUNICATION Strategies

ACTING ETHICALLY

Brainstorm with the class for situations on which to test the questions for acting ethically. (Examples: Should I allow my friend Bob to drive home, knowing that he's overtired? Should I cheat on the Spanish test?) For each situation, pose the five questions listed on this page and invite students to discuss the issues involved. Finally, ask students which of the five questions they found most useful in defining their personal standards. **L1**

Visual Instruction

Answer Ethical communicators keep confidences and are honest, considerate, and truthful.

MEETING INDIVIDUAL NEEDS

GIFTED AND TALENTED

Use of Language Some types of communication are illegal: It is against the law to use language that defames or harms another person unjustly and language that creates a clear and present danger (such as inciting an audience to riot). What constitutes ethical communication is not determined by law but resides in value judgments about rightness and wrongness.

Activity Have students work together to find articles in newspapers and magazines that provide examples of illegal, ethical, or unethical use of language. You might encourage them to also examine recent Supreme Court decisions about the First Amendment. Ask them to place each article in a category and to explain why they believe the communication should be considered as illegal, ethical, or unethical.

COMMUNICATION
PRACTICE LAB

Identifying a Competent Communicator

Have students follow the four steps in the Communication Practice Lab on this page to apply their understanding of what constitutes a competent communicator and identify examples of the three characteristics in action. Suggest that students locate print or video records of the person's speeches, broadcasts, writing, or other communications. Be sure students can support their opinions with specific examples. Guide the class to form an original definition of communication competency based on the examples they have collected. **L2**

GLENCOE
Online

For additional Practice Labs for this section, have students visit the *Glencoe Communication Applications* Web site at **communicationapplications.glencoe.com.** Click on Communication Practice Lab 2–2. **L1**

Language Tip

Sound logic is based on inductive or deductive reasoning. Both require three elements: *data* (evidence, assumptions, assertions), which provide the basis for a *conclusion* (the inference drawn or to be proven), and a *statement* showing how the conclusion follows from the data. If you gather evidence that allows you to make a generalization, you are using inductive reasoning. If you begin with a generalization and proceed to a logical conclusion based upon it, you are using deductive reasoning.

COMMUNICATION
PRACTICE LAB

Identifying a Competent Communicator

To understand the characteristics of a competent communicator, follow these steps.

Step 1 On your own, choose a well-known person you regard as a competent communicator.

Step 2 In your school library, online (with supervision) or using resources at home, research supporting information about the individual and his or her effectiveness as a communicator.

Step 3 Make a list of the characteristics of a competent communicator found in this section. For each, give one example of the individual's competent communication behaviors.

Step 4 As a class, review the choices and communication behaviors each reflects.

You will want to know all the facts and issues that are involved in your project so that you can speak effectively about them and gain support for your proposal. If you are planning a professional presentation, you need to be well informed about your topic in order to support your information and to answer questions from the audience.

Logical Responsible communicators also develop reasoning skills and use logical reasoning to draw conclusions and reach decisions. They avoid faulty judgment and poor decision making. If your boss at your weekend job at the bagel shop asks why you think sales are dropping, you may need to draw conclusions based on your observations. Perhaps the dough lately has been of lesser quality. Customers may gripe about an increase in price, a change in the hours of operation, or poor service. Competent communicators apply logic to their interactions to solve problems.

Accountable Responsible communicators take personal responsibility for their information, their decisions, and their actions. This is sometimes called "owning" or "owning up" to your words, behaviors, and actions.

Competent communicators own up to, or admit and take responsibility for, their actions and decisions, whether or not these are appropriate or inappropriate, effective or ineffective. Responsible communicators are up front about being late or making a mistake in counting a day's receipts and take responsibility for the consequences.

Owning your own communication eliminates statements like "It's her fault" or "He made me do it." It leads to comments like "I'm sorry. This won't happen again" or "I learned my lesson this time. I'll try to do a better job next time."

Owning communication can also include being open with feelings, ideas, or suggestions when asked. "You know, I really feel we're on the wrong path here" may be the remark of a group member willing to risk owning and sharing ideas with others.

Reliable Responsible communicators are reliable, or dependable. They can be trusted to keep their word even if a decision may not be to their benefit. They establish consistent patterns of behavior that make their actions predictable to others.

60 *Glencoe Communication Applications*

INTERDISCIPLINARY CONNECTION

Math Messages sent in code are an interesting and complex example of communication. The sender-receiver wants only a specific receiver-sender to understand the message, so he or she encodes it using a system no one else should be able to decipher. To crack a code requires mathematical and logical skills in addition to knowledge of the language on which the code is based.

Activity Have students work in pairs to invent a code and use it to create a message. Ask partners to post their messages around the room. Give the class time to study several codes and try to decipher their messages. Lead a class discussion of the logic used to crack the codes. Then, discuss the ethics of intercepting and decoding messages not intended for you. How might such interception harm the sender-receiver and the intended receiver-sender?

At home, school, and work, reliable individuals have more responsibility, more freedom, and more trust. A supervisor who believes an employee to be reliable will assign that employee a task with confidence. The supervisor knows that the employee's past performance indicates that he or she does the task well, will do exactly what is being asked, and will do the work on time. Your principal may ask you to arrive early in the day to set up the materials for a school assembly. The principal knows you are reliable and can be depended upon to do what is asked. Your parents may impose fewer curfews and give you more freedom if your previous actions confirm that you act reliably. Reliability is a valued characteristic in relationships.

Accessible Competent communicators tend to value positive relationships with peers, supervisors, and clients. They are open and approachable, and others see them as accessible. Accessible communicators are seen as caring, likable, and pleasant to be around.

Think for a moment about someone you would describe as easy to talk to and open to ideas from others. Which characteristics account for how you view that person as a communicator? You probably view the person as friendly, someone who likes people. Other traits might include being a good listener, having a good sense of humor, and being courteous and considerate of others. People who are seen as open, sincere, genuine, and pleasant to be around tend to be very accessible.

Competent communicators make appropriate choices and use effective communication strategies to accomplish tasks and maintain relationships. You could say, for example, that a speaker's use of visual aids was effective in his or her presentation. You would mean that the visual aids supported the points the speaker made. You would also mean that the speaker used the visual aids skillfully. You might also remark that a friend's pep talk at a critical moment worked effectively to reassure your lack of confidence.

Parents must have confidence that the person providing care for their child, such as the young man shown here, is reliable and responsible. **How can a person establish a reputation of being reliable?**

61

Ice Cubes and Hot Tamales
Point out that it is difficult to communicate with someone if you cannot approach him or her. Lead the class in a discussion of traits that make a person approachable. Create a continuum on the board with characteristics of people who seem indifferent or cold on one end and those with quick tempers and low-boiling points on the other. Have students place their "approachable" traits in the middle of the continuum. Invite a volunteer to explain how these traits also relate to creating and maintaining relationships. **L1**

Visual Instruction
Answer Students may respond that they can establish a reputation for reliability by demonstrating that they can be trusted and establishing a consistent, predictable pattern of behavior.

3 ASSESS

Assign Section 2 Assessment as a homework or in-class activity.

🔴 Use *Interactive Tutor Self-Assessment Software* to review Section 2.

Section 2–2 Quiz

| SECTION QUIZ 2–2 | EXPLORING THE COMMUNICATION PROCESS Communicating for Success | | SCORE |

Matching Match each item in the left column with the best selection from the right column. Write the letter of the item on the line provided. *(10 points each)*

_____ 1. intrapersonal communication   a. communication within a group or team

_____ 2. interpersonal communication   b. a speaker trying to persuade an audience

_____ 3. small-group communication   c. self-talk

_____ 4. one-to-group communication   d. communication between two people

_____ 5. mass communication   e. electronic or print transmissions of messages

Multiple Choice In the blank provided, write the letter of the item that best answers each question. *(10 points)*

_____ 6. Which of the following is a reason to use self-talk?
a. to persuade a friend to do what you want
b. to think about something and decide what it means
c. to lead a small group's discussion
d. to inform a group about your opinion on an issue

_____ 7. On what level does all communication begin?
a. intrapersonal communication
b. interpersonal communication
c. one-to-group communication
d. mass communication

_____ 8. Which of the following states a problem with mass communication?
a. The media may be sharing misinformation.
b. Mass communication can only be used in emergency situations.
c. Computer technology changes too rapidly.
d. The cost of advertisement forces an increase in products' prices.

_____ 9. Which of the following is an example of a competent communicator being ethical?
a. a car salesman not telling the customer the true mileage of the car
b. an employee who is asked to supervise others when the boss is away
c. a student who admits making a mistake
d. a coworker who keeps confidences

_____ 10. Which of the following is not an example of a competent communicator being responsible?
a. a student being able to answer questions after a class presentation
b. a student admitting he did not study for a test
c. a student who never cheats on homework or tests
d. a student who can be trusted to help a classmate understand an assignment

INTERDISCIPLINARY CONNECTION

Social Studies Ask students to describe the types of interactions they have observed in open discussions at meetings. What kinds of communicator characteristics were exhibited?

Activity Have students work together to prepare a survey form to find out about behaviors people may or may not exhibit as communicators. Ask students to devise a rating scale with one end indicating Competent Communicator and the other end indicating Weak Communicator. When their form is completed and copied, individual students in the group can use it to survey five people. Groups reconvene to compile their data. Each group should prepare a short summary of their findings for the class.

Reteaching Activity 2-2

Enrichment Activity 2-2

4 CLOSE

Have students recall the five levels of communication from memory and rank them 1–5 according to personal proficiency and frequency of use. Ask them to set a goal to improve in one of these levels and state specific actions they will take to improve their competency in this type of communication.

Extra-Credit Project

Ask students to select a character in a movie available on videotape and analyze the character's communication competency. Have students prepare written notes with examples that show the character's ethics, responsibility, and accessibility in communicating with others. Ask that they write a paragraph evaluating how the character's communication style and traits helped or hindered in relationships with others.

Is it possible to make ethical and responsible communication choices, be accessible, and use effective communication strategies and still not get desired results? Yes, even the most-skilled communicators do not always get the results they seek. However, the odds are strong enough for you to make the effort to develop effective skills.

While on your road to becoming a competent communicator, you may stumble. Rest assured, however, that each setback will get you closer to your goal of effective communication. As American author Elbert Hubbard once observed, "Constant effort and frequent mistakes are the stepping stones to genius."

Section 2 Assessment

GLENCOE *Online*

Visit the *Glencoe Communication Applications* Web site at **communicationapplications. glencoe.com** and click on **Self-Check and Study Guide 2.2** to review your analysis of the action of the communication process.

Review Key Terms

1. Define each term and write it in a sentence: intrapersonal communication, self-talk, interpersonal communication, small-group communication, one-to-group communication, mass communication, mass media.

Check Understanding

2. What are the five levels of communication, and how do you use them to communicate?

3. What are the characteristics of competent communicators, and how do they impact the quality of the communication?

4. **Analyze** How do competent communicators display responsibility?

APPLICATION *Activity*

Presenting an Argument Choose one of the following sentences and list three reasons why you think the statement is true or false.

• There always is a reason behind communication.

• Communication is irreversible.

• Communication cannot be duplicated.

• It is impossible not to communicate.

• For communication to occur, it must have feedback.

Using your list, prepare a two-minute argument to convince your classmates to agree with your position. Include examples to support each of your claims and answer questions from the class.

Present your argument to the class. Then vote to see who agrees and who disagrees with you. What might you do to make your communication more effective and to convince more listeners of your position?

Section 2 Assessment Answers

1. Accept all reasonable sentences.
2. Use intrapersonal to reason or think; interpersonal to communicate with a person or informal group; small-group to interact with teams informally or formally; one-to-group for speaker to present to audience; mass communication to transmit messages to the general public.
3. Ethical, responsible, and accessible are characteristics of competent communicators that help

them convey accurate, ethical, useful messages and get the most value from messages received.
4. Competent communicators display responsibility by being informed, reliable, and accountable.

Application Activity Effectiveness of students' arguments will be based upon their application of the qualities of an effective communicator, their experiences, and their opinions.

Communication Self-Assessment

Analyzing Your Ability to Transmit Meaningful Messages

How Do You Rate?

On a separate sheet of paper, use the key to answer the following questions. Put a check mark at the end of each skill you would like to improve.

KEY: **A** Always **R** Rarely
   U Usually **N** Never
   S Sometimes

1. When I have difficulty understanding, or decoding information, I ask questions.
2. I use reason and logic, as opposed to emotion, as I reach decisions.
3. When I disagree with others or try to persuade them of my viewpoint, I consider what matters to them as well as what I would like to accomplish.
4. I use respectful language.
5. I avoid making false or misleading statements.
6. When I give information to others I take responsibility for accuracy and completeness.
7. I can be trusted to share my ideas and stand behind what I say, taking on accountability for what I say.
8. When I give a presentation or a talk, I try to use all possible means to reach my audience.
9. I try to be accessible to other people.
10. I communicate without defensiveness or competitiveness.

How Do You Score?

Review your responses. Give yourself 5 points for every A, 4 for every U, 3 for every S, 2 for every R, and 1 for every N. Total your points and evaluate your score.

41–50 Excellent You may be surprised to find out how much you can improve your skills.

31–40 Good In this course, you can learn ways to make your skills better.

21–30 Fair Practice applying the skills taught in this course.

1–20 Needs Improvement Carefully monitor your improvement as you work through this course.

Setting Communication Goals

If you scored Excellent or Good, complete Part A. If your score was Fair or Needs Improvement, complete Part B.

Part A
1. I plan to put the following ideas into practice:
2. I plan to share the following information about communication with the following people:

Part B
1. The behaviors I need to change most are:
2. To bring about these changes, I will take these steps:

Exploring the Communication Process **63**

Communication Self-Assessment

Have studens respond to the survey statements using the key provided on this page, then evaluate their communication skills using the scoring rubric. Based on their scores, have students complete either Part A or B of the goal-setting activity. Suggest that they write their specific goals on a separate sheet of paper and post it in a location where they will see it often and use it to improve their skills.

Communication Journal Activity

Point out to students that to accomplish goals, one must make them specific and concrete and review them often to assess progress. Have students use their goals from this activity to create an organized plan for improvement in communication and write their plan in their Communication Journals.

Communication Tip

When communicating with someone whose ideas differ from your own, the use of a simple, direct, nonconfrontational tone is helpful. Sarcasm and retorts only increase antagonism and reduce the chances that real communication will occur. As students may have heard, "Sometimes, it isn't what you say but how you say it that affects the reaction."

EXTENDING THE CONTENT

Essential Communication Skills in the Workplace A survey conducted by the San Diego Community College's Continuing Education Centers showed that the skills ranked most essential to success on the job are as follows: listening (89%); asking questions (89%); controlling anger (82%); respecting others' points of view (77%); writing (66%).

Activity Have students correlate each of these skills with one or more of the questions in the survey they have taken. Ask that they note their responses to each category of question and evaluate areas in which their workplace communication skills will need improvement.

Communication Through Writing

Using Correctness in Writing

Objectives:

• To revise business writing to reflect appropriate style, format, grammar, and mechanics.

• To identify the purpose and audience for a business communication and tailor language to both.

Teaching Suggestions and Strategies

Connection to the Workplace

Effective, accurate communication is so important to many businesses and organizations that they frequently produce style manuals as guides for their written communications.

Particularly in international corporations that do business around the world, understanding the values and attitudes of other cultures is key to success. Training of employees may include orientation to the differences in customs, language, and beliefs in countries where they will do business.

In any organization, the value of correct written communications is clear. The ability to use language that is correct, to the point, and considerate of others is a prized skill.

Using Correctness in Writing

Have you ever read something that you felt was confusing or insensitive? Have you ever written something that was misinterpreted? If you answered yes to either question, you know that written communication sometimes can have unintended results.

The Importance of Correctness Because your writing is a reflection of yourself and your organization, it is important to state your message clearly, effectively, and with sensitivity. The best way to accomplish this is by following the rules of correctness. Correctness in writing means accurately presenting information for the intended reader(s) and for the desired result.

To write with correctness, remember to follow these four basic steps.

1. **Define the Purpose of the Writing** What is the main reason for your written communication? Are you writing a document to inform? Persuade? Motivate? Entertain? Try to keep this purpose in mind as you write to help you stay on task.

2. **Determine the Style and Format for the Writing** Businesses and other organizations typically have a preferred format and style for most types of writing, including e-mail, letters, faxes, and reports. Be sure to use the framework appropriate to your specific task. A memo, for example, may need to be written on company letterhead and sent to a certain group of individuals.

3. **Target the Writing to the Audience** Depending on attitudes, cultures, and experiences, people sometimes have different perceptions of the same words and phrases. Your writing should use language that is appropriate for the specific audience. This includes avoiding stereotypes such as gender bias. For example, rather than referring to a mailman, a better choice would be letter carrier.

 For additional information about business writing, see the Language Handbook section of the Communication Survival Kit in the Appendix.

CRITICAL THINKING ACTIVITY

Divide the class into groups of four or five students. Assign each group a writing assignment with a specific context—for example, write a letter to the editor about safety in your school, a speech for a candidate for class president, or a formal request asking a famous person to attend and speak at graduation ceremonies. Each group is to determine the audience, purpose, style, and format for the writing. Require groups to write out these steps, then create an outline and introductory paragraph using the style, grammar, and mechanics appropriate to the task.

Communication Through Writing

4. Use Correct Grammar and Mechanics

Always proofread your work carefully. Check for typographical errors and mistakes in spelling and grammar. Finally, make sure your message is complete and easy to understand.

Imagine that you are writing a letter to persuade someone to donate to the cancer research fund where you work. Your letter might look something like this.

Helping People Cancer Research Foundation
P.O. Box 1234
Dallas, TX 75225

July 5, 2002

Ms. Opal Wells
359 Magnolia Boulevard
Macon, GA 31201

Dear Ms. Wells:

This month marks the beginning of Helping People Cancer Research Foundation's tenth annual funding drive. This year, we hope to raise $50,000 for cancer research. Your past donations have helped us in many ways, including the development of a new drug that may help prevent some types of cancer.

The enclosed brochure describes some of our ongoing research, such as finding a better way to detect cancer in its early stages. We also are continuing to develop more effective and patient-friendly surgeries and treatments.

We truly appreciate your past contributions and hope we can count on your gift again this year. Whatever amount you choose to give will be greatly appreciated. Thank you for playing such a vital role in the ongoing battle against cancer.

Sincerely,

Your Signature

Your Typewritten Name
Public Relations Assistant

WRITING Activity

Imagine that you work for a travel agency, and a customer has asked one of your coworkers for information about traveling to Rome, Italy. The coworker has written a response and wants you to edit it. Rewrite the letter to make it more correct.

Hi, Mr. Wu,

In response to your letter, here are some tips regarding your upcomming trip to italy. First, the official language in Rome is Italian. While most shop, hotel, and restaraunt folks speak some English, romans are delighted when visitors try to speak a few words or phrases in Italian.

While your there, I figure you'll want to visit some old churches. Italian churches are definitely the most beautiful things you've ever seen. When touring a church, just dress like you normaly would at your own church. To show respect, though, it's important that your and your wife's shoulders are covered. Tank tops, sleeveless shirts, and sleevelessdresses are not acceptable.

Finally—and you'll hate this—tipping is customary everwhere in Rome. In hotels, tips of 20 percent of the cost of services may be added to you're bill. In most restaurants, a 15 percent tipp is added to your bill. And if you liked the service, an additional 10 percent is expected.

Hope this information helps. Let me know if their is anything else I can do. Have a great vacation in Rome!

Sincerely,

Arlene Bettis

Teaching Activity

Ask students to list the last three writings they have completed and describe each. How did they address each of the four areas discussed in this lesson? Which might they improve? Encourage students to share editing and proofreading techniques they have found useful in correcting errors in their rough drafts.

WRITING Activity

Student revisions should include corrections of errors in punctuation, spelling, grammar, and format as well as reworking of language to avoid excessive informality and slang and converting to typewritten form. Suggest that students use the sample as a guide.

Grammar Tip

Dangling modifiers are phrases that do not logically modify any word in the sentence. To correct these errors, rewrite the sentence, adding a noun to which the dangling modifier clearly refers. Often, you must add or move other words to make your meaning clear.

Additional Resources

Appendix, "Guide to Business Communication"

Glencoe Writer's Assistant CD-ROM

Glencoe Interactive Grammar Software

Grade 9 Writer's Choice, Unit 2

GRAMMAR PRACTICE

Correcting Dangling Modifiers

Have students rewrite each sentence to correct the dangling modifier. Answers may vary.

1. After working feverishly all week, the annual report was finished. *(After . . . week, we finished the annual report.)*
2. Hoping to raise $50,000 for research, your gift in any amount is greatly appreciated. *(Hoping . . . research, we greatly appreciate any gift you choose to give.)*
3. Being exhausted after our long flight, the alarm clock didn't even register. *(Being . . ., we didn't even hear the alarm clock.)*

GLENCOE TECHNOLOGY

 MindJogger Videoquiz

Use *MindJogger* to review the Chapter 2 content.

Reviewing Key Terms

1. false; communication is a constantly changing, interactive process between two or more people.

2. false; the sender-receiver initiates communication and sends the message to the receiver-sender.

3. true

4. false; a personal exchange would be a preferred communication channel between salesperson and customer.

5. true

6. false; communication has occurred when there is verbal and/or nonverbal feedback.

7. false; you acquire a message by decoding.

8. true

GLENCOE Online

Visit the *Glencoe Communication Applications* Web site at **communicationapplications. glencoe.com** and click on **Chapter 2 Activity** for additional practice in becoming a more competent communicator.

Reviewing Key Terms

Read each statement. On a separate sheet of paper, answer True or False. If the statement is false, rewrite the sentence to make it true.

1. Communication is a never-changing process between two people.

2. The receiver-sender initiates communication and sends the message to the sender-receiver.

3. The sender-receiver is unaware of the fact that he or she is sending an unintentional message.

4. A printed brochure would be a preferred channel of communication between a salesperson and a special customer.

5. Hunger is an example of internal noise that can interfere with communication.

6. It is unsafe to assume that communication has occurred until there is some kind of nonverbal cue.

7. You acquire a message through the encoding process.

8. One reason communication is transactional is that communicators bargain and negotiate with one another.

Reviewing Key Concepts

1. Explain why communication is a continuous process.

2. What are the five principles of communication?

3. What are the components of the communication process and what is the function of each?

4. What are the three basic functions of feedback in the communication process?

5. How do the content, feelings, and relationship between communicators affect a message?

6. What does channel do to a message?

7. Name three barriers to communication; are they internal or external?

8. Describe the process sender-receivers and receiver-senders typically follow to send and receive a message.

9. What factors influence a well-communicated message?

10. What are the characteristics of a competent communicator?

Reviewing Key Concepts

1. Answers may include because a first communication sets off a chain of interactions extending indefinitely into the future.

2. Communication is transactional, complex, unavoidable, continuous, and learned.

3. *Context* provides the occasion for communicating and the relationship of communicators; *environment* provides the space in which communication occurs; *climate* provides the emotional atmosphere; *communicators* are senders and receivers at the heart of the process; *message* conveys meanings and feelings; *channel* provides the medium for sending a message; *noise* and *barriers* impede transmission of communications; *feedback* tells the senders what was received and the receiver's reaction.

4. Feedback assures that communication has occurred, allows adjustment of communication, and provides insights into how effective communication was.

Assessment and Activities

Reading and Critical Thinking Skill

1. **Applying** You are dissatisfied with the way your boss schedules teenagers to work on holidays. Which channel would be an effective one to use to challenge your schedule? Explain your answer.

2. **Synthesizing** You are trying to decide how to convince your boss to give you next Saturday off so you can attend a concert with friends. On which level of communication are you focusing?

Skill Practice Activity

Researching Online Research the e-mail addresses of companies or groups dedicated to supplying information about a hobby or interest you have. Draft an e-mail message that lists your name, e-mail address, and the type of information you would like to find out about your chosen hobby. Ask each company or group to provide you with information and the dates of events dedicated to people who have the same hobby or interest. With your teacher's permission, send your e-mail message.

Cooperative Learning Activity

Creating a Gestures Chart As a class, brainstorm a list of socially acceptable gestures used by teens in everyday communication. Display the list on the chalkboard or on an overhead transparency and add a sketch of each gesture. In groups of four to six people, choose a country such as France, Japan, Brazil, or Saudi Arabia and look for the meanings for the same gestures in that country. You may wish to consult travel guides, books on cultural etiquette, or geography texts to search for this information. Create a chart showing how each gesture is used in your chosen country and present the chart to the class.

Chapter Project

Planning On a sheet of paper, list the objectives found at the beginning of the two sections of this chapter. Cut the list into strips so that there is only one objective on each strip. Fold each strip and place it into a container or on a desk. Form groups of four or five students. Have a group member select one objective for the group. Together write a skit including characters, dialogue, and stage directions that communicates the information needed to meet your chosen objective.

Presenting Present your group skit to the class. After the skit, analyze as a class the messages conveyed by individual actors in each skit. Categorize each message as intentional or unintentional.

Cooperative Learning Activity

Creating a Gestures Chart

Remind students that gestures can include motions of the body as well as the limbs—for example, a bow, a double take. Complex gestures or those difficult to illustrate might be represented by a series of drawings. Students with access to the Internet may find it a good resource for multicultural meanings of gestures. Students might try keywords such as *nonverbal communication signals or international communication.*

---

5. Answers may include effects on manner in which message is delivered, openness of receiver to message, whether message will be misinterpreted.

6. Channel conveys the message.

7. Interior barriers: ignorance, prejudice, defensiveness, competitiveness; exterior barriers: foreign language, unclear speech, cultural differences

8. Sender takes in sensory data and encodes it, transmits message; receiver acquires message, decodes information, assigns meaning, and provides feedback.

9. Communication skills and relationship skills

10. Competent communicators are ethical, responsible, and accessible.

Reading and Critical Thinking Skill

1. Accept answers for which students give reasonable explanations. A face-to-face dialogue or a written communication might be wisest.

2. Intrapersonal

Skill Practice Activity

Researching Online

Direct students to use a search engine to locate Web sites dedicated to their favorite hobby or interest. The sites generally show e-mail addresses that can be copied and used later or clicked on to send an immediate message. Web sites for hobby magazines and corporations may also provide an interactive "Ask an Expert" page or a subdivision with FAQs (frequently asked questions).

Chapter Project

Encourage groups to establish a range of characters to illustrate a variety of types of communication.

67

Chapter 3 Planning Guide

SECTION RESOURCES

Daily Objectives

Section 1

1. Identify and explain the three steps of the perception process
2. Describe the factors that influence selective perception
3. Describe the factors that influence personal perception
4. Use perception checks to clarify and confirm understanding
5. Explain the importance of gathering and using accurate and complete information as a basis for perception choices

Reproducible Resources

 Reproducible Lesson Plan 3-1
 Application Activities 3-1
 Guided Reading Workbook Activity 3-1
 Vocabulary Activity 3*
 Reteaching Activity 3-1*
 Enrichment Activity 3-1*
 Graphic Organizer Transparency Strategies and Activities 3-1

Multimedia Resources

 Graphic Organizer Transparency 3-1
 Chapter 3 Teaching Transparency
  Interactive Tutor Self-Assessment
 PuzzleMaker
 ExamView® Pro Testmaker
Interactive Lesson Planner
Communication in Action Video Chapter 3
MindJogger
communicationapplications.glencoe.com
Presentation Plus!

Section 2

1. Identify and analyze common influences on self-concept
2. Analyze the relationship between self-fulfilling prophesy on communication and personal performance
3. Explain the effects of self-fulfilling prophesy on communication and personal performance
4. Analyze and use the Johari window to evaluate personal interaction with others

 Reproducible Lesson Plan 3-2
 Application Activities 3-2
 Guided Reading Workbook Activity 3-2
 Vocabulary Activity 3*
 Reteaching Activity 3-2*
 Enrichment Activity 3-2*
 Graphic Organizer Transparency Strategies and Activities 3-2

 Graphic Organizer Transparency 3-2
 Chapter 3 Teaching Transparency
 Interactive Tutor Self-Assessment
 PuzzleMaker
 ExamView® Pro Testmaker
 Interactive Lesson Planner
Communication in Action Video Chapter 3
MindJogger
communicationapplications.glencoe.com
Presentation Plus!

Use Glencoe's *Presentation Plus!* multimedia teacher tool to easily present dynamic lessons that engage and motivate your students. Using Microsoft PowerPoint®, you can customize the presentations to create your own personalized lessons.

* Also available in Spanish

 Blackline Master   CD-ROM   Software

Transparency   Videodisc   Videocassette   Web site

Chapter 3 Planning Guide

FOR THE TEACHER

Self-Perception

How do your students perceive themselves? How do others perceive them? Have them take ten minutes to write down adjectives and nouns that they would use to describe themselves. They should try to name only positive attributes. When the lists are finished, have students set their sheets aside. Assign each student a partner and have them take ten minutes to write adjectives and nouns that they would use to describe their partners, using only positive attributes. Have them exchange their lists and compare what they wrote about themselves with what their partners wrote. Are their self-perceptions similar to their partners' perceptions of them?

After reading Section 2, focus on the different dimensions of self identified in the chart on page 84. Have students try to place both sets of descriptions into the chart under the appropriate dimensions of self.

CHAPTER RESOURCES

Resources for the Teacher

- *You've Got to Be Believed to Be Heard* by Bert Decker with James Denney, St. Martin's Press, 1992
- *What to Say When You Talk to Yourself* by Shad Helmsletter, MJF Books, 1986
- *Sense Ability: Expanding Your Sense of Awareness for a Twenty-First Century Life* by Doris Wild Helmering, Eagle Book, 1999

Resources for the Student

- *Creative Communication* by Victor Annigan, R & E Publishers, 1993
- *Knowing Yourself: Learning About Your Skills, Values and Planning Your Life* by Susan Christopherson and J. Michael Farr, JIST Works, 1990
- *Frames of Reference* by Carol Rudman, Ph.D., Peterson's/Pacesetter Books, 1995

Block Scheduling

Block scheduling differs from traditional class scheduling in the amount of time allotted to each period. The extended time frame provided by block scheduling affords you the opportunity to implement a greater number of research-oriented and activity-intense projects to motivate and involve your students. Activities that are particularly suited to use within the block-scheduling framework are identified throughout this chapter by the following designation:

KEY TO ABILITY LEVELS

Teaching Strategies have been coded for varying learning styles and abilities.

L1 **BASIC** activities for all students

L2 **AVERAGE** activities for average to above-average students

L3 **CHALLENGING** activities for above-average students

ELL **English Language Learner** activities

Chapter 3 Resource Manager

The following materials may be used when teaching the chapter. Materials for specific lessons are also shown at point-of-use in the margins of the Teacher's Wraparound Edition.

TEACHING TRANSPARENCIES

Chapter 3 Teaching Transparency

Graphic Organizer Transparency 3-1

Graphic Organizer Transparency 3-2

APPLICATION ACTIVITIES

Chapter 3, Section 1

Chapter 3, Section 2

Chapter 3, Cumulative

REINFORCEMENT AND REVIEW ACTIVITIES

Vocabulary Activity 3

Guided Reading Activity Workbook 3-1, 3-2

Reteaching Activities 3-1, 3-2

67C

Chapter 3 Resource Manager

ASSESSMENT AND EVALUATION

Section Quizzes 3-1, 3-2

Chapter 3 Test, Forms A & B

Performance Assessment Activity 3

ENRICHMENT AND EXTENSION

Technology Application Activity 3

Enrichment Activities 3-1, 3-2

SPANISH RESOURCES

- Spanish Chapter and Unit Tests
- Spanish Vocabulary Activities
- Spanish Section Quizzes
- Spanish Reteaching Activities
- Spanish Enrichment Activities

MULTIMEDIA

-   Interactive Tutor Self-Assessment
-   ExamView® Pro Testmaker
- PuzzleMaker
-   Communication in Action Videodisc and Videocassette
- MindJogger
- Interactive Lesson Planner
- Presentation Plus!
- Writer's Assistant
- Glencoe Interactive Grammar
- communicationapplications.glencoe.com

ORAL PRESENTATION ACTIVITIES

Activities 1, 8, 9

TEACHER PLANNING AND SUPPORT

- Reproducible Lesson Plans
- Interactive Lesson Planner
-   Presentation Plus!

The Communication Process and You

"Whether you think you can or think you can't—you are right."
—Henry Ford, American automobile manufacturer

WHY IT'S IMPORTANT

Communication begins within you. How you perceive yourself, your experiences, and the world around you lays a foundation for social and professional communication.

 To better understand yourself as a communicator, view the **Communication in Action** Chapter 3 video lesson.

WHY IT'S IMPORTANT

Ask a volunteer to read aloud the quotation by Henry Ford. Then, have students scan the text headings for Chapter 3. Ask: **Why do you think that what a person thinks or believes about whether he or she will succeed is a predictor of what is likely to happen?** *(A possible answer may be that what a person tells himself or herself over and over often affects the person's attitudes and actions.)*

Section 1

Understanding Intrapersonal Communication

GUIDE TO READING

Objectives

1. Identify and explain the three steps of the perception process.
2. Describe the factors that influence selective perception.
3. Describe the factors that influence personal perception.
4. Use perception checks to clarify and confirm understanding.
5. Explain the importance of gathering and using accurate and complete information as a basis for perception choices.

Terms to Learn

perception
selective perception
personal perception
perception check
feed-forward

I am the voice. I will lead, not follow. I will believe, not doubt. I will create, not destroy. I am a force for good. I am a leader. Defy the odds. Set a new standard. Step up!"

Did you know that you communicate messages to yourself all the time? Author and speaker Anthony Robbins recommends including positive messages like the one above in your communication with yourself about yourself. Telling yourself that you can succeed could help you create a more positive self-image. This, in turn, could give you the confidence and motivation you need to succeed. Your own self-image, along with the way you perceive others, plays a large role in shaping your communication choices and influences your effectiveness as a communicator.

Most children, like the one shown here, dream of their future careers. How can communicating positive messages to yourself help you succeed?

The Communication Process and You **69**

RESOURCE MANAGER

Teaching Tools
- Interactive Lesson Planner
- Reproducible Lesson Plan 3–1
- Application Activities 3–1

Reproducible Masters
- Guided Reading Activity Workbook 3–1
- Enrichment Activity 3–1
- Reteaching Activity 3–1
- Section Quiz 3–1
- Transparency Strategies and Activities Booklet 3–1

Transparencies
- Graphic Organizer Transparency 3–1
- Chapter 3 Teaching Transparency

Technology Resources
- Interactive Tutor Self-Assessment Software
- Presentation Plus! Software
- ExamView® Pro Testmaker
- PuzzleMaker Software
- communicationapplications.glencoe.com

1 FOCUS

Bellringer
Direct students to read silently the opening quotation. Discuss with students the identity of "I" in the quotation and to whom "I" is speaking. Ask whether the statement is positive or negative and why that might be important to "I." *(The "I" is a person talking to himself or herself. The statement is positive and designed to help the person think and act in a positive way.)*

You may use Graphic Organizer Transparency 3–1 to introduce this section.

Graphic Organizer Transparency 3–1

Grammar Tip

Quotation marks are used to set off the words of a speaker or of a quotation from a book, tape, or other work. In the introductory paragraph, the quotation marks represent both the words of a speaker—the "I"—and a quotation from Anthony Robbins. The opening quotation marks do not appear because of the decorative lettering.

Visual Instruction

Answer Students may say that communicating positive messages to oneself can help a person create a positive self-image, gain confidence, and have positive motivation.

2 TEACH

The Value of Effective Communication

Most people give little thought to effective communication until communication becomes important. Effective listening might be needed to understand the details of a special assignment or an emergency weather report. Effective speaking may be important when talking to someone you would like to get to know or for a job interview. Communication becomes especially important on the job. On the chalkboard, write the question "What types of communication skills will I need in the professional world to which I aspire?" Have students identify the careers or occupations they hope to have. List these on the chalkboard. As a class, discuss the kinds of communication skills needed for each. **L1**

Visual Instruction

Answer The source of self-talk is an individual's thoughts and opinions as he or she thinks.

Guided Reading Activity 3–1

Name _____ Date _____ Class _____

THE COMMUNICATION PROCESS AND YOU
Understanding Intrapersonal Communication

GUIDED READING
Activity 3–1

As you read Section 1, answer the following items.

1. List five instances when you use self-talk.

2. List the three steps of the perception process.

3. List the four factors that influence your selection of stimuli.

4. List the four steps in making more effective perception selections.

5. Define personal perception and list the factors that influence personal perception.

6. What does the word *prejudice* literally mean?

7. What happens if you have not learned how to listen effectively?

8. The secret to checking perception is what?

9. The sayings "Think before you speak" and "Look before you leap" refer to what?

10. What are the three methods of interpersonal perception checking?

11. "Let me see if I understand this recommendation correctly" is an example of what type of statement?

COMMUNICATION BEGINS WITH YOU

When you were younger, you may have been asked what you wanted to be when you grew up. Over time, you probably learned that this question actually meant, "What kind of job or profession do you hope to have?" Regardless of your answer, you probably pictured yourself as a grown-up in some sort of professional capacity.

Today, if you were asked what you hope to become, you might answer differently. In addition to answering with a career choice, you might also picture yourself assuming social roles in your church, community, or other organizations. Envisioning yourself with a fulfilling job and in positive social roles can help you pinpoint the type of person you might like to become.

However, to define who you are and establish what identities you would like to assume requires more than just wishful thinking. Start by asking yourself some important questions. "Who am I?" "What do I want to do with my life?" "What knowledge and skills do I need to reach my professional and social goals?" Answering these questions can help you determine the types of technical and communication skills you will need to establish a successful identity in the social and professional world.

Intrapersonal Communication

Effective communication skills are critical to achieving professional and social success. You might think that communication is interaction between two or more people. However, have you ever considered that, in addition to being able to communicate successfully with others, you need to learn to communicate effectively with yourself? This type of communication is known as intrapersonal communication, the first, or basic, level of communication. It begins with an understanding of who you are and what you think of yourself.

Self-Talk

Intrapersonal communication is a form of self-talk, or inner speech. It includes the questions and comments you make to yourself. "Should I look for a ride to school or catch the bus?" "Wow! I did that really well!" "Is my presentation for work good enough to impress my boss, or should I practice one more time?" Because these types of thoughts are stated only to yourself, they are examples of self-talk.

Self-talk is a powerful influence in your life. How you view things in your mind very much affects your attitude and your ability to reach your goal. If, for example, you believe that you cannot run that last lap, your brain

■ **Athletes like Karl Malone may use positive self-talk to achieve greater success. What is the source of self-talk?**

---

probably will convince your body that you can't do it. If, on the other hand, you give yourself a personal pep talk, your brain may help your body respond more positively.

Even though you may be unaware of it, you use self-talk all the time. This includes when you

- think things through
- interpret events
- interpret the messages of others
- respond to your own experiences
- respond to your interactions with others

Researchers are convinced that, whether spoken aloud or processed mentally, more positive self-talk can increase your focus, concentration, and performance. Sports psychologists note that athletes who talk positively to themselves—during practice, in competitions, or even during injury rehabilitation—experience greater success than those who do not.

Similarly, people who are afraid or under intense pressure often are able to reduce their stress by repeating calming words to

*inter*NET
A C T I V I T Y

Self-Talk Whether positive or negative, self-talk can have a powerful influence on your behavior and others' responses to you. Log on to the Internet and access a dependable World Wide Web search engine to search for sites related to self-talk. Then think about the type of self-talk that was helpful to you during your first week as a high school student. Use your own experience and the information from the Web to develop a one-page guide for incoming freshmen. Include a definition of self-talk and give examples and advice for using self-talk effectively.

themselves. Why? This type of positive self-talk helps them focus on achieving the task at hand and helps block out distracting internal and external noise.

"It's all according to your point of view. To me, you're a monster."

"Reprinted with permission from Modern Maturity. Copyright American Association of Retired Persons."

THE PERCEPTION PROCESS

The process you use to assign meaning to data about yourself or the world around you is called perception. Much of self-talk is based on your perceptions. People seldom share precisely the same perceptions. Since each person is unique, his or her perceptions are highly personal and individualized.

The Communication Process and You **71**

Sensory Cues

Senses provide cues that guide behavior and influence communication choices. List the five senses—seeing, hearing, smelling, tasting, and touching—in a column. Ask students to give examples of how cues received through each sense could affect communication. For example, what might be said after hearing the telephone ring? **L3**

Tuning Out

During the process of selective perception, we tune out certain information in order to focus on something more important. Point out that tuning things out is sometimes a conscious choice and sometimes an unconscious choice. Have students identify situations in which people often tune out. Why is this done? What might they be tuning in to? **L2**

■ **Visual Instruction**

Answer Students may indicate that communicators have to decide what stimuli to focus on and what stimuli to ignore.

You form your perceptions by acquiring data, focusing on specific parts of that data, and deciding how to organize and interpret the data you selected. These three steps of the perception process are

- sensory perception
- selective perception
- personal perception

Sensory Perception

As you learned in Chapter 2, sensory perception is the physical process of taking in data through the senses. Seeing, hearing, smelling, tasting, and touching all are physical senses that provide links between you and the world. They allow you to take in information and to learn. They allow you to respond to the data—to communicate with yourself and others about what you experience. Think about how you know when it is time to go to school or to work. You probably look at a clock and interpret the time, communicating to yourself your interpretation of the data you collected. You may feel a chill in the air or listen to a weather report forecasting cool conditions that day. You may then use your sensory perceptions to decide that you should wear a jacket when you go outside. Every day our

72 *Glencoe Communication Applications*

senses send us hundreds of cues that guide our behaviors. Our senses also guide our communication choices.

Selective Perception

The second step of the perception process is selective perception. Selective perception is the mental process of choosing which data or stimuli to focus on from all that are available to you at any given time. We are constantly bombarded with information—far more than we are able to take in. So, we constantly are making decisions about which information to focus on and which to ignore. Our selective perception, then, influences what we notice.

Imagine that a mowing crew is cutting the grass outside your classroom window. The noise of the mower and the voices of the crew catch your attention so you focus on them for a moment. During this short sensory vacation away from the classroom, you acquire literally dozens of different stimuli.

However, what classroom data did you tune out when you turned your attention outside? Did you miss a communication opportunity by not hearing your name as your teacher called on you to answer a question? The important things to remember about selective perception are that you have a choice about what you tune in or tune out and that the choices you make influence your communication. Every time you choose to focus your attention on a particular stimulus, you screen out dozens of other cues to which you might have paid attention.

■ **The stimuli people create around you in a movie theater sometimes make it hard to concentrate on the movie itself.** What communication decisions must be made in regard to all the stimuli we receive?

MULTIPLE LEARNING STYLES

Musical Incoming information comes in many forms and to all the senses. Musical learners remember tunes and lyrics and are especially attuned to musical stimuli.

Activity Ask students to watch a series of commercials, noting the music used within each commercial. Ask students to analyze the music and its use. Does the music set the tone for the commercial? Is it used for background? Does the music have lyrics? Are the lyrics original or are they from a previously published work? How does the music affect their perception of the product and its worth?

Figure 3–1 Factors That Influence Selective Perception

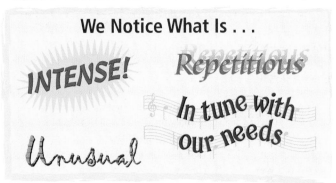

Making Perception Choices From the example on the previous page, you can see that you make conscious choices hundreds of times a day about what you perceive. You also make perception choices subconsciously. In other words, you make many choices that you do not even realize you are making.

It takes focused communication energy to select and concentrate on the most important stimuli. Understanding what influences your selections can help you make appropriate communication choices for yourself, the occasion, and the task.

Factors That Influence Selections As shown in Figure 3–1, there are several factors that influence your selection of stimuli. Four important ones are intensity, repetition, uniqueness, and relevance to our individual needs, interests, and motivations. Stimuli that display these characteristics tend to have a greater influence on our perception choices than other stimuli.

Intensity As a rule, the more intense or dramatic the stimulus, the more likely we are to notice it. For example, you are more likely to notice someone screaming than someone talking quietly in the corner of a room. Unfortunately, the most intense or noticeable data may not always be the most important.

Repetition People also tend to notice repetitious stimuli. The ticking of a clock or the constant drip of water from a faucet may become so distracting that you cannot seem to hear anything else. Advertisers and politicians know that the messages most often repeated are the ones people tend to believe. By saturating the media with memorable images, phrases, and slogans, they constantly bombard consumers with their message. The idea is that the more we hear—and, in turn, are influenced by—a message, the more likely we are to buy the product or vote for the candidate.

Uniqueness People usually notice things that are new, unusual, unexpected, or unique. This can have either a positive or negative effect. Performers often rely on a new look or gimmick to catch the public's attention and to boost their popularity. This may be necessary to remain noticed in the constantly changing world of entertainment. However, in the business world, many companies frown on employees who draw attention to themselves through their appearance.

Many companies want to present a specific company image and may require employees to wear uniforms or a specific style of clothing anytime they are working or representing the company. Many schools also have dress codes, and some social situations call for a specific look or image. In each situation, eliminating unusual data or stimuli is designed to focus people's attention on what is more important—the company's product or the task of learning.

The Communication Process and You   **73**

Picturing Perception Choices
Point out the way the artist has depicted the four perception choices in the graphic. Challenge students to do a similar drawing for each perception stimulus. After the drawings are completed, let students explain their interpretations to a group of classmates. **L1**

Repetition and Perception
Repetition is sometimes used in politics to affect people's perceptions of individuals or parties. Politicians running for office often have a slogan or theme that is repeated over and over. Sometimes, to influence public opinion on a debate, a party will adopt a theme for the day or week for which everyone talking to the media recites the same phrase. Have students watch several Sunday talk shows and list some of the phrases repeated over and over. Who is making the statements? Why? During a class discussion have students share their results and observations. **L2**

COOPERATIVE LEARNING ACTIVITY

We perceive things through all five of our senses. However, the sense of hearing sometimes strongly influences our perceptions. A dripping faucet can become annoying, but a failure to perceive the siren of an approaching ambulance when driving can be serious.

Ask students to select a time during the day to just listen. Suggest that they find a comfortable place, close their eyes for a minute or more, and then list all the sounds they hear. In class, ask students to identify something that they were surprised to have heard. What influenced their ability to perceive that sound in this particular situation? Why might they not have heard it otherwise?

Why Do I Have to Listen to This?

Although a person may not always consciously ask this question when evaluating things perceived by the senses, the person often acts on the answer. Ask students to identify situations in which they have stopped paying attention to something. Why did they stop? Which sense or senses were perceiving the information? **L2**

Don't Think of a Pink Elephant!

One of the steps for developing selective perception skills is to screen out distractions and noise. This takes practice because once a noise or other distraction becomes part of the conscious mind, people sometimes have great difficulty screening out the distraction. To demonstrate this, tell students you will give them a direction that they are to follow. Then say, "Don't think of a pink elephant." Have students describe the results. Then, discuss with students what techniques they have used to erase noise and other distractions from their mind so that they can concentrate on other things. **L2**

COMMUNICATION *Strategies*

DEVELOPING SELECTIVE PERCEPTION SKILLS

Ask students to suggest good work habits to follow when studying or doing homework. What things would make their study time most productive? List the ideas on the board. Have students compare their suggestions to the steps for developing selective perception skills. Which ones are similar? Why might the two lists be similar? What ideas from one list could be added to the other? **L2**

Relevance We often notice things that mirror our own interests, needs, and motivations. This can influence data selections. If you are in the market to buy a car, you probably will begin noticing cars similar to the one you want. You may see this model more often as you travel to school or work, and you may begin noticing more advertisements for that type of car. You have subconsciously begun focusing on data that meet your specific needs at that time.

Not only do we tend to notice things that are relevant to our interests and needs, but we also tend to tune out stimuli that we think do not pertain to us. For instance, a coach may notice certain details about a ball game that spectators are likely to miss. However, he or she may be totally unaware that threatening storm clouds are moving in overhead. By focusing his or her attention on the game, the coach overlooks information that may be necessary to keep the team safe.

Sometimes, the most important data is not the data that is the most intense, repeated, unusual, or related to your needs and interests. By studying your own perception patterns and analyzing what types of data are most important in a given situation, you can learn how to focus your communication energy for maximum effectiveness.

Managing Selective Perception

Think about how air traffic controllers, truck drivers, machinists, or surgeons must focus their attention on the job. Allowing themselves to become distracted for even an instant could lead to tragedy. While the consequences might not be quite as extreme, the same rule applies to most people, whether they are on the job or at school. In order to perform more effectively, individuals can learn to screen out distractions and focus on the task at hand by using the following suggestions.

COMMUNICATION *Strategies*

DEVELOPING SELECTIVE PERCEPTION SKILLS

- ✓ Stay alert.
- ✓ Make conscious choices about what is and what is not important data.
- ✓ Screen out distractions and noise that may interfere with concentration.
- ✓ Monitor your selection patterns and choices and set goals for improvement.

The first step in making more effective perception selections is to stay alert. It can be easy, at times, to let your mind wander. For example, have you ever watched the news so you could find out what the weather would be like the next day and yet still miss it? Staying alert can help you avoid this type of oversight.

The second step is to ask yourself what you need to focus your attention on. Obviously, if you are in class, you should focus on the class and avoid daydreaming. Similarly, if you are driving a car, you should make a conscious decision to keep your attention on the road. Talking and choosing what music to play can be entertaining but should not draw your attention from driving safely to your destination.

Third, screen out distractions and noise. This means taking control of your mental processes. Much of your effectiveness as a competent communicator is related to your ability to concentrate and hold your focus on whatever needs your attention at the moment. This may take practice, but it is an important and valuable skill.

GIFTED AND TALENTED

Perceiving Commercials Commercials are good examples of how companies with products to sell capitalize on the perceptions of people.

Activity Have students check their perceptions and filtering systems. Encourage students to tape-record a commercial or provide a videotape of a commercial. After viewing the tape, students should write down what they thought was said in the commercial. Then, students should replay the tape to assess what was really said. How does what was really said compare to what students thought was said? Have students write a brief summary of the commercial they watched, their findings, and suggestions for why descrepancies in actual messages and perceived messages may occur.

■ **Figure 3–2 What Do You See?**

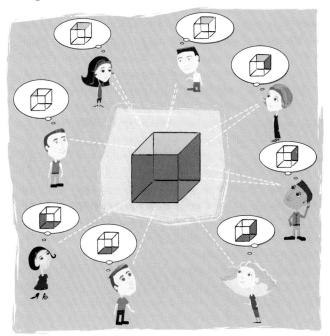

The product of this part of the process is your personal perception. Personal perception is your own understanding of reality. As shown in Figure 3–2, it is the reality you construct for yourself as you organize and interpret data and as you create and assign meaning to events, people, and objects around you. Your personal perceptions become the basis for the judgments and decisions you make. They also determine the appropriateness of your communication choices.

Factors That Influence Personal Perception Your perceptions are as personal and unique as you are. As shown in Figure 3–3 on the next page, a number of different factors affect your personal perceptions.

Finally, monitor the way you select data. If you realize that you have some weak patterns, correct them. Use self-talk to raise your level of awareness and to tune out distractions. Then set goals to make more effective choices in specific professional and social situations. Developing better skills in selective perception will help you become a more competent communicator.

Personal Perception

The third step of the perception process involves organizing and sorting the data to which to pay attention. During this filtering process, you create meanings for the events, people, and objects around you. You tell yourself what is happening, interpret what the data means to you, and decide how to respond to each set of data.

What Do You See?
After students read through the information in the first column, focus on the drawing, Figure 3–2. Have students tell how each person in the drawing might answer the question What do you see? Why might the answers be so different? How does this drawing help explain the concept of personal perception? **L2**

A Filtering Process
The authors of the text have called the concept of personal perception a filtering process. Discuss with students what a filter is. Then, ask what things are a part of their filters. For example, what things affect whether they like a movie or television show? What things affect how they feel about certain issues related to the school or community? What other words might the authors have used other than *filter* that would make the same point? **L3**

🌐 **GLOBAL COMMUNICATION**

Making Assumptions

It is important to remember that one individual's behavior does not necessarily represent the values, beliefs, or practices of an entire culture. Consider how you might feel if one student from your school were chosen at random to represent all American high school students. What is one cultural assumption you made in your selection? Did you base this assumption on fact or opinion? How might you avoid making this type of assumption in the future?

The Communication Process and You **75**

🌐 **GLOBAL COMMUNICATION**

Making Assumptions

In working through this activity, be sure students know what an assumption is. Discuss with them whether it would be possible to choose one person to represent all high school students. Why would the choice always be flawed? In answering the questions in the activity on the student page, students may say mistaken assumptions in the past may have been the result of a limited amount of knowledge about a culture. Students should understand that their cultural knowledge should come from facts, not opinions. **L2**

INTERDISCIPLINARY CONNECTION

Social Studies American movies are shown throughout the world. For better or worse, each movie portrays a part of the American culture. Personal perceptions of Americans by people in other countries is sometimes formed by the images they see on movie screens.

Activity Have students choose three movies they have enjoyed. Remind students to use classroom-appropriate examples. Ask them to make a list of what they feel were accurate portrayals of American culture and what inaccurate portrayals were present. Discuss the results. Then, ask how the students' personal perceptions might have affected their lists. 📦

Bias—Positive and Negative

Bias is part of a person's filtering system. Most people tend to think of bias as negative because it can often have unfair consequences. However, bias might also be positive. As a group, discuss positive and negative examples of bias. Would students agree with a person who said, "I don't have a biased bone in my body?" Why or why not? **L2**

Great Expectations

Draw the following diagram on the chalkboard:

Expectation → Event → Result = Judgment/Communication

Point out that everyone has expectations about a wide variety of things, from how good the Thanksgiving turkey will taste to how a person thinks someone should act. Call attention to the diagram and discuss what it is meant to show. Have students identify some examples of times when they have had expectations. Were the results what they expected? How did the result influence the judgments they made or the communication that followed? Was it positive or negative? Ask students why making judgments or communication choices based on expectations may not be a good thing to do. **L2**

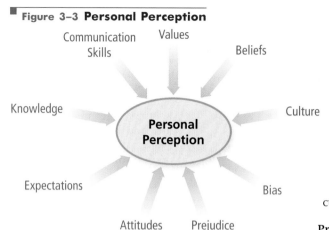

■ **Figure 3–3 Personal Perception**

Values Values reflect your priorities. They help you answer the questions "What do you think is important?" and "How important do you think it is?" For example, you may value strong family relationships, friendship, and honesty. When you select specific data to focus on, you filter it through these values. This helps you determine how information applies to you and what judgments or decisions you will make in order to use it.

Beliefs People often feel so strongly about their beliefs—thoughts and ideas they accept as true—that they will fiercely defend them. Your beliefs are a part of the system through which you filter incoming information. They help you decide whether to accept or reject information. They also help you determine how the information affects your decisions and communication choices.

Culture You can be part of a family culture, a community culture, or even an organizational culture. Different parts of the country and the world, different religions, and different ethnicities form and practice their own cultures. Culture affects virtually every aspect of your life and your communication. It is a strong influence on how you

view, organize, and interpret the information and messages you receive.

Bias Another influence on perception is bias. Bias is a consistent attitude, viewpoint, or pattern of perception through which we view the world. Biases can be positive or negative. In either case, they result from our personal experiences and also from our cultural perspectives.

Prejudice Perception also can be influenced by prejudice. Prejudice is a preconceived judgment. Broken down into its syllables, prejudice literally means to *pre-judge*. It means to judge based only on opinion, not on fact. Facts can be verified or proven; opinions are beliefs that cannot be proven.

Prejudices usually stem from negative emotions such as fear, hate, suspicion, and distrust. They are based on opinion, on a lack of information rather than on fact. When prejudices are not acknowledged and eliminated, they can present barriers to logical judgment and effective communication.

Attitudes A person's attitude generally is classified as either positive or negative. It is the way we choose to respond to various situations. Attitude is a powerful force in influencing our perceptions, our decisions, and our communication with others.

Expectations What you expect something to be like and what you expect from others also influences your perceptions. For example, if a movie does not meet the promises made in its advertisements, you may be disappointed. If a friend's actions exceed your expectations, you may be delighted. In either case, you are basing a judgment on what you expected rather than on what actually happened. The fact that your

---

MEETING INDIVIDUAL NEEDS — MULTIPLE LEARNING STYLES

Visual-Spatial We perceive information in many forms and through all the senses. Visual-spatial learners are especially attuned to visual stimuli, and their personal perception filtering system may be more highly developed. As a result, they may be able to detect what information is being filtered.

Activity Ask students to work in pairs in front of a television set. Have them watch a series of commercials with the sound off. Ask each person to give his or her initial reaction—either positive or negative—to the product or person. What influenced the individuals to make the evaluations they did? Then, have students refer to Figure 3–3. Which factors shown in the diagram may have affected their judgments? Why? 📖

expectations were or were not met is a questionable basis for making judgments or communication choices. Your expectations may not reflect what an acceptable outcome might be.

Knowledge Knowledge also influences your perceptions. What you know and what you do not know influence how you organize and interpret information. If you have studied music, acting, dance, athletics, or painting, you are likely to view a performance or work of art differently from someone who has not had training in that field. The expression "Knowledge is power" relates to the fact that the more knowledge you have, the better you can understand information, process and filter ideas, make decisions and judgments, and communicate with others.

Communication Skills Your communication skills also affect how you view the world. If you do not understand the words others use, you cannot decode or interpret their messages as effectively. If you have not learned how to listen effectively, you may have difficulty acquiring the messages of others and organizing and interpreting them.

To understand ourselves, it is vital to understand the different factors that influence our perceptions. Of course, the amount of influence each factor has on your filter system can vary. However, by monitoring these factors closely, you can ensure that your self-talk, decisions, and communication choices are as effective as possible.

Analyzing Perceptions

Everyone sees himself or herself, others, events, and the world in general from a different viewpoint. Therefore, it is easy to understand why each person's perceptions are unique. Our communication is influenced by our perceptions of ourselves and others, what we talk about, and the setting in which the communication takes place. This explains why two people in the same room can have completely different perceptions of the same event. As a communicator, it is important to understand not only our own perception process, but to recognize that others can experience the same event but interpret it differently.

Examine **Figures 3–4** and **3–5.** Do you and your classmates all perceive the same information about these drawings?

Think about the class you are in right now. No two people in your classroom are experiencing the exact same class. One person may view the class as interesting while another perceives it as dull. One student may feel uncomfortable participating in classroom

■ Figure 3–4 **Face or Vase?**

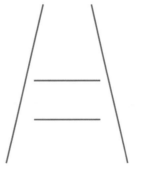

■ Figure 3–5 **Which Line Appears Longer?**

The Communication Process and You **77**

C O M M U N I C A T I O N
P R A C T I C E   L A B
Examining Different Perceptions

Have students follow the four steps in the Communication Practice Lab on this page to help appreciate how different observers in different roles experience and perceive the same event. When listing the factors that influenced perceptions, students may want to refer to Figure 3–3 on page 76. How do perceptions vary because of role? Finally, discuss with students why understanding that people have different perceptions can help them communicate more effectively. **L2**

GLENCOE
Online

For an additional Practice Lab for this section, have students visit the *Glencoe Communication Applications* Web site at **communicationapplications.glencoe.com**. Click on Communication Practice Lab 3–1. **L1**

Culture and Perception
Draw a word web on the chalkboard, using Cultural Barriers to Communication as the title for a center circle. Discuss with students why people from other cultures may have perceptions of certain people or events that differ from those they hold. Write reasons in circles surrounding the center circle as they are given. **L2**

C O M M U N I C A T I O N
Examining Different Perceptions
P R A C T I C E   L A B

To understand how people can have different perceptions of the same event, follow these steps:

Step 1 As a class, act out the following scenario: While moving a cash register from one counter to another, two workers accidentally drop it, damaging it severely. Several coworkers and customers observe the incident.

Step 2 Take turns describing what each student observed. Was everyone's perception of the event exactly the same? Discuss why or why not.

Step 3 On the chalkboard, list factors that may have influenced people's perceptions.

Step 4 Using this list, arrive at a group consensus about what actually occurred. How did the class reach agreement?

---

discussions while another enjoys the opportunity to interact with classmates. The perceptions and attitudes that each student forms are unique and will affect his or her performance and communication in class.

If perceptions can vary among students in the same classroom, you can imagine how much they can vary among people of different backgrounds and cultures. This can lead to some barriers to communication. People with different perceptions tend to make different kinds of communication choices, draw different conclusions, and make different judgments.

It is these types of differences that account for many of the conflicts and misunderstandings people encounter in personal, professional, and social situations. One way to overcome these problems is to continually check your own perceptions to make sure they are as accurate as possible. This can help you function more effectively as a competent communicator.

USING PERCEPTION CHECKS

How do you know you really saw what you think you saw or heard what you think you heard? In many cases, you can't. However, you

can learn to use perception checks to improve your accuracy in gathering and using information as a basis for making your communication decisions.

A perception check is a question that helps you determine the accuracy and validity of your perceptions. The secret to checking perceptions is never to assume that what you perceived as the truth is the actual, absolute truth.

You need to base your communication choices on accurate perceptions. To do this, you can use two kinds of perception checks: intrapersonal and interpersonal.

Intrapersonal Perception Checks

Like your communication, your perception checks begin within you. Start the process by checking the accuracy of your self-talk. To do this, ask yourself questions based on the steps of the perception process.

Begin by questioning your sensory perception. If you were a witness to a car accident, you might ask yourself the same types of questions a police officer or attorney might ask. "Could I actually see the accident well?" "Was the sun in my eyes" "Was it dark, making details hard to see?"

78   *Glencoe Communication Applications*

REAL-WORLD CONNECTION

Selective Perception on the Job Selective perception is used throughout the day on most jobs. The ability to use selective perception effectively can sometimes mean the difference between doing okay and doing very well.

Activity Help students arrange to observe a person in a work environment such as a busy office or in a home with small children. What were some examples of selective perception this person used or seemed to use? What were the results? Did the person seem to be aware of the choices? How could students tell? When the observations have been completed, have students share the results with the class. What conclusions can be drawn?

After checking appropriate details of your sensory perception, question your selective perception. Ask yourself, "Was I actually looking at the accident at the moment of the crash, or did I hear the screech of brakes or the cars colliding and then change my focus to look at the cars? Was my attention distracted, even for a split second? Did I actually see all of what happened?"

Finally, question your personal perception. You might ask, "What influenced my interpretation of the accident? Have my conclusions been influenced by a similar experience I had? Was I influenced by any biases or prejudices about the circumstances of the accident?"

How, then, do sensory perception, selective perception, and personal perception relate to communication? Using perception checks helps you safeguard the accuracy of your self-talk and avoid making wrong assumptions about the things that you observe. Perception checks help you check for accuracy before taking action or communicating your perceptions to others. To help you understand how perception checks can help you become a more competent communicator, think about the sayings "Think before you speak" and "Look before you leap."

Intrapersonal perception checks do not always provide firm proof that your perceptions are accurate. In fact, they may raise additional questions that make you say, "I'm still not sure." When you can't clear up your perceptions yourself, your next step is to perform some interpersonal perception checks.

COMMUNICATION *Strategies*

QUESTIONS FOR CHECKING PERCEPTION

- ✓ Do I stay alert?
- ✓ Do I strive for sensory awareness?
- ✓ Am I making conscious choices about what to tune in and what to tune out?
- ✓ Do my choices focus on what is most important rather than what is most obvious?
- ✓ Am I easily distracted?
- ✓ Am I aware of factors that influence my self-talk?
- ✓ Do I ask myself "Is this really what I saw or heard or merely what I told myself I saw or heard?"
- ✓ Do I compare my perceptions to the perceptions of others to check for accuracy?

Interpersonal Perception Checks

One of the basic guidelines you can use to check perceptions is to clarify meanings so you will not misunderstand someone else's messages. Other guidelines are to analyze others' points of view and to take responsibility for your own communication. Developing skills in these areas can give you real power in professional and social situations where accurate perceptions are vital.

Clarifying Your Perceptions of Others' Messages
Interpersonal perception checks involve asking others about their perceptions of an event. For instance, you might ask someone else who witnessed the same car accident you did to explain his or her perception of what occurred. Comparing your perceptions to the other person's can help you both get a clearer picture of what actually occurred.

Similarly, after hearing your boss explain a new project during a staff meeting, you feel you may have misunderstood some of the

The Communication Process and You **79**

When?
Doing an in-depth perception check before making a communication decision usually is not practical. However, there are times when such checks are necessary. Ask students to give some specific, real-world examples of when perception checks are helpful and when they are essential. Why do some situations require such an analysis? **L3**

COMMUNICATION *Strategies*

QUESTIONS FOR CHECKING PERCEPTION

Before students read the list of questions, ask them why such a list for checking perception may be useful. Then, direct students to answer the questions on a sheet of paper. Have students evaluate their skills at checking perception. Did they answer most of the questions with a "Yes"? Ask students to choose one question to which they answered "No" and to list three ways they could try to improve the skill. After a week, have students report back to the class on their progress. **L1**

MEETING INDIVIDUAL NEEDS

INCLUSION STRATEGIES

Learning Disabled Sensory and selective perception may be difficult for some students. Therefore, perception checks may prove a useful aid in improving communication with others and in improving self-talk.

Activity Intrapersonal perception checks can have an influence on a person's self-talk. Ask students if they agree or disagree with this statement and why. Review the list of questions found under Communication Strategies on this page. How might intrapersonal perception checks, such as the one shown, help a person develop more positive self-talk? Why might this happen? Let students work in small groups to brainstorm some specific examples of how careful intrapersonal perception checks can improve self-talk.

Imagine

Clarifying perceptions of others' messages can be a powerful tool in succeeding professionally. Students who have done some kind of work—whether it be homework assignments, household chores, baby-sitting, or a part-time job—know that there are times when the words of another may need clarification. Let students work in groups to prepare skits of such situations and to act out how a person would go about clarifying perceptions. When each group is ready, have the members present their skit to the class. Ask the class to evaluate each skit by identifying a suggestion they might find useful in future situations. **L2**

3 ASSESS

Assign Section 1 Assessment as a homework or in-class activity.

🔘 Use *Interactive Tutor Self-Assessment Software* to review Section 1.

THE INVESTIGATION

HE WAS A REAL TALL GUY DRESSED NORMALLY WITH LIGHT, DRY HAIR.

HE WAS A HEALTHY, GOOD LOOKING YOUNG KID... BUT DRESSED RATHER SHABBILY.

HE WAS REAL BIG AND REAL OLD.

HE WAS A WELL-DRESSED SORT, A LITTLE OVERWEIGHT AND WITH A LOT OF HAIR.

I REMEMBER HE HAD A LARGE HEAD AND HE SMELLED FUNNY.

HE WAS SURELY A WESTERNER.

HE WAS A SCRAWNY LITTLE SHORT-HAIRED TWERP FROM BACK EAST.

HE HAD DARK HAIR AND A CUTE NOSE. A REAL DOLL.

HE WAS A ROUGH, FURRY GUY WITH LITTLE BEADY EYES. PROBABLY INEDIBLE.

(Reprinted by permission of John Jonik from Psychology Today.*)*

point of view. Asking someone else how he or she feels about an event can provide you with valuable insight. In some cases, it can make you aware of issues or special circumstances that you might not have considered before. After analyzing the other person's point of view, you can confirm, clarify, or you might even decide to change your own perceptions as necessary.

Taking Responsibility for Your Own Communication

A third basic method of interpersonal perception checking is to take responsibility for your own communication. When you feel someone else has not fully understood your message, it is your responsibility to check that person's perceptions. By asking questions, you can confirm what the person does or does not understand.

Also, if you're not sure you fully understand someone else's message, use questions to clarify your own understanding. Making a "feed-forward" statement shows that you take responsibility for needing more information. To **feed-forward** is to offer an explanation that you want to make or a reason or explanation for a question, request, or offer.

For instance, if you need clarification in a meeting, you might make a feed-forward statement such as "Let me see if I understand this recommendation correctly." Then you could ask "Is this what we're recommending?" and restate the recommendation as you understand it.

You might also use a feed-forward method to clarify perceptions related to your own memory. If, for example, you are uncertain about the time and place of a prom

details. You might ask a coworker about his or her perceptions of the information. This can help you clear up any misunderstandings and proceed more effectively.

Whether clarifying your own perceptions or the perceptions of others, it is important to be as accurate and easy to understand as possible. In other words, make clear requests, give accurate directions, ask appropriate and purposeful questions, and respond appropriately to the requests, directions, and questions of others.

Analyzing Others' Points of View

A second method of interpersonal perception checking is to try to analyze the other person's

80

MEETING INDIVIDUAL NEEDS

MULTIPLE LEARNING STYLES

Interpersonal Using feed-forward is not only a way of taking responsibility for one's own understanding and communication, it is also a form of tact. By using feed-forward, a person can put someone else at ease when asking for a clarification rather than putting him or her on the defensive. A feed-forward statement tells the listener why you are asking the question.

Activity Let students work in pairs to identify situations in which feed-forward statements could be used in their everyday communications to help them understand the communications of others better and to put other people at ease. Tell students to come up with specific phrases they could use to preface their questions, such as, "I want to be sure I understand this correctly." When pairs are ready, have them present some of their situations and the phrases they came up with. 📖

committee meeting, you might call a friend and say, "I'm sorry. I forgot today's announcement. Can you tell me when and where the meeting will be held?" Again, you are taking responsibility for your perception and asking a question to clear up your confusion.

By taking responsibility for a potential misunderstanding, asking a question, and restating the issue as you understand it, you create a climate for clarification. Your purpose is

obvious: You wish to clarify understanding, not start a dispute or argument.

Perception checking is just one more skill that can help make your intrapersonal communication more effective. It is your intrapersonal communication skills that form the basis for your interpersonal, group, and one-to-group interactions. In other words, how you view yourself and the world around you has a great impact on how you communicate with others.

Section 1 Assessment

Visit the *Glencoe Communication Applications* Web site at **communicationapplications. glencoe.com** and click on **Self-Check and Study Guide 3.1** to review your understanding of intrapersonal communication.

Review Key Terms

1. Define each term and write it in a sentence: perception, selective perception, personal perception, perception check, feed-forward.

Check Understanding

2. Explain perception as a process.

3. Describe the four factors that influence selective perception and give an example of each.

4. Identify the nine factors that influence personal perception. Choose one factor and describe how it affected your personal perception of a past event or issue.

5. Imagine that, while shopping at the mall, you saw someone snatch a woman's purse. How might you check your perception of the event? Why?

6. **Drawing Conclusions** Why is it important to make sure your perceptions are as accurate and complete as possible before acting on them?

APPLICATION *Activity*

Checking Perceptions Imagine that your boss just walked into your office and said, "I know the project you're working on is important. This report is important too. Finish it as soon as possible." Write a list of questions you might ask yourself to clarify your perception of what he or she said. Next, write a list of questions you might ask your boss. Be sure to use feed-forward statements when appropriate. Finally, share your questions as a class and discuss how to tactfully question unclear communication.

The Communication Process and You **81**

4 CLOSE

Have students reread the opening paragraph for Section 1 on page 69. Ask students to identify ways positive self-talk and accurate perceptions can help shape their communication choices and influence their effectiveness as communicators.

Extra-Credit Project

Have students keep a record of feed-forward questions they hear during the course of a day in their classes, in social situations, or with their family. Have them share some of the best examples with the class.

Section 1 Assessment Answers

1. Accept all reasonable sentences.

2. The perception process involves a person taking in information through sensory perception, using selective perception to decide on which information to focus, and organizing and sorting the information using personal perception.

3. The four factors that influence selective perception are intensity, repetition, uniqueness, and relevance. Accept all correctly applied examples.

4. values, beliefs, culture, bias, prejudice, attitudes, expectations, knowledge, and communication skills. Students' choices of factors and descriptions will vary.

5. Students' perceptions will vary.

6. Accept all reasonable answers.

Application Activity The completed activity should consist of two lists of questions: questions the students might ask themselves that may be informal and pointed and questions to ask the boss.

Applying Reading Skill

Monitoring Comprehension

Comprehension is the most important part of reading. We read to comprehend. The purpose of reading something is to find out what was written. Sometimes, when reading purely for pleasure, it is enough simply to read the story or article. Sometimes, however, a more in-depth kind of comprehension is needed. For example, if studying for a quiz or getting ready to write a report, a reader needs a thorough understanding of the material. Certain techniques can help a reader monitor comprehension—help a reader make sure the information is understood. Review the four steps with students. Ask which ones they use or have used and how the techniques helped them. Encourage students to add to the list tips of their own. **L1**

Practicing the Skill

1. A typical statement of the main idea might be that government and the nation's economy are tied closely together.

2. Notes students take will vary but will probably focus on the statistics included in the information.

3. Lists will vary and may include dates followed by number of government workers.

Application Activity

Student answers for this activity will vary greatly and, in general, will reflect how well students comprehended the material. Let students share the results of the activity with a classmate.

MONITORING COMPREHENSION

When you comprehend something, you understand it completely. Monitoring your reading comprehension can help you get the most out of everything you read.

Learning the Skill

Step 1 Look for the Main Idea. After reading a few paragraphs, start thinking about the main idea of a selection. You can gather clues about the main idea by examining the main title and subheads and any introductory or background material. After you have determined the main idea, think about what it means. You may even wish to write it down as a reminder.

Step 2 Underline Important Ideas. If you are allowed to write on what you are reading, use a highlighter to mark important information. As you read, underline any ideas, facts, and supporting details you will want to remember. Highlighting allows you to quickly review material. This can be especially helpful when studying for tests, writing papers, or preparing presentations.

Step 3 Take Brief Notes. When a sentence or idea is complex or confusing, rewrite it in a way that makes sense to you. Also, take notes on the main ideas and supporting details of what you are reading. Writing information in your own words boosts comprehension and helps you remember what you have read.

Step 4 Make Lists. Sometimes it is important to remember instructions or other information in a specific sequence.

Rewriting the information in list form can help you remember the proper sequence. Lists also are helpful for remembering a series of dates, places, names, or events.

Practicing the Skill

Read the following selection from a recent economics text. Rewrite the main topic, or idea, in your own words. Then, take notes on the most important information. Create lists as necessary.

Government at every level—local, state, and federal—is closely tied to the U.S. economy. Over the past 50 years or so, that government has grown significantly larger. In 1929, the U.S. government at all levels employed just over 3 million civilian workers. During the Depression, however, more government services were needed. As a result, the government grew. In 1999, about 2.7 million people worked for the federal government alone. With state and local employees added in, the government employed a total of 19.6 million workers by the end of the twentieth century. The U.S. government had increased to six times its size while the population had only doubled. This has had a great impact on our nation's economy.

APPLICATION *Activity*

Close your book and ask yourself what you remember about the four steps for monitoring comprehension. On a separate sheet of paper, make a list of these steps. Rely on your memory to explain each step in your own words.

MEETING INDIVIDUAL NEEDS

INCLUSION STRATEGIES

Less-Proficient Readers Good readers can often be effective mentors for students who need help with comprehension skills.

Activity Pair a good reader with a less-proficient reader. Allow the less-proficient reader to provide an actual reading assignment for another class or for this class. Have the pair review the steps in monitoring comprehension described in the lesson. Then, suggest that the proficient reader model how to accomplish each step, guiding the partner to express the main idea and offering personal tips on how to take notes and make lists while reading. Finally, have the partners quiz each other on the content of the material they covered.

Section 2

Understanding Self as a Communicator

GUIDE TO READING

Objectives

1. Identify and analyze common influences on self-concept.
2. Analyze the relationship between self-concept and interpersonal communication.
3. Explain the effects of self-fulfilling prophecy on communication and personal performance.
4. Analyze and use the Johari window to evaluate personal interaction with others.

Terms to Learn

self-concept
self-fulfilling prophecy
self-disclosure

Imagine you are prepared for an important job interview. You have studied the company's background, possess the right skills for the position, and look and feel your best. You are confident that the job is yours. On the way into the interviewer's office, however, you realize that you are wearing two different shoes. Now you feel very self-conscious. Does this change the situation? How?

One step to building better communication skills with others is to take a close look at your own self-concept. Self-concept, also known as self-perception, is the view you have of yourself. It is the person you think you are, formed from your beliefs and attitudes. Your self-concept also is influenced by other factors, such as how you think others see you and the person you were in the past, are today, and would like to be in the future.

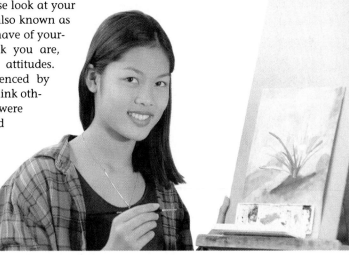

Displaying your work with confidence indicates positive self-concept. Self-concept plays an important role in developing communication skills. What factors influence self-concept?

The Communication Process and You **83**

RESOURCE MANAGER

Teaching Tools

- Interactive Lesson Planner
- Reproducible Lesson Plan 3–2
- Application Activities 3–2

Reproducible Masters

- Guided Reading Activity Workbook 3–2
- Enrichment Activity 3–2
- Reteaching Activity 3–2
- Section Quiz 3–2
- Transparency Strategies and Activities Booklet 3–2

Transparencies

- Graphic Organizer Transparency 3–2
- Chapter 3 Teaching Transparency

Technology Resources

- Interactive Tutor Self-Assessment Software
- Presentation Plus! Software
- ExamView® Pro Testmaker
- PuzzleMaker Software
- communicationapplications.glencoe.com

CHAPTER 3
Section 2

1 FOCUS

Bellringer

Ask students to read the objectives and opening quotation of the section. Have them write their answers to the questions. Then discuss the students' responses, focusing on the role self-concept might play in the communication process. *(Students may say that they would feel very self-conscious and that they may end up trying to avoid being near the person. Because the person no longer feels confident, his or her verbal and nonverbal communication is likely to be affected.)*

You may use Graphic Organizer Transparency 3–2 to introduce this section.

Graphic Organizer Transparency 3-2

Your Own Expectations | Others' Expectations

Grammar Tip

Apostrophes are used to indicate ownership. An *'s* is used for singular nouns and for plural nouns not ending in -s (company's background, interviewer's office). Use an apostrophe alone for plural nouns ending in -s (companies' stocks, interviewers' skills).

Visual Instruction

Answer Students might identify the following as factors that influence self-concept: your beliefs and attitudes; how other people see you; how you think others see you; how you see yourself in the past, today, and in the future.

2 TEACH

Changing Self-Concepts

Self-concept changes. It can change from day to day and even moment to moment. While each person has a basic idea of who he or she is, over time that image and the image others have of the person can change. Discuss with students why a person's self-concept might change. Encourage specific examples for each reason given. **L1**

You Are the Voice!

Review with students the Anthony Robbins quotation on page 69 and also the idea of self-talk. Discuss with students how self-talk and self-concept are related. Are they the same thing? Which one influences the other? Does each have an influence on how you feel about yourself? Who ultimately decides how you feel about yourself? **L2**

Guided Reading Activity 3–2

GUIDED READING
Activity 3–2

THE COMMUNICATION PROCESS AND YOU
Understanding Self as a Communicator

Name _____ Date _____ Class _____

As you read Section 2, complete the sentences below.

1. Self-concept, also known as _____, is the view you have of _____.
2. The three factors that have the greatest influence on self-concept are how you _____ that you are seen and treated by _____, your own _____ and _____ that you set for yourself, and how you _____ yourself to others.
3. The messages you receive from others impact your self-_____, as well as your self-_____.
4. If you have a positive concept of yourself in a certain situation, your _____ is likely to be highly _____. However, if you allow negative interactions to influence your _____, your communication may be _____ successful.
5. A positive self-concept is the key to success in _____ and _____ situations. To accentuate positives, identify your _____, focus on areas that need _____, and boost your concept of your _____ self.
6. To change negatives _____, you must begin by setting _____, then self-monitor or _____ on your changes. Once you have done this, obtain _____ or support from others.
7. A self-_____ prophecy is a _____ of an event that shapes your _____, making the _____ more likely to occur. These prophecies can come from the expectations you establish for _____ or from what you think _____ expect of you.
8. Successful people often _____ their _____. This helps to build positive _____.
9. Self-_____ is the deliberate _____ of significant _____ about _____ that is not readily apparent to _____. It should _____ your interpersonal relationships, _____ your communication, and _____ your communication bonds.
10. The _____ window helps communicators identify what they know about _____ and _____. The four areas in the window are _____, _____, _____, and _____.

UNDERSTANDING SELF-CONCEPT

You are a unique person, made up of many different dimensions that form a kind of "core" self. In addition, other influences impact who you are. How you feel about each of these different parts of yourself makes up your self-concept. The list on this page explains some of the different dimensions of your self-concept.

As your experiences and relationships with others change, your self-concept can change in specific areas. For example, your concept of your social self may change as you mature and are involved in a wider variety of social situations. Your perception of your artistic self may change dramatically after writing a poem, drawing a cartoon, singing for an audience, or demonstrating your creativity in some other way.

In addition, one part of your self-concept can become more important than the others at any given time. If you make a perfect score on a test, your concept of your academic ability may soar. If you find yourself feeling awkward around a group of people you don't know, your social self may influence you to believe that you are miserable and you want to leave.

Your self-concept is responsible for that little voice that tells you, "You're doing great" or "You're not doing so well right now." The important thing to remember is that you control that little voice. In fact, in the words of Anthony Robbins, "You are the voice!" How you perceive yourself—positively or negatively—impacts your life in many ways, including how you communicate with others.

Factors That Influence Self-Concept

Your self-concept is influenced by many factors, such as your own experiences and relationships. However, the following three factors tend to have the greatest influence on self-concept:

SELF-CONCEPT

Dimension of Self	Defined by . . .
Real Self	Your "core" self; who you really are
Perceived Self	Who you see yourself to be
Ideal Self	Who you want to be now or in the future
Public Self	The self you freely disclose to others; who you are in public situations
Private Self	The self you do not share with others; who you are in private
Professional Self	Who you are in your job or profession
Social Self	Who you are when you interact with other individuals, in groups, in society, or in social situations
Intellectual Self	Who you are as a student and a learner; the part of you that acquires and uses knowledge
Emotional Self	The part of you that uses and processes feelings
Physical Self	Who you are physically, including your concept of your own body, athletic ability, gracefulness and coordination, level of attractiveness, and physical health and well-being
Artistic Self	The part of you that is creative or artistic

84 *Glencoe Communication Applications*

INTERDISCIPLINARY CONNECTION

Language Arts Self-concept can be affected both positively and negatively. Over time, experiences and relationships can cause a person's self-concept to change.

Activity Ask students to write two brief anecdotes in their journals. Have them write one that describes how a negative feeling about oneself was changed to a positive feeling. The other anecdote should tell about how a positive feeling was turned into a negative one. Encourage students to write a conclusion to each anecdote, explaining what brought about the change—internal or external factors—and if the self-concept changed again at a later time and why.

COMMUNICATION PRACTICE LAB

Analyzing Your Self-Concept

To better understand your self-concept, follow these steps:

Step 1 On a sheet of paper, draw a large circle. Label this circle **Self.**

Step 2 Review the chart of different selves on page 80 and choose all the selves that represent you.

Step 3 Within the large circle, draw smaller circles and label them as the different selves that make up you. The size of each circle should reflect that self's importance to you.

Step 4 Indicate how you perceive each part of yourself by marking a plus for a

positive feeling or a minus for a negative feeling within each circle.

Step 5 Analyze your drawing to gain insight about your self-concept. In what areas do you feel really good about yourself? Which areas do you feel need improvement?

Step 6 Make a personal improvement plan for those areas you would like to make more positive. Try to list behaviors that you can practice; set goals for yourself to master the positive behaviors. Making a plan and acting on it will improve your self-concept and your ability to communicate effectively with others.

- How you perceive that you are seen and treated by others
- Your own expectations and the standards that you set for yourself
- How you compare yourself to others

As you can see, two of the three main influences on self-concept focus on your relationships with others. This is why it is important to develop effective skills for communicating with others.

The messages you perceive as positive or negative from other people, especially those whom you admire and respect, impact your self-concept and your self-esteem. In turn, your self-concept and self-esteem greatly affect the messages you send.

Importance of Self-Concept

Your self-concept lays the foundation for your communication with others on a one-to-one basis, in groups, and in one-to-group

situations. You are likely to repeat certain patterns of communication in specific situations. For example, your concept of your social self affects how you communicate when you are with friends. If you have a positive concept of yourself in that situation, your communication is likely to be very effective. You may tend to fall into a relaxed pattern of communication that makes your interactions predictable and enjoyable.

On the other hand, if you frequently seem to clash with another student or a coworker, your communication behavior may be following a different sort of "script." Each time you meet, your communication may become defensive or hostile, based not only on a specific interaction but on your previous negative interactions that have influenced your self-concept. Because of this, your interactions are less successful than they would be if you were to identify and break the cycle of your behavior.

The chart on the next page describes four specific scripts people tend to follow when interacting with others. Which script you

The Communication Process and You **85**

Communication and Self-Concept

Relationships with others can greatly influence how we feel about ourselves. Let students work in small groups. Have them create a list of ways communication skills can affect a person's self-concept both positively and negatively. **L3**

Communication Tip

Knowing what communication pattern you are most likely to follow in certain social situations can help you improve your communication skills. For example, if you know you are nervous and avoid eye contact when meeting someone for the first time, you can change this habit. Knowing how you are likely to react can help you get better at communicating with others.

COMMUNICATION PRACTICE LAB

Analyzing Your Self-Concept

Have students follow the six steps in the Communication Practice Lab to help them analyze their self-concept and assess areas where they might like to make changes. As a class, discuss how the final product of one large circle with smaller circles of varying sizes within it will look. When the activity has been completed, let students compare their circles with those of classmates. Let partners share ideas on how each might reach a goal that has been set. **L2**

INCLUSION STRATEGIES

Special Needs One factor that affects self-concept is our perception of how we are seen and treated by others. Be sure students understand that this factor does not say how other people *do* perceive us but how *we think* they do.

Activity Ask small groups of students to discuss different ways in which the actions or words of another can be perceived in different ways. Have each group make a chart of two columns. In the first column, they should list a behavior or reaction of another person and in the second column, the different ways that behavior might be perceived. You could start them out with behaviors such as a head shake "No," a smile, a failure to say hello, and a suggestion that is ignored. Let students discuss why the same behavior can be perceived in so many different ways.

For an additional Practice Lab for this section, have students visit the *Glencoe Communication Applications* Web site at **communicationapplications.glencoe.com.** Click on Communication Practice Lab 3–2. **L1**

Scripts

What is a "script"? You might explain to students that a script is a coherent sequence of events expected by the individual either as a participant or as an observer. For example, we have a particular script in mind when ordering at a restaurant. Let students suggest other times that scripts may come into play during their daily lives. **L3**

TECHNOLOGY *Activity*

Graphing Self-Concept Review with students the various dimensions of self-concept shown in the self-concept chart on page 84. Remind students that they will be creating two sets of rankings—order of importance and order of ability. Ask students to make predictions as to how they think these two sets of rankings will compare and to give reasons for their opinions.

After the charts have been completed and the final questions dicussed, you might suggest that students set specific goals and develop a step-by-step plan to improve their skills in the areas that they feel are most important. **L2**

Key to Success

A self-concept can give a person confidence which in turn can help a person succeed in personal, professional, and social situations. On the chalkboard, write the headings Personal, Professional, and Social. Ask volunteers to choose a heading and to give examples of how confidence due to a positive self-concept can help them succeed in their communication efforts. **L2**

INTERACTION SCRIPTS

Script	Roles	Outcome of Interaction
I'm OK, you're OK.	I see us both as positive influences on the interaction	Positive; A win-win script
I'm OK, you're not OK.	I see myself as positive, you as negative	Possibly negative; A win-lose script
I'm not OK, you're OK.	I see myself as negative, you as positive	Possibly negative; A lose-win script
I'm not OK, you're not OK.	I see us both as negative influences on the interaction	Negative; A lose-lose script

follow depends largely on how you see yourself in relationship to the other person. The roles you both assume then influence the outcome of your interaction with that person.

Building a Positive Self-Concept

Having a positive self-concept can give you the confidence you need to communicate effectively. This kind of confidence is a key to success in personal, professional, and social situations.

Most of us are pleased with at least some aspects of ourselves. In those areas that we view positively, we tend to have confidence in ourselves. This can help develop assertiveness and a sense of accomplishment. Negative views of self, on the other hand, may be expressed as a lack of confidence or a sense of inadequacy or ineffectiveness.

How do you accentuate your positive perceptions about yourself and minimize the negative ones? The secret lies in identifying your strengths. Learning to draw from your strongest communication skills can help you improve upon the less effective ones. It also can help you build confidence and develop assertiveness, tact, and courtesy with others.

First, think about the parts of yourself in which your self-concept is the strongest. If you have completed the Communication Practice Lab on page 85, look at the circles containing pluses. Are you particularly confident of your communication skills in social situations? Are you proud of your intellectual ability?

Next, focus on the areas in which you feel you need improvement. In the activity on page 85, these are the circles containing minuses. Do you wish you could speak more confidently around your peers? Would you like to improve your decision-making ability? You can use your strengths in other areas to improve these skills.

If, for example, you feel that your emotional self influences too many of your decisions and actions, you might use your strengths in another area to make changes. You might make the conscious decision to rationally consider the facts surrounding any future decision or action. In this way, you use

TECHNOLOGY *Activity*

Graphing Self-Concept Choose five different dimensions of yourself, such as artistic self and public self. Assign points to rank these five selves in order of personal importance to you. Total points should equal 100. Using charting or graphing software, create a pie graph to show this ranking. Next, create a graph that shows how you rank your abilities in the same five areas. Does your current self-concept reflect what you think is most important? How might you make these two rankings as similar as possible?

COOPERATIVE LEARNING ACTIVITY

How does a person say, "I'm OK, you're not OK"? Usually not with those exact words, but such self-concepts are projected during communication. Ask students to work in pairs. Have them "script" one of the four interaction scripts in which an "I'm OK" or an "I'm not OK" message is sent. When they have completed their script and have had time to practice it, let them act it out in front of the class. Have classmates identify which of the four scripts was being portrayed and how.

your strong intellectual self-concept to offset "minuses" in your emotional self-concept.

The physical self is sometimes the easiest self to change. To boost your concept of how attractive you are, draw on your creative strengths. You might simply decide to smile more often. Or, you might experiment with changes to your clothing or hair to project a more stylish or positive image. Once you change a behavior to influence your self-concept, it is important to validate or confirm the effectiveness of the change. What kind of feedback, if any, did you receive? Have you addressed the real issue or does another area deserve more attention?

Setting Goals for Change Moving from negatives to positives is not always easy. You can begin by picturing yourself with strong skills in the areas where you currently

The poem suggests that an adult's self-concept in large part is the result of the relationships and experiences of childhood. Describe the effect of a positive self-concept on the communication process.

Children Learn What They Live
by Dorothy Law Nolte

If children live with criticism,
They learn to condemn.

If children live with hostility,
They learn to fight.

If children live with fear,
They learn to be apprehensive.

If children live with pity,
They learn to feel sorry for themselves.

If children live with ridicule,
They learn to feel shy.

If children live with jealousy,
They learn to feel envy.

If children live with shame,
They learn to feel guilty.

If children live with encouragement,
They learn confidence.

If children live with tolerance,
They learn patience.

If children live with praise,
They learn appreciation.

If children live with acceptance,
They learn to love.

If children live with approval,
They learn to like themselves.

If children live with recognition,
They learn it is good to have a goal.

If children live with sharing,
They learn generosity.

If children live with honesty,
They learn truthfulness.

If children live with fairness,
They learn justice.

If children live with kindness and consideration,
They learn respect.

If children live with security,
They learn to have faith in themselves and in those about them.

If children live with friendliness,
They learn the world is a nice place in which to live.

Application Activities 3-2

APPLICATION ACTIVITIES CHAPTER 3, Section 2

Picturing Change

Students may have difficulty deciding what kinds of goals to set and what actions to consider reasonable in order to fight against negative self-concepts. They may also have trouble believing that anything will work. You might use an example to model the kinds of goals that can be set and how success can be pictured. Let students suggest other possible ideas for goals and how they could be reached. **L2**

Goal-Setting Journal

Suggest that students begin a goal-setting journal that they keep over time to record changes they wish to make. They might begin by making a list of attributes they would like to have and identifying steps to take to develop them. **L3**

Visual Instruction

Answer Students may say that a person who has a positive self-concept is more relaxed and is, therefore, often a more effective communicator.

MEETING INDIVIDUAL NEEDS

ENGLISH LANGUAGE LEARNERS

Wisdom of the Ages In most cultures, there are bits of wisdom handed down from generation to generation through stories or sayings. Some of these deal with self-concept and making changes. A fable such as "The Tortoise and the Hare" shows two types of self-concept and the value of one over the other. Sayings such as "Be true to yourself" or "I'm not getting older, I'm getting better" contribute to the idea that improvement and being the best you can be are achievable goals and continue over a lifetime.

Activity Let students work in small groups. Ask each group member to share examples of stories or sayings from his or her culture that touch on the issues of self-concept and changing for the better.

ELL

BUSINESS BRIEF

Dale Carnegie gained fame and fortune teaching businesspeople communication strategies. He lived what he taught. His maxim "Believe that you will succeed, and you will" expresses the importance of positive visualization.

You Get What You Expect

We can convince ourselves that we are winners or losers. You might use the following as an example: You believe that no matter how much you study for a math test you are going to fail, so you don't study and you do fail. You then say, "I'm lousy in math." Ask students to list in a journal some ways that their positive ideas about themselves have helped them succeed and how negative ideas about themselves have contributed to failure. **L1**

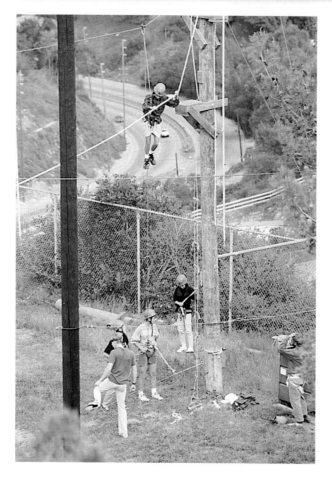

Challenges like rope climbing require setting goals and believing in yourself to achieve success. **Identify some of the guidelines for goals.**

To make sure you are moving in the right direction, you sometimes may need feedback, assistance, or support from others. The key is to believe that you can achieve anything you set your mind to. Picturing yourself as a success is a strong first step toward achieving your goal.

SELF-FULFILLING PROPHECY

You may have heard it said that we create our own destiny. Carefully checking our perceptions and correcting false assumptions, as outlined in **Figure 3–6,** allow us to make appropriate communication choices. Sometimes we fail to use our communication skills to improve our perception of the world. Instead, we decide what our viewpoint is, collect data to support that viewpoint, and discard any data that disagrees with it. Once we have formed perceptions based on this very subjective process, we then communicate with others as if our viewpoint were the absolute truth, not simply our own perspective.

A self-fulfilling prophecy is a prediction or expectation of an event that shapes your behavior, making the outcome more likely to occur. There are two kinds of self-fulfilling prophecies. The first comes from your own self-concept and the expectations you establish for yourself. We tend to behave as consistently as

need improvement. Think about what it will take for you to get to that point. Once you have determined what actions you need to take, set specific goals and write them down. Then post your goals someplace where you will see them every day. Remember, writing down your goals and using positive self-talk can go a long way toward improving your self-concept.

In addition to setting goals, change also requires self-monitoring and reflection. Do your methods of improvement seem effective? Are you consistently making an effort to improve?

INTERDISCIPLINARY CONNECTION

Logical-Mathematical In sports, odds of winning are sometimes calculated. Certain football teams, for example, are expected to win, while other teams are viewed as likely losers. Sometimes, such predictions can have an effect on the outcomes. Underdogs sometimes work harder to win. Perspective winners sometimes slack off.

Activity Have students gather a list of winners predicted for a certain sport. What teams are expected to win and why? Then, have students compare the predictions with the final results. If the outcome was not as predicted, what brought about the change? In interviews following an upset win, what do players say were the reasons for the win? Do any of the reasons have to do with fulfilling personal expectations or the expectations of others?

Figure 3-6 Self-Fulfilling Prophecy

possible with the person we see ourselves to be. The second kind of self-fulfilling prophecy comes from what you think others expect of you. We tend to be especially sensitive to the expectations of people we admire and respect.

Fulfilling Your Own Expectations

Imagine that you are going to audition for a role in the upcoming school theatrical production. As you study the lines and prepare for the audition, your own self-concept will play an important role in how well you do. If you see yourself as capable and able to perform the role, you will enter the audition with a positive outlook. You will expect success. On the other hand, if you have doubts about your ability to perform the role, you will probably approach the tryout without confidence. Either of these expectations could construct a self-fulfilling prophecy.

Fulfilling the Expectations of Others

Just as we tend to live up to our own expectations of ourselves, we also are influenced by the expectations others have for us. Avery

Johnson, the point guard for the 1999 National Basketball Association Champion San Antonio Spurs, was not seen by many fans as a great point guard. A former teammate from another team had commented that no team could win a championship with Avery Johnson at point guard. Even so, Avery Johnson became the hero of the final game when he made a jump shot in the closing seconds of the game to win the game for the team.

Later, Avery Johnson talked about his not too successful career in basketball. He said that he always believed in himself. He tried and worked hard. More important, Coach Popovich believed in him more than he believed in himself. Avery Johnson had confidence in himself. Moreover, he was boosted to success by a coach who believed he could play

Practice for the Workplace

Using Skills in the Workplace Sometimes, a strength or skill in one area can help you succeed in a seemingly unrelated area. For example, skills that allow you to write or draw creatively also may help you think of creative solutions. When interviewing for a job, be prepared to point out how all your strengths and skills can be useful in the workplace.

BUSINESS PRACTICE *Activity*

What skills, talents, or personality traits do you possess that might benefit you in the workplace? List your top five strengths and the possible workplace benefits of each. Then, with a partner, take turns acting out a job interview. When it is your turn to be interviewed, point out all the relevant on-the-job uses for your skills. When you are the interviewer, ask questions that require your partner to back up his or her claims.

The Communication Process and You **89**

Self-Perception

Have students identify a situation in which they want to succeed. The situation can be a simple one, such as speaking to a new classmate they think might be interesting to talk with, asking a parent for permission to do something, or performing well during a band tryout. Ask them to close their eyes and picture themselves succeeding at the task. Then, have them write about the experience. What did they do that made the event a success? What did they say? How did they feel during the interaction? How did this come across to them as they viewed themselves in the scene. Let volunteers share their results with the class. **L2**

Practice for the Workplace

Using Skills in the Workplace

Before students read the information, name some jobs and ask students to list as many skills as they can think of that might be useful for each job. You might use these jobs as possibilities: computer-game designer, order taker at a fast-food restaurant, checker in a supermarket, salesclerk in a clothing store, mechanic in an auto repair shop, or telemarketer. As students make suggestions, ask them to explain the reasons why they think each skill would be useful. After the obvious skills have been named, ask them to expand the list by naming and justifying other skills.

Remind students that for the Business Practice Activity each partner is to take a turn as the interviewer and the person being interviewed. Students' individual strengths will differ but should be applied in a way that will be useful in the workplace. **L1**

INTERDISCIPLINARY CONNECTION

Language Arts Help students evaluate what is and what is not appropriate self-disclosure in certain situations.

Activity Have students use their sense of humor to write "That's good. That's Bad" skits, using this model: A person applied for a job in a candy factory. After the interview, the applicant discussed the interview with a friend.

Applicant: I told them I was punctual and a hard worker.   Friend: Oh, that's good.

Applicant: I also told them I would be their best product sampler.   Friend: Oh, that's bad.

Let students share their skits with the class.

Role Models

Role models—people who are respected, loved, or admired—can affect expectations we have for ourselves. Ask students to construct webs, using Role Models as the label for the center circle of the web. In circles surrounding the web, have them identify people they view as role models and the positive ways these people have influenced the students' expectations of themselves. **L2**

The Future You

Ask students to visualize themselves ten years from now. What will they be doing? Will they own a restaurant or be a manager in a store? Will they be doing construction work, teaching, or working in an office? Will they be in school getting an advanced degree? How do they see their future? Suggest that students write a brief paragraph about what their plans are for the future. Encourage them to enclose their visionary paragraph in an envelope and keep it. They may enjoy reading their vision many years from now. As an alternative to writing a paragraph about the future, students could superimpose a picture of themselves in the working or school environment in which they envision themselves in ten years. Magazines and other print materials as well as computer graphics could be sources of environmental pictures for the activity. **L1**

Visual Instruction

Answer Visualizing success can give a speaker the self-confidence he or she needs to make an effective presentation.

basketball. He fulfilled a coach's expectations by playing like the player he thought the coach believed him to be.

Believing in yourself does not always guarantee success, but it is very difficult to succeed without having the confidence needed to do well. We look for ways to reinforce our own perceptions and expectations, and we look for ways to reinforce what we perceive to be the perceptions and expectations of others.

Visualizing Success

How can you begin to manage outcomes and predict your own success? Successful people often visualize their success. They picture themselves succeeding in whatever they do. Once they "see" themselves winning an award, becoming a faster runner, or making a new friend, the path between where they are and where they want to be becomes clearer. This can make the individual more focused and the goal more attainable.

Public speakers often are advised to think ahead of time how they want to behave as a speaker. Perhaps they want to have a good command of information, to appear confident and poised, and to relate to the audience in a relaxed and sincere manner. Visualizing themselves acting in this way can give speakers the confidence they need to make their vision a reality.

Mentally "seeing" yourself as a success in a professional or social situation can build positive expectations for you to fulfill. Setting realistic goals and continually building skills can help put you on the path to success.

SELF AS AN INTERACTOR

The level to which you express yourself to others is your level of self-disclosure. Self-disclosure is the deliberate revelation of significant information about yourself that is not readily apparent to others. Self-disclosure can be tricky, however, because it can be either appropriate or inappropriate for a particular time, place, or circumstance.

Understanding Self-Disclosure

To make self-disclosure a positive element of communication requires analysis. You need to know what facts, opinions, or feelings are appropriate to reveal under the circumstances. Why and how you disclose information about yourself that most people don't know is important.

A graduate realizes the success she had visualized during her school years. What can a speaker accomplish by visualizing success?

MULTIPLE LEARNING STYLES

MEETING INDIVIDUAL NEEDS

Visual-Spatial What makes someone an effective communicator? How much and what kind of self-disclosure is involved?

Activity Ask students to choose a popular figure whose communication skills are important. Students might consider talk-show hosts, politicians, or actors. Ask students to make a word web with the name of the person in the center and the qualities that make the person an effective communicator placed in circles around the name. After the word webs have been completed, have students work in small groups to compare their webs. Do any of the communicators have qualities in common? If so, what are they?

Figure 3–7 The Johari Window

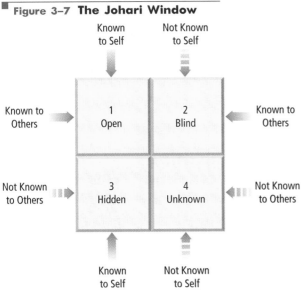

Analyzing Your Interaction Style

As you interact with others in a variety of situations, you make different choices about what to disclose. These choices are based on what information is already known and what is not known. The Johari window, shown in **Figure 3–7,** is a four-part diagram communicators use to identify what they know about themselves and others. It is helpful for analyzing and evaluating the effectiveness of your communication.

The diagram looks like a window with four panes. The panes help you analyze your communication with yourself and your interaction with others.

Imagine that you've just started an after-school school part-time job at a preschool. The lead teacher in your classroom praises how well you interact with the youngsters in your care. You reveal that you have several younger brothers and sisters and always have enjoyed playing with them. This example of self-disclosure is positive and appropriate. Insight into your background and work-related experiences will give others confidence in your ability. It may also open doors to other opportunities that otherwise may not have been offered to you.

It is important to carefully consider the purpose of any self-disclosure, its appropriateness, and the communication goals you hope to reach when deciding what and how much to disclose. The goal of self-disclosure should be to enhance your interpersonal relationships, improve your communication, and strengthen your communication bonds. Wise choices for self-disclosure will help you achieve this.

The Johari Window The Johari window is particularly helpful for analyzing your communication with others, including what you are willing to disclose. First, consider what you know about yourself, and what types of things you may not know completely. Then, think about what others know and do not know about you.

Area 1: Open The things that you know about yourself and that you allow others to know about you are included in this area. Area 1 is called the open area because many of a person's behaviors, motivations, feelings, likes, and dislikes are openly communicated to others.

Area 2: Blind This is known as the blind area. It includes information known to others but not to you. For example, you may not notice that you tend to cut off other speakers before they have finished talking. In this area, you also are blind to what others perceive about you.

The Communication Process and You **91**

Self-Disclosure

Discuss appropriateness of self-disclosures. Then, have the class brainstorm a number of scenarios in which students might disclose information about themselves. Ask students working in small groups to choose three of the scenarios and identify examples of appropriate and inappropriate self-disclosures for them. Groups can share their examples with the class and discuss why they identified the disclosures as they did. **L2**

Johari Window

Draw a Johari window on an overhead transparency and display the drawing. As a class, list things that might be included in each category shown on a window pane. As the students read the information about each pane of the Johari window, have them verify whether the information written proves to be accurate and, if not, what changes might be needed. **L2**

Johari Window Analysis

The Johari window can be used to analyze characters from favorite television programs and books. Ask students to choose a character and to use the Johari window to analyze what the character knows about him- or herself and what others know about the character. Suggest that students first analyze a character from a relatively simple story. For example, they might analyze the ugly duckling from Hans Christian Andersen's *Ugly Duckling.* **L2**

CRITICAL THINKING ACTIVITY

Have students list their everyday roles, such as student, sibling, daughter or son, and friend. Ask students to identify one positive and one negative example of themselves in each of the roles. Encourage them to visualize how they can improve their negative examples and then implement that visualization. Ask that they write a short paper indicating how the visualization did or did not help them improve.

Open vs. Hidden

While traits included in the Open section of the Johari window may help us communicate and connect with others, there are certain things people like to keep hidden. Those pieces of information fall into the Hidden section. Ask students to list some things that might fall into the Hidden category. Point out that the suggestions may include things that are both positive and negative. Discuss reasons people choose to disclose certain things about themselves while they keep other things hidden. Finally, discuss why individuals may want to keep some positive things hidden. **L3**

Pane to Pane

On the chalkboard, draw a Johari window. Discuss each interaction style identified in the chart Common Interaction Styles on page 93. Ask students to indicate which panes would contain the most and the least information. For example, for the interaction style listed first, much information would be in the Hidden pane and little information would be in the Open pane. **L1**

Voltaire on Speech

Voltaire was a French author and philosopher during the eighteenth century. He wrote in *Dialogue 14*: "Men use thought only to justify their wrongdoings, and speech only to conceal their thoughts." Ask students to discuss what Voltaire might have meant by this statement. Students might also hypothesize which interaction style someone who used speech in this way might have. **L3**

Feedback from others may make you aware of this information. When this happens, it moves out of the blind area into the open area because everyone knows it. You may or may not decide to adapt or change your behavior based on this information.

Area 3: Hidden This is the area of hidden information. It represents the things you know or believe about yourself but that you do not choose to share with others. For example, some people don't share certain information about their background or family. Others may not disclose personal information such as age, hobbies, or accomplishments.

Should you disclose everything you know about yourself? Probably not, especially if you think others are not willing to accept your disclosures or if you feel that too much risk is involved. However, your willingness to disclose and deal openly and honestly with information about yourself can be an important asset to communication.

Area 4: Unknown This is the area of unknown information—things that neither you nor others know or acknowledge. A subconscious fear or a yearning would be placed in this area. In addition to complete unknowns, this area may include things that you simply do not remember. Even though old memories may be forgotten, they can still affect your communication with others.

Your Own Johari Window Practice creating your own Johari window. Start by making a list of things that relate to you. Your list might include your goals, strengths, weaknesses, ideas, beliefs, fears, insecurities, perceived needs, values, personal facts, such as your age and height—anything you think is important about you. Then draw a blank Johari window on a sheet of paper. Number the window panes from 1 to 4 and label them **Open, Blind, Hidden,** and **Unknown.**

Next, sort the items from your list into their proper areas. For example, if your goal is to be a photographer and you often talk about that goal, you would list "want to be a photographer" in the Open area (1). If you do not want people to know you made a failing grade on your algebra test, you would write "algebra test" in the Hidden area (3).

Evaluating Interaction Styles

When you have finished plotting your Johari window, analyze the information you have generated. This will help you see just how willing you are to disclose information and learn from others' feedback.

What does it mean if you have few open items but a great deal of hidden information? What if your blind area contains more items than any of the other areas? Analyzing your Johari window can help you understand your approach to interaction and, if necessary, take steps to change it.

First, examine which areas of your window contain the most items. Based on that information, you can use the following guidelines to get a general idea of your interaction style. Keep in mind that your personal style may combine the characteristics of two or more areas.

A large number of items listed in this area may mean:

Open You are willing to disclose a great deal of information about yourself. You also know much about yourself through personal insight and feedback from others.

Blind You may be reluctant to seek feedback from others or learn from it. You also may not be using self-reflection to know more about yourself.

COOPERATIVE LEARNING ACTIVITY

One of the panes of a Johari window is called "Open." This section includes things the person knows about himself or herself and what others know about the person.
Let pairs of students who know each other fairly well work together. Have one partner name something he or she believes others know about him or her. Let the partner name another. Then, let the pair switch roles. Have them continue this five times. What did each partner learn about what he or she thinks is known about him or her and what actually is known? Was any information disclosed that would have fallen into the "Blind" pane of the Johari window? **L3**

Hidden You have a great deal of personal information that you are not willing to disclose. You also may be providing little feedback to others.

Unknown A low interaction level may be keeping you and others "in the dark" about certain valuable information about yourself. Through reflection and self-analysis you can discover more about yourself.

The chart below contains descriptions of four common types of communicators. Compare the information to your own Johari window. While these models may not exactly match your interaction style, they can give you some insight into how others may perceive you and into the effects of your self-disclosure and feedback habits. The models of the common interaction styles also can help you analyze the effectiveness of others' communication styles.

Changing Interaction Style If you wish to change your interaction style, it is important to set goals. To begin, make a list of items you would like to move from one area of your Johari window to another. For example, if you need to tell your parents about your failing grade on the algebra test before report cards are sent home, you might set a goal to move your algebra test from the Hidden area (3) to the Open area (1). If you don't understand why you failed the test, you could write algebra test in the Unknown area (4). You might set a goal to move it to Open (1), and make an appointment with your teacher to discuss the test.

In each case, meeting your goal depends on your communication. You may need to open up in your interactions with others. On the other hand, you may need to talk less about yourself and pay closer attention to the messages and feedback you receive from others. You may also need to practice new ways to seek additional information and reduce the number of unknowns in your Johari window.

Whatever your interaction style, it is important to remember that you are in control. The more information you have in your open area, the better chances you have of interacting successfully with others.

COMMON INTERACTION STYLES

Interaction Style	Disclosure/Feedback	Possible Results
Spend little time disclosing information or giving and receiving feedback; much information in Hidden area; often perceived as quiet, shy, introspective, or withdrawn	They know little about others; others know little about them	Close relationships may be difficult due to a lack of shared information
Spend much time receiving feedback from others, but disclose little about themselves; may be perceived as mysterious, secretive, or unapproachable	They know a great deal about others; others know little about them	Close relationships may be difficult because communication is so one-sided
Spend much time disclosing information and giving feedback, but not open to feedback from others; may be perceived as great talkers or as uncaring people	They know little about others; others know a great deal about them	Close relationships may be difficult because communication is so one-sided
Disclose information openly and appropriately; freely give and accept feedback; may be perceived as friendly, open, and sensitive to others	They know a great deal about others; others know a great deal about them	Openness of both parties make conditions excellent for close relationships

The Communication Process and You **93**

Evaluating Results

Review together the four possible results of the common interaction styles described in the chart on this page. Then, divide the class into four groups. Assign each group one of the interaction styles described in the chart. Have each group prepare specific examples of the interaction style and why the possible results are usually positive or usually negative. As a class, discuss why three of the four possible interaction styles usually result in negative communication results. **L3**

3 ASSESS

Assign Section 2 Assessment as a homework or in-class activity.

🔷 Use *Interactive Tutor Self-Assessment Software* to review Section 2.

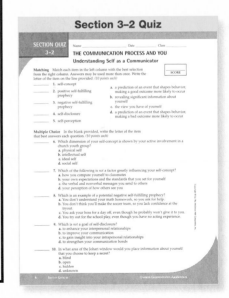

REAL-WORLD CONNECTION

Open Interactors Some jobs require a strong Open interaction style. In these jobs, the person must be open, revealing certain personal information in order to be effective.

Activity Write this question on the chalkboard: What kinds of jobs require an Open interaction style? Have students work in small groups. Ask them to prepare a two-column chart. In the first column, have them list jobs that require an Open interaction style. In the second column, have them tell why an Open interaction style is needed. For example, students might list a comedian as a job requiring an Open interaction style. Students might point out that some of the best comedians poke fun at themselves by revealing personal information.

Reteaching Activity 3-2

Enrichment Activity 3-2

4 CLOSE

Ask students to return to the opening of the section on page 83. Reread the opening paragraph and focus on the questions at the end of it. Review what students previously gave as answers. Ask students to explain, using information they learned in the section, why the students may have answered as they did.

Extra-Credit Project

Setting goals and determining steps for change can be difficult for students. Challenge students to create an outline showing how to set a goal and how to identify steps needed to achieve the goal. Students can determine their own ways of organizing the information either by using a graphic or by using sets of questions or both.

Now that you have an understanding of intrapersonal communication, you can begin to analyze your perception and the perception of others in communication situations. Making continual perception checks and clarifying the meaning of your messages and those of others will guide you to make appropriate communication choices.

Building a positive self-image, setting goals for yourself, and visualizing yourself as a success in meeting those goals will also help assure that you act as an effective communicator. The more you know and analyze your self as an interactor in social and professional contexts, the closer you will be to becoming a more competent communicator.

Section 2 Assessment

GLENCOE Online

Visit the *Glencoe Communication Applications* Web site at **communicationapplications. glencoe.com** and click on **Self-Check and Study Guide 3.2** to review your understanding of yourself as a communicator.

Review Key Terms

1. Define each term and write it in a sentence: self-concept, self-fulfilling prophecy, self-disclosure.

Check Understanding

2. Identify three factors that tend to influence self-concept. Give an example of each.

3. Explain how self-concept influences our choice of "script" when interacting with others.

4. Differentiate between the two kinds of self-fulfilling prophecy. What is the effect of each on communication and personal performance?

5. **Predicting** Imagine that you currently have many items listed in the Hidden area of your Johari window. How are others likely to perceive you? How might their perceptions change if you move items from the Hidden area to the Open area?

APPLICATION *Activity*

Using Feedback to Improve Self-Concept Divide into groups of four or five students. Cut a sheet of paper into smaller squares so that you have one square for each member of your group. Other group members should do the same. On the squares, write something positive about each member of your group, fold the paper, and write the person's name on the outside. Finally, exchange papers. Were you previously "blind" to some of these positive perceptions of you? Discuss as a class how you might use this feedback to improve your self-concept.

Section 2 Assessment Answers

1. Accept all reasonable sentences.
2. how you perceive yourself to be seen and treated by others; what expectations and standards you set for yourself; and how you compare yourself to others. Specific examples of each will vary.
3. How we feel about ourselves can affect how we feel about others and how we interact with them.
4. We can fulfill our own expectations about ourselves or can fulfill the expectations of others by becoming what they think of us.

5. Others might see such a person as unaware, uncaring, or self-absorbed. Moving some items from the Hidden area to the Open area may make the person seem more caring, more sensitive to others, and more interesting.

Application Activity Be sure the writing of the traits is kept anonymous and that the students understand that something positive is to be written.

Communication Self-Assessment

Analyzing Your Communication Style

How Do You Rate?

On a separate sheet of paper, use the key to answer the following questions. Put a check mark beside each skill you would like to improve.

KEY: **A** Always   **R** Rarely
       U Usually   **N** Never
       S Sometimes

1. I use positive self-talk to build my confidence and my performance.
2. I listen wisely by staying alert and tuning out distractions.
3. I understand that people can perceive the same situation differently. I use this information to avoid misunderstandings.
4. I try to use methods that will help me to improve my communication style.
5. I am aware of my own biases and prejudices.
6. I regularly check and evaluate my perceptions before I take action.
7. I use feed-forward statements and take responsibility for my need for clarification.
8. My positive self-concept helps me build good working relationships.
9. I visualize myself as a success in areas where I need improvement.
10. I deal honestly and openly with others but avoid taking too much risk in what I disclose to others.

How Do You Score?

Review your responses. Give yourself 5 points for every A, 4 for every U, 3 for every S, 2 for every R, and 1 for every N. Total your points and evaluate your score.

41–50 Excellent You may be surprised to find out how much you can improve your skills.

31–40 Good In this course, you can learn ways to make your skills better.

21–30 Fair Practice applying the skills taught in this course.

1–20 Needs Improvement Carefully monitor your improvement as you work through this course.

Setting Communication Goals

If you scored Excellent or Good, complete Part A. If your score was Fair or Needs Improvement, complete Part B.

Part A
1. I plan to put the following ideas into practice:
2. I plan to share the following information about communication with the following people:

Part B
1. The behaviors I need to change most are:
2. To bring about these changes, I will take these steps:

The Communication Process and You **95**

Communication Self-Assessment

Have students respond to the statements using the key on the page. Then, have them score their responses using the How Do You Score? scale. Based on the scoring results, assign either Part A or Part B of the goal-setting activity. Have each student write his or her responses on an index card. Remind students that the goals should be specific, concrete, and attainable.

Communication Journal Activity

Encourage students to write their goals in their communication journal. Along with the goals and other plans, they may want to write the reasons they feel it is important to achieve the goals listed.

Communication Tip

Suggest that students set up a timetable for reviewing their goals and a time frame in which they hope to accomplish them. For example, a student may want to achieve a certain goal in a month and may review weekly how progress is going.

EXTENDING THE CONTENT

The Art of Avoiding Miscommunication Feed-forward can sometimes be an important way of eliminating communication problems before they happen by putting people at ease about answering questions. Explaining why a question is needed is the key. Feed-forward statements get at the answers needed without causing perception or self-concept problems.

Activity Ask students to create a three-column chart in a journal or notebook. Have them use the categories School, Family, and Friends as column headings. Tell students to make entries throughout a one-week period. Have them list feed-forward statements that they used or that they heard used that helped avoid confusion or misunderstandings. After the assignment is completed, let students share some of their results and their conclusions with the class.

Clarity and Conciseness in Writing

Objective: To write clear and concise instructions

Teaching Suggestions and Strategies

Connection to the Workplace

Explain that in business, written communication within a company or outside the company is common. Being able to write with clarity and conciseness is a skill that is valued in the workplace because clear communication often means fewer misunderstandings.

Written communication in the workplace often takes the form of instructions and information—what time to be at a meeting and where, how to operate the copying machine, whom to contact with questions or problems, what to include in a progress report, or what steps to follow when closing out a cash register for the day. When these instructions or sets of information are clear and to the point, employees are able to do their jobs more efficiently and effectively. This saves the company time and money.

Clarity and Conciseness in Writing

Clarity and conciseness make your writing easier to read. In writing, clarity means simplicity. Similarly, conciseness means writing something in the fewest possible words. You can perfect writing clearly and concisely by following the tips below.

Use Action Verbs Action verbs show the subject engaging in some form of mental or physical activity. They are direct and straightforward. Passive verbs make sentences wordy and more difficult to read. Consider the differences in the following sentences:

- My friends and I enjoyed the concert.
- The concert was enjoyed by many people, including four of my friends and me.

Which of these sentences is more concise? Clearer? More direct? In the first example, the people are taking direct action. In the second example, they are no longer the subject. The new subject, concert, passively receives the action.

Use Colorful Adjectives and Adverbs Adjectives tell more about a noun or pronoun and help turn a bland sentence into one that paints a vivid mental picture. Adverbs tell more about a verb, verb phrase, adjective, or another adverb. You can use them to add detail to a sentence.

Read the following sentences. Which one provides more precise information?

- I need a person to help me carry a box.
- I need a strong person to help me carry this heavy computer box into my office down the hall.

Using adjectives and adverbs in the second sentence made the meaning much clearer.

Combine Sentences to Avoid Redundancy When parts of two sentences are similar or very closely related, you may be able to combine them. This eliminates unnecessary words. Which of the following examples seems more concise?

- The man who came into the room was handsome. When he stormed into the room, he was angry.
- The handsome man angrily stormed into the room.

For additional information about business writing, see the *Language Handbook* section of the Communication Survival Kit in the Appendix.

CRITICAL THINKING ACTIVITY

Challenge students to identify real-world situations in which they were required to communicate something in writing. They might mention situations in the home, such as writing directions to help someone get to a certain place; on the job, such as how to clean a grill; between friends, such as a note about a homework assignment; or for a school activity, such as a handout for an upcoming event or election.

Ask students to bring in samples of these written communications. Then, let students work in groups to evaluate the written materials available by focusing on the clarity and conciseness of the information. Was the information clear? Was it to the point? Was anything confusing? What could be changed to improve the overall effectiveness of the material?

Communication Through Writing

Use Basic Editing Skills To make sure your writing is clear and concise, be sure to give it a thorough edit. For example, is all the information in the correct sequence? Have you eliminated highly technical language and slang? Can you make long sentences shorter or replace long words with words of fewer syllables? Use a thesaurus to avoid overusing certain words, and always check your spelling, punctuation, and grammar for errors.

The following letter is an example of clear and concise business writing.

ACCU-COMP COMPUTER SERVICE
1212 Sprocket Drive
Fort Worth, Texas 76133

May 2, 2002

Mr. Mark McCovey
693 Morningside Ave.
Lakewood, NJ 08701

Dear Mr. McCovey:
I would be happy to answer your question about increasing your computer's speed. If I understand correctly, your main goal is to gain faster access to Internet information.
Basically, three elements of your computer system help determine this speed. They are the

1. speed (in megahertz) of the computer
2. speed (in kilobytes per second) of the computer's modem
3. amount (in megabytes) of Random Access Memory, or RAM, available for use

I have enclosed a brochure explaining more about computer speed. Don't let the technical language confuse you. In short, the higher the number, the faster the computer.

If I can answer any other questions or assist in upgrading your system, please let me know.

Sincerely,
Richard Clemons
Richard Clemons,
Account Representative

WRITING Activity

Use the following steps to write clear and concise instructions to a classmate:

- Choose a partner in your class. Write a letter to him or her explaining how to use a computer printer, photocopier, video camera, or other device.
- Use a business-style format for your letter. Make the steps of your instructions as clear and concise as possible.
- Use action verbs whenever possible.
- Use adverbs and adjectives to make your instructions more descriptive.
- Be sure the steps of your instructions are in the correct sequence.
- Consider the reader. Avoid using slang or highly technical language that may be difficult to understand.
- Combine sentences as necessary to avoid redundancy.
- Avoid vague language and long, complex sentences.
- Proofread your letter and correct any errors in spelling, punctuation, and grammar.
- Exchange papers with your partner and read the instructions. Circle any language that seems unclear to you. Discuss with your partner how you might make your letters clearer and more concise.

The Communication Process and You **97**

Teaching Activity

Ask students if they have ever had to read instructions that were totally incomprehensible and impossible to follow. What were the instructions for? What did the students do in order to accomplish the task?

Point out the information in the opening paragraph that describes the difference between clarity (simplicity) and conciseness (putting something in the fewest words). Discuss why both characteristics are needed when writing a set of instructions. Then, challenge students to write instructions on how to get from one place to another in the school. Give students a few minutes after the initial writing to edit for clarity and conciseness. Which student was able to write the clearest, most concise instructions? How was that accomplished?

WRITING Activity

Student instructions should reflect the suggestions made in the bulleted list, be written in the correct format of a business letter, and have been edited and proofread before being given to a partner for comment.

Grammar Tip

To help make writing concise, use the active voice rather than the passive voice. In active voice, the subject performs the action; in passive voice, the subject is acted upon. Note that fewer words are needed to say, "The speaker offered a good analogy," than to say, "A good analogy was offered by the speaker."

Additional Resources

Appendix, "Guide to Business Communication"

Glencoe Writer's Assistant CD-ROM

Glencoe Interactive Grammar Software

Grade 9 Writer's Choice, Lesson 5.3

GRAMMAR PRACTICE

Passive to Active Voice
Have students rewrite each sentence, changing the passive verb to an active verb.

1. The list of instructions was submitted by the students. *(The students submitted the list of instructions.)*
2. The camera was placed on the tripod by the photographer. *(The photographer placed the camera on the tripod.)*
3. Repairs were made to the car by the mechanic. *(The mechanic repaired the car.)*
4. The test was passed by my friend and me. *(My friend and I passed the test.)*
5. A screwdriver was used by me to open the back of the computer. *(I used a screwdriver to open the back of the computer.)*

CHAPTER 3 Assessment and Activities

GLENCOE
TECHNOLOGY

MindJogger Videoquiz

Use *MindJogger* to review the Chapter 3 content.

Visit the *Glencoe Communication Applications* Web site at **communicationapplications. glencoe.com** and click on **Chapter 3 Activity** for additional practice in understanding your part in the communication process.

Reviewing Key Terms

1. self-concept
2. feed-forward
3. personal perception
4. self-fulfilling prophecy
5. perception
6. self-disclosure
7. perception check
8. selective perception

Reviewing Key Terms

On a separate sheet of paper, write the vocabulary term that fits each description. The number of spaces indicates the number of letters in each answer (hyphens do not count).

1. How you see yourself
   - - - - - - - - - - -

2. A type of statement that offers a reason for a question you want to ask
   - - - - - - - - - -

3. Your own version of reality
   - - - - - - -   - - - - - - - - - -

4. A positive or negative view that shapes the outcome of an event
   - - - - - - - - - - - - -   - - - - - - - -

5. The basic process of assigning meaning to the things you experience
   - - - - - - - - - -

6. Sharing information about yourself that people would not otherwise know
   - - - - - - - - - - - - - -

7. A question to help determine whether things happened exactly the way you think they did
   - - - - - - - - - -   - - - - -

8. Choosing what to focus on and what to ignore
   - - - - - - - - -   - - - - - - - - - -

Reviewing Key Concepts

On a separate sheet of paper, answer the following questions in complete sentences.

1. What is another name for intrapersonal communication, and what does this process involve?

2. What is the first step in the perception process? Give three examples of this type of perception.

3. What negative consequence may occur when you focus on a specific set of data? How can you avoid this problem?

4. Why is it important to visualize success when setting personal goals?

5. What effect can too little self-disclosure have on your relationships? Too much self-disclosure?

Reviewing Key Concepts

1. Another name for intrapersonal communication is self-talk. It involves the things we say to ourselves.

2. Sensory perception is the first step in the perception process. Accept any three examples involving the senses of seeing, hearing, smelling, tasting, or touching.

3. Focusing on one set of data can cause misperception. Analyzing perceptions by using perception checks can help avoid this problem.

4. By visualizing success, a person is more likely to achieve it.

5. Too little self-disclosure can make a person seem cold and aloof. Too much disclosure can make a person seem uncaring about other people.

Assessment and Activities

Reading and Critical Thinking Skills

1. **Synthesizing** Reread the information on the factors that influence personal perception. Using all nine factors, create a brief description of a competent communicator.

2. **Drawing Conclusions** Explain why it is important to keep an open mind when using perception checks.

3. **Analyzing** Imagine that you are not confident of your public speaking ability. Write one goal for improving your self-concept in this area. Analyze and briefly describe a plan for reaching this goal.

4. **Applying** Imagine you are a team leader who has assigned projects to two team members. Later, one of them tells you, "That's not fair!" Use the concepts from this chapter to respond as a competent communicator.

Skill Practice Activity

Writing Clearly and Concisely On a sheet of paper, rewrite the following paragraph to make it clear and concise.

One way to improve your interaction style is by moving items around in your Johari window. Items can be moved from the Blind area to the Open area. To do this, you really ought to be willing to (a) recognize feedback from others and (b) accept feedback from others. Either verbal or nonverbal is the way this feedback may be. Both verbal and nonverbal feedback can help a competent communicator.

Cooperative Learning Activity

Using Sensory Stimuli On the chalkboard, create a chart of the five senses. Then, in groups of three or four students, write a short script that uses as many of these senses as possible to convey messages. As two or three group members perform the script for the class, have another member place a check mark in the chart each time a sensory stimulus is used. As a class, analyze ways to use sensory stimuli to convey messages.

Chapter Project

Planning Choose one person with whom you would like to improve your communication. List any negative perceptions or communication patterns influencing your interactions with that person. For each negative one, list a positive perception, behavior, or communication skill you could use to improve your interactions. Before this class meets again, use these skills in an interaction with the chosen person. Afterward, note how he or she responded.

Presenting Describe to the class the problems you were experiencing as a result of negative communication patterns. Then, describe the positive communication skills you substituted and the reaction to each. Predict how you think these new patterns might affect your future communication.

Chapter Project

Remind students that they will be setting a specific goal and specific strategies to use to improve communication with one individual. Stress that during the implementation of their strategy, they need to focus on the response of the individual. Discuss ways that misperceptions can be avoided. When students present their results, some may have experienced no change, in other words a continued negative communication. The class could discuss possible reasons for the continuing problem and additional strategies to use.

Reading and Critical Thinking Skills

You may wish to assign one or all of the activities for students to complete, or you may want to allow students to select an activity they would like to do.

1. Students' descriptions should provide ways in which each factor can help improve communication.

2. Students may respond that it is important to keep an open mind because perceptions may vary from time to time or that their perceptions of other's perceptions may be faulty.

3. Students may note that they do not feel confident about their presentation style, content knowledge, or comfort when speaking publicly. Solutions could be respectively practicing and adapting different styles, doing additional research and using notes, and pretending that the audience is only one or two people.

4. Students may suggest using self-talk before responding and questioning strategies to assess the worker's perceptions as means of identifying the problem and trying to solve it.

Skill Practice Activity

One possible revision of the paragraph follows. Accept other reasonable revisions.

One way to improve your Johari window is to move items around from the Blind area to the Open area. To do this, you need to be willing to recognize and accept feedback from others. This feedback may be verbal or nonverbal. Either form of feedback can help a competent communicator.

Cooperative Learning Activity

After the activity has been completed, list as a class the ways sensory stimuli were used to convey messages and which of the ways were most effective.

Chapter 4 Planning Guide

SECTION RESOURCES

Daily Objectives	Reproducible Resources	Multimedia Resources

Section 1

1. Define oral language and identify its characteristics
2. Describe the characteristics of speech sound
3. Compare and contrast pronunciation, articulation, and enunciation
4. Analyze communication challenges presented by dialect
5. Explain how oral language choices can affect individuals on a personal level and on a cultural level

 Reproducible Lesson Plan 4-1
 Application Activities 4-1
 Guided Reading Workbook Activity 4-1
 Vocabulary Activity 4*
 Reteaching Activity 4-1*
Enrichment Activity 4-1*
Graphic Organizer Transparency Strategies and Activities 4-1

  Graphic Organizer Transparency 4-1
 Chapter 4 Teaching Transparency
  Interactive Tutor Self-Assessment
 PuzzleMaker
 ExamView® Pro Testmaker
 Interactive Lesson Planner
 Communication in Action Video Chapter 4
MindJogger
communicationapplications.glencoe.com
Presentation Plus!

Section 2

1. Analyze the characteristics of power language
2. Analyze and apply standards for using formal, technical, and informal language appropriately
3. Compare and contrast the functions of oral language
4. Identify and describe the types of language to avoid in oral communication

 Reproducible Lesson Plan 4-2
 Application Activities 4-2
 Guided Reading Workbook Activity 4-2
 Vocabulary Activity 4*
 Reteaching Activity 4-2*
 Enrichment Activity 4-2*
 Graphic Organizer Transparency Strategies and Activities 4-2

  Graphic Organizer Transparency 4-2
Chapter 4 Teaching Transparency
 Interactive Tutor Self-Assessment
 PuzzleMaker
 ExamView® Pro Testmaker
Interactive Lesson Planner
  Communication in Action Video Chapter 4
 MindJogger
communicationapplications.glencoe.com
Presentation Plus!

Use Glencoe's *Presentation Plus!* multimedia teacher tool to easily present dynamic lessons that engage and motivate your students. Using Microsoft PowerPoint®, you can customize the presentations to create your own personalized lessons.

* Also available in Spanish

 Blackline Master   CD-ROM   Software
 Transparency   Videodisc   Videocassette   Web site

Chapter 4 Planning Guide

FOR THE TEACHER

Oral Language

Organize the class into groups of three or four and have them spend a few minutes thinking of information or questions that one person might need to share with another—for example, your house is on fire; I'm lost; you're driving the wrong way down the street; where can I find something to eat. When each group has five or six good ideas, have them write them onto strips of paper, fold them, and put them in a hat.

Next, have someone write on the board the following list of people: a 3-year-old child; a visitor who speaks very little English; a college professor; a high school student with an attitude. Ask four or five willing actors from the class to stand up and demonstrate the rich variety of oral language. Have volunteers choose one of the phrases out of the hat and select a character listed on the board to be the "speaker." Remind the class to listen carefully to what the actors say and how they say it—their word choice and pronunciation—and try to guess which character each has selected.

Block Scheduling

Block scheduling differs from traditional class scheduling in the amount of time allotted to each period. The extended time frame provided by block scheduling affords you the opportunity to implement a greater number of research-oriented and activity-intense projects to motivate and involve your students. Activities that are particularly suited to use within the block-scheduling framework are identified throughout this chapter by the following designation:

CHAPTER RESOURCES

Resources for the Teacher

- *Leading Out Loud: the Authentic Speaker, the Credible Leader* by Terry Pearce, Jossey-Bass Publishers, 1995
- *Modern American Usage* by Jacques Barzun (ed.), Hill and Wang, 1966
- *Speaking with Confidence: A Guide for Public Speakers* by Wanda Vasallo, Betterway, 1990

Resources for the Student

- *The Elements of Style* by William Strunk Jr. and E. B. White, Macmillan, 1979
- *How to Speak, How to Listen* by Mortimer J. Adler, Macmillan, 1983
- *What to Say When You Don't Know What to Say* by Alice Fleming, Macmillan, 1982

KEY TO ABILITY LEVELS

Teaching Strategies have been coded for varying learning styles and abilities.

L1 **BASIC** activities for all students

L2 **AVERAGE** activities for average to above-average students

L3 **CHALLENGING** activities for above-average students

ELL **English Language Learner** activities

Chapter 4 Resource Manager

The following materials may be used when teaching the chapter. Materials for specific lessons are also shown at point-of-use in the margins of the Teacher's Wraparound Edition.

TEACHING TRANSPARENCIES

Chapter 4 Teaching Transparency

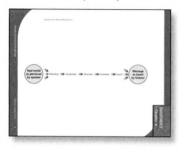

Graphic Organizer Transparency 4-1

Graphic Organizer Transparency 4-2

APPLICATION ACTIVITIES

Chapter 4, Section 1

Chapter 4, Section 2

Chapter 4, Cumulative

REINFORCEMENT AND REVIEW ACTIVITIES

Vocabulary Activity 4

Guided Reading Activity Workbook 4-1, 4-2

Reteaching Activities 4-1, 4-2

Chapter 4 Resource Manager

ASSESSMENT AND EVALUATION

GLENCOE'S
ASSESSMENT
ADVANTAGE

Section Quizzes 4–1, 4–2

Chapter 4 Test, Forms A & B

Performance Assessment Activity 4

ENRICHMENT AND EXTENSION

Technology Application Activity 4

Enrichment Activities 4–1, 4–2

ORAL PRESENTATION ACTIVITIES

Activity 11

SPANISH RESOURCES

- Spanish Chapter and Unit Tests
- Spanish Vocabulary Activities
- Spanish Section Quizzes
- Spanish Reteaching Activities
- Spanish Enrichment Activities

MULTIMEDIA

- Interactive Tutor Self-Assessment
- ExamView® Pro Testmaker
- PuzzleMaker
- Communication in Action Videodisc and Videocassette
- MindJogger
- Interactive Lesson Planner
- Presentation Plus!
- Writer's Assistant
- Glencoe Interactive Grammar
- **communicationapplications.glencoe.com**

TEACHER PLANNING AND SUPPORT

- Reproducible Lesson Plans
- Interactive Lesson Planner
- Presentation Plus!

CHAPTER **4**

 GLENCOE
TECHNOLOGY

 MindJogger Videoquiz

Use *MindJogger* to preview the Chapter 4 content.

VIDEODISC
Communication in Action

Have students view the Chapter 4 video and complete the Chapter 4 video lesson in the *Glencoe Communication in Action Strategies and Activities* booklet.

 Also available in VHS.

GLENCOE
Online

Direct students to communication applications.glencoe.com. Have students read the **Overview–Chapter 4** to identify three concepts they will study in the chapter. Ask a volunteer to list on the chalkboard or an overhead projector all concepts as they are offered.

Discovering the Power of Oral Language

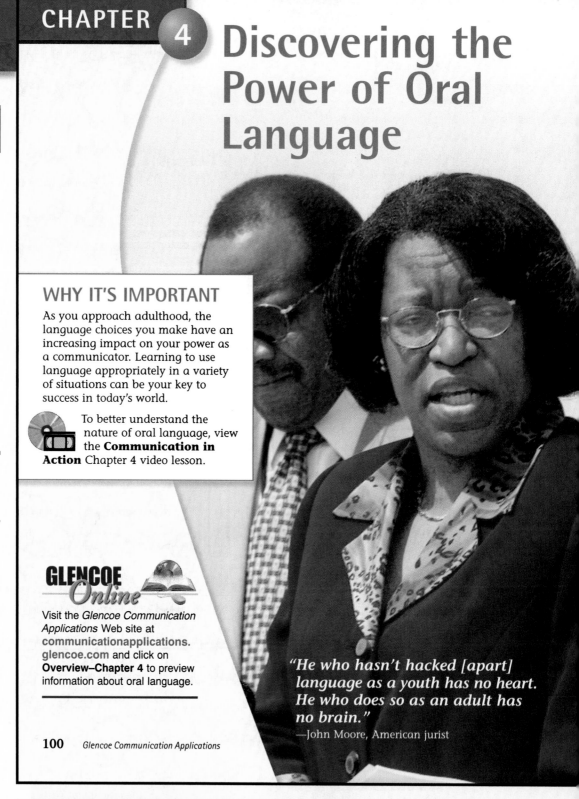

WHY IT'S IMPORTANT

As you approach adulthood, the language choices you make have an increasing impact on your power as a communicator. Learning to use language appropriately in a variety of situations can be your key to success in today's world.

To better understand the nature of oral language, view the **Communication in Action** Chapter 4 video lesson.

GLENCOE
Online

Visit the *Glencoe Communication Applications* Web site at **communicationapplications. glencoe.com** and click on **Overview–Chapter 4** to preview information about oral language.

"He who hasn't hacked [apart] language as a youth has no heart. He who does so as an adult has no brain."
—John Moore, American jurist

100   *Glencoe Communication Applications*

WHY IT'S IMPORTANT

Have students read the quotation. Ask them what they think it means to "hack apart" language. *(Students may suggest that it means using language in different ways as one learns about it.)*
Ask: **Why is it a good idea to hack apart language while young but not when old?**
(Experimentation with words is natural for youth; however, adults are expected to be in command of their speech.) Lead students to understand that people are often judged on their abilities to express themselves. It pays to practice the skills of oral language while in school.

Section 1

The Nature of Oral Language

GUIDE TO READING

Objectives

1. Define oral language and identify its characteristics.
2. Describe the characteristics of speech sound.
3. Compare and contrast pronunciation, articulation, and enunciation.
4. Analyze communication challenges presented by dialect.
5. Explain how oral language choices can affect individuals on a personal level and on a cultural level.

Terms to Learn

oral language
vocabulary
structure
grammar
diction
pronunciation
articulation
enunciation
dialect

Speech is learned, purposeful behavior. Think about all the ways you use speech and oral language in a single day. You may talk with friends, have a serious conversation with a coworker, or ask and answer questions in a class discussion.

While each of these situations is different, they all incorporate spoken language. Have you ever given serious thought to how you talk? Speech is something you depend on every day to reach out to friends, express your ideas and feelings, accomplish your goals, and meet your needs. Are you taking it for granted? Looking carefully at language from a new perspective can give you new insight and a new appreciation for the potential power of language.

Oral language provides the means for a supervisor to effectively explain a process to another employee. What does the spoken language allow you to do?

1 FOCUS

Bellringer
Give students five minutes to jot down the names of everyone they can remember speaking to during the course of the day. Ask them to identify the type of conversation they had with each individual. Which form of speech was the most frequent? Which did the students have to think about beforehand? Discuss the importance of speech during a typical day. *(Students are likely to note that informal greetings and conversations among friends, coworkers, and families are the most common forms of speech. Class discussions and lectures are also common for students.)*

You may use Graphic Organizer Transparency 4–1 to introduce this section.

Graphic Organizer Transparency 4–1

Characteristics of Oral Language

Visual Instruction
Answer Reach out to friends, express ideas and feelings, accomplish goals, and meet needs

RESOURCE MANAGER

Teaching Tools
- Interactive Lesson Planner
- Reproducible Lesson Plan 4–1
- Application Activities 4–1

Reproducible Masters
- Guided Reading Activity Workbook 4–1
- Enrichment Activity 4–1
- Reteaching Activity 4–1
- Section Quiz 4–1
- Transparency Strategies and Activities Booklet 4–1

Transparencies
- Graphic Organizer Transparency 4–1
- Chapter 4 Teaching Transparency

Technology Resources
- Interactive Tutor Self-Assessment Software
- Presentation Plus! Software
- ExamView® Pro Testmaker
- PuzzleMaker Software
- communicationapplications.glencoe.com

2 TEACH

Encoding Oral Language

Point out that encoding language so that only a few listeners have access to it is a common way of maintaining secrecy or exclusivity or rapport among groups, ranging from groups of teenagers to intelligence agencies. Ask students to identify some classroom-appropriate examples of slang they and their friends use. Do adults understand the terms and their meanings? Invite volunteers to speak to the class in a system that encodes English and encourage students to decode their speech. **L2**

Grammar Tip

When a parenthetical clause separates a subject from its verb, the clause is set off by commas. An example is the punctuation for the parenthetical clause "if you remember" under the head Encode and Decode.

Guided Reading Activity 4–1

Figure 4–1 Characteristics of Oral Language

Real world as perceived by speaker ➡ Meaning ➡ Vocabulary ➡ Structure ➡ Grammar ➡ Sound ➡ Message as heard by listener

DEFINING LANGUAGE

Language is a system used for human communication. Like other systems, language consists of specific interrelated components and processes that interact to achieve a desired result or purpose. Oral language is language that is spoken and heard rather than written and read.

Language Has Rules

Like other systems, language is governed by rules that make the system work and give it order. The rules also make it possible for us to understand one another. In the case of oral language, the conventions or rules may be different from the rules you have learned to use for writing. The conventions for oral language are seldom taught directly, such as by saying, "This is how we talk." Rather, new speakers learn rules for oral language as they listen to others and learn to speak and use the language. No one explains to a child learning to talk, "Every sentence must have a subject and verb." Yet the child learns to understand and use words and put them together to form complete thoughts that are consistent with the ways language is used in the child's culture.

Language Is Like a Code

Each language system has its own set of agreed-upon conventions and rules that regulate the system and make it different from other languages. A language system is often referred to as a code. Each code has its unique

system of sounds, symbols, and structures as determined by the rules that govern the use of the particular language. Think of English, French, Spanish, and other languages as different codes because each has its own set of sounds, word symbols, and structures that make the language unique.

Encode and Decode Understanding language as code can further your understanding of the terms *encode* and *decode*. *Encode*, if you remember, means to assign meaning and language to data. In other words, it means putting data into code or into language. *Decode* means to assign meaning to someone else's words. Literally, *decode* means to take meaning from language.

Differences Between Oral and Written Language It may be helpful to think about oral language and written language as two separate codes. Oral language is sometimes considered the primary code because it is the language you learned first, the one you use every day, and the language you use most often. Writing is a secondary code because it is based on an attempt to describe speech sounds. Writing preserves thought and speech. In addition, it provides a code to substitute for speech when speech is not possible.

The two systems—oral language and written language—are interdependent and interrelated. Sometimes they overlap because they have the same set of rules. However, there are differences in the way they approach language. Standards for oral communication are based on appropriateness, while standards for writing are based on correctness. Speech

---

ENGLISH LANGUAGE LEARNERS

MEETING INDIVIDUAL NEEDS

The World of Languages It is difficult for native English speakers to understand the unsettling feeling of not being able to communicate fluently in English with others. Simulate for them the experience of many English language learners.

Activity Ask English language learners to teach the class several phrases or sentences from their own languages. Have students teach the class their languages by repetition and gesture, getting their "students" to repeat the phrases or sentences in chorus until they are comfortable with the sounds. (Modeling this process for them will make it easier.) After the lessons, discuss the experience of exposure to a system of word symbols that is not one's own. **ELL**

choices should be appropriate for the specific situation or context. Writing should be correct according to rules for the specific form.

THE CHARACTERISTICS OF ORAL LANGUAGE

At the beginning of your study of communication, you learned that systems have specific components and processes that interrelate and work together to make the system work. In order to understand language as a system, you need to look at the specific series of characteristics and processes that interact to make the language system work. As shown in Figure 4-1, the characteristics of the oral language system are meaning, vocabulary, structure, grammar, and sound.

Meaning

The first characteristic of language is meaning. You learned earlier that the data we observe in the world around us has no meaning of its own except that which we assign. In addition, the word symbols we use to talk about or describe the data have no meaning other than those we give them. We communicate with others based on the meanings we assign to things around us and the symbols we use to communicate those meanings.

When people share knowledge and understanding of language, they are able to communicate effectively. Think, for example, about how hard it can be for a patient and a doctor to communicate with each other. The doctor may ask specific questions about symptoms in order to diagnose the illness. The doctor's questions and language will reflect the doctor's knowledge as a medical expert. The patient, on the other hand, may have difficulty interpreting and responding meaningfully to the doctor's questions because of

lack of knowledge about medicine and lack of familiarity with the words the doctor uses. A broad base of knowledge and meaning on a wide range and variety of subjects, along with knowledge about language, provides a base for effective communication.

Vocabulary

The second characteristic of language, vocabulary, is closely associated with meaning. Vocabulary is all the word symbols that make up a particular code or language. Your personal vocabulary is the total collection of word symbols you know and use to think, to express yourself, and to listen and respond to others. Having a large and flexible vocabulary is important because language

- is symbolic
- has standards for appropriateness
- adds interest to communication

Symbolic Nature of Language

Word symbols have no meanings of their own; instead, the meaning of a symbol resides within individuals. Symbols are always open to

Just as the American flag symbolizes the United States of America, word symbols represent ideas and meaning used in communication. *What is the relationship between word symbols and vocabulary?*

Discovering the Power of Oral Language **103**

Vocabulary
Point out that English has the largest vocabulary of any of the world's languages. The most complete English dictionary lists 500,000 words, but some scholars estimate that there may be another 500,000 not included in this publication. Have students calculate how many words per week they would have to learn in order to acquire a vocabulary of 25,000 words in twelve years of public schooling. **L1**

Appropriateness
Point out that we are constantly making decisions about the appropriateness of the language we use. Most of these decisions are made without conscious thought. Ask students to think of situations during the course of the day in which they have adjusted their language to suit their company or purpose. What might have happened if they had used other words or phrases to express themselves? **L2**

Important Reasons for Building Vocabulary
Have students read the bulleted reasons for building vocabulary. Ask which they consider to be the two key points and invite volunteers to explain their choices to the class. Point out that increasing one's vocabulary involves more than simply knowing the meaning of words. Learning how to use new words appropriately is as important as memorizing their definitions. **L2**

Visual Instruction
Answer Vocabulary is all the word symbols that make up a particular code or language.

Visual Instruction

Answer Another artist who uses artistic language is a poet.

Singers use artistic language to compose and perform their music. Identify another type of artist who uses artistic language.

interpretation. If you asked ten people what a symbol such as the American flag means, you would probably get ten different answers.

Similarly, if you were to ask ten English speakers what the word symbol "low" means, you may hear it defined as a measurement of depth, a level of sound, a state of depression, or even the sound a cow makes. The uncertain and fragile nature of words as symbols for conveying meaning is echoed in Humpty Dumpty's words, "When *I* use a word, it means just what I choose it to mean; neither more nor less."

The problem with words as symbols for communicating meanings is that we cannot know what a particular word symbol means to

someone else. The arbitrary nature of symbols means that the more symbols we have at our disposal to express a specific concept or meaning, the more apt we are to choose symbols that are understood by listeners. If you want to communicate your meanings clearly to others, a large collection of word symbols will assist you.

Standards for Appropriateness A second reason for building a large and flexible vocabulary is to communicate appropriately in a variety of situations. For this purpose you will need a large collection of word symbols that are appropriate for expressing who you are, what you mean and feel, and what you are really like. You will also need a wide variety of word symbols to meet the needs of your listener, your occasion, and your task. In this sense, your vocabulary can be compared to your wardrobe. You know that you need a variety of clothing to meet the demands of your lifestyle. You may need casual clothes for casual occasions, special clothes for work or school, clothes for attending or participating in public or social events, and perhaps more formal clothes for formal occasions. Occasionally, you may choose to wear something unusual or "artsy" to express your creative side.

The same is true of language. You need different kinds of language and a large collection of word symbols to communicate appropriately in different contexts and situations. You might speak casually with friends and family, use special terminology at work or school, and use more standard language for formal situations. On some occasions, you may even use artistic language such as poetry or song to express your creativity.

Adds Interest to Communication A large and flexible vocabulary can add interest, originality, vitality, and clarity to your communication. What did you have for lunch yesterday? Was it broth, soup, or stew? It might not matter to you now, but knowing the

REAL-WORLD CONNECTION

Specialized Vocabulary Most of the words in the English vocabulary are never heard outside certain contexts; yet within those contexts they are essential to precise communication. Lead students to understand the importance of specialized vocabulary in the functioning of many trades and professions.

Activity Have students research the specialized vocabulary of a trade, sport, craft, or profession that interests them. (Point out that there are innumerable choices, from the obvious, technology, to the less familiar, oboe-reed making!) Ask students to design an illustrated poster featuring at least ten of their words. Have them present their vocabulary research to the class.

WHY IT'S IMPORTANT TO BUILD YOUR VOCABULARY

Your language makes an impression on others and influences their perceptions of who you are and what you are like.

Language depends heavily on context and is subject to standards for appropriateness. Meeting standards shows skilled use of language.

A large vocabulary allows you to express yourself clearly and effectively in a wide range of situations with a wide variety of people.

The ability to express yourself clearly and interpret and respond to the messages of others appropriately and accurately is vital in professional and social contexts.

Building a large vocabulary is an easy way to add interest and personality to your image as a communicator.

difference and using the most appropriate word would matter when you order from a menu. Certainly, distinguishing the three dishes and knowing the appropriate word symbol for each are important to the server and the chef. As your lifestyle expands into professional and social contexts, you will discover a need to expand your vocabulary along with your wardrobe to meet the norms of new situations. Several major reasons for making a serious effort to build and increase your vocabulary are found in the chart above.

Structure

Structure, the third characteristic of language, is the way the different parts of a language are arranged. Both words and sentences must follow an accepted structure in order to carry meaning from a speaker to a listener.

Words have syllables that go in a particular order and influence the function and meaning of the word. For example, in English the word symbol *form* can be used to describe an outward shape or appearance. If you add the syllable *al* to the end, however, you create the new word *formal.* In so doing you change both the function and the suggested meaning of the word to describe something that follows an established

custom. Add the syllable *in* to the beginning of the word, and you create *informal,* a word that means the exact opposite of *formal.* Each syllable must be added at the correct place to carry a specific meaning. *Alformin* makes no sense and cannot be recognized as an English word. The parts must be in the right order. The conclusion you can draw is that the way to build words in a language is regulated by the particular code or structure of the language.

Structure is also important in making statements and asking questions. Speakers learn to arrange words in sentences so that

Practice for the Workplace

Communication Tools Just as the words we choose can affect our communication, the channel of delivery also can affect the way we communicate. Choosing the most appropriate channel of communication for a specific situation can greatly influence the effectiveness of a message.

BUSINESS PRACTICE *Activity*

Read the following list of communication channels found in most schools. Then, speak to a businessperson in your community and identify channels in the business world that might parallel these channels.
- school newspaper
- school announcements
- student handbook
- club meetings
- state conferences
- distance learning classes
- e-mail
- flyers

Discovering the Power of Oral Language **105**

Practice for the Workplace

Communication Tools Point out that effective workplace communication includes gathering information from a variety of sources to get a complete picture. *(Students may find the following parallels between the school communication channels listed and the channels conventionally used in the business world: school newspaper/organizational newsletter; school announcements/electronic bulletin boards; student handbook/institutional policies and procedures; club meetings/committee meetings; state conferences/national conventions; distance learning classes/video conferencing; e-mail/e-mail; flyers/memos.)* **L2**

Structure

Ask students how they learned the structure of the language. *(Students may answer by modeling, repetition, or trial and error.)* Invite volunteers to make any general statements about the structure of English. What rules would they be able to tell a visitor to an English-speaking country about how the language is put together? Finally, challenge students to identify a way in which they have altered their manner of speaking as a result of something they have learned from an English teacher in school. Lead students to understand that we acquire much of our knowledge of the language not by conventional teaching but by a process of absorption with our earliest experiences. **L2**

MEETING INDIVIDUAL NEEDS — GIFTED AND TALENTED

Language Structure Encourage students to think critically about the structure of language by having them develop one of their own.

Activity Ask pairs of students to develop a simple form of language, using a different vocabulary, structure, and grammar from any other language with which they are familiar. Ask them to create a vocabulary of at least fifty words and to devise a system for making statements, asking simple questions, and speaking of events in the past and future. Have them prepare a visual display to accompany a classroom presentation. Finally, ask pairs to conduct a brief conversation in their language. Invite comments and discussion from the class.

Grammar

Ask students why schools teach grammar when most people pick up the structure of the language and can make themselves understood in oral speech without formal training. *(Answers may include that formal instruction in grammar provides insights into the language and its formal and informal use.)* Point out that knowing the rules of a language can sometimes prevent confusion. On the chalkboard, write the sentence "Barking angrily, the news crew filmed the police dogs attacking the demonstrators." Ask what is wrong with the example *(Barking angrily is a misplaced modifier, suggesting that the news crew is barking)*. Explain that the only reason we understand what is happening in this ungrammatical description is that we know people don't usually bark. Lead students to understand that knowledge of how a language works enables us to communicate precisely and with variety of expression. **L1**

Speech Sounds

Point out that everyone has a unique way of producing speech sound. Invite two or three volunteers to read the same paragraph on this page. Encourage other members of the class to analyze their delivery, describing differences in their sounds. Ask students whether they believe that the sound of a person's speech influences their opinion of him or her. Do mispronunciations, accents, or slurred words give the listener a message? If so, is the message a truthful one or an example of a harmful prejudice? Discuss with the class their responses to the way people speak. Lead students to understand the complexity of our reaction to speech sound. **L2**

their thoughts are stated clearly for audiences to understand and remember. People who interview others learn to structure questions clearly so they can get the answers they desire. People who are being interviewed learn to structure answers to questions clearly so they can give appropriate responses to the specific questions asked. In the workplace, in the classroom, and in interpersonal situations, clear and appropriate language structures are important to clear communication.

Grammar

Grammar, the fourth characteristic of language, is the basic understandings and rules that regulate the use of a language. These rules identify all the different components of a language, explain their functions, and dictate the way they are used in communication.

Not all languages observe the same rules of grammar. For example, in Spanish, nouns precede adjectives. A Spanish speaker would say *la mesa grande,* "the table large." In English, adjectives precede nouns. English speakers would therefore say "the large table." Learning the rules that regulate a particular code is important to using a language appropriately and skillfully.

Grammar, meaning, vocabulary, and structure are interrelated parts of a language system. If you could watch your encoding process in slow motion, you would realize that you first assign meaning to data and then choose language symbols or vocabulary to express what you want to say. After that, you have to structure your ideas into the complete thought you want to express. Finally, you formulate the statement to incorporate the grammar of the code so you can make a literate, articulate statement. All four steps tend to occur subconsciously and simultaneously as you speak and express your ideas.

"GOT IDEA. TALK BETTER. COMBINE WORDS. MAKE SENTENCES."

Reprinted by permission of Sidney Harris.

Sound

Sound is central to the very idea of oral language. In fact, *oral* means uttered or spoken. Speech sound is the observable characteristics of oral language. Every oral language has its own sounds that represent its unique set of word symbols. Without sound, the words cannot convey meaning orally.

Importance of Sound Sounds not only are vital for understanding the words of a language, they also affect the interpretation of messages. That is, the way you sound affects the messages you send to others. What your spoken words convey to others is an important part of your image and effectiveness as a communicator.

Sound and Image Fair or not, individuals often are judged and labeled according to the way their speech sounds. Speakers, for example, can gain or lose credibility because of the way they sound. A speaker who is articulate

CRITICAL THINKING ACTIVITY

At no other point in history have people been exposed to the variety of oral language as they are today. Encourage students to become critical listeners. Have students videotape at home a few minutes of public speaking from film or television that they are prepared to critique. Remind them that there is a wealth of material, from comedy monologues and infomercials to C-Span coverage of the Senate. Direct students to take notes on their selected clips with an eye for image and diction as described in the text. Have them present their examples to the class, drawing their audience's attention to at least five points in the speaker's delivery that they consider to be strengths or weaknesses. Discuss the video clips and analyses with the class.

and clear can give a speech that has little or no worthwhile content and still be perceived as credible by listeners. This theory has been demonstrated in a number of experiments and often is referred to as the Dr. Fox Hypothesis.

During a convention, a group of highly respected psychiatrists, psychologists, social workers, and educators attended a speech by Dr. Myron Fox. Dr. Fox delivered a stirring half-hour discussion on "Mathematical Game Theory Applied to Physical Education." At the conclusion of Dr. Fox's speech, questionnaires were distributed, allowing the audience to evaluate the presentation they had just heard. The completed questionnaires revealed an overwhelmingly positive response to the session. Listeners indicated that they found the lecture to be informative and interesting.

What's so unusual about that? Dr. Fox was a fraud. He had been portrayed by a professional actor coached in the art of intelligent-sounding language and double-talk. His lecture was a series of jokes, contradictory statements, and references to unrelated topics. Yet he spoke with enough eloquence and style to convince listeners of his credibility.

The message of this story is that how you sound is an important part of the message you convey. It takes focused thought, appropriate language, and clear, articulate speech to communicate effectively with others.

CHARACTERISTICS OF SPEECH SOUND

Everyone who speaks shapes the sounds of his or her speech in a unique way. However, although everyone's speech sounds different, there are some general guidelines we all should try to follow when it comes to forming words.

The way your words sound can affect the messages you send. For instance, if you sloppily run together the words of a formal introduction, you may be perceived as lazy or disrespectful. If you continually mispronounce words during a job interview, you could be perceived as uneducated or careless. If you speak with a heavy regional accent, people may have trouble understanding you.

By following some important guidelines, you can make sure that your speech sounds are as clear and correct as possible. As shown in **Figure 4–2** below, these guidelines relate to diction—which includes pronunciation, articulation, and enunciation—and also to dialect.

Diction

At some point in your life, you probably have heard a speaker who pronounced words incorrectly, did not complete words, or changed the sound so much that he or she seemed to be saying another word entirely. If so, you might say that the person had poor diction.

Diction is the degree of clarity and distinctness in a person's speech. It is the way his or her words are spoken. A person with good diction speaks clearly and uses appropriate and effective speech sounds to get his or her meanings across. Your own diction is determined by the choices you make in pronunciation, articulation, and enunciation.

■ **Figure 4–2 Characteristics of Speech Sound**

Discovering the Power of Oral Language **107**

Problems with Articulation

Ask students to read the descriptions of the four articulation problems given in the text. Have they ever heard any of these examples of poorly articulated words? What other examples can they think of that fit into these categories? Challenge students to consider the following problem: Who decides how a word should sound? Lead them to understand that there is a very fine distinction between a genuine mistake in articulation and a cultural assumption about correct pronunciation. **L2**

COMMUNICATION PRACTICE LAB

Eliminating Pronunciation Errors

Which words did students most frequently mispronounce? Is there any word about which a majority of the class disagreed with the dictionary? What might the reasons for this be? *(Students may suggest that in their part of the country a "faulty" pronunciation is acceptable.)* During discussion in Step 4, ask students if some errors in pronunciation are more acceptable than others. Are there certain words that one should never mispronounce? **L2**

GLENCOE Online

For an additional Practice Lab for this section, have students visit the *Glencoe Communication Applications* Web site at communicationapplications.glencoe.com. Click on Communication Practice Lab 4–1. **L1**

Pronunciation Pronunciation is the standard set for the overall sound of a word. The pronunciations of most words are listed in the dictionary. Often, the preferred or most-used pronunciations are listed first, followed by other ways people might pronounce the word. For example, the preferred pronunciation of *often* is "ah • fun." However, so many people say "ahf • tun" that many dictionaries list this as a second or alternative pronunciation. When a dictionary lists multiple pronunciations of a word, it is a good idea to use the one that is listed first.

Other words have only one correct pronunciation. Consider the word *athlete,* for instance. The dictionary lists its pronunciation as "ath' • leet" with no alternatives. Therefore, if you have a habit of saying "a' • thuh • leet," you are mispronouncing the word. It is important to know that a mispronounced word can confuse the meaning of a message and reflect poorly on a speaker's credibility or image. On the other hand, clear, appropriate word pronunciation is the mark of a knowledgeable and literate communicator.

Articulation It is not enough to simply pronounce a word. It also is important to articulate it. Articulation is the act of clearly and distinctly uttering the consonant sounds of a word. There are four kinds of articulation problems that can interfere with speech. They are omission, addition, substitution, and slurring.

Omission Sometimes, people omit, or leave out, certain consonant sounds within a word. For example, a person who says "bi'ness" instead of "business" is omitting the *s* from the middle of the word. Similarly, saying "he'p" instead of "help," "dolla'" instead of "dollar," or "'Uston" instead of "Houston" is an articulation problem related to the omission of a consonant sound.

Addition The opposite of omission is addition. This type of problem occurs when a person adds extra consonant sounds to a word. For example, if you say "warsh" instead of "wash" or "Florider" instead of "Florida," you have added an inappropriate *r* sound that does not belong.

Substitution Another common articulation problem is substitution. This occurs when a speaker substitutes one consonant sound for another. If you say "idn't" instead of "isn't," you are substituting a *d* for an *s* sound. Saying

COMMUNICATION PRACTICE LAB

Eliminating Pronunciation Errors

To eliminate mispronunciations in your speech, follow these steps:

Step 1 As a class, brainstorm a list of words that are commonly mispronounced. Ask your teacher for additional suggestions. Write each term on the chalkboard or an overhead transparency. Explain the meaning of each term as it is listed.

Step 2 Discuss as a class how you think each word should be pronounced correctly.

Step 3 Use a dictionary to look up the correct pronunciation of each word. Were your predictions on target?

Step 4 As a class, discuss how mispronouncing words might affect your image as a communicator in different situations.

MEETING INDIVIDUAL NEEDS — MULTIPLE LEARNING STYLES

Musical Point out that not all the speech sounds we hear are in the form of speech. As long as there has been poetry, musicians have been setting words to music. Even so, the spoken word and the sung word do not always sound the same.

Activity Have students bring to school a classroom-appropriate recording of a song that they feel includes some interesting variations in diction from the language as it is conventionally spoken. Ask them to distribute a word sheet to the class and have the class analyze the singer's pronunciation, articulation, and enunciation. Encourage students to consider factors that might explain these differences. Does the act of singing alter the way words are sounded?

"mirrow" rather than "mirror" substitutes a *w* for an *r* sound, and saying "liddle" rather than "little" substitutes a *d* for a *t* sound. Substitution sometimes is described as "lazy speech" because instead of the correct sound, the speaker has used a consonant sound which requires less effort to produce than the originally intended sound.

Slurring A fourth type of articulation problem occurs when consonant sounds are slurred, or run together. This occurs when speakers simply slide over a group of sounds, pronouncing some but failing to give proper emphasis to others. Slurring results in unclear speech that listeners may find difficult to understand. An example of slurring is shown in the center column of the chart below. The clear articulation of each sentence is shown in the right column.

One entertaining way to test your articulation skills is by repeating tongue twisters. If you can rapidly repeat "rubber baby buggy bumpers" or "She sells sea shells by the seashore" without substituting or omitting sounds, you have great articulation skills! However, if you're like most people, you may occasionally get your tongue tangled. When that happens, just keep trying. With enough practice, you may be able to sharpen your skills and become a more articulate speaker.

DICTION

	Slurred Diction	Clear Diction
Speaker 1	"Jeet?"	"Did you eat?"
Speaker 2	"Novyu?"	"No. Have you?"
Speaker 1	"Nopedyuwanna?"	"Nope. Do you want to?"
Speaker 2	"Surefyurgonna."	"Sure, if you're going to."

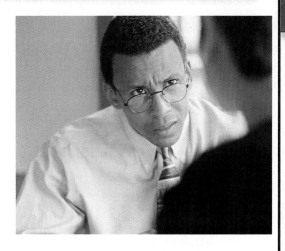

The gentleman in the photograph appears to be having a difficult time understanding the speaker. If a person has poor diction, he or she will not be an effective communicator. **What four articulation problems can interfere with speech?**

Enunciation Just as articulation relates to consonant sounds, enunciation refers to vowel sounds. Enunciation is the act of clearly and distinctly uttering the vowel sounds of a word.

Sometimes, vowel sounds can become distorted. This may be the result of faulty placement of the teeth, tongue, or lips as a vowel sound is formed. For example, if you say "git" instead of "get," it may be because the jaw and lips are not properly opened to shape the short *e* sound. A closed jaw or flattened lip opening will instead form a short *i* sound. If you look in a mirror while you repeat "git, get, git, get, git, get" you can see the different mouth shapes for both vowel sounds. Failing to shape your mouth to form the short *e* sound also may cause you to say "pin" rather than "pen," "jist" rather than "just," and "inyone" rather than "anyone." Most of the time, poor enunciation is subconscious. By paying attention to vowel sounds, you can learn to enunciate clearly and effectively.

Discovering the Power of Oral Language **109**

Tongue Twisters
Students may know other tongue-twisting tests of articulation. Write examples on the board and invite volunteers to try them at speed. Can any student say, "The Leith police dismisseth us" three times quickly? Point out that the famous "sea shells" twister has a second line that makes it even more challenging: The shells that she sells are seashore shells. Ask students if they can identify what it is that makes a tongue twister difficult to articulate. **L1**

The Oral Language System
Have students study the chart in Figure 4–2. Ask them which of the elements comprising oral language they have studied in school or otherwise consciously learned? Which have they picked up intuitively? *(Students may respond that vocabulary and grammar are standard school subjects; a few may also have been taught the elements of diction.)* Discuss with the class whether speech and diction are important enough to be a part of the standard school curriculum. **L1**

Visual Instruction

Answer Four articulation problems that can interfere with speech are omission, addition, substitution, and slurring.

MEETING INDIVIDUAL NEEDS

ENGLISH LANGUAGE LEARNERS

Problem Words Point out that every language has its unique system of sounds. Native speakers of any language grow so accustomed to their own speech habits that they often find it extremely difficult to duplicate all the sounds of an acquired language.

Activity Have English language learners share with the class words in English that they find difficult to pronounce or articulate. Ask them to prepare a list of words from their own language that native English speakers find difficult to say. Have volunteers from the class experiment with these problematic sounds. Encourage students to analyze the reasons some sounds are more difficult than others. **ELL**

Dialect in a Global Culture

Point out that as the world becomes more closely linked by modern channels of communication, the need to be mutually understood grows increasingly important. Remind students that English is the official language used by pilots of international flights to communicate with flight control operators. Ask how dialect might cause difficulties in this area. *(Students may suggest that imprecise communication in flight control could prove fatal.)* In what other fields might dialect-free speech be particularly critical? *(Students may suggest disaster relief or warfare.)* **L2**

■ Visual Instruction

Answer The Navaho language only existed in oral form, so it was impossible for the enemy to translate.

■ **During World War II, young Navajo Indians, or "code talkers," used their native language to transmit intelligence messages for the Allies.** Why was this practice successful in preventing enemies from breaking the codes?

Dialect

Dialect can be used to describe two different aspects of speech. First, dialect can refer to a language that exists only in oral form. During World War II, for example, the Navajo language was exclusively oral. Also, very few people outside the Navajo nation spoke the language. Because of this, young Navajo Indians used their native language as a code for transmitting intelligence messages for the Allied Forces. The "Code Talkers," as they were called, successfully prevented enemy intelligence from breaking Allied codes. Because there was no print representation of the Navajo language, the messages were virtually impossible for the enemy to translate.

The second aspect of dialect probably is the most common and is the focus of this study. Dialect is a unique combination of speech sounds that identify speech with a particular group of people. The dialect of a specific region may have different vocabulary, grammar, and pronunciations from dialects of other regions. Some dialects—such as Mandarin and Cantonese, both of which are versions of Chinese—can be so distinctive that

speakers of one may not be able to speak or understand the other. On the other hand, some dialects are similar enough that they simply are referred to as accents.

Regional Dialect The so-called "southern drawl" is a regional dialect characterized by prolonged vowel sounds, soft consonant sounds, and some unique vocabulary such as *y'all* or *fixin'*. A person who speaks this dialect generally is easily identified as being from the southern United States. By the same token, a person may be usually identified as a New Yorker if he or she tends to drop hard consonant sounds within some words, drops *r*'s from the ends of some words, and uses unique vocabulary such as *youse* or *wit'*.

Ethnic and Cultural Dialect Dialect also can relate to the speech characteristics of various ethnic or cultural groups. Sometimes, these groups may continue to use some of the characteristics of their first or native language when speaking another language. For example, a native speaker of Japanese who has not yet mastered the sounds of Spanish may continue to use some characteristics of his or her own language and perhaps even inject Japanese words when speaking Spanish. This creates a personal dialect that, at times, may be difficult for the native speaker of Spanish to understand.

In today's global society, people from all regions of the world communicate with each other across all sorts of language, ethnic, and cultural lines. Because all these variations can work against the effectiveness of communication, it is important for your speech to be as clear as possible. For English speakers in the United States, speech educators generally recommend developing a general American dialect that is relatively free of regional or ethnic influence.

Although strong regional, ethnic, or cultural dialects may be perfectly acceptable for informal communication within the culture, they may be less appropriate for more general contexts. For example, if you listen to a national news cast, you will seldom find the anchor using a regional dialect.

To function effectively in most professional and social contexts, individuals need to develop diction that is clear and easy to understand by a variety of listeners. Generally speaking, this kind of speech reflects appropriate use of language and diction that is relatively free of diverse dialects.

PUTTING LANGUAGE INTO PERSPECTIVE

Now that you have defined oral language and explored its components and characteristics, you may be wondering, "How does all this affect me?" It helps to understand that speech is highly personal and cultural in nature.

Personal Implications of Oral Language

Now that you understand some of the ways your speech influences how you are perceived by others, you may want to give some thought to the image you want your language to project.

Projecting Image The first step toward determining your image is to ask yourself, "Who am I, really?" Of course, the answer will not be simple. You are made up of many different aspects, each of which may have its own language needs. So, you might want to begin by considering what type of language is most appropriate for the "personal you" in interpersonal relationships and academic settings. You also may want to start developing language skills for the "professional you" and the you who is involved in social projects and organizations.

All of these aspects of you, your activities and pursuits, require different sets of language skills. To equip yourself, it is a good idea to become a collector of words, improving your personal vocabulary and speaking skills.

■ The girl's style of dress distinguishes her "personal image" from her "professional image." Language is also instrumental in creating your image. Give an example of when it is appropriate to use "personal you" language.

Projecting Image

Ask students if they are aware of molding their speech styles to suit the image they wish to project. As an exercise in self-awareness, ask them the following question: How would you introduce yourself to these people: the coach of a varsity team for which you are trying out, the cutest guy or girl at a party, or the dean of a college you would like to attend? Invite volunteers to act out a scene of their choice. Have students analyze the performance. What image did the performer intend to convey? **L2**

■ Visual Instruction

Answer Possible answers: when with family and friends, at school, with teammates

EFFECTIVE LANGUAGE STRATEGIES

After students have reviewed the checklist for effective language strategies, discuss one tactic they might use to increase their vocabularies. Suggest that they might keep a journal in which they note new words they encounter (they might want to note the context as well as the word). After they hear a new word, they should learn the definition and practice using the word in their own speech and writing. **L1**

GLOBAL COMMUNICATION

Gender Differences

Point out that a major concern among educators is the tendency of male students to be more assertive in the classroom, directing a teacher's attention away from the needs of female students. Some have advocated single-sex schooling as a solution to this perceived imbalance. Ask students to share their experiences of gender differences in education. Do they feel they would thrive in a single-sex environment? **L1**

Conveying Attitudes As you begin thinking about language skills, remember that your speech conveys powerful messages about your attitudes and feelings toward your listener. Therefore, it is important to remind yourself of the interpersonal signals you are sending. As a competent communicator, you not only need to develop language skills that help you clearly and efficiently complete tasks such as asking and answering questions, giving directions, and explaining information. You also need to complete these tasks with courtesy, civility, and respect for others.

Determining Success It would be difficult to overestimate the role of language in determining your success in professional contexts. In fact, studies have shown that many employers value strong verbal skills more than any other communication skill in their employees. In addition, as you have been involved in interpersonal relationships, you probably have experienced some of the effects of language skills in social contexts. Most of us realize that there are times when saying the right thing in the right way can make a world of difference.

EFFECTIVE LANGUAGE STRATEGIES

✓ Increase your knowledge base.

✓ Build your vocabulary.

✓ Experiment by using new words.

✓ Practice using clear statements and asking clear questions.

✓ Use clear diction.

✓ Strive to use language effectively and build positive relationships.

GLOBAL COMMUNICATION

Gender Differences

Researchers claim that American women engage in more supportive, tentative, and emotionally expressive communication than males, who are more direct, assertive, and fact-oriented. Remember this when you interact with people from other countries or cultures. There are not only culturally determined differences in communication styles, but also gender differences within cultures. How do men and women you encounter communicate their attitudes differently?

One way to begin building language skills is to increase your knowledge base in the personal, professional, and social arenas of your life. As you expand your knowledge, you also expand your vocabulary by learning new terms, words, and expressions related to the subjects you are studying. In addition, it is helpful to continually build your general vocabulary. The goal is to develop an interesting, precise, and flexible word bank that will energize your language and serve you well in personal, professional, and social contexts.

Whenever possible, experiment with using new words. You also might practice different ways to structure statements and explanations and ask and answer questions to get the results you want. Remember to incorporate and practice the language of courtesy to demonstrate respect for others. You might enjoy experimenting with different language tactics to see what kinds of results you get. One obvious reward of new language skills is likely to be a new appreciation for and enjoyment of language itself.

EXTENDING THE CONTENT

Rapport Versus Report Talk In *You Just Don't Understand: Men and Women in Conversation*, author Deborah Tannen distinguishes between the "rapport" talk of females and the "report" talk of males. According to Tannen, females tend to use more supportive language and to express their emotions more frequently than males. Men, on the other hand, focus more on facts. Their language is oriented toward action and not emotion. A man will more likely offer advice than sympathy.
Activity Read the preceding passage to students, or give them a copy of it, and allow them ten minutes to record their responses in their journals. Invite volunteers to read their entries. Encourage the class to discuss gender differences in speech.

Cultural Implications of Oral Language

Language is so closely related to culture that some scholars insist that language *is* culture. This theory is based on the notion that culture affects how we think and, therefore, how we use language. Given the complexities of today's multicultural society, this idea has some special implications.

Historical Research In the early 1800s, German scholars Jakob and Wilhelm Grimm began gathering the stories that would eventually become the well-known *Grimm's Fairy Tales.* The brothers Grimm traveled from province to province and community to community throughout Germany listening to people as they told the stories of their culture. What the brothers Grimm discovered was that, although many of the stories' minor details changed from region to region, the tales were essentially the same. Names and details changed, perhaps, but the wolves, witches, dwarves, lost children, maidens, and princes all seemed to share common adventures from version to version of the famous stories.

As they gathered their stories, the Grimms became fascinated with the differences in language that they encountered. They began to record not only the stories but also how people spoke in different cultures and regions. The brothers wrote detailed phonetic descriptions of different storytellers' speech patterns and language choices throughout the land. The Grimms' comparative study of speech is still used today as a basic study in oral language.

Grimm's Law The Grimms' study resulted in what is known as Grimm's law, which has some important implications in today's society. First, the Grimms refuted the notion that one speech pattern was superior to another. They concluded instead that the oral language used in each area of Germany best served the needs of the people within that culture. Each was effective in allowing the people to verbally communicate with one another.

Expanding upon this idea, they also suggested that there are no grammatical errors within an oral culture. Remember that grammar relates to the agreed-upon conventions for using language. So if the people's established rules are not being violated, no error has occurred. However, before you celebrate the idea that you can talk any way you want, think carefully about the last four words of the Grimms' rule: "within an oral culture." A literal translation of the Grimms' conclusion suggests that the agreed-upon language is appropriate only as long as you remain in the culture. The translation also suggests that once you cross a cultural line, the language choice may not be appropriate.

Jakob and Wilhelm Grimm, authors of *Grimm's Fairy Tales*, studied different cultures and language throughout Germany. What did Grimm's law imply about oral language?

Discovering the Power of Oral Language **113**

3 ASSESS

Assign Section 1 Assessment as a homework or in-class activity.

🔊 Use *Interactive Tutor Self-Assessment Software* to review Section 1.

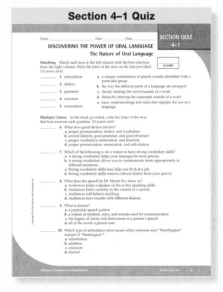

Visual Instruction

Answer No one speech pattern is superior to another; the oral language used in the cultural area serves the needs of the people within that culture; there are no grammatical errors within an oral culture; an agreed-upon language is appropriate only as you remain in that culture.

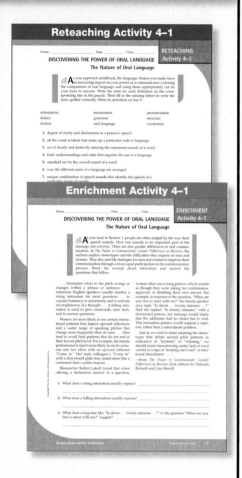

Reteaching Activity 4–1

DISCOVERING THE POWER OF ORAL LANGUAGE
The Nature of Oral Language

As you approach adulthood, the language choices you make have an increasing impact on your power as a communicator. Learning the components of oral language and using these appropriately can be your keys to success. Write the term for each definition on the corresponding line in the puzzle. Then fill in the missing letters to write the term spelled vertically. Write its definition on line 9.

articulation   enunciation   pronunciation
dialect   grammar   structure
diction   oral language   vocabulary

1. degree of clarity and distinctness in a person's speech
2. all the word symbols that make up a particular code or language
3. act of clearly and distinctly uttering the consonant sounds of a word
4. basic understandings and rules that regulate the use of a language
5. standard set for the overall sound of a word
6. way the different parts of a language are arranged
7. unique combination of speech sounds that identify the speech of a particular group of people

Enrichment Activity 4–1

DISCOVERING THE POWER OF ORAL LANGUAGE
The Nature of Oral Language

As you read in Section 1, people are often judged by the way their speech sounds. How one sounds is an important part of the message one conveys. There are also gender differences in oral communication. In *The Power to Communicate: Gender Differences as Barriers*, the authors explore stereotypes and the difficulties they impose on men and women. They also provide strategies for men and women to improve their communication through a more equal participation in the communication process. Read the excerpt about intonation and answer the questions that follow.

. . . Intonation refers to the pitch swings or changes within a phrase or sentence. . . . American English speakers usually employ a rising intonation for most questions . . . to express hesitancy or uncertainty, and to indicate incompleteness of a thought. . . . A falling intonation is used to give commands, state facts, and to answer questions.

Women are more likely to use certain intonational patterns that feature upward inflections and a wider range of speaking pitches that change more frequently than do men. . . . Men tend to avoid final patterns that do not end at their lowest pitch level. For example, the female professional is much more likely to invite someone into her office with a downward inflected "Come in." Her male colleague's "Come in" with a downward glide may sound more like a command than a polite request.

[Researcher Robin] Lakoff found that when offering a declarative answer to a question, women often use a rising pattern, which sounds as though they were asking for confirmation, approval, or doubting their own answer. For example, in response to the question, "When are you free to meet with me?" the female speaker may reply "In about . . . twenty minutes . . .?" Had she replied "In twenty minutes." with a downward pattern, her message would imply that the addressee had no choice but to wait. This intonation pattern would support a superior, rather than a subordinate position. . . .

Just as we need to resist adopting the stereotypes that define several pitch patterns as indicative of "hysteria" or "whining," we should resist characterizing males' lack of vocal variety as a sign of "keeping one's cool" or emotional detachment . . .

—from *The Power to Communicate: Gender Differences as Barriers* (2nd edition) by Deborah Borisoff and Lisa Merrill

1. What does a rising intonation usually express? _____

2. What does a falling intonation usually express? _____

3. What does a response like "In about . . . twenty minutes . . .?" to the question "When are you free to meet with me?" suggest? _____

4 CLOSE

Have students review their responses to the opening paragraph of this section on page 101. Which type of speech do they feel they most need to practice? How would they begin to improve their oral language skills?

Extra-Credit Project

Ask students to imagine that they have been chosen to speak for two minutes on "the importance of education" to an assembly of parents and educators. Ask them to explain how context affected the choices they made.

114

Diversity The implications of Grimm's law are significant. How many times do you cross cultural lines each day? How can you anticipate your future involvement with diverse cultures in the future? Of course, some of us are more affected by cultural crossovers than others. However, almost everyone encounters cultures different from their own on a regular basis.

In many cases, an individual may experience vastly different language cultures at home and at school. For instance, if Spanish is the primary language spoken at home and English is the primary language spoken at school, a person may have to make several major language transitions each day. Along the same line, street language or school slang probably will not be appropriate in the culture of most organizations or workplaces. Casual language used with your friends might not cross cultural lines and work effectively with some adults. Moreover, your regional language and dialect may not be acceptable in certain professional, public, or social situations. As with any other aspect of communication, the standards for your language choices should be appropriate for yourself, the listener, the occasion, and the task.

Section 1 Assessment

GLENCOE
Online

Visit the *Glencoe Communication Applications* Web site at **communicationapplications. glencoe.com** and click on **Self-Check and Study Guide 4.1** to review your understanding of the nature of oral language.

Review Key Terms

1. Define each term and write it in a sentence: oral language, vocabulary, structure, grammar, diction, pronunciation, articulation, enunciation, dialect.

Check Understanding

2. Define oral language and briefly explain each of its characteristics.

3. Describe the two main characteristics of speech sound.

4. How are pronunciation, articulation, and enunciation alike? How are they different?

5. Describe one communication problem that might result from using a strong dialect. What is one possible solution to this problem?

6. **Apply** Explain one way your oral language choices might affect you on a personal level and on a cultural level in your future.

APPLICATION *Activity*

Analyzing Dialect Working in groups of three or four, select a dialect and brainstorm a list of common words that might be considered part of that dialect. As a class, list your words in a chart and classify each as regional, ethnic, or cultural. Brainstorm how you might replace each word with more standardized language. Were there any words you had difficulty replacing? Why?

Section 1 Assessment Answers

1. Accept all reasonable sentences.
2. Oral language is a system of symbols, rules, and sounds used for human communication. The symbols, or words, are arranged according to rules of structure and grammar and then expressed as speech sounds to convey meanings.
3. The two characteristics are diction and dialect. *Diction* is the degree of distinctness and clarity in a person's speech. Good diction involves proper pronunciation, articulation, and enunciation of words. *Dialect* is a unique combination of speech sounds that identify speech with a particular group of people. It is made up of the vocabulary, grammar, and pronunciations of a specific region.
4. All are elements of diction. Pronunciation relates to the way a whole word sounds, while articulation deals only with the consonant sounds of a word, and enunciation deals only with the vowel sounds of a word.

RECOGNIZING BIAS

Just as there is a need to send clear messages in social and professional contexts, there also is a need to be aware of the messages being sent by others. Sometimes those messages contain bias statements. A bias is a prejudice. It prevents you from looking at a situation in a reasonable or truthful way.

Learning the Skill

To recognize bias, follow these steps:

* Analyze the sender's message in terms of his or her views and possible reasons for making the statement.
* Try to notice language in the message that reflects an emotion or opinion. This may include words such as *all, never, best, worst, might,* or *should.*
* Look for imbalances in the message. Does it give only one viewpoint and fail to provide equal coverage of other possible viewpoints?
* Identify statements of fact. Factual statements usually answer who, what, where, and when.
* Identify the bias in the message.

Practicing the Skill

Read the advertisement in the next column and answer the questions that follow.

1. Who is the sender of the message?
2. What are the sender's reasons for sending this message?
3. List any words or phrases that indicate emotion or opinion.
4. List any factual statements.
5. Identify the bias in the message.

Best Desks, Incorporated makes only the very highest quality office furniture. Once you have used a Best Desks ergonomically designed chair, you will never want to use any other furniture. Our desks are made of solid wood and always are attractive and comfortable. Our padded chairs can be adjusted to your size and to the height of your desktop. Our prices are among the lowest in the industry. In addition, when you buy from Best Desks, you receive two <u>free</u> gifts: an attractive desk clock and a useful desk calendar.

APPLICATION *Activity*

Choose an editorial from a newspaper. In groups, read your chosen editorials aloud. As you read, emphasize any emotional or opinionated words through tone or expression you use. As a group, go through the steps to identify the bias in each editorial.

Recognizing Bias

Many students will accept bias in advertising as an essential part of the free-enterprise system. Few consumers expect advertisements to give the whole truth about a product or service. Another type of bias that is much harder to detect, however, is the research conducted by qualified professionals for industries or interest groups that can gain from specific findings. Point out that the drug and food industries routinely commission scientists to test their products, publicizing research that comes out in their favor. Ask students whether they believe this sort of self-promotion is ethical.

Practicing the Skill

The manufacturer, Best Desks, Incorporated, is the sender of this message. The manufacturer is hoping to persuade consumers to purchase a desk. Phrases indicating emotion or opinion include "the very highest quality," "you will never want to use any other furniture," and "always are attractive and comfortable." The word *best* in the company name is itself an opinion, as are the words "attractive" and "useful" used to describe the free gifts. The phrase "Our prices are among the lowest" sounds like fact but fails to identify the number of other desks in the comparison. The chairs are padded and adjustable. The desks are made of solid wood. Buyers receive two free gifts. By using unsupported superlatives to describe Best Desks and by failing to give any information about similar products on the market, this advertisement is clearly biased in favor of the manufacturer.

Application Activity

Point out that one of the difficulties in assessing bias in an editorial is knowing what facts have been left out. Ask students if there is information they would still like to know before forming opinions about the issues covered by their editorials.

Section 1 Answers, continued

5. Answers may include that it may be hard for someone from a different region to understand your speech. One possible solution is to reduce or eliminate the regional words, pronunciations, and grammar styles in one's own language.

6. Answers should reflect an understanding that language choices often affect personal image and may help or hinder one's ability to interact effectively with people from diverse cultures.

Application Activity Students may find that some words are difficult to replace because they represent things and ideas that are unique to a particular region, ethnicity, or culture.

1 FOCUS

Bellringer

Have students list the communication methods of animals, including insects. Write a master list of methods on the board. Are these methods more or less sophisticated than those of a kindergarten student? Explain your answer. *(Students' answers may include that although children in kindergarten have relatively unsophisticated communication skills for humans, they have communication skills far superior to members of other species. A child has the ability to form complex thoughts and use language that other animals do not have.)*

You may use Graphic Organizer Transparency 4–2 to introduce this section.

Graphic Organizer Transparency 4–2

Levels of Usage	Definition	When Is It Used?
Formal Language		
Technical Language		
Standard Language		
Informal Language		
Ungrammatical Language		

Grammar Tip

The semicolon is used instead of the comma to separate items in a series when the items already contain commas. An example occurs in the third paragraph of this section, in the sentence beginning, "Language has allowed . . ."

Visual Instruction

Answer Language and sophisticated thought

Developing Skills for Power Language

GUIDE TO READING

Objectives

1. Analyze the characteristics of power language.
2. Analyze and apply standards for using formal, technical, standard, and informal language appropriately.
3. Compare and contrast the functions of oral language.
4. Identify and describe the types of language to avoid in oral communication.

Terms to Learn

formal language
technical language
jargon
standard language
informal language
colloquialism
slang
ungrammatical language
social ritual
denotation
connotation
filler
tag

*T*hink about the world of nature. What is the most sophisticated communication you can think of in the animal kingdom? How does that compare to the communication skills of a typical human of kindergarten age?

Through language, human beings have the power to communicate as no other animal can. True, some animals are capable of communicating a wide variety of messages—"Watch me," "Go away," "I'm hungry," "I'm sad," or "Run!" to name a few. However, these types of messages are on a level of communication that most humans achieve early in their language development. Even Koko, a much-studied primate who not only speaks "Gorilla" but also some human sign language, is only able to communicate a limited range of ideas through her "speech."

It is through sophisticated thought and language that human beings are set apart from other animals. Language has allowed us to communicate specific, complex messages; preserve and study others' ideas; and use tools such as persuasion, manipulation, honesty, and conviction to influence those around us. In other words, language is power. Certainly, if this idea is true, we all need to learn how to use that power to help meet our personal needs and goals.

Koko, the well-known gorilla, developed language skills through the use of human sign language. *What sets humans apart from animals?*

Glencoe Communication Applications

RESOURCE MANAGER

Teaching Tools
- Interactive Lesson Planner
- Reproducible Lesson Plan 4–2
- Application Activities 4–2

Reproducible Masters
- Guided Reading Activity Workbook 4–2
- Enrichment Activity 4–2
- Reteaching Activity 4–2
- Section Quiz 4–2
- Transparency Strategies and Activities Booklet 4–2

Transparencies
- Graphic Organizer Transparency 4–2
- Chapter 4 Teaching Transparency

Technology Resources
- Interactive Tutor Self-Assessment Software
- Presentation Plus! Software
- ExamView® Pro Testmaker
- PuzzleMaker Software
- communicationapplications.glencoe.com

UNDERSTANDING AND USING POWER LANGUAGE

Why do people communicate? We all communicate to meet specific needs and goals. As you learn more about communication, you will discover ways to use "power language" to efficiently meet these needs and goals. Power language is a valuable tool for enhancing your image as a communicator. Power language is also valuable for achieving positive results and promoting effective relationships.

Characteristics of Power Language

Think about the most effective communicator you know. Whether this person is a teacher, parent, businessperson, or celebrity of some sort doesn't matter. What is important is his or her ability to get to the point, meet the listener's needs, and achieve positive results from communication. In other words, this person is skilled in using power language.

You too can learn to use power language in your day-to-day communication. The following chart describes the traits displayed in power language.

CHARACTERISTICS OF POWER LANGUAGE

Language Displays . . .	How	Effect on Communication
Clarity	Speech is precise, clearly organized, and grammatical. Speech is easy to understand.	Speaker may develop an image as a knowledgeable, efficient communicator. Understanding may be enhanced by ability to speak effectively.
Courtesy and Tact	Speaker listens empathically, negotiates with respect, disagrees without being disagreeable, and focuses discussions on issues rather than on people.	Showing respect and consideration to others promotes positive relationships. Speaker is considered a real "pro" in social and professional interactions.
Ownership of Thoughts and Feelings	Speaker takes responsibility for thoughts and feelings. Speaker uses "I" messages to express opinions, ideas, and feelings: "I was bored" rather than "That was boring."	When the speaker is seen as responsible, self-confident, and nonjudgmental, clarity and understanding are promoted. Speaker is viewed as someone who gets things done rather than a "blamer."
Inclusion of Others	Speaker listens empathically and personalizes speech with direct references to others: "What do you think about this issue?" "I'd really like to hear your opinion."	Including others helps establish a common ground and paves the way for cooperation and understanding. Speaker is seen as open-minded and interested in others.
Vividness and Imagery	Speaker expresses ordinary ideas in new and imaginative ways. Imagery is used to help people visualize complex ideas.	Speech is interesting and memorable. People look forward to hearing what the speaker has to say.
Appropriate Usage	Speaker uses a level of language that is appropriate for the specific context.	Speaker is often viewed as reasonable, thoughtful, and with a strong command of the language. Others trust him or her to communicate appropriately.

Discovering the Power of Oral Language **117**

2 TEACH

Characteristics of Power Language
Have students read the six characteristics of power language and their descriptions. Which of these items would require extra practice in order for a speaker to achieve competence? *(Students may suggest* Clarity *or* Vividness and Imagery.*)* Which require thought and care? *(Students may suggest* Courtesy and Tact *or* Inclusion of Others.*)* Ask students to list each item under the column headed Language Displays in what they consider to be order of importance. Keep a tally of the students' votes on the chalkboard and discuss the results. **L2**

BUSINESS BRIEF

The most effective speakers know when not to speak. "Sometimes it's good for both parties to keep quiet for a few moments. . . . Nonstop conversation may be an indication that something is seriously wrong," wrote Mary Kay Ash of Mary Kay Cosmetics. Ask students to comment on the role of silence in the repertoire of the power speaker.

Guided Reading Activity 4–2

GUIDED READING Activity 4–2	Name _____ Date _____ Class _____
	DISCOVERING THE POWER OF ORAL LANGUAGE Developing Skills for Power Language

As you read Section 2, answer the following items.

1. List the characteristics of power language: _____

2. How are formal and informal languages different? _____

3. Give the two names used to define a language associated with a particular profession, activity, or field of study.

4. List the four standards for using standard speech _____

5. Define colloquialism and slang, and discuss the limitations of each. _____

6. What are the five functions of oral language? _____

7. List four forms of social rituals. _____

8. How does a denotation differ from a connotation? _____

9. List the seven types of troublesome language you should avoid _____

10. How do fillers and tags affect a speaker's message? _____

INTERDISCIPLINARY CONNECTION

Science The study of how animals communicate is part of the larger field of ethology. Point out that although other species lack our intellectual capacity and the sophisticated oral vocabulary accompanying it, many compensate with a repertoire of scent and body language that leaves humans far behind.

Activity Ask students to research the means of communication practiced by one species of animal. Have them determine the importance of communication among individuals of the species, the type of information conveyed, and a typical "vocabulary list" of sounds or gestures. Encourage students to provide audiovisual aids to illustrate their findings and ask them to present their research to the class. Discuss with students the role of communication among species other than humankind.

Formal Language

Invite students to share experiences in which they have been exposed to formal language. (Remind them that many religious, political, and legal processes employ traditional verbal formulas.) Ask students what they believe the purpose of formal language to be. Lead students to understand that formal language can signify respect, while it also imposes verbal rules that are clearly understood by all parties. **L2**

DID YOU KNOW?

Henry Martyn Robert, an American army engineer, wrote *Robert's Rules of Order* in 1876. He based his system on the traditional rules of the British Houses of Parliament.

■ Visual Instruction

Answer Language that conforms to a highly structured set of rules, usually in situations requiring rigid protocol and form

■ Most governmental proceedings, such as the council meeting shown, involve aspects of formal language. **What is formal language?**

Power language is not as mysterious as it sounds. In short, it is clear, interesting, effective language. You already are familiar with much of what it takes to use power language. It involves mastering the components of language you read about in Section 1. It also emphasizes the diction and dialect habits you read about earlier and the easy-to-understand concepts of courtesy, ownership, inclusion, and vividness. Still, there is something more to power language. It also requires a thorough understanding of when to use different types of language.

UNDERSTANDING LEVELS OF USAGE

Skilled communicators learn early on that certain types of language strategies are appropriate for different situations. They also learn to avoid language that is inappropriate for a particular context. For example, you wouldn't use highly technical computer jargon to talk to most four-year-olds, nor would you use street slang to communicate in a job interview.

Speech has five basic levels of usage, each with its own type of language. These levels of language and usage are

- formal
- informal
- technical
- ungrammatical
- standard

Standards for Using Formal Language

Formal language is language that conforms to a highly structured set of rules; that is, there are strict standards dictating its use. Formal language typically is reserved for situations that require rigid protocol and form. Most legal proceedings and many religious services use some type of formal language. Certain social

118 *Glencoe Communication Applications*

COOPERATIVE LEARNING ACTIVITY

Point out that conducting a meeting using formal rules of order requires civility and cooperation. Allow students to experience the procedure firsthand with the following exercise. Have students research the rules of order governing meetings. Ask them each to make a page of notes including what they consider to be the essential procedures. In class, have them form pairs to compare their findings; then, appoint a chair to informally establish the rules that will govern the debate. Assign students a topic about which they all have an opinion. (A school or local issue may be the most productive.) Instruct the chair to convene the meeting and allow students to debate and vote on the issue and finally to adjourn the meeting according to the rules they have established. After the debate, discuss the experience of using formal language.

club meetings and political ceremonies also may adhere to a strict set of language rules.

Perhaps the clearest example of formal language is parliamentary procedure, which applies strict rules to all group communication. The formality involved in parliamentary procedure is really quite extensive. First, it requires a working knowledge of *Robert's Rules of Order*, which lists all the necessary guidelines for parliamentary-style meetings. In these meetings, participants address the presiding officer by his or her formal title and ask to be recognized before speaking to the group. They also structure each statement formally. For instance, you might say "I move that we . . ." before making a suggestion or motion.

Standards for Using Technical Language

Technical language is language associated with a particular profession, activity, or field of study. Another name for technical language is jargon. Medicine, law, finance,

Videoconferencing is an effective channel often used by members of the medical profession. Medical professionals utilize technical language frequently. What are some other fields that rely on technical language?

*inter*NET
A C T I V I T Y

Etymology The etymology of a word is a history of the uses of the word and how its definition or usage has changed over the years. The meaning of many words, including names, slang, technical language, and greetings, can be traced back hundreds of years. Do an Internet search using the word *etymology* to find the meaning of words you use on a daily basis.

technology, and sports are just a few fields that depend heavily on jargon. You probably also have encountered various types of technical language in the classes, clubs, and organizations to which you belong. Any time you take a course in a new area of study, enter a new activity, or take a new job, you probably will encounter a new technical vocabulary.

Technical language often can be misunderstood by those outside the profession or group. In addition, the same term can mean something quite different when used in a different context. The term *pound,* for example, can stand for a specific thickness of fishing line in a sporting goods store, a measurement of weight in math class, or a unit of currency at a bank.

The Changing Nature of Technical Language Even if you have a background in a specific field, you still are likely to encounter new vocabulary from time to time within that setting. Technical language tends to change rapidly and continually. Sometimes, things change so quickly that communicators simply make up new terms to meet specific needs. If these temporary terms remain useful over a period

Discovering the Power of Oral Language **119**

*inter*NET
A C T I V I T Y

Etymology Give students some practice for this assignment by looking up the etymology of a few words in class. Borrow an etymological dictionary from the library and choose words of interest to the class. Discuss how these words have come to acquire their current usage. **L2**

DID YOU KNOW?

The word *jargon* itself has an interesting etymology. It derives from the French *jargon*, meaning "the chattering of birds" and shares its origin with the words *gargle* and *gurgle*. The point is that, for most people, jargon represents meaningless noise.

Communication Tip

Students should realize that *jargon* is often used in a negative sense. The first definition in most dictionaries is "nonsensical talk." There is a good reason for this. Technical language must be used carefully, not as an excuse for confusing outsiders or making oneself seem important. Much jargon can be translated into Standard English. When communicating with the general public, one's first responsibility is precise, intelligible speech and writing.

Visual Instruction

Answer Law, finance, technology, and sports

MEETING INDIVIDUAL NEEDS
MULTIPLE LEARNING STYLES

Linguistic Jargon is sometimes essential, sometimes unnecessary. Students should realize that as professions become increasingly specialized, people are hearing more and more technical language. Encourage students to develop a critical ear for the correct use of jargon.

Activity Have students bring to class a piece of writing that relies upon jargon to convey information. Suggest to them that legal documents, computer manuals, literature about sound equipment or automobiles, and rock music reviews may all fall into this category. Have them choose a short passage from their selection and rewrite it in words that an average person would understand. Invite students to read their two passages to the class. Ask the class to evaluate the translations. Discuss with students under what circumstances jargon is necessary.

Standard Language

Students should realize that most high school English departments concentrate on teaching standard language. Ask students why standard language is so central to education. *(Possible answers: Having a universal form of expression makes misunderstandings less likely. The ability to communicate in standard language serves as a proof of education.)* Have students assess their own abilities to communicate successfully in standard speech and writing. On a scale of one to ten, ask them to rate their own achievements, with ten serving as their ideal language goal. **L2**

Colloquialisms

Point out that some colloquial expressions are so much a part of a regional culture that people may not even realize they are using them. Bostonians, for example, don't think twice when they say they are going "down to Maine," yet this expression stems from the days when sailing ships sailed downwind along the coast. Ask students if they have ever been made aware of their own colloquial expressions when traveling to other parts of the country. Make a list of their suggestions on the chalkboard. **L2**

■ **Visual Instruction**

Answer They do not translate well outside of the original culture.

---

of time, they may become incorporated into the group's standard jargon. Eventually, they may even find their way into the public's vocabulary.

Applying Technical Language

Knowing and using technical language can be vital to your success in many specialized activities or in the workplace. As you become more accustomed to using technical language in various contexts, you will realize that certain standards govern its use. For instance, technical language generally should be avoided when you are speaking with people outside your field. For example, use technical language sparingly when speaking with customers, clients, patients, audience members, or others whom it might confuse. If certain forms of jargon are unavoidable, be sure to explain the term carefully so the listener can understand.

Standards for Using Standard Language

Standard language is the language used by the majority of knowledgeable communicators within a specific language. It is what

■ **One colloquialism used in the agricultural community is "till the cows come home."** What is important to remember when utilizing colloquialisms?

most people refer to as "correct" speech. The standards for using standard speech include a precise vocabulary, appropriate use of language structures, adherence to the rules of the language, and clarity of diction. Standard language is the level of usage recommended for most professional and social contexts. It is often called "power language" because it is the level of usage that most directly affects your success in most situations.

Standards for Using Informal Language

Informal language is the type of language most often used in casual situations and close interpersonal relationships. It would be incorrect to assume that because language is informal, it has no rules. The standards for using the two most common types of oral language—colloquialisms and slang—are analyzed here.

Colloquialisms A colloquialism is a term associated with a specific regional culture. Most regional dialects contain a number of individual colloquialisms, which often are firmly entrenched in the speech traditions of the people. For example, many colloquialisms in the United States stem from the nation's agricultural roots. You may have heard someone speak of "going to bed with the chickens" to describe going to bed early or staying somewhere "till the cows come home" to describe staying a long time. Both are widely used examples of informal language.

Limitations of Colloquialisms Almost every culture has a number of colloquialisms rooted in its speech. These terms, phrases, and sentences usually are familiar to most people within a culture and may even be prized for adding a local flavor to the language. It is important to remember, however, that colloquialisms often do not translate well outside of their original culture. They can be easily

---

GIFTED AND TALENTED

A Standard Language Some people believe the stability of the country depends on English as a unifying force; others argue that diversity in language is just as beneficial. Encourage students to address these issues, paying particular attention to the views of English language learners.

Activity Have students debate the pros and cons of establishing English as the official language. Ask them to research the arguments from print sources or the Internet. Choose two teams of three or four students each and have them debate the issue. Allow the other students to contribute their views at the end of the debate. Make sure that English language learners have the opportunity to express their opinions on the controversy. Ask students at the end of the discussion if their views were altered by any arguments they heard.

misinterpreted or completely meaningless to anyone from a different regional culture.

Using Colloquialisms For this reason, colloquialisms are best reserved for informal communication with close friends or casual relationships within the culture. Generally speaking, they are not appropriate for use in interviews, conversations related to professional or social business, or public presentations. Although some situations may allow a "folksy" or "homespun" communication style, it is important not to overuse these informal terms. Heavy reliance on colloquial language may give others the impression that a communicator has limited language skills or education.

Slang Slang is a second type of informal language. It can be described as temporary language because it typically is used for only a brief period of time by a limited group of people.

Slang can be compared to a fad in clothing. Both stem from popular culture, and neither tends to last for very long. A slang term used in a movie or popular song may become popular for two or three years but eventually fades away as enthusiasm for that movie or song declines. Slang often results from a need to make language more fun or interesting or to find new ways to express ideas and feelings. It often is associated with young people who invent new language terms to communicate within their own groups.

Limitations of Slang Slang presents some definite limitations to communication. While it often is used to help define who belongs to the "in" crowd, it also excludes outsiders from understanding or participating in conversations. Also, like certain items of fad clothing, it can be unbecoming when used by people who obviously do not belong to the intended user group. For example, an adult speaker who tries to use teen slang in a speech to a

high school audience may appear to be insincere or out of touch. His or her use of slang may unintentionally have the opposite effect of what was desired.

A third limitation of slang is its temporary nature. What is "cool" one year may be "bad" the next, "hot" six months later, and "phat" before the end of the school term. So, by the time you work a slang term into your everyday speech, it may no longer be popular. Allowing a slang term to linger too long in your vocabulary can result in tired, lackluster language. Terms such as "Awesome!" "No way!" and "Chill out!" have become overused and boring over the years. So, remember, choosing to use slang can make you appear out of date and out of touch very quickly.

Using Slang Even though slang can be fun to use at times, it should be used sparingly. As informal language, it often does not measure up to the standards of appropriate communication. As a general rule, try to limit that use of slang to communication with

Discovering the Power of Oral Language **121**

TECHNOLOGY *Activity*

Language Choices Context is a major factor in determining the level of language chosen by the sender. For one week, keep a log of the language levels you observe and look for patterns in how technical, formal, or colloquial the messages are. Do you observe a difference between local and national newscasters? Between e-mail messages from friends and form letters or business correspondence your family may receive through the mail? Between communication among friends in a sitcom and how information is presented in a documentary? Between disc jockeys on a top-forty radio station and an easy-listening station? Are the language choices made in each context appropriate? Why or why not?

TECHNOLOGY *Activity*

Language Choices Have students form groups to compare their language notes. Ask if they can make any generalizations from their research. *(Possible generalizations: Larger audiences require more formal language, as in national versus local news. Informal language requires less concentration on the part of the listener, as in sitcom versus documentary. Solicitations for money by mail are often written using informal, friendly language.)* Discuss the relationship between context and language choice. **L2**

Slang
Point out that slang is generally short lived. Ask students to recall slang that they had used in the past but would no longer use today. Make a list of outdated slang expressions on the board. Ask students what they would think of someone who routinely used these words today. Lead them to consider the purpose and limitations of slang. **L1**

> **DID YOU KNOW?**
>
> The word *slang* stems from the Scandinavian *slengjeord*, meaning "an insulting word." Its root is the Icelandic *slyngva*, meaning "to sling." The sense is that slang words are thrown, often insultingly, at the listener.

MULTIPLE LEARNING STYLES

Linguistic Students may be surprised to learn that slang is even a subject of scholarly research. Point out that there are dictionaries of slang and colloquial expressions that make for fascinating browsing.

Activity Play a game of Call My Bluff using slang. Ask students to compile from library or Internet sources a list of ten slang words or expressions that are no longer current. In class, have students working in groups compare their lists, choosing two or three terms that they feel are particularly interesting or unusual. Direct the groups to write one of their selected terms on the chalkboard and have each member offer a possible definition, only one of which is the correct one. Have the class vote on the definition that seems most plausible.

Ungrammatical Language

Students may argue that everyone uses ungrammatical speech. Lead students to understand that the habit of speaking ungrammatically can have consequences that affect one's career and reputation. Students should know that practicing grammatical speech at all times is a wise precaution for occasions when it is important to make a good impression. **L1**

The Five Functions of Oral Language

Have students read the five bulleted items in the box on page 122. Ask students to think back over their day for examples of speech functions they have encountered. Make a list on the chalkboard of situations that the students feel correspond with each function. **L2**

friends in informal situations. Over time, relying too heavily on slang can have a crippling effect on your ability to express yourself effectively. It can begin to creep into other areas of your speech where it is inappropriate. Slang always should be avoided in business-related situations and usually is unacceptable for discussions and public presentations.

Ungrammatical Language

Ungrammatical language is language that does not use expected standards of grammar or mechanics. Ungrammatical phrases such as "I seen" or "they was" can detract from a communicator's credibility. It is important to try to eliminate this type of language from your speech because it can detract from your message and tarnish your credibility as a speaker.

Choosing Your Speaking Style

In Section 1, your vocabulary choices were compared to the choices you make about what to wear in different situations. Earlier in this section, slang was compared to fad clothing. However, the comparison doesn't end there.

Just as you may be known for wearing a particular style of clothing, you probably are known for your style of speech. While both of these reveal information about you to others, your language probably tells more about you than your clothes.

The level of usage that you choose for most situations helps define your overall image as a communicator. If you follow the rules of usage for standard language in most situations, use formal and technical language when appropriate, limit your use of informal language to casual settings, and eliminate ungrammatical language from your speech, you will build an image as a competent communicator.

FUNCTIONS OF ORAL LANGUAGE

Once a communicator has mastered the components of language, refined the characteristics of his or her speech, and determined appropriate levels of usage for different contexts, the power language process is almost complete. The remaining step is to understand the true functions of language that are shown in **Figure 4–3** and use them to their fullest extent.

Expressing and Responding to Feelings

An important aspect of gaining power through language is the ability to put your feelings into words. Equally important is your ability to respond to others' feelings.

Expressing Feelings Sometimes, perhaps due to cultural upbringing or lack of confidence, individuals have trouble expressing their feelings to others. As a result, they may go to great lengths to avoid letting others know how they feel. Learning to state and label feelings in a rational way, however, can be very empowering.

For example, knowing how to calmly and effectively express your feelings can help change a frustrating situation. Instead of simply enduring the situation until you are completely fed up, you might say, "I was

■ **Figure 4–3 The Five Functions of Oral Language**

- Expressing and responding to feelings
- Informing
- Controlling or persuading
- Participating in social rituals
- Creating and imagining

REAL-WORLD CONNECTION

Ungrammatical Language Lead students to understand also that it is crucial to be able to recognize ungrammatical language so that it can be avoided when necessary.

Activity Have students make a note of ungrammatical oral language that they have identified over the course of a day. Suggest that they find examples from at least three sources, such as television, radio, family, friends, song lyrics, and overheard conversation. Ask students working in groups to give three examples of ungrammatical speech, each representing a different problem. Make a list on the chalkboard, noting the context in which the remark was made. Discuss the impact of ungrammatical language.

The child in the center is clearly experiencing frustration. An important part of oral language is finding an effective way of expressing one's feelings. How can you deal with a frustrating situation effectively?

and provide answers that are clear and effective. The key to providing information to others is using clear language that is appropriate for the speaker, listener, occasion, and task. Instructions, reports, and other types of spoken information are most effective when they are tailored to the specific context. Clarity also is the key to seeking information from others. The ability to phrase questions so that they focus directly on the information needed is a mark of a skilled communicator.

frustrated by his lack of cooperation," or "I was angry about the interruption." No one can fault you for calmly and honestly stating your feelings. Rather, your words may open the door to discussion and prevent irrational outbursts of emotion.

Responding to Feelings A certain amount of power also lies in listening and responding appropriately to the feelings of others. For example, if you have learned to say, "I'm sorry you were disappointed" rather than "You shouldn't be disappointed," you are more likely to gain people's trust and respect. Both statements express concern over someone's disappointment, but each sends a different message about your attitude toward both the person and the situation.

Giving and Seeking Information

In professional and social contexts, a major function of language is giving and seeking information. Students and teachers, supervisors and employees, group leaders and group members all need to be able to ask questions

Controlling and Persuading

A great deal of personal power lies in your ability to influence others. Whether you are serving customers, talking your boss into giving you a raise, or convincing a friend to see a particular movie, you are attempting to persuade or influence others. Much of your effectiveness in making suggestions or requests depends on the language you use. Also, giving commands or making demands of others requires special skills. It takes competent communication skills and knowledge to get others to achieve the results you want while still preserving the relationship. This balancing act requires not only clarity, directness, and self-confidence but also courtesy, tact, and integrity. As you continue to work though this text, you will have an opportunity to practice some of these skills.

Participating in Social Rituals

Believe it or not, much of your personal power lies in the way you interact in everyday social rituals. A social ritual is a communication situation that is frequently repeated in

Discovering the Power of Oral Language **123**

Expressing Feelings
Remind students that for some people, expressing feelings is as natural as breathing; for others, it is extremely difficult. Point out that many cultures have very strong traditions regarding the expression of emotion. Invite English language learners to share how their cultures deal with the issue of feelings. **L1** **ELL**

Giving Information
When giving information, students should realize that what is "clear language" for one listener may be obscure or inappropriate for another. Have them practice by considering how they would give information in the following situations: Someone who has never used the Internet wants instructions; someone wants to know what he or she should eat for a balanced diet; a visitor wants to know what the most interesting sights in the area are. Ask students to imagine that they must provide this information to two people: a middle-aged professional and a six-year-old child. Invite volunteers to model how they would tailor their information for these listeners. Discuss their performances with the class. **L3**

■ **Visual Instruction**
Answer State and label your feelings in a rational way.

MULTIPLE LEARNING STYLES

Interpersonal Students should realize that stating their needs clearly and directly is only part of personal speech. Understanding the feelings and thoughts of the person they are addressing and adjusting their language appropriately is just as important.

Activity Brainstorm with the class for a list of challenging situations in which you might be in a position to influence or persuade your listener. (Remind students that home, school, work, and recreation provide innumerable moments when the power of language can be used to one's advantage.) Have students practice role playing these situations with partners or in groups. Invite volunteers to perform their skits. Discuss with the class which performances they found most convincing. Encourage them to analyze the elements that make speech persuasive.

Social Rituals
Have students describe typical social rituals in which they engage on a daily basis. Ask them to imagine what would happen if they failed to participate in these interactions. How would their behavior affect the attitudes of others toward them or their own feelings toward peers and coworkers? Have students who work at after-school jobs describe social rituals that their employers insist they follow. Do they feel that automatic interactions such as "Have a nice day" serve a purpose? **L1**

Sharing Creative Ideas
Remind students that imaginative, creative language can sometimes sell ideas that are unnecessary or even harmful. They would be interested to hear that P. T. Barnum, one of America's great entrepreneurs, once got people to pay good money to view the "invisible fish"—in reality an empty aquarium. Legends abound of hawkers who sold *aqua pura* (pure water) and other useless "medicines" to a gullible public. Ask students if they can think of occasions when they have been swayed by the creative power of words. **L1**

Visual Instruction
Answer Social rituals provide a basis for interpersonal relationships and are characterized by courtesy, good manners, and civility.

The two individuals are practicing the social ritual of shaking hands. **Explain how social rituals help one to become a competent communicator.**

daily social interaction. For example, if you exchange a friendly "good morning" with the same people as you arrive at school or work every day, you are taking part in a social ritual. Making and acknowledging introductions, giving and accepting compliments, engaging in short personal conversations with coworkers, and giving and responding to praise and suggestions all are forms of social rituals.

Social rituals usually follow a pattern and sometimes call for using social etiquette. They provide the basis for interpersonal communication in the workplace and group situations. They also are the first stepping stone to developing relationships with others. Social rituals usually are characterized by courtesy, tact, good manners, and civility—all of which are keys to success as a competent communicator.

Creating and Imagining

The ability to imagine and create is vital to success in almost any area of life. Creativity gives you the ability to find new solutions, generate new ideas, and envision new alternatives—some of the most valuable skills in professional and social contexts. However, all the imagination and creativity in the world is fairly useless if you cannot adequately express your ideas.

So, how do you describe an idea that is new and different? How do you persuade others to share your vision? Expressing ideas or describing products that have not yet taken form requires an imaginative and creative use of language. You may find yourself searching for new descriptive terms, learning to ask thought-provoking questions, or using language that reflects imagery, energy, and conviction.

LANGUAGE TO AVOID

As a skilled communicator, you not only need to know what language is appropriate for a specific context but also what language to avoid. Language plays an important role in establishing the climate for communication, determining the impact of communication, and defining the quality of relationships. Therefore, as shown in the chart on the next page, it is important to avoid words and strategies that can result in negative or defensive responses from listeners.

MEETING INDIVIDUAL NEEDS — MULTIPLE LEARNING STYLES

Linguistic How many imaginative ideas have failed to materialize because their creators were poor at expressing themselves? It is likely that the world would be a different place if all of its thinkers and inventors had been powerful communicators.

Activity Have students prepare a powerful, persuasive speech of no more than three minutes in length, selling an idea that we now take for granted—the car, the wheel, the fast food restaurant, the solar system—to a skeptical audience. Encourage them to research their subject in order to re-create the historical context in which their idea first came to light. When students have delivered their pitches, have the class vote on the ideas that they would "buy." What made some speeches more persuasive than others? Discuss with students the art of sharing creative ideas.

Understanding Denotations and Connotations

One thing to remember as you begin to fine-tune your language skills are that words have denotations and connotations. A denotation is a word's objective description or meaning. A word's connotation, on the other hand, is the emotions or feelings with which it is associated. A word's denotation is found in the dictionary, its connotation is not. If, for example, you are talking about a particular dwelling, you might

STRATEGIES FOR AVOIDING TROUBLESOME LANGUAGE

Language	Description	Alternative Language Strategy
Sexist	Sexist language implies that something is more suited to a specific gender. It groups men or women into a category and perpetuates gender-based stereotypes.	Use descriptive language that replaces gender related terms with general terms. Examples of sexist/nonsexist language include: mankind/humankind, chairman/chair, fireman/firefighter, housewife/homemaker, congressman/representative
Racist	Racist language applies labels or behavioral characteristics to an entire race of individuals. It is the language of prejudice and stereotypes and is extremely offensive.	Racist language is never appropriate. Use personal names and descriptions that do not refer to ethnic identity.
Profane or Obscene	Profane language is vulgar, irreverent, or abusive language that can be considered defensive in social and professional contexts. Dependence on profanity or obscenity can damage a speaker's credibility.	This type of language is never appropriate. Learn to express and assume ownership for feelings. Say, "I am angry" or "I am frustrated" when these feelings arise.
Judgmental	Judgmental language implies an inappropriate evaluation or critique of someone or something. Qualitative words such as *good*, *bad*, *worthwhile*, or *worthless* may imply that you are sitting in judgment of someone or their behavior. *Why* questions are sometimes seen as defensive and can convey judgment on the speaker's part.	Try to assume ownership of your remarks and use descriptive, supportive words that give information in an objective way. For example, instead of saying, "That was a good introduction," the critic would say, "Your introduction really caught my attention" (giving information focused on a specific criterion for an effective introduction). Also, ask information seeking questions that begin with *how*, *what*, *when*, *where*, and *who* whenever possible.
Accusatory	Using "you" messages improperly can make a speaker sound bossy or judgmental. The listener may feel as if he or she is being accused or attacked.	Instead of saying sentences like "You need to clean this up," try saying, "I'm uncomfortable with the way this place looks."
Assumptive	Assumptive language implies that everyone shares your views, opinions, or concerns. Overusing words such as *we*, *everyone*, *everybody* and forms of the verb *to be* can trigger the response "No, I don't," and quickly put listeners on the defensive.	Try using qualifiers such as *may be*, *can be*, or *appears to be*.
Absolute	Absolutes assume that there are no exceptions. Absolute language is risky for two reasons: few things stay the same forever, and there are exceptions to every rule.	Avoid words such as *every*, *always*, *never*, or *will*. Instead, use less-rigid terms such as *most*, *usually*, *seldom*, or *may*.

Strategies for Avoiding Troublesome Language

Direct students to read the seven descriptions of language to avoid. Ask if they think all of the categories represent language that is equally inappropriate. Have them rank the headings in the order of seriousness, explaining their choices in a sentence or two. Take a class-wide poll of how students ranked the types of language. Discuss the problems involved with troublesome language and the difficulties of finding a means of speech that is acceptable to all. **L2**

Communication Tip

Offensive language, like all speech, is partly defined by context. Words that are spoken with no ill intent may seem racist or sexist in certain situations. What is important is that the speaker keeps the listener in mind at all times. A speaker's sensitivity to the context of his or her speech is the best safeguard against causing offense.

CRITICAL THINKING ACTIVITY

Was Shakespeare anti-Semitic? Was Mark Twain racist? Are the Harry Potter books profane? When does language become so troublesome that literature or speech featuring it must be banned from school systems? Students should be aware that the line distinguishing acceptable from unacceptable language is very vague.

Give students the following questions: Should books be banned from high school reading lists because of language or content? If so, who should make the choices? If not, what should be done about those who are offended by the content? Ask students to address these questions, not in a formal essay, but in a thoughtful reflection of 200 to 500 words. Have them form groups of four or five and read their reflections to one another. As a class, discuss their observations.

Connotation

Point out that there are few exact synonyms in the English language. Almost every word has a shade of meaning that suits it for a particular purpose. Students who use a dictionary or thesaurus to strengthen their vocabularies may not be familiar with the connotation of the new words they select. This can lead to unintentional problems in communication. As a class exercise, write on the board the following groups of words: *pause, intermission, recess; high, towering, lofty; love, fondness, infatuation; fault, weakness, vice; dismiss, fire, drop.*

Point out that the three words in each group are given in the dictionary as synonyms. Ask students if they would use them in exactly the same manner. Invite volunteers to choose two words from each group and to compose sentences using them. How would they describe the different connotations of these words? **L3**

Fillers and Tags

Point out that the beginnings and ends of our spoken messages are places one typically finds unnecessary words and sounds. Some people habitually start a sentence with "Well, um" or "I mean, like." Others end their phrases with a grunt or an irrelevant giggle. These mannerisms are seldom noticed by the speaker, although they can become irritating to the listener, especially on occasions requiring powerful, precise speech. Suggest to students that they are doing their friends a favor by politely drawing their attention to mannerisms that detract from effective communication. **L1**

refer to it as either a "house" or a "home." The word *house* denotes a particular kind of structure but does not imply any particular feeling about that structure. On the other hand, the connotations of the word *home* tap into images and feelings that may have little to do with the structure itself.

Using words that have strong emotional associations often requires careful analysis of the listener and the occasion. For instance, if you are describing a dog to a veterinarian, he or she probably will understand that your use of the word *mutt* simply denotes a mixed-breed dog. However, if you are speaking to the dog's owner, calling the dog a "mutt" may result in hurt feelings. The owner may focus on the negative connotations of *mutt* as a lowly or worthless animal and may become defensive. Developing your vocabulary so that you better understand the connotations of various words will help you communicate your intentions more clearly to others and avoid unintentionally offending them.

Avoiding Troublesome Language

Understanding possible negative connotations in your speech is a good way to start avoiding troublesome language. There are other steps you can take as well. As you found out from the chart on page 125, problematic language can negatively affect communication. Some of the most troublesome words are short, simple ones that we use frequently without giving thought to the effect these terms have on our listeners.

A connotation of the word home could bring to mind a scene like the one shown. Why is it important to understand connotations?

Avoiding Powerless Language

You've gained knowledge about how to speak and use language appropriately for each situation, apply the functions of language to your advantage, and avoid offending your listeners. You're well on your way to mastering power language. However, there is still one important adjustment to make. Now it is time to eliminate powerless language from your speech patterns.

Powerless language tends to be vague and accomplishes very little. It does nothing to enhance others' perceptions of a speaker, and therefore does not contribute to powerful speech. In fact, it actually can erode a speaker's power by making him or her seem indecisive or lacking in confidence.

Fillers You probably already are familiar with the form of powerless language known as fillers. A filler is a word or phrase

COOPERATIVE LEARNING ACTIVITY

Encourage students to appreciate the importance of connotation in language. Point out that words with exactly the same denotation can often have a positive, negative, or neutral connotation, which determines how we use them.

Write the following pairs of words on the chalkboard: *clean/cleanse, nerd/intellectual, jock/athlete, slender/skinny, bright/radiant, melody/tune, sad/melancholy, bad/diabolical, learning impaired/stupid, scent/odor.* Have students form groups and ask them to identify the connotation of the words within each pair as neutral, positive, or negative. Give each group paired words to use in sample sentences. Have them share their sentences with the class and discuss the importance of understanding connotation.

used to cover up hesitancy in speech. Some common fillers are "uh," "um," "like," "so," "you know," and "totally." When these words are used to fill gaps in speech, they not only add no value to the message, but they also detract from the speaker's image as a competent communicator.

POWERLESS LANGUAGE FILLERS

Message With Fillers	Message Without Fillers
"Well, I, uh, want to, you know, graduate with, uh, honors, you know, because I, like, want to, uh, get a good job or, uh, maybe even, like, go to, uh, college."	"I really want to graduate with honors because I want to get a good job or perhaps even go to college."

Tags A *tag* is a statement or question added to the end of a statement to invite approval or cooperation from others. Like fillers, tags can make speakers appear as if they lack confidence or knowledge. When concluding a presentation, you probably would not want to say, "It's time to go, don't you think?" This might make you sound as if you lack self-assurance or as if you are uninformed about when to end. Saying "It's time to go," or "I think it's time to go," or even asking "Don't you think it is time to go?" projects a much more powerful image than does a statement with a tag.

Vague Wording Vague, unproductive sentences often rely heavily on words such as *it*, *they*, or *but*. These sentences tend to be "throw-aways," providing little information and detracting from your power as a communicator.

For example, overusing the words *it* and *they* tends to make communication impersonal, abstract, and without detail. The result is that communicators may lose interest. For instance, consider which sentence might mean more to you on the job: "They need you to sign it," or "Our office manager and the people in accounting need you to sign this purchase order." By including relevant details, you can make your speech more valuable to listeners.

COMMUNICATION PRACTICE LAB

Avoiding Fillers

To practice ridding your speech of meaningless fillers, follow these steps:

Step 1 Form a group with two or three other students and brainstorm several questions on a topic with which you are all familiar.

Step 2 Have one group member ask another a question from your list.

Step 3 The second person must give a thirty-second response that does not contain the words "uh," "like," or "you know." Pauses can be no longer than one second.

Step 4 Have the third group member time the response, stopping immediately if a filler or long pause is used.

Step 5 Take turns timing and trying to respond without using fillers. Who had the best time in your group? In the class?

Discovering the Power of Oral Language **127**

GLENCOE
Online

For an additional Practice Lab for this section, have students visit the *Glencoe Communication Applications* Web site at communicationapplications.glencoe.com. Click on Communication Practice Lab 4–2. **L1**

COMMUNICATION PRACTICE LAB

Avoiding Fillers

Extend this exercise by inviting volunteers to represent their groups in front of the class. Each performer should be given a choice of questions generated by another group. Time and assess the performances, as directed in Step 3. At the end of the activity, point out that if one must stop to think while speaking, a pause is always more effective than a meaningless filler word or sound. **L2**

3 ASSESS

Assign Section 2 Assessment as a homework or in-class activity.

Use *Interactive Tutor Self-Assessment Software* to review Section 2.

Section 4–2 Quiz

SECTION QUIZ 4–2

DISCOVERING THE POWER OF ORAL LANGUAGE
Developing Skills for Power Language

Matching Match each item in the left column with the best selection from the right column. Write the letter of the item on the line provided. *(10 points each)*

_____ 1. formal language
_____ 2. technical language
_____ 3. informal language
_____ 4. standard language
_____ 5. ungrammatical language

a. language associated with a particular profession or field
b. language used by the majority of skilled communicators within a specific language
c. language that does not use expected standards of grammar or mechanics
d. language most often used in casual situations
e. language that conforms to a highly structured set of rules

Multiple Choice In the blank provided, write the letter of the item that best answers each question. *(10 points each)*

_____ 6. Which of the following is *not* a characteristic of power language?
a. Speech is precise, logically organized, and grammatically correct.
b. Speech is personalized and includes others.
c. Speaker avoids "I" messages.
d. Speaker expresses ordinary ideas in new and imaginative ways.

_____ 7. What is a word's *objective* description or meaning called?
a. its colloquialism
b. its slang
c. its connotation
d. its denotation

_____ 8. In what type of communication situation are you participating when you say "good morning" to someone every day?
a. social ritual
b. filler
c. tag
d. colloquialism

_____ 9. How is profanity an example of troublesome language?
a. It unfairly groups people based on gender.
b. It may make the listener feel like he or she is being attacked.
c. It implies that the speaker is judging others.
d. It shows a lack of imagination in a speaker's credibility.

_____ 10. What is the type of powerless language in which "uh" is inserted in speech?
a. filler
b. tag
c. vague wording
d. troublesome

REAL-WORLD CONNECTION

How We Really Speak Point out that casual conversations are full of the sort of problems that impede powerful speech.

Activity Have students record a conversation with friends or family. A car ride, family dinner, or coffee break at work might make suitable occasions. (Make sure that students ask permission to use a recording device before starting the project.) Have them listen to the tape carefully and transcribe a page of speech that includes problems such as fillers, fragments, and ungrammatical constructions. In class, have students form groups and ask them to share their excerpts. In a general discussion, ask students to analyze the speech problems they typically found and to identify those that were most harmful to effective communication.

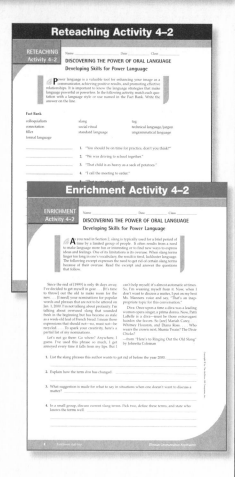

Reteaching Activity 4–2

RETEACHING
Activity 4-2   DISCOVERING THE POWER OF ORAL LANGUAGE
Developing Skills for Power Language

Enrichment Activity 4–2

ENRICHMENT
Activity 4-2   DISCOVERING THE POWER OF ORAL LANGUAGE
Developing Skills for Power Language

4 CLOSE

Have students review their responses to the Bellringer on page 116. Then, ask them what they have learned about human communication skills and needs that set people apart from animals.

Extra-Credit Project

Have students talk with a person whom they consider to be a powerful and effective speaker. Suggest that they discuss topics such as vocabulary, diction, levels and functions of language, and language to avoid. Ask students to give assessments of what makes a powerful speaker.

Another hallmark of vague language is the repeated use of the word *but*. Frequently placing the word *but* between statements results in a message "wipeout" that can be time-consuming and frustrating to listeners. For example, if you say "I'll try to be there, but don't wait for me," or "She's a hard worker, but she doesn't get along with her coworkers," the second statement confuses or contradicts the meaning of the first. Consequently, this type of language can make you seem like an indecisive or confused speaker.

The words and expressions you use can be your best ally or your worst enemy. Choosing and using power language is a real asset to everyday communication. It not only can help you get the results you want from your interactions with others, but it also can help you achieve the goal of becoming a competent communicator.

Section 2 Assessment

Visit the *Glencoe Communication Applications* Web site at **communicationapplications. glencoe.com** and click on **Self-Check and Study Guide 4.2** to review your understanding of using power language.

Review Key Terms

1. Define each term and write it in a sentence: formal language, technical language, jargon, standard language, informal language, colloquialism, slang, ungrammatical language, social ritual, denotation, connotation, filler, tag.

Check Understanding

2. Writing one sentence for each characteristic, describe how you might use each characteristic of power language in your daily communication at school.

3. Which type or types of language might be most appropriate to use in a job interview? Which might be least appropriate? Why?

4. Which function of oral language serves mainly the interests of the speaker rather than the listener? Explain your answer.

5. **Evaluating** Which types of troublesome language do you consider the worst? Why?

APPLICATION *Activity*

Becoming a Powerful Speaker On a sheet of paper, write the one characteristic of power language that most needs improvement in your current speaking style and why. Then, write a three-step plan detailing how you might improve this speaking skill over the next week. Share your plans as a class and discuss real-world opportunities for testing your skills.

Section 2 Assessment Answers

1. Accept all reasonable sentences.
2. Ask questions with clarity. Show courtesy to other students. Take ownership of feelings about school. Include personalization when talking to classmates. Answer questions with vivid language. Use appropriate language in class.
3. Standard and, possibly, technical language would demonstrate a mastery of language and a knowledge of the industry. Formal language might make conversation difficult, informal language might show disrespect, and illiterate language might make one seem unqualified.
4. Controlling and persuading allows the speaker to have a certain amount of power over the listener.
5. Answers may focus on sexism, racism, and absolutes. They can result in misleading or harmful messages.

Application Activity Students' plans should indicate reasonable and effective steps towards improvement.

Communication Self-Assessment

Analyzing Your Oral Communication Skills

How Do You Rate?

On a separate sheet of paper, use the key to respond to the following statements and assess your communication style. Put a check mark beside each skill you would like to improve.

Key: **A** Always **R** Rarely
U Usually **N** Never
S Sometimes

1. I choose my words carefully when I communicate with others.

2. When I don't know how to pronounce a word, I ask someone to pronounce it for me or I look it up in the dictionary.

3. I clearly articulate my consonants.

4. I seldom slur my words.

5. I regularly try to add new words to my vocabulary.

6. When I disagree with someone, I carefully select my words when I respond.

7. I use the word "I" to express my opinions, ideas, and feelings.

8. I try to be imaginative when I explain something.

9. I avoid sexist, racist, and profane language.

10. I try not to speak in absolutes.

How Do You Score?

Review your responses. Give yourself 5 points for every A, 4 for every U, 3 for every S, 2 for every R, and 1 for every N. Total your points and evaluate your score.

41–50 Excellent You may be surprised to find out how much you can improve your skills.

31–40 Good In this course, you can learn ways to make your skills better.

21–30 Fair Practice applying the skills taught in this course.

1–20 Needs Improvement Carefully monitor your improvement as you work through this course.

Setting Communication Goals

If you scored Excellent or Good, complete Part A. If your score was Fair or Needs Improvement, complete Part B.

Part A 1. I plan to put the following ideas into practice:

2. I plan to share the following information about communication with the following people:

Part B 1. The behaviors I need to change most are:

2. To bring about these changes, I will take these steps:

Have students respond to the ten statements using the key on this page, then evaluate their listening strengths. Based on their scores, assign either Part A or Part B of the goal-setting activity. Discuss with the class ways students might go about strengthening individual areas in their oral language skills.

Communication Journal Activity

Have students choose one of the skills they checked for needing improvement in the self-assessment quiz. Ask them to make a daily entry in their Communication Journals, describing their difficulties or progress in this area. At the end of the week, encourage students to share their journals with a partner and discuss ways they can continue to improve their communication skills.

Communication Tip

Some students may believe that effective speaking is a gift rather than a skill that can be developed. Lead them to understand that practice in speaking, just as in any other physical or mental discipline, is essential to powerful communication and can lead to significant improvement.

MEETING INDIVIDUAL NEEDS

GIFTED AND TALENTED

Oral Language Skills Suggest to students that among the people most reliant on the oral language skills are politicians. Some, such as the President of the United States, are rarely out of the public eye; others are particularly conspicuous during the campaign period.

Activity Have students "adopt" a politician for a set period of time (a week or a month, perhaps). Ask them to follow their subject's progress on television or in the newspaper, taking special note of the oral language skills discussed in this chapter. Have students keep a record of their subject's strengths and weaknesses, including representative examples of his or her skills. Students should prepare a presentation, including audiovisual aids, highlighting their findings and evaluating their politician's command of oral language.

Communication Through Writing

Formatting Business Messages

Objectives: To learn how to correctly format business communications, including e-mails, letters, and faxes

Teaching Suggestions and Strategies

Connection to the Workplace

Students should be aware that how a person communicates in business, as in all other forms of communication, depends partly upon the context of the message. Generally speaking, a letter or e-mail addressed to people with whom you are not very familiar should be formally formatted. Explain to students that this is a courtesy to the readers. Since you do not know them well, you do not wish to offend them with a familiarity that might be misinterpreted. Just as you would avoid dressing casually or speaking colloquially at a formal interview, so you should use a standard format for comparable business communications.

Point out that there are times, however, when a more casual approach to formatting is appropriate. If your relationship with a coworker is such that you can send an e-mail or memo saying simply, "How about talking over the design at lunch tomorrow?" you probably won't need to do much more than sign your name. Even in this case, however, students should realize that a date must be somewhere on the communication.

Formatting Business Messages

Every day, millions of business messages are written throughout the world. These include letters, e-mail messages, faxes, brief notes, and memorandums, or memos. The format of these messages can vary from handwritten notes to memos to published reports and legal correspondence. Although the ways in which these messages are relayed can vary, all identify the date, sender, and recipient and provide some sort of address along with the content of the message.

Format of a Letter One effective format for a business letter is shown here.

Format of an E-Mail Message An e-mail message is sent from one computer to another through an internal network or through an e-mail provider. Usually, the date and the sender's e-mail address are automatically shown at the top of each message. Also, a greeting is optional if the recipient is clearly identified in the "To" field. One effective format for an e-mail message is shown here.

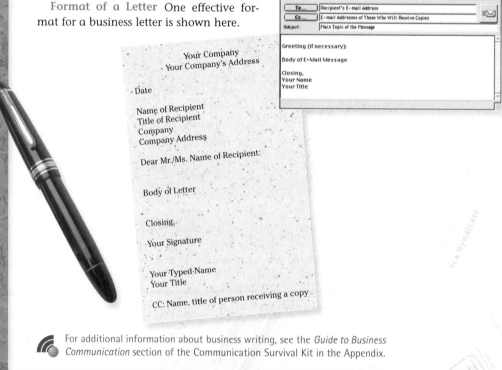

For additional information about business writing, see the *Guide to Business Communication* section of the Communication Survival Kit in the Appendix.

REAL-WORLD CONNECTION

Formatting in the Business World Students will have learned that every business has its own culture. Lead them to understand that this extends to how a company formats its letters, memos, and e-mails.

Activity Have students bring to school at least two samples of communications used by a local business or institution. Accept e-mails, business letters, memos, or fax cover sheets. Divide the samples into categories and assign groups of students to compare the formats. Have volunteers from each group present their findings to the class, comparing and contrasting models of formatting.

Format of a Fax Cover Sheet Each facsimile, or fax, you send should have a cover sheet that provides important information about the attachment, sender, and recipient. One effective format for a fax cover sheet is shown here.

FACSIMILE TRANSMITTAL SHEET

To:	From:
Company:	Date:
Fax #:	Fax #:
Phone #:	Phone #:
Re: Main Topic of Fax	Pages:
CC: (Names of those who will receive copies)	

Body of Fax Cover Sheet

Below is an example of an effectively formatted memorandum.

MEMORANDUM

Subject: New Order Forms
Date: Mon, Mar 12, 2004
From: M_Mitchard_J&HDallas@network.com
To: L_Nguyen_J&HChicago@network.com
CC: J_Riley_J&HNewYork@network.com

All staff:

From now on we will be using new forms to order office supplies. Our office managers are in the process of distributing these forms now. Look for one in your inbox very soon. Please be sure to carefully follow all directions on the form. These new order forms will help our data entry team use our new computerized ordering system more efficiently. Thanks for your help!

Sincerely,
Melody Mitchard
Office Mgr., J&H Headquarters

WRITING Activity

Take the following ideas into consideration as you unscramble the e-mail message below. Write the message in the correct format on a separate sheet of paper.

- You are in charge of filling orders for a company that sells outboard motors over the Internet.

- Customers typically order products through an e-mail link on your Web site.

- Payment must be received in full before items will be shipped.

- Due to a computer malfunction, you receive the following scrambled e-mail order.

CC: W_Brown@LakeGenevaResort.com

Thank you,
Lisa Brooke
Purchasing Dir.

To: J_Garland@BoatWorks.com
Subject: Merchandise order

I am interested in buying a 10-horsepower outboard motor from your company. I have chosen motor #5512 from p. 34 of your Fall 2004 catalog. I have sent $1,732.84 by wire transfer to cover the cost of the motor plus sales tax and shipping and handling.

Please ship the motor to the following address:
　　　ATTN: Lisa Brooke
　　　Lake Geneva Resort
　　　1529 Hobart Lane
　　　Geneva, New York 12345

Date: Thurs, Sep 04, 2004
From: L_Brooke@LakeGenevaResort.com

Teaching Activity

Students may believe that the letter is becoming extinct in the age of e-communication. Point out that although business letters may occupy a less central position in the commercial world than in the past, they still must know how to construct a business letter. Ask pairs of students to write a business letter to you, including your correct title and "business" address. The letter must follow the format outlined on page 130.

WRITING Activity

If students have difficulty completing the work by themselves, have them work with a partner to write the e-mail in the correct order.

Grammar Tip

In most sentences, the subject comes before the predicate. In the case of the command or request, however, the predicate constitutes the entire sentence, with the pronoun *you* understood to be the subject.

Additional Resources

Appendix, "Guide to Business Communication"

Glencoe Writer's Assistant CD-ROM

Glencoe Interactive Grammar Software

Grade 9 Writer's Choice, Lesson 21.4

GRAMMAR PRACTICE

Identifying Commands or Requests

Have students identify the four in-text commands or requests on pages 130 and 131 in which the pronoun *you* is understood to be the subject.

The footnote on page 130 beginning, "For additional information, see . . ."

The first sentence under Writing Activity on page 131: "Take the following ideas . . ."

The second sentence under Writing Activity on page 131: "Write the message . . ."

The sentence in the scrambled e-mail beginning "Please ship the motor. . . ."

CHAPTER 4 Assessment and Activities

GLENCOE TECHNOLOGY

MindJogger Videoquiz

Use *MindJogger* to review the Chapter 4 content.

GLENCOE *Online*

Visit the *Glencoe Communication Applications* Web site at **communicationapplications. glencoe.com** and click on **Chapter 4 Activity** for additional practice in developing powerful oral language.

Reviewing Key Terms

1. Connotation is the degree of clarity and distinctness in a person's speech. False, Diction

2. All the sounds in a language make up its vocabulary. False, words

3. True

4. Pronunciation is the general understandings and rules that regulate the use of a language. False, Grammar

5. Medicine, law, finance, technology, and sports are just a few fields that depend heavily on specialized language or slang. False, jargon

6. Grammar is a system of symbols, rules, and sounds used for human communication. False, Oral language

7. Articulation is the act of leaving out certain consonant sounds within a word. False, Omission

8. Pronunciation is the act of clearly and distinctly uttering the vowel sounds of a word. False, Enunciation

9. The "southern drawl" is an example of a regional diction. False, dialect

10. Enunciation is the way a specific word sounds. False, Pronunciation

Reviewing Key Concepts

1. They all communicate meaning and are all made up of symbols, rules, and sound.

Reviewing Key Terms

On paper, write whether each statement is true or false. If the statement is false, copy the statement, underline the word that makes it false, and write a substitute that makes it true.

1. Connotation is the degree of clarity and distinctness in a person's speech.

2. All the sounds in a language make up its vocabulary.

3. The most basic rules of a language relate to the structure of words and sentences.

4. Pronunciation is the general understandings and rules that regulate the use of a language.

5. Medicine, law, finance, technology, and sports are just a few fields that depend heavily on specialized language or slang.

6. Grammar is a system of symbols, rules, and sounds used for human communication.

7. Articulation is the act of leaving out certain consonant sounds within a word.

8. Pronunciation is the act of clearly and distinctly uttering the vowel sounds of a word.

9. The "southern drawl" is an example of a regional diction.

10. Enunciation is the way that a specific word sounds.

Reviewing Key Concepts

1. How are all oral languages similar?

2. What is a major difference between oral language and written language?

3. Give examples of two situations for which you would use different kinds of language.

4. Why is it important to build strong vocabulary?

5. What allows you to add interest and personality to your messages?

6. List the three functions of grammar.

7. What are two drawbacks of mispronouncing words?

8. What is the level of language usage recommended for most professional and social contexts?

9. What are the five functions of oral language?

10. How do denotations and connotations differ?

2. Writing is the visible representation of oral language.

3. Answers may include casual speech for speaking with friends on a sports team and formal speech for participating in a school debate contest.

4. To be able to communicate more effectively with a greater number of people is one reason for building one's vocabulary.

5. A broad vocabulary

6. Grammar identifies all the different components of a language, explains their function, and dictates the way the components are used in communication.

7. A mispronounced word can confuse the meaning of a message and reflect poorly on a speaker's image.

8. Standard language

Reading and Critical Thinking Skill

1. **Applying Information** How do you determine which pronunciation to use for the word *harass* when a dictionary lists two pronunciations?

2. **Cause-Effect** What are the results when a speaker expresses ordinary ideas in imaginative ways and uses imagery to help people visualize complex ideas?

3. **Making Contrasts** How do the articulation errors of addition and substitution differ?

4. **Summarization** Sum up five guidelines for speaking clearly and effectively.

5. **Classifying Information** At what level of language does a speaker use *Robert's Rules of Order*?

Skill Practice Activity

Recognizing Bias Identify the bias in the following quotes. On a separate sheet of paper, rewrite the quotes avoiding troublesome words.

"The republican is the only form of government which is not eternally at open or secret war with the rights of mankind." Thomas Jefferson

"The trade of critic, in literature, music, and the drama, is the most degraded of all trades." Mark Twain

Cooperative Learning Activity

Powerful Language With a partner, hold a ten-minute discussion about language usage in your school. List some of the powerful and troublesome language that you hear from students. Prepare a list of suggestions for making students' language more powerful. Share your list with other members of the class.

Chapter Project

Planning Throughout one school day, record on audiotape everything you say. Transcribe your words and then evaluate your diction according to the following criteria: Which words did I mispronounce? In which words did I omit consonant sounds? In which words did I add consonant sounds? In which words did I substitute one consonant for another? In which words did I slur consonant sounds? In which words did I fail to enunciate?

Make a list of words that show poor diction. Practice saying them correctly.

Presenting Try to use all the words on your list during the course of one school day. Be conscious of your pronunciations, articulations, and enunciations. Congratulate yourself if you get through the day saying all the words on your list correctly.

Chapter Project

Help students by pointing out examples in the text of transcribed speech, for instance, *y' all* and *fixin'*. Ask them to try to recognize and transcribe their diction problems accurately. Suggest they ask friends or family to help them identify problems on the tape.

9. Expressing and responding to feelings, informing, controlling or persuading, participating in social rituals, and sharing creative ideas

10. Denotations are a word's objective meanings and connotations are emotions or feelings with which the word is associated.

Reading and Critical Thinking Skill

1. **Applying Information** Follow the one that is listed first.

2. **Cause-Effect** The speech is interesting and memorable, and people look forward to hearing what the speaker has to say.

3. **Making Contrasts** Addition occurs when a speaker adds an extra consonant to a word, while substitution replaces one consonant sound with another.

4. **Summarization** Make appropriate language choices. Draw from a precise vocabulary. Follow the rules of grammar. Practice proper diction. Eliminate elements of dialect.

5. **Classifying Information** Formal language

Skill Practice Activity

Recognizing Bias

Revisions will vary. The following responses are samples:

The republican form of government is less often at war with the rights of humans than many other kinds of governments.

I might feel degraded if I made my living criticizing literature, music, and drama.

Cooperative Learning Activity

Powerful Language

Students' observations will differ. Remind them to listen for questions at the end of statements, for fillers, and for vague wording.

Chapter 5 Planning Guide

SECTION RESOURCES

Daily Objectives

Section 1

1. Describe nonverbal communication
2. Explain the functions of nonverbal communication
3. Describe the characteristics of nonverbal communication

Section 2

1. Explain how nonverbal skills can convey the confidence, poise, assertiveness, and immediacy needed for a positive image in professional and social contexts
2. Describe the types of nonverbal communication and their effects
3. Describe the four characteristics of voice

Reproducible Resources

 Reproducible Lesson Plan 5-1
 Application Activities 5-1
 Guided Reading Workbook Activity 5-1
 Vocabulary Activity 5*
 Reteaching Activity 5-1*
 Enrichment Activity 5-1*
 Graphic Organizer Transparency Strategies and Activities 5-1

 Reproducible Lesson Plan 5-2
 Application Activities 5-2
 Guided Reading Workbook Activity 5-2
 Vocabulary Activity 5*
 Reteaching Activity 5-2*
Enrichment Activity 5-2*
Graphic Organizer Transparency Strategies and Activities 5-2

Multimedia Resources

 Graphic Organizer Transparency 5-1
 Chapter 5 Teaching Transparency
 Interactive Tutor Self-Assessment
 PuzzleMaker
 ExamView® Pro Testmaker
 Interactive Lesson Planner
 Communication in Action Video Chapter 5
 MindJogger
 communicationapplications.glencoe.com
 Presentation Plus!

 Graphic Organizer Transparency 5-2
 Chapter 5 Teaching Transparency
 Interactive Tutor Self-Assessment
 PuzzleMaker
 ExamView® Pro Testmaker
 Interactive Lesson Planner
 Communication in Action Video Chapter 5
 MindJogger
 communicationapplications.glencoe.com
Presentation Plus!

Use Glencoe's *Presentation Plus!* multimedia teacher tool to easily present dynamic lessons that engage and motivate your students. Using Microsoft PowerPoint®, you can customize the presentations to create your own personalized lessons.

* Also available in Spanish

 Blackline Master   CD-ROM   Software

 Transparency   Videodisc   Videocassette   Web site

Chapter 5 Planning Guide

FOR THE TEACHER

Body Talk

Students should clip pictures of people from magazines, choosing those that communicate through facial expression, dress and grooming, movement and gestures, or kinesics (posture and tension). Have the class divide the pictures into four piles as each best fits into one of the above categories. Direct students to participate in one of four groups to make a collage of the pictures and write balloons above each person indicating what he or she communicates through facial expression, posture, clothing, or gestures.

After collages are complete, each group should select a leader to explain how the group decided on what was being communicated in each picture.

CHAPTER RESOURCES

Resources for the Teacher

- *Nonverbal Communication in Human Interaction* by Mark L. Knapp and Judith A. Hall, HBJ College and School Division, 1996
- *Successful Nonverbal Communication: Principles and Applications* by Dale G. Leathers, Allyn & Bacon, 1996
- *Reading People: How to Understand People and Predict Their Behavior—Anytime, Anyplace* by Jo-Ellan Dimitrius and Mark Mezzarella, Random House, 1998

Resources for the Student

- *Delivering Dynamic Presentations: Using Your Voice and Body for Impact* (The Essence of Public Speaking Series) by Ralph Hillman, William Thompson (Editor), Yoda Hillman, Derek Hanson, Allyn & Bacon, 1999
- *Casual Power: How to Power Up Your Nonverbal Communication & Dress Down for Success* by Sherry Maysonave, Bright Books Inc., 1999
- *How to Read a Person Like a Book* by Gerard I. Nierenberg, Hawthorn, 1971

Block Scheduling

Block scheduling differs from traditional class scheduling in the amount of time allotted to each period. The extended time frame provided by block scheduling affords you the opportunity to implement a greater number of research-oriented and activity-intense projects to motivate and involve your students. Activities that are particularly suited to use within the block-scheduling framework are identified throughout this chapter by the following designation:

KEY TO ABILITY LEVELS

Teaching Strategies have been coded for varying learning styles and abilities.

L1 **BASIC** activities for all students

L2 **AVERAGE** activities for average to above-average students

L3 **CHALLENGING** activities for above-average students

ELL **English Language Learner** activities

Chapter 5 Resource Manager

The following materials may be used when teaching the chapter. Materials for specific lessons are also shown at point-of-use in the margins of the Teacher's Wraparound Edition.

TEACHING TRANSPARENCIES

Chapter 5 Teaching Transparency

Graphic Organizer Transparency 5-1

Graphic Organizer Transparency 5-2

APPLICATION ACTIVITIES

Chapter 5, Section 1

Chapter 5, Section 2

Chapter 5, Cumulative

REINFORCEMENT AND REVIEW ACTIVITIES

Vocabulary Activity 5

Guided Reading Activity Workbook 5-1, 5-2

Reteaching Activities 5-1, 5-2

Chapter 5 Resource Manager

ASSESSMENT AND EVALUATION

GLENCOE'S
ASSESSMENT
ADVANTAGE

Section Quizzes 5–1, 5–2

Chapter 5 Test, Forms A & B

Performance Assessment Activity 5

ENRICHMENT AND EXTENSION

Technology Application Activity 5

Enrichment Activities 5–1, 5–2

SPANISH RESOURCES

- Spanish Chapter and Unit Tests
- Spanish Vocabulary Activities
- Spanish Section Quizzes
- Spanish Reteaching Activities
- Spanish Enrichment Activities

MULTIMEDIA

- Interactive Tutor Self-Assessment
- ExamView® Pro Testmaker
- PuzzleMaker
- Communication in Action Videodisc and Videocassette
- MindJogger
- Interactive Lesson Planner
- Presentation Plus!
- Writer's Assistant
- Glencoe Interactive Grammar
- **communicationapplications.glencoe.com**

ORAL PRESENTATION ACTIVITIES

Activities 7, 12

TEACHER PLANNING AND SUPPORT

- Reproducible Lesson Plans
- Interactive Lesson Planner
- Presentation Plus!

CHAPTER **5** Understanding Nonverbal Communication

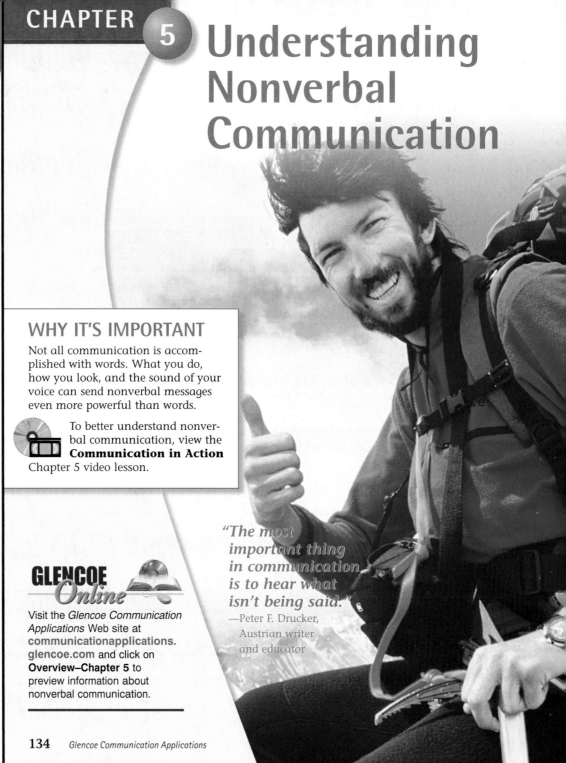

WHY IT'S IMPORTANT

Not all communication is accomplished with words. What you do, how you look, and the sound of your voice can send nonverbal messages even more powerful than words.

To better understand nonverbal communication, view the **Communication in Action** Chapter 5 video lesson.

"The most important thing in communication is to hear what isn't being said."
—Peter F. Drucker, Austrian writer and educator

Visit the *Glencoe Communication Applications* Web site at **communicationapplications. glencoe.com** and click on **Overview–Chapter 5** to preview information about nonverbal communication.

134 *Glencoe Communication Applications*

WHY IT'S IMPORTANT

Invite students to comment on the photo and discuss how much they count on body language signals to understand what others are telling them. You might have students compare face-to-face communication with telephone conversation to gauge this. Ask a volunteer to read aloud the quotation above and have students explain what it means to them. Ask: **What are some ways to communicate without using words?** *(Students may suggest that facial expressions, posture, body movements, clothes, accessories, hairstyle, and distance send messages.)*

Principles of Nonverbal Communication

GUIDE TO READING

Objectives

1. Describe nonverbal communication.
2. Explain the functions of nonverbal communication.
3. Describe the characteristics of nonverbal communication.

Terms to Learn

nonverbal communication
ambiguous

*H*ave *you ever felt as if you weren't in the mood to talk? Maybe you were tired or upset or just in a quiet mood. Regardless of your reason, you may have taken a break from talking to your family or friends. What did your lack of speech communicate to them? Think about the statement "You cannot not communicate." Do you agree or disagree? Why?*

What was your first reaction to the statement above? If you are like many people, you may have thought, "Of course I can avoid communicating. All I have to do is keep my mouth shut!"

However, that's not exactly true. Even if you don't talk to anyone around you—don't say hello, ask questions, or even answer questions—you still are communicating. Your facial expressions, body language, and even the way you use distance and space all send messages to others. Surprisingly, these messages often speak louder than words.

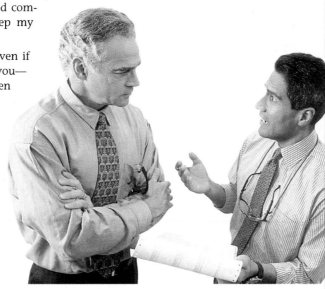

Body language is an example of nonverbal communication. Identify the ways in which the two men shown are using nonverbal communication.

Understanding Nonverbal Communication **135**

1 FOCUS

Bellringer

Ask students to vote by a show of hands whether they agree or disagree with the quoted statement on page 134. Display several photos of teens interacting but not talking. Have students suggest what message each participant is sending. Vote again to find out whether any votes have changed.

You may use Graphic Organizer Transparency 5–1 to introduce this section.

Graphic Organizer Transparency 5–1

Visual Instruction

Answer One is crossing his arms across his body while the other is using a hand gesture to make his point. They are both using facial expressions and exhibiting space and distance in their stances.

RESOURCE MANAGER

Teaching Tools
- Interactive Lesson Planner
- Reproducible Lesson Plan 5–1
- Application Activities 5–1

Reproducible Masters
- Guided Reading Activity Workbook 5–1
- Enrichment Activity 5–1
- Reteaching Activity 5–1
- Section Quiz 5–1
- Transparency Strategies and Activities Booklet 5–1

Transparencies
- Graphic Organizer Transparency 5–1
- Chapter 5 Teaching Transparency

Technology Resources
- Interactive Tutor Self-Assessment Software
- Presentation Plus! Software
- ExamView® Pro Testmaker
- PuzzleMaker Software
- communicationapplications.glencoe.com

2 TEACH

Words in a Vacuum

Play a portion of a video in which two or more characters interact verbally. First, play it with the screen covered and have students describe what they think is going on. Then, play it with the screen uncovered. Ask students to change or add to their descriptions. Discuss how the visual clues helped them to understand what the characters were communicating. **L1**

Guided Reading Activity 5–1

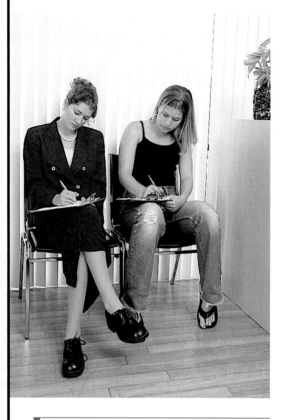

| Name _____ Date _____ Class _____ | GUIDED READING |
| UNDERSTANDING NONVERBAL COMMUNICATION | Activity 5–1 |

Principles of Nonverbal Communication

As you read Section 1, complete the sentences below.

1 _____ communication is a system of symbolic behaviors that includes all forms of communication except 2 _____. There are three categories for these behaviors: 3 _____, 4 _____, and 5 _____. Most of the meaning in messages is conveyed 6 _____ rather than through words.

Nonverbal behaviors often support, or 7 _____, verbal messages. Sometimes, however, your nonverbal cues can make your verbal messages less 8 _____. Nonverbal messages can also be used as a 9 _____ for verbal messages. There is a risk in relying on nonverbal messages instead of words, often leading to confusion or varied interpretations.

Messages about 10 _____ and 11 _____ are almost always communicated nonverbally. Through these nonverbal messages we reveal how we feel about others and the relationships we have with them.

Nonverbal communication is most often sent and received on a 12 _____ level. In addition, we tend to process, interpret, and 13 _____ to the nonverbal messages of others on this same level. This communication is also highly 14 _____, meaning it depends on the situation in which it occurs. A 15 _____ communicator takes into account the special 16 _____ surrounding another's actions before interpreting the behavior and making a snap 17 _____ based on those interpretations.

Nonverbal symbols have no specific meanings of their own but are often interpreted 18 _____ by different people. They are said to be 19 _____, meaning they are open to interpretation and often 20 _____. These cues also tend to happen very 21 _____.

There is also a distinct 22 _____ nature to nonverbal communication. Using an appropriate tone of voice; making direct 23 _____ eye contact; or greeting someone with a handshake, hug, or kiss all vary among cultures.

Visual Instruction

Answer The woman on the left is dressed professionally and sitting very poised, giving the impression that she is very serious about the position. The one on the right is dressed very sloppily and sitting in a very unpoised fashion, giving the impression that she doesn't care about the position.

WHAT IS NONVERBAL COMMUNICATION?

Nonverbal communication is a system of symbolic behaviors that includes all forms of communication except words. A symbolic wave of the hand, for example, can mean "Hello," "Good-bye," "Go ahead," "I'm over here," or a number of other things, depending on the context or situation. A laugh can symbolize such emotions as humor, nervousness, or sarcasm, just as a sigh can symbolize sadness, wishfulness, anger, or impatience.

Think about all the ways you convey messages and feelings without words. These are your nonverbal behaviors. Nonverbal behaviors can be organized into three categories:

- sounds, including the voice and vocalizations that substitute for speech
- body language
- environmental factors such as time, touch, distance, and objects and artifacts

Studies in nonverbal communication have concluded that anywhere from 65 to 93 percent of meaning communicated from one person to another is communicated nonverbally. Although these numbers vary, they all point to one important fact: Most of the meaning in messages is conveyed nonverbally rather than through words.

Nonverbal communication can be a powerful tool or a real hindrance to a communicator. That is why it is important to understand it and learn how to use it effectively.

FUNCTIONS OF NONVERBAL COMMUNICATION

Nonverbal communication represents a wide range of behaviors and is a vast area of study. However, we can identify two main functions of nonverbal communication:

- It relates to verbal communication.
- It conveys emotional and relationship dimensions of a message.

Relates to Verbal Communication

Nonverbal cues may exist on their own, or they may accompany a person's words. As mentioned earlier, waving hello is a form of

Two young women indicate interest in a job position by filling out an application. Identify what their nonverbal clues suggest about their interest in the job.

MEETING INDIVIDUAL NEEDS
ENGLISH LANGUAGE LEARNERS

Using Nonverbal Cues to Communicate Students who are learning English may enhance their ability to send messages accurately by practicing the use of nonverbal cues customary to English-speaking people. Since these cues may differ in the students' native cultures, students may require explanations as well as demonstrations of behaviors that can substitute for spoken messages.

Activity Pair students who are learning English with proficient English speakers and have them practice giving each other pointers about shaking hands, making direct eye contact, smiling, sitting forward, staying relaxed, and so on. If necessary, model the appropriate nonverbal behavior for students. Volunteer pairs might demonstrate positive nonverbal communication cues for the class. **ELL**

GLOBAL COMMUNICATION

Nonverbal Messages

Look around your classroom. Is someone sitting with the arms crossed over the chest? How many people are slouching or have their feet resting on another chair? Have you ever pointed to objects in a room or waved your hand to get someone's attention? Do you expect others to maintain eye contact with you when you are speaking to them? What messages do each of these nonverbal actions convey? Find someone in your community who works with international clients. Ask that person what these nonverbal behaviors suggest to people who are not from the United States.

nonverbal communication. In addition, your voice, the facial expressions you use, and your accompanying hand gestures and body movements also are forms of nonverbal cues.

Reinforces a Verbal Message

Nonverbal behaviors often support, or reinforce, verbal messages. For example, imagine that a job applicant tells an interviewer, "I really want this job. I also believe that I have the qualifications you're looking for." As she speaks, she seems relaxed, but she still sits up straight in her chair. Her speech is clear and firm, and her voice is businesslike and sincere. She makes direct eye contact with the interviewer. Her dress and grooming also convey a businesslike appearance.

In this situation, all the applicant's nonverbal cues clearly support her words. They reinforce her message, making it seem more believable to the interviewer.

Contradicts Verbal Messages

On the other hand, some nonverbal cues can make verbal messages less believable. Suppose another job applicant meets with the interviewer. She also says that she wants the job and thinks she is qualified. However, as she speaks, she fidgets uncomfortably in the chair. She hesitates in her answers, and her voice often is so soft it is difficult for the interviewer to hear. In addition, the applicant keeps looking around the room, avoiding direct eye contact with the interviewer.

In this case, the person's words—taken alone—would convey confidence and a desire to get the job. Her nonverbal behaviors, however, seem to contradict her stated message. They suggest that the applicant may not be as confident of her abilities as her words imply. Her actions may even imply that she is being dishonest about how well suited she is for the job.

It is important to note that, when a nonverbal message contradicts a verbal message, the receiver usually will believe the nonverbal message. At best, the receiver will be confused about the meaning that is being conveyed.

Acts as a Substitute for a Verbal Message

Nonverbal messages often are used as a substitute for verbal messages. For instance, a highway worker may stand at an intersection wearing a hard hat and waving a red flag to slow traffic. This person does not need to tell individual drivers to slow down for construction because his or her dress and actions convey that information.

Similarly, if a new student asks you, "Where is the principal's office?" you may simply smile and point to the second door on the left. You may use a quick handshake to say hello or a pat on the back to express approval. If you think about your day-to-day communication, you probably use a variety of nonverbal behaviors as a substitute for spoken messages.

Understanding Nonverbal Communication   **137**

GLOBAL COMMUNICATION

Nonverbal Messages

Invite volunteers to demonstrate each of the nonverbal messages listed in the feature. Discuss what they communicate in Western culture. Suggest that students try an online search or check with a professor of international business studies if they cannot find local businesses with international ties.

Communication Tip

Bodily action defines the meaning of your message. Thinking actively about what you are saying will help you produce expressions, gestures, and movements that reinforce your idea. You may need to learn to consciously control distracting mannerisms.

Mismatched Verbal and Nonverbal Messages

With a volunteer or another staff member, demonstrate nonverbal cues that contradict verbal messages about accepting a date, liking a gift, and not being hurt when jamming your toe. Ask students to tell which message they believed—the verbal or the nonverbal one—and explain why. **L2**

Grammar Tip

Complementary parts of a sentence or an outline should be constructed with the same grammatical structure. Notice the major subheads under Functions of Nonverbal Communication on pages 136 and 138. Both begin with a singular present tense verb (Relates, Conveys).

MULTIPLE LEARNING STYLES

Linguistic Students who enjoy telling stories, jokes, and riddles can readily relate to the importance of body language in communicating meaning. Discuss examples of nonverbal communication that are important to creating humor and suspense or emphasizing emotion and reaction.
Activity Have each student select a story, joke, or riddle to tell the class. Students should first write the words they will say and practice them in front of a mirror, adding body and voice cues that enhance the message. Have students hand out copies of their materials for the class to read silently. After students perform, have audience members evaluate what was added by the nonverbal aspect of the performance.

All Nonverbal All the Time?

Point out to students that substituting nonverbal for verbal communication can be helpful in certain situations (when talking is off limits or when communicating with someone whose language you don't speak), but it leaves a lot to be desired where subtlety of meaning is concerned. Have a small group of students leave the room while you describe a scenario (for example, a person who is nervously waiting to be questioned about a crime) and what it intends to communicate. Then, have the group return. Pantomime the scenario and have each group member interpret its "message." What information was unclear without words? **L2**

DID YOU KNOW?

If your receiver listens to you with hand on chin, head slightly tilted, eyeglasses or pen in mouth, and ear turned toward you, he or she is probably listening closely and evaluating your message.

Visual Instruction

Answer Because nonverbal messages are received on the subconscious level, they can be open to many different interpretations.

A police officer directs traffic by using nonverbal communication. **What is the risk involved when using nonverbal communication?**

Unfortunately, there is some risk in using nonverbal messages as a substitute for words. Nonverbal messages can be open to many different interpretations. Because nonverbal cues are received on the subconscious level, are highly personal, are highly cultural, and often are fleeting, they can be confusing and difficult to interpret.

Conveys Emotional and Relationship Dimensions of Message

In Chapter 2 you learned that there are three dimensions, or components, of a message. Most messages have an intellectual component, an emotional component, and a relationship component.

Communicators usually use their best available verbal skills to express what they mean. The remaining two dimensions of a message that relate to feelings, however, almost always are communicated nonverbally.

Messages About Feelings Imagine that the school board has called a meeting to discuss making your school a closed campus. Under this policy, students would not be allowed to leave the school grounds for lunch or free periods. Individuals who oppose the plan and those who support it are both registered to speak.

As the meeting progresses, speakers for both sides begin to shout at one another. One listener sneers and laughs as someone with an opposing view speaks. Even if these individuals' verbal messages remain fair and reasonable, their meanings are overshadowed by strong feelings of hostility implied in the nonverbal behavior. In the end, the meeting becomes disruptive and must be adjourned.

During this meeting, no one actually said, "I'm angry." However, the speakers' sharp voices and other nonverbal cues conveyed that message loudly and clearly. The feeling component of a message is most often conveyed and read by others in terms of nonverbal behaviors.

138 *Glencoe Communication Applications*

INTERDISCIPLINARY CONNECTION

History The introduction of videotape in the twentieth century has allowed for recording both the verbal and nonverbal components of political speeches. Viewing key moments on tape (or film) gives students a chance to apply concepts about nonverbal communication to real-life situations.
Activity Play a video segment showing a prominent politician responding to media questions, making a speech, or participating in a debate about a sensitive topic (for example, Nixon's resignation speech). Have students work in small groups to identify body language and analyze its meaning. Discuss whether the nonverbal and verbal cues match or contradict each other.

Messages About Relationships

Individuals seldom speak openly about their feelings or their relationships with others. For example, a teacher might find it difficult to tell students, "I enjoy having you in my class." Similarly, you might hesitate to tell a coworker, "I really don't like working with you."

We often reveal how we feel about others and our relationships with them through nonverbal messages. We may depend on a touch, a glance, or a smile to convey "I really like you" or "I really appreciate your friendship." On the other hand, we may avoid eye contact, frown, or fold our arms to convey "I don't want to talk to you" or "I don't enjoy your company. You really annoy me."

CHARACTERISTICS OF NONVERBAL COMMUNICATION

Imagine this situation. As you and a friend step into the checkout line at the grocery store, you suddenly realize that you've cut in front of a gentleman with a cart full of groceries. When you start to apologize, he says, "No. By all means, you go first." Now you feel bad because you think his tone was sarcastic. Your friend, on the other hand, thinks the man was sincere and that he let you go first because you had only an item or two to purchase.

Figure 5–1 Characteristics of Nonverbal Communication

Subconscious — Contextual

Nonverbal Communication

Cultural — Ambiguous

What actually happened? Only the message sender knows for sure. Nonverbal communication can be open to a variety of interpretations, any of which may or may not be valid. This is because nonverbal communication has some unusual characteristics. As illustrated in **Figure 5–1**, it is by nature subconscious, contextual, ambiguous, and cultural.

Subconscious

Nonverbal communication is most often sent and received on a subconscious level. In other words, we are usually not aware of the messages we send nonverbally. In addition, we tend to process, interpret, and respond to the nonverbal messages of others on the subconscious level.

For instance, think about the Academy Awards. The camera zooms in on the nominees' faces as the winner's name is announced, but only one jumps up and rushes to the stage. The others smile politely and applaud, but their disappointment is painfully clear to millions of viewers. The expression in their eyes, the slump of their shoulders, or the looks exchanged with friends send subconscious messages to others.

The same is true of most people. While you may pay great attention to how you look for a certain occasion, you may not always think about your tone of voice, posture, facial expressions, or gestures. However, if a receiver observes the behavior, he or she will assign meaning to it. All of the nonverbal messages, conscious or subconscious, send messages about you, your attitude, and your feelings. The impression you wanted to convey with your careful grooming may be completely shattered by a hurt look or a slumped posture of which you are not even aware.

Understanding Nonverbal Communication **139**

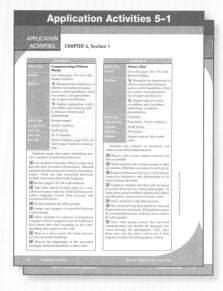

DID YOU KNOW?

Most people talk at a rate between 140 and 180 words per minute. However, slowing one's rate of speech does not necessarily improve audience understanding. The best rate for a listener depends upon how well words are articulated and how the voice is varied at a given speed.

Teaching Nonverbal Characteristics

After students have read Section 1, divide the class into four groups and assign each group one of the characteristics of nonverbal messages to teach to the class. In their groups, students can agree on a brief explanation of the characteristic and brainstorm several examples to illustrate it. After each group's presentation, discuss questions the presentation has raised.
L2

INCLUSION STRATEGIES

Less-Proficient Readers Struggling readers can gain confidence and demonstrate concepts in this section by focusing on one concept at a time, thus limiting vocabulary and increasing comprehension.

Activity Assign each subsection to a small group and have members read it together, pausing to demonstrate the nonverbal cues it discusses. When the group feels knowledgeable about the material, have one or more members summarize it for the class.

■ **Students raising their hands to ask questions in a classroom represent contextual nonverbal communication.** *What affects how we interpret nonverbal communication?*

Not only are most nonverbals and the messages they send transmitted on a subconscious level, but they also tend to be interpreted on the subconscious level by the receiver. Imagine that you see a man push in front of a person in a wheelchair as they both are entering a building. You may later relate the incident to someone else and remark that you do not like the man—without realizing the source of your dislike. You probably did not stop to analyze the reason for your feelings or to question whether you interpreted his behavior appropriately. You simply made your judgment subconsciously.

Contextual

Like other forms of communication, nonverbal communication is highly contextual. In other words, it depends on the situation in which it occurs.

Think again of the man who pushed his way into the building. What if you learned that he was a doctor rushing to the aid of a heart-attack victim? Would this change your interpretation of his behavior? Now you might not consider him rude or inconsiderate. In fact, you might think of him as considerate for successfully dodging the wheelchair when he was in such a hurry.

The roles, norms, and standards of every context vary. These, in turn, affect how we interpret nonverbal communication. A competent communicator works to take into account the special circumstances surrounding another's actions before interpreting the behavior and making a snap judgment based on those interpretations.

Ambiguous

In Chapter 4 you learned that meanings lie in people rather than in language. Nonverbal symbols have no specific meanings of their own. They may be interpreted differently by different people. Therefore, they are said to be ambiguous. Ambiguous means they are open to interpretation and often confusing. For example, if you are talking to someone whose arms are folded, you may get the impression that he or she is angry. Another person may think the person is bored. What if that individual is simply feeling chilly and is trying to get warm?

Not only are nonverbal cues ambiguous and open to interpretation, but they also tend to happen very quickly. Studies show that facial expressions usually last only a split second. A flick of a wrist, a stamp of the foot, or a shrug of the shoulders also happens quickly and may be difficult to catch. A sigh or a pause may go unnoticed or be misinterpreted.

The best advice for interpreting and assigning meaning to nonverbal messages is to strive to increase your awareness and sensitivity to the nonverbal messages of others. In other words, try to process messages on the conscious rather than the subconscious level. If you find yourself feeling confused or uncertain about the cues you receive, you can use intrapersonal and interpersonal perception checks to try to clarify your interpretations and check your responses.

Cultural

Nonverbal communication also has a distinctly cultural nature. A particular nonverbal message commonly used in one culture may send a completely different message in another culture. For instance, a loud tone of voice is much more acceptable in some cultures than it is in others. Other cues such as direct or indirect eye contact; greeting someone with a handshake, hug, or kiss; or what are considered acceptable or unacceptable styles of dress also vary among different cultures.

Cultural differences in nonverbal communication are so important in international relations that the U.S. State Department has specially trained experts in the field. Their task is to counsel ambassadors and other diplomats who travel to other countries about specific nonverbal cultural differences.

The impact of culture on nonverbal communication was clearly illustrated in 1995 when a U.S. congressman accidentally offended Iraqi leader Saddam Hussein while attempting to negotiate the release of two American hostages. After shaking hands

COMMUNICATION PRACTICE LAB

Considering Context

To practice interpreting nonverbal communication according to its context, follow these steps:

Step 1 Divide the following contexts among five equal groups of students:
- A cubicle in an office
- A hospital waiting room
- A car
- A witness stand in a courtroom
- A first date

Step 2 Have one member of each group act out the following nonverbal behavior for his or her group: fidgeting, glancing around the room, tapping one foot, sighing repeatedly.

Step 3 Have each group discuss its interpretation of these behaviors and arrive at a consensus.

Step 4 As a class, share your interpretations. How did they differ? Why? Discuss the effect of context on nonverbal communication.

Understanding Nonverbal Communication **141**

3 ASSESS

Assign Section 1 Assessment as a homework or in-class activity.

🔊 Use *Interactive Tutor Self-Assessment Software* to review Section 1.

Section 5–1 Quiz

MULTIPLE LEARNING STYLES

Interpersonal Use students' cooperative and social skills to assist in reviewing important concepts in the section.

Activity Pair students and have them take turns creating fill-in-the-blank questions for their partners to answer or providing examples for them to classify. Have pairs conclude their reviews by summarizing for the class what they learned about nonverbal communication.

Reteaching Activity 5–1

Enrichment Activity 5–1

4 CLOSE

Ask students to reread the section's opening paragraph and think about the statement "You cannot not communicate." Ask them to write an original statement that includes this meaning and relates it to nonverbal messages.

Extra-Credit Project

Have students observe a teacher or family member during conversation and note any nonverbal messages the person sends subconsciously and unintentionally. Ask students to record their observations and what is being communicated in a journal entry.

with the Iraqi leader, the congressman sat down and crossed his legs. At this point, Hussein immediately stood up and walked out of the room.

The congressman had unwittingly insulted Hussein by showing him the sole of his foot. In some Arab cultures, the bottom of the foot is considered to be the lowest, dirtiest part of the body. As one writer stated, the congressman unfortunately started the negotiations off "on the wrong foot."

Culture is just another factor that influences the way nonverbal communication is interpreted. Remember, nonverbal cues can mean different things to different people. They also can change meanings in different contexts and happen so fast you may miss part or all of them. Therefore, the best advice for interpreting or assigning meanings to nonverbal messages is to be careful and consider the context, the relationship, and the communication.

Section 1 Assessment

Visit the *Glencoe Communication Applications* Web site at **communicationapplications. glencoe.com** and click on **Self-Check and Study Guide 5.1** to review your understanding of the principles of nonverbal communication.

Review Key Terms

1. Define each term and write it in a sentence: nonverbal communication, ambiguous.

Check Understanding

2. Compare and contrast verbal and nonverbal communication.

3. What are the two main functions of nonverbal communication? Explain each function.

4. Describe the four characteristics of nonverbal communication.

5. **Analyze** Imagine that you missed your bus and are late for class. As you are explaining your reason for being late to the principal, she begins slowly shaking her head back and forth. Name two ways you might interpret this nonverbal cue. What characteristic of nonverbal communication does this example illustrate?

APPLICATION *Activity*

Interpreting Nonverbal Behaviors Choose one student to act out a ten- to fifteen-second scenario for the class. The scenario should nonverbally convey some emotion or attitude. Individually, write your interpretation of the student's actions. Then, share your ideas as a class. Were most students' interpretations similar? What cues led you to your specific interpretation? What did the student intend to convey with his or her actions? Were you close?

Section 1 Assessment Answers

1. Accept all reasonable sentences.
2. Verbal communication consists of words; nonverbal of all other forms of communication, accounting for most of the meanings communicated.
3. (1) Relates to verbal communication by reinforcing, contradicting, or substituting. (2) Conveys emotion and relationship meanings of messages.
4. Often sent and received at subconscious level; contextual (its meaning depends on situation); ambiguous (open to interpretation); cultural

(variously interpreted in different cultures).

5. Interpretations may include "Your tardiness is not going to be excused," "That bus causes nothing but trouble for our students," or "I don't believe you." The example illustrates ambiguity of nonverbal cues.

Application Activity Answers should reflect reasonable interpretation of students' nonverbal behaviors. Students may discover that some behaviors are highly ambiguous.

Technology Skill

Using a Word-Processing Program

Word-processing software can be used to create, edit, print, and store electronic documents.

Learning the Skill

- Open your word-processing program, then click on the *File* pull-down menu in the top left-hand corner of your screen.
- Click on the word *New* from the *File* menu. This brings up a screen that allows you to create a new document.
- Label the document by selecting *Save As* or *Name* from the *File* menu. Enter the new name of the document when you are prompted.
- Establish margins for your new document by clicking on *File* and selecting *Setup* or *Page Setup* and responding to the prompts.
- You are now ready to begin entering information into your new document. Find the cursor and start typing.
- Proofread, correct, and then save the document by clicking on *File,* then *Save.*
- Print the document by clicking on *Print* from the *File* menu. Store the document by selecting *Close* from the *File* menu.

Practicing the Skill

Read the steps below to sharpen your word-processing skills.

Step 1 Open your word-processing program and create a new document in which you will summarize the characteristics of nonverbal communication.

File Menu

New — Click here to create new document.

Name/Save As — Give your document a title.

Setup/Page Setup — Establish margins here.

Save — Keep changes to your document up-to-date.

Print — Print your document out on paper.

Close — Click here to store your document.

Step 2 Label the new document.

Step 3 Establish margins for your document.

Step 4 Type the information into the document.

Step 5 Proofread and save your work.

Step 6 Print the document, then store it.

APPLICATION *Activity*

Assume that you have been asked to give the introduction at a banquet honoring your favorite teacher, who has been recognized as the teacher of the year in your district. Use a word-processing program to write and edit the introduction, print the document, and save it as a file on a computer.

COOPERATIVE LEARNING ACTIVITY

Group students and have them teach one another how to use different word-processing programs. Each group should make a chart comparing differences in commands, command locations, and procedures among the programs they learned. If possible, students should use the computer to create their charts.

Using a Word-Processing Program

Point out that word-processing programs vary in minor ways in their commands and procedures. All have a pull-down help menu that can be used to answer questions about how functions of the program work.

Have students practice inserting, deleting, and moving information within the files they have created until they feel comfortable doing this. Other functions that students should master are selecting a block of type, italicizing and boldfacing type, changing font size, changing leading (spacing), and creating numbered and bulleted lists.

Practicing the Skill

Students will need to scan Section 2 to create their lists. You may want to complete this step as a class, summarizing on the board the ways to convey messages with body talk. If each student begins with the same text, it will be easier to make points about entering and formatting text to the whole class. Demonstrate how to highlight and move blocks of text so that students can reorder their six types efficiently.

Application Activity

Student responses will vary. A sample response is given.

Ladies and Gentlemen,
Thank you for coming here this evening to honor a great teacher and coach, Mr. Shepherd. I have had the pleasure of being a student in Mr. Shepherd's classes for two years. During that time, he has helped me become a better student, a better athlete, and, most importantly, a better person. He is dedicated to the math and business classes that he teaches, the sports that he coaches, and especially the people who are near him every day both in the school and the community. It is my honor to introduce to you Mr. Damien Shepherd. Thank you.

1 FOCUS

Bellringer
Write on the board the sentence "He/She is a real professional." Ask students to write the first person who comes to mind when they read this. Have them explain why this person seems professional. Read the opening paragraph aloud and have students answer the question. Discuss traits that make a person seem professional.

You may use Graphic Organizer Transparency 5–2 to introduce this section.

Graphic Organizer Transparency 5–2

Nonverbal Communication	Positive	Negative
1. Varying the inflection in your voice		
2. Speaking too loudly		
3. Varying the tempo of your speech		
4. Using many empty vocalizations		
5. Wearing professional attire		
6. Appearing well groomed		
7. Sitting or standing in a slouched position		
8. Using empty gestures		
9. Making direct eye contact		
10. Invading someone's personal space		
11. Using a firm handshake		
12. Arriving late to an appointment		

Application Activities 5–2

APPLICATION ACTIVITIES   CHAPTER 5, Section 2

[Application activities worksheet]

Visual Instruction

Answer By projecting certain messages about yourself and your abilities as a communicator

---

Section 2

Using Nonverbal Communication to Create a Professional Image

GUIDE TO READING

Objectives

1. Explain how nonverbal skills can convey the confidence, poise, assertiveness, and immediacy needed for a positive image in professional and social contexts.
2. Describe the types of nonverbal communication and their possible effects.
3. Describe the four characteristics of voice.
4. Recognize the importance of effective nonverbal strategies such as a firm handshake, direct eye contact, and appropriate use of space and distance.

Terms to Learn

pitch	tone	kinesics
range	rate	artifacts
inflection	tempo	

Imagine that you are a restaurant manager. At staff meetings, you notice that one server always seems to complain loudly and often leaves angry. Another server typically sits silently near the back of the group. A third server can be counted on to participate with enthusiasm and offer helpful suggestions. Which of these waiters is projecting a professional image?

As you develop competence and effectiveness as a communicator, you will face many challenges. Some of these challenges will take place in your school, community, or possibly in a business context. One of the most important challenges will be participating effectively with coworkers, supervisors, or customers in business conversations, discussions, and presentations. To make your communication in these situations as effective as possible, you will want to convey a professional image.

Barbara Walters exhibits a professional image. How can you create a positive professional image through nonverbal communication?

144 *Glencoe Communication Applications*

RESOURCE MANAGER

Teaching Tools

- Interactive Lesson Planner
- Reproducible Lesson Plan 5–2
- Application Activities 5–2

Reproducible Masters

- Guided Reading Activity Workbook 5–2
- Enrichment Activity 5–2
- Reteaching Activity 5–2
- Section Quiz 5–2
- Transparency Strategies and Activities Booklet 5–2

Transparencies

- Graphic Organizer Transparency 5–2
- Chapter 5 Teaching Transparency

Technology Resources

- Interactive Tutor Self-Assessment Software
- Presentation Plus! Software
- ExamView® Pro Testmaker
- PuzzleMaker Software
- communicationapplications.glencoe.com

CHARACTERISTICS OF A POSITIVE PROFESSIONAL IMAGE

A positive professional image and presence can be important to your success in professional and social contexts. It means that others see you as poised and confident. It also means that you consistently conduct yourself in a businesslike manner in the workplace. Finally, a professional image means that you can be depended on to communicate appropriately and effectively in any situation that may arise.

Through nonverbal communication, you can project certain messages about yourself and your abilities as a communicator. With enough practice and skill, you can create a professional image that projects all of the following characteristics:

- confidence
- poise
- assertiveness
- immediacy

Image That Projects Confidence

A strong voice and an attentive and positive attitude project an image of confidence. These nonverbal cues show that you believe in yourself and your communication skills. Confidence conveys to others that you believe you can accomplish tasks successfully and that you can build and maintain positive relationships.

Image That Projects Poise

People who are known for their poise generally have an ability to "read" any situation and act appropriately. They don't hesitate in their speech and are seldom uncertain about how to act in a given context. They also tend to keep their cool in a stressful situation.

Poise stems from an understanding of communication situations and a strong sense of appropriateness and correctness. Poise sends the nonverbal message that you are in control of your communication and the situation.

■ **These young ladies are projecting a positive professional image.** What does an image that projects confidence convey to others?

Understanding Nonverbal Communication **145**

2 TEACH

Professional Image

Point out that a person need not always feel confident to project an image of confidence. By practicing positive attitude, voice, appearance, and movement, one can gradually attain this image. With experience and time, the inner feeling of confidence grows. Have students list voice and action traits that show confidence and work in pairs to practice using them in role-playing an interview situation. **L2**

DID YOU KNOW?

Share these common feelings and how they are revealed in body language.

Uncertainty/Indecision: Closed eyes, pinching bridge of nose, chewing or biting lips, sideways eye movement, pacing, concerned or puzzled look, slightly tilted head

Nervousness: Unable to maintain eye contact, frequent blinking, shifting from foot to foot, fidgeting

Boredom: Staring into space, jingling objects in pockets or hands, looking at watch, adjusting clothing, tapping or jiggling foot

Suspicion/Dishonesty: Avoiding eye contact, glancing sideways, hands near or touching nose, ears, or mouth while speaking, gestures not matching words, body poised to move away

---

EXTENDING THE CONTENT

What Body Language Reveals Business interactions require people to read body language to understand what others are feeling. Share with students the information in Did You Know? on this page. You might want to write the information on the board for students to refer to later.
Activity Have students use the information in the Did You Know? to evaluate nonverbal messages sent by students and adults they observe. Have students write a paragraph explaining what was communicated nonverbally in one of the encounters they observed.

■ **Visual Instruction**

Answer Confidence conveys that you believe in yourself and your communication skills.

Attention Span and Professional Image

Ask students whether they find that they are easily distracted or cannot pay attention long enough to "get the message" in class, conversation, or at work. Explain that attention span can be improved with practice and conscious effort. Help students see that focus is critical to making others feel that they have worth to you and are being heard. Have the class brainstorm a list of techniques they might use to practice and improve their active listening. Write these on a poster and post it in class. Set aside five minutes each day for a week as time for students to use these techniques as they listen to one other person. **L2**

Guided Reading Activity 5–2

GUIDED READING
Activity 5-2   Name _____ Date _____ Class _____
UNDERSTANDING NONVERBAL COMMUNICATION
Using Nonverbal Communication to Create a
Professional Image

As you read Section 2, answer the following items.

1. What are the four characteristics of a professional image? _____
2. What are the three main types of nonverbal communication? _____
3. List the four sound characteristics your voice has that make it unique. _____
4. What are the three forms of pitch, and which is the one you would use for normal speech? _____
5. What does it mean to speak in a monotone? _____
6. How do rate and tempo differ? _____
7. What are a few examples of vocalizations? What is the function of vocalizations? _____
8. What are the four factors of body talk? _____
9. What are the three concepts to keep in mind when dressing professionally? _____
10. What nonverbal signals do your muscle tone and tension send? _____
11. How does a gait differ from a gesture? _____
12. Making direct eye contact is a sign of what? _____
13. What are the four types of distances that describe spatial communication? _____
14. List the three ways you can manage your time more effectively. _____
15. What is an artifact? _____

Types of Nonverbal Communication

Refer students to the table on this page to summarize the aspects of voice, body language, and use of environment that communicate who they are to others. As they review the table silently, have students inventory how they illustrate each of these items today. Is there anything they want to change? **L2**

Image That Projects Assertiveness

Assertiveness suggests a strong sense of purpose. It means that you are confident of yourself and your opinions or beliefs and are not afraid to take a stand when necessary. An assertive individual will not allow a pushy salesperson, a bullying coworker, or an inconsiderate friend to treat him or her unfairly. Instead, that person will project verbal and nonverbal messages that convey logical reasoning and command respect.

Unlike an aggressive person, an assertive individual does not try to impose his or her ideas on others, forcing them to change or take action against their will. Rather, an assertive person uses tact and persuasiveness to take a stand and, if necessary, win others over to his or her way of thinking.

Image That Projects Immediacy

A competent communicator has a sense of immediacy in interacting with others. A communicator who has the quality of immediacy is perceived by others as approachable, friendly, and open. When you bring a problem to this person, you usually feel satisfied that you have his or her full attention. Immediacy—especially when used in combination with confidence, poise, and assertiveness—is a valuable aspect of projecting a professional image.

As these characteristics illustrate, image depends on more than just strong verbal skills. It also relies heavily on effective nonverbal

communication. In the following pages, you will learn more about the role nonverbal communication plays in creating and maintaining a positive professional image.

TYPES OF NONVERBAL COMMUNICATION

Have you thought about how the way you laugh, the way you dress, how you use space, and how you protect your territory convey nonverbal messages about you? Perhaps you have not considered how your use of time sends messages about your priorities, your attitudes, and your feelings about relationships. All of these are ways you communicate nonverbally.

There are three main types of nonverbal communication: voice, body talk, and environmental cues. Within each of these broad categories are a number of subcategories. The following table lists a wide variety of nonverbal cues that people use in everyday communication.

TYPES OF NONVERBAL COMMUNICATION

Voice	Body Talk	Environmental Cues
Pitch	Dress and grooming	Space and distance
Range and inflection	Posture	Territory
Volume	Muscular tone and tension	Touch
Quality and tone	Movement and gesture	Time
Duration: Rate and tempo	Facial communication	Artifacts
Pause and silence	Eye communication	Color
Laughter		Fragrance and odor
Vocalizations		

MEETING INDIVIDUAL NEEDS

INCLUSION STRATEGIES

Learning Disabled Students with severe disabilities will benefit from tactile and kinesthetic activities that deal with the concepts in the section.

Activity Review the aspects of nonverbal communication displayed in the table on this page. Assign each student one of the voice, body talk, or environmental cues listed in the table. Have students use the text to learn about this aspect, then find pictures, CDs, or videos that illustrate how their aspect affects communication. Use the chalkboards to create three large sections. As students present their information, have them write their subjects in the appropriate sections and add illustrations or objects as examples.

VOICE AS NONVERBAL COMMUNICATION

Voice, as shown in **Figure 5–2**, is the human sound that is used to transmit oral language from sender to receiver. The speaking voice that carries words is often accompanied or replaced by other vocal cues, such as a sigh or a laugh.

Voice is an important aspect of your overall communication. Studies generally agree that when voice is involved in communication, it accounts for 38 percent of the message received by the receiver. When voice is involved in communication, it is one of the most influential kinds of nonverbal cues. For this reason, a pleasant speaking voice can be very important to creating a professional image.

Characteristics of Voice

Imagine that a supervisor called to say, "You need to get your report in on time." The meaning of the words probably would be clear. However, you would need to pay attention to the supervisor's voice to decide whether the call was a gentle reminder, a brief scolding, or a stern warning. Your response would be influenced not only by the meaning of the person's words but also by the characteristics of his or her voice.

■ **Figure 5–2 From Voice to Speech**

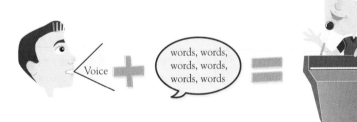

■ **Figure 5–3 Characteristics of Voice**

As sound, your voice has the same four characteristics, illustrated in **Figure 5–3**, as all other sounds. They are the following:

- pitch
- volume
- tone
- duration

The way these characteristics blend in your speaking makes your voice unique and different from all other voices.

Pitch Pitch is one of the most important characteristics of voice because it is so closely tied to the emotion of a message. Pitch is the highness or lowness of sound on a musical scale. Think about how you respond to the pitch of a musical instrument or singing voice. Whether the music energizes you, makes you feel peaceful and calm, or makes you feel sad or happy and "upbeat" probably depends to a large extent on the use of high and low pitch. Similarly, the pitch of your voice affects others' interpretation and emotional response.

High Pitch People often associate a high-pitched voice with external factors such as stress, fear, tension, excitement, frustration, or uncertainty.

Understanding Nonverbal Communication **147**

INTERDISCIPLINARY CONNECTION

Science Students can refer to physical science textbooks to explain how the vocal cords produce sound waves and what causes the sound to vary in pitch *(frequency)*, volume *(decibels)*, and tone *(timbre)*.

Activity Assign an interested group of students to research and report on vocal sounds as wave phenomena. Require students to use audiovisual aids to help them explain the concepts. For example, diagrams might show how the sound wave pattern alters as pitch changes from high to low.

The Speaking Voice

Review with students the definitions for pitch, volume, tone, and duration of voice. Record and play for students short excerpts from broadcasts by national newscasters. Include men and women. Ask students to describe these four qualities in each of the voices and to compare and contrast them. Which voice do most students prefer listening to? Have them explain why, using the terms you defined. Have students summarize the main idea of this subsection in their own words. **L3**

DID YOU KNOW?

The vocal cords in the larynx produce sound by vibrating as sound passes over them. During the adolescent growth spurt, boys' larynxes enlarge and the vocal cords grow longer and thicker, deepening the pitch of the voice. Boys' voices "crack" and they have difficulty controlling pitch while still growing because the vocal cords have not yet adjusted to the larger voice box.

Communication Tip

When leaving a voice message on the telephone, be sure to speak slowly and pronounce words clearly. Spell your name if necessary. Remember that the listener will have to replay the message several times if your voice is unclear.

BUSINESS BRIEF

In *NonVerbal Selling Power*, Gerhard Gschwandtner describes body language that expresses confidence to a prospect: Stand with feet about a foot apart, arms at your side and shoulders relaxed. Stand 1 1/2 to 4 feet away. Have no object covering the front of your body. Shake hands straight up and down and smile.

Setting the Volume

Many teenagers prefer to listen to their music with the volume turned up (and may have already incurred some hearing loss because of this practice). They may have difficulty assessing an appropriate volume for professional speaking. Point out to them that listeners will give them cues about whether they need to turn their voice volumes up or down. (Leaning forward and tilting the ear toward the speaker indicate too soft a voice; shrinking back, covering ears, or frowning may indicate that the voice is too loud and grating.) Have students take turns reading aloud from the text in their natural voices as classmates note whether they can hear the reader adequately. Have classmates give each reader written feedback. **L1**

DID YOU KNOW?

Your voice affects listeners more than what you say. In persuasive speeches, 76 percent of effectiveness is attributable to delivery (the way you talk), while only 24 percent is due to content. Numerous studies have proven that listeners decide whether a speaker is truthful, competent, credible, and trustworthy just from the sound of his or her voice.

Visual Instruction

Answer Volume determines whether a speaker is understood and how the listener receives the message.

High pitch can also indicate fatigue, youth, uncertainty, or a low energy level. Occasional use of high pitch can add variety, humor, and enthusiasm.

Medium Pitch Medium pitch is the pitch you use when you speak normally in conversations, discussions, and presentations. A medium pitch usually conveys calmness and confidence and can be used to emphasize the intellectual content of a message.

Low Pitch Low-pitched voices often are described as rich, deep, or resonant. Low pitch can express a wide range of emotions from sadness to uncertainty and from tenderness to concern. Because they are usually pleasant to listen to, low-pitched voices can be a real asset in professional and social conversations, discussions, and presentations. However, consistent use of low pitch in long discussions and

Mexican President Carlos Salinas and Canadian Prime Minister Brian Mulroney lean in to hear one another better. How does volume affect communication?

presentations can lull listeners to sleep and cause them to lose interest in what the speaker has to say.

Range and Inflection Vocal range and inflection are both associated with pitch. **Range** relates to the variations possible for a speaker to reach—from the highest pitch possible to the lowest pitch possible. **Inflection** is the rising and falling of pitch that adds variety to speaking. A person's inflection often reveals the meaning and feeling underlying his or her message.

Individuals who speak consistently at the same pitch without variety in range and inflection are said to speak in a monotone. Unfortunately, few things kill the impact and effectiveness of a message like a monotonous voice that lacks animation and inflection.

Volume It is the speaker's responsibility to be clearly heard and understood by listeners in conversations, discussions, and presentations. Being understood depends on clear, articulate sounding of words. Being heard depends on using appropriate volume for the situation.

Listeners tend to be sensitive to the volume of the messages they receive. For instance, you may view a loud, boisterous speaker as rude or overbearing. On the other hand, if a speaker consistently talks too softly, you may view him or her as incompetent, inconsiderate, shy, or lacking confidence.

As a general rule of thumb, use listener feedback to judge the appropriateness of your volume. If you notice listeners leaning

---

MULTIPLE LEARNING STYLES

MEETING INDIVIDUAL NEEDS

Musical Range, tone, rate, and tempo are vocal qualities that relate both to the speaking and the singing voice. Students who participate in choir or other musical groups can demonstrate for classmates how these qualities affect perceptions of what is said or sung.

Activity Have students prepare a how-to talk in which they demonstrate techniques for lowering pitch, improving resonance, and varying volume and rate in order to make the voice more pleasant to listen to. After listening, classmates should ask questions, then pair off to practice the techniques they observed.

forward or turning one ear toward you to hear better, speak a little louder. You also might use perception checks to help you find the right volume and ensure that your message is heard.

Tone The human voice is unique because of its tone. Tone is a specific vocal quality. Think of how you would describe the tone of a bell, a siren, or an alarm. Some bells produce rich, mellow sounds, but others sound weak and small. Sirens often are shrill. An alarm may be harsh and grating. Like these sounds, voices often are thought of as pleasant or unpleasant depending upon their tone.

The good news is that almost everyone can develop a pleasant speaking voice. Competent communicators usually want to develop voices that are rich, melodic, resonant, and full. One tip for developing the full resonant voice is to breathe deeply for speech and speak from the diaphragm like actors and singers.

Duration Almost everyone has encountered a speaker who raced through his or her words so quickly a listener could hardly keep up. You probably also have heard speakers plod along so slowly you wondered if they would ever finish a sentence. Duration has two related components: rate and tempo. Rate refers to how fast or how slowly an individual speaks. Tempo refers to the rhythmic quality of a person's speech. Tempo results from variations in an individual's rate of speech.

The rate of a person's speech can have a significant effect on listeners. For example, if a speaker talks too fast, listeners may have difficulty following and understanding the message. If a speaker goes too slowly, listeners may tire of the slow pace and lose interest. The key is variety. Speeding up and slowing down the rate of speech appropriately can

TECHNOLOGY *Activity*

Hearing Yourself Speak How you say something is just as important as the words that you use to say it. Assume that you have just won a free dinner with your favorite media celebrity or athlete. The famous person wants to know why you are such a big fan. With a classmate, develop a series of questions that the celebrity might ask. Using an audio recorder, tape your answers to the questions. Listen to the recordings of yourself and your partner. Analyze each voice's pitch, range, tone, and rate. Are your answers convincing? Record your responses again while concentrating more on the sound of your voice and compare the results.

help you create a tempo that holds listeners' interest and helps them understand your message.

How do you know whether or not your rate and tempo are suitable in a given situation? The answer once again is to analyze the feedback from your audience. If you have a question, use perception checks and adapt your rate to meet the needs of your listeners.

Cues That Accompany Speech

Speech is often accompanied by a variety of attributes or vocalizations, such as pause and silence, laughter, sighs, sobs, or other sounds. Such vocal cues may be intentional or unintentional messages about meanings and feelings.

Pauses and Silence When you pause in your speech, it typically is only for a brief period of time. Silence usually refers to a longer

Understanding Nonverbal Communication **149**

Hearing Yourself Speak Explain that breathing, relaxation, support, pronunciation, rate, emphasis, and phrasing are all elements with which students can experiment to alter the way their voices sound and are perceived by others. Suggest that students check the tape before recording to be sure it is not damaged or too loosely wound. Remind them to note changes they made in each recording, so that they will be able to recall how they produced the sound they like best. **L1**

Grammar Tip

When a subordinate clause is placed first in a complex sentence, it is set off by a comma. (*If a speaker talks too fast,* listeners may have difficulty. . . .) If it follows the independent clause, it is not. (You have heard speakers plod along so slowly you wondered *if they would ever finish.*)

Language Tip

Good articulation is the art of speaking so that every sound is clear and distinct. To improve articulation, move your lips and tongue energetically, take care in forming beginning and ending sounds of words, tape-record yourself and listen critically, and watch listeners for feedback.

COOPERATIVE LEARNING ACTIVITY

By working with word combinations, such as tongue twisters, that are difficult to say, students can build skills in precise speaking. Have students practice tongue twisters like the following and make up more of their own. They should begin repeating them slowly and gradually increase the speed at which they speak while keeping sounds crisp, clear, and distinct.

Six sick slick slim sycamore saplings; a box of biscuits, a batch of mixed biscuits; three free throws; which wristwatches are Swiss wristwatches?; the boot black bought the black boot back; a noisy noise annoys an oyster; twelve twins twirled twelve twigs; Ed had edited it; strange strategic statistics; the ochre ogre ogled the poker.

Laughter is an effective nonverbal cue. How does laughter contribute to communication?

period of suspended sound. Pauses punctuate speech by setting off specific units of thought. They can also be used deliberately to provoke thought, develop curiosity or suspense, create a dramatic effect, or raise questions.

You may have heard the expression "Speech is silver; silence is golden." In other words, you often can communicate more with silence than you can with sound. Silence, including pauses, can indicate a willingness to listen. It also can communicate a willingness to defer to another speaker or to consider a matter carefully before speaking. Silence can be used to express approval, disapproval, or total apathy. It also can be used to demonstrate courtesy, respect, or profound emotion.

Laughter Laughter can be an extremely effective nonverbal cue. It can clearly convey humor, friendliness, acceptance, and good feelings. Depending on the context, however, it also can convey cruelty or sarcasm. Either way, laughter can add a wealth of meaning to

a conversation, discussion, or presentation. The key to using laughter is appropriateness and a few simple rules that are shown in the Communication Strategies checklist.

Vocalizations When you make sounds without forming words with meaning, you are vocalizing. Sounds such as sighs, whines, or throat clearing are all examples of vocalizations. Vocalizations send messages about a sender's feelings. A sigh, for example, may be interpreted as wishfulness, boredom, or fatigue. It also could indicate pleasure or complete relaxation. Random or overused vocalizations such as "um" or "ah" tend to clutter speech and interrupt a smooth and meaningful transfer of information from sender to receiver.

COMMUNICATION *Strategies*

SENDING POSITIVE MESSAGES WITH LAUGHTER

✓ Analyze the context. Is it appropriate to laugh in a particular situation?

✓ Listen to your laugh. Is it pleasant and controlled? Generally avoid overly loud, raucous laughter.

✓ Laugh *with* others, not at them.

✓ Learn to laugh at yourself. Lighten up and take little mistakes, miscues, and failures in stride.

✓ Use laughter to promote good-natured humor and goodwill.

To communicate more clearly, become aware of the vocalizations you tend to use. Analyze them and evaluate their effect on your communication. If you find that ineffective vocalizations clutter your speech, you can develop your awareness and try to eliminate them from your speech.

Voice Production

Voice can be a determining factor in a job interview, making a sale, or persuading a group to adopt your point of view and take action. It can project an image on the telephone, and it can determine whether others enjoy being around you or not. Remember that with analysis, work, and practice, almost everyone can have an effective voice that is easy to listen to. Some tips for improving the quality of your voice are found in the Communication Strategies checklist.

COMMUNICATION *Strategies*

IMPROVING VOICE

✓ Breathe deeply using the diaphragm to control exhaling air.

✓ Stand and sit tall when you speak to allow your sound waves to resonate, but be sure not to draw your shoulders upward to your neck. Let your shoulders remain relaxed and unmoving while you breathe.

✓ Speak from the diaphragm instead of the chest or head.

✓ Become aware of how sounds are properly shaped in the oral cavity.

✓ Create clear speech sounds by using the hard and soft palate.

COMMUNICATION *Strategies*

IMPROVING VOICE

Display a chart or overhead transparency showing the diaphragm, lungs, nasal cavity, and other parts of the vocal apparatus. Discuss the role of each part in creating voice quality. Ask volunteers to model the various techniques listed in the chart. Have each volunteer first speak while breathing, sitting, standing, or shaping sounds incorrectly, then repeat the message using correct technique. Have the class describe differences they hear. Provide pairs of similar sounding words (such as *battle/paddle, sinker/singer, noose/news, cease/seize, medal/metal, few/view, owe/hoe, witch/which*) and have students practice saying them clearly. Have listeners write the words, so that speakers get feedback on how well they did. **L2**

■ **Visual Instruction**

Answer Voice production can determine how well you do in an interview or a persuasive argument, whether others enjoy being around you, and how effective your skills are on the telephone.

■ **Members of a choir must be aware of voice production.** How can voice production impact one's communication success?

REAL-WORLD CONNECTION

Professional Singers Explain that singers perform breathing and articulation exercises daily, in addition to constantly monitoring their posture. Through training, they are able to enrich and even transform their tone, pitch, range, and other voice elements to develop a professional singing voice.

Activity Have students watch videos of a number of singing professionals, from opera stars to country music stars, and read articles about their training. Invite students to share what they learned with classmates.

Work Wardrobes

Canvass students to find out who have jobs. Invite working students to describe appropriate dress for their work. Invite all students to describe how the adults they know dress for work. Match professions with wardrobe details in a chart on the board until students are able to see a pattern of acceptable dress codes for such major divisions as business administration, restaurant service, sales, and so on. Point out that excessive amounts of jewelry and scents and poor grooming are not acceptable in any job. **L2**

BUSINESS BRIEF

Dress for Success

Mr. McCarthy of McCarthy & Company, a national firm providing career-transition assistance for the corporate world, recommends two tailor-made suits for the interview process. Of course, the suits also form the basis for the employment wardrobe. He advises business professionals to "dress each day as if you were expecting to run into and chat with the president of the company."

BODY TALK AS NONVERBAL COMMUNICATION

In addition to voice, another type of nonverbal communication is body talk. If voice is the nonverbal language of sound, body talk is the nonverbal language of silence. Body talk is the visual messages we send with our physical presence. It includes the following factors:

- personal appearance
- kinesics
- movement and gesture
- facial communication

Personal Appearance

What do you first notice when you are introduced to someone new? Studies indicate that most people respond first to what they see (body talk and environmental cues); second, to what they hear (voice); and third, to what they understand (words and other nonverbal cues we process as messages).

Because we base so much of our first impressions on what we see, personal appearance can have a great impact on communication. In fact, some aspects of appearance can tend to block out other messages. For instance, an interviewer might be so distracted by an applicant's inappropriate attire that he or she cannot concentrate on the applicant's answers.

For this reason, remember to "watch your nonverbals" when interacting in professional and social contexts. In these situations, making a good impression and conveying a professional image can be vital to your success.

Dress Your choices about how you dress can substantially influence the way others view and respond to you. Because of this,

your attire can add to or detract from the image you want to project in social and professional contexts.

A major factor to keep in mind is that appropriate dress for professional and social situations depends to a large extent on an organization's culture. Organizational expectations for attire may be carefully laid out in employee policy manuals or may be part of your employee orientation and training. On the other hand, clothing choices may be left up to your own best judgment. In either case, you will want to project a positive, professional image to others at all times.

It is important to note that clothing need not be brand-new or expensive to be appropriate and professional. Rather, it should be well maintained and in good taste. Three concepts to keep in mind when dressing professionally are *classic, clean,* and *conservative.*

Of course, not all workplaces require a classic or conservative style. Many creative fields allow or even encourage more expressive forms of dress. For instance, an advertising agency, a contemporary art gallery, or any fashion-related business may set different standards for personal appearance on the job. Keep in mind that appropriate dress depends to a large extent on organizational culture and protocol.

Grooming Grooming, as shown in **Figure 5–4**, can be very important to your professional image. It shows others whether or not you take pride in your appearance. It also implies that you want to look and be your best—and, therefore, are likely to be a conscientious, responsible worker.

Hair Hair should always be clean and, in most cases, conservatively styled. The classic hairstyle for men typically is a short haircut with short sideburns. For women, classic hairstyles are typically neatly trimmed and well styled or pulled away from the face. Fad

---

CRITICAL THINKING ACTIVITY

Just because an employer does not provide a dress code does not mean that the employer does not assume employees will dress to a certain standard. He or she may expect a newly hired person to observe other employees and conclude what type of dress is appropriate. Group students and give each group a job and workplace description (for example, field representative for a seed and agricultural chemical company, sales clerk in a fashionable clothing store, computer consultant for a national corporation). Each group is to decide on the corporate culture for their firm and dress accordingly. Have the class observe each group's clothing and accessories and explain how they would dress for an interview at this company.

Figure 5–4 *Personal Appearance: Grooming*

haircuts and unnatural hair colors should be avoided in all but the most unconventional organizations.

If you are in doubt about the norms for hairstyle or hair color for a job that you want, it may be wise to investigate the organizational culture as part of your interview preparation. Ignoring organizational or community norms can lead to negative stereotyping, which may ultimately keep you from getting a job or may cause you problems at work. The general rule is to choose a neat, simple hairstyle that is becoming to you and does not get in your way as you work.

Face Facial grooming should follow the same guidelines. If you are a male, observe whether sideburns, mustaches, and beards are worn in your workplace. If they aren't, they may be inappropriate even if they are not officially forbidden. In many workplaces, the less facial hair the better.

If you are a female, facial grooming should consist of conservative makeup styles and colors. If you are in doubt, observe the makeup choices of the most successful employees in the organization. Then, use these standards as a basis for making choices of your own.

For either gender, multiple piercings or visible tattoos may be unacceptable in a workplace. As a general rule, females should wear only one earring per ear. For males, earrings may or may not be appropriate, depending on the company. For both genders, any other piercings should be left unadorned while at work. Many businesses require that tattoos remain covered while employees are on the job.

All of these guidelines relate to conveying a professional appearance to employers, coworkers, and the public. However, body talk goes far beyond hair, face, and clothing. It also includes the physical presence you command. How you sit, stand, and move also has an impact on the image you project.

Kinesics

Kinesics refers to the use of the body in communication. It typically is the first thing people think of when they hear the term "body language" or "body talk." It is the nonverbal messages we send with our bodies.

Understanding Nonverbal Communication **153**

Hair
Bring to class and display images that illustrate changes in popular (but not shock value) hairstyles for men and women over several decades. Guide students to see that, while hairstyles may vary, keeping hair neat, clean, and healthy is a constant in looking well groomed. **L1**

Communication Tip
If you have trouble coming up with a way to use gestures in your presentation, try adding phrases like "on the other hand" or talking about how many points you have made or how large or small something is.

Appearance Choices
Many schools have a dress code or policy. In addition, grooming requires a minimum standard of cleanliness. Ask students to do a self-evaluation of their own appearances. Encourage them to consider the dos and don'ts of their appearances based on dress codes, grooming standards, and personal choices. Do they conform to basic grooming standards? What message does their appearance send about them? Would they like to change the message? How could they change the message? Suggest that students develop a checklist for checking their appearance every day before they leave for school. **L2**

MEETING INDIVIDUAL NEEDS
MULTIPLE LEARNING STYLES

Visual-Spatial Appearance is important to many teens. Take advantage of their natural investment in looking their best by having them create visuals that illustrate the dress, hairstyle, and accessories that establish various types of image. Discuss with students ways they acquire "data" about what articles to combine to create a suitable outfit.

Activity Have students locate or draw pictures showing the total look suitable for specific jobs and occasions and assemble them on a poster. You may wish to have students select the subject or assign one to each student. Examples might include president of a greeting card corporation, independent CPA, an athlete accepting an award from a charity, and a financial officer delivering the annual report for stockholders.

Effects of Posture

Explain that good posture is achieved by properly aligning body parts relative to one another. Good posture helps one move with ease and prevents injury to bones, muscles, and ligaments in addition to projecting a positive image. Point out that achieving good posture requires becoming aware of the body parts (head, chest/torso, pelvis/hips, legs, feet), thinking of them as separate blocks of weight, and learning how to align them directly on top of one another. Ask students to find a reference (text or physical education teacher, for example) and learn correct positioning for each body part. Have students demonstrate proper placement and balance and contrast poor posture for the class. **L2**

Visual Instruction

Answer A gesture is a movement of any part of the body that reinforces a message or substitutes for speech.

Grammar Tip

Gerunds are -ing forms of verbs that function as nouns. In the sentence "Sitting tall creates much the same effect," the subject is a gerund.

The speaker above draws the audience's attention with a gesture. **What is a gesture?**

Posture Generally, a straight but relaxed posture sends a message of confidence and purpose. Standing tall as you enter a room, speak to a client or coworker, or make a point in a discussion can help you create an image that says, "I have everything under control." Good posture not only makes your clothes fit better, but it also gives you an air of confidence, poise, and immediacy.

Sitting tall creates much the same effect. The receptionist who sits tall at his or her desk can easily use direct eye and facial communication with customers and clients. Such direct contact is more difficult when a seated person stays slumped over his or her work. Good sitting posture also helps prevent much of the fatigue tension in the shoulders and back that often accompanies desk jobs.

Muscular Tone and Tension Your comfort level in a given situation generally is revealed through your muscular tone and tension. These nonverbal signals send a variety of messages about your feelings, emotional state, and level of well-being.

Have you ever been advised to "settle down" or "loosen up" when you were feeling tense about something? Maybe you have commented that a friend was "uptight" about an upcoming interview or test. Such expressions illustrate how body tone and tension reveal our emotions. Taut muscles, a stiff neck, and jerky movements may indicate that you are stressed or ill at ease. Muscles that are more relaxed may indicate that you are comfortable and in control of the situation, confident and poised.

Analyzing Your Own Signals You can learn to be more aware of your own muscular tone and tension. Pain at the base of your neck or between your shoulders can indicate that you need to take a break and relax. In addition, feedback from others may give you clues about whether or not you are sending messages about being open and friendly.

If you think you tend to send messages of anger, tension, or fatigue, you can learn some simple relaxation techniques to help you convey a more positive image. You can use these at your desk or before a presentation to eliminate tension. If tension or anxiety is a chronic problem, you will need to investigate more complex techniques.

REAL-WORLD CONNECTION

Dance and Mime Dancers, mimes, and pantomimes learn numerous techniques for controlling movement and gestures in order to communicate specific ideas and emotions. Discuss ways that different dancers students have seen express feelings or send messages. Ask students to explain why pantomime involves so many subtle gestures. *(It cannot rely on words to assist in giving meaning.)*

Activity Ask students to interview dance or theater instructors to learn specific movement techniques that they can explain to the class. You may want to suggest that presenters locate or make a videotape in order to demonstrate the concepts they present. Have audience members give feedback about what they learned so that presenters can evaluate their effectiveness.

Movement and Gestures

Imagine participating in a meeting at work. You are professionally dressed and groomed, relaxed, standing tall, and projecting a confident professional image. However, you can shatter this image in an instant with uncontrolled, overly aggressive, or hesitant movement and gestures.

Movement Movement generally refers to gait. Gait describes the way you walk or move from one place to another. Studies show that gait can reveal a great deal of information about an individual's mood and attitude. Practicing a confident gait can help you project a positive image. You can begin by standing tall and moving with assurance and poise. Try not to make overly aggressive and long strides, shuffle or drag your feet, or make many hesitant movements.

Gestures A gesture is a movement of any part of the body that reinforces another message or acts as a substitute for speech. For instance, tapping the foot may suggest nervousness or impatience. Holding both hands palm-up at shoulder level can mean "Who knows?" or "I don't get it." A wink, a nod, a wave, or any other of a wide variety of movements can send intentional or unintentional messages that affect communication.

It is important to note that gestures tend to be highly cultural in nature. For example, in the United States, a nod of the head usually indicates agreement or consent. In parts of Greece, Turkey, and some other countries, however, nodding the head means "no."

One problem with gestures is that they often develop into personal mannerisms that can become distracting or annoying to others. You may know someone who repeatedly points his or her index finger to emphasize a point or continually nods his or her head in agreement while listening to others speak.

interNET
ACTIVITY

Nonverbal Communication Online Computer-mediated communication is considered an impersonal channel of communication because so few nonverbal cues are available. As a result, many conventions and symbols have been developed by computer users to illustrate the emotions that accompany their writing. Typing in capital letters, for example, is considered shouting. Symbols added to the written text such as ;-), a wink, are called *emoticons.* Do an online search using the term *emoticons.* Compile a list of at least ten of these symbols and their meanings and share them with the rest of the class.

Perhaps you know someone who uses "empty," or meaningless, gestures such as smoothing his or her clothes, straightening his or her hair, fidgeting, making doodles on notepads, or playing with pencils or other small objects. In these instances, this person has performed the movement so often, he or she is no longer conscious of using the gesture at all.

To become more aware of any gestures you may be overusing, carry on a conversation with a friend in front of a mirror. Watch your reflection to see if there are any mannerisms you would like to eliminate. Then, practice speaking without them. Eventually, you can break old habits and eliminate unnecessary gestures from your communication. You also may want to add certain gestures to bring interest and clarity to your communication.

Understanding Nonverbal Communication **155**

interNET
ACTIVITY

Nonverbal Communication Online
Students' responses may include the following emoticons:

:-)	Smile; happiness
: (or : - (	Frown; sadness
:)	Have a nice day
;-)	Wink; denotes pun or sly joke
:-o	Yelling or screaming or shock
:-()	Can't or won't stop talking
:-D	Big, delighted grin
:-P	Sticking out your tongue
:-} or :-]	Sarcastic smile
%-)	Confused but happy
%-(	Confused and unhappy
:'-(	Crying
:'-)	Crying happy tears
*	Kiss
{} or []	Hug

Communication Tip

Presenting a serious subject with a big smile or suggesting enthusiasm when your face is blank sends a confusing message. Practice your speeches before a mirror to help you check how well your facial expressions match your thoughts.

Comedic Gestures

Comedians who do impressions of other people often incorporate into their impressions movements and gestures associated with that person. Many people have distinctive mannerisms or ways of doing things. Encourage each student to study someone he or she knows—a classmate or family member, for example. Ask them to watch for distinctive gestures or ways of moving that they can associate with the person. Ask students to identify the gestures or movements of the person and the contexts in which they are used. **L2**

MEETING INDIVIDUAL NEEDS

MULTIPLE LEARNING STYLES

Bodily-Kinesthetic Students who enjoy expressing themselves through physical motion should excel in showing how movement, gesture, and facial expression communicate ideas and feelings without words.

Activity Have students make up situations to be acted out without speaking, such as walking on ice, playing a game of table tennis, and warming yourself by a campfire on a cold night, and summarize them on 3" x 5" cards. Ask each student to draw a card, take a minute to decide how to act it out, then give a thirty-second role play, with audience members guessing the scenario and the actor's feelings about it.

Eye Contact

Ask students to estimate how much of the time they maintain eye contact in the following situations:

Talking with a parent

Talking with a close friend

Answering a question in class

Talking with the boss

Have them check their habits of eye contact for a day as they socialize and work with others, summarizing what they learn in journal form. You may want to suggest that students rate themselves—*Effective eye contact, Some eye contact, Little eye contact*—and write a goal for improving this communication skill. **L2**

Communication Tip

In conversation, it is best to avoid extremes of eye contact. Too much is distracting; not enough communicates lack of interest.

DID **Y**OU **K**NOW?

Research has shown that in two-person conversations, speakers gaze at their listeners an average of 38 to 41 percent of the total conversation time. Listeners look at speakers 62 to 75 percent of the total time.

Facial Communication

Next to vocal characteristics, facial expression may be the most noticeable and important aspect of nonverbal communication. Certainly, it can display a wider range of emotions more accurately and immediately than any other form of body talk. Expressions such as "I never forget a face," "You should have seen the look on your face," or "Put on your game face," all emphasize the fact that people tend to be very aware of faces and their important role in communication.

Many times, facial expressions may last only a split second. Yet, even in that short period of time, they can communicate some of our most subtle and complex feelings. Like other aspects of nonverbal communication, facial expressions are highly personal and cultural. However, in the United States, many of the more obvious facial expressions tend to be interpreted in a similar manner.

Eye Communication In communication, the eyes are capable of sending powerful nonverbal messages. People use the eyes to make contact with others, to maintain and regulate interaction, and to provide space or distance when others get too close or a situation becomes overly emotional or intense.

Eye communication is strongly influenced by culture. In the United States, many communicators value direct, personal eye contact. You may have been told by an adult, "Look at me when I talk to you." You may have heard someone say, "I don't think he was telling the truth. He wouldn't even look me in the eye." However, children of Native American,

■ **Facial communication involves expressions like the ones shown.** How do facial expressions help one communicate?

MULTIPLE LEARNING STYLES

MEETING INDIVIDUAL NEEDS

Intrapersonal Students who prefer working independently can show their understanding of nonverbal communication concepts by keeping a learning log.

Activity Encourage students to make a conscious effort to observe ways in which people around them communicate through their personal appearance, body language, and use of space. Ask that they keep a daily log or diary of their observations and thoughts about how other people interpret these signals. Students might draw from their journals to write as an extra-credit project a short story about nonverbal communication.

African, Asian, or Hispanic descent may have been taught to look down when addressing elders to demonstrate respect.

Many people believe that the eyes are a form of "window" to a person's inner intentions and feelings. Therefore, great importance is often placed on eye communication. The messages you send with your eyes most certainly will be interpreted as your "true" feelings about yourself and your interpersonal relationships.

Eye Communication Importance

Eye communication tends to be very important in professional and social contexts. Making direct eye contact often will be viewed as a sign of honesty and credibility. Avoiding eye contact may be seen as a sign of dishonesty or an effort to hide certain feelings. Because these assumptions are so widespread, learning to use eye communication appropriately can be the difference between success and failure in some situations.

Eye communication is an important aspect of body talk. However, body talk—and voice, as you learned earlier—are not the only ways people send nonverbal messages. The way we alter or work within our surroundings also says something about us.

ENVIRONMENTAL CUES AS NONVERBAL COMMUNICATION

Environmental cues can reveal much about a person's feelings and relationships and can be vital to projecting a positive professional image. Some of the environmental aspects of nonverbal communication may surprise you. For example, the way you use space, distance, and territoriality communicates messages about you and your relationships. How you manage time and allocate time to others also

sends nonverbal messages. Similarly, touch, color, and fragrance communicate much about your feelings and relationships.

Spatial Communication

Spatial communication refers to your perception and use of space. Using space appropriately in professional and social contexts involves balancing personal and interpersonal needs with efficiency. Individual perceptions and needs related to space and territory can vary widely.

In addition, the kind of space you need to do your work well may vary from the needs of other people. Regardless of the situation, human beings tend to have definite spatial perceptions, needs, and preferences. How we use space and observe and respect the spatial needs of others is an important factor in working with other people. It can be a source of conflict or, if used appropriately, can help to promote positive relationships.

Space and Distance

Like other aspects of nonverbal communication, the way you use space and distance is highly personal and strongly influenced by your cultural background. Generally speaking, however, there are four types of distances that describe spatial communication, as illustrated in **Figure 5–5** on the next page.

Intimate Distance Intimate distance is up to eighteen inches from your body. You might use this space when you make a quiet or confidential comment to someone or when you carry on a private conversation. You also may work within your intimate distance when sharing a book, working closely with one of your friends, or giving someone a hug.

Because intimate distance is the area closest to the body, communication within this range tends to be very personal. Most people

Understanding Nonverbal Communication **157**

How Close Is Too Close?

Explain that we all have an invisible "territory" around us that we consider private. Whom we allow to invade this territory, how closely, and for how long says much about how we feel about them and react to them. Ask students to work in groups to discuss and role-play reactions to each of the following persons invading your intimate space:

a new acquaintance   a boss
an interviewer   a coworker
a family member   a close friend
a classmate you know casually

Ask the class to debate which range is a comfort zone of spatial communication for each of these. **L3**

Communication Tip

Since moving in too close causes embarrassment and discomfort, it hinders communication. Be aware of your use of space so that you don't make others uncomfortable.

MULTIPLE LEARNING STYLES

MEETING INDIVIDUAL NEEDS

Logical-Mathematical Discuss with students the dynamics of spatial communication in a classroom. Have them consider ways their feelings and reactions in your classroom are affected by the space and its arrangement. Relate this concept to the precise dimensions of your room and its setup by having students measure the classroom.

Activity Ask students to reproduce the shape of the classroom to scale using graph paper. They should show the positions of desks, tables, chairs, and other furniture, measuring the space that separates them. Then, direct students to create color-coded zones around their desk showing intimate distance, personal distance, social distance, and public distance.

Mark That Distance

To help students visualize the differences in the spatial lengths of intimate, personal, social, and public distances, have students use measuring tools and masking tape to mark the classroom floor for each type of distance. Discuss which ranges overlap and why. Ask students to give examples of relationships in which each distance might be appropriate. **L1**

Adjusting Space

Discuss with students times when they may have felt uncomfortable because someone had entered their comfort zones or were at too great a distance in intimate, personal, social, or public situations. Ask them to recall or suggest ways to adjust the space so that they were or could be more comfortable. *(Students may suggest backing up when someone stands too close to them in a personal situation, for example.)* **L2**

feel uncomfortable with someone in their intimate distance unless they have invited him or her into that space.

Personal Distance Personal distance extends from eighteen inches to four feet from the body. This area is your own space in which to move freely.

Whom do you allow to enter your personal space and under what circumstances? Typically, people allow friends, family members, and some coworkers to enter their personal space comfortably. However, if someone else gets too close, you may feel that he or she is "invading your space." If, for example, you begin to feel uncomfortable when a salesperson or other stranger approaches, it may be because he or she has come into your personal space.

Social Distance Social distance extends from about four feet to twelve feet from the body. This distance still allows communicators to see and hear one another easily, while maintaining enough distance to avoid highly personal interaction. Social distance is logically the most appropriate distance for interpersonal and small group interactions in professional and social contexts.

Social distance shows respect for a person's individual space when a close relationship has not yet

been established. Therefore, it often is used for making and acknowledging interpersonal introductions, business conversations, and informal presentations.

Public Distance Public distance extends from about twelve feet to twenty-five feet or more. It is far less interpersonal than any of the

■ **Figure 5–5 Spatial Communication**

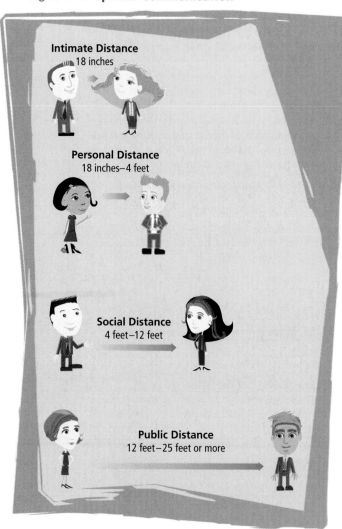

Intimate Distance
18 inches

Personal Distance
18 inches–4 feet

Social Distance
4 feet–12 feet

Public Distance
12 feet–25 feet or more

MULTIPLE LEARNING STYLES

Visual-Spatial Television programs often provide examples of space and distance relationships and violations of such relationships.

Activity Have students watch a courtroom or police show on television. Ask them to analyze how characters in the show use spatial relationships. For example, in a courtroom scene, a lawyer questioning a witness may get closer and closer to a witness as the questioning becomes more intense. Ask students to identify examples of the use and violation of space by characters and analyze what the motivation for the use or violation of space might be. Encourage students to summarize their analyses in a written report and share their findings with classmates.

other types of distances. Public distance is most often used for formal presentations. At a public distance, special lighting and sound-projection equipment may be needed to allow the presenter and audience to see and hear one another clearly.

Presenters sometimes choose to come out from behind a podium or down off a stage to achieve more personal interaction with an audience. However, depending on the kind of meeting or program and the size of the audience, public distance may be most appropriate for a formal presentation.

Violating Distance Norms Using distance inappropriately can create embarrassment, discomfort, and conflict. For instance, asking a personal question at a public distance and expecting a public answer containing private information can cause everyone in the area to feel uncomfortable. By the same token, invading a stranger's personal or intimate space may make him or her uncomfortable, defensive, or afraid. As a general rule, fit your use of space to the context of the situation.

Territory Sometimes, people will identify a space or territory, claim it, and protect it as their own. You probably have done this yourself at some point. Have you ever entered a classroom to find someone sitting in "your" chair? Even though there may have been no prescribed seating plan, you might have selected a space and then occupied the same place every day. Therefore, you felt it was your territory.

Workers often personalize their cubicles or office spaces by arranging them a certain

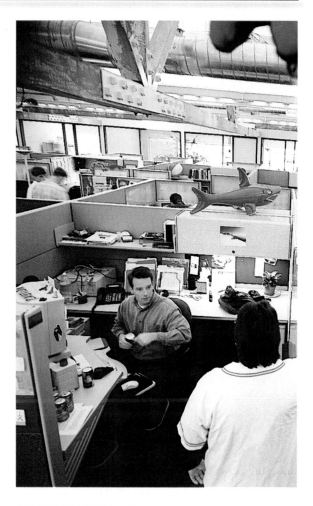

Employees in an office setting usually personalize their office space. **Why?**

way, decorating them with art or photos from home, and otherwise adding their own special touches. This nonverbal behavior makes it very clear that "This space is mine." They may also claim a certain chair for staff meetings or a certain coffee mug in the break room and may become offended if someone intrudes on their territory.

Understanding Nonverbal Communication **159**

Territorial Claims

After they read pages 157–161, have students close their texts and write explanations of spatial communication, territory, and time communication as they relate to them personally. Ask them to describe a space they have claimed as their own territory (such as a locker or a bedroom) and how they have personalized it. Invite students to share their writings with the class. **L2**

■ Visual Instruction

Answer to establish their own territory

> **DID YOU KNOW?**
> Research has shown that, used correctly, color can increase motivation, concentration, learning, retention, and recall by 55 to 78 percent.

Close Encounters

Discuss with students situations in which people may have their personal spaces invaded but accept it because of the situation. For example, often personal space is invaded in an airplane, on a crowded bus, and in a ticket line. Ask students to consider ways that people adjust to such situations. *(Possible answers include keeping arms close to one's body, looking out a window, leaning toward someone they know rather than a stranger, indicating that one does not wish to engage in conversation by reading or doing paperwork.)*

INTERDISCIPLINARY CONNECTION

Life Science Wild animals operate under stricter rules of territoriality than people do. Understanding how this concept works for animals, such as the wolves, birds, and even house pets, can help students understand its significance in the human community.

Activity Assign a group of interested students to research territorial behavior among various species of animals. Each student can choose a separate species to research. The group may be able to create or rent a video that demonstrates reactions when one member of the species invades another's territory. After the group's presentation, open the floor to discussion about similarities in human territoriality.

Shake on It

Have each student shake hands with all other students in class. Ask students to describe different handshakes they experienced. How did they react to each? Write the following types of handshakes on the board. Have students summarize what each most likely communicates.

Palm-down thrust: force other person's palm into lower position *(denotes control)*

Glove (or politician's) handshake: envelops hand with both hands *(intends to show trust and honesty but effect often opposite; too intimate for stranger)*

Elbow grasp: grab hand in one hand, elbow in other *(denotes suspicion, mistrust; too intimate for first meeting)*

Dead fish: cold, clammy, limp *(suggests weak character or boredom, lack of interest)*

Fingertip grab: miss hand and catch fingers *(suggests lack of confidence)*
L3

Communication Tip

A good, firm handshake inspires confidence, but all the previously described handshakes should be avoided.

Violating Territory Norms Sometimes, real hostilities over territory can develop among coworkers. Imagine how a secretary might feel, for example, if coworkers often borrowed the stapler from his or her desk without asking first. What if they periodically opened the secretary's desk drawers to look for needed supplies? He or she probably would become annoyed or even angry because the coworkers were not respecting the secretary's space. In fact, when you are visiting coworkers' workspaces, it is considered good manners even to keep your gaze averted from their computer screen and from papers on their desk unless the purpose of your visit is to discuss those matters. To develop positive interpersonal relationships in the workplace, it is important to respect others' privacy and personal territory.

Sending Nonverbal Messages How you use and maintain your territory or workspace sends a variety of messages about you. Your use and control of space can give others any of the following messages:

- **I'm organized.** When books, papers, and other materials are systematically arranged, you send a message that you are in control of your space and are well organized.

- **I'm disorganized.** A messy desk or workspace filled with random papers, trash, and other clutter sends a message that you may be struggling with work and are not well organized.

- **I take pride in my space.** Keeping your office or workspace neat and personalizing it show that you want your space to reflect all your best qualities. In some organizations, there may be policies about what may or may not be displayed in a work area; however, within the available limits, you can nearly always make your mark.

- **I don't like it here.** A messy office or one that looks exactly as it did the day you moved in tells others that you don't value that space and don't care to make it your own.

- **You're welcome in my space.** Often, a person will use a bowl of candy, a comfortable chair, or some novelty item to make people want to spend time in his or her workspace.

Touch To touch or not to touch has become a critical question for people in the workplace and social organizations. In recent years, rules and norms have taken a definite shift toward "Don't touch." Touching can be considered harassment and intimidation and can cause serious emotional and legal issues.

However, this does not exclude all forms of touch. Certainly, a firm handshake can be considered an appropriate gesture for both men and women. The handshake has become a standard gesture used in professional and social contexts for making and acknowledging introductions and for extending congratulations or recognition. In many professional and social situations, a handshake is usually considered more appropriate than hugs, pats, and other forms of contact.

Time Communication

In today's busy world, the excuse "I just didn't have time!" has become commonplace in professional and social contexts. When people fail to appear at meetings, carry out responsibilities, meet deadlines, or return calls, they often claim that they just didn't have enough time to do what was expected. In reality, these people may actually have had enough time, but they just managed it inappropriately.

MULTIPLE LEARNING STYLES

Visual-Spatial Students will better retain the concepts they take in visually and demonstrate by illustration.

Activity Have students look through magazines and clip pictures that illustrate messy or organized work spaces. Students can work in groups to categorize the pictures and write captions about what the use of space communicates.

Sending Messages with Time

How you manage time is a form of nonverbal communication. If you have a friend who is consistently late for dates or meetings, you may begin to wonder if that person cares about you very much. Similarly, if your employer pays you late every month, you probably will conclude that salary issues don't mean that much to him or her, and you may even look for another job.

How you use time sends strong messages about you, your perceptions of others, your relationships with them, and your attitude about responsibilities. Therefore, learning how to manage time can be vital to building a professional image and succeeding in professional and social contexts.

Time Management

As you begin learning to manage your time, consider this: Not everyone has the same amount of money, talent, or physical ability, but everyone has the same amount of time. We all have exactly twenty-four hours every day. How you use your time reflects your priorities and sends messages about your effectiveness as a student, an employee, and a communicator.

Second, try not to think of time as something that is constantly moving. Instead, think of it as an object that stays in one place. You can arrange its parts however you wish.

Arranging "Slices" of Time

If you begin to think of time as a kind of circle graph reflecting one twenty-four-hour day, as illustrated in **Figure 5–6,** you can start thinking of different activities as individual slices of the total pie. For instance, you probably need eight hours of sleep each day. So, one-third of your pie is already filled in, leaving you with sixteen hours. You probably also need about eight hours for work or school. That leaves eight hours for recreation, homework, household responsibilities, meals, and relationships.

Suddenly, managing your time sounds a lot like budgeting your money, doesn't it? The idea is the same for both. You have a limited amount of something, and you must arrange it carefully to get the most from it.

Noting Special Time Commitments

Once you have learned to arrange your time, it is important to make a note of special commitments such as meetings, appointments, and deadlines so you won't forget them. In professional and social contexts, it is vital not only to remember your commitments but also to be prompt and punctual.

Learning to Say "No"

If, after learning to manage your time, you still find yourself running behind schedule, you may need to make some changes. Consider whether you have too many time commitments. You might need to learn how to decline politely when others ask you to take on extra responsibilities. Alternatively, if you feel you must participate, you might say "I can do that, but I won't be able to get it done until next week." Knowing how to divide your time and stay within your limits is a major part of being a responsible friend, group member, or employee.

■ **Figure 5–6 Slices of Time**

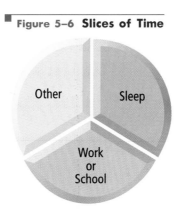

Understanding Nonverbal Communication **161**

Managing Your Time

Discuss with students the messages that are sent by
- being chronically late
- overscheduling yourself
- allowing interruptions when in conversation with others

Explain that many people are sometimes overwhelmed by all they have to do, but everyone has the same amount of time to budget. As a class, brainstorm ideas for managing time for priority activities. *(Students may suggest keeping a calendar with activities, homework, and work; prioritizing activities and eliminating less important ones; combining activities; making backup plans and staying flexible.)* Ask students to act on one or more of these suggestions and report the results. **L2**

Communication Tip

Provide students with a circle graph divided into twenty-four segments. Ask students to estimate how much time they spend on sleep, school, meals, recreation, homework, household and job responsibilities, and relationships. Have them block in these activities on the graph. Discuss what they learned from the graph and have them fill in a second one showing how they would prefer to use their time. **L2**

MEETING INDIVIDUAL NEEDS
INCLUSION STRATEGIES

Special Needs To stay on task, special-needs students need high-motivation materials that apply the concepts of the section to their daily lives.

Activity As a class, brainstorm a list of the "ten most important messages" to communicate to others. Post the list in the classroom and, as students read the section, apply the ideas about voice, body talk, and environment cues to these specific messages. How would students communicate them nonverbally? For example, have students demonstrate ways to use voice, facial expression, and body language to send the message "I am concerned about you."

Practice for the Workplace

Subtle Clues Ask students to list three personal artifacts that help define them. Have students decide what messages the artifacts send about them.

In order to minimize disruptions, assign one small group of students to each location. Each group can report results to the class.

(Students' responses to this exercise should demonstrate their understanding that each area's artifacts reflect the activities that take place there. Students should also be conscious of the effects of colors on each location.) **L2**

GLENCOE *Online*

For an additional Practice Lab for this section, have students visit the *Glencoe Communication Applications* Web site at **communicationapplications.glencoe.com.** Click on Communication Practice Lab 5–2. **L1**

Other Types of Environmental Cues

Besides distance, territory, touch, and time, you also send messages with other aspects of your surroundings. Think about how you personalize your room at home, your locker or backpack, even your own appearance. These environmental cues all say something special about you.

Artifacts and Objects Most people surround themselves with artifacts and objects that communicate a variety of messages. Artifacts are articles of adornment you use to decorate yourself or your surroundings. Jewelry and accessories are artifacts. Clothing may be considered an artifact. Pictures on walls, visual themes or motifs, trophies, favorite books, and posters all are artifacts people use to decorate their rooms and offices.

Objects include all the materials that you keep in your space or take with you to classes, meetings, presentations, or other events. A backpack and a notebook may be objects that stay with you all day at school. The way you maintain or personalize each of these sends messages about your personality, likes, and dislikes. A briefcase and date book may communicate that an employee is highly organized and professional. The personal photos

Figure 5–7 Cool and Warm Colors

Cool Colors

Warm Colors

162   *Glencoe Communication Applications*

Practice for the Workplace

Subtle Clues The artifacts that you surround yourself with are nonverbal clues to your interests and values. Other people assign meaning to the artifacts you display. The items in your backpack, your locker, your car, or your home reflect your interests and values. Professionals know that others will interpret the artifacts observed in their offices. For example, you would expect to find different artifacts in a dentist's office than you would in a travel agent's office.

BUSINESS PRACTICE *Activity*

Visit your school's main office, the gymnasium's office area, the cafeteria, the library, a science classroom, an art room, and the instrumental or vocal music room. Observe the artifacts found in each location. Report your observations and the interpretations of your findings to the class.

on a person's desk may indicate that he or she has a strong sense of home and family.

In social and professional contexts, objects and artifacts generally should be kept in good repair. They also should be attractively arranged and logically organized. As with dress, three key words to remember are *classic, clean,* and *conservative.* Keeping these things in mind will help you project the best possible image of the professional you.

Color What is your favorite color? Do you tend to buy clothes, artifacts, and objects in

EXTENDING THE CONTENT

Color and Mood Share the following information about colors and their effects with students— green: eases stress, helps gain self-respect, soothes anger; blue: helps overcome hurt, resolves conflict, helps self-acceptance; purple: helps accept responsibility, relaxes and soothes fears, helps tune in to inner voice; red: color of courage, self-esteem, sexual expression, mental clarity; orange: soothes anxiety, resolves conflicts, reveals emotions; yellow: resolves conflicts, contributes to feelings of harmony

Activity Have students note the colors used in various public places (for example, stores, offices, libraries, museums). Ask them to explain why these colors might have been used and what effects they may have on people who visit these places.

that color? Have you ever been attracted to a color because it was associated with a certain meaning or feeling?

Advertisers and manufacturers fully understand the nonverbal messages sent by color. Advertisers use color to grab your attention or to convey an overall feeling about a product. Fashion designers use color to attract attention and to create a specific effect with clothing. Decorators, lighting consultants, and others often use color to create a specific mood and atmosphere.

For example, interior designers sometimes use light blue walls or room accessories to create a calming effect. Soft, gold-toned lights may be used to evoke a warm feeling of home. Navy, gray, brown, and black tend to project a formal mood and, therefore, are most often chosen for formal professional attire. See **Figure 5–7** for a visual description of cool and warm colors in a spectrum.

Fragrance and Odor Of all the senses, the sense of smell is believed to provide the most direct link to the emotion center of the brain. It has great power to instantly evoke memories, feelings, and permanent impressions. In short, fragrance and odor can send powerful nonverbal messages.

In recent years, an entire industry has developed around so-called "aroma therapy." This is the intentional use of certain smells to promote relaxation, energy, comfort, or other emotional states. For instance, realtors often recommend that homeowners bake bread or an apple pie when a potential buyer is scheduled to visit because most people have fond memories of the smell of warm apple pie or freshly baked bread. The theory is that the aroma will provoke warm images of family and home and make the individual want to buy the house. In many cases, the theory seems to be effective.

Today, many businesses and meeting places deodorize the premises to avoid inappropriate or unpleasant responses. Unless you're in the food or fragrance business where smell could attract customers, business environments should, for the most part, be kept odor free. The same advice as that given for clothing and artifacts applies to the appropriate use of

COMMUNICATION PRACTICE LAB

Interpreting Messages from Color

To practice recognizing the nonverbal messages sent by different colors, follow these steps:

Step 1 Working in groups of three or four, choose one of the following objects and draw it five times on a sheet of white paper:
- an expressionless face
- a mid-length jacket
- a square sign on a signpost

Step 2 Color the first four objects on the sheet of paper these colors: red, blue, green, and yellow. Leave the last object white.

Step 3 As a group, discuss the nonverbal messages sent by each object. Below each, write what you think that color of object represents. For example, if you had drawn a red flower, you might have said it represents romance.

Step 4 As a class, discuss your interpretations of each object. How did color influence your interpretations? How might you use colors in other ways to communicate nonverbal messages?

Understanding Nonverbal Communication **163**

COMMUNICATION PRACTICE LAB

Interpreting Messages from Color

Have students follow the four steps in the Communication Practice Lab on this page to analyze the nonverbal messages sent by different colors. Guide the class to see that colors suggest meanings because we give them symbolic significance. They also have a psycho-biological impact causing physiological responses. **L1**

Student interpretations may include

Color	Face	Jacket	Sign
red	anger	firefighter jacket	stop; danger
blue	coldness	police uniform	hospital
green	jealousy	army uniform	highway info
yellow	sickness	raincoat	yield; caution
white	fright	lab coat	speed limit; parking

3 ASSESS

Assign Section 2 Assessment as a homework or in-class activity.

➊ Use *Interactive Tutor Self-Assessment Software* to review Section 2.

Section 5–2 Quiz

REAL-WORLD CONNECTION

Fragrances The detection and appreciation of various fragrances or odors varies from person to person. Students should find that many different odors emanate from places in their community and their homes.

Activity Suggest that students go on a fragrance/odor hunt in their community and around their homes. Students may find aromas emanating from the food courts or perfume counters at a mall and cooking and cleaning odors within the home. Have students record odors and fragrances they notice and note whether or not they found them appealing. They might also state why they did or did not find the odors appealing. Students might survey others to determine whether they agree with their assessments of the odors.

4 CLOSE

Have students reread the opening paragraph of the section. For each of the servers described, ask students to explain the voice, body talk, and environmental cues that communicate positively or negatively.

Extra-Credit Project

Ask students to pick one of the three types of nonverbal communication and create a video or display that illustrates how people respond to nonverbal cues, such as different voice qualities, eye contact, scents, and colors.

---

fragrance by individuals in professional and social contexts. Fragrance should be light, conservative, and sparingly used. Cleanliness and personal hygiene can prevent unpleasant odors. Remember that you don't want to project any smell that might cause you to alienate a client, lose a sale, or offend a boss or coworker.

Nonverbals: voice, body talk, and the use of environmental cues are powerful influences on the professional image you project. Remember, nonverbal cues represent about 90 percent of what you communicate. Using that 90 percent to convey positive, appropriate messages will help establish you as a competent communicator.

Section 2 Assessment

Visit the *Glencoe Communication Applications* Web site at **communicationapplications. glencoe.com** and click on **Self-Check and Study Guide 5.2** to review your understanding of creating a professional image through nonverbal communication.

Review Key Terms

1. Define each term and write it in a sentence: pitch, range, inflection, tone, rate, tempo, kinesics, artifacts.

Check Understanding

2. What are the characteristics of a positive professional image? Explain how you might demonstrate one of these characteristics using nonverbal skills.

3. What are the three main categories of nonverbal communication? Choose one category and describe how those types of nonverbal signals might affect communication between an interviewer and a job applicant.

4. Using the four characteristics of voice, describe how a person might contradict a spoken message with his or her nonverbal vocal cues.

5. **Synthesize** Describe an appropriate use of handshake, eye contact, space, and distance when meeting your new boss for the first time. What might be the overall effect of this behavior?

APPLICATION *Activity*

Enhancing Relationships Working with a partner, brainstorm a list of nonverbal cues and behaviors that put you at ease and make you feel closely bonded with another individual. Then, brainstorm a list of cues and behaviors that have the opposite effect. Finally, choose a topic and conduct a one-minute interaction that employs only those nonverbal behaviors that help enhance an interpersonal relationship. Share your conclusions as a class.

Section 2 Assessment Answers

1. Accept all reasonable sentences.
2. Confidence, poise, assertiveness, immediacy; answers should reflect appropriate nonverbal behaviors for students' chosen characteristics.
3. Voice, body talk, environmental cues; answers should reflect an understanding of nonverbal communication.
4. Answers should reflect logical ways a verbal message might be contradicted nonverbally.
5. A firm handshake displays confidence; direct eye contact conveys honesty and credibility; respecting the boss's personal space and maintaining a social distance show respect and may keep the boss from feeling uncomfortable in your presence. The overall effect might be one of competence and professionalism.

Application Activity Students may conclude that close range, using touch, laughter, relaxed posture, positive facial expression, and direct eye contact can enhance interpersonal relationships.

Communication Self-Assessment

Evaluating Your Nonverbal Communication Skills

How Do You Rate?

On a separate sheet of paper, use the key to respond to the following statements. Put a check mark at the end of each skill you would like to improve.

KEY: A Always   **R** Rarely
       U Usually   **N** Never
       S Sometimes

1. I know how to use body language and the sound of my voice to support what I say.
2. I try not to use nonverbal communication as a substitute for verbal communication.
3. When I am with people of a different culture, I try to learn all I can about their nonverbal communication customs.
4. I use confidence, poise, assertiveness, and immediacy to manage situations.
5. I use a variety of pitches, tones, and tempos when I speak.

6. In business settings, my dress and grooming are appropriate to the norms of the organization.
7. In tense situations, I use feed-forward statements or humor.
8. When I want to convey honesty and credibility, I use eye contact.
9. To avoid making other people feel uncomfortable, I respect their social, personal, and public space.
10. I manage my time commitments promptly and on schedule.

How Do You Score?

Review your responses. Give yourself 5 points for every A, 4 for every U, 3 for every S, 2 for every R, and 1 for every N. Total your points and evaluate your score.

41–50 Excellent You may be surprised to find out how much you can improve your skills.

31–40 Good In this course, you can learn ways to make your skills better.

21–30 Fair Practice applying the skills taught in this course.

1–20 Needs Improvement Carefully monitor your improvement as you work through this course.

Setting Communication Goals

If you scored Excellent or Good, complete Part A. If your score was Fair or Needs Improvement, complete Part B.

Part A   1. I plan to put the following ideas into practice:

       2. I plan to share the following information about communication with the following people:

Part B   1. The behaviors I need to change most are:

       2. To bring about these changes, I will take these steps:

Understanding Nonverbal Communication   **165**

Have students respond to the survey statements using the key provided, then evaluate their presentation organizational skills using the scoring rubric. Based on their scores, have students complete either Part A or B of the goal-setting activity.

Communication Journal Activity

Point out to students that to accomplish goals, one must make them specific and concrete and review them often to assess progress. Have students write specific goals in their Communication Journals.

Communication Tip

Remind the class that progress toward accomplishing their goals will come only with practice and encourage them to apply the skills in presentations.

CRITICAL THINKING ACTIVITY

Ask students to think of a person they know who is a great communicator. Have they ever analyzed how much of this person's effectiveness is due to nonverbal communication? Review the chapter headings, having students list nonverbal communication skills this person uses well. Ask students to use the survey on this page to evaluate those skills, substituting "he" or "she" for "I." Then, have students compare these results with their own. Where are they similar? Where do they differ most? Explain that by using this person as a role model, they may be able to improve their skills more quickly.

Communication
Through Writing

Writing a Business Letter

Objectives: To learn the format of a business letter; to compose a business letter

Teaching Suggestions and Strategies

Connection to the Workplace

Explain that, while most business letters are generated from the workplace, individuals also need to write business letters from time to time

- to inquire about or apply for jobs
- to order, return, or complain about purchases of goods or services
- to write letters to the editor
- to sell a service, an idea, or an object to someone

The ability to write a succinct, effective business letter is an advantage both in the workplace and in personal life.

Review the parts of the business letter, having students locate each part in the example on page 167 as they read. Use the overhead projector to display various styles for the body of the letter: pure block, block, and indented.

Writing a Business Letter

No matter what career path you follow, you will almost certainly be required to write a business letter at some point. A business letter is a tool that is used universally because it has many applications. A business letter can request information, serve as an introduction, resolve problems, or clarify issues. Use a business letter when the contents are too formal or detailed for an e-mail or telephone call. Refer to the sample on the next page as you read about the parts of a business letter described below.

The Heading The heading is the first element of a letter. It includes a date line, which usually follows the sender's name and mailing address. Put the heading at the top of the letter, even with the left margin. The lines within the heading should be single-spaced. Double-space only after the last line. Many companies have personalized stationery that shows the company name and address at the top of the page. If this is the case, you need only include the date after the address.

The Opening The opening includes the inside address, which is the address of the person or business designated to receive the letter, and the salutation, or greeting, which begins the letter.

This information, like the heading, should be even with the left margin of the paper. The opening should be spaced in the same way as the header.

The Body The most important part of the business letter is contained in the body. This is where the reader gets your message. The body is sometimes preceded by a subject line, which tells the recipient what the letter is about before he or she begins to read. Identify the purpose of the letter, then decide how you will proceed. If the purpose of your letter is to solve a problem, for example, you would first describe the problem, then provide a solution. The lines within each paragraph should be single-spaced, but you should double-space between paragraphs. Many business letters use a block style. This means that the paragraphs within the body are not indented. While the block style is very popular, indenting the paragraphs is also acceptable as a style choice.

The Closing The closing signals the end of the letter. It first shows respect for the recipient, then it gives the writer's name and title. The most commonly used closing is *Sincerely*. Other closings are *Regards* and *Very truly yours*. Triple-space after the closing and type the signature block. The person whose name is typed here will sign the letter. If you are enclosing additional material, write the word

For additional information about business writing, see the *Guide to Business Communication* section of the Communication Survival Kit in the Appendix.

MEETING INDIVIDUAL NEEDS

INCLUSION STRATEGIES

Less-Proficient Readers Students who have difficulty reading may struggle with spelling and grammar in producing original writing. Use a collection of student-generated business letters from your past classes or from another teacher's class for students to analyze.

Activity Provide students with copies of several business letters. Have students label each part and note the style used to format the letter. Then, ask students to write a business letter, inputting it on computer. Students can check spelling and grammar using their word-processing programs, then exchange letters with their partners for proofreading.

Communication Through Writing

enclosures followed by the number of items to be sent. List the names of any persons who will receive copies of the letter. Make sure the appropriate person signs the letter.

Proofreading the Letter Check your letter for spelling and grammar mistakes. Make sure the format of the letter is correct. Make changes only if they are necessary to improve the appearance of the letter.

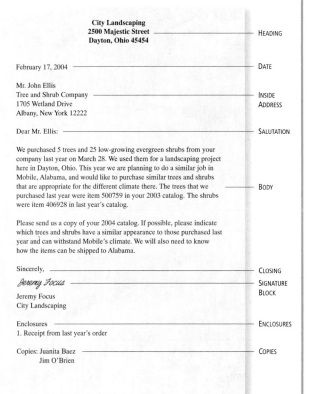

City Landscaping
2500 Majestic Street
Dayton, Ohio 45454 ———— HEADING

February 17, 2004 ———— DATE

Mr. John Ellis
Tree and Shrub Company ———— INSIDE
1705 Wetland Drive   ADDRESS
Albany, New York 12222

Dear Mr. Ellis: ———— SALUTATION

We purchased 5 trees and 25 low-growing evergreen shrubs from your company last year on March 28. We used them for a landscaping project here in Dayton, Ohio. This year we are planning to do a similar job in Mobile, Alabama, and would like to purchase similar trees and shrubs that are appropriate for the different climate there. The trees that we ———— BODY
purchased last year were item 500759 in your 2003 catalog. The shrubs were item 406928 in last year's catalog.

Please send us a copy of your 2004 catalog. If possible, please indicate which trees and shrubs have a similar appearance to those purchased last year and can withstand Mobile's climate. We will also need to know how the items can be shipped to Alabama.

Sincerely, ———— CLOSING
Jeremy Focus ———— SIGNATURE
                    BLOCK
Jeremy Focus
City Landscaping

Enclosures ———— ENCLOSURES
1. Receipt from last year's order

Copies: Juanita Baez ———— COPIES
        Jim O'Brien

WRITING *Activity*

Assume that you are a work-study student with an automotive firm and your supervisor asks you to write a letter that he will sign. The letter is about an automobile recall. Be sure to include all of the points listed below.

- Your supervisor is John Anders, Assistant Vice President.
- The company for which you work is Detroit Motor Company, 99 Automobile Lane, Detroit, Michigan 48222.
- A problem has been discovered regarding the black, maroon, and navy paint used on all models.
- The defective paint was used on vehicles manufactured between March 1 and November 22, 2000. The paint may seriously crack, which could cause the cars to rust.
- Apologize to the customer for any inconveniences caused by the problem.
- Offer a free repainting job to all owners of these cars. Ask them to return their cars to the nearest Detroit Motor Company Service Center.
- The letter should be ready to send on December 15 of this year.

GRAMMAR PRACTICE

Capitals and Punctuation in a Business Letter
Have students capitalize and punctuate correctly.

mr. robert ludlow	*(Mr. Robert Ludlow)*	dear mr. ludlow	*(Dear Mr. Ludlow:)*
emagic corp.	*(Emagic Corp.)*	thank you for your . . .	*(Thank . . .)*
55 technology way	*(Technology Way)*	very truly yours	*(Very . . . yours,)*
chicago, il 60606	*(Chicago, IL)*	maya smithfield	*(Maya Smithfield)*

Communication Through Writing

Teaching Activity
Explain to students that the reason for a business letter is to communicate efficiently; time is valuable. Ideas, information, or requests should be phrased as directly and succinctly as possible. It is a good idea to edit business letters after composing them, asking yourself, "Is my purpose clearly stated? Is every sentence I have included necessary to make my point? Would my point be more effective if more sentences used active voice? Is my language correct and my attitude courteous and professional? Does the letter follow format correctly? Is it appealing to the eye and easy to read?"

Have students read the sample letter on this page and answer these questions as though they had written the letter. Ask them to evaluate the letter's tone, word choices, and length in view of its purpose.

WRITING *Activity*

Students' letters should be dated December 15 of the current year, and include a made-up opening. The body of the letter should consist of at least three paragraphs: one to explain the problem and its time frame, one to apologize (and assure of company integrity), and one to offer the solution. Closings may vary.

Grammar Tip

All the words in the heading and opening and the first word in the closing are capitalized. A colon follows the salutation of a business letter; a comma follows the closing.

Additional Resources
Appendix, "Guide to Business Communication"

Glencoe Writer's Assistant CD-ROM

Glencoe Interactive Grammar Software

Grade 9 Writer's Choice, Lesson 6.5

GLENCOE TECHNOLOGY

MindJogger Videoquiz

Use *MindJogger* to review the Chapter 5 content.

Reviewing Key Terms

1. h
2. g
3. a
4. c
5. b
6. f
7. e
8. d

Visit the *Glencoe Communication Applications* Web site at **communicationapplications. glencoe.com** and click on **Chapter 5 Activity** for additional practice in nonverbal communication.

Reviewing Key Terms

Read each definition. On a separate sheet of paper, write the number of the description and the letter of the term that fits the description best.

1. Articles of adornment used to decorate oneself or one's surroundings

2. The use of the body in communication

3. A system of symbolic behaviors that includes all forms of communication except words

4. The distance between the highest and lowest pitch someone can produce

5. Something that has more than one meaning

6. The rhythmic quality of someone's speech

7. A specific vocal sound or quality

8. Rising and falling speech

a. nonverbal communication	**e.** tone
b. ambiguous	**f.** tempo
c. range	**g.** kinesics
d. inflection	**h.** artifacts

Reviewing Key Concepts

1. List the three major categories of non-verbal behaviors.

2. What are three main functions of nonverbal communication?

3. List four qualities that describe the nature of nonverbal communication.

4. What four qualities project a professional image?

5. How can a speaker with a monotone voice increase the effectiveness of his or her message?

6. Give four examples of vocal cues that accompany speech.

7. What six factors does body talk include?

8. What three adjectives should you keep in mind when dressing for a job interview?

Reviewing Key Concepts

1. Sounds, body language, and environmental factors

2. Reinforce, contradict, or substitute for verbal messages

3. Subconscious, contextual, ambiguous, cultural

4. Confidence, poise, assertiveness, immediacy

5. Learn to vary range, inflection, and volume.

6. Pauses and silence, laughter, sighs, throat clearing

7. Personal appearance including dress and grooming, kinesics including posture and muscular tone and tension, movement and gestures, facial expression

8. Classic, clean, conservative

Assessment and Activities

Reading and Critical Thinking Skill

1. **Classifying Information** Into which major category of nonverbal behavior does a frown fall?

2. **Synthesis** How might you use nonverbal behavior to communicate the idea of a bird to someone who speaks a different language?

3. **Applying Information** A fire starts in the cafeteria, and a student runs from room to room shouting, "Fire!" Would the student's voice most likely be high-pitched, medium-pitched, or low-pitched? Explain your answer.

4. **Cause-Effect** What may be the result of ignoring a company's norms in dressing for a job interview?

5. **Making Comparisons** Research the use of eye communication in two cultures. You might make your choice from one of the following: Native American, African, Asian, Hispanic.

Skill Practice Activity

Recalling Information On a sheet of paper, draw a four-column chart. Label the four columns Intimate Distance, Personal Distance, Social Distance, and Public Distance. Then write each description below in the correct column: a teacher lecturing the class, a principal speaking at an assembly, a gossiping friend, a waving neighbor, a hugging parent, an angry parent, and a salesperson giving a pitch.

Cooperative Learning Activity

Nonverbal Communication and Culture With a partner, choose a country and research its culture. List significant nonverbal messages and their meanings in that culture. For example, white is the color of mourning in Japan. Write the name of the country at the top of a poster. Then, illustrate the nonverbal messages on the poster and display the poster in class.

Chapter Project

Planning Think of a career that you would like to pursue. Compile a list or find photographs of at least five artifacts that represent that occupation. Do not reveal your career choice or the artifacts that represent it to your classmates.

Presenting Reveal your photographs or the artifacts on your list to your classmates one item at a time. After each item is revealed, let the rest of the class guess what career you have chosen. If the class guesses your occupation, let them try to identify the remaining items.

Understanding Nonverbal Communication **169**

Chapter Project

Point out that many artifacts are useful in a number of different careers. For example, a briefcase might signify a career in sales, teaching, or business administration, among others. Have students brainstorm a list of all the artifacts they can think of for their chosen career, then analyze each item, asking, "Is this object particularly significant to this career?" Their final five should, as a group, communicate something unique about the career and suggest its value to society. Students might enjoy demonstrating their artifacts' uses to give clues to the class.

Reading and Critical Thinking Skill

1. **Classifying Information** Body language

2. **Synthesis** Answers may include imitating its song, flapping arms like wings, or showing its colors through clothing.

3. **Applying Information** High-pitched, which indicates stress and fear

4. **Cause-Effect** An unfavorable impression, concern by the employer about your fitting in, or failure to be considered on the basis of your merits

5. **Making Comparisons** Mainstream U.S. businesspeople view failure to make direct eye contact as a sign of dishonesty or desire to hide something. Young people from several minority cultures view lowering the eyes as a sign of respect for elders.

Skill Practice Activity

Recalling Information

Possible answers: Intimate Distance—gossiping friend, hugging a parent. Personal Distance—angry parent. Social Distance—salesperson giving a pitch, waving neighbor. Public Distance—teacher lecturing, principal speaking.

Cooperative Learning Activity

Nonverbal Communication and Culture

Have partners organize their examples into Voice, Body Talk, and Environmental Cues sections. After the class has looked at all posters, discuss which type of nonverbal communication differs most from country to country.

Chapter 6 Planning Guide

SECTION RESOURCES

Daily Objectives

Section 1

1. Explain the importance of listening in professional and social contexts
2. Identify the four steps of the listening process and describe their related functions
3. Analyze the factors that can affect listening
4. Apply specific suggestions to improve listening in each step of the process
5. Describe the importance of feedback in the listening process

Section 2

1. Compare and contrast the characteristics of active, passive, and impatient listening
2. Evaluate the results of active, passive, and impatient listening
3. Describe the four kinds of listening
4. Determine the most appropriate kind of listening for a given situation

Reproducible Resources

 Reproducible Lesson Plan 6-1
 Application Activities 6-1
 Guided Reading Workbook Activity 6-1
 Vocabulary Activity 6*
 Reteaching Activity 6-1*
 Enrichment Activity 6-1*
 Graphic Organizer Transparency Strategies and Activities 6-1

 Reproducible Lesson Plan 6-2
 Application Activities 6-2
 Guided Reading Workbook Activity 6-2
 Vocabulary Activity 6*
 Reteaching Activity 6-2*
 Enrichment Activity 6-2*
 Graphic Organizer Transparency Strategies and Activities 6-2

Multimedia Resources

 Graphic Organizer Transparency 6-1
 Chapter 6 Teaching Transparency
 Interactive Tutor Self-Assessment
 PuzzleMaker
 ExamView® Pro Testmaker
 Interactive Lesson Planner
 Communication in Action Video Chapter 6
 MindJogger
 communicationapplications.glencoe.com
Presentation Plus!

 Graphic Organizer Transparency 6-2
 Chapter 6 Teaching Transparency
 Interactive Tutor Self-Assessment
 PuzzleMaker
ExamView® Pro Testmaker
Interactive Lesson Planner
 Communication in Action Video Chapter 6
 MindJogger
 communicationapplications.glencoe.com
 Presentation Plus!

Use Glencoe's *Presentation Plus!* multimedia teacher tool to easily present dynamic lessons that engage and motivate your students. Using Microsoft PowerPoint®, you can customize the presentations to create your own personalized lessons.

* Also available in Spanish

 Blackline Master   CD-ROM   Software

 Transparency   Videodisc   Videocassette   Web site

Chapter 6 Planning Guide

FOR THE TEACHER

Active Listening

Have students work with a partner to practice active listening. Ask the class to agree on the criteria that the active listener must meet: for example, does not interrupt; maintains eye contact; shows attentiveness by leaning forward, smiling, and nodding; gives appropriate feedback through facial expressions, gestures, and responses.

Have students sit facing their partners. One person talks while the other listens. The speaker talks for a minute uninterrupted about the way he or she would most like to spend Saturday night. After they complete the exercise, ask students to write answers to these questions:

- (listener) Was it difficult to listen without interrupting? Why?
- (speaker) How did the listener's responses help you to keep talking?

Have students share their written answers with the whole class.

CHAPTER RESOURCES

Resources for the Teacher

- *The Lost Art of Listening: How Learning to Listen Can Improve Relationships* (The Guilford Family Therapy Series) by Michael Nichols, Guilford Press, 1996
- *The 7 Habits of Highly Effective People: Powerful Lessons in Personal Change* by Stephen Covey, Simon & Schuster, 1993
- *Coercion: Why We Listen to What 'They' Say* by Douglas Rushkoff, Riverhead Books, 1999

Resources for the Student

- *Brain Dancing: Work Smarter, Learn Faster and Manage Information More Effectively* by Patrick Magee, Magee Research, 1998
- *"Listening Skills Needed in Diverse Workplace"* by Paul Bauck, in Small Business Weekly, Seattle, May 25, 1998
- *Listening: The Forgotten Skill* (A Self-Teaching Guide) by Madelyn Burley-Allen, John Wiley & Sons, 1995

Block Scheduling

Block scheduling differs from traditional class scheduling in the amount of time allotted to each period. The extended time frame provided by block scheduling affords you the opportunity to implement a greater number of research-oriented and activity-intense projects to motivate and involve your students. Activities that are particularly suited to use within the block-scheduling framework are identified throughout this chapter by the following designation:

KEY TO ABILITY LEVELS

Teaching Strategies have been coded for varying learning styles and abilities.

L1   **BASIC** activities for all students

L2   **AVERAGE** activities for average to above-average students

L3   **CHALLENGING** activities for above-average students

ELL   **English Language Learner** activities

Chapter 6 Resource Manager

The following materials may be used when teaching the chapter. Materials for specific lessons are also shown at point-of-use in the margins of the Teacher's Wraparound Edition.

TEACHING TRANSPARENCIES

Chapter 6 Teaching Transparency

Graphic Organizer Transparency 6-1

Graphic Organizer Transparency 6-2

APPLICATION ACTIVITIES

Chapter 6, Section 1

Chapter 6, Section 2

Chapter 6, Cumulative

REINFORCEMENT AND REVIEW ACTIVITIES

Vocabulary Activity 6

Guided Reading Activity Workbook 6-1, 6-2

Reteaching Activities 6-1, 6-2

Chapter 6 Resource Manager

ASSESSMENT AND EVALUATION

GLENCOE'S ASSESSMENT ADVANTAGE

Section Quizzes 6-1, 6-2

Chapter 6 Test, Forms A & B

Performance Assessment Activity 6

ENRICHMENT AND EXTENSION

Technology Application Activity 6

Enrichment Activities 6-1, 6-2

ORAL PRESENTATION ACTIVITIES

Activities 18, 19

SPANISH RESOURCES

- Spanish Chapter and Unit Tests
- Spanish Vocabulary Activities
- Spanish Section Quizzes
- Spanish Reteaching Activities
- Spanish Enrichment Activities

MULTIMEDIA

- Interactive Tutor Self-Assessment
- ExamView® Pro Testmaker
- PuzzleMaker
- Communication in Action Videodisc and Videocassette
- MindJogger
- Interactive Lesson Planner
- Presentation Plus!
- Writer's Assistant
- Glencoe Interactive Grammar
- **communicationapplications.glencoe.com**

TEACHER PLANNING AND SUPPORT

- Reproducible Lesson Plans
- Interactive Lesson Planner
- Presentation Plus!

CHAPTER **6**

Toward Effective Listening

WHY IT'S IMPORTANT

Effective listening skills not only are the key to knowledge and understanding, but they also increase our own creativity and our value to others.

To better understand how to listen effectively, view the **Communication in Action** Chapter 6 video lesson.

GLENCOE *Online*

Visit the *Glencoe Communication Applications* Web site at **communicationapplications. glencoe.com** and click on **Overview–Chapter 6** to preview information about listening effectively.

"The key to success is to get out into the store and listen to what the associates have to say. . . ."
—Sam Walton, founder of Wal-Mart

WHY IT'S IMPORTANT

Ask a volunteer to read aloud the quotation above, then have students scan the text headings for Chapter 6. Ask: **In what ways is listening a more complex and useful skill than you imagined on first thought? Why is it important for businesspeople to learn effective listening techniques?**
(Students likely had not considered the active role a good listener plays in effective communication. Answers may include to determine customer's needs, to analyze personnel issues, and to interact with staff.)

Understanding the Listening Process

GUIDE TO READING

Objectives

1. Explain the importance of listening in professional and social contexts.
2. Identify the four steps of the listening process and describe their related functions.
3. Analyze the factors that can affect listening.
4. Apply specific suggestions to improve listening in each step of the process.
5. Describe the importance of feedback in the listening process.

Terms to Learn

listening	understanding
hearing	interpreting
attending	responding

During a typical day, we communicate in many different ways, including through writing, reading, speaking, and listening. Which of these activities do you think takes up the largest part of your communication time? You may be surprised by the answer.

You may think you spend the largest portion of your communication time speaking. However, if you are at all typical, your answer should be *listening*. Listening is our most-used communication skill. In fact, a study of people from various occupational backgrounds showed that 70 percent of their waking time was spent in communication. Of that time, as shown in **Figure 6–1** on the next page, writing consumed 9 percent, reading absorbed 16 percent, talking accounted for 30 percent, and listening occupied 45 percent. That means we spend much more time listening than we do speaking!

This student utilizes his listening skills while working on the computer. What is the most-used communication skill?

Toward Effective Listening **171**

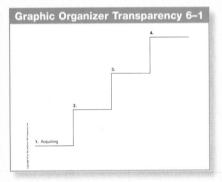
RESOURCE MANAGER

Teaching Tools
- Interactive Lesson Planner
- Reproducible Lesson Plan 6–1
- Application Activities 6–1

Reproducible Masters
- Guided Reading Activity Workbook 6–1
- Enrichment Activity 6–1
- Reteaching Activity 6–1
- Section Quiz 6–1
- Transparency Strategies and Activities Booklet 6–1

Transparencies
- Graphic Organizer Transparency 6–1
- Chapter 6 Teaching Transparency

Technology Resources
- Interactive Tutor Self-Assessment Software
- Presentation Plus! Software
- ExamView® Pro Testmaker
- PuzzleMaker Software
- communicationapplications.glencoe.com

2 TEACH

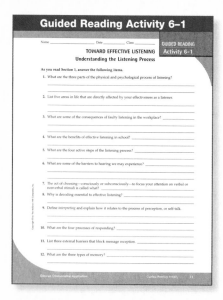

Guided Reading Activity 6–1

Effective Listening Techniques

Point out that learning techniques that foster effective listening lead to many personal and professional benefits. On the chalkboard or an overhead transparency, write the column headings *Ineffective Listening* and *Effective Listening* and the row headings *At Work, At School,* and *In the Community.* Guide students to complete the chart as a class, citing real-life examples. **L1**

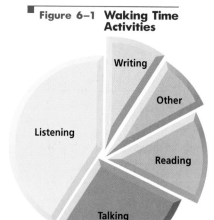

■ **Figure 6–1 Waking Time Activities**

WHY LEARN ABOUT LISTENING

Because we spend so much of our time listening, it is important that we learn to listen well. Unfortunately, effective listening tends to be the least taught and least understood communication skill. Parents and teachers often assume that if a child can hear well, he or she can listen well too. Listening skills are assumed to develop naturally. Therefore, little attention is given to training children to listen effectively.

Generally, the little training we do receive is negative and often the result of trial and error. For instance, if you have ever allowed your attention to wander in class, you may have been instructed to "Sit up and pay attention!" If you "tuned out" while a parent was speaking, you may have been told "Look at me when I talk to you." In both situations, you may have been jolted into paying attention, but you probably learned little about avoiding the problem again in the future.

A recognized authority in listening, Dr. Ralph Nichols, once conducted tests to see just how effectively most people listen. His

tests revealed that immediately after the average person listens to someone speak, he or she remembers only half of what was said—no matter how carefully the person thought he or she was listening. The tests further indicated that after only eight hours, the average listener tends to forget an additional one-half to one-third of what he or she originally grasped of a speaker's message. Unfortunately, remembering only about twenty-five percent of a test review or a supervisor's instructions can cause a great deal of trouble in the real world.

Defining Listening

A first step toward understanding listening is to realize that listening, like other aspects of communication, is a process. It consists of specific sets of skills that can be identified and learned. Your understanding of this process begins with an examination of the meaning of listening. Listening as a process includes much more than just hearing sounds and understanding language. Rather, listening is a physical and psychological process that involves acquiring, assigning meaning, and responding to symbolic messages from others.

Importance of Listening

The primary reason for listening is to acquire oral messages from others. These messages are vital to the way we function in our everyday lives. Many of the most important aspects of your life are influenced by your skills—or lack of skills—in listening. For instance, the quality of your friendships depends, in large measure, on your ability to listen well. Making appropriate listening choices also affects the strength of family bonds. Following are just a few of the areas in life that are directly affected by your effectiveness as a listener, as shown in **Figure 6–2.**

ENGLISH LANGUAGE LEARNERS

Idioms English contains many idioms, which are difficult for people who do not speak English to understand. For example, *you bet* is used in many situations, yet few nonnative speakers realize that it has nothing to do with betting. Idioms are one stumbling block to listening comprehension for English language learners.

Activity Pair students who are learning English with English-proficient partners to read a short story or essay and locate idioms. On 3" x 5" cards, pairs should list idioms, define them, and use them in context. When both partners know the meanings of their idioms, have them present them and illustrate their meanings in a fragment of dialogue. **ELL**

School You probably are well aware of the importance of listening in school. Your ability to participate in class discussions, ask meaningful questions, give relevant answers, carry out detailed homework instructions, and score well on tests relates directly to your ability to listen. One recent study of college students stresses the importance of listening in school. According to the report, faulty listening, more than any other factor, determines student failure in colleges and universities.

Relationships Listening skills also play a vital role in interpersonal relationships. For example, good listeners tend to be valued as friends because they are perceived as sensitive and caring. When someone listens closely to the message another is sending, he or she conveys a sense of acknowledgment, concern, and respect for the other person. As a result, effective listeners tend to be trusted and may be sought out as leaders. In their own lives, the ability to listen well may help them avoid certain conflicts and form close, productive interpersonal relationships.

Social Groups and Organizations Listening skills also play a vital role when participating in social contexts. Making and acknowledging introductions and asking for and following directions all require special listening skills. Listening skills also play a vital role in your ability to participate effectively in social and community organizations. Your own personal effectiveness and how you are perceived by others in these groups may be influenced by your listening ability. Whether participating in a youth group, a city council meeting, or a legislative body, members who listen effectively tend to make better decisions and are more likely to influence the outcome of individual or group goals.

Public Dialogue Another level of social interaction involves listening to speeches and other forms of public messages. Effective listening skills allow you to better understand and remember what you hear, which helps you make better decisions. They also help you participate more effectively in public dialogues both as a citizen and as a consumer.

The Workplace Being able to listen well can be vital to your success on the job. Listening skills are important to businesses because they help employees be more productive. This, in turn, can create greater profits for the company. Reports from the Department of Labor as well as from several major corporations all underscore a direct relationship between listening ability, productivity, and job performance.

Costs to Business There are an estimated one hundred million workers on the job in the United States today. One report points out that if each worker were to make a simple ten-dollar mistake as a result of poor listening, the overall cost would add up to a billion dollars. Sound hard to believe? Actually, that estimate may be low. Faulty listening is estimated to cost American industry approximately eighty-six billion dollars per year.

We all make inappropriate listening choices from time to time. As a result of poor listening skills, you may find yourself redoing homework or asking a teacher or another student to

■ **Figure 6–2 Areas of Life Affected by Listening**

Toward Effective Listening **173**

BUSINESS BRIEF

Paul Bauck, writing in *Small Business Weekly*, points out that a cause of employee dissatisfaction is the failure of managers to respect or listen to them. Conversely, learning to listen and show respect for staff inspires loyalty. He cites three keys for managers to make staff feel respected and listened to: (1) Be aware of biases in one's own thinking, (2) keep an open mind about alternative ways of thinking, and (3) ask five consecutive questions about a thing you don't agree with to try to understand why someone believes as he or she does.

Listening as a Process
Invite a volunteer to define *process*. (*A series of actions or operations carried out to achieve a desired end or result.*) Ask students to review their experiences and cite evidence to show that listening is a dynamic process, not merely a taking in of sound. (*Students may suggest that a person who is distracted does not get meaning from what you say although they technically do hear your words or that individuals may respond differently upon listening to the same message.*) **L2**

MULTIPLE LEARNING STYLES

Logical-Mathematical Showing concretely and graphically how little is retained from what is heard can help students understand the importance of effective listening skills.

Activity Have students work in pairs. Give each pair random lists of fifteen vocabulary words. Have one partner read the list to the other who then recalls as many of the terms as possible. Have pairs relax and talk for several minutes, then have the listener again write as many of the terms as he or she can. Repeat the procedure with new terms, having students reverse roles. After partners record scores, tally results for the class and draw a conclusion about the curve of forgetting.

Are You Listening?

Invite volunteers to relate personal experiences of faulty listening that led to inconvenience, misunderstanding, or accident. Discuss situations in which failure to listen closely can become a serious or life-threatening problem. **L1**

Visual Instruction

Answer Students' answers may include any of the following: in school, effective listeners tend to find classes more interesting, become actively involved, make better grades; in business, effective listeners tend to enjoy rewards for productivity, are valued by coworkers, get better jobs.

---

repeat instructions. On the job, faulty listening can lead to revising letters or reports, rescheduling appointments, researching incorrect information, and rerouting shipments, among other errors. Each of these mistakes not only costs a company money but also trickles down as costs to the consumer.

Cost to Consumers Any time business suffers a consistent loss, it is likely to pass the cost along to consumers through higher prices and extra charges. One recent report suggests that at least 10 percent of the cost of consumer goods is added on by businesses to absorb the cost of faulty listening in the workplace.

Inconvenience Faulty listening leads not only to more expensive products but also to inadequate services. At one time or another,

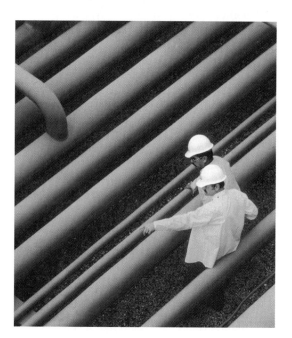

you probably have been inconvenienced by an inefficient worker who made a mistake because he or she just wasn't listening. Perhaps a server at your favorite lunch spot brought you a hamburger with mayonnaise and pickles when you clearly ordered a cheeseburger with mustard and no pickles. As a result, there was an extra cost. Either you suffered the "cost" of eating a meal that was not to your liking, or the restaurant management suffered the cost of replacing part or all of the first burger.

Safety Issues However, not all costs are so easily absorbed. Sometimes, the faulty listening skills of highly trained professionals can lead to tragedy. One such incident occurred in 1982 as a commercial airliner was taking off from Washington International Airport. In this instance, the pilot failed to heed a message from his copilot that the jet's engines were not delivering enough take-off power. As a result, seventy-eight people died when the plane left the runway and plunged into the icy Potomac River.

Benefits of Effective Listening

Just as faulty listening can have costly results, effective listening skills can produce great rewards. Individuals who have reputations as effective listeners tend to build successful relationships. In school, effective listeners tend to find classes more interesting, become more actively involved, and make better grades. Businesses with employers who are effective listeners are usually rewarded not only with increased sales and more satisfied customers but also with increased productivity and overall profits. Employees who are good listeners are usually valued by coworkers. They also tend to get better jobs, receive more promotions, and have more satisfactory work experiences than their coworkers with poor listening skills.

MULTIPLE LEARNING STYLES

Interpersonal Students who are skilled in person-to-person communication can help illustrate the communication management skills needed to build confidence and take a leadership role.
Activity Script several conflict scenarios or have volunteers write them ahead of time for your approval. Select students to serve as peacemakers for each conflict. Have these students leave the classroom while you give other students conflict situations to act out. Have peacemakers return, listen to the dialogue, and then sit down with the pair. A peacemaker should ask questions about the problem and what each person wants, listen carefully, summarize the situation, and propose a compromise that the parties can accept.

Effective communication between airplane pilot and copilot is imperative for a safe flight. *What is the first step to becoming an effective listener?*

Misconceptions About Listening

Listening well can benefit you in many ways throughout your life. However, as important as these skills may be, they still tend to be underappreciated and misunderstood. Understanding exactly what listening is—and is not—can help you analyze your skills and develop better listening habits. Some of the common misconceptions known about listening are listed in the table below.

ANALYZING THE LISTENING PROCESS

The invisible, complex phenomenon we know as listening is more than merely hearing sounds or understanding language. Rather, listening is a process that involves making sense of verbal and nonverbal messages. Study **Figure 6–3** on page 176, which displays a model of the listening process. As a process, listening involves four active steps that build upon one another. These include

- acquiring
- attending
- understanding
- responding to messages from others

LISTENING MISCONCEPTIONS

Misconceptions	Fact
Listening and hearing are the same thing.	Hearing is the physical first step in the listening process and does not imply understanding.
Listening is easy or automatic.	Listening is a complex process that requires energy, effort, and skills.
Listening develops naturally.	Listening consists of learned skills and behaviors that can be learned, relearned, improved, and refined.
Anyone can listen well if he or she really tries.	You can exert effort in the listening process, but if you don't have the needed skills, you may not be able to listen effectively.
The speaker is primarily responsible for the message and for the success of the interaction.	In effective communication, the speaker and the listener share responsibility. For communication to be successful, listeners may have to compensate for a sender's lack of ability in transmitting messages.
If that's what I heard, then that's what you said!	Listeners cannot assume they have understood messages correctly and should use perception checks to clarify messages.
Attitude and listening are unrelated.	Attitude is a very important factor in listening and retaining information.
People remember most of what they hear.	Listening and memory are related, but failure to remember may or may not indicate faulty listening.

Toward Effective Listening **175**

CHAPTER 6
Section 1

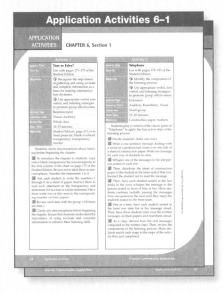

Application Activities 6–1

Just the Facts
Refer students to the table Listening Misconceptions. Ask which misconceptions they believed to be true. Guide students to see what makes these statements false. Invite students to give examples from their experience, particularly of listener responsibility and attitude. **L1**

Communication Tip

Good listeners gain more from conversations as well as from radio and TV programs and classes. Effective listening will help you build a storehouse of information and allow you to relate better to people with varied interests.

■ Visual Instruction

Answer Analyze specific skills and strategies to help you listen more effectively.

MEETING INDIVIDUAL NEEDS

INCLUSION STRATEGIES

Less-Proficient Readers Having a limited vocabulary constitutes a real listening handicap. Students who are unfamiliar with words used in conversation or in class are often embarrassed to ask for clarification, but without knowing meaning, they are unable to listen effectively.

Activity Have students write down words they hear throughout the day whose meaning they do not know. They should include a brief description of the context in which the words were used. Ask students to share their lists of words in class. Establish the words' spellings and have students look up their meanings. Set up conversation groups in which students use these words as often as possible during class.

Steps to Listening

Introduce and explain the four steps of the listening process outlined on this page: acquiring, attending, understanding, and responding. List the steps on the chalkboard. As you describe each, write key words and examples of each step under the heading. Encourage students to copy this organizer into their notebooks for future reference. **L2** 📦

Lend Me an Ear

Using the model shown on this page, have students trace the steps in hearing. Point out that the electrical impulses received by the brain enable us to assign meaning to sounds. Sound waves themselves do not have meaning. Ask a volunteer to explain why a damaged auditory nerve causes deafness. **L1**

Communication Tip

Take notes when listening to a lecture. Try to create a system of codes for your notes, such as underlining or numbering important points.

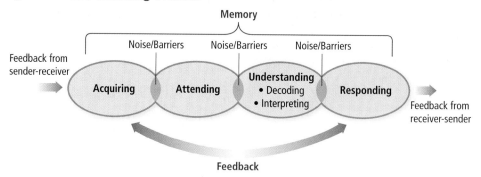

Figure 6–3 The Listening Process

Acquiring

The listening process begins with acquiring. As you learned in Chapter 2, acquiring is the act of picking up some type of stimulus through the senses. Usually, the first sense involved in listening is hearing, or the physical process of receiving sound. Sound can come from someone's voice or from some nonverbal cue, such as a knock on the door. As shown in **Figure 6–4**, the outer ear, which serves as antennae to aid sound reception, first picks up sound waves. These waves are then relayed to the middle ear, where they are amplified and passed to the inner ear. The inner ear transforms this acoustical energy into electrical impulses and relays the impulses to the brain for processing.

Hearing Ability It was once thought that all people hear in exactly the same way. Today, we know that the physical ability to receive sound waves varies from one person to another. Not everyone can distinguish different sounds, levels of volume, or high and low pitches.

Noise and Barriers to Hearing In addition to our individual hearing ability, many other factors affect our ability to acquire sounds in specific situations. Loud noises, such as traffic, blaring music, jet engines, sirens, and ringing telephones, also can interfere with hearing and sometimes cause hearing loss. Even chronic ear infections and repeated doses of certain kinds of antibiotics can damage hearing.

Other factors can also interfere with hearing. Visual and auditory messages can conflict, causing listeners to question what they hear. A speaker can use inappropriate or distracting physical movements that overshadow his or her spoken message. A speaker's voice can be harsh or irritating and cause listeners to lose concentration.

Figure 6–4 Model of the Human Ear

Outer Ear   Middle Ear   Inner Ear

176 *Glencoe Communication Applications*

INTERDISCIPLINARY CONNECTION

Science Have students trace, with the help of anatomical visuals, the physical and neurological processes involved in hearing. Discuss the concepts of waves, amplitude, and electrical impulses as they relate to hearing.

Activity Provide students with an illustrated poster showing the outer, middle, and inner ear as well as the auditory nerve and brain. Have them work in groups of four or five, taking turns explaining how sound waves enter the ear, the role of each part of the ear, and the role of the nervous system in assigning meaning to sounds and responding to them. With the class, discuss injuries and problems that could prevent a person from hearing.

Even the attitude or emotions that a receiver is feeling can interfere with the hearing process. You can, for example, become so angry that you literally do not hear the words someone speaks. Despite an individual's physical ability to hear, when other factors create noise or barriers that keep a person from hearing the message, listening will be blocked in this initial step of the process.

Attending

Are you interested in entering a particular field of business someday? If so, you are likely to listen more intently to discussions about that line of work. You also are more likely to participate in those discussions. On the other hand, if you consider a topic to be boring, irrelevant, or unimportant, you are more likely to "tune out" the speaker. Both of these situations involve a choice on your part. You are choosing which information you will attend and which you will not. Attending is the act of choosing— consciously or subconsciously—to focus your attention on verbal or nonverbal stimuli.

Choosing to Attend Many people assume that paying attention is automatic. If that were the case, however, you would never daydream or allow your mind to wander. Instead, you can learn to play an active role in focusing your attention on a message. When you decide to attend to a message, you use selective perception. You focus on specific stimuli that are being received at a particular time. If you choose not to attend to a message, you may give in to distractions or simply ignore those stimuli.

What are some of the elements that affect your ability to attend? Your own needs, interests, attitudes, and knowledge at a given time affect your choice of whether you will attend to or ignore a message. For example, if you have chosen and been accepted to a particular college, you probably will pay little attention to a speaker who is a recruiter from another university. Your lack of interest in this information affects your attending choices.

Specific needs also affect these choices. Imagine that a supervisor at work tells you to present a report on your project in a meeting as soon as she finishes her opening remarks. How much attention do you think you will give to the supervisor's opening remarks? Probably very little. Instead, you may feel it is more important to mentally review what you want to say in your report. Just the stress of being called on to give an impromptu speech can be an extreme barrier to attending to other messages. Barriers to attending can, however, be overcome. You can use the points listed in the Communication Strategies checklist on this page to help you become a more attentive listener.

COMMUNICATION Strategies

IMPROVING ATTENDING SKILLS

- ✓ Evaluate the communication situation by determining what is important and what should be attended.

- ✓ Adjust your attitude to expect the message to be interesting or rewarding.

- ✓ Turn off other thoughts and focus your energy on the sender's message.

- ✓ Determine what you have to gain from focusing your attention and listening.

- ✓ Ignore outside distractions. Bring your attention back to the speaker when you realize that your mind is wandering.

- ✓ Stay focused and maintain your concentration.

Toward Effective Listening **177**

Drowned Messages

How do body language and tone that are inappropriate to a message alter the way the message is heard? Assign several students to present a dialogue with a clear message, such as a manager hiring a new employee she clearly likes. Instruct the presenters to use movements and tone that contradict what is expected to go with this message. For example, the manager might act threatening and the new employee fearful. Have audience participants write a summary of what they heard. Then, have the performers repeat the role play, substituting appropriate body language and tone, and have the audience report any changes in what they heard. **L3**

COMMUNICATION Strategies

IMPROVING ATTENDING SKILLS

Ask volunteers to model for the class the effective attending skills noted in the checklist on this page. Copy the checklist and post it in the classroom. Have students add other strategies they find effective. Ask students to use as many of these strategies as possible during a full school day. On the next day of class, chart and rank which strategies were practiced and which ones students found most effective. **L1**

COOPERATIVE LEARNING ACTIVITY

Many occupations, such as air-traffic control, teaching, and managing, rely on careful listening for success. Divide the class into groups of four or five. As a class, brainstorm a list of occupations requiring effective listening skills. Then, ask each group to select and research one of the occupations and take notes about the importance of listening in that field. Have groups present their findings orally to the class as the listeners apply effective listening techniques.

Powers of Concentration

Explain that "tuning out" is a major problem for listeners who find a topic boring or fail to see how it affects them. Discuss ways in which students can motivate themselves to focus on material that they do not automatically consider interesting. Techniques include adopting a positive listening attitude, preparing physically and mentally to listen, and finding personal reasons to listen. Have students try adjusting their posture to one of alert concentration and to note differences in their ability to attend. Point out that one can't become a good listener without making a commitment to use good listening behaviors. **L2**

COMMUNICATION *Strategies*

IMPROVING DECODING SKILLS

Compile various library and classroom resources that help build vocabulary and have volunteers scan them to note their scopes and organizational plans. After listening to reports from volunteers on these resources, students can assess which they would like to use or write their own plans for building a stronger listening and speaking vocabulary. Ask students to describe actions they can take to make classes a way of improving their language skills. **L2**

TECHNOLOGY *Activity*

How Do I Sound? Radio and TV broadcasters are hired, in part, based on several vocal variables. Have you ever changed a TV or radio station or psychologically tuned out a presentation because the speaker's voice was irritating? Find out how your voice sounds to others by making an audio recording of yourself. Recite a nursery rhyme, read a paragraph out of a book, and tell a joke. Play the recording and listen critically. Would others find you easy to listen to? Do you have a monotonous sound? Do you talk too fast? Do you speak clearly? How can your presentation be improved? Record the same readings again and listen for improvements.

Understanding

Why do you talk to others? You probably want them to understand the messages you send and who you are as a person. Why do you listen? You listen because you want to comprehend what others are saying, form relationships, and build mutual trust and understanding. Understanding is a complex mental process that involves decoding the symbolic message received from others and then interpreting and assigning a personal meaning to that message.

Decoding To understand what someone says, you must first decode it. Decoding was defined earlier as a listener's assigning meaning to a sender's words and nonverbal cues. Decoding involves listening carefully to a speaker's words to try to understand the meaning the speaker intends to convey. Next, you interpret or filter the message based on your own experiences. Decoding is essential to effective listening because without it you cannot understand the language of the speaker.

Such factors as knowledge, culture, and language skills affect your ability to decode messages. Remember that language is code, and different languages have different codes or word symbols for the same meaning. If someone were to speak to you in a language that you had never learned, you probably would have trouble decoding the message.

Even words of the same language can be unfamiliar or mean different things to different people. If you are in a class and the teacher uses a term you don't recognize, you may be facing a decoding gap in your listening process. It can be extremely difficult to understand a concept if you don't know the meaning of the terms used to describe it.

Interpreting Decoding the words and nonverbal cues is only the initial step in understanding a sender's message. The receiver also has to interpret the meanings or feelings the speaker is expressing. Interpreting is a process in which you personalize the sender's message to determine meaning for you. It relates to the process of perception, or self-talk, in which you tell yourself what the speaker is saying.

COMMUNICATION *Strategies*

IMPROVING DECODING SKILLS

- ✓ Build your speaking and listening vocabularies to help with listening.
- ✓ Use perception checks to clarify a sender's use of words and nonverbal behaviors.
- ✓ Assume responsibility for your own listening and language skills rather than always expecting others to adjust their messages for you.

INTERDISCIPLINARY CONNECTION

Language Arts Paraphrasing, or restating a speaker's remarks in one's own words to the speaker's satisfaction, is an important language arts skill businesspeople use daily to enhance communication.

Activity Divide the class into pairs of students. One person will play the role of the speaker and will talk about one of the following "How to" activities: how to perform a specific task, how to advance in a particular career, or how to operate a specific piece of equipment. The listening partner will paraphrase the speaker's remarks. Have partners exchange roles, then discuss barriers that interfered with their ability to attend.

COMMUNICATION *Strategies*

CHECKING INTERPRETATIONS

✓ Check factors in your "filter system" that influence your interpretation of messages. Remember, factors like feelings and needs can change momentarily.

✓ Make a habit of asking yourself, "Is this what the sender is really saying or is this merely what I am hearing?" and "Are there other interpretations that I am overlooking?"

✓ Ask questions to gain more information and increase your understanding before finalizing your interpretation.

✓ Take responsibility for your personal interpretations and remain open and flexible to adapt and adjust.

It has been said that the message lies in the receiver. It is the receiver who determines the meaning of the actual message. Your knowledge or lack of knowledge, attitudes, values and needs, culture, language, beliefs, biases, prejudices, expectations, and self-concept all are important elements that influence your personal interpretation of the sender's message. How can you know if your interpretation and understanding are correct? Often, you can't be sure. You can, however, be reasonably sure that it is unlikely that any two people will interpret a particular message in exactly the same way.

Students interpret the teacher's message by personalizing the message to determine its meaning. Identify factors that influence personal interpretation of a message.

Word symbols used by speakers are inexact and depend on the context in which they are given. Each listener's interpretative "filter system" is unique. The guidelines in the Communication Strategies checklist will help you interpret messages to prevent future misunderstandings.

Responding

Once you have arrived at your own personal understanding—or misunderstanding—of a message, you will respond to it. Responding is the listener's internal emotional and intellectual reaction to a message. The verbal and nonverbal feedback is the listener's external response to the message. Generally, when you respond to a message, you go through the following processes:

- You first respond emotionally to the message. At this point, you determine how you feel about it.

- You respond intellectually to the message. You decide what you think about your feelings and the message.

- You analyze and evaluate your response to the message.

- You encode choices about what to say or do in response to your understanding of the message and your reaction to it.

COMMUNICATION *Strategies*

CHECKING INTERPRETATIONS

Point out to students that leaders in business often listen to people whose views differ markedly from their own. Being aware of their personal biases and how biases affect their thinking allows leaders to listen to alternative points of view with an open mind and perceive ways the unique knowledge of each employee can be used. To illustrate, have a small group, with members having very different points of view, present an impromptu panel on an issue selected by the teacher. A prerequisite for each member of the group is to state personal bias and agree to ask questions that attempt to understand rather than to respond with disapproval or anger when responding to an opposing viewpoint. **L3**

■ Visual Instruction

Answer Knowledge, attitudes, values, needs, language, culture, beliefs, biases, prejudices, expectations, and self-concept

MEETING INDIVIDUAL NEEDS — INCLUSION STRATEGIES

Special Needs These students may need to build their tolerance for sitting still and listening with attention over time. Generally, however, lectures or presentations will need to contain interactive portions to hold their interest.

Activity After students have read and discussed the section Analyzing the Listening Process (pages 175–183), divide the class into four groups and assign each group a subsection. Their job will be to summarize and illustrate the main points of the listening process creatively. You might suggest that groups plan interactive activities, skits, or comedic examples and involve as many senses as possible.

Practice for the Workplace

Responding Options Encourage students to work in groups to analyze the situations. Ask them to decide what the problem or difficulty is and how to address it in an appropriate manner. *(Answers will vary; possible responses are shown: (1) You could tell the customer what your most popular orders are if they need suggestions. If they change their order, make sure you write it down each time they start over, then repeat it back before ending the call. (2) Listen to the shopper's complaint so you understand the situation. Listen for clues about when the suit was purchased, how it was paid for, and how it is damaged. (3) Listen to the person who is complaining and try to find out why he or she is concerned about the coworker's tardiness.)*

Reacting to Messages To help understand the responding process, imagine the scenario outlined in **Figure 6–5**. You have just learned that you failed a history test even though you had studied hard for it. Your first emotional reaction is shock and disbelief. Then you react intellectually and tell yourself, "There must be something wrong." You scan the paper and the comments made by the teacher. You decide to remain after class to ask the teacher about your grade and if you can do some extra work to raise the grade. You have just gone through the entire responding process. You reacted emotionally to the grade. Then you thought about the grade and decided to talk to your teacher to ask for extra work.

COMMUNICATION *Strategies*
IMPROVING RESPONDING SKILLS

- ✓ Monitor, analyze, and evaluate your emotional and intellectual reaction.
- ✓ Consider possible alternative reactions.
- ✓ Consider basic standards of appropriateness and balance the rewards and consequences of alternative responses.
- ✓ Take responsibility for your chosen response.
- ✓ Consider all responses before giving feedback.
- ✓ Adapt and adjust your messages according to the feedback you receive.
- ✓ Choose words that are clear to the listener.

Practice for the Workplace

Responding Options It is important to analyze the messages of others and remember that you have several options when responding to them. Interpretation and analysis are especially important in the workplace.

BUSINESS PRACTICE *Activity*

Consider how you would use effective listening skills to respond to each of the following scenarios. In groups of three, take turns responding. Focus on how effectively listening would help you respond appropriately in each situation.

1. A couple calls and orders a pizza. You take the call. They do not know exactly what they want and change their order several times.

2. A shopper asks to exchange a suit that was already damaged when purchased. The style is no longer available.

3. A coworker complains to you about another employee who is always late.

Analyzing Reactions You have reacted emotionally to the situation and intellectually decided what kind of action you want to take and what message or feedback you want to send. Now, suppose the scenario continues. Your teacher scans your paper and responds with feedback, "I don't think extra work is the answer. However, you can take another version of the test." The cycle begins again. This time your emotional reaction to the teacher's feedback may be one of real frustration, perhaps even anger. You may then think to yourself one of the following: "Oh well, it's not that important. It's just one grade, after all;" "She doesn't like me anyway, and that's why she won't let me do extra work;" or "Even though I don't want to retake

MULTIPLE LEARNING STYLES

Visual-Spatial Discovering your students' dominant learning styles can enhance the learning process and maximize retention of key information. Because much information is presented visually, all learners can benefit from practicing with visuals.

Activity Ask students to think about the process they follow when they are listening to someone speak. On the chalkboard, draw a flowchart of the listening process in a format different from that shown in the text on page 176, such as a vertical format with connecting arrows. Have students copy the diagram in their notebooks and complete it. Have visual learners refer to the diagram of the listening process, as needed, in your study of this section.

the test, it looks like my only option. I'll just have to study more." The choice is yours. Which are the most appropriate emotional and intellectual responses for you? Which responses probably are inappropriate? Why? What kind of feedback would accompany your response?

If you look at the first reaction, your mental self-talk may be saying, "Forget it, it doesn't matter." The second reaction might mean, "What difference does it make? She doesn't like me and I'll make a bad grade in this class anyway." The third response still reflects your feelings of anger, but your self-talk says, "I

don't want to retake this test. It may not even help my grade, but it looks like my only option. I'll have to study more and try." In each case the scenario features the same feeling but results in a different intellectual response to those feelings.

In order to analyze the three reactions, this student would need to pause to weigh and consider the most appropriate response, he or she could make—the one in keeping with the goals for the course. Which response would send the most positive message about his or her attitudes about self, school, or the class?

■ **Figure 6–5** **Reacting to Messages**

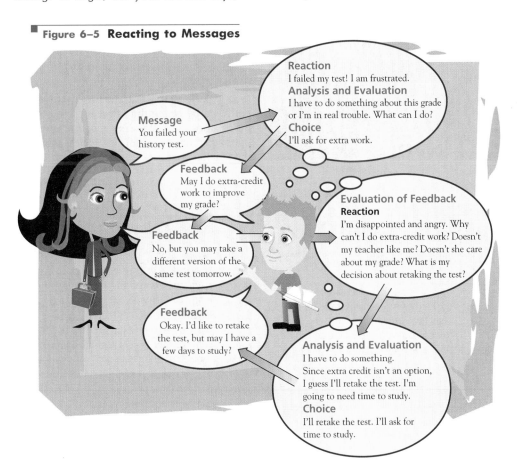

Toward Effective Listening **181**

Learning to Respond Appropriately

Have students work with a partner to discuss possible responses to a specific situation, such as being told a piece of gossip, having someone blame you for losing something, or being asked by a friend to lend him or her money. Ask that they make notes on each type of response and describe the likely results. Have pairs role-play each situation, showing the outcome with different responses. Ask the class to give their reactions and evaluate which response was most appropriate. **L3**

Appropriate Responses in the Workplace

Explain that learning to control immediate emotional reactions is vital in the workplace, where interactions with customers, supervisors, and colleagues are unavoidable. Have students brainstorm possible responses to several workplace communications and rank them from most appropriate to least appropriate. Possible situations include handling a rude, pushy customer in a checkout line and responding to a supervisor's complaint about your work. **L3**

INTERDISCIPLINARY CONNECTION

Changing the Course of History Moments in history when the fate of a nation hinged on a single response can provide students an entertaining opportunity to visualize the importance of weighing the most appropriate feedback to a communication.

Activity Have students scan a history text or library book to read about a meeting of minds that changed the course of history for a country. Students can act out the scene, write a brief description of it, or invent a dialogue that might have taken place. Require students in the audience to analyze the response of one of the people involved and offer an alternative that might have changed the outcome.

Grammar Tip

Conjunctions are joining words that show a relationship between sentence parts they join. Correlative conjunctions, for example, *either/or* and *both/and*, work in pairs to join words or word groups of equal weight. On page 183, this sentence contains a correlative conjunction: "They *not only* show your skill as a listener *but also* may determine your success in social and professional interactions."

COMMUNICATION PRACTICE LAB

Training Your Memory

Have students follow the six steps in the Communication Practice Lab to illustrate the impact of intervening information and repetition on memory. Caution students to use unrelated objects and avoid unfamiliar vocabulary in each list in order to control the difficulty. Explain that most people forget more if asked to take in additional information before studying the initial list adequately. On the other hand, repetition tends to increase memory. Have students record and graph their results for each technique. **L3**

This audience is responding and providing feedback to the speaker. How?

To help you learn to respond and provide feedback appropriately, you can use the same standards you learned in Chapter 1. Which choice is more appropriate and productive for me, for my listener and our relationship, for the occasion (history class) and the task (passing the test)? Before giving feedback, competent communicators analyze and evaluate their responses and the situation before deciding what to do and say about their responses.

Providing Feedback Despite your emotional and intellectual reaction or response, you still have a choice about the feedback you give. You've heard, "Think before you speak," and "Look before you leap." That advice could be important at this point in the responding process. The saga of the history class has not ended. The disappointed student has not provided feedback to the teacher.

COMMUNICATION PRACTICE LAB

Training Your Memory

To practice improving your memory, follow the steps below:

Step 1 On a sheet of paper, create three lists of ten objects each. Try to make the objects as unrelated as possible, such as *chalkboard, bicycle, dog,* and so on.

Step 2 With a partner, take turns completing the following test. Begin by slowly reading your first list to your partner. When you have finished, ask your partner to repeat as many objects as possible from the list. Put a check mark beside each item recalled.

Step 3 Repeat Step 2, using your second list.

Step 4 Now, ask your partner to go back and name the items from the first list. How many can he or she remember?

Step 5 Finally, read your third list to your partner. After reading each item, allow your partner to repeat the word three times before moving on.

Step 6 At the end of the third list, have your partner repeat every word he or she can remember. Did repeating the word increase his or her memory? Discuss your results as a class.

MEETING INDIVIDUAL NEEDS — MULTIPLE LEARNING STYLES

Linguistic Linguistic learners use words effectively and are sensitive to the ways that word choice and semantics affect the messages that are sent. Students can use this skill to evaluate responses and rework them to make feedback clear and effective.

Activity Have volunteers brainstorm communication situations in which an emotional response might lead to conflict. Assign small groups one situation and have them write the first response that comes to mind. Ask the class to evaluate and rework responses until their wording is clear and helps resolve rather than expand conflict. Inform students that they will study conflict-resolution strategies in Chapter 12.

To provide a happier ending, we might assume that the student chose the third response. The student still must make choices about giving feedback. Should the student say, "Okay, I'll take the test," or merely ask, "When can I take the test?" Remembering that competent communicators need to use both task and interpersonal skills, the student might say, "I'm really disappointed in my grade. I really did study. I appreciate your giving me another chance. May I have a few days before I retake the test to look over my notes?" Carefully choosing the verbal and nonverbal feedback you want to give is a vital last step in the responding process.

Importance of Giving Appropriate Feedback Feedback is one person's observable response to a message. A speaker generally cannot be certain that oral communication has occurred until he or she receives some kind of observable feedback from the listener. As an effective listener, you have the responsibility to provide appropriate feedback. Feedback gives the speaker some idea about whether or not the message was received. Finally, feedback also gives the speaker clues about how the listener decoded, interpreted, and reacted to the message the speaker sent.

Benefits of Appropriate Responses and Feedback Carefully considering all responses and providing constructive, realistic feedback are hallmarks of a competent communicator. They not only show your skill as a listener but also may determine your success in social and professional interactions. For example, if you discuss politics at a social gathering, you should consciously stay calm if you want to make your point. Getting angry or lashing out at a guest who does not share your opinion may only make you look like an ineffective communicator.

Responding and Providing Feedback Appropriately in the Workplace One airline company recognizes the importance of careful response choices in the workplace. This company stresses the value of humor in the workplace and routinely tests applicants to see how they might respond to an unpleasant stimulus. First, job applicants are given a typical scenario involving an unhappy passenger. They then are asked how they might resolve the conflict using humor. Again, responding appropriately to the unpleasant stimulus reveals an applicant's communication skill level. Making carefully crafted decisions to keep cool or to use humor appropriately in difficult situations can be a valuable asset to any effective communicator.

 GLOBAL COMMUNICATION

Cultural Distinctions

People sometimes are distracted by internal listening barriers when communicating with people from other cultures. These barriers often exist because the listener has had few opportunities to observe people from different regions or cultures. Look for opportunities to learn about the cultures of other people. Watch a national news broadcast for one week, search the Internet for photos, scan your textbooks, recall movies you have seen, and cut out newspaper photos that show different cultures. Identify five visible regional or cultural characteristics and tell how they could affect your ability to listen when in conversation with someone from another culture.

 GLOBAL COMMUNICATION

Cultural Distinctions

Invite students to describe their conversations with people from other cultures. Does the feature accurately capture their reactions? How did language differences create barriers to communication? Assign the feature activity to the class. (*Examples of differences students might identify: accents, jewelry, make-up or tattoos, hairstyles, hand gestures, clothing. Students might say that cultural differences distract them from their conversational goals, and they may need to make a conscious effort to ignore those differences.*) **L2**

DID YOU KNOW?

The average person speaks at a rate of about 150 words a minute, but listeners can understand messages presented at a rate of 380 words per minute.

 GIFTED AND TALENTED

Improving Memory In *Brain Dancing*, Patrick Magee suggests various methods for improving memory: Use short periodic reviews at intervals of 10 minutes after introduction, 24 hours later, 1 week later, and 1 month later. Use imagination to associate what is to be remembered with a visual "peg." Map in your mind the material as you read or listen. Combine the key words in a concept in a graphic way that shows their relationship. Articulate the new material by talking it over or by explaining the content of your mind map as if you were teaching a class. Associate strong emotions with each main point and identify words that trigger each emotion.

Activity Have students select one technique and try it out for a week, keeping detailed notes in a journal.

Barriers to Listening

As students look at Figure 6–6, they should classify each barrier as internal or external and select three that they think are the most difficult barriers to overcome. Ask students to explain their choices. **L2**

Communication Tip

When learning names or other important information you want to retain, associate the information with a visual image. Take time to see it clearly in your mind's eye and think about the connection between them. For example, you might visualize the person you just met holding a jar full of shiny pennies to help you remember her name is Penny.

GLENCOE Online

For an additional Practice Lab for this section, have students visit the *Glencoe Communication Applications* Web site at **communication.applications.glencoe.com**. Click on Communication Practice Lab 6–1. **L1**

Figure 6–6 Barriers to Listening

Biases · Needs · Attitudes · Beliefs · Anger · Fear · Unfamiliar Language · Fatigue · Prejudices · Hearing Problems · Ignorance · Tuning Out · Communication Overload · Stress

Barriers to Listening

FACTORS THAT AFFECT THE LISTENING PROCESS

Imagine that a coworker walks up to you in a hallway and says, "You won't believe what happened in the management meeting today." What type of reaction would you have? What types of listening behaviors would you show? What kind of listening do you think your friend expects? How you react to your coworker's statement depends on your listening skills.

What factors cause us to listen poorly at times? Why do we listen effectively at other times? The listening process is influenced by three key factors. They are as follows:

- noise
- barriers
- memory

Noise

The first critical factor that affects the listening process is noise—the internal and external distractions that interfere with listening and concentration. Noise can exist in every step of the listening process—hearing, acquiring, attending, and responding. The truck driver who is having a stressful day or the store clerk who is eager to meet friends after work may experience internal noise that can result in mistakes and difficulty in listening. Internal noise such as confusion, impatience, or annoyance may drown out valuable incoming messages.

Similarly, external noise can distract you and keep you from fully understanding a message. Trying to listen to a lecture when a room is too warm or too cold can create noise that makes it difficult to concentrate. Static on a telephone line or people talking loudly nearby are examples of external noise that may reduce listening efficiency.

MEMORY

Category	Explanation	Example
Immediate	Recalling information for a brief period of time	"Yes, Joe called a few minutes ago."
Short Term	Recalling information for carrying out a routine of daily task	"The homework assignment is to practice giving the presentation in front of a mirror."
Long Term	Recalling information from past experience	"I was very nervous my first day on the job."

INCLUSION STRATEGIES

MEETING INDIVIDUAL NEEDS

Less-Proficient Readers Encourage students to use periodic reviews of the chapter sections rather than waiting to review all the material the day before a test. You may also want to model mind mapping of key concepts signaled by major headings in each section, placing key words in a graphic structure that shows their relationship concretely.

Activity Have students review the main concepts of a section with a partner the day after reading it and again one week later. Have them create mind maps of the ten concepts they consider most important in the section and articulate them to their partners. A mind map might link important terms by arrows or a word web.

Barriers

Barriers to the listening process, like barriers to other aspects of communication, can prevent or block effective communication. Some of these barriers are shown in **Figure 6–6**. Speech problems, incompatible language, and reduced hearing ability are some of the external barriers that block message reception. External barriers tend to be harder to eliminate than noise because they involve more complex or long-term problems.

You also might experience internal barriers in the listening process. Internal barriers often result from ignorance, intolerance, fear, or traumatic experiences. They tend to be deeply rooted attitudes, biases, prejudices, and beliefs that interfere with listening.

Memory

Memory, or the process of retaining or recalling information, affects all aspects of the listening process. Without memory, there would be no knowledge and no learning. In addition, memory often is an incentive for listening. You may listen closely to an introduction to remember someone's name. You may listen to a lecture to remember facts that will show up on your next quiz. You may listen to a trainer to remember how to operate a new piece of machinery.

Memory is not always so straightforward, however. Like other aspects of listening, memory can be selective. For instance, you may choose what you wish to remember, remember an incident only as you wish to remember it, or eliminate or suppress certain memories if you do not wish to be reminded of them.

Three Types of Memory As shown in the Memory chart, memory can be classified into three categories: immediate memory, short-term memory, and long-term memory. Your ability to remember can be affected by many different factors, including not paying attention or being easily distracted. Others include mental or physical health problems, denial or suppression of memories, fatigue and stress, and communication overload. The tips in the Communication Strategies checklist are designed to help you improve your memory skills.

Using Feedback to Analyze Listening

One way to analyze your and others' listening is to look at the feedback. If the feedback does not appear appropriate, it might be because of one of the following situations.

- The receiver cannot or did not hear the message.

- The receiver may lack appropriate verbal or vocabulary decoding skills.

- The receiver may interpret the message as unrelated to him or her, or as uninteresting, offensive, or irrelevant.

Toward Effective Listening **185**

3 ASSESS

Assign Section 1 Assessment as a homework or in-class activity.

🔊 Use *Interactive Tutor Self-Assessment Software* to review Section 1.

Section 6–1 Quiz

MULTIPLE LEARNING STYLES

Visual Visually oriented students find graphics helpful in analyzing and understanding information.
Activity Have students make a web with a central circle titled *Reasons for Inappropriate Feedback*. Ask them to extend each reason for inappropriate feedback from the central circle. Then, they can give an example of each reason or an approach to elicit favorable feedback in response to the reason extending from its circle.

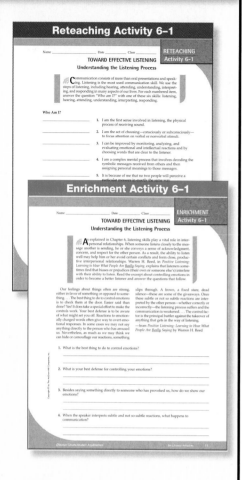

Reteaching Activity 6–1

TOWARD EFFECTIVE LISTENING
Understanding the Listening Process

Enrichment Activity 6–1

TOWARD EFFECTIVE LISTENING
Understanding the Listening Process

4 CLOSE

Refer students to the objectives on page 171 and have them summarize what they learned about each of these areas in studying this section.

Extra-Credit Project

Have students discuss listening strategies with a parent or adult friend and hold a conversation with the adult, after which both write down a summary of what they heard the other person say. Have the student compare the versions, list differences, and write a paragraph explaining why they differ.

- The listener's knowledge, attitude, feelings, or culture may be the source of unique or inaccurate interpretations of the intended message.

- The listener's response may reflect unique elements of personality, personal bias, or past experiences with which the sender is unfamiliar.

- Internal or external noise or barriers may interfere with listening and cause a discrepancy between expectations and responses.

- The listener may not remember the message.

- For any number of reasons, the listener may choose to give feedback that the speaker considers inappropriate.

You can use these checks to help you create an atmosphere of understanding. As you put these concepts to work in your life, remember that effective listening is a win-win situation. Not only does the speaker succeed in getting the message across, but you also have the opportunity to grow and learn.

Section 1 Assessment

GLENCOE *Online*

Visit the *Glencoe Communication Applications* Web site at **communicationapplications. glencoe.com** and click on **Self-Check and Study Guide 6.1** to review your understanding of the listening process.

Review Key Terms

1. Define each term and write it in a sentence: listening, hearing, attending, understanding, interpreting, responding.

Check Understanding

2. Relate the following to the importance of listening in professional and social contexts.

   Courage is what it takes to stand up and speak; courage is also what it takes to sit down and listen.

   —Winston Churchill

3. Identify the four steps of the listening process and describe their related functions.

4. Of the factors that affect listening, which do you think is the hardest to change? Why?

5. Give one specific suggestion for improving effectiveness in each step of the listening process.

6. **Cause–Effect** How might communication be different if no one ever provided feedback? Explain your answer.

APPLICATION *Activity*

Creating a Chart Talk with a parent or friend about the importance of listening effectively at his or her work or school. Ask how much total time he or she spends listening each day. Next, ask the person to describe effective and ineffective listening experiences he or she has had. Create a chart that lists the person's answers for both of these categories and share your findings as a class.

186   *Glencoe Communication Applications*

Section 1 Assessment Answers

1. Accept all reasonable sentences.
2. It is important to admit that we don't know everything. Rather, we can learn much from listening to others.
3. Acquire or hear the sounds of a message; choose which of these sounds to attend to; decode the sounds to understand the message; respond.
4. Barriers might be hardest to change because they tend to be long-held beliefs and attitudes.
5. Answers will vary but should reflect understanding of each step of the listening process.
6. Answers should reflect that there would be no assurance that messages have been received or interpreted correctly.

Application Activity Students may conclude that they should adopt the listening habits involved in the positive experiences and avoid those involved in the negative experiences.

RECALLING INFORMATION

Listening is useful only if you can recall what you heard. Recall is the ability to remember. It helps you put new information to use.

Learning the Skill

Follow these guidelines when you listen to a lecture or speech.

- **Focus your attention on the speaker.**
- **Be prepared to take notes.**
- **Listen for concepts.** Concentrate on the main points or concepts of the presentation. Concepts are different from facts. For example, a blueprint for building a skyscraper is a concept. The number of floors that will be in the skyscraper is a fact.
- **Ask questions.** If something is unclear to you, ask questions. If you don't have a chance to do this during the presentation, write your question down so you can ask it at a later time.
- **Listen critically.** Even if you think you already agree or disagree with a speaker's message, you should listen to the entire presentation. You can't be critical of a presentation if you haven't listened to it completely. To better understand the concepts being presented, pay close attention to the graphics and visual aids. Try to determine how this information might be useful.
- **Listen for emphasis and repetition.** Speakers use special voice tones and physical gestures when they want to emphasize an important idea. Watch and listen for these variations. Also, listen for ideas that are repeated. Speakers often repeat important aspects of a presentation.

Practicing the Skill

Read the sample presentation, then answer the questions that follow.

If we do not vote to build a subway system, we will be making the biggest mistake of our lives. We need a subway system because our roads are too crowded. Over 90 percent of us depend on our roads for transportation. We need a subway system because almost 60 percent of us sit in traffic jams at least once a week. Our roads are getting more crowded every day. We need a new means of transportation. We need a subway system.

1. Read the first sentence again. What is your initial reaction to this statement? Do you think what the speaker says is true?

2. What is the main concept of this presentation? How do you know?

3. What are some facts that the speaker uses in the presentation?

4. What questions would you ask if you were at this presentation?

APPLICATION *Activity*

With three or four other students, create a list of the ways you study for tests. Describe how you use class notes, homework, quizzes, and readings from the text. Have your group share its list with the rest of the class. Then, listen to the ideas presented by the other groups. Combine all the lists into one master list explaining how to study for a test.

Toward Effective Listening **187**

Recalling Information

Point out to students that the main ideas or concepts in a talk are revealed through the facts and examples. By asking themselves, "What overall truth is revealed by these facts?" they can better grasp concepts a speaker wants to communicate. Seldom does a speaker expect listeners to recall all the facts. However, listening to get "the big picture" is a learned skill requiring both active listening and an ability to step back from the details and summarize what is being communicated. Stimulation of multiple senses helps recall. For this reason, many presenters use visual aids or even involve audience participation. Ask students to tell about a speech or presentation they remember vividly and explain why. **L1**

Practicing the Skill

Have students discuss their responses to the questions.

1. Many students will think this is an overstatement.

2. Repetition makes clear that the main concept is the need to build a subway system.

3. Crowding of the roads, dependence of 90 percent of the population on the roadways, large percentage of population affected by weekly traffic jams

4. Students might ask: Why is a subway system the best solution? What would a subway system cost? Where would the money come from? How would it help long-distance commuters? What other solutions are possible? What would these solutions cost?

Application Activity

As groups share their study tips, point out that tests are a way of showing recall of what one hears and reads. Review the master list, having volunteers tell which tips help listening recall and which help reading recall. Remind students that note-taking skills are essential in college, where many professors lecture regularly.

1 FOCUS

Bellringer

Ask students to think of a time when they felt a friend or family member was not really listening to them. What listening signals were they looking for that they did not receive? *(Students may respond that they expected the complete attention of the listener and wanted verbal confirmation that their message had been received and considered.)* After discussing the first paragraph, have students read the next two paragraphs and describe different kinds, or levels, of listening they do each day. *(Students are likely to identify active listening situations, as in a class discussion, in which they listen and respond and passive situations, as when listening to a radio commercial, in which they listen but do not respond.)*

You may use Graphic Organizer Transparency 6–2 to introduce this section.

■ Visual Instruction

Answer The listening process changes because each listening situation can have different purposes and characteristics, requiring a different kind of listening.

Section 2

Developing Listening Skills

GUIDE TO READING

Objectives

1. Compare and contrast the characteristics of active, passive, and impatient listening.
2. Evaluate the results of active, passive, and impatient listening.
3. Describe the four kinds of listening.
4. Determine the most appropriate kind of listening for a given situation.

Terms to Learn

active listening
passive listening
impatient listening
critical listening
deliberative listening
empathic listening
appreciative listening

As you are searching frantically for a pen, one of your friends begins telling you about a movie he saw last night. You continue to rummage through your locker, occasionally mumbling "Uh-huh" or "Nope" when asked a question. After a few minutes, your friend says "Forget it. You're not even listening." You're sure you were acquiring, attending, understanding, and responding. So what's the problem?

Listening is listening, isn't it? If you can recall what your friend said about the movie, then weren't you listening effectively? The truth is, while your listening style may have been effective, your friend may not have seen it as appropriate. He probably wanted to participate in an interactive conversation with you. However, your lack of participation made the conversation too one-sided for his purposes.

In this section, you will learn that, although the listening process always is the same, it can have different purposes and characteristics from one situation to the next. Each purpose requires a different kind of listening. Each kind, in turn, requires its own set of communication skills.

■ **Close friendships are built on effective listening.** Why does the listening process change from one situation to the next?

188 *Glencoe Communication Applications*

RESOURCE MANAGER

Teaching Tools

- Interactive Lesson Planner
- Reproducible Lesson Plan 6–2
- Application Activities 6–2

Reproducible Masters

- Guided Reading Activity Workbook 6–2
- Enrichment Activity 6–2
- Reteaching Activity 6–2
- Section Quiz 6–2
- Transparency Strategies and Activities Booklet 6–2

Transparencies

- Graphic Organizer Transparency 6–2
- Chapter 6 Teaching Transparency

Technology Resources

- Interactive Tutor Self-Assessment Software
- Presentation Plus! Software
- ExamView® Pro Testmaker
- PuzzleMaker Software
- communicationapplications.glencoe.com

CHARACTERISTICS OF LISTENING

Imagine you and a friend disagree about who is the best singer of all time. What types of listening behaviors do you use as you debate the issue? Now think about your listening behaviors as you sit through a long meeting. In both cases, you are listening, but you probably take a more active role in one situation than in the other.

The listening process usually uses the same steps in the same sequence. However, the way that you listen varies according to the context and what you want to get out of the communication. You can listen three ways: actively, passively, or impatiently.

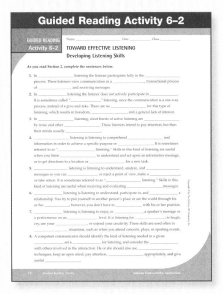

■ **Active listening is important to a child's education.**
Identify three ways to listen.

Active Listening

In active listening, the listener participates fully in the communication process. When you listen attentively, provide feedback, and strive to understand and remember messages, you are being an active listener.

Active listeners view communication as a dynamic, transactional process of sending and receiving messages. They see themselves as active participants in conversations, group discussions, and group decision-making processes. Generally, active listeners expect

listening to be rewarding and enjoyable. They demonstrate their enthusiasm by asking questions and giving positive, supportive feedback.

Competent communicators tell themselves, "There's something in this message for me. How can I gain the most from this interaction?" They realize that active listening results in certain valuable rewards. For example, active listeners typically make better grades than those who take more passive roles. They also tend to get more enjoyment and useful

Peanuts reprinted by permission of United Features Syndicate, Inc.

Toward Effective Listening **189**

CHAPTER 6
Section 2

2 TEACH

Guided Reading Activity 6–2

GUIDED READING
Activity 6-2

Name _____ Date _____ Class _____

TOWARD EFFECTIVE LISTENING
Developing Listening Skills

As you read Section 2, complete the sentences below.

1. In _____ listening the listener participates fully in the _____ process. These listeners view communication as a _____, transactional process of _____ and receiving messages.

2. In _____ listening the listener does not actively participate in _____. It is sometimes called "_____" listening, since the communication is a one-way process, instead of a give-and-take. There are no _____ for this type of listening, which results in boredom, _____, and a general lack of interest.

3. In _____ listening, short bursts of active listening are _____ by noise and other _____. These listeners intend to pay attention, but then their minds usually _____.

4. _____ listening is listening to comprehend _____ and information in order to achieve a specific purpose or _____. It is sometimes referred to as "_____ listening." Skills in this kind of listening are useful when you listen _____ to understand and act upon an informative message, or to get directions to a location or _____ for a new task.

5. _____ listening is listening to understand, analyze, and _____ messages so you can _____ or reject a point of view, make a _____ or take action. It is sometimes referred to as "_____ listening." Skills in this kind of listening are useful when receiving and evaluating _____ messages.

6. _____ listening is listening to understand, participate in, and _____ a relationship. You try to put yourself in another person's place or see the world through his or her _____; however, you don't have to _____ with his or her position.

7. _____ listening is listening to enjoy, or _____ a speaker's message or a performance on an _____ level. It is listening for _____ to laugh, cry, use your _____, or extend your creativity. These skills are used often in _____ situations, such as when you attend concerts, plays, or sporting events.

8. A competent communicator should identify the kind of listening needed in a given _____, set a _____ for listening, and consider the _____ with others involved in the interaction. He or she should also use _____ techniques, keep an open mind, pay attention, _____ appropriately, and give useful _____.

The Listener as Active Participant

After students read about the three ways of listening, have volunteers demonstrate each listening style as another person explains how to complete a task. Write the headings *Active Listening, Passive Listening,* and *Impatient Listening* on the chalkboard. Ask students to list defining qualities and an important benefit or disadvantage of each type of listening. Have students copy this table into their notebooks and refer to it as they study the section. **L2**

■ **Visual Instruction**

Answer You can listen actively, passively, or impatiently.

REAL-WORLD CONNECTION

Identifying Ways of Listening in Social Situations Students can learn to evaluate and improve their own listening skills by watching others.

Activity Have students observe the listening behaviors of a single person in a group setting—for example, in conversations at lunch, club or team meetings, and classroom settings. Ask them to identify which way of listening (active, passive, impatient) is applied in each situation they observe and then to list the behaviors by which they identified the type. Have each student select one of his or her observations to analyze and write a paragraph explaining why he or she thinks the person listened as he or she did and how communication was affected.

■ Visual Instruction

Answer Active listeners tend to make fewer mistakes, resulting in better performance, higher productivity, and increased value as employees.

Communication Tip

A reason many listeners' minds wander as they listen is because they can complete a sentence mentally before the speaker can complete it verbally. Boredom sets in, and they begin to daydream. Listeners can maintain their focus by summarizing the main points being made or by asking themselves questions to stay on task.

Application Activities 6–2

There are generally no rewards for passive listening. The results most often are boredom, apathy, and a general lack of interest in the people or topics involved in the communication.

Impatient Listening

In impatient listening, short bursts of active listening are interrupted by noise and other distractions. Impatient listeners usually intend to pay attention—and may even be successful for short periods of time—but then they allow their mind to wander in some way. Types of impatient listening are described in the following chart.

Impatient listeners fail to assume responsibility for promoting understanding in communication. They often make mistakes or forget details or instructions because they have "tuned out" the speaker and "tuned in" to some distraction or other interest. Impatient listeners may shift their gaze, nod, or give verbal comments such as "Right," or "Uh-huh" at inappropriate times. This "fake listening"

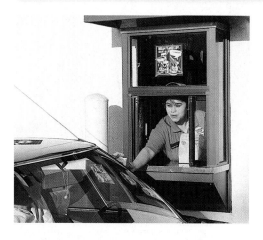

The fast-food employee shown must practice active listening skills in order to do the job effectively. **Identify ways in which active listening makes a productive employee.**

information from conversations and group discussions. On the job, active listeners tend to make fewer mistakes, resulting in better performance, higher productivity, and increased value as employees.

Passive Listening

In passive listening, the listener does not actively participate in interactions. Passive listeners think they can absorb information even when they do not contribute to the interaction. They tend to view communication as a one-way process and place the responsibility for successful communication on the speaker.

Passive listening is sometimes called "lazy" listening. Passive listeners often perceive themselves as message receivers rather than as interactors. The communication context is viewed as a one-way process rather than as a give-and-take. Passive listeners often view listening as easy or automatic and see little need to invest energy or effort in the process. They may easily become bored or distracted, ask few questions, or give negative nonverbal feedback.

190   *Glencoe Communication Applications*

TYPES OF IMPATIENT LISTENING

Type	Description
Anticipatory Listening	Listener anticipates what the speaker will say and then rushes ahead in his or her mind to plan a response
Defensive Listening	Listener's main goal in listening is to argue or disagree
Combative Listening	Listener's main goal in listening is to "win" or to put down a speaker
Distracted Listening	Listener pays attention to the first part of a statement, assumes what the speaker will continue to say, then stops listening and starts thinking about something else

MEETING INDIVIDUAL NEEDS — MULTIPLE LEARNING STYLES

Bodily-Kinesthetic Some students learn and express ideas best by using the whole body. Having these students demonstrate the three styles of listening enables others to solidify their understanding by greater visual stimulation.

Activity Divide the class into four groups and assign each group one type of impatient listening to role-play. Each group is to choose the topic for, participants in, and location of the listening occasion. Have them decide how their role play will illustrate the type of listening, write the script, and stage a skit of a minute or less. As the class observes each skit, have students tell at what point they realized the listener wasn't "getting the message."

COMMUNICATION

Demonstrating Listening Characteristics

PRACTICE LAB

To understand the advantages and disadvantages of listening actively, passively, and impatiently, follow these steps:

Step 1 As a class, brainstorm a list of listening occasions at home, at school, with friends, in organizations, and on the job. Ideas might include listening to a homework assignment or conversing with friends about what movie to see. List your ideas in a single column on the chalkboard.

Step 2 In a second column, list whether you would typically listen actively, passively, or impatiently in each situation.

Step 3 As a class, discuss the advantages and disadvantages of your usual listening choices.

Step 4 In a third column, list the most appropriate listening choice for each listening occasion. Discuss the reasons for your answers. Do you notice any patterns in this column?

---

effort is intended to mask a lack of concentration or interest. Instead, it is a dead giveaway that the listener is not paying attention.

Listening Flaws

Competent communicators avoid relying heavily on passive listening or using it inappropriately. They also avoid impatient listening whenever possible. Generally speaking, both of these characteristics can be classified as faulty listening habits.

On the other hand, effective listening skills include focusing attention on the message, clarifying meanings, and actively promoting understanding. Your challenge is to become an active listener whenever possible, participating fully in the communication process.

KINDS OF LISTENING

Just as you may listen in different ways—actively, passively, or impatiently—you also may have different goals for listening. Depending on your goal and the context of the

communication, you may choose a different kind of listening.

The four major kinds of listening include critical listening, deliberative listening, empathic listening, and appreciative listening. Each has

The listener shown above is exhibiting signs of **impatience.** Describe an impatient listener.

Toward Effective Listening **191**

COMMUNICATION
PRACTICE LAB

Demonstrating Listening Characteristics

Have students follow the four steps in the Communication Practice Lab on this page to analyze their listening patterns and the effects of these patterns. Help students to evaluate the appropriateness of their listening choices. Ask that volunteers explain what they may lose if they choose a passive or impatient listening role in an important communication situation, such as a customer complaint or a distress call from a friend. **L2**

GLENCOE *Online*

For an additional Practice Lab for this section, have students visit the *Glencoe Communication Applications* Web site at **communicationapplications.glencoe.com.** Click on Communication Practice Lab 6–2. **L1**

Communication Tip

To take notes as you listen critically in class, write down only key words and phrases. This allows you to continue to listen while you write. Highlight, star, or underline main ideas to make reviewing easier. Rewrite and refine your notes soon after the class. This helps you recall what you heard and makes it easy to understand your notes later.

■ Visual Instruction

Answer Impatient listeners intend to listen and pay attention but allow their minds to wander.

MEETING INDIVIDUAL NEEDS

INCLUSION STRATEGIES

Learning Disabled To make vocabulary less difficult, reword the four purposes for listening: listening to get a message (comprehension); listening to decide or act (judgment); listening to understand a person (personal meanings/feelings); listening to enjoy (performance).

Activity Write the kinds of listening on the board. Read each subsection of Section 2 aloud, substituting the new wording for critical listening, evaluative listening, empathic listening, and appreciative listening. Ask volunteers to describe situations in which each type of listening is needed. Discuss how the tips for each listening strategy can be applied.

Listening to Evaluate and Decide

Ask students to think of different persuasive messages they listen to each day. Invite volunteers to frame questions they ask themselves in order to analyze the arguments they hear. *(Examples might include "What reasons are given? Do they make sense? Has the speaker oversimplified the issue? Manipulated my emotions unfairly? Are the facts and figures accurate? Are they misleading? Is the speaker's logic sound?")* Point out the value of reserving judgment when you do not have all the information you need. **L2**

■ Visual Instruction

Answer The main purpose of listening critically is to comprehend ideas and information in order to achieve a specific purpose or goal.

COMMUNICATION *Strategies*

TIPS FOR CRITICAL LISTENING

After reviewing the tips with students, ask them to identify ways in which they can apply the skills to classroom interactions. *(Students may suggest that doing reading and other assignments before class and using effective listening strategies are ways they can apply the tips to classroom interactions.)*

These future chefs are listening critically to a lecture. What is the main purpose of listening critically?

a unique purpose, requires a specialized application of listening skills, and has its own rewards. When used effectively, each kind of listening can help you communicate successfully in social and professional contexts.

Critical Listening

The first kind of listening is probably very familiar to you. You use critical listening every day in school as well as in other areas of your life. Critical listening is listening to comprehend ideas and information in order to achieve a specific purpose or goal. Critical listening is sometimes referred to as "comprehensive listening" because your reason for listening is to comprehend or understand the sender's message.

Critical listening skills are particularly useful when you listen actively to understand and act upon an informative message. For example, when you listen to a lecture in class, you use critical listening because your goal is to acquire and understand information. You also use critical listening when you listen to announcements that inform you about upcoming school or social events. Critical listening skills also are important when listening to directions to a location or instructions for a new task.

Deliberative Listening

Deliberative listening is listening to understand, analyze, and evaluate messages so you can accept or reject a point of view, make a

COMMUNICATION *Strategies*

TIPS FOR CRITICAL LISTENING

- ✓ Identify the goal or purpose for listening.
- ✓ If possible, gather information about the topic before the listening experience to build a vocabulary and have background information available.
- ✓ Focus your attention on the sender's verbal and nonverbal messages.
- ✓ Organize the information to grasp the speaker's main idea and supporting details.
- ✓ Use perception checks to form appropriate responses.
- ✓ Consciously store the information in your memory bank.
- ✓ Ask questions, give appropriate feedback, and take appropriate action.

CRITICAL THINKING ACTIVITY

As deliberative listeners, students must sort out and evaluate a speaker's arguments. Have students select a videotaped persuasive speech, an advertisement, or a customer complaint they have handled on the job and evaluate it to identify any of the following flaws: irrelevant evidence (details that don't develop the point); oversimplifying the issue (assuming that an issue has only two sides); begging the question (staging a position that needs to be proved as though it were already proved); red herrings (introduction of a topic to distract from central issue and hide a weak argument); cause-and-effect errors (falsely assuming that because one event happened first, it caused another). Ask students to prepare a script of the spoken message they analyzed, highlight errors in reasoning, and attach an explanation of each error. 📑

decision, or take action. This kind of listening sometimes is referred to as "evaluative listening" because the listener's purpose is to analyze and evaluate information as a basis for future action.

You use deliberative listening skills when receiving and evaluating persuasive messages. Persuasive messages may range from a friend's plea of "I need help!" to a customer's request or complaint. In each case, you need to analyze and evaluate the message because you are expected to take some kind of action. What kind of help are you being asked to provide? Are you actually capable of helping your friend or should you refer him or her to someone else? What does the customer expect you to do to solve the problem? Would it be ethical or wise to do what the customer is asking? Listening to persuasive messages requires the listener to evaluate the message and deliberate, or think over, the position or action he or she is being asked to take.

Empathic Listening

Have you ever listened to a friend tell a story and felt that you could completely understand what the friend was going through? If so, you had empathy for that person. In other words, you understood and appreciated his or her situation. As you listened to the friend's story, you probably used empathic listening. Empathic listening is listening to understand, participate in, and enhance a relationship.

Even though empathic listening frequently is used in interactions between two people or in a small group, it can be used appropriately in larger group, social, professional, and public contexts. Regardless of the setting, the goal of empathic listening is to develop understanding and appreciation of the meanings and feelings expressed by a message sender.

COMMUNICATION Strategies
TIPS FOR DELIBERATIVE LISTENING

✓ Identify your goal or purpose for listening.

✓ If possible, gather information before the listening experience to provide a basis for evaluation, deliberation, and judgment.

✓ Listen specifically to understand, analyze, and evaluate the message.

✓ Organize your listening to grasp the speaker's claim or idea, the use of supporting information, the reasons to support the speaker's claim, and the use of emotional appeals and persuasive strategies.

✓ Observe the speaker's use of language and nonverbal cues to identify, analyze, and evaluate his or her attitudes or feelings. Then, determine whether these behaviors support or counteract the speaker's message.

✓ Analyze the speaker's motivation or intent.

✓ Reflect on your own responses and reasons for accepting or rejecting the speaker's message.

✓ Form reasoned responses and give appropriate feedback. Delay action if necessary.

✓ Reserve judgment if you are unsure of all the facts.

✓ When you feel you have enough information, make responsible decisions and take prudent action.

Toward Effective Listening **193**

COMMUNICATION Strategies
TIPS FOR DELIBERATIVE LISTENING

Introduce the tips for deliberative listening and review those for critical listening. Have the class explain which type of listening seems more complex and why *(deliberative listening because it requires evaluation and action in addition to receiving and processing messages)*. Have students brainstorm a list of occasions when they have had to use deliberate listening. Write the list on the board. Encourage students to use the tips consciously for a week and note any differences in their abilities to make decisions.

DID YOU KNOW?

Good listeners listen with their faces. Much of our time is spent in tuning out the abundance of information that is thrust at us. When listening, show by your body language that you are making yourself a receiver and make your face the satellite dish. The facial animation and emotion with which you react to the speaker make you a better listener and enhance the speaker's message-sending capability.

EXTENDING THE CONTENT

Making Yourself a Responsive Listener The Canadian Association of Student Activity Advisors gives the tips listed below for monitoring and improving your listening.
Activity Have students monitor these reactions and act on the suggestions for a full day, then report any improvement they noticed in their communication. (1) If you are listening intently, you should feel tired after your speaker has finished. (2) When you find yourself drifting away, change your body position and establish eye contact. (3) Lead with your face and make it react to what the person is saying. Make it an active and contoured catcher of information. (4) When listening, talk only to use receptive language, such as "I see," or to ask questions to clarify ideas. (5) Refrain from arguing mentally or prejudging what the speaker is saying.

COMMUNICATION *Strategies*

TIPS FOR EMPATHIC LISTENING

- Listen carefully to the speaker's words to understand the meaning of the speaker's message and the feelings he or she is expressing.
- Observe the speaker's nonverbal behaviors to analyze his or her feelings about the listener or the relationship involved and the context or situation.
- Monitor your understanding of the speaker, the message, and the situation.
- Analyze your own responses, feelings, biases, or prejudices toward the speaker, the message, or the situation.
- Use personal perception checks such as, "Is this what the speaker really is saying, or is this just what I am hearing and telling myself about the speaker's message?"
- Try to paraphrase the sender's message.
- Ask questions to help the sender clarify his or her meanings and feelings.

When you listen empathically, you try to put yourself in another person's place or see the world through his or her eyes. Empathic listening does not, however, mean listening to agree or to sympathize with those meanings and feelings. As an empathic listener you may find yourself saying, "I think I understand what you are saying, and I appreciate your concern, but I'm not sure I share your position on this issue."

Skills in empathic listening are essential for full participation in communication. They also are the key to developing productive personal relationships.

Appreciative Listening

Appreciative listening is listening to enjoy, or appreciate, a speaker's message or a performance on an artistic level. It is listening for fun—to laugh, cry, use your imagination, or extend your creativity. You most likely use appreciative listening skills in social situations, such as when you attend concerts, plays, dance presentations, or even sporting events. You also use appreciative listening or viewing when you attend movies or watch television, listen to music, or go to the theater.

The main goal of appreciative listening is enjoyment. Not only can appreciative listening help a person relax or escape from everyday stress, but it also can inspire and provide an outlet for personal growth and fulfillment.

The audience is practicing appreciative listening while being entertained by the musicians. *What is the goal of appreciative listening?*

Using the Four Kinds of Listening

Why do you need to know about the four major kinds of listening? It's no secret that people pay the most attention to what is interesting or important to them. When you

COMMUNICATION *Strategies*

TIPS FOR APPRECIATIVE LISTENING

- Listen with the goal of enjoying and appreciating.
- Consider selecting some listening experiences especially to expand your knowledge and understanding of art, philosophy, nature, or a particular sport.
- Before the listening experience, investigate the style and format of the performance and the techniques and skills used by the performers. Understanding the form, rules, or conventions of what is being performed may enhance your understanding, enjoyment, and appreciation.
- Become familiar with background information and critiques of the players or actors themselves to get the maximum results from your listening investment.
- Avoid distractions and keep your focus on the performance.
- Avoid making judgments about the performance until it is over.
- Respond appropriately to the ideas, feelings, and skills of the performers.
- Give appropriate and considerate feedback.

*inter*NET
A C T I V I T Y

Classical to Current You have probably heard someone say, "I don't like classical music!" How do you know if you have not tried it? You can find sample sound clips on the Internet by entering any of these words or phrases in your Internet search engine: music, jazz, German music, country music, classical music, dance music, reggae, blues, folk music, opera. Find and listen to any two types of music you have never heard before. Can you identify the different instruments? Does music ever have an impact on your mood? Why do you appreciate one type of music more than another? Why do you listen to music?

understand the goal of listening in a specific situation, you can pay attention to the things that are most important for reaching that goal. For instance, the goal of listening to a sales presentation is to evaluate the information so you can make a decision. Understanding this goal can help you concentrate on the information that is most important to making that decision.

Identifying the appropriate kind of listening for each situation is a valuable life skill. It not only helps you achieve the results you want but also helps others see you as an effective listener. Listening skills are highly valued in personal relationships, in school, in organizations, and on the job. Most importantly, they help you function effectively as a competent communicator. As a communicator, keep in mind the following when you are listening to the messages of others.

Toward Effective Listening **195**

COMMUNICATION *Strategies*

TIPS FOR APPRECIATIVE LISTENING

Discuss the tips with the class, asking students to list occasions when learning about the style or techniques of a performance beforehand was helpful. Have each student select a television program, movie, or live performance, approved by you, that represents a new experience. Students should investigate the genre or the style of the performance and its techniques. They should apply the tips for listening during the performance. Require students to note their research findings and responses to the performance in a journal. **L2**

3 ASSESS

Assign Section 2 Assessment as a homework or in-class activity.

Use *Interactive Tutor Self-Assessment Software* to review Section 2.

Section 6–2 Quiz

SECTION QUIZ 6–2

Name _____ Date _____ Class _____

TOWARD EFFECTIVE LISTENING
Developing Listening Skills

SCORE

Matching Match each item in the left column with the best selection from the right column. Write the letter of the item on the line provided. *(10 points each)*

_____ 1. active listening
_____ 2. critical listening
_____ 3. appreciative listening
_____ 4. empathic listening
_____ 5. deliberative listening

a. listening to enjoy
b. listening to understand and enhance a relationship
c. listening to comprehend ideas and information to achieve a goal
d. listening to analyze messages so you can make decisions or take action
e. listening to fully participate in the communication process

Multiple Choice In the blank provided, write the letter of the item that best answers each question. *(10 points each)*

_____ 6. What type of listeners often see listening as a one-way process and do not put much effort into it?
a. impatient listeners
b. passive listeners
c. critical listeners
d. active listeners

_____ 7. In what type of listening does the listener try to argue with the speaker?
a. impatient listening
b. passive listening
c. defensive listening
d. active listening

_____ 8. What type of listening should you use when you are given directions?
a. deliberative listening
b. empathic listening
c. appreciative listening
d. critical listening

_____ 9. What type of listening would you use to evaluate a persuasive message?
a. deliberative listening
b. empathic listening
c. appreciative listening
d. critical listening

_____ 10. What type of listening would you use to become more creative?
a. deliberative listening
b. empathic listening
c. appreciative listening
d. critical listening

MEETING INDIVIDUAL NEEDS

GIFTED AND TALENTED

Writing Lyrics Provide an opportunity for gifted students to write their own lyrics to music you select.

Activity Have students listen to a short musical piece that you selected. Ask them to write classroom-appropriate lyrics for the music. Encourage students to read, sing, or chant the lyrics to the music. Perhaps they could produce copies of their lyrics for other class members, who then perform with the lyric writer.

Reteaching Activity 6-2

Enrichment Activity 6-2

4 CLOSE

Ask students to jot down their listening strengths and weaknesses in the following areas:

1. acquiring, attending, understanding, and responding to messages they hear
2. critical, deliberative, empathic, and appreciative listening

Have each student write specific goals for improving in each area. They can be taped to a notebook or posted in a locker and checked periodically.

Extra-Credit Project

Ask students to talk to five teachers about how teachers determine if students in their classes are listening to their presentations. Create a list of these behaviors and share these with the remainder of the class.

- Try to identify the kind of listening needed in a given situation and then adapt to it.
- Set a goal for listening. Decide what you can gain from your listening experience. What is your specific listening task?
- As a part of your goal, consider the relationship with others involved in the interaction. Plan how you can use listening to protect or enhance the relationship.

- Use memory techniques to remember useful parts of the sender's message.
- Keep an open mind. Avoid prejudging what the sender is saying until you have heard everything he or she has to say.
- Be an interactive listener by paying attention, responding appropriately, and giving useful feedback.

Section 2 Assessment

Visit the *Glencoe Communication Applications* Web site at **communicationapplications. glencoe.com** and click on **Self-Check and Study Guide 6.2** to review your understanding of the characteristics and kinds of listening.

Review Key Terms

1. Define each term and write it in a sentence: active listening, passive listening, impatient listening, critical listening, deliberative listening, empathic listening, appreciative listening.

Check Understanding

2. Describe the characteristics of active, passive, and impatient listening. How are these characteristics similar to each other? How are they different?

3. Imagine that a friend is giving you complex directions to a shopping mall in another city. How should you listen— actively, passively, or impatiently? Why?

4. Consider critical, deliberative, empathic, and appreciative listening. Describe the main goal of each kind of listening.

5. **Apply** Imagine that you are a teacher listening to a student explain why she did not complete her report on time. The student wants an extra day to finish the report. What kind of listening would you use and why?

APPLICATION *Activity*

Listening with Purpose Working in four groups, listen to a volunteer read a short magazine article or, if a television is available, observe a single report from a newscast. Each group should listen to the performance using a different kind of listening—critical, deliberative, empathic, or appreciative. Discuss what types of information each group listened for and your resulting impressions of the performance. Did each group get something from the experience?

196   *Glencoe Communication Applications*

Section 2 Assessment Answers

1. Accept all reasonable sentences.
2. Active: participates fully in communication process; passive: does not participate fully; impatient: short bursts of active listening are interrupted by distractions. All involve the listener receiving messages, but not all involve the listener asking questions and giving feedback.

3. Active listening would allow you to ask questions and confirm information so that you do not get lost.
4. Critical: gathering information and determining whether it makes sense; deliberative: evaluating information so you can make a choice; empathic: understanding someone's situation; appreciative: enjoying for fun or to expand creativity

Communication Self-Assessment

Evaluating Your Listening Skills

How Do You Rate?

On a separate sheet of paper, use the key to respond to the following statements. Put a check mark at the end of each skill you would like to improve.

Key: A Always   **R** Rarely
        U Usually   **N** Never
        S Sometimes

1. I listen carefully to others in order to be a more successful communicator.

2. When I hear words that I don't know, I try to find out their meanings.

3. I realize that as a listener I share the responsibility for understanding the person speaking.

4. When a speaker presents a viewpoint different from mine, I work at understanding what is said rather than "tuning out" or becoming defensive.

5. To improve my listening skills, I maintain eye contact with the speaker and ignore outside distractions.

6. I choose my responses by evaluating the situation and weighing the consequences of my feedback.

7. I use memory skills like concentrating, taking notes, and organizing ideas when I listen to a presentation.

8. To help me listen more actively, I tell myself, "There's something in this message for me."

How Do You Score?

Review your responses. Give yourself 5 points for every A, 4 for every U, 3 for every S, 2 for every R, and 1 for every N. Total your points and evaluate your score.

31–40 Excellent You may be surprised to find out how much you can improve your skills.

21–30 Good In this course, you can learn ways to make your skills better.

11–20 Fair Practice applying the skills taught in this course.

1–10 Needs Improvement Carefully monitor your improvement as you work through this course.

Setting Communication Goals

If you scored Excellent or Good, complete Part A. If your score was Fair or Needs Improvement, complete Part B.

Part A   **1.** I plan to put the following ideas into practice:

          2. I plan to share the following information about communication with the following people:

Part B   **1.** The behaviors I need to change most are:

          2. To bring about these changes, I will take these steps:

Communication Self-Assessment

Have students respond to the ten statements, using the key provided, then evaluate their communication skills using the scoring rubric. Based on their scores, have students complete either Part A or Part B of the goal-setting activity. Suggest that they write their specific goals on a separate sheet of paper and post it in a location where they will see it often and use it to improve their skills.

Communication Journal Activity

Point out to students that to accomplish goals, one must make them specific and concrete and review them often to assess progress. Have students use their goals from this activity to create an organized plan for improvement in listening and write their plan in their Communication Journals.

BUSINESS BRIEF

The Better Business Bureau advises that to handle customer complaints effectively, a businessperson must listen carefully and calmly. He or she should note on what date the problem occurred, what product or service was involved, what caused the complaint, and what the complaint is; hear what the customer expects and understand how he or she feels; respond in a clear, specific manner and avoid blaming the computer or "them" or saying "I can't"; formulate a solution that allows for both technical and emotional issues.

Section 2 Answers, continued

5. Students may answer *empathic* because the teacher might understand and appreciate the student's situation even if he or she doesn't approve of it or *deliberative* because the teacher needs to determine whether or not to take the action the student is requesting.

Application Activity The critical listening group might focus on the information in the report or article; the deliberative group might decide whether it agrees with the reporter or writer's point of view; the empathic group might identify with the characters; the appreciative group might focus on the setting, wording, or images invoked.

Note Taking

Objectives: To practice taking notes while listening; to evaluate and improve note-taking skills

Teaching Suggestions and Strategies

Connection to the Workplace

Point out to students that many occupations involve jargon, or a specialized vocabulary that has meaning within the workplace. In meetings and work sessions, where these terms are used, workers may find it helpful to know abbreviations to make note taking easier. In addition, in the workplace, many presenters give the audience an outline covering their major points and may provide copies of the graphs that they will show on tables or in slides. Many employees use these forms to follow major points and concepts and to add their own notes about pertinent details.

Grammar Tip

Abbreviations may be picked up from notes and used in papers or reports. Be sure to capitalize abbreviations formed from proper nouns (U.S. Congress) and those related to dates and times (A.M., B.C.). Many abbreviations are followed by a period. Two exceptions are ZIP code abbreviations of state names (AR = Arkansas) and organization names formed from initial letters (NASA, IRS).

Note Taking

Note taking is a way of recording the important parts of a speech or presentation. Taking notes also helps you recall information. You should take notes

- in class
- during an interview
- at business presentations
- in press briefings
- when learning a new skill
- when doing research

The guidelines explained below will help you get the most out of your notes.

Survey the situation. When you begin, write down the date, time, and place of the presentation. Record the topic of the lecture, and list the names of the people presenting the information.

Listen carefully. Follow the speech as closely as possible. Presenters usually tell the audience which parts of their speech are the most important. Write down the main ideas as they are introduced. Leave space between the main points to add supporting information as it is given.

Know what to write. How you take notes will mainly be determined by the kind of information being presented. If you are taking notes on a history lecture, your focus will probably be on important people, events, and dates. At a business meeting, you might find it useful to record information shown in graphs or charts. When learning a new skill, you'll want to record all of the steps necessary to complete that process. Most of the time, your notes will resemble an informal outline. There will be main points and subpoints, mostly written in a very brief style.

Keep your notes short and to the point. Don't try to write down every word the speaker says. Instead, try to write as little as possible while still getting the main ideas. You can do this in many different ways. One method is abbreviating long words or phrases. If you are at a lecture about the United States Department of Agriculture, for example, you could use the initials *USDA*. Also, common words like *a, an,* and *the* can be left out of your notes. When possible, use symbols to represent numbers, money, and percentages. Use a plus sign instead of the word *and*. Another way to take shorter notes is to paraphrase what is being said. When you paraphrase information, you are putting it into your own words. Use short sentences when you paraphrase.

Stay alert. Keep your attention focused on the speaker. If there are loud noises or

 For additional information about business writing, see the *Guide to Business Communication* section of the Communication Survival Kit in the Appendix.

CRITICAL THINKING ACTIVITY

Many students lack the experience as listeners to confidently determine which information represents key concepts. Brainstorm a list of cues that can help listeners determine what they should be writing down. *(The list may include pre-listening research, the speaker's introductory statements, the fact that main ideas often come at the beginning of a "paragraph" [subsection of a talk] and are repeated at the end of it; tracking visuals; and practicing to gain confidence and discernment.)* Have students interview each other about a topic or skill the interviewee knows well. Encourage interviewees to use visuals. The interviewer's job is to take notes that capture main ideas and steps in processes. Ask interviewees to review the notes Thnd point out any steps or concepts that are missing. Then, have students reverse roles and repeat the process.

other distractions, you will have to listen more carefully. You may have to ask the presenter to speak louder or pause until the disturbance stops. Ask questions if you do not understand the information being presented.

Taking Notes at a Business Seminar Suppose you attend a seminar on documenting Internet research sources. Your notes might look something like the ones shown below. Which suggestions for taking notes have been followed in this example?

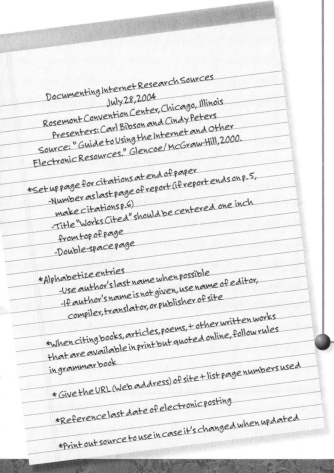

Documenting Internet Research Sources
July 28, 2004
Rosemont Convention Center, Chicago, Illinois
Presenters: Carl Bibson and Cindy Peters
Source: "Guide to Using the Internet and Other Electronic Resources." Glencoe/McGraw-Hill, 2000.

*Set up page for citations at end of paper
  -Number as last page of report (if report ends on p. 5, make citations p. 6)
  -Title "Works Cited" should be centered one inch from top of page
  -Double-space page

*Alphabetize entries
  -Use author's last name when possible
  -If author's name is not given, use name of editor, compiler, translator, or publisher of site

*When citing books, articles, poems, + other written works that are available in print but quoted online, follow rules in grammar book

* Give the URL (Web address) of site + list page numbers used

*Reference last date of electronic posting

*Print out source to use in case it's changed when updated

WRITING Activity

Turn back to the section titled "Critical Listening" on page 190, then follow these instructions with a classmate. Use this activity to improve your note-taking skills.

- Assume that this information is being presented in a seminar or workshop. Read this selection aloud while your partner takes notes, then switch roles (your partner reads the same information while you take notes).

- After you have both taken notes, switch papers.

- Read your partner's notes. Find the date, time, and location of the presentation and circle this information. If this information is not in your partner's notes, write it at the top of the page.

- Locate the main idea and put a star to the left of it. If you cannot find the main idea, write it in.

- Look for abbreviated words or symbols. Circle any examples that you find.

- Underline any paraphrased information.

- Return the notes to your classmate.

- Discuss any shortcuts or abbreviations you learned from the activity.

Teaching Activity

Have students discuss when they take notes and how they use their notes. Invite volunteers to share what is most difficult about taking notes. *(Many students may cite their inability to listen to and write down information at the same time.)* Point out that trying to write down too much detail in notes can cause problems. The listener is distracted by "getting it all down" and cannot listen closely. Hasty notes are often illegible. Explain that a better technique is to think before listening about which types of information you want to record, write down only key points, and rewrite notes after listening to summarize what is most important. Give students a five-minute lecture on a topic of your choice. Have them take notes and then compare these notes with classmates, noting any differences.

WRITING Activity

Sample Answer
10/26/2001
Communications Class
5th Period

Critical Listening
- listening to understand message
- used to understand + act on info
- important when listening to directions

Tips for Critical Listening
- identify listening goals
- prepare yourself for listening
- focus on sender's messages
- organize info
- ask questions + take action

GRAMMAR PRACTICE

Abbreviations

Have students write the correct abbreviation for each word or phrase listed.

1. anno Domini *(A.D.)*

2. before Christ *(B.C.)*

3. ante meridiem *(A.M.)*

4. post meridiem *(P.M.)*

5. Federal Bureau of Investigation *(FBI)*

6. North Michigan Avenue *(N. Michigan Ave.)*

7. District of Columbia *(D.C. or DC)*

Additional Resources

Appendix, "Guide to Business Communication"

Glencoe Writer's Assistant CD-ROM

Glencoe Interactive Grammar Software

Grade 9 Writer's Choice, Lesson 27.1

CHAPTER 6 Assessment and Activities

Visit the *Glencoe Communication Applications* Web site at **communicationapplications. glencoe.com** and click on **Chapter 6 Activity** for additional practice in listening effectively.

Reviewing Key Terms

1. Listening
2. attending
3. Hearing
4. interpreting
5. responding
6. Active
7. impatient
8. critical
9. deliberative
10. empathic

Reviewing Key Terms

On a separate sheet of paper, write the communication term that completes each statement.

1. _____ is a physical and psychological process involving acquiring messages, assigning meaning to them, and responding.

2. The act of choosing to pay attention to verbal or nonverbal stimuli is called _____ .

3. _____ is a filtering process that begins when sound is relayed to your brain.

4. When you personalize a sender's message to determine meaning, you are _____ .

5. The listener's intellectual and emotional reaction to a message is called _____ .

6. _____ listening includes listening attentively, providing feedback, and trying to understand and remember.

7. Listening only to argue or disagree is a type of _____ listening.

8. The goal of _____ listening is to comprehend the listener's message.

9. The purpose of _____ listening is to analyze and evaluate information as a basis for future action.

10. An important goal of _____ listening is to enhance a relationship.

Reviewing Key Concepts

1. Are listening and hearing the same thing? Why or why not?

2. What are the four active components of listening?

3. Explain the roles of the outer ear, middle ear, and inner ear in the process of hearing.

4. List six ways to improve your attending skills.

5. What other process must come first before you can interpret a message?

6. What are usually the consequences of passive listening?

7. List the four factors that influence listening.

8. What style of listening would you choose when a sales person is trying to sell you a product?

Reviewing Key Concepts

1. No; hearing is the first physical step in the listening process; it doesn't imply understanding or include response.

2. Acquiring, attending, understanding, responding

3. The outer ear picks up sound waves; the middle ear amplifies them; the inner ear transforms waves into electric impulses and sends them to the brain.

4. Evaluate what is important; have a positive attitude toward the message; focus on the message; decide what you will gain; ignore distractions; maintain concentration

5. Decoding, or assigning meaning to the message

6. Boredom, lack of interest

7. Noise, barriers, memory

8. Deliberative

Assessment and Activities

Reading and Critical Thinking Skill

1. **Synthesis** Imagine you are a flight attendant. A passenger complains that the airplane's aisle is too narrow. How would you respond to resolve the conflict with humor?

2. **Cause-Effect** What results when a listener fails to give appropriate feedback?

3. **Classifying Information** Under which key factor that influences the listening process would you classify an intolerance for bluegrass music?

4. **Applying Information** Which style of listening should a student choose during a lecture given in class?

Skill Practice Activity

Recalling Information Adapt the tips suggested for improving memory to prepare for your next exam.

- Concentrate on the teacher's words as he or she lectures.
- Jot down the important points in notes.
- After the lecture, paraphrase, rehearse, repeat, or write the information to seal it in your memory.

- Form mental associations and organize elements of information into related memory clusters.
- Memorize facts in small portions, rather than cramming for the exam the night before.

After you receive your graded exam, compare the grade to one you received before you tried to improve your memory skills.

Cooperative Learning Activity

Graphing the Effects of Noise Make three lists, each including ten simple words. Have the rest of the class prepare sheets of paper for a spelling test. Choose a music CD that your teacher has previewed, then read the list of the words for the class to spell while the CD is playing. Turn off the CD and present the second list of words to the class. Say the words on the third list quickly in succession. Grade the tests and analyze the scores. Then draw a conclusion about oral tests and noise based on the analysis.

Chapter Project

Planning Test the theory that many people's longest-lasting memories are formed between the ages of seventeen and twenty-five. Interview an adult from your parents' or grandparents' generation. Ask him or her to describe the ten most memorable events of his or her life. Then, note the age of the speaker at the time of each event.

Presenting As a class, combine the data from the interviews. Plot the number of events remembered for each age between one and fifty on a large graph displayed in the classroom and use this graph to reach a conclusion about the validity of the experts' theory.

Toward Effective Listening **201**

Reading and Critical Thinking Skill

1. **Synthesis** Answers will vary but might suggest a gentle joke that reminds of the physical limitations and need to adapt on an aircraft. Sarcasm or anxiety-producing answers are not acceptable.

2. **Cause-Effect** The speaker terminates the communication or tries a different approach to get through.

3. **Classifying Information** Barriers

4. **Applying Information** Critical

Skill Practice Activity

Recalling Information

You may want to have students practice note taking in your class as they view a film or listen to a lecture. Have students compare notes and practice paraphrasing important points. Some students may need pointers on using imagery and organizing "bites" of information logically to assist in recall.

Cooperative Learning Activity

Graphing the Effects of Noise

As they prepare the experiment, be sure students are aware they must control elements such as the difficulty of the word lists and the speed and clarity with which words are read. Have students work in a small group to design and complete a graph showing the high, low, mean, and median scores for each ten-word quiz.

Chapter Project

Also have students categorize and group the events cited. Do they conform to a pattern? That is, are certain life events (such as graduations, career decisions, marriages, births of children, deaths of family members) mentioned by all respondents? Discuss as a class the relationship between age and the nature of an event in establishing its importance to the individual.

After students have completed the project, have them assess the listening skills they used. How do they think this chapter helped them in their interviews?

Sentence Structure
Multiple-Choice
Theme: Communication Technology

Teaching Strategy

Encourage students to read each underlined section of the passage and try to identify an error *before* looking at the answer choices.

If students have trouble seeing the error, they can look at the directions to remind themselves of the possibilities. The underlined section could have any of the following:
• incomplete sentences
• run-on sentences
• sentences that should be combined
• nothing wrong at all

You may also want to ask students to decide what they could do to make the underlined section better.

Students should then read through each answer choice and determine if it contains one of the errors listed above. If it does, it can be eliminated. If it does not, it should be left as a possible "best answer."

If students carefully read the underlined section a few times and there is no sign of an incomplete, run-on, or choppy sentence, they should still read through the choices thoroughly to be sure they are all "worse" than the original.

Read each passage. Some sections are underlined. The underlined sections may be one of the following:

> •**Incomplete sentences**
>
> •**Run-on sentences**
>
> •**Correctly written sentences that should be combined**
>
> •**Correctly written sentences that do not need to be rewritten**

Choose the best way to write each underlined section and mark the letter for your answer. If the underlined section needs no change, mark the choice "Correct as is."

Thomas Edison was a masterful inventor, Edison was also very skilled at improving
(1)
existing inventions. His first invention was a gadget that made communication

easier, and believe it or not, it nearly cost him his job.

Invented by Samuel Morse in 1838. The telegraph allowed the first reliable form
(2)
of long-distance communication. As a young boy, Edison was fascinated by the

telegraph. At the age of sixteen. Edison moved to Canada to become a telegraph
(3)
assistant. His job was to report to Toronto every hour by telegraph signal. Young

Edison came up with a better idea. He converted the telegraph's mechanism so that

it would transmit and receive automatically. Edison's boss discovered him asleep at
(4)
his station. Edison was almost fired. Edison's invention was later used as part of the

automatic telegraph, improving worldwide communication.

 Test-Taking Tip

It is important for students to think critically about the underlined section before looking at the answer choices. If students read the answer choices immediately, they can often be confused by more than one choice that "sounds" good.

 Test-Taking Tip

Students need to have eagle eyes when reading the answer choices. They may all look similar, but there is an important difference between a period and a comma!

1 A Thomas Edison was a masterful inventor, and he was also very skilled at improving existing inventions.

B Thomas Edison was a masterful inventor. And Edison was also very skilled at improving existing inventions.

C Thomas Edison was a masterful inventor, he was also very skilled at improving existing inventions.

D Correct as is

2 F Invented by Samuel Morse in 1838, the telegraph allowing the first reliable form of long-distance communication.

G Invented by Samuel Morse in 1838, the telegraph allowed the first reliable form of long-distance communication.

H Invented by Samuel Morse in 1838, the telegraph. It allowed the first reliable form of long-distance communication.

J Correct as is

3 A At the age of sixteen, Edison moved to Canada, it was to become a telegraph assistant.

B At the age of sixteen, Edison moved to Canada. To become a telegraph assistant.

C At the age of sixteen, Edison moved to Canada to become a telegraph assistant.

D Correct as is

4 F Edison's boss discovered him asleep at his station, but Edison was almost fired.

G Edison's boss, who discovered him asleep at his station, was almost fired.

H When Edison's boss discovered him asleep at his station, Edison was almost fired.

J Correct as is

STOP

THE PRINCETON REVIEW

Test-Taking Tip

Number 4 is a difficult item for many students because there is no clear violation of sentence structure rules. Many students may be tempted to choose J, "Correct as is," because the sentences are not fragments or run-ons. Remind them that there is a third "error": short, choppy sentences that need to be combined. This is an error in style more than structure, and students need to be aware that they must strive to retain the meaning of the original.

Answers and Analyses

1. A The original section contains a run-on sentence because two complete sentences are joined with a comma, so choice D should be eliminated. Choice A fixes this problem by inserting *and* after the comma. It also improves the flow of the sentence by replacing the second *Edison* with *he*. Choice B is not the best answer because although it fixes the comma splice, it retains the choppiness of the original. Choice C is still a run-on sentence.

2. G The underlined section contains an incomplete sentence because "Invented by Samuel Morse in 1838" contains no subject, so choice J should be eliminated. Choice F is also incomplete because the progressive form of "allow" cannot stand on its own. Choice G improves the section by making the fragment into an introductory clause set off by a comma. Choice H retains the error of an incomplete sentence.

3. C Students should be able to identify the error for this item because it is similar to the one just discussed. The underlined section contains an incomplete sentence, so choice D should be eliminated. Choice A corrects it but contains a run-on sentence. Choice B corrects it but also contains a new incomplete sentence. Choice C corrects it by making the fragment into an introductory phrase followed by a comma.

4. H Choice F does not make a logical connection between the two sentences, and choice G means something entirely different from the original. Choice H shows the connection between the two sentences more clearly than the original, implying causation. Choice J, "Correct as is," can be eliminated only because choice H will make the section better than the original.

Unit Objective
Students will learn to identify and demonstrate appropriate social and professional skills in interpersonal communication.

Unit Overview
Unit 2 provides students with the skills to develop proficiency in a variety of interpersonal contexts, from informal social exchanges to formal communication at work. Students will study and practice verbal, nonverbal, and listening skills in order to increase their confidence and effectiveness as friends, family members, colleagues, and participants in the interviewing process.

Internet Address Book
Record useful Internet addresses in the space below for quick reference.

_____

_____

_____

_____

_____

_____

_____

_____

_____

_____

_____

_____

_____

_____

UNIT 2
Interpersonal Communication

204

VISUAL INSTRUCTION ACTIVITY

Have students examine the photograph on pp. 204–205. Invite volunteers to describe what they notice about the woman in the picture. *(Students may comment on her confident smile, her well-groomed appearance, her steady eye contact, and the printed material conveniently at hand.)* Ask: **What do you think is the most important aspect of effective communication with others at work?** *(Answers may include acting confidently, looking good, knowing your subject thoroughly, coping with differences of opinion, learning to say what you mean without causing offense, and identifying the line between professional and social relationships.)*

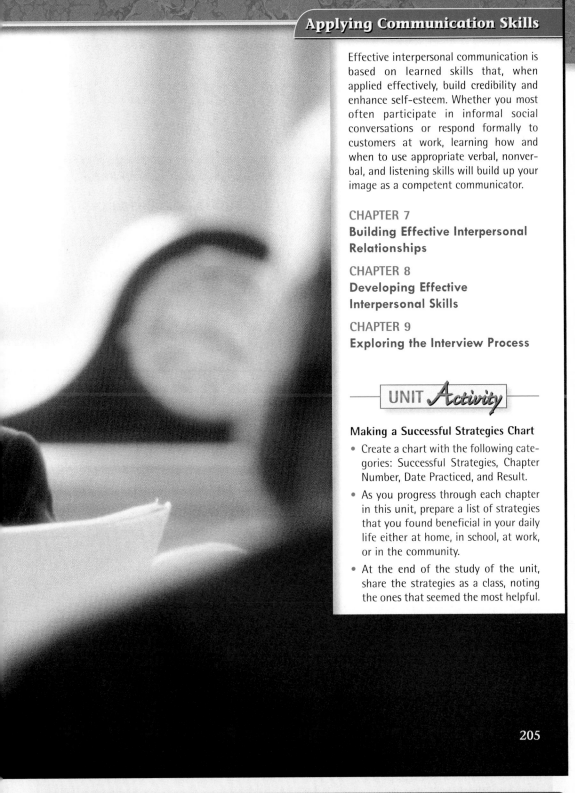

Applying Communication Skills

Effective interpersonal communication is based on learned skills that, when applied effectively, build credibility and enhance self-esteem. Whether you most often participate in informal social conversations or respond formally to customers at work, learning how and when to use appropriate verbal, nonverbal, and listening skills will build up your image as a competent communicator.

CHAPTER 7
Building Effective Interpersonal Relationships

CHAPTER 8
Developing Effective Interpersonal Skills

CHAPTER 9
Exploring the Interview Process

UNIT *Activity*

Making a Successful Strategies Chart
- Create a chart with the following categories: Successful Strategies, Chapter Number, Date Practiced, and Result.
- As you progress through each chapter in this unit, prepare a list of strategies that you found beneficial in your daily life either at home, in school, at work, or in the community.
- At the end of the study of the unit, share the strategies as a class, noting the ones that seemed the most helpful.

205

Introducing the Unit
Write the words *international, interstate,* and *Internet* on the chalkboard, and ask students what they think the prefix *inter-* means. Elicit from students the meaning "between." Point out that interpersonal communication refers to verbal and nonverbal exchanges between two people. Brainstorm with the class for skills that might be involved in interpersonal communication and write their answers on the board. Ask how these skills might be necessary in social or professional contexts. Point out that Unit 2 contains information on interpersonal communication that will help students achieve their goals in all areas of their lives.

Unit Assessment
After students have completed Unit 2, assign the Unit 2 Assessment in the *Glencoe Communication Appplications Chapter and Unit Tests.*

Testmaker Use the *Glencoe Communication Applications ExamView® Pro Testmaker* software to create a customized Unit 2 test.

UNIT *Activity*

Point out to students that practical communication strategies are provided throughout the text. Assign the following strategies as needed:

Improving Attending Skills, p. 9
Improving Memory Skills, p. 15

For additional strategies, see the "Guide to Business Communication" in the Communication Survival Kit on pages 635–659.

COMMUNICATING IN THE COMMUNITY

Give students firsthand experience with the interviewing process by inviting an executive from a local business or an administrator from a college or university to conduct model interviews in your class with student volunteers. Inform students beforehand of the interview's subject in order to allow them time for preparation. Ask your guest for an assessment of the volunteers' performances. Invite students to comment on the procedure and to ask for tips on successful interviewing.

Chapter 7 Planning Guide

SECTION RESOURCES

Daily Objectives	Reproducible Resources	Multimedia Resources

Section 1

1. Identify the types of interpersonal relationships in professional and social contexts
2. Explain the importance and purpose of each type of interpersonal relationship
3. Describe the five characteristics of productive interpersonal communication

 Reproducible Lesson Plan 7-1
 Application Activities 7-1
 Guided Reading Workbook Activity 7-1
 Vocabulary Activity 7*
 Reteaching Activity 7-1*
 Enrichment Activity 7-1*
 Graphic Organizer Transparency Strategies and Activities 7-1

 Graphic Organizer Transparency 7-1
 Chapter 7 Teaching Transparency
 Interactive Tutor Self-Assessment
 PuzzleMaker
 ExamView® Pro Testmaker
 Interactive Lesson Planner
 Communication in Action Video Chapter 7
 MindJogger
 communicationapplications.glencoe.com
 Presentation Plus!

Section 2

1. Identify and describe four types of personal style
2. Determine your own current personal style
3. Explain how differences in personal style can affect interpersonal relationships

 Reproducible Lesson Plan 7-2
 Application Activities 7-2
 Guided Reading Workbook Activity 7-2
 Vocabulary Activity 7*
 Reteaching Activity 7-2*
 Enrichment Activity 7-2*
 Graphic Organizer Transparency Strategies and Activities 7-2

 Graphic Organizer Transparency 7-2
 Chapter 7 Teaching Transparency
 Interactive Tutor Self-Assessment
 PuzzleMaker
 ExamView® Pro Testmaker
 Interactive Lesson Planner
 Communication in Action Video Chapter 7
 MindJogger
 communicationapplications.glencoe.com
Presentation Plus!

Use Glencoe's *Presentation Plus!* multimedia teacher tool to easily present dynamic lessons that engage and motivate your students. Using Microsoft PowerPoint®, you can customize the presentations to create your own personalized lessons.

Also available in Spanish

 Blackline Master
 Transparency
 CD-ROM
 Videodisc
 Software
Videocassette
Web site

Chapter 7 Planning Guide

FOR THE TEACHER

Being Positive and Supportive in Interpersonal Communication

Ask students to take an inventory of their interpersonal relationship competence: Have them list and describe five occasions in the last week when they responded to someone with sincere praise or compliments, listened attentively to what someone else was saying, used perception checks to make sure they understood someone, gave encouraging or hopeful feedback, avoided using evaluative ("you should . . .") language, responded in terms of possibilities.

Direct students to form small groups with classmates and spend five to ten minutes daily in conversation. During this time, students should make a conscious effort to improve in one or more of these areas as they interact with classmates. At the end of a week, ask students to inventory their positive and supportive interactions again. Have them write about any changes they have noticed in their responses to each other.

CHAPTER RESOURCES

Resources for the Teacher

- *You Just Don't Understand: Men and Women in Conversation* by Deborah Tannen, Random House, 1991
- *Listening to Conflict: Finding Constructive Solutions to Workplace Disputes* by Erik J. Van Slyke, AMACOM, 1999
- *The 7 Habits of Highly Effective People: Powerful Lessons in Personal Change* by Stephen Covey, Simon & Schuster, 1993

Resources for the Student

- *What Type Am I? Discover Who You Really Are* by Renee Baron, Penguin USA, 1998
- *Be Your Own Executive Coach: Master High-Impact Communication Skills for Dealing with Difficult People, Improving Your Personal Image, etc.* by Peter Delisser, Chandler House Press, 1999
- *Changing the World: One Relationship at a Time: Focused Listening for Mutual Support and Empowerment* by Sheryl Karas, Crossing Press, 1998

Block Scheduling

Block scheduling differs from traditional class scheduling in the amount of time allotted to each period. The extended time frame provided by block scheduling affords you the opportunity to implement a greater number of research-oriented and activity-intense projects to motivate and involve your students. Activities that are particularly suited to use within the block-scheduling framework are identified throughout this chapter by the following designation:

KEY TO ABILITY LEVELS

Teaching Strategies have been coded for varying learning styles and abilities.

L1 **BASIC** activities for all students

L2 **AVERAGE** activities for average to above-average students

L3 **CHALLENGING** activities for above-average students

ELL English Language Learner activities

Chapter 7 Resource Manager

The following materials may be used when teaching the chapter. Materials for specific lessons are also shown at point-of-use in the margins of the Teacher's Wraparound Edition.

TEACHING TRANSPARENCIES

Chapter 7 Teaching Transparency

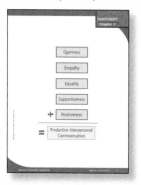

Graphic Organizer Transparency 7-1

Graphic Organizer Transparency 7-2

APPLICATION ACTIVITIES

Chapter 7, Section 1

Chapter 7, Section 2

Chapter 7, Cumulative

REINFORCEMENT AND REVIEW ACTIVITIES

Vocabulary Activity 7

Guided Reading Activity Workbook 7-1, 7-2

Reteaching Activities 7-1, 7-2

Chapter 7 Resource Manager

Section Quizzes 7-1, 7-2

Chapter 7 Test, Forms A & B

Performance Assessment Activity 7

ENRICHMENT AND EXTENSION

Technology Application Activity 7

Enrichment Activities 7-1, 7-2

SPANISH RESOURCES

- Spanish Chapter and Unit Tests
- Spanish Vocabulary Activities
- Spanish Section Quizzes
- Spanish Reteaching Activities
- Spanish Enrichment Activities

MULTIMEDIA

- Interactive Tutor Self-Assessment
- ExamView® Pro Testmaker
- PuzzleMaker
- Communication in Action Videodisc and Videocassette
- MindJogger
- Interactive Lesson Planner
- Presentation Plus!
- Writer's Assistant
- Glencoe Interactive Grammar
- **communicationapplications.glencoe.com**

ORAL PRESENTATION ACTIVITIES

Activities 8, 9

TEACHER PLANNING AND SUPPORT

- Reproducible Lesson Plans
- Interactive Lesson Planner
- Presentation Plus!

CHAPTER **7**

Building Effective Interpersonal Relationships

WHY IT'S IMPORTANT

The secret to "getting along" with others is to learn how to interact productively with them on an interpersonal basis. To do this, you'll need to learn some special skills in communication.

To better understand interpersonal relationships, view the **Communication in Action** Chapter 7 video lesson.

GLENCOE Online

Visit the *Glencoe Communication Applications* Web site at **communicationapplications. glencoe.com** and click on **Overview–Chapter 7** to preview information about interpersonal relationships.

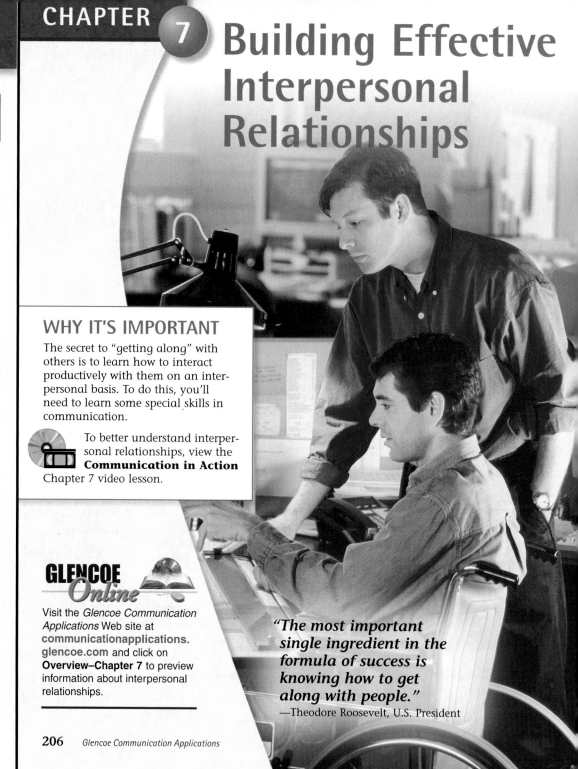

"The most important single ingredient in the formula of success is knowing how to get along with people."
—Theodore Roosevelt, U.S. President

WHY IT'S IMPORTANT

Invite students to comment on the photo and give their impressions of the similarities and differences between workplace relationships and friendships. Ask: **Why are some people able to get along with others well, while others seem to be in constant conflict?** *(Students may suggest that those who get along have genuine liking for and interest in others and communicate those attitudes well, while others may have poor self-image or unresolved anger that surfaces in their interactions with others.)*

Section 1

Understanding Interpersonal Relationships

GUIDE TO READING

Objectives

1. Identify the types of interpersonal relationships in professional and social contexts.
2. Explain the importance and purpose of each type of interpersonal relationship.
3. Describe the five characteristics of productive interpersonal communication.

Terms to Learn

integrating

*P*icture the beginning of a typical day. You get up, get dressed, and say good morning to someone in your family. Perhaps you discuss the day's plans as you eat breakfast. Then, it's off to school, where you communicate with various friends, classmates, and teachers all day. However, what if you never were allowed to speak with others on a one-to-one basis?

It's hard to imagine not communicating with others on a one-to-one basis—or at least in very small groups. How many times a day do you interact with teachers, coworkers, or fellow students? As you learned in Chapter 2, this level of one-to-one communication is called interpersonal communication. While most interpersonal communication occurs between only two individuals, it sometimes may refer to interaction among three family members, friends, or coworkers. It also includes one-to-one talk in formal interviews and professional conversations. It is through these types of interpersonal interactions that we build relationships and carry on the meaningful business of the day in professional and social contexts.

Interpersonal communication occurs between coworkers. What is the purpose of interpersonal communication in social and professional contexts?

Building Effective Interpersonal Relationships **207**

1 FOCUS

Bellringer
Have students volunteer their answers to the question asked in the opening paragraph. *(Students might respond that it would be nearly impossible not to communicate with an individual because some communications, such as requesting someone to pass something at a table, requires one-on-one communication.)* Then, ask students to describe the kind of face-to-face, one-on-one communication situation with which they are most comfortable. Which kind makes them most uncomfortable? Have them read the section to identify and characterize the types of interpersonal contact they just named.

You may use Graphic Organizer Transparency 7–1 to introduce this section.

Graphic Organizer Transparency 7–1

Visual Instruction

Answer Interpersonal communication can help build relationships and carry on meaningful business of the day.

RESOURCE MANAGER

Teaching Tools
- Interactive Lesson Planner
- Reproducible Lesson Plan 7–1
- Application Activities 7–1

Reproducible Masters
- Guided Reading Activity Workbook 7–1
- Enrichment Activity 7–1
- Reteaching Activity 7–1
- Section Quiz 7–1
- Transparency Strategies and Activities Booklet 7–1

Transparencies
- Graphic Organizer Transparency 7–1
- Chapter 7 Teaching Transparency

Technology Resources
- Interactive Tutor Self-Assessment Software
- Presentation Plus! Software
- ExamView® Pro Testmaker
- PuzzleMaker Software
- communicationapplications.glencoe.com

2 TEACH

Relating for Success

Remind students that President Theodore Roosevelt believed interpersonal communication was the single most important ingredient in success. Have students brainstorm a list of positive effects of good one-on-one communication skills in the workplace. Then, have students read the section to add to the list. **L2**

Guided Reading Activity 7–1

Name_____ Date_____ Class_____
GUIDED READING Activity 7-1

BUILDING EFFECTIVE INTERPERSONAL RELATIONSHIPS
Understanding Interpersonal Relationships

As you read Section 1, answer the following items.

1. Why are relationships at work and in social organizations important? _____

2. List the three types of relationships necessary for getting work done in a professional context.

3. Open and direct communication in the workplace between managers and employees has what three benefits? _____

4. What are some of the ways companies can promote positive employee relationships?

5. Why is customer loyalty so important to a company? _____

6. What are the three types of interpersonal relationships between members of an organization?

7. A lack of positive one-to-one interaction between members and leaders can lead to what three results? _____

8. What is the main purpose of member-to-member relationships? _____

9. What are the five characteristics most needed for effective interpersonal relationships?

10. What does *empathy* mean? _____

11. How should one try to speak to be supportive? _____

12. What three qualities indicate positiveness in an individual? _____

▪ Visual Instruction

Answer Employers look for individuals who work and relate well with others and who can form productive interpersonal relationships.

THE ROLE OF INTERPERSONAL COMMUNICATION

In Chapter 1, you learned that communication skills are vital to your success in professional and social contexts. However, of all your communication skills, interpersonal skills may be the most important to your employability, productivity, and career success. Interpersonal skills also play a significant role in the relationships that you develop.

Applicants who demonstrate strong interpersonal skills in interviews have a definite advantage over less-skilled communicators. Similarly, individuals who work and relate well with coworkers help promote goodwill and positive morale in the workplace. They also are more likely to keep their jobs or be promoted than peers who lack interpersonal skills.

On the other hand, poor human-relations and interpersonal skills can actually cause a person to lose his or her job. Employers and social organizations usually seek individuals who can form productive interpersonal relationships. The bottom line in workplace and social contexts is that harmonious, positive interactions produce a climate of cooperation. Cooperative relationships help improve morale, enhance success, and increase productivity.

RELATIONSHIPS IN PROFESSIONAL AND SOCIAL CONTEXTS

Relationships are formed and nurtured through interpersonal interactions. In fact, the quality of your interpersonal communication determines the quality and nature of your relationships. In other words, if your

Interpersonal communication skills can determine career success. *What type of applicants do employers and social organizations look for?*

communication is positive, the relationship that results is likely to be positive and productive. If your communication is hostile, rude, or otherwise perceived as negative, the relationship most likely will be negative, strained, or even hostile.

There are two important considerations regarding relationships in professional and social contexts. First, why are relationships important? Second, what kinds of relationships are necessary and appropriate at work and in various social contexts?

Importance of Relationships

Relationships at work and in social organizations are important because the people who work together in these settings are interdependent. That is, they must depend on one another and combine their tasks and skills to see that work is done efficiently.

For example, a supervisor may depend on his or her administrative assistant to send out

---

INCLUSION STRATEGIES

Special Needs Teenagers are highly motivated to develop rewarding relationships with their peers. Use their interest in this area to hold their attention as they read by engaging them in role-playing and observing activities that apply the relationship concepts expressed in the chapter.

Activity Assign employed students to develop skits involving relationships with employees, fellow workers, and the public. Students who participate on teams or in organizations can do the same for relationships with leaders and other members. After they complete Section 1, have students revise their skits to apply one or more characteristics of productive interpersonal communication (openness, empathy, and so on).

a memo to employees about a change in policy on the job. The employees then work together to adapt their individual tasks and functions to conform to the new policy. Similarly, in a social organization, a committee may establish procedures and goals for a community fund-raiser. The members of the organization then work together to see that the goals are reached.

Individuals in professional and social contexts not only are interdependent in their tasks and functions, but they also share resources and supplies. This means they must cooperate to keep budgets in line. As an employee or member of an organization, you may find yourself sharing a workroom, a locker, a fax machine, office supplies, tools, lunch room, and secretarial and accounting services with others. You also will need to share your time and have others share their time with you in order to meet the goals of the company, conduct daily business, meet deadlines, and work cooperatively.

Types of Professional Relationships

Relationships in professional contexts typically are determined by a company's culture and by the different roles individuals fill in the company's hierarchy. In other words, your day-to-day communication with others at work probably will be shaped by your role or function within the company. Professionals usually communicate role to role, depending on their job or function within the organization. There generally are three types of relationships necessary for getting work done in a professional context. These are relationships between

- management and employees
- employees and other employees
- employees and clients or the public

As you study each of these professional relationships, pay particular attention to the importance of each and to the purpose each serves to help the organization achieve its goals.

Communication Tip

Effective flow of messages in the workplace is crucial and requires an atmosphere of mutual understanding and trust. For real communication to occur, interactions among workers need to be based on sincere empathy—honest recognition of the needs and fears of the receiver.

COMMUNICATION PRACTICE LAB

Practicing Interdependent Communication

Provide students with an example description to show how to provide details that do not give away the object's identity. Students may discover that perception checks, empathy, descriptive language, and certain types of questioning strategies were most effective. Negativity, closed questions, and an impatient attitude probably were least effective. **L2**

COMMUNICATION PRACTICE LAB

Practicing Interdependent Communication

To practice communicating effectively in an interdependent relationship, follow these steps:

Step 1 Choose a partner.

Step 2 Have one partner describe an object in as much detail as possible. The partner should not name the object or hint at its identity through his or her clues and descriptions.

Step 3 The second partner should then attempt to draw the described object on a clean sheet of paper. Use a pencil to erase any mistakes.

Step 4 Exchange as much information and feedback as necessary to create an

accurate drawing of the described object. Remember, the describer cannot reveal the identity of the object or assist in the drawing.

Step 5 When you have completed your drawing, share it with the class and reveal what the object is supposed to be.

Step 6 As a class, discuss the types of communication skills you used when working interdependently with your partner. Which skills were most effective and which created problems?

GLENCOE Online

For an additional Practice Lab for this section, have students visit the *Glencoe Communication Applications* Web site at **communicationapplications.glencoe.com**. Click on Communication Practice Lab 7–1. **L1**

Building Effective Interpersonal Relationships **209**

CRITICAL THINKING ACTIVITY

Professional and social relationships among characters on TV sitcoms tend to be oversimplified and stereotypical. Invite students to list their "top five" pairs of characters on favorite TV shows. Be sure the list includes one or more pairs whose relationship is primarily business or professional. Discuss qualities in a character that make him or her stereotyped versus realistic. Have each student select one of the pairs from the list and watch them in action on one or more episodes, taking notes about how they interact and what their relationship is like. Ask students to create charts or write essays explaining what makes the relationship stereotyped rather than realistic.

Corporate Lines of Communication

Ask students why communications between a CEO of a corporation and employees tend to be one-way. *(Students may suggest that one CEO cannot relate one-on-one with thousands of employees; the large size of the corporation makes it unlikely that he or she would encounter most employees or have time to seek them out. Important messages therefore are written and communicated via e-mails, employee handbooks, and so on.)* Ask students to direct you in drawing a diagram on the chalkboard showing possible lines of communication in a large corporation and to suggest what kinds of relationships exist among the individuals who communicate interpersonally. **L2**

DID YOU KNOW?

The opening stage of a relationship, the initiation stage, when interactors are concerned with making a favorable impression on each other, may be as short as 10–15 seconds. At this stage, many people make judgments about whether to include or exclude the other from a possible relationship.

Grammar Tip

Who is a pronoun that can serve as the subject of a subordinate clause; the clause itself may work as a unit to modify another word in an independent clause. *Applicants **who** demonstrate strong interpersonal skills in interviews have a definite advantage.* The underlined clause modifies the subject in the clause *Applicants have a definite advantage.*

Management and Employees The culture, philosophy, and size of an organization usually determines the norms and protocol for communication between management and employees. In large companies, communication between upper-level management and employees may be indirect. This communication takes the form of written company policies, salaries, or benefits that establish the tone of the workplace.

For example, a chief executive officer for a large company may communicate concern for employees by providing generous sick-leave and health benefits, on-site child care, and extra vacation time as compensation for working overtime. His or her employees might then perceive the CEO as being generous and considerate. Therefore, the relationship between employees and upper-level management at that company is likely to be warm and mutually rewarding.

Communication between lower- or mid-level managers and employees tends to be more direct, immediate, and ongoing. It is more of a give-and-take type of relationship. For instance, it is the duty of all employees and managers to see that the company runs smoothly, work is carried out efficiently, and the clients' and customers' needs are met.

Managers and employees must be able to communicate clearly on a day-to-day basis and cooperate as a team to accomplish all of these goals.

Importance Positive relationships between managers and employees are important for a variety of reasons. As in any other interpersonal situation, the way individuals interact and form relationships establishes a climate for communication. When this climate is positive, morale is boosted, and the mood and tone of the workplace are improved. This typically results in increased productivity and higher job satisfaction.

Purpose The purpose of positive relationships between managers and employees is to keep open the lines of communication in the workplace. Open and direct communication helps clarify expectations, procedures, policies, and deadlines. It also invites participation, suggestions, and constructive feedback. Finally, it promotes a general sense of understanding and well-being on the job and generates a climate of mutual ownership in company decisions. In short, positive relationships between various levels of management and employees make businesses operate more efficiently and successfully.

DILBERT reprinted by permission of United Feature Syndicate, Inc.

COOPERATIVE LEARNING ACTIVITY

Explain that, according to communication theory, we use interpersonal communication for four basic needs: (1) to gain information about others so we can interact with them more effectively; (2) to better understand what others say in a given context; (3) to establish our identity in terms of the role we play in a relationship or the public image we present; (4) to express and satisfy interpersonal needs, such as the need to prove our abilities or experience affection. Group students by fours or fives and have each group watch a different video excerpt to note the interpersonal interactions it includes. Have the group categorize each interaction that members observe into one of the four areas defined above and write a brief description of it. Groups can create a table and compare the numbers and types of interactions represented.

Employees and Other Employees

The everyday work of a company is most often carried out by its rank-and-file employees. Even though these individuals are not members of management, they fill different roles and command different amounts of authority depending on their job functions.

Your school, for example, probably has teachers, a secretarial staff, a maintenance staff, a food-service staff, and other employee personnel. Each has a designated role within the school's overall hierarchy. Each has his or her area of expertise or authority. In order to carry out the business of your school, all these different employees need to work in cooperation with each other.

Most of the time, employees work productively together to accomplish the goals of a company. They form positive relationships that allow them to communicate with each other and function more productively in their jobs. Sometimes, however, differing levels of authority and responsibility can lead to problems among fellow employees. Tensions and competitiveness can create barriers to effective communication.

To avoid these problems, employees need to view themselves as valued members of a team. In a team, each person has a different role that is equally vital to the team's success. Therefore, it is expected that other team members will have different responsibilities and areas of authority. Once employees learn to understand and appreciate each other's contributions in the workplace, they may find it easier to form positive and productive employee-to-employee relationships.

Importance Positive employee relationships can be so important that some companies sponsor special events to encourage employees from all divisions to get to know one another better. These events may include company softball or basketball tournaments,

Tension and competitiveness in the workplace can create barriers to effective communication between employees. How can tension and competitiveness be avoided?

parties, picnics, or other social gatherings. The hope is that, through these events, employees will develop closer, more positive interpersonal relationships.

Purpose Employees who form positive relationships with coworkers have a better understanding of their interdependence with others on the job. This makes them more likely to cooperate and communicate productively in the workplace. It also adds to employees' enjoyment of their jobs. As a result, they tend to do better work. In general, employees—and the company as a whole—benefit from positive productive relationships in the workplace.

Employees and Clients or the Public

One-to-one communication between the employee and the individual customer can have a great influence on a company's success. Most companies realize that their overall image is a reflection of these interpersonal relationships. Because this is so important,

Building Effective Interpersonal Relationships **211**

Team Concepts in the Workplace

Ask students to name a situation in their school, social, or work lives in which they consider themselves part of a team. Encourage them to describe the qualities that are helpful in working with others in these situations. You might also ask members of your school's staff to visit the class and speak for several minutes about how the staff cooperate to accomplish their work and goals. As a class, brainstorm a list of all the jobs performed in the school. Have volunteers draw lines between those that require interaction, explaining their interdependence. **L1**

Visual Instruction

Answer Employees must view themselves as valued members of a team and learn to appreciate and understand others' contributions.

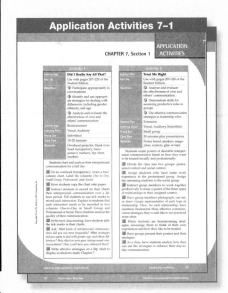

Application Activities 7–1

businesses often train employees to interact with customers in a way that projects certain positive attributes.

One way employees send positive messages to customers or the public is by the way they dress on the job. Dress codes project an organization's philosophy about its relationship with customers. It may reflect a very professional level of communication, or it may convey a message of informality and friendliness, inviting a more casual relationship with customers. Similarly, employees usually are trained to use a pleasant voice on the telephone and handle troublesome phone calls with courtesy and efficiency. Sales associates also are trained to listen carefully and to deal with clients in a professional manner.

Importance Positive interpersonal relationships between employees and clients or the public are important because of their effect on business. If customers perceive that they have a positive relationship with a certain employee, they may be more likely to take their business to him or her.

A nurse builds an interpersonal relationship with her patient. **How does a client benefit from an interpersonal relationship with a business?**

Practice for the Workplace

Word-of-Mouth Advertising Have you ever been unhappy with the food or service at a restaurant? If you were like most customers, you probably told all of your friends about your negative experience. If that restaurant is suggested to your friends in the future, they will probably recall that you did not enjoy it. With that in mind, they will probably go to another restaurant. This is a powerful form of advertising known as word-of-mouth. Word-of-mouth is just that—words, usually in the form of an assessment, from the mouths of others. This type of information affects many of the decisions we make as consumers each day.

BUSINESS PRACTICE *Activity*

Why do you choose one store or business over another? Visit three different local businesses in the next week. Observe the actions of the employees in these businesses. Were you greeted when you entered the store? Were the employees eager to assist you? Did the sales people answer your questions correctly the first time? Did you get exactly what you wanted? How were the employees dressed? Write down examples of why you would or would not recommend these businesses to others. What areas need the most improvement and why? Share your evaluations with the rest of the class.

However, businesses aren't the only ones who benefit from these positive relationships. Forming interpersonal relationships with clients can make an employee's job more enjoyable. Customers usually benefit from better, more personalized service. Finally, open lines of communication reduce misunderstandings and lead to faster solutions when problems arise.

Purpose The main purpose of positive employee-customer relationships is to create goodwill and a feeling of loyalty. Employees who feel a sense of loyalty to their company and customers are likely to do better work and may stay with the company longer. When individual customers or the public in general feel loyal to a company, they are more likely to choose its products over a competitor's. They also tend to spread good news about the firm, generating new business. Finally, a loyal customer is more likely to be a repeat customer—which results in a better bottom line for any company.

Joan Baez works with others in a social organization. Identify why it is important for a leader to establish open lines of communication with members in a social organization.

Types of Social Relationships

When you talk with a friend or play a game of basketball with someone you just met, you are interacting on an interpersonal level in a social context. You probably have a lot of social relationships in your life. However, one type of social relationship that you may be less familiar with is your interaction with other members of an organized group or club.

These social relationships are special because they often include people of different ages, ethnicities, and backgrounds who have come together to accomplish a common goal. They also may share certain interests that they want to support in some public way. The interpersonal relationships between members of an organization can have a great impact on achievement of the group's goals. Three important relationships in this context are between

- leadership and members
- members and other members
- members and the public

Leadership and Members Much like in the workplace, most social organizations have leaders who make sure work stays on track and goals are accomplished. Open lines of communication between leaders and members make it easier to convey information, share ideas, and solve problems. They also allow leaders to communicate their commitment and enthusiasm for a project to build group cohesiveness.

Individual members of organizations also form interpersonal relationships with their leaders. This allows members to clarify information, share ideas, and work interdependently to achieve the organization's goals. Positive relationships also serve as a motivator, keeping group members' interest and enthusiasm high and making members more productive.

Importance Effective interpersonal relationships between leaders and members are essential for the success of any organization. Without these close ties, it can be much more difficult to work as a cohesive unit to achieve

Building Effective Interpersonal Relationships **213**

■ Visual Instruction

Answer Establishing open lines of communication makes it easier to convey information, share ideas, and solve problems. It allows leaders to communicate their commitment to and enthusiasm for a project.

Paraphrasing Professional Relationships

After they have read pages 208–213, have students close their textbooks and recall the three levels of interpersonal relationships on the job. Invite volunteers to explain each in their own words. **L2**

DID YOU KNOW?

Lack of recognition by leaders has a negative impact on employee productivity. Studies show that encouragement and recognition play a major role in stimulating creativity in research and development organizations.

Language Tip

Many people tend to express the negatives rather than the positives about a new suggestion or idea. Experts speculate that this is because most of us haven't been taught to look first at the strengths of an idea. Rather than gravitating automatically toward the negative when presented with a new idea, look first for its strengths and express those strengths using words with positive connotations.

MEETING INDIVIDUAL NEEDS — MULTIPLE LEARNING STYLES

Interpersonal Student leaders frequently have already developed good social relationships and skills for interpersonal communication. Invite several such students to talk informally to the class about techniques they have found helpful in building positive attitudes and cooperation among organization members.

Activity Have the class ask questions of the student presenters, then brainstorm a list of social groups to which they or members of their families belong. Ask each student to select one of these groups and write a paper explaining how he or she fits into it. Students might include diagrams showing their relationships to leadership, other members, and the public.

Focus on a Group Goal

Remind students that friendship with group members is often a side benefit of working with an organization to meet its goals. Survey the class to see how many belong to organizations. Have them list friends who are also members and put a star beside names of those who became friends after they joined the organization. Assign students randomly to groups; give each group a task to accomplish together, such as moving an object a set distance without using hands. After they accomplish their goals, ask groups how their interpersonal communications changed as they worked on their tasks. **L3**

DID YOU KNOW?

Men and women tend to use different styles in face-to-face communication. Men use "report talk" with a purpose such as exchanging information, maintaining their status, or impressing others. Women use "rapport talk" to create intimacy rather than necessarily for a specific purpose.

■ Visual Instruction

Answer Setting aside personal interests makes it easier to focus on the group goal.

---

organizational goals. For example, when a school board member makes a decision that is unpopular with teachers, the quality of the teachers' work may be affected and students' education can suffer.

Problems also can occur if members do not build productive relationships with their leaders. A lack of positive one-to-one interaction between members and leaders can disrupt the communication within the organization. This can result in a lack of interest or direction, low morale, and ineffectiveness.

Purpose All of these potential problems relate directly to the need for open, supportive channels of communication between leaders and members in social organizations. The purpose of positive interpersonal relationships on this level is to build a sense of interdependence and to facilitate the achievement of goals. If the goal is to plan a special event, respect for a leader's direction may be essential to get everything ready in time.

Members and Other Members

Many times, members of social organizations may represent similar interests, ethnic groups, ages, and socio-economic levels. These common qualities provide a basis for communication and interpersonal relationships. In some social organizations, on the other hand, members may represent a wide variety of cultures and interests. Whether their interests are similar or different, members may have varying levels of communication skills.

Importance Reaching organizational goals and advancing specific causes depends on the interpersonal relationships of group members. Social organizations often sponsor events specifically to promote personal relationships and goodwill between group members. A church may have a pie supper or potluck dinner to bring members together. A team or committee may have a picnic. A large organization may hold a banquet to encourage interaction.

■ **Individuals are diverse and therefore may have different interests than other group members.** Why must an individual set aside his or her own personal interests when working with a group?

Most of these occasions are intended as icebreakers to allow people to get to know one another outside of the context of group work.

Purpose The first guideline for any organizational member is to set aside his or her own personal interests and focus on the group goal. Therefore, the main purpose of member-to-member relationships is not to benefit the individual—even though this is a common side effect. Rather, the main purpose in this context is group cohesiveness. When individual members use skills in assertiveness, confidence, tact, courtesy, respect, and ethics to build cooperative relationships, they create a positive environment for reaching group goals and operating a successful organization.

Members and the Public

You don't have to be a specialist in advertising or public relations to understand that public image plays a large role in the success of an organization. Each member of an organization serves as the group's ambassador. Each member affects public perception of the organization through his or her relationships within the community. In turn, this public perception can influence the success of the organization.

EXTENDING THE CONTENT

Building Confidence to Communicate Assertively Paulette Dale, professor of Speech Communications at Miami Dade Community College and internationally known lecturer and consultant, addresses the need for assertive expression in her book *Did You Say Something, Susan?* She points out that many people use their lack of confidence as an excuse to avoid speaking up.
Activity Ask each student to interview an adult who he or she thinks models positive assertiveness and communication skills. Instruct students to prepare interview questions that are open-ended and will encourage the person to explain how he or she gained self-confidence in speaking up. Have students share with the class any techniques or tips they learned.

For example, if a committee member gossips with a friend about internal conflicts in an organization, the friend may decide not to make a donation to the group's cause. A team member who constantly complains to outsiders about group members' lack of interest may unwittingly discourage someone else from joining the team.

For this reason, leaders and individual members of social organizations should communicate positively with the public. They should consistently promote the organization throughout the community. In other words, the motto "Say something good, or say nothing at all" is good advice for members who want their organization to be a success.

Importance Positive relationships between organization members and the public are important for two reasons. First, creating a sense of goodwill with the public can generate much-needed funding or support or both for the group's cause. It also can promote a sense of cooperation in the community that helps eliminate certain barriers to the group goal.

Second, interpersonal relationships between group members and outsiders benefit the public. Open lines of communication allow members of the community to contribute ideas regarding the organization's work. Also, many organizations repay supportive communities by building parks, contributing money or volunteers to local events, or providing special services for the public.

Purpose The purpose of productive relationships between organizational members and the public is to create goodwill for the group and support for the group's goals. That is why it is important to always keep in mind that others view you as a representative of your organization. The image you project with your behavior and communication skills is likely to shape others' overall opinion of the organization. In short, your relationships with the public can play a large part in the success or failure of your organization.

CHARACTERISTICS OF PRODUCTIVE INTERPERSONAL COMMUNICATION

The communication choices you make every day have a great impact on your interpersonal relationships. Typically, negative, unproductive communication leads to unproductive relationships. On the other hand, positive, productive communication tends to lead to productive relationships. Thus, the question becomes, "What kind of communication skills do I need to develop to build productive relationships?"

Communication in most productive relationships seems to share some basic characteristics. These characteristics help the individuals involved feel valued and understood. If any characteristic is missing, the relationship tends

■ **Figure 7–1 Characteristics of Productive Interpersonal Communication**

Openness

Empathy

Equality

Supportiveness

+ Positiveness

= Productive Interpersonal Communication

Building Effective Interpersonal Relationships **215**

Improving Productivity in Interpersonal Communication Skills
Have students study Figure 7–1 on this page and devise a statement that summarizes its main idea. Ask students to privately make note of the qualities listed here that are personal strengths and those that they would like to improve. Then, have them read pages 215–219, jotting down ideas that occur to them as they read for how they can improve in these areas. **L2**

BUSINESS BRIEF

The PPC technique was developed by Dr. Firestien, Dianne Foucar-Szociki, and Bill Shepard. It is a tool for encouraging innovation and improvement in business by responding to a new idea by

1. first enumerating its PLUSES (strengths, advantages)
2. then discussing its POTENTIALS (possible spin-offs for future gains)
3. last addressing CONCERNS posed by the idea. Concerns are addressed, however, not with judgmental comments but with challenges: not "That costs too much" but "How might you reduce the cost?"; not "They'll never go for it" but "How might you get management's support?"

This type of response by business leaders has been shown to inspire employees, improve relationships, and stimulate business growth.

MEETING INDIVIDUAL NEEDS — MULTIPLE LEARNING STYLES

Linguistic Students should be encouraged to use their oral language skills to express their understanding of what they read. With this material, participation in small-group discussion can also help them build skills in interpersonal communication.

Activity Assign students who express knowledge naturally by speaking to lead discussion on one of the five characteristics of productive interpersonal communication. Leaders might prepare open-ended questions for their groups. Remind them that a goal is to get everyone in the group to contribute ideas. Have each group summarize for the class its ideas on the importance of their skill and how it can be improved.

COMMUNICATION *Strategies*

KEEPING COMMUNICATION OPEN IN RELATIONSHIPS

Ask students to recall how to make "I" statements, listen actively, and make perception checks. (If necessary, review these concepts.) Invite two volunteers to demonstrate the difference in communication when one uses blaming "You" statements while the other uses self-disclosure in "I" statements. Another pair might demonstrate contrasts between poor listening and active listening (including elements of body language, attention, and attitude). Ask the class to explain which demonstrations invited open communication and to tell why.

COMMUNICATING EMPATHICALLY IN RELATIONSHIPS

Also have volunteers model the tips for communicating empathically noted in the chart on this page. Define and model yourself any techniques about which students seem uncertain. Have them try consciously using one or more of these tips in their communications with friends, and report whether communication seemed improved. Invite the class to discuss which tips were most helpful and explain why. **L2**

COMMUNICATION *Strategies*

KEEPING COMMUNICATION OPEN IN RELATIONSHIPS

- Use "I" messages to demonstrate ownership of all your thoughts and ideas.
- Use active listening skills and provide appropriate feedback to show your interest in others' ideas.
- Use intrapersonal and interpersonal perception checks to make sure you clearly understand others' messages.
- Carefully reflect on the messages that have been communicated so you can adapt and make appropriate decisions.

COMMUNICATING EMPATHICALLY IN RELATIONSHIPS

- Use appropriate facial expressions, eye contact, and an attentive posture to demonstrate interest in the other's messages.
- Respect the other person's feelings about personal space and physical contact.
- Use tentative but supportive language to show that you don't necessarily know all the answers but are willing to help find them.
- Use perception checks and descriptive language to help the other person express exactly what he or she is feeling.
- Listen without judging the other person's feelings or actions as right or wrong.

---

to suffer. Once you learn about these characteristics, you can use your knowledge to evaluate your own interpersonal communication. As Figure 7–1 on page 215 shows, the five characteristics most needed for effective interpersonal relationships are as follows:

- openness
- empathy
- equality
- supportiveness
- positiveness

Openness

In productive social and professional relationships, communication tends to be open. Open communication typically displays the following traits:

- willingness to share ideas and feelings and to disclose appropriately to others
- willingness to listen carefully and to consider the ideas and feelings of others
- willingness to reflect on the effectiveness of communication and adapt it to be more productive

Effective communicators recognize equality in communication. What does it mean to have equality in communication?

MEETING INDIVIDUAL NEEDS

MULTIPLE LEARNING STYLES

Bodily-Kinesthetic Explain that the way in which two people relate can generally be perceived by carefully observing their body language as they communicate. Just as empathy, openness, and equality in communication improve relationships, positive feelings between two people are likely to result in open, empathic, and equal interchanges.

Activity Ask students who communicate effectively through body language to play the parts of communicators and model postures, gestures, and facial expressions that communicate empathy and equality. Then, have other students volunteer to role-play speaker-listener scenarios. As they role-play the situations they are given, allow members of the class to freeze frame the action and change actors' body language as needed to improve these qualities.

Empathy and supportiveness are characteristics for building a social relationship. How does empathy strengthen an interpersonal relationship?

Empathy does not demand that you agree or disagree with the other person's views. It simply allows you to say, "I think I understand how you're feeling." When you are able to understand and appreciate another's position, ideas, and opinions, your relationship is likely to be more harmonious and productive. The Communication Strategies checklist describes what you can do to make your communication empathic.

Equality

Competent communicators tend to view one another as equals. In professional and social contexts, individuals often have different jobs, responsibilities, status, and authority. They may have unique talents, abilities, strengths, and weaknesses, and represent a blend of different genders, ethnicities, and ages. However, equality in communication does not imply sameness. Rather, it embraces personal and cultural differences.

Equality in communication means all participating individuals have equal respect, rights, and opportunity. It asserts that individuals, regardless of their status or ability, have equal dignity as human beings. Communicators who value equality in relationships often have a general attitude of "I'm OK, and you're OK too." An underlying sense of equality lays a firm foundation for win-win communication and relationships. The following checklist provides tips for communicating with an attitude of equality.

Supportiveness

In productive relationships, the individuals involved are supportive of one another. That is, they care about and respect one another. They also encourage and help each other reach their personal and organizational goals.

Analyzing the Johari window in Chapter 3 provided some insight into the need for openness in communication. As you examined the various degrees of openness reflected by the four windows, you discovered that open communication leads to productive interpersonal relationships. On the other hand, closed communication—which is characterized by hesitancy to disclose, unwillingness to listen to others, and being closed to change and information about self—can seriously damage relationships.

Empathy

In addition to openness, productive relationships require empathy. Empathy, or the ability to understand and appreciate, involves feeling *with* someone rather than feeling *for* someone. In other words, you are putting yourself in someone else's position and seeing the world through his or her eyes.

Building Effective Interpersonal Relationships **217**

Establishing Equality in Relationships

Have the class list judgmental statements that they hate hearing. *(Students may list "You always . . . [let me down, break things, show up late]," "Why can't you . . . [be more like your brother/sister, listen to what I say, do it now instead of later]," "You shouldn't . . . [say something like that, put off your work].")* For each one listed on the board, have students suggest a positive, nonjudgmental way of communicating the real concern. Ask volunteers to role-play a teenager and parent communicating using the strategies in the list on page 218. Then, have the class identify the strategies that were used and evaluate their effectiveness. **L2**

Visual Instruction

Answer Empathy strengthens an interpersonal relationship by building trust and loyalty.

REAL-WORLD CONNECTION

Congruent Communication Educational psychologist Haim Ginott advised about the need for *congruent communication*—using the language of acceptance rather than rejection to make communication congruent with objectives. By belittling, shaming, blaming, and ridiculing, Ginott reasoned, we disable the persons we are labeling and cause them to seal off their minds.

Activity Have students read and learn more about the educational and communication theories of Ginott and other educational psychologists. Ask that they look for studies, data, and articles that discuss ways of creating a positive environment for learning. In class discussion, relate these techniques to concepts of interpersonal communication. Have groups of students apply congruent communication techniques to offering and receiving criticism about a recent assignment or project.

COMMUNICATION *Strategies*

BEING SUPPORTIVE IN RELATIONSHIPS

As a class, read the list of strategies for being supportive in relationships. After each, ask students to express one way that strategy shows caring, respect, encouragement, or help for the person. *(For example, students might note that describing an idea as creative rather than evaluating it negatively avoids hurting the communicator's feelings and allows for its potential, even if the listener does not think it is workable.)* **L1**

GLOBAL COMMUNICATION

Status, Respect, and Courtesy

Students' responses may include the following examples. Shaking hands is a way of showing courtesy. Beginning an introduction with the name of the person of higher status is a way of showing respect and acknowledging status. Seating the most powerful person at the head of the table acknowledges status. Using a title such as Dr. to address people shows respect. Saluting officers of higher rank in the military shows respect and acknowledges the difference in power. Standing when someone of higher status enters the room shows respect. **L1**

As with empathy, you do not always have to agree with the other person or approve of his or her behavior to be supportive. For instance, a supportive teacher may care deeply about a student and do everything possible to help that student reach his or her goals. Still, the teacher may disapprove of that student's disruptive behavior and failure to complete assignments. The teacher may encourage the student to reach his or her potential by offering after-school tutoring or counseling.

A supportive employee will find ways to help coworkers do their jobs effectively. For instance, he or she may volunteer to help out when a coworker is given the responsibility of hosting a company picnic. He or she may offer to help prepare the food, provide transportation, or do some other task to make the coworker's job easier and ensure the picnic's success.

Supportiveness in professional and social relationships can work wonders in building trust and loyalty. It also tends to be contagious. When you are consistently supportive of others, you are more likely to be supported in your own endeavors. The Communication Strategies checklist offers some tips for being supportive in your social and professional relationships.

GLOBAL COMMUNICATION

Status, Respect, and Courtesy

Some people from Japan customarily bow when greeting one another as a formal sign of respect and courtesy. Bowing is also a way to recognize the status of the other person. Identify five verbal or nonverbal actions that people in other cultures, including your own, use to show respect and to acknowledge the status of others.

COMMUNICATION *Strategies*

BEING SUPPORTIVE IN RELATIONSHIPS

✓ Whenever possible, use descriptive rather than evaluative language.

✓ Try to speak in terms of possibilities, not certainties.

✓ Avoid "preaching" and using negative communication strategies such as "you" statements, "why" questions, labels, and names.

✓ Be an active, attentive listener.

✓ Give appropriate nonverbal feedback.

✓ Use perception checks to show interest and to clarify understanding.

ESTABLISHING EQUALITY IN RELATIONSHIPS

✓ Make sure your verbal and nonverbal messages demonstrate respect, courtesy, and tact.

✓ Avoid evaluative, judgmental language or language that may put the other person on the defensive. This includes terms such as "should," "ought," "must," "right," and "wrong," as well as "you" statements and "why" questions.

✓ Demonstrate a willingness to listen carefully to others without interrupting or responding with judgmental statements.

✓ Use "feed forward" statements to personalize messages.

✓ Use perception checks to show interest and clarify understanding.

INTERDISCIPLINARY CONNECTION

Language Arts Students may be familiar with characters from literature or movies who model one or more of the traits of productive interpersonal communication. Lead the class in a discussion of relationships in a story the class has read recently. Point out the relationship that best illustrates the skill of empathy or support.

Activity Have students select and read another story in order to analyze the way in which the main character relates to others. Ask students to write an essay explaining how the character models one or more of the positive communication traits.

Positiveness

Positive interpersonal interactions tend to build productive relationships. Positiveness can be described several ways. First, positiveness is based on positive attitudes and communication that moves relationships and tasks toward mutually rewarding results. Positiveness is often marked by optimism, confidence that you and other individuals will be able to accomplish goals, and a general sense of well-being.

Individuals who demonstrate positiveness often encourage others through their own enthusiasm and tend to see some element of hope or humor in even the most difficult situations. Positive communication focuses more on the solution than the problem. It also provides constructive suggestions and well-deserved praise to help others reach their goals. The checklist on the right describes some ways you can encourage positiveness in your own relationships. Try to follow these strategies to become a more positive communicator.

COMMUNICATION *Strategies*

BEING POSITIVE IN RELATIONSHIPS

✓ Adjust your attitudes so that you consistently look on the bright side of things.

✓ Always expect the best from yourself and others.

✓ Be generous with sincere compliments and praise.

✓ Be an active listener, demonstrating true concern for others.

✓ Use nonverbal signals that show you are interested and in a pleasant frame of mind.

✓ Provide feedback that encourages others and gives them a sense of hope or accomplishment.

TECHNOLOGY *Activity*

Sending Copies of E-Mails To show support for a person, you can write a letter of recommendation to his or her supervisor. A letter of recommendation acknowledges accomplishments or recognizes good deeds. Copies of the letter are usually sent to the person for whom you wrote the recommendation and their other supervisors. Write a letter of recommendation for a teacher, friend, coach, or volunteer at your school. Create the letter as an e-mail message and have your teacher check the content and the format. With your teacher's approval, send a copy of the document to the subject of the letter and at least three people to whom that person reports.

INTEGRATING INTERPERSONAL SKILLS WITH TASK SKILLS

As a competent communicator in the workplace or in social settings, you will face many challenges. One of these will be balancing the communication skills necessary to carry out tasks effectively with the interpersonal skills necessary to build productive relationships. While clarity, efficiency, and accuracy may be useful for carrying out tasks, people skills such as empathy, supportiveness, and equality are more useful for strengthening relationships.

The most successful communicators learn to integrate their interpersonal skills with

Building Effective Interpersonal Relationships **219**

COMMUNICATION *Strategies*

BEING POSITIVE IN RELATIONSHIPS

After students read the list of strategies, ask them to listen carefully for the rest of the day to responses they hear others give, rating them *positive, negative,* or *neutral* in attitude. Have students comment about which kind of responses got the best results. **L2**

TECHNOLOGY *Activity*

Sending Copies of E-Mails Students should understand that spelling and grammar must be correct. Check the letters for these types of errors. Check e-mail addresses for accuracy. **L2**

3 ASSESS

Assign Section 1 Assessment as a homework or in-class activity.

● Use *Interactive Tutor Self-Assessment Software* to review Section 1.

Section 7–1 Quiz

MEETING INDIVIDUAL NEEDS

INCLUSION STRATEGIES

Less-Proficient Readers Students who have difficulty retaining what they read will benefit greatly from review activities that require them to find and restate in their own words the main concepts of the reading.

Activity Group students by twos or threes and ask them to think of themselves as experts on interpersonal relationships. Each team will be asked to present a program on interpersonal communication for a talk show. Each group should work together to locate main points from the text and rephrase them in group members' own words. Allow groups to perform their presentations for each other.

Reteaching Activity 7–1

RETEACHING Activity 7–1

BUILDING EFFECTIVE INTERPERSONAL RELATIONSHIPS
Understanding Interpersonal Relationships

Relationships at work and in social organizations are important because the people who work together in these settings must depend on one another. They must combine their tasks and skills to see that work is done efficiently. In the following activity, the six types of work and social relationships discussed in Section 1 are listed. Discuss the importance and purpose of each.

Relationship	Importance	Purpose
1. Management and employees		
2. Employees and other employees		
3. Employees and		

Enrichment Activity 7–1

ENRICHMENT Activity 7–1

BUILDING EFFECTIVE INTERPERSONAL RELATIONSHIPS
Understanding Interpersonal Relationships

As you read in Section 1, rank-and-file employees most often carry out the everyday work of a company. Most of the time, employees work productively together to accomplish the goals of a company. Sometimes, however, differing levels of authority and responsibility can lead to problems among fellow employees. Read "Fresh Static in the A.M." from *People Weekly*. It describes the problems between two high-ranking employees from NBC. Then, answer the questions that follow.

4 CLOSE

Refer students back to the opening paragraph of the section and have them revisit what would be missing if all interpersonal contact were eliminated. As a class, sum up the importance of interpersonal communication to individuals, to the workplace, and to society.

Extra-Credit Project

Have students analyze one work or school relationship and one social or personal relationship, comparing and contrasting the communication style they use in each and explaining similarities and differences.

---

task skills. **Integrating** means to blend things so that they function together as a whole. Most communicators find that using a balance of skills often provides more personal satisfaction than continually focusing on task skills alone. That is, you might achieve your goals through the use of task-oriented skills. However, you can enjoy working with others and develop satisfying relationships along the way through the use of interpersonal skills.

As the previous chapters have shown, the hallmark of a competent communicator is an ability to use skills with versatility and appropriateness. Learning to size up a specific situation and use the most appropriate skills helps you grow as a communicator and build a reputation as a valued friend and colleague.

Section 1 Assessment

Visit the *Glencoe Communication Applications* Web site at **communicationapplications. glencoe.com** and click on **Self-Check and Study Guide 7.1** to review your understanding of interpersonal relationships.

Review Key Terms

1. Define this term and write it in a sentence: integrating.

Check Understanding

2. Name three types of interpersonal relationships that occur in professional contexts and three types that occur in social contexts.

3. Give a real-life example of one type of social or professional relationship. Then, explain the importance and purpose of your example relationship.

4. Imagine that you and your best friend are both hired by the same company. Compare and contrast appropriate interpersonal interaction on the job and away from the workplace.

5. **Predict** Imagine that a coworker—with whom you have a positive interpersonal relationship—has been denied a promotion because he frequently misses work. He is upset and asks for your input on the situation. Explain how you might use all five characteristics of productive communication in your discussion.

APPLICATION *Activity*

Identifying Types of Relationships Divide the class into two equal groups: one focusing on professional relationships, the other on social. With your group, brainstorm a list of job titles in a chosen company or position titles in a chosen social organization. Write your group's ideas on the chalkboard in two equal columns. Then, draw lines to randomly match up the titles in the two columns. Finally, label each match with one of the types of relationships you studied in this section. Which type of relationship was most common? Do you think that is accurate in most cases?

Section 1 Assessment Answers

1. Accept all reasonable sentences.
2. Professional: management and employees, employees and other employees, and employees and clients or the public; social: leadership and members, members and other members, and members and the public.
3. Accept all reasonable answers.
4. Interaction in the workplace should follow the norms and protocols for professional relationships.
5. Students may respond that they would remain open to the coworker's thoughts and feelings, listen and respond empathically, treat the coworker as an equal, be supportive of his wish to do better, and remain positive.

   Application Activity Students may match a number of management-to-employee or leader-to-member relationships but should realize that each employee or group member is likely to have more relationships with peers than with authority figures.

— USING THE CONTEXT TO DEFINE WORDS —

Everyone has seen or heard words that they do not recognize. When you encounter a word that you have not seen or heard before, there are strategies you can use to determine that word's meaning. These strategies are based on the use of the context, or words and sentences positioned near the unfamiliar term. The information below explains how to use the context to determine the meaning of a word.

Learning the Skill

Context clues are the hints that we gather from the words surrounding an unknown term. These clues enable you, as a reader or listener, to make an "educated guess" at the meaning of the undefined word.

One context clue is the word itself. To find the meaning of an unfamiliar word, first determine its part of speech. Then, look for other uses of these parts of speech within the context. Sometimes, a similar word will be used in the same sentence. Try one of those words in place of the one you don't know. If the sentence makes sense and is still grammatically correct, you likely have found the meaning of the unknown word.

If you are still uncertain of the word's meaning, use the other parts of speech near or next to the word in the sentence. Other parts of speech can help you determine the meaning of a word. Nouns and verbs can provide clues for each other. In turn, adjectives and adverbs provide clues for nouns and verbs.

Unfortunately, you will not be able to guess the correct meaning of every word, even when you use context clues. If you are still unsure about an undefined term, you have two options. First, you can look up the meaning of the word in a dictionary. This may be necessary for words that are exceptionally technical, outdated, or rarely used. Your other option is to skip the word and hope that you will find its meaning within some later context. This technique is unreliable, so it should be used only when absolutely necessary.

Practicing the Skill

This chapter focuses on building interpersonal relationships. Some words that characterize good interpersonal relationships are used in the following sentences. Use the context clues to determine the meaning of the underlined word in each sentence.

1. The senator, proud of his reputation for honesty, is a <u>veracious</u> communicator.

2. Donating those coats was a very <u>altruistic</u> deed.

3. Our supervisor sets a good example because she is always <u>affable</u> when talking to customers.

4. Friends who are supportive <u>embolden</u> each other to try new things.

5. Effective interpersonal communicators participate <u>fervently</u> in lively conversations.

APPLICATION *Activity*

Reread the paragraphs on page 210 that describe relationships between management and employees. Using the context within these paragraphs, provide definitions for the following terms: *compensation, morale, perceive, mutually,* and *tone.*

Using the Context to Define Words

You may wish to point out several ways writers provide context clues:

- giving a definition or restating in an appositive, possibly introduced by *that is* or *in other words.*
- including familiar synonyms.
- providing an example, introduced by *for instance, such as, especially.*
- comparing or contrasting a new word with a familiar word, using signal words *like, as, unlike, rather than.*

Have students skim the chapter to find examples of each type of context clue. **L1**

Practicing the Skill

Have volunteers point to clues by which they discovered the meanings of new words. Ask other students to look up each word in the dictionary so the class can check their guesses.

1. truthful, honest
2. unselfish, charitable
3. friendly, agreeable
4. encourage, inspirit
5. intensely, enthusiastically

Application Activity

Students' responses to this activity may be similar to the examples shown here.

Compensation—payment for work

Morale—the mood of people working together

Perceive—to form an opinion of someone or something based on what is known of the subject

Mutually—have the same effect on more than one person or group of persons

Tone—the general mood or attitude of a certain place

MEETING INDIVIDUAL NEEDS

ENGLISH LANGUAGE LEARNERS

Meaning in Context Encourage English language learners to develop a context within which to attack new vocabulary. For example, they might use what they already know about the subject matter; the familiar words in the sentence; root words within the new word; and pictures, graphs, and other visual clues surrounding an unfamiliar word to create a meaningful context.

Activity Have students choose a brief magazine article on communication or personal style and highlight unfamiliar words. Pair students who are learning English with English-proficient readers and have them read the article aloud together. As they read, students can discuss reasonable definitions for the highlighted terms and check them in a dictionary. Students should add the new words they learn to their vocabulary notebooks. **ELL**

1 FOCUS

Bellringer

Write the word *style* on the chalkboard and ask students to jot down words and phrases that describe their own personal style. Brainstorm on the board a list of famous personalities and have students suggest adjectives that describe the communication style of each.

You may use Graphic Organizer Transparency 7–2 to introduce this section.

Graphic Organizer Transparency 7–2

STYLE	SPEAKS	LISTENS	HOW TO SPEAK TO
Dominant			
Influencing			
Steady			

Application Activities 7–2

Visual Instruction

Answer Personal style is pattern of communication choices that reflect a person's individuality.

Personal Style in Interpersonal Relationships

GUIDE TO READING

Objectives

1. Identify and describe four types of personal style.
2. Determine your own current personal style.
3. Explain how differences in personal style can affect interpersonal relationships.

Terms to Learn

personal style
dominant style
influencing style
steady style
conscientious style

You probably have heard statements like "She always wears the latest style!" or "That's an interesting style of architecture," or "This author has a great writing style"—but have you ever thought of style as the way someone communicates with others?

In the first section of this chapter you learned that a competent communicator faces the challenge of integrating task skills with interpersonal skills in professional and social contexts. To communicate effectively and appropriately within these contexts, it is helpful to try to understand how you generally speak and listen to others and how others can communicate most effectively with you. Both of these situations are based on your personal style.

Personal style is a pattern of clear and consistent communication choices that reflects a person's individuality and distinguish him or her from other individuals. Your personal communication style describes how you relate to others and the world around you. It refers to your attitudes, your use of language, your nonverbal expressions, and your use of listening skills. In short, your personal style is a blueprint of who you are.

Oprah Winfrey exhibits her personal style while interacting with guests on her television show. What is personal style?

RESOURCE MANAGER

Teaching Tools

- Interactive Lesson Planner
- Reproducible Lesson Plan 7–2
- Application Activities 7–2

Reproducible Masters

- Guided Reading Activity Workbook 7–2
- Enrichment Activity 7–2
- Reteaching Activity 7–2
- Section Quiz 7–2
- Transparency Strategies and Activities Booklet 7–2

Transparencies

- Graphic Organizer Transparency 7–2
- Chapter 7 Teaching Transparency

Technology Resources

- Interactive Tutor Self-Assessment Software
- Presentation Plus! Software
- ExamView® Pro Testmaker
- PuzzleMaker Software
- communicationapplications.glencoe.com

IDENTIFYING PERSONAL STYLE

The first and most important rule about personal style is that no single style is better than any other. They are just different. Once you understand that, you can learn to analyze your own and others' styles and adapt your communication to be more effective. You also can learn to integrate personal styles to accomplish goals more efficiently.

Finally, understanding people's personal communication styles can help you predict and avoid many different kinds of conflict. For instance, it can help you learn not to take certain types of communication personally. It also can help you avoid finding fault or blame when you encounter someone with a different personal style.

Four Types of Personal Style

Have you ever taken a "personality test" just for fun? If so, you may have been surprised to find that, for the most part, you fit the profile of a general personality category.

Of course everyone is unique. Therefore, no behavioral category will describe you perfectly. However, in most cases, your basic traits can identify you as a particular personality type. The same is true for communication types.

The following information about personal communication style is widely used by businesses for making decisions about hiring, promotions, assignments, training, and counseling. It often is used by social organizations to organize teams and assign persons to groups where their style will complement the style of others and strengthen the effectiveness of a group. Individuals also tend to make day-to-day communication choices based on

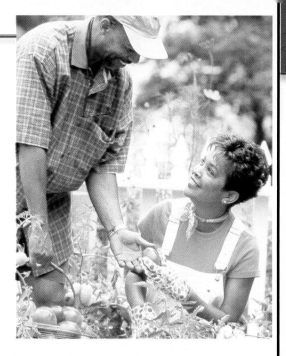

One's personal communication style describes how that person communicates with others. **What is included in one's personal communication style?**

a basic understanding of personal style—even if they are unfamiliar with the study of personal style.

As you read the description of each style, you probably will recognize yourself and other people you know. It may be helpful to note that most people tend to have one predominant style. This is referred to as your "high" style, which describes your usual approach to conducting business and dealing with others. It also is important to note, however, that most people also exhibit characteristics from other styles. In fact, we probably all exhibit some degree of each of the four types of personal style shown in the following list:

- dominant
- influencing
- steady
- conscientious

Building Effective Interpersonal Relationships **223**

2 TEACH

Guided Reading Activity 7–2

GUIDED READING
Activity 7-2

Name _____ Date _____ Class _____

BUILDING EFFECTIVE INTERPERSONAL RELATIONSHIPS
Personal Style in Interpersonal Relationships

As you read Section 2, complete the sentences below.

A 1 _____ style is a pattern of clear and consistent communication choices that reflects a person's 2 _____ and distinguishes him or her from other individuals. Your personal communication style refers to your attitudes, your use of 3 _____, your 4 _____ expressions, and your use of 5 _____ skills.

No personal style is better than any other; they are just 6 _____. Once you understand that, you can learn to analyze your own and others' styles and adapt your communication to be more 7 _____. The four personal styles are 8 _____, 9 _____, 10 _____, and 11 _____.

A 12 _____ style of communication is one that is fast-paced and more task-oriented than people-oriented. 13 "_____" want to get things done but may have little patience for 14 _____. They will often 15 _____ detail work to others and will do anything necessary to overcome 16 _____.

The influencing, or 17 "_____," style, is a fast-paced, 18 _____-oriented style. Interactors tend to be 19 _____, enthusiastic, outgoing, spontaneous, and 20 _____. They get results by influencing 21 _____ others.

About 35 percent of the population makes up the 22 _____ personality style. These people tend to be slow-paced and both 23 _____- and 24 _____-oriented. They are cooperative and 25 _____ and can be counted on to get the job done. High S's are good 26 _____ players and have a calming effect on others.

The final personality style is the 27 _____ style. These people are 28 _____-paced and task-oriented. They are highly analytical 29 _____ who love detail. They are 30 _____, guarded in relationships, and tend to avoid risks.

You may be less likely to clash with others if you realize that all four personality styles are necessary to get work done in 31 _____ and 32 _____ contexts.

Personality and Personal Style

Point out to students that for many centuries people have recognized the existence of four varying temperaments and four distinct ways of functioning. Rather than attempting to make everyone more like us in style, we should recognize people's differences, appreciate the different contributions they have to make, and learn ways of communicating effectively with them. Have students read the section for two purposes: (1) to note the basic differences in temperament exhibited by each type of personal style and (2) to consider and list positive contributions each type can make to the workplace or to a relationship. **L3**

Visual Instruction

Answer Personal communication style includes attitudes, use of language, nonverbal expressions, and listening skills.

EXTENDING THE CONTENT

Analyzing Temperament The Myers-Briggs Type Indicator (MBTI) assesses personality traits as indicated by the following inferences: extroversion or introversion (ways to gain energy); sensing or intuition (ways to gather information); thinking or feeling (ways to make decisions); and judging or perceiving (ways to deal with the outer world.)

Activity Assign teams of students one of the following MBTI topics to research at the library or online: extroversion and introversion, sensing and intuition, thinking and feeling, and judging and perceiving. Each topic should be presented to the class using both visual and verbal elements.

High D Style

The High D category of communication style corresponds to the intuitive-thinking temperament defined by the Myers-Briggs Type Indicator. In addition to being energized by contact with people, this type of communicator has talents for seeing the big picture and conceptualizing. He or she communicates clearly and precisely. Ask students to review the characteristics in the chart on page 224. Which do they think enhance communication? Which hamper it? Discuss why High D style workers make good leaders. *(They have the big picture, get right to the point, inspire others, delegate jobs well.)* **L2**

DID YOU KNOW?

Over 2,500 years ago, Greek physician Hippocrates described four types of personality: *sanguine* (fun-loving, happy-go-lucky, faces life with gusto, loves a challenge), *choleric* (orderly, critical, controlling, traditional, structured, likes making decisions, able to take charge), *phlegmatic* (peace-loving, patient, indecisive, positive, affirming communicators who seek harmony), and *melancholic* (withdrawn, serious, objective, readily sees the big picture, good at analyzing, has insight into logic and principles of systems).

"HIGH D" CHARACTERISTICS

How the High D Speaks	• Direct and to the point • Can be blunt and critical • Can be sarcastic • Gives instructions for the big picture but often omits details that must be accomplished before the project can get under way • Inspires others but can be overly optimistic in the actual carrying out of the plan • Does not hide accomplishments and can be self-centered in his or her talk • Will escalate conflict • Can be manipulative in order to get desired results • Will close off all communication except through a messenger when highly stressed • Sometimes needs to be confronted to get his or her attention—you may have to push back to gain respect
How the High D Listens	• Not a patient listener; seldom seeks others' opinions • Wants brief answers • Wants the bottom line first and reasons or contingencies second • Will ask questions if he or she wants more detail • Is more interested in task-oriented information than in people issues
How to Speak to a High D	• Provide direct answers; be brief and to the point. • Ask "what" questions, never "how" questions. • Stick to business; outline the possibilities for the person to get results, solve problems, or be in charge. • Stress the logic of specific ideas or approaches. • Agree with the facts and ideas, not the person. • Provide facts and figures about the probability of success or the effectiveness of options. • Show how the person will reach his or her goals.

Dominant ("High D") Style

According to research, about 15 percent of all people have a highly dominant personal style. A dominant style of communication is one that is fast-paced and more task-oriented than people-oriented. Highly dominant communicators, or "High D's," often appear very businesslike and want others to quickly get to the point of their messages. High D's generally like others to be efficient and decisive. They want to get things done but may have little patience for details. For this reason, they often delegate detail work to others who they feel are competent.

High D's typically are "movers and shakers"—outgoing risk-takers whose goal is to get results. If something gets in the way of reaching a desired result, a High D will do whatever is necessary to overcome the obstacle. High D's typically are skilled at providing direction to others. Therefore, they often are sought out as leaders.

■ **This drill sergeant exemplifies a dominant style of communication.** Describe how High D's generally appear to others and how they want others to communicate.

GIFTED AND TALENTED

Personal Styles of Famous Figures Challenge students to apply to famous people what they learn about characteristics of distinct personal styles. Point out how great leaders with very different temperaments have achieved greatness. For example, Churchill and Gandhi were opposite in style, but each managed to save his nation—Churchill through political wheeling and dealing and tactical maneuvering; Gandhi by diplomacy, benevolence, and rebuilding relationships.

Activity Have each student select a biography or historic account about a historical figure or celebrity and read it to note the individual's characteristic communication style. Each should then categorize the famous person as *dominant, influencing, steady,* or *conscientious* and make a poster that illustrates ways the person characterizes this type.

"HIGH I" CHARACTERISTICS

How the High I Speaks	• Friendly initiator of communication • Spontaneous and often humorous • Makes positive and enthusiastic remarks • Physically expressive with face, tone of voice, and gestures • Often promises more than he or she can deliver • Uses excuses liberally • Influences and persuades others through verbal praise • Makes judgments intuitively rather than by analyzing the data • A physical communicator, shaking hands, giving hugs, patting shoulders • Has a real need to express himself or herself verbally and at length
How the High I Listens	• Responsive • Encourages speakers verbally and nonverbally • May interrupt in order to compare experiences, not to dominate • Very empathic because of his or her high degree of emotionality • May hear only what he or she wants to hear • May not hear negatives • May react too quickly to a speaker's first few words and then inappropriately offer comments out of context
How to Speak to a High I	• Be a good listener. • Provide a chance for him or her to verbalize about ideas, people, and his or her intuitions. • Speak in democratic terms such as "we" or "the team," rather than "I'm the boss. You do what I say." • Give the big picture without getting bogged down in details. However, be sure you put the details in writing. • Provide testimonials from people he or she sees as important and prominent. • Provide extra incentives, since he or she enjoys being recognized as a leader. • Lead the High I step-by-step to conclusions. He or she may tend to jump to conclusions and not be analytical. • Be willing to converse about items of mutual interest before getting down to business. • Be very realistic. High I optimism does not need support from you. • Give clear instructions, then get a firm commitment through a handshake or in writing. • Confront the High I only as a last resort. Persuasion and encouragement work better. • Accept his or her failures and encourage rather than punish.

Influencing ("High I") Style The influencing style is sometimes referred to as the "interactor" style. Another 15 percent of the population falls into this category. An *influencing style* of communication is one that is fast-paced and more people-oriented than task-oriented. Highly influencing communicators, or "High I's," tend to be extroverted, enthusiastic, outgoing, spontaneous, and optimistic. High I's often appear very stylish and like stimulating conversation. They sometimes have difficulty with boring or routine tasks. They get results by influencing and persuading others.

High I's often are valued and sought out by others because of their fun-loving, optimistic nature. Yet, they also enjoy having others recognize their achievements with compliments and other methods of recognition. For example, because a High I is often a friendly initiator, he or she might walk into a team, committee, or other type of group meeting, smile, introduce himself or herself to new people, and welcome the newcomers to the meeting. A High I might then make a comment about one of the positive accomplishments the group or an individual had recently made.

High I Style

Using the Myers-Briggs Type Indicator (MBTI), the High I type can be described as fun-loving and facing life with gusto. They generally trust information gained indirectly, through inference, analogy, and imaginative leaps and make quick decisions based on values, harmony, and mercy. Have students brainstorm a list of jobs or public functions for which a High I would be well suited. *(Students may suggest sales representative, educator, performance artist, mental health professional, or religious leader.)* **L2**

INTERDISCIPLINARY CONNECTION

Life Science Have students ever wondered if animal species exhibit distinct personality traits? Invite students to describe personalities of pets they have. How might they go about proving scientifically that certain animals exhibit specific patterns of personality?

Activity Have interested students read articles in science journals about studies of animal personality traits. After students report on what they learned in class, you may want to assign several students to design an experiment to assess personality in a specific species, such as dogs or cats.

High S Style

The High S type parallels the MBTI temperament characterized by preferences for making judgments based on values, harmony, and mercy; indecisiveness; and dealing with the outer world by taking in information. These individuals are positive, affirming communicators who seek harmony above all else. After students have read the text and studied the chart for High S style, ask them to list traits that make this individual valuable as an employee. *(Students may mention loyalty, practicality, good listening skills, tendency to think things through, and capacity to make plans that are logical and orderly.)* **What traits make it unlikely that a High S would make an outstanding CEO?** *(Students may suggest difficulty in making decisions and saying negative things that must be said, and the reluctance to give evaluative feedback or to compromise.)* **L2**

"HIGH S" CHARACTERISTICS

How the High S Speaks	• Usually not the initiator of conversation or new ideas; likes the stability of a group, so he or she often refers to work situations as "we" or "our" business • Gives practical advice • Prefers to ask "how" questions rather than "if" or "when" questions because he or she is not comfortable initiating decisions • Always takes time to think things over • Is very faithful and loyal—sometimes to a fault—when it comes to people in institutions • May not communicate well under stress, keeping thoughts and feelings to self and becoming silent or noninvolved • Will not attack, suppressing own anger; however, will hold a grudge • Stores up a list of grievances, ultimately making him or her suspicious of others • Can overuse kindness when assertiveness would have been more effective • Often will not say "no" when it needs to be said • Presents well-thought-out, logical, orderly, step-by-step plans • Can be blunt when disagreeing with others or defending self • Withholds expression of true feelings and rarely expresses much enthusiasm • Tends to think in terms of either/or rather than compromise
How the High S Listens	• Patient, empathic listener because of his or her people involvement • Prefers honesty and openness • Tends to withhold evaluative feedback; has excellent insights—although he or she won't share unless asked • Often creates an open-door atmosphere in which sharing thoughts about work as well as family and personal issues is acceptable • Controls emotional expression so the speaker feels accepted • Can be a wonderful conversationalist because he or she is a wonderful listener
How to Speak to a High S	• Provide a sincere, personable, and agreeable environment. • Show sincere interest in the person and, particularly, in his or her family. • Ask "how" questions to get his or her opinions. • Draw out his or her goals systematically. • Present new ideas or departures from the status quo in a non-threatening manner and show the benefits to the High S. • Clearly define goals in any new plans and point out how the High S fits into those plans. • Provide personal assurance and reassurance. • Give the High S constant, specific appreciation. • Refrain from aggression, ultimatums, and conflict. • Always use logical, systematic, rational systems when explaining or asking for cooperation. • Give him or her time to process information and make decisions. • Be loyal and supportive.

Steady ("High S") Style About 35 percent of the population has a personal communication style known as the steady, or "High S," style. The steady style tends to be slow-paced and both people- and task-oriented. As a result, these communicators typically are cooperative and efficient and can be counted on to get the job done. High S's are fairly reserved, pay attention to detail, love structure, and are very stable. They also are good team players, even though they may appear somewhat pessimistic. High S's tend to appear casual and conforming. Because High S's reach their objectives by cooperating, they tend to have warm personalities and a calming effect on others.

Conscientious ("High C") Style About 35 percent of the population falls into the conscientious, or "High C," category of personal style. The conscientious style tends to be slow-paced and task-oriented. High C's are highly analytical perfectionists who love detail. They also tend to be introverts, guarded in their

MULTIPLE LEARNING STYLES

Visual-Spatial Students who think in visual images and enjoy drawing can add a personal element to the analysis of personal interaction styles by helping the class "see" each type.

Activity As they study the characteristics of the dominant, influencing, steady, and conscientious styles, ask students to sketch what the office of each would be like: What is on the walls? What is on the desk? How is the person dressed? How does he or she stand and gesture when interacting with coworkers? Have students create a collage or poster-size illustration combining elements that reveal the traits and personal qualities of one of these types.

"HIGH C" CHARACTERISTICS

How the High C Speaks	• May pass the buck if you go to him or her for answers • May yield a position in order to avoid controversy • Becomes defensive when threatened • Exact about details; feels quality is extremely important; may talk at great length about details that don't seem important to other styles of communicators • Asks many, many detailed questions to clarify the other person's position • Slow to respond because he or she must process all the information • Extremely critical of own work and, often, highly critical of others who do not meet his or her expectations • Influences others by collecting and organizing factual data and logical presentations • Seldom admits to true emotional reactions and will withhold insights and opinions until he or she feels it is safe to share them • Seldom gives positive feedback of appreciation to others • Has a special talent for organizing and communicating instructions correctly • Follows life's rules and fulfills commitments • As a method of analysis, he or she often will seek someone's opinion only to argue with it or move on to seek someone else's opinion • Very cautious about expressing opinions or making recommendations until all data have been checked and rechecked • Enjoys intellectual argument as a way of exercising his or her reasoning abilities • May seem to take little initiative or contribute few ideas; fears criticism and may keep to self to feel protected
How the High C Listens	• Attentive, intuitive listener; sensitive to the feelings of the speaker • May miss the main point and get off on tangents • Will ask many, many questions—which, at times, may begin to feel like an attack • Will need to hear the same things repeatedly, reprocess the same information, and ask the same questions • Will take criticism or comments personally although they were not aimed directly at the High C
How to Speak to a High C	• Take time to prepare your case logically in advance. • Provide straight pros and cons of the ideas and support ideas with accurate data. • Provide exact job descriptions with precise explanations of how each fits into the big picture. • Provide reassurance that no surprises will occur. • Provide a step-by-step approach to the goal. • Be specific if agreeing; if disagreeing, disagree with the facts, not the person. • Be prepared to provide many explanations and answer "how" and "if" questions in a patient, persistent manner. • Encourage verbal independence as well as job independence. • Provide many assurances that you value quality and accuracy. • Refrain from antagonistic responses that breed withdrawal and avoidance. • Offer as much reassurance and support as possible; assure the High C that everything will be all right.

relationships and avoiding risk at all costs. Because of this, High C's tend to seek the safety of rules and regulations and appear very formal and conservative. They follow rules and meet deadlines conscientiously and expect others to do the same. They get results by working within the guidelines or prescribed structure to ensure quality and accuracy. High C's sometimes prefer to work alone rather than in groups, but often they are sought out for advice about routine and details.

Building Effective Interpersonal Relationships **227**

High C Style

Individuals who are dominant High Cs fit into the MBTI category of people who prefer taking in information and making decisions based on factual information gained through the five senses and prefer making decisions whenever possible. This type is orderly, structured, and conservative in approach. They are analytical and serious and objective. After they study the list of characteristics for the High C style, ask students to list occupations or work-related roles that suit the "High C." *(Students may mention fields that require imagining possibilities for things or systems—such as research, engineering, and architecture.)* Have students list five teachers whom they have found effective. Students should analyze the lists of characteristics for each personal style and choose the one that suits each teacher best. Ask students to share what they discovered. Did most teachers fit into one category? **L3**

Communication Tip

Introverts may have trouble holding their own in meetings and discussions on the job because they tend to take longer to think answers through and consider all the possibilities. However, the Internet gives them a way to express themselves on their own terms, because they can take as much time as needed to frame responses without interruption by extroverts. Online interaction may even give introverts some communication advantages.

INTERDISCIPLINARY CONNECTION

Social Studies As a class, discuss the social roles played by political leaders, business leaders, and cultural and religious icons in America. Do students think many examples of people in these roles today fit into particular types?

Activity Have students select one high profile individual in one of the three categories you discussed and research this person's life and contributions. After fitting the pieces together, students should categorize the individual as having a *dominant, influencing, steady,* or *conscientious* temperament. Ask that students present a short talk to the class explaining their choices.

GLENCOE *Online*

For an additional Practice Lab for this section, have students visit the *Glencoe Communication Applications* Web site at communicationapplications.glencoe.com. Click on Communication Practice Lab 7–2. **L1**

■ Visual Instruction

Answer Interpersonal conflict can be avoided by adapting behavior from one relationship to another and realizing a person's communication style is their natural orientation toward getting work done.

COMMUNICATION
PRACTICE LAB

Personal Style

Have students follow the six steps in the Communication Practice Lab on page 229 to give students a working understanding of personal style categories and determine which best describes them. Students should conclude that dominant communicators spur the class forward and keep it on task, influencers make class time enjoyable by adding enthusiasm and humor, steady communicators make sure things remain calm and group work gets done, and conscientious communicators make sure the work is accurate and conforms to school and class rules. **L2**

■ Interpersonal conflict occurs between a referee and coach. **How can one avoid interpersonal conflict?**

Analyzing Style to Prevent Interpersonal Conflict

You may have heard people talk about personality conflicts. Many times, these problems reflect a conflict in personal communication style.

Consider, for example, the pace at which each style works. This factor alone can cause different styles to come into conflict in the workplace. For instance, the fast-paced High D who cares little about details and thinks only about results may come into direct conflict with the slower-paced High S who is detail-oriented. The fast-paced, outgoing High I and the slow-paced, structure-oriented High C may annoy one another when working together.

Determining Your Personal Style

You may have characteristics of all the personal styles described. However, you can try to get an idea of which style best describes you by completing the Communication Practice Lab on the next page. Once you do this, you may have a better idea of how to handle conflicts in communication situations with others who have a style different from yours.

Avoiding Conflict
If you examine the tables provided for each personal style, you probably will see a number of areas in which conflicts are likely to occur. These may include pace, attention or lack of attention to details, openness, willingness to change, and people versus task orientation.

MEETING INDIVIDUAL NEEDS
MULTIPLE LEARNING STYLES

Musical Students with musical training can explain to the class ways in which music expresses different qualities—for example, optimism versus pessimism, light-hearted versus serious. Play excerpts from classical pieces and have students practice describing the "character" of the music.
Activity Invite students to compose songs honoring each of the four types of personal style. Students should use rhythm, melody, and other musical tools as well as lyrics to express the styles. Have students perform their songs for the class and ask classmates to offer feedback.

To avoid conflict, you may find it helpful to adapt your own communication behavior slightly from relationship to relationship. For example, if you are a High I and your boss is a High C, you can use your knowledge of the two styles to avoid problems. You might make a special effort to get your reports done quickly and efficiently. You also might have a coworker check your work for accuracy before you give it to the boss.

If you are a High D, you might try to be more aware of your tendency to be overly aggressive in pursuit of results. You might make a point of developing empathic listening skills and work toward developing sensitivity and empathy for your slower-paced counterparts who, after all, are really responsible for getting the work done.

Another thing that can help you avoid conflict is realizing that a person's communication style is his or her natural orientation toward getting work done. It really has nothing to do

interNET
ACTIVITY

Analyzing Your Personality To understand yourself better, you can analyze your personality. Conduct an Internet search using *personality tests* as your search term. You will find several surveys, questionnaires, and personality profiles. These tests are scientifically designed to try to pinpoint your personality type. They are usually in a multiple-choice format. Review at least three different personality assessment tests or surveys. What do the tests have in common? What is different about each test? Ask your guidance counselor which tests are used the most. For what purposes are the results of personality tests used?

interNET
ACTIVITY

Analyzing Your Personality Students' responses may be similar to the examples provided here. Most personality inventories consist of multiple-choice questions, often based on hypothetical situations. Answers may be based on a frequency scale, such as "Always" to "Never." Test results are compiled and expressed in different ways. Some tests may have dozens of questions while others may have just a handful. Two well-known tests are the Myers-Briggs Type Indicator (MBTI) and the Minnesota Multiphasic Personality Inventory (MMPI/MMPI-2). These tests are used by colleges and universities, the legal system, and doctors. Psychologists can review test results and provide expert opinions to people in other professions. **L3**

3 ASSESS

Assign Section 2 Assessment as a homework or in-class activity.

❶ Use *Interactive Tutor Self-Assessment Software* to review Section 2.

COMMUNICATION

PRACTICE LAB

Personal Style

To practice determining your own personal style, follow these steps:

Step 1 Divide the class into four groups.

Step 2 Work with your group to develop a list of fifteen adjectives that describe one specific personal style. (Be sure each of the four groups describes a different style.) Describe how a person of that style might be perceived by coworkers, bosses, or other group members.

Step 3 Present your group's list of adjectives to the class and write them on the chalkboard. Discuss all the lists as a class and make any necessary changes.

Step 4 On a separate sheet of paper, copy the Personal Style Profile and Scoring Sheet found on pages 647 and 648 of

the Appendix. Take the profile and determine which style best describes you. Write that style on a sheet of paper. Then, below that style, write the remaining three styles in the order that they describe you.

Step 5 Choose four adjectives that describe you and your personal style. Compare these adjectives to the ones the class listed under that style.

Step 6 Compare personal styles as a class. Discuss how all four styles work interdependently to help your class function and get work done.

Building Effective Interpersonal Relationships **229**

MEETING INDIVIDUAL NEEDS
INCLUSION STRATEGIES

Learning Disabled For disabled students, you may want to provide an audiotape of the chapter which they can read along. Create and display simplified poster-size versions of the personal styles characteristics charts so students can refer to them readily during activities and discussion.

Activity Have students watch portions of a video (excerpts from movies, television shows, or corporate videotapes) that show people interacting socially and in the workplace. Discuss and replay these to have students observe how each illustrates the characteristics of a productive interpersonal relationship or one of the four personal styles.

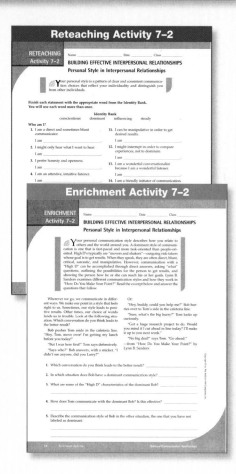

Reteaching Activity 7-2

RETEACHING
Activity 7-2
BUILDING EFFECTIVE INTERPERSONAL RELATIONSHIPS
Personal Style in Interpersonal Relationships

Enrichment Activity 7-2

ENRICHMENT
Activity 7-2
BUILDING EFFECTIVE INTERPERSONAL RELATIONSHIPS
Personal Style in Interpersonal Relationships

4 CLOSE

Have students write a journal entry explaining the "blueprint" of their personal style, using the section content as a guideline.

Extra-Credit Project

Ask students to interview a counselor, administrator, or teacher who has mediated student conflicts to learn that person's beliefs about the role different communication styles and poor interpersonal communication skills play in creating conflict. Students can present their findings in an oral report or skit.

with that person's perception of you. This realization can help you depersonalize the individual's actions and better understand him or her.

Finally, you may be less likely to clash with others if you realize that all four styles are necessary to get work done in professional and social contexts. We need High D's to get us going and keep us on task. We need the optimism, energy, and humor of High I's to establish a positive and creative atmosphere on the job. We need High S's to calm us down—and sometimes slow us down—so we can do the job right. We need High C's to keep us on task and in line with the rules. Regardless of which style you identify with, you are a valuable force in the workplace.

Section 2 Assessment

GLENCOE Online

Visit the *Glencoe Communication Applications* Web site at **communicationapplications. glencoe.com** and click on **Self-Check and Study Guide 7.2** to review your understanding of personal style in interpersonal relationships.

Review Key Terms

1. Define each term and write it in a sentence: personal style, dominant style, influencing style, steady style, conscientious style.

Check Understanding

2. Name each type of personal style and describe its main characteristics.

3. Which style most closely describes you? Explain how you might use that communication style effectively in the workplace.

4. **Predict** Imagine that you are a High C and your partner on a class project is a High I. How do you think these different styles might affect your working relationship? How might you both adapt your communication behavior to work together productively?

APPLICATION *Activity*

Integrating Personal Styles Choose a partner with a personal style that is different from your own. (If none is available, choose someone whose secondary styles are in a different order.) Next, imagine the two of you must work together as boss and employee. Discuss how you each might adapt your behaviors to avoid conflict and better meet each other's communication needs. Then, switch roles. Share your conclusions with the class.

Section 2 Assessment Answers

1. Accept all reasonable sentences.
2. Dominant: fast-paced, task-oriented, little patience for details; influencing: fast-paced, people-oriented, outgoing, optimistic; steady: slow-paced, people- and task-oriented, reserved, cooperative, detail-oriented; conscientious: slow-paced, task-oriented, introverted, focused on accuracy and detail, perfectionistic
3. Answers should reflect an understanding of the specific strengths of each personal style.
4. The High C might become frustrated with the High I's perceived lack of focus or attention to detail; the High I might see the High C as too serious. To adapt, the High C might try to relax and have a little more fun with the project, and the High I might try to work more diligently.

Application Activity Students should suggest adapting their own pace, giving more attention to accuracy and detail, and being willing to share ideas, among other things, based on the particular styles involved.

Communication Self-Assessment

Interpersonal Communication Skills

How Do You Rate?

On a separate sheet of paper, use the key to respond to the following statements. Put a check mark at the end of each skill you would like to improve.

KEY: A Always   **R** Rarely
        U Usually   **N** Never
        S Sometimes

1. I try to maintain a positive attitude in my relationships with others.
2. I use "I" messages in my interpersonal communication to show ownership of my thoughts and ideas.
3. I use active listening skills and provide appropriate verbal and nonverbal feedback in my interpersonal communication.
4. I use supportive language to show my willingness to help find answers to questions.
5. I use perception checks to make sure I clearly understand others' messages.
6. I try to listen without being judgmental, and I try to avoid preaching.
7. I avoid evaluative language.
8. I use feed-forward statements to personalize messages.
9. I give frequent and specific compliments and praise.
10. I try to understand each person's interpersonal style and adapt my communication to it.

How Do You Score?

Review your responses. Give yourself 5 points for every A, 4 for every U, 3 for every S, 2 for every R, and 1 for every N. Total your points and evaluate your score.

41–50 Excellent You may be surprised to find out how much you can improve your skills.

31–40 Good In this course, you can learn ways to make your skills better.

21–30 Fair Practice applying the skills taught in this course.

1–20 Needs Improvement Carefully monitor your improvement as you work through this course.

Setting Communication Goals

If you scored Excellent or Good, complete Part A. If your score was Fair or Needs Improvement, complete Part B.

Part A
1. I plan to put the following ideas into practice:
2. I plan to share the following information about communication with the following people:

Part B
1. The behaviors I need to change most are:
2. To bring about these changes, I will take these steps:

Building Effective Interpersonal Relationships **231**

Communication Self-Assessment

Have students respond to the statements, using the key provided, then evaluate their presentation organization skills using the scoring rubric. Based on their scores, students should complete either Part A or Part B of the goal-setting activity.

Communication Journal Activity

Point out to students that to accomplish goals, one must make them specific and concrete and review them often to assess progress. Have students write specific goals in their Communication Journals.

Communication Tip

Remind the class that progress toward accomplishing their goals will come only with practice. Encourage students to apply the skills presentations they make.

CRITICAL THINKING ACTIVITY

As a class, discuss actions and thought processes one of the personal style types values most. For example, a High C values a logical, factual approach to problem solving, exactness and quality in details, following rules and honoring commitments. Divide the class into four groups and assign each group one personal style type. Have the groups list values this style most likely holds. Create a whole class chart on the board, adding each group's list as it is completed.

Communication Through Writing

Writing a Letter of Complaint

Objectives: To learn proper tone and content for a letter of complaint; to write a letter of complaint

Teaching Suggestions and Strategies

Connection to the Workplace

Explain that businesses want people to be pleased with their products and services. That is why they exist. An unhappy client or customer can damage a business's reputation through bad word-of-mouth advertising. Therefore, most businesses have personnel or a department for handling customer relations. Tell students that if they have a complaint to make about a bill for services or a faulty product, they should read the document that came with the billing or the product. It probably gives the appropriate contact number and/or address and may also outline procedures for making returns or complaints.

Writing a Letter of Complaint

A letter of complaint is a way of expressing unhappiness with the quality of a product or service. You might write a letter of complaint to ask that a damaged product be replaced, request compensation for inferior goods, or avoid a similar problem in the future. Some suggestions for writing a letter of complaint are provided below.

Be Specific. Explain the problem you are writing about in as much detail as possible. State the problem clearly and specifically so that the recipient understands all of the important details. For example, a manufacturer would not know where to look for a problem if you wrote only, "Your products don't work!" Provide the make and model number of the product, where and when it was purchased, and then carefully describe the problem you're having with it.

Be Objective and Polite. Maintain a friendly, positive tone in your letter. Avoid threats, insults, and strong emotional responses. Don't make an enemy of the person who reads your letter. He or she needs clear, logical information in order to solve your problem. Do not blame a specific person or group of people.

If you can suggest that a simple misunderstanding is at fault, you are more likely to receive a prompt, courteous, and satisfying reply.

Use Proper Procedure. Manufacturers often have specific procedures for returning merchandise. Make sure that you abide by these policies. If you are asked to send an item back in its original package, be sure to do so. If you are asked to send proof of purchase, do this as well.

Ask for the Compensation You Want. Most companies want to change your unfavorable opinion of them before you tell others about your negative experience. Let companies know what actions you expect them to take. If you would like a replacement for a defective product, say so. If you received poor or unfriendly service, ask that the sales staff be spoken to about their professional etiquette. If you would like your money back for an inferior product, make this clear. If an item has been repaired but still does not work, let the company know if you want a proper repair job or if you would prefer to get your money back.

Keep a Copy of Your Letter. If you need to write to the same company again, attach copies of all previous correspondence.

 For additional information about business writing, see the *Guide to Business Communication* section of the Communication Survival Kit in the Appendix.

MULTIPLE LEARNING STYLES

MEETING INDIVIDUAL NEEDS

Intrapersonal Encourage students to keep a file or a journal outlining their experiences in communicating dissatisfaction with products and services. The log can become a tool for learning how to communicate assertively without causing ill will.

Activity Ask students to make note of their concerns and fears as they wrote each letter of complaint they sent, the type of response they received, and how satisfactory it was to them.

Communication Through Writing

The following is a letter of complaint about a defective part in an automobile. Note how the customer is specific, objective, politely goes through the proper procedures, and asks for compensation.

575 Olympic Street
Seattle, WA 98060
January 28, 2003

United Motors, Inc.
8415 Sandhill Road
Lafayette, IN 47901

Dear United Motors, Inc.:

I am writing to inform you that your new Pacesetters may have a design flaw in the steering column assembly. According to the mechanic who repaired mine, the wiring is bundled so tightly that it is no wonder a cable frayed and parted after only a few weeks of wear.

On the morning of January 22, 2003, with all four members of my family aboard, I was turning our new Pacesetter from southbound Orion onto Burlington Boulevard in Seattle. All of a sudden, I was trying to steer a car that had no power steering. If traffic had not been unusually light, I might not have been able to guide the car safely to the berm. My family and I were lucky to escape harm.

I bought the car new at your dealership last November 19. At the time of the incident, the odometer read 1,455 miles.

Westgate Automotive, Inc., repaired the steering column assembly and promised that the car would be safe to drive, but I am not satisfied. I want to have the car thoroughly examined by your own experts because neither my wife nor I trust it as we used to. We also think you should reimburse us for the repairs.

Yours truly,
Drew Brooks
Drew Brooks

WRITING *Activity*

Use the steps outlined earlier and the following facts to write an effective letter of complaint.

- You bought a toy truck from Land of Toys at 1771 West Elm Street in your town last week.

- You are enclosing a copy of the receipt.

- The first time the child played with it, both front tires fell off.

- You want either a refund or a new toy truck.

Write your letter of complaint and then share it with a classmate. Read your classmate's letter, and suggest improvements if you can. If you were an employee of Land of Toys, how would you respond to the complaint letter you wrote? Why

Teaching Activity

Ask students to list three products or services they have purchased that did not live up to their expectations. What problem(s) resulted? What would they like the business or manufacturer to do to make it right? Display a product and give a brief explanation for a defect or failure in the product. Have students work in pairs to outline the points they would make in a letter of complaint to the manufacturer. After students compare their outlines, select the best points and, as a class, draft a letter.

WRITING *Activity*

Student letters should be formatted as the sample indicates and should include all the bulleted points in the list. Remind students to maintain a polite and positive tone in their writing.

Grammar Tip

Prepositional phrases act as adjectives that modify nouns and pronouns and adverbs that modify verbs, adjectives, and other adverbs.

Additional Resources

Appendix, "Guide to Business Communication"

Glencoe Writer's Assistant CD-ROM

Glencoe Interactive Grammar Software

Grade 9 Writer's Choice, Lesson 6.4

GRAMMAR PRACTICE

Prepositional Phrases as Adjectives and Adverbs

Have students underline each prepositional phrase and draw an arrow from it to the word it modifies. Then, have them write *adjective* or *adverb* in the blank to show what kind of modifier the phrase is.

1. I purchased the ring from your store last month. _____ *(adv., modifies purchased)*

2. The stone in the center has chipped. _____ *(adj., modifies stone)*

3. It was to be a gift for my mother. _____ *(adj., modifies gift)*

4. This damage is disappointing to me and her. _____ *(adv., modifies disappointing)*

5. I appreciate your prompt attention to this problem. _____ *(adj., modifies attention)*

GLENCOE TECHNOLOGY

MindJogger Videoquiz

Use *MindJogger* to review the Chapter 7 content.

Reviewing Key Terms

1. The conscientious style of communication is slow-paced and more task-oriented than people-oriented.

2. A person with a dominant style of communication tends to be critical and sarcastic.

3. A person with a steady style of communication is generally both people- and task-oriented.

4. true

5. The influencing style of communication often includes spontaneity and humor.

6. true

Reviewing Key Concepts

1. Relationships of management to employees, employees to other employees, and employees to clients or the public

2. To improve morale, enhance success, increase productivity

3. By sponsoring special events such as company softball or basketball tournaments, parties, picnics

4. Students may suggest this outfit is too informal and suggests unskilled or unprofessional attitudes, which could make patients feel anxious and uncertain about the doctor. The pleasantness of the voice might communicate a caring, supportive attitude toward patients.

GLENCOE Online

Visit the *Glencoe Communication Applications* Web site at **communicationapplications. glencoe.com** and click on **Chapter 7 Activity** for additional information about interpersonal communication.

Reviewing Key Terms

Read each statement. On a separate sheet of paper, write whether the statement is true or false. If the statement is false, rewrite it so that it reads true. Underline the words that you substitute to make statements true.

1. The dominant style of communication is slow-paced and more task-oriented than people-oriented.

2. A person with a steady style of communication tends to be critical and sarcastic.

3. A person with a conscientious style of communication is generally both people- and task-oriented.

4. Integrating means to blend things so they function as a whole.

5. The conscientious style of communication often includes spontaneity and humor.

6. Personal style is a pattern of clear and consistent choices that reflects a person's individuality.

Reviewing Key Concepts

1. What are the three types of relationships in a professional context?

2. Give three purposes for open and direct communication in the workplace.

3. How do some companies encourage employees to get to know one another better?

4. A receptionist at a doctor's office dresses in jeans and T-shirts and uses a pleasant phone voice. What kinds of messages is this worker sending to clients who visit the office or call on the phone?

5. What is the main purpose of trying to maintain a positive employee-customer relationship?

6. How do positive relationships with leaders in a social organization motivate members?

7. List the five characteristics of an effective interpersonal relationship.

8. Identify and briefly describe the dominant characteristics of each type of personal style.

5. Positive employee-customer relationships bolster business.

6. They make members work with renewed effort and enthusiasm to achieve goals.

7. Openness, empathy, equality, supportiveness, positiveness

8. Dominant: fast-paced, task-oriented, little patience for details; influencing: fast-paced, people-oriented, outgoing, optimistic; steady: slow-paced, people- and task-oriented, reserved, cooperative, detail-oriented; conscientious: slow-paced, task-oriented, introverted, focused on accuracy and detail, perfectionistic

📻 Reading and Critical Thinking Skill

1. **Cause-Effect** What is often the effect when one person's communication with another is rude?

2. **Making Comparisons** How is communication between upper-level managers and employees different from that between lower- or mid-level managers and employees?

3. **Synthesis** A student brings home a report card with five Cs and one D. Formulate a question or comment that this student's parent might make that avoids evaluative, judgmental language.

4. **Classifying Information** Which style of communicator wants brief, direct answers?

📻 Skill Practice Activity

Using Word Context Clues A reader can often guess the meaning of an unfamiliar word based on the context, or the passage in which the word is used. Write your definition of the underlined word based on its context:

Because High S's <u>attain</u> their objectives by cooperating with others, they tend to have warm personalities and a calming effect on the group.

📻 Cooperative Learning Activity

Evaluating Communication Styles With a partner, create a survey that determines a person's communication style. Write multiple-choice items for which each answer represents a different style. Base the items on the charts in Section 2. Work on the item stems with your partner. Share the task of writing the answers by writing the options for two styles and letting your partner write the options for the others. Use the following item as a model.

When carrying out a plan, you tend to be

A. overly optimistic (High D)

B. spontaneous and humorous (High I)

C. thoughtful, orderly, and logical (High S)

D. exact about details (High C)

Chapter Project

Planning Share with the class the survey that you created for the Cooperative Learning Activity. As a class, select the best questions from each pair of students and combine them into a new survey. Make copies of the survey and distribute them to teachers, counselors, and other adults in your school. Collect the completed surveys and evaluate the results.

Choose a communication style and write a brief article about its characteristics. List ways to interact with this style as a competent communicator.

Presenting As a class, choose the best article about each communication style. Publish the four articles as a series in the school newspaper or as a separate communications handbook.

📻 Reading and Critical Thinking Skill

1. **Cause-Effect** Students may suggest that rudeness causes resentment and creates or heightens conflict.

2. **Making Comparisons** Communications between middle managers and employees are more direct, immediate, and day-to-day.

3. **Synthesis** Answers should show understanding of the importance of supportive, positive "I" statements that show concern and do not label.

4. **Classifying Information** Dominant-style communicator

📻 Skill Practice Activity

Using Word Context Clues

Likely answers may include *accomplish, reach, achieve.*

📻 Cooperative Learning Activity

Evaluating Communication Styles

You may want to suggest that students find parallel items across the four charts on pages 224–227 and use phrases from these to construct their survey items. Point out that questions are most useful when they point to differences among the four styles in a single area, such as listening or physical reactions.

Chapter Project

As a class, while creating the new survey, discuss what each question reveals about the communication styles. Create a chart on the board for tallying survey results and have the class work together to compile data. Lead a class discussion about what the survey shows, then have students write their articles. Students might also publish the series of articles on the Web and invite other schools to give feedback.

SECTION RESOURCES

Daily Objectives	Reproducible Resources	Multimedia Resources

Daily Objectives

Section 1

1. Describe strategies for participating appropriately in conversations
2. Devise clear and appropriate requests
3. Describe strategies for giving clear and accurate directions
4. Recognize the importance of appropriate and purposeful questions
5. Respond appropriately to the requests, directions, and questions of others

Reproducible Resources

 Reproducible Lesson Plan 8-1
 Application Activities 8-1
 Guided Reading Workbook Activity 8-1
 Vocabulary Activity 8*
 Reteaching Activity 8-1*
 Enrichment Activity 8-1*
 Graphic Organizer Transparency Strategies and Activities 8-1

Multimedia Resources

 Graphic Organizer Transparency 8-1
 Chapter 8 Teaching Transparency
 Interactive Tutor Self-Assessment
 PuzzleMaker
 ExamView® Pro Testmaker
 Interactive Lesson Planner
Communication in Action Video Chapter 8
MindJogger
communicationapplications.glencoe.com
Presentation Plus!

Section 2

1. Explain professional protocol for making introductions
2. Describe professional protocol for using the telephone
3. Compare and contrast professional etiquette for offering and receiving criticism
4. Analyze and evaluate the effectiveness of your own and others' communication
5. Use appropriate strategies for dealing with diversity

 Reproducible Lesson Plan 8-2
 Application Activities 8-2
 Guided Reading Workbook Activity 8-2
 Vocabulary Activity 8*
 Reteaching Activity 8-2*
 Enrichment Activity 8-2*
 Graphic Organizer Transparency Strategies and Activities 8-2

 Graphic Organizer Transparency 8-2
 Chapter 8 Teaching Transparency
 Interactive Tutor Self-Assessment
 PuzzleMaker
 ExamView® Pro Testmaker
 Interactive Lesson Planner
Communication in Action Video Chapter 8
MindJogger
communicationapplications.glencoe.com
Presentation Plus!

Use Glencoe's *Presentation Plus!* multimedia teacher tool to easily present dynamic lessons that engage and motivate your students. Using Microsoft PowerPoint®, you can customize the presentations to create your own personalized lessons.

* Also available in Spanish

 Blackline Master   CD-ROM   Software

Transparency   Videodisc   Videocassette   Web site

Chapter 8 Planning Guide

FOR THE TEACHER

Interpersonal Skills

Ask each student to list five different types of conversations he or she has had today. Tell students to note the person or group with whom they held the conversation, the general topic or purpose of the conversation, and whether it was what they would consider an informal conversation or a more formal one. Suggest that they make a chart to organize this information.

Then, ask them to recall their own part in each conversation they have labeled "informal" and each one they have labeled "more formal." Invite discussion about what students recall about the way they talked in those conversations. Was their choice of words different for formal and informal conversations? Was their tone of voice different? Why? What made a conversation more formal than others? Was it the individuals or kinds of people to whom they spoke? Was it the topic or purpose?

CHAPTER RESOURCES

Resources for the Teacher

- *BusinessSpeak: Using the Gentle Art of Verbal Persuasion to Get What You Want at Work* by Suzette Haden Elgin, McGraw-Hill, 1995
- *Great Connections: Small Talk and Networking for Businesspeople* by Anne Baber and Lynne Waymon, Impact Publications, 1992
- *How to Say It at Work: Putting Yourself Across with Power Words, Phrases, Body Language, and Communication Secrets* by Jack Griffin, Prentice Hall, 1998
- *Working Woman's Communications Survival Guide: How to Present Your Ideas with Impact, Clarity, and Power and Get the Recognition You Deserve* by Ruth Herrman Siress, with Carolyn Riddle and Deborah Shouse, Prentice Hall, 1994

Resources for the Student

- *How to Talk So People Listen: The Real Key to Job Success* by Sonya Hamlin, Harper & Row, 1988
- *Success with the Gentle Art of Verbal Self-Defense* by Suzette Haden Elgin, Prentice Hall, 1989

Block Scheduling

Block scheduling differs from traditional class scheduling in the amount of time allotted to each period. The extended time frame provided by block scheduling affords you the opportunity to implement a greater number of research-oriented and activity-intense projects to motivate and involve your students. Activities that are particularly suited to use within the block-scheduling framework are identified throughout this chapter by the following designation:

KEY TO ABILITY LEVELS

Teaching Strategies have been coded for varying learning styles and abilities.

L1 **BASIC** activities for all students

L2 **AVERAGE** activities for average to above-average students

L3 **CHALLENGING** activities for above-average students

ELL **English Language Learner** activities

Chapter 8 Resource Manager

The following materials may be used when teaching the chapter. Materials for specific lessons are also shown at point-of-use in the margins of the Teacher's Wraparound Edition.

TEACHING TRANSPARENCIES

Chapter 8 Teaching Transparency

Graphic Organizer Transparency 8–1

Graphic Organizer Transparency 8–2

APPLICATION ACTIVITIES

Chapter 8, Section 1

Chapter 8, Section 2

Chapter 8, Cumulative

REINFORCEMENT AND REVIEW ACTIVITIES

Vocabulary Activity 8

Guided Reading Activity Workbook 8–1, 8–2

Reteaching Activities 8–1, 8–2

Chapter 8 Resource Manager

ASSESSMENT AND EVALUATION

Section Quizzes 8-1, 8-2

Chapter 8 Test, Forms A & B

Performance Assessment Activity 8

ENRICHMENT AND EXTENSION

Technology Application Activity 8

Enrichment Activities 8-1, 8-2

ORAL PRESENTATION ACTIVITIES

Activities 13, 14, 18

SPANISH RESOURCES

- Spanish Chapter and Unit Tests
- Spanish Vocabulary Activities
- Spanish Section Quizzes
- Spanish Reteaching Activities
- Spanish Enrichment Activities

MULTIMEDIA

- Interactive Tutor Self-Assessment
- ExamView® Pro Testmaker
- PuzzleMaker
- Communication in Action Videodisc and Videocassette
- MindJogger
- Interactive Lesson Planner
- Presentation Plus!
- Writer's Assistant
- Glencoe Interactive Grammar
- **communicationapplications.glencoe.com**

TEACHER PLANNING AND SUPPORT

- Reproducible Lesson Plans
- Interactive Lesson Planner
- Presentation Plus!

Developing Effective Interpersonal Skills

WHY IT'S IMPORTANT

Whether you are speaking to someone you would like to have as a friend or an employer, the quality of that relationship depends, in part, on the appropriateness of your speech.

To better understand interpersonal communication, view the **Communication in Action** Chapter 8 video lesson.

GLENCOE *Online*

Visit the *Glencoe Communication Applications* Web site at **communicationapplications. glencoe.com** and click on **Overview–Chapter 8** to preview information about interpersonal skills.

"The trouble with . . . is [he/she] lacks the power of conversation but not the power of speech."
—Bernard Shaw, British author

WHY IT'S IMPORTANT

Ask a student to read aloud the quotation from Bernard Shaw. Let students discuss it briefly. Then, have students preview the chapter by reading the headings and subheadings and looking at the photographs and captions. Ask: **What are interpersonal skills? How do you think interpersonal skills are related to the "power of conversation" Shaw speaks about?** *(Answers may reflect that interpersonal skills include the ability to converse well, which Shaw claims someone lacked even though he or she had the power of speech.)*

Section 1

Communicating Interpersonally

GUIDE TO READING

Objectives

1. Describe strategies for participating appropriately in conversations.
2. Devise clear and appropriate requests.
3. Describe strategies for giving clear and accurate directions.
4. Recognize the importance of appropriate and purposeful questions.
5. Respond appropriately to the requests, directions, and questions of others.

Terms to Learn

open-ended question
closed question
paraphrase

*W*hat if you were to meet the President of the United States? Would you greet him the same way that you greet your best friend? Of course not. You have built a more interpersonal relationship with your friend. Together you have developed a unique way of speaking and listening to each other.

As you learned in Chapter 2, interpersonal communication takes place anytime messages are exchanged between two or more people. Interpersonal communication within social and professional contexts can take place at home, at school, in the community, or at work. Every day you communicate with a number of different people. You talk to members of your family, friends, teachers, other group members, and, possibly, coworkers and employers.

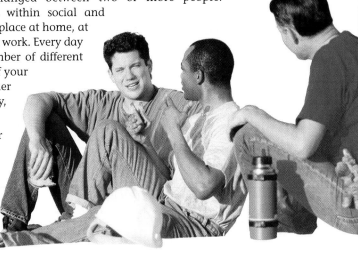

Although the purpose for your communication may vary from contact to contact, one goal remains constant: You want your communication to be as successful as possible. To accomplish this, you need to learn techniques for participating effectively in conversations.

Interpersonal communication takes place between these coworkers as they have lunch. What goal remains constant for communication in any relationship?

Developing Effective Interpersonal Skills **237**

1 FOCUS

Bellringer
Lead a brief discussion about the differences between how students greet a friend and how they might greet the president of the United States. *(Students are likely to conclude that they would be much more formal in meeting and greeting the president than they would when greeting their friends.)*

You may use Graphic Organizer Transparency 8–1 to introduce this section.

Communication Tip

By definition, communication takes place only when one party receives and responds to a message sent by another party. Talking or writing is not communicating unless someone understands and responds, even if the response is private (as with reading).

Visual Instruction

Answer The goal of wanting the communication to be successful remains constant.

RESOURCE MANAGER

Teaching Tools
- Interactive Lesson Planner
- Reproducible Lesson Plan 8–1
- Application Activities 8–1

Reproducible Masters
- Guided Reading Activity Workbook 8–1
- Enrichment Activity 8–1
- Reteaching Activity 8–1
- Section Quiz 8–1
- Transparency Strategies and Activities Booklet 8–1

Transparencies
- Graphic Organizer Transparency 8–1
- Chapter 8 Teaching Transparency

Technology Resources
- Interactive Tutor Self-Assessment Software
- Presentation Plus! Software
- ExamView® Pro Testmaker
- PuzzleMaker Software
- communicationapplications.glencoe.com

2 TEACH

Small Talk

Point out that small talk comes easily to some people, but others have difficulty trying to think of something to say. Students who consider themselves among the latter group might benefit from copying the "Common Topics for Small Talk" chart at the bottom of page 239. Encourage pairs of such students to practice small talk together. **L2**

Visual Instruction

Answer Light, social "chitchat" that begins a conversation

Communication provides the means for one employee to explain a procedure to another. **What is small talk?**

BECOMING AN EFFECTIVE CONVERSATIONALIST

Conversations help people in an organization understand the organization's culture. In addition, conversations help people do their jobs more effectively. In social and professional organizations, conversations allow a free flow of information. They also enable people to clarify job tasks; persuade employees, coworkers, or superiors to do something; or ask for opinions on work-related issues. Finally, conversations are useful for providing guidance on procedures or policies in the workplace or organization.

Initiating Conversations

Some people find it easy to begin conversations. If you are not one of these people, it may seem awkward or difficult for you to begin talking with someone. However, by following a few simple steps, you can become a good conversationalist.

Begin with Small Talk. In many social and business situations, conversations begin with what is called "small talk." Small

talk is the kind of light, social "chitchat" that initiates a conversation. Small talk simply breaks the ice and sets the tone for the communication.

Small-Talk Topics

Small talk can span a broad range of topics, but it is all similar in one respect. Small talk almost always takes on a superficial, somewhat distant tone. In other words, it does not involve strong opinions, feelings, or great detail. In general, topics for small talk tend to revolve around three categories: environment, personal characteristics, and biography.

Guidelines for Small Talk Small talk is a starting point for developing valuable social and professional relationships. To use small talk effectively for these purposes, use the guidelines in the Communication Strategies checklist on the following page.

Check Nonverbal Signals. Before you initiate any conversation, check the nonverbal signals you and your receiver are sending. If your nonverbal messages show confidence and poise, they can help to make a positive impression on the person with whom you'll be conversing. If the other person appears distant or uninterested, perhaps he or she is not interested in small talk.

Take the Lead. Often, the hardest part of small talk is the first few words. Fortunately, the more you take the initiative, the easier it gets. So, how do you start? It's simple. Just say something. Introduce yourself. Offer a sincere compliment. You might make this

---

Guided Reading Activity 8–1

Name _____ Date _____ Class _____

DEVELOPING EFFECTIVE INTERPERSONAL SKILLS — GUIDED READING Activity 8–1

Communicating Interpersonally

As you read Section 1, answer the following items.

1. Define "small talk" and state its function. _____
2. List three common topics for small talk. _____
3. Explain how open-ended questions differ from closed questions. _____
4. What are some of the topics to avoid when keeping small talk "safe?" _____
5. List the four purposes of questions used to maintain conversation. _____
6. What is *tact*? _____
7. What are the four ways of listening carefully in conversations? _____
8. What three steps should you take when making a persuasive request? _____
9. What three steps should you take in giving clear and accurate directions? _____
10. What are the four effective questioning strategies? _____
11. List the four strategies that can help you to follow directions. _____

ENGLISH LANGUAGE LEARNERS

MEETING INDIVIDUAL NEEDS

Learning "Small Talk" Students without much confidence in their verbal abilities may be intimidated by the need for small talk discussed in this section. That group is likely to include not only English language learners but also students whose dominant learning style is not verbal or auditory.

Activity Let students work with partners they are comfortable with to practice small talk. They can begin with school-related topics and then expand their practice to include the suggestions in the "Common Topics for Small Talk" chart at the bottom of page 239. **ELL**

COMMUNICATION Strategies

INITIATING CONVERSATION WITH SMALL TALK

✓ Check nonverbal signals.

✓ Take the lead.

✓ Ask open-ended questions.

✓ Stick to safe topics.

✓ Don't rush or skip the small talk.

initial contact by commenting on the weather, saying something humorous, or even asking the time.

Ask Open-Ended Questions. Once you have made initial contact, move into small talk by asking open-ended questions. An open-ended question is broad in scope, requiring more than a single-word answer such as "Yes" or "No." Open-ended questions draw answers from a person and help shy or reluctant conversationalists take an active role in the dialogue.

Open-ended questions are much more effective than closed questions in the context of a conversation. A closed question is one that requires a very specific answer, often just one word. A closed question such as "Did you see the big game last night?" requires only a "Yes" or "No."

Stick to Safe Topics. Another tip for effective small talk is to keep the conversation "safe" and light. You can talk about school, work, sports, hobbies, or other interests that you might have in common. However, you should avoid

personal or controversial topics such as politics, religion, personal beliefs or values, criticisms, or topics that can be misinterpreted as reflecting bias or harassment.

Don't Rush or Skip the Small Talk. Small talk is an important buffer that allows both parties to warm up to more purposeful communication. Although it should be kept fairly brief, rushing through small talk or skipping it entirely can make your communication seem abrupt, awkward, or even rude.

Maintaining Conversations

During the small-talk phase of a conversation, the parties form opinions and impressions and decide whether they want to maintain the communication. If they decide that the communication is not worth their time, they may excuse themselves from the situation or simply stop contributing to the exchange. If they wish to maintain the conversation, the tone and topic is likely to become more meaningful, moving toward the real reason for the contact. Your goal is to maintain the conversation so it can move to a level necessary to achieve the reason for the conversation. The basic strategies for participating effectively in conversations are found in the Communication Strategies checklist on the next page.

COMMON TOPICS FOR SMALL TALK

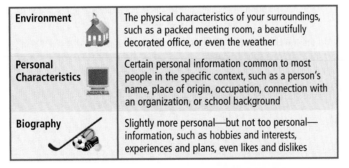

Environment	The physical characteristics of your surroundings, such as a packed meeting room, a beautifully decorated office, or even the weather
Personal Characteristics	Certain personal information common to most people in the specific context, such as a person's name, place of origin, occupation, connection with an organization, or school background
Biography	Slightly more personal—but not too personal— information, such as hobbies and interests, experiences and plans, even likes and dislikes

Developing Effective Interpersonal Skills **239**

COMMUNICATION Strategies

INITIATING CONVERSATION WITH SMALL TALK

Have students discuss possible additions to the list of ideas for beginning a conversation with small talk. Explain that students will read about each of the listed strategies as they proceed through this section. Encourage them to add to the list strategies they find effective. **L2**

Communication Tip

Make sure the person you are talking with realizes that you are listening when he or she is talking. Indicate your interest and attention by maintaining eye contact. Be sure to comment or otherwise reflect on what the person has said.

Small-Talk Topics

Newspapers can be a good source of topics for small talk. Give each group of four students a copy of a major daily newspaper. Have each member of the group scan a section of the paper for small-talk topics. Students should highlight or cut out articles or features that seem appropriate. The group members then must agree on whether each topic is safe for small talk and explain why. Groups should share their results with the class. Did groups make the same choices? Did their choices vary widely? **L2**

COOPERATIVE LEARNING ACTIVITY

Tell students to imagine that they are employees of a sports equipment retail store who are getting together for a dinner meeting during which they will plan strategies for selling during the pre-Christmas holiday season. Divide the class into teams of four or five students each. Ask each team to practice making small talk with one another as though they are just arriving for the meeting. Then, have all groups mix and carry out what they have practiced with members of other teams.

Appropriate Topics
Discuss with students that the appropriateness of topics depends on time, place, situation, and the people involved in the conversation. Encourage them to list appropriate, and perhaps inappropriate, conversation topics for various situations. Suggest such situations as a family dinner, a school dance, and a parent-teacher-student meeting.

Choose Only Appropriate Topics.
People who converse effectively often develop a set of proven topics to choose from. So, what topics are appropriate for maintaining a conversation in social and professional situations? That depends in part on the purpose and context of your communication. Is this a business meeting of new clients? Are you at a staff meeting at your workplace? Is this a club gathering or social event? While your small talk and conversation do not necessarily have to relate directly to the context, you will want to choose topics that would be of interest to someone in that specific group. Also, try to choose topics that you know something about. This allows you to contribute something of value to the conversation.

Ask Effective Questions.
Knowing information about many different topics allows you to ask effective questions. Questions are probably the most powerful tool you can use to maintain a conversation. People enjoy talking about themselves and voicing their own opinions. They may even see questions as a type of compliment that says, "I think you're interesting. Tell me more." Questions allow you to put the other person in the spotlight. You

COMMUNICATION *Strategies*

PARTICIPATING EFFECTIVELY IN CONVERSATIONS

- Choose appropriate topics.
- Ask effective questions.
- Use tact and courtesy.
- Demonstrate confidence and assertiveness.
- Demonstrate immediacy.
- Practice ethical communication.
- Balance speaking and listening.

show respect for that person's knowledge and opinions by asking him or her to share information and insights with you.

Use Tact and Courtesy.
Tact is knowing what to do or say—or *not* do or say—to maintain a positive professional exchange. A tactful person uses a considerate, courteous, and respectful tone to manage difficult communication situations without offending others. He or she understands that communication is powerful. It can help solve problems or make them worse, depending on the message and how it is communicated. In addition, a tactful communicator also understands that people prefer to be treated with courtesy in day-to-day communication. The best way to call out courteous behavior from other people is to be courteous yourself.

USING QUESTIONS TO MAINTAIN CONVERSATION

Purpose of Question	Example
Draws others into the conversation	"I'm thinking about taking that class. Do you think I should?"
Obtains information	"How do you feel about our new automated telephone system?"
Directs the conversation toward or away from a specific topic	"I just thought of something. When do we sign up for the new workshop?"
Maintains or ends an interaction	"That's a great report. What else have you prepared for the meeting?" *or* "This has been very informative, hasn't it? Let's talk again next time."

MULTIPLE LEARNING STYLES

Linguistic Students who talk easily and with natural verbal charm can act as mentors and coaches for others in the class as they learn to be effective conversationalists.

Activity Ask students with strong auditory and verbal skills to volunteer their help. You might ask two or three to model a conversation that includes some of the elements discussed in this section, such as small talk, effective questions, balanced speaking and listening, and so on.

Tact can be a valuable skill in professional and social contexts. When a conversation moves toward a new topic—particularly if it is unusual or controversial—pay close attention to verbal and nonverbal feedback. Look for signs of interest or boredom, agreement or disagreement. If the other person seems uncomfortable, you may wish to steer the conversation elsewhere.

Sometimes, you will be the one who feels uncomfortable or disagrees. To tactfully disagree with someone else's opinion, try to find some part of the statement with which you can agree. Then, gently and courteously lead into your perspective by saying something like, "I can see what you're saying, but what about . . . ?" You may even want to compliment the other person by saying, "That's a unique way to look at the issue. I can tell you really feel strongly about it." Either of these methods can help you maintain the positive climate of a conversation.

Demonstrate Confidence and Assertiveness. In conversation, it is important to offer your ideas about a topic in a clear, direct manner. Include in these comments

A student driver questions his instructor to learn more about driving. Besides gathering information, what do questions allow one to do?

GLOBAL COMMUNICATION
Appropriate Conversations

Although some people who live in the United States openly discuss their personal relationships and family activities, people from other cultures might consider questions about these topics intrusive. Many people from cultures outside the United States do not discuss their families, personal relationships, religious beliefs, or political opinions in the workplace. Why do you think these subjects are so sensitive? What are some other topics that might be considered offensive?

some statements of how you hope the other person will respond to your proposal or information. For instance, if someone asks you for a report on the status of your project, you might respond with a statement such as, "I will have that to you within the hour if that is acceptable to you." Your response indicates your confidence in meeting the request, and provides a window for the listener to respond.

In addition, there are other practices that will indicate confidence and assertiveness. To show the other person that you are focusing on the conversation, use some of the suggestions given in Chapter 5, such as nodding, making appropriate gestures, and maintaining a conversational posture that is neither threatening nor distant.

Developing Effective Interpersonal Skills **241**

GLOBAL COMMUNICATION
Appropriate Conversations

Encourage students whose backgrounds are in other cultures to share their knowledge about acceptable and unacceptable topics of conversation in those cultures. Let the class as a whole discuss why certain personal topics might be sensitive or offensive. Students can make a list of broad general topics to avoid when speaking with people of other cultures. **L2**

■ **Visual Instruction**

Answer Questions allow one to put others in the spotlight and to show respect for the knowledge and opinions of others.

Tactful Responses
Model for students ways of tactfully handling differences of opinion or responses to questions in several situations. For example, what would you say if someone asks your opinion about a shirt he or she plans to buy and you don't like? *(Possible response is "I like the way the shirt fits you, but the color is not quite right for you.")* Then, ask students to think of scenarios in which two people have differing opinions about a topic. They should identify the scenarios and write down something that one of the persons says about the topic. They then should exchange papers with partners. Each student is to write a tactful response to the person in their partner's scenario. Volunteers may wish to share the responses for discussion with the class. **L2**

EXTENDING THE CONTENT

Civics Point out to students that most people who are leaders in their field learn to be effective speakers and conversationalists; communication with others is crucially important to them.
Activity Have students follow television coverage of political leaders and note their verbal and nonverbal interaction with others. Do the speakers use direct eye contact? Do they avoid fillers? Do they respond to questions asked? Do they listen to one another? Students can assess what they observe and then report to the class the ease of communication that some leaders display as they interact with one another and citizens.

COMMUNICATION *Strategies*

DEMONSTRATING IMMEDIACY IN CONVERSATIONS

Point out to students that immediacy means that you seem approachable to others. Go over the list in the box of ways to demonstrate immediacy. Let students suggest other strategies. Ask volunteers to list nonverbal responses that demonstrate immediacy. *(Answers may include nodding one's head, murmuring positive "mmm-hmmms," and so on.)* **L1**

Balanced Speaking and Listening

Most people have been involved in conversations or meetings in which more than one person is speaking at a time. The result can be mere distraction or total chaos. Encourage students to draw up a list of rules for participation in conversations and meetings to avoid multiple speakers. To prompt suggestions, offer rules such as "Do not participate in one-on-one comments during a group meeting" and "Wait for one person to finish talking before you begin." **L2**

Demonstrate Immediacy. Remember that immediacy means that you are approachable. In conversations in social and workplace contexts, you want to show the other person that you are interested in what he or she has to say. The Communication Strategies checklist can serve as a guide to demonstrating immediacy in conversations.

Practice Ethical Communication. Each person has a different set of ethical standards based on his or her priorities and values. Even so, some basic assumptions apply to communicating ethically. Generally speaking, communicators should be able to assume the following:

- What is being said in conversation is both true and complete as far as the communicators know.

- One person is not trying to deceive the other about shared information or opinions on the topic.

- Information given in confidence will be considered private and not revealed to others.

- Verbal and nonverbal messages are consistent with the meanings they communicate.

Balance Speaking and Listening. Generally, in a conversation, people enjoy revealing insight into their own experiences and opinions. However, both parties can't talk all the time, or you'd drown each other out. The art of carrying on a conversation depends on the participants' ability to maintain a balanced flow of talk.

Although this responsibility can often be shared, it is more than likely that one person will stand out as the dominant speaker. If that person is you, encourage the other participant to contribute to the conversation. If the other person is speaking more, listen carefully and

COMMUNICATION *Strategies*

DEMONSTRATING IMMEDIACY IN CONVERSATIONS

- ✓ **Establish and maintain eye contact while the other person is speaking.**

- ✓ **Respond nonverbally to show you are listening to and considering what the other person is saying.**

- ✓ **Restate the other person's comments before adding your own.**

- ✓ **Avoid distracting behaviors, such as looking at your watch or your papers or notes while the other person is talking.**

- ✓ **Keep your voice at a comfortable volume that is easy to hear but not too loud.**

try to contribute when you can. Remembering the roles and responsibilities of effective speakers and listeners will help your conversations flow easily.

Listening in Conversations

Careful listening is key to maintaining conversations. Because people enjoy talking about themselves, they usually appreciate a good listener. To be an effective listener in a conversation, it is important to be able to restate the speaker's ideas in your own words. Ask questions that show you are listening and are interested in what the speaker is saying. Try to remember the person's name when you first meet, then repeat it later in the conversation. Use appropriate eye contact and other nonverbal communication to demonstrate your interest. Also, be sure to allow someone to finish speaking before you take your turn.

242 *Glencoe Communication Applications*

MEETING INDIVIDUAL NEEDS — INCLUSION STRATEGIES

Special Needs People with hearing impairments understandably have special problems with conversation. However, most learn communication techniques that would be useful for those without such problems to know.

Activity Ask hearing-impaired students to teach the class how to have conversations with them. What do they need people to do and to remember when talking with people who have hearing impairments?

Listen to What Is Said. What kinds of topics interest the speaker? To find out, listen to his or her opinions, attitudes, and concerns regarding the topics that are discussed. These topics can serve as a basis for further conversation. Use your listening skills to prepare you to comment intelligently and ask good questions. In this way, you will become an active participant in the conversation.

Listen Empathically. Often, what a person says is not as important as what he or she is feeling. When you listen empathically, you pay attention to the feeling component of the message. As you read in Chapter 6, empathic listening involves listening to understand the emotions attached to a message. While you do not necessarily have to agree with or sympathize with those feelings, as an effective listener you should demonstrate an appreciation for the situation.

Listen to What Is Left Unsaid. To listen empathically, it is important to listen actively to what is left unsaid in a conversation. Nonverbal communication behaviors, such as posture and tone of voice, provide valuable clues to how a person really feels. Does the person stand tall or allow his or her shoulders to droop? Is the voice excited or dull and flat? Do the eyes look directly at you, or are they downcast?

Imagine that a friend is telling you about a job interview he just had. Your friend may say "Oh, it went really well." However, you notice that his voice is flat and his eyes are focused on your feet. You get the feeling that, despite your friend's words, the interview didn't go as well as he would have you believe. This is because his verbal and nonverbal messages don't match. When this happens, people tend to believe the nonverbal message.

Now imagine that another friend, who also interviewed, says the same words, but her response is more animated and enthusiastic. Her tone of voice is excited, she stands confidently, and she shares some of the interviewer's questions with you. Despite using the same words, your two friends' messages are very different. Paying attention to nonverbal details is a valuable part of listening. It allows you to gain insight into a conversation so you can continue it appropriately.

Listen Before You Speak. While observing nonverbal cues may help you interpret what is said, avoid making assumptions. It is important to confirm your initial perceptions because first impressions aren't necessarily accurate.

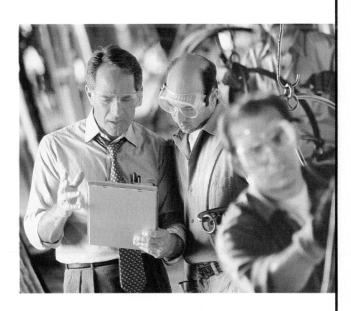

Careful listening in conversations is imperative to being a competent communicator. Identify the ways in which you can show that you are listening effectively in a conversation.

Developing Effective Interpersonal Skills **243**

The Importance of Listening

Recall with students what they learned in Chapter 6 about the importance of effective listening. You might want to review the four steps of the listening process: acquiring the message, attending or paying attention to it, understanding and interpreting, and responding. Ask students to discuss why listening is an important part of interpersonal communication. **L2**

BUSINESS BRIEF

In 1996 a team of researchers in New Zealand began a study of spoken communication in the workplace. They hoped to identify the characteristics of effective interpersonal communication, diagnose possible causes of miscommunication, and explore implications of the findings for human resource development programs.

Preliminary results of the research indicate that (1) there are no simple rules for effective communication; (2) skilled communicators use a variety of strategies to make sure interaction is successful, including adjusting their language according to whom they are talking and what they are talking about; and (3) the most direct way of communicating is not necessarily the most effective. Ask students to consider and discuss these ideas.

■ Visual Instruction

Answer To show you are listening and interested, ask questions, use appropriate eye contact and other nonverbal communication, and allow the other person to finish speaking before you speak.

MEETING INDIVIDUAL NEEDS — MULTIPLE LEARNING STYLES

Bodily-Kinesthetic Students with kinesthetic learning styles may need to physically act out how they would behave as an attentive listener.

Activity Have pairs of students pantomime a conversation in which they take turns "talking" and "listening." Show them, if necessary, how to position themselves and use gestures to communicate that they are listening.

Consider a conversation you might have with a teacher who is the advisor for your school newspaper. As you discuss the editorial section together, the teacher may frown while listing the different articles. You "read between the lines" and wonder if the teacher disapproves of some of the topics. If you fail to investigate what the teacher is feeling, you may make a false assumption. Perhaps the advisor is frowning simply because of a headache. To confirm your suspicion, you might ask if he or she has any issues to share about the editorial page. This allows for open discussion and resolution of any questions.

REQUESTS, DIRECTIONS, AND QUESTIONS

Often, communication extends beyond small talk to sharing information with a purpose or goal. People exchange information, make requests, give and receive directions, and ask and respond to questions. This is part of everyday interaction, whether you are at work, at school, or at home. The ability to communicate effectively in this capacity is crucial to both your personal and professional success.

Making Clear and Appropriate Requests

Whenever you ask for something, you are making a request. Sometimes, you may find it necessary to request information, such as when you ask a teacher what grade you made on a quiz. Asking incorrectly might not yield the exact information you need. Requests also may

BEFORE REQUESTING INFORMATION, CONSIDER . . .

Who has the information I need?	Not everyone in an organization has the same knowledge base or access to resources. Be sure to make your request of the person who can be the most helpful.
What is my specific question?	The more specific your question, the less margin for error. State exactly what information you need.
Why am I making this request?	Briefly explaining why you need to know something can give a person insight into exactly what you need.
When do I need the answer?	Be sure to share your deadline for a response. The best information in the world is of little use if it's a day too late.
How do I need the information?	In what form should the information be provided? Do you need a photocopy of the source, a signed report, or just a verbal answer? Describing how you need the information can save valuable time and effort.

244 *Glencoe Communication Applications*

WHEN MAKING A PERSUASIVE REQUEST . . .

Describe the problem unemotionally	Give a clear description of the situation, conveying the facts, not your personal feelings. Whining or being rude or angry will not help you persuade the listener. Instead, use your description to help the listener understand the need for change.
Suggest a solution	Act as a problem solver, offering a reasonable solution to the situation. Be specific and remain calm. Issuing threats can make the listener defensive and may reduce your chances of finding an acceptable solution.
Explain the consequences	Even if you're thinking, "Do it or else," don't say that. Instead, point out the benefits of fulfilling your request and creating a win-win solution. If the listener refuses to comply, calmly outline consequences that are realistic and appropriate.

be used to persuade someone to do something. Done improperly, this type of request can sound like a demand, and you may not get the response you seek. You can see that it is important to learn how to make effective requests.

Requests for Information Have you ever heard the saying "If you ask the wrong question, you'll get the wrong answer"? This is never more true than when you make a request for information. Reviewing who, what, why, when, and how before you make a request can help you get the information you seek.

Imagine that your friend is wearing a cap with your school logo on it. You'd like one too. If you ask, "Where'd you get that?" your friend may simply reply, "Downtown." However, if you ask, "Can you tell me where you bought that cap? I'd like to buy one myself after school," you'll be more likely to get a useful response. This question employs all the details necessary to effectively request information. Whether you are the speaker or the respondent in requests for information, make sure that your questions and responses are as clear and thorough as possible. Remember, you get what you ask for!

Requests to Persuade Persuasive requests do not ask for information. Instead, they request that some action be taken. Because you are asking another person to do something, persuasive requests can be tricky. If stated ineffectively, they may be perceived as whiny or demanding. Careful phrasing of persuasive requests can help you avoid these problems.

■ A customer uses a persuasive request when discussing with the car salesperson the problems she is having with her new car. How does a persuasive request differ from a request for information?

Persuasive Requests
To help students understand persuasive requests, invite them to share personal examples from their own lives during which they were either the requester or the receiver of a persuasive request. To get them started, you may want to offer an example, such as your feeling defensive or cooperative when someone demanded that you do something or requested it persuasively. Point out that persuasive requests are basically a matter of good manners and of trying to understand the other person's point of view while making your request. **L2**

Communication Tip
Remind students that nonverbal communication and body language are very important when making requests of any kind. Tone of voice should remain polite and calm, never belligerent, challenging, or angry.

■ Visual Instruction
Answer Persuasive requests do not ask for information; rather, they ask that someone do something.

INTERDISCIPLINARY CONNECTION

Language Arts Persuasive writing is a genre found in many publications. Newspaper editorials try to persuade readers to consider a certain point of view, as do letters to the editor. Reviews of books and theatrical or musical performances similarly persuade audiences to judge them as the reviewer has. Business letters often have a persuasive purpose, too.

Activity Ask each student to draft a business letter that is a persuasive request for a company to refund money for an unsatisfactory purchase.

GLENCOE
Online

For an additional Practice Lab for this section, have students visit the *Glencoe Communication Applications* Web site at **communicationapplica-tions.glencoe.com**. Click on Communication Practice Lab 8–1. **L1**

DID YOU KNOW?

James Boswell, born in 1740 and famous as the biographer of Samuel Johnson, once said, "I think no innocent species of wit or pleasantry should be suppressed: and that a good pun may be admitted among the smaller excellencies of lively conversation."

Imagine that you have just purchased a car that is not performing well. It is most likely that you will use a persuasive request to correct the problem. For instance, you might take the vehicle back to the dealership and say, "This car is a lemon. I want another one now, or you'll be hearing from my lawyer!" While this approach certainly would get the salesperson's attention, it also might result in your being escorted off the car lot.

A more effective request would follow the guidelines you read in the chart. You might instead say, "I just drove this car off the lot, and it stalled at every red light on my way home. I noticed that you have another car like mine on the lot. Would you like to give me that one, or would you prefer to loan me a vehicle at no charge while you repair this one?" This not only explains the problem but also suggests a logical solution.

If the salesperson refuses both of the solutions you offered, you might then ask to speak with a manager, say that you will be writing a letter to the company, or even explain that you will be withholding payment until a satisfactory solution has been reached. By remaining calm and reasonable, you have presented an effective persuasive request.

Giving Clear and Accurate Directions

From time to time, you may be asked to give someone directions. Sometimes, these directions will be geographic, involving getting from one place to another. Other times, the directions will be instructional, indicating how to do something. In either case, the foundation for good directions is communicating a logical sequence of steps to achieve a desired result.

Organize the Steps. In order to give directions, you must first understand the process clearly. Sometimes, this is more difficult than it sounds. Have you ever been asked to give directions to a particular place and

COMMUNICATION
PRACTICE LAB
Making a Persuasive Request

To practice making appropriate persuasive requests, follow these steps:

Step 1 As a class, brainstorm a list of problems you have encountered as consumers. This might include receiving defective merchandise, being treated poorly by a salesperson, or other problems.

Step 2 Working with a partner, choose one of the problems from the list. Then determine who will role-play the customer and who will play the company or store representative.

Step 3 Act out a scenario in which the customer makes a persuasive request to solve the problem. The store representative should respond realistically to the request.

Step 4 Adjust the request as necessary to get the desired response from the store representative. Note the adjustments that you made.

Step 5 Carefully observe as volunteers act out their scenarios for the class. Was the customer's request effective? Was the store representative's response realistic?

Step 6 As a class, discuss the adjustments that made your requests more effective. Did you notice any common changes?

MEETING INDIVIDUAL NEEDS
MULTIPLE LEARNING STYLES

Visual-Spatial Visually oriented students are often more comfortable giving geographic directions by drawing a map than by describing the sequence of actions verbally.

Activity Suggest that such students actually draw a map, such as one showing directions from the school to a local mall or other spot. Then, they can look at the map while they rehearse how to describe the directions verbally. Tell students that in the future they may be able to visualize a map without actually having to draw it before they attempt to give someone directions.

Figure 8–1 Steps in Directions

My Favorite Chocolate Cake
from the kitchen of Mary

Preheat oven to 325°
Grease (2) 8-inch cake pans
Mix ingredients
Bake @ 325° for 35 minutes

realized that you don't know the names of certain key streets? Sometimes, you may know how to perform a certain process without understanding how to describe it.

As shown in Figure 8–1, you can begin creating clear and accurate directions by listing all the necessary steps and then arranging them in order. Often, that order is time-related, as in "do this, then this, then this." For example, you explain how to bake a cake beginning with pre-heating the oven and ending with spreading the frosting. It would be very confusing to a listener to hear how to frost the cake, then how to grease the pan, then to preheat the oven, all out of order. Usually, directions for accomplishing a task need to be arranged according to the sequence in which they are to be performed.

Avoid Assumptions. One of the most important things to remember about giving effective directions is to avoid assumptions. For example, don't assume everyone speaks the specialized jargon associated with a particular field. A computer technician may speak too technically to be helpful, or a doctor may confuse patients with complex medical terms. As a result, they may miscommunicate information or frustrate the people who are trying to follow their directions.

Making assumptions can also cause you to skip steps in a process. Even though you may be very familiar with a process, don't assume the listener is. Rather, phrase your directions as though the listener is performing the process for the first time.

Use Details. For clear, accurate directions, use general language, but provide specific detail. In other words, don't just say, "Turn the knob." Say, "Turn the blue knob to the left one-quarter turn." To make sure you are providing adequate detail, pay attention to feedback. Does the listener look confused? Is he or she hesitating? One effective way to check understanding is to ask the listener to restate your directions in his or her own words. This allows you to clarify any areas of confusion and ensure that your directions are as effective as possible. Also, be careful using pronouns. Make sure you define *it, he, we,* and *they* carefully. Don't assume the listener understands.

Asking Appropriate and Purposeful Questions

Often, people hesitate to ask questions because they do not know what question to ask or how to ask it. For example, imagine that the manager at your office shows you four different forms, explains quickly when and how to fill out each, and directs you to begin using them immediately to organize some files. You understand that you need to use the forms, but you are unsure of how to actually complete the assignment. Worse still, you are afraid that if you ask questions, your manager will think that you were not paying attention or that you are not competent to complete the job. What do you do?

First, do not be afraid to ask questions. Remember the old saying "The only bad question is one that is never asked." Then, remind yourself that it is better to ask questions than

Developing Effective Interpersonal Skills **247**

Giving Directions
Giving clear directions is a very important skill necessary in many activities. Let students work in pairs to practice. Have one partner describe to the other exactly how to get to the first partner's home (or another real place, if students prefer) from school. The partner who listened should then draw a map or write the directions as clearly as he or she heard them. The first partner can check the accuracy of the directions he or she gave by looking over the written response. Then, partners can switch roles. **L2 ELL**

Language Tip

Remind students that, when giving directions, they should clarify the sequence of steps by using words such as *first, then, next, after,* and *finally.*

CRITICAL THINKING ACTIVITY

Discuss with students the written directions that often come with a toy, device, or appliance that needs to be assembled or used in a certain way. Such directions are notoriously difficult to understand and awkwardly written. Ask students to bring to class examples of written directions. Have them evaluate the directions for clarity and accuracy, reviewing the guidelines on pages 246–247. Then, have students rewrite the directions to improve them.

Asking Questions Effectively

You may want to point out to students that purposeful questions are the opposite of the open-ended questions that are part of the small talk used to begin a conversation. Purposeful questions usually require a specific answer in order to clarify the questioner's understanding of something. It is part of the skill of asking effective questions to phrase requests in such a way that the other person will provide the information you need in response. Provide practice in developing purposeful questions by giving students a topic for which they brainstorm examples of purposeful questions. **L2**

Responding

Remind students that they are as likely to be on "the other side" of questioning as they are to be the questioner. Responding to requests often requires an application of the Golden Rule—"to treat others as we would wish to be treated." You may want to allow pairs of students to act out several scenarios of inappropriate and appropriate interchanges based on what they have read about appropriate requests and responses. **L1**

to do a job wrong. The following chart provides you with some effective tips for asking appropriate and purposeful questions.

Responding Appropriately to Requests and Questions

Requests and questions are examples of communication for a specific purpose. They are intended to seek information or bring about change. If the person asking the question or making the request is unskilled in these forms of communication, they may instead sound like demands or criticisms. The most effective way to respond to a request or a question is to reply using the level of courtesy you would have liked the speaker to use.

EFFECTIVE QUESTIONING STRATEGIES

Strategy	Explanation	Example
Rephrase the message	Restate in your own words what you heard the speaker say. This allows him or her to correct any misunderstandings.	"Let me see if I understand you correctly. I add the figures in these two columns to find the total sales?"
Ask for clarification	Sometimes, a speaker will assume you are familiar with certain jargon and background information. If you are not, ask the speaker to explain.	"I'm sorry. I'm not familiar with that term. Could you clarify it for me?"
Ask for more details	Often, more information can help you better understand a concept. Ask specific questions to get specific details.	"Which products were involved in this comparison study?"
Confirm through examples	Verify that you understand with an example that summarizes or illustrates what you have heard.	If you are baby-sitting and the parents say the children can stay up for "a while," ask, "Is 9:30 OK, or is that too late?"

Responding Appropriately to Requests A request that begins with a forcefully stated solution, particularly if it is followed by some type of real or implied threat, is likely to be perceived not as a request but as a demand. However, you do not have to respond with the same level of emotion. Imagine that you work in the customer service department of a major clothing store. A customer waves a damaged item in front of you and yells, "I'm so tired of bad quality. Look at this! You need to replace it now!"

Stay Objective. As an employee and as an effective communicator, it is your responsibility to filter out the hostile emotion in a request. Focus on the message—no matter how emotionally it was communicated to you.

Assess the Situation. Determine what the problem is so you can decide what course of action is necessary. What is the item? When was it purchased? Exactly what is wrong with it? Did the customer damage it, or does it really have a fault? What is really the problem?

Use Problem-Solving Style. To respond best to requests—whether friendly or aggressive—try to use a problem-solving style of communication. After assessing the current situation, suggest that the person describe some possible solutions. Depending on your store's policy, you might say, "I can see the tear in the vest, and

REAL-WORLD CONNECTION

Responding on the Job Ask students who have had part-time or summer jobs to recall occasions when they needed to respond to a request or a question on the job.

Activity Have volunteers relate their examples to the rest of the class, explaining how they responded to the requests or questions and whether they now think their responses were appropriate and why. Invite the class to discuss the examples based on the information provided on pages 248–249.

■ **This student appears to be listening defensively.** How do defensive listeners tend to hear questions?

I apologize for your inconvenience. What can we do to make this right for you?" Join in brainstorming solutions, if possible.

State Consequences. Finally, carefully and objectively state the consequences you are trying to achieve. You might say, "I understand that you are upset, ma'am, and I very much want for you to be a satisfied customer. Could we replace the defective part or give you one of our other products instead?" Reassure the person that you are seeking a positive outcome.

Requests are part of everyday interaction whether at work, school, or home. Maintain a descriptive and objective tone and use a problem-solving style when responding to requests, no matter how harsh or unreasonable they may appear to you. This will help you build an image as a fair and competent communicator.

Responding Appropriately to Questions When responding to questions, it also is crucial to be an active—not defensive—listener. Defensive listeners sometimes hear questions as if they were criticisms.

To answer questions effectively, first determine exactly what information is being requested. Did the person just not hear clearly? You may be able to simply repeat the information. Perhaps the listener needs for you to define your terms or clarify your meanings. Maybe he or she is asking for additional information. Knowing what kind of information is needed will help you to respond appropriately to the question.

Inappropriate Questions Sometimes, you will be asked inappropriate questions. When this happens, ask yourself whether it would be unwise or unethical for you to provide the requested information. For instance, if a coworker asks you how much you earn per hour, it might be unwise to answer. The coworker might resent your wage or start feeling superior, depending on how much you make. By the same token, it would be unethical to reveal how much a friend makes per hour. Remember, you do not have to answer inappropriate questions.

When You Don't Know an Answer Occasionally, you might be asked a question for which you do not have an answer. In these cases, ask yourself who might be the best person to answer the question. Who has knowledge on the topic or access to accurate resources? Who can most efficiently communicate the answer to the question? If you suspect that no one else knows the answer either, consider how you might obtain the information for the questioner. No one knows the answer to every possible question. However, knowing when to redirect a question to a

Developing Effective Interpersonal Skills **249**

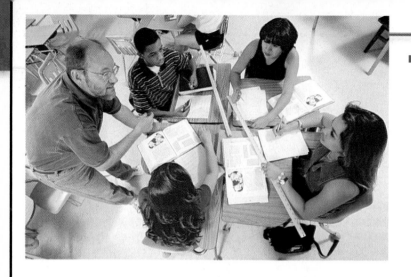

Responding to Directions

Point out to students that their first response to directions must be to make sure they understand them. Do they know exactly what to do? They need to clarify whatever is not clear. Although some directions, such as the sequence of turning off lights before going out and locking the door, can be figured out through common sense, that is not always the case. Remind students that before they begin to follow directions, they must know what to do. **L2**

3 ASSESS

Assign Section 1 Assessment as a homework or in-class activity.

❶ Use *Interactive Tutor Self-Assessment Software* to review Section 1.

more knowledgeable source or to say "I don't know, but I'll find out," will make you a valuable resource.

RESPONDING APPROPRIATELY TO THE DIRECTIONS OF OTHERS

How many times a week does someone give you an instruction or provide you with directions? How many times each day? Following directions is a crucial part of being an effective family member, student, and employee. Whether the directions involve going somewhere or completing a task, you are expected to listen to the steps and follow them.

Listen Without Judgment

Sometimes, people are their own worst enemies when it comes to following directions. Instead of listening actively, they begin thinking of other things. They may assume they have heard it all before, or predetermine that the directions will be impossible to remember or unpleasant to follow. Think about when your teacher explains an assignment. As he or she gets to the second step, you may think,

"Why are you repeating these directions?" Later, you may discover that you have done the assignment incorrectly because you did not listen with an open mind.

Listen for Steps or Main Points

Directions usually are explained in a particular order—usually in a time-related sequence or according to a certain grouping. Imagine directions for closing up a business at night. The directions may be given in a particular order in time. For example, secure the back room, lock the cash register, turn off the lights, and set the alarm. If you complete these steps out of order, you might set off the alarm or find yourself walking around in the dark. While you may be able to get by without remembering all the tiny details of directions, you need to listen carefully for the steps or main points.

Paraphrase

Even if you think you have understood a set of directions, it is important to check your own understanding. You can do this by paraphrasing.

Visual Instruction

Answer One should listen without judgment, listen for steps or main points to paraphrase, and ask the speaker to explain.

INCLUSION STRATEGIES

Less-Proficient Readers Point out to students that they must be particularly careful when reading directions to follow. It is especially important for students to paraphrase the directions in their own words. They also must not hesitate to ask for clarification of anything they did not understand completely.

Activity Have students work with more proficient readers. Together, they can find a set of directions, ask questions to clarify the directions, and respond to the questions. Students then restate the directions in their own words, showing their levels of understanding.

To paraphrase is to repeat a message in your own words. As the speaker gives you directions, briefly repeat each step to yourself. If you cannot repeat the steps, it probably means that you did not understand the instructions well enough to follow them.

Ask the Speaker to Explain

Sometimes, noise can impact how a message is received. If you are unsure you have correctly understood a message, ask for confirmation. You may need to ask the speaker to repeat the message. Perhaps he or she needs to define some technical terms, or you may need to ask for more explanation. One thing is certain. Pretending to understand and remember directions is not an effective communication strategy. In some circumstances, it can even threaten your health or safety. It is always better to confirm what you know and ask for any extra information you may need. Responding to questions in this manner shows that you are a responsible and competent communicator.

Section 1 Assessment

Visit the *Glencoe Communication Applications* Web site at **communicationapplications. glencoe.com** and click on **Self-Check and Study Guide 8.1** to review your understanding of communicating interpersonally.

Review Key Terms

1. Define each term and write it in a sentence: open-ended question, closed question, paraphrase.

Check Understanding

2. What are seven strategies for participating effectively in conversations?

3. Imagine you are served an improperly cooked meal in a restaurant. Request a solution to this problem.

4. What three things should you remember when giving clear and accurate directions?

5. Why is it important to ask appropriate and purposeful questions when you are unsure of something?

6. **Apply** Imagine that a classmate asks you about a school policy that you are not familiar with. How might you respond appropriately?

APPLICATION *Activity*

Analyzing Interpersonal Communication On a sheet of paper, list at least five people you see almost every day. Choose one day of the week and monitor how effectively you converse with these people. Next to each person's name, list the communication skill you used to initiate or maintain a conversation with him or her. Use the Communication Strategies checklists on pages 240 and 242 as a guide. Study your analysis, then design a personal strategies checklist to improve your conversation skills.

Developing Effective Interpersonal Skills **251**

4 CLOSE

Have students reread the opening paragraph on page 237. Considering what they have learned in this section, how might students make small talk with the president of the United States differently than they would with a best friend? What might be the topics discussed?

Extra-Credit Project
Suggest that pairs of students work together to prepare skits demonstrating examples of effective and ineffective interpersonal communication as described in this section.

Section 1 Assessment Answers

1. Accept all reasonable sentences.
2. Choose appropriate topics; ask effective questions; use tact and courtesy; demonstrate confidence and assertiveness; demonstrate immediacy; practice ethical communication; balance speaking and listening.
3. Answers will vary but should reflect the basic strategies of describing the problem unemotionally, suggesting a solution, and explaining the consequences.

4. Organize the steps, avoid assumptions, and use details.
5. It is better to ask questions than to misunderstand or get the information wrong.
6. Suggest that you find out the answer together. You might go to the principal's office, for example, or ask a teacher.

Application Activity Students' analyses and personal strategies checklists should reflect what they have learned in this chapter as well as self-knowledge.

Technology Skill

Using Voice Mail

Explain that voice mail is used both in business and with personal telephones. In business, it can be used to receive messages from incoming callers, send information to employees or clients, and screen or transfer calls.

When you are calling a business and need to leave a message, be sure to state your name, organization, and the time and date of your call. At the beginning and again at the end of the message, give the telephone number where you can be reached. Speak slowly and clearly so your message will be easily understood.

Practicing the Skill

1. You may want to have students work in teams or small groups.

2. Suggest that students obtain a savings account balance from a bank, for example, or magazine subscription rates from a publisher.

3. Direct students to hang up and try another number if the company does not seem to have an automated telephone answering system, since the purpose of this activity is to practice using voice mail.

4. Make sure students leave their phone number as well as their name and the time and date of their call.

Application Activity

You may want to allow students to present their outgoing voice-mail announcements orally to the class. Let them vote on which they like best and why.

USING VOICE MAIL

Voice mail is an automated telephone answering system that companies use to conduct business more efficiently. While voice mail is useful for businesses, it also offers many conveniences for callers.

Learning the Skill

If you call a place of business that has voice mail, keep the following in mind:

- You can respond to voice mail prompts only if your telephone uses tones to communicate. If you have a rotary dial or pulse phone, you are usually instructed to wait for an operator.

- You'll need to listen carefully to a menu of choices.

- You must be prepared to leave a message. Before you call, arrange a list of points you want to discuss with the other party.

If you use voice mail to manage your calls at work or at home, follow these suggestions:

- Make your greeting short but pleasant. Explain why you are unable to take any calls. Tell your callers what information you want them to include in their messages. Always speak slowly and clearly.

- Check your messages frequently and return calls promptly.

- If your message gives several options for routing a call, make sure they are clearly stated and not confusing to callers.

Practicing the Skill

Compare and contrast the voice mail for five companies.

Step 1 Browse through a newspaper or magazine to locate five toll-free telephone numbers.

Step 2 Decide what kind of information you want from each company.

Step 3 Call each organization. Listen carefully to the automatic announcement for directions on how to proceed.

Step 4 If you are required to leave a voice message, be cordial and speak clearly.

APPLICATION *Activity*

Assume that your school has voice mail and you will be using it to manage calls about the school play. Write an outgoing announcement that gives the following information: which play is to be performed, when the play will be staged, how to purchase tickets, how to get to the school, where drivers should park their cars, and how to speak to a person if the caller needs other information.

MEETING INDIVIDUAL NEEDS

GIFTED AND TALENTED

Gifted Point out to students that when they are leaving a voice-mail message, they should be careful not to obscure their message by background noise.

Activity Record several messages in your school voice mailbox, leaving different messages without background noise and with a variety of background noises. Tape-record the messages. Have students listen to the tape and discuss what happens to the message when background noise is present. Encourage students to write a list of "rules" for leaving voice mail. Suggest such rules as "All radios and televisions should be turned off."

Section 2

Applying Professional Etiquette and Protocol

GUIDE TO READING

Objectives

1. Explain professional etiquette and protocol for making introductions.
2. Describe professional etiquette and protocol for using the telephone.
3. Compare and contrast professional etiquette for offering and receiving criticism.
4. Analyze and evaluate the effectiveness of your own and others' communication.

5. Identify and use appropriate strategies for dealing with differences, including differences in culture, gender, ethnicity, and age.

Terms to Learn

etiquette
protocol
constructive criticism
descriptive communication
evaluative communication

Imagine that you found an advertisement for the ideal summer job. You applied for the job, aced your interview, and were hired. Now you're just waiting for the job to begin. You are looking forward to this job—particularly because your interview with the boss went so well.

Imagine that the weekend before your new job begins, you are at the grocery with one of your teachers buying supplies for a band picnic. Suddenly, you see your future boss right there in the vegetable aisle. A second later, she sees you too. Now what should you do?

In the seconds that follow, a thousand questions crowd your brain: "Should I say something or shouldn't I?" "What should I say?" "Does she remember me?" "Should I introduce my teacher?" "How formal should I be?" All of these questions center on how to communicate appropriately in a professional context.

■ **Etiquette and protocol are used when making introductions like the one shown.** What role do etiquette and protocol play in the workplace?

Developing Effective Interpersonal Skills **253**

RESOURCE MANAGER

Teaching Tools
- Interactive Lesson Planner
- Reproducible Lesson Plan 8–2
- Application Activities 8–2

Reproducible Masters
- Guided Reading Activity Workbook 8–2
- Enrichment Activity 8–2
- Reteaching Activity 8–2
- Section Quiz 8–2
- Transparency Strategies and Activities Booklet 8–2

Transparencies
- Graphic Organizer Transparency 8–2
- Chapter 8 Teaching Transparency

Technology Resources
- Interactive Tutor Self-Assessment Software
- Presentation Plus! Software
- ExamView® Pro Testmaker
- PuzzleMaker Software
- communicationapplications.glencoe.com

1 FOCUS

Bellringer
After students have read the opening paragraph to themselves, invite discussion. Ask students to brainstorm for reasons the interview might have gone so well. Review with them possibly pertinent points made in Section 1 about appropriate interpersonal communication. *(Students might suggest that the interview went well because the participants were polite and honest and used effective speaking and listening strategies.)*

You may use Graphic Organizer Transparency 8–2 to introduce this section.

Grammar Tip

Various punctuation marks, such as periods, commas, and dashes, are used to indicate a pause. A dash, such as the one in the last sentence of the opening paragraph on this page, signifies a longer or more dramatic pause than a comma does, but a shorter one than a period indicates.

■ Visual Instruction

Answer Etiquette and protocol provide guidelines for interpersonal communication in the workplace.

2 TEACH

Guided Reading Activity 8-2

GUIDED READING
Activity 8-2

Name _____ Date _____ Class _____

DEVELOPING EFFECTIVE INTERPERSONAL SKILLS
Applying Professional Etiquette and Protocol

As you read Section 2, complete the sentences below.

1. _____ is an established code of behavior or courtesy _____ is a code of _____ that is written and prescribed by an _____
2. When performing any introduction, it is important to use your best Consider the _____ and the individuals involved and back up your decision with the rules of _____
3. Knowing how to correctly answer the telephone makes you a valuable relations source. You should speak _____ and _____, _____ yourself and your employer, be a responsible _____ develop a plan for _____ and _____ calls, and take accurate _____
4. Constructive criticism is a _____ evaluation done in a way that brings about _____ change. This type of criticism is valued because it helps people to _____
5. _____ communication is talk that paints a picture of the facts of a _____ This is the first step that helps you ease into a _____ without appearing to attack the person unfairly.
6. _____ communication is talk that tells how you interpret a _____ and how you feel about a situation. As you complete this step of the process, you should remember that you are evaluating the specific _____ and not the _____
7. When you are _____ to criticism, you put up an _____ barrier to communication. This prevents you from _____ and becoming more effective.
8. To get the most from criticism, you should ask for a description of the _____ the criticism, try to agree with the critic's _____, listen for the desired _____ and focus on the positive _____ of change.
9. The four factors that often affect people's perceptions and communication are _____, _____, and _____

How you communicate in such situations could affect how you are perceived, not only as a person, but also as a student and as an employee. Although there are no hard and fast rules, there are some generally accepted guidelines to help you make appropriate choices in a situation like this one. These guidelines are based on what is considered to be socially acceptable behavior for a specific context.

PROFESSIONAL ETIQUETTE AND PROTOCOL

In interpersonal communication, there are certain rules for interacting with supervisors, coworkers, teachers, classmates, and even the parents of classmates. Because these relationships tend to be more distant than our close friendships, rule violations are viewed more seriously. Mistakes can result in a lasting bad impression, a lost opportunity, a complaint from a customer, or a reputation as a poor communicator.

For these reasons, it is important to understand and follow the rules of professional etiquette and protocol. **Etiquette** is an established code of behavior or courtesy. There are different forms of etiquette for different contexts in life. Sometimes this code is written, and sometimes it isn't. **Protocol** is a code of etiquette that is written and prescribed by an organization. This particular form of etiquette typically is used for official dealings, such as business or governmental operations. The armed services, in particular, are known for prescribed behavior or protocol. For example, enlisted personnel are required to salute officers, all personnel must wear hats outdoors, and officers are not supposed to socialize with enlisted personnel.

Most other social and professional organizations do not have such rigorous, formal rules of protocol. In many cases, the expectations for your interactions may be unstated—

at least until you violate them. Inappropriate behaviors can result in personal humiliation, lost customers, offended coworkers, and embarrassed employers. They also can affect your future with the organization.

How are you supposed to know what behavior is appropriate for any situation? In general, you do the thing that is the most courteous and polite for the situation at hand. There are some fairly set standards for several of the most common professional interpersonal situations. Try to keep in mind that these standards reflect the accepted norms for these behaviors. There may be situations when you need to adapt these recommended standards to be appropriate to yourself, a listener, the occasion, or the task.

Etiquette and Protocol in Making Introductions

What do you do when your boss walks out to meet a customer or client you just greeted and the two have not met before? Obviously, you have to introduce one to the other. Whose name do you say first, and how do you identify each of them? Is it the same as introducing a new coworker to your boss? How do you introduce a friend to your boss or coworker? As you can see from the chart below, according to etiquette the person who deserves the most respect in the situation is named first. You are actually presenting the other person to the one who is more respected. At work, a client usually will be introduced first, followed by your boss or other superior, coworkers, family members, and then friends. When introducing people outside the workplace, you usually introduce the person you are with to the person you encounter.

Exceptions to the Rules As with all forms of communication, the appropriateness of an introduction depends on the context. Sometimes, introductions will vary slightly from the examples in the chart. This is especially true in very informal situations and when more than one rule of etiquette applies. If you are on a first-name basis with one or both parties in an introduction, state the individuals' first names as well as their last names. When people fit into multiple categories, always defer to the person with the most power. For instance, if you are introducing a new female coworker to a male president of the company, state the president's name first, then the woman's name.

ETIQUETTE FOR MAKING INTRODUCTIONS

When Introducing . . .	Tradition	Order of Introduction	Example
Your boss to a client	Respect is shown to the client.	State the client's name first, then your boss's name.	"Ms. Sanchez, I'd like you to meet our manager, Mr. Jones."
Your boss to a new coworker	Respect is shown to your boss.	State your boss's name first, then your coworker's.	"Mr. Tong, this is our new staff member, Stacy Adams."
Your friend to your boss or a coworker	At work: Respect is shown to your boss or coworker.	At work: State your boss's or coworker's name, then your friend's.	"Ms. Majors, I would like you to meet my friend Elizabeth Maddox."
	Outside of work: Equal respect is shown to your friend and your boss or coworker.	Outside of work: State your friend's name, then your boss's or coworker's. Then, introduce your friend to your boss or coworker.	"Elizabeth, I would like you to meet my boss, Ms. Majors. Ms. Majors, this is my friend Elizabeth Maddox."
A junior businessperson and a senior businessperson	Respect is shown to the person with the most experience.	State senior businessperson's name first, then the junior businessperson's name.	"Ms. (company vice president), allow me to introduce Mr. (salesperson)."
Anyone and a guest of honor	Respect is shown to the person with the most power or authority.	State the guest of honor's name first, then the other person's name.	"Mr. (governor), please allow me to introduce our high school principal, Ms. Greene."

Developing Effective Interpersonal Skills   **255**

Making Introductions
Explain to students that the rules of etiquette for making introductions are frequently misunderstood or confused by many people. Students will be well served to memorize useful parts of the chart on this page. If necessary, work through the chart with students so they can see the logic of the chain of command in each case. Be sure to model various scenarios requiring introductions. **L2**

The Importance of Etiquette
Acknowledge to students that some of today's small companies—especially those in the computer field—are very casual, and formal rules of etiquette may not be practiced so carefully in them. Point out to students that, nevertheless, it is always better to err on the side of formality rather than informality until you are confident of what is expected in a certain group. **L2**

BUSINESS BRIEF

You may want to share with students several books on business etiquette. There are many available. Among them are *Letitia Baldrige's New Complete Guide to Executive Manners* by Letitia Baldrige (New York: Macmillan International, 1993), *Do's and Taboos Around the World for Women in Business* by Roger E. Axtell (New York: Wiley, 1997), and *Business Protocol: How to Survive and Succeed in Business* by Jan Yager (New York: Wiley, 1991).

REAL-WORLD CONNECTION

Making Introductions Students will introduce people to each other throughout their lives in many situations, not all of them in business.

Activity Have students complete this extension of the chart on this page:

When Introducing . . .	Tradition	Order of Introduction
A man and a woman	Respect is shown to the woman.	State the woman's name first, then the man's name.
A child or young adult and an adult	Respect is shown to the adult.	State the adult's name first, then the child's name.

COMMUNICATION Strategies

USING EFFECTIVE TELEPHONE SKILLS

You may want to have pairs of students act out business telephone conversations to demonstrate effective telephone skills. Invite students to add to the list other strategies they believe are effective and useful to remember. **L2**

interNET ACTIVITY

Cultural Etiquette Let students work in pairs or small groups on available school computers. Some students may prefer to do this Internet search at home, reporting individually on their results. Allow students from different cultural backgrounds to volunteer their own knowledge of cultural expectations as well. **L1**

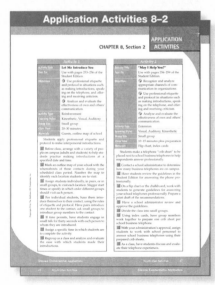

Application Activities 8–2

When performing any introduction, it is important to use your best judgment. Consider the context and the individuals involved and back up your decision with the rules of etiquette. Making wise choices will help you distinguish yourself as a competent communicator and help the person who is being introduced know with whom he or she will be meeting or speaking.

Etiquette and Protocol in Using the Telephone

Another area of communication where rules of etiquette apply is on the telephone. Although you may have been talking on the phone since you were very young, you may not have been doing so effectively. Your family and friends may have learned to ignore a lack of phone etiquette on your part. Business associates and clients, however, will expect you to be a competent communicator, following the rules of etiquette in your phone conversations.

Knowing how to use appropriate telephone skills can improve your effectiveness with clients and customers and in other business interactions. Correctly answering the telephone can also make you a valuable public relations source.

COMMUNICATION Strategies

USING EFFECTIVE TELEPHONE SKILLS

✓ Speak clearly and pleasantly.

✓ Identify yourself and your employer.

✓ Be a responsible listener.

✓ Develop a plan for making calls.

✓ Develop a plan for receiving calls.

✓ Take accurate notes.

256   *Glencoe Communication Applications*

interNET ACTIVITY

Cultural Etiquette Social and professional etiquette consists of written and unwritten rules that reflect cultural expectations as well as official policies and procedures. Search the Internet using the following terms: *airplane travel etiquette, dining etiquette, disability etiquette, gift-giving etiquette,* and *etiquette for making proper introductions.* Create a list of "Dos and Don'ts" based on the expectations that most people in the United States have regarding these issues. Compare your findings with those of your classmates.

If communicating on the telephone appropriately is so important to professional and organizational success, how do you do it? Just as in other types of professional interactions, there are not always defined rules. However, whether you are speaking to a person, to voice mail, or to some other type of recording system, you can follow some basic rules of etiquette and protocol when using the telephone. These skills are given in the Communication Strategies checklist.

Speak Clearly and Distinctly. Although this rule seems obvious, people sometimes forget to practice it. Have you ever called a company and been unable to understand the person who answered the phone? As **Figure 8–2** on the following page shows, the person who answered may have spoken too quickly, too softly, mumbled the greeting or the name of the company, or perhaps used slang terms that were difficult for you to understand. It is very likely that this person did not make a positive impression on you. You do not want to

MEETING INDIVIDUAL NEEDS   MULTIPLE LEARNING STYLES

Interpersonal Explain to students that when they are making a business call, it is wise to use a similar style as that of the person they are speaking to. Some people are busy and efficient and prefer a direct approach with little social chat or small talk. Others like a more sociable approach. Being a careful listener can help you figure out the style of the other person.

Activity Have small groups of students choose a business scenario, write a script for communication within the scenario, and role-play it. To avoid duplicate scenarios, you may wish to assign role-play situations to groups or to approve those suggested by students before they begin working on their scripts.

create this same impression for yourself or your organization. Instead, make sure that you speak clearly and distinctly and use a pleasant tone. Also, if your listener is trying to write down what you say, adjust your pace accordingly.

Identify Yourself and Your Employer. As a general rule, when answering the phone, give both your first and last names and the name of your employer or organization. This assures the caller that he or she has reached the right number. Many companies also want you to identify the department or office in which you are located. It is usually appropriate to say something like, "Hello, this is Jane Smith in Receiving."

The purpose of clear identification is to make the speaker and the company recognizable and traceable. The caller should be able to refer to you by name and call you back later, if necessary. This person also should see you as a pleasant and helpful representative of the company. During a phone call, you are, indeed, the voice of your company or organization.

Be a Responsible Listener. When you answer the phone, you often are the first contact the caller has with your company or your department. No one expects you to be able to solve every problem or answer every question, but you do need to know how to handle each inquiry efficiently.

Develop a Plan When Making Phone Calls. When you need to make a telephone call for your company or organization, take the time to organize the materials you will need to make the call efficiently. It may help you to create a quick list of topics that you want to cover during the call. When you have reached the person, identify yourself and ask if he or she has time to talk with you.

■ Figure 8–2 Speak Clearly and Distinctly

mumble mumble mumble . . .

What is this person saying?

If the Person Is Available If the person is available, preview the purpose of your call, saying something like, "I have two questions" or, "There are three projects I need to discuss." Try to keep the conversation organized and on track, limiting small talk as much as possible. After you have received the information you need, briefly summarize the conversation and ask if you are clear on all the information. Then, conclude the call by thanking the person for his or her information and time.

If the Person Is Not Interruptible If the person responds that he or she does not have time to speak at that time, ask for a time when he or she might be available. It may also help if you can estimate how much time your conversation will last. "When would be a good time for me to speak with you about my current project? I will need about fifteen minutes to get your answers to two or three important questions." This helps the person plan enough time to respond. Once the person names a time for you to call back, it is important for you to remember to do so at that time.

Developing Effective Interpersonal Skills **257**

Telephone Etiquette
Review with students the points of business telephone etiquette addressed on pages 256–259. As necessary, explain to students why each point is important to remember and carry out. In each case, help students understand what it might be like to be on the other end of the call. **L1**

Summarizing
At the end of a business call, it is important for both people to summarize the points they have made during the conversation. That way they both know that they agree about what has been said and what action each will take next. Have students ask a business representative about ways he or she summarizes a call. Encourage them to share the information with the class. **L3**

Plan Your Call
Discuss the purposes for business calls students might make. For example, they might call to place a catalog order, to inquire about an employment opportunity, or to ask for directions to a place of business. Then, model how you would prepare to place a catalog order over the phone. Point out that there is information that you must provide when placing the order and show how a list can help you have the information ready when needed. Information about you includes your name, address, and method of payment. Information about the product may include name, order number, size, and color. You may wish to have students role-play placing orders over the phone. If so, provide catalogs that they can use to choose products and product information. Have one student play the part of the person placing the order and another student play the part of the person taking the order. **L2** **ELL**

MULTIPLE LEARNING STYLES

MEETING INDIVIDUAL NEEDS

Linguistic Explain that the quality of one's voice is particularly important on the telephone.
Activity If students have difficulty assessing how they sound on the phone, suggest they turn on a tape recorder when they make a phone call. They should listen to the tape; assess the quality of their voice and speech, perhaps with your input; and practice improving these qualities if necessary.

COMMUNICATION
Strategies

**EFFECTIVELY HANDLING
HOSTILE TELEPHONE CALLS**

Remind students that in a business context, they do not have the option of simply hanging up on a hostile caller as they might if they were at home. Point out that they are the company as far as the person on the other end of the line is concerned, and they must do their best to calm the person down, keep him or her as a satisfied customer, and solve the problem. Have students review the points in the chart on this page. Encourage students to add to the list. **L2**

Communication Tip

Remind students that handling telephone calls on the job requires a more formal approach than they might use for personal calls at home, just as other business interactions are more formal than personal ones. You may want to use this opportunity to mention that making and taking personal calls while on the job can often be a delicate situation: Some companies actively discourage personal phone calls, and all realize that employees are using company-paid time while making and taking personal calls. Although most employers realize that some personal calls during the workday are unavoidable, employees usually serve their own business image best by making and taking as few as possible.

Prepare to Receive Phone Calls. When you receive a phone call, prepare by having paper and pen or pencil ready. Find out the full name of the caller and write it down. Next, ask about the purpose of the call. If you will need to put the person on hold temporarily or call him or her back, write down the complete phone number, including the area code.

If the caller asks a question you cannot answer, route the caller to someone who can. Then, check the phone's indicator lights to make sure the transferred call has been picked up and not left on hold or lost in the wilderness of voice mail. If the call is not picked up after one minute, redirect it yourself. A well-answered call can lead to a positive evaluation of both you and your company.

Documenting the Call When dealing with business matters, you may find it helpful to document phone calls. Documentation can help you verify any information you receive and can serve as a reminder to follow up on the purpose of the call. Many companies use a preprinted form like the one in **Figure 8-3**

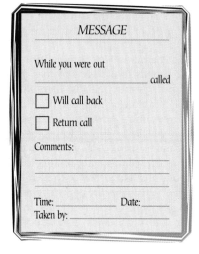

■ **Figure 8–3 Telephone Message Form**

258   *Glencoe Communication Applications*

COMMUNICATION
Strategies

**EFFECTIVELY HANDLING
HOSTILE TELEPHONE CALLS**

- Remain calm.
- Listen empathically.
- Keep your responses objective.
- Acknowledge the caller's anger or hostility.
- Let the caller know that you want to help.
- Respond with clear, logical messages that reflect empathy with the caller.

on which you can record information vital to a conversation. If your company does not use a preprinted form, you may want to develop one for yourself. This can help you track the caller, the caller's phone number, the date and time of the call, and any information that results from the conversation.

Answering the Telephone for Someone Else When answering the telephone for a supervisor or another employee, be sure to take accurate, organized notes. If the person the caller wishes to speak with is not available, simply say that he or she cannot take the call at that time. There is no need to reveal details about why the person cannot take the call.

If you have been asked to screen calls, do so with tact and courtesy. Try to avoid making promises for other people, such as "She'll call you as soon as she gets back to the office." Also, avoid making comments about policies or programs about which you lack knowledge or authority. Finally, remember to remain professional on the phone even if the person is upset and hard to deal with.

REAL-WORLD CONNECTION

Business Telephone Etiquette In a business situation, a telephone should never be allowed to ring more than three times before being answered.

Activity Arrange, if possible, for students to individually observe a receptionist or company telephone operator or to intern for a single day as a receptionist or operator for a business. Have them assess the duties of the receptionists and log the number of incoming calls and visits the receptionists handle during the day. If they answer a business phone that has rung more than three times, they should apologize to the person who is calling. Encourage students to share their observations or experiences with the class.

Dealing With Hostile Telephone Calls Some of the most difficult phone calls to deal with involve angry or hostile callers. Effective communication strategies in these instances are extremely important to the relationship between the person making the call and your company or organization. Use the Communication Strategies checklist on the left as a guide to handling hostile calls.

Etiquette and Protocol in Giving Criticism

In a perfect world, all people would do their jobs effectively and efficiently, generating absolutely no need for negative feedback. The real world is not quite so simple, though. Sometimes, in order to do your own job well, it becomes necessary to give criticism. When you criticize people in a manner that helps them to learn and grow, you are offering constructive criticism. **Constructive criticism** is a negative evaluation done in a way that brings about positive change. Often, people value this type of criticism because it helps them to improve. To keep criticism positive and constructive, however, it is necessary to follow certain rules.

Describe the Facts. Few people truly enjoy being criticized. However, by structuring your criticism a certain way, you reduce its unpleasantness and make the communication as productive as possible.

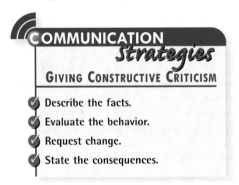

COMMUNICATION *Strategies*
GIVING CONSTRUCTIVE CRITICISM

- Describe the facts.
- Evaluate the behavior.
- Request change.
- State the consequences.

First, it is important to remember that constructive criticism always begins with descriptive communication—not an evaluation. **Descriptive communication** is talk that paints a picture of the facts of a situation. Starting with a simple description of the facts helps you ease into the criticism without looking as though you are attacking or judging the person unfairly.

To begin, simply describe the exact behavior or set of behaviors that are the root of the issue. At this point, try not to use any words that imply an evaluation. This can be a little tricky because so many common words fall into that category. In general, avoid words such as *good, bad, better, worse, right, wrong,* and so on.

It can be much easier to apply a label to someone than to describe the behaviors that led you to that evaluation. For example, it might be simpler to tell someone, "You are acting like a slacker," than it would be to describe his or her unmotivated behaviors. However, with a little practice, you can learn to describe the facts of a situation without passing judgment on the person.

For example, instead of calling the person a slacker, you might say, "You rarely offer to do any work other than what is strictly required." Using this kind of description not only avoids evaluation, but it also lets the person know how to improve his or her behavior. This is the only way criticism can be constructive.

Evaluate the Behavior. After you have clearly and objectively described the troublesome behavior, it is appropriate to evaluate it. **Evaluative communication** is talk that tells how you interpret a behavior and how you feel about a situation. At this point, you might say, "It seems as if you don't care much about this job anymore. Unfortunately, the quality of your work is suffering because of your attitude."

Developing Effective Interpersonal Skills **259**

COMMUNICATION *Strategies*
GIVING CONSTRUCTIVE CRITICISM

Ask students to brainstorm situations in which one person might find it necessary to give constructive criticism to another. *(Answers will probably be situations in which one person has authority over another: the coach of a team player, a teacher of a student, or, in a business situation, a supervisor of an employee).* In most cases, students will not be in a position to do this currently. However, ask them to "put themselves in the place" of a person who must provide constructive criticism. Have them review the list on this page. Suggest they add to it any ideas they think might also be useful. **L2**

Telephone Etiquette

Discuss telephone etiquette for businesses. Role-play with a student volunteer how to answer business calls using the information on pages 258 and 259. Ask the student to play the roles of a business associate, a friend, and a dissatisfied customer for different role plays. Demonstrate for students ways of taking and handling the call for each type of caller. Also, show students how to take a message and what information to include on the message. Then, have volunteers take turns initiating calls, answering calls, and taking messages. **L1**

CRITICAL THINKING ACTIVITY

We have all experienced telephone calls in which we were treated rudely. To draw students' attention to ways not to behave on the phone, let them discuss instances of rude telephone behavior they have experienced. You may want to mention examples such as someone on the other end of the telephone eating or interrupting to talk to someone else. Have students list the behaviors and rate them on a rudeness scale of 1 to 5, with 5 being the most rude behavior. You may also wish to ask students whether they think specific technology-related behaviors, such as interrupting a phone conversation to take a "call waiting" call, are rude, and why or why not.

Compare and Contrast

Suggest that students look at the Communication Strategies on pages 259 and 261. Point out that together, these two lists identify the course of a conversation between two people whose purpose is for one person to provide criticism of another's behavior. Ask students to compare and contrast the two lists. How are the recommended behaviors alike? How are they different? *(One strategy is for giving and one for receiving constructive criticism. Both strategies depend on tact and consideration to be effective.)* **L2**

■ Visual Instruction

Answer Defensiveness interferes with growth and improvement.

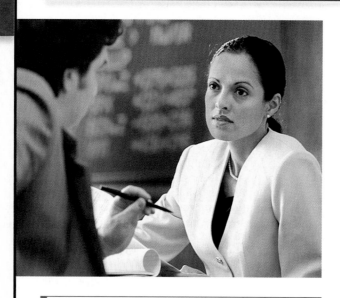

A young woman receives constructive criticism during an annual review. What can happen if one becomes defensive when receiving constructive criticism?

As you complete this step of the process, it is important to remember that you are evaluating the specific behavior and not the person. While a person may be unmotivated or unproductive at work, he or she still is a valuable human being. Try to keep your criticism from becoming personal.

Request Change. Immediately following a brief, direct evaluation, return to descriptive communication. This time, however, focus on the specific behavioral change you want to see. To avoid any misunderstandings, be as specific as possible in your description. For instance, if a worker has not been completing his or her duties, you might say, "Our company policy is that breaks end on time and the employee immediately returns to the sales floor. I'd appreciate it if you would be careful about this in the future." This type of detailed instruction tends to be much more effective than a general request to "shape up."

State the Consequences. Finally, you need to tell the person what will or may happen as a result of his or her behavior. Remember, you have clearly described two different behaviors: one that is the problem and another that is the solution. Now you need to mention the possible negative consequences if the problem behavior continues. For instance, "If you continue to return late from breaks, I will have to take that time out of your pay."

The focus of this step, however, should be on the positive consequences of change. You might say, "Being prompt and eager to work will help identify you as an enthusiastic employee. That's the type of person who gets promoted." Constructive criticism is based on the assumption that people want to grow and develop. By giving them some instruction for change, you can help them become more effective.

Etiquette and Protocol in Receiving Criticism

While criticism does focus on a need for change, that need can be viewed as either negative or positive. Viewing the criticism as a negative judgment can cause you to respond defensively. However, viewing it constructively can help you see the situation as an opportunity to better yourself.

When you are defensive to criticism, you put up an emotional barrier to communication. You close yourself off from change and, instead, may try to justify your own behavior or even launch a counterattack. A defensive response prevents you from growing and becoming more effective as a result of the criticism.

260   *Glencoe Communication Applications*

COOPERATIVE LEARNING ACTIVITY

Constructive criticism can help a person identify areas needing improvement and strategies for improving them. The delivery and reception of criticism is an important aspect of effective communication. Divide students into teams of four. Have each team develop a skit or scenario in which one person offers constructive criticism to another, following the guidelines on pages 259–262. Ask each team to choose two members to act out the skit for the whole class. Let students discuss the skits and evaluate the effectiveness of the roles of giving and receiving criticism effectively.

A constructive response does just the opposite. Even if the criticism itself is not expressed constructively, you can still respond in a positive way. There are several strategies you can use to get the most out of criticism.

Ask for a Description of the Facts. It can be difficult to make positive changes if you do not understand exactly what behaviors are the problem. Therefore, if a critic says that you are not doing your work, tells you that you are selfish, or accuses you of having a bad attitude, politely ask the person what caused him or her to arrive at that conclusion. If the person cannot give you any specifics, adopt a problem-solving attitude. Ask probing questions such as "When did you begin noticing this?" or "Has the problem seemed to get worse lately?" to help narrow the person's broad criticism to specific behaviors that you can change.

Paraphrase the Criticism. Stating the person's criticism in your own words can serve several purposes. First, it helps ensure that you have understood correctly. If you get off on the wrong track, the critic can clear up any misunderstandings immediately.

Second, paraphrasing can help buy time while you control your emotions. If you have received a particularly harsh criticism, you may need to compose yourself before offering a response. Rephrasing the criticism less harshly can help take the edge off of it. It also may help the critic see that his or her language is more negative than it needs to be.

If Possible, Agree With the Critic's Assessment. Some criticism is constructive; some may be unjustified. To the extent that it is possible, agree with the factual description of your problem behavior without adding any qualifiers. Qualifiers often begin with "but . . ." or "that's because. . . ."

Employees who are tardy to work may receive criticism from a supervisor. **What are the benefits of paraphrasing a criticism?**

Learning to Take Criticism

Listening to yourself being criticized is a very difficult situation for most people. Nevertheless, it happens routinely in business situations as supervisors attempt to teach their employees proper skills and behavior on the job. Discuss with students how they can learn to handle criticism in a professional and effective manner. **L1**

COMMUNICATION *Strategies*

RECEIVING CRITICISM EFFECTIVELY

Students are likely to be able to empathize more with receiving criticism than giving it. Review with them the items listed in the chart. Encourage discussion of why these behaviors are effective. Ask them to add any strategies they feel might be useful. **L2**

■ **Visual Instruction**

Answer Paraphrasing helps ensure that the message was understood and gives time to the person being criticized to control his or her emotions.

CRITICAL THINKING ACTIVITY

Part of the standard interaction between teacher and students is constructive criticism by the teacher of the students. Post copies of the Communication Strategies for Giving and Receiving Criticism Effectively. When you have a session with a student, draw his or her attention to the strategies and agree that both of you will try to practice them.

GLENCOE
Online

For an additional Practice Lab for this section, have students visit the *Glencoe Communication Applications* Web site at **communicationapplications.glencoe.com.** Click on Communication Practice Lab 8–2. **L1**

Language Tip

When dealing with people whose first language is not English, it is important to be aware of your own language use. For example, avoid talking too fast or too slowly—either can be difficult to understand. Pronounce words clearly without running them together, for example, "I dunno" or "gimme," as is common in spoken English. These can be difficult for a listener to understand.

If you have been taking longer breaks than you should have, avoid qualifying your behavior with statements such as "But I had a ton of homework this week that I was trying to finish up during my breaks." Instead, just say, "Yes, sir (or ma'am), I have been late returning from breaks this week."

Even if you feel that a certain behavior should not be judged negatively, you may be able to agree with the principle involved. For instance, if you were late only once because you spent your break helping your manager, you probably would not want to agree that you have made a habit of being tardy. Instead, you might say, "Yes, sir (or ma'am), I agree that people who always return late from breaks look like slackers."

Listen for the Desired Change. To view criticism as an opportunity for change, you need to know exactly what change the critic thinks is necessary. Once there is a clear understanding of what behavior is the source of the problem, there needs to be an equally clear understanding of the proposed solution.

Actively listen for a description of the desired behavioral change. If you do not hear it, ask the critic for specific changes he or she would like to see.

Stay Focused on the Positive Consequences of Change. Perhaps the least pleasant part of criticism is hearing what may happen if problem behavior continues. The person making the criticism may warn or even threaten you with these negative consequences. Remember to stay calm and listen actively and politely. You can use these consequences later as a motivating force to help you change.

However, as a competent problem-solver, you will want to focus most of your energy on the benefits of change. What will happen if you change in the manner that the critic has described? Will the critic be more pleased with your performance? Will you improve your image as a valuable employee? Will you increase your chances for promotion? These questions help you put the past behind you and move ahead with positive growth and change.

COMMUNICATION

Responding Appropriately to Criticism

PRACTICE LAB

To practice an appropriate response to criticism, follow these steps:

Step 1 As a class, brainstorm a list of criticisms that students might hear from parents, teachers, or employers.

Step 2 In groups of four or five, choose a few of the criticisms from the list and write them on a sheet of paper. Think of an appropriate scenario in which an annoyed employer might state these criticisms to a teenage worker.

Step 3 Working as a group, write a script of the employer's criticism and the teenage worker's response. Be sure to follow the protocol for giving and receiving criticism.

Step 4 Present your scripted scenarios to the class.

Step 5 As a class, evaluate the effectiveness of both the critic and the teenager. Did both parties seem to view the criticism as an opportunity for positive change?

MEETING INDIVIDUAL NEEDS

ENGLISH LANGUAGE LEARNERS

Cultural Differences Every culture has its own way of doing things. Yet, most have many things in common.

Activity Invite students from other cultures to share with the class some examples of the differences between their native cultures and the one they now live in. Those who are confident may be willing to provide anecdotes of problems they have had with "culture clashes" as examples of the need for sensitivity. Encourage all students to discuss ways that the cultural standards and practices are alike and different. **ELL**

Diversity in the workplace leads to a wealth of ideas. How does a person's culture impact his or her communication?

APPROPRIATE STRATEGIES FOR DEALING WITH DIFFERENCES

The United States always has been a richly diverse nation, with people from many different backgrounds and traditions living and working together. Sometimes, however, this variety can breed conflict in the workplace. People often feel threatened by ideas and people that are new or different to them. Sometimes, people prefer to shut out information that does not fit in with their personal perspective of the world.

Our taste in food often follows this same pattern. You may not like some new flavors the first time you try them. However, over time, you may grow to appreciate many different flavors. Diversity among human beings is similar. Just as a strong flavor might jump out at you at first but later add to the uniqueness of a dish, so might a person's most obvious differences seem striking and objectionable at first. However, over time, as you become more accustomed to these differences, you may come to appreciate the richness that they provide.

The trick is to be open to other peoples' perspectives. That does not mean that you need to agree with their ideas. Nor does it mean that you must do things someone else's way, rather than your own. However, skillful communicators are willing to keep an open mind when it comes to diverse ideas.

As you become a more experienced communicator, you will find that differences exist on many levels. What's more, each of these areas can have an effect on communication. Four factors that often affect people's perceptions and communication are the ones listed here:

- culture
- ethnicity
- gender
- age

Developing Effective Interpersonal Skills **263**

Dealing with Cultural Differences

Remind students that the effective interpersonal skills that are the topic of this chapter imply interaction with all people in all situations. Point out that it may be initially difficult to interact effectively with people whose cultural backgrounds are different from one's own. However, such interaction is likely to be more and more necessary as global business dealings become more common. Point out that although the "golden rule" is always a good one—treating others as you wish to be treated—sometimes, it is easy to stumble if someone in another culture would not wish to be treated in exactly that way. You may want to invite students from different cultural backgrounds to offer examples. **L2**

BUSINESS BRIEF

Every culture has its acceptable gestures—and its unacceptable ones. Such body language can often lead to misunderstandings. For example, people in some Asian cultures believe that the spirit enters the body at the top of the head; therefore, any gesture to touch another person's head is simply not done. Other gestures, such as snapping your fingers, slapping a person's back, pointing with your index finger, whistling, and so on are frowned upon in some cultures. Warn students to be careful of body language when dealing with people of other cultures.

Visual Instruction

Answer The way that one approaches communication and its standards of etiquette and protocol is affected by one's cultural background, which establishes the "right" way of doing things in one's culture.

CRITICAL THINKING ACTIVITY

Encourage students to spend several days observing and noting elements of cultures other than their own around them in school, on television, and in movies, newspapers, and advertisements. Have them analyze their lists in small groups. Which elements are now part of mainstream American culture? *(Answers may include foods such as tacos and pizza, clothing, media such as animation, and so on.)* What does this reveal about today's American culture? Why?

Avoiding Stereotypes

As students discuss interacting effectively with people of various ethnic backgrounds, you may want to bring up the issue of avoiding stereotypes. If necessary, remind students that a stereotype is an unfair and illogical generalization that all people of a certain cultural or ethnic background share certain (usually negative) characteristics. **L1**

Acknowledging Cultural Differences

Make sure students realize that dealing with cultural differences does not mean ignoring them and assuming or pretending that others will feel comfortable being treated as you would treat people of your own culture. On the contrary, it is very important to understand and respect the expectations of people from another culture. Otherwise, you may unintentionally offend them. **L2**

Visual Instruction

Answer People may communicate differently with people of opposite genders. Some cultures have rules and norms for the way that men and women communicate, although North American cultures make few distinctions.

Culture

In Chapter 1, you read that a culture is the life patterns of a specific group of people. It is the rules, norms, customs, values, and beliefs that allow people to define themselves—and be defined by others—as members of a particular group. Among other things, a person's cultural background may influence his or her language, food, dress, leisure activities, work ethic, traditions, and family role. It also may affect the way he or she approaches conflict, decisions, and communication. In addition, culture can affect the rules of etiquette and protocol that a person follows. In short, a person's culture strongly influences the way he or she perceives the world.

As you have grown, you have come to identify with one or more specific cultures. Your communication reflects the assumption that these cultural rules, norms, and customs are the "right" way of doing things for you. However, other cultures often can open our eyes to different and perhaps better ways of doing things.

To deal effectively with cultural differences, you need to be open to new ideas, avoid rushing to judgment, and see diversity

Elizabeth Dole is an accomplished speaker and politician. In what ways can gender influence communication?

264   *Glencoe Communication Applications*

INTERDISCIPLINARY CONNECTION

History During the 1950s through the 1970s, different ethnic, gender, and social groups worked to end discriminatory practices in the United States. Part of their efforts focused on language and how it helped to perpetuate discriminatory practices and stereotypical images.

Activity Ask students to do some research to find out about the 1960s and 1970s in the United States. Have students find out what they can about the social history that began to "raise consciousness" so people could be aware of such unfair discrimination and could attempt to change such practices.

as opportunity. As today's business world becomes increasingly global, those who are able to communicate effectively with people of different cultural backgrounds will surely enjoy great opportunities for advancement and success.

Ethnicity

Sometimes, when certain cultural groups share a national origin, language, religion, or other characteristic, they are referred to as an ethnic group. Very often, the people in a specific ethnic group also share certain physical traits. For this reason, people tend to judge a person's ethnicity according to the way he or she looks.

However, basing even part of a person's identity on his or her physical features can create problems. First, you may offend someone by incorrectly identifying his or her ethnicity or nationality. Second, you may tend to shape your communication to fit some unjust ethnic stereotype. This kind of mass generalization can easily lead to misunderstanding. It can also lead to communication failure.

As a rule of thumb, avoid basing your communication choices on a person's ethnicity. Instead, concentrate on communicating appropriately and effectively—just as you would in any communication context.

Gender

People typically identify themselves as belonging to a specific gender, male or female. Certain aspects of that gender influence your perceptions and communication. For instance, you may communicate a certain way with people of your same gender and a slightly different way with people of the opposite gender. To make matters even more complicated, cultural rules and norms for your gender may influence your communication.

Most cultures have developed certain rules and norms for the way males and females communicate. North American cultures typically make few distinctions between the way men and women communicate. Of course, some stereotypes still exist. For example, an outspoken woman may be viewed by some as overbearing while an outspoken man may simply be viewed by those same people as assertive. Still, the goal in communication—especially in social and professional contexts—is for men and women to behave as equals.

Sometimes, however, this attitude may come into direct conflict with the norms of other cultures. For instance, in some Asian or Muslim cultures, females are expected to defer to males. Therefore, even if a female outranks a male colleague, businessmen from one of these cultures may insist on negotiating with the male. This type of behavior may seem extremely unjust to a businesswoman from the United States. However, if she insists on doing the negotiating herself, she runs a high risk of offending the businessmen and causing the negotiations to fail.

As a competent communicator, it is important for you to recognize when a culture has different gender rules for communication. You can then adapt your communication to make it appropriate for the context. This will help you communicate as effectively as possible in any culture.

Age

Sometimes, society groups people together according to their age whether they like it or not. Just as you should not stereotype people of different ethnicities, you also should not stereotype people of different ages. People of all ages have their own unique perceptions and ways of communicating. Some teenagers tend to be extremely mature, very serious, and strikingly formal. By the same token,

Developing Effective Interpersonal Skills   265

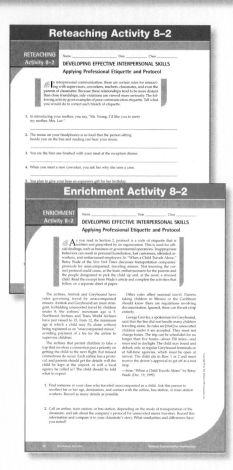

some elderly people are whimsical, young at heart, and up to date on the latest trends.

Rarely would every person in a particular age group perceive things the same way. Therefore, your communication choices should not be based on a person's age. Stereotyping others on the basis of age is just as dangerous as any other kind of stereotyping. It almost always has a harmful effect on communication.

Section 2 Assessment

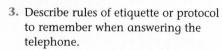

Visit the *Glencoe Communication Applications* Web site at **communicationapplications. glencoe.com** and click on **Self-Check and Study Guide 8.2** to review your understanding of applying professional etiquette and protocol.

Review Key Terms

1. Define each term and write it in a sentence: etiquette, protocol, constructive criticism, descriptive communication, evaluative communication.

Check Understanding

2. What is the main rule of etiquette or protocol to remember when making introductions?

3. Describe rules of etiquette or protocol to remember when answering the telephone.

4. Compare and contrast the rules of etiquette for giving and receiving criticism.

5. What is one effective way to evaluate others' communication skills in an organization? How might you evaluate your own skills?

6. **Synthesize** When communicating with diverse peoples, which of the following should you pay most attention to: culture, ethnicity, gender, or age? Why?

APPLICATION *Activity*

Recognizing the Impact of Diversity On a sheet of paper, list the following categories related to your culture: gender, race, age, religion, native language, number of people in household, favorite holiday, favorite food, what you hope to be, and what is most important to you. Beside each category, write an answer that applies to you and another answer that is very different from yours. Now, imagine that you must carry on a fifteen-minute conversation with the second person you described. What would be most interesting and most difficult about your conversation? Discuss your ideas as a class.

4 CLOSE

Have students turn back to page 253 and reread the opening paragraphs. In light of what they have learned in Section 2, how would they handle meeting their future boss in the supermarket with their teacher? What would they say and do? Why?

Extra-Credit Project

Have students describe a business scenario they have faced in a part-time job or in what they imagine will be their first job. Ask them to incorporate several strategies they have learned for professional etiquette and protocol.

Section 2 Assessment Answers

1. Accept all reasonable sentences.
2. Always name the person who deserves the most respect first.
3. Speak clearly and pleasantly, identify yourself and your employer, be a responsible listener, develop a plan for making calls, develop a plan for receiving calls and take accurate notes.
4. Answers will vary but should reflect what students learned about the etiquette of giving and receiving criticism as summarized in

Communication Strategies on pages 259 and 261.
5. Answers may vary but might include evaluating one's communication skills in terms of how effectively others think that person communicates.
6. You should keep in mind the perspectives of all other cultures, ethnicities, gender, and ages. It is important to avoid all kinds of stereotyping.
Application Activity Students' two sets of answers should reflect differences between their own culture and another with which they have some familiarity.

266

Communication Self-Assessment

Evaluating Your Interpersonal Communication Skills

How Do You Rate?

On a separate sheet of paper, respond to the following statements. Put a check mark at the end of each skill you would like to improve.

KEY: **A** Always   **R** Rarely
       U Usually   **N** Never
       S Sometimes

1. I am able to build unique, interdependent, and irreplaceable relationships.
2. My interpersonal skills include the ability to start conversations with open-ended questions.
3. I can maintain conversations because I know how to ask tactful questions, and I can balance listening with talking.
4. I listen empathically and ask questions if I don't understand nonverbal clues.
5. When I request information, I define what I want, why I am making the request, and when I need the information.
6. When I give directions, I assume the person is performing a task for the first time.
7. When I respond to questions, I listen actively and avoid making judgments.
8. I make introductions according to the etiquette and protocol of the situation.
9. I am able to accept constructive criticism by focusing on the value of making changes.
10. In work situations, my communication follows the norms set by my superiors.

How Do You Score?

Review your responses. Give yourself 5 points for every A, 4 for every U, 3 for every S, 2 for every R, and 1 for every N. Total your points and evaluate your score.

41–50 Excellent You may be surprised to find out how much you can improve your skills.

31–40 Good In this course, you can learn ways to make your skills better.

21–30 Fair Practice applying the skills taught in this course.

1–20 Needs Improvement Carefully monitor your improvement as you work through this course.

Setting Communication Goals

If you scored Excellent or Good, complete Part A. If your score was Fair or Needs Improvement, complete Part B.

Part A
1. I plan to put the following ideas into practice:
2. I plan to share the following information about communication with the following people:

Part B
1. The behaviors I need to change most are:
2. To bring about these changes, I will take these steps:

Developing Effective Interpersonal Skills **267**

Communication Self-Assessment

Have students respond to the ten statements, using the key on this page. Then, have them evaluate their interpersonal communication skills. Based on their scores, assign either Part A or Part B of the goal-setting activity. On an index card or sheet of paper, students should concretely define their communication goals to improve their current levels of skill.

Communication Journal Activity

Point out to students that people who write down their goals and review them regularly are more likely to accomplish their objectives than people who merely think of areas of improvement. Have students list their goals in their Communication Journals.

Communication Tip

Suggest that students keep a list of the questions and their answers in a folder that they can review frequently. They can add their own communication goals to the list. You may want to recommend that students review these lists and update them as they attain some of those goals.

MEETING INDIVIDUAL NEEDS

INCLUSION STRATEGIES

Learning Disabled Students with learning disabilities may have little confidence in their conversational ability. They and many other students may benefit from additional practice.

Activity Encourage students to choose partners with whom they feel especially comfortable. Have the pairs practice their conversational skills for several weeks—before and after class and whenever possible. You may wish to videotape or tape-record the initial and several subsequent conversations so that students can observe and assess their own improvements.

Communication Through Writing

Writing a Résumé

Objective: To create a résumé

Teaching Suggestions and Strategies

If possible, provide sample résumés for students to view. Anonymous samples are available in books on résumé writing. You may also ask parents and others to donate copies of their own résumés.

Connection to the Workplace

Tell students that résumés are expected by any employer who has a job opening. Nevertheless, a résumé does not get a job for anyone. Instead, a résumé piques the interest of an employer and is instrumental in getting the job applicant a personal interview. Most employers want to know whether the applicant can do the job the employer has available. They are interested in the information in the résumé to see whether it describes experience and aptitude that fits the position. In a personal interview, the employer discovers whether the applicant has the communication skills necessary for the position.

Writing a Résumé

A résumé is a summary of your employment qualifications and work experience that is used to present your credentials to possible employers. Just as effective small talk can set the tone for a good conversation, a well-written résumé can positively influence your chances for getting the job that you want. Employers use résumés to assess your educational background, review your employment history, and evaluate your organizational skills. If your résumé shows that you can be an asset to an employer, you are likely to be offered a job interview. Your résumé should make a positive first impression for you. Use the following pointers to write an effective résumé.

Identify Yourself. Your full name, address, and telephone number are essential parts of your résumé. If you have a fax number or an e-mail address, include that as well. This information must be accurate and should be featured prominently at the top of the document. Make it as easy as possible for employers to contact you. If possible, supply the number of a phone that has an answering machine or voice mail.

State Your Objective. This part of the résumé follows your identification. Use this space to identify the position for which you would like to be considered. You may also want to briefly state your personal and professional goals or summarize your special abilities in this section.

Describe Your Educational Background. State the names of the schools you attended, your areas of study, and the degrees that you earned. Start by listing the academic degree you earned most recently or your current course of study, then work backward. Since you have not yet completed high school, include your projected graduation date. Mention any academic honors that you have received. Your education is a valuable asset—use it to your advantage.

List Your Work Experience. Your work history is an important part of your résumé because it shows potential employers that you know how to interact with other people on a professional level. List the jobs you have held by starting with the most recent one and working backward. Explain the positions you held at each place of employment and the duties for which you were responsible. Include part-time jobs and internships as well as any full-time jobs you have had.

Mention Special Interests and Volunteer Work. Volunteer work suggests to employers that you have good social skills and are willing to dedicate yourself.

For additional information about business writing, see the *Guide to Business Communication* section of the Communication Survival Kit in the Appendix.

MEETING INDIVIDUAL NEEDS

MULTIPLE LEARNING STYLES

Visual-Spatial Students with a visual learning style often have design and artistic talent. Such students will appreciate the need to present a résumé in an attractive and readable format.

Activity Draw students' attention to the sample résumé on page 269 and have them note the way it is set up on the page with headings in bold type and bulleted lists. Ask students to pay special attention to the graphic design of their own sample résumés and to share them with the rest of the class.

Mention your special interests and hobbies. This information tells potential employers that you are a well-rounded person.

Give References. A reference is a person you know, such as a teacher or a work supervisor, who knows you well enough to discuss your work habits with potential employers. Ask your references for permission to use their names and advise them that they may be contacted. When listing a reference, provide the person's name, title, business address, and business phone number. If you do not include the names of references on your résumé, make sure the employer knows that you have references available. Put your reference information at the end of your résumé.

Gina M. Pandelli
230 Patterson Avenue
Ft. Collins, Colorado 80525
Phone: 970-555-8025
Fax: 970-555-3699
E-mail: gmpandelli@isp.com

Objective
To obtain a position as a teller with a national bank that will enable me to use my education and work experience to the fullest extent

Education
Mountainside High School
- Graduated May 1999
- Business-preparatory curriculum
- Honor Roll student
- Student Council treasurer

Work Experience
Gourmet Grocers, 10/97–present
Cashier
- Helped customers check out and purchase groceries
- Bagged items for customers
- Assisted with store opening and closing duties

Activities
Mountainside High School
- School newspaper staff
- Vocal music accompanist
- Varsity track and field
Volunteer at Larimer County Animal Shelter

References
Andrew Sparks, DVM
Veterinarian, Larimer County Animal Shelter
284 Springs Road, Ft. Collins, CO 80525
970-555-7387

Mr. Douglas McKee
Teacher, track coach, Mountainside High School
860 Mountaineer Lane, Ft. Collins, CO 80525
970-555-7866

WRITING Activity

Imagine that you have heard about a summer job that you really want to have. Write your résumé for this job, using the following points as guidelines:

- Put your full name, home address, and telephone number at the top of the résumé. Include your e-mail address or fax number if you have one.

- Indicate the job opening in which you are interested and why. If possible, explain how this job can accommodate your personal or career goals.

- Provide your educational background, including schools, subjects studied, graduations, extracurricular activities, academic honors, and leadership roles.

- Give the names of your past employers and the dates during which you were employed.

- Describe your responsibilities at your past jobs.

- Include your interests and activities.

Developing Effective Interpersonal Skills **269**

Teaching Activity

Have students assess the sample résumé. Does it meet the criteria established on pages 268–269? How? What kind of job does the applicant want? Do students think the résumé might get her an interview with a bank? Why or why not? *(The applicant is looking for a position as a bank teller. Students may respond that the résumé might help the applicant get a job interview because it shows she has worked with money and has demonstrated responsibility through her activities.)*

WRITING Activity

Students' résumés should follow the general format shown in the model and include the items listed in the assignment. Let students share and discuss their résumés.

Grammar Tip

A declarative sentence has a subject and a verb and states a complete thought. When a declarative sentence is written, it ends with a period. An imperative sentence gives a command or makes a request. It usually begins with a verb, and its subject is not stated but rather is understood as "you." It also expresses a complete thought. An imperative sentence can consist of only one word: for example, "Stop!" When an imperative sentence is written, it ends with a period unless its sense is very urgent, in which case it can end with an exclamation mark.

GRAMMAR PRACTICE

Declarative and Imperative Sentences

Have students identify the following sentences as declarative or imperative.

1. A résumé is a summary of your qualifications and experience. *(declarative)*

2. Identify yourself. *(imperative)*

3. Make it easy for employers to contact you. *(imperative)*

4. Use this space to identify the position for which you want to be considered. *(imperative)*

5. You may want to include your professional goals on your résumé. *(declarative)*

Additional Resources

Appendix, "Guide to Business Communication"

Glencoe Writer's Assistant CD-ROM

Glencoe Interactive Grammar Software

Grade 9 Writer's Choice, Lesson 1.4

CHAPTER 8 Assessment and Activities

GLENCOE
TECHNOLOGY

MindJogger Videoquiz

Use *MindJogger* to review the Chapter 8 content.

Visit the *Glencoe Communication Applications* Web site at **communicationapplications. glencoe.com** and click on **Chapter 8 Activity** for additional practice in interpersonal skills.

Reviewing Key Terms

1. c
2. f
3. a
4. b
5. d
6. g
7. e
8. h

Reviewing Key Terms

Read each definition. On a separate sheet of paper, write the number of the description and the letter of the term that fits the description best.

1. Helps a shy conversationalist participate
2. Etiquette used for official business or government dealings
3. Describes communication that has no specific individual reference or connection
4. Something that is satisfying within itself
5. Requires a very specific, one-word answer
6. A negative evaluation that brings about positive change
7. Repeat a message in your own words
8. People's willingness to accept differences in status within an organization

a. impersonal
b. intrinsic reward
c. open-ended question
d. closed question
e. paraphrase
f. protocol
g. constructive criticism
h. power distance

Reviewing Key Concepts

1. List the six characteristics of interpersonal communication.
2. What makes a relationship irreplaceable?
3. How do most conversations begin?
4. What are four strategies for participating effectively in a conversation?
5. What nonverbal communication behaviors provide the most valuable clues to how a speaker feels?
6. What effective questioning strategy is being used when a speaker asks, "Will a ten-page paper on *The Scarlet Letter* be satisfactory, or should it be longer?"
7. Imagine that you are invited to an awards dinner to be honored for establishing a food pantry in your community. How would you acknowledge a public introduction by the mayor to a roomful of civic leaders?
8. Give two reasons for identifying yourself and your company when answering phone calls.

Reviewing Key Concepts

1. unique, irreplaceable, interdependent, self-disclosing, rewarding, and scarce
2. uniqueness
3. with small talk
4. (1) Choose an appropriate topic. (2) Ask effective questions. (3) Use tact. (4) Balance speaking and listening.
5. Students' responses should include posture, eye contact, and tone of voice.
6. open-ended questioning
7. Students' answers will vary but should be similar to the following response: "Thank you, Mr. or Ms. Mayor. I am honored to be with such a distinguished group tonight."
8. (1) Clear identification assures the caller that he or she has reached the correct party. (2) The caller knows whether he or she has reached the correct business; he or she can retrace the call if he or she is disconnected.

Assessment and Activities

Reading and Critical Thinking Skill

1. **Applying Information** Describe the characteristics of a unique relationship.

2. **Classifying Information** Under which topic of small talk would you classify a discussion about the temperature?

3. **Synthesis** Suppose you are the dominant speaker in a conversation about automobiles. Synthesize a question that encourages another participant to contribute to the conversation.

4. **Making Contrasts** How do requests for information and persuasive requests differ?

5. **Recognizing Cause and Effect** What are two possible effects of violating the rules of professional etiquette with a potential employer?

Skill Practice Activity

Evaluating Criticism Read the following criticism from a teacher to a student. On a separate sheet of paper, rewrite the paragraph using strategies for constructive criticism.

"Your essays are getting worse, and you obviously spend little time on them. If your lazy thinking and writing persist, your grade in this class will suffer. Improve the quality of your next paper. Otherwise, you'll fail this course."

Cooperative Learning Activity

Giving Directions As a class, organize into small groups. As a group, choose a site within the school building and write a set of directions from the classroom to that site. Address a short letter to the members of another group and leave it at the selected site. Exchange sets of directions with another group. Follow the directions you now have and retrieve the letter from the site selected by the other group. Return to the classroom and evaluate the directions you used.

Chapter Project

Planning Select a video in which culture, ethnicity, gender, or age affects the communication between two characters. Possible choices are *The Searchers, Prince of Egypt, Yentl,* and *Treasure of the Sierra Madre.* As you watch the video, write descriptions of several scenes in which characters deal ineffectively with their differences. Afterwards, rewrite the dialogue of one of the scenes to make the characters more open to new ideas and less likely to stereotype each other.

Presenting In class, show scenes from the video in which characters are dealing ineffectively with differences. Read your rewritten dialogue to the class and sum up how the movie would end differently if the characters used effective communication. Discuss whether the rewrites make the movie more or less entertaining.

Developing Effective Interpersonal Skills **271**

Reading and Critical Thinking Skill

1. **Applying Information** Students' answers should explain that people who share a unique relationship view each other as being special in some way, talk to each other in a way that others cannot identify with, and rarely need to clarify their words or thoughts with each other.

2. **Classifying Information** environmental

3. **Synthesis** Students' responses may be similar to the following question: "Which car manufacturer do you think has improved most over the last decade?"

4. **Making Contrasts** Requests for information seek answers while persuasive requests ask for action.

5. **Recognizing Cause and Effect** Students' answers should include at least two of the following responses: a lasting bad impression, a lost opportunity, and a reputation as a poor communicator.

Skill Practice Activity

Evaluating Criticism

Students' responses may be similar to the following example. "Your essays are unorganized and full of misspellings. If they continue to show poor planning and little attention to details such as spelling, your grade in this class will suffer. For your next essay, make an outline and follow it. Use a dictionary while you write. Otherwise, your grade will be a D."

Cooperative Learning Activity

Giving Directions

Before students write their directions, remind them to arrange the steps in order, avoid assumptions, and provide specific details. When they return to the classroom, have them ask these questions: Were the directions arranged in order? Did any part of the directions assume knowledge the reader did not have? How could the directions have been made clearer?

Chapter Project

Students' projects will vary with the video that each chooses. You may want to show a scene from *The Searchers* in which John Wayne denigrates Native Americans. As a class, rewrite the dialogue so that Wayne's character appears more open-minded. Have students use this rewrite as a model for their own rewrites. Encourage students to work together and act out rewritten scenes for the class.

Chapter 9 Planning Guide

SECTION RESOURCES

Daily Objectives

Section 1

1. Analyze the roles in the interview process
2. Describe the different types of interviews and identify an appropriate situation for each
3. Explain the importance of communicating effectively in interviews

Section 2

1. Identify and describe the components of the interview process
2. Explain the steps needed to prepare for an interview
3. Distinguish the basic components of an interview
4. Explain the importance of the activities in the post interview

Section 3

1. Explain why appropriateness is important in an interview
2. Develop appropriate questions for an interview
3. Recognize unlawful interview questions
4. Determine what constitutes appropriate dress and demeanor for an interview

Reproducible Resources

 Reproducible Lesson Plan 9-1
 Application Activities 9-1
 Guided Reading Workbook Activity 9-1
 Vocabulary Activity 9*
 Reteaching Activity 9-1*
 Enrichment Activity 9-1*
 Graphic Organizer Transparency Strategies and Activities 9-1

 Reproducible Lesson Plan 9-2
 Application Activities 9-2
 Guided Reading Workbook Activity 9-2
 Vocabulary Activity 9*
 Reteaching Activity 9-2*
 Enrichment Activity 9-2*
 Graphic Organizer Transparency Strategies and Activities 9-2

 Reproducible Lesson Plan 9-3
 Application Activities 9-3
 Guided Reading Workbook Activity 9-3
 Vocabulary Activity 9*
 Reteaching Activity 9-3*
 Enrichment Activity 9-3*
 Graphic Organizer Transparency Strategies and Activities 9-3

Multimedia Resources

 Graphic Organizer Transparency 9-1
 Chapter 9 Teaching Transparency
 Interactive Tutor Self-Assessment
PuzzleMaker
 ExamView® Pro Testmaker
 Interactive Lesson Planner
 Communication in Action Video Chapter 9
 MindJogger
 communicationapplications.glencoe.com
Presentation Plus!

 Graphic Organizer Transparency 9-2
Chapter 9 Teaching Transparency
 Interactive Tutor Self-Assessment
PuzzleMaker
 ExamView® Pro Testmaker
 Interactive Lesson Planner
 Communication in Action Video Chapter 9
 MindJogger
communicationapplications.glencoe.com
Presentation Plus!

 Graphic Organizer Transparency 9-3
 Chapter 9 Teaching Transparency
Interactive Tutor Self-Assessment
PuzzleMaker
 ExamView® Pro Testmaker
 Interactive Lesson Planner
 Communication in Action Video Chapter 9
MindJogger
 communicationapplications.glencoe.com
Presentation Plus!

* Also available in Spanish

Chapter 9 Planning Guide

FOR THE TEACHER

Interviewing

Ask students to imagine that they are on a committee that has the responsibility of hiring a person to organize their school's college and career fair. Write five questions that they would ask an applicant for the job. Then, have them meet with a small group of classmates. Instruct the groups to pool their questions and decide on the ten that will best help them carry out their responsibility.

Direct the students to work in pairs with one member of each pair acting as an interviewer and one as an interviewee. Each pair should carry out its interview, using the questions their group developed, in front of the group. As a group, ask students to discuss the most and least effective techniques used by interviewers and interviewees.

CHAPTER RESOURCES

Resources for the Teacher

- *The Essential Book of Interviewing* by Arnold B. Kanter, Random House, 1995
- *Interview for Success* by Caryl Rae Krannich and Ronald L. Krannich, Ph.D.s, Impact Publications, 1997
- *Knock 'Em Dead 2000: The Ultimate Job-Seeker's Handbook* by Martin Yate, Adams Media Corporation, 2000

Resources for the Student

- *From Campus to Corporation: Successful Career Strategies for Students* by Stephen Strasser, Ph.D., and John Sena, Ph.D., Career Press, 1993
- *If You're Clueless About Getting a Great Job and Want to Know More* by Seth Godin and Beth Burns, Dearborn Financial Publishing Inc., 1998

Block Scheduling

Block scheduling differs from traditional class scheduling in the amount of time allotted to each period. The extended time frame provided by block scheduling affords you the opportunity to implement a greater number of research-oriented and activity-intense projects to motivate and involve your students. Activities that are particularly suited to use within the block-scheduling framework are identified throughout this chapter by the following designation:

KEY TO ABILITY LEVELS

Teaching Strategies have been coded for varying learning styles and abilities.

L1 **BASIC** activities for all students

L2 **AVERAGE** activities for average to above-average students

L3 **CHALLENGING** activities for above-average students

ELL **English Language Learner** activities

 Blackline Master   CD-ROM

 Software   Transparency

Videodisc   Videocassette

 Web site

 Use Glencoe's *Presentation Plus!* multimedia teacher tool to easily present dynamic lessons that engage and motivate your students. Using Microsoft PowerPoint®, you can customize the presentations to create your own personalized lessons.

Chapter 9 Resource Manager

The following materials may be used when teaching the chapter. Materials for specific lessons are also shown at point-of-use in the margins of the Teacher's Wraparound Edition.

TEACHING TRANSPARENCIES

Chapter 9 Teaching Transparency

Graphic Organizer Transparency 9–1

Graphic Organizer Transparency 9–2

Graphic Organizer Transparency 9–3

APPLICATION ACTIVITIES

Chapter 9, Section 1

Chapter 9, Section 2

Chapter 9, Section 3

Chapter 9, Cumulative

REINFORCEMENT AND REVIEW ACTIVITIES

Vocabulary Activity 9

Guided Reading Activity
Workbook 9-1, 9-2, 9-3

Reteaching Activities
9-1, 9-2, 9-3

Chapter 9 Resource Manager

ASSESSMENT AND EVALUATION

GLENCOE'S
ASSESSMENT
ADVANTAGE

Section Quizzes 9–1, 9–2, 9–3

Chapter 9 Test, Forms A & B

Performance Assessment
Activity 9

ENRICHMENT AND EXTENSION

Technology Application
Activity 9

Enrichment Activities
9–1, 9–2, 9–3

SPANISH RESOURCES

- 📁 Spanish Chapter and Unit Tests
- 📁 Spanish Vocabulary Activities
- 📁 Spanish Section Quizzes
- 📁 Spanish Reteaching Activities
- 📁 Spanish Enrichment Activities

MULTIMEDIA

- Interactive Tutor Self-Assessment
- ExamView® Pro Testmaker
- PuzzleMaker
- Communication in Action Videodisc and Videocassette
- MindJogger
- Interactive Lesson Planner
- Presentation Plus!
- Writer's Assistant
- Glencoe Interactive Grammar
- **communicationapplications.glencoe.com**

TEACHER PLANNING AND SUPPORT

- Reproducible Lesson Plans
- Interactive Lesson Planner
- Presentation Plus!

CHAPTER 9

Exploring the Interview Process

WHY IT'S IMPORTANT

An interview generally is a small window of time in which you have the opportunity to present your "best" self to others. When you understand and master the interview process, you should be able to positively impact the outcome of many situations.

To better understand the nature of interviews, view the **Communication in Action** Chapter 9 video lesson.

272 *Glencoe Communication Applications*

"The important thing is to never stop questioning."
—Albert Einstein, American physicist

WHY IT'S IMPORTANT

Ask for a show of hands of students who have participated in a job interview. Then, ask how many expect to participate in a job interview sometime in the future. Point out that effective interviewing is a learned skill. Ask: **How might learning this skill affect your future?** *(Answers may include that it will enable them to present themselves better at job interviews and thus help increase the likelihood of getting the jobs.)*

Section 1

The Nature of Interviews

GUIDE TO READING

Objectives

1. Analyze the roles in the interview process.
2. Describe the different types of interviews and identify an appropriate situation for each.
3. Explain the importance of communicating effectively in interviews.

Terms to Learn

interview
interviewer
interviewee
information-gathering interview
survey interview
investigative interview
exit interview
information-giving interview
performance appraisal
counseling interview
employment interview

*Y*ou've found an ad in your hometown newspaper for part-time employment at a popular fast-food restaurant. The hours are perfect, the pay is good, and you feel that you have all the necessary skills and abilities to perform the tasks. You're qualified, but is the job yours?

People often believe that the only important consideration in getting a job is whether they can do the work. However, being qualified may not be enough. If you cannot communicate your qualifications and do not know how to conduct yourself during an interview, you may not be hired.

On the other hand, if you learn to communicate effectively and conduct yourself appropriately in an interview, you may increase your chances of getting the job you want. Not only can interviewing skills help you in the job market, but they also may help you communicate successfully in a variety of other situations.

For instance, when you question the president of your senior class for a yearbook story, conduct a telephone poll of local citizens, or try to get the perfect summer job, you are engaged in an interview situation. Although each type of interview is different, they all have set roles and a specific purpose.

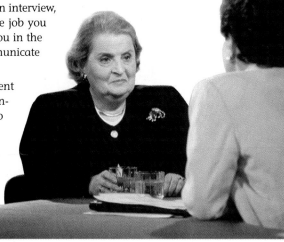

A television journalist interviews Madeleine Albright. How are all types of interviews similar?

Exploring the Interview Process **273**

---

1 FOCUS

Bellringer

Ask students to consider several types of important information that an employer can obtain from a job applicant during an interview. Have students write one question they would ask if they were an employer interviewing job applicants. Then, have them write one question they would want to be asked if they were applying for a job.

You may use Graphic Organizer Transparency 9–1 to introduce this section.

Graphic Organizer Transparency 9–1

Application Activities 9–1

Visual Instruction

Answer All types of interviews involve two parties in which one party has a set purpose and the other gives information.

RESOURCE MANAGER

Teaching Tools

- Interactive Lesson Planner
- Reproducible Lesson Plan 9–1
- Application Activities 9–1

Reproducible Masters

- Guided Reading Activity Workbook 9–1
- Enrichment Activity 9–1
- Reteaching Activity 9–1
- Section Quiz 9–1
- Transparency Strategies and Activities Booklet 9–1

Transparencies

- Graphic Organizer Transparency 9–1
- Chapter 9 Teaching Transparency

Technology Resources

- Interactive Tutor Self-Assessment Software
- Presentation Plus! Software
- ExamView® Pro Testmaker
- PuzzleMaker Software
- communicationapplications.glencoe.com

2 TEACH

Observing Interviews

Point out that students can frequently observe interviews on television. Ask students to describe a specific interview they have seen on TV in which the interviewer clearly set a goal and structure, asked well-prepared questions, and controlled the direction of the interview. Then, ask volunteers to describe a specific interview in which these responsibilities were not carried out. What were the results in each case? **L1**

■ Visual Instruction

Answer Interviewing allows one to make a well-informed choice by obtaining the information necessary for that choice.

Guided Reading Activity 9–1

Name _____ Date _____ Class _____

EXPLORING THE INTERVIEW PROCESS
The Nature of Interviews

GUIDED READING
Activity 9–1

As you read Section 1, complete the sentences.

1. An _____ is a formal two-party communication in which at least one of the participants has a set _____. The two roles in this process are the _____, who asks the questions, and the _____, who answers the questions.
2. The interviewer's responsibilities are to set the _____ and _____ of the interview, prepare and ask _____, and control the _____ of the discussion.
3. The interviewee's responsibilities are to provide complete, clear, well-thought-out, and _____ answers, and to gather additional _____.
4. In _____ interviews, an interviewer obtains information from an interviewee. There are two types of these interviews: _____, in which the interviewer gathers information from a number of people, and _____, in which the interviewer uses questions to find out unknown information.
5. An _____ interview is used to determine _____ a person has decided to _____ an organization.
6. There are two forms of _____ interviews, in which an interviewer gives information to an interviewee. They are a _____ interviews, which is an evaluation of how well you have achieved your goals and _____ over a set period of time, and a _____ interview, in which the interviewer helps the interviewee decide on a course of action.
7. An _____ interview is a process for judging whether a _____ candidate is qualified and well suited for a position. The employer investigates a prospective employee's _____ to determine if he or she is best suited for the job.
8. Communication _____ and a knowledge of _____ can be more important to a successful interview than grade-point average or work _____.
9. A _____ is a brief history of a person's education and work experience. Often employers will review this first and then grant an _____ if he or she feels the person is suitable for the job.
10. Besides interviewing on site at the company, interviews can be held at a job center, in a _____ conference room, or elsewhere. Most off-site interview locations are chosen for their convenience to the _____ or the _____.

ROLES IN THE INTERVIEW PROCESS

An interview is a formal two-party communication in which at least one of the participants has a set purpose. Interviewing allows you to give and receive information through the use of questions and answers. This specific type of communication calls for using excellent listening skills, asking appropriate questions, and giving appropriate answers. It also requires an understanding of the roles people assume in an interview.

There are two main roles in the interview process: the interviewer and the interviewee. The interviewer is the one who determines the purpose of the interview and ensures that the discussion remains focused on the purpose. The interviewee is the one who provides information to the interviewer. In order to have a successful interview, both parties must participate fully. In other words, both must ask questions, listen to each other's responses, and then provide feedback to each other.

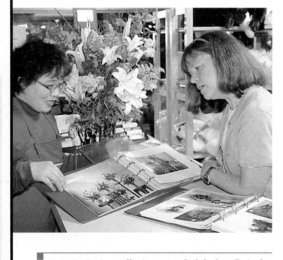

Interviewing is an effective way to find the best florist for a formal event. What does interviewing allow one to do?

Imagine that you are on the planning committee for your senior prom. Your task is to interview local florists and select one to create flower arrangements for the tables. As the interviewer, your main responsibility is to ask questions that will help you determine which florist will best meet your needs. Closely tied to this is another important responsibility: You also need to listen carefully to the florists' answers.

In this interview, both parties must participate and listen even though their goals are different. As the interviewer, you will provide information to each florist about your expectations regarding color, style, budget limitations, and date of delivery. As the interviewee, the florist needs to listen to your needs and respond by showing you examples of floral arrangements that meet those needs. In turn, you need to listen to what each florist has to say and decide which one has the most to offer. Although these roles overlap somewhat, each participant in the interview has a specific set of responsibilities.

The Interviewer

In most cases, the interviewer drives the interview. In other words, he or she has the responsibility of setting up the interview and carrying it out. The interviewer's main responsibilities are to set the goal and structure of the interview, prepare and ask questions, and control the direction of the discussion.

Set a Goal. A goal defines what you would want the outcome of the interview to be. For example, if you were to interview a veterinarian about his or her career field, your goal might be to find out what type of education and experience are required. A different goal might be to find out about new advances in animal medicine. In the workplace, an interviewer might have a goal to hire an employee to work the evening shift.

INTERDISCIPLINARY CONNECTION

Social Studies Point out that information about government, including legislation, elections, and international politics, is frequently presented on television in the form of interviews.
Activity Have students view an interview regarding government on a television news program or talk show. Have them prepare an overview of the interview. The overview should indicate the interview participants, the interviewer's goal, some sample questions and answers, a summary of the information presented, and an evaluation of the interviewer and the interviewee. Have students share their reports in small groups.

■ **Figure 9–1 Interviewer Controls Direction**

Responsibilities of Interviewers

On the chalkboard, write the four main responsibilities of interviewers. Then, have volunteers define each responsibility. Ask other volunteers to give an example of each responsibility from their observation or from their own experience. **L1**

Grammar Tip

Often, when two words are used as a single modifier before a noun, the words are hyphenated, as in *follow-up interviews* and *customer-service skills*. When the words are used after a noun or are not used as a modifier, as in "My experience is in customer service," they are not hyphenated.

Develop the Structure. The structure of an interview is the manner in which it is conducted. Most interviews involve only the interviewer and the interviewee. However, a team or group interview may be set up so that a group of people ask questions of the interviewee. This is often done in a job interview if the applicant would be working with a team or would be supervised by several bosses. Another structure might be to have the initial interview with one person and then follow-up interviews with other individuals if the first interview was successful.

Prepare and Ask Questions. A qualified interviewer does not simply arrive at an interview ready to "wing it." Instead, he or she will prepare a list of appropriate questions ahead of time. The interviewer will then ask these questions to help meet the goal of the interview.

If the goal of an interview is to determine whether the interviewee has good customer-service skills, the interviewer probably will prepare and ask questions that revolve around customer-service situations. If the goal of an interview is to determine whether a new school rule is appropriate, the interviewer's

questions might focus on why the rule was created, how it will be enforced, and what the expected results are.

Control the Direction of the Discussion. As **Figure 9–1** indicates, in an interview, the interviewer keeps the discussion focused and moving toward the goal. He or she makes sure that the interviewee actually answers the specific questions and does not avoid them or talk around them.

Suppose an interviewer were to ask, "Why did you leave your last job?" and the interviewee replied, "I really want to work here." The interviewee avoided the question. It is the responsibility of the interviewer to maintain focus and get the interview back on track.

The Interviewee

Many people mistakenly believe that, because the interviewer controls the direction of the interview, he or she is the only one responsible for successful communication. It is important to understand, however, that interviewees also have the responsibilities of providing clear, complete, and appropriate answers and of gathering information.

Exploring the Interview Process **275**

COOPERATIVE LEARNING ACTIVITY

Have each student prepare a list of three questions regarding extracurricular activities that could be asked of all students. Encourage students to be as specific as possible. For example, they could ask, "Which activity that you participate in do you think will be most useful for you in a future career?" Then, have pairs of students take turns interviewing each other based on their questions. Instruct students to focus on controlling the direction of the interview when they are serving as interviewers. After both students have completed their interviews, have the pairs repeat the interviews. This time, instruct interviewees to answer questions in an unsatisfactory manner, as in the example on this page. Challenge the interviewers to regain control of the interview and to obtain satisfactory answers.

Improving Vague Answers

Discuss the importance of being not only clear, but also specific and thorough in answering interview questions. Read the following responses that might be provided in a job interview. Ask students to tell how each one might be made more specific.

"My favorite activities are sports related."

"As a camp counselor, I had a variety of duties."

"I do well in most of my classes." **L2**

ractice for the Workplace

The Importance of Perspective
Have students identify the perspective of each of the following questions as *interviewer* or *interviewee:*

Do you object to working after 9:00 P.M.? *(interviewer)* Does the job require working after 9:00 P.M.? *(interviewee)* Is the workday steady, or are there periods with very little work to do? *(interviewee)* Would you dislike a job that had some hectic periods and some very slow periods? *(interviewer)* Do you offer training of the skills required for the job? (interviewee) Do you already know how to use a cash register? *(interviewer)*

After discussing the entire chapter, you can ask students to review the questions generated in this exercise to determine whether they asked illegal questions, if they think they should include more structure, and label the types of questions they generated. **L2**

■ **Visual Instruction**

Answer In order to learn more about the company and job to determine whether the position fits his or her needs

Provide Clear, Complete, and Appropriate Answers. Imagine that an interviewer asks you what duties you had in your last job. To answer, you simply say, "I had a lot of different responsibilities." Did you thoroughly answer the interviewer's question? This type of vague answer doesn't really tell the interviewer anything about your specific experience.

It is the responsibility of the interviewee to provide clearly worded, well-thought-out answers. Clear, complete answers help the interviewee convey information to the interviewer without any need for interpretation. In addition, thinking about your response before actually voicing it can help you avoid making misleading or confusing statements.

To provide appropriate answers in an interview, it is essential to listen. Often, interviewees concentrate too much on what they want to say in an interview and too little on

276 *Glencoe Communication Applications*

ractice for the Workplace

The Importance of Perspective As you prepare for a job interview, whether as the interviewer or the interviewee, it is helpful to consider the other person's point of view. Try to visualize the interview from more than one perspective. If you are preparing to hire a cook for a restaurant, for example, you may consider asking an applicant if he or she has any experience making pasta sauces. The cook, preparing for the same interview, might ask to see what pasta sauces are on the menu. Both parties have similar concerns, but they are viewed from different perspectives.

BUSINESS PRACTICE *Activity*

Suppose you are the owner of a limousine service in a major city. You need to hire a new driver. Develop a series of questions you would ask the applicants. Next, as a potential applicant for the same job, develop a list of questions you would ask the interviewer. Are the two sets of questions related in any way? Do the two sides have any mutual concerns? Compare your results.

what they need to hear. Remember, to answer a question appropriately, you need to hear and understand it first.

Gather Information. Although an interviewee's main responsibility is to provide information, he or she also may need to gather certain information. This responsibility occurs most often when interviewing for a job.

■ **Job responsibilities for employees in a grocery store range from running the cash register to bagging groceries. Why is it important for an interviewee to gather information during an interview?**

MULTIPLE LEARNING STYLES

Musical Using the question-and-answer format of interviews creatively can help students learn how to and how not to answer questions in an interview.

Activity Have small groups of students write a short song illustrating a job interview situation. Instruct them to write two versions of their song: one in which the interviewee answers all questions clearly and thoroughly, and one in which he or she does not. When the songs have been written, have members of each group perform the *Do* and *Don't* versions of their songs for the class.

The purpose of a job interview is not only to allow an interviewer to learn more about an individual. It also is designed to help the interviewee learn more about the company and the job. By asking specific, appropriate questions, an interviewee can better determine whether a company or position fits his or her needs.

For example, suppose you are interviewing for a part-time cashier position at a local grocery store. The manager explains that the job will require you to work fifteen hours per week, including some weekends. As a member of your school band, you have a standing Friday evening commitment during football season. If you tell the manager that you are unavailable Friday evenings and ask if that is a problem, you'll have a better idea if the position is a good choice for you. Your question also will help the manager decide whether you are right for the company. Realistically, if one of the two people in the interview finds that the situation is not a good match, it may be best not to offer or take a position just to have a job.

It is clear that interviewers and interviewees have specific responsibilities in interview situations. It also is clear that, in order to have a successful interview, both must be effective communicators. Listening carefully, asking questions, and answering clearly and appropriately all are important communication skills that can make or break an interview. Other factors in determining the role and responsibility of interviewer and interviewee are the type of interview being conducted and its purpose.

TYPES OF INTERVIEWS

From what you have read so far in this section, you probably have concluded that not all interviews are alike. A job interview, for example, would be different from interviewing the principal about a new rule or interviewing florists for the prom. Interviews vary because they are conducted for different reasons. Thus, interviews are categorized by type. The three main types of interviews are as follows:

- information-gathering
- information-giving
- employment

COMMUNICATION PRACTICE LAB

Determining Roles and Responsibilities

To practice determining your specific role and responsibilities in an interview, follow these steps:

Step 1 Imagine that you are a staff member of your school newspaper and you are going to interview a fellow student about an accomplishment. You have arranged to meet tomorrow to discuss it. On a sheet of paper, write your role and the other student's role in the interview.

Step 2 List each party's main goal or purpose for the interview.

Step 3 List two specific responsibilities for each party in this interview situation.

Step 4 Share your answers as a class and discuss how your goals and responsibilities might change if the roles were reversed.

Exploring the Interview Process **277**

MEETING INDIVIDUAL NEEDS — MULTIPLE LEARNING STYLES

Linguistic Students may have forgotten about interviews they have participated in or may think narrowly of interviews as always being in employment situations. Writing summaries of interviews they have participated in can help students recall previous interview experiences and learn from them.

Activity Ask students to recall any of the three types of interviews in which they have participated. Have them write a summary of one memorable interview. Instruct them to identify their role as interviewer or interviewee, state the purpose of the interview, summarize the body of the interview, and describe the outcome.

GLENCOE Online

For an additional Practice Lab for this section, students can visit the *Glencoe Communication Applications* Web site at **communicationapplications.glencoe.com.** Click on Communication Practice Lab 9–1. **L1**

Survey Interviews

Ask students to brainstorm topics for which survey interviews are often used. They may know of general kinds of surveys, or those in which they or their parents have participated. Also have students discuss ways in which the interviews are conducted.

(Examples include surveys about election candidates, political issues, television programs, movies, radio stations, restaurants, and stores. Interviews may be conducted in person by appointment, on the street, on the phone, or on exiting a store, theater, or polling place.) **L2**

DID YOU KNOW?

The Gallup Organization conducts surveys before elections to predict the percentage of votes for each candidate. In twelve presidential elections between 1936 and 1984, the average error in the final poll was less than .03 percent.

Language Tip

In writing résumés and cover letters and participating in job interviews, use strong action verbs such as *accomplished, initiated,* and *created* to describe your previous experience.

Information-Gathering

An information-gathering interview is one in which an interviewer obtains information from an interviewee. The interviewer usually does this through a survey or an investigation.

Survey Interviews Survey interviews gather information from a number of people. The information is used to draw conclusions, make interpretations, and determine future action. Survey interviews also are used to find out consumers' reactions to a product. For example, you might be asked in a grocery store to taste several different juice drinks, such as the ones shown in **Figure 9–2**, and give your opinion about which one you like best. This information helps the juice drink companies understand what consumers like and dislike about their product. They can then make changes, if necessary, to better meet the customers' needs.

Survey interviews also are used to gather information about people's reactions to change or new ideas. For example, imagine your school is thinking about changing its dress code to specify uniforms. The student council may conduct a survey interview to find out how the student body and parents will feel about the change. The information they gather may influence the way the school puts its new uniform rule into effect. You will receive information about preparing a survey in Chapter 14.

Investigative Interview An interview in which the interviewer uses questions to find out unknown information is known as an investigative interview. This information often is used to determine the cause of an event.

The types of questions generally asked in an investigative interview are *Who, What, When, Where, Why,* and *How.* For example, suppose a student in a neighboring school was awarded a four-year scholarship to a famous university. Your school guidance counselor wants to investigate how the student won the scholarship to determine if students at your school might be eligible. To make that determination, the counselor, or interviewer, might ask the following questions:

- *"Who* was the recipient of the scholarship?"
- *"What* were the criteria for the award?"
- *"When* was the deadline for applications?"
- *"Where* did the student obtain the information?"
- *"Why* was the student chosen?"
- *"How* will the scholarship monies be distributed?"

A business will often use investigative interviews among its employees to discover what is needed for the development of products and services. Journalists depend upon investigative interviews to develop the lines of information upon which they base their stories. Detectives and lawyers depend heavily upon investigative interviews while attempting to solve crimes or develop cases.

Another type of investigative interview is called an exit interview. An exit interview is used to determine why a person has decided to

■ **Figure 9–2 Product Samples**

FRESHER FRUIT JUICE

VERY VEGETABLE JUICE

REAL-WORLD CONNECTION

Survey Organizations Several organizations are dedicated to gathering information through surveys. For example, the Gallup Poll conducts survey interviews on political issues, political candidates, and lifestyle issues. Nielsen Media Research gathers information through surveys about the public's reading, listening, and viewing habits. It is especially well-known for its television surveys.

Activity Have students research, on the Internet or in a library, a survey organization such as the two mentioned above to find out what kinds of information they gather, who they survey, and how they conduct survey interviews. Have students share their findings in oral reports.

A reporter holds an investigative interview. **What types of questions are asked in an investigative interview?**

leave an organization. Companies often conduct exit interviews at the end of employment or involvement of a person in an organization to determine why employees leave for other jobs. If they discover that several employees have left because of a troublesome manager or a poor benefits package, they may decide to make changes before others leave. Schools also might arrange exit interviews to determine why students resign from school clubs and organizations. Exit interviews can give them the information they need to keep their membership strong.

Information-Giving

An information-giving interview is one in which an interviewer gives information to an interviewee. Two commonly used information-giving interviews are performance appraisals and counseling interviews.

Performance Appraisal

An evaluation of how well you have achieved your goals and objectives over a set period of time is called a performance appraisal. As **Figure 9–3** shows, when you get your grade card, you have received a type of written performance appraisal. This type of interview most often occurs face-to-face, such as when an employer talks to an employee about job performance.

Counseling Interview

A counseling interview generally occurs when an interviewer helps the interviewee decide on a course of action. For example, you might talk to a school counselor about scheduling your classes or choosing a college. A social worker or family counselor may use counseling interviews to help individuals solve difficult personal problems. In both cases, the counselor shares his or her expertise with the interviewee to achieve a positive result.

Figure 9–3 School Performance Appraisal

SUBJECT	GRADE
Language Arts	A+
Algebra	A+
Physical Science	A+
World History	A+

Exploring the Interview Process **279**

Asking Investigative Questions

Discuss the importance of investigative interviews in many careers. Ask students to name people besides journalists, detectives, and lawyers who must use investigative interviews in their work. *(Answers may include doctors and nurses, insurance employees, and school administrators.)* Have students think of a local, national, or international news issue that interests them. Ask them to write a list of investigative questions they could use to gain a thorough knowledge of the issue. **L3**

Visual Instruction

Answer Who, what, when, where, why, and how questions are asked in an investigative interview.

BUSINESS BRIEF

In her book *Interviewing*, Arlene S. Hirsch offers specific advice for mealtime interviews. She advises, "Don't order the most expensive meal on the menu, don't start eating before your host, don't order food that's likely to splatter, like soup or pasta, and use good manners at all times." Ask students to offer other advice for people who have a job interview in a restaurant.

GIFTED AND TALENTED

Investigative Interviews Students may have specific careers that they are interested in researching and perhaps pursuing someday. They can use investigative interviews to find out more about a chosen career.

Activity Have students choose a career that interests them and write a list of investigative questions they could use to interview a person in that career. Encourage students to use at least one of each kind of question—who, what, when, where, why, and how—to get as much specific information as possible from the interviewee. Then, you may wish to have students use their questions to actually interview a person in their chosen career. If so, they may share reports on their interviews in small groups. Otherwise, they may share their lists of questions with their groups.

Importance of Job Interviews

Emphasize the importance of making a good first impression by having good interview skills. Discuss how first impressions affect individuals in everyday life. Ask the following questions: What qualities in a new acquaintance make you want to know the person better? What characteristics in an acquaintance might discourage you from knowing the person better? What experiences have you had in which your first impression was mistaken? What led to a mistaken first impression? Point out that in a job interview, an interviewee has the opportunity to make the first impression as positive as possible. **L1**

3 ASSESS

Assign Section 1 Assessment as a homework or in-class activity.

⊕ Use *Interactive Tutor Self-Assessment Software* to review Section 1.

By permission of Mell Lazarus and Creators Syndicate.

Employment

A common type of interview is an employment interview. An employment interview is a process employers use to judge whether a job candidate is qualified and well suited for a position. During an employment interview, an employer investigates a prospective employee's experience, motivation, education, and personality, among other considerations, and decides who of the interviewees is best suited for the job.

Importance People often do not realize how important employment interviews can be. However, in a poll of personnel executives, the Bureau of National Affairs discovered that the employment interview was the single most important factor in landing a job. The executives went on to say that communication skills and a knowledge of interviewing were even more important to a successful interview than grade-point average or work experience.

Employers use interviews to size up the whole individual. Does this person know how to communicate in a professional environment? Will he or she be able to make sound decisions? Does the applicant know how to communicate appropriately and effectively? Does he or she possess the interpersonal skills to work well with others in this office? Is he or she qualified to meet the responsibilities of

the job? Because so many of your qualities are being evaluated in a short period of time, it is important to make your best possible impression on the interviewer. For this reason, it is critical to master the skill of interviewing effectively.

Building Skills Now is the time to develop strong interviewing skills. The way to build these valuable skills is through study and practice. To begin, take a look at how companies advertise job openings to attract the right candidates. Notices for employment can be found in newspapers' classified advertising sections, on radio and television, through your school counselor, by word of mouth, on school or community bulletin boards, or on the Internet. Careful study of these employment ads may indicate what you need to be prepared for in an interview.

Some positions require that applicants phone first or send a brief letter with a résumé. A résumé is a brief history of your education and work experience. In many cases, an employer will review an applicant's résumé first and then only grant an interview if he or she feels the person is suitable for the job. A well-written résumé not only may get you through the door, but it may give you a strong base of information to expand upon in the interview itself.

280 *Glencoe Communication Applications*

Section 1 Assessment Answers

1. Accept all reasonable sentences.
2. In both roles, parties give and receive information and are involved in achieving the goal of the interview. However, it is the responsibility of the interviewer to set a goal for the interview and then to control the interview so that it achieves that goal. An interviewee's role is to listen carefully to the interviewer and to provide any information that will help him or her achieve the goal.
3. Information-gathering interview: a reporter interviewing a fire chief about the cause of a fire; information-giving interview: a sales manager giving a performance appraisal to a salesperson; employment interview: a student interviewing for a part-time job as a pizza delivery driver.
4. Many other characteristics besides job experience are evaluated during an employment interview. If you learn to communicate effectively and conduct yourself professionally in an interview,

Employment Interview Variations

Most of the time, employment interviews are conducted on-site, which means at the company where the job is being offered. However, some employment interviews may be held at a job fair, in a hotel conference room, on the telephone, at a convention center, over dinner or sodas at a restaurant, or elsewhere. Most off-site interview locations are chosen for their convenience to the interviewer or the interviewee.

In this section you have learned about the roles of the participants in an interview and about the different types of interviews. You also may have noticed that every type of interview has a specific purpose. However, how is this purpose met? Each type of interview has a special interview process, or order of events. Understanding this process will help you prepare for your own interviews in the community and the workplace.

Section 1 Assessment

GLENCOE Online

Visit the *Glencoe Communication Applications* Web site at **communicationapplications. glencoe.com** and click on **Self-Check and Study Guide 9.1** to review your understanding of the nature of interviews.

Review Key Terms

1. Define each term and write it in a sentence: interview, interviewer, interviewee, information-gathering interview, survey interview, investigative interview, exit interview, information-giving interview, performance appraisal, counseling interview, employment interview.

Check Understanding

2. Compare and contrast the roles of an interviewer and an interviewee.

3. Describe the three types of interviews and give one real-life example of each.

4. Explain the following statement: Communication skills can be even more important than your qualifications when interviewing for a job.

5. **Analyze** You have been selected to write a professional profile of your communication applications teacher for the school newspaper. What type of interview would you use? Give three questions you might ask as the interviewer.

APPLICATION *Activity*

Developing Interview Goals Imagine that you would like to create a student-run computer help desk at your school. Before presenting your idea to the principal, you want to find out students' reactions to the idea. Create two columns on a sheet of paper. Label one column *Students* and one *Principal* and write the type of interview you might conduct with each. Then, in each column, list a goal you might have as the interviewer in that situation.

Exploring the Interview Process **281**

Section 1 Answers, continued

you may be selected over someone with more experience who communicates less effectively.
5. An investigative, or information-gathering, interview; students' questions should be structured to gather specific information about their teacher's professional education and experience.

Application Activity Students: Information-gathering survey, find out if students would use the center and volunteer to help run it; Principal: Information-giving interview, convince the principal to support the idea.

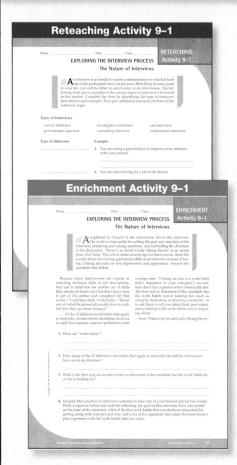

Reteaching Activity 9–1

EXPLORING THE INTERVIEW PROCESS
The Nature of Interviews

Enrichment Activity 9–1

EXPLORING THE INTERVIEW PROCESS
The Nature of Interviews

4 CLOSE

Have students reread the italicized paragraph on the first page of Section 1. Ask them to list three things they have learned about job interviews that might help them obtain the job described in the opener.

Extra-Credit Project

Have students work with a partner or small group to develop a survey topic and survey questions. Then, have them decide how to conduct survey interviews and administer the survey. Instruct students to come up with a specific, timely survey subject, such as the need for additional lunch options in the school cafeteria or for a multi-theater movie complex in the community.

Skimming for Information

Discuss specific situations in which skimming is a useful skill: to find out whether a particular text is useful for one's purpose, to preview a text before reading it in detail, to study for a test, or to look for specific information.

Point out that in an employment situation, an employer might skim résumés in order to screen applicants. What steps might an applicant take to get the employer's interest if he or she knows this is the case? *(Possible answers include making the résumé neat and easy to read; using key words and phrases that describe previous work experience; using eye-catching words and phrases such as* created, initiated, *or* energetic.*)* **L2**

Practicing the Skill

1. Emphasize that an employee handbook provides an employee with information about the employer's policies and expectations. The handbooks may describe rules and regulations, benefits, working hours, and so on.

2. If possible, have a variety of company and school district employee handbooks available for students to skim.

3. The information is most likely to be found in Chapter 8, Compensation Practices, and Chapter 10, Vacations and Holidays.

Application Activity

Summaries should mention the major elements of the policies and procedures without using unnecessary detail.

Applying Reading Skill

SKIMMING FOR INFORMATION

Skimming means quickly reading through a body of information in order to pick out key points or concepts.

Learning the Skill

Follow the guidelines listed below when skimming different materials.

- When skimming a book, start by looking at the table of contents or the index to get an overview of the entire body of information. Notice the titles of major chapters or sections, headings within sections, and lists. Use the index to find specific topics.

- If you are skimming an essay or other scholastic report, pay attention to the title and any major divisions.

- When skimming a memorandum, fax, or e-mail message, check the beginning of the message for a heading such as *Re:* or *Subject.*

Once you get to the main body of any source, always look for words or topics that are related to the specific information for which you are looking. Find the topic sentence in each paragraph. Always check information that is displayed in graphs, tables, charts, artwork, and photograph captions.

Practicing the Skill

Many companies supply their workers with employee handbooks. The handbooks provide information on company policies and practices. Assume that your supervisor has asked for volunteers to work on Thanksgiving Day. You are not sure what your company's policies are regarding holidays and overtime pay. In which chapters from the following employee handbook would you find information about these policies?

Employee Handbook

Table of Contents

APPLICATION *Activity*

Obtain a copy of the handbook that describes the policies and procedures of your school. Skim the handbook's table of contents to find your school's attendance policies and procedures. Write a brief paragragh that summarizes this information.

MEETING INDIVIDUAL NEEDS

INCLUSION STRATEGIES

Less-Proficient Readers Students may need further instruction and practice in skimming a text. **Activity** Find a page in this book that includes pictures, graphic aids, and several subheads. Demonstrate how to use each of these elements to gain an understanding of the general meaning of the page. Also point out two or three topic sentences. Explain that these give a general idea of the subject matter of the paragraphs in which they appear. Have volunteers summarize the information found on the page. Then, ask students to skim the page to find a particular fact or quotation. Finally, ask students to locate a book in the library on job hunting or job interviews. Have them bring to class one specific tip from the book or article on participating successfully in a job interview.

Section 2

Understanding the Interview Process

GUIDE TO READING

Objectives

1. Identify and describe the components of the interview process.
2. Explain the steps needed to prepare for an interview.
3. Distinguish the basic components of an interview.
4. Explain the importance of the activities in the post interview.

Terms to Learn

interview process
highly closed question
primary question
secondary question
leading question
neutral question

direct question
indirect question
factual question
opinion question
hypothetical question

*W*hat would happen if you worked at a fast-food establishment where none of the employees were assigned specific tasks? Who would take people's orders? Who would order supplies? Would several people rush to get beverages while no one cooked hamburgers? How effective do you think this operation would be in the long run?

Clearly, if no one were assigned specific duties, the process of operating a fast-food restaurant would be inefficient. Customers and employees alike probably would become frustrated and go elsewhere.

Like a fast-food restaurant, almost every endeavor needs a plan or structure that the participants understand and follow. An interview is no different. It consists of more than just two people showing up to talk to each other. Instead, it is a planned process. The interview process is a sequence of actions that results in an effective interview. This process includes preparation, the actual interview, and the post interview.

The efficiency of a fast-food restaurant is determined by the process by which the food is prepared and served.
What does the process of the interview include?

Exploring the Interview Process **283**

2 TEACH

Setting Goals

Discuss the importance of setting goals. Have students write a brief description of a goal they have set for themselves in the past few months. For example, they may have set goals relating to schoolwork, sports activities, or jobs. Instruct students to summarize whether the goal was met or not. If so, how was it met? When students are finished writing, ask them to consider and discuss how setting a goal affects the success of any undertaking. **L1**

COMMUNICATION Strategies

PREPARING FOR AN INTERVIEW

Read and discuss the steps described. Then, have students work in small groups. Assign each group one of the following hypothetical interviews: interviewing a new teacher for an informative article in the school newspaper, interviewing students to find out the most popular movies and television shows, interviewing someone to care for your family's yard, interviewing a power company executive to find out the reasons for recent power outages. Have groups complete the first two steps on the list. Encourage them to complete the remaining steps after they have read and discussed the rest of the section. **L2**

PREPARING FOR AN INTERVIEW

If your English class assignment is to write a composition about a classic novel, you probably would not begin writing before you had read the book. Just like writing an English composition, an interview requires a lot of thought and preparation.

Set a Goal

The first step in preparing for an interview is to set a goal. To do this, determine what you want the outcome of the interview to be. For instance, if one of your friends has asked your advice about an argument she is having with her brother, you will need to be prepared for a counseling interview. Your goal might be to get your friend to resolve her conflict with her brother.

Goal of the Interviewer As you learned earlier in this section, it is the responsibility of the interviewer to determine the goal of the interview. A clear goal helps him or her decide how to approach the situation.

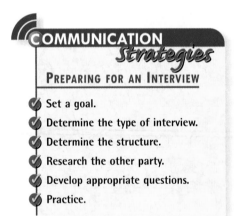

COMMUNICATION Strategies

PREPARING FOR AN INTERVIEW

- ✓ Set a goal.
- ✓ Determine the type of interview.
- ✓ Determine the structure.
- ✓ Research the other party.
- ✓ Develop appropriate questions.
- ✓ Practice.

284 *Glencoe Communication Applications*

Goal of the Interviewee Like the interviewer, the interviewee also should decide what he or she wants to accomplish in the interview. Imagine you are a reporter for the local television station. Your assignment today is to interview one of the candidates running for the office of mayor. Your goal as the interviewer is to gain as much objective information about the candidate as possible. On the other hand, the interviewee has an important goal, too. That person wants to prove to local viewers that he or she is the best candidate for the office.

Determining the Type of Interview

How you prepare for an interview depends upon the type of interview situation you are involved in. This is a key step in preparing for an interview and usually is the responsibility of the interviewer.

As the interviewer, it is important for you to analyze the situation and use context clues when determining which type of interview to conduct. Choose the type of interview that will best enable you to reach your goal. For example, if your goal is to find out how many students have computers at home, it may be too time-consuming to conduct an investigative interview with every student. Instead, a survey interview might be appropriate.

However, if you are going to interview the captain of the school football team for the yearbook, you may determine that the most appropriate type of interview is an investigative interview. This type of interview will enable you to gather all the information needed to write a complete story. Once you have determined the best type of interview to conduct, you can adapt the structure and your research accordingly.

MEETING INDIVIDUAL NEEDS — INCLUSION STRATEGIES

Special Needs Students with physical disabilities may be especially familiar with the importance of setting goals.

Activity Have students make a chart showing goals they have set, worked toward, and did or did not reach in dealing with their disability. Instruct students to include information on the steps they took to reach each goal. They should also include future goals and how they plan to attain them. Students may wish to share their completed charts with classmates.

Larry King talks with Ross Perot in a prearranged interview. What is a scheduled interview?

Determine the Structure

Another important preparation step is to determine the structure of the interview. Again, this step typically is the responsibility of the interviewer. Because the different structures can produce very different results, it is important that interviewers base their choice on the goal of the interview. For instance, where will the interview take place? Who will be present?

A prearranged interview is one that is arranged in advance. If you are researching a topic and must interview a person who has information about your topic, make sure that you arrange the interview several days in advance. Call and ask the person for some time to discuss your topic at his or her convenience. Try to let the person know approximately how much time you will need for the interview. Give the person your phone number or a way in which he or she can contact you if the interview appointment cannot be kept. Call to confirm the appointment the day before the interview and remind the person about the topic of the interview.

Which format will produce more useful results? Would a scheduled interview, a non-scheduled interview, or one that is a little of both be the most useful?

Scheduled Interviews A scheduled interview is one in which the questions are standardized, such as in a survey or poll. A scheduled interview might include questions such as "How many juice drinks do you drink each week?" Generally, there is little flexibility for expanding upon specific questions or answers. Because of this, a scheduled interview typically takes less time than other types of interviews. It also gives the interviewer more control over the interview and its outcome.

Scheduled interviews usually strive to ask each interviewee the same questions in the same manner. Answers also tend to be limited to either a specific type—"In what year were you born?"—or even specific words—"Would you describe yourself as a heavy sleeper or a light sleeper?" Because answers are so limited, they are fairly easy to quantify. For instance, it is easier to group answers to a question such as "Do you prefer red or blue?" than it is to group answers to "What is your favorite color?"

When conducting the interview, remember to be flexible with your questions. The person you are interviewing may disclose some interesting pieces of information that you may not have heard before, or you may want to ask a question about an answer that you get. In these or other cases, you may want to get away from your plan and go with the moment. However, keep in mind that it may take you away from the original purpose of the interview.

While it may take substantial expertise to develop effective questions for a scheduled interview, the interview itself requires little interviewer skill. Information is gathered according to a strict set of guidelines, leaving little opportunity for interviewer discretion.

Exploring the Interview Process   **285**

Conducting a Scheduled Interview

Discuss the characteristics of a scheduled interview and the way in which it is conducted. Ask students to mention some topics that would be appropriate for scheduled interviews. Possible topics include the movie- or television-viewing habits of students in their school. Then, choose one or two of the topics and have others generate questions that would be useful to gain information on the topics. Ask students to improve any questions that are not limited enough or are too flexible. Discuss the best time and place for the interviews. **L2**

■ Visual Instruction

Answer A scheduled interview is one in which the questions are standardized, such as in a survey or poll.

MULTIPLE LEARNING STYLES

MEETING INDIVIDUAL NEEDS

Logical-Mathematical Scientists may use scheduled interviews to gather information as they research a particular problem or question. They may begin with a hypothesis that guides their questioning. They can use scheduled interviews to gain specific information to support or refute their hypothesis.

Activity Have students develop a scientific question that can be researched through a survey or poll. For example, they may want to find out if students who routinely get fewer than eight hours of sleep per night tend to get sick more than others. Ask students to make up a series of questions that could be asked in scheduled interviews, to conduct their survey, and to compile their results. They can share their hypotheses, questions, and results with the class.

Nonscheduled and Moderately Scheduled Interviews

After discussing these two types of interviews, have students work with a partner to create a scenario for one of these two kinds of interviews. Encourage volunteers to present their scenarios. Ask the class to decide which kind of interview is being enacted. **L2**

Interviewers' Research

Point out that television interviewers must spend much time in research. Have students watch or videotape a morning talk show and list the various interviews conducted by each interviewer on the program. Then, ask them to make a note summarizing the kind of research that was necessary in order for the interviewer to ask intelligent questions and respond to the interviewee. Have students compare their findings with the entire class. **L2**

■ Visual Instruction

Answer An interviewer in a nonscheduled interview must keep the interview on track and moving forward toward a goal.

BUSINESS BRIEF

In his book *The Essential Book of Interviewing*, Arnold B. Kanter says, "The most serious interview mistakes both interviewers and interviewees make are made before the interview." Then, he quotes Yogi Berra: "If you don't know where you are going, you will wind up somewhere else." Have students discuss the meaning of these statements and how they might apply to the interview process.

One example of a nonscheduled interview is a salesperson checking up on a client to evaluate the client's satisfaction with a product. What must an interviewer in a nonscheduled interview do to make the interview a success?

Nonscheduled Interviews Nonscheduled interviews, on the other hand, generally have a topic but may not involve a standardized set of questions. An example of a nonscheduled interview might be a sales representative casually calling a client to make sure he or she is satisfied with a particular product.

Finally, because of their flexible, changing nature, nonscheduled interviews require considerable skill on the part of the interviewer. He or she must know how to keep the interview on track and moving forward to meet a specific goal.

Moderately Scheduled Interviews Scheduled interviews and nonscheduled interviews tend to represent two extremes regarding structure—one is highly structured, and the other has little structure at all. Often, the most useful interview structure lies somewhere in between.

A moderately scheduled interview combines useful aspects of both scheduled and nonscheduled interviews. An interviewer may develop a set of questions to use as a guide, but he or she will venture away from the list as needed to pursue an interesting thought or an unusual answer. While the list of questions helps ensure that the most important information is covered, the interviewer is free to discover other information that might otherwise have been overlooked.

Regardless of which type of interview the interviewer chooses, it is important for both participants to be well prepared. An important part of that preparation involves learning as much as possible about the other party.

Research the Other Party

Before you enter into an interview, it is important to find out as much as possible about the other party who will be participating. This will give you the foundation needed to engage in a successful interview. Although both parties need to prepare for each type of interview, the majority of the responsibility usually falls on one party. Whether that is the interviewer or the interviewee depends on the type of interview.

Information-Gathering Research In an information-gathering interview, it is primarily the interviewer's responsibility to prepare research. He or she is the one trying to obtain as much information as possible from the interviewee. To prepare for the interview, you will need to know some background on both the topic and the interviewee. For example, if you are preparing to interview a police officer about crime prevention, you might want to read up on crime statistics in your area and across the country. You also might

---

MEETING INDIVIDUAL NEEDS — GIFTED AND TALENTED

Interviewing People of Accomplishment Students likely know of individuals in a particular field, such as art, music, literature, science, politics, or journalism, whom they particularly admire and would like to interview.

Activity Have students imagine that they have the opportunity to interview an accomplished person whom they admire. Ask them to determine a specific topic for the interview and then make a list of facts or background information that they would need to research in order to conduct a successful interview. Have them write a list of questions for the interview.

want to find out about the officer's professional history, such as how long he or she has served on the force and any special honors or awards he or she has received.

Information-Giving Research

As with an information-gathering interview, in an information-giving interview, the responsibility for most of the research falls on the interviewer. In order to present accurate and complete information to the interviewee, the interviewer needs to be able to support his or her evaluation.

One common type of information-giving interview is a performance appraisal. During a performance appraisal, the manager, or interviewer, needs to be able to explain why he or she is or is not satisfied with the quality of the employee's work. To do this, the manager needs to have enough research and data to support his or her conclusion.

Although the interviewer will do most of the research for an information-giving interview, it is important for the interviewee to conduct research as well. By learning something about the topic and the speaker beforehand, the

interviewee will have a better basis for understanding and critically examining any information he or she receives.

Employment Research

An employment interview also requires preparation by both parties. However, the primary research responsibility lies with the interviewee. As an interviewee, it is important for you to research both the company and the job for which you are interviewing.

Researching the Company Usually, you can find information about individual companies at the public library, through current employees, on the Internet, or through a city's Better Business Bureau. If a company is new or very small, it is important to research at least current trends and leaders in the company's industry. Most of the time, however, you will be able to find at least some information on the businesses in your community.

As you conduct your research of the company, keep in mind the questions on the next page.

■ A reporter interviews a police officer to gather information on a breaking story. **What is the responsibility of the interviewer in an information-gathering interview?**

Exploring the Interview Process **287**

Researching a Company

On the chalkboard, write the ways to find out about a company: at the library, through current employees, on the Internet, through the Better Business Bureau, or by researching current trends and leaders in the company's industry. Then, mention the following companies and have students tell the best way or ways to research them: a national fast-food restaurant with a local franchise *(through current employees, on the Internet, by researching current trends);* a locally owned clothing store *(through current employees, Better Business Bureau);* a national bookstore chain *(through current employees, on the Internet, by researching current trends);* a new local telemarketing firm *(through current employees, Better Business Bureau, researching current trends).* **L2**

■ Visual Instruction

Answer In an information-gathering interview, the interviewer's responsibility is to research background on the topic and the interviewee.

MULTIPLE LEARNING STYLES

Interpersonal In a performance appraisal, it is particularly important for the interviewer to be polite and tactful. Students with strong interpersonal skills will readily recognize the best tone to use in this kind of interview.

Activity Have students work in pairs. Try to make sure at least one participant in each pair has strong interpersonal skills. Have the pairs choose one of the following scenarios and enact a performance-appraisal interview between the two parties: a teacher and a student whose work needs improvement; a coach and a team player whose attitude is not positive; a restaurant manager and a waiter who is rude to customers. Have volunteer pairs enact their interviews for the class. Discuss ways for the interviewers to get their points across without being rude or insulting.

Researching a Company and a Job

Have students read and discuss the questions for researching a company and for researching a job. Then, have the class generate a list of questions to ask current employees of a company. Write these questions on the chalkboard. Point out that these questions might be less formal than the ones listed in the book. However, they also must be appropriate and not too personal. Examples include: How long have you worked for the company? What is your favorite part of working for the company? What do you think is the best benefit of working for the company? What have you learned that will help you in future jobs? **L2**

 GLOBAL COMMUNICATION

Gathering Information

If the class includes students from other countries or who have lived or traveled extensively in other countries, pair them with others for interviews. Students' questions may include the following examples: What are the major industries? What major products are imported or exported? What kinds of work do people do? What language do most people speak? Do many people speak English? How do people travel to work or school? What is the country's population? Do most of the people live in urban or rural areas? What is the dining or social etiquette?

Before applying for a bank teller position, it is wise to familiarize yourself with the job responsibilities. **What factors should you keep in mind when researching a position?**

1. When and by whom was the company founded?
2. Who runs the company now?
3. What is the company's main line of business?
4. Have any recent changes or developments occurred at this company or in this line of business?
5. Who is the competition?
6. Approximately how many employees work for this company?
7. How does the company train its employees?
8. What employee benefits does the company offer, such as sick leave, medical insurance, vacation time, and retirement?

Researching the Job In addition to learning some basic information about the company, you need to research the job itself.

As you conduct your research, keep the following questions in mind.

1. What are the primary responsibilities of the job?
2. What role would I play in this position?
3. What skills typically are required for this type of position? Will I need any special training?
4. Where might this type of job lead in the near future? In the distant future?
5. What kind of employee performance appraisal system does the company use?

Suppose you are applying for a job as a bank teller. Prior to the interview, you will need to find out what a teller's primary

 GLOBAL COMMUNICATION

Gathering Information

If you are going to conduct business in a country you have never visited before, the best way to learn about it is to ask people who have lived there. Find people in your community who have lived in other countries by consulting with international companies, ethnic businesses, military bases, the chamber of commerce, or local universities. Develop a list of questions for a moderately scheduled information–gathering interview designed to learn more about other countries and their customs. Use the interview questions to ask the people in your community about another culture. Share your interview results with the rest of the class.

Visual Instruction

Answer You should find out the primary job responsibilities, the types of skills required, and the types of equipment you will be expected to use.

REAL-WORLD CONNECTION

Researching a Company and/or Job Many students may know of a specific company or a specific job that interests them. They can use the skills they have learned to research these career opportunities now.

Activity Have students make notes of the lists of questions on this page and add at least two of their own questions to each list. Then, have them schedule an interview with an employee of a company that interests them or one who works in a job that interests them. Instruct them to gather information about the company and/or job through the interview. They may share the results of their interviews in small groups.

responsibilities are. Your main duty might be processing customer transactions, or the job could include doing daily audits, or balancing a cash drawer. You will also need to find out what your role would be when performing the tasks. For example, you may be the person to whom customers are directed when they have a problem with their deposit.

Also, you need to find out what types of skills a bank teller needs and what types of equipment you will be expected to use. In many cases, tellers use a special computer system to process transactions. How might your current skills help you quickly learn to use this system?

Benefits of Research Besides providing you with valuable background information, research has other benefits as well. First, it will help you decide whether this particular company and job are a good match for your skills and goals. Does this company seem stable and ethical? Is it a safe environment? Am I qualified for this job? Will I be challenged in this position? Answering yes to these questions may help you feel enthusiastic about interviewing for the position.

Research also can help you feel confident in your interview. Learning about the job's responsibilities can help you match them to your own skills and experience. This allows you to enter the interview confident that you can do the job and do it well.

Interviewer's Responsibilities Although the biggest burden of research in an employment interview rests upon the interviewee, the interviewer also needs to do research. As the interviewer, you need to make sure the interviewee has the qualifications and skills necessary to justify an employment interview. You also will need to carefully review the information the interviewee has provided, such as an application for employment, a résumé, or a cover letter. As **Figure 9–4** shows, once you have done your research, you are ready to formulate the questions that you want to ask during the interview.

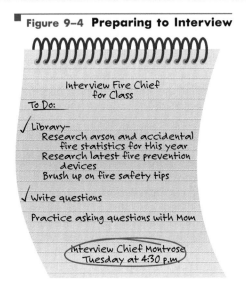

■ **Figure 9–4 Preparing to Interview**

> Interview Fire Chief for Class
>
> To Do:
> ✓ Library–
>   Research arson and accidental fire statistics for this year
>   Research latest fire prevention devices
>   Brush up on fire safety tips
> ✓ Write questions
>   Practice asking questions with Mom
>
> Interview Chief Montrose Tuesday at 4:30 p.m.

Develop Appropriate Questions

Based upon their research, both parties in a successful interview should develop questions as part of the preparation process. To determine which questions are appropriate, you will need to make a list of what you already know versus what you need or want to know. Then, you can better develop questions to bridge this gap.

Interviewee Questions As the interviewee, your questions should help you achieve your goal for the interview. The goal, of course, depends upon the type of interview.

Information-Gathering Interviews In an information-gathering interview, your goal probably will be to provide accurate, interesting, and complete information to the interviewer. You may want to ask questions about how your information will be used. You also may want to ask perception-checking questions throughout the interview to make sure your meanings are clearly understood.

Exploring the Interview Process **289**

Researching a Job
As you discuss researching companies and jobs, have students make an informal chart describing the jobs they have had. Instruct them to describe each job and then list the responsibilities, skills, and equipment of each one. After students have completed their charts, ask them whether they ever had a job in which their responsibilities and necessary skills were unclear when they began. How did that affect their experience? How does previous knowledge of a job affect the employment experience? **L2**

BUSINESS BRIEF

In *Job Interviews for Dummies*, Joyce Lain Kennedy offers the following tips for researching a company on the Internet: locate a company's Web site; check research sites that review companies, such as those of business publications; use the company name as a keyword to locate articles about the company; look up the company on trade group sites; network with others online.

ENGLISH LANGUAGE LEARNERS

Researching Jobs and Companies Students who are learning English may want to research additional aspects of a company or a job that interests them.

Activity Have students work in small groups and brainstorm ways to find a company and a job that fit their needs and skills. For example, they may find a demand for their language skills in companies that offer bilingual services for customers. On the other hand, they may not be ready to apply for jobs that require strong English skills. Suggest that interviewing current employees of a company that interests them can help them decide whether their language skills are a good fit for the company. Point out that language requirements may vary greatly in various jobs within a company, so being honest with an interviewer about one's language proficiency is essential. **ELL**

Interviewee and Interviewer Questions

Have students take turns reading aloud the sample interviewee questions. Ask students to characterize the questions. *(They are specific, to the point, and show knowledge of the company and the position.)* Then, have them read the sample interviewer questions in Figure 9–5 and characterize them. *(They are fairly general and are designed to elicit specific information about the interviewee's work habits, experience, and plans for the future. They allow the interviewee room to exhibit his or her personality.)* **L1**

Interview Types

Write the three different types of interviews—information-gathering, information-giving, and employment interviews—on the board. Help students identify what the goal of the interviewer and the interviewee is in each type. Write the goals on the board. *(Information-gathering interview: interviewer goal is to gather as much information as possible; interviewee goal is to provide accurate and complete information. Information-giving interview: interviewer goal is to be an information source for the interviewee; interviewee goal is to learn as much as possible from the interviewer. Employment interview: interviewer goal is to evaluate a candidate's suitability for the position needing to be filled; interviewee goal is to provide honest and relevant information to demonstrate how and why he or she would be the best candidate for the position.)* **L1**

Information-Giving Interviews In an information-giving interview, your goal should be to learn as much as possible from the interviewer. Therefore, your questions probably will center around the topic. These might even include asking the interviewer about his or her own experiences as they relate to the topic.

Employment Interviews The questions you ask in an employment interview can be extremely important. They help the interviewer better understand who you are and where your motivations and interests lie. In an interview, it is important to ask questions that are relevant, respectful, and appropriate for the situation. In most cases, this means you would not ask about salary or certain benefits unless the interviewer brings up the topics first. On the other hand, you will show initiative by asking intelligent questions about the company, the position, and your specific responsibilities.

For instance, imagine that you are preparing to interview for a position as an assistant video technician. You know that the position requires someone who can maintain and operate video editing equipment as well as assist in other video production tasks. You also know that the company provides training on its specific video equipment, but you are interested in knowing more. Your questions for the interview might include these:

1. What specific editing equipment does this company use?

2. Will the company provide tuition reimbursement if I take courses to learn new editing techniques or programs?

3. Will I ever travel with the videographer to shoot and edit video on location?

4. In addition to my regular responsibilities, will I ever participate in planning the shoots or actually shooting a video myself?

As an interviewee, you should make sure that your questions reflect a basic understanding of the company and the position but show an eagerness to learn more. They also should imply a desire to work hard and to stay with the company for a significant length of time. In general, view your questions as another opportunity to make a good impression on the interviewer.

Interviewer Questions As the interviewer, your questions will direct the course of the interview. Sample interviewer questions are shown in **Figure 9–5**. As was the case for the interviewee, the nature of your questions will depend upon your goal and the type of interview in which you are involved.

Information-Gathering Interviews In an information-gathering interview, it is the interviewer's responsibility to gather as much information as possible from the interviewee. Your questions will probably center around a central theme or topic and should be based on the research you have done.

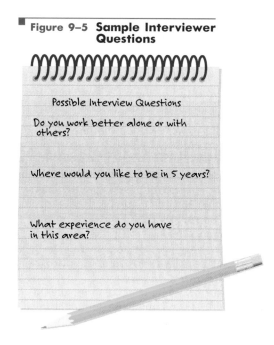

Figure 9–5 Sample Interviewer Questions

Possible Interview Questions

Do you work better alone or with others?

Where would you like to be in 5 years?

What experience do you have in this area?

EXTENDING THE CONTENT

Typical Interview Questions Employment interviewers may use one or more "typical" questions, such as those shown on Figure 9–5. Preparing answers to these may be useful.

Activity Share the following typical employment interviewer questions with students. Have them write brief answers to the questions. What are your strengths? What are your weaknesses? What is your greatest accomplishment? What did you like most and least about your last job? What are your career goals? What would your coworkers say about you?

Seeing Is Believing One way to practice your job interviewing skills is to videotape yourself in a mock interview. Identify a career that you would like to pursue; then, choose a partner and develop ten employment interview questions for each other. Have a third student record your interview with a video camera. Watch both interviews and analyze your questions, your answers, and your nonverbal communication. Try watching the interviews with the sound turned off to more easily see and analyze nonverbal behaviors. What do you see on tape that you didn't notice before? Having seen yourself on tape, what would you try to improve upon during an actual interview?

Information-Giving Interviews In an information-giving interview, your goal is to be an information resource for the interviewee. As you explain your topic or ideas, you may want to use perception-checking questions to make sure the interviewee understands what you are saying. Depending on the tone you have set, you also may wish to ask the interviewee to contribute some of his or her own ideas to the interview.

Employment Interviews In an employment interview, the interviewer's questions should be designed to evaluate the interviewee's personality, qualifications, potential, and goals, among other things. If you are interviewing a number of individuals for the same position, you may decide to ask each a similar set of questions. However, try not to be so focused on following a routine that you fail to follow up on unusual answers or comments given by the interviewee. Many interviewers find it helpful to discuss possible questions with those who will be working directly with the newly hired person. In general, the more you can find out about each interviewee, the better equipped you will be to make a final hiring decision.

Practice

Once you have determined the goal, type, and structure of the interview, researched the other party, and developed your questions, it is time to put all these elements together. Practice allows you to experiment with the flow of the interview, correct any missteps, and adjust your behavior for maximum impact and effectiveness when it counts.

Practice Interviewing. As the interviewer, it is important for you to practice what you want to say during the beginning, middle, and end of the interview. Keep the goal of the interview in mind and practice getting the discussion back on track when it strays. In addition to practicing what you will say, take time to focus on your nonverbal behavior. Make sure it sends the right message. You also may wish to choose the clothing you plan to wear to the interview and make sure it is clean and

This person is practicing in front of a mirror before an interview. **How does practicing help an interviewee?**

Conducting Employment Interviews

Students may picture themselves exclusively in the role of interviewee when they study interviewing skills. Point out that there are a variety of situations in which they might serve in the role of employment interviewer. Have students give some real or hypothetical examples. Possibilities include a school newspaper editor choosing a photographer, an individual hiring a yard worker or child-care worker for one's family, and a camp supervisor hiring counselors. Have students write a list of interviewer questions for one of these situations or one they think of themselves. **L2**

Seeing Is Believing To analyze verbal communication more easily and with fewer distractions, suggest that students listen to the audio portion of the recording with the picture turned off. After students have performed their videotape interviews, ask each pair to show portions of the videotapes to the class and point out two or three interesting items they noticed as they studied their interviews.

■ Visual Instruction

Answer Practice allows an interviewee to experiment with the flow of the interview, correct any missteps, and adjust his or her behavior for maximum impact and effectiveness.

MEETING INDIVIDUAL NEEDS — INCLUSION STRATEGIES

Learning Disabilities Students may have difficulty answering questions in an interview situation and may therefore be intimidated by the entire interview process.
Activity Help students gain confidence answering questions orally by offering the following advice: (1) Encourage students to improve their decoding and language skills. (2) Have them write a list of frequently asked interview questions and then write out their answers. (3) Encourage them to practice their questions and answers with a partner several times. (4) Suggest that partners critique each other's weaknesses. (5) Students who give rambling or vague answers should practice condensing their thoughts. (6) Those who tend to give excessively brief answers should work on expanding their responses.

Interview Openings

Discuss the importance of the opening portion of an interview. Point out that it is similar to a social situation in which a person meets someone for the first time. A smile, a firm handshake, and politeness make a good first impression. Have students stand up. Instruct each one to turn to a student nearby and role-play meeting an interviewer for the first time. Have them repeat the role-playing with another student. **L1**

COMMUNICATION PRACTICE LAB

Practicing an Interview

Before students prepare for their role playing, you may wish to model an interview for them. As you do, emphasize the importance of business etiquette and body language during the interview process. Students' interviews will vary but should show adequate preparation. **L2**

For an additional Practice Lab for this section, students can visit the *Glencoe Communication Applications* Web site at **communicationapplications.glencoe.com**. Click on Communication Practice Lab 9–2. **L1**

---

ready to wear. Practice your note-taking skills. Practicing your role as an interviewer will help you participate in the actual interview with confidence and remain focused on your goals.

Practice Being Interviewed. As the interviewee, you will want to be prepared to respond appropriately to any situation that may arise in an interview. One way to practice this is to make up questions that you think the interviewer might ask. Have a parent or friend pretend to be the interviewer and ask you the questions so you may practice your answers. Also enlist that person's help in evaluating your nonverbal behavior. Try to use nonverbal cues that communicate honesty, openness, respect, and enthusiasm. In Section 3 of this chapter, nonverbal behaviors will be discussed.

THE ACTUAL INTERVIEW

Just as with an English composition, a business letter, or a speech, an interview has a definite beginning, middle, and end. These components are referred to as the *opening*, the *body*, and the *closing*. Analyzing how each of these components work together will help you participate more effectively in any interview.

The Opening

The opening of the interview begins with both parties establishing a rapport, or harmonious relationship, with one another. A typical beginning has both parties introducing themselves. Sometimes, this step is followed by a handshake and a few moments of "small talk" or polite conversation. The purpose of this is to develop an atmosphere of goodwill and to put both parties a little more at ease in what often is a stressful situation. Generally, this brief, initial conversation will set the tone for the rest of the interview.

Once the tone has been set, it is important for the interviewer to review the purpose of the interview. This will help both parties keep their comments on track during their

COMMUNICATION PRACTICE LAB

Practicing an Interview

To practice participating in an interview, follow these steps:

Step 1 As a class, brainstorm possible interview situations. Then, with a partner, choose one of these situations and write it on a sheet of paper.

Step 2 Determine the type of interview and write it on the sheet of paper.

Step 3 On the same sheet, write the interviewer's and interviewee's goals for the interview. Also, describe the structure and how you might research each party.

Step 4 Write three questions for the interviewer and three for the interviewee and label each with the type of question it models.

Step 5 Describe your interview situation to the class. Then, with one partner acting as the interviewer and one acting as the interviewee, practice your interview.

Step 6 As a class, discuss the strengths and weaknesses of each pair's preparation.

INTERDISCIPLINARY CONNECTION

Language Arts Some students enjoy approaching a subject through creative writing. Challenge these students to write a creative dialogue depicting a job interview.

Activity Have students write a dialogue depicting two people participating in a job interview. Suggest that students think of a plot or theme for their piece. For example, they may want to show an interview in which many things go wrong or for which the interviewee is not prepared. Also suggest that students define the character traits of the two people in the dialogue before writing. Have volunteers share their dialogues with the class.

TYPES OF QUESTIONS IN AN INTERVIEW

Question Type	Definition	Example
Open-ended	Broad in scope, giving the respondent a great deal of freedom in his or her answer	Tell me about yourself.
Closed	Seeks a very specific answer	What hours are you available to work?
Highly closed	Not only seeks a specific answer but may even provide answers from which to choose	Would you prefer to work mornings, afternoons, or evenings?
Primary	Begins a new topic	Tell me about your hobbies.
Secondary	Helps the interviewer better understand the answer to a primary question	Why do you like that particular hobby?
Leading	Suggests the desired answer	You do want to work weekends, don't you?
Neutral	Implies no specific or "right" or "wrong" answer	Would you like to work weekends?
Direct	Straightforward; asks exactly what the interviewer wants to know and leaves no room for ambiguity	Can you work Friday evenings?
Indirect	Seeks specific information without directly asking for it	What do you usually do on Friday evenings?
Factual	Seeks information that can be proven	Where do you attend high school?
Opinion	Asks for the respondent's judgment about something	What is your opinion about employees who steal?
Hypothetical	Asks how a respondent might react in a given situation	If you knew someone were stealing from the company, what would you do?

The Body

The body is the main part of the interview. During this time, the conversation turns to specific questioning. Unlike casual conversation with your friends, conversation during an interview is planned. The interviewer asks questions that have a specific purpose in mind. The interviewee also carefully considers each answer to make sure it is appropriate and accurate and contributes to the goal of the interview.

In a balanced interview, both parties speak and listen. The interviewer will both ask and answer questions of the interviewee. Similarly, the interviewee not only will answer questions but also may have questions to ask of the interviewer. Both parties make decisions based upon the information they receive. They do this by analyzing the answers to many types of questions.

There are several types of questions that may be asked during an interview. Some might not even seem like questions at all at first glance. The chart lists some of the different types of questions and gives an example of each.

As an interviewer, understanding the different types of questions may help you get the exact information you need. As an interviewee,

discussion. The interviewer also may wish to explain the structure and length of the interview so the interviewee will know what to expect. The interviewee's primary responsibility during the opening of the interview is to listen, respond appropriately, and try to make a good first impression.

Exploring the Interview Process **293**

Types of Questions
Discuss the types of questions in an interview as shown on the chart. Have students write an additional example that might be used by an employment interviewer for each question type. Have volunteers read their examples. **L2**

Questions and Answers
In 1903, British philosopher George E. Moore wrote, "It appears to me that in Ethics, as in all other philosophical studies, the difficulties and disagreements, of which history is full, are mainly due to a very simple cause: namely to the attempt to answer questions, without first discovering precisely what question it is which you desire to answer." Remind students that ethics is the philosophical study of the nature of right and wrong. Then, encourage students to discuss what they think Moore meant by this statement. *(Students may suggest that questions can be interpreted to have many levels of meaning, from the simple meaning of the direct words to more subtle and underlying meanings behind the words.)* Ask them to consider how the questions they choose to answer might differ from those posed. Suggest that each student write a question and exchange it with a partner who rephrases the question to conform to how he or she would choose to answer it. Students can then discuss the similarities and differences in the questions. **L3**

COOPERATIVE LEARNING ACTIVITY

Have each student write on a small piece of paper a job title for a job that would be appropriate for someone in his or her age group. Encourage students to be creative yet realistic in their job titles. Some possible choices are amusement park performer, pet-shop assistant, and floral arranger. Put all the job titles in a box and have students draw one. Give them time to write one interview question of each type on the chart for the job they chose. Then, working in pairs, each student can conduct his or her interview based on the job title chosen.

Interview Thank-You Letters

Ask a student to read aloud the thank-you letter shown in Figure 9–6. Ask students to name the features that will make a good impression on the potential employer and explain why. *(The writer compliments the company on specific qualities, communicates that she knows the traits the company looks for in employees, reminds the employer of her strong points, and thanks the employer for her time.)* **L2**

3 ASSESS

Assign Section 2 Assessment as a homework or in-class activity.

🌐 Use *Interactive Tutor Self-Assessment Software* to review Section 2.

knowing what types of questions you may be asked can help you answer more appropriately. In both cases, you may want to record answers given in the interview. Careful note-taking skills will help you do this. In any case, providing clear, concise answers adds to your overall effectiveness in any interview.

The Closing

The closing is a summary of what occurred during the body of the interview. In an information-gathering interview, the interviewer also may take this opportunity to summarize and verify what he or she has learned from the interviewee. For example, a college interviewer may say, "I understand that you want to earn a degree in education. You currently have a high school grade-point average of 3.3. You plan to work part time while attending school and will live on campus." This summary gives the interviewee a chance to correct any information that has been misunderstood.

This also is the time to discuss plans for future action. Usually, the interviewer will initiate these plans. He or she might say, "I will contact you by mail within two weeks." If no future plans are mentioned, the interviewee might ask if he or she may make a follow-up call to the interviewer in a few days. Whether the interview has gone well or not, both parties should express appreciation to each other for their time and consideration. It is important to leave the interview on a friendly note.

THE POST INTERVIEW

As you may have guessed from its name, the post interview is what happens following the interview. This is a key time for reconnecting with the interviewer and reminding him or her of your strong points.

■ Figure 9–6 **Sample Thank-You Letter**

386 Lakeview Street
Columbus, Ohio 12312
(614) 123-4567

November 23, 2002

Jessica Jones
Banking Center Manager
Franklin National Bank
252 Main Street
Columbus, Ohio 12312

Dear Ms. Jones:

Thank you for taking time to discuss possible employment opportunities at Franklin National Bank. I realize that Franklin National Bank has a reputation for excellence in customer service and desires energetic and effective tellers to continue this proud tradition. I believe my skills meet the needs of your company.

As we discussed, having spent two years as a cashier at East End Market has shown me the importance of quality customer service. It is for these reasons that I wish to be considered for a teller position.

I look forward to hearing from you next week. Thank you for your time and consideration.

Sincerely,

Andrea M. Smith

Andrea M. Smith

A follow-up thank-you letter or other type of business communication is a crucial part of the post interview. In this brief communication, you should summarize what you discussed in the interview and thank the interviewer for taking time to meet with you. The tone of your thank-you should be warm but professional, similar to the one modeled in the letter in **Figure 9–6.**

The post interview also is the best time to analyze how the interview went. After participating in an interview, ask yourself what went right, what went wrong, and how you can improve next time. The following is a list of several questions you may wish to include in your analysis.

INCLUSION STRATEGIES

Less-Proficient Readers Some students may need to review and practice the writing of a business letter such as the thank-you letter.

Activity Have students study the sample letter as you review the various parts of a business letter: heading, inside address, salutation, body, closing, and signature. Point out the title used for the person being addressed and the punctuation that follows the salutation and the closing. Have students refer to the sample as they write thank-you letters of their own. Instruct them to invent job interview situations for which they are writing the letters.

- Was I adequately prepared for the interview?
- Did I ask clear, appropriate questions?
- Were my responses accurate and complete?
- Did I listen carefully?
- Did I seem confident during the interview?

- (Employment interviews only) Based on this interview, would I hire me?
- What behaviors, questions, or answers would I change for the next interview?

Each time you participate in an interview and evaluate your role, you learn more about the interview process. The more you learn, the better a participant you will become.

Section 2 Assessment

Visit the *Glencoe Communication Applications* Web site at **communicationapplications. glencoe.com** and click on **Self-Check and Study Guide 9.2** to review your understanding of the interview process.

Review Key Terms

1. Define each vocabulary term and write it in a sentence: interview process, highly closed question, primary question, secondary question, leading question, neutral question, direct question, indirect question, factual question, opinion question, hypothetical question.

Check Understanding

2. Identify and describe the three components of the interview process.

3. Imagine that you will be interviewing for a position as a counselor at a summer camp. Describe how you will prepare for the interview.

4. During which component of the interview would each of the following be most likely to occur? Explain your answers.
   - Questions about the interviewee's experience and qualifications
   - A summary of information
   - Small talk and introductions

5. **Predict** Imagine you have interviewed two candidates for the same job. The first sends a thank-you letter reminding you of his or her qualifications. The second sends no letter. How might this affect your decision? Explain.

APPLICATION *Activity*

Applying the Interview Process Imagine that a recruiter from your favorite college is coming to speak to your class. Each student interested in attending the college will be given fifteen minutes to speak individually with the recruiter. Working in a groups of three or four students, complete each of the following. Then, discuss your answers as a class.

- List three things you should do to prepare for your interview with the recruiter.
- Prepare five questions for the interview.
- Describe when and how you will follow up with the recruiter.

Exploring the Interview Process **295**

Section 2 Assessment Answers

1. Accept all reasonable sentences.
2. Opening: parties become acquainted; body: main part of the interview; closing: summary of body.
3. Answers should include setting a goal, predicting the type and structure of the interview, conducting research, developing questions, and practicing.
4. Questions occur during the body; Closing: verify and summarize information; Opening: sets the tone for the interview

5. While students shouldn't base the decision on the letter alone, it might make the candidate seem more professional. No letter might reflect negatively on the other candidate.
Application Activity Students' answers will differ but should reflect an understanding of each step of the interview process.

Reteaching Activity 9-2

RETEACHING Activity 9-2 Name _____ Date _____ Class _____
EXPLORING THE INTERVIEW PROCESS
Understanding the Interview Process

You have just received a phone call from the manager of a jewelry store where you applied for a job. She wants you to come in for an interview next week. You now have to prepare yourself for the big event! Complete the following interview preparation list, filling in what you need to do to be ready for this interview.

1. Set a goal.

2. Determine the type of interview.

3. Determine the structure.

Enrichment Activity 9-2

ENRICHMENT Activity 9-2 Name _____ Date _____ Class _____
EXPLORING THE INTERVIEW PROCESS
Understanding the Interview Process

As an interviewee, it is important for you to research both the company and the job for which you are interviewing. Section 2 suggests that an interviewer can find information about individual companies at the public library, through current employees, on the Internet, or through a city's Better Business Bureau. The following passage by Robert Huber describes the process of doing such research. Read the explanations and answer the questions that follow.

1. Imagine you are interviewing for an entry-level position at an investment firm. Based on the excerpt above, describe what you could do to research the company before your interview.

2. Talk to an adult who has been through a career-oriented interview. Record the preparation that this person did for the interview.

4 CLOSE

Have students complete the following sentence without reviewing the beginning of Section 2: *An interview is like a fast-food restaurant because both _____.* Have several students read their answers. Point out that according to the beginning of the section, the two are alike because both require a plan or structure in order to be effective and efficient. Discuss other interesting answers that may shed light on the interviewing process.

Extra-Credit Project

Have students locate a human resources manager or other company manager who frequently conducts job interviews. Suggest that students conduct their own interview of the manager, asking questions to find out what the manager looks for in an interviewee. Ask students to prepare a written report summarizing the manager's main points.

1 FOCUS

Bellringer

Ask students to close their eyes and imagine a person their age wearing each of the following outfits: a black leather jacket and blue jeans; baggy khaki pants and a baseball cap; a knee-length skirt and a navy blazer; a pair of shorts and a tank top. Then ask: Which of these is an appropriate outfit? *("Appropriate" dress depends on the occasion. Shorts and a tank top would be inappropriate for a job interview; a skirt and blazer would be inappropriate for the beach.)* Emphasize that the idea of appropriateness does not mean that some kinds of dress are always in bad taste, but that people should dress in order to feel comfortable and make others comfortable in a particular context.

You may use Graphic Organizer Transparency 9–3 to introduce this section.

Graphic Organizer Transparency 9–3

	Interview for a music store sales associate position	
	Appropriate	**Inappropriate**
1. Dress professionally.		
2. Smile.		
3. Appear indifferent.		
4. Be enthusiastic.		
5. Answer a cellular phone call during the interview.		
6. Be on time.		
7. Make eye contact.		
8. Listen carefully.		
9. Appear arrogant.		
10. Be friendly.		
11. Appear confident.		
12. Use slang and informal language.		
13. Mumble.		
14. Project a positive attitude.		
15. Chew gum.		
16. Complain about a previous employer.		
17. Slouch in your chair.		
18. Ask about your duties and responsibilities.		
19. Become angry about illegal questions.		
20. Lie about why you left your previous job.		

Visual Instruction

Answer You can be sure to make a good impression in an interview situation by dressing, behaving, and speaking appropriately.

Appropriateness in Interviews

GUIDE TO READING

Objectives

1. Explain why appropriateness is important in an interview.
2. Develop appropriate questions for an interview.
3. Recognize unlawful interview questions.
4. Determine what constitutes appropriate dress and demeanor for an interview.

Terms to Learn

demeanor   discriminate
body language

*L*ook at the clock and count off one minute. It's not a very long period of time. It's not long enough to listen to a whole song. It's probably not even long enough to walk from one class to the next. However, when you meet someone for the first time in an interview, he or she forms an opinion about you within just one minute.

This phenomenon is called a first impression. In an interview, a good first impression can be critical. Some experts believe that up to 50 percent of an interviewer's hiring decision may be determined by his or her first impression of the interviewee. So, how can you be sure you will make a good impression? One way is to dress, behave, and speak appropriately.

PERSONAL APPROPRIATENESS IN INTERVIEWS

During an interview, appropriateness is necessary for making a positive first impression. As you learned in Chapter 1, appropriateness is what is acceptable or the norm for a given situation. Generally speaking, a person who does not act appropriately in a specific context is likely to be perceived negatively by others.

It is important to make a good first impression when meeting someone for the first time. How can you be sure to make a good first impression in an interview situation?

RESOURCE MANAGER

Teaching Tools

- Interactive Lesson Planner
- Reproducible Lesson Plan 9–3
- Application Activities 9–3

Reproducible Masters

- Guided Reading Activity Workbook 9–3
- Enrichment Activity 9–3
- Reteaching Activity 9–3
- Section Quiz 9–3
- Transparency Strategies and Activities Booklet 9–3

Transparencies

- Graphic Organizer Transparency 9–3
- Chapter 9 Teaching Transparency

Technology Resources

- Interactive Tutor Self-Assessment Software
- Presentation Plus! Software
- ExamView® Pro Testmaker
- PuzzleMaker Software
- communicationapplications.glencoe.com

For example, it may be appropriate to yell and shout for your team at a sporting event. However, if you were to engage in this type of behavior in the school library, you probably would be in trouble—or at least be asked to leave. Loudness in the library is not appropriate.

Just as certain kinds of conduct need to be followed in the library, certain guidelines of appropriateness should be followed by both parties in an interview—especially in an employment interview. Among these are guidelines regarding appropriate appearance, demeanor, and questioning techniques.

Appropriate Dress and Appearance

As you learned in Chapter 15, clothing and overall appearance carry a strong non-verbal message. It is hard to overestimate the impact of clothing and overall appearance when you first enter an interview situation. As unjust as it may seem, people do tend to judge a book by its cover. That is, they tend to form their initial impressions based on physical appearance.

COMMUNICATION Strategies

FIRST-IMPRESSION CHECKLIST

✓ Do you have a confident posture?

✓ Are you smiling?

✓ Are you dressed appropriately?

✓ Are your clothes neat and clean?

✓ Do you appear clean and well groomed?

✓ Do you seem relatively calm?

✓ Do you seem outgoing and enthusiastic?

Figure 9–7 Appropriate Dress for an Interview

From the moment the interviewer first sees you, he or she begins forming judgments about who you are and whether you are right for the job. Before you ever even speak, you will be evaluated on several important points.

Each of these factors is important to making a good first impression. However, when surveyed, job recruiters have named clothing as the most important factor in shaping their initial impressions of applicants.

Dress How you dress for a specific interview will, of course, depend upon the context. You might dress more casually when interviewing for a lifeguard position than you would for a summer internship at a law firm. Jeans and a knit shirt might be all right for the lifeguard interview, but you surely would be underdressed at the law firm. If you think you might have to demonstrate your skills, such as in the case of applying for a welding or machinist position, make sure you have your work clothes available. **Figure 9–7** shows some appropriate styles of dress for more formal interviews.

If you are unsure of how to dress for an interview, keep this rule in mind: Overdressed is usually better than underdressed. In other words, if you happen to dress too formally, you probably will be perceived as trying to make a good impression—which is a definite plus. If, however, you happen to be dressed too casually, you may be perceived as disrespectful, rebellious, or just plain lazy. In any case, the interviewer probably will see you as someone who exercises poor judgment.

Exploring the Interview Process **297**

2 TEACH

COMMUNICATION Strategies

FIRST-IMPRESSION CHECKLIST

Read and discuss the first-impression checklist. Point out that each item hints at a specific character trait, such as self-confidence, self-respect, and friendliness. Have students imagine they are going into a job interview at this very moment. Which of the items on the checklist would they need to quickly adjust or would they like to have more time to prepare for?

Guided Reading Activity 9–3

EXPLORING THE INTERVIEW PROCESS
Appropriateness in Interviews

As you read Section 3, complete the sentences below.

MEETING INDIVIDUAL NEEDS   MULTIPLE LEARNING STYLES

Visual-Spatial Discuss the fact that fashion design and clothing styles are a form of art in which everyone participates to some extent.

Activity Have students design one or more outfits appropriate for a job interview for a job they would like to have. Students can illustrate their outfits with pictures cut out of magazines. Particularly artistic students may wish to design and draw their own examples.

Demonstrating Demeanor

Discuss the personality traits—friendliness, poise, and confidence—that an interviewer usually wants to communicate. Then, ask volunteers to demonstrate for the class facial expressions, posture, and body language that demonstrate each of these traits and its opposite. You might want to continue and have students demonstrate traits such as timidity, boredom, and lack of ambition. **L2**

DID YOU KNOW?

According to *Job Hunting for Dummies* by Max Messmer, a survey conducted by Robert Half International asked executives which traits aside from ability and willingness to work impressed them most during a job interview. 38 percent said verbal skills, and 24 percent said enthusiasm. In third place were honesty/integrity and past experience/accomplishments, both of which were mentioned by 7 percent of the executives.

Personal Appearance Although clothing usually makes the most memorable first impression, its influence can be overshadowed. Unfortunately, this probably means that some other aspect of a person's appearance was so distracting that it caused the interviewer to temporarily forget how the person was dressed.

Think about things that can be a major distraction when you meet someone for the first time. Poor hygiene, an overpowering scent of cologne, too much makeup, an unusual hair color or style, uncombed hair, or even bad breath may cause you to form a poor opinion of someone you have just met.

The rule of thumb regarding personal appearance in an interview is to always be clean and neat. Keep hair and nails neutral. Jewelry should be kept to a minimum. Wear appropriate clothing. That means dresses and skirts should be of a modest length, and pants should fit neatly. Avoid sweatshirts, tank tops, halter tops, spaghetti straps, shorts, sandals, and sneakers unless you are absolutely sure they are appropriate for an interview context.

Appropriate Demeanor

Typically, the first thing an interviewer will notice is your physical appearance. However, this will be followed closely by your demeanor, or outward behavior, and your verbal communication skills. For this reason, it is important to enter any interview situation poised, confident, and friendly. Use appropriate speech and body language to show that you are a professional who would be an asset to any company.

Friendliness Close your eyes and think about one person who makes you feel comfortable and welcome whenever you are around him or her. Imagine for a moment that you are meeting that person on the street or in the hallway of your school building. How does this person greet you? You probably imagine a smile and a sincere, friendly greeting. When you are trying to make a positive first impression, it is important to be friendly. Make eye contact with the other person, offer a firm handshake, and extend a sincere greeting. For example, you might say, "Hello, Mr. Brown. It's so good to meet you."

Poise and Confidence Along with friendliness, it is important to project a poised and confident attitude. A person who has an air of confidence may be perceived as mature and as having certain leadership abilities. One way to display confidence in an interview situation is to adequately prepare. You are working toward that goal now by reading this chapter. Research, practice, and the other preparation techniques you have read about are all ways to gain confidence and poise in an interview.

It is important to note, however, that although you want to be confident, you don't want to appear arrogant. An arrogant person is one who believes he or she knows everything. Arrogance, as opposed to confidence, can create a negative image.

INTERVIEWING DOS AND DON'TS

Do	Don't
Look professional.	Chew gum.
Make good eye contact.	Wear too much fragrance.
Be specific.	Wear excessive jewelry.
Be flexible.	Lie.
Listen carefully.	Mumble.
Be enthusiastic.	Brag.
Speak clearly and concisely.	Interrupt.
Smile.	Look at your watch.

MEETING INDIVIDUAL NEEDS — MULTIPLE LEARNING STYLES

Bodily–Kinesthetic Dramatizing "Dos" and "Don'ts" of job interviewing can be both fun and helpful.

Activity Have students work in small groups. Instruct them to act out the dos and don'ts of interviewing listed on this page. Encourage students to experiment with formats. For example, they may wish to have a narrator who reads each item as it is acted out. They may wish to pantomime a piece of advice or create a scene with dialogue to illustrate it. Encourage creativity.

Verbal Skills How you speak is another manner to consider when interviewing. Unless the job requires it, avoid using slang in an interview. Also avoid using speech fillers such as "you know," "uh," "um," and "like." Above all, do not interrupt or raise your voice to an interviewer. The key is to present yourself as a pleasant, intelligent, well-qualified professional.

When you ask or answer questions in an interview, make sure your speech is clear and straightforward. Before you answer a question, think about your answer. It is common to be nervous in an interview, which often can cause you to speak too loudly or too softly. It also can cause your speech to speed up. When this happens, put on the brakes. Take a deep breath, speak in a normal tone, and take your time. A well-thought-out answer says volumes about you as a competent communicator.

Body Language In Chapter 5, you learned that body talk is a powerful communicator. Body language is how people nonverbally express feelings and attitudes. For example, imagine that you have arrived early for a 7:00 A.M. interview. Five minutes before

COMMON REASONS FOR REJECTING JOB APPLICANTS	
Poor appearance	Overbearing, aggressive
Poor voice, diction, grammar	Lack of purpose, career goals
Little enthusiasm, passive, indifferent	Unwilling to start at the bottom
Late for interview, disrespectful	Lack of courtesy, proper etiquette
Talks too much, rambles	Poor eye contact, extreme nervousness
Unable to handle silence	Lack of poise, confidence
Negative attitude	Lack of leadership skills
Couldn't sell himself/herself to employer	Condemnation of previous employer
Talked about salary	Didn't ask for the job

your appointment, the interviewer apologizes and says it will be at least a half hour before she can meet with you. Even though you may respond politely, if you fold your arms across your chest or slump down in your seat, your body language may demonstrate that you are disappointed or angry.

During an interview, the way you use your body will send important messages. As you enter the interview situation, use positive body language. Smile. Stand tall. Your posture should be relaxed but erect. Greet the

COMMUNICATION PRACTICE LAB

Analyzing Body Language

To better understand the messages sent by nonverbal behaviors, follow these steps:

Step 1 As a class, brainstorm ten to fifteen examples of appropriate body language and list them on the chalkboard.

Step 2 Beside each behavior, write under what circumstances it might be exhibited by an interviewer or interviewee.

Step 3 Discuss why each would be appropriate in an interview situation.

Step 4 Have a pair of volunteers act out an interview using the appropriate behaviors you listed.

Step 5 As a class, draw conclusions about the possible effects of various body language in an interview situation.

Exploring the Interview Process **299**

MULTIPLE LEARNING STYLES

MEETING INDIVIDUAL NEEDS

Intrapersonal In *Job Interviews for Dummies,* Joyce Lain Kennedy suggests that job applicants create "commercials" that introduce themselves and advertise their own best qualities. Challenge students to prepare for interviews by creatively assessing themselves.

Activity Tell students to imagine that they will be asked to tell an interviewer about themselves. Have students write a "commercial" that would tell the interviewer engaging and pertinent facts about themselves. Suggest that they consider facts such as their favorite school subjects, their job history, the accomplishments and talents they are most proud of, hobbies, and college and career goals. Urge them to put the information in a coherent, compelling paragraph.

Improving Verbal Skills

Ask students to name some current slang terms that are classroom appropriate. Write them on the chalkboard. Then, have the class suggest words and phrases that express the slang expressions in a way that would be appropriate in a job interview. Point out that slang is similar to casual dress styles: Although it is not inappropriate in many contexts, it does not give a positive impression in an interview. Have students jot down a few slang terms that they use often and then write them in a more formal style. **L1**

COMMUNICATION PRACTICE LAB

Analyzing Body Language

Students should conclude that appropriate body language can help make all conditions favorable for achieving the interview's goals.

GLENCOE *Online*

For an additional Practice Lab for this section, students can visit the *Glencoe Communication Applications* Web site at **communicationapplications. glencoe.com.** Click on Communication Practice Lab 9–3. **L1**

BUSINESS BRIEF

In *Job Interviews for Dummies,* Joyce Lain Kennedy quotes four classic guidelines for dressing for an interview: "Dress one step up from what you'd typically wear to work in that position"; "Dress 10 percent better than you ordinarily would"; "Dress for the position you'd like to have, not for the one you do have"; "Dress the best you're ever going to look in the job you want."

Interviewee and Interviewer Questions

Ask volunteers to read aloud the interviewee questions. Ask students to name some questions they *don't* find on the list, such as those regarding salary, vacation time, and other benefits. Point out that these kinds of questions should usually be asked only after a job offer has been made. Have students work in pairs. Instruct them to take turns asking and answering the list of interviewer questions. Suggest that partners offer one another constructive criticism on their answers. **L2**

Communication Tip

Be aware of subtle differences in the way you phrase questions as an interviewee. You may want to seem especially confident and urge the interviewer to visualize you in the job you are seeking. Therefore, you might say, "What would my duties be?" instead of "What are the duties of this position?" However, if you don't wish to seem too forward or overconfident, you may want to stick to the more objective phrasing.

interviewer appropriately. Confidently approach the chair where you will sit and settle into it as comfortably as possible.

Sit tall in the chair, making sure not to slump. Your feet should be flat on the floor so that you are balanced and comfortable. You can lean slightly forward, making appropriate eye contact. If someone is asking a question, maintain eye contact with that person. However, when you answer, your eye contact should be with everyone in the room. Your hands should lie quietly in your lap when you are not using them to make graceful, appropriate gestures while you speak. If you have a pen for taking notes, be sure that you hold it only when you are writing. Avoid playing with any object since this communicates anxiety and lack of confidence. Overall, your body should show that you are interested, attentive, and ready to participate fully in the interview.

APPROPRIATE QUESTIONS IN INTERVIEWS

An appropriate question is one that is suitable based on the situation. In order to determine if a question is suitable, you need to analyze the context and norms for that particular situation.

Interviewee Questions

In a job interview, you are the guest of the interviewer. He or she ultimately controls how much information is exchanged. However, by preparing and asking appropriate questions, you can help ensure that you will get the information you need about the job and the company.

In Section 1, you read about preparing useful questions. Following are some appropriate questions you may wish to use as a guide.

- What are the specific duties of this position?
- How might you describe a typical day in this position? At this office?
- Is this a new position, or has it recently been vacated?
- How much travel is normally involved?
- With whom will I be working most closely?
- What type of computer technology is involved in this position?
- Is any special training provided?
- Is performance reviewed on a regular basis?
- What else can I tell you about my qualifications?
- When do you expect to make a decision?

Interviewer Questions

What types of appropriate questions can you expect to hear from the interviewer? Following are some questions commonly asked in employment interviews.

- Tell me about yourself.
- What is one of your weaknesses/ strengths?
- How will your specific experience and qualifications help you do this job?
- Why did you leave your last job?
- What is the most important thing you learned from your last job or from school?
- What did you like most about your last job/school? What did you like least?
- What have you done that shows initiative (taking charge) or a willingness to work?

REAL-WORLD CONNECTION

Overcoming Stage Fright Point out that in a job interview, an individual is "on stage" in a way. Therefore, he or she may undergo stage fright and be unable to perform as well as possible.
Activity Invite an experienced actor or stage director to class to share methods for overcoming stage fright. Your guest may be a drama teacher, a community actor or director, or a student who is an experienced actor. Encourage the class to consider and practice the methods used by actors to feel comfortable on stage, such as breathing, stretching, and visualization exercises.

- Why do you want to work for this company?
- Why should we hire you for this position?
- When are you available to start?
- May we contact your references?

Laws Governing Employment Questions

Many laws govern what questions are and are not legal in employment interviews. Basically, employers may not legally ask for information that can be used to discriminate on the basis of race, color, religion, sex, disabilities, marital status, national origin, or age. To **discriminate** means to treat differently based on reasons other than individual merit, or quality.

A few examples of illegal interview questions are shown in the table. Note that simply asking the question is not illegal. However, it becomes illegal if the question leads to an act of discrimination. For this reason, most interviewers consider these questions inappropriate and avoid them entirely.

ILLEGAL INTERVIEW QUESTIONS

Questions Related to . . .	Example
Birthplace, nationality, or ancestry	"Pasquale—is that a Spanish name?"
Gender or marital status	"Is that your maiden name?"
Race or color	"Are you considered to be part of a minority group?"
Religion or religious days observed	"Does your religion prevent you from working weekends or holidays?"
Physical challenges or disabilities	"Do you have any use of your legs?"
Health or medical history	"Do you have any pre-existing health conditions?"
Pregnancy or child care	"Do you plan to have children?"

Responding to an Unlawful Question Of course, just because a question is illegal doesn't mean it won't be asked. That's why it is important to know how to respond to unlawful questions in an interview. There are several ways to answer unlawful questions. They include the following.

- Simply answer the question.
- Note that you think the question is illegal but answer anyway.
- Ask the interviewer about the appropriateness of the question. "Why? Is my religion a factor in whether or not I will be hired?"
- Refuse to answer directly, but rationalize that your answer would have no bearing on your ability to do the job.
- Ask the interviewer how the question relates to the job and whether it really is lawful.
- Redirect the focus of the discussion from the question to something else, such as the job requirements.
- Refuse to provide the information.
- End the interview and leave.

Choosing a Specific Response If you are asked a question that is not legal, how do you know which of these responses to use? There are several factors to think about. First, consider why the interviewer asked the question. Many interviewers may not realize that certain questions are unlawful. The interviewer who asks about nationality or family may simply be trying to make conversation.

A second consideration is how badly you want the job.

Exploring the Interview Process **301**

Dealing with Illegal Questions

Have students study the chart showing illegal interview questions and ask volunteers to read each possible way of responding to an unlawful question. Have the class discuss the advantages and disadvantages of each kind of response. **L1**

DID YOU KNOW?

One question that is illegal for an interviewer to ask in an employment interview is "Have you ever been arrested?" because an arrest does not mean that guilt was established. Another illegal inquiry is "How's your health?" which is forbidden by the Americans with Disabilities Act.

3 ASSESS

Assign Section 3 Assessment as a homework or in-class activity.

🖊 Use *Interactive Tutor Self-Assessment Software* to review Section 3.

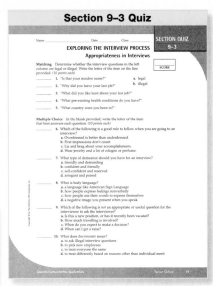

CRITICAL THINKING ACTIVITY

Have students work in small groups in which they create a skit based on an employer asking one or more interview questions that are illegal. Point out that students should start by imagining a specific (though imaginary) company and employment interviewer. They should then create one or more characters as interviewees. Urge students to be creative in deciding whether to show a variety of possible responses by an interviewee or simply illustrating one response. Have each group present their skit to the class. Encourage the class members to discuss each situation and the interviewees' responses. Were they effective? What other responses might have been better?

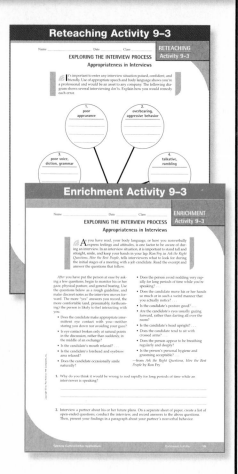

Enrichment Activity 9–3

4 CLOSE

Have students reread the italicized paragraph that opens Section 3. Then, ask students to close their books and in one minute list the characteristics that an interviewer typically notices about an interviewee in the first minute after meeting.

Extra-Credit Project

Have students research the history of laws against employment discrimination in the United States. Ask them to present their findings in an oral report.

If you feel that the interview is going well and you would like the position, you may decide to answer the question.

A third consideration is how comfortable you feel with the interviewer. If the interviewer is your age or has children your age, you may feel more comfortable discussing age issues.

Finally, consider your own personal style. You may or may not be willing to confront the interviewer or walk out on the interview. You may prefer to go ahead and answer the question but then refuse to take the job if it is offered.

Ethics in Interviewing

You can see the ethical stance interviewers need to take when asking questions. How does ethics apply to the interviewee? Imagine that you were fired from your previous job. If the interviewer asks why you left, how should you answer? The best choice is to tell the truth, briefly explaining any special circumstances or simply that you made a mistake and have learned from the experience. In all questions, honesty is best. If an employer finds that you have lied, nothing else you say will be believable.

Section 3 Assessment

GLENCOE Online

Visit the *Glencoe Communication Applications* Web site at **communicationapplications. glencoe.com** and click on **Self-Check and Study Guide 9.3** to review your understanding of appropriateness in interviews.

Review Key Terms

1. Define each term and write it in a sentence: demeanor, body language, discriminate.

Check Understanding

2. Explain why appropriateness is important in an interview.

3. Write two specific questions you might ask when interviewing for a job as an editorial assistant at a small newspaper.

4. If an interviewer asked you "Would you have any problem working on Christmas Day?" how might you respond? Explain.

5. Might it be appropriate to wear jeans and a nice shirt to an interview for a construction job? Explain why or why not.

6. **Analysis** Think of an instance when you met someone for the first time. What type of impression did that person make? Describe what about their dress, appearance, and demeanor helped to create this impression.

APPLICATION *Activity*

Determining Appropriate Dress Working with a partner, discuss what type of dress would be appropriate for each of the following interview situations:
- You apply for an internship in the state capitol building.
- You audition as a singer in a local band.
- You meet a new neighbor who needs a baby-sitter.
- You apply for a summer job in your local parks and recreation department.

Section 3 Assessment Answers

1. Accept all reasonable sentences.
2. Appropriateness is vital for a positive first impression.
3. Questions should be appropriate for the context.
4. Accept any reasonable responses.
5. Some students may say *yes* because the context of the interview probably will be fairly informal. Others may believe that dressing up might give them the edge over other applicants.

6. Answers will describe individual experiences. Accept any reasonable response.
Application Activity Possible answers:
Internship: formal business attire such as a suit;
Singer: clothing appropriate to the style of music;
Baby-sitter: modest casual wear; Parks job: perhaps slacks/skirt with a nice shirt

Communication Self-Assessment

Evaluating Your Interview Skills

How Do You Rate?

On a separate sheet of paper, respond to the following statements. Put a check mark at the end of each skill you would like to improve.

KEY: A Always   **R** Rarely
       U Usually   **N** Never
       S Sometimes

1. When I am an interviewer, I have a goal and questions.

2. In an interview, I listen carefully and answer questions directly.

3. I try to make the best impression possible in an employment interview.

4. To prepare for being an investigative interviewer, I plan questions ahead.

5. I prepare for performance evaluations by learning about my interviewer, reviewing my job description, and preparing a summary of my past work.

6. I do research about the company before an employment interview.

7. As I prepare for an interview, I think about what I want to say, focus on non-verbal behaviors, and practice the interview with someone, if possible.

8. I know how to recognize unlawful interview questions.

9. I wear appropriate clothing and choose proper demeanor when I am interviewed.

10. I am able to show poise and confidence in an interview.

How Do You Score?

Review your responses. Give yourself 5 points for every A, 4 for every U, 3 for every S, 2 for every R, and 1 for every N. Total your points and evaluate your score.

41–50 Excellent You may be surprised to find out how much you can improve your skills.

31–40 Good In this course, you can learn ways to make your skills better.

21–30 Fair Practice applying the skills taught in this course.

1–20 Needs Improvement Carefully monitor your improvement as you work through this course.

Setting Communication Goals

If you scored Excellent or Good, complete Part A. If your score was Fair or Needs Improvement, complete Part B.

Part A 1. I plan to put the following ideas into practice:

         2. I plan to share the following information about communication with the following people:

Part B 1. The behaviors I need to change most are these:

         2. To bring about these changes, I will take these steps:

Exploring the Interview Process   **303**

Communication Self-Assessment

Have students respond to the ten statements using the key on this page, then evaluate their interview skills. Based on their scores, assign either Part A or Part B of the goal-setting activity. On an index card or sheet of paper, students should concretely define their communication goals to improve their current level of skill.

Communication Journal Activity

Point out to students that people who write down their goals and review them regularly are more likely to accomplish their objectives than are people who merely think of areas of improvement. Have students list their goals in their Communication journals.

COOPERATIVE LEARNING ACTIVITY

Researching Interview Skills Many books have been written about job hunting and job interviews. Students can survey the literature on interviewing and improve their knowledge of interview skills.

Activity Have pairs of students go to a public library and find books on interviewing skills. Instruct them to skim the books and choose one or two they find are the most informative and engaging. They should write a review of the book or books that tells a prospective reader the best features. Ask them to include two or three facts or tips about interviewing that are new to them. Have students write, make copies, and distribute their reviews or present them orally.

Writing a Cover Letter

Objective: To create a résumé cover letter

Teaching Suggestions and Strategies

Connection to the Workplace

Discuss the tips for writing a cover letter in each subhead. Point out the importance of good writing skills and knowledge of the correct form for business letters even in this age of e-mails and other electronic communication.

Ask students to share their own experiences and advice on cover letters. Also discuss the following additional tips: If you know someone in the company or have spoken with a company employee in the process of researching the job, mention the person in the first paragraph. Use strong verbs to make your previous experience and accomplishments sound compelling. Emphasize the accomplishment listed on your résumé that you would like the employer to notice.

Grammar Tip

The case of personal pronouns depends on their use in a sentence. Pronouns used as subjects include *I, you, he, she, we,* and *they*. Pronouns used as objects are *me, you, him, her, us,* and *them*.

DID YOU KNOW?

According to Max Messmer in *Job Hunting for Dummies,* 60 percent of executives in a survey said that cover letters are as important or more important than résumés.

Writing a Cover Letter

A résumé sent in with an application for work is often general and impersonal. A cover letter sent with your résumé, however, acts like a personal introduction when directed to the individual responsible for hiring new workers. Getting an interview is the ultimate goal of sending the cover letter and résumé. To write an effective cover letter, follow the procedures below.

Provide the Context. Let the employer know how you heard about the job opening. Do this near the beginning of your cover letter.

Catch the Reader's Attention Quickly. Classified advertisements in major newspapers or journals may attract hundreds of responses. Most of these responses will be discarded. Therefore, you need to give the employer a reason to call or remember you. Do this by asking a question or making a clever statement at the beginning of your letter. If you don't capture the attention of the reader right away, your full letter and résumé may not be read.

Describe Your Previous Accomplishments. Show the employer that your qualifications meet the job requirements. Since companies are interested in people who are achievers, show the reader that you take initiative. Explain to the employer how you can use your skills to fulfill the objectives outlined in the job description. By doing this, you relate your past experiences to the kind of talent the employer needs. You can refer to your résumé to support your claim.

End by Requesting an Interview. One way to ask for an interview is to say you will call on or near some future date. Suggest that you would enjoy having the opportunity to meet and talk with this person. You can also ask the potential employer to contact you. If you use this approach, provide an accurate telephone number with a message service or other reliable means of contact so the employer will be able to reach you.

Check Format and Appearance. Write your cover letter on standard $8\frac{1}{2}" \times 11"$ stationery using the format shown in the sample letter on the following page. Your cover letter should be centered on the page, and it should be only one page long. Make sure that you proofread your cover letter. Be sure to correct all errors in spelling, punctuation, and grammar before you send the letter.

 For additional information about business writing, see the *Guide to Business Communication* section of the Communication Survival Kit in the Appendix.

REAL-WORLD CONNECTION

Cover Letters What *really* gets the attention of employers in a cover letter? Challenge individuals or pairs of students to find out.

Activity Have students contact someone they know, such as an executive or human resources manager, who receives many résumés and cover letters from job applicants. Ask them to conduct a telephone interview to find out what most effectively captures the manager's attention in a cover letter. Students may also ask their interviewee to quote from impressive letters. Instruct students to take notes of their interview and then to present their findings to the class in an oral report.

Communication Through Writing

WRITING *Activity*

You have learned about an entry-level position in a real estate office. Your guidance counselor informed you of this position. Use the following information to write a cover letter. Write your letter using the information you have learned in this feature and in the rest of Chapter 9.

- Applicant must have courteous phone skills and be able to direct calls to a busy staff of real estate agents.

- Applicant will need excellent word processing skills.

- Job description includes typing weekly ads about properties for sale and submitting them to a Sunday newspaper.

- You have learned many word processing programs and feel comfortable with them.

- You have had some experience answering a busy telephone in your high school business office.

- Last summer you worked for a temporary office service using your word processing skills.

- You had one two-week assignment last summer working in the advertising department of a local paper.

April 9, 2002

Hector Cruz
4510 Elm Drive
Chillicothe, Missouri 64601

Mr. Elmer Todd
Human Relations
City of St. Louis International Bank
1157 Avenue of the Arch
St. Louis, Missouri 62035

Dear Mr. Todd:

Are you interested in hiring a Spanish/English speaking person to work as a receptionist in your bank this summer? When I read your ad in the St. Louis *Post-Dispatch*, I was eager to answer because I enjoy working with people and speak Spanish and English fluently.

My résumé is enclosed. You might be interested in the fact that I am president of the Spanish Club at Chillicothe High School. I have held this position for two years. You might also note from my résumé that I spent last summer working as a travel guide in St. Louis translating English into Spanish for many Spanish-speaking groups.

I am very interested in discussing this position with you. I will telephone you early next week to talk about this possibility.

Sincerely,

Hector Cruz

Hector Cruz

Reading the Sample Letter

Point out the correct form for the date, heading, address, greeting, body, and closing of the business letter. Then, have volunteers read each paragraph in the body of the letter. Have students explain the purpose of each statement.

WRITING *Activity*

Students' letters should include all the specific information listed, have a strong opening and a conclusion requesting an interview, follow the format shown in the sample letter, and be free of grammatical and mechanical errors.

Communication Tip

As in a job interview, it is always a good idea to show in a cover letter that you are familiar with the company to which you are applying. You might mention specific recent developments and how you heard about them.

Additional Resources

Appendix, "Guide to E-Business Communication"

Glencoe Writer's Assistant CD-ROM

Glencoe Interactive Grammar Software

Chapter 9 Writer's Choice, Lesson 6.1

GRAMMAR PRACTICE

Subject and Object Pronouns

Have students choose the word or phrase that correctly completes each sentence.

1. The other counselors and (I, me) supervised eighty children. *I*

2. (Him and me) (He and I) discussed the sales position at your company. *He and I*

3. No one sold more magazine subscriptions than (I, me). *I*

4. The sales manager worked closely with (her and me) (she and I). *her and me*

5. You and (me, I) should meet in person and talk about my extensive design experience. *I*

CHAPTER 9 **Assessment and Activities**

 MindJogger Videoquiz

Use *MindJogger* to review the Chapter 9 content.

GLENCOE Online

Visit the *Glencoe Communication Applications* Web site at **communicationapplications. glencoe.com** and click on **Chapter 9 Activity** for additional practice in the interview process.

Reviewing Key Terms

1. False: The <u>interviewer</u> determines the purpose of the interview.

2. True

3. False: Investigative is a kind of information-<u>gathering</u> interview.

4. False: A <u>performance appraisal</u> is an evaluation of how well an employee has achieved his or her goals over time.

5. True

6. False: An <u>exit</u> interview is used to determine why a person has left an organization.

7. True

8. True

Reviewing Key Concepts

1. Both must ask questions, listen to each other's responses, and provide feedback.

2. (1) setting a goal, (2) developing a structure for the interview, (3) setting the tone, (4) preparing and asking questions, and (5) controlling the direction of the questions

3. The interviewee can avoid making misleading or confusing statements.

4. Who, What, When, Where, Why, and How

Reviewing Key Terms

Read each statement. On a separate sheet of paper, write whether the statement is true or false. If the statement is false, rewrite the statement so that it reads true. Underline the word or words that you substitute to make it so.

1. The interviewee determines the purpose of the interview.

2. Survey interviews gather information from a number of people.

3. Investigative is a kind of information-giving interview.

4. A counseling interview is an evaluation of how well an employee has achieved his or her goals over time.

5. A highly-closed question can provide options or a specific answer.

6. An employment interview is used to determine why a person has left an organization.

7. The interview process includes preparation, the actual interview, and the post interview.

8. An example of discriminating is turning down a job applicant for an office position because he or she belongs to a certain race.

Reviewing Key Concepts

1. In what three ways do interviewer and interviewee participate fully in an interview?

2. What are five major responsibilities of an interviewer?

3. How does thinking about a response before voicing it help an interviewee?

4. What six types of questions does an interviewer generally ask in an investigative interview?

5. Name the two kinds of information-giving interviews.

6. List six steps in preparing for an interview.

7. How does practice help the participants before an interview?

8. What are two elements of the interviewee's post interview?

5. A performance appraisal, a counseling interview, and a persuasive interview

6. (1) Set a goal. (2) Determine the type of interview. (3) Determine the structure. (4) Research the other party. (5) Develop appropriate questions. (6) Practice.

7. Practice allows participants to experiment, correct any missteps, and adjust their behavior for maximum impact and effectiveness.

8. A thank-you letter to the interviewer and an analysis of the interview

Reading and Critical Thinking Skill

1. **Applying Information** An interviewer greets you, the interviewee, with a smile, a handshake, and an offer of coffee. What responsibility is the interviewer carrying out by these actions?

2. **Synthesis** How should an interviewee respond to the ambiguous question "Can you walk long distances?"

3. **Cause-Effect** What is generally the result of sending a poorly written résumé?

4. **Classifying Information** How would you classify the following question: "At which office would you prefer to work—Dallas, Houston, or Oklahoma City?"

5. **Making Comparisons** Which type of interview generally takes more time—a scheduled or an unscheduled? Why?

Skill Practice Activity

Skimming Get an employee handbook from a business in your area, or use your school's handbook of policies. Skim the handbook for information about sick leave or procedures to follow when you are sick and unable to go to work or school. Provide a list of these policies. Discuss as a class the procedures you used to find the policies in the handbook.

Cooperative Learning Activity

Modeling Appropriate Dress Organize into groups of four. As a group, select an employment ad from the classified section of the newspaper. Then search magazines and catalogues for appropriate dress in an interview for that job. Create a poster with the title of the job at the top. Cut out the photographs of the clothing, and glue the photographs onto the poster. Beside each type of dress, explain why the outfit is appropriate for the interview.

Chapter Project

Planning Choose a company at which you would like to interview in the future. Start your preparation now by finding answers to the research questions on page 288.

Presenting Arrange the information you have researched on a flyer. Place the name of the company at the top of the flyer and include bold headings for each classification of facts. Add the facts in brief phrases. Remember to include the company's address and phone number. Make copies of your flyer and distribute them to interested classmates.

Exploring the Interview Process **307**

Reading and Critical Thinking Skill

1. **Applying Information** setting the tone

2. **Synthesis** Students' answers may vary. Responses should be similar to the following example: An interviewee should request clarification, such as "How far—less than or more than a mile?"

3. **Cause-Effect** The interviewer may decide the applicant is unsuitable for the job and therefore won't arrange an interview.

4. **Classifying Information** Highly closed

5. **Making Comparisons** An unscheduled interview usually takes more time because, unlike a scheduled interview, the tone is conversational and more difficult for the interviewer to control.

Skill Practice Activity

Skimming

Encourage students to try to find employee handbooks from companies. Ask students what particular skimming technique helped them the most.

Cooperative Learning Activity

Modeling Appropriate Dress

Groups' posters will vary with the kinds of jobs they choose. Remind students that dressing too formally for an interview is always better than dressing too casually. Display the posters in the classroom and spend some class time asking students to evaluate each group's appropriate attire.

Chapter Project

Students can use the Internet and ask the librarian about sources for individual companies. Set aside time for a job fair in your classroom at which students can distribute their informational flyers about companies.

THE PRINCETON REVIEW

Standardized Test Practice

**English Usage
Multiple-Choice
Theme: Professional
Communication**

Teaching Strategy

Encourage students to read the passage and each time they see a blank, come up with their own word to fill it. Then, students can look at the choices and eliminate those that do not fit.

Having their own hypothesis about what should fill the blank will help them quickly see which choices are wrong.

Answers and Analyses

1. **A** This item tests students' use of verb tense and agreement. Choice A agrees in tense and number with the rest of the sentence. Choice B does not agree with the singular subject of the sentence, which is *an employer*. Choices C and D are in tenses that do not match the rest of the sentence.

2. **H** This item tests students' use of verb tense and agreement. Choice F is not the right tense for the sentence because the surrounding sentences are in the present tense and there is no reason to switch. Choice G does not agree with the plural subject, *businesses*. Choice H agrees with the subject of the sentence and also keeps to the present tense. Choice J does not agree with the plural subject.

3. **B** The item tests whether students will choose a pronoun that agrees with its antecedent. The antecedent in this case is *people*, so the pronoun must be third person plural: *they*.

4. **H** This item tests students' use of superlatives and comparatives. The blank should be filled with the correct form of the superlative: *hard*.

5. **D** This item tests students' use of adjectives, adverbs, and comparatives. The blank requires an adverb because it modifies a verb, *communicate*. The only adverb choice is also a comparative: *more effectively*.

Read each passage and choose the word or group of words that belongs in each space. Mark the letter for your answer.

Looking for a summer job can be difficult and stressful. It is important to realize that you can always find an employer who __(1)__ a vacancy if you keep searching. Remember, thriving businesses often __(2)__ new positions as they grow and prosper. In addition, existing positions are continually becoming available, for a number of reasons. People are promoted to new positions, or sometimes __(3)__ move on to other companies. All of these factors contribute to the availability of jobs in the marketplace.

Finding a vacancy may be the __(4)__ part of the process, but it is not the last. Do not forget to prepare for your job interview. Research the organization ahead of time, so you know what they are looking for in an employee. Make a list of your accomplishments and strengths. You will be able to communicate your desires and abilities __(5)__ if you plan ahead.

1 **A** has
   B have
   C is having
   D had

2 **F** created
   G creates
   H create
   J is creating

3 **A** we
   B they
   C you
   D it

4 **F** hard
   G more hard
   H hardest
   J most hardest

5 **A** effective
   B eff700effiver
   C more effectiver
   D more effectively

THE PRINCETON REVIEW **Test-Taking Tip**

If students are tempted to look at the answer choices first, tell them to cover them with one hand as they read the passage. That way, they can think of their own word for a blank before looking at the choices.

Read each passage and decide which type of error, if any, appears in each underlined section. Mark the letter for your answer.

> When Cynthia recieved her first writing assignment from the *Washington High*
> (1)
> *School Observer, she was* excited. She decided to interview a local nutritionist for an
>
> article about keeping fit. To prepare for the interview, Cynthia asked some of her
>
> fellow students what they did to stay in shape. "On Mondays and Thursdays I go
> (2)
> to the gym after school, said her friend Louisa."
>
> Joe, a member of the school Football Team, said, "I get plenty of exercise at
> (3)
> practice every day."
>
> At the library, Cynthia discovered a cookbook containing healthy recipes for the
> (4)
> following: pasta, fish, meat, and even desserts. Later, she called a health club in the
>
> area and asked about their membership fees. Cynthia spent some time reading the
> (5)
> materials that she borrowed from the library: and created a long list of questions to
>
> ask the nutritionist. When it was time for the interview, Cynthia was ready!

1 A Spelling error
B Capitalization error
C Punctuation error
D No error

2 F Spelling error
G Capitalization error
H Punctuation error
J No error

3 A Spelling error
B Capitalization error
C Punctuation error
D No error

4 F Spelling error
G Capitalization error
H Punctuation error
J No error

5 A Spelling error
B Capitalization error
C Punctuation error
D No error

STOP

Interpersonal Communication **309**

English Mechanics
Multiple-Choice
Theme: Preparing for Interviews

Teaching Strategy

Students should try to find the error on the first reading. If they don't see anything, they should then look specifically for a spelling error, then capitalization, and finally punctuation. If they've read the underlined section four times and still see nothing wrong, they should choose "No error."

Answers and Analyses

1. **A** *Received* is spelled incorrectly. Remind students of the spelling rule, "*i* before *e* when the sound is *ee*, except after *c*." If students are worried about spelling, remind them that it counts for only a few points on most standardized tests.

2. **H** The quotation marks should appear after the word *school*. Quotation marks should surround only the quoted material, not the information about who said what.

3. **B** The words *football team* should not be capitalized because they are not a proper adjective or noun.

4. **J** There is no error in the underlined section. Remind students that when "no error" is one of four answer choices, they should not be afraid to choose it. It is usually correct approximately one-fourth of the time.

5. **C** The colon is used incorrectly in this sentence. Remind students that in a sentence, a colon is usually used to introduce a list or explanation.

THE PRINCETON REVIEW **Test-Taking Tip**

Students need to have sharp eyes when reading the underlined sections. The errors in items like these often involve the placement of one letter or punctuation mark.

Unit Objective
Students will learn to identify and demonstrate knowledge of group dynamics in social and professional contexts, including how to manage conflict and acquire leadership skills.

Unit Overview
Unit 3 equips students to understand and participate effectively in the groups that form the basis of their social and professional lives. Students will learn to identify types of groups and their functions, to demonstrate their abilities as group members, to practice the skills of conflict management, and to analyze leadership styles.

Internet Address Book
Record useful Internet addresses in the space below for quick reference.

_____

_____

_____

_____

_____

_____

_____

_____

_____

_____

_____

_____

_____

_____

_____

_____

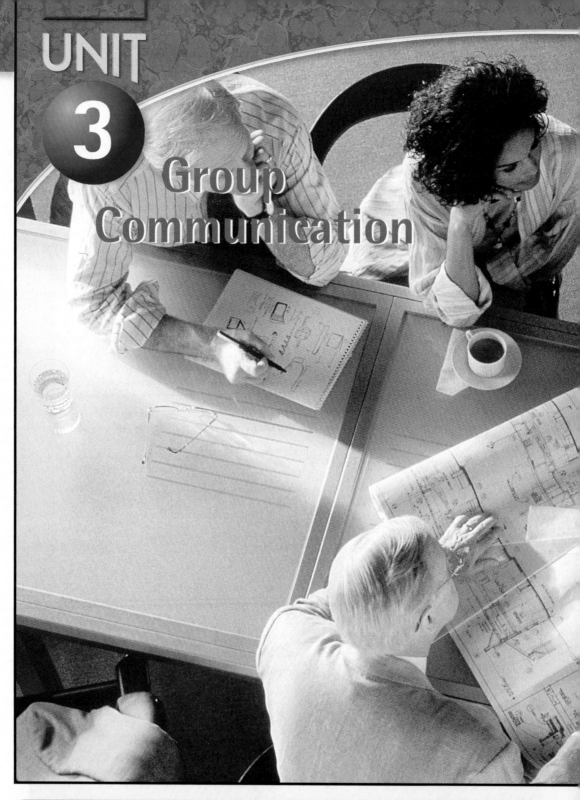

UNIT 3
Group Communication

VISUAL INSTRUCTION ACTIVITY

Have students examine the photograph on pp. 310–311. Ask them to describe what they believe is occurring in this situation. *(Students may suggest that the man on his feet is leading a team of coworkers in a group project.)* Ask: **What skills should one possess in order to lead an effective group at work? What skills does one need to be a productive group member?** *(Students may respond that a leader must be informed, organized, imaginative, skilled in handling conflict, a clear communicator, and a good listener. They may attribute many of the same qualities to group members, while adding adaptability, willingness to take responsibility, and a sense of humor.)*

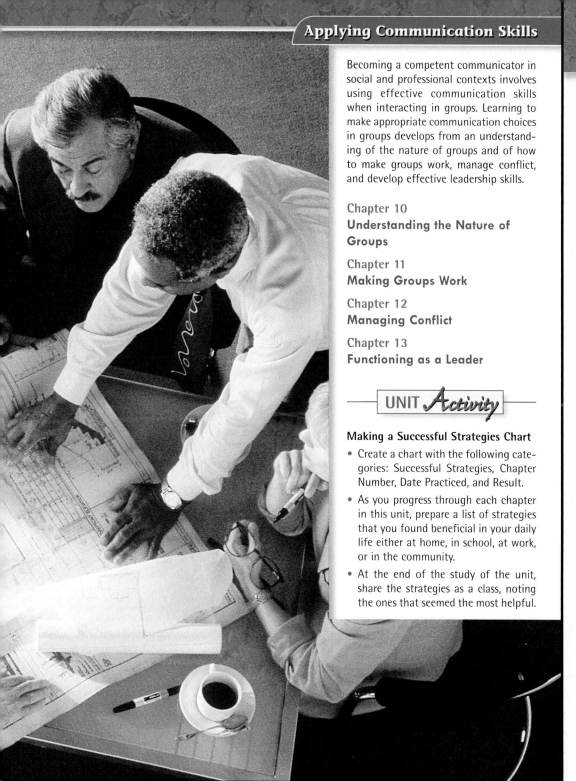

Applying Communication Skills

Becoming a competent communicator in social and professional contexts involves using effective communication skills when interacting in groups. Learning to make appropriate communication choices in groups develops from an understanding of the nature of groups and of how to make groups work, manage conflict, and develop effective leadership skills.

Chapter 10
Understanding the Nature of Groups

Chapter 11
Making Groups Work

Chapter 12
Managing Conflict

Chapter 13
Functioning as a Leader

UNIT *Activity*

Making a Successful Strategies Chart

- Create a chart with the following categories: Successful Strategies, Chapter Number, Date Practiced, and Result.
- As you progress through each chapter in this unit, prepare a list of strategies that you found beneficial in your daily life either at home, in school, at work, or in the community.
- At the end of the study of the unit, share the strategies as a class, noting the ones that seemed the most helpful.

Introducing the Unit

Write on the chalkboard: *I work productively with other people.* Ask students to apply this statement to themselves, rating themselves from one (poor) to ten (excellent). Invite them to share their strengths or weaknesses in this area with their fellow students. Inform them that employers are particularly interested in candidates who successfully work as members of a team. Ask students why they think this should be the case. What is it about efficient groups that make them more productive than individuals working alone? Point out that many of the skills necessary for effective group communication are discussed in Unit 3.

Unit Assessment

After students have completed Unit 3, assign the Unit 3 Assessment in the *Glencoe Communication Appplications Chapter and Unit Tests*.

Testmaker Use the *Glencoe Communication Applications ExamView® Pro Testmaker* software to create a customized Unit 3 test.

UNIT *Activity*

Point out to students that practical communication strategies are provided throughout the text. Assign the following strategies as needed:

Improving Attending Skills, p. 9
Improving Memory Skills, p. 15

For additional strategies, see the "Guide to Business Communication" in the Communication Survival Kit on pages 635–639.

COMMUNICATING IN THE COMMUNITY

Encourage students to experience how groups function by asking them to attend a meeting where a committee is deliberating or a task force is debating strategy. Point out that while many bodies meet behind closed doors, there are often opportunities for the public to observe groups in action. The school committee, zoning board, town council, finance committee, or other local organizations may hold regular public meetings. Alternatively, have students inquire if a local business would admit observers to meetings—an editorial meeting at a newspaper, for instance, or a sales meeting at a local manufacturing firm. Have students take notes on the order of the meeting, the roles of the members, and the decisions reached. Invite volunteers to share their observations with the class.

Chapter 10 Planning Guide

SECTION RESOURCES

Daily Objectives

Section 1

1. Identify the four characteristics of a group
2. Explain how groups are important to organizations
3. Explain how groups are important to individuals
4. Create an effective group goal statement
5. Distinguish between the two main kinds of groups
6. Compare and contrast the purposes of task groups and social groups

Section 2

1. Explain why the group function of planning is important to organizations
2. Identify the three main considerations involved in planning
3. Describe the six steps of the problem-solving process
4. Explain why brainstorming is useful for generating new, creative ideas

Reproducible Resources

 Reproducible Lesson Plan 10-1
 Application Activities 10-1
 Guided Reading Workbook Activity 10-1
 Vocabulary Activity 10*
 Reteaching Activity 10-1*
 Enrichment Activity 10-1*
 Graphic Organizer Transparency Strategies and Activities 10-1

 Reproducible Lesson Plan 10-2
 Application Activities 10-2
 Guided Reading Workbook Activity 10-2
 Vocabulary Activity 10*
 Reteaching Activity 10-2*
 Enrichment Activity 10-2*
Graphic Organizer Transparency Strategies and Activities 10-2

Multimedia Resources

 Graphic Organizer Transparency 10-1
 Chapter 10 Teaching Transparency
 Interactive Tutor Self-Assessment
 PuzzleMaker
 ExamView® Pro Testmaker
 Interactive Lesson Planner
 Communication in Action Video Chapter 10
 MindJogger
 communicationapplications.glencoe.com
Presentation Plus!

 Graphic Organizer Transparency 10-2
 Chapter 10 Teaching Transparency
 Interactive Tutor Self-Assessment
 PuzzleMaker
 ExamView® Pro Testmaker
 Interactive Lesson Planner
 Communication in Action Video Chapter 10
 MindJogger
 communicationapplications.glencoe.com
Presentation Plus!

Use Glencoe's *Presentation Plus!* multimedia teacher tool to easily present dynamic lessons that engage and motivate your students. Using Microsoft PowerPoint®, you can customize the presentations to create your own personalized lessons.

* Also available in Spanish

 Blackline Master   CD-ROM   Software

Transparency   Videodisc   Videocassette   Web site

Chapter 10 Planning Guide

Working in Groups

Have students think about how the following statement applies to them: I am a team player. Ask: Do you work and play well with others? Do you feel your creative abilities stimulated by the responses of a friend or classmate? Have students rate themselves as team players from one (decidedly not) to ten (any team, anywhere).

Next, form groups of three or four and have each group discuss the following question: What three inventions would you like to see developed in the next fifty years? At the end of a time period you have determined, have each group write a description of the three inventions they proposed. Have groups share their ideas with the class.

Finally, have students reflect on the group project they have just experienced by considering the following questions: Did your group work well together? Did you feel that your participation was valuable? Could you have done better by yourself? Have students compare their recent group experiences with their self-assessment ratings. Discuss the value of working in groups.

CHAPTER RESOURCES

Resources for the Teacher

- *Creativity in Small Groups* by Paul A. Hare, Sage Publications, 1992
- *Groups, Theory and Experience* by Rodney W. Napier and Matti K. Gerstenfeld, Houghton Mifflin, 1989
- *The Thinking Manager's Toolbox: Effective Processes for Problem Solving and Decision Making* by William J. Altier, Oxford University Press, 1999

Resources for the Student

- *Going to Work: A Unique Guided Tour Through Corporate America* by Lisa Birnbach, Random, 1988
- *How to Meet, Think and Work to Consensus* by Daniel A. Tagliere, Pheiffer, 1992
- *Understanding a Company* by Jeffrey B. Little, Chelsea House, 1988

Block Scheduling

Block scheduling differs from traditional class scheduling in the amount of time allotted to each period. The extended time frame provided by block scheduling affords you the opportunity to implement a greater number of research-oriented and activity-intense projects to motivate and involve your students. Activities that are particularly suited to use within the block-scheduling framework are identified throughout this chapter by the following designation:

KEY TO ABILITY LEVELS

Teaching Strategies have been coded for varying learning styles and abilities.

L1 **BASIC** activities for all students

L2 **AVERAGE** activities for average to above-average students

L3 **CHALLENGING** activities for above-average students

ELL **English Language Learner** activities

Chapter 10 Resource Manager

The following materials may be used when teaching the chapter. Materials for specific lessons are also shown at point-of-use in the margins of the Teacher's Wraparound Edition.

TEACHING TRANSPARENCIES

Chapter 10 Teaching Transparency

Graphic Organizer Transparency 10-1

Graphic Organizer Transparency 10-2

APPLICATION ACTIVITIES

Chapter 10, Section 1

Chapter 10, Section 2

Chapter 10, Cumulative

REINFORCEMENT AND REVIEW ACTIVITIES

Vocabulary Activity 10

Guided Reading Activity Workbook 10-1, 10-2

Reteaching Activities 10-1, 10-2

Chapter 10 Resource Manager

ASSESSMENT AND EVALUATION

Section Quizzes 10-1, 10-2

Chapter 10 Test, Forms A & B

Performance Assessment Activity 10

ENRICHMENT AND EXTENSION

Technology Application Activity 10

Enrichment Activities 10-1, 10-2

SPANISH RESOURCES

- Spanish Chapter and Unit Tests
- Spanish Vocabulary Activities
- Spanish Section Quizzes
- Spanish Reteaching Activities
- Spanish Enrichment Activities

MULTIMEDIA

- Interactive Tutor Self-Assessment
- ExamView® Pro Testmaker
- PuzzleMaker
- Communication in Action Videodisc and Videocassette
- MindJogger
- Interactive Lesson Planner
- Presentation Plus!
- Writer's Assistant
- Glencoe Interactive Grammar
- **communicationapplications.glencoe.com**

ORAL PRESENTATION ACTIVITIES

Activities 13, 14

TEACHER PLANNING AND SUPPORT

- Reproducible Lesson Plans
- Interactive Lesson Planner
- Presentation Plus!

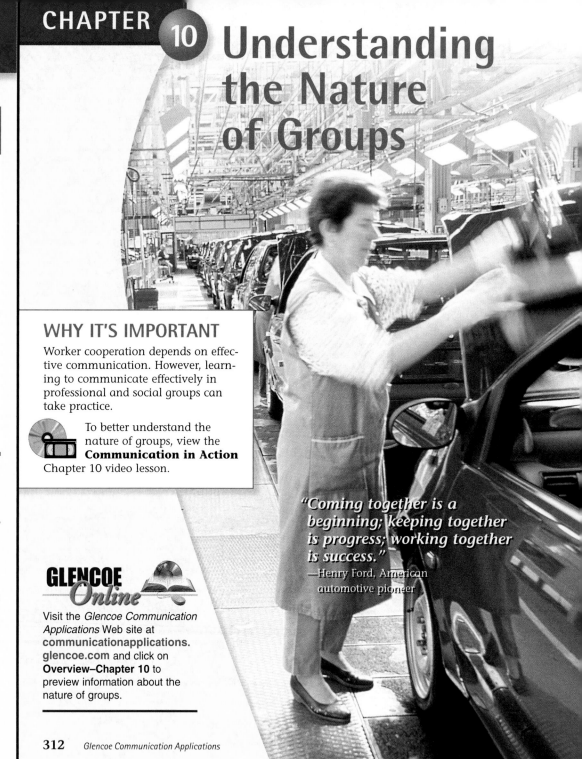

CHAPTER 10 Understanding the Nature of Groups

WHY IT'S IMPORTANT

Worker cooperation depends on effective communication. However, learning to communicate effectively in professional and social groups can take practice.

To better understand the nature of groups, view the **Communication in Action** Chapter 10 video lesson.

"Coming together is a beginning; keeping together is progress; working together is success."

—Henry Ford, American automotive pioneer

WHY IT'S IMPORTANT

Have students read the Henry Ford quotation above and ask them what important word Ford uses three times. *(together)* Encourage them to consider the significance of Ford's statement by asking the following question: **What does "working together" have to do with communication?** Lead students to the idea that one cannot work successfully in a group without effective communication.

Section 1

Understanding Groups

GUIDE TO READING

Objectives

1. Identify the four characteristics of a group.
2. Explain how groups are important to organizations.
3. Explain how groups are important to individuals.
4. Create an effective group goal statement.
5. Distinguish between the two main kinds of groups.
6. Compare and contrast the purposes of task groups and social groups.

Terms to Learn

group
committee
team
advocacy group
group goal
prescribed goal
emergent goal

task group
information-gathering group
policy-making group
action group
social group
informal social group
formal social group

The expression "Two heads are better than one" illustrates why so many organizations use groups to meet their goals. However, another expression, "A camel is a horse put together by a committee," indicates that working in groups is not always easy or effective!

Groups are a major part of both our professional and social lives. We often identify ourselves by the groups and organizations in which we are involved. Organizations also use groups to meet their goals. Because groups are such a large part of our lives, it is important to understand exactly what they are. It is also important to know how they are used in professional and social contexts.

DEFINITION OF A GROUP

A group is a small number of people who identify and interact with one another because of a common interest, bond, or goal.

This definition applies to many different types of groups as well as to groups with different purposes and functions.

Members of a marching band form a group that works together to perform an entertaining show. Define group.

Understanding the Nature of Groups **313**

---

1 FOCUS

Bellringer
Have students read the opening paragraph of the section silently. Then, ask them to write down in their own words what they think the two sentences in quotation marks mean and to explain whether they agree with them or not. Invite students to share their answers with the class. Discuss the benefits and difficulties of working in groups. *(Students may suggest for the first statement, "More people will bring with them a variety of ideas and skills, making a job easier;" for the second statement, they may suggest, "More people create conflict and confusion, resulting in undesired outcomes.")*

You may use Graphic Organizer Transparency 10–1 to introduce this section.

Graphic Organizer Transparency 10–1

Grammar Tip

Quotation marks are used to set off the words of a speaker or quotations from a book or other work. In the introductory paragraph, the quotation marks represent quoted adages. Quotation marks are signals that the words that follow are not the author's but are from another source.

Visual Instruction

Answer Students may say that a group is a small number of people who identify and interact with one another because of a common interest, bond, or goal.

RESOURCE MANAGER

Teaching Tools
- Interactive Lesson Planner
- Reproducible Lesson Plan 10–1
- Application Activities 10–1

Reproducible Masters
- Guided Reading Activity Workbook 10–1
- Enrichment Activity 10–1
- Reteaching Activity 10–1
- Section Quiz 10–1
- Transparency Strategies and Activities Booklet 10–1

Transparencies
- Graphic Organizer Transparency 10–1
- Chapter 10 Teaching Transparency

Technology Resources
- Interactive Tutor Self-Assessment Software
- Presentation Plus! Software
- ExamView® Pro Testmaker
- PuzzleMaker Software
- communicationapplications.glencoe.com

2 TEACH

Formation of Groups

Encourage students to share their personal experiences as members of groups. Ask whether their participation was voluntary or required. Have them assess their experiences. Did groups provide the satisfaction or achieve the results they had anticipated? Could the same purpose have been achieved without a group effort? **L1**

Characteristics of a Group

Ask students to review the four defining characteristics of groups. Have them form pairs and direct them to create a chart showing how these characteristics apply to an organized group at their school. Invite students to share their findings with the class. Make a master chart on the chalkboard, pointing out differences and similarities among the lists. **L2**

Groups Within Organizations

An easy way to understand how groups function within organizations is to think about a marching band. Although a marching band is a single musical organization, it is divided into different instrumental groups. Each member of each group has a common goal or task: to play—accurately and skillfully—the notes in a musical composition. As a result, the group has created a product that is greater than the sum of its parts.

Members of each section of a marching band will rehearse together to learn the notes for their specific instruments. Their notes will be different from the notes for the other groups. When the whole band plays together, the resulting sound from all these groups doing different things at the same time is a complete song, which is the goal of the band. In the same way, both individuals and organizations use groups to accomplish parts of an overall goal. These goals are often ones that would be difficult for someone to achieve individually.

Formation of Groups

Participation in a group can be either required or voluntary. An employer, governmental representative, or other authority may appoint someone to serve in a group. This would be the case if your boss appointed you to a special marketing team.

Other times, people become involved in a group because they want to be a part of what that group is doing. For example, if you are interested in improving the school's homecoming activities, you might volunteer to serve on the planning committee. If you are interested in the security of the neighborhood where

you live, you might ask others who share your interests to form a neighborhood watch group. Regardless of whether participation is voluntary or required, we belong to groups in both our professional and social lives to accomplish specific goals.

Names of Groups

Just as the different sections in a marching band have different names, the groups used in social and professional organizations have a variety of names. These names are derived from the organization itself or from the nature of the particular group. Three names for different groups are committee, team, and advocacy group.

Committee A committee is a group with a specialized task that is part of the basic structure of an organization. A committee that is a permanent part of an organization is called a standing committee.

Team A team is a small group that usually is given the power to make and implement decisions. Teams may be made up of a

Figure 10–1 Characteristics of a Group

1. Limited size
2. Shared goal — Goal
3. Face-to-face meetings
4. Meetings over time

ENGLISH LANGUAGE LEARNERS

MEETING INDIVIDUAL NEEDS

Creating Multi-Cultural Groups Many English language learners feel isolated from the mainstream community by the twin barriers of language and cultural differences. Organizations can promote understanding and communication among members of different cultures.

Activity Have students form groups of four or five, making sure that English language learners are represented in as many groups as possible. Direct each group to propose a school club that would bring together English language learners and mainstream students. Have them write a brief statement of purpose for their club and describe how they would advertise for new members, when the club would meet, and what activities it would pursue. Ask groups to describe their clubs to the class, and discuss whether they think their proposals would succeed. **ELL**

variety of people from different levels and departments in an organization. Organizations may give their teams different names too, such as management teams, work/study teams, and quality-control teams.

Advocacy Group An advocacy group is a group set up specifically to support, protect, defend, or lobby for a cause or group. Advocacy groups are highly specialized. They may exist either independently or within an organization.

CHARACTERISTICS OF A GROUP

A group is more than just a collection of people who happen to be in the same place at the same time. People standing on the corner waiting for a bus or people who happen to be eating at the same restaurant at the same time are not classified as a group. Rather, as Figure 10–1 shows, people in groups display a specific set of characteristics.

Limited Size

The membership of a group is limited. In fact, the best size for a group is four to six people. Imagine trying to listen to ideas and suggestions from every student in your school when planning your school prom. The process probably would be extremely frustrating. It also would be time-consuming. This is why organizations as a whole are not well suited for the kind of interaction and decision making that groups do.

With a limited size, most members of a group have the chance to voice their ideas in a typical meeting. Also, when membership is limited in a small group, members can fully explore issues and examine many different

Figure 10–2 Sample Group Goals

Research → Research dress codes from other schools and make a recommendation for a dress code at our school.
Expected outcome

Research → Discover what causes our products to be broken during shipping and handling and then design packaging that prevents breakage.
Expected outcome

plans of action. They can then bring their work back to the larger group for approval, implementation, or evaluation.

The most productive group work is done when a limited number of people work together to discuss an issue fully, share different ideas, and explain the reasoning behind opposing ideas. This allows group members to seek new alternatives. It also allows for better combinations of ideas as members agree upon a common solution.

Shared Goal

Members of a group share a common purpose or goal. Before a group can work effectively, its members must understand and agree upon this goal. They then have to decide how best to accomplish it.

A group goal identifies what specific tasks are to be accomplished and what the expected group outcome is. A group goal statement might look like one of the two statements in Figure 10–2.

Both of these examples define what tasks are to be done. They also point out whether or not the group will simply make a recommendation or actually implement some action.

Types of Group Goals Sometimes, a group's goal may be prescribed. A prescribed goal is one that is assigned by a person in

Understanding the Nature of Groups **315**

BUSINESS BRIEF

Alfred P. Sloan Jr., served as president of General Motors for more than thirty years. He was a pioneer in recognizing the importance of committees in policy making. "I have never issued an order since I became operating head of this corporation," he wrote in 1924. "Policies should be performed by the men who make them. . . . A group of men who have invented a policy together understand the policy." Ask students to suggest some strengths and possible weaknesses of this form of management.

Group Goals
Have students review the two examples of group goals shown on this page. Ask them to imagine serving on committees with these goals. How might having to implement a course of action differ from making a recommendation? Encourage students to come up with goals they would be willing to undertake as part of a group. **L2**

COOPERATIVE LEARNING ACTIVITY

A high school provides opportunities to observe the functions of many groups. Changes are constantly occurring in curriculum, administration, scheduling, discipline, and student privileges. Many policy decisions in a school arise from the recommendations of groups appointed to address specific problems. With the class, list issues that are current at your school. (Examples: senior privileges, daily schedule, dress code, curriculum changes) Then, have students form groups of four or five, assign them one of the issues, and ask them to imagine that they have been appointed to recommend policy changes in that area. Give them a few minutes to come up with a list of ideas they would want to discuss as part of such a task force. For each idea, encourage students to list an associated problem that they might have to address. Have groups share their ideas with the class.

Working as a Group

Have students review the bulleted tasks for the media literacy class. Do they agree that this is a goal suitable for a group project? Which specific tasks would be particularly suited to cooperative efforts? Which to individuals? Discuss students' answers with the class. **ELL**

Visual Instruction

Answer Students may indicate that as members of a group bond they begin to depend upon one another to accomplish their goal.

Application Activities 10–1

This group is working on a common goal by creating a commercial. **What takes place when group members bond?**

authority. Often an organization's president, a manager, or a committee chairperson will appoint a group and issue the group goal at the same time. At other times, a group's goal may be emergent. An emergent goal is a goal set by the group itself. When a group sets its own goal, it may do so over a period of time or at its first meeting. Regardless of who sets the group goal, its main purpose is to guide a group in its work.

Importance of Group Goals

Sharing a common goal helps group members think of themselves as a group. This means they probably know one another by name. They also recognize that their group is a special unit working toward a common goal. Finally, they feel a sense of commitment and loyalty to the group, leading to a more effective group effort.

As members begin bonding as a group, they also begin to depend upon one another to accomplish their goal. In other words, they recognize that they need the input and assistance from other members to achieve the group goal. Rather than one person working alone, it is the group's charge to complete the task together.

A group in a media literacy class might have a project assignment due in two weeks. The group's goal could be to produce a persuasive thirty-second commercial to promote an upcoming school event. To accomplish its goal, the group might work together to complete a number of tasks:

- Gather all pertinent information about the event.
- Write a persuasive script.
- Determine the location of each individual video shot.
- Cast all the acting parts.
- Rehearse the script and video shots.
- Obtain the necessary video equipment and shoot the actual commercial.
- Edit the commercial and reshoot any necessary footage.

All these tasks help accomplish the group goal of making the thirty-second commercial. It's likely that no one member would be able to carry out all of these tasks within the time limitations. The members must depend upon one another to accomplish the goal together.

Face-to-Face Meetings

The third characteristic of a group is that the members generally meet face-to-face.

Benefits of Face-to-Face Meetings

Meeting face-to-face is important because it allows each member to be aware of both the verbal and nonverbal messages that other members send. Face-to-face interaction also allows members to recognize who is and who is not participating fully. This can help the group know who needs to be encouraged to contribute ideas.

Meeting face-to-face also tends to encourage spontaneous interaction that can lead to more creative ideas and solutions. Members can modify or adjust their messages based on

316 *Glencoe Communication Applications*

MEETING INDIVIDUAL NEEDS | **MULTIPLE LEARNING STYLES**

Interpersonal Many groups, including high school classes, are made up of individuals who are strangers to one another. Knowledge about one's peers is essential for developing trust.

Activity Arrange students' desks in a circle and ask for volunteers to correctly identify all their classmates by both first and last names. Then, have students pair up with a neighbor and ask each other whom they most admire, what they are most afraid of, and where they would most like to be. Each student will then introduce his or her partner to the class. Finally, ask for volunteers to go around the circle again, naming students and listing as much of the information as they can remember. (Note: Although a typical "first day" activity, it is often worth repeating a bonding exercise like this further into the year.)

interaction with others. When people meet face-to-face, they can give and get direct and immediate feedback, which helps them understand the verbal and nonverbal messages of others.

When Meeting Face-to-Face Is Not Possible Although the benefits are clear, it is not always possible for group members to meet face-to-face. In such cases, groups often use other methods to meet and exchange information. These may include contact via interoffice memos, postal mail, e-mail, teleconferencing, or videoconferencing. Each of these methods allows group members to maintain communication and continue progress toward the group goal even when they can't get together.

In today's busy world, teleconferences and videoconferences have become attractive methods of business communication. Both can be less expensive than face-to-face meetings that require travel arrangements for a number of group members. Also, electronic meetings often can be much more convenient for busy group members. Because no travel time is involved, meetings can be called, conducted, and adjourned relatively quickly. This often happens in a fraction of the time that it would take for members to all assemble face-to-face.

It is important to note, however, that convenience does have its costs. The direct and immediate interaction and exchange of ideas and nonverbal messages often are lost when the group cannot communicate directly. That's why the work of groups is generally more successful when conducted face-to-face.

Meetings Over Time

Rarely can the work of a group be completed in only one meeting. Therefore, groups usually meet over a period of time. Groups typically follow a specific cycle of meetings: orientation meetings, action meetings, and implementation meetings. The chart below describes this cycle.

THE IMPORTANCE OF GROUPS

Groups are important to social and professional organizations as a whole. They also are important to individuals within those organizations. In general, groups have the potential to benefit everyone involved.

Communication Tip

One of the difficulties of communicating in writing—either by memo, ordinary mail, or e-mail—is that your tone of voice and facial expression cannot contribute to the message. What might be intended as a joke ("What a stupid idea!" for example) will not always be taken as one in writing. Keep your written communication to colleagues straightforward. Save sarcasm for occasions when your smile can soften the message.

Group Meeting Cycle

Have students review the steps in the cycle of meetings illustrated on this page. Ask them to divide a piece of paper into three columns labeled Orientation, Action, and Implementation. Then, have students consider groups with the following goals: creating a new baseball field, organizing a school dance, and improving cafeteria food. Allow students to work in pairs, encouraging them to fill in as many activities as they can under each column for these group goals. Make master charts on the board for each of the activities. **L2**

GROUP MEETING CYCLE

Meeting Cycle	Duration	Function	What Happens in This Cycle
Orientation	1–2 meetings	• to introduce members • to discuss group goals • to determine members' talents and expertise	This cycle helps the group develop productive working relationships.
Action	middle set of meetings	• members work on group goals • members gather information and interact on how to complete the group goal • members come to a conclusion on how to complete the goal	The group members have established their areas of expertise and are able to work from their strengths to complete the group goal.
Implementation	last few meetings	• implement solution, or • present findings to a designated management group	Group members are now at the end of their task and will either implement the solution or report their findings to another group.

Understanding the Nature of Groups **317**

MEETING INDIVIDUAL NEEDS
MULTIPLE LEARNING STYLES

Bodily-Kinesthetic While most people would agree that face-to-face meetings are more productive than long-distance methods of doing business, it is not always easy to specify the advantages. Point out that a number of visual elements supplement verbal communications.

Activity Ask for volunteers to perform for the class a variety of highly charged communications: I got into Stanford; I failed the chemistry final; Your dog just had a fight with a skunk. Allow them a few moments to prepare a wordless skit for each situation, advising them not to mime their messages but to act them out, lip-synching if they wish. Have students perform their skits in pairs and ask their classmates to guess what message they are communicating. Have the class discuss the role of nonverbal elements in communicating and receiving information.

COMMUNICATION
PRACTICE LAB

Creating a Group Goal Statement

Answers for possible goal statements may include these:

- Research type and cost of necessary computer hardware and software, prepare persuasive presentation for school board, and give presentation.

- Survey students in your high school to find out what might interest them in working part-time and what your company might do to attract those students.

Extend this exercise by asking students how they would allocate tasks to complete the projects. In how many days do they estimate they could accomplish their goals?

GLENCOE Online

For an additional Practice Lab for this section, have students visit the *Glencoe Communication Applications* Web site at **communicationapplications.glencoe.com**. Click on Communication Practice Lab 10–1. **L1**

Benefits to Everyone?

The text states that groups have the potential to benefit everyone. Ask students to discuss situations in which groups have not benefited certain individuals or groups but have had the opposite effect. Have students list examples and tell what could be done within groups and outside groups to prevent similar situations in the future. **L3**

COMMUNICATION
PRACTICE LAB

Creating a Group Goal Statement

To write an effective group goal statement, follow these steps.

Step 1 Form a group of four to six students and create a statement that describes a group goal for each situation below. Make sure your statements identify the specific research to be done and the expected group outcome.

- Your technology department wants the school board to buy ten new computers for the lab.

- The manager at your part-time job asks employees to help find ways to get more students interested in working part time for the company.

Step 2 When your group's goal statements are complete, have one person write them on the chalkboard.

Step 3 Take turns explaining why each statement will produce the desired results.

Benefits to the Organization

Groups are a necessary part of large social and professional organizations. Organizational leaders who use groups know that they can provide very important benefits for the organization. These benefits include members or employees who are more creative, involved, motivated, and ultimately, more productive. The quality of the work also often increases when it is conducted in groups.

Benefits to the Individual

Organizations are not the only ones who benefit from groups. Participating in groups can help individuals in many aspects of their lives. This may include improving the conditions in which they work and developing better social and professional relationships.

KINDS OF GROUPS

Most groups—those that are established and work independently and those that exist within organizations—can be divided into two basic kinds: task groups and social

groups. These two main types of groups have very different purposes and operate in different ways.

Task Groups

The Macintosh computer, the stealth bomber, and even the painted ceiling of the Sistine Chapel all were created by different types of groups. However, each of these groups has a common element: Each was a type of task group.

Definition A *task group* is a group that is given a specific job, or a task, to complete. A task group may have a different name. Sometimes, it may be called a task force. At other times, it might be named a committee, team, or advocacy group. A task group might exist for only a short period of time, or it may meet for years. The amount of time depends upon the task it has been assigned. After the task has been completed, the group is dissolved.

Purpose A task group's purpose is to complete an objective or a job. Sometimes, a task group will be given the charge of finding out all the information about a problem

REAL-WORLD CONNECTION

Groups in the Workplace Point out that working in groups is central to many trades and professions. There are few adults who have not been asked to work cooperatively at some point in their careers.

Activity Ask the class for a sampling of thoughtful questions to ask adults about their experiences in working with groups. Make sure to include questions about the composition and goals of the group, its duration and outcome, as well as the participant's reflections on the experience. Using these prompts, create a standardized questionnaire for the students to give to an adult acquaintance. Have students write a summary paragraph of their research and share their findings with the class.

and then suggesting possible solutions. Other times, it may be charged with creating a new policy or procedure or to perform some other type of action to solve a particular problem.

Some task groups have a very clear objective. For example, if a group is appointed to determine how satisfied parents are with the elementary school's new dress code, the task is very clear. Other times, groups do not have a clear objective to follow. A task group might be formed to anticipate what changes customers and clients might like to see in a company's product.

Some engineers at Saturn Corporation were asked to build a prototype of a three-door coupe. They were given a standard two-door car. In addition, they were given a saw and

IMPORTANCE OF GROUPS

Benefit to the Organization	Explanation
Productivity	• Individual members are motivated to perform well in front of their peers. • Individual members report that they communicate more with their group members than with employees in other departments/divisions of the organization.
Accuracy	• All group members examine each others' work, catch errors, and suggest corrections.
Creative Energy	• In groups, people tend to be more creative and enthusiastic about their work. • People tend to approach a project with more interest and excitement when it is a group endeavor.
Organizational Commitment	• Group members report higher morale than other organizational members not involved in any groups. • Group members report a higher satisfaction with their jobs and higher commitment to the organization than those not involved in groups.
Community Presence	• Community group members represent their organizations to the whole community. • These individual group members, representing their organizations, make the organization seem to be involved in and concerned about the welfare of the community at large.

Benefit to the Individual	Explanation
Political Influence	• Our U.S. political processes depend upon citizen participation to function democratically. • Individuals can influence governmental regulations by participating in town meetings, school board meetings, and civic and local planning groups.
Career Advancement	• Successful group participation skills help people in civic, political, and professional groups. Doing well in groups at a job increases the chances of promotion. • Doing well in groups of professional and social associations helps people network for career positions across the country.
Job Satisfaction	• Employees involved in groups report being more satisfied with their jobs and their companies. • Employees involved in groups report less work stress and more pleasant and safe work environment than those not involved in groups at work. • Employees involved in groups report they are encouraged to use their creativity and initiative, which raises their morale at work.

Understanding the Nature of Groups **319**

Task Groups

Invite students to suggest other familiar products, inventions, or works of art that they feel were probably created by groups. Then, have them list important creations that they believe owe their existence to one man or woman. Ask them what they feel constitutes the difference between the group-generated and the individually inspired creations. *(Students may suggest that group projects tend to be bigger and more complex, involving physical size or a range of expertise beyond the reach of a single person.)* **L2**

Benefits to the Organization and the Individual

Have students review the benefits to organizations described in the chart on this page. Ask how they would explain these effects. For example, what is it about the group experience that makes participants more productive? *(Students may suggest that team pride, friendships, mutual cooperation, exchange of ideas, and individual competition all play a part in this effect.)* Have students review the benefits to individuals and follow a similar discussion procedure as was used for discussing benefits to the organization. **L3**

Grammar Tip

A dash can be used to signal a sudden change in thought or to emphasize supplemental information when a comma does not seem sufficient. Dashes are used on page 318 in the first sentence under the heading Kinds of Groups.

3 APPLY

Comparing Group Communication Methods Have students follow the instruction for the Technology Activity. Since most groups in the business world must come up with written explanations of their conclusions, ask each group to provide a few sentences summarizing their plan. Have the groups compare their summaries and ask them which aspect of the procedure—the brainstorming, discussing, or writing— they found most suited to the method of communication they were assigned. **L2**

Types of Task Groups

Ask students to imagine that they are school superintendents in charge of a large school district. Under what circumstances might they need to form groups of the three types listed on the chart? What would be the function of these groups? *(An information-gathering group might be formed to survey parents' reactions to employing security guards in a school; a policy-making group might establish a city-wide school dress code; an action group might address the problem of smoking on school grounds.)* Have students share their ideas and discuss their examples with the class. **L3**

TECHNOLOGY *Activity*

Comparing Group Communication Methods As a class, form three or four groups. Each group will identify a traditional school activity and come up with a plan for changing it. Group One should complete its task through a face-to-face meeting. Group Two should conduct all group interactions by writing memos or letters to each other. Group Three should be divided in half, with the two halves simulating a teleconference. Ask for permission to use two speakerphones at your school for your teleconference. Group Four, if feasible, should interact through e-mail.

When all groups are finished, compare your solutions and the time needed to accomplish the group goal. What were the advantages and disadvantages of each method?

---

the outline of a door marked with masking tape. Engineers were then told to cut on that car until they came up with a way to make the idea work. When the engineers finished, they had sawed an extra door on the driver's side that allowed drivers to easily put things in the back seat.

Types of Task Groups

Organizations use various types of task groups to accomplish different organizational goals. Each of these has a different purpose for the organization. These groups may be divided into three main types:

- information-gathering groups
- policy-making groups
- action groups

Information-Gathering Groups

All types of groups have to gather extra information or conduct research in order to accomplish their goals. An **information-gathering group** is designed specifically to gather data. After the group has gathered its information, it provides it to an administrative or managerial group or an organization for consideration. The information-gathering group has completed its task and accomplished its goal when it has turned in a summary report.

Sometimes, the duties of an information-gathering group extend beyond gathering, compiling, and reporting information. This type of group also may be asked to suggest decisions, solutions, or alternative courses of action for the organization. Financial institutions such as banks, credit unions, and savings and loans

TYPES OF TASK GROUPS

	Type of Task Group	Characteristics	Power
	Information-gathering group	Designed specifically to gather information and relay that information to the organization	Only has power to make recommendations; does not implement its decisions
OFFICIAL HANDBOOK	Policy-making group	Creates procedural rules that all members of the organization must follow; evaluates the effectiveness of those rules	Has power to implement, enforce, review, and change policies as needed
TITLE ROLL SCENE TAKE	Action group	Plans and takes action to solve a problem, create or improve something, or effect change	Has power to implement its decisions and evaluate their effectiveness

---

MEETING INDIVIDUAL NEEDS   **MULTIPLE LEARNING STYLES**

Logical-Mathematical Families don't generally form task groups to obtain information or to establish policies, but even on a domestic level, intelligent decisions are based on the same steps that corporations employ.

Activity Brainstorm with the class for a list of major decisions that a family makes. Have students form groups and write these decisions in a column on the left side of a piece of paper. They should then divide the paper into three more vertical columns headed Information-Gathering, Policy-Making, and Action. Ask them to fill in under each column the work that would typically be accomplished by a task group of that category. Choose one of the decisions and make a master chart on the chalkboard. Discuss the role of planning in the decision-making process.

Most companies have travel policies stating that employees must provide receipts in order to be reimbursed for travel expense. **What is the responsibility of a policy-making group?**

often maintain loan committees. These types of information-gathering groups research the loans the institution already has made. They also compute which future loans should be made. Loan committees then provide this information to the officers of the institution so they can make the wisest lending decisions possible.

Organizations also regularly use a different kind of information-gathering group. These are called learning or study groups. These groups' task is to stay current on information that affects the organization. Group members often attend training programs, gather current information, and bring that information back to the organization. They may even plan workshops or training sessions to share the new information with other employees.

Policy-Making Groups Think about the rules you follow every day at school or on the job. Did you ever wonder where those rules came from? Chances are that a policy-making group created them. A policy-making group has the task of creating procedural rules that all organizational members must follow. A policy-making group might be responsible for deciding which skills and level of education or training an applicant must have to be hired. It might also decide on policies—such as hiring procedures, how to deal with customers or clients, or how often employees are expected to travel for the company.

Because policies are rules, policy-making groups need to be aware of some guidelines. Effective policies include a statement of what will happen if these guidelines are not followed. For example, many organizations require employees to travel to different cities

for their work. A company may have a travel policy stating that to be reimbursed for travel expenses, employees must turn in all receipts for food, travel, and hotel costs incurred while away on company business. The policy also might state that if employees lose their receipts, the organization will not reimburse them for any of their expenses. Therefore, it is to the employees' advantage to collect and organize their receipts.

Policy-making groups also are in charge of reviewing how current policies are working. Often, policy decisions will be reviewed a year or so after they have been put into effect. This allows groups to evaluate whether their decisions are providing the intended result.

Understanding the Nature of Groups **321**

BUSINESS BRIEF

Wal-Mart founder Sam Walton, like many business leaders, placed special emphasis on the importance of teamwork. "If you want to build an enterprise of any size at all," he wrote, "it almost goes without saying that you absolutely must create a team of people who work together." Read this statement to students and ask them to suggest how teamwork might be important in Walton's field, the retail industry.

Information-Gathering Groups

After students have read the section on information-gathering groups, write on the chalkboard the following quotation by the 19th-century showman P.T. Barnum: "He who is without a newspaper is cut off from his species." Tell students that Barnum wrote this in an essay entitled "The Art of Money-Getting." Ask them what they think making money has to do with a newspaper and how this is related to the importance of information gathering in the business world. **L2**

Policy-Making Groups

Invite an administrator to talk to your class about school policies, how they are created, and what forces make them change. In preparation for this presentation, have students review the school's student handbook or similar publication of rules and disciplinary procedures. Encourage students to prepare questions about specific issues that interest them. Make sure that the ensuing discussion touches upon the role of groups in the policy-making process at your school. **L1**

■ **Visual Instruction**

Answer Students may answer that the responsibility of a policy-making group is to create procedural rules for organizational members.

MEETING INDIVIDUAL NEEDS
ENGLISH LANGUAGE LEARNERS

Comparing School Policies The rationale for school policies is not always comprehensible to young people; for some English language learners, school rules make little sense at all. Point out that educational policies are formulated from a number of sources—parents, politicians, standardized exams, and social mores. These will necessarily differ from country to country.

Activity Invite English language learners to share with the class policy differences between the school they are currently attending and ones they, or their parents, have attended in other countries. Lead the class in a discussion of how policies are created and how cultural and social differences affect them. **ELL**

Quality Control

Ask students for their reaction to the anecdote of the fruit baskets. Point out that the best solutions are often very simple. Can they think of other problems, at school or at work, where the services of a quality-control team would be useful? Encourage examples and invite students to come up with solutions.

Social Groups

Point out that most people belong to a social group at some time in their lives—many to more than one. Invite students to name social groups to which they belong and ask them to explain how they are different from task groups. Then, challenge them to think of cases in which the roles of task and social groups overlap. *(Many groups that are not related to an individual's profession are still task driven—the school newspaper or a social committee, for example.)* **L2**

Action Groups An action group is appointed to plan and implement a specific course of action. Action groups often are charged with solving organizational problems. They can also develop products, improve the quality of products or services, or promote higher morale and productivity in the organization. The most common type of action group in an organization is a team.

Quality-Control Team Organizations sometimes use a type of action group called a quality-control team. This team is expected to check on the quality of work within the organization. It also does creative problem solving for the organization.

One international hotel chain had spent $6,196 on fruit baskets that were provided to corporate clients as free gifts during their stay. However, the fruit in many of these baskets was left uneaten. Since the hotel wanted to provide this service but did not want to waste money, a quality-control team in the hotel was asked to investigate and suggest a solution.

The team found that the fruit often spoiled as it sat in unoccupied rooms. Also, some guests didn't take the baskets because they did not understand that they were free. To solve these problems, the quality-control team recommended that the baskets be sealed and to be delivered to rooms only after guests checked in. This process kept the fruit from spoiling as quickly and added a personalized touch. It also made it clear that the fruit was a free gift. As a result, the hotel reduced waste and increased corporate guests' satisfaction.

Self-Managed Work Team Another type of action group is a self-managed work team. A self-managed work team is a group that works on its own to complete a particular job for an organization. These teams select their own leaders and complete their tasks with little or no supervision. They then bring back a finished product or other result. Members are assigned to this team because of the unique talents they can contribute to the group task.

Social Groups

Not all groups are task driven. Think about the groups to which you belong. In some groups, you probably don't expect anything more than friendship with the other members. You do get certain personal benefits from being part of these groups, but they do not have any particular task or job to do.

Definition A social group is a group that someone joins for purely personal reasons. Joining a social group is voluntary. People often join to engage in something in which they have an interest. Social groups can exist independently or be part of an organization, such as a company, school, neighborhood, or religious association. Study groups, neighborhood street hockey teams, "Monday Night Football" watchers, and your school's yearbook staff are all social groups. These groups typically have casual memberships that tend to fluctuate as members come and go.

Purpose The purpose of social groups is to allow members to follow some mutually agreeable activity with the help of a general support system. Exercise classes, poetry groups, and cycling clubs are also social groups, so long as the members participate as much for the company of the other members as for the skills they are learning. Like task groups, social groups have goals. These goals are usually related to the relationships group members desire to maintain.

MEETING INDIVIDUAL NEEDS — MULTIPLE LEARNING STYLES

Visual-Spatial Unlike task groups, to which members are appointed, social groups rely upon their reputation and the appeal of their activities to attract recruits. Without new members, they will eventually cease to exist. Point out to students that one of the ways a social group survives is by publicizing its activities.

Activity Have students design a poster advertising for new members for one of the school's clubs, teams, or musical groups. Successful designs will combine essential information with a strong visual element. Have students present their posters to the class.

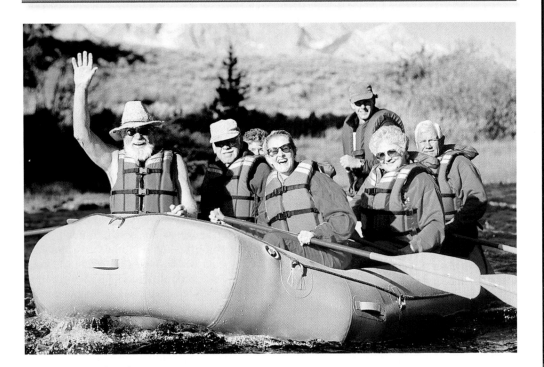

■ Social groups are people joining together to share in something they mutually enjoy, such as rafting. **What are some of the social groups you are involved in?**

Grammar Tip

One use of the hyphen is to connect words in compound adjectives, such as *well-liked, fifteen-year-old,* or *sea-green.* There are several kinds of examples of compound adjectives on this page. Ask students how many they can find. *(part-time, self-defense, decision-making, problem-solving)*

Kinds of Social Groups

Ask students what they believe the difference in atmosphere would be between informal and formal social groups. *(Students may respond that a formal group might be less relaxed, obliging members to behave as representatives of the company.)* **Why would an employer wish to establish formal social groups within an organization?** *(Students may mention the benefits of improved teamwork and morale among employees. The group could also enhance public relations by showing the human side of a large employer, as well as giving its name extra currency in the community.)* **L2**

■ **Visual Instruction**

Answer Students' answers will vary but may include social groups such as sports teams, musical groups, and special-interest groups.

Some of the groups you belong to at school may not be related to your career goals. For example, you may hope to have a career in the computer field someday, but you also may be a member of your school band. Being in the band might not teach you much about your future career, but it can support your interest in music. It also can give you an opportunity to be around people you like. Therefore, band is one of your social groups. Several of the people who work with you at your part-time job might decide to take a self-defense class together one night each week. This, too, is a social group. The class probably has nothing to do with your work, but it allows you to spend time with coworkers you like while you all learn about self-defense tactics.

Some of your social groups will be made up of people with whom you work. Others will be made up of people from your neighborhood, church, or community. These groups can help you build valuable decision-making and problem-solving skills while participating in an enjoyable activity that is unrelated to your job.

Kinds of Social Groups

There are two kinds of social groups within organizations: informal and formal. An informal social group is one in which membership may be encouraged, but not required, by an organization. A formal social group is one in which the organization chooses members to participate in community activities.

Understanding the Nature of Groups **323**

MULTIPLE LEARNING STYLES

Linguistic Point out that all of us have been involved in social groups, however briefly, at some stage in our lives. From Little League to Girl Scouts, many people spend a substantial proportion of their days learning and cooperating with other people. Remind students that informal interactions with our peers contribute to life's zest and often give us stories to tell.

Activity Have students write a personal narrative about a memorable experience—good or bad—that they have had as a member of a social group. Ask them to describe, using vivid details, what made this a particularly joyful or painful experience. Have volunteers read their narratives to the class.

Formal to Informal

Sometimes, formal groups may become informal ones. For example, some members of a Little League team might become friends and play together in the neighborhood, forming a "club." Let students suggest other examples from their own lives of situations where they have become a member of an informal group because of first having been a part of a formal group. **L2**

3 ASSESS

Assign Section 1 Assessment as a homework or in-class activity.

🖰 Use *Interactive Tutor Self-Assessment Software* to review Section 1.

Section 10–1 Quiz

Visual Instruction

Answer Students may say that a formal social group has a regular meeting time, officers, rules for joining and participating, and agendas or schedules while an informal social group is one in which membership may be encouraged but is not required.

Informal Social Groups Participation in informal social groups is not required by an organization. However, an organization may encourage its members to join a social group to build morale and help form relationships across different departments or divisions. Members of an organization might form physical-fitness groups, softball leagues, or other clubs that are made up of only organizational members. If employees at a company begin meeting at a local gym after work to play a casual game of racquetball, they have formed a social group. No one requires their attendance, but they enjoy the game and develop new friendships with coworkers.

An informal group might form at first because all the members have the same lunch schedule and happen to choose the same place to eat. These members may then begin inviting a few more friends, making it a regular practice to meet for lunch on a certain day. Eventually, the group might expand the lunch activity to include some sort of exercise,

and the lunchtime meeting might become more structured for the group. At this point, the group has developed a social purpose of meeting with a particular group of people on a regular—perhaps even daily—basis.

Formal Social Groups An organization also might create formal social groups. These groups often have a regular meeting time, officers, rules for joining and participating, and agendas or schedules for their meetings.

Many company-sponsored sports teams fall into this category. If an organization is quite large, it may have several departmental sports teams, such as bowling, golf, or softball. These teams compete against other departmental teams from within their own organization or from outside organizations. If an organization is small, it might form a single company team to compete against teams from other companies in community tournaments.

Formal social groups may grow out of informal ones. For example, members of a lunch

---

A company team working on a community project could be either a formal or informal social group. What is the difference between formal and informal social groups?

Section 1 Assessment Answers

1. Accept all reasonable sentences.
2. Limited size: allows all members to participate equally; shared goal: provides a common task to pull members together; face-to-face meetings: allow for full verbal/nonverbal participation; meetings over time: allow the group to complete a task interdependently.
3. Workers are more productive, work more accurately, have increased creative energy, and are more committed to the organization.
4. May increase an individual's political influence, career advancement, and job satisfaction.
5. Students' goal statements should reflect an understanding of the purposes of both types of groups. The two statements are alike in that they both specify what the group is to do. They are different in that one calls for information while the other calls for new policies or policy changes.

group might decide to start devoting one lunch hour per week to a non-profit community organization such as Habitat for Humanity—a group that builds homes for low-income families. If this informal effort is successful the first year, the group may strive to make it more formal in following years. This might lead to

management recognizing the effort and forming a "Habitat Team" in the organization. Thus, the informal social group has become a formal social group within the organization. A company also may encourage members to belong to various non-profit civic groups to support community projects.

Section 1 Assessment

Visit the *Glencoe Communication Applications* Web site at **communicationapplications. glencoe.com** and click on **Self-Check and Study Guide 10.1** to review your understanding of the nature of groups.

Review Key Terms

1. Define each of the following terms and write it in a sentence: group, committee, team, advocacy group, group goal, prescribed goal, emergent goal, task group, information-gathering group, policy-making group, action group, social group, informal social group, formal social group.

Check Understanding

2. List the characteristics of a group. How does each characteristic contribute to a group's effectiveness?

3. Describe how groups are important to an organization.

4. Describe how groups are important to individuals.

5. Create one group goal statement for an information-gathering group and one group goal statement for a policy-making group. How are the two statements alike? How are they different?

6. Describe the two main kinds of groups and give an example of each.

7. **Comparison** How are purposes of the two main kinds of groups alike and different?

APPLICATION *Activity*

Working as a Quality-Control Team In a group of four to six students, assume that you are a quality control team with the power to implement recommendations. As a team, solve the following quality-control issue: How do you get more parents involved in your high school events and organizations? Create a group goal statement and write an outline detailing how your quality-control team should proceed to investigate and solve this issue. As a group, use this outline to prepare and deliver a four- to six-minute group presentation on how to resolve the issue.

Understanding the Nature of Groups **325**

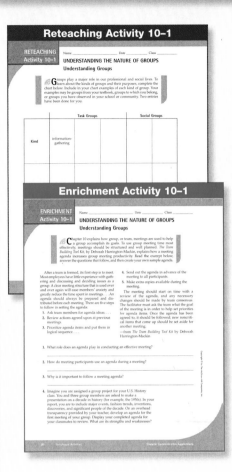

4 CLOSE

Have students reread the opening paragraph at the beginning of Section 1 on page 313. In the light of what they know about groups, ask the following questions: "When are two heads better than one?" and "Under what circumstances does a committee put together a camel rather than a horse?"

Extra-Credit Project

Ask students to interview the human resources manager of a large employer to find out what task or social groups are regularly sponsored by that organization. Have students create a list of their findings and share them with the class.

Section 1 Answers, continued

6. A task group is given a specific job or task to complete. (Examples: groups formed to gather information or take action) A social group is a group someone joins for personal reasons. (Examples: a formal or an informal social group)

7. Both task and social groups allow group members to interact with others who share a common interest. However, task groups are formed to complete some specific goal, while social groups have no such goal.

Application Activity A goal statement might be, "Do the research and then inform sponsors of high school events and organizations about how they might adjust their event schedules and advertising to appeal to more parents." Outlines will vary.

Making an Inference

Point out that while we make inferences all the time, those that are based on faulty or misinterpreted information can be embarrassing or even harmful. Remind students that racial and religious prejudices often arise from faulty inferences. The assumption that a person of another skin color or one who worships differently from you is going to behave in a certain way is probably based upon misinformation. Good inferences are made with an open mind from all the available information. **L2**

Practicing the Skill

1. An IT job is available. You have the skills necessary.

2. Companies used to look primarily for technical knowledge; now they are increasingly interested in the personality of the applicant.

3. Because more attention is being paid to personal qualities, technical skills alone may not be sufficient to land a good job.

4. It is wise to be aware of communication and interpersonal skills when applying for a job.

Application Activity

Students should not ignore the significant role of the weather, but they should bear in mind that other evidence may be related to the accident rate: day of the week, time of day, age of driver, role of drugs, condition and type of vehicle. They might also need to know what constitutes "bad weather." Light rain might have little effect, while a single snow storm or flood might account for all the weather-related accidents.

Critical Thinking Skill

MAKING AN INFERENCE

An **inference** is a reasoned judgment or conclusion based on a set of circumstances or facts.

Learning the Skill

No one wants to make incorrect inferences, especially when working in a group where others can witness your mistakes. The following four steps are an effective process for making intelligent, informed inferences.

Step 1: Observe

Step 2: Review What You Know

Step 3: Draw Conclusions

Step 4: Test Your Inference

Step 1 Observe. When working in a group, pay careful attention, listen to others, read, research, and check facts to enhance your observation skills.

Step 2 Review What You Know. After making your observations, compare them to what you have observed in the past.

Step 3 Draw Conclusions. One of the best ways to make accurate inferences is to use your own common sense. Evaluate conclusions to see if they are logical.

Step 4 Test Your Inference. Whenever possible, try to gather specific information that will prove or disprove your conclusion.

Practicing the Skill

Read the quote below and answer the questions that follow.

A great IT [information technology] job has opened up at a local company, and you have the technical skills for the position. Unfortunately, that may not be enough. . . . At one time, companies placed a premium on technical skills and worried less about communication and interpersonal skills. . . . To assess the personality of IT job candidates, some companies are using behavioral interviewing . . . style of questioning that elicits descriptions . . . that may reveal how a candidate will perform in the future.

1. What observations has the writer made?

2. What generalizations were made?

3. What are the reasons behind the writer's inference?

4. What inferences did you make after reading the article?

APPLICATION *Activity*

Imagine that you are the chief of police in a small community. The city council has asked you to write a report on the main cause of automobile accidents in your town and to suggest ways to reduce accidents. Your research shows that 55 percent of accidents over the past two years occurred during bad weather. Would it be accurate to conclude that bad weather causes traffic accidents? Why or why not? How might these conclusions affect your suggestions? Discuss your conclusions as a class.

MEETING INDIVIDUAL NEEDS

INCLUSION STRATEGIES

Learning Disabled Students who have difficulty grasping the concept of making inferences should realize that they utilize these skills many times a day. Point out that an inference is really a technical name for a conclusion based on one's past knowledge.

Activity Give students a number of simple prompts and ask them to draw logical inferences. *(Prompt: John enters the room soaking wet. Inference: It's raining.)* Encourage students to think of less-likely inferences as well. *(John is wet because a friend poured a bucket of water on his head as a joke.)* Ask what makes one inference more likely than the other, and discuss the advisability of limiting yourselves to one possibility. Finally, have students think of their own prompts and test one another's inferring skills.

Section 2

Functions of Groups

GUIDE TO READING

Objectives

1. Explain why the group function of planning is important to organizations.
2. Identify the three main considerations involved in planning.
3. Describe the six steps of the problem-solving process.
4. Explain why brainstorming is useful for generating new, creative ideas.

Terms to Learn

problem
problem solving
criteria
brainstorming
decision making

Statements such as "None of us is as smart as all of us" and "Two heads are better than one" point out the advantages of working in groups. How have groups served a useful function in your life?

All task and social groups engage in planning, problem solving, or both. Why are these functions so well suited to groups? Each requires creativity. And the more knowledge and experience available, the more ideas generated.

worked on a group project for a class at school. You had to plan what each person would contribute and how often the group would meet. You also had to plan when each task would be completed to get the entire project done.

PLANNING

One major function of a group is planning for some event, action, or change. You probably have participated in group planning for some event, action, or change. Think of the last time you

Groups such as the one shown are ideal for planning and problem solving. Why is it better to have a group working on solving a problem instead of an individual?

Understanding the Nature of Groups **327**

Bellringer
Ask students to read the opening paragraph of this section. Give them a few moments to think about the groups to which they have belonged. (Remind them that groups can go back to their preschool T-ball team.) Then, have them write the following prompt on a piece of paper: The best group I ever belonged to was ___ because ___. Ask them to complete the sentence. Encourage students to share their memories with the class. Discuss the importance of group activities in their lives and in the broader social context.

You may use Graphic Organizer Transparency 10–2 to introduce this section.

Graphic Organizer Transparency 10–2

Visual Instruction

Answer Students might say that when more people are working on solving a problem there may be more ideas on how to solve it.

RESOURCE MANAGER

Teaching Tools

- Interactive Lesson Planner
- Reproducible Lesson Plan 10–2
- Application Activities 10–2

Reproducible Masters

- Guided Reading Activity Workbook 10–2
- Enrichment Activity 10–2
- Reteaching Activity 10–2
- Section Quiz 10–2
- Transparency Strategies and Activities Booklet 10–2

Transparencies

- Graphic Organizer Transparency 10–2
- Chapter 10 Teaching Transparency

Technology Resources

- Interactive Tutor Self-Assessment Software
- Presentation Plus! Software
- ExamView® Pro Testmaker
- PuzzleMaker Software
- communicationapplications.glencoe.com

2 TEACH

Visual Instruction

Answer Planning is important for professional organizations because the business climate constantly changes.

Guided Reading Activity 10–2

Name _____ Date _____ Class _____

UNDERSTANDING THE NATURE OF GROUPS
Functions of Groups

GUIDED READING
Activity 10-2

As you read Section 2, answer the following items.

1. What are the three things a group needs to consider when planning properly?

2. Explain how Japanese group meetings may differ from American group meetings.

3. List the four factors to consider when planning an occasion.

4. What are the six steps to problem solving?

5. What word means "the standards or conditions that any solution must meet in order to be acceptable"?

6. What is the most valuable feature of brainstorming?

7. There are several ways for a group to make its final decision. What are the three discussed?

8. What are the five steps used in implementing a solution?

Considerations in Planning

Have students review the chart on page 329 illustrating questions a committee must ask in order to plan properly. Ask if these issues are relevant to the type of planning that an individual also has to make. Encourage students to think of situations in their own lives when they have had to make plans involving some of the same questions. *(Students may suggest that buying a car, planning a party, or arranging a vacation with friends would involve much the same process.)* **L1**

Businesses use groups to plan and organize work. Why is planning important to a professional organization?

Importance of Planning

Social and professional organizations depend on groups to plan the work they want to do. Without planning, social organizations can lose sight of their purpose. Businesses may not make a profit and have to close their doors.

Planning in Professional Organizations
Planning is important for professional organizations because the business climate constantly changes. Companies have to plan how they are going to adapt to those changes to stay in business. They need to plan what, when, how, and who will produce, sell, and distribute their products or services. They will also plan for special events in the organization and for other company actions. Finally, they need to make both short-term and long-term plans. Some companies even have master-plan committees who do nothing but make long-term plans.

Planning in Social Organizations
Just as professional organizations have to adapt to change, so do social ones. Many communities have permanent planning commissions whose job is to predict how conditions may change over time. Commissioners might be involved in planning new schools, roads, parks, or other community services. Communities must also plan for civic events and for actions that will affect the entire city.

Considerations in Planning

A committee whose main function is planning is not usually responsible for implementing the plans it develops. Rather, its job is to envision the result of the plan and what should be done to achieve that result. Since the group plan will be implemented within either a professional or social

CRITICAL THINKING ACTIVITY

"If you're going to drain the swamp, you don't consult the frogs," a politician once explained when giving reasons for not including the public in a controversial government project. Point out that most major planning decisions will leave at least some people dissatisfied. The difficult question is how to judge whether a plan's eventual benefits will compensate for the losses incurred. Have students form groups and ask them to consider the following projects (or others of your devising): constructing a dam, locating a landfill, building a football stadium, widening a highway, constructing a chemical plant. Ask students to list the advantages and possible drawbacks of each scheme. Who would likely protest? What action could be taken to address their problems? Is there an ideal solution? Encourage students to look at all angles of each project and invite them to debate the issues. 📦

context, the group should carefully consider the people, the occasion, and the task involved in any plan.

Consider the People. Who will be involved in the event or change proposed by your plan? A planning group should carefully consider all organizations, departments, or individuals that will be affected by a plan. The group also needs to consider the group itself and its goals.

By considering everyone who will be affected, the group can base its decisions on the most complete knowledge available. It also ensures that the group will fully consider all the consequences of its plan. For example, imagine that a group is planning to have all new employees attend a software training seminar. After speaking with several new employees, the group finds that most already know how to use that software. However, more senior employees feel they are the ones who really need the training. The planning group might then decide to make the training voluntary and offer it to all employees.

Get the Support of the People. For a plan to achieve its goal, it must have the support and positive participation of the people affected. One way to build support for a plan is to show how it will ultimately benefit those

GLOBAL COMMUNICATION
To Speak or Not to Speak?

When is it wise to speak up in group meetings and when is it better to remain silent? The answer to this question may differ from culture to culture. Some cultures, such as the Japanese, may respect silence while Americans typically are uncomfortable with long periods of silence. The Japanese sometimes find silence to be useful in decision making and problem solving, especially when they are uncertain about the response of other group members. How do you respond to silence in a group setting? Why?

involved. For example, when planning a community celebration, the planning group could show merchants how many tourists they expect the event to draw into the community. Support for a plan can be built by reducing people's fears. For example, a planning group might identify those employees most likely to be affected by a company's reorganization and then address their fears. By making a special effort to inform these employees in advance, the group can help remove any perceived threats.

Identify the Target Audience. The planning committee also will need to identify the target audience for an event and plan how to attract that audience. For a concert event, the committee might decide to provide discount admission coupons at area stores. For a

PLANNING

To Plan Properly	Issues to Consider
Consider the People Involved	Who is needed to implement the plan? Who is affected by the plan? How will we motivate people to participate in the plan?
Consider the Occasion	What is the purpose of the action being planned? When and where will it take place?
Consider the Task	Have we considered the impact of the plan? How much time is needed to accomplish all parts of the plan? How many people must be involved in the plan? How much money will the plan cost?

Understanding the Nature of Groups **329**

Consider the Occasion

Brainstorm with the class a hypothetical school event that would require careful planning to coordinate activities. (Examples: celebrating International Students Day or Martin Luther King Jr. Day; organizing a tribute to a retiring teacher; celebrating the school's 50th birthday) Discuss how a planning group would approach this event, with specific reference to the five bulleted questions on this page. ELL

Considering Location and Facilities

Have students consider the importance of location and the need for facilities for a number of possible events. (Examples: a rock concert, a memorial service, a graduation ceremony, a freshman dance or a senior prom) Ask them what information they would need in order to choose an appropriate location and to assess what support facilities to provide.

(Students may suggest that the number of people attending the event is key to planning. Other factors might include the expected weather conditions, the length of the event, and the ages of the attendees.) **L2**

Visual Instruction

Answer Some factors students might suggest would include who will attend, what the purpose of the occasion is, and what must be accomplished as the group's task.

---

business conference, the committee might mail invitations to related businesses throughout the region. By focusing its efforts, the committee can make sure that it reaches the people who will be most interested in attending.

Consider the Occasion. Planning groups need to consider the occasion—the actual event or action being planned. Some factors to consider are the occasion's purpose, timing, location, and impact. The planning group might need to begin by asking the following questions:

- Why is this event taking place?
- What is the desired outcome?
- Does this event or activity conflict with other ongoing or traditional events?
- Will the proposed location of the event create any special difficulties?
- Have we adequately thought about the impact of the event on the community?

Consider the Purpose. Suppose a community decides to hold a summer festival to encourage tourism or to honor some historical occasion. One of the first responsibilities is to examine how the event will accomplish the stated purpose. The planning group may want to look at what other communities have done or consider some other approach. This might include establishing a new park or community center or restoring a historic building.

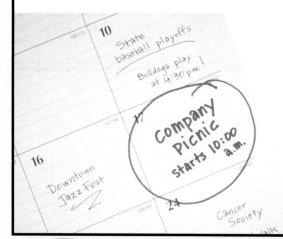

Consider the Timing. Event-planning committees also should look closely at community or organizational calendars to plan a successful event. The group should determine what other activities are occurring at or around the same time to avoid scheduling conflicts. If a community plans a walkathon for a local charity during the school district's spring break, it might have a small turnout for the event. Similarly, a company that plans its annual employee picnic for the same weekend on which the local high school baseball team is in the state playoffs might find that attendance at their picnic will suffer.

Consider the Location. The proposed location of an event is another factor that should be examined. Any proposed location should have adequate space and support facilities for the number of people expected to attend. Utility services such as electricity and water might be required. There also might be a need for security or police officers at the event. In addition, details such as parking, availability of food services, and rest areas also must be considered when choosing a location.

Consider the Task. A planning group also takes into consideration the task. The task includes everything that must be done to implement the plan. The planning group must consider how the work will be done, when it will be done, and who will do it.

Event-planning committees then should decide when each part of the work is to be completed and by whom. They also should consider whether there is enough time in which to accomplish the task. These two considerations can be accomplished by developing a time line. One method for creating a time line is to

---

When planning an event, it is important to consider other events taking place on or around the same day. List the factors a planning group should keep in mind when planning an event.

MULTIPLE LEARNING STYLES

MEETING INDIVIDUAL NEEDS

Logical-Mathematical Visual representations of a group project are often an essential part of the planning process. From a general's battle plans to an editor's book plans, the use of maps, graphs, charts, and other graphic aids gives instant, easily understandable information.

Activity Have students imagine that they are responsible for producing the school yearbook. List with them the important steps that are part of that process, including obtaining individual photos, group photos, blurbs, and team records; advertising; printing; and distribution. Then, have students form pairs and ask them to create a time line indicating the points at which each of these stages must be completed. Have students share their efforts and create a master time line on the chalkboard. Compare the class's time line with the one your school yearbook committee employs.

start from the event date and then work backward in time. By incorporating how long it will take to accomplish each part, the committee can establish the start date of the task.

Sometimes, a plan may require more people than are available in an organization. Also, a plan may be too costly for the resources that are available. If the task itself is not realistic given the money, labor, or time available, then the planning will have to be adjusted.

PROBLEM SOLVING

Organizations and businesses face a wide range of problems every day. A problem is a difficulty or uncertainty—a difference between the way something should be and the way it is. A business's problems might include determining how to cut costs, increase employee satisfaction, or keep up with the competition. An individual's problems might include how to improve grades or stick to a budget.

Definition

Problems can affect how an organization or individual meets its goals. Problems that go unsolved also can allow harmful situations to continue or worsen. Because of the need for effective solutions, problem solving is the second major function of groups. Problem solving is the act of understanding the nature of a dilemma, creating alternative solutions, determining which solution is best, and implementing that solution. Problem solving is a creative activity that is best accomplished through a step-by-step process.

Steps in the Process

Organizations and individuals frequently face problems in both professional and social contexts. These problems can cause emotional responses and may keep people from reaching the best solution. Therefore, it is valuable to apply a systematic process for

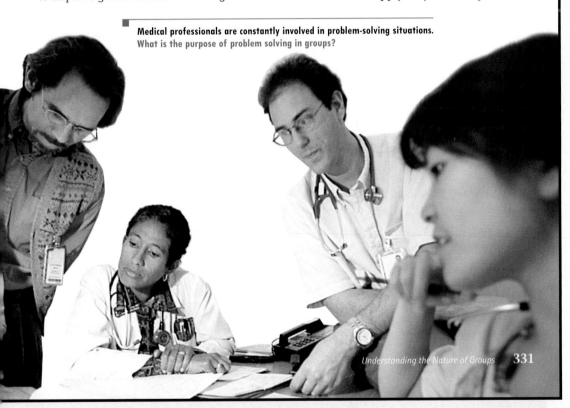

Medical professionals are constantly involved in problem-solving situations. What is the purpose of problem solving in groups?

Understanding the Nature of Groups 331

Problem Solving
Point out that people engage in problem solving throughout their lives. A six-year-old may debate how to reach a cookie jar; a seventy-year-old may fret about how to stretch a pension. Introduce the subject by inviting students to share a problem they have recently solved. Ask them to explain the process that they used in solving the problem. L1

■ Visual Instruction

Answer Students may say that since problem solving in groups incorporates the ideas of different individuals, it facilitates finding answers to complex problems.

INTERDISCIPLINARY CONNECTION

Social Studies How can we improve race relations? How can we decrease crime? How can we revitalize education? How can we preserve our environment? Point out that governing a country is a continuous exercise in problem solving. Encourage students to see the same problem-solving methods at work in all levels of society, from the classroom to Capitol Hill.

Activity Have students choose an issue of national importance that is likely to remain under discussion for some time. Ask them to research this issue, defining the problem and listing the solutions that have been put forward. Have them present their findings to the class, including their own choice of solution. Invite other students to come up with alternative solutions or to challenge the speaker's conclusion.

Define the Problem

Ask students to think of problems they would like solved at their school and to create a problem/question format. (Problem: The yearbook is operating at a big loss. Question: How can we make the yearbook profitable?) Point out that after further investigation, more than one question may arise. Ask students how they would establish which questions truly reflect the problem. **L2**

COMMUNICATION *Strategies*

SIX STEPS TO PROBLEM SOLVING

Have students review the six steps shown on the page. Ask them which steps they believe most people leave out, or speed over, in making simple personal decisions. Test their ideas by asking them to solve a typical problem that they might experience in the course of a day. Invite students to break down their problem solving into the steps illustrated under Communications Strategies. Which stages took the most time? Which did they neglect? **L2**

*inter*NET
ACTIVITY

Absenteeism Advise students that they may well find several thousand entries in a keyword search as broad as this. Suggest that they work in small groups or pairs and each choose half a dozen different sites to investigate. **L2**

---

moving logically and unemotionally to a solution. These steps are found in the Communication Strategies list below. Although the steps are in sequence, all six steps do not have to be done each time. Sometimes, the problem has already been defined, and the group's goal is to analyze it and solve it. In addition, all steps of the process are of equal importance.

Define the Problem. The first step is to define the problem facing the group. This can be accomplished by talking about the problem either with the group or with those involved in the problem. You cannot solve a problem that is unclear to you.

Sometimes, the problem to be solved is very clear. If management's prescribed goal is for the group to work out employees' work and vacation schedules for the next year, the problem is defined clearly. However, if the group has developed an emergent goal to improve employee morale, the problem will need to be defined before solutions can be found.

A problem's definition should fully describe what the group needs to accomplish. The problem statement often is written in the form of a question, such as "How can the company

COMMUNICATION *Strategies*

SIX STEPS TO PROBLEM SOLVING

- ✓ Define the problem.
- ✓ Analyze the problem.
- ✓ Establish criteria for the best solution.
- ✓ List all possible solutions.
- ✓ Choose the best solution.
- ✓ Implement the solution.

---

*inter*NET
ACTIVITY

Absenteeism "How many days of school or work have you missed in the last year?" You may be asked this question in a future job interview. Employee absenteeism costs United States businesses approximately $20 billion per year. As a result, special committees are often formed to gather information or develop ways to address employee absenteeism. Using a reliable Internet search engine, enter the keywords "employee absenteeism" to learn more about this dilemma. Summarize the information you find in your own words. Share your findings with the class.

raise employee morale?" This goal of this statement is to keep the group members on track as they search for a solution.

Sometimes, a problem is not exactly what it appears to be at first. A broad problem must be more narrowly defined. Consider, for example, that you have been assigned to a group of students to research the problem of an increasing number of locker thefts at your school. To move from the broad problem— "How can we stop thefts from student lockers?"—to a defined problem statement, your group might ask the following:

- Is there a specific time of day or location at which more or fewer locker thefts occur?

- Is one particular student group targeted more than others are?

- Are the lockers being broken into in any specific part of the school?

CRITICAL THINKING ACTIVITY

Remind students that asking the right questions is one of the most important exercises in critical thinking. Have students form groups and give them the following problem: What do you serve 150 people for lunch? Point out that this question gives almost no information. The students' job will be to formulate the questions that will enable them to define and analyze the problem and to establish criteria for solutions. *(Questions students may ask include: Who are the people? How much money is at our disposal? Where is the event to take place?)* Encourage students to pursue various possibilities based on hypothetical answers. *(Example: If the people are over the age of 70, we will have to serve food that is easy to chew!)* Invite groups to discuss their analyses with their classmates.

After answering these questions, your group may discover that 90 percent of all locker thefts are from the student lockers in the gym area. With that information, your group can formulate a defined problem statement focusing on a particular location of the thefts, such as, "How can we stop thefts from student lockers in the gym area?" This more accurate definition of the problem can now focus the group's work and energy and allow the group to proceed logically to the next step.

Analyze the Problem. The next step is to analyze the problem. You will try to discover its causes, how far-reaching the problem is, what conditions are contributing to the problem, and other information that may help lead to solutions.

To begin, determine what information the group needs to know. Group members can start by sharing their own knowledge and experiences that relate to the problem. Next, generate research questions about specific areas in which your group lacks information. Each member should take one or more of the research questions and find an answer to it prior to the next meeting. Members might find this information by conducting interviews or reviewing written materials available in the organization, or they might get it from the Internet or a library. At the next meeting, all members should share the answers to their question(s) and consider the answers and comments given by the other group members.

The group that has been formed to solve the problem of locker thefts in the school gym area will have several things to consider. This group might first determine if there is a

specific time in which the thefts typically occur. It also might consider what is different about the gym and how that may contribute to the problem. As the group poses these questions, other issues that need investigating may present themselves. This may lead to questioning how well the locker room is supervised and how isolated the lockers are. Finally, it might consider if these lockers have a different locking system than those in other parts of the building.

The group's analysis of the problem is a vital step in the problem-solving process. This group might discover that most of the gymnasium thefts occur after school while athletic teams are practicing. It may find inadequate supervision in the gym. It might also discover that the padlocks indeed are less secure than combination locks.

Groups may be called upon to solve problems like theft in the locker room. What steps are involved in analyzing a problem?

Understanding the Nature of Groups **333**

Analyze the Problem
Before students read this section, write on the chalkboard a statement by Henry Ford II: "In business, recognizing the problem is just as important as knowing the method that will solve it." Ask students whether they agree with this remark. Follow up by asking whether it is possible to have problems without being aware of them. Ask students who answer "Yes" to support their answers. **ELL**

■ Visual Instruction

Answer Students might say that the steps in analyzing a problem include determining what information the group needs to know, generating research questions, and finding and sharing the answers to the research questions.

Personal Problem-Solving Methods The text provides a detailed analysis of how problems can be solved effectively in group situations. However, individuals solve problems all the time both alone and in groups often without realizing it. Most people have developed their own techniques for solving problems.

Activity Ask students to work in pairs. Suggest that students identify problems they have recently solved either in group situations, such as in their family, or alone. Have them analyze the process they used and describe it to their partner. How do the personal methods compare to the techniques outlined in the text? Let students discuss this with their partner. **ELL**

Establish Criteria

Ask students to imagine that they are planning big parties at their houses. What criteria might they have to set in order to formulate a solution that would satisfy friends, parents, and neighbors? *(Answers might include lots of snacks, a mix of music, room to dance, a limit to numbers, no music after midnight, no uninvited guests, no alcoholic beverages, guests to stay in restricted areas of the house, full clean-up afterwards.)* **L2**

Grammar Tip

While the plurals of most English nouns are formed simply by adding *-s* or *-es,* there are a number of exceptions. Point out that the word *criteria* is plural; its singular form is *criterion.* A similar exception, is *phenomenon,* the plural of which is *phenomena.*

Practice for the Workplace

Promoting a Sense of Community
After students complete the exercise, suggest that they choose two or three of their best activities to develop further. Have the class present these to an administrator as a formal proposal for building community at your school. **L2**

Establish Criteria for the Best Solution. After the group understands the problem and the conditions that contribute to it, it needs to identify the characteristics of a good solution. These characteristics are known as the criteria of the solution. Criteria are the standards or conditions that any solution must meet in order to be acceptable. A criteria list for the locker-theft problem is shown in Figure 10–3.

This list of criteria should be generated before the group discusses any possible solutions. If the group tries to set criteria after it already is looking at a possible solution, it may tend to formulate criteria to fit that particular solution. Instead, the criteria should reflect what is both desirable and possible within the organization. Sometimes, the criteria are imposed, while other criteria can come from the members themselves.

After the group has listed all the criteria, it should double-check to make sure everything important is covered and there are

Figure 10–3 List of Criteria

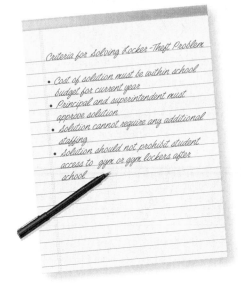

Criteria for Solving Locker-Theft Problem

- Cost of solution must be within school budget for current year
- Principal and superintendent must approve solution
- Solution cannot require any additional staffing
- Solution should not prohibit student access to gym or gym lockers after school

Practice for the Workplace

Promoting a Sense of Community How does it feel to move to a new city, attend a new school, join a new club, or begin a new job? It is normal to be concerned about how to meet new people and how they will respond to you.

BUSINESS PRACTICE *Activity*

Planning committees in the workplace are responsible for developing activities that promote a sense of community, commitment, and inclusion among employees. In groups of five or six, work as a planning committee. Make a list of activities that would result in cooperation and a sense of teamwork among students at your school. Present your ideas to the remainder of the class. As a class, discuss which activities offered at your school might also be available in the workplace.

no unnecessary criteria. Some groups might even choose to rank the criteria in order of importance. In general, the fewer criteria statements the better. This keeps the group from eliminating too many possible solutions.

Occasionally, a group may identify some criteria that are essential and others that are preferable but not essential. If, for example, the group were aware of a budget limit, then a non-negotiable criterion would be cost. On the other hand, if there are ample resources for a solution, the cost criterion could be eliminated. Without this criterion, the group would not have to eliminate potentially costly solutions from its list. Therefore, the group would have more possibilities from which to choose the best solution.

List All Possible Solutions. After the group has had time to consider all the criteria carefully, it can begin looking for a

COOPERATIVE LEARNING ACTIVITY

When trying to reach a solution to a problem, it is important to identify the criteria upon which the ultimate solution will be based. However, at times determining which criteria are essential and which are not essential is not always easy.

Give students a problem to solve or allow the class to devise one to use for this activity. They might choose to plan an end-of-school picnic, determine what new course to add to the curriculum, or decide how to raise money for new computers. Then, let students work in small groups and list the criteria needed to solve the problem. After students have made a list, have them evaluate it. Which criteria, if any, should be eliminated? Have them discuss what the basis will be for determining which criteria are essential and which criteria are not essential.

solution. This step may be most effective if it is conducted in a separate meeting after all the criteria have been developed. Otherwise, a member may be so busy thinking about the criteria that he or she does not offer possible solutions.

During this step, members of the group need to be highly creative. The purpose of this step is to generate as many ideas as possible. One way to do this is through brainstorming.

Brainstorming is a process of quickly listing all ideas that come to mind regarding a specific topic. Although group members often contribute ideas in the course of everyday meetings, brainstorming refers to a particular technique. This technique begins with a warm-up session that helps familiarize members with the process. During the warm-up,

members toss around ideas about a nonsense topic. Any topic will do as long as it is not related to the main group topic.

After the warm-up session, the actual brainstorming can begin. The most valuable feature of brainstorming is that you generate ideas before you judge any of them. Group members do not critique their own or others' ideas, no matter how silly or impractical those ideas might seem. The process demands that group members list ideas spontaneously— offering new ideas, building upon each other's ideas, and even combining ideas before evaluating them.

The group should continue brainstorming and listing ideas as long as it is productive— usually for no more than thirty minutes. Compare brainstorming to popping popcorn.

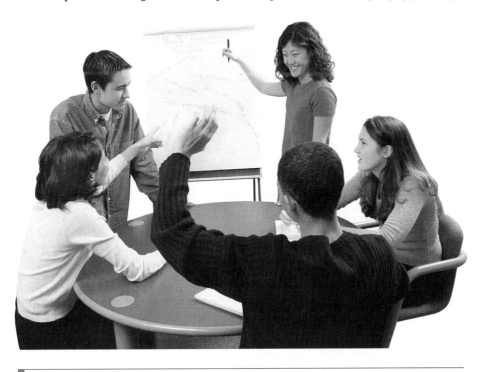

The students above are brainstorming. What is the most important rule for brainstorming in a group format?

Understanding the Nature of Groups **335**

Identifying Essential Criteria

Suggest to students that financial considerations often restrict essential criteria in problem-solving solutions. Ask the class to give examples in which money would limit the solutions. *(Examples: how to improve cafeteria food; how to explore the solar system; how to win the war against drugs)* Then, invite students to think of solutions that would not necessarily be restricted by financial constraints. *(Examples: how to be a better student; how to improve relations with the next-door-neighbors)* **ELL**

Communication Tip

Point out that brainstorming is an important technique for students to know as part of the writing process. The first stage, known as prewriting, consists of collecting information and generating ideas about a topic. Brainstorming, freewriting, and making lists can all contribute to this part of the process.

■ Visual Instruction

Answer Students may say that the most important rule for brainstorming in a group is not to judge any of the ideas before the brainstorming process is completed.

MEETING INDIVIDUAL NEEDS
MULTIPLE LEARNING STYLES

Visual-Spatial Students who learn best by visualizing their ideas may prefer a graphic version of the brainstorming process. Described variously as clustering, webbing, or making a network tree, this technique shows the relationship between thoughts and helps many students narrow a topic for writing or discussion.

Activity Assign students a general subject—vacations, teenagers, or food, for example. Have them write this in a circle in the center of a piece of paper. Then, invite students to list other topics as they occur to them, enclosing them in circles and connecting them with lines in a network of freely associated ideas. Point out that their ideas can go in several directions, like strands of a web or the branches of a tree. Have students return to those ideas that interest them most.

Choosing the Best Solution

To suggest that the "perfect" solution is not always possible, tell students the fable of the mice and the cat. The mice wanted an early warning that the cat was approaching and came up with the solution of tying a bell around the cat's neck. Only one problem: Which mouse was going to tie the bell? Ask students to suggest other possible "warning devices" the mice could use or create. **L1**

For an additional Practice Lab for this section, have students visit the *Glencoe Communication Applications* Web site at **communicationapplica-tions.glencoe.com.** Click on Communication Practice Lab 10–2. **L1**

When the popping slows, it's time to stop the cooking process. Similarly, when the ideas begin to slow down significantly, it's time to stop brainstorming.

After the session, the group should take a moment to clarify all the ideas that were listed, marking out any duplicates. It is not a good idea for the group to start checking these suggestions against the criteria at this meeting. Instead, the group should just post the full list of ideas and adjourn the meeting.

Choose the Best Solution. Once all suggested solutions have been listed, the group can go back and find the best solution for the problem based on the established criteria. This step is a decision-making activity. **Decision making** involves examining a set of alternatives and using reason and logic to select the best one. Decision making does not involve creating any additional alternatives. The brainstorming session has already done this.

During the decision-making session, the group first should review all the ideas to be evaluated, making sure everyone understands each idea. Next, members should carefully check all brainstormed solutions against the criteria. It usually is helpful to have a criteria checklist to make this task easier. **Figure 10–4** below is a sample criteria checklist for the locker-theft problem.

In addition to considering how well each possible solution meets the criteria, the group should ask itself three questions.

1. Does the solution achieve all the desired results? If it solves only part of the problem, your group may need to change or eliminate the solution.

2. Is the implementation of this solution within the group's power? Even if it is a good solution, the group must have the ability to implement it. Otherwise, your group may need to change or eliminate the solution.

3. Are there serious disadvantages to this solution? If a solution will create additional problems, your group may need to change or eliminate the solution.

■ **Figure 10–4 Criteria Checklist**

REAL-WORLD CONNECTION

Assessing Solutions Point out that solutions to social and scientific problems are not always easy to assess. Even when a solution has been chosen, the results are sometimes open to interpretation. **Activity** Have students research a major social or scientific "solution" of recent years (Examples: SDI, the Endangered Species Act, school vouchers, laws allowing the carrying of concealed weapons, "three strikes and you're out" laws). Have them prepare a presentation describing why this policy was established and what its results have been. Remind them to include how both supporters and critics interpret the results. Finally, invite students to include their own opinion. Was the policy they studied a true solution or was it the beginning of yet another problem?

COMMUNICATION
PRACTICE LAB

Brainstorming Ideas

Point out that combining several people's creativity and energy results in a greater variety of ideas than one person could produce during the same period of time. Create a variation of this brainstorming activity by turning the session into a contest. Give each group a piece of paper and a single writing implement. On the word *Go*, the person with the paper writes an idea and passes it quickly to the left. The next student writes down another idea and passes the list on in turn. This continues until the students receive the signal to stop. Have each group count their ideas (allow no repetitions) and declare a winner. Discuss the ideas generated with the class. **L2**

COMMUNICATION
PRACTICE LAB

Brainstorming Ideas

To practice conducting a warm-up brainstorming session, follow these steps.

Step 1 Working in groups of five or six, generate ideas for five minutes on one of the following topics or a topic of your own. Have any new topics approved by your teacher.
- New game shows you'd like to see on TV
- How to spend one million dollars
- Uses for a paper plate

Step 2 List your ideas on a sheet of paper. List at least twenty ideas.

Step 3 After your ideas have been generated, discuss as a class some of the most unusual ideas. How difficult was it to keep from criticizing others' ideas? Do you think you could have generated such a diverse list on your own in the same period of time? Why or why not?

After checking the solutions against the criteria and answering the implementation questions, the group may then cross off those ideas that do not fit. Some solutions might meet all the criteria but be unacceptable because of the implementation questions. In this stage of decision making, the group should consider combining ideas or modifying them before discarding them.

Once the group's ideas have been focused, it is time to choose the best solution. Group members should fully discuss all the remaining suggestions. They then should choose the idea or combination of ideas that best meets the criteria.

There are several ways for a group to make its final decision. The most desirable method is to reach a collective decision, or consensus, that every member is willing to support. If this does not seem possible after sufficient discussion, the group may decide to vote. Group members might also decide to ask an expert to listen to the issues and make a decision. Regardless of the decision-making method used, the final step in the process cannot be completed until a solution is chosen.

Implement the Solution. This is the last step in the problem-solving process. In this step, the group should list, in chronological order, all the tasks or jobs necessary to put the solution into effect. The group also should identify the resources necessary to make the plan work. If, for example, cost were a non-negotiable criterion, the implementation plan would need to demonstrate that the solution falls within the established budget.

Next, the group should specify individual responsibilities. Who will do each of the listed tasks? What are the deadlines for completing these tasks? What is the timeline for the plan's overall completion? Understanding these basic guidelines can play a large part in the overall success of the solution.

The implementation plan also should include a system for evaluating the effectiveness of its solution. This evaluation plan should include ways to assess the results of the solution. It should list specific standards for this evaluation as well. Finally, it is important to include a realistic time line for the evaluation.

Understanding the Nature of Groups **337**

3 ASSESS

Assign Section 2 Assessment as a homework or in-class activity.

Use *Interactive Tutor Self-Assessment Software* to review Section 2.

Section 10–2 Quiz

MEETING INDIVIDUAL NEEDS
INCLUSION STRATEGIES

Special Needs Implementing solutions to problems may mean face-to-face contact with authority figures. Some students may find it difficult to communicate with these individuals.

Activity Let students work in small groups. Allow them to choose a problem and solution that have been discussed during the course of the chapter. As a group, have them identify the ways they could go about implementing solutions. As part of the discussion, the group should identify the different roles group members would need to play. For example, someone may need to write letters; others may be needed to deliver an oral presentation to the appropriate person; some students may be needed to create charts, posters, or other graphics. Help students realize that part of group work is helping all members contribute from beginning to end.

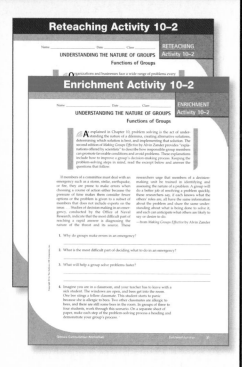

Reteaching Activity 10–2

Enrichment Activity 10–2

4 CLOSE

Have students refer back to the first paragraph of Section 2 on page 327. Ask them whether any of the groups they have belonged to served to solve problems as described in this section. Invite volunteers to give examples from their experiences showing how "two heads are better than one."

Extra-Credit Project

Ask students to interview an adult serving on a committee or task group. What three important problems has his or her group recently had to solve? What were the solutions and how did they achieve them? Have students present their findings to the class.

As a final step, the group should put into place a plan for dealing with possible emergencies. Emergencies might include running over budget, having a key group member quit or move away, or taking more time than was planned. By anticipating and planning for these types of difficulties, a group can ensure that its plan will be implemented successfully.

Once the group's implementation plan has been finalized, it should be clearly explained in a report. This is a communication task for the group. The final report should be submitted to the parent organization. For example, the locker-theft group could use the information from its chart to write up a recommendation, justifying the reasoning behind each step. This report could then be turned in to the school's administration, thus completing the group's problem-solving task. In this way, the group has not only found a solution but also has carefully thought out every step toward putting it into effect.

Section 2 Assessment

Visit the *Glencoe Communication Applications* Web site at **communicationapplications. glencoe.com** and click on **Self-Check and Study Guide 10.2** to review your understanding of the functions of groups.

Review Key Terms

1. Define each of the following terms and write it in a sentence: problem, problem solving, criteria, brainstorming, and decision making.

Check Understanding

2. Why is the group function of planning important to an organization?

3. Identify the three main considerations involved in planning and give an example of each.

4. Explain the six steps of the problem-solving process.

5. **Drawing Conclusions** Why might brainstorming be an effective tool for solving problems?

APPLICATION *Activity*

Planning a Campus Radio Station Imagine that you are a member of a team charged with creating a new radio station format at your school. Working in groups of four to six people, list the different areas you should consider as you plan the new format. Base your list on a consideration of the people, occasion, and task. Once you have created your list, come to a group consensus on which are the three most important considerations. If you have trouble forming a consensus, use the problem-solving strategies you read about in this section. After all groups have completed their lists, share them as a class. Create a class list of ideas for creating a station at your school.

338   *Glencoe Communication Applications*

Section 2 Assessment Answers

1. Accept all reasonable sentences.
2. If an event is not well planned, it might not be a success. If an organizational change is poorly planned, it might have a bad effect on the organization, waste money or cause a loss of profits.
3. People, occasion, and task; examples will vary.
4. Describe the problem; analyze the problem; establish the criteria for the solution; brainstorm possible solutions; compare all possible solutions

to the criteria and choose one; implement the chosen solution.
5. Answers may include that brainstorming is nonjudgmental and frees individuals to think in new ways.

Application Activity Lists should include determining whether there is support, what resources might be picked up, how to obtain any necessary equipment or music resource, how to staff, and so on.

Communication Self-Assessment

Analyzing Your Group Communication Skills

How Do You Rate?

On a separate sheet of paper, use the key to answer the following questions. Put a check mark at the end of each skill you would like to improve.

Key: **A** Always   **R** Rarely
          U Usually   **N** Never
          S Sometimes

1. When I work in a group, I talk about thirty percent of the meeting time.

2. I am more comfortable when I speak face-to-face with people.

3. I express my opinions in a group whether or not I think the group will agree with me.

4. When I am on a committee or task force, I am willing to do research for the group.

5. I offer information I have about our group work at the proper point on the agenda.

6. I enjoy moving forward to meet group goals.

7. When there is tension in the group, I try to relieve it by asking people to clarify their differences.

8. If someone violates a group norm, I speak to them about this privately.

9. When new members join the group, I am eager to welcome them and bring them up to date on our work.

10. In a group, I tend to be the one who brings our group back to its goal.

How Do You Score?

Review your responses. Give yourself 5 points for every A, 4 for every U, 3 for every S, 2 for every R, and 1 for every N. Total your points and evaluate your score.

41–50 Excellent You may be surprised to find out how much you can improve your skills.

31–40 Good In this course, you can learn ways to make your skills better.

21–30 Fair Practice applying the skills taught in this course.

1–20 Needs Improvement Carefully monitor your improvement as you work through this course.

Setting Communication Goals

If you scored Excellent or Good, complete Part A. If your score was Fair or Needs Improvement, complete Part B.

Part A 1. I plan to put the following ideas into practice:

2. I plan to share the following information about communication with the following people:

Part B 1. The behaviors I need to change most are:

2. To bring about these changes, I will take these steps:

Understanding the Nature of Groups **339**

Have students respond to the ten statements using the key; then, have them evaluate their group communication skills as described in How Do You Score? Based on their scores, assign either Part A or Part B of the goal-setting activity. Have students rank the ten quiz questions in order of difficulty, according to their self-assessments. Discuss with the class the areas of greatest difficulty.

Communication Journal Activity

Remind students that although they may not be members of an organized group, they regularly engage in group activities, whether eating lunch in the cafeteria or walking home with friends. Have students record in their Communication Journals their participation in groups of three or more people over the course of a week. Have them choose one of these occasions and write an entry describing and assessing their role as group communicators.

Communication Tip

Point out that many of the skills valued by groups can be practiced by students in their daily communication with others. Encourage students to identify an area in which they need improvement and to find ways of practicing that skill in everyday situations.

INTERDISCIPLINARY CONNECTION

Language Arts Point out that in the world of business, not all successful leaders follow the same communications philosophy.

Activity Write on the chalkboard the following statements by Alfred P. Sloan Jr., former head of General Motors, and Lee Iacocca, former head of Ford and Chrysler: "We do not issue orders. I have never issued an order since I have been the operating head of this Corporation. . . . Our policies come from the bottom." (Sloan) "What's to admire about consensus management anyway? By its very nature, it's slow. It can never be daring. There can never be real accountability—or flexibility." (Iacocca) Have students discuss the pros and cons of both of these statements.

Communication Through Writing

Writing a Memo

Objective: To create a memorandum

Teaching Suggestions and Strategies

The Need for Memos

Although the telephone and face-to-face meetings are convenient and quick, they do not always serve for occasions when information must be transmitted to a number of individuals simultaneously. Point out that because a memo is intended for several readers, its style must be suitable for all recipients. A personal reference or a joke that is meaningful to one reader might be unintelligible, or perhaps offensive, to another. For this reason, the writer must stick to the facts and keep language clear and concise.

In organizations where all employees have regular access to personal computers, the e-mail memo has replaced the written sheet. If your high school is one of the many that have not caught up with the information age, share with your students a written memo you have received and discuss how effectively it serves its purpose.

Writing a Memo

A memorandum is a communication circulated within a company. A shorter name for a memorandum is a *memo*. Memos provide employees with important information and updates. Memos can range in length from one paragraph to two or three pages.

Using the Appropriate Style Although a memo may look somewhat like a letter, its style is quite different. A memo is strictly informative and is intended to get right to the point. Typically, it does not include a greeting or closing. The wording of a memo also may be direct or indirect. Most memos use a direct style, summarizing the subject matter in the first paragraph. Then, if necessary, more detail is provided in additional paragraphs. A memo should give only the most important information on a topic.

Occasionally, a memo may have a more indirect style. This style often is effective for conveying bad news or trying to persuade someone to do something he or she may not want to do. In these cases, the first paragraph might explain a special situation or the reasons why a decision has been made. Then the memo can move on to the main information.

Tips for Effective Memos To make your memos useful and easy to read, follow these guidelines.

- Include all the necessary information in the heading. If others besides the main recipient will receive a copy of the memo, list their names beside cc: in the heading. The abbreviation *cc* means *copies.*

- Use a block style for paragraphs.

- Refer to only one topic in each paragraph.

- Do not use highly technical language.

- Use bulleted lists for important points and to convey more complex information.

- Handwrite your name, initials, or a P.S. on the memo for a personal touch.

- Proofread your work, correcting any errors in grammar or spelling.

Now, imagine that you are a sales manager whose staff must begin using a new form. To inform them of this change, you have written the following memo.

For additional information about business writing, see the *Guide to Business Communication* section of the Communication Survival Kit in the Appendix.

MULTIPLE LEARNING STYLES

Bodily-Kinesthetic Remind students that they are constantly adapting their tone in spoken and written communication to suit the occasion, the subject, and the audience. Explain that tone is particularly important in business communication. A memo, for example, should not be formal, but it must be direct and clear, using the standard rules of English grammar.

Activity Divide the students into groups and give them the following prompts: 500 employees are going to lose their jobs; the company is moving to Canada/Mexico; three vice presidents are being investigated for fraud. For each prompt, have groups prepare this news as they might hear it from a colleague and then as they might receive it in a brief memo. Have groups perform their skits and read their memos. Discuss how the tone differs with the situation.

Communication Through Writing

Date: June 15, 2004
To: All Sales Agents
From: Marcy McDonald
      Purchasing Manager
Subject: New Purchasing Procedure

As of today, June 15, 2004, purchasing order forms 123-A are outdated. We are substituting forms 123-B. Look for the new forms in your inbox today. Each of you will receive a dozen new forms.

The reason we are making this change is that we have changed our accounting procedures.

If you compare the old and new forms, you will see few differences between them. The only difference is that you will order Real Estate Contracts on line 10 of the new form (as opposed to line 1 on the old form).

Things for you to do:
• Find all copies of form 123-A in your files.
• Compare the old form with the new one.
• In addition, note the change on line 10.
• Toss out all copies of form 123-A.
• File copies of 123-B.

P.S. Sam, thanks for recommending this idea. It will make all of our jobs easier.

WRITING Activity

Imagine that you are an office manager for a company in a large office building. A security officer has informed you that employees at your company are illegally parking in the building's 15-minute loading and unloading zones. Using a word-processing program, follow these steps to write a memo to all employees.

• Create the heading for your memo.

• Send a copy of the memo to Mark Fields, Chief of Security.

• Using a block paragraph style, write a paragraph summarizing the reason for your memo.

• In another paragraph, remind employees that parking is allowed only along the street, in the outdoor lot, and on floors B, C, and D of the parking garage. Use a bulleted list for this information.

• In a third paragraph, explain that illegally parked cars will be towed at the owner's expense.

• Proofread your memo, correcting any errors.

• Print your memo.

• Handwrite your initials beside your name in the heading.

Understanding the Nature of Groups   341

Teaching Activity

Many students will never have had to write information in memo form. To those who question this lesson's relevance, point out that the skills needed to impart clear, straightforward information are always valuable.

Have students study the sample memo on this page and ask them to use it as a model for a memo of their own, addressed to a group of friends. Encourage them to write on any subject they like—an upcoming party, a football game, or an after-school job opportunity, for example. Insist, however, that their content be clear, their grammar standard, and their language free of slang. Invite volunteers to read their memos to the class.

WRITING Activity

Have students peer edit their memos before printing, asking editors to be particularly aware of the appropriateness of grammar and vocabulary.

Grammar Tip

The indefinite pronouns *each, either, neither,* and *one,* along with all indefinite pronouns ending in *one, thing,* or *body,* are singular in number. In Standard English other pronouns referring to them must also be singular.

Additional Resources

Appendix, "Guide to Business Communication"

Glencoe Writer's Assistant CD-ROM

Glencoe Interactive Grammar Software

Grade 9 Writer's Choice, Lesson 5.1

GRAMMAR PRACTICE

Agreement with Indefinite Pronouns

Have students write the correct personal pronoun in the blank space.

1. Each employee must park in ___ own space. *(his; her; his or her)*

2. Neither woman knew why ___ had not received a memo. *(she)*

3. Either man will do ___ best to give the employees a fair deal. *(his)*

4. Everybody knows ___ job in this organization. *(his; her; his or her)*

5. Anyone challenging our CEO at a meeting will get ___ in trouble. *(himself; herself; himself or herself)*

CHAPTER 10 Assessment and Activities

GLENCOE TECHNOLOGY

 MindJogger Videoquiz

Use *MindJogger* to review the Chapter 10 content.

Visit the *Glencoe Communication Applications* Web site at **communicationapplications. glencoe.com** and click on **Chapter 10 Activity** for additional practice in identifying the nature and function of groups.

Reviewing Key Terms

1. information-gathering
2. criteria
3. committee
4. advocacy group
5. problem
6. group goal
7. prescribed goal
8. social group
9. task group
10. decision-making

Reviewing Key Terms

On a separate sheet of paper, write the communication term that completes each statement.

1. A(n) _____ is a group designed specifically to gather data.
2. In order to be acceptable, a solution to a problem must meet certain _____ .
3. A(n) _____ is a group that is part of the basic structure of an organization.
4. A(n) _____ is set up to promote, protect, defend, or lobby for a cause or group.
5. The difference between the way something should be and they way it is a(n) _____ .
6. A(n) _____ tells what specific research is to be done and what outcome to expect.
7. A person in authority assigns a(n) _____ .
8. Someone joins a(n) _____ for purely personal reasons.
9. The purpose of a(n) _____ is to complete an objective or a job.
10. The activity of a group choosing the best solution for the problem is a(n) _____ activity.

Reviewing Key Concepts

1. Individuals often use groups as a source of identity, and organizations use groups to accomplish goals.

2. 1. limited membership; 2. shared goal, interest, or bond; 3. face-to-face meetings; 4. meetings over time

3. With a limited membership, members of a group have time to express their ideas, to listen to the others' ideas, and to avoid hasty votes as the way to settle disagreements.

4. A sample goal would be to research the areas that need to be cleaned, then take action to clean them up. (These could include cleaning up the neighborhood playground, furnishing a large trash can for the site, or emptying the trash periodically.)

5. Unlike meeting on the telephone or sending e-mail, meeting face-to-face allows each member to see the nonverbal messages that other members are sending.

Reviewing Key Concepts

On a separate sheet of paper, answer the following questions in complete sentences.

1. Why do individuals and organizations use groups?
2. What are the four characteristics of a group?
3. How does limited membership help a group agree?
4. Create a statement that describes a group goal for a neighborhood cleanup committee.
5. Name one advantage meeting face-to-face has over telephone or e-mail.
6. How does working in groups benefit an organization?
7. How does working in groups benefit the individual?
8. Define the three main types of task groups.
9. Why might a company encourage its employees to join nonprofit civic groups?
10. What are the two main functions of groups?

6. The organization benefits by increased productivity, commitment to the organization, accuracy, creative energy, and community presence.

7. The individual benefits by gaining political influence, career advancement, and job satisfaction.

8. The three main types of task groups are information-gathering, policy-making, and action groups.

9. Answers may include: to gain positive publicity for the company or to broaden the employees' contacts within the community.

10. The two main functions of groups are planning and solving problems.

Assessment and Activities

Reading and Critical Thinking Skill

1. **Inference** What can you infer from the following statement by an employee: "As a group member, I get to contribute so much that I wouldn't dream of looking elsewhere for work"?

2. **Cause-Effect** What effect does group work have on employee morale?

3. **Summarization** Summarize the three main considerations a group whose main function is planning must address to implement its plan.

4. **Analysis** How does a problem-solving group determine what information it needs to know?

Skill Practice Activity

Making an Inference Read the following information taken from a memo and answer the questions below.

> To: Paloma Gonzalez, Lynn Tse, and Pamela Walker—customer service team
> Enclosed are certificates to mark your five years as a team. Our company enjoys an excellent standing in the community because our employees are committed to their work. Recently, a rare 'unsatisfied' customer called to praise your team for your conscientious efforts to correct a delivery error.

> With these certificates, the company wishes to thank you for your loyalty. We hope you are with us for many more years.

1. What observations are made?

2. Which of the following statements is an inference based on the memo?

   a. The customer service team adds to the company's good standing.

   b. Despite the company's excellent reputation and loyal employees, many customers call to complain.

Cooperative Learning Activity

Picturing an Organization Form teams of four to six people. As a team, consult the yellow pages in a phone book to find a business that probably has several levels of management and other employees. Brainstorm to name the kinds of groups the business might need to operate and the kinds of workers each group might need. Use the lists to create a diagram of the business's organization.

Chapter Project

Planning As a class, brainstorm a list of all the workshops, seminars, and summer camps that help students get information about or training in school activities. Form groups of four or six. Each group selects one information or training opportunity and gathers all the information it can find on the event.

Presenting Each group uses the information to create a brochure for students who might benefit from the event.

Understanding the Nature of Groups **343**

Chapter Project

Brochures might include a time line with a registration deadline as well as the date and time of the event. It might also include a map from the school to the event site and list available means of transportation, such as bus, train, or car pool. Finally, the brochure could include a questionnaire to help students who participate in the event evaluate its effectiveness.

Reading and Critical Thinking Skill

1. Group members develop a high level of commitment to the goals of an organization if allowed to participate.

2. Group work raises morale by giving employees the feeling that the company encourages their creativity and initiative.

3. A planning group must address how the work will be done, when it will be done, and who will do it.

4. First, members share information they already have; then, they generate research questions about areas in which they lack information; finally, they research those areas.

Skill Practice Activity

1. The company enjoys an excellent standing in the community in part due to the customer service team and that a customer praised the team.

2. a.

Cooperative Learning Activity

The process of creating the diagram gives students an opportunity to assume productive roles in groups and to use appropriate verbal, nonverbal, and listening strategies, for example, during brainstorming and while putting together the rough draft of the diagram.

The following is a simple example of a possible diagram.

Hardware Store

Owner

Manager

Clerks   Stockers   Cleaning Crew

Chapter 11 Planning Guide

SECTION RESOURCES

Daily Objectives

Section 1

1. Distinguish between prescribed and emergent norms
2. Identify and describe the three major roles group members play
3. Analyze and adapt group dynamics to achieve productive group participation
4. Describe appropriate skills and strategies for participating effectively in group discussions

Section 2

1. Use appropriate verbal strategies to promote group effectiveness
2. Use effective and describe ineffective nonverbal behaviors in group meetings
3. Use a variety of listening strategies to contribute to group effectiveness
4. Identify and analyze the role of the group chairperson
5. Analyze the participation and contributions of group members and evaluate group effectiveness

Reproducible Resources

 Reproducible Lesson Plan 11-1
 Application Activities 11-1
 Guided Reading Workbook Activity 11-1
 Vocabulary Activity 11*
 Reteaching Activity 11-1*
 Enrichment Activity 11-1*
 Graphic Organizer Transparency Strategies and Activities 11-1

 Reproducible Lesson Plan 11-2
 Application Activities 11-2
 Guided Reading Workbook Activity 11-2
 Vocabulary Activity 11*
 Reteaching Activity 11-2*
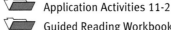 Enrichment Activity 11-2*
Graphic Organizer Transparency Strategies and Activities 11-2

Multimedia Resources

 Graphic Organizer Transparency 11-1
 Chapter 11 Teaching Transparency
 Interactive Tutor Self-Assessment
 PuzzleMaker
 ExamView® Pro Testmaker
Interactive Lesson Planner
 Communication in Action Video Chapter 11
MindJogger
 communicationapplications.glencoe.com
 Presentation Plus!

 Graphic Organizer Transparency 11-2
 Chapter 11 Teaching Transparency
 Interactive Tutor Self-Assessment
 PuzzleMaker
 ExamView® Pro Testmaker
Interactive Lesson Planner
 Communication in Action Video Chapter 11
 MindJogger
 communicationapplications.glencoe.com
 Presentation Plus!

Use Glencoe's *Presentation Plus!* multimedia teacher tool to easily present dynamic lessons that engage and motivate your students. Using Microsoft PowerPoint®, you can customize the presentations to create your own personalized lessons.

* Also available in Spanish

 Blackline Master   CD-ROM   Software

 Transparency   Videodisc   Videocassette   Web site

Chapter 11 Planning Guide

FOR THE TEACHER

Groups

Ask students to list three to five groups in which they are members. If necessary, point out that the family is one group and your class is another. Sports teams, community-service groups, and clubs are other possibilities. Groups need not be formally organized; a bunch of friends who interact regularly can also be considered a group for this activity.

Have students keep their own groups in mind as the class discusses groups. What are some different kinds of groups? Does every group have a leader? Are all leaders formally established or do they seem to emerge from the group? How do group members interact? Do all members seem to have an equal voice in the group's activities? Do all members take an active part? Why or why not? Why are groups important? What does it take to be an effective member of a group?

CHAPTER RESOURCES

Resources for the Teacher

- *Finding a Way to Win: The Principles of Leadership, Teamwork, and Motivation* by Bill Parcells, Doubleday, 1995
- *How to Run a Successful Meeting—In Half the Time* by Milo O. Frank, Simon and Schuster, 1989
- *Teamwork: Involving People in Quality and Productivity Improvements* by Charles A. Aubrey, Unipub/Quality Resources, 1988
- *Workplace Wars and How to End Them: Turning Personal Conflicts into Productive Teamwork* by Kenneth Kaye, American Management Association, 1994

Resources for the Student

- *Who's Got the Ball?: And Other Nagging Questions About Team Life: A Player's Guide for Work Teams* by Maureen O'Brien, Jossey-Bass, 1995
- *The Winner Within: A Life Plan for Team Players* by Pat Riley, Putnam's Sons, 1993
- *Inside Teams: How 20 World-Class Organizations Are Winning Through Teamwork* by Richard S. Wellins, Jossey-Bass, 1994

Block Scheduling

Block scheduling differs from traditional class scheduling in the amount of time allotted to each period. The extended time frame provided by block scheduling affords you the opportunity to implement a greater number of research-oriented and activity-intense projects to motivate and involve your students. Activities that are particularly suited to use within the block-scheduling framework are identified throughout this chapter by the following designation:

KEY TO ABILITY LEVELS

Teaching Strategies have been coded for varying learning styles and abilities.

L1 **BASIC** activities for all students

L2 **AVERAGE** activities for average to above-average students

L3 **CHALLENGING** activities for above-average students

ELL **English Language Learner** activities

Chapter 11 Resource Manager

The following materials may be used when teaching the chapter. Materials for specific lessons are also shown at point-of-use in the margins of the Teacher's Wraparound Edition.

TEACHING TRANSPARENCIES

Chapter 11 Teaching Transparency

Graphic Organizer Transparency 11-1

Graphic Organizer Transparency 11-2

APPLICATION ACTIVITIES

Chapter 11, Section 1

Chapter 11, Section 2

Chapter 11, Cumulative

REINFORCEMENT AND REVIEW ACTIVITIES

Vocabulary Activity 11

Guided Reading Activity Workbook 11-1, 11-2

Reteaching Activities 11-1, 11-2

Chapter 11 Resource Manager

Assessment and Evaluation

Section Quizzes 11-1, 11-2

Chapter 11 Test, Forms A & B

Performance Assessment Activity 11

Enrichment and Extension

Technology Application Activity 11

Enrichment Activities 11-1, 11-2

Oral Presentation Activities

Activities 13, 14

Spanish Resources

- Spanish Chapter and Unit Tests
- Spanish Vocabulary Activities
- Spanish Section Quizzes
- Spanish Reteaching Activities
- Spanish Enrichment Activities

Multimedia

- Interactive Tutor Self-Assessment
- ExamView® Pro Testmaker
- PuzzleMaker
- Communication in Action Videodisc and Videocassette
- MindJogger
- Interactive Lesson Planner
- Presentation Plus!
- Writer's Assistant
- Glencoe Interactive Grammar
- **communicationapplications.glencoe.com**

Teacher Planning and Support

- Reproducible Lesson Plans
- Interactive Lesson Planner
- Presentation Plus!

343D

CHAPTER 11

Making Groups Work

WHY IT'S IMPORTANT

By developing the Macintosh computer, which made personal computing easier than ever before, Steven Jobs's team made a huge impact on the universe of personal computing. And it proved once again that effective groups can accomplish great things.

To better understand how communication affects the productivity of groups, view the **Communication in Action** Chapter 11 video lesson.

GLENCOE Online

Visit the *Glencoe Communication Applications* Web site at **communicationapplications. glencoe.com** and click on **Overview–Chapter 11** to preview information about making groups work.

"*Make a dent in the universe.*"
—Steven Jobs

WHY IT'S IMPORTANT

Have a volunteer read aloud Steven Jobs's quotation on this page. Then, have students skim the chapter, reading the headings and subheadings. Ask: **Why is it important for businesspeople to work in groups effectively? How might that help them "make a dent in the universe"?** *(Answers may include that most tasks are done cooperatively, and often teams and groups move a company forward.)*

Section 1

Interacting in Groups

GUIDE TO READING

Objectives

1. Distinguish between prescribed and emergent norms.
2. Identify and describe the three major roles group members play.
3. Analyze and adapt group dynamics to achieve productive group participation.
4. Describe appropriate skills and strategies for participating effectively in group discussions.

Terms to Learn

group norm
prescribed norm
emergent norm
initiator
facilitator

agitator
groupthink
group dynamics
group discussion

*T*hink about how you might be expected to behave in an English class. Now think about how you might act in athletics. Are there different expectations about your behavior in each type of school activity? What do you think accounts for these differences?

The degree to which your behavior changes from one type of activity to another depends on a number of factors. Two of these are the rules set by your teacher or coach and the roles you choose to play as a participant in the activity. Rules and roles play a large part in the way we communicate with others in almost any group setting.

IDENTIFYING GROUP NORMS

Whether you join a group on your own or are assigned to one, you will be expected to follow some group norms while working in that group. Group norms are the informal, often unstated rules about what behavior is appropriate in a group. If you

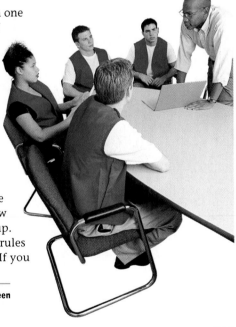

Group norms determine the interaction that takes place between people when they are at work. Define group norms.

Making Groups Work **345**

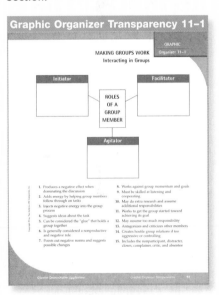

1 FOCUS

Bellringer
Have students read the opening paragraph of the section to themselves. Discuss the influence of different groups on individual behavior described in the paragraph. Then, direct discussion to students' answers to the two questions. *(Answers may include that there are different expectations for behavior in different group settings, perhaps because different types of activities take place.)*

You may use Graphic Organizer Transparency 11–1 to introduce this section.

Graphic Organizer Transparency 11–1

MAKING GROUPS WORK
Interacting in Groups

Initiator   Facilitator

ROLES OF A GROUP MEMBER

Agitator

Visual Instruction

Answer Group norms are the informal, often unstated rules about appropriate group behavior.

RESOURCE MANAGER

Teaching Tools

- Interactive Lesson Planner
- Reproducible Lesson Plan 11–1
- Application Activities 11–1

Reproducible Masters

- Guided Reading Activity Workbook 11–1
- Enrichment Activity 11–1
- Reteaching Activity 11–1
- Section Quiz 11–1
- Transparency Strategies and Activities Booklet 11–1

Transparencies

- Graphic Organizer Transparency 11–1
- Chapter 11 Teaching Transparency

Technology Resources

- Interactive Tutor Self-Assessment Software
- Presentation Plus! Software
- ExamView® Pro Testmaker
- PuzzleMaker Software
- communicationapplications.glencoe.com

2 TEACH

Behavior in Groups
Remind students that the behavior expected of individuals varies within different groups. You may want to begin an ongoing discussion of the reasons following those norms can be important to an individual. Encourage students to develop an understanding of the importance of groups to the individual. **L1**

Making Predictions
As students read about prescribed and emergent norms, discuss with them the consequences of individuals not following one of the other types of norms when they are part of a group. Ask what effect such behavior might have on the group and on the individual. *(Answers may include that the group will be disrupted and not be able to pursue its purpose; the individual may be excluded from the group.)* **L2**

▪ Visual Instruction

Answer The categories of norms are prescribed norms (written or unwritten norms routinely taught to new group members) and emergent norms (group norms that develop as result of the interaction and personalities of group members).

For an additional Practice Lab for this section, have students visit the *Glencoe Communication Applications* Web site at **communicationapplications.glencoe.com.** Click on Communication Practice Lab 11–1. **L1**

---

work as a stocker at a grocery store, you probably have certain duties when you begin each workday or shift. You might be expected to punch a time clock, put on a uniform, or check with a supervisor to find out what specific tasks are assigned to you that day.

As a student, you also are expected to do certain things each morning as you begin your school day. For example, you probably are expected to dress appropriately, arrive on time, gather your books and materials for your first class, and proceed to that classroom at the designated time. By behaving in this way, you are following the group norms for the student body at your school.

As you can see, the norms for one group may be very different from those for another group. However, despite their differences, most group norms can be classified into two categories. They are either prescribed norms or emergent norms.

Prescribed Norms
A **prescribed norm** is a rule for appropriate behavior that is routinely taught to new group members. Prescribed norms may be written or unwritten.

In School Both schools and workplaces have prescribed norms. For instance, at the beginning of the school year, some teachers give students a list of rules, or prescribed norms, for their specific classroom. This establishes the norms for students' behavior in class.

In the Workplace In the workplace, prescribed norms usually include a specific time for the workday to begin and end or when people usually have lunch. Members of the armed services have prescribed norms about which uniforms to wear on different occasions. A coach might establish norms such as how long practice will last, what uniforms will be worn for home games, and how players are expected to behave when traveling to games in other cities.

▪ Members of the armed services adhere to a strict dress code. One individual shown above appears to be going against the dress norm. Identify the two categories of group norms.

MEETING INDIVIDUAL NEEDS
MULTIPLE LEARNING STYLES

Tactile-Kinesthetic Dominant learning styles can influence the way students incorporate information in school. Many students of this age are affected by the need for physical movement, which can lead to a tactile-kinesthetic learning style coming to the forefront, even temporarily.
Activity Ask students to recall how they learned what behaviors were expected in certain groups. Invite pairs of students to act out those acceptable behaviors as they enter a room and then participate in several different kinds of groups: an athletic team practice, an English class, a cafeteria, and so on.

GLOBAL COMMUNICATION

Culture in Meetings

The group norms followed in meetings often vary from culture to culture. In Brazil, for example, the norm is to engage in conversation about family and friends before moving on to the business part of a meeting. A person unfamiliar with this norm might dive right into business matters first and be considered cold and unfriendly. Think about the activities and interactions that might take place in meetings. What other group norms might clash in a business meeting involving people from different cultures?

Emergent Norms

Not all norms are as basic and enduring as the prescribed norms just described. Some develop as the group grows and changes. An emergent norm is any group norm that develops from the group interaction and the mix of the group members' personalities. These norms usually are unwritten and arise from some need that is determined by the group members.

If a teacher assigns a group project, the group goal and project deadline would be prescribed. However, the way in which the group chooses to complete the project; details about where, when, and how often the group will meet; and decisions about who will complete each task will emerge as a result of the group working together.

Imagine that the employees of a fast-food restaurant establish the norm that they will celebrate each other's birthdays by giving cards rather than gifts. If one member of the group brings a gift, the emergent norm of the group has been violated. The behavior is not appropriate for that group's norms.

Emergent group norms make a big difference in how a group works. Positive emergent norms can make group membership more pleasant and can help the group achieve its goal. Negative emergent norms, on the other hand, can be harmful to the group. When it

Guided Reading Activity 11-1

COMMUNICATION

Classifying Norms

PRACTICE LAB

To learn how to distinguish prescribed norms from emergent norms, follow these steps:

Step 1 As a class, brainstorm a list of group norms. Then, write the list on the chalkboard.

Step 2 Copy the list of norms onto a sheet of paper.

Step 3 For each norm, ask yourself "Would this norm be taught to all new group members?" If so, write *Prescribed* beside that norm.

Step 4 For each remaining norm, ask "Is this norm a result of group members' interactions and personalities?" If so, write *Emergent* beside that norm.

Step 5 Compare your answers as a class and discuss any differences of opinion. Then discuss whether each norm might have a positive or negative effect on a group and why.

Making Groups Work 347

GLOBAL COMMUNICATION

Culture in Meetings

Invite students with experience, heritage, or insight into any other culture to offer other examples of cultural differences in meetings. Let them discuss the group norms that might clash in a meeting involving people from other cultures. Point out that businesspeople who interact with others around the world must learn and respect the norms of other cultures.

COMMUNICATION
PRACTICE LAB

Classifying Norms

Have students follow the five steps in the Communication Practice Lab on this page to distinguish between prescribed norms and emergent norms. Students may find this task easier if they choose a familiar group to keep in mind as they follow the steps. Guide the class to realize that understanding the difference between the types of norms can help them analyze their own participation.

REAL-WORLD CONNECTION

International Business Communication Point out to students that customs and expectations of people from different cultures can interfere with business dealings when people from one culture do not understand or know the expectations of people from another.

Activity Have students do some research to discover some examples of the variations of cultural expectations that might affect business communication such as e-mail, letters, phone calls, and—most importantly—face-to-face meetings. Ask students to report the results of their research to the class.

Group Roles

As students discover the three different roles individuals typically play within a group—initiator, facilitator, and agitator—have them list characteristics of each role in a box on the board. You may want to encourage them to add specific examples of each they observe during their own participation in groups during the time they are working on this chapter. Suggest that students keep a copy of these lists for their future reference. **L1**

Application Activities 11-1

COMMUNICATION *Strategies*

DISPLAYING POSITIVE INITIATOR BEHAVIORS

Ask students to add their own ideas to the list of positive initiator behaviors in the chart on this page. Make a master list on the board or chart paper and have students add to it as they continue to participate in groups and realize what positive initiator behaviors are effective.

---

becomes the norm to be late or to complain about the task, the group is likely to become less effective. It doesn't take long for new norms to emerge in a group.

Sometimes problems arise in a group because discussion of emergent norms happens so rarely. If a norm is not written, a person may be breaking a norm and not know it. Others in the group may assume the person knows so they don't say anything. Fortunately, however, these norms usually can be changed quickly through group discussions and action.

Productive groups set productive group norms. The members also are productive in their group roles. In other words, they interact in ways that help accomplish the goal. For instance, people in productive groups either agree with each others' ideas or disagree respectfully. They also critically examine the work of others without being rude or sarcastic. Finally, they promote the task of the group without being impatient with other members. In short, productive group members act as competent communicators.

GROUP ROLES

Have you been a part of a group whose members really seemed to work well together? In this type of group, the work tends to be shared among all group members. Members also seem to genuinely enjoy working on the group task and working with each other, and there is a lot of positive energy.

In committees, teams, and other groups some members will have formal roles such as chairperson or manager. However, all members have communication roles that indicate the way they function in a group. The three roles that members are likely to play are initiator, facilitator, and agitator. In a single group session, it is possible that one person might switch from one role to another so that he or she actually plays all three roles during

COMMUNICATION *Strategies*

DISPLAYING POSITIVE INITIATOR BEHAVIORS

✓ Get the discussion started.

✓ Offer ideas about the task.

✓ Try to bring energy to the interaction.

✓ Point out negative norms and suggest possible ways to change them.

✓ Ask others to contribute their skills or talents to the task.

the session. In a productive group, members take turns playing these three roles to keep the group balanced and to keep it moving toward the achievement of its goal.

Initiator

Within a group, a member may play the role of an initiator. An initiator works to get the group started toward achieving the group goal. An effective initiator contributes positive task energy to the group.

Positive Initiator Behaviors A person playing the role of initiator can contribute to the group by displaying certain positive behaviors.

An initiator in a group of students planning a school dance might suggest different tasks to group members based on their individual talents. He or she might ask someone who plays in a band to plan how and where to set up the sound equipment and band platform. The initiator also might ask a skillful writer to compose an article about the dance for the school newspaper.

COOPERATIVE LEARNING ACTIVITY.

Much human activity is carried out by groups—in business, politics, education, the arts, and so on. Students need to become aware that group participation is a frequent human activity and not just something described in a textbook. They also need to learn how to monitor their own behavior in groups in order to become effective group members.

Divide the class into groups of four to six students each. Ask each group to assign itself a purpose, perhaps by mimicking a group some students already belong to, such as an athletic team. Have each group tackle a problem the "real" group might have, with members deliberately taking turns playing the roles of initiator, facilitator, and agitator.

Sometimes, the role of the initiator can be assumed by a member of a group who is not the group leader. Think about a time when you were in a group meeting and realized it was time to begin. However, the group leader may have been busy talking with another member, unaware that the group was ready to start the discussion. To avoid wasting time, someone else in the group needed to assume the role of initiator by saying, "Hey, it's late. Should we get started?" By helping to begin the discussion, this person provides positive energy to the group.

Negative Initiator Behaviors

Initiators also can contribute negative energy to a group. If an initiator is too aggressive and tries to control what everyone in the group does, his or her actions may backfire. Often, this creates a hostile relationship among group members instead of encouraging a spirit of cooperation.

Initiators who dominate a discussion also have a negative effect on a group. When other members are not allowed to contribute, they often quit trying. This can stop the free exchange of ideas that is so important to productive groups.

Finally, initiators may display negative behavior by ignoring the feelings of others while trying to get the task done. Although it is important to keep the group moving toward its goal, it also is important to recognize the value and contributions of each individual member.

Facilitator

Another role a group member may play is that of a facilitator. A facilitator is a person who also adds energy to the group by helping group members follow through on tasks. The facilitator is the glue that holds a group together. This person often offers to do the tasks necessary for the group to achieve its goal.

Positive Facilitator Behaviors

The facilitator can contribute greatly to the effectiveness of the committee, team, or group. To do this, he or she should display certain positive behaviors.

An effective facilitator is one who listens and cooperates. He or she also supports other members of the group. A facilitator may volunteer to do extra research, make key changes to a report, make phone calls, write letters, or assume other responsibilities needed to help the group reach its goal.

Think about a time when you tried to contribute a comment during a particularly lively group discussion. You may have had

During community meetings such as the one shown here, individuals sometimes act as initiators. **Describe an effective initiator.**

Making Groups Work **349**

Categorizing Group Roles

Ask a volunteer to begin two columns on the chalkboard: Initiator and Facilitator. Point out that the word initiate means "to begin something" and that the word facilitate means "to make something easy." You may want to have these words and definitions written under the appropriate headings. Invite discussion of the relationship of these definitions to the terms *initiator* and *facilitator* in terms of people's roles in groups. **L2**

Grammar Tip

Similar ideas should be expressed in a similar way. Such parallelism helps a reader understand the similarities. Note the example of parallelism in the Communication Strategies checklist on page 348: the items listed are parallel, because they are all presented as imperative sentences.

Visual Instruction

Answer An effective initiator listens, cooperates, and supports other members of the group.

Communication Tip

When you become a member of a group, make sure you understand what the goal or purpose of the group is. This will allow you to concentrate only on that purpose as you act within the group.

INTERDISCIPLINARY CONNECTION

Social Studies Recall with students the role of groups in the history of the United States, such as the group of men who drafted the Declaration of Independence. Point out that in current state and federal governments, groups such as legislatures meet to carry out the business of government.

Activity Ask students to follow the news about their state government activity or the federal Congress for a week. Have them write an analysis of which persons played the roles of initiator, facilitator, and agitator during the observation period. Ask them to explain their analysis in their report.

COMMUNICATION *Strategies*

DISPLAYING POSITIVE FACILITATOR BEHAVIORS

Discuss with students that a person who plays the role of facilitator in a group is often—though not always—the group leader who directs the action. After they have reviewed the chart on this page, ask students for examples of other positive facilitator behaviors. Discuss why people who act as facilitators are necessary to a group. *(Answers may include that facilitators keep things moving toward the accomplishment of the goals of the group.)*

Negative Group Roles

Discuss with students that people who play negative roles in a group prevent the group from moving its agenda forward. Review with students that even the generally positive group roles of initiator and facilitator may have negative behaviors associated with them, often when positive behaviors are exaggerated. For example, the positive initiator role of getting things started can become negative if the person insists on continuing to control the flow of conversation and others' actions. Point out that the role of agitator in a group is almost always a negative role. People who play such roles in a group are usually harmful to the group and to its agenda. **L2**

---

some difficulty making yourself heard. You may have leaned forward, possibly gestured for silence from the rest of the group, and started speaking. However, after only one or two words, someone else may have started speaking, taking the group discussion in another direction.

If someone had assumed the role of facilitator in the group, your comment might not have been lost. A facilitator would have heard that you had been cut off before you had an opportunity to be heard. He or she might

COMMUNICATION *Strategies*

DISPLAYING POSITIVE FACILITATOR BEHAVIORS

- ✓ **Direct the discussion.**
- ✓ **Assume responsibility for completing tasks to attain the group goal.**
- ✓ **Ask for group members' ideas on the task.**
- ✓ **Support group members' participation by complimenting their work when appropriate in the group.**
- ✓ **Notice when facial expressions and other nonverbal feedback indicate a member has a problem that needs to be addressed.**
- ✓ **Ask for input from all group members who haven't yet spoken on the topic.**
- ✓ **Summarize the main points of discussion for other group members.**
- ✓ **Provide humor and relieve tension among members as needed.**

350   *Glencoe Communication Applications*

---

have redirected the discussion by saying something like, "I think you had a comment to make when we were talking about the cost of this project. I'd like to hear your idea."

Negative Facilitator Behaviors Like an initiator, a facilitator sometimes may display negative behaviors. One common negative facilitator behavior is assuming too much responsibility and not delegating to others. A facilitator also may be so concerned about keeping the peace in a group that useful disagreements do not develop. Some conflict can benefit a group, causing group members to examine the issues more closely.

Agitator

Some roles generally are considered to be nonproductive and negative. People who play the role of agitator inject negative energy into the group process. There are six identifiable roles typically adopted by agitators: nonparticipant, distracter, clown, complainer, critic, and absentee. These six types of agitators are described in the following chart.

Negative Agitator Behaviors As you can see, most agitator behaviors are negative. An agitator works against the group's momentum. Some may even aggressively work against the group goals. Constantly criticizing and antagonizing other group members can create conflict and disrupt the group process. If an agitator argues for the sake of argument or disagrees just to be disagreeable, barriers to group effectiveness result.

Dealing With Agitators Agitators who actively create negative energy and those who contribute only a low level of energy both become a drain on the positive energy of a group. They create dissension and frustration and hold back group progress. The general rule for dealing with the negative behaviors of

---

MEETING INDIVIDUAL NEEDS

ENGLISH LANGUAGE LEARNERS

Group Participation English language learners may lack confidence in their ability to participate effectively in groups because of their limited understanding of the language. However, point out to them that it is their thinking skills that are most important to use in group activities.

Activity Ask students to brainstorm techniques they can use to help themselves become effective initiators and facilitators in the groups they belong to. Let them work together in a mock group to practice their ideas. **ELL**

TYPES OF AGITATORS

Type	Characteristics	Effect on Group
Nonparticipant	• Unconcerned with meeting group goal • Does not contribute ideas • Invests a low level of energy to group activities and meetings • Often may be late to meetings or fail to complete tasks on time • May do work of poor quality	• Can drain positive energy from the group and lower group morale • May create frustration and dissatisfaction among other group members who have to take over nonparticipant's share of responsibilities
Distracter	• Has difficulty focusing on the business of the meeting • Equates group time with social time • May be enthusiastic and energetic, but energy is misdirected • Tends to stay off the purpose, off the topic, and off the task	• Continual interruptions can be very disruptive • Can get other members off track • Can be annoying to group members trying to focus on the task
Clown	• Diverts attention from a task he or she does not find interesting • May disrupt the group's progress with jokes, wisecracks, sarcasm, or teasing	• Can provide comic relief, but typically overdoes it • Actions interfere with group's goal and purpose
Complainer	• Has a negative attitude • Repeatedly voices doubts or opposition to whatever the group is doing • Shares his or her bad attitude with the rest of the group	• Creates an atmosphere of negative thinking that can be difficult for a group to overcome
Critic	• Constantly points out what is wrong with others' ideas • Makes a habit of putting down others' suggestions • Seldom makes suggestions of his or her own	• Creates an atmosphere of hurt feelings, defensiveness, and anger among group members • Some members may not participate for fear of being criticized
Absentee	• Is a frequent "no show" for group meetings • Often will not respond to telephone calls or other contact from group members	• Even in his or her absence, injects negative energy into the group dynamics • Other members must step up to fulfill the absentee's responsibilities

agitators is simply to move on before the agitator's negative energy has a chance to influence the group. Once the group has moved on, the problem becomes that of the agitator, not of the group as a whole.

Positive Agitator Influences There are exceptions to this rule, however. Occasionally, it may be good for an agitator to slow the momentum of the group. If, for example, the group has missed an important detail while making its decision, it may take an agitator to draw attention to the oversight. In this case, the agitator has caused the group to reexamine its work as it progresses, rather than waiting until a real mistake has been made.

Imagine that a committee has been formed to explore changes in a company's vacation policy. Most members quickly agree that employee vacations should be restricted to the summer months. An agitator in the group might say, "Shouldn't we give some

Making Groups Work **351**

interNET
ACTIVITY

Groupthink Students may work in pairs or small groups to carry out this activity, perhaps in the school computer lab. Ask them to report not only the results of their search for "groupthink" but also the search engines and keywords they used to find the information.

Visual Learning

Ask students to interpret the cartoon illustration in Figure 11–1. What kind of person is in the sound-proof booth? Why? *(A negative agitator is probably in the booth to remove him from the meeting.)* What effect is the sound-proof booth having on the group? *(The group seems to be proceeding calmly.)* When sound-proof booths are not available, how might a group best handle a negative agitator? *(Answers may include simply talking to the person and pointing out how obstructive his or her behavior is to the group as a whole.)*
L2

consideration to individuals who want time with their families during winter holidays or who enjoy ski vacations?" With this challenge, the agitator has stopped the momentum of the group. Instead of agreeing too quickly on a solution, a more complete discussion can now occur. The agitator's comment also may have given courage to other members of the group. Those members who were silently concerned about the group's decision now have another opportunity to speak up and make their feelings known.

Groupthink Even though agitators cause a disruption in the group momentum, groups with no agitators may perform poorly. Groupthink is the name for poor decision-making in a group because group members have a stronger desire to agree with one another than to solve the problem.

■ **Figure 11–1 Dealing with Agitators**

interNET
ACTIVITY

Groupthink Log on to the Internet and access a reliable World Wide Web search engine. Conduct a search using the keyword *groupthink* and explore the results. Note three facts about avoiding groupthink and share them with the class.

A group of people who are afraid of disagreeing with one another or who want very much to be agreeable may become a victim of groupthink. If this group had a member who could play the agitator role positively, the group would have a better chance of making good decisions. It also would avoid making decisions that might cause additional problems.

Assuming Productive Group Roles

Although the roles of group members at first may seem very distinct, they are not set in stone. At one point in a discussion, you may be an initiator trying to move the group discussions along toward the goal. Later, you might be a facilitator encouraging a silent member to participate. At another point in the discussion, you may be an agitator, trying to get the group to consider an alternate idea. You also may have to find a way to deal with the apathetic or uncooperative agitator to safeguard the momentum of the group.

COOPERATIVE LEARNING ACTIVITY

Agitators who persist in interrupting group activity should be approached with a calm but firm attitude. Caution students to recall that in dealing with people who are confrontational, it is best not to become angry or confrontational oneself; to do so is to risk increasing the level of frustration and anger without successfully solving the problem. Have students brainstorm and role-play ways in which groups can handle problems involving agitators.

The key to assuming successful group roles is balance. Productive groups need members who can play all three roles and understand which role is appropriate at any given time. When should you change group roles? Ask yourself these two important questions: "Are we making progress?" and "What role do I need to assume to help move the group forward?"

ANALYZING GROUP DYNAMICS

As you move from committees to teams to other kinds of groups, changing your behavior in each situation, you are responding to group dynamics. Group dynamics is the energy created as group members communicate and interact with each other in committees, teams, and other groups.

Interaction among group members may be either positive or negative. Positive group interaction moves the group toward accomplishing its goal and building cohesion among group members. Negative interaction creates barriers that can prevent the group from reaching its goal. These barriers also provide obstacles to unity within the group.

■ **Figure 11–2 Factors Affecting Group Dynamics**

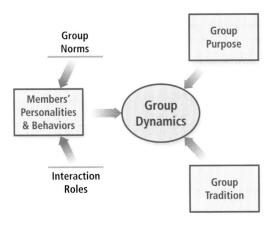

As **Figure 11–2** shows, group dynamics is the unique combination of group members' different personalities and behaviors, the group purpose, and the group tradition. Because each of these elements can change, group dynamics tend to be active, unpredictable, and constantly evolving.

Group members often influence one another's behavior, which can change the dynamics of the group. This typically occurs when they form and perform group norms or when they assume different group roles.

Impact of Norms on Dynamics

In a group, both prescribed and emergent norms should lead to achieving the group task and purpose. They also should contribute to a sense of unity within the group. A group's norms have a definite effect on the nature and quality of interaction among group members. For example, if a norm for committee members is to be courteous and direct with each other, members have a safe environment for voicing their ideas. This may make their interaction more comfortable. If the

Making Groups Work **353**

Connecting Visuals to Text
Ask students to consider probable reasons why the Far Side cartoon was placed on this page. Invite brief discussion, asking what the cartoon seems to illustrate *(the phenomenon known as "groupthink")*. **L3**

Grammar Tip

The phrase *group dynamics* is plural in form but singular in meaning. Therefore, in a sentence the subject *group dynamics* takes a singular verb: "Group dynamics is the energy . . ." and "Group dynamics is the unique combination. . . ."

THE FAR SIDE   By GARY LARSON

The entire parliament fell dead silent.
For the first time since anyone could remember,
one of the members voted "aye."

norm, such as the time and place or the level of formality, creates a problem within the group, the members should discuss the issue and look for a way to change the norm.

Impact of Roles on Dynamics

All group members should try to remain aware of which roles are needed during a meeting. Once a need has been determined, the members should do their best to fill that vacant role. A productive group needs a good balance of all three roles—initiators, facilitators, and agitators—performed competently. When there are too many or too few people filling one specific role, the group dynamics suffer.

Too many initiators can lead to power struggles. Too few initiators, however, can stall a meeting or send it off track. Too many facilitators may cause the group's work to stall if nobody takes action, even though everyone is willing to help. With too few facilitators, less assertive members may not be heard. Too many agitators in a group can create disruption and focus the group's energy on its disagreements. Too few agitators, on the other hand, may keep a committee from fully examining its decisions. The group may fail to consider alternative points of view.

When every group member assumes productive roles as they are needed, group dynamics often change for the better. This type of positive adaptation can help a group to function effectively and successfully.

GROUP DISCUSSION

Have you ever been to a meeting that never seemed to get down to business? Perhaps side conversations and activities made the meeting last twice as long as necessary? Using effective group discussion skills could have solved both of these problems.

In Chapter 1, you read that different contexts require different communication skills. In the context of personal interaction, communication may require conversation skills or small-talk skills. However, in the context of a group, communication requires the appropriate use of discussion skills.

Importance of Discussion

During a meeting, it is important to hear information and opinions of all group members. This can be accomplished through group discussion.

Group discussion occurs when three or more people exchange ideas on a specific topic for a specific purpose. A discussion is

---

EXTENDING THE CONTENT

Working in Business Groups Because working in groups is so important to the success of business, many people are evaluated in their jobs on the basis of their performance in groups. They can be evaluated either on the basis of their individual performance within a group, or their group can be evaluated and that evaluation might be made part of the individual employee's record.

Activity Suggest that students draw up a "report card" for group participation that includes the activities mentioned in this section, as well as others they think might be important. Have them use the report card to evaluate their own contribution to a group and the group's success.

different from a conversation, in which people informally exchange random observations, ideas, and opinions. Rather, a discussion is focused on a particular topic. It is organized around a central idea and has a specific reason for occurring. Group discussion also engages every member of the group.

Many times in a professional or social group setting, the topics of discussion are determined ahead of time. Some groups may organize these discussion topics in a formal agenda like the one in Figure 11–3.

Many groups do not prepare agendas for their meetings but may follow a fairly predictable order of topics in their meetings. These topics may relate to the type of group it is, its task, or its purpose. Whether or not these topics are written down, they serve as a guide for group discussion.

Characteristics of Effective Discussions

You probably know from experience that not all discussions go smoothly. In fact, some are much more effective than others. Effective discussions in committees, teams, and other groups share some important qualities. They are

- interactive
- focused
- organized
- cooperative

Interactive Group discussions generally are not effective unless everyone participates. For maximum participation, group members should remember to do the following:

Prepare ahead of time. This ensures that each member will have something valuable to contribute during the group session.

Take turns speaking. If two or more members speak at once, no one can hear everything that is being contributed to the discussion. A facilitator can help make sure everyone gets a turn to speak.

Listen carefully. Remember that others have prepared for the meeting as well. They may have important information and ideas to contribute to the discussion. Listening can mean keeping an open mind until different views are completely voiced before beginning to criticize. Listening carefully helps you stay more informed and aware in the group

■ Figure 11–3 **Formal Agenda**

POOLS Inc.

Discussion of Possible Market Expansion

Monday, March 12, 2003
Conference Room A
8:30 A.M.–10:30 A.M.

Benefits of market expansion 8:30–8:45
Susan Margolis, President

Possible expansion areas 8:45–9:15
Mark Pulos, Vice President, Marketing

Cost/benefit analysis 9:15–9:30
Ian Bernsen, Vice President, Accounting

Employee suggestions 9:30–9:45

Group discussion of all options 9:45–10:20

Wrap-up, plans for next stage 10:20–10:30
Susan Margolis

Making Groups Work **355**

The Importance of Discussion

Explain to students that classroom discussions are pertinent examples of group discussions. Point out that such discussions focus on a specific topic, engage all members of the group, and otherwise fulfill the definitions of a group discussion. Use this insight as students proceed to address discussions as a topic of effective groups. **L1**

BUSINESS BRIEF

Basketball superstar Michael Jordan, in *I Can't Accept Not Trying*, says: "Managers, like coaches, have to find ways to utilize individual talents in the best interests of the company. It's a selfless process. In our society, sometimes it's hard to come to grips with filling a role instead of trying to be a superstar. We tend to ignore or fail to respect all the parts that make the whole possible. Talent wins games, but teamwork and intelligence win championships." Ask students whether they think Jordan's insights into teamwork in basketball are applicable elsewhere. Have them explain their reasons. **L2**

CRITICAL THINKING ACTIVITY

Explain to students that the sequence of the presentations for the Pools, Inc. agenda shown in Figure 11–3 follows a certain logic: the benefits of expansion would logically be discussed before possible expansion areas, for example. Ask students to evaluate the Pools, Inc. agenda in terms of the sequence and time allotted for each topic. Make sure they realize that time allotments are usually estimates, and the presentations may not take up exactly the time provided for them. However, such time suggestions are a helpful tool for managing the length of the meeting. Have students draft similar agendas for two or three real groups they participate in, perhaps including your own classroom agendas for a day. Ask them to note how the actual meeting did or did not conform to the proposed agenda.

Comparing Group Discussions

Ask students to think of various class discussions they have participated in as they consider the characteristics of effective discussions. Invite them to offer specific examples of the four main qualities of effective group discussions. You may want to begin by suggesting, for example, that interactive discussions in class depend on students' preparation by having done their homework, thought about the topic, and so on. **L2**

Communication Tip

According to Max DePree, Chairman Emeritus of Herman Miller, Inc., "There may be no single thing more important in our efforts to achieve meaningful work and fulfilling relationships than to learn to practice the art of communication."

■ Visual Instruction

Answer The initiator acts to keep the group moving toward achieving its goal.

discussion. Your nonverbal behavior also should show that you are interested in what others have to say.

Contribute to the discussion. You can contribute by offering information, opinions, or suggestions about the topic. You also can contribute by asking others for their information, suggestions, and opinions.

Assume different roles as needed. Group members should act as initiators and facilitators and use questioning skills to keep the group moving toward achieving its goals.

Focused Group sessions are most effective when they focus on one topic at a time. Group discussion allows all group members to fully explore the information about one topic before moving to the next one. The goal is to

use each group member's critical evaluation skills to fully explore a topic before coming to a conclusion. First, the chairperson of the group or an initiator should introduce the topic to be discussed. He or she might then suggest how to start the discussion. If the initiator doesn't do this, a facilitator might make the suggestion and then keep the group on topic. For example, if a member strays from the topic, the facilitator might say something like, "Good idea, but we haven't finished with fund-raising ideas yet. Let's remember your suggestion for our next meeting." By being both direct and courteous, the facilitator can help the discussion stay productive and on track.

Organized Unlike conversation or small talk, which may jump from topic to topic, effective group discussion progresses from one

Members of a group assume different roles to keep the discussion focused. What role does the initiator play?

MEETING INDIVIDUAL NEEDS — INCLUSION STRATEGIES

Less-Proficient Readers Students who have some reading difficulties will benefit from examining the structure of nonfiction material, especially textbooks such as this one.
Acitivity Draw their attention to the headings and subheadings on pages 355 and 356. Show them that the items in the bulleted list in the first column on page 355 become headings on pages 355 and 356. Explain that the fact that these are identical indicates they are of equal importance. Continue by pointing out the five subheadings under "Interactive." Again show students that these five headings are alike. Let students leaf back through the chapter, noting similar headings. Have them write them in outline form.

logical point to the next to get the group's work accomplished. The goal of this sequence is to achieve a specific purpose. Whether a group is planning or problem solving, its interaction will be more effective if discussion is organized.

Cooperative To be effective, interaction in a committee or team should be cooperative. Group members should focus discussion time on achieving the group's stated goals. The degree to which members feel positive toward the group, its goals, and the other group members affects how cooperative the nature of any group discussion will be.

EFFECTIVE GROUP DISCUSSION

No one is born a discussion expert. On the contrary, participating appropriately in a group discussion is a learned skill. Quite simply, to be most effective in a committee, team, or other group discussion, you must learn how to adequately prepare for it. Preparing to participate in a group discussion involves some basic communication behaviors.

Become Informed

If you are participating in a committee, team, or other group and know the topic ahead of time, research it before the group meeting. You may want to read more about it in books, periodicals, or special publications.

You also may want to talk with someone who is familiar with the topic to get his or her ideas and perspectives. Finally, you may wish to gather information from videotapes, newscasts, the Internet, or special televised programs that deal with your topic. Throughout your research, concentrate on finding factual information about the topic that might be useful to your group.

COMMUNICATION Strategies

PREPARING TO PARTICIPATE IN A DISCUSSION

- Become informed.
- Formulate ideas.
- Prepare materials.

Formulate Ideas

Prior to the group meeting, take time to think about what ideas you can contribute to the group task. Come to your committee, team, or other group meeting with questions to ask about the topic, ideas to contribute, and suggestions to make.

Use your reasoning skills to formulate ideas and questions about the topic. Depending on your group's task, you may need to think about the long-term and short-term effects of taking a particular action or adopting a particular policy. Think about how your ideas or proposals might affect different members of your group or other groups. Consider cost, time, workers, and other practical issues involved in implementing your ideas. You might even want to anticipate potential arguments to your suggestions. Once you have considered all these factors, you can properly formulate and organize your ideas to present to your group.

Prepare Materials

If, after researching and considering the topic, you have developed new ideas or suggestions, you may want to prepare certain materials to help explain them to the group. These materials might include handouts, fact sheets, charts, or graphs that clarify your position.

Making Groups Work **357**

COMMUNICATION Strategies

PREPARING TO PARTICIPATE IN A DISCUSSION

Ask students to add to the list in the chart on this page other preparatory strategies they have found useful. For example, it may be very helpful to list thoughtful questions that may keep the group on track toward its basic purpose. **L2**

DID YOU KNOW?

As early as the Paleolithic Age (beginning about 750,000 years ago), people worked in cooperative groups of twenty or thirty people. Everyone worked together to feed the group, although most groups were nomadic and wandered to find food.

Section 11–1 Quiz

COOPERATIVE LEARNING ACTIVITY

Explain that presentation tools such as posters and transparencies can help enhance group discussions. Suggest that students review the information included in the text under the major heading Effective Group Discussion. Ask small groups of students to prepare two presentation tools that could enhance their discussion of the topic. Encourage them to explore the usefulness of illustrations, charts, diagrams, and other visuals as presentation tools.

---

3 ASSESS

Assign Section 1 Assessment as a homework or in-class activity.

🖱 Use *Interactive Tutor Self-Assessment Software* to review Section 1.

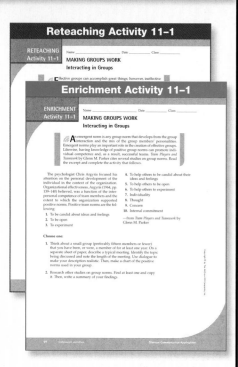

4 CLOSE

Ask students to reread the opening paragraph on page 345 and to recall their answers to the questions. Based on what they have learned in this section, how might their answers be different now? Have students answer the questions again, amplifying what they think accounts for the differences in behavior in different groups.

Extra-Credit Project

Ask students to list three or four committees, teams, or other groups they are part of. Have them use what they have learned in this section to assess the effectiveness of each group and to analyze the type of role they usually play in each group. Let students share their results with the class and/or with other members of their committees, teams, or groups.

You also will want to consider that other group members will be bringing their own ideas and information to the group. You may want to preview all the topics on the agenda and have a list of questions and ideas that you want to voice. Do you have questions about other members' work on the group task? Be prepared to play the initiator or agitator role. Do you have extra information that might be helpful to the group regarding the topic? Be prepared to play the facilitator or initiator. By preparing adequately and participating actively in the group discussion, you will help your group achieve its task and purpose.

Section 1 Assessment

GLENCOE *Online*

Visit the *Glencoe Communication Applications* Web site at **communicationapplications. glencoe.com** and click on **Self-Check and Study Guide 11.1** to review your understanding of the interaction in groups.

Review Key Terms

1. Define each term and write it in a sentence: group norm, prescribed norm, emergent norm, initiator, facilitator, agitator, groupthink, group dynamics, group discussion.

Check Understanding

2. Explain the difference between prescribed and emergent norms. Give an example of each.

3. Identify and describe the three major roles group members play.

4. Why is it important to maintain a balance of the roles assumed by group members?

5. How might you adapt group dynamics to help a group function more productively?

6. **Apply** How might you prepare for a discussion on possible guest speakers for this year's graduation ceremony at your school?

APPLICATION *Activity*

Determining Group Roles Work with a group of three students to play "What's My Role?" Have one student write the following words on separate strips of paper: *initiator*, *facilitator*, and *agitator*. Fold the strips of paper, mix them up, and have each student in your group choose one. As a group, determine a possible discussion topic for a business meeting. Then, taking turns with the other groups in your class, play your group's assigned roles in a one- to two-minute discussion of that topic. Perform your discussion for the whole class. When you have finished, the rest of the class should vote on which student was playing each role. Finally, reveal your roles to the class.

Section 1 Assessment Answers

1. Accept all reasonable sentences.
2. Prescribed norms are rules for behavior that are taught to new members; emergent norms are rules for behavior that develop from the group interaction and the mix of members' personalities. Examples will vary.
3. The three major roles group members play are initiator—a person who gets the group started toward action; facilitator—a person who helps

members follow through on their tasks; and agitator—a person who disrupts the group's work but may also draw attention to oversights.
4. The balance of roles is important in order to move the group forward to complete its agenda or purpose. The absence or exaggeration of any role can hinder the group's progress.
5. Answers may include that an individual can change his or her role within a group as necessary to help a group move forward.

Technology Skill

VIDEOCONFERENCING

Videoconferencing uses video and audio signals to allow people in different locations to participate in a meeting. During videoconferencing, special cameras send live video images over phone lines to distant locations.

Learning the Skill

Videoconferences require preplanning. Read the planning steps below.

1. **Set the Conference Date and Time.** Contact all groups involved in the conference and arrange a meeting time.

2. **Get to Know the Participants.** Call participants before the actual meeting.

3. **Prepare an Agenda.** Create and send an agenda listing the date, time, and purpose of the meeting and detailing what needs to be accomplished.

4. **Use the Technology Effectively.** To keep communication clear, make sure all participants are visible in the camera's range. Remind everyone to speak clearly and avoid side conversations.

PLANNING

Set Date and Time
↓
Know Participants
↓
Prepare Agenda
↓
Use Technology Effectively

Practicing the Skill

Imagine that you are planning a videoconference among a marketing group in Houston, a design group in San Diego, and a production group in Tokyo, Japan. The purpose of the meeting is to share ideas about creating and marketing a new hand-held video game. Follow these steps for your videoconference.

Step 1 Imagine that, after speaking with all participants, the best time for the meeting is Thursday at 4:30 P.M. central standard time. Calculate the meeting time for each participating group. Include these times on your agenda.

Step 2 Create an agenda for your meeting. Include items that you think might be important to discuss in this type of meeting.

Step 3 Share your agenda with the class. Combine students' ideas to create a master agenda for the class.

Step 4 As a class, work in three groups—one for each group involved in the meeting. Hold a mock videoconference, taping the proceedings with a video camera.

Step 5 Watch the tape of your meeting. How could you make your next videoconference more effective?

APPLICATION *Activity*

Explain the advantages or disadvantages of videoconferencing in the following situations: interviewing for a job in another city, and people located in different cities brainstorming ideas for the development of a new product.

Making Groups Work **359**

Videoconferencing

Make sure students understand that videoconferencing is becoming a common meeting technique as businesses and their customers and suppliers expand. Point out that it is usually much cheaper in both time and money for people to meet through a videoconference than to travel to a meeting. Explain that this is another example of the development of technology helping business do business. **L1**

Practicing the Skill

1. Encourage students to search the Internet for the times in Houston, San Diego, and Tokyo when it is 4:30 P.M. CST.

2. Point out that students' agendas should allocate certain topics to the appropriate group.

3. Make sure the agendas are not too long or detailed. You may want to suggest a time limit of one hour for the videoconference.

4. Students' mock videoconferences should follow their agendas. You may want to have them appoint someone to lead the conference, explaining that this would be a logical way for a business meeting to be organized.

5. As students debrief their own videoconference, help them identify the group roles that various people played during the conference.

Application Activity

Have students compare their lists of advantages and disadvantages of videoconferencing in the situations. How is a job interview different from a brainstorming session? How can these differences impact the effectiveness of a videoconferencing format?

Section 1 Answers, continued

6. Answers should include becoming informed, perhaps about who might be guest speakers and why; formulating ideas, perhaps how many speakers and why; and preparing materials, perhaps background information on suggested speakers.

Application Activity Each group's discussion should clearly include an example of a student playing the role of initiator, facilitator, and agitator. As the class votes to identify which student was playing each role, resolve any differences of opinion by letting students discuss their understanding of the actions of each type of role.

1 FOCUS

Bellringer

Have students read the opening paragraph to themselves and consider answers to the two questions. Discuss their responses and the importance of actively contributing to groups. *(Answers are likely to include that the fourth person is not participating appropriately or making a positive contribution. Some students may feel that the group can be effective without the nonparticipating member; others will feel that unless all members contribute, the group is not effective.)*

✎ You may use Graphic Organizer Transparency 11–2 to introduce this section.

Graphic Organizer Transparency 11–1

MAKING GROUPS WORK
Participating in Groups

GRAPHIC
Organizer 11–2

Group Problem	Group Effectiveness Strategy to Use
1. Receiving unclear or irrelevant answers.	1. Ask specific and clear questions. (V)
2. Hurt feelings when someone's ideas are rejected.	2.
3. Lack of effective communication of ideas.	3.
4. Criticism causes hard feelings and becomes personal.	4.
5. The beginnings of meetings are delayed.	5.
6. Some members' clothing and hair styles become a distraction to others.	6.
7. Some members are reading while someone else is talking.	7.
8. Some members are forced to stand or sit outside the main group.	8.
9. You are speaking in a large room and not everyone can hear.	9.
10. People leave the room during another's talk.	10.
11. Group members are not understanding the information being presented.	11.
12. Group members are not focusing on the speaker.	12.

Visual Instruction

Answer To work with a group effectively requires communication skills involving verbal, nonverbal, and listening strategies.

Section 2

Participating in Groups

GUIDE TO READING

Objectives

1. Use appropriate verbal strategies to promote group effectiveness.
2. Use effective and describe ineffective nonverbal behaviors in group meetings.
3. Use a variety of listening strategies to contribute to group effectiveness.
4. Identify and analyze the role of the group chairperson.
5. Analyze the participation and contributions of group members and evaluate group effectiveness.

Terms to Learn

task need
maintenance need

Imagine that you are part of a small group whose goal is to develop new product ideas. At the beginning of the meeting, three of the four group members sit around the table and begin to brainstorm ideas. The fourth member turns her chair away from the table and works on a report she has to turn in later that day. You and the other group members feel resentful that she is not helping the group do its work. Is the fourth person participating appropriately and making a positive contribution to the group? Is this group being effective?

If you were a member of this group, how might you improve the situation? What will it take for the group to become productive? By learning how to apply your communication skills in a group, you will learn how to answer these questions. You will learn methods for overcoming challenges to group productivity and effectiveness. You will also learn how to use effective verbal, nonverbal, and listening strategies in teams, committees, or other groups. Finally, you will have some guidelines to analyze the effectiveness of your participation and the participation of other members in committees, teams, or other groups.

Participating in groups at work offers challenges and rewards. What kind of skill must one develop in order to work with a group effectively?

360   *Glencoe Communication Applications*

RESOURCE MANAGER

Teaching Tools

- Interactive Lesson Planner
- Reproducible Lesson Plan 11–2
- Application Activities 11–2

Reproducible Masters

- Guided Reading Activity Workbook 11–2
- Enrichment Activity 11–2
- Reteaching Activity 11–2
- Section Quiz 11–2
- Transparency Strategies and Activities Booklet 11–2

Transparencies

- Graphic Organizer Transparency 11–2
- Chapter 11 Teaching Transparency

Technology Resources

- Interactive Tutor Self-Assessment Software
- Presentation Plus! Software
- ExamView® Pro Testmaker
- PuzzleMaker Software
- communicationapplications.glencoe.com

COMMUNICATION Strategies

**USING EFFECTIVE
VERBAL STRATEGIES**

✓ Ask clear questions.

✓ State your ideas, opinions, and position.

✓ Use courtesy and tact.

✓ Provide constructive criticism.

EFFECTIVE VERBAL STRATEGIES IN GROUPS

Your responsibility as a productive group member is to assume the role of initiator, facilitator, or agitator appropriately as needed. This helps your group, regardless of its purpose, take care of the task needs and the maintenance needs of the group.

A task need is a need that relates directly to the business and goals of the group. Task needs are met when members give and seek information that will help move the group toward accomplishing its goal.

A maintenance need relates to the feelings of group members and their relationships to one another. Maintenance needs are met when members are satisfied with their position in the group and the way members are interacting. The effective verbal strategies in the Communication Strategies checklist can help you meet your group's task and maintenance needs.

Ask Clear Questions

Computer programmers often repeat this important work rule: "Garbage in, garbage out." In other words, if you give a computer an unclear or faulty command, the computer won't perform the way you want it to. The same concept applies to asking questions. If you are not specific about what you want to know, you aren't likely to get the right information you need.

Ask Specific Questions. Consider the conversation below between two members of a company's planning committee.

Martina Says:
"Robert, do you have any comments about these plans?"

Martina Means:
"It's time for you to share your research on the cost of each plan."

Robert Says:
"No. I don't have anything to add right now."

Robert Means:
"I know what each plan costs, but I have no other comments. I wonder when she'll ask me for those cost figures?"

Martina and Robert are not communicating effectively. In order to communicate effectively, one should always ask clear questions. Why is it important to be specific when asking a question?

Making Groups Work **361**

Nonverbal Communication

Remind students that effective communication includes more than simply the words one uses. Properly phrased questions and clear statements of one's ideas are not enough to communicate properly in a group. It is equally important to communicate in a respectful tone of voice and with a nonthreatening body stance. Ask students to model several different ways to use tone of voice and body stance to communicate different intentions for the same question or statement, such as "Will you please research the cost of each plan?" or "We cannot hold another meeting until next month." **L2**

Guided Reading Activity 11-2

Grammar Tip

Rhetorical questions are those for which no answer is expected. The first two sentences in the bottom paragraph of page 360 are rhetorical questions; students are not expected to answer them until later when they have the information necessary for the answers.

In this conversation, Martina did not directly ask for the information she wanted. Likewise, Robert did not draw conclusions about what Martina really wanted to know. To avoid this type of misunderstanding, Martina could have been more specific. At the previous meeting, she might have asked Robert, "Will you please research the cost of each plan and then distribute the figures to everyone at our next meeting?" Then, at the next meeting, Martina could have asked Robert, "Will you now share with the group your information about the cost of each plan?"

Other Uses for Questions Questions are not only used to get information. They also can be used to move the discussion forward. For example, an initiator might ask, "Shall we now consider the real nature of the problem?" or "Have we considered the disadvantages of such a program?" Regardless of whether they are seeking information or directing a discussion, well-formed questions help meet the task needs of a group.

Questions also can be used to help meet the maintenance needs of a group. For instance, a facilitator might ask, "Have we heard from everyone on this issue?" An initiator might ask, "Would you begin our discussion of this phase of the plan? I know you have some innovative ideas." In both cases, the question promotes cohesion by involving all members in the group task.

State Your Ideas, Opinions, and Position

Usually, you are a member of a committee, team, or other group because you have some experience, knowledge, or ability to offer regarding the group task. That means, what you know and think about the group task matters. Also, building group enthusiasm and support for your ideas can help bring

Questions can direct group members to communicate their ideas to one another. What are other uses for questions in group situations?

members together, meeting the maintenance needs of the group. In either case, your information and opinions must be stated clearly and persuasively to be effective.

As you prepare for each group meeting, think about the topics to be discussed and what you might contribute. Also, consider the other group members. Will some members be opposed to your ideas? If so, try to anticipate their concerns and address them as you give your information. You might say, "I know that some members are concerned about the state of our current budget, so I think we should make this purchase after the new budget comes into effect this January because . . ." This statement then could be followed by a list of reasons why you support making the purchase.

As you state your opinions and ideas, you may be involved in an information-giving interaction. This type of interaction advances the task by providing information or opinions for the group's consideration. You might

---

MEETING INDIVIDUAL NEEDS

MULTIPLE LEARNING STYLES

Auditory-Verbal Students who learn best auditorially will benefit from acting out the effective verbal strategies listed in the checklist on page 361.

Activity After you have covered pages 361–365 and students have learned in more detail what these strategies are, ask volunteers to choose one of the four strategies and act it out during a classroom discussion. Encourage listeners to discuss the effectiveness of each example.

say, "I have learned that three of our competitors have tried this plan. Here is what they discovered. . . ."

On the other hand, you may be involved in information-seeking interactions. You might say, "I would be interested in hearing what you found out in your research on this issue." This statement not only advances the task, it also serves a maintenance function by acknowledging an interest in this person's ideas.

Use Courtesy and Tact

The third effective verbal strategy is the use of courtesy and tact. Courtesy and tact can make a great impact on the cohesiveness of a committee, team, or group.

Courtesy By using courteous verbal and nonverbal language, you show respect to the other members of the group. After a short time, you'll realize that courteous language is contagious. Other members will tend to follow your lead in being courteous. Courtesy should become an emergent norm for every group.

One practical use of courtesy in a group is to praise group members for effective contributions—especially if you are filling the facilitator role. An important part of giving praise is to make it genuine and specific to the behavior or idea, not just a general statement.

Tact In group interactions, tact is a way of dealing with others so that good relations are maintained in the group. Tact is especially important when a group is discussing a controversial topic or when there are strong feelings on either side of an issue.

Tact is useful when you must disagree with someone but do not want to hurt that person's feelings or make him or her angry. For instance, if you think a group member is slowing the group down by being overly cautious about every decision, you might say, "I agree that we should be cautious, but I would like us to consider this idea."

To be tactful, try to use diplomatic language and choose your words and tone of voice carefully. Your goal is not to offend others; your goal is to accomplish a task cooperatively. Both tact and courtesy are vital to maintaining unity in a group. In this way, they fulfill important maintenance needs in a group.

Utilizing courtesy and tact can further effective communication. Compare the two photos above. Which photo suggests that a person is using courtesy and tact? Explain.

Making Groups Work **363**

Having Self-Confidence
A contributing factor to many students playing the nonparticipant agitator role in groups is their lack of self-confidence. Often students feel intimidated by bolder or more verbal group members. They may also feel that their own contributions will not measure up to those of others. Suggest that students who feel such hesitation make a list for themselves of the experience, knowledge, and abilities they have that qualify them for active membership in the group. Help with suggestions if students have difficulty, or suggest that students work in pairs to make such lists about each other. You may want to allow small groups of such students to practice being more assertive by meeting together and testing their skills. **L1**

Visual Instruction

Answer The bottom right photo shows two people being courteous and tactful by facing one another and being close to the same eye level.

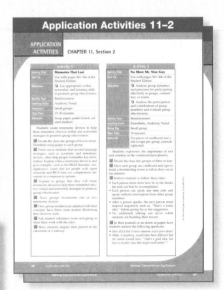

Application Activities 11–2

MULTIPLE LEARNING STYLES

MEETING
INDIVIDUAL
NEEDS

Tactile-Kinesthetic Body language, facial expressions, and gestures are important communication strategies, especially during group interactions. Point out that even "please" and "thank you" can be misinterpreted as negative if they are said in a rough tone of voice with negative facial expressions.

Activity Students talented in kinesthetic expression can pantomime scenarios in which one person "says" something to another in the group in a respectful and in a disrespectful way.

Current Examples

Examples of certain kinds of behaviors are more pertinent to a business committee or team. Some students may not be able to "translate" these into examples that are more meaningful to them now. Work with students to develop examples of quotations and behavior that might be used appropriately in groups students currently participate in, such as athletic teams, class discussion groups, and so on. **L2**

COMMUNICATION *Strategies*

PROVIDING CONSTRUCTIVE CRITICISM

Make sure students understand that criticizing others is often difficult. Learning to give constructive criticism is a necessary skill, however, particularly when participating in a group. Ask students to add points they feel might be helpful to the list in the chart on this page. Ask a volunteer to make a master list that can be photocopied and distributed to each student. Students can refer to the list for helpful hints when they are in a position to provide constructive criticism to someone.

Language Tip

It is human nature to mimic the language used by people nearby. That is how children learn to talk, and it is how slang is communicated so quickly among teenagers and jargon among people who work together. This very phenomenon is useful in promoting courteous language in groups, too.

COMMUNICATION *Strategies*

PROVIDING CONSTRUCTIVE CRITICISM

- Separate the speaker's information from any feelings you might have about him or her. Do not disagree just because you don't like the speaker.

- Try to restate the other person's point of view before adding your own comments.

- Calmly and objectively state why you disagree. Do not verbally attack the person who gave the information.

- Do not interrupt other speakers.

- If your concerns already have been answered by another group member, graciously state your agreement. Don't waste the group's time by repeating what already has been said.

- When possible, use tentative language to soften your disagreement. For instance, you might say, "Would it be just as effective if we . . . ," or "Perhaps we could look at this from another point of view as well."

- Offer an observation and then a suggestion. For example, say, "Somehow I think we have gotten off the topic. Perhaps we could finish the original discussion first and then come back to this topic."

- If there is a part of the other person's work that you can compliment or agree with, do so.

Provide Constructive Criticism

Constructive criticism is often difficult to give. If you disagree with comments made by other members, make an effort to disagree without being disagreeable. Remember that constructive criticism has two important elements: praise for appropriate choices, behaviors, and results; and positive suggestions for improvement when improvement is needed.

Offering constructive criticism requires courtesy, tact, and careful consideration of the other person. Following are some important ideas to consider when offering constructive criticism.

EFFECTIVE NONVERBAL STRATEGIES IN GROUPS

Your nonverbal behavior is as important to a group discussion as your verbal comments. In other words, what you do is just as important as what you say! Following are some nonverbal behaviors that require your special attention during group interactions. These are

- dress and grooming
- time
- space and distance
- eye contact
- volume and tone
- gestures and movement

Dress and Grooming

If you are preparing to attend a group meeting, first plan your dress and grooming so that you will fit in with the rest of the group. Is this a casual group or is it the norm to dress more formally? If you are in a group at school, there may be a time when you wear a special shirt or sweatshirt to a meeting.

COOPERATIVE LEARNING ACTIVITY

Because providing constructive criticism can make a group member feel awkward and uncomfortable, students will benefit from role-playing. Divide students into groups of four or five. Have each group give itself a team or committee identity for the activity, such as basketball team members or holiday decorating committee members. Ask them to suppose one person has neglected his or her assigned duties or performed badly. Students should work together to practice providing constructive criticism.

If you are in doubt about what to wear, it is better to dress too formally than too casually, such as the young man in **Figure 11–4**. As for grooming, always appear clean and neatly groomed when participating in business or group activities.

Time

How you use time transmits a message to others around you. If you arrive late to a group meeting, your actions may indicate that the meeting is not important to you. Lateness also indicates that you are unconcerned about wasting other group members' time as they sit and wait for you.

If you miss a meeting entirely without notifying someone in advance, you convey the message that both the group and the group task are unimportant to you. Finally, if you leave the meeting early, you send the same negative message.

Space and Distance

People tend to divide space equally among the people who are occupying that space. For instance, if four people will be meeting around a square table, each person probably would sit at a different side of the table. If the table were round, the group probably would mentally divide the table into fourths, with each person taking one-fourth of the space. Crowding into another group member's space without good reason can make that member uncomfortable and, therefore, would be inappropriate behavior.

Some informal group meetings might take place in a living room, in an empty classroom, in a coworker's office, or in some other type of room that isn't equipped with a large, round table. When this happens, try to arrange the group so that everyone can see and be seen by the other members.

Eye Contact

At home, at school, or at work, eye contact commands attention. We use our eyes as nonverbal traffic signals. In a group setting, not only should members be able to see one another, but they also should work at maintaining eye contact with the other group members. Because of this, you should not examine printed materials while group members are speaking unless they are guiding you through those materials. If you are the one speaking, be sure to look at all the members of the group—one by one—on a regular basis.

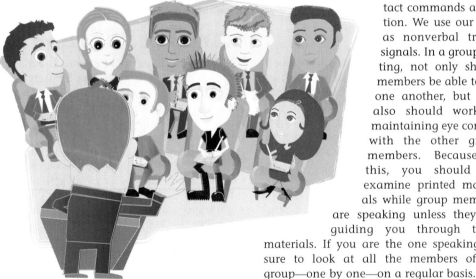

■ **Figure 11–4 Appropriate and Inappropriate Dress**

Appropriate Appearance
Explain to students that one reason for making sure you are appropriately dressed is to avoid undue attention to yourself and therefore distract others from the purpose of the meeting. It is important to blend in with the group as a whole. Point out that suggestive or revealing clothing is never appropriate in a business meeting. Along similar lines, make sure students understand that good grooming includes reasonable hair styles (including facial hair), subdued makeup, jewelry that does not make noise, and only subtle perfumes and colognes. Ask students to suggest additional points to remember. **L2**

Importance of Place
Point out to students that the physical arrangement of people in a group can be very important. No one wants to feel left out or singled out. When someone is forced to sit or stand outside the main group, he or she is likely to participate less than the other members. Therefore, it is important that everyone has a place to sit or stand in the group's main "circle." One exception is that the acknowledged leader (even a temporary one) might stand in front of the group in order to command attention. Ask students to provide examples of comfortable group arrangements with which they are familiar.

MEETING INDIVIDUAL NEEDS

MULTIPLE LEARNING STYLES

Tactile-Kinesthetic Students who learn well by physical movement will benefit from "walking through" the placement of people for a group meeting.

Activity Have students arrange tables and chairs in various ways and then sit in the chairs to demonstrate effective and ineffective placement. Let students discuss why some arrangements seem better than others.

Communication Tip

Most people do not realize how they sound to others. To help students judge their own volume and tone, tape-record part or all of a class discussion in which you encourage all to participate. As you play back the tape, ask students to listen to themselves as though they are members of the audience. They can jot down their evaluation of themselves to refer to later. **L2**

Visual Instruction

Answer Volume should be high enough so that all group members can easily hear what is being said.

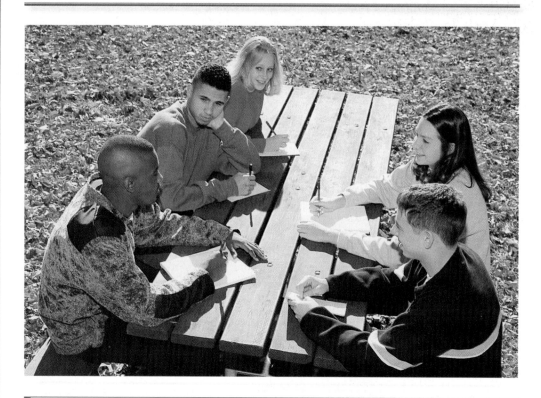

During group interactions, it is important that all members are able to hear and see each other. What is the general rule with regard to voice volume when interacting with a group?

Volume and Tone

Most importantly, all group members need to be able to hear the discussion. Therefore, it is your responsibility to speak loudly enough for all to hear. This may require you to project your voice more loudly than you are accustomed to speaking. If this makes you a little uncomfortable, just remember: No one will complain about being able to hear you. However, they might become very frustrated if they can't. As a general rule, address a group as if you were speaking specifically to the people farthest away from you. If those people can hear you, the rest can too.

Gestures and Movement

Gestures and other body movements can add emphasis to your verbal message. Speakers also use gestures to complement their verbal message. As a listener, try to avoid any distracting movements or gestures that may take attention away from whomever is speaking.

In formal groups or groups that have a large number of members, you may have to raise your hand to be recognized. However, this usually is not the case with smaller, informal groups such as committees and teams. Generally speaking, it is not appropriate for you to move away from the group or leave the room while another member is speaking.

INTERDISCIPLINARY CONNECTION

Drama Students skilled and talented in dramatics can make an impressive presentation to the rest of the class on effective nonverbal strategies to use in groups.

Activity Divide students into two groups, if possible. Let one group act out a committee meeting in which all members use effective nonverbal strategies. The other group can act out a committee meeting in which members break all the rules and do not use the effective nonverbal strategies. Alternatively, have the same group of students act out both scenarios.

EFFECTIVE LISTENING STRATEGIES IN GROUPS

In a group setting, effective nonverbal posture and eye contact can help you listen well. To better focus on a speaker, use all three types of listening skills—critical, deliberative, and empathic—that you learned about in Chapter 6. These effective listening strategies can help you understand and properly respond to what is being said in a group discussion.

Using Critical Listening Skills

When you use critical listening skills, you are not only listening for information but also evaluating the value and meaning of that information. Is the person's information logical? Is it accurate and useful? Do you agree with the message?

The next time a classmate speaks as a member of a group, use your critical listening skills to answer the following questions:

- What are the speaker's main ideas and how are they supported?
- Is the group member expressing facts, personal opinions, or informed or expert opinions?
- Is the information current and appropriate to the situation?
- Is there any evidence that contradicts the speaker?

As you listen, note any concerns you have about the speaker's information. Then, when he or she has finished speaking, ask questions.

Using Deliberative Listening Skills

As a deliberative listener, you should assume that a group member is offering information

COMMUNICATION PRACTICE LAB

Listening Deliberatively

To practice listening so that you know how to learn and take action, follow these steps.

Step 1 On a sheet of paper, list ideas about how you might organize a canned-food drive at your school. Spend no more than five minutes writing your ideas.

Step 2 Working with a partner, take turns explaining your plan as if you were presenting it to a group of volunteers. Presentations should last three minutes.

Step 3 As your partner explains his or her ideas, ask yourself these questions:

- What does he or she want the group to do?
- What supporting information is he or she offering to persuade me to do these things?
- What questions do I have?
- What are the advantages and disadvantages of this plan?

Step 4 Ask your partner any questions you may have.

Step 5 After you have both presented your plans, discuss as a class the benefits of deliberative listening.

Making Groups Work **367**

Communication Tip

Well-known novelist Henry James once advised a nephew on how he should live his life: "Three things in human life are important. The first is to be kind. The second is to be kind. And the third is to be kind." Ask students to consider how this advice might be incorporated when providing constructive criticism on nonverbal strategies in communication.

COMMUNICATION PRACTICE LAB

Listening Deliberatively

Direct students to follow the steps in the Communication Practice Lab on this page in order to practice listening deliberatively. If necessary, review with students the part of Chapter 6 that discusses deliberative listening. Discuss with students any other suggestions for good listening techniques that might help members of groups be more attentive listeners.

GLENCOE *Online*

For an additional Practice Lab for this section, have students visit the *Glencoe Communication Applications* Web site at **communicationapplications.glencoe.com**. Click on Communication Practice Lab 11–2. **L1**

REAL-WORLD CONNECTION

Cultural Differences Verbal and nonverbal strategies are important whenever people deal with one another, particularly in groups. However, different cultures often have different ways of doing things, and behavior that is considered courteous and tactful sometimes varies.

Activity Invite students who are knowledgeable about other cultures to demonstrate how a committee member might interact with others during a meeting, showing such things as facial expressions, gestures, and tone of voice, as well as words.

Types of Listening Skills

The three types of listening skills—critical, deliberative, and empathic—were discussed in detail in Chapter 6. They are reviewed on the following several pages in this chapter of the student's text. Ask a volunteer to write the three types on the board as headings for a chart. Ask other volunteers to list under each heading helpful hints for each type of listening. **L2**

■ Visual Instruction

Answer Strategies for listening empathically include interpreting the feelings transmitted by nonverbal communication and listening for the feelings behind the message as well as the words.

---

he or she wants the group to act upon in some manner. With that attitude, the next time a group member speaks, try to learn what he or she is trying to tell you.

As you listen to the speaker's message, ask the following questions:

- What does this group member want me to do?
- What supporting information is he or she offering to persuade me to do this?
- Do I have questions about this information?
- What are the advantages and disadvantages to the group if I do as the member asks?

Using Empathic Listening Skills

When you listen empathically, you listen for the speaker's feelings and provide him or her with emotional support. To be an empathic listener in a group setting, assume that all group members are trying to offer helpful information

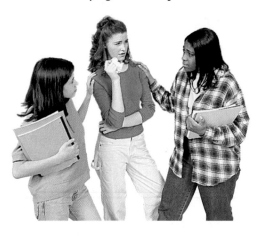

■ You are listening with empathy when you listen to a friend tell you about his or her feelings and you offer emotional support. **Identify two strategies to listening emphatically.**

and to make progress on the group task. When all group members display this attitude, a caring atmosphere is created. As a result, the group grows more cohesive.

To listen empathically to another group member, there are two main things to remember:

- Watch the speaker's nonverbal communication. What does it indicate about his or her feelings?
- Listen to the message. How does the speaker seem to feel about information he or she is sharing?

Empathic listening can be valuable in a variety of group situations. For instance, imagine that a hard-working group member was assigned to gather information from the school principal regarding a specific security policy at the high school. However, the principal was only willing to reveal a portion of that information. As a result, the group member could not complete the assignment before the next group meeting.

This could have several different effects on the group member. He or she might feel angry, helpless, or disappointed about presenting incomplete information to the group. This, in turn, could make him or her avoid eye contact with the others, seem unenthusiastic, or send other negative nonverbal cues.

You might show empathy by saying, "You seem upset that you didn't get the information we needed. I know you did the best you could. Where do you think we might get the rest of the information we need?"

With this response, you have affirmed that he or she could not force the principal to give any more information. In addition, you have asked his or her opinion about how to finish the task. For effective empathic listening, try to put yourself in the speaker's position. It is important for you to respond to how the speaker feels about the information as well as to the information itself.

INTERDISCIPLINARY CONNECTION

Language Arts The techniques students learn in language arts classes about detecting bias and propaganda techniques can help them as they listen critically and deliberatively to speakers in group meetings.

Activity Have students pay special attention to bias and propaganda techniques used by speakers in a team, committee, or other group meeting. Ask them to report to the class examples they observed.

DISCUSSIONS AND CONSENSUS BUILDING IN GROUPS

A chairperson is someone who has been appointed or elected to organize a group or preside over it. The chairperson, sometimes referred to as the chair, not only should use all the skills normally used by group members, but he or she also has some additional responsibilities that require special skills. Among these skills is the ability to plan an effective meeting.

Planning the Meeting

One of the responsibilities of a group chairperson is planning the meeting. This involves making all the necessary arrangements for the meeting, delegating responsibilities to others when necessary. First, the chair must arrange the time and place of the meeting. Then, he or she most likely will need to create a meeting agenda to organize the group discussion.

Arranging Time and Place As a group's chairperson, it is important to remember that meeting times should take into consideration all members' schedules. Of course it may be impossible to accommodate every member's schedule, but it is courteous to ask members for their scheduling suggestions, when possible. The group chair or someone chosen by the chair also is responsible for determining a meeting place and setting up the room appropriately. As you arrange the time and place of your meeting, keep in mind these considerations.

Setting Agendas Whether in an informal or a formal group, the chairperson has a plan for how the meeting should proceed from topic to topic. In informal group meetings, if you are the chair and do not wish to create a formal agenda, you should at least

Practice for the Workplace

Effective Listening in Groups Surveys in the workplace reveal that listening is one of the most important communication skills in business. It also is the foremost communication skill employees wish they had been taught in school. Listening can help make a group more effective and productive on the job. Discuss as a class how you can identify an effective listener or a poor listener.

BUSINESS PRACTICE *Activity*

Imagine that you are a member of a group developing an Internet marketing plan for a CD and video store. Working with a partner, take turns brainstorming ideas for your marketing plan. Each time one partner makes a suggestion, the other partner should restate the idea in his or her own words. How accurate were your statements? How could you listen more effectively?

make a list of the goals to be accomplished in the meeting. For some informal meetings and most formal meetings, you should prepare and distribute a written agenda, if possible, a day or two before the meeting.

Meeting agendas typically include

- any announcements that should be made at the meeting

- a reading of the last meeting's minutes (This mostly applies to formal groups, such as a zoning committee, school board, or board of directors.)

- any topics which were not completely discussed or resolved at the last meeting

- the topics to be discussed at the meeting

- a request for any special announcements members may have

Making Groups Work **369**

Practice for the Workplace

Effective Listening in Groups Invite students to list techniques for good listening, such as looking at the speaker, concentrating on what is being said, asking pertinent questions at an appropriate time, and so on. Point out that one good technique is being prepared by having some idea of what the speaker will talk about, by thinking and/or reading about the topic in advance, and by being prepared to interact with the speaker about the topic. Finally, ask students to discuss why being a good listener is important to the success of a group. *(Students' restatements will vary but should include the main idea of the original suggestion.)*

REAL-WORLD CONNECTION

Hearing from an Expert Because students often have difficulty relating what they are learning in school to the "real world," it will be helpful for them to hear from someone in business about the crucial need for effective listening strategies.

Activity Work with students to identify and invite one or two parents or community members to address the class about the role of listening in their workplaces. Have students brainstorm topics and questions they want the experts to discuss and communicate these to the guests several days before their presentation.

COMMUNICATION *Strategies*

ARRANGING THE SETTING FOR YOUR MEETING

Discuss with students who might be responsible for arranging the setting of a meeting. *(Answers may include the chairperson of the group, a volunteer, or someone asked previously by the group to do it.)* Ask students to brainstorm any additional points to remember when arranging the setting. Discuss in what ways setting can affect a meeting both positively and negatively.

Language Tip

You may want to point out to students that until recent years, the word *man* was often used to refer to people in general. Because this practice effectively excluded women and girls, people have tried to make language more inclusive. One example is that the word *chairman* is often changed to *chairperson* or simply *chair* so it does not imply that the person is assumed to be male.

COMMUNICATION *Strategies*

ARRANGING THE SETTING FOR YOUR MEETING

✓ Make sure every member will be able to see every other member in the meeting.

✓ Obtain enough chairs for all members to be seated at the table.

✓ Regulate the room temperature to be comfortable for most members.

✓ Make sure the room is ready to be used at the appointed time.

✓ Locate and provide any presentational equipment needed by group members. This may include a videocassette player, flip chart, overhead projector, computer with presentation software, or other audio-visual aids.

Chairing the Discussion

Once the group is gathered and ready to perform its task or engage in its social process, the chairperson will need to exercise some special verbal, nonverbal, and listening skills. Although the chair's primary responsibility is to meet the task needs of the group, he or she also should pay attention to building consensus and meeting the group's maintenance needs.

Chairperson as Initiator The chairperson has several roles to play during a group discussion. As the initiator, you should call upon members to give information or ideas. You also should encourage other members to comment on those ideas. Your goal is to allow a full discussion that results in all the members agreeing, or coming to a consensus, on some course of action for the group.

Chairperson as Facilitator To encourage full discussion, the chairperson also should play the role of facilitator. He or she should observe members' interactions and nonverbal cues. If a member wishes to comment or appears to disagree with some point of discussion, the chair should encourage that person to offer his or her ideas and opinions. The chair also should be aware of members who are not contributing to the discussion and try to get them to participate.

Also in the facilitator role, the chairperson is responsible for maintaining order in the meeting. If a member is discourteous or argumentative, the chairperson should step in and reinstate the courtesy norm for the group.

Chairperson as Agitator An effective chairperson occasionally may need to display positive agitator behavior. This may be necessary if members seem to be accepting information without fully considering it. In this instance, the leader may need to challenge the assumptions of the speaker or call upon other group members to critically examine the information.

Nonverbal Responsibilities and Skills In a group setting, it is important for the chairperson to try to maintain eye contact with any group member who is contributing information or ideas. This tells the member that the chairperson is listening and trying to understand the information. Smiling, nodding, and providing other types of acknowledgment indicate to members that their contributions are appreciated.

Listening Responsibilities and Skills All members, especially the chairperson, should listen critically, deliberatively, and empathically to the group discussion. Critical listening helps the chairperson determine the quality of information given by group members. Deliberative listening helps him or her determine whether or not to be

EXTENDING THE CONTENT

Chairing a Group Share the following quotation with students: "Potent leadership is a matter of being aware of what is happening in the group and acting accordingly," wrote John Heider in *The Tao of Leadership*.

Activity Ask students to relate the quotation to what they have learned about the responsibilities of the chairperson of a group. Why would it be so necessary for a potent (or powerful) chairperson to be aware of what is happening in the group? How would knowing what is happening lead to appropriate actions on the part of the chair? Let students discuss their insights.

persuaded by members' suggestions. Empathic listening also can be helpful in a variety of group situations.

For instance, if a group's task is especially challenging, it may cause group members to become frustrated. Similarly, group members may become frustrated if they have personal disagreements with one another. Group members with numerous outside responsibilities also may become discouraged when too much group work is added to their heavy workload. A chairperson who is listening empathically addresses these concerns when they come up in the group meeting.

EVALUATING GROUP EFFECTIVENESS

Competent communicators regularly evaluate their own effectiveness and the effectiveness of their group. As a group member, are you doing all you can to help the group complete its task? Is the group operating in a

In some group formats, a chairperson is chosen to preside over or organize the group. Identify some of the responsibilities of a chairperson.

COMMUNICATION Strategies

MANAGING CONFLICT AND BUILDING CONSENSUS AS A CHAIRPERSON

✓ **Paraphrase a concern or complaint to a speaker's satisfaction.** For example, when paraphrasing, you may wish to say, "I hear you saying that you disagree with the plan. Is that correct?" This demonstrates that you have understood the point the group member wished to make. If there is a disagreement between members, summarizing the different points of view helps clarify on which points the members agree and disagree.

✓ **Ask questions that allow a speaker to give a full analysis of the issue.** This helps prevent misunderstandings.

✓ **Open the discussion to the other group members,** asking if they share the same concern or complaint. If several members do, this item may need to be discussed fully in a future group meeting. If only one or very few members share this problem, you may be able to work out a solution with these members alone.

way that will achieve positive results? To begin making these evaluations, examine the group results and the process the group follows to achieve those results. This not only will reveal the group's strengths and weaknesses but also will help you find new ways to build your own group participation and leadership skills.

Making Groups Work **371**

Selecting a Group Chairperson

As students discover the responsibilities of a chairperson, encourage them to consider what kinds of skills and capabilities a chair should have. Point out that the chair of a group is usually elected by that group, and therefore it is the responsibility of the group to choose someone who will serve their interests. Invite students to list characteristics of a good chairperson. You may want to point out that a popular person may make a good chair, but it is not his or her popularity that qualifies that person. Have students volunteer other examples. **L3**

COMMUNICATION Strategies

MANAGING CONFLICT AND BUILDING CONSENSUS AS A CHAIRPERSON

Invite students to add their own ideas to the list of strategies for managing conflict listed in the chart on this page. Encourage them to relate successful strategies they have used or observed in meetings of groups they have attended. Discuss with students why it is important to manage conflict and to achieve consensus in a group meeting.

▪ Visual Instruction

Answer Among the responsibilities of the chairperson is keeping the group on task, calling for ideas and information, encouraging people to express themselves, encouraging thoughtful consideration of ideas, and listening critically to group discussion.

CRITICAL THINKING ACTIVITY

Have students list teams, committees, organizations, and other kinds of groups with which they are familiar. They can include groups they know about but are not part of, such as the United States Senate and House of Representatives. Then ask them to identify how each group is organized. How is the chair chosen? What other officers are there? What are the duties of the officers? How does the group choose its officers, plan its meetings, and set its agenda? Encourage students to provide examples of the chair (or other members) acting as initiators, facilitators, and agitators. You may want to invite students to evaluate the effectiveness of each organization on the basis of its success in carrying out its goals.

COMMUNICATION *Strategies*

ANALYZING GROUP RESULTS FOR GROUPS THAT PLAN

Remind students that when they analyze, they consider individual aspects of a situation or event and determine how they affect the whole. The same process is used to evaluate group effectiveness in accomplishing goals. They can use the analysis process to identify and address problems and to help make the group interaction more effective.

COMMUNICATION *Strategies*

ANALYZING GROUP RESULTS FOR GROUPS THAT SOLVE PROBLEMS

- Was the group able to identify the nature and extent of the problem?
- Did the group set up criteria for the solution that were achievable?
- Did the group measure all possible solutions against the criteria?
- Did the chosen solution solve the problem without creating other problems?
- Was the chosen solution put into effect according to the group's recommendation?
- Has the problem been solved or has it reoccurred?

ANALYZING GROUP RESULTS FOR GROUPS THAT PLAN

- Was enough consideration given to the people who would be affected by the plan?
- Was enough consideration given to the occasion for which the plan was made?
- Was enough consideration given to the task or tasks involved in the carrying out of the plan?
- Was the event or change implemented according to the plans?
- Was the response of the people involved positive?
- Were the timing, location, and impact of the occasion well received?
- Were all tasks adequately performed?

Analyzing Group Results

One way to evaluate a group's effectiveness is by determining whether it achieved the desired results. Evaluating the results of a group's work requires the collection of certain information. This may include following up to see if a problem was completely solved, listening to feedback from people affected by a plan, or taking note of unforeseen consequences. The questions in the Communication Strategies checklist can help you evaluate the group's work based on the results it achieved.

Evaluating the Group Process

Your goal each time you participate in team, committee, or other group discussion is to use group skills effectively. Learning to evaluate your own participation and the participation of others is necessary if you are to improve your group communication skills.

The Effectiveness of Your Participation The most important evaluation you will make is to determine how effective you were in the group process. The evaluation of your own effectiveness will lead you to understand both your strengths and your challenges as a communicator in group discussion. You can use the following questions to guide the evaluation of your participation in a group, committee, or team.

1. Was I able to determine when emergent norms were not productive?
2. Was I able to help change harmful norms?
3. Was I able to assume the roles of initiator, facilitator, and agitator appropriately?
4. Did I make appropriate and timely contributions to the group discussion?
5. Did I use appropriate verbal and nonverbal strategies?
6. Did I use effective listening skills?

COOPERATIVE LEARNING ACTIVITY

Divide students into groups of three or four. Ask these groups to work independently to evaluate a school team, committee, or club. Each group should ask permission to visit the committee they will evaluate to observe at least one of its meetings. The group should list the criteria it used for evaluation, make a group roles chart like the one shown on page 373, and add any other information they think is important. Each group should draft a final report of its evaluation and share its results with the class.

GROUP ROLES CHART

Member	Initiator	Facilitator	Agitator
Julio		✓ ✓ ✓ ✓ ✓ ✓	
Ken	✓		✓ ✓ ✓
Rae	✓ ✓ ✓ ✓ ✓	✓	✓
Kwan	✓	✓ ✓ ✓	

7. Did I perform needed research and group assignments?

8. Did I help meet both the task and the maintenance needs of the group?

9. Did I adhere to both prescribed and emergent group norms?

The Effectiveness of Others' Participation Once you have looked at your own participation, you need to look at other members of the group. Your purpose in this stage of evaluation is not to pass judgment on anyone but to identify characteristics of the participation of others that might have influenced your own.

You can answer the same questions about others' participation as you asked about yourself. Answering these questions will help you identify members who were the most effective and members who may need help in group situations. Most importantly, however, you may also identify behaviors that you want to use again and behaviors that you want to avoid as you work in committees, teams, and other groups.

Evaluating the Group Dynamics
The overall effectiveness of a group process does not just depend on how effectively individual group members performed. The quality of the group dynamics also affects how effective a group will be. To evaluate the quality of the group dynamics, you will need to answer the following questions:

1. Were the emergent and prescribed norms productive and helpful to the group?

2. Did members provide a good balance in the roles they assumed?

3. Were group members' interactions positive, helping to meet both task and maintenance needs?

4. Were negative interactions dealt with in a constructive and positive manner?

5. Did all members participate and contribute to the discussion?

6. Did all members exercise good listening skills?

7. Was there enough positive energy in the group discussion?

Information for Evaluating Evaluating the effectiveness of a team, committee, or other group requires that you have information. You will need to be very aware of your own and others' participation in the group and be honest in your assessment of that participation. You will also need to be aware of the overall group dynamics.

There are several ways you can collect data you will need for this evaluation. You could audiotape or videotape several sessions of the group. You and other members could listen to and watch those tapes in order to discover the level and quality of everyone's participation.

Another useful device for collecting information about performance is to use a group roles chart like the one shown above. It allows you to

Making Groups Work **373**

Evaluating Groups
Ask students to list on the board groups they belong to, such as the school band, athletic teams, and so on. Then, divide students into teams, with the members of each team also being members of one of the groups listed on the board. For example, three members of your class who all play in the school band might form a team of band members for this activity. Ask each team to evaluate the group to which members belong according to the activities and criteria on pages 372–374.

DID **Y**OU **K**NOW?
Some school districts are attempting to develop local and national norms for evaluation standards in various areas of the curriculum. However, most school districts have their own standards for evaluation, norms for grades, and grading patterns for formal student evaluations.

3 ASSESS

Assign Section 2 Assessment as a homework or in-class activity.

❶ Use *Interactive Tutor Self-Assessment Software* to review Section 2.

Section 11–2 Quiz

CRITICAL THINKING ACTIVITY

Point out to students that the questions evaluating group dynamics all require a *yes* or *no* answer and the wording of the questions implies that a *yes* answer indicates positive results. Explain that evaluation tools like this one can be even more helpful if more detail is included. Suggest that students add an explanation to each answer, perhaps by giving an example.

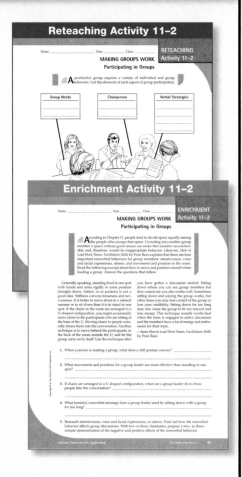

4 CLOSE

Have students turn back to page 360 and reread the opening paragraph. Considering what they have learned in Section 2, how would they answer the questions differently? Why?

Extra-Credit Project

Have students follow the guidelines in Section 2 to evaluate the effectiveness of a school group to which they do not belong. You may have to help students get permission from faculty advisers to observe the group during several meetings in order to carry out their analysis.

count the number of times each member interacts during the group meeting. You could complete a group roles chart while watching a videotape of one or two meetings. The group could also invite an observer to chart group interaction while the discussion was taking place. A debriefing session afterwards could help you and other members of the group evaluate the effectiveness of your work. The goal of such a session is to get information that can be very useful in improving your interaction skills.

The information from a group role chart and a self-assessment checklist provides group members with feedback on how they interact in the group. Often, group members are surprised to find that their actual group behavior is quite different from how they thought they acted.

As a competent communicator, you will want to use all the information gathered during your evaluation of group process. This information helps you build better group interaction skills and eliminate negative interactions.

Section 2 Assessment

Visit the *Glencoe Communication Applications* Web site at **communicationapplications. glencoe.com** and click on **Self-Check and Study Guide 11.2** to review your understanding of participating in groups.

Review Key Terms

1. Define each term and write it in a sentence: task need, maintenance need.

Check Understanding

2. Use an effective verbal strategy in an example scenario. Explain your answer.
3. Give six examples of effective nonverbal strategies for group members.

4. Give an example of one type of listening skill and how it has helped you function effectively in a group.
5. Why is the role of group chairperson important?
6. **Synthesis** Why is it important to evaluate your own effectiveness and the effectiveness of your group?

APPLICATION *Activity*

Acting as Group Chairperson Imagine that you are the chairperson of a six-member group at your school. Choose one of the following group tasks and prepare your group for the first group meeting.

- Plan how to raise money for someone in the community who needs kidney dialysis or some other costly medical treatment.
- Solve the problem of low student attendance at high school athletic events.

Assume that your group must meet after school hours somewhere on school property. How will you prepare yourself, other group members, and the meeting location for this meeting? Write a paragraph explaining your answer.

Section 2 Assessment Answers

1. Accept all reasonable sentences.
2. Students should choose one of the strategies listed in the checklist on page 361.
3. dress and grooming, time, space and distance, eye contact, volume and tone, and gestures and movement
4. Answers may vary within critical, deliberative, and empathic listening skills. Accept logical descriptions of effective functioning.

5. Answers may include that the chairperson is most responsible for the effectiveness of the group.
6. Students should acknowledge the improvement of group and personal effectiveness as a goal.

Application Activity Students' paragraphs should include plans for arranging the time and place of the meeting, setting the agenda, and so on.

Analyzing Your Participation in Groups

How Do You Rate?

On a separate sheet of paper, use the key to answer the following questions. Put a check mark by each skill you would like to improve.

KEY: **A** Always   **R** Rarely
       U Usually   **N** Never
       S Sometimes

1. When I am in a group meeting, I try to keep eye contact with the person speaking.
2. I give and seek information that contributes to the unity of the group.
3. I track nonverbal communication and try to find out what it indicates.
4. I prepare for group meetings and present my suggestions by anticipating group objections.
5. When I act as an initiator, I try to let the group reach a decision on its own before I interject my own thinking.
6. When a person in the group is an agitator, I cause the meeting to go forward.
7. When I am a facilitator, I try to cause full discussion in a group.
8. When I express disagreement, I do so calmly and objectively.
9. As a group member, I listen critically to learn what I think about suggestions given.
10. I believe it is important to evaluate how my group works together and how well we reach our goals.

How Do You Score?

Review your responses. Give yourself 5 points for every A, 4 for every U, 3 for every S, 2 for every R, and 1 for every N. Total your points and evaluate your score.

41–50 Excellent You may be surprised to find out how much you can improve your skills.

31–40 Good In this course, you can learn ways to make your skills better.

21–30 Fair Practice applying the skills taught in this course.

1–20 Needs Improvement Carefully monitor your improvement as you work through this course.

Setting Communication Goals

If you scored Excellent or Good, complete Part A. If your score was Fair or Needs Improvement, complete Part B.

Part A 1. I plan to put the following ideas into practice:
            2. I plan to share the following information about communication with the following people:

Part B 1. The behaviors I need to change most are:
            2. To bring about these changes, I will take these steps:

Making Groups Work   **375**

Communication Self-Assessment

Have students respond to the ten statements, using the key on this page. Then, have them evaluate their participation in groups. Based on their scores, assign either Part A or Part B of the goal-setting activity. On an index card or sheet of paper, students should concretely define their communication goals to improve their current level of skill.

Communication Journal Activity

Point out to students that people who write down their goals and review them regularly are more likely to accomplish their objectives than are people who merely think of areas of improvement. Have students list their goals in their Communication Journals.

Communication Tip

Suggest that students keep a list of the questions and their answers in a folder that they take with them to various group, committee, or team meetings. They can review their own participation frequently by looking at the questions.

MEETING INDIVIDUAL NEEDS   **MULTIPLE LEARNING STYLES**

Visual Students who learn best visually may benefit from seeing the Key presented as a continuum. Draw a horizontal line on the board.

Activity At the far left end of the line, write the word *Always*. At the far right end of the line, write the word *Never*. Space equally between those ends three slash marks labeled from left to right *Usually*, *Sometimes*, and *Rarely*. If possible, write the first letter of each of the words (A, U, S, R, N) in brightly colored chalk.

Communication Through Writing

Writing a Meeting Agenda

Objective: To create the agenda of a meeting

Teaching Suggestions and Strategies

Discuss with students the types of written agendas used in some of the group meetings they attend. If possible, ask them to bring examples. You might also encourage them to bring sample agendas from other group meetings, such as those parents attend at work or elsewhere.

Connection to the Workplace

Explain that written agendas serve several purposes: they help attendees prepare for the meeting, they remind presenters of how much time is scheduled for their part of the meeting, they give everyone an overview of the purpose of the meeting, and they alert everyone to the need to monitor the time in order to accomplish the goals of the meeting. For all these reasons, written agendas are often used for business meetings. They are used especially for meetings attended by many people and for meetings that are organized formally.

Writing a Meeting Agenda

In meetings, people communicate with one another to share ideas and relay progress on specific activities. To keep this communication on track, it is a good idea to have a meeting agenda. A meeting agenda is an order of discussion that allows all group members to know the sequence and direction of a meeting. It also provides a springboard for discussion so the group may make decisions, vote, reach consensus, and take action.

Determine the Type of Meeting. What type of meeting is needed to accomplish your group goal? Is the purpose of the meeting to make decisions, solve problems, resolve conflicts, or accomplish some other goal? Will your meeting be formal—that is, conducted according to parliamentary procedure—or informal? Once you have determined the purpose, you can begin structuring your agenda.

Specify the Meeting Basics and Order Agenda Items. First, the agenda's title should reflect the basic purpose of the meeting. Additionally, the time and place of the meeting should be specified. Next, you may begin listing the items to be discussed.

In a formal meeting, the items on an agenda might not be listed in the order in which they are discussed. The chairperson may accept requests to give certain items priority in the meeting. In an informal meeting, however, the most important items are usually listed first on the agenda. This way, if time is limited, at least the most possible time can be dedicated to the main points of the meeting.

Set Time Limits. For both formal and informal meetings, the agenda should include a time limit for each topic. It also should include the estimated length of the overall meeting so attendees can schedule their time accordingly.

Encourage Member Participation. When group members actively participate in meetings, they often feel more committed to the work being done. If group leaders wish to have everyone participate in specific activities and discussions, these items should be listed on the agenda. The agenda also should note whether participants are to prepare any information before the meeting begins. For this reason, it is a good idea to send a copy of the agenda to all expected attendees beforehand. Well-prepared group members result in more productive meetings.

For additional information about business writing, see the *Guide to Business Communication* section of the Communication Survival Kit in the Appendix.

ENGLISH LANGUAGE LEARNERS

MEETING INDIVIDUAL NEEDS

Organizing English language learners might need extra practice with expressing meeting goals in agendas. Let students who have difficulty with English work together to discuss what meeting agendas are, their purpose, and their parts.

Activity Work with English language learners to make sure they understand and can put into their own words the goals listed as subheadings on this page. You may wish to encourage these students to work together on the Writing Activity on page 377 so they can work at their own pace.
ELL

Communication Through Writing

Following is an example agenda for a sales manager's meeting at a clothing manufacturing company. See if you can identify all the basic elements of an effective meeting agenda.

Introducing the Casual on Friday Collection

February 25, 2003
8:00 A.M.–5:00 P.M.
The Conference Lodge
Louisville, Kentucky

Fashion Show . . . . 8:00 A.M.
(Develop notes/questions)   Main Ballroom

Morning Break . . . . 10:00 A.M.

Guest Speaker: Marta Bianco . . . . 10:30 A.M.
(Followed by question/answer session)   Main Ballroom

Lunch . . . . 12:00 P.M.
     Poolside Cafe

Marketing Presentation . . . . 1:30 P.M.
(Followed by question/answer session)   Suite 450

Afternoon Break . . . . 3:00 P.M.

Discussion: Sharing Ideas About Selling . . . . 3:30 P.M.
     Suite 1000

Free Time . . . . 5:00 P.M.
(Fill out meeting evaluation)

Dinner and Live Music . . . . 6:30–9:00 P.M.
     Main Dining Room

WRITING Activity

Imagine that you are a manager at an employee recruitment firm called Super Staffers. Create an agenda for an informal planning meeting. The purpose of the meeting is to plan an upcoming job fair. A job fair is usually a day-long event in which area businesses set up information booths and interview prospective employees. People attend the fair to explore job opportunities with these companies.

- Use the agenda on this page as a guide to create an agenda template of your own.
- Create a descriptive title for your meeting.
- Specify that the meeting will last from 9:00 A.M. to 5:00 P.M. on this coming Tuesday. The meeting will be held in Conference Room B at the Super Staffers office in your hometown.
- Point out that members of your staff will be asked to share information about local employers who might participate in the job fair.
- Tell attendees how much time they will have to share their information.

Besides these items, your agenda should list the other details of the meeting. This may include group discussions, lectures, breaks, and other activities. By the end of the meeting, the group should have planned, voted, and assigned duties to accomplish the upcoming job fair. When you have completed your agenda, share it with the class.

Teaching Activity

Ask students whether meetings they have attended with written agendas were more efficient than those that did not have written agendas. Invite discussion of the reasons why those with written agendas usually go more smoothly. Point out that groups always have a purpose, and an agenda for a group meeting shows how the group will achieve its purpose for that meeting.

WRITING Activity

Students' agendas should follow the general format shown in the model and include the items listed in the assignment. Let students discuss their agendas. You may want to allow some students to work in pairs or small groups to draft their sample agendas.

Grammar Tip

Words, phrases, or clauses in a series are separated by commas. Most authorities recommend the inclusion of a comma before the conjunction at the end of the series in order to help clarify the series for the reader.

Additional Resources

Appendix, "Guide to Business Communication"

Glencoe Writer's Assistant CD-ROM

Glencoe Interactive Grammar Software

Grade 9 Writer's Choice, Lesson 5.1

GRAMMAR PRACTICE

Commas in a Series

Have students add commas where they belong.

1. The people coming to the meeting include Sarah Tom and Jaunita. (*Add commas after* Sarah *and* Tom.)
2. We need to write an agenda find a place to meet and decide on the time. (*Add commas after* agenda *and after* meet.)
3. The club needs to plan our holiday party find a place to hold it choose a committee to decorate and find a date that everyone likes. (*Add commas after* party, it, decorate.)
4. For the party, should we have cheese and crackers sandwiches peanuts soft drinks or all of those things? (*Add commas after* crackers, sandwiches, peanuts, *and* soft drinks.)

CHAPTER 11 Assessment and Activities

GLENCOE TECHNOLOGY

 MindJogger Videoquiz

Use *MindJogger* to review the Chapter 11 content.

Reviewing Key Terms

1. initiator
2. group discussion
3. maintenance need
4. groupthink
5. agitator
6. group dynamics
7. initiator
8. emergent norm

Reviewing Key Concepts

1. Group norms are the rules about what behavior is appropriate in a group. A positive norm, such as everyone being on time, helps the group be positive and productive. A negative norm, such as late arrival being acceptable, has the opposite effect.

2. Because an initiator helps the group move toward achieving its goals, he or she can have a positive effect on group dynamics. Accept all answers that students can defend.

3. The statement defines an agitator as being negative and nonproductive.

4. A group member should be aware of what is on the agenda, be prepared to offer information or ask pertinent questions, and know how to play a suitable role during the discussion.

GLENCOE Online

Visit the *Glencoe Communication Applications* Web site at **communicationapplications. glencoe.com** and click on **Chapter 11 Activity** for additional practice in making groups work.

Reviewing Key Terms

On a separate sheet of paper, write the vocabulary term that fits each description. The number of spaces indicates the number of letters in each answer.

1. Group member who gets the discussion started - - - - - - - - -

2. Different from a conversation because it is an exchange of ideas on a specific topic for a specific reason - - - - - - - - - - - - - -

3. A need that promotes unity in the group - - - - - - - - - - - - - - - -

4. Group members' strong desire to agree with one another, even if it means making a poor decision - - - - - - - - -

5. Group member who questions others' decisions, facts, or research - - - - - - - -

6. The energy created as group members communicate and interact with one another - - - - - - - - - - - -

7. Group member who may negatively affect the group by dominating the discussion - - - - - - - - -

8. Rule of behavior that develops from group interaction - - - - - - - - - - - -

Reviewing Key Concepts

On a separate sheet of paper, answer the following questions in complete sentences.

1. What are group norms? Give an example of a positive norm and a negative norm.

2. What is one way an initiator's actions might influence group dynamics?

3. What is meant by the statement "An agitator goes against the momentum of a group"?

4. What steps should a group member take to prepare for discussion?

5. How might you use tact to inform a group member that his or her habit of interrupting others is inappropriate behavior in group discussions?

6. Why do you think feedback is an important tool for evaluating group results?

7. Describe one way to collect information for evaluating group process.

5. Answers will vary, but students should reflect most of the points in the Communications Strategies checklist on page 364.

6. Students' opinions may vary, but most will think that feedback is important because many people discover their actual behavior in groups is different from what they think it is.

7. Although students' answers will vary, some will choose to describe the use of a group roles chart such as the one on page 373.

Reading and Critical Thinking Skill

1. **Predicting** Imagine that several members of a group have begun skipping meetings. How might the group change this harmful norm?

2. **Inferring** Why is it important for a facilitator to understand people's nonverbal behaviors?

3. **Applying** As the president of a fan club, what question might you ask the treasurer to find out about the state of the club's finances?

4. **Making Comparisons** Explain the difference between criticizing and offering constructive criticism.

Skill Practice Activity

Writing a Meeting Agenda Imagine that you are the chairperson of a citizen group charged with cleaning up litter and debris around a local lake. During your first meeting, the group will need to determine individual tasks such as which areas to clean up, where to begin the cleanup, how to dispose of different types of debris, and what tools will be needed. Write an agenda for this meeting.

Cooperative Learning Activity

Evaluating Group Results Working with four or five other students, imagine that your group is charged with cleaning up around a local lake. Participate in a five-minute discussion about the cleanup. If you completed the *Skill Practice Activity* above, base your discussion on one or two points from your agenda. As you discuss, notice how the roles of initiator, facilitator, and agitator are being filled. Also, notice the effectiveness of group members' verbal, nonverbal, and listening skills. Finally, work together to write a one-page evaluation of the group process. Share your group evaluations as a class.

Chapter Project

Planning Divide your class into three groups. Decide which group will give a five- to ten-minute presentation on verbal skills, which will present nonverbal skills, and which will present listening skills. Once you have chosen a topic, work with your group to brainstorm a list of effective and ineffective skills in that area. Divide the list, assigning each listed skill to two or three students. Work with group members to research your assigned skill. Use visual aids and brief skits or dramatizations to effectively demonstrate and explain your assigned skill.

Presenting As a group, present your dramatizations and visual aids to the rest of the class. Explain why each skill is effective or ineffective and what impact it can have on a group. Ask your classmates if they have any questions.

Making Groups Work **379**

Reading and Critical Thinking Skill

1. Although answers may vary, most students will see that the group can change this harmful norm by group discussion of the group's norms and expectations.

2. A facilitator must understand people's nonverbal behaviors in order to figure out what their real messages are and respond to them appropriately.

3. The president is likely to ask the treasurer to present a report on the group's income and expenditures for a specified period.

4. Constructive criticism separates the feelings toward a person from the information provided by that person; it does not attack the person, but rather the information. Other kinds of criticism often include an emotional reaction to the person.

Skill Practice Activity

Students' agendas will vary but should include information about where and when the meeting will be held, as well as appropriate items as directed. Students should follow the general plan for writing an agenda presented in Communication Through Writing on pages 376–377.

Cooperative Learning Activity

Encourage the class to work together as a group as they share their small-group evaluations.

Chapter Project

Ask teams to evaluate each other's presentations. Invite students to discuss all the presentations as a way of summarizing the chapter.

Chapter 12 Planning Guide

SECTION RESOURCES

Daily Objectives

Section 1

1. Describe possible advantages and disadvantages of conflict
2. Determine the level on which a conflict exists
3. Analyze how relationships and interdependence impact conflicts
4. Determine types of conflict

Section 2

1. Describe possible losses and gains in conflict resolution
2. Classify forces behind conflict resolution as helpful or hindering
3. Justify a decision to resolve conflict
4. Compare and contrast conflict-resolution strategies
5. Organize a conflict-resolution meeting
6. Develop strategies for coping with unresolved conflict

Reproducible Resources

 Reproducible Lesson Plan 12-1
 Application Activities 12-1
 Guided Reading Workbook Activity 12-1
 Vocabulary Activity 12*
 Reteaching Activity 12-1*
 Enrichment Activity 12-1*
 Graphic Organizer Transparency Strategies and Activities 12-1

 Reproducible Lesson Plan 12-2
 Application Activities 12-2
 Guided Reading Workbook Activity 12-2
 Vocabulary Activity 12*
 Reteaching Activity 12-2*
 Enrichment Activity 12-2*
 Graphic Organizer Transparency Strategies and Activities 12-2

Multimedia Resources

 Graphic Organizer Transparency 12-1
 Chapter 12 Teaching Transparency
 Interactive Tutor Self-Assessment
 PuzzleMaker
 ExamView® Pro Testmaker
Interactive Lesson Planner
 Communication in Action Video Chapter 12
 MindJogger
 communicationapplications.glencoe.com
 Presentation Plus!

 Graphic Organizer Transparency 12-2
 Chapter 12 Teaching Transparency
 Interactive Tutor Self-Assessment
 PuzzleMaker
 ExamView® Pro Testmaker
Interactive Lesson Planner
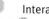 Communication in Action Video Chapter 12
 MindJogger
 communicationapplications.glencoe.com
 Presentation Plus!

Use Glencoe's *Presentation Plus!* multimedia teacher tool to easily present dynamic lessons that engage and motivate your students. Using Microsoft PowerPoint®, you can customize the presentations to create your own personalized lessons.

* Also available in Spanish

 Blackline Master
 CD-ROM
 Software
 Transparency
Videodisc
 Videocassette
Web site

Chapter 12 Planning Guide

Chapter 12 Resource Manager

The following materials may be used when teaching the chapter. Materials for specific lessons are also shown at point-of-use in the margins of the Teacher's Wraparound Edition.

TEACHING TRANSPARENCIES

Chapter 12 Teaching Transparency

Graphic Organizer Transparency 12-1

Graphic Organizer Transparency 12-2

APPLICATION ACTIVITIES

Chapter 12, Section 1

Chapter 12, Section 2

Chapter 12, Cumulative

REINFORCEMENT AND REVIEW ACTIVITIES

Vocabulary Activity 12

Guided Reading Activity Workbook 12-1, 12-2

Reteaching Activities 12-1, 12-2

Chapter 12 Resource Manager

ASSESSMENT AND EVALUATION

Section Quizzes 12-1, 12-2

Chapter 12 Test, Forms A & B

**Performance Assessment
Activity 12**

ENRICHMENT AND EXTENSION

**Technology Application
Activity 12**

**Enrichment Activities
12-1, 12-2**

ORAL PRESENTATION ACTIVITIES

Activities 1, 3–6, 15, 16

SPANISH RESOURCES

- Spanish Chapter and Unit Tests
- Spanish Vocabulary Activities
- Spanish Section Quizzes
- Spanish Reteaching Activities
- Spanish Enrichment Activities

MULTIMEDIA

- Interactive Tutor Self-Assessment
- ExamView® Pro Testmaker
- PuzzleMaker
- Communication in Action Videodisc and Videocassette
- MindJogger
- Interactive Lesson Planner
- Presentation Plus!
- Writer's Assistant
- Glencoe Interactive Grammar
- **communicationapplications.glencoe.com**

TEACHER PLANNING AND SUPPORT

- Reproducible Lesson Plans
- Interactive Lesson Planner
- Presentation Plus!

Managing Conflict

WHY IT'S IMPORTANT

Conflict plays a part in all of our lives. Learning how to manage conflict can help you be sure that it doesn't play the starring role.

To better understand how to manage conflict, view the **Communication in Action** Chapter 12 video lesson.

"How many a dispute could have been deflated into a single paragraph if the disputants had dared to define their terms."
—Aristotle, Greek philosopher

WHY IT'S IMPORTANT

Have students read the quotation. Ask: **What is Aristotle saying about the role communication plays in conflict management?** *(Students may respond that disputes, or conflicts, could be shortened or resolved if the participants clearly stated why they were disagreeing.)* Ask students how this can be applied to conflicts with which they are familiar.

Section 1

Diagnosing Conflict

GUIDE TO READING

Objectives

1. Describe possible advantages and disadvantages of conflict.
2. Determine the level on which a conflict exists.
3. Analyze how relationships and interdependence impact conflicts.
4. Determine types of conflicts.

Terms to Learn

conflict over facts
conflict over values
conflict over policies

You may know someone who always seems to be "looking for a fight." You probably know someone else who will go to great lengths to avoid the smallest disagreement. Which is the better approach to conflict? Neither one is very productive in the long run.

It takes courage, along with well-developed communication skills, to confront conflict. People who are afraid of disagreement can be as destructive to relationships as people who are consistently confrontational. Letting your problems simmer inside of you can eventually make you angry, resentful, or perhaps argumentative. However, these actions aren't always directed at the person your original conflict involves. Often, unresolved conflict interferes in other relationships, both at home and at work. The key lies not with having conflict, but managing it.

UNDERSTANDING CONFLICT

As you learned in Chapter 1, conflict is a struggle between two or more parties who sense interference in achieving their goals. At various times, you may find yourself in conflict with other people or with an organization if its needs or values directly contradict your own. Your conflict may be an obvious one, with loud arguments and slammed doors. It may be less emotional, marked by calm discussion. It may even continue unnoticed by others, simmering below the surface.

■ **In order to build effective relationships, one must develop conflict management skills. What is conflict?**

Managing Conflict **381**

1 FOCUS

Bellringer
After students have read the opening paragraph of this section, have them assess their own attitudes toward conflict. Ask them to rate themselves from one to ten, with one representing a desire to avoid conflict at all costs and ten indicating a highly confrontational nature. Have them form pairs and explain their ratings to their partners. Invite volunteers from the full spectrum of ratings to share their self-evaluations with the class.

📖 You may use Graphic Organizer Transparency 12–1 to introduce this section.

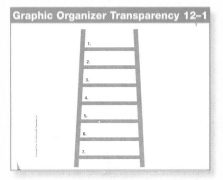

Graphic Organizer Transparency 12–1

■ **Visual Instruction**

Answer Students may define *conflict* as a struggle between two or more parties who sense interference in achieving their goals.

RESOURCE MANAGER

Teaching Tools
- Interactive Lesson Planner
- Reproducible Lesson Plan 12–1
- Application Activities 12–1

Reproducible Masters
- Guided Reading Activity Workbook 12–1
- Enrichment Activity 12–1
- Reteaching Activity 12–1
- Section Quiz 12–1
- Transparency Strategies and Activities Booklet 12–1

Transparencies
- Graphic Organizer Transparency 12–1
- Chapter 12 Teaching Transparency

Technology Resources
- Interactive Tutor Self-Assessment Software
- Presentation Plus! Software
- ExamView® Pro Testmaker
- PuzzleMaker Software
- communicationapplications.glencoe.com

2 TEACH

Conflict Is Inevitable

Give students two minutes to write a list of conflicts to which they have been a party during the last year, reminding them that these may include internal conflicts as well as conflicts among people. Have students form pairs and share their lists. Have volunteers share conflicts with the class and explain whether, and how, these have been resolved. **L1** 🗍

Conflict May Be Beneficial

Encourage students to respond to the Chinese symbol for *crisis*. Ask them to think of situations in which danger and opportunity are both potential results. Invite volunteers to share crises in their own lives that held these possibilities. **L3**

Guided Reading Activity 12–1

GUIDED READING Activity 12-1	Name _____ Date _____ Class _____
	MANAGING CONFLICT
	Diagnosing Conflict

As you read Section 1, answer the following items.

1. Define *conflict*. _____
2. Explain how conflict can be a beneficial part of your life. _____
3. What is the first step in diagnosing a conflict? _____
4. When does interpersonal conflict occur? _____
5. List three forms of group conflict. _____
6. Explain how organizational change can foster conflict. _____
7. How does conflict with a family member differ from conflict with a supervisor? _____
8. When parties are involved in a conflict, what does *interdependence* mean? _____
9. What type of conflict involves a disagreement over something that can be proven true or false? _____
10. What is a conflict over values? _____
11. What type of conflict requires the willing cooperation of the administration or management of an organization in order to be resolved? _____
12. List five sources of conflict. _____
13. Name three crisis situations and discuss what you should do about them. _____

Just as conflicts may take on many appearances, they also may involve a variety of relationships. You may deal with internal conflict. That is, you may have conflicting emotions, loyalties, or goals within yourself. Conflicts also can occur between two individuals, such as coworkers, family members, or friends. In addition, conflicts may occur between an individual and a group, or between and among different groups and organizations.

Whether your conflicts are emotional or rational, angry or calm, external or internal, they can be managed in much the same way. Once you understand what conflicts have in common, you'll be well on your way to examining, diagnosing, and resolving the conflicts that arise in your social and professional lives.

Conflict Is Inevitable

While most people would prefer not to have conflicts, they are a part of life. Over the years, you'll find it impossible to escape conflict in your personal relationships or working

Conflict may occur in any relationship. How can conflict be beneficial?

environment. Therefore, in order to be successful, you must learn to diagnose the conflicts in your life and work to manage them.

Conflict May Be Beneficial

Although conflict typically is thought of as negative, it can sometimes be beneficial. The seemingly contradictory nature of conflict is clearly illustrated in the Chinese language. In Chinese, the symbol for the word *crisis* consists of two characters. One character represents danger, and the other represents opportunity. Just as in a crisis situation, the outcome of conflict can be either negative or positive.

Danger

Opportunity

The frustration of a conflict situation often motivates people to confront and solve problems that face their relationships or working environment. By working through a conflict, you are likely to learn something about yourself and the others around you. The process of finding a constructive resolution for a conflict may help you feel revitalized or empowered as a problem-solver. The organizations you belong to also may benefit from improved organizational policies and procedures. This, in turn, can lead to streamlined processes, higher profits, and better working conditions.

Conflict May Be Destructive

If a conflict is not effectively managed, it can damage or destroy relationships and, potentially, entire

Visual Instruction

Answer Students may say that through conflict, people often learn things about themselves and others.

CRITICAL THINKING ACTIVITY

"People learn from their failures. Seldom do they learn anything from success," wrote Harold Geneen, former president of ITT. "No man can learn to be a crack shot unless he wastes some ammunition," wrote Richard W. Sears, of the famous mail-order company. Is failure the first step to wisdom? Write on the board the statement by Geneen and ask students whether they tend to agree or disagree with it. Have them form groups according to their views on the subject and ask them to come up with reasons for their opinions. Direct them to include at least two hypothetical situations or specific examples from real life to support their views. Ask each group to nominate one or two speakers and have the speakers form teams to debate the issues in front of the class. Invite the class to contribute their views at the conclusion of the debate. 🗍

organizations. Friendships can end. At work, morale can suffer, which can cause a decrease in productivity and quality. Employees with pent-up frustrations may be abrupt or even rude to customers. They may put less effort and energy into their work, either consciously or subconsciously.

In addition, the benefits of working to resolve conflict are not absolute. They often come at a price. For example, you may feel like a problem-solver each time you resolve a conflict with a coworker. However, if this is the fourth conflict you have been involved in this month, you may gain a reputation as a troublemaker. At this point, you might want to do some self-analysis. When conflicts occur too often between the same two parties—even if each conflict is successfully resolved—the relationship is likely to suffer. The emotional toll of constant tension or repeated problems with another can easily overshadow the benefits of any single conflict.

STEPS FOR DIAGNOSING CONFLICT

To develop skills for managing the conflicts in your life, you need a systematic procedure to diagnose them. By breaking down a conflict into its separate elements, you can make it seem less overwhelming. The steps in Figure 12–1 can help you systematically diagnose each conflict you face.

Identify the Conflict

Have you ever found yourself well into an argument and then realized you were unable to remember what you were arguing about? Have you ever snapped at a family member over something insignificant, when your real source of irritation was a problem at school? Conflict often has a way of hiding or

Figure 12–1 Steps for Diagnosing Conflict

- Identify the conflict.
- Determine the level of the conflict.
- Analyze the relationships involved.
- Determine the level of interdependence.
- Analyze the type of conflict.
- Identify the source of conflict.
- Analyze the severity of the conflict.

disguising itself. After all, it's much easier to wage a minor battle with your little sister than to tackle an issue with your teacher or boss. The first step toward resolving a conflict is identifying the actual conflict at hand.

Start diagnosing your conflict by stating and describing the problem. Along with the problem-solving skills you read about in Chapter 11, the questions in the following activity can help you clarify the conflict from your point of view.

A clear definition of the conflict at hand is essential. Knowing what is really bothering you can help you eliminate emotional distractions. Then, once you've identified the issue at the heart of your conflict, you're ready to move on to managing it!

Managing Conflict **383**

Application Activities 12–1

MULTIPLE LEARNING STYLES

Bodily-Kinesthetic Suggest to students that our days are punctuated by conflict but that we rarely are in a position to look at these clearly because we are so often the participants. Remind them that someone else's conflict is generally much simpler to identify than our own.

Activity List with the class conflicts that typically occur during the course of a day. (Examples might include conflicts with parents about grades, activities, or friends; with siblings about sharing or noise; with friends about relationships and recreation.) Ask for pairs of volunteers to improvise a situation of their choice in front of the class. Have other students comment on the scenes performed. How are they typical? What other variations might they include? Can, or should, situations such as these be avoided?

Determine the Level of the Conflict

Ask students to read the five bulleted descriptions of conflict level. What do they notice about the progression of the list? *(The number of people involved tends to increase with each level.)* Invite students to comment on the text's recommendation to manage conflict "on the smallest level possible." **L2**

DID YOU KNOW?

The Latin prefix *inter-* means "between," while *intra-* means "within." Thus, interstate highways go between states, while intrastate roads remain within state borders. The same principle applies to interpersonal and intrapersonal levels of conflict.

For an additional Practice Lab for this section, have students visit the *Glencoe Communication Applications* Web site at **communicationapplications.glencoe.com.** Click on Communication Practice Lab 12–1. **L1**

■ Visual Instruction

Answer Students might say that a good rule to follow is to manage conflict on the smallest possible level.

■ Businesses that promote competition between employees can inadvertently cause conflict by pitting employee against employee. **What is a good rule to use when handling conflict?**

Determine the Level of the Conflict

Conflict can occur on any of the five levels of communication:

- intrapersonal
- interpersonal
- group
- organizational
- environmental

Each time additional people or groups are brought into a conflict, the level of that conflict progresses. An effective rule of thumb is to manage conflict on the smallest level possible. That means that it is most desirable to handle a conflict by yourself or with the fewest people necessary to come to a true resolution.

Intrapersonal Conflict All conflicts begin on the intrapersonal level with your perception of a situation. Some situations may be purely intrapersonal; that is, no other individuals, groups, or policies are involved. For example, you may be in conflict over whether to keep a higher-paying job or accept another with better potential for promotion. This conflict is an internal one. In other words, you must decide for yourself. Even with outside advice, this type of conflict remains intrapersonal.

Here's another example. Imagine that, at your office, you and your coworkers share telephone-answering duties. You may feel that you answer the phone for one or more of your coworkers much more often than they do for you. If you have not yet spoken to your coworkers about what you perceive to be a problem, this conflict is still on the intrapersonal level. Is this an important conflict to you? Are you willing to "get over it" and just let things continue as they are now? Is the conflict important enough for you to consider quitting your job?

You must analyze your own needs in this situation and determine whether or not you will resolve the conflict yourself or share your feelings with your coworkers. If you choose to discuss the conflict, you take it to the next level of communication.

Interpersonal Conflict Interpersonal conflict occurs when two or more people openly express their perceptions of a problem. Once a conflict becomes interpersonal, it is more complex than before. There are at least two sets of goals, needs, values, and feelings to be considered and dealt with.

INTERDISCIPLINARY CONNECTION

Social Studies Point out that conflicts comprise much of what is delivered to the public as news, whether it is fighting with words at political meetings or fighting with guns across the globe. Remind students that the same questions suggested in the Communication Practice Lab on page 385 apply as equally to arguments between nations as to those between siblings.

Activity Have students choose a conflict that has been in the news at some point during the past two or three years. Ask them to research its origins and the points of view expressed by the parties involved. Have students prepare a presentation in which they analyze their conflict, explaining whether or not it has been resolved. Encourage them to illustrate their presentation with a poster or audio-visual material. Invite students to compare and contrast the conflicts they have researched.

In the earlier telephone example, your coworkers may surprise you with their perception of the situation. They may each believe that they, too, do more than their share of answering the telephone! On the other hand, your coworkers may think your answering the phone more often is a sign that you prefer to answer it. They may even be irritated at you for answering more than your share of the calls. You should be prepared to listen to very different perceptions of the situation from the others' points of view.

Group Conflict Group conflict may occur in different ways. It may involve one group member who perceives a conflict between himself or herself and the rest of the group. Conflict also may occur between or among subgroups within the same group. Additionally, conflict can occur between or among different groups within an organization. If properly managed and resolved, conflict actually can strengthen a group. If improperly managed, that same conflict can have the power to destroy the group.

Imagine that you have a new player on your high school hockey team. If the rest of the team has played hockey together since you were in elementary school, group conflict may occur as the new player tries to fit in. Since the rookie doesn't know the formations and lines most often used by this team, his or her awkwardness at practices may cause the group to feel resentment or anger. This kind of group conflict is much more complex than interpersonal conflict; the individual may feel as if everyone else is working together against him or her. The person also may feel excluded and victimized. Adding to the complexity of the situation is the fact that not just one or two sets of emotions and needs are at stake. In this case, there are many.

Equally complex are clashes between subgroups within a larger group or between groups in the same or a different organization. The afternoon shift at the restaurant where you work may clash with the morning shift over the cleanliness of the break room; the Spanish Club may feel threatened by the French Club's continual use of the school's language lab. When many people share their opinions and feelings regarding an uncomfortable situation, emotions can escalate, making resolution more difficult.

COMMUNICATION PRACTICE LAB

Identifying Conflict

To identify the true source of a conflict, follow these steps:

Step 1 List any conflicts you have been involved in over the last month.

Step 2 Choose one of the conflicts listed. Write what you remember or know about the conflict.

Step 3 Answer the following questions about the conflict you have described: What did you want? What prevented you from getting it? Which of your goals, needs, values, or emotions were involved? What people and/or policies were involved?

Step 4 How did your answers in Step 3 compare with your description in Step 2? Were you honest with yourself and others about the true issue or issues in conflict? If the conflict has not been resolved yet, you may wish to use this information and the skills you'll learn in this chapter to bring it to a close.

Managing Conflict **385**

Interpersonal Conflict

Point out that people frequently feel misunderstood during the course of interpersonal conflicts. "If only the other party would see it my way," they reason, "things would work out." Brainstorm with the class for typical sources of conflict—relationships, noise, privacy, regulations. Have students form pairs and ask them to assume roles in a conflict, pretending that they are the parties involved. Invite pairs to address the class, with each individual giving his or her version of the conflict. Have the class discuss the conflicts and make suggestions for resolution. **L2**

COMMUNICATION PRACTICE LAB

Identifying Conflict

Ask students what lesson this exercise is intended to teach. *(Students may respond that people have difficulty being objective about their real reasons for participation in a conflict.)* How might asking the questions posed in Step 3 help resolve a conflict? *(By analyzing our participation in the conflict, we equip ourselves to make rational decisions.)* **L2**

MEETING INDIVIDUAL NEEDS
MULTIPLE LEARNING STYLES

Musical "Try to see it my way," sang the Beatles, and they were not the only group to have expressed conflict in music. Point out that popular songs encompass much of human experience; it is not surprising that conflict should be a major theme in the music we listen to every day.
Activity Have students bring to class three recorded examples of music that address the subject of conflict. Ask them to play excerpts to the class and to describe their choices. What sorts of conflict are the singers describing? Is there a promise of resolution?

Organizational Conflict

Organizational conflict is a favorite theme for Hollywood filmmakers. Honest police officers, corporate whistle blowers, maverick teachers, and independent students have all played starring roles. Ask students to recall the plots of movies that have involved conflicts between the organization and the individual. How were these conflicts resolved? What is the attraction of such themes? **L3**

Sometimes, organizations hold competitions that can unintentionally turn into conflict situations. Companies that hold competitions to determine star sales representatives may unintentionally pit employee against employee, department against department, or work shift against work shift. The competitive conflict may have its benefits: increased productivity, sales, and bottom line. However, it also can result in employee resentment, backbiting, anger, and job dissatisfaction.

Organizational Conflict Organizational conflict occurs between an organization itself and individuals or groups of individuals within that organization. For instance, individuals or groups may determine that the organization uses unfair policies. When employee advocacy groups come into conflict with an organization's management, it usually is over policy matters such as hiring practices, benefits, or salary rates.

Other sources of organizational conflict may be unsafe, outdated, crowded, or otherwise inefficient conditions at a worksite. A construction site may be without first-aid equipment, or several lab technicians may have to share one computer. Employees may demand that the organization make changes to improve conditions, opening a conflict between labor and management divisions.

Sometimes, organizational change fosters conflict. Any time a company changes how work is done, employees may need to be retrained. They also may need to be motivated to embrace these new work conditions. When these important steps are ignored, employee frustration, confusion, resentment, and, ultimately, conflict can occur. Left unresolved, all these conflicts can be very costly.

Environmental Conflict If a conflict is environmental, it is important to identify it quickly. Many times, we blame other people when our conflict is truly environmental. For example, you and the two students in your class who share an area of a biology lab may be in constant conflict. While you believe it is their rudeness or lack of organization that is the cause of the conflict, it may actually be the result of too little personal working space. The cramped quarters may be amplifying any differences in work style and adding tension to your working relationship. Understanding that the conflict has nothing to do with your classmates but rather with your surroundings helps take some of the emotion out of the situation.

At any of these different communication levels, you may make the decision not to engage the conflict but just to cope with the situation as it stands. However, if you do choose to resolve the conflict, the next step is to analyze what relationships are involved.

THE BORN LOSER reprinted by permission of Newspaper Enterprise Association, Inc.

MEETING INDIVIDUAL NEEDS

ENGLISH LANGUAGE LEARNERS

Ethnic Conflict Conflict is very often the result of misunderstanding. Few areas create more misunderstanding than differences in culture and language. English language learners are likely to be particularly sensitive to conflicts resulting from ethnic and linguistic differences.

Activity Have students research a conflict among ethnic or national groups within a society, either in the United States or abroad. Ask them to discover the viewpoints of both sides of the issue in order to be able to express them clearly for the class. Invite English language learners to use examples from their own national backgrounds or from their personal experiences in the United States if they wish. Have students present their findings to the class. Encourage students to discuss what lessons can be learned from conflicts among ethnic or national groups. **ELL**

Analyze the Relationships Involved

Is there a difference between a conflict with a family member and one with a good friend? What is the difference between a conflict with another player on your team and one with your coach?

The relationships of the parties involved in a conflict matter a great deal. Regardless of the outcome of your family dispute, you probably will still be considered a family member. However, can you be certain that your friendship will withstand any conflict? Likewise, a conflict between teammates may be uncomfortable and result in poor teamwork at times, while a serious conflict with the coach can put you on the bench or off the team entirely.

People Involved Determining who is involved in the conflict and what relationships they have with one another is important. In the workplace, conflict tends to be more serious if those involved work in the same department rather than in different ones. It can become even more difficult if they hold different levels of authority, such as a supervisor and an employee.

Relationships of Those Involved The relationships of those involved in a conflict often have a major impact on whether or not it can be resolved. In some cases, conflict with a supervisor may be better left alone. You might decide that coping with it intrapersonally is preferable to addressing it openly and risking your future at your job. Likewise, ruining a lifelong friendship may be too great a price to pay to resolve a minor difference. It is important to take an honest look at how you feel about that person, how much you want to maintain the relationship, and what each person's role is in the

TECHNOLOGY Activity

Analyzing the Message Channel Technology can have a significant impact on communication. A receiver often will interpret a message based partly on the channel of communication chosen to communicate it. When discussing a conflict, how is a face-to-face meeting different from a discussion through e-mail, voice mail, or memos? Discuss your answers in groups of four or five.

relationship. You then want to weigh the risks of pursuing a resolution or coping with the conflict.

Determine the Level of Interdependence

How interdependent are the parties involved in a specific conflict? That is, how much do they need one another in order to get their work done? It is more important for two basketball teammates to resolve their differences than it is for a basketball player and a tennis player to resolve theirs.

So, how do you determine the interdependence of parties in conflict? First, analyze how much space and equipment they must share and how much time they must spend together. Also, determine whether or not one of the participants has some control or supervisory power over the other. It is particularly important to resolve differences if the cooperative decision making is a major function of the parties involved, such as with the administrators at your school.

Imagine a situation in which two coworkers are in conflict because they must share a telephone, a computer, and other office equipment. The costs of not resolving their

Managing Conflict **387**

Environmental Conflict

Students will likely respond to the idea that school is a rich source of environmental conflict—from the school bus, to the classroom, to the cafeteria. Invite them to share anecdotes relating how their school environment contributes to conflict. Encourage the class to come up with solutions to these areas of conflict. **ELL**

TECHNOLOGY Activity

Analyzing the Message Channel If students feel that they need more information in order to interpret the significance of the communication channels proposed here, ask them to consider the following scenario:

You have just attended a meeting in which there was considerable conflict. Afterwards, you call the district manager's secretary to schedule an appointment to discuss this issue.

Have students evaluate the following possible responses by the manager, who leaves a voice mail asking for additional comments, schedules a face-to-face meeting with you, sends everyone at the meeting an e-mail requesting comments, writes a personal memo to you requesting additional input, sends a fax to all meeting participants requesting additional input, announces by memo that another meeting is scheduled for next week. Then, have them complete the activity in the student text.

MEETING INDIVIDUAL NEEDS

GIFTED AND TALENTED

Social Conflict Point out that the causes of social conflict are not always easy to establish. Scholars disagree on the extent to which environmental aspects play a part, as culture and heredity are also factors in the equation. Encourage students with an interest in important issues and the skills for academic research to investigate this area further.

Activity Have students research the relationship between conflict and the environment in which people live. Ask them to locate and study at least three scholarly sources confirming or disputing the idea that social conflict has at its roots environmental factors. Have students summarize and analyze their research in a brief paper. Ask them to present their findings to the class.

Determine the Level of Interdependence

Ask students to consider the role of interdependence in conflicts they have experienced. Encourage them to recall conflicts at home or school, with friends, adults, or peers. How did the degree of interdependence affect the way they dealt with these conflicts? Did the status of the person with whom they were in conflict make this situation more or less difficult? Was the conflict resolved, and if so, how? **L2**

Conflicts Over Facts

"The fact is this." Ask students how often they have heard a parent, teacher, friend, or boss express a conflict beginning with these words. However, this may be only half the story. Encourage students to understand the importance of airing all the facts when attempting to resolve a conflict. Ask them to form pairs and consider the following "facts": You took the car without asking; You are failing algebra; You went out with another guy/girl; You called in sick for work, but someone saw you at the movies that evening.

For each of these scenarios, have students come up with other, mitigating facts, which might change their accuser's mind. **L2** 📦

■ Visual Instruction

Answer Students might say that interdependence is determined by analyzing how much space and equipment is shared, how much time is spent together, and whether one or more participants has supervisory control.

---

conflict may be that one of them refuses to share what the other needs. In this case, each person's ability to do his or her job is likely to be affected by the conflict. Therefore, it may be to everyone's advantage to address the conflict.

Analyze the Type of Conflict

The next step in the analysis of a conflict is to look at the type of conflict it is. Most conflicts occur over differences in factual information, personal values, or policies. Analyzing your conflict can help you classify it in one of

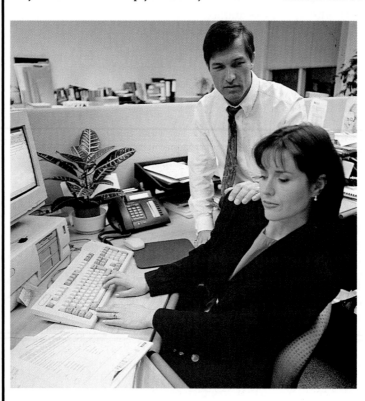

Interdependence between coworkers can lead to conflict. *What causes most conflicts to occur?*

these categories and better understand what issues are at stake.

Facts A conflict over facts is a disagreement over something that can be proven to be true or false. These conflicts are the easiest to resolve because they are the result of inadequate information or misinterpretation. Once you uncover the facts, the conflict is settled. If the conflict is over whether or not you can purchase a new copy machine for your department or club, looking at the funds provided in the budget probably will provide the answer. Once those in conflict understand the factual information, the conflict can be resolved.

Conflicts over facts also are the easiest to avoid altogether. Making sure you have gathered as much information as possible can help you avoid unnecessary conflict. It also can save you from the potential embarrassment of appearing uninformed.

Values As you learned in Chapter 1, a value is something you find important. A conflict over values is a disagreement over priorities. Unlike facts, values and opinions are not verifiable. Rather, they are deeply personal and rooted in what someone believes.

Imagine that you and a classmate are in conflict over when to work on an assigned team project. You place a priority on time with your family; you'd rather not meet on Saturday or Sunday. Your

---

COOPERATIVE LEARNING ACTIVITY

Anger is only effective when managed. Have students form groups of four. Ask each group to designate one student as coordinator, one as recorder, one as writer, and one as presenter. Ask them as groups, led by their coordinators, to brainstorm for specific situations in which an expression of anger might be appropriate. (Remind students that their situations can range from friends, family, work, and school to politics and social issues.) Have the recorder jot down the group's ideas, then ask each group to choose the scenario that they feel most persuasively justifies an expression of anger. Direct the writer, with the group's assistance, to compose a dramatic monologue, expressing the speaker's feelings in a rational, yet honest manner. Complete the assignment with performances by the presenters, reading their groups' monologues to the class. 📦

COMMUNICATION Strategies

IDENTIFYING SOURCES OF CONFLICT

- Is there a difference in perspective due to roles?
- Is there a power struggle?
- Are there unclear guidelines?
- Is there a difference in personal style?
- Is there some external stress or burnout?

partner, on the other hand, values school athletics and would rather not meet during game time.

Each person in a conflict over values will be emotionally involved in and committed to his or her personal stance. Therefore, each person in the conflict needs to listen empathically and try not to be judgmental or accusatory about other points of view. If you decide to resolve the conflict using the strategies found later in this chapter, it will help if you take into account the feelings and emotions of each person involved.

Policies A conflict over policies is a disagreement that deals with differences over how to best complete a task. Such a conflict does not concern the end goal of the task, but rather how to get to that goal. For example, a goal at your workplace might be to hire the best-qualified managers for the company. The hiring policy might require that all job openings be advertised nationally to attract a large group of qualified applicants from across the country. On the other hand, your employees might feel that experienced workers who have done well in

your company should be given more consideration than "outsiders" whose true work record and abilities are unknown. Everyone agrees that the company needs good managers; they disagree on how to go about hiring those managers.

Resolving a conflict over policies generally requires the willing cooperation of the administration or management of an organization. Therefore, when you diagnose this type of conflict, be sure to include an analysis of the people who will need to be consulted and involved if you try to resolve this conflict.

Identify the Source of the Conflict

One of the most important steps in diagnosing a conflict is identifying what produced the conflict in the first place. Remember that all people perceive things differently. Therefore, no two people will perceive a conflict the same way. As part of your perception check, ask the questions in the Communication Strategies checklist to get to the source of the conflict.

Roles Some conflicts may be caused by roles. The role you play in a particular situation tends to give you a perspective that is different from that of someone in another role. Employers and employees may view what happens at work differently. Coaches, athletes, and parents may all view the purpose of school sports differently. Conflict may result from these different points of view.

Power Struggle The conflict might be over a struggle for power. You and a coworker may be competing for recognition, rewards, bonuses, or promotions. Competitive activities often lead to conflict because both of you may not be able to achieve the same prize.

Managing Conflict **389**

COMMUNICATION Strategies

IDENTIFYING SOURCES OF CONFLICT

Before they read the related section of text, have students read the checklist on this page. Ask them to infer what is meant by the terms *role*, *power struggle*, *unclear guidelines*, *personal style*, and *external stress*. Brainstorm for situations in which the sources of conflict listed might lead to an actual conflict. Then, direct students to continue reading. Discuss the accuracy of their inferences with the actual description provided by the text. **L3**

Values

Point out that everyone has values and that most of us are willing to accept the values of others or at least to work out compromises to accommodate them. Ask students if they feel there are some values that are completely incompatible. What are they? Do these result in conflicts for which there is no resolution? Why or why not? **L2**

Policies

Point out that school policies often have understandable aims but that these are not always apparent to the students. Brainstorm with the class for policies of central importance to your school (examples: detention, curriculum requirements, cafeteria rules, parking regulations, clothing policies). What is the point of these policies? Are they a source of conflict? Can students think of other policies that might achieve the same ends while diminishing conflict? **L1**

Unclear Guidelines

Students constantly receive guidelines from teachers and administrators. Have them share instances of conflicts that arose from misinterpreted instructions. Ask students to assess whether the problem lay with the guidelines themselves or with their own skills at understanding and carrying them out. **L2**

Personal Style

Point out that siblings, friends, coworkers, and schoolmates rarely have exactly the same personal styles as students themselves do. Invite students to recall instances of conflicts arising from differences in attitude. Were the conflicts resolved? What made them important or negligible? **L2**

BUSINESS BRIEF

While stress is difficult to avoid at school or work, one way to reduce its effects is by regular aerobic exercise. "In working with thousands of creative people, I now recommend a regular exercise program as the single best way both to increase resistance to stress and to facilitate personal creativity," explains Thomas E. Backer, a professor at the UCLA School of Medicine. Ask students to comment on the role of exercise in their lives.

Garfield ®
by Jim Davis

Unclear Guidelines If you have not been given clear guidelines on how to proceed with a task, you may make some mistakes in trying to do your job. When this happens, your expectations for a task may differ from that of a supervisor, causing conflict. You may get angry with your supervisor because you feel he or she should have given a better explanation of your responsibilities. Your supervisor may be upset with you for taking too much time or using the wrong materials. He or she may have thought you would ask questions if you were unclear about how to do this part of your job.

Personal Style Sometimes, the source of a conflict simply may be different personal styles. Different cultural backgrounds, personal biases, or prejudices all can lead to conflict situations. You like to talk through problems; your coworker likes to work through problems alone. You may enjoy listening to music while you work, but the coworker in the next cubicle prefers silence. Since we don't often identify or talk about all the pieces that make up our personal style, we may expect others to behave as we do. These unmet expectations can lead to conflict situations.

External Stress Often, external stress can creep into unrelated situations and cause conflict. Feeling "burned out" at your job or school may cause you to become irritable and create conflict at home. In the same way, family issues may follow you to the office or school, creating problems there.

Analyze the Severity of the Conflict

Now that you've identified and described the conflict and analyzed the people and issues involved in it, your final step is to determine how serious the conflict is to you. To do this, imagine the degrees of severity, as shown in **Figure 12–2**.

After completely diagnosing and understanding a conflict, you may find that you are no longer bothered by it. You may recognize, for example, that the conflict stems from the different roles you and the other person play. You may be willing to allow that person to continue his or her behavior because it is reasonable in the context of his or her role. On the other hand, you may have discovered the facts underlying the dispute and can now put the conflict to rest. If so, you may determine that there is no longer a conflict and, therefore, decide to take no action on the issue. You have resolved the conflict on the intrapersonal level.

MEETING INDIVIDUAL NEEDS
MULTIPLE LEARNING STYLES

Interpersonal Lead students to understand that it is perfectly natural for relationships to change from day to day. The more we understand our roles in these changes, the greater is our ability to anticipate conflict or to manage conflicts that have already arisen.

Activity Have students create an annotated line graph of their relationships with a person they see daily. Ask them to choose someone with whom they are close (a sibling, a good friend, a parent) and to draw a line graph expressing the high and low points of that relationship over the course of a week. For each day, have students write a description of the relationship, noting what caused highs or lows in the profile. Have students form pairs and share their graphs.

At the interpersonal level, you may determine that there is a problem, but you don't find it to be serious enough to bother others with it. Perhaps you view this as something that happened only once under special circumstances and is not likely to happen again. If the conflict is due to differences in interpersonal style, you now may feel you know how this person acts. Therefore, you think you can avoid clashes in the future without bringing the issue to the other person's attention.

On the other hand, as the result of your diagnosis, you may view your problem as being fairly serious. You still have the option of coping with the conflict yourself, or you may choose to address it with the other parties involved. If you decide that the price of confronting the other party is greater than the benefit of having the conflict resolved, you may decide to just cope.

If you view the conflict as potentially devastating to you, consider whether or not you are engaged in a crisis situation. If so, you may want to have others trained in this type of crisis to help you diagnose and resolve the conflict. At times, people are trapped in serious situations which are outside their direct control. Abuse, harassment, and discrimination are crisis situations. In these cases, you may want to consult a social service organization or a trained counselor or minister. Another alternative would be to report this problem to a special office within your organization. Personnel or human resources departments typically help employees deal with such issues. Some employees belong to unions that help them resolve such conflicts.

TO RESOLVE OR NOT TO RESOLVE

Each step in the analysis of conflict is important because it shows a very different aspect of the issue that is troubling you. You do not need to complete each one in order to resolve your conflict, however. At any step along the way you may decide that the risks involved in confronting the others involved or in pursuing a resolution are simply too great. If your job is on the line or a family relationship is in jeopardy of being strained, you may decide to let the issue go and learn to cope with the situation as it stands.

On the other hand, you may decide at any step in the diagnosis process that a conflict definitely needs resolution. For example, in analyzing the interdependence of coworkers involved in a conflict you may realize that without resolution, very little work will get done. At that time, there would be no further need for

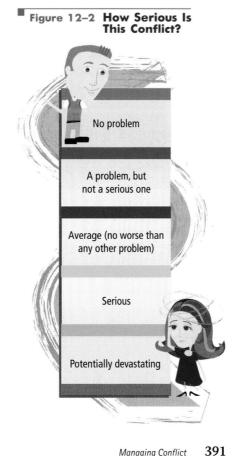

Figure 12-2 How Serious Is This Conflict?

No problem

A problem, but not a serious one

Average (no worse than any other problem)

Serious

Potentially devastating

Managing Conflict **391**

Reteaching Activity 12–1

Enrichment Activity 12–1

4 CLOSE

Have students review the ratings they gave themselves after reading the first paragraph of this section. Ask them to comment on how they feel information in this section may have changed the way they deal with conflict.

Extra-Credit Project

As illustrations in this section suggest, conflict is often a source of humor. Have students cut out from the daily or Sunday newspaper five separate comic strips dealing with conflict. Ask them to diagnose the conflicts, following as far as possible the steps recommended in the text. Have them create a poster illustrating and explaining their analyses.

analysis. Instead, you should act to resolve the conflict between the coworkers. Napoleon Bonaparte, emperor of France, is quoted as having said, "Take time to deliberate, but when the time for action has arrived, stop thinking and go in." Any stage in your analysis may be the one that moves you to stop thinking about your conflict and to start resolving it.

GLENCOE *Online*

Visit the *Glencoe Communication Applications* Web site at **communicationapplications. glencoe.com** and click on **Self-Check and Study Guide 12.1** to review your understanding of diagnosing conflict.

Review Key Terms

1. Define each term and write it in a sentence: conflict over facts, conflict over values, conflict over policies.

Check Understanding

2. Describe two advantages and two disadvantages of conflict.

3. Imagine a group of your coworkers is concerned about your company's policy regarding overtime hours. At what level is this conflict occurring?

4. How might the relationship and the interdependence between a supervisor and his or her employee affect their conflicts?

5. **Classify** Imagine that you and a partner must complete a history report together. Your partner suggests copying a report her sister wrote several years ago. You say that is cheating and that you should work together each night to finish the report. What type of conflict is this? Why?

APPLICATION *Activity*

Charting a Diagnosis Think of a conflict you have experienced. You may wish to refer back to the list you created in the Communication Practice Lab. Create a chart that shows how each of the nine diagnosis steps applies to your conflict. Use your chart to determine at which stage you could have ended the conflict analysis. At that stage, would you have chosen to resolve the conflict, cope with it, or acknowledge that the conflict no longer existed? Explain the reason for your choice.

1. Accept all reasonable sentences.
2. Advantages: conflict can motivate people to solve problems; one can learn about oneself. Disadvantages: conflict can damage relationships; productivity can decrease. (Accept other reasonable answers.)
3. This conflict is occurring at the organizational level.

4. Answers will vary but may include that sometimes conflicts must remain intrapersonal if a job is at stake.
5. This is a conflict of values. You believe that it is wrong to pass off someone else's work as your own. Your partner does not share this value.

Application Activity Students should be prepared to explain how the conflict ended and to indicate whether they might have handled it differently based on the information in this chapter.

FINDING THE MAIN IDEA AND SUPPORTING DETAILS

To fully understand the things that you read, it is important to know how to recognize the main idea or ideas. The main idea is a sentence that tells what the whole paragraph, story, article, or other written work is about.

Closely related to the main idea are the supporting details. Supporting details confirm the main idea and provide additional information, clarity, interest, or proof.

Learning the Skill

To find the main idea and supporting details, it is important to first ask yourself, "What is the purpose of this information?" Before beginning to read the text, glance at any titles or visual aids that might be included. Photos, illustrations, charts, graphs, tables, and other visuals are added to a text to enhance the main idea or ideas. Study these graphics before beginning a new section of text to help you anticipate what you will learn. Look for a common theme among sentences or paragraphs.

Finally, look for sentences that tell something about the main idea. Each time you learn something more about the main idea, you have found a supporting detail. To understand this relationship better, write the main idea at the top of a sheet of paper. Then, list each supporting detail below the main idea.

Practicing the Skill

Read the following advertisement for a veterinary hospital and answer the questions that follow.

1. What is the main idea of this ad?
2. What other information in the ad supports that idea?
3. What information is not necessary to the ad?

Purr-fect Care Veterinary Hospital

Your pet will receive the very best care at Purr-fect Care Veterinary Hospital. Specializing in small-animal care, our veterinarians treat your pet as if it were their own. Plus, each member of the Purr-fect Care support staff is trained to provide you with all the information you need. We also work hard to keep our kennels comfy and clean. Puff, the Purr-fect Care mascot, says,

"Come on in. We'll take the 'ow' out of 'meow.'"

APPLICATION *Activity*

Study an advertisement from a newspaper or magazine. Write the main idea of the ad at the top of a sheet of paper. Then, in one column below the main idea, list all the supporting details. In a second column, list any nonsupporting details found in the ad. Share your lists as a class.

Finding the Main Idea and Supporting Details

Students have probably been taught that the main idea of a paragraph is expressed in a topic sentence. They should realize, however, that not every paragraph has a topic sentence. Sometimes, the main idea may be revealed by the use of supporting details alone. If a student wants to describe how tough football practice is, for instance, he doesn't have to write, "Practice is really hard work." By vividly describing the daily workout, the athlete can imply the main idea just as powerfully as if it had stated it in a topic sentence. **L2**

Practicing the Skill

1. That a pet will receive good care at the Purr-fect Care Veterinary Hospital.
2. Supporting details include trained, caring staff; small animal specialists; clean, comfy kennels.
3. The final "quote" from the mascot is unnecessary but contributes to the ad's fun.

Application Activity

Make sure students realize that many ads employ far more than words to persuade the public. Point out that some of the most persuasive supporting details are in the visual images, not in the text.

MEETING INDIVIDUAL NEEDS

MULTIPLE LEARNING STYLES

Linguistic The main idea of a piece of writing must be strongly implied by the supporting details. **Activity** Have each student cut out and bring to school a short, interesting article from a magazine or newspaper. Ask them to copy one or two sentences that best express the main idea (check to see if they have been accurate). Then, have them "white out" the same sentences in their printed copy. Have students form groups and distribute articles to each group, making sure that the original owner does not receive his or her own article. Ask students to read all the articles distributed to their group and to discuss the wording of sentences to replace the ones that have been deleted. Ask students to compare their reconstructed sentences with the originals. Use an example from each group to discuss how main ideas may be inferred from supporting details.

1 FOCUS

🔔 Bellringer

Have students read the opening paragraph of this section and ask them to recall a time when they have made a decision to confront a friend in an attempt to resolve a conflict. Why did they make the decision? How did it work out? Would they adopt the same policy today? Invite volunteers to share experiences with the class.

✏️ You may use Graphic Organizer Transparency 12–2 to introduce this section.

Graphic Organizer Transparency 12–2

Resolution Strategy	Advantage	Disadvantage
1.		
2.		
3.		
4.		
5.		
6.		

■ Visual Instruction

Answer Students might give answers such as "What is left to be done? Why is there a conflict? What can be done to resolve it?"

Confronting Conflict

GUIDE TO READING

Objectives

1. Describe possible losses and gains in conflict resolution.
2. Classify forces behind conflict resolution as helpful or hindering.
3. Justify a decision to resolve conflict.
4. Compare and contrast conflict-resolution strategies.
5. Organize a conflict-resolution meeting.
6. Develop strategies for coping with unresolved conflict.

Terms to Learn

avoidance	compromise
accommodation	negotiation
coercion	collaboration

Imagine your history class group project is due next Monday. You think your group should work together every night until you complete the project. Another member argues that the group should just wait and work together all day Saturday. You've analyzed the people and the issues involved in the conflict. But now what do you do?

Now that you've analyzed the different elements of the conflict, it's time to decide on a course of action. Do the benefits of resolving the conflict outweigh the costs of confronting your friends? The answer may help you determine whether to try to resolve it or to cope with it. If you decide to resolve the conflict, you will need to know how to analyze the forces behind resolution and determine which resolution strategy to use. In any case, you'll need to develop a plan and polish your communication skills.

OUTCOMES OF CONFLICT RESOLUTION

Before you begin to resolve a conflict, you'll want to consider what you and the other people involved have to gain or lose. If

Part of working on a group project involves taking responsibility for your part of the work. If there is conflict in a group, what questions would you ask to decide on a course of action for dealing with the conflict?

RESOURCE MANAGER

Teaching Tools
- 🔋 Interactive Lesson Planner
- 📁 Reproducible Lesson Plan 12–2
- 📁 Application Activities 12–2

Reproducible Masters
- 📁 Guided Reading Activity Workbook 12–2
- 📁 Enrichment Activity 12–2
- 📁 Reteaching Activity 12–2
- 📁 Section Quiz 12–2
- 📁 Transparency Strategies and Activities Booklet 12–2

Transparencies
- 📷 Graphic Organizer Transparency 12–2
- 📷 Chapter 12 Teaching Transparency

Technology Resources
- 🔋💾 Interactive Tutor Self-Assessment Software
- 🔋 Presentation Plus! Software
- 🔋💾 ExamView® Pro Testmaker
- 🔋 PuzzleMaker Software
- 💻 **communicationapplications.glencoe.com**

the others have nothing to gain and something to lose by resolving the conflict, your work toward finding a resolution is likely to be opposed. However, if you can imagine a resolution that allows everyone to gain something, you may have a better chance at bringing the conflict to an end.

Identifying Gains

Imagine that you and a coworker are in conflict over the use of an office computer. Computer time currently is decided on a first-come, first-served basis, which means one of you is left waiting a great deal of the time.

Since you currently use the computer more than half of the time, you may want to keep the situation as it is. Resolving it means you risk losing some computer time. On the other hand, if giving up some computer time will greatly improve your relationship with your coworker, you might be willing to work it out. You'll want to look at the conflict from all sides to see what everyone has to gain from the present situation as well as what each party might gain from a resolution.

Social gains, such as enjoying a pleasant working environment or making a positive impression on someone, may be worth some sacrifices. At home, you might do some chore that you dislike, such as folding the laundry, because it makes your family members, whom you care about, happy. Work gains also are important incentives for conflict resolution. Two coworkers in conflict may be less helpful to one another on a major project than they would be if the conflict were resolved.

Identifying Losses

What will a resolution cost you and the others involved in a conflict? Is there some way that this conflict works in your favor? If so, you may lose that benefit if you

Being late for a meeting can cause conflict with group members. What costs must you consider when deciding whether or not to resolve a conflict?

successfully resolve the conflict. Is there some danger involved in confronting the other party or parties in the conflict? If the person you're in conflict with is your supervisor at work, you may put a possible promotion or even your job in jeopardy. Is it possible that the other person will be angered by your confrontation and create different problems for you? For instance, if you confront a coworker today, will he or she undermine you in a future project?

Imagine that you and a close friend work together on the yearbook staff. Your friend always arrives late for group meetings and rarely completes his assigned tasks. Should you confront him over his conflict with the group? Would your friendship, both with him and with mutual friends, possibly suffer? If he doesn't distinguish between your roles as

Managing Conflict **395**

2 TEACH

Identifying Gains
Point out that gains are not always evident when you are exploring the possibility of conflict resolution. Lead students to understand that the cessation of conflict-related stress may itself outweigh any material loss entailed by a resolution. Invite volunteers to share with the class experiences they have had when the resolution of a conflict resulted in unexpected gains. **L2**

Visual Instruction

Answer Students should consider the possible gains and losses both for themselves and others involved in the conflict.

EXTENDING THE CONTENT

Conflicts in Fiction and Film No one in literature has had a more famous decision to make regarding a conflict than Shakespeare's Hamlet. However, he is just one of many characters in fiction and film whose conflict propels the plot to either a tragic or happy ending. Studying the decisions of fictitious characters is a good way of broadening students' understanding of conflict.

Activity Ask students to recall a film or book in which a character's decision to resolve or not to resolve a conflict is central to the plot. Have them summarize their character's dilemma for the class. Ask them to include an evaluation of the decision and to speculate what would have happened if the character had acted in another manner. What would they themselves have done under similar circumstances? Encourage the class to ask questions after each presentation.

COMMUNICATION *Strategies*

DECIDING WHETHER TO RESOLVE A CONFLICT

Have students read the checklist on resolving a conflict. Suggest that while all situations are different, they can all be analyzed in the same manner. Ask students to consider the sources of conflict listed below, discussing each one in relation to the checklist: your friend refuses to talk to anyone about an eating disorder, your boss wants you to do extra work without pay, your sister borrowed your CDs without asking. Which situations might warrant a resolution? **L2**

Grammar Tip

Conjunctive adverbs, such as *therefore, however, furthermore, moreover, nevertheless,* and *subsequently,* often introduce statements or serve to link main clauses. These clauses must be separated by a semicolon or period. Conjunctive adverbs also occur in common expressions such as *that is* and *for example.* These are generally set apart with a comma from the rest of the clause they introduce. Under the heading Forces That Help Resolution, there are four consecutive sentences that begin in this manner.

members of the yearbook staff and as friends, he may have trouble with the confrontation. However, he might appreciate your talking to him privately so that he's not embarrassed by a group confrontation. Try to consider both the possible benefits and costs to your goals before deciding whether to cope with or to resolve the conflict.

FORCES BEHIND RESOLUTION

Imagine that you are involved in a conflict over limited supplies at your job. Your coworkers are generally cooperative, and you anticipate they would be willing to find a solution to this problem. However, your boss is not generally open to new ideas and has reacted defensively to suggestions from the staff in the past. Many forces are at work behind the situation. They can either help you achieve a resolution or make the process much more difficult.

COMMUNICATION *Strategies*

DECIDING WHETHER TO RESOLVE A CONFLICT

✓ **Look at the severity of the conflict. Is it serious?**

✓ **Determine whether resolving the conflict will result in gains or losses.**

✓ **Analyze the risks involved. Is a resolution worth the risk?**

✓ **Analyze what forces might support or hinder a resolution.**

✓ **Determine what information and communication skills are necessary to proceed toward a resolution.**

Forces That Help Resolution

After examining the office-supplies conflict, you may find that conditions are favorable for a resolution. For example, one argument may be that budgets are being cut throughout your company. Therefore, there is only a limited amount of money available for supplies. However, after investigating the issues, you have discovered that your company already has purchased plenty of supplies. Furthermore, you think you have developed a plan for sharing them that should not inconvenience other departments. If you were to analyze what is in favor of finding a resolution, you might note that

- most of the time everyone in the office tries to cooperate and work together
- there seem to be enough resources for everyone
- you have a plan you think will work

Each of these points is a positive force that would help you resolve your office-supplies conflict. However, before you begin working toward a resolution, you need to consider one more thing: What might work against the resolution of this conflict?

Forces That Hinder Resolution

Sometimes, a specific set of circumstances can present a barrier to conflict resolution. Some potential barriers to resolving the office-supplies conflict might include that

- your boss is not generally open to new ideas for the company
- your boss is anticipating more budget cuts in the near future
- your boss sometimes reacts defensively to suggestions from staff members

MEETING INDIVIDUAL NEEDS — MULTIPLE LEARNING STYLES

Interpersonal Analyzing the severity of a conflict requires observation and empathy. Students who are skilled at understanding the fears, feelings, and beliefs of others will know that much can be learned from accurate people-watching.

Activity Prepare a few minutes of selected video clips from films or television programs in which the characters are experiencing some form of conflict. Play these to the students with no sound and ask them to infer from nonverbal clues what the characters are feeling, thinking, and even saying. Allow students to make notes based on their observations; then, have them form groups to discuss the most likely scenarios. Invite groups to share their views with the class. Finally, play the clips again, this time with sound. Discuss how students read, or misread, the situations.

Each of these barriers may present quite a challenge. At this point, you'll need to ask yourself if pursuing the solution in the face of these difficulties is worthwhile.

Once you have a clear idea of the forces at work behind your conflict, the time has arrived for a decision. Should you try to resolve it or learn to cope with it?

CHOOSING A RESOLUTION STRATEGY

Imagine that you have weighed the possible outcomes of a conflict resolution. Because the positives outweigh the negatives, you have decided to try to resolve the conflict. However, you still have another decision to make. What strategy will you use to reach a resolution?

There are many different ways to approach a conflict. Consider the advantages and disadvantages of each before choosing the one that's right for your situation. The six most commonly used resolution strategies are

- avoidance
- compromise
- accommodation
- negotiation
- coercion
- collaboration

Avoidance

One way to deal with a conflict is to avoid it altogether. Avoidance is keeping away from or withdrawing from something. Avoidance

RESOLUTION STRATEGIES

Consider	When One of These Is True
Avoidance	• The issue is trivial. • You cannot win. • The negatives of confrontation outweigh the benefits of resolution. • It is possible to unobtrusively avoid the others involved.
Accommodation	• You find out you were wrong and others were right. • The issue is less important to you than to the others involved. • Harmony is more important to you than the issue.
Coercion	• It is imperative that you have your way on the issue. • You are willing to live with the consequences of coercion. • You have sufficient perceived power to force your will upon the others.
Compromise	• Your goals are more important, but you can give in on some issues. • You can achieve a temporary settlement for a complex issue. • It becomes clear that no party will give up its entire position.
Negotiation	• You have something to trade for what you want to accomplish. • The others involved are willing to bargain.
Collaboration	• All involved have concerns that are too important to be compromised or negotiated away. • A long-term relationship between/among the parties is important. • A goal is to build consensus among all parties. • The others involved are willing to collaborate.

can be physical or psychological. At times, there are advantages to using avoidance. Sometimes, however, avoidance can be a negative resolution strategy.

Physical Avoidance You might choose physical avoidance of your conflict. That is, you may try to stay away from the others involved in the conflict. This is different from coping because you are not deciding to "live with" the current situation. Rather, you are taking action to end the conflict.

Managing Conflict **397**

Avoidance

Point out that avoidance is one of the most commonly employed strategies in conflict resolution, though not always for good reasons. Before they read ahead, ask students to suggest some of the advantages and disadvantages of avoidance. What makes it an attractive strategy for some people? **L2**

BUSINESS BRIEF

Some businesses thrive on conflict. "I never hesitated to promote someone I didn't like," wrote Thomas J. Watson Jr., former Chairman of IBM. "I looked for those sharp, scratchy, harsh, almost unpleasant guys who see and tell you about things as they really are." Encourage students to discuss Watson's theory that what you don't like to hear may be good for you. What might be the disadvantages of seeking advice from friends?

Application Activities 12–2

CRITICAL THINKING ACTIVITY

Not all situations fit easily into one of the resolution strategies listed on this page. Have students form groups of three or four and ask them to spend five minutes listing situations that might need to be resolved. While they are working, write the following headings at separate points on the chalkboard: *Avoidance, Accommodation, Coercion, Compromise, Negotiation,* and *Collaboration.* Then, assign each group to a workstation at the board and ask them to copy onto the board a situation from their list that would best be solved by the manner described in the heading. At a given signal, have them move around the room from station to station, matching situations to headings. After each heading has several situations, discuss their choices and what alternatives would have been worth considering.

Physical Avoidance

Ask students what they think about physical avoidance. How many of them have ever adopted this policy as a means of conflict resolution? Have them think of situations in which avoidance would be the most appropriate means of dealing with conflict. What are its benefits? What are its disadvantages? *(Students may suggest that avoidance serves to eliminate the problem altogether. They may also suggest that someone who avoids a problem physically may be perceived as a coward.)* Can students think of situations when physical avoidance is not a possible option? **L2**

Psychological Avoidance

Ask students if they have ever participated in a conflict in which one of the parties chose to ignore or deny the issue under dispute. How did they feel about the experience? In their opinion, was this a successful way of dealing with the conflict? **L3**

■ Visual Instruction

Answer Students might answer that conflict accommodation is maintaining harmony with others by giving in to their wishes.

For example, you may be in conflict with a friend who is raising money for a charity event. Every day, the friend asks you for a contribution, even though you have explained it is not in your budget. You are becoming increasingly irritated by the friend's requests. However, by choosing to avoid the friend and not return his or her phone calls, you are resolving the conflict. The friend is no longer able to bother you. Once the event is over, you can stop avoiding your friend and resume your relationship.

Psychological Avoidance Avoidance also can be psychological. You can choose to ignore whatever the others say or do that brings up a conflict by refusing to respond to their words or actions. You might even deny that there is a conflict at all.

Problems with Avoidance Because avoidance is a one-sided approach to conflict resolution, it can have some negative effects. Instead of resolving a conflict, avoidance actually may intensify it. If the parties involved in the conflict are highly interdependent, avoidance can create even more problems. For instance, even though you may avoid discussing the issue in conflict, you cannot force others to stop discussing it. This can make you appear detached or uninformed and can provide fuel for harmful gossip and rumors. Avoidance may not be the best choice if you must be in continual contact with the others involved.

Avoidance may require a strong self-image. It can take a great deal of positive self-talk to manage the resentment and frustration you may feel from others involved in a conflict. Without managing your feelings, you may reach a point at which the avoidance of one conflict creates new conflicts intrapersonally and in many other contexts in your life.

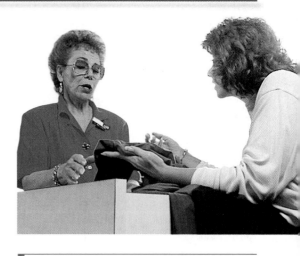

■ **Businesses utilize accommodation to resolve conflicts with customers.** Define conflict accommodation.

Advantages of Avoidance Even though avoidance as a strategy has its drawbacks, there are some circumstances in which it might be a wise response. Avoidance tends to work more easily in social contexts than at work. However, if your boss tends to put you down each time you make a suggestion, you might choose to remain silent for a while. This can help you avoid conflict until you can determine what to do about the situation.

Accommodation

Conflict accommodation is maintaining harmony with others by giving in to their wishes. This is a variation of the avoidance strategy. In effect, you are avoiding conflict by choosing to do what the others want done in the situation, regardless of your ideas or feelings. To accommodators, relationships are more important than issues.

There are some good reasons to choose accommodation as a conflict-resolution strategy. You might choose this strategy if you discover you have made a mistake. Admitting your error

---

MEETING INDIVIDUAL NEEDS — MULTIPLE LEARNING STYLES

Visual-Spatial Point out that in an age of increasing internationalization, universal symbols have become a common language, from road signs to the icons on computer screens. Improving one's visual literacy is an important element in gaining communication skills. Students with a strong visual-spatial sense can enhance the class's appreciation of communication concepts.

Activity Have students read the table on page 397 and discuss with them the six resolution strategies. Ask them to imagine that the organizers of an international convention on conflict resolution want to use symbols for each of the six steps. Tell students that they have entered a competition to design the symbols. Have them create posters illustrating their symbols and invite them to explain their designs to the class as if they were presenting their submission to the convention organizers.

and accommodating the others would be a sign of strength and intelligence. You might also choose accommodation if the issue you disagree upon is of relatively little importance to you and seems to be of great importance to someone else. You might also choose accommodation if the rewards for putting up with the others' demands are greater than the cost of asserting your rights. For example, you might put up with a rude, but reliable, customer in order to keep his or her repeat business.

A disadvantage to choosing accommodation is the possibility that you will resent having to accommodate the other person, particularly if you feel he or she does not often accommodate your wishes. If so, resentment may build and harm your relationship in the long run. Also, if you choose accommodation to resolve a conflict over values, you are likely to both resent the other person and be angry with yourself for not living up to your personal standards. Accommodation, in these instances, may be very costly to you.

Coercion

Coercion is another way to resolve conflict. Coercion is trying to force others to go along with your wishes. If you are a manager or supervisor, you may use your position of authority to make others agree with your decisions. Coercion is only possible if one person involved in a conflict is perceived as more powerful than the others.

The obvious advantage to coercion is the possibility of getting your way. The disadvantages are equally obvious. People forced into an agreement won't like it and may even try to retaliate against you some other time. This may take many different forms, including not cooperating with you in the future because you coerced them on this issue.

Even those who agree with you on the issue may be offended by your tactic of forcing their cooperation. If so, they may speak out against your methods and join those who oppose you. At best, coercion may let you "win" this issue, but you are very likely to pay a price for it later.

Compromise

Compromise is a resolution choice that may not be as costly as coercion, accommodation, or avoidance. Compromise is settling differences by having each party give up something. When you compromise, you say that you are willing to "give in" on certain issues if the others involved will make similar sacrifices.

COMMUNICATION PRACTICE LAB

Choosing Accommodation

To practice using accommodation as a conflict resolution strategy, follow these steps:

Step 1 Working with a partner, create a list of adjectives you might use to describe an accommodator.

Step 2 Discuss which of these adjectives might be considered positive attributes, such as *generous*, and which might be negative, such as *wimpy*.

Step 3 With your partner, brainstorm a situation when accommodation would be a good choice for conflict resolution.

Step 4 Act out your chosen situation for another set of student partners. First, portray the accommodator in a way that highlights the positive aspects of accommodation. Then, switch roles and portray the negative aspects of accommodation.

Managing Conflict **399**

COMMUNICATION PRACTICE LAB

Choosing Accommodation

Invite pairs of volunteers to act out their accommodation situations for the class. Which role did the students find more convincing, the positive or the negative? Ask the performers which side they found easier to present. **L2**

GLENCOE Online

For an additional Practice Lab for this section, have students visit the *Glencoe Communication Applications* Web site at communicationapplications.glencoe.com. Click on Communication Practice Lab 12–2. **L1**

DID YOU KNOW?

The word *coerce*, meaning "to compel," originates from the Latin verb *coercere*. It is formed from the prefix *co-*, meaning "together," plus *arcere*, meaning "to enclose." *Arcere* stems from the noun *arca*, Latin for a chest or box. Students might agree that very few people would voluntarily allow themselves to be enclosed in a box together!

INTERDISCIPLINARY CONNECTION

History Warfare represents a state of conflict in which all options except coercion have been eliminated. As is the case with any coerced settlement, the treaties that end wars sometimes result in bitterness and further conflict. History offers important lessons in conflict resolution.

Activity Have students consult a social studies teacher or librarian for examples of conflicts in history that have been resolved as a result of coercion. Ask students to research a subject of their choice and to prepare a presentation giving the background of the conflict, the circumstances of its resolution, and its long-term results. Could this conflict have been handled differently? Were its results entirely beneficial for the victor? Compare the results of the conflicts presented and discuss with the class the historical lessons to be learned from coercive policies.

GLOBAL COMMUNICATION

Competition vs. Cooperation

Point out that in an era of global trade, representatives from different cultures are frequently meeting to discuss treaties and strategies. Ask students if they would expect those from other cultures to accept American workplace values. Whose responsibility is it to learn about other cultures? Can Americans respect people of different cultural backgrounds while encouraging them to express their opinions? Lead students to understand that "different" is not the same as "inferior" and that the norm in any one culture is not always the best way to resolve differences. **L2**

BUSINESS BRIEF

Lee Iacocca, outspoken former head of Chrysler Corporation, believes that American and Japanese management styles have more in common than most people think. "I know the Japanese fairly well," he writes. "In my dealings with them, they talk a lot about consensus, but there's always one guy behind the scenes who ends up making the tough decisions. . . . When the chips are down, the yen stops at the top guy's desk." Ask students if they share Iacocca's opinion that decisions must ultimately be made by individuals.

■ Visual Instruction

Answer Students may say that compromise is a good choice when there is no hope of attaining what you really want and you are willing to settle for a little less.

GLOBAL COMMUNICATION

Competition vs. Cooperation

American, Swedish, and Norwegian cultures are sometimes described as individualistic, direct, independent, and competitive and sometimes may challenge authority. Japanese, Arabic, and Latin American cultures typically avoid openly challenging authority and practice indirect communication approaches and cooperative problem solving. Imagine two people from these diverse cultural categories having a difference of opinion on an issue. What conflict resolution strategies would you use to encourage a solution?

Generally, the compromisers cooperate on all issues except for those that are most important to them. Compromise is a very common strategy among political factions and groups that make budget decisions.

Compromise is a worthwhile choice when you have no hope of attaining everything you really want and are willing to settle for a little less. Before deciding on entering a compromise, you should be sure about what you are willing to give up and what you refuse to sacrifice.

The advantage of compromise is that usually each person involved is at least partially pleased with the resolution. The disadvantage is that it may result in a "watered down" version of what might have been accomplished without compromise.

You might choose to use a compromise strategy if you reach a stalemate and cannot move on until an issue is resolved. If you feel you cannot give up any part of your position simply to reach agreement, compromise may not be the best choice.

Negotiation

Conflict negotiation is bargaining with others to gain what you want. As with the compromise strategy, negotiation requires you to determine what you are and are not willing to give up in the final solution. Unlike the compromise strategy, however, all trade-offs may not be directly related to the conflict issue. For example, labor negotiators bargaining for a pay increase may accept better benefits or vacation time instead. Similarly, when negotiating with your brother or sister over mowing the lawn, you may agree to do that chore if he or she will loan you his car for one day. Negotiation often involves giving up your entire position on an issue in order to get something else.

■ The Congress of the United States practices compromise when passing a bill. When is compromise a good choice?

MEETING INDIVIDUAL NEEDS   ENGLISH LANGUAGE LEARNERS

Diversity in Conflict Resolution   Newcomers to this country do not automatically adopt American approaches to conflict resolution. Many English language learners are surprised, and sometimes offended, by the strategies they encounter in their new culture.

Activity   Invite students from among the English language learners in your class (or volunteers from the larger school community) to form a panel and to share with other students the difficulties they have faced in resolving conflicts with the mainstream culture. Do they find Americans too outspoken and individualistic? Encourage members of the class to ask questions about the panel's observations. Lead students to appreciate the need for knowledge and understanding in a diverse society.

ELL

In negotiation, you assertively bargain for the best deal you can get. The others involved do the same. The goal is to grant something that each person involved wants. Negotiation only works if each party is willing to trade with the others in the dispute.

Negotiation is a more assertive approach to conflict resolution than compromise because it is competitive. Each party gives up items equally in a compromise. However, negotiation involves trying to make the most favorable deal for yourself that you can.

Collaboration

Put simply, collaboration is working together to achieve some result. People who choose to collaborate believe that working with others will create the best possible solution to the conflict. Collaboration does not involve competition. Rather, collaborators know that they will have to work together over a long period of time. Therefore, they try to maintain positive relationships with the others involved in a conflict. The parties involved genuinely try to understand what each other wants out of the interaction. They also try to explain clearly what they want. They then work together to accomplish all goals.

In collaboration, everyone agrees that there is a problem. They also all agree that the problem is causing an undesirable conflict. No one likes having the conflict, so they agree to work together to find a way to resolve it.

IMPLEMENTING STRATEGIES

Once you have chosen the strategy that will best resolve your conflict, you may think the difficult part is over. What happens if one of the others involved has chosen a different strategy? It's important to learn how to bring everyone together in a conflict-resolution meeting

interNET
ACTIVITY

Negotiating As a class, brainstorm a list of school issues and then choose one that seems to be of most concern to students. Use information found in your text and through a reliable Internet search engine to prepare to negotiate a win/win solution to the conflict. Set up a meeting between the parties involved. Develop a plan to bring the concerned parties together. Then, prepare a list of ten meeting guidelines for distribution to meeting participants.

where you can share strategies and choose one that meets the most needs. After all, if everyone agrees with the plan, they will be more likely to work toward making it happen.

Preparing for a Conflict-Resolution Meeting

At times, the best plans for conflict resolution may be ruined by poor attitudes, unrealistic expectations, or poor communication skills. By taking action early, you can help ward off these barriers to resolution.

Assume a Positive Attitude. Before undertaking a conflict-resolution meeting, arm yourself with a win/win attitude. That is, come to the meeting with the attitude that everyone can gain something by working together. Rid yourself of biases and try to see others' points of view in a positive light.

To do this, try to think of others in positive terms—and always speak of them that way. Avoid being defensive. Instead, try to be

Managing Conflict **401**

Collaboration

Lead students to understand that there are situations in which collaboration can be a controversial method of conflict resolution. Point out that in Europe during World War II the term *collaborator* came to mean "one who cooperated with the occupying Nazi forces" and that fifty years later people were still being brought to justice for collaboration. Ask students why they believe people might collaborate with unjust, or even violent, parties. **L3**

interNET
ACTIVITY

Negotiating Issues might include dress code, computer-use policies, attendance policy, prom activities, security measures (surveillance cameras, metal detectors) and open/closed campus rules. In determining their ten guidelines for participants, students can conduct an Internet search on "school conflict" or "conflict resolution" for suggestions on negotiating procedures. **L2**

MULTIPLE LEARNING STYLES

MEETING INDIVIDUAL NEEDS

Linguistic "Jack Sprat could eat no fat; /His wife could eat no lean./And so between them both/They licked the platter clean." Point out that this old nursery rhyme is a good example of a negotiated settlement: Both sides end up feeling that they are winners. Remind students also of Aesop's fable about the fox and the stork, in which negotiation failed to take place and both sides lost. (The fox invited the stork to supper and gave him soup in a flat dish, which the stork, with its long bill, could not eat. In retaliation, the stork served the fox soup in a long, thin tube, which left the fox hungry.)

Activity Ask students to write a fable or rhyme for children in which negotiation or compromise takes place (or fails to do so). Have them share their creative writings with the class.

Assume a Positive Attitude

Point out that it is often difficult to act positively toward a person or group with whom you are in conflict. Your own stress level may be high, and you may rightfully blame the other party for your discomfort. Ask students what may happen if anger or negative behavior takes over. Lead students to understand that negative behavior may well end the whole process. Anger has its place, but not in a conflict-resolution meeting. The person who can remain calm and objective is likely to be in the best position to negotiate to his or her advantage. **ELL**

Visual Instruction

Answer Students may indicate that staying positive, being reasonable, acting courteously, and communicating clearly can help in the meeting.

---

objective and open-minded. Also, make up your mind to cooperate with others in the meeting.

Behave Realistically. Make sure you understand what you are trying to resolve so that you can offer realistic solutions. Also, as you found out in Chapter 3, realize that your point of view, or your perception, may not be shared by others in the conflict. The more reasonable your proposal and behavior, the more acceptable your ideas will seem.

Plan for the resolution to take time. It requires patience to listen carefully to the issues and to propose realistic solutions. Understand that the conflict may not be resolved in one meeting. Be realistic about what you can accomplish each time you meet.

Communicate Clearly. In a conflict, you and the other parties involved already disagree. You do not want to complicate matters

COMMUNICATION *Strategies*

COMMUNICATING TO ACHIEVE A RESOLUTION

- ✓ Listen actively.
- ✓ Seek clarification when you don't understand.
- ✓ Use frequent perception checks.
- ✓ Express your ideas as clearly as possible.
- ✓ Pay attention to feedback and clear up misunderstandings early.
- ✓ Be courteous.
- ✓ Use nonverbal behavior that is appropriate for achieving a resolution.

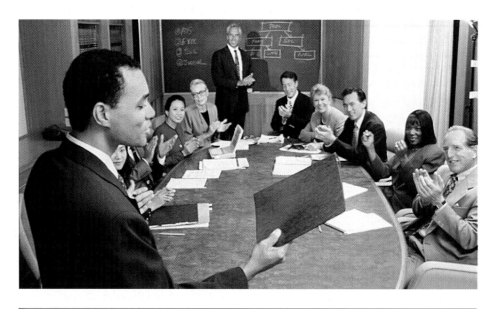

■ **Conflict resolution is affected by the communication skills of group members.** What communication skills will help you in a conflict resolution meeting?

EXTENDING THE CONTENT

Managing Other People's Anger In *Smart Moves*, a book of advice for businesspeople, authors Sam Deep and Lyle Sussman give the following steps for "defusing another person's anger": Determine not to get angry yourself; get on the same physical level as the other person; keep quiet; express concern nonverbally; listen to understand; speak in a calm voice; ask questions.

Activity Write these seven points on the chalkboard and ask students what they believe the purpose of the guidelines to be. In a class discussion, analyze why these tactics might have the effect of reducing anger in another person. Encourage students to share experiences in which they have used these or related methods to calm down an adversary.

with poor communication and frequent misunderstandings. To avoid these problems, remember the important suggestions in the Communication Strategies checklist on the previous page.

Conducting the Meeting

Sometimes, conflict resolution takes place in a formal meeting called just for that purpose. Other times, however, this meeting may be much less formal. For example, imagine that you typically see the person you're in conflict with at the same time each day at work. You may try to initiate the conflict resolution on one of these occasions, rather than scheduling a more formal meeting.

Take the Initiative. Before a formal or informal meeting can begin, someone must take the first step. By initiating the discussion, you show your willingness to work toward a resolution of the conflict.

After your initial statement or question, you may choose to patiently listen to what the others have to say about the conflict. This can serve as a valuable perception check, helping to clarify the issues at stake.

Remember to remain as objective as possible during the discussion. At times, the ideas and responses of others may surprise you. Use critical listening skills to discern the basis for their points of view. Also, use deliberative listening to consider what the others want you to do about the conflict. Finally, use empathic listening skills to try to understand how the others feel about the conflict.

Often, it is valuable to use a feed-forward technique to prepare the others to hear your point of view. For example, you might say, "If I understand correctly, you said . . ." Then, state your feelings clearly, avoiding defensive or accusatory language. Use this opportunity to resolve any misunderstandings the others may

have about your point of view. Convey a general attitude that you are open to other ideas and genuinely want to achieve a solution.

Employ a Resolution Strategy. Your next step in the meeting is to decide upon or implement an appropriate resolution strategy either by suggesting one yourself or by developing it as a group. Remember that even though you may decide on one particular strategy, this decision may change over the course of resolving the conflict. For example, everyone may begin with a desire to collaborate. However, at some point, you may hit a stalemate, try to negotiate, and finally determine that the best chance of resolving the conflict is through compromise. For this reason, try to remain flexible and positive about the conflict-resolution process as it unfolds.

Managing Conflict **403**

Practice for the Workplace

Choices and Consequences In the workplace, as in school, you will have to make choices in determining the best way to resolve conflict. Unresolved conflict can be stressful and it is important that you assertively, but not timidly or aggressively, express yourself in order to get your needs met in the workplace.

BUSINESS PRACTICE *Activity*

In groups of three or four, develop three types of responses—timid, assertive, and aggressive—to the scenarios given below.

- Other students repeatedly ask to copy my homework. This bothers me, but I also don't want to make them mad at me.
- My friend and I carpool to work. He is late at least twice each week, which makes me late and often gets me in trouble.
- My coworker repeatedly asks me to put his name on the weekly reports that I develop.

Practice for the Workplace

Choices and Consequences Point out that timid people, who hesitantly express their opinions, may end up feeling resentful because their needs do not get met. Aggressive people, who make demands in a threatening fashion, may feel guilty and frustrated. An assertive approach involves a controlled and honest expression of one's feelings and opinions. These three approaches can be exemplified as follows and applied to the second bulleted example under the Business Practice Activity:

"I was late to work again last week." (timid)

"You idiot! You always make me late for work. You can't be trusted." (aggressive)

"I need to be on time. If you can be at my house by 7:45 each day, we can continue to carpool; otherwise, you will have to find another ride to work." (assertive)

Discuss the probable effects of the different approaches. **L2**

BUSINESS BRIEF

Mary Kay Ash, founder of Mary Kay Cosmetics, believed that listening was an essential business skill: "When someone enters my office to speak with me, I don't allow anything to distract my attention. . . . I look directly at the person. Even if a gorilla were to walk into the room, I probably wouldn't notice it." Discuss with students the importance of giving people one's undivided attention in conflict resolution.

CRITICAL THINKING ACTIVITY

Many familiar sayings describe various aspects of the conflict resolution process. Have students review their knowledge of the conflict-resolution process by forming pairs and matching the following proverbs: **1.** Tit for tat., **2.** Soft words win hard hearts., **3.** Come let us reason together., **4.** Might makes right., **5.** Half a loaf is better than none., **6.** One who fights and runs away lives to fight another day., with the appropriate strategies in the second column: **A.** avoidance, **B.** accommodation, **C.** coercion, **D.** compromise, **E.** negotiation, **F.** collaboration Discuss with students their answers. Which of the proverbs do they find most convincing? Can they think of other well-known sayings that describe conflict-resolution strategies? *(Answers: 1. E; 2. B; 3. F; 4. C; 5. D; 6. A)*

Know When to End

Point out that high school classes are a sort of business meeting—with education as the business. Ask how it is that some classes seem endless while others of exactly the same length go by rapidly. Have students share their classroom experiences. Invite them to comment on factors influencing their ability to concentrate and levels of stress. What can a good teacher do to encourage a smooth, effective "meeting?" What are the responsibilities of the student? **ELL**

Communication Tip

Peer mediation is an increasingly popular means of reducing conflicts at high schools and universities. By this process, students trained in conflict resolution act as facilitators at meetings between fellow students who are in a dispute. Encourage students to learn more about this form of conflict resolution by searching under the keywords "peer mediation" on the Internet.

■ Visual Instruction

Answer Students may suggest that they come to the meeting with a win/win attitude, rid themselves of biases, think of others in positive terms, avoid being defensive, be objective and openminded, and make up their minds to cooperate.

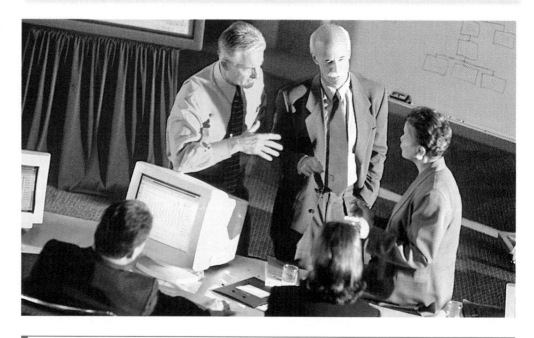

■ **Meetings can be used to generate ideas for conflict resolution.** What are some strategies for assuming a positive attitude during a meeting?

As you work toward a resolution, remember that all sides need to cooperate in the effort. You'll be more successful if everyone stays flexible, considers a variety of options, and works toward a logical and reasonable resolution to the conflict.

Know When to End. There is little to be gained in very lengthy "marathon" meetings. Particularly in the case of collaboration, but also in compromise and negotiation, you may create too many alternatives to sort out at one meeting. In these cases, summarize all the alternatives generated and suggest postponing a decision on any of them until another meeting time. This allows both sides to fully consider all the possibilities.

Another reason to avoid lengthy meetings is that people generally do not work well under stress for long periods of time. The emotions, concentration level, and intense discussion involved in resolving a conflict can create a great deal of stress. After a while, tempers can flare and communication can become careless. For this reason, it is best to limit conflict-resolution meetings to no more than one hour. Then, if you must postpone the final decision, do so on a positive note. Be sure to congratulate everyone for working hard to resolve the conflict.

If Conflict Flares During the Meeting If one or more parties become too emotionally involved in the conflict discussion, communication can become hostile or otherwise unproductive. In some instances, the discussion can actually renew the conflict or introduce new areas of disagreement. If any of these situations occurs, end the interaction quickly. If possible, you should delay

INCLUSION STRATEGIES

Learning Disabled Key to the success of any meeting is the ability of its participants to listen. Lead students to understand that listening, like speaking, is a skill that requires practice.
Activity Have students arrange their desks in a circle. Ask them to review the chapter they have just been reading and invite them to reflect on it. Reflections may include observations on what they have learned, aspects of the subject about which they would like to know more, personal anecdotes relating to material in the text, and so on. Ask for volunteers to give their reflections. After several students have had a chance to speak without interruption, stop the process and say, "Can anyone repeat what one of your classmates has just said?" Try to obtain summaries of each student's reflections. Repeat the process with a fresh round of observations.

setting another meeting time until after everyone has had a chance to cool down.

If a Stalemate Is Reached It is possible that your conflict-resolution meeting will result in a stalemate. Particularly during compromise or negotiation, the members may reach a point where they "dig in" and refuse to budge on an issue. At this point, you can remark that this particular issue seems to be the main point under contention and may need a little more thought. Again, end on a friendly note. Restate that you are confident that the conflict can be resolved in some mutually-agreeable way and set another meeting time.

If Agreement Is Reached Congratulations! If you were able to find a solution, get everyone involved in implementing it. Often, even when compromise and negotiation are used, the solution will not be enthusiastically approved by everyone. However, by helping everyone focus on their obvious gains—as well as the benefit of no longer having to deal with the conflict—you will gain their cooperation in quickly and easily implementing the resolution.

COPING WITH UNRESOLVED CONFLICT

Unfortunately, not all conflicts are resolved. Sometimes, even your best attempt at conflict resolution can fail. No resolution strategy comes with a guarantee of success. Also, after your initial analysis of a conflict, you may decide to skip the resolution process altogether. When a conflict goes unresolved, you may have to cope with the difficult people and difficult situations involved in it.

The Communication Strategies checklist points out just a few strategies for coping with unresolved conflict. You likely have developed a few of your own that meet your specific

needs. Whatever strategy you use, it is important to move on. Situations usually don't improve if you dwell on the negative.

To let a conflict go and get on with your work or relationship, it helps to focus on intrapersonal management. Be sure that you

COMMUNICATION Strategies

COPING WITH UNRESOLVED CONFLICT

- Develop an attitude of self-confidence, respect for the others involved, and understanding of both your position and theirs.
- Maintain a realistic perspective about the situation. Try to keep the big picture in mind.
- Maintain a respectful attitude toward others who disagree with you, viewing them as your equals. This will help you avoid bitterness and disillusionment.
- Try to be supportive of others and continue to care for them. This may help you salvage worthwhile relationships.
- Be positive. Look for something good even in a bad situation. This can help you put the conflict behind you.
- Realize that you are bigger than this one conflict. While it may impact your life in some way, it does not determine your destiny.
- Learn from this adversity, growing in self-understanding and wisdom. This will help you move on to greater things.

Managing Conflict **405**

COMMUNICATION Strategies

COPING WITH UNRESOLVED CONFLICT

Point out that unresolved conflict is not the same as defeat, but it can feel very similar. Encourage volunteers to describe experiences they have had when a resolution was not achieved. How did they feel about themselves and about the other parties in the conflict? **ELL**

3 ASSESS

Assign Section 2 Assessment as a homework or in-class activity.

✪ Use *Interactive Tutor Self-Assessment Software* to review Section 2.

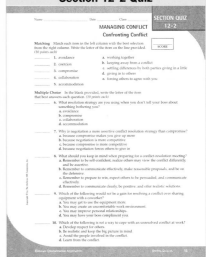

Section 12–2 Quiz

MULTIPLE LEARNING STYLES

Logical-Mathematical With its complex rules and game-flavored vocabulary, such as *win/win* and *stalemate*, it is not difficult to think of conflict resolution in terms of a competition. Use this connotation to your advantage when reviewing the chapter with your students.

Activity Have students form creative teams and ask them to design a game for two or more players using the terms and concepts contained in this chapter. Suggest a simple card game with a specially designed deck or a board game. Encourage groups to create games in which the players' understanding of the terms assists their play. Have groups present their games to the class and allow students time to experiment with them.

Reteaching Activity 12-2

MANAGING CONFLICT
Confronting Conflict

Enrichment Activity 12-2

MANAGING CONFLICT
Confronting Conflict

4 CLOSE

Have students read the opening paragraph of this section again and review their responses to the Bellringer. In the light of their reading about conflict resolution, would they now proceed to resolve the conflict with their friend differently? Ask them to explain their answers.

Extra-Credit Project

Have students interview three adults about their experiences with conflict resolution. Ask students to analyze the conflicts in terms of the concepts covered in this chapter. Have them evaluate the way these conflicts were handled. Were the resolutions successful? Would they have suggested different tactics? Have students present their findings to the class.

---

have a positive mind-set. Don't waste time thinking about a past conflict, but rather look to the future. Allowing an unresolved conflict to rule your emotions not only may destroy valuable relationships or enthusiasm but also can harmfully affect other aspects of your life. Learning to cope when situations aren't ideal is a very valuable life lesson—one that you may be called upon to use more often than you'd like. As you develop the skills of a competent communicator, you will have a knowledge base to draw from when faced with conflict situations in professional and social contexts.

Section 2 Assessment

Visit the *Glencoe Communication Applications* Web site at **communicationapplications. glencoe.com** and click on **Self-Check and Study Guide 12.2** to review your understanding of confronting conflict.

Review Key Terms

1. Define each term and write it in a sentence: avoidance, accommodation, coercion, compromise, negotiation, collaboration.

Check Understanding

2. What might be gained by confronting your neighbor about his or her barking dog? What might be lost?

3. Think of a recent conflict. List at least two forces at work behind that conflict. Classify each as helpful or hindering to the resolution of your conflict.

4. Imagine that one of your coworkers does not always wash his or her hands when preparing customers' sandwiches. Should you try to confront your coworker and resolve the conflict? Why or why not?

5. How are accommodation and compromise alike? How are they different?

6. Imagine that you are in conflict with the other members of your soccer team over where to purchase your new jerseys. What steps should you take to prepare a conflict-resolution meeting with your teammates?

7. **Apply** Imagine that you have a basic personality conflict with your boss. Because of the risks involved, you decide to cope with the conflict rather than to resolve it. Describe five things you can do to effectively cope with this unresolved conflict.

APPLICATION *Activity*

Coping With Conflict Talk with a parent or friend about a time when it was necessary for him or her to cope with a conflict. Inquire about specific intrapersonal management skills that helped make the situation tolerable. Share your findings as a class. Notice which skills were most used and brainstorm as a class how to develop or improve those skills for yourselves.

Section 2 Assessment Answers

1. Accept all reasonable sentences.
2. Gain: the noise might be eliminated. Loss: your neighbor might become increasingly hostile.
3. Accept reasonable answers.
4. Accept answers that indicate students can identify the gains and losses of conflict resolution.
5. Both accommodation and compromise involve giving in to the other party; accommodation is one-sided, compromise involves sacrifices by both sides.
6. Analyze the conflict; choose a suitable strategy; approach the meeting positively and realistically.
7. One should remain self-confident, realistic about the situation, respectful and supportive of others, and positive in attitude.

Application Activity Encourage students to think of adult role models who have particular competence in these areas and to assess how qualities such as self-confidence, realism, respect, and a positive outlook can enrich every aspect of one's life.

Communication Self-Assessment

Evaluating Your Conflict Management Skills

How Do You Rate?

On a separate sheet of paper, respond to the following statements. Put a check mark beside each skill you would like to improve.

KEY:	**A** Always	**R** Rarely
	U Usually	**N** Never
	S Sometimes	

1. I approach conflict from the point of view that it is a manageable part of life.

2. Before I act, I break conflicts down into sub-elements.

3. I think it's okay not to work at resolving some conflicts.

4. I carefully analyze my relationship to another person before I react to a conflict situation.

5. I analyze the source of the conflict before I decide how I will approach it.

6. I decide to confront a conflict only when I think the benefits of taking action outweigh the costs.

7. To me, negotiation and collaboration are better ways to resolve conflict than avoidance and accommodation.

8. If I were to chair a conflict resolution meeting, I would stop the meeting immediately if tempers started to flare.

How Do You Score?

Review your responses. Give yourself 5 points for every A, 4 for every U, 3 for every S, 2 for every R, and 1 for every N. Total your points and evaluate your score.

31–40 Excellent You may be surprised to find out how much you can improve your skills.

21–30 Good In this course, you can learn ways to make your skills better.

11–20 Fair Practice applying the skills taught in this course.

1–10 Needs Improvement Carefully monitor your improvement as you work through this course.

Setting Communication Goals

If you scored Excellent or Good, complete Part A. If your score was Fair or Needs Improvement, complete Part B.

Part A
1. I plan to put the following ideas into practice:
2. I plan to share the following information about communication with the following people:

Part B
1. The behaviors I need to change most are:
2. To bring about these changes, I will take these steps:

Managing Conflict **407**

Have students respond to the eight statements using the key on this page, then evaluate their listening strengths. Based on their scores, assign either Part A or Part B of the goal-setting activity. On an index card or sheet of paper, have students concretely define their communication goals to improve their current level of skill.

Communication Journal Activity

Have students keep a record in their Communication Journals of any conflicts occurring or resolved over the course of a week. Ask them to explain what strategies they intend to use to resolve emerging conflicts and how earlier conflicts have reached a settlement.

Communication Tip

Point out that while conflicts are inevitable in life, the personal qualities recommended on page 405 for coping with unresolved disputes may serve to prevent some conflicts from occurring in the first place.

INCLUSION STRATEGIES

MEETING INDIVIDUAL NEEDS

Less-Proficient Readers Images of conflict are a constant accompaniment to modern life, from the sulking model to the martial arts expert. Point out that the more aware we are of the visual messages that surround us, the more we will be able to detach ourselves from their influence.

Activity Have students clip out images of conflict from magazines and newspapers and ask them to design a poster collage. Suggest that they search for pictures representing a wide range of emotions and situations—from disapproval to anger—from the living room to the boardroom. Alternatively, suggest that they take a thematic approach: conflicts with parents, spouses, friends, in sports or business. Have students present their collages to the class, explaining the images and the rationale for their designs.

Communication Through Writing

Responding to Letters of Complaint

Have you ever written a letter of complaint? If so, what type of response did you receive? The way an organization responds to complaints can affect its professional reputation and, ultimately, its ability to attract customers.

Often, dissatisfied consumers send complaint letters to businesses. Sometimes, these letters are to voice a concern about some aspect of the company. Other times, the customer is seeking compensation for inferior merchandise or service. By responding appropriately to letters of complaint, a company can build good public relations and, hopefully, avoid losing a customer. When you respond to a letter of complaint, be sure to follow these steps.

Restate the Problem. What is the specific reason why the customer is unhappy? Was he or she treated poorly? Did the merchandise not live up to its promise? Focusing on the problem and restating it at the beginning of the response letter shows the customer that you are taking the complaint seriously.

Express Your Regrets. Let your customer know you are sorry the problem occurred. This affirms that you want him or her to be satisfied. This statement can be brief and may appear early in the letter or in the closing.

Explain What Actions You Will Take. Tell the customer how you will correct the problem, whether it is by making changes at the business or by compensating the customer. Before stating what will be done, be sure you know the company policy regarding this type of complaint. The customer may be entitled to a refund or credit, or he or she may have to trade the unsatisfactory merchandise for something else of equal value. For complaints about poor service, the company might offer to do the job over or provide a gift certificate for a free service in the future.

Thank the Person for Writing. Your customer has done you a service by writing a letter of complaint. He or she could have simply walked away, refused to do future business with your company, and complained about your company to other potential customers. Sometimes, the only way a business can know about a problem is through customer complaints. This can help a company know whether to recall an unsafe product, remove a product from the shelves, lower prices, or improve services.

 For additional information about business writing, see the *Guide to Business Communication* section of the Communication Survival Kit in the Appendix.

Responding to Letters of Complaint

Objective: To respond appropriately to letters of complaint about products or services

Teaching Suggestions and Strategies

Connection to the Workplace

On the chalkboard write the phrase "The customer is always right." Ask students if they have heard this expression and invite volunteers to explain what it means. *(One explanation: A businessperson should always behave towards customers as if whatever claims they make are justified.)*

Next, ask students if they consider the advice to be true. Lead them to understand that the statement is a practical example of business wisdom. If you were to express it truthfully, the sentence would be expanded to read, "You will lose business if you do not behave as if the customer is always right."

Encourage students to comment on this philosophy. How is it important to keep this in mind when responding to a letter of complaint? *(Students may respond that taking the complaint seriously and offering a reasonable compensation leaves the writer feeling good about him- or herself as well as about your company.)*

Finally, ask students how they should respond to a customer whom they suspect to be wrong—someone who may be misusing a product or whose intention seems to be personal gain. Point out that even under these circumstances, civility is the best policy. Remind students that you don't have to give up anything, or admit liability, to express regrets about a customer's dissatisfaction.

 MEETING INDIVIDUAL NEEDS

MULTIPLE LEARNING STYLES

Bodily-Kinesthetic Complaints in writing allow recipients to consider their responses and to word them tactfully. This is not the case with the telephone complaint. Emotional callers can tax the skills of company representatives, who must adopt a reasonable, understanding tone.

Activity List with the class typical situations in which a consumer might complain about a product or service. Then, ask for pairs of volunteers to stage an impromptu telephone complaint line for the class. Assign each pair one of the situations developed by their fellow students. Ask one partner to play the consumer and one the company representative. Seat partners so they are not able to see each other and have them act out the assigned scenario in a pretend telephone conversation. Discuss the performances with the class.

Communication Through Writing

The following letter is an example of an appropriate response to a letter of complaint.

United Motors, Inc.
8415 Sandhill Road
Lafayette, IN 47901

March 14, 2003

Mr. Drew Brooks
575 Olympic Street
Seattle, WA 98060

Dear Mr. Brooks:

I recently received your letter stating your dissatisfaction with your new United Motors automobile. We at United Motors understand the high cost of repairing your car's steering column and apologize for the inconvenience this has caused. It is our goal to resolve this problem to your satisfaction.

For your safety, we request that you take your car to the nearest United Motors dealership as soon as possible. This will allow our repair technicians to ensure that your car will be fully repaired to the highest standards. Any necessary repair work will, of course, be free of charge. Also, please send me a copy of the original bill for repairing the steering column assembly. We will reimburse you for this cost.

Thank you for pointing out this problem. Letters such as yours give United Motors the opportunity to provide better service to our valued customers.

Sincerely,

Janet Green

Janet Green
Director, Customer Relations
United Motors, Inc.

WRITING *Activity*

Use the steps outlined earlier and the following facts to write a letter of response to a dissatisfied customer.

- The customer bought a new set of your company's dishes at a local department store last December. Some of the plates now show dark scratches from use with stainless steel utensils.

- Marks-Be-Gone is a stoneware cleaner that sells for under $10 and is very effective at removing discoloration. The product is available in the kitchenware department of most department stores.

- Your company's policy is to give customers a free sample of Marks-Be-Gone and a $2-off coupon for a full-size bottle of the cleaner.

- If the customer is still dissatisfied after using Marks-Be-Gone, the company will replace the dishes.

Write your response letter and then share it with the class. As a class, discuss how you might respond to various students' letters if you were the customer who issues the complaint.

Managing Conflict **409**

Teaching Activity

Ask students to read the model response to a customer complaint. Point out the three-part formula: paragraph one restates the problem; paragraph two outlines a course of action; paragraph three thanks the writer for bringing the matter to the company's attention.

Have students practice this technique by altering the nature of the customer's complaint. Ask them to imagine that owners of the same type of vehicle complained about the following circumstances:

- Gas consumption is not as good as advertised.
- The upholstery is stained from a grape juice spill.
- One of the headlights burned out and was expensive to repair because the whole unit had to be replaced, not just the individual bulb.

Have students pair up and compose a response to one of these complaints. Invite them to share their letters with the class. Discuss the issues raised and the skills required to handle them.

WRITING *Activity*

Students' responses should restate the customer's complaint and clearly present the terms of the manufacturer's offer. Responses should conclude with regrets that the customer has not been entirely satisfied and a courteous acknowledgment of his or her interest in the product.

Additional Resources

Appendix, "Guide to Business Communication"

Glencoe Writer's Assistant CD-ROM

Glencoe Interactive Grammar Software

Grade 9 Writer's Choice, Lesson 6.1

GRAMMAR PRACTICE

Commas in Compound Sentences

Have students indicate whether commas are necessary and where.

1. Ms. Green received the letter and responded to it promptly. *(unnecessary)*
2. Mr. Brooks was clearly upset with the steering fault but he made no demands of the company. *(necessary; after* fault*)*
3. Ms. Green might have offered Mr. Brooks a rental car while his was being repaired or she might have accepted a return of his vehicle. *(necessary; after* repaired*)*
4. United Motors has stringent quality control yet thousands of vehicles have to be recalled each year. *(necessary; after* control*)*
5. Mr. Brooks got his vehicle repaired but will not buy another one from United Motors. *(unnecessary)*

GLENCOE TECHNOLOGY

MindJogger Videoquiz

Use *MindJogger* to review the Chapter 12 content.

 GLENCOE Online

Visit the *Glencoe Communication Applications* Web site at **communicationapplications. glencoe.com** and click on **Chapter 12 Activity** for additional practice in managing conflict.

Reviewing Key Terms

1. False; change *policies* to *values*.

2. True

3. False; change *facts* to *values*.

4. True

5. False; change *coercion* to *accommodation*.

6. True

7. True

8. False; change *negotiation* to *compromise*.

9. False; change *compromise* to *negotiation*.

10. False; change *competition* to *collaboration*.

Reviewing Key Concepts

1. Ineffectually managed conflict can damage or destroy relationships and organizations. Morale can suffer; productivity may drop.

2. There are many sets of emotions and needs at stake. The individual may feel excluded or victimized.

3. The relationships of those involved have a major impact.

Reviewing Key Terms

Read each statement. On a separate sheet of paper, write whether the statement is true or false. If the statement is false, change the word that will make it true and underline the word that you substitute.

1. A conflict over policies is a disagreement over priorities.

2. A conflict over facts is a disagreement over something that can be proven true or false.

3. Each person in a conflict over facts will be emotionally involved in his or her stance.

4. Avoidance is dealing with a conflict by withdrawing from it.

5. Maintaining harmony with others while giving in to their wishes is called coercion.

6. If you discover that you have made a mistake, choosing accommodation to settle conflict is a sign of strength.

7. Coercion is only possible if one person is perceived as more powerful than the others involved in a conflict.

8. Negotiation is settling conflicts by having each party give up something.

9. In compromise, trade-offs may be unrelated to the conflict issue.

10. Competition means working together to find a way to resolve conflict.

Reviewing Key Concepts

1. What may happen if conflict is ineffectively managed?

2. Why is a conflict between a group and an individual more complex than an interpersonal conflict?

3. What often has the biggest impact on whether a conflict can be resolved?

4. Which type of conflict is easiest to resolve? Why?

5. What term describes the source of conflict between two friends who are competing for a place on the school basketball team?

6. Identify a conflict you have with a parent or teacher. Name one force that will help and another that may hinder the conflict's resolution.

7. How might a person use psychological avoidance to resolve a conflict?

4. Conflicts over facts are the easiest to resolve because they are the result of inadequate information.

5. A power struggle is the source of conflict between friends competing for a place on the basketball team.

6. Accept reasonable responses.

7. One might ignore the sources of conflict or deny that a conflict exists.

Assessment and Activities

Reading and Critical Thinking Skill

1. **Summarizing** Summarize steps used to diagnose conflict.

2. **Classifying Information** Dirk and his brother are angry because each borrows the other's CDs without asking. At what level of communication is their conflict?

3. **Making Comparisons** Of the following strategies—coercion, accommodation, and compromise—which is least costly? Why?

4. **Inferring** What can you infer about the personalities of people who prefer to negotiate rather than compromise?

Skill Practice Activity

Finding the Main Idea and Supporting Details Identify the main idea and the supporting details in the following paragraph. On a separate sheet of paper, restate them in your own words.

While most people would prefer not to have conflicts, they are a part of life. Over the years, you'll find it impossible to escape conflicts in your personal relationships or working environment. Therefore, in order to be successful, you must learn to diagnose the conflicts in your life. Once you have the diagnosis, you can begin to work to manage them.

Cooperative Learning Activity

Analyzing the Relationships Involved in a Conflict As a class, organize into groups. Each group should have a copy of an advice column from the newspaper. The members of each group should choose and discuss a letter from the column that describes a conflict. The discussion should determine who is involved in the conflict and what relationships these individuals have with one another. As a group, decide which resolution strategy should be suggested to resolve the conflict. Provide reasons for the choice of strategy.

Chapter Project

Planning Design a conflict management workshop. For each major section in Chapter 12, write note cards that cover the main ideas and supporting details in the material. Make posters or overhead transparencies that list the steps for diagnosing conflict and the different resolution strategies. Plan audience participation.

Presenting Give the workshop for your family or close friends. Speak to them from your note cards and use your visual aids to emphasize important points. After you have spoken to your family or close friends about conflict, record your family's or friends' responses to the workshop and report them to the class.

Managing Conflict **411**

Chapter Project

Before students present their workshop to an actual audience, you might want to provide time for them to practice with a classmate. Encourage the classmate to give constructive criticism—identifying both positive points and places where change might improve the presentation. Remind students that upon receiving suggestions, it is up to them to decide whether or not they want to implement the changes.

Reading and Critical Thinking Skill

1. **Summarizing** To diagnose a conflict, identify it, determine the level of conflict, analyze the relationships involved, determine the level of interdependence, analyze the type of conflict, identify the source of conflict, and analyze the severity of the conflict.

2. **Classifying Information** Interpersonal

3. **Making Comparisons** Compromise is least costly. Each person in the conflict comes away with something. In the other two strategies, one person loses.

4. **Inferring** Students may say that such a person believes strongly in what he or she wants. They may also be seen as stubborn or unbending.

Skills Practice Activity

Finding the Main Idea and Supporting Details

Main Idea: While most people would prefer not to have them, conflicts are a part of life.

Supporting Details: It is impossible to escape conflicts. Learn to diagnose them. Work to manage them.

Restatement: Conflicts are a part of life. While it is impossible to escape conflicts, if you learn to diagnose them, you can begin to work on managing them.

Cooperative Learning Activity

Analyzing the Relationships Involved in a Conflict

Have a variety of advice columns from which students can choose. Be sure groups identify both the relationships involved in the conflict and a resolution strategy.

Chapter 13 Planning Guide

SECTION RESOURCES

Daily Objectives

Section 1

1. Distinguish between appointed and emergent leaders
2. Describe the three approaches for identifying potential leaders
3. Determine which leadership style is the most effective in specific situations

Section 2

1. Explain the importance of preparation and communication skills for effective leadership
2. Analyze the six types of power
3. Recognize seven communication methods shared by effective leaders

Reproducible Resources

 Reproducible Lesson Plan 13-1
 Application Activities 13-1
 Guided Reading Workbook Activity 13-1
 Vocabulary Activity 13*
 Reteaching Activity 13-1*
 Enrichment Activity 13-1*
 Graphic Organizer Transparency Strategies and Activities 13-1

 Reproducible Lesson Plan 13-2
 Application Activities 13-2
 Guided Reading Workbook Activity 13-2
 Vocabulary Activity 13*
 Reteaching Activity 13-2*
 Enrichment Activity 13-2*
Graphic Organizer Transparency Strategies and Activities 13-2

Multimedia Resources

 Graphic Organizer Transparency 13-1
 Chapter 13 Teaching Transparency
 Interactive Tutor Self-Assessment
 PuzzleMaker
 ExamView® Pro Testmaker
 Interactive Lesson Planner
Communication in Action Video Chapter 13
MindJogger
communicationapplications.glencoe.com
Presentation Plus!

 Graphic Organizer Transparency 13-2
 Chapter 13 Teaching Transparency
 Interactive Tutor Self-Assessment
 PuzzleMaker
 ExamView® Pro Testmaker
 Interactive Lesson Planner
 Communication in Action Video Chapter 13
 MindJogger
communicationapplications.glencoe.com
 Presentation Plus!

Use Glencoe's *Presentation Plus!* multimedia teacher tool to easily present dynamic lessons that engage and motivate your students. Using Microsoft PowerPoint®, you can customize the presentations to create your own personalized lessons.

* Also available in Spanish

 Blackline Master   CD-ROM   Software

Transparency   Videodisc   Videocassette   Web site

Chapter 13 Planning Guide

FOR THE TEACHER

Leaders and Leadership

Write the following prompts on the board and have students copy and take a couple of minutes to complete them:

A leader is someone who . . .

An effective leader should possess the following three characteristics . . .

A leader exists because . . .

Allow partners to share and discuss answers and develop a single list between the two. On the chalkboard, create three separate stations, one for each of the prompts. Have each pair write their ideas at the appropriate locations. When everyone's list is on the board, discuss the similarities and differences in responses. Try to develop a class consensus on the nature of leaders and leadership.

CHAPTER RESOURCES

Resources for the Teacher

- *Lesson from the Top: the Search for America's Best Business Leaders* by Thomas J. Neff and James M. Citrin, Currency/Doubleday, 1999
- *Maximum Leadership: The World's Leading CEOs Share Their Five Strategies for Success* by Charles M. Farkas, Holt, 1996
- *Titan: The Life of John D. Rockefeller, Sr.* by Ron Chernow, Random, 1998

Resources for the Student

- *How to Be a Star at Work,* Times Business: Random, 1998
- *I'd Like the World to Buy a Coke* by David Greising, Wiley, 1998
- *Self-Made Women* by Diane Jennings, Taylor, 1987

Block Scheduling

Block scheduling differs from traditional class scheduling in the amount of time allotted to each period. The extended time frame provided by block scheduling affords you the opportunity to implement a greater number of research-oriented and activity-intense projects to motivate and involve your students. Activities that are particularly suited to use within the block-scheduling framework are identified throughout this chapter by the following designation:

KEY TO ABILITY LEVELS

Teaching Strategies have been coded for varying learning styles and abilities.

- **L1** **BASIC** activities for all students
- **L2** **AVERAGE** activities for average to above-average students
- **L3** **CHALLENGING** activities for above-average students
- **ELL** **English Language Learner** activities

Chapter 13 Resource Manager

The following materials may be used when teaching the chapter. Materials for specific lessons are also shown at point-of-use in the margins of the Teacher's Wraparound Edition.

TEACHING TRANSPARENCIES

Chapter 13 Teaching Transparency

Graphic Organizer Transparency 13-1

Graphic Organizer Transparency 13-2

APPLICATION ACTIVITIES

Chapter 13, Section 1

Chapter 13, Section 2

Chapter 13, Cumulative

REINFORCEMENT AND REVIEW ACTIVITIES

Vocabulary Activity 13

Guided Reading Activity Workbook 13-1, 13-2

Reteaching Activities 13-1, 13-2

Chapter 13 Resource Manager

ASSESSMENT AND EVALUATION

GLENCOE'S ASSESSMENT ADVANTAGE

Section Quizzes 13-1, 13-2

Chapter 13 Test, Forms A & B

Performance Assessment Activity 13

ENRICHMENT AND EXTENSION

Technology Application Activity 13

Enrichment Activities 13-1, 13-2

SPANISH RESOURCES

- 📁 Spanish Chapter and Unit Tests
- 📁 Spanish Vocabulary Activities
- 📁 Spanish Section Quizzes
- 📁 Spanish Reteaching Activities
- 📁 Spanish Enrichment Activities

MULTIMEDIA

- 💿 💾 Interactive Tutor Self-Assessment
- 💿 💾 ExamView® Pro Testmaker
- 💾 PuzzleMaker
- 📼 💿 Communication in Action Videodisc and Videocassette
- 📼 MindJogger
- 💿 Interactive Lesson Planner
- 💿 Presentation Plus!
- 💿 Writer's Assistant
- 💿 Glencoe Interactive Grammar
- 🖥 **communicationapplications.glencoe.com**

ORAL PRESENTATION ACTIVITIES

Activities 1, 5, 10, 14–16

TEACHER PLANNING AND SUPPORT

- 📁 Reproducible Lesson Plans
- 💿 Interactive Lesson Planner
- 💿 Presentation Plus!

CHAPTER **13** # Functioning as a Leader

WHY IT'S IMPORTANT

It's not easy to be a leader. Becoming a positive and effective leader requires you to examine and emphasize your strengths and work hard to improve your weaknesses, all while working to organize and inspire your followers.

To better understand effective leadership, view the **Communication in Action** Chapter 13 video lesson.

GLENCOE *Online*

Visit the *Glencoe Communication Applications* Web site at **communicationapplications. glencoe.com** and click on **Overview–Chapter 13** to preview information about effective leadership.

412 *Glencoe Communication Applications*

"A leader takes people where they want to go. A great leader takes people where they don't necessarily want to go but ought to be."

—Rosalynn Smith Carter, former U.S. First Lady

WHY IT'S IMPORTANT

Invite a volunteer to read aloud the statement about leadership by Rosalynn Carter. Ask: **What qualities distinguish the great leader from the merely capable leader, according to Mrs. Carter's definition?** *(Possible answer: A great leader has the wisdom to know that the difficult path may sometimes be the right one and has the skill to lead people in that direction.)*

Section 1

Identifying Leaders

GUIDE TO READING

Objectives

1. Distinguish between appointed and emergent leaders.
2. Describe the three approaches for identifying potential leaders.
3. Determine which leadership style is the most effective in specific situations.

Terms to Learn

leader
appointed leader
emergent leader
trait approach
style approach

authoritarian leader
democratic leader
laissez-faire leader
balanced leader
functional approach

Imagine that your debate team advisor has come down with the flu the week of your state tournament. Instead of your teammates all working together to get ready for the big event, practice turns into a chaotic argument.

How can this group function without its leader? Do you consider yourself a leader? Are only teachers, bosses, or presidents leaders? Leadership is not only earned through a promotion or an election. Very often, the quick actions of a confident group member propel him or her into a position of leadership.

these leaders were appointed to their positions. An appointed leader is given his or her leadership position by a person in authority.

TYPES OF LEADERS

A leader is someone who influences or inspires others to act in specific ways to accomplish a common goal. Many leaders are easy to identify. The chair of the homecoming committee, the principal at your school, and the manager at your local movie theater are all obvious leaders. All of

Political candidates campaign to convince voters to choose them as their leader. What is a leader?

Functioning as a Leader **413**

1 FOCUS

Bellringer
Ask students how they think they would respond in the situation described in the opening paragraph. Encourage volunteers to describe incidents from their own lives when order broke down due to lack of leadership. What role did they take in the situation? Were they pleased or dissatisfied with their behavior? Discuss with the class the importance of leadership.

You may use Graphic Organizer Transparency 13–1 to introduce this section.

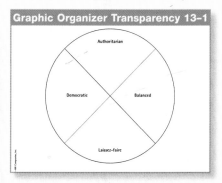

Language Tip

Avoid using the masculine pronouns *he*, *him*, and *his* to indicate people in general. Refer instead to both genders, as the authors do in the last sentence on this page, or change the subject from singular to plural and use the pronouns *they*, *them*, and *their*.

Visual Instruction

Answer A leader is someone who influences or inspires others to act in a specific way to accomplish a goal.

RESOURCE MANAGER

Teaching Tools
- Interactive Lesson Planner
- Reproducible Lesson Plan 13–1
- Application Activities 13–1

Reproducible Masters
- Guided Reading Activity Workbook 13–1
- Enrichment Activity 13–1
- Reteaching Activity 13–1
- Section Quiz 13–1
- Transparency Strategies and Activities Booklet 13–1

Transparencies
- Graphic Organizer Transparency 13–1
- Chapter 13 Teaching Transparency

Technology Resources
- Interactive Tutor Self-Assessment Software
- Presentation Plus! Software
- ExamView® Pro Testmaker
- PuzzleMaker Software
- communicationapplications.glencoe.com

2 TEACH

Guided Reading Activity 13–1

GUIDED READING Activity 13–1 — Name ___ Date ___ Class ___
FUNCTIONING AS A LEADER
Identifying Leaders

As you read Section 1, answer the following items.

1. Describe the difference between an appointed leader and an emergent leader ___

2. What are the four common traits that most leaders have? ___

3. How do most successful leaders choose their styles? ___

4. What are the four major styles leaders might choose? ___

5. Where is authoritarian leadership most effective? ___

6. How is a democratic leadership style different from an authoritarian style? ___

7. What type of leader has a distinctly "hands-off" style? ___

8. How can a balanced leader be most effective? ___

9. What does the functional approach to leadership suggest? ___

■ Visual Instruction

Answer The trait approach assumes that leaders share certain personality traits that help them lead successfully.

However, not all leaders are appointed by a supervisor or boss. An emergent leader is chosen by peers or members of his or her group because of his or her personality, power in the group, or the special circumstances of the group task. Emergent leaders may be chosen officially, such as in an election of class officers or the chair of a PTA committee. They also may be chosen informally. For example, a classmate who steps forward to organize a class trip may attract many followers. Simply by choosing to go along with your classmate's plans, you informally have chosen him or her as your leader.

SUCCESSFUL LEADERS

In many organizations, leaders are appointed, promoted, or elected to their positions. What makes these specific individuals get selected? The answer is that they exhibit the characteristics of a leader. There are three ways to determine what type of person typically makes a successful leader:

- leadership traits
- leadership styles
- leadership functions

COMMUNICATION
Strategies

EMERGING AS A GROUP LEADER

✓ Participate early, often, and with quality and purpose in group meetings.

✓ Demonstrate your ability to do a job well.

✓ Don't push too hard to get your way.

✓ Provide a solution for group dilemmas.

■ Some leaders, like the first woman vice president of Ecuador, Rosalia Arteaga, are chosen through election. Explain the trait approach.

Leadership Traits

Can you tell who will make a good leader just by observing his or her personality? The trait approach assumes that leaders share certain personality traits that help them lead successfully. Many times, the necessary traits for leadership are determined by the type of job that needs to be done. These traits may vary from job to job and from organization to organization. A few traits, though, seem to be common in most leaders in a variety of types of organizations. These traits are as follows:

- effective communication skills
- the desire to be a leader
- originality or creativity
- intelligence

While these qualities are present in most leaders, they are not a guarantee of leadership. Why? Even though some individuals may exhibit these traits, they may be weak in other important areas, such as sensitivity to

---

MEETING INDIVIDUAL NEEDS — **GIFTED AND TALENTED**

The American Presidency Point out that few public figures have as great a responsibility to exhibit leadership skills as does the President of the United States.

Activity Have students choose an American president to research. (Avoid duplicates by giving each student a short list of names to choose from.) Ask them to become familiar with the qualities that made their presidents leaders. They should focus their evaluations on their subjects' abilities in the following areas: effective communication skills, the desire to be a leader, originality or creativity, and intelligence. Invite them to present their findings to the class, encouraging them to support their assessments with specific examples from their president's biography, words, and accomplishments. Discuss with the class the traits evident in leaders of the United States.

others, ability to organize self and others, knowledge of the organization, and leadership style. Strengths in all these areas can help you utilize your leadership traits to the fullest.

Developing Leadership Traits What if you have a great desire to be a leader, and you're intelligent and creative, but your interpersonal communication skills need work? On the other hand, what if you are often seen as a leader, but your strengths lie in other areas? There are two important points to consider.

First, as the old saying goes, good leaders are made, not born. By constantly working to improve your skills, you may build the strengths you need to serve as a leader.

Second, a leader is simply someone who leads. Therefore, if your skills allow you to lead others effectively, you must be doing something right. The leadership traits listed here may give you some direction for continued improvement since they are ones that researchers have identified as common to most leaders.

Leadership Style

The style approach to leadership assumes that the leader's communication method and use of power with followers determines his or her success. Most successful leaders choose styles that parallel the traditions and policies of their organization. There are at least four major styles that leaders might choose. They are as follows:

- authoritarian
- democratic
- laissez-faire
- balanced

Authoritarian A leader who uses power to force followers to do what he or she wants them to do is an authoritarian leader. Authoritarian leadership is used very effectively by military organizations, prison systems, and any type of organization that needs the power to make quick decisions or to have strong control over the group.

COMMUNICATION

Analyzing Leadership Traits

To analyze and strengthen your leadership traits, follow these steps:

Step 1 Make a four-column chart and label each column with one of the leadership traits listed on page 414.

Then, in each column, list examples of each trait as it applies to you. For example, under *Originality and Creativity*, you might write "Thought of theme for Prom."

Step 2 Using your chart, rate yourself from one to ten (with ten being the highest) on how well you display each leadership trait.

PRACTICE LAB

Step 3 Identify which trait is your strongest and which is your weakest.

Step 4 As a class, brainstorm specific ways to develop or strengthen each of the personality traits most often found in leaders. For example, to build up your intelligence, you might take a study skills or a speed-reading class.

Step 5 On your own, apply your classmates' suggestions to any weaknesses you determined in Step 3. Develop a plan for improving your skills so that you can be an effective leader.

Functioning as a Leader **415**

CRITICAL THINKING ACTIVITY

When is a leader not a leader? Is everyone in the public eye skilled at influencing or inspiring others? Encourage students to think critically about the distinctions between fame and leadership with the following exercise. Brainstorm names of prominent people whom students consider to be leaders. Write the names on the chalkboard. Then, have students form groups to evaluate each individual as a leader in the light of the definition given at the beginning of this section: A leader is someone who influences or inspires others to act in specific ways to accomplish a common goal. Have groups rank their candidates in order of leadership skills. Write their conclusions on the board and examine areas of disagreement. Conclude the activity by discussing with the class the qualities of leadership.

Leadership Traits

Have students assess the four bulleted traits listed on this page. Ask them to assign each trait a number from one to four, with one being most important and four, least important. On the chalkboard, make a master list of their rankings and discuss with the class the qualities of leadership. **L2**

COMMUNICATION
PRACTICE LAB
Analyzing Leadership Traits

Have students bring to class the plans they made in Step 5 and report on one strategy for personal improvement that they would like to share with their peers. **L1**

For an additional Practice Lab for this section, have students visit the *Glencoe Communication Applications* Web site at **communicationapplications.glencoe.com**. Click on Communication Practice Lab 13–1. **L1**

3 ASSESS

Assign Section 1 Assessment as a homework or in-class activity.

✪ Use *Interactive Tutor Self-Assessment Software* to review Section 1.

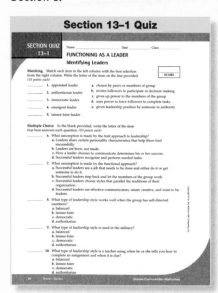

Democratic A democratic leadership style is very different from an authoritarian style. A **democratic leader** invites followers to participate in decision making, trying to get a majority to agree with and commit to decisions. Most organizations only experience crisis or extreme stress from time to time. Therefore, they often have time to deliberate about how to proceed with the organization's tasks. For example, newspapers often are led democratically. Rather than the publisher or one editor making all the decisions about content, the publisher, editors, and reporters typically work together to decide what news stories to cover.

Laissez-faire Laissez-faire is a French term meaning "to let people do as they choose." A **laissez-faire leader** gives up his or her power to the members of the group. He or she leads with a distinctly "hands-off" style. A laissez-faire leader provides the members of his or her group with the task or purpose of the

group and then steps back to let the group accomplish the task or purpose on their own. The group will generally meet together only two or three times, but individual members will keep the leader informed of their individual progress toward the completion of the project. This type of leadership style is effective only when a group is comprised of self-directed members who are capable of working on a project alone or in a subcommittee. For example, the chairperson of the prom committee can be a laissez-faire leader if he or she has strong group members who head up subcommittees such as time and place, entertainment, and refreshments.

Balanced A fourth style of leadership is one that is balanced according to the grid in **Figure 13–1.** A **balanced leader** strives for an equal focus on both tasks and relationships in order to be most effective.

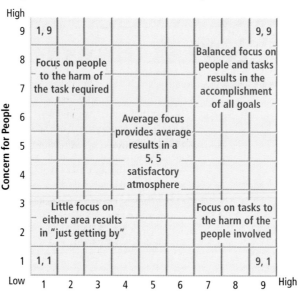

Figure 13–1 Balanced Leadership Grid

416   *Glencoe Communication Applications*

Leaders who are overly concerned with getting a task done may have a tendency to "run over" the people who are connected with the work. At the other extreme are leaders who are overly concerned with what everyone involved might think or feel about the work. These leaders may be more preoccupied with the relationship issues of the group and may not get very much work done. Leaders who typically get the most done are those who can get tasks accomplished while being sensitive to the relationships and feelings of those connected to the tasks.

A balanced leader can, in times of crises, initiate ways to complete the task. When time is not so critical, the leader needs to be able to facilitate discussion, spending more time listening to how group members feel and thinking about how to best complete a task.

Functional Leadership

The functional approach to leadership suggests that successful leaders both recognize and actively perform needed tasks. In other words, leaders see a job that needs to be done and either do it or get it done by others. Very often, emergent leaders are born out of this kind of assertiveness or take-charge attitude. A person who has leadership potential needs to work hard to develop the behaviors and communication skills necessary for success as a leader.

Section 1 Assessment

Visit the *Glencoe Communication Applications* Web site at **communicationapplications. glencoe.com** and click on **Self-Check and Study Guides 13.1** to review your understanding of identifying leaders.

Review Key Terms

1. Define each term and write it in a sentence: leader, appointed leader, emergent leader, trait approach, style approach, authoritarian leader, democratic leader, laissez-faire leader, balanced leader, functional approach.

Check Understanding

2. How are appointed and emergent leaders different?

3. Describe the three approaches for identifying potential leaders.

4. **Predict** Imagine that your school yearbook staff must finish the layout for the advertisement section by tomorrow. The yearbook editor has chosen the democratic style of leadership during this stressful time. How do you think staff members might respond to his or her requests? How effective will his or her chosen style be in this situation?

APPLICATION *Activity*

Preparing a Campaign Poster Imagine that you are running for a class office. Apply the three approaches for determining effective leadership to yourself. Then, prepare a poster for your campaign, highlighting your strengths.

Functioning as a Leader **417**

Section 1 Assessment Answers

1. Accept all reasonable sentences.
2. An appointed leader is given his or her position by someone in authority, while an emergent leader is selected, either informally or officially, by peers or members of his or her group.
3. The trait approach assumes that leaders share certain personality traits that make them successful. The style approach assumes that how a leader chooses to communicate with followers determines his or her success. The functional approach suggests that successful leaders both recognize and actively perform needed tasks.

4. Answers should reflect that some staff members may resent having to discuss every little issue when they are trying to meet a deadline. Using a democratic leadership style may be less effective than one of the other styles in this specific situation.

Application Activity Posters should emphasize how the traits, styles, and actions of students show that they will be successful in leading the class.

4 CLOSE

Have students review the incidents they recalled in response to the Bellringer on page 413. What sort of leadership traits or styles do they feel would have been necessary to restore order to the situation that they described?

Extra-Credit Project

Ask students to interview three adults whom they consider to be effective leaders. Have them ask their interviewees for their views on leadership in terms of a leader's traits, styles, and functions. Have students write a summary of their findings, comparing and contrasting the views of their three subjects.

Critical Thinking Skill

Predicting Outcomes

Point out that the ability to make predictions depends entirely on one's knowledge and understanding of current information. Students should recognize that each of the Steps 1 to 3 under Learning the Skill involves a different means of acquiring information.

Practicing the Skill

Student responses may include the following examples: You already know what your prices are, how much money you make on each pizza, how much money you need to make to stay open, how much you pay your employees, and what your utility bills are each month. You would probably want to know the prices at other pizza shops and how much they charge for delivery. You can research this information by calling the other pizza shops and asking them. If you raised prices or charged for delivery in the past, you can use that information to help make your prediction. You could also ask people in the area which option they would prefer: the price increase or the delivery charge. If you make the wrong decision, you might lose customers who were still loyal to you instead of the competition.

Application Activity

Student responses may include the following examples but will vary greatly:

If you make the wrong decision, the fund-raising campaign could get off to a bad start. If the campaign starts poorly, it will probably not raise enough money to build a new gymnasium.

One thing to consider is how many people would be at the game because you could tell a lot of people about the fund-raiser at one time. Also, people at a basketball game would probably support a new gymnasium.

PREDICTING OUTCOMES

A leader often has the responsibility to provide guidance when the outcome of a decision may not be completely apparent. When you predict an outcome you are trying to determine how an event will turn out before it takes place. Although no one can be completely sure of any future event, there are ways to help you make more accurate guesses and, therefore, become a more skillful leader.

Learning the Skill

Use the following steps to predict outcomes:

Step 1 Start with what you know. Carefully review the information with which you are already familiar. Then decide what other information you will need to make a good prediction.

Step 2 Research what you want to know. Try to determine how people will feel about an event and why. Find out everything you can about similar situations and look for patterns. You can use surveys or opinion polls to determine a variety of people's thoughts about an idea.

Step 3 Study the past. It is often useful to use information from the past, especially if you are doing something that has been attempted before. Study the history leading up to the event, and guess what should happen based on that information.

Step 4 Consider the cost of being wrong. When you are predicting an outcome, remember to consider the effects of a poor prediction.

Practicing the Skill

Suppose you own a small pizza shop. Increased competition has recently hurt your business. You have decided you'll have to either raise your prices or start charging for delivery service in order to increase your profits. Answer the following questions to predict an outcome for your business.

1. As the owner, what are some things you already know about your business?

2. What else do you need to know before making your decision? How can you research this information?

3. If you make the wrong decision, how will it affect your business?

APPLICATION *Activity*

You are a student council member at your high school and you need to set a date on which to start a month-long fund-raising campaign that will support the building of a new gymnasium. You have the choice of starting your fund-raising campaign on the same night as a basketball game or the following week.

1. When should you host the event? Why did you make that choice?

2. What is the cost of making a wrong decision?

3. What information did you consider in making your decision? Why did you consider this information?

MEETING INDIVIDUAL NEEDS

MULTIPLE LEARNING STYLES

Bodily-Kinesthetic Point out that since leadership is largely about action, one of the best ways of appreciating the qualities of a leader is through role play.

Activity Brainstorm with the class for crises in which immediate action would have to be taken. (Encourage students to think about a broad range of scenarios.) Choose several realistic situations and ask volunteers from the class to form performing groups. Have each group designate an emergent leader and ask them to perform one of the crisis scenarios, encouraging performers to realistically re-create the emotions the occasion requires. The leader's role will be to establish order and purpose in a chaotic situation. After the performances, discuss the role of a leader in emergencies.

Leading Others

GUIDE TO READING

Objectives

1. Explain the importance of preparation and communication skills for effective leadership.
2. Analyze the six types of power.
3. Recognize seven communication methods shared by effective leaders.

Terms to Learn

power
resistance
legitimate power
reward power

coercive power
expert power
informational power
referent power

Think about General Norman Schwarzkopf, professional quarterback John Elway, the Reverend Jesse Jackson, and former prime minister Margaret Thatcher. What do all of these leaders have in common? What sets each of them apart from their followers?

Schwarzkopf, Elway, Jackson, Thatcher—each of these names brings to mind exceptional leadership qualities. These leaders all possess certain traits and styles that have made them successful, whether leading an army or a sports team. Each of these leaders exhibited intelligence and knowledge about his or her organization and program, creativity in solving problems, and communication and sociability skills that matched the needs of the situation. Jesse Jackson, for example, is known for his gift of public speaking, while John Elway used incredible drive to inspire his football teammates to greatness both on and off the field. What is it, then, that ties these leaders together?

Jesse Jackson, who exhibits a gift for public speaking, possesses many leadership qualities. Identify other leaders in society.

Functioning as a Leader **419**

1 FOCUS

Bellringer

Make sure that students are familiar with the leaders mentioned in the opening paragraph. If not, brainstorm for suitable figures widely recognized as leaders. Give students a minute to jot down answers to the questions. (*Students might suggest that all the leaders have demonstrated the ability to effectively convey their ideas and have taken active roles in carrying them out.*)

You may use Graphic Organizer Transparency 13–2 to introduce this section.

Graphic Organizer Transparency 13–2

BUSINESS BRIEF

"I learned early, in business as well as politics, that people love a leader. They like decisive action," wrote T. Boone Pickens, founder of Mesa Petroleum. Ask students to comment on this powerful generalization.

Visual Instruction

Answer Students' answers will vary.

RESOURCE MANAGER

Teaching Tools

- Interactive Lesson Planner
- Reproducible Lesson Plan 13–2
- Application Activities 13–2

Reproducible Masters

- Guided Reading Activity Workbook 13–2
- Enrichment Activity 13–2
- Reteaching Activity 13–2
- Section Quiz 13–2
- Transparency Strategies and Activities Booklet 13–2

Transparencies

- Graphic Organizer Transparency 13–2
- Chapter 13 Teaching Transparency

Technology Resources

- Interactive Tutor Self-Assessment Software
- Presentation Plus! Software
- ExamView® Pro Testmaker
- PuzzleMaker Software
- communicationapplications.glencoe.com

419

2 TEACH

Guided Reading Activity 13–2

(Guided Reading Activity 13–2 worksheet — FUNCTIONING AS A LEADER, Leading Others)

SKILLS FOR EFFECTIVE LEADERSHIP

Once you have been appointed to lead or have emerged as a leader, what do you do next? A good first step might be to examine your knowledge and specific skills as they relate to the position you are in. If you are like most people, you will realize that successful leadership requires strong skills in preparation and communication.

Preparation

An important aspect of leadership is motivating followers to do whatever is necessary to accomplish specific goals. Effective leaders first make sure they understand what needs to be done before asking their followers to take action. This requires planning ahead for the tasks or events facing the group.

To adequately prepare, leaders should do the following:

- plan tasks
- evaluate followers
- evaluate resources
- plan communication

COMMUNICATION *Strategies*

PLANNING TASKS

✓ Examine the task.

✓ Break the task down into separate, smaller steps.

✓ Construct a time line for the task.

✓ Suggest ways to accomplish each step.

Figure 13–2 Publicizing an Event

CAR WASH
WHEN: SATURDAY
WHERE: SCHOOL PARKING LOT
• DONATIONS WELCOME
• PROCEEDS WILL HELP PAY FOR MARCHING BAND UNIFORMS

Plan Tasks. A leader's first step in preparation is to plan what needs to be done. You read about planning procedures in Chapter 10. The Communication Strategies checklist on this page summarizes the most important elements of planning.

Evaluate Followers. What are the talents of the people involved in the task? If certain individuals already have demonstrated talent in certain areas, use those talents! This not only makes for smooth work, but it also builds the self-confidence of those group members. Being called upon as an expert can help motivate them to do their jobs as effectively as possible. For example, suppose you were the leader of a project planning a special event at school. To publicize the event, you might call on one of the group members who has artistic talent to create flyers or posters, such as the one in **Figure 13–2.** Leaders in social and professional organizations who use the talents of group members effectively often have greater success achieving group goals.

Just as it is important to be aware of individual group members' strengths, it also is important to analyze their weaknesses. Suppose you have a job that must be completed quickly and know someone who could do very good work on this task. However, that person is not very good at meeting deadlines. You should probably find someone else to do

■ **A factory supervisor gives instructions to employees.**
What should a leader do in order to adequately prepare to communicate?

the work. What help do you think a specific group member will need to accomplish his or her part of the task? Knowing this can help you plan for any special training or support workers might require along the way.

Evaluate Resources. A leader must be prepared to seek out anything needed to accomplish the goals of the group. For example, it is the responsibility of a highway construction project leader to request new equipment if older equipment breaks or wears

out. Successful leaders in any group not only anticipate what supplies, equipment, and physical space are required for a job but also seek to provide workers with needed tools to complete the job.

Plan Communication. Finally, to adequately prepare, a leader needs to determine how and what to communicate. For example, a factory supervisor not only needs to share new instructions with the workers, but he or she also will report the group's progress to upper management. The leader is a communication link between his or her group and other leaders in the organization. This link also may extend beyond the group or organization to the community as a whole. A leader may communicate on behalf of his or her followers on many different levels, through a variety of channels, and in a number of different contexts.

Communication

Leadership is more than just envisioning a goal and then making sure the work gets done to reach that goal. It also involves communication. An effective leader takes steps to

🌐 GLOBAL COMMUNICATION

Giving Gifts

In the United States, policies concerning the acceptance of gifts by employees are often stated in a company's handbook. Americans representing their organizations in other countries, however, must be aware of cultural traditions regarding gifts. For example, while clocks or watches are a common workplace gift in the U.S., this gift might not be appropriate in China because a clock is a symbol of bad luck to some people there. Survey teachers, friends, and relatives who have worked with people from other cultures. Find five examples of occasions when it is appropriate to offer gifts in other cultures. Are there people to whom you should not give gifts? Are there things that should not be presented as gifts, like the clocks mentioned in the example?

Functioning as a Leader **421**

REAL-WORLD CONNECTION

Communication in the Workplace Point out that communication is central to most employment. The more people who are involved in a workplace, the more important an organized process of communication becomes.

Activity Ask students to interview adults whose jobs involve some aspect of leadership. (Remind them that their subjects need not be at the top of their organization; many jobs require leadership skills.) Have them discover what channels of communication their subjects regularly use at work. How do communication skills enhance their performance? Have students present their findings to the class. 📖

Evaluate Followers

Point out to students that many movies and television programs have been based on groups of individuals who possess remarkable individual talents. Together, they make an unbeatable team. Encourage students to share experiences they may have had in groups with people whose abilities complemented their own and helped achieve success. **L1**

Evaluate Resources

Brainstorm with the class for a list of the supplies necessary—from floppy disks to floor polish—to keep their school operating. Point out that supplying a school system with the materials necessary for education is a complex process, extending from individual teachers to the superintendent of schools. Explain your role in the chain of command. Invite an administrator to speak to the class about the larger picture. **L1**

🌐 GLOBAL COMMUNICATION

Giving Gifts

Ask students why companies would have strict rules regarding employees accepting gifts. Have them try to define the difference between a gift and a bribe. *(Students may suggest that a gift is a simple expression of goodwill, while a bribe is a donation of some value, offered with the expectation of services in return.)* Lead students to understand that the line between a gift and a bribe is not always easy to draw. Point out that in some cultures, employees routinely supplement their incomes with what they would call gifts but others would call bribes. **L2**

■ **Visual Instruction**

Answer A leader should determine how and what to communicate.

Figure 13–3 Effective Leaders Consider the Appropriate Channel

ensure clear communication on all levels of the group. Depending upon the type of group and the nature of the task, a leader may need to do some or all of the following:

- gather and analyze feedback from followers
- conduct problem-solving or other group meetings
- provide performance reviews
- preside over meetings
- explain (and perhaps demonstrate) new tasks
- represent the group to others
- speak out in favor of needed organizational changes

Each of these tasks requires effective communication skills on the part of the leader. They may require the leader to create and express messages to followers, peers, supervisors, or even the community. They also may require him or her to listen critically, deliberatively, and empathically to others. Most of all, these communication tasks require a leader to demonstrate ethical judgment about what to say and when to say it.

Good judgment is especially necessary when performing the first three communication tasks listed above. Listening to feedback, solving

problems, and evaluating others' performance can involve sending and receiving negative messages as well as positive ones. Dealing with negative messages can pose a special challenge to leaders who feel threatened when followers disagree with them. If you find yourself in this situation, use the perception checks you read about in Chapter 3 and the conflict management skills you learned in Chapter 12 to work through any difficulties.

The last four tasks listed above can require, in addition to other communication abilities, special skills in diplomacy, or the art of reaching an agreement that suits all parties. As a leader, you may find that your position will be very threatening to some people. An effective leader will be sensitive to the feelings of others and will try to anticipate ways to help them feel more comfortable with his or her leadership. To keep these people working effectively toward the group goal, you may need to experiment with different styles and methods of communication.

As **Figure 13–3** shows, a successful leader will consider the special needs of group members when determining the best ways to organize and communicate his or her wishes to them. For example, it may be helpful to use more than one communication channel to introduce new procedures or policies at work. Some employees may be satisfied to read about the change in a memo, while others might prefer to hear about it in a small group meeting, receive detailed written instructions about the change, attend a training session on the new process, or even have the opportunity to be trained individually. The leader should determine, given the context, which method or methods of communication will be most effective for the group and then carry out that plan.

USING POWER

Power is available at some level to all leaders. Power is the ability of one person to get others to behave in a particular way or to carry out certain actions. How willingly followers work with a leader may be determined by the type of power that leader uses.

The six main types of leadership power are as follows:

- legitimate power
- reward power
- coercive power
- expert power
- informational power
- referent power

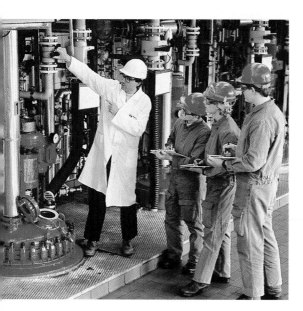

It is necessary for a supervisor to practice effective communication skills in order to lead or train others. How does an effective leader handle others who may feel threatened by his or her position?

TECHNOLOGY *Activity*

Creating a Spreadsheet Leaders, such as company managers, must keep detailed records of many workplace activities. In many businesses, all incoming calls are logged by a receptionist. Other businesses require all visitors who enter their building to sign in at a security desk. Information like this is sometimes entered into a database. The data can be recorded and analyzed using spreadsheet software. Think of three types of information that you could record and analyze over a period of time. Choose one of them and create a log or database by recording this information for one month. After one month, review your data and provide a one-page analysis of the information you gathered.

As a leader, the type of power you choose will affect the amount of resistance you are likely to encounter from others in the organization. Resistance is the force generated within a person that keeps him or her from accepting another's use of power. Power is something that one person allows another to have. Leaders depend upon their followers to acknowledge their power. Followers may choose to ignore or deny a leader's power. However, if power is used well, most followers will offer very little resistance to a leader's requests.

Legitimate Power

Within any organization, some individuals will be given specific titles or offices. With these assignments come certain responsibilities and

Functioning as a Leader **423**

TECHNOLOGY *Activity*

Creating a Spreadsheet Brainstorm with students for types of information suitable for recording in their databases. Areas to consider include stock market information (many possibilities), daily intake of foods categorized by type, class homework and test scores, income and expenditures, school club financial records, and physical fitness schedule. **L2**

Using Power
Assign each student one of the six types of leadership power bulleted on this page. Give students a few minutes to read the text about their allocated type of power and take notes. Then, ask them to form groups and compare notes with other students assigned the same subject. Invite a volunteer from each group to introduce their assigned topic to the class. **L2**

Power in School
Point out that from a very early age people exert power. Ask students to share their experiences about how their peers have used power in the school setting, from kindergarten to high school. What makes a grade-schooler or a high school student powerful? Has the power structure of school society changed during their years in school? What similarities and differences do students perceive between power in the school world and in the adult world? **L1**

Visual Instruction

Answer An effective leader is sensitive to the feelings of others and tries to anticipate ways to help others feel more comfortable.

EXTENDING THE CONTENT

Power in Words Point out that power has been a subject of continual fascination and conflict among men and women, from politicians to PTA members, and in organizations, from Congress to street gangs. Encourage students to examine the observations that people have made on this intriguing topic.

Activity Have students use the Internet or a dictionary of quotations to find five statements that interest them about the nature of power. Ask them to present one of their statements to the class, explaining why they chose it and whether they agree with it. Look for common themes or conclusions in the class's collective findings.

Using Legitimate Power

Have students form pairs and ask them to think of specific examples of power being used both appropriately and inappropriately in the following settings: at home, at work, at school. Ask them to share their scenarios with the class. Discuss the uses of power and ways to detect and discourage its abuse. **L2**

Using Reward Power

Ask students to describe situations in which a person in a position of power rewarded them for performing well. Do they feel that this strategy resulted in their being better employees or students? Have they ever been in a position to reward a subordinate for good behavior? What were the results? Lead from these anecdotes to a discussion of the advantages and drawbacks of reward power. **L2**

decision-making powers. Legitimate power is the power assigned to anyone who holds a particular position, office, or title. For example, principals have legitimate power to oversee teachers and students. Supervisors often have the power to hire and fire workers in their department. Legitimate power allows supervisors to demand that employees come to work on time, follow company policies, and complete their work according to some standard of quality. If employees fail to meet these requirements, the supervisor may legitimately use his or her own judgment to correct the problem.

Using Legitimate Power Appropriately It is possible for a leader to abuse legitimate power by the way he or she uses it. For instance, a leader may have the legitimate power to call meetings whenever he or she wishes. However, yelling for an employee to "Get in here now!" would be inappropriate in most cases. The leader may be overstepping his or her power by being rude or overbearing while making what would otherwise be a reasonable demand.

Another misuse of legitimate power occurs when a leader tries to extend his or her influence beyond where it is appropriate. For instance, a supervisor at work cannot legitimately require you to join a particular political party, social organization, or recreational association. It may be within his or her power, however, to ask you to belong to professional associations that would help you stay current on developments in your career field.

Employees both understand and expect supervisors to use their legitimate power to get work accomplished. To use that legitimate power in a way that provokes the least resistance, leaders should be courteous in explaining their expectations to employees. A good rule of thumb is to try to give instructions in the same way you would like to have them given to you.

Reward Power

Reward power is the ability to repay others in exchange for complying with a given direction. Rewards at work might include pay raises, promotions, improved workspace, or special recognition, such as the Employee of the Month award shown in Figure 13–4. Unlike legitimate power, everyone in an organization—not just the leader—has some amount of reward power. For example, almost any employee has the power to reward coworkers by helping out with a different project, sharing office equipment, or simply making the work environment especially friendly and pleasant.

Using Reward Power Appropriately One danger with reward power is that it can appear to be bribery. Few people like to feel they can be bought. To use rewards appropriately, the reward should directly reflect the task completed. For example, if an employee finds an innovative way to use computers to ease everyone's workload, an appropriate reward might be to update the office computers and give that employee the best system.

Coercive Power

Coercive power can be thought of as the opposite of reward power. Coercive power is the ability to force others to do something by

■ Figure 13–4 **Use of Reward Power**

Employee of the Month

Robin Juarez
June 2002

INTERDISCIPLINARY CONNECTION

Behavioral Science Point out that leadership is not a human phenomenon. Students should understand that many species of mammals wield power in a way that is remarkably similar to our own practices.

Activity Have students research the power structure among a species of advanced social animals such as wolves or primates. Ask them to examine the type of leaders that control group activities and the power they use to maintain their roles. Have students present their findings to the class, comparing and contrasting the use and abuse of power in human society with that in the species of animal they studied. Conclude with a discussion about the role of power in the animal kingdom.

A supervisor gains respect from employees by being courteous when explaining expectations. **What is reward power?**

imagine that the special events committee at your school failed to arrange for the custodial department to clean up after the fall dance. The committee's sponsor might require members to remain after the dance and take down decorations and clean up the area. If the committee members learn from this the importance of careful planning and responsibility for tasks, the coercion might work.

Expert Power

A group's designated leader may not be the person with the most knowledge about a particular project, task, or situation. Expert power is held by the person who knows the most about the work that must be done.

Imagine that you are a part of a small group whose task is to design and produce publicity for an upcoming fund-raiser at your school. One group member can draw well, another is an announcer on a local radio station, and a third works for the student newspaper. You, in turn, have experience in producing computer-generated, full-color flyers. Each group member holds some expert power over the others.

Using Expert Power Appropriately One drawback of expert power is having a leader who doesn't recognize the expertise of his or her workers or who refuses to allow the experts to act. Equally dangerous is a leader who assigns expert status to someone who is not truly an expert. A wise leader will determine the true expertise of his or her group members and give them the freedom to do what each does best.

Informational Power

Just as expert power consists of knowing how to do something very well, informational power consists of knowing where to learn about it. In other words, informational power

punishing them if they do not comply. If the person making the demand can withhold pay raises, deny promotions, change your job to include some unpleasant duty, or even fire you, that person has coercive power over you.

Like reward power, almost everyone has some level of coercive power. Your coworkers have the ability to make your work environment either pleasant or unpleasant depending on how they treat you at work. Team members can make meetings tedious by arguing over every item on the agenda, if they choose to do so. However, while your peers can make some aspects of your tasks inconvenient or unpleasant, they probably can't punish you with any severe consequence.

Using Coercive Power Appropriately The use of coercive power usually is not the most effective way to lead a group. Followers may become resentful or angry toward a coercive leader. This negativity usually results in a leader who gets little respect and a lot of resistance from followers.

While it generally is undesirable to use coercion, a leader may find that it is the most effective last resort for getting a particular job done. The best use of coercion is to allow the consequences of doing a bad job fall upon those who did the poor work. For example,

Functioning as a Leader **425**

Using Coercive Power
Students will be familiar with the use of coercive power. Ask them to give examples of how they have experienced coercive power at home, school, work, or in social contexts. Do they agree with the text that this is "not the most effective way to lead a group"? Under what circumstances do they feel coercive power is necessary and effective? **L1**

Visual Instruction
Answer Reward power is the ability to repay others in exchange for complying with given instructions.

Using Expert Power
Point out that the state and federal governments are largely run by people appointed for their expertise in key areas. Brainstorm with students for the titles of important positions in the cabinet of the President of the United States. Ask them to suggest areas in which each official must be an expert. *(Examples include the Secretaries of State: international affairs, Defense: military matters, Interior: resources and environment, Commerce: business affairs, Agriculture: farm policy, and the Attorney General: law.)* **L2**

COOPERATIVE LEARNING ACTIVITY

"To make the punishment fit the crime" was the aim of Gilbert and Sullivan's Mikado in the comic opera of the same name. Point out that judges are increasingly passing imaginative sentences on criminals in an effort to bring home the consequences of antisocial behavior. Brainstorm with the class a punishment that is custom made for the crime committed. *(Example: A bicycle thief is sentenced to work for a charity that rebuilds bikes for needy children.)* Ask groups of students to develop a list of five such crimes and punishments. Ask each group to present its ideas to the class. Encourage students to share their views about creative sentencing.

Using Informational Power

Point out that ethical standards sometimes come into conflict with the law when confidentiality and privacy issues are involved. On the board, write the words *Psychiatrist, Lawyer,* and *Newspaper Reporter.* Brainstorm with the class scenarios in which people in these professions might be under pressure to reveal confidential information. *(Possible situations: Did a psychiatric patient have violent delusions? Did a legal client reveal the whereabouts of an accomplice? Where did a reporter get confidential information about a corporation's illegal activities?)* Discuss with students the complexities of confidentiality. **L2**

Practice for the Workplace

Power and Leadership Answers may include custodian: has access to all areas of the building, knows the floor plan; receptionist: can determine who has access to the company's highest ranking officials, can control access to important information; security officer: has access to all areas of the building, can control access to the building; company accountant: has access to a company's financial records; senior employee: has knowledge and power due to length of employment, can help train younger employees; computer network administrator: has access to all information stored as computer files, can grant access to network.

Visual Instruction

Answer Followers refer power onto an individual, making the leader powerful through their willingness to follow.

is held by individuals who have access to needed information. These individuals are not necessarily experts in the subject, but they have either a position or some special skill that allows them to get the information that is needed. In a mock trial, a participant who knows how to conduct research using government documents will be useful in providing statistical information. Likewise, a new employee just hired from a competing firm may possess valuable information about what that competitor is developing.

Using Informational Power Appropriately The more an individual knows how to access scarce or difficult-to-locate information, the more valuable he or she can be. However, that person must be careful not to violate ethical standards in revealing specific information or sources of information. An effective leader will not ask that person to provide information that might

Practice for the Workplace

Power and Leadership Everyone takes on leadership responsibilities and is empowered in different situations. Think about the following list of people in your school and identify the types of power each one possesses.

Counselors	Students
Teachers	Cafeteria manager
Principal	Coaches
Librarian	Club advisors
Team captains	Music section leaders
Class valedictorian	Student council president
Newspaper/Yearbook editors	

BUSINESS PRACTICE *Activity*

Sometimes people who seemingly have little power within a company can be your greatest sources of information. Consider the following employees. What types of power do they possess?

Custodian	Company accountant
Receptionist	Senior employee
Security officer	Computer network administrator

harm any relationships he or she wishes to maintain. This usually includes information that was given to the individual in confidence.

Revealing confidential information might very well cost the person a friendship, a business contact, or some other valuable relationship. Not only might this cause significant personal conflict for that person, but it also erodes his or her power. A person retains informational power only as long as he or she can keep the confidence of potential sources and continue to provide information.

Mother Teresa was a referent leader. Describe how a person gains referent power.

Intrapersonal Students should understand that the exercise of power is generally not a dramatic event. Point out that almost every human transaction involves the use of power by one of the parties.

Activity Ask students to keep a chart for one complete day recording situations in which they have either exercised power or been the subject of someone else's power. Have them divide their chart into two columns for each set of circumstances. (Encourage them to examine their day minutely.) Students should attempt to identify what type of power was applied in each case, using the definitions given in the text. Have students present excerpts from their power charts. Discuss with the class the role of power in everyday activities.

Referent Power

Most leaders hope to gain the respect of their followers. Referent power is the influence held by someone who is respected, liked, or otherwise admired by his or her followers. The name "referent" comes from the fact that the followers refer power onto the individual. They make the leader powerful through their willingness to follow him or her. A leader has referent power only if followers hope to become like him or her.

Of all the types of power, referent power is the most desirable for a leader to hold. Leaders with this power don't have to point out who is in charge, resort to rewards or threats, or claim some special expertise or information connections to get others to follow. Workers accept this leader's direction because they want to help the leader accomplish the work and are pleased to work for and with that person.

Most friends hold a certain amount of referent power over each other. You probably do what your friends ask because of your respect and affection for them, not because you fear them or hope to be rewarded. The same is true when it comes to your heroes as well. Anyone you admire as a hero has referent power over you. When you look up to someone for their athletic ability, musical talent, or knowledge about something, you have given him or her referent power.

Using Referent Power Appropriately Unlike legitimate, reward, and coercive power, which partially stem from a position you hold, referent power is given exclusively by the followers. As a result, they can choose to withdraw it at any time. If you have referent power over others and then disappoint them by doing something unethical or by letting them down when they are counting on you, you probably will lose some or all of that power. To maintain this type of power, you should always try to work in the best interests of those who admire, trust, and respect you.

COMMUNICATION PRACTICE LAB

Understanding Power

To analyze and understand power, follow the steps outlined here:

Step 1 As a class, brainstorm a list of leaders, including local, national, and world leaders, school officials, and other students. Write your list on the chalkboard.

Step 2 Working in groups of three or four, choose one person whom you believe to be the most effective leader on the list. Make sure you do not choose the same leader as another group in your class.

Step 3 Analyze how your chosen leader uses each of the six types of power you just read about.

Step 4 List the six types of power on a sheet of paper in the order you think your leader uses them. Then, assign a percentage value to each type. For instance, 30 percent of your chosen leader's influence may be legitimate power. Create a circular graph using the percentages you assigned.

Step 5 Share your graphs as a class. Which type of power is used most by the leaders your class chose? Which type is used the least? Do most effective leaders use every type of power at some point? Why or why not?

Functioning as a Leader **427**

EXTENDING THE CONTENT

Practicing Referent Power Point out that self-improvement books are often concerned with the acquisition of referent power. In *How to Win Friends and Influence People,* the classic best-seller on self-improvement, Dale Carnegie suggests six strategies to make people like you: (1) become genuinely interested in other people, (2) smile, (3) remember a person's name, (4) be a good listener, (5) talk about the other person's interests, and (6) make the other person feel important. **Activity** Have students copy these guidelines and ask them to practice some or all of them at least once a day. Students should keep a daily journal recording their experiences. In class, have students form groups and share their research. Invite volunteers to present their experiences to the class. Discuss the importance of referent power and the practicality of developing it.

COMMUNICATION PRACTICE LAB

Understanding Power

Students should understand that a leader's effectiveness does not necessarily correspond to the number of people over whom he or she exerts power. The local mayor may be a more effective leader than the president of the United States, and the high school chorus director may be more effective than both of them.

After students have shared their graphs, ask them to discuss whether it is possible for everyone to agree on what constitutes effective leadership. Are effective leaders always admired? Do people respond equally to a leader's use of power? *(Answers will vary.)* **L2**

GLENCOE Online

For an additional Practice Lab for this section, have students visit the *Glencoe Communication Applications* Web site at **communicationapplications.glencoe.com.** Click on Communication Practice Lab 13–2. **L1**

Using Referent Power

Point out that a person with referent power is commonly known as a role model. Have students think of someone whom they consider a role model. Ask them to explain what qualities of this individual led them to refer power to him or her. Discuss with the class what causes a person to be admired and whether referent power is always a good quality. **L2**

COMMUNICATION *Strategies*

LEADING EFFECTIVELY

Ask students to review the checklist of leadership strategies. Before they read ahead, have them choose any two of the items on the list, shut their books, and write down a sentence or two explaining why they think these might be important. Invite students to share their thoughts with the class. After finishing the section, students should return to these first impressions and discuss leadership strategies in light of their reading. **L2**

Make Others Feel Important

Ask students to describe a situation in which a leader made them feel important. What strengths in themselves were enhanced as a result of this attention? Did they perform better as a result?

Any leader may lose his or her power in the eyes of followers. Making numerous mistakes or poor decisions, treating others unfairly or rudely, or requiring that followers adhere to a set of standards that the leader does not personally follow all may diminish a leader's power. It is important for a leader to be aware of and to adjust to feedback from followers so that he or she may lead as effectively as possible.

EFFECTIVE COMMUNICATION METHODS FOR LEADERS

So far in this section, you have analyzed and addressed your communication and preparation skills and looked at the wide variety of power that a leader can have over his or her followers. You now have the knowledge base you need to perfect your leadership skills.

Effective leaders focus the energy of their followers on the mission, or the vision, of the organization and inspire their followers to do their best work. Remember that the purpose of

COMMUNICATION *Strategies*

LEADING EFFECTIVELY

- ✓ Make others feel important.
- ✓ Promote a vision.
- ✓ Focus workers on the task.
- ✓ Treat others with respect.
- ✓ Admit mistakes.
- ✓ Criticize others only in private.
- ✓ Stay visible to your followers.
- ✓ Celebrate achievement.

428 *Glencoe Communication Applications*

---

an organization of people is to combine their talents to accomplish much more than any of them could possibly accomplish by acting alone. Leaders should facilitate the strategic plan—that is, they should try to create the best working situation and conditions so that all the members of the organization can do their best work.

What distinguishes a good leader from a great one? How can you be like those leaders who have made such a difference in your own life? If you examine these leaders' communication methods closely, you will find some common ideas. The Communication Strategies checklist on this page lists a few of their secrets for leading effectively.

Make Others Feel Important

The purpose of any organization is to combine the talents of all the members to accomplish more than any one of them could possibly accomplish on his or her own. Effective leaders try to find each member's particular strength and use it. By emphasizing the strengths of the members rather than your own skill as a leader, you will encourage each follower to give the best he or she has to offer.

Promote a Vision

Effective leaders focus the energy of their followers on the mission of the organization and inspire their followers to do their best work. Not only does an effective leader provide a blueprint of the goals at hand; he or she also shows the value of those goals to his or her followers.

For example, one major corporation has a motto that places a value on the safety and health of customers. The motto is framed and placed in all offices and break rooms, typed on notices to employees, and often quoted in meetings.

INCLUSION STRATEGIES

MEETING INDIVIDUAL NEEDS

Less-Proficient Readers Point out that for many people, learning is enhanced by visual aids. As a result, lecturers typically supplement their presentations with an array of memorable visual aids.

Activity Have students examine the visuals in the chapter and note the kind of information each gives. Then, invite students to imagine that a speaker for a leadership workshop has asked them to prepare a visual aid illustrating one of the communication strategies listed on this page. They may create this with an original design or drawing or with illustrations from periodicals. Have students present their visual aids to the class, explaining the choices they made in the design process.

An effective leader provides structure to guide the work. What else does an effective leader do?

Focus Workers on the Task

An effective leader creates a structure to guide the work to its completion. In addition, an effective leader continually gives information to and seeks information from employees while the work is progressing.

Initiate a Structure. Workers usually want to be certain of which of their duties are of the most importance, how quickly they should proceed with the work, what standards of quality are expected, and the process by which they should do the work. Any time you do an assignment for a teacher, you probably want to know what the end goal is, whether it is a speech, a research paper, or some type of project. You will want to know how you are to proceed on the project, when it is due, and how it will be graded. The assignments leaders give their workers should be as clear as the assignments your teachers give you.

Request and Give Feedback on the Work's Progress. Effective leaders ask workers for their opinions about how the work is proceeding, whether they need additional equipment to do the job, what is going well, and what is causing them difficulty on the job. A leader can also do perception checks to be sure that what he or she hoped to communicate to the workers is what they also understand to be important about the job. If there are problems to be solved during the work progress, the leader collaborates with the workers and they implement whatever solution is decided upon.

Treat Others With Respect

It is always important to treat others the way you wish to be treated. Treating followers with kindness and respect will lessen any resistance you might encounter. On the contrary, it will probably increase the respect others have for you.

Admit Mistakes

You will seem more approachable and likable if you are willing to admit your errors. Your honesty will also encourage followers to take chances without fear of failure. Finally, if your followers suspect that you are covering up your own errors, they are likely to try to cover up their own as well.

Criticize Others Only in Private

Some have said, "Public praise, private criticism." Public criticism has the tendency to embarrass everyone involved, not just the person being criticized. It also reflects poorly on you as a leader. On the other hand, public praise encourages everyone to do his or her best for continued success.

Functioning as a Leader **429**

Admit Mistakes

Point out that there are successful and less successful ways of admitting mistakes. A good leader will take responsibility for his or her misjudgments without appearing weak or overly self-critical. Model for the class a good and a bad way in which a teacher might acknowledge a mistake (Example: not having grades ready on time). Ask students to assess your performance. Then, brainstorm with the class for situations in which students might have to admit a mistake. Encourage volunteers to act out these scenarios. Invite responses from the class on their performances. **L1**

3 ASSESS

Assign Section 2 Assessment as a homework or in-class activity.

🔵 Use *Interactive Tutor Self-Assessment Software* to review Section 2.

Visual Instruction

Answer An effective leader gives information to and seeks information from employees.

MEETING INDIVIDUAL NEEDS

MULTIPLE LEARNING STYLES

Logical-Mathematical Point out that too often people take on jobs without a very clear idea of what their boss expects. Students should realize, however, that considerate employers prepare a written job description, clearly setting out all the responsibilities of the employment.

Activity Have students write a description of jobs that they have done. (Point out that these do not have to be paid work but can include any duties for which they have been responsible.) Students' job descriptions should give clear and precise instructions concerning hours, duties, benefits, and possible extra responsibilites. Students may wish to categorize and chart the information. Encourage them to share their descriptions with the class. 📦

Reteaching Activity 13–2

FUNCTIONING AS A LEADER
Leading Others

Enrichment Activity 13–2

FUNCTIONING AS A LEADER
Leading Others

4 CLOSE

Have students review their answers to the questions posed in the opening paragraph on page 419. Ask them to describe the types of power and communication methods these leaders use. After reading the chapter, would students now revise their initial answers?

Extra-Credit Project

Have students select five people whom they consider to be effective leaders. These may be public figures, friends, or relatives. Ask each student to create an illustrated poster, featuring his or her selection and indicating the qualities that make that person a role model of leadership.

Stay Visible to Your Followers

Staying in touch allows for a free flow of information as well as a constant source of feedback and ideas. Talking to followers, visiting work sites, asking questions, and observing interactions all provide a leader with valuable insight into current conditions and how to improve them.

Celebrate Achievement

When you reward the accomplishment of a goal, you encourage followers to work that much harder on future goals. While failures can be examined carefully and learned from, successes should be celebrated openly and enthusiastically.

One thing is certain: You will have many opportunities in life to lead others. You may be called upon to lead as the result of an official election or a job promotion. Alternatively, your call to leadership may be less formal. You may lead your family through a difficult decision or your study group through a tough problem. In any case, you'll find it important to keep in mind these valuable skills for being an effective leader.

Section 2 Assessment

Visit the *Glencoe Communication Applications* Web site at **communicationapplications. glencoe.com** and click on **Self-Check and Study Guide 13.2** to review your understanding of leading others.

Review Key Terms

1. Define each term and write it in a sentence: power, resistance, legitimate power, reward power, coercive power, expert power, informational power, referent power.

Check Understanding

2. What two skill areas are most important for effective leadership?

3. Identify the source of each type of leadership power.

4. **Classify** Think of the different ways your teacher communicates in a typical class period. Classify each task by the communication method it best illustrates.

APPLICATION *Activity*

Communicating Effectively as a Leader Talk with a parent or older friend about leadership positions he or she has held. Ask the person to describe different types of power and specific communication methods he or she found most effective in that leadership role. Write a brief summary of how that person's experience illustrates the concepts of this section. Discuss your conclusions as a class.

Section 2 Assessment Answers

1. Accept all reasonable sentences.
2. Preparation and communication
3. Legitimate power comes directly from a leader's position. Reward power is based on whatever the leader can give to a follower who complies with requests. Coercive power stems from whatever the leader can take away or whatever punishment the leader can give those who fail to follow directions. Expert power comes from knowledge of a particular task or subject. Informational power comes from the ability to access needed information. Referent power comes directly from followers' respect or admiration.
4. Answers should reflect an understanding of the behaviors required for effective leadership.

Application Activity Answers should reflect an understanding of how power can help or hinder a leader and how certain actions are required for all effective leaders.

Evaluating Your Leadership Skills

How Do You Rate?

On a separate sheet of paper, use the key to respond to the following statements. Put a check mark at the end of each skill you would like to improve.

Key: A Always   **R** Rarely
       U Usually   **N** Never
       S Sometimes

1. I am seen as a leader when I participate in groups.

2. When I work in a group, I try not to be so concerned about pleasing people that nothing gets done.

3. I know how to motivate people to accomplish specific goals.

4. When I have legitimate power, I use it wisely. I am not rude or overbearing.

5. My leadership style is balanced. In times of crisis I can make a decision, but at other times I am a facilitator.

6. I choose experts to lead my group only when I know they have true competence.

7. I try to establish referent power so that workers enjoy working with me.

8. When I am in a leadership role, I give the members of my group the opportunity to do what each does best.

9. I deliver criticism to group members only in private.

10. I work hard to develop the communication skills needed for leadership success.

How Do You Score?

Review your responses. Give yourself 5 points for every A, 4 for every U, 3 for every S, 2 for every R, and 1 for every N. Total your points and evaluate your score.

41–50 Excellent You may be surprised to find out how much you can improve your skills.

31–40 Good In this course, you can learn ways to make your skills better.

21–30 Fair Practice applying the skills taught in this course.

1–20 Needs Improvement Carefully monitor your improvement as you work through this course.

Setting Communication Goals

If you scored Excellent or Good, complete Part A. If your score was Fair or Needs Improvement, complete Part B.

Part A 1. I plan to put the following ideas into practice:

2. I plan to share the following information about communication with the following people:

Part B 1. The behaviors I need to change most are:

2. To bring about these changes, I will take these steps:

Functioning as a Leader **431**

Communication Self-Assessment

Have students respond to the ten statements, using the key on this page, then evaluate their leadership skills. Based on the scores, assign either Part A or Part B of the goal-setting activity. On an index card or sheet of paper, students should concretely define their communication goals to improve their current levels of skill.

Communication Journal Activity

Point out that observation and evaluation are important first steps to acquiring leadership skills. Have students keep a record in their Communication Journals of effective and ineffective examples of leadership they have witnessed during the course of a day. Invite them to share their journal observations with the class.

Communication Tip

Point out that there are many skills involved in effective leadership. Attempting to master all of them at once may result in confusion and disappointment. Encourage students to select one or two behaviors they need to improve and to observe their successes and setbacks in those areas.

MEETING INDIVIDUAL NEEDS · ENGLISH LANGUAGE LEARNERS

Language and Leadership Although many great speakers have been leaders, not all great leaders are naturally gifted at making speeches. Encourage English language learners to understand that there are many leadership skills they can acquire without complete fluency in English. **Activity** Ask groups of students to review the key points in Sections 1 and 2 of this chapter, considering the following questions: Which aspects of leadership do they feel require the greatest command of language? Which aspects can be mastered without total fluency in English? What behaviors would they advise an English language learner to practice in order to assume leadership in an English-speaking context? Have groups prepare notes on their observations and ask them to present their suggestions to the class. Discuss with students the role of language in leadership. **ELL**

Communication Through Writing

Writing a Meeting Summary

Objectives: To create a summary of a meeting

Teaching Suggestions and Strategies

Connection to the Workplace

Students may question why meeting summaries are necessary in an age of recording devices that capture every word and gesture. Point out that very few participants want to revisit a meeting in its entirety. What is necessary is a document that tells the reader at a glance the essential facts and substance of that meeting. The summary remains an ideal method for communicating this information.

Other students may question the need for an official summary at all. "Can't people just take notes of what happened at the meeting for themselves?" they may ask. Point out that taking notes for one's own use is an excellent idea; however, one person's recollection of a meeting is rarely the same as another's. This can cause difficulties when decisions have been made and responsibilities have been allocated. Assigning one person to record the essential facts frees others to participate more fully and to engage in the discussion without the distraction of having to take notes.

Lead students to understand that skill is involved in preparing a meeting summary. Long, rambling reports are time-consuming and dull to read. A good summary is both complete and brief. It requires careful attention to detail and excellent critical skills.

Writing a Meeting Summary

Meetings are held every day throughout the world. Any meeting that addresses important issues should document its activities. A **meeting summary** is a record of a meeting.

Formality Some meeting summaries are written in a more formal style than others. The degree of formality depends on the participants, the issues, and the environment in which the meeting is held. Many companies have formal summaries, called minutes, prepared after meetings of boards of directors or major committees. Less formal summaries are prepared for other types of meetings, such as weekly team meetings or project planning meetings.

Meeting Details When writing a meeting summary, you must carefully attend to the communication taking place during the meeting. Focus on the people, the issues, and the verbal and nonverbal messages being relayed. Maintain eye contact with each speaker and ignore any distractions. Be an active listener.

Meeting Notes If you are responsible for preparing a meeting summary, you will need to take accurate notes of the meeting's activities. Include the following details in your notes:

- The name of the group holding the meeting and the reason for the meeting. Note any specific goals.

- Date, time, and place of the meeting. This information is an important part of the summary. If someone misses a meeting, he or she can use this information later as a reference point to trace progress. Identify yourself as the writer of the summary.

- Who was present and absent. These lists may be important if a question of who attended arises later.

- Reports presented and major points of discussion. State the facts objectively. Listen to the discussion and ask questions when something is unclear. Any decisions that are made should be stated accurately in your summary.

- Follow-up. Include any decisions, assignments, and deadlines made during the meeting. This will remind people of the responsibilities they have taken on as a result of the meeting.

Once you have your notes, you can develop them into a meeting summary like the one that follows. You can then use the summary as a record of the proceedings of the meeting.

 For additional information about business writing, see the *Guide to Business Communication* section of the Communication Survival Kit in the Appendix.

MEETING INDIVIDUAL NEEDS

MULTIPLE LEARNING STYLES

Linguistic Point out that the person writing a summary must make important decisions about which information to discard and which to preserve. Determining what is important about a meeting or speech is a skill that requires practice.

Activity Prepare for the class a fifteen-minute tape recording of a television or radio talk show or phone-in. Play it for the students, asking them to take careful notes; then, have them prepare a summary of the taped segment. Have students form pairs, asking them to share and revise their summaries. Invite volunteers to read their summaries to the class. Discuss what students chose to include and discard. With the help of the class, make a list of essential information from the taped segment.

VIP Company
Company Supplies Task Force
MONTHLY MEETING SUMMARY
June 14, 2002

TIME AND PLACE: 1:30–2:00 p.m.
           Conference Room C
PRESENT: Josephina Myers, Thomas Blevins,
           Christina Jones, Dillon Smith,
           Tanisha Evans
SUMMARY BY: Dillon Smith
REPORTS: Christina presented the Company
           Supply Budget Report to the team.

After the report was presented, Thomas led a discussion about the amount of money that is available for supplies. He noted that the budget has been reduced, yet suppliers have increased their prices on many of the major items the company purchases, such as paper and pens.

Christina said that her department is using more supplies than in the past. Tanisha stated that one of the suppliers has a new catalog.

It was decided after the discussion that Tanisha and Thomas would research other suppliers to find out if the company can buy supplies at a lower cost. A report of their findings will be presented at next month's meeting.

Discussion was then held about the quality of the new disks that were ordered last month. Everyone agreed that the disks were of higher quality than those used in the past. This factor will be considered as we search for new suppliers.

WRITING Activity

Use the following steps to create minutes of a class session, a club that you belong to, or a workplace meeting that you have attended.

- State the name of the group.
- State the reason for meeting.
- State the date, time, and place of the meeting. Identify yourself as the writer of the summary.
- List the people who attended and those who were absent from the meeting.
- Briefly describe any reports presented and tell who presented them.
- Briefly describe the major points of discussion, noting each speaker's remarks. Avoid making any judgmental comments on the discussion.
- Report any votes taken during the meeting, and detail the result of the voting.
- Describe any follow-up that will be accomplished after the meeting, and include everyone's responsibilities.

Functioning as a Leader   433

Teaching Activity

Ask students if they have ever had to explain to someone what happened at a meeting. What were the results of that interaction? Tell students that summaries are a convenient way to record the activity of group meetings.

Have students read carefully the sample notes shown on this page. Then, ask them to write a brief summary of the first ten minutes of the class. In groups, have students compare the summaries. Discuss the differences and accuracy of the summaries. Ask students what might account for the differences. (Students may suggest that individuals have different perceptions of what occurs at any given event. They may also point out that an individual's skills in writing and understanding will influence his or her interpretation.)

WRITING Activity

Student summaries should include each of the items on the list and should be formatted as in the sample.

Grammar Tip

Number refers to the form of a word that indicates whether it is singular or plural. A verb must agree with its subject in number.

Additional Resources

Appendix, "Guide to Business Communication"

Glencoe Writer's Assistant CD-ROM

Glencoe Interactive Grammar Software

Grade 9 Writer's Choice, Lesson 2.6

GRAMMAR PRACTICE

Subject-Verb Agreement

Have students write the correct verb from the choice in parentheses.

(Has, Have) the members been informed about the meeting? *(Have)*

She and Dillon (sits, sit) near the window. *(sit)*

The meeting always (opens, open) with a reading of last week's summary. *(opens)*

All of the members (is, are) going to attend. *(are)*

(Does, Do) he always write the summaries of your meetings? *(Does)*

CHAPTER 13 Assessment and Activities

GLENCOE TECHNOLOGY

MindJogger Videoquiz

Use *MindJogger* to review the Chapter 13 content.

Visit the *Glencoe Communication Applications* Web site at **communicationapplications. glencoe.com** and click on **Chapter 13 Activity** for additional practice in functioning as a leader.

Reviewing Key Terms

1. h
2. e
3. c
4. g
5. f
6. d
7. b
8. a

Reviewing Key Concepts

1. Possible responses are school principal, army colonel, and city manager.

2. (1) Participating early and often in group meetings, (2) demonstrating an ability to do a job well, (3) not insisting on his or her way, and (4) providing solutions for group dilemmas.

3. (1) Effective communication skills, (2) the desire to be a leader, (3) originality or creativity, and (4) intelligence.

4. The kind that does most of its work under crisis or stressful circumstances, such as the army or a prison

5. A balanced leader gets tasks accomplished while being sensitive to the feelings of those connected with the tasks.

Reviewing Key Terms

Read each definition. On a separate sheet of paper, write the number of the definition and the letter of the term that fits the definition best.

a. balanced leader   **e.** style approach
b. laissez-faire leader   **f.** power
c. authoritarian leader   **g.** democratic leader
d. resistance   **h.** emergent leader

1. Is chosen by peers of his or her group
2. Identifies leaders by how they choose to communicate with followers
3. Forces followers to do what he or she wants
4. Invites followers to join in decision making
5. Ability of one person to get others to behave in a particular way
6. Force that keeps a person from accepting another's use of power
7. Gives up his or her power to the followers
8. Strives to be more effective by focusing equally on tasks and relationships

Reviewing Key Concepts

1. Give examples of appointed leaders.
2. In what four ways might a person emerge as a group leader?
3. What four traits are common among leaders?
4. In what kind of organization does the authoritarian leader work best?
5. Why does a balanced leader typically get more done than other kinds of leaders?
6. When does a balanced leader need to act as an initiator rather than a facilitator?
7. Why should a leader analyze the weaknesses of group members?
8. Why is a leader's good judgment especially necessary when listening to followers' feedback?

6. When time is critical to completing a task
7. Knowing weaknesses can help a leader plan for any special training or support workers might need.
8. Listening to feedback can involve sending and receiving negative as well as positive messages. This poses a challenge when followers disagree with a leader and a leader has to manage a conflict.

Assessment and Activities

Reading and Critical Thinking Skill

1. Classifying Information Mr. Byrnes is the principal of Hamilton High School. When a teacher or student asks for direction, he says, "Do what you think best." What is Mr. Byrnes's leadership style?

2. Summarization Sum up the steps an effective leader uses to plan ahead for the tasks facing his or her group.

3. Synthesis Imagine you are the leader of a group that must solicit members for a school club on a day especially set aside for school club recruitment. Synthesize a list of the resources you will need to have a successful membership campaign.

Skill Practice Activity

Predicting Outcomes Seniors at Montcalm High School have traditionally skipped school on the Friday before homecoming weekend. This year the school has a new principal who is unaware of the tradition. Nevertheless, the seniors stay away from school on Friday. Compare the methods an authoritarian principal and a democratic principal might use to exert leadership when the seniors return to school on Monday. Which methods do you think would be more successful? Why?

Cooperative Learning Activity

Planning Tasks As a class, organize into groups of three. Each group should decide on a simple craft, such as making paper flowers, that uses materials already in the classroom. Each member should assume that he or she is the group leader and write out a plan for accomplishing the task. In constructing your plan, follow the four steps given in the chapter. Take turns as a group following one another's plan. Then rate the plans from one to three, one being the most efficient.

Chapter Project

Planning Choose a school or social organization to which you belong and follow the strategies for emerging as a leader:

Participate early and often in group meetings.
Demonstrate your ability to do a job well.
Don't push too hard to get your way.
Provide solutions for group dilemmas.

Keep a journal of your efforts and the feedback you get from other group members.

Presenting Share your journal entries with other members of the class who are participating in the project. Compare your approaches and decide whether to adopt methods that worked for them.

Chapter Project

Encourage students working on the project by supplying them with copies of the following form for their journal pages:

Organization: _____ Describe: _____

Date: _____ _____

Check at least one: _____

____ Participate early and often in group meetings. _____

____ Demonstrate your ability to do a job well. _____

____ Don't push too hard to get your way. _____

____ Provide solutions for group dilemmas. _____

Reading and Critical Thinking Skill

1. Classifying Information Laissez-faire

2. Summarization (1) Planning tasks, (2) evaluating followers, (3) evaluating resources, and (4) planning communication

3. Synthesis Answers may include the following list: a folding table, markers and posterboard for a display, prizes for a raffle, raffle tickets for the drawing, pamphlets about the organization, a sign-up sheet, and volunteers to work the table.

Skill Practice Activity

Predicting Outcomes

Students' answers will vary. The description of the authoritarian principal's methods should include forcing the students to do what the principal wants them to do. The description of the democratic principal's methods should include asking the students how they should be disciplined. Students probably will agree that the democratic principal's methods are more appropriate because the incident is not a crisis.

Cooperative Learning Activity

Planning Tasks

Remind students of the parts of planning a task: (1) examine the task, (2) break the task into steps, (3) make a schedule for the task, allowing enough time for each step, (4) suggest ways to accomplish each task. Have a representative from each group explain what made the group's "number one" plan the best.

THE PRINCETON REVIEW

Standardized Test Practice

Mathematics
Multiple-Choice
Themes: Professional Presentations, Interpersonal Communication, and Cross-cultural Interaction

Answers and Analyses

1. C Think about the perfect squares that are around $\sqrt{150.6}$. $\sqrt{144}$ is 12 and $\sqrt{169}$ is 13. That means that $\sqrt{150.6}$ must be between 12 and 13

2. G Ignore the irrelevant information in the question. If Sarah covers 7 points in 2 hours, then we know she covers 3.5 points in one hour. Divide 168, the number of points she needs to cover, by 3.5, the number of points she can cover in one hour. It will take her 48 hours to cover all her points.

3. C Lines p and q are parallel and are intersected by line l. This intersection creates four angles. $\angle 2$ and $\angle 4$ are supplementary angles. This means the sum of their measurements is 180°. We subtract the measurement of $\angle 2$ from 180° to find the measurement of $\angle 4$. $180° - 81° = 99°$

4. G First, make sure that all measurements are in the same units. Since all the measurements are in inches except for the length of the box, we should convert that measurement to inches. 1 foot = 12 inches; therefore, the length of the box is 12 inches. Look at the ratios of the measurements. The total volume of the box is $6 \times 6 \times 12$, or 432 in^3. The total volume of each pamphlet is $6 \times 3 \times 1$, or 18 in^3. Now all we have to do is divide. $432 \div 18 = 24$. Therefore, 24 pamphlets can fit in the box.

1 $\sqrt{150.6}$ is between which pair of consecutive integers?

A 28 and 29

B 27 and 28

C 12 and 13

D 9 and 10

2 Sarah is preparing to present a three-month series of lectures on value and belief systems. In the past, it has taken her 2 hours to cover 7 main points. If she has 168 main points to cover, how many hours will it take her?

F 108

G 48

H 24

J 12

3 Lines p and q are parallel. If the measure of $\angle 2$ is 81°, what is the measure of $\angle 4$?

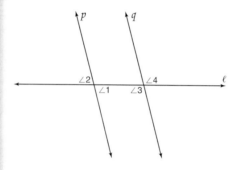

A 9°

B 81°

C 99°

D 109°

4 Tom has put together a conflict mediation pamphlet for his classmates. He will pack the pamphlets vertically in a box

that is 6 inches high, 6 inches wide, and 1 foot long. If each pamphlet is 6 inches high, 3 inches wide, and 1 inch thick, how many pamphlets will Tom be able to fit into the box?

F 18

G 24

H 36

J 378

5 Margot has taken a poll of how many hours in one day that her friends spend outside of school with people from the same high school. Her friends agreed to keep track of the time that they spent. The times were 3.7hrs, 3.9hrs, 4.5hrs, 3.1hrs, 4.7hrs, 4.6hrs, and 3.3hrs. What was the median amount of time that these seven friends spent?

A 3.3hrs

B 3.9hrs

C 4.0hrs

D 4.6hrs

6 The Cross-Cultural Club had a bake sale. They sold 40 empanadas for $8.75 total, two multinational cook books for $10.90 each, and a dozen packs of greeting cards in several languages for $24.00 total. How much money did the Cross-Cultural Club make at the bake sale?

F $24.70

G $43.65

H $54.55

J $395.80

K Not Here

5. B The median in mathematics is just like the median of the middle of a road. In a series of numbers ordered from least to greatest, the median is the number that falls in the middle of the series. For this question, we have to rearrange the numbers to put them in order: 3.1, 3.3, 3.7, 3.9, 4.5, 4.6, 4.7. The median is 3.9 hours.

6. H To find how much money the club made, we need to find the total amount of money they made selling each of the three items and then add those totals together. They made a total of $8.75 selling empanadas and a total of $24.00 selling greeting cards. They sold 2 cookbooks for $10.90 each for a total of $21.80. Add those three totals together for a grand total of $54 55

7 Martin and Francis are playing a game called "Guess What Strategy I'm Using." Francis is the first to explain 4 different conflict resolution strategies. Today, Martin correctly identified the 4 strategies in 28.3 seconds. Yesterday, he correctly identified the 4 strategies in 48.1 seconds. How much faster did Martin identify the strategies today?

  A 19.2 sec

  B 19.8 sec

  C 20.2 sec

  D 20.8 sec

  E Not Here

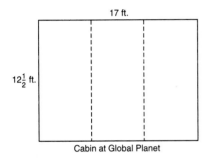

17 ft.

$12\frac{1}{2}$ ft.

Cabin at Global Planet

8 The cabins at Global Planet, a camp for teens, are each $12\frac{1}{2}$ feet by 17 feet. They will each be divided into thirds, as shown, for the three campers.

If the three campers per cabin can share the space equally, what are the dimensions of one camper's area?

  A $4\frac{1}{3}$ ft. by $5\frac{2}{3}$ ft.

  B $6\frac{1}{2}$ ft. by $8\frac{1}{2}$ ft.

  C $5\frac{2}{3}$ ft. by $12\frac{1}{2}$ ft.

  D $5\frac{2}{3}$ ft. by 13 ft.

9 A youth anti-violence seminar paid $412 for 192 non-violence posters. Which is the best estimate of how much the seminar paid per poster?

  F $2.00

  G $.25

  H $2.50

  J $3.00

  K $3.50

10 Toby makes 11 phone calls to get 5 job interviews. What proportion could be used to determine the number of phone calls, *n*, needed for 13 interviews?

  A $\frac{13}{11} = \frac{n}{5}$

  B $\frac{5}{13} = \frac{n}{11}$

  C $\frac{5}{11} = \frac{13}{n}$

  D $\frac{5}{11} = \frac{n}{13}$

  E $\frac{11}{5} = \frac{n}{13}$

11 At the beginning of the school year, Meredith drew a diagram that included the names of her immediate friends. After interacting with the rest of her classmates for the rest of the year, Meredith made another diagram to include her new friends. If Meredith doubled the number of friends that she originally started with and ended up with 58 friends at the end of the year, which equation can be used to find *y*, the number of friends that Meredith had at the beginning of the year?

  F $3y = 58$

  G $58(y + 2) = 0$

  H $y = 58 \times 2$

  J $106 - y = 58$

  K $2y = 58$

STOP

7. B Yesterday Martin identified 4 strategies and today he also identified 4 strategies. Since these numbers are equal, all we need to do to find the time difference is to subtract the shortest time from the longest time.
$48.1 - 28.3 = 19.8$ seconds
He identified the strategies today 19.8 seconds faster than yesterday.

8. C The diagram shows us each camper will have $\frac{1}{3}$ of the 17 feet length which is
$17 \div 3 = 5\frac{2}{3}$ ft.
All of the sections will still be $12\frac{1}{2}$ feet wide. This means the dimensions of each camper's area is $5\frac{2}{3}$ ft by $12\frac{1}{2}$ ft.

9. F These numbers are easy to estimate. $412 is about $400, and 192 posters is about 200 posters. Divide the total estimated cost of the posters by the estimated number of posters. $400 divided by 200 posters is $2.00 per poster.

10. E Set up a fraction (phone calls/interviews) to determine the ratio of the number of calls to interviews. Toby made 11 calls and got 5 interviews, so the ratio is $\frac{11}{5}$. If the number of calls needed to get 13 interviews is unknown, then the proportion is $\frac{11}{5} = \frac{n}{13}$.

11. K Meredith had *y* number of friends at the beginning of the year. She then doubled that number, so she now has 2*y* friends. We know she now has a total of 58 friends, so the correct equation is $2y = 58$.

Unit Objective

Students will learn to identify and demonstrate skills in the presentation process, from preparation to evaluation.

Unit Overview

Unit 4 provides students with knowledge of the presentation process, including information on preparing, researching, practicing, delivering, and evaluating presentations. Students will learn to analyze occasion and purpose in order to prepare effectively. They will have the opportunity to apply all the steps of the process, including the delivery of presentations designed to inform, persuade, and motivate an audience.

Internet Address Book

Record useful Internet addresses in the space below for quick reference.

_____

_____

_____

_____

_____

_____

_____

_____

_____

_____

_____

_____

_____

_____

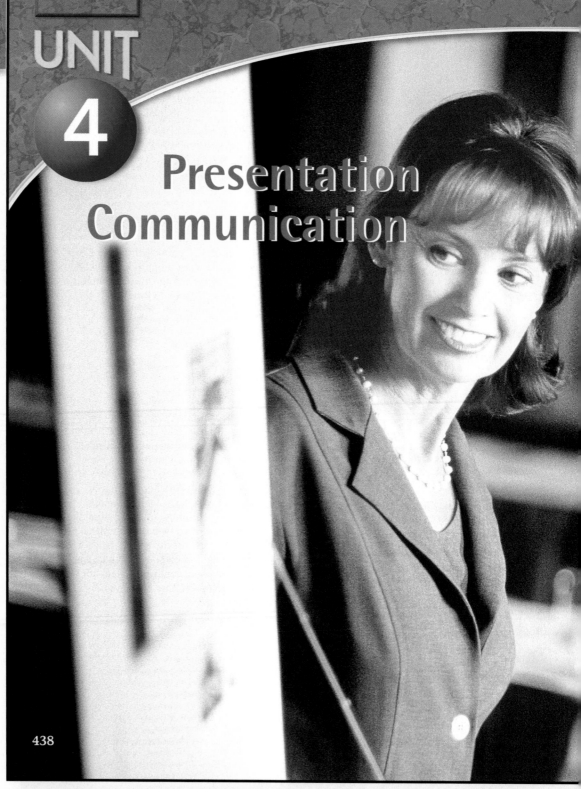

UNIT 4
Presentation Communication

438

VISUAL INSTRUCTION ACTIVITY

Have students examine the photograph on pp. 438–439 and identify the situation. *(A woman is giving a professional presentation with the aid of a flip chart.)* Ask: **What might be some specific reasons for giving a presentation at work?** *(Answers may include informing colleagues about a proposed project, offering instruction in a new technology, or inspiring employees to exceed last year's sales figures.)* Ask: **What do you find most challenging about the presentation process?** *(Answers may include doing the research, organizing the material, speaking effectively, using visual aids, or overcoming stage fright.)*

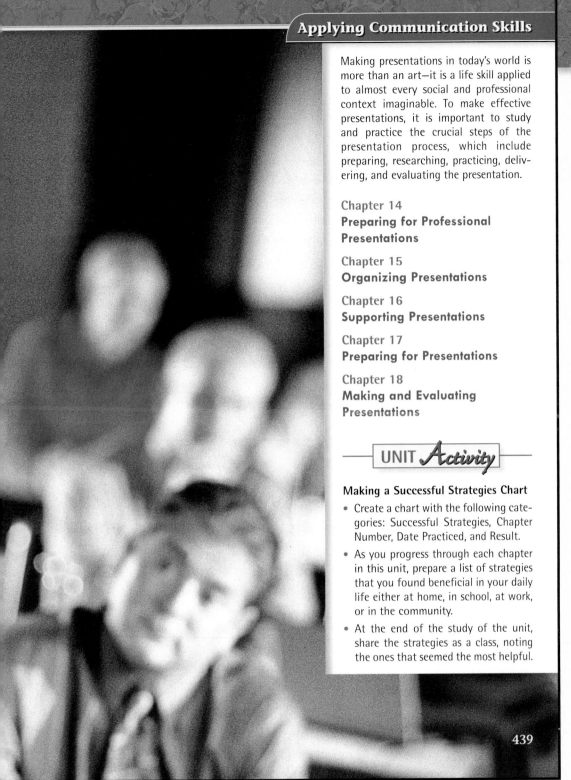

Making presentations in today's world is more than an art—it is a life skill applied to almost every social and professional context imaginable. To make effective presentations, it is important to study and practice the crucial steps of the presentation process, which include preparing, researching, practicing, delivering, and evaluating the presentation.

Chapter 14
Preparing for Professional Presentations

Chapter 15
Organizing Presentations

Chapter 16
Supporting Presentations

Chapter 17
Preparing for Presentations

Chapter 18
Making and Evaluating Presentations

UNIT *Activity*

Making a Successful Strategies Chart

- Create a chart with the following categories: Successful Strategies, Chapter Number, Date Practiced, and Result.

- As you progress through each chapter in this unit, prepare a list of strategies that you found beneficial in your daily life either at home, in school, at work, or in the community.

- At the end of the study of the unit, share the strategies as a class, noting the ones that seemed the most helpful.

439

Introducing the Unit

Ask students when they can recall last attending a presentation. Point out that they are attending one at this moment, with their teacher as presenter! Brainstorm with the class for presentations that people typically experience over the course of a year, at school, work, or home. Lead them to understand that there are many different kinds of presentations, some requiring almost no preparation, others requiring lengthy research and rehearsal. Point out that to be effective, even the most casual presentation requires the acquisition and application of the skills described in Unit 4.

Unit Assessment

After students have completed Unit 4, assign the Unit 4 Assessment in the *Glencoe Communication Appplications Chapter and Unit Tests*.

Testmaker Use the *Glencoe Communication Applications ExamView® Pro Testmaker* software to create a customized Unit 4 test.

UNIT *Activity*

Point out to students that practical communication strategies are provided throughout the text. Assign the following strategies as needed:

Improving Attending Skills, p. 9
Improving Memory Skills, p. 15

For additional strategies, see the "Guide to Business Communication" in the Communication Survival Kit on pages 635–659.

COMMUNICATING IN THE COMMUNITY

Invite a local businessperson or administrator to give your class a presentation on delivering effective presentations. Ask him or her to discuss the importance of research, organization, practice, oral style, and support material. How does your guest cope with communication apprehension? What role do presentations play in his or her organization? Make sure students have questions prepared to ask their guest.

Chapter 14 Planning Guide

SECTION RESOURCES

Daily Objectives	Reproducible Resources	Multimedia Resources

Daily Objectives

Section 1

1. Compare and contrast formal and informal presentations
2. Describe a presenter's responsibilities
3. Analyze the context for a professional presentation

Reproducible Resources

 Reproducible Lesson Plan 14-1
 Application Activities 14-1
 Guided Reading Workbook Activity 14-1
 Vocabulary Activity 14*
 Reteaching Activity 14-1*
 Enrichment Activity 14-1*
 Graphic Organizer Transparency Strategies and Activities 14-1

Multimedia Resources

 Graphic Organizer Transparency 14-1

 Chapter 14 Teaching Transparency

 Interactive Tutor Self-Assessment

 PuzzleMaker

ExamView® Pro Testmaker

Interactive Lesson Planner

 Communication in Action Video Chapter 14

MindJogger

communicationapplications.glencoe.com

Presentation Plus!

Section 2

1. Explain the relationship between context and the selection and limitation of a topic
2. Describe how to limit a topic by classification
3. Determine the purpose of a professional presentation
4. Compare and contrast the characteristics of the three purposes of presentations: informative, persuasive, and motivational

Reproducible Resources

 Reproducible Lesson Plan 14-2
 Application Activities 14-2
 Guided Reading Workbook Activity 14-2
 Vocabulary Activity 14*
 Reteaching Activity 14-2*
 Enrichment Activity 14-2*
 Graphic Organizer Transparency Strategies and Activities 14-2

Multimedia Resources

 Graphic Organizer Transparency 14-2

 Chapter 14 Teaching Transparency

 Interactive Tutor Self-Assessment

PuzzleMaker

 ExamView® Pro Testmaker

 Interactive Lesson Planner

 Communication in Action Video Chapter 14

MindJogger

communicationapplications.glencoe.com

Presentation Plus!

Section 3

1. Recognize the importance of gathering and using accurate and complete information as the basis for making communication decisions
2. Explain how to use surveys and questionnaires to secure information about a topic
3. Determine appropriate sources of information for a presentation
4. Analyze sources for qualifications, credibility, competence, and accuracy

Reproducible Resources

 Reproducible Lesson Plan 14-3
 Application Activities 14-3
 Guided Reading Workbook Activity 14-3
 Vocabulary Activity 14*
 Reteaching Activity 14-3*
 Enrichment Activity 14-3*
 Graphic Organizer Transparency Strategies and Activities 14-3

Multimedia Resources

 Graphic Organizer Transparency 14-3

 Chapter 14 Teaching Transparency

 Interactive Tutor Self-Assessment

 PuzzleMaker

 ExamView®Pro Testmaker

 Interactive Lesson Planner

Communication in Action Video Chapter 14

MindJogger

communicationapplications.glencoe.com

 Presentation Plus!

*** Also available in Spanish**

Chapter 14 Planning Guide

FOR THE TEACHER

Creating a Mini-Presentation

Explain to the students that everyone has some area of expertise. It might be folding shirts just right for display at a department store, kicking field goals, or making a perfect spaghetti sauce. Tell them to spend a moment thinking of an area in which they are an "expert." Then, have them choose partners and share their special skills with each other. Direct them to take detailed notes as their partner talks and to ask questions to make sure they understand the process.

Inform them that their assignment will be to prepare a one-minute presentation on the information they have just received. Remind them to organize their notes so that their description will be clear to their audience. Ask them to try to think of a suitable opening and concluding sentence. Then, tell the students to get together with the same partners, rehearse their presentations, and make revisions where necessary. If they feel confident in their research and rehearsals, ask the students to deliver the presentation to the class. Have them discuss with their classmates the problems and satisfactions of giving presentations.

CHAPTER RESOURCES

Resources for the Teacher

- *The American Library Association Guide to Information Access: A Complete Resource Handbook and Directory* by Sandy Whitely (ed.), Random House, 1994
- *How to Develop and Write a Research Paper* by Phyllis Cash, Arco, 1988
- *How to Give a Speech* by Margaret Ryan, Watts, 1994

Resources for the Student

- *How to Make a Speech* by Steve Allen, McGraw, 1986
- *Knowing Where to Look: The Ultimate Guide to Research* by Lois Horowitz, Writer's Digest, 1988
- *Using the Internet, Online Services, and CD-ROMS for Written Research and Term Papers* by Charles Harmon (ed.), Neal-Schuman, 1996

Block Scheduling

Block scheduling differs from traditional class scheduling in the amount of time allotted to each period. The extended time frame provided by block scheduling affords you the opportunity to implement a greater number of research-oriented and activity-intense projects to motivate and involve your students. Activities that are particularly suited to use within the block-scheduling framework are identified throughout this chapter by the following designation:

KEY TO ABILITY LEVELS

Teaching Strategies have been coded for varying learning styles and abilities.

L1 **BASIC** activities for all students
L2 **AVERAGE** activities for average to above-average students
L3 **CHALLENGING** activities for above-average students
ELL **English Language Learner** activities

 Blackline Master   CD-ROM

 Software   Transparency

 Videodisc   Videocassette

 Web site

 Use Glencoe's *Presentation Plus!* multimedia teacher tool to easily present dynamic lessons that engage and motivate your students. Using Microsoft PowerPoint®, you can customize the presentations to create your own personalized lessons.

Chapter 14 Resource Manager

The following materials may be used when teaching the chapter. Materials for specific lessons are also shown at point-of-use in the margins of the Teacher's Wraparound Edition.

TEACHING TRANSPARENCIES

Chapter 14 Teaching Transparency
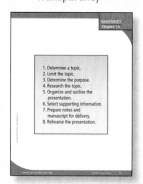

Graphic Organizer Transparency 14–1

Graphic Organizer Transparency 14–2

Graphic Organizer Transparency 14–3

APPLICATION ACTIVITIES

Chapter 14, Section 1

Chapter 14, Section 2

Chapter 14, Section 3

Chapter 14, Cumulative

REINFORCEMENT AND REVIEW ACTIVITIES

Vocabulary Activity 14

Guided Reading Activity Workbook 14–1, 14–2, 14–3

Reteaching Activities 14–1, 14–2, 14–3

Chapter 14 Resource Manager

ASSESSMENT AND EVALUATION

Section Quizzes 14–1, 14–2, 14–3

Chapter 14 Test, Forms A & B

Performance Assessment Activity 14

ENRICHMENT AND EXTENSION

Technology Application Activity 14

Enrichment Activities 14–1, 14–2, 14–3

ORAL PRESENTATION ACTIVITIES

Activities 1–3

SPANISH RESOURCES

- Spanish Chapter and Unit Tests
- Spanish Vocabulary Activities
- Spanish Section Quizzes
- Spanish Reteaching Activities
- Spanish Enrichment Activities

MULTIMEDIA

- Interactive Tutor Self-Assessment
- ExamView® Pro Testmaker
- PuzzleMaker
- Communication in Action Videodisc and Videocassette
- MindJogger
- Interactive Lesson Planner
- Presentation Plus!
- Writer's Assistant
- Glencoe Interactive Grammar
- **communicationapplications.glencoe.com**

TEACHER PLANNING AND SUPPORT

- Reproducible Lesson Plans
- Interactive Lesson Planner
- Presentation Plus!

CHAPTER **14**

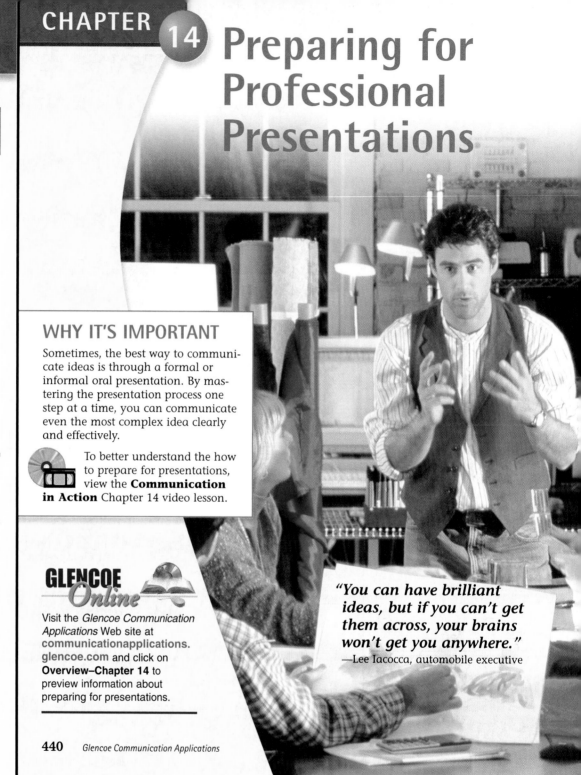

Preparing for Professional Presentations

WHY IT'S IMPORTANT

Sometimes, the best way to communicate ideas is through a formal or informal oral presentation. By mastering the presentation process one step at a time, you can communicate even the most complex idea clearly and effectively.

To better understand the how to prepare for presentations, view the **Communication in Action** Chapter 14 video lesson.

"You can have brilliant ideas, but if you can't get them across, your brains won't get you anywhere."
—Lee Iacocca, automobile executive

WHY IT'S IMPORTANT

Have students read the quotation above. Ask: **What do you feel are the most important skills to learn in communicating your ideas to others.** *(Answers may include careful research, enthusiasm, organization, and practice.)* Ask students to preview the contents of Chapter 14 by reading the headings and have them think of other important aspects of the presentation process.

Introducing Professional Presentations

GUIDE TO READING

Objectives

1. Compare and contrast formal and informal presentations.
2. Describe a presenter's responsibilities.
3. Analyze the context for a professional presentation.

Terms to Learn

professional presentation
formal presentation
informal presentation
ethos
demographics

Help Wanted: Individual with strong communication skills to make frequent presentations before small and large groups. Must be able to inform, persuade, and motivate. Salary negotiable. Position open immediately.

Would you consider responding to an advertisement like this one? If the answer is no, why not? If you are like thousands of others, you may fear making a presentation almost more than anything else. What makes you uncomfortable speaking in public?

If you have ever given a presentation, you may have felt awkward being the center of attention. You might also be unsure about the information you were presenting. Whatever your discomfort, there are ways to overcome it through practice and preparation. The ability to produce and give quality oral presentations is a basic social and professional skill.

Public speaking is a necessity in some careers. Name two ways to overcome anxiety with regard to public presentations.

Preparing for Professional Presentations **441**

Bellringer

Give students five minutes to write a paragraph or two on the following subject: *How I feel about speaking in public.* When they have finished, ask them to rank themselves from 1 to 10 on the basis of how comfortable they feel in giving presentations, with 1 for "very comfortable" and 10 for "total stage fright." Have students who scored themselves from 1 to 5 find a partner in the 6 to 10 range and ask them to read their paragraphs to each other. Ask for volunteers to share their ideas with the class. Conclude with a discussion about what makes people uncomfortable speaking in public.

You may use Graphic Organizer Transparency 14–1 to introduce this section.

Graphic Organizer Transparency 14–1

Speaker
Audience
Occasion
Task

Visual Instruction

Answer Responses may include learning techniques for effective presentations and practicing in front of audiences as much as possible.

RESOURCE MANAGER

Teaching Tools

- Interactive Lesson Planner
- Reproducible Lesson Plan 14–1
- Application Activities 14–1

Reproducible Masters

- Guided Reading Activity Workbook 14–1
- Enrichment Activity 14–1
- Reteaching Activity 14–1
- Section Quiz 14–1
- Transparency Strategies and Activities Booklet 14–1

Transparencies

- Graphic Organizer Transparency 14–1
- Chapter 14 Teaching Transparency

Technology Resources

- Interactive Tutor Self-Assessment Software
- Presentation Plus! Software
- ExamView® Pro Testmaker
- PuzzleMaker Software
- communicationapplications.glencoe.com

2 TEACH

Formal and Informal Presentations

Ask students to recall two recent occasions when they have had to make both a formal and an informal presentation. Have them jot down answers to the following questions: What were the subjects? How much notice were they given? How much preparation did the presentations take? How would they compare the two occasions? Lead the class in a discussion comparing and contrasting types of presentations, based on the students' written answers. **L1**

🌐 GLOBAL COMMUNICATION

Oral Cultures

Have students consider the extent to which information is still communicated by word of mouth. Ask them to make a chart of how they receive information during the course of a day, including in it a wide range of informational material, from how to get to the bowling alley to causes of the Civil War. Have them break their chart down into the following categories: *direct speech, television, print, radio, Internet, other.* Using their charts as a starting point, discuss the importance of oral communication. **L2** 📄

PROFESSIONAL PRESENTATIONS

A **professional presentation** is an informed, organized oral statement made to a group of professional or social peers, supervisors, clients, or members of the general public. Most presentations in professional and social contexts fall into one of two categories: formal or informal.

Formal Presentations

A **formal presentation** is scheduled in advance and usually involves individual or team research and audiovisual, or AV, support. Formal presentations usually require a carefully structured format and outline. They also require formal language strategies and delivery techniques. These presentations might be made by a salutatorian at a high school graduation, by a corporate executive to stockholders at an annual meeting, or by project managers requesting funding for a specific project. Sales presentations, product demonstrations, reports to executive boards, committee project reports, and assigned classroom presentations all are examples of formal presentations.

Informal Presentations

An **informal presentation** may occur on a daily or ongoing basis. It usually is shorter and more spontaneous than a formal presentation and may involve a smaller audience.

You might give an informal presentation to your teacher or boss when you are casually asked for an update on your current project. At work, informal presentations might occur when showing a new employee around the office, when explaining a bill to a client, or when telling the principal your opinions on a proposed change in school policy. Each of these situations requires you to make an informal presentation on relatively short notice.

🌐 GLOBAL COMMUNICATION

Oral Cultures

In ancient oral cultures that did not have a systematic form of writing, minstrels, poets, and storytellers created and narrated stories that described traditional practices and recounted historical events. What aspects of ethos do you think these presenters conveyed? How do we capture and preserve cultural traditions today?

PRESENTER'S RESPONSIBILITIES

As in other forms of oral communication, the competent speaker has a specific set of responsibilities that relate to the context of his or her presentation. These responsibilities include developing basic speaking skills and creating an image as a competent presenter.

Basic Skills

The basic skills most needed by professional presenters fall into five categories. These are:

- selection
- organization
- style
- memory
- delivery

Selection A presenter's first responsibility is to select topics, ideas, and supporting information carefully. Topics and ideas should be well supported through sufficient research. It also is critical that topics and ideas be carefully tailored to meet the

---

🔵 MEETING INDIVIDUAL NEEDS — MULTIPLE LEARNING STYLES

Linguistic Point out that word of mouth is still an important means of conveying information in our society but that it requires both speaking and listening skills to be reliable and effective.

Activity Have students bring to school copies of a daily newspaper or a weekly newsmagazine. Give them time to find an article of at least 500 words in length that interests them. Ask them to read the article carefully; then, have them form groups and summarize their articles to each other, without notes or reference to the original. Finally, ask for a volunteer from each group to retell, fluently and convincingly, the information he or she received from a teammate. Discuss with the class the nature of receiving and presenting oral information based on this exercise.

demands of a particular audience, occasion, and task. If the topic has been selected for you, you still need to select additional ideas and support information that are appropriate to the topic.

Organization Presenters are responsible for making sure their presentations are put together well. Effective presenters take time to learn how to properly organize their presentations for maximum effectiveness.

Style It is important for speakers to use appropriate language in their presentations. Selecting the words and language style for a presentation is like selecting the clothing you will wear to a certain event. Just as some types of clothing are appropriate to specific situations, so are some types of language. Effective presenters evaluate what is needed and then use language that is appropriate for their topic, audience, task, and occasion.

Memory Presenters need to possess a variety of speaking and language skills that they can adapt to different speaking situations. This allows them to "think on their feet" as specific needs arise during a presentation. You can accomplish this by mentally filing away information and ideas on a topic as you do your research. Committing information to memory provides you with a bank of knowledge that you can draw from during a presentation whenever you need it.

Delivery Presenters also are responsible for using appropriate verbal and nonverbal skills. For example, even the best-prepared presentation can fail if the presenter does not speak loudly enough. Additionally, if a speaker does not establish eye contact, an audience may feel ignored or unimportant or become skeptical. In many cases, the success or failure of a presentation is determined by the presenter's delivery skills.

An Appropriate Image

In addition to developing and polishing essential speaking skills, a responsible presenter gives careful consideration to the image he or she conveys to an audience. Aristotle, a Greek philosopher, taught that a speaker's image is directly related to whether or not an audience will accept and believe a message. If an audience has a poor image of a speaker, it may not believe his or her message. A speaker with a credible image is more likely to be believed.

Aristotle stressed that a speaker has a responsibility to develop and convey a positive ethos. Ethos is the image a presenter displays to an audience. There are four main aspects of ethos that presenters should try to

Aristotle taught that a speaker was more believable if he or she established a positive ethos, as General Schwarzkopf has done. Identify the four aspects of ethos that a presenter should consider.

Preparing for Professional Presentations **443**

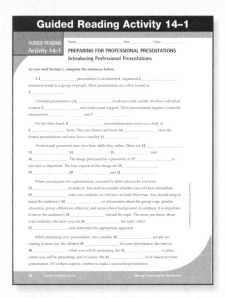

Guided Reading Activity 14–1

Looking at the Basic Skills
Have students review the skills described on this page. Ask them to rank the skills from 1 to 5 in what they believe to be the order of importance. On the chalkboard, make a table of the rankings and encourage a class discussion, leading students to understand the importance of all the basic speaking skills. **L2**

Dɪᴅ Yᴏᴜ Kɴᴏᴡ?
The art of persuasion was one of the many fields in which the Greek philosopher Aristotle (384-322 B.C.) was an authority. He also wrote about politics, history, literature, psychology, physics, chemistry, biology, botany, and zoology. His treatise on logic is still studied as an important philosophical text. A pupil of Plato and the tutor of Alexander the Great, Aristotle's teaching dominated European thought and education until the eighteenth century.

■ **Visual Instruction**

Answer A presenter should consider knowledge, character, good intent, and genuineness.

The Speaker's Image

Have students consider what the word *image* means to them by asking them to jot down ways in which people acquire a public image. (*Possible answers include wealth, unusual clothing, untruthfulness, honesty, beauty, romance, defiance, and so on.*) Ask if students believe in the image that public figures create for themselves. How much is real? How much is self-promotion? Point out that in an age of skepticism and media hype, creating a positive ethos is often a challenging task for a contemporary speaker. **L2**

BUSINESS BRIEF

Harold Geneen, former President of ITT, was renowned as an able, aggressive business leader—"The Michelangelo of Management," as one admirer called him. He was also a fierce critic of egotism in the corporate world. "At the top level, I've known some chief executives to compete with one another in the length and model of their limousines" he wrote. "That is ego gratification." Ask students whether they believe that image and performance are complementary or conflicting partners to a successful career.

---

consider: knowledge, character, good intent, and genuineness. In his teachings, Aristotle discussed the first three aspects. Modern researchers have added the fourth.

Knowledge An audience has the right to expect complete and accurate information in a presentation. Therefore, a presenter should be well informed about his or her subject. It is the presenter's responsibility to study all aspects of a topic so that he or she can speak ethically. In addition to being informed, a presenter must let the audience know that he or she is knowledgeable about the subject matter. For example, before proceeding with a presentation on grandparenting, General Norman Schwarzkopf might explain his relationship with his own grandchildren.

Character For an audience to believe a message, it must feel that the presenter is of sound character. That is, the listeners must believe a presenter would not intentionally mislead them by telling untruths or omitting important information. They must trust the presenter to believe his or her message.

Good Intent A presenter should demonstrate good intentions when relating a message to an audience. Listeners will be more receptive if they feel that a speaker has their best interests at heart. They also want to feel that information is being presented fairly and that the speaker sincerely cares about the outcome of the presentation.

Genuineness Today's audiences also want speakers who are genuine, sincere, and truly interested in the audience and the topic. They want to believe that the emotions, attitudes, and ideas presented are those of the presenter; this helps them trust both the speaker and the message. However, audiences tend to reject the ideas of presenters they think are arrogant or insincere.

CONTEXT OF THE MESSAGE

As you prepare a presentation, you will make choices that reflect your ideas and knowledge about a topic. These choices are based on the specific context of your presentation. This includes what you know about yourself as a speaker, your audience, the occasion for your presentation, and the task, or purpose, you want to accomplish.

Consider the Speaker

When you begin to prepare a presentation, think about why you were selected to make it. Are you an authority who will have immediate credibility with the audience, or will you need to build your audience's trust? Are you a recognized member of the group to which the presentation will be made or will you have to select information that establishes who you are? Have you been selected to make the presentation because of your role on a project at work? What will you or your organization gain from this presentation?

After answering these questions, consider your own personal interest in the topic. How long have you been involved with this particular topic? How extensive is your knowledge of the subject? What do you have to gain from the presentation? The answers to these questions will help you make choices that will build your personal ethos with your audience and set the stage for your presentation.

Consider the Audience

Many of the responsibilities of the presenter are based on a thorough analysis of the audience. Therefore, the more you know about your audience, the better choices you can make to meet your responsibilities.

MEETING INDIVIDUAL NEEDS — MULTIPLE LEARNING STYLES

Bodily-Kinesthetic A good speaker is capable of creating a feeling of confidence in his or her audience. Knowledge, credibility, good intent, and genuineness are not always easy to identify. **Activity** Ask for four or five students who enjoy acting to form a panel to challenge the class. Instruct each member of the panel to tell an unusual story involving himself or herself, with the provision that only one of these stories is to be true. Have the panel confer to decide on their strategy. After they have presented their stories, ask the class to guess which student told the truth. Discuss the reasons they guessed as they did, linking the discussion to how speakers attempt to create a positive ethos. This game can be played in several variations, including the real or fictitious definitions of unusual words. 📦

Audience Demographics One important consideration for a speaker is the demographics of the audience. As shown in **Figure 14–1**, **demographics** is information about a group's age, gender, education, group affiliations, ethnicity, and sociocultural background.

You can use audience demographics to make generalizations about listeners' interests and needs. For example, if your goal is to get approval for a skating park in your community, you might first study the demographics of area residents to get an idea of who you need to convince. To get help convincing community leaders, you could meet with local students and make a presentation that focuses on the fun, recreational aspects of skateboarding and in-line skating. You also might make a presentation to local business people pointing out how the park might keep young people from skating on public sidewalks and streets.

In both cases, your goal as a presenter is the same: build support for a public skating

interNET
ACTIVITY

Demographics Speakers must consider the demographics of their audiences. Use a reliable search engine or log on to **www.census.gov** to find information about the demographics of your community or state. How would demographics affect your giving a speech to community leaders in your community or state?

park. However, by knowing your audience's unique perspectives and concerns, you can customize your message for maximum effectiveness. In other words, you can focus on what is most important to each group.

Age People of different ages typically have different interests. Because of this, they may be interested in different aspects of a topic. For instance, when the audience is a group of young employees, a presentation about a company's benefits package might focus more on family benefits and disability protection. A benefits presentation to a group of older employees may focus more heavily on retirement options and long-term medical care.

Gender Although gender once was a major consideration in audience demographics, attitudes about gender roles have drastically changed. Today, it is important not to make judgments about your audience based on gender. One possible exception is if the topic is based on statistics that categorize men

■ **Figure 14–1 Elements of Demographics**

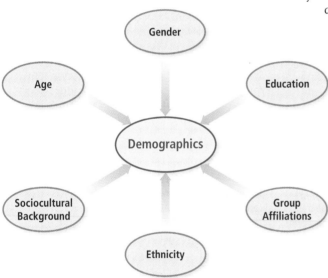

Preparing for Professional Presentations **445**

Considering the Audience
Have students review the six elements of demographics displayed in Figure 14–1. Which do they believe would most powerfully influence a speaker's presentation? Discuss how demographics affect the speaker's message and the way it is delivered. **L2**

interNET
ACTIVITY

Demographics Ask the class to cite instances in which demographics plays a key role in presenting persuasive messages. *(Answers may include the campaign speeches of political candidates, advertisements pertaining to political issues in a specific region, or commercials for adolescent products airing during television programs oriented toward young adults.)* Lead the students in a discussion of specific examples of such demographically oriented persuasive messages on a local or national level. Taking into account the demographic information found on the www.census.gov Web site, debate which messages are most effective and why. **L2**

Gender
Making generalizations about the roles and attitudes of men and women may no longer be wise, but does gender still influence communication? Ask students to consider whether they communicate differently with members of the opposite sex. Do they feel that there are good reasons for considering men and women as distinct audiences, or are gender distinctions the result of tradition and prejudice? **L1**

COMMUNICATION Strategies

PREDICTING AUDIENCE ATTITUDE

Point out that knowing how another person is feeling may well influence the way you approach him or her. Ask students to imagine that they have been called to the principal's office under one of the following three circumstances: they are going to be praised; they are going to be punished; they don't know why. Have volunteers model their behavior for each of these alternative scenarios. Ask how this role-playing exercise is related to the importance of predicting audience attitudes. **L2**

Gathering Audience Information

Ask students to share experiences about being new to a group, school, or summer camp. How did they behave, and why? What would have made them feel more comfortable? Point out that a speaker without information about his or her audience is in a similar situation to the new student at a school—uncertain and insecure. **L1**

Communication Tip

Varying your voice in pitch and volume is an important technique for keeping an audience's attention. Even the most interesting ideas will fail to make an impact when delivered in a monotone. When preparing for a presentation, make a note of passages that require special emphasis and practice speaking them.

COMMUNICATION Strategies

PREDICTING AUDIENCE ATTITUDE

- ✓ Will they agree or disagree with what I have to say?
- ✓ Will their initial reaction to the topic be positive or negative?
- ✓ Are they already familiar with the topic?

---

and women differently. For example, auto insurance companies use data about age and gender to determine car insurance rates. Based on statistics, young male drivers under the age of twenty-five usually pay more for auto insurance coverage. That is because this group, statistically, is more likely to be involved in an auto accident than a member of another age group or gender. In general, however, making generalizations about gender not only may offend your audience, but they also may be inaccurate.

Education Sometimes, audiences with a higher level of education may have a broader knowledge base on a specific topic. However, listeners who have a great amount of interest or experience in a topic may be just as knowledgeable, regardless of their level of education. It is important to find out how much an audience actually knows about a topic so you can either provide more information or avoid talking down to them.

Group Affiliations Knowing which groups audience members identify with can help you understand their common interests. It also can help you select examples and ideas that will relate to those interests. This information also can help you quote appropriate authorities to establish your credibility on a topic.

Sociocultural and Ethnic Backgrounds The sociocultural background of an audience helps you better understand the listeners' experience with your topic. Audiences from different backgrounds may have different ways of looking at a topic. For example, an audience from a neighborhood in a very large city may think of mass transit as a necessity while an audience from a rural area may feel that mass transit is an unnecessary expense for its community. Audiences with differing social, economic, ethnic, or cultural backgrounds may have different ways of identifying with a topic based on how they are affected by it.

Audience Attitude In addition to knowing the demographics of your audience, it is important to determine in advance how listeners feel about the topic. Ask yourself the questions in the Communication Strategies checklist to help predict their attitude.

The answers to these questions will help you predict how your audience will accept what you have to say. If you think they might initially disagree with your main topic, you might focus on certain aspects of the topic with which everyone can agree. If your audience already knows something about a topic, your goal may be to share new information.

Gathering Audience Information The more information you can discover about your listeners, the more you can adapt the topic, select information, and determine the appropriate approach to suit their needs and expectations. You want to put yourself in your audience's shoes. What do they need to know? What is their interest level? One way to find out this information is to contact several members of the audience before presenting. Discuss your plans with them to find out if you are on the right track. Another, but sometimes more difficult, way to get information about your audience is to administer an audience survey prior to preparing your presentation. The

---

CRITICAL THINKING ACTIVITY

Remind students that speakers are not always in a position to say what their audience wants to hear. Politicians, military leaders, executives, and even rank-and-file employees sometimes have to convey bad news. Point out that selling the unpopular message is a true test of a speaker's skills. Brainstorm with the class for situations in which the speaker's message is unlikely to find favor with the audience. (Examples: A CEO announces the closure of a plant; a principal announces a longer school day; a general gives news of a defeat.) Make a list of these situations on the chalkboard and ask the class to consider strategies for conveying such information. Discuss ways in which a speaker could persuade an audience not to blame the messenger for the message.

information you get from the survey can provide you with important insight into your audience's attitudes and knowledge about your subject.

Considering the Occasion

What is the occasion for your presentation? Is it a special ceremony to honor some person or the accomplishment of a goal? The beginning of a special campaign or sales drive? An informational presentation? Given in the morning or evening? Given around a small conference table or at a particular work site? The more you know about the occasion, the better you will be able to adapt your message and choose appropriate ideas and information.

Attendance Why are people gathering to hear your presentation? Is it a regularly scheduled social meeting, or is it a business meeting that employees are required to attend? Knowing the occasion helps you determine whether the audience is there because it wants to be or because attendance is required.

Usually, audience members who attend because they want to be there will be more interested in your topic than those who are required to attend. It is your responsibility as a presenter to include both groups and motivate them to listen to what you have to say in your presentation.

Time Time, especially in a business setting, is an important context consideration. As you can see in **Figure 14–2** on page 448, you need to think about how much time is allotted for your presentation and at what time of day you will make it. A five-minute presentation requires a much more specific topic than a twenty-minute presentation. It would be difficult to fully explain an entire budgeting process in only five minutes. However, if you've been allotted twenty or thirty minutes, you can easily cover more information. Because of these considerations, a shorter presentation may take more time to prepare than a longer one. It can take considerable effort to limit a topic to the bare essentials.

COMMUNICATION PRACTICE LAB

Considering the Context

To practice taking context into consideration when preparing to present, follow these steps:

Step 1 Imagine that you have been asked to speak about a school organization to which you belong. The organization can be athletic, academic, work-related, social, or community-based. Create a brief description of the information you will present and how you will present it.

Step 2 Determine how the following circumstances might affect your presentation.

- You are giving a fifteen-minute presentation in the high school auditorium to a group of students who will be freshmen next year.
- You are giving a five-minute presentation in a high school classroom to a group of parents.

Step 3 Make lists of ways you might adjust your presentation based on each context in which it will be given.

Step 4 Discuss your lists as a class. Did most students make similar presentation choices?

Preparing for Professional Presentations **447**

EXTENDING THE CONTENT

Speaking at the Right Speed In *Smart Moves* authors Sam Deep and Lyle Sussman suggest that rate of speaking is an important factor in keeping an audience motivated to listen. "Don't stray below 120 words per minute, except for effect," they advise. "The best motivational speakers average closer to 200 wpm. Going below 120 wpm will cause your listeners' minds to wander."
Activity Have students form pairs, and ask them to take turns timing each other reading aloud a passage from this book (or any other written passage). Allow them to practice until they feel confident they can read at rates of about 120 and 200 words per minute. Invite volunteers to demonstrate these rates in front of the class and discuss the effect of the two speeds on the audience.

Reasons for Attending a Presentation

Ask students to recall presentations that they have particularly enjoyed. What made them enjoyable? Were students required to attend any of these presentations? Discuss how an audience's reason for attendance can affect the presenter's task. **L1**

COMMUNICATION PRACTICE LAB
Considering the Context

After students follow the steps described, ask them which presentation they would have found easier to make and why. Invite volunteers to model a third presentation on the same subject but in the following context: A four-year-old child asks you to describe something you do at school. Discuss how this context alters the nature of the presentation. **L2**

Application Activities 14–1

For an additional Practice Lab for this section, have students visit the *Glencoe Communication Applications* Web site at **communicationapplications.glencoe.com**. Click on Communication Practice Lab 14–1. **L1**

Holding an Audience's Interest

Students often complain that it is difficult to maintain full attention during a school day. Ask them what techniques teachers have successfully used to keep them alert and on task. **L1**

3 ASSESS

Assign Section 1 Assessment as a homework or in-class activity.

✪ Use *Interactive Tutor Self-Assessment Software* to review Section 1.

Section 14–1 Quiz

■ Figure 14–2 **Time Considerations**

Allotted Time   Time of Day

As noted, another consideration is the time of day during which you will make your presentation. What will the audience be doing before and after your presentation? An audience will tend to compare your presentation to another it has just heard. If listeners are eagerly anticipating whatever comes afterward, you may have a hard time holding their attention.

Will your presentation occur first thing in the morning? Audience members may arrive late or need time to adjust to the workday. Will you present just before or after lunch? If your presentation is just before lunch, listeners may be too hungry to concentrate. If it is right after lunch, they may be sleepy or easily bored. What if your presentation occurs at the end of the day? In this instance, listeners' attention may drift to what they will be doing after work.

As you can see, all these time periods can impact a presentation. There is no ideal time for a presentation. As a presenter, you will always face the challenge of maintaining your audience's attention. Regardless of when you give your presentation, try to be as interesting and enthusiastic as possible and pay attention to your audience's responses to you. Provide breaks during long

presentations, pause periodically to allow opportunities for questions, and use visuals to keep your audience focused on the topic.

Location Consider where you will be giving your presentation. The location affects your delivery and possibly any visual aids you plan to use. Will you be presenting to a small group around a conference table? To a large group in a small room? To a small group in a large room? There are many variations on room and group size, and each presents a special set of needs. For example, the larger the audience, the more formal the presentation because there may be less opportunity for audience interaction. However, your presentation may not be held in a room at all. A five-minute informal presentation at a company picnic will require you to make different presentation choices than will a five-minute formal presentation in an executive conference room.

There are other location concerns as well. What noise can you expect in the area designated for your presentation? Are phones likely to ring? Can you overhear others in

The location can greatly affect the delivery of a presentation. What possible problems should speakers consider if their presentation is to be held outdoors?

Visual Instruction

Answer Responses may include noise from cars, trains, airplanes, and construction workers, as well as generally poor acoustics.

Section 1 Assessment Answers

1. Accept all reasonable sentences.

2. Formal and informal presentations are both informed, organized oral statements made to groups of professional or social peers, supervisors, clients, or members of the general public. An informal presentation is usually shorter and more spontaneous than a formal presentation, which is scheduled in advance and requires careful planning and formal delivery techniques, often with audiovisual support.

3. A presenter is responsible for developing basic speaking skills and creating an appropriate image. The five skills most needed by presenters involve selection and organization of material, effective style, memory, and appropriate delivery. The presenter develops image by cultivating the following four areas: knowledge, credibility, good intent, and genuineness.

4. A presenter should consider the speaker, the audience, the occasion, and the task.

the next room? If you must give a presentation in a setting that is uncomfortable or distracting to your audience, try to focus on the positive elements surrounding the presentation.

Effective presenters try to be considerate of their audience as they communicate their message. Keep your message lively, allow for frequent breaks, and encourage participants to stretch regularly during longer sessions. When you do this, your listeners will appreciate your thoughtfulness and will reward you with their attention.

Considering the Task

A fourth context consideration is the task itself, or the nature or reason for the presentation. What are you being asked to do, and what will it take for you to accomplish it? Will your presentation need to be formal or informal? A five-minute presentation highlighting why a client should buy your product is different from a short presentation to someone who has never heard of your product. Although the goal in both of these situations is to get the client to buy the product, the form of each presentation will be dramatically different.

Section 1 Assessment

Visit the *Glencoe Communication Applications* Web site at **communicationapplications. glencoe.com** and click on **Self-Check and Study Guide 14.1** to review your understanding of preparing for presentations.

Review Key Terms

1. Define the following terms and write each in a sentence: professional presentation, formal presentation, informal presentation, ethos, demographics.

Check Understanding

2. How are formal and informal presentations similar? How are they different?

3. What are the responsibilities of a presenter? Explain.

4. **Synthesis** What should a presenter consider before preparing a presentation and why?

APPLICATION *Activity*

Developing Evaluation Criteria You hear all kinds of presentations—so many that you likely are unaware that each is, in fact, a presentation. School announcements, oral reports, and even your teachers' lectures are all types of presentations. Think about a recent presentation you experienced. Now, consider the responsibilities of the presenter. What criteria might you develop to evaluate whether that person has met his or her responsibilities as a presenter? Apply these criteria. Which responsibilities were met and which were not? Discuss your criteria as a class. Together, make a class list of criteria for determining whether or not a presenter has met his or her responsibilities. Copy your list in your notebook for future reference.

Preparing for Professional Presentations **449**

4 CLOSE

Have students recall the rankings they gave themselves before starting to read Section 1, on the subject of speaking in public. On the basis of what they have read since then, invite them to specify the areas in which they feel they need the most practice. Discuss how they might effectively go about developing the necessary skills.

Extra-Credit Project

Ask students to interview someone whose job involves frequent professional presentations. Have them inquire which skills are the interviewee's strengths and weaknesses, how he or she prepares for a presentation, and how he or she adapts a message to the context of the presentation. Have students write up their findings and present them to the class.

Section 1 Answers, continued

Speaker: to know why you have been chosen to make a presentation.
Audience: to understand the demographics of those you are addressing in order to effectively convey your message.
Occasion: to adapt your ideas and choose appropriate information.
Task: to understand what you are being asked to do and what you must do to accomplish it.

Application Activity Encourage students to create their criteria list by reviewing the section and including a checklist for the basic skills and aspects of image described in the text as necessary for a presenter. They should also include an assessment of whether the presenter has considered the four areas of context discussed in this section: the speaker, the audience, the occasion, and the task.

1 FOCUS

Bellringer

Have students read the opening paragraph of this section silently. Ask them what they think is meant by "a journey of a thousand miles." *(One explanation: a long and difficult undertaking)* Have them consider "thousand-mile journeys" they have taken in their lives. How did they feel when contemplating the task ahead? How did they tackle and overcome the problem? What did they learn from the experience?

✍ You may use Graphic Organizer Transparency 14–2 to introduce this section.

Graphic Organizer Transparency 14–2

	Informative Presentation	Persuasive Presentation	Motivational Presentation
Presenter's Goal or Purpose			
Examples			
Roles to Assume			
Words That Describe the Information Presented			

■ Visual Instruction

Answer The first step is to determine a general topic for the presentation.

Beginning the Presentation Process

GUIDE TO READING

Objectives

1. Explain the relationship between context and the selection and limitation of a topic.
2. Describe how to limit a topic by classification.
3. Determine the purpose for a professional presentation.
4. Compare and contrast the characteristics of the three purposes of presentations: informative, persuasive, and motivational.

Terms to Learn

informative presentation
persuasive presentation
motivational presentation

An ancient Chinese proverb states that "a journey of a thousand miles begins with but a single step." When confronted with the idea of making a presentation, you may have no idea where to begin. Like a journey of a thousand miles, a presentation also begins with a single step.

You already have learned that many of your daily communication activities are accomplished through a series of steps or processes. Just as there is a process for giving and receiving information and a process for listening, there is also a process for preparing an oral presentation.

UNDERSTAND THE PROCESS

When considering the steps involved in organizing an effective presentation, it may be helpful to think of the process in reverse. In other words, before you can give a presentation, you need to plan and organize it. Before you can plan and organize it,

---

Whether you are Jimmy Carter, former president of the United States, or a student giving a speech for the first time, one thing remains constant: Process is important to preparing for a presentation. What is the first step in the presentation process?

450 *Glencoe Communication Applications*

RESOURCE MANAGER

Teaching Tools
- Interactive Lesson Planner
- Reproducible Lesson Plan 14–2
- Application Activities 14–2

Reproducible Masters
- Guided Reading Activity Workbook 14-2
- Enrichment Activity 14–2
- Reteaching Activity 14–2
- Section Quiz 14–2
- Transparency Strategies and Activities Booklet 14–2

Transparencies
- Graphic Organizer Transparency 14–2
- Chapter 14 Teaching Transparency

Technology Resources
- Interactive Tutor Self-Assessment Software
- Presentation Plus! Software
- ExamView® Pro Testmaker
- PuzzleMaker Software
- communicationapplications.glencoe.com

you need to research it. Finally, before you can research a presentation, you determine and organize a topic and a purpose.

By approaching presentations in a step-by-step way, you focus on one part of the presentation at a time. You have time to pay attention to the details that inexperienced or untrained presenters may overlook. If you become confused, you can go back a step to clarify the choices you have made so far. The result can be a presentation that is clear and to the point and accomplishes its task. An added benefit is that you can approach a presentation knowing that you are fully prepared. If you are well prepared, you may experience less communication apprehension.

Preparing for a presentation involves nine basic steps, as shown in **Figure 14–3.** The first four of these steps are covered in this chapter. The remaining steps will be explained in Chapters 15 through 18.

DETERMINE A TOPIC

The first step in the preparation process is to determine a general topic for your presentation. As you read in Section 1, your topic

should be one in which you are interested and qualified to speak. It also should be a topic that is relevant to the audience. In addition, it should be suitable for the occasion and meet the requirements for your task.

Many speakers in professional and social contexts have their topic chosen for them. Former President Jimmy Carter is often asked to speak about his experiences during the Mid-East Peace Accords. An employee may be

---

■ Figure 14–3 **Steps of the Presentation Preparation Process**

1. Determine a topic.
2. Limit the topic.
3. Determine the purpose.
4. Research the topic.

5. Organize and outline the presentation.
6. Select supporting information.
7. Prepare notes and manuscript for delivery.
8. Rehearse the presentation.

COMMUNICATION

PRACTICE LAB

Determining a Presentation Topic

To practice determining a presentation topic, follow these steps:

Step 1 Brainstorm a list of topics about which you are qualified to speak or interested in presenting. Your list might include classes, sports, jobs, relationships, or personal experiences.

Step 2 Beside each item on your list, jot down why you are interested in the topic. What qualifies you to speak on that

topic? Is it experience, interest, or something else?

Step 3 Exchange lists with a partner. One-on-one, explain your qualifications and knowledge of each topic.

Step 4 Have your partner draw a check mark next to each topic you appear qualified to present.

Step 5 Switch roles and repeat steps 3 and 4.

Preparing for Professional Presentations **451**

---

2 TEACH

Selecting a Topic
Point out that talk shows on radio and television regularly select guests who have a message of current interest—politics, sports, crime, or scandal. Ask students to recall recent shows they have seen or heard whose guests were clearly chosen for the message they had to deliver. **L1**

Steps in Preparing a Presentation
Have students read the eight steps in the presentation process shown on this page. Ask them which they feel would generally take the most time. Which steps could sometimes be omitted? Which do they feel are their personal strengths and weaknesses? How does the nature of a presentation determine the way one prepares for it?

COMMUNICATION
PRACTICE LAB
Determining a Presentation Topic

After they have completed the five steps described in the Communication Practice Lab, invite pairs of students to explain what led them to check certain topics on their partner's list. What was it that persuaded them that their partner was qualified to make a presentation on those subjects? Did the partner agree with this assessment? **L2**

GLENCOE *Online*

For an additional Practice Lab for this section, have students visit the *Glencoe Communication Applications* Web site at **communicationapplications.glencoe.com.** Click on Communication Practice Lab 14–2. **L1**

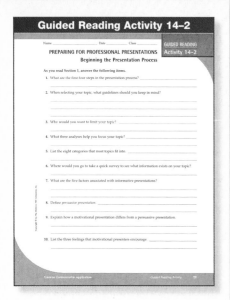

Adjusting to Your Audience

Inquire how students would put knowledge of their audience to practical use. Discuss strategies for adjusting presentations under the following circumstances:

- There are two or three members of the audience who know as much about the subject as you do.
- The audience knows nothing about you.
- Several members of the audience are likely to disagree with what you have to say.
- The audience is required to attend this presentation.
- Everyone in the audience is older than you are.

In your discussion, point out that each speaker has his or her own style; there may be no one way to respond to these situations. **L2**

■ Visual Instruction

Answer A speaker should analyze the audience and the task.

---

asked to update a supervisor on the project he or she is working on. The captain of the football team may be asked to speak about the team. In short, individuals usually are asked to speak on a topic because of who they are, what they do in the workplace or community, or what they know about the topic.

Other times, however, you are responsible for choosing your own topic. In these instances, speak about what you know. You will make the best presentations about topics with which you are personally involved in some way. You have a commitment to the topic. Therefore, the first consideration for selecting a topic is for the topic to suit the speaker: YOU!

LIMIT THE TOPIC

Once you know the general topic for your presentation, consider how you can focus it for your specific audience, occasion, and task. When you limit a topic, you narrow it to a specific aspect of the general topic. Limiting the topic will help the audience follow, understand, and remember what you have to say.

Apply Your Analyses to Narrow the Topic

Before you began preparing your presentation, you analyzed the specific audience, occasion, and task. As shown in **Figure 14–4**, these analyses will help you focus your topic.

Analyzing the Audience The more you know about an audience, the more directly your presentation can relate to it. For example, when presenting a company's policy on summer hours, a presenter might narrow the topic by referring to benefits that employees might not have considered. Explaining how different options might benefit different workers, such as part-time staff and working parents, can also help the presenter relate directly to the audience.

Analyzing the Occasion Similarly, the more you understand about the occasion for your presentation, the better you can prepare for what your audience expects. Analyzing the occasion can help you avoid situations like the one encountered by a recent group of premed students. The group was scheduled to speak at a local luncheon meeting just before lunch was served. Unfortunately, the group's presentation about the importance of donating organs included

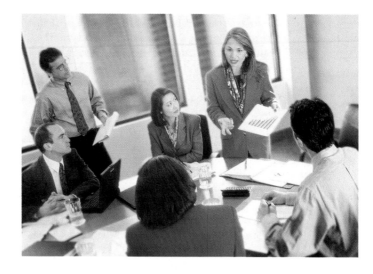

■ **When preparing a presentation, it is always a good idea to consider the occasion in relation to your topic.** *What else should the speaker analyze before preparing for a presentation?*

MEETING INDIVIDUAL NEEDS — MULTIPLE LEARNING STYLES

Visual-Spatial Point out that sometimes our ideas literally take shape on a piece of paper. Visual learners may find that their best thoughts start off as doodles.

Activity Ask students to choose a general subject about which they feel they could prepare a presentation. Select one subject at random from their choices and model the following technique on the chalkboard: Draw a simple representation of the topic on the board—a basketball, a fish, a book. Brainstorm with the class for related subtopics. *(Example: fishing – trout fishing – fly fishing – dry flies – tying your own flies.)* Write each new idea inside the outline, circle it, and draw lines to connect it to the previous one. Have students create similar graphics for their own subjects. Ask volunteers to recreate their visuals on the board.

Figure 14–4 Narrowing a Topic

Limited Topic		Category	
Campus and plans for expansion			Places
History of college and academic traditions			Events
Faculty members and their academic reputations			People
Improved admissions procedures			Processes
University's position on academic integrity and ethics			Policies

a very graphic explanation of how donated organs are harvested. Needless to say, few audience members felt much like eating at the conclusion of the presentation. These students did not do a good job of limiting their topic for the occasion of the presentation.

Analyzing the Task Another important factor is your analysis of the task that you want to accomplish. Imagine that you have been asked to be the keynote speaker at a picnic to kick off a community fund-raising drive. The audience includes many people who have taken time off from work to attend. The picnic is held on a warm day in May in a park with little shade. After speaking for almost an hour about your personal political views, you begin to wonder why people are walking away from your presentation.

This problem could have been avoided with a better analysis of the context of the presentation. Given the warmth of the afternoon sun, the audience's time considerations, and the reason for the presentation, you might have made wiser choices. Your keynote address should have been brief, focused on community spirit, and intent on building support for the cause.

Classify the Topic

If, after considering the audience, occasion, and task for your presentation, you still are not sure about how to limit a topic, try classifying it. Almost any topic fits into one of the following categories:

- people
- places
- things
- events
- problems
- processes
- policies
- concepts

Think about a college president who has been asked to give a ten-minute presentation on the state of the school. The presentation might focus on the campus and plans for expansion, the history of the college and its academic traditions, the faculty members and their academic reputations, improved admissions procedures, or the university's position on academic integrity and ethics. To help determine these potential topics' classifications, you might create a classification chart like the one shown here.

Once you have classified the various aspects of a topic, consider which best fit you, your audience, the occasion, and the task. Develop your presentation about one of these limited aspects of the overall topic.

Survey the Availability of Information

Another consideration when focusing your topic is how much information is available. A presenter's responsibilities include being well informed about a topic. No matter how good a topic may seem, if little information is available to the presenter, the presentation is likely to suffer.

How do you determine whether enough information is available to make an effective

Preparing for Professional Presentations **453**

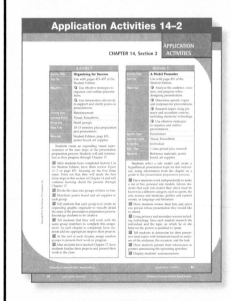

Determine the Purpose

Review the meanings of the three purposes listed in the text: to inform, to persuade, to motivate. Have students form pairs and ask them to make a note of presentation topics suitable for each of these purposes. Create a master list of topics under the categories *inform, persuade, and motivate* on the chalkboard. Discuss whether the class feels they are classified correctly. **L2**

Informative Presentations

Have students read the five bulleted qualities that comprise a good informative presentation. Ask which of these points are easy to assess and which might require critical judgment or knowledge on the part of the audience. **L2**

BUSINESS BRIEF

According to Andrew S. Grove, CEO of microchip manufacturer Intel, "Information-gathering is the basis of all other managerial work, which is why I choose to spend so much of my day doing it." Discuss this statement with students. What is the importance of information to the manager of a business? **L2**

■ **Visual Instruction**

Answer The main goal is to increase the audience's knowledge by providing new information.

---

presentation? Do a quick survey in the local library to see what information you can find in its books and magazines. Also, enter keywords about your topic in a search engine on the Internet. This quick survey can help you assess the amount of information that is readily available. It also may help you discover different aspects of your topic that you might not have considered previously.

Once you have limited your topic to the one aspect that is most appropriate and acceptable to your audience on this specific occasion, you are ready to move on to the next step in the process. Now you can begin to consider the purpose of your presentation.

DETERMINE THE PURPOSE

You have looked at the various elements of your task, considering length, nature, formality, and overall purpose. Now you need to determine the specific purpose you will try to accomplish in the presentation. Most professional presentations have one of the following purposes: to inform, to persuade, or to motivate.

Purpose: Informative Presentation

An informative presentation conveys ideas and information in a clear, accurate, and objective manner to gain the audience's interest. When you give an informative presentation, you assume the role of a teacher or newscaster. Your goal is to increase your audience's knowledge by providing them with new information. Informative presentations convey information that is

- easy to understand
- accurate
- interesting
- relevant
- objective and without bias

Many different situations call for informative presentations. When an employee gives a status report on a current project, his or her purpose is to inform. Similarly, when someone explains how to use a specific piece of equipment, or when your teacher introduces new material in class, he or she is making an informative presentation.

Purpose: Persuasive Presentation

A persuasive presentation attempts to get an audience to voluntarily change its thoughts, beliefs, or actions on a topic. Just as

Television newscasters give informative presentations every time they relay the news to their viewers. **What is the main goal of an informative presentation?**

REAL-WORLD CONNECTION

Assessing Broadcast Information Remind students that there is no guarantee that all information they receive is accurate and bias-free. Encourage students to become critical listeners to the information they routinely receive on television or radio.

Activity Ask students to make an audio recording of a news story or other informative presentation, no more than five minutes in length, from television or radio. Have them form groups of four or five, making sure each group is equipped with a tape recorder. Direct groups to listen to their tapes and to consider whether the presentations are easy to understand, accurate, interesting, relevant, and without bias. Ask each group to select a recording to present to the class, along with their comments. Have students discuss the experience of listening critically.

in an informative presentation, the presenter should provide thorough information to support his or her message. However, in a persuasive presentation, the speaker then attempts to convince the audience to take some action based on the information provided during the presentation.

The difference between informing and persuading an audience is the difference between explaining an idea and encouraging others to support it. Persuasive presentations urge one or more of the following:

- acceptance of facts, values, or ideas
- action
- changes in attitude or behavior

A persuasive presentation may urge an audience to vote for a specific issue or contribute to a specific cause. A speaker may try to persuade an audience to accept his or her viewpoint or values about something. Candidates for political office, for example, give persuasive presentations so voters will be inclined to vote for them. A presenter's goal also may be to change audience members' attitudes on a topic. For example,

TECHNOLOGY Activity

Persuasion and Context Technology is responsible for many of the messages we receive each day. Consider the following channels of communication and determine the effectiveness of each in persuading you to join a health club: a funny television ad, an enthusiastic telephone solicitor, a direct mail ad, a door-to-door sales rep, an Internet ad, voice mail from a friend, a magazine ad, a colorful billboard, and a sales representative who speaks to your class. Think about what motivates you to pay attention to various forms of persuasive messages. How can you incorporate those strategies into your oral presentations?

someone might give a presentation to convince people that soccer has replaced baseball as America's favorite sport.

Many of the everyday presentations that you hear from salespeople, politicians, friends, and family members are persuasive presentations. When someone tries to influence your

COMMUNICATION

Recognizing Persuasive Presentations

To practice recognizing the characteristics of persuasive presentations, follow these steps:

Step 1 As a class, separate into three groups.

Step 2 Divide the following categories among the groups so that each group has a different category:
- acceptance of facts, values, or ideas
- action
- changes in attitude or behavior

PRACTICE LAB

Step 3 Brainstorm a list of at least ten persuasive topics based on your group's chosen category. Choose a volunteer or volunteers to write down the topics as they are suggested.

Step 4 Share your lists as a class. Discuss the types of information that would be needed to give a persuasive presentation on these topics. Which category might present the largest challenge for persuading an audience?

Preparing for Professional Presentations **455**

Persuasive Presentations

Invite students to describe recent occasions when they have responded to a persuasive message by changing their minds, actions, or behavior. For those who claim that they are never influenced by persuasion, remind them of their constant exposure to such messages, from advertising to parental lectures. Ask students why the message they responded to was successful and whether their change was temporary or long lasting. **L1**

TECHNOLOGY Activity

Persuasion and Context Have the class consider each of the channels of communication. Lead students to understand the importance of analyzing persuasive presentations with questions such as the following: Are there any of these methods that students believe they would never respond to? Are there some that would not have an immediate effect but might over the long term? Which could they ignore; which would they have to receive? Which techniques would they be more likely to believe without question? Have students bring to class two examples of persuasive communications: one they find effective, and one they would not respond to. Invite them to share their findings with the class.
L2

COMMUNICATION
PRACTICE LAB

Recognizing Persuasive Presentations

Have students follow the four steps in the Communication Practice Lab on this page to recognize the characteristics of persuasive presentations. As a class, discuss any topics that have more than one goal. Have students discuss how overlapping persuasive goals might affect persuasive presentations.

MEETING INDIVIDUAL NEEDS
MULTIPLE LEARNING STYLES

Musical Point out that many of the most effective persuasive messages we receive are in the form of brief songs, commonly known as commercial jingles. Remind students that messages often have sugar coatings.

Activity Have students compose a brief, persuasive musical message, advertising a product, a service, or a campaign. Ask them to record their jingles and to play them for the class or to perform them "live." (Students who are not prepared to compose original music should bring to class recorded examples of two musical messages that they find effective.) Have students discuss the decisions they made in composing their jingles. Those who chose professional selections should be prepared to explain how the music effectively conveys the message.

Motivational Presentations

Ask students to describe a motivational presentation that they have recently experienced. Point out that such messages are often brief and unrehearsed. Parents and teachers regularly try to motivate young people. Have students explain whether the presentation had the intended effect. **L1**

3 ASSESS

Assign Section 2 Assessment as a homework or in-class activity.

Use *Interactive Tutor Self-Assessment Software* to review Section 2.

Section 14–2 Quiz

Visual Instruction

Answer Motivational presentations tend to rely more on emotion than on information to make their point.

buying habits, asks you to donate to a specific cause, or convinces you that something is right or wrong, that person is giving a persuasive presentation.

Purpose: Motivational Presentation

A motivational presentation inspires or encourages an audience. Motivational presentations usually are more persuasive than informative. Although motivational and persuasive presentations may seem similar, motivational presenters tend to rely more on emotion than on information to make their point. These presentations are designed to directly affect the audience in some way. Motivational presentations encourage one or more of the following feelings:

- happiness
- confidence
- self-worth

Some examples of motivational presentations are speeches that encourage students to stay in school until they graduate or to volunteer in a community program. Others might include encouraging sales personnel to meet a monthly or yearly goal, giving players an emotional pep talk at half-time of

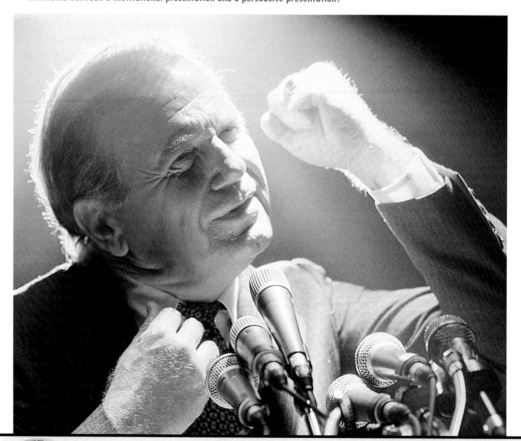

Motivational speakers use their presentations to inspire or encourage the audience. What is the difference between a motivational presentation and a persuasive presentation?

MEETING INDIVIDUAL NEEDS

MULTIPLE LEARNING STYLES

Interpersonal Motivational speaking is not just the domain of professionals. We are continually giving and receiving encouraging messages. While motivational presentations need not be formal or lengthy, they require a skill that goes beyond a casual "Look on the bright side."

Activity Have students imagine a situation in which they might need to deliver a motivational address. (For those who have difficulty coming up with an idea of their own, suggest the following: a friend is refusing to try out for the cheerleading squad; a parent has lost a job; a younger sibling has given up doing any work at school.) Ask them to prepare an address of one to two minutes, reminding them that the best speeches are informed, encouraging, and passionate. After students have delivered their speeches, have them discuss the skills involved in motivational presentations.

a football game, or providing a positive evaluation for a hard-working employee. Many motivational presentations focus on improving job performance or goal achievement.

Competent speakers determine the purpose for their presentation—to inform, persuade, or motivate an audience. These presenters then use their knowledge of the context—information about the content, audience, occasion, and task—to guide how they prepare for their presentations. Once they have determined the basics, they are ready to move on to the next step of the presentation process: research.

Section 2 Assessment

Visit the *Glencoe Communication Applications* Web site at **communicationapplications. glencoe.com** and click on **Self-Check and Study Guide 14.2** to review your understanding of the beginning of the presentation process.

Review Key Terms

1. Define each of the following terms and write it in a sentence: informative presentation, persuasive presentation, motivational presentation.

Check Understanding

2. What considerations should influence the selection and limitation of a topic?

3. Create five different limited topics from the general presentation topic "the environment." How would each limited topic be classified?

4. What is the main difference between informative presentations and persuasive presentations? Between informative presentations and motivational presentations?

5. **Apply** Imagine that at this year's graduation ceremony, the high school principal gives a speech encouraging young people to give back to their school. He or she suggests that students volunteer their time and money to organize and set up a scholarship fund for deserving students. What is the purpose of this presentation?

APPLICATION *Activity*

Choosing and Limiting a Topic List at least three topics on which you are qualified to speak. If you completed the Communication Practice Lab on page 451, refer to the list you created earlier. Next, choose one of the topics to use for a three-minute presentation to your class. Consider the context of your presentation and limit your topic appropriately. Then determine the purpose of the presentation. Finally, list some of the available resources for researching your topic. As a class, share your topics, your reasons for choosing them, and how you plan to gather information.

Preparing for Professional Presentations **457**

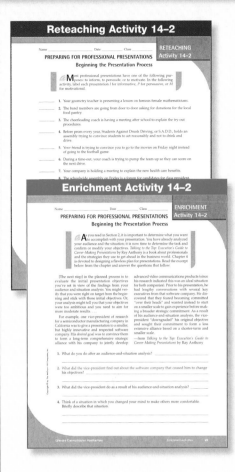

4 CLOSE

Have students review their responses to the opening paragraph of this section on page 450. If a presentation can be compared to "a journey of a thousand miles," how far into the journey would they say they have traveled? Do they now feel more confident of finishing?

Extra-Credit Project

Have students follow the steps outlined in this section to select and limit a topic for presentation in each of the three categories discussed: informational, persuasive, and motivational. Ask them to provide a brief written description of their research and to present their findings to the class.

Section 2 Assessment Answers

1. Accept all reasonable sentences.

2. You should choose a topic in which you are interested and knowledgeable. It should be suitable to the occasion and relevant to the audience. In limiting the topic, apply your analyses of the audience, the occasion, and the task. Classify the topic into a suitable category and survey the availability of information.

3. Accept any reasonable topics.

4. An informative presentation conveys ideas and information; a persuasive presentation encourages others to think or act in a certain way. A motivational presentation is concerned with inspiration and encouragement.

5. The purpose is to persuade students to accept an idea and to take action.

Application Activity Students should be prepared to explain how they have limited their topic.

1 FOCUS

Bellringer

Have students read the opening paragraph of this section and ask them to describe a presentation that really kept them interested and informed. What was it about the information that made the occasion memorable?

✎ You may use Graphic Organizer Transparency 14–3 to introduce this section.

Graphic Organizer Transparency 14-3

Primary Source   Secondary Source

1. Includes personal experiences and insight you yourself may have
2. Must be used ethically and responsibly
3. The most up-to-date information available
4. Needs to be timely to be useful
5. Must be credible and relevant
6. Sources include interviews, surveys, and questionnaires
7. Should not be biased
8. Often comes from books, magazines, newspapers, radio, or TV
9. Used to discover new ideas as well as support old ones
10. Also called secondhand information
11. Needs to be carefully evaluated
12. Effective communication depends on how you use it
13. Comes from someone other than the original source

Visual Instruction

Answer Student responses may include that accurate, relevant, interesting, and up-to-date information is essential to an effective presentation.

Section 3

Researching the Presentation Topic

GUIDE TO READING

Objectives

1. Recognize the importance of gathering and using accurate and complete information as a basis for making communication decisions.
2. Explain how to use surveys and questionnaires to secure information about a topic.
3. Determine appropriate sources of information for a presentation.
4. Analyze sources for qualifications, credibility, competence, and accuracy to support a presentation.

Terms to Learn

secondary source
primary source
sample

---

*T*hink about the last time a speaker made a presentation and you really learned something valuable. How did you feel about the presenter and the information that was shared with you?

Effective communicators know that much of their communication success depends on the information they use. Reliable, current, unbiased, interesting information lays the foundation for an effective presentation.

RESEARCH THE TOPIC

What information will you need for your presentation? One way to determine this is by reviewing the decisions and considerations you already have made. What do you know about your audience, occasion, and task to indicate the kinds of information you will need? What information will your audience expect you to know in order to make your point and to accomplish your purpose?

A well-informed presenter is one who has done research, like this student in the library. What provides the foundation for an effective presentation?

458 *Glencoe Communication Applications*

RESOURCE MANAGER

Teaching Tools

- Interactive Lesson Planner
- Reproducible Lesson Plan 14–3
- Application Activities 14–3

Reproducible Masters

- Guided Reading Activity Workbook 14–3
- Enrichment Activity 14–3
- Reteaching Activity 14–3
- Section Quiz 14–3
- Transparency Strategies and Activities Booklet 14–3

Transparencies

- Graphic Organizer Transparency 14–3
- Chapter 14 Teaching Transparency

Technology Resources

- Interactive Tutor Self-Assessment Software
- Presentation Plus! Software
- ExamView® Pro Testmaker
- PuzzleMaker Software
- communicationapplications.glencoe.com

COMMUNICATION
Strategies

QUESTIONS TO GUIDE RESEARCH

- What is the value of my topic to my audience and me? What do they want to know? What do I want to tell them?

- What is the most current information about my topic?

- What is unique or unusual about my topic?

- What is the background of my topic?

- Who are the people associated with my topic? What are their contributions and how much influence have they had? How has this topic affected them?

- To what other topics does my topic relate?

- What forces have contributed to or distracted from the development of my topic?

- What are the strengths and weaknesses of my topic?

After considering these questions, you may find that you know or have much of the information you need. Your responses to the questions in the Communication Strategies checklist should give you an idea of additional information you will need to gather.

Research is a process of discovery that is best approached with an open mind. Looking only for information that supports your ideas can

---

Today's technology, such as the Internet, has made research more convenient. **Describe an effective researcher.**

---

cause you to overlook something important. It also can make you appear biased and, if you only choose to reveal certain facts, deceptive or unethical when questioned. An effective researcher looks for all kinds of information about his or her topic. You might discover a new or different aspect of your topic that you had not previously considered, or you might even discover that your initial ideas were flawed or incorrect. An effective presenter uses research as a tool to discover new ideas as well as to confirm old ones.

LOCATING INFORMATION

What is the first thing you usually do when you need to find information or conduct research for a specific project or class? Imagine that you want to buy a car. You might head to the library or log on to the Internet and look for information about the make, model, and year of the car. You might look for books, articles, and reports that other people have written about your topic. The information you get is from secondary sources.

Preparing for Professional Presentations **459**

---

2 TEACH

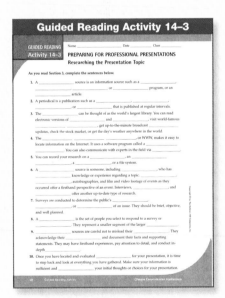

COMMUNICATION
Strategies

QUESTIONS TO GUIDE RESEARCH

Have students review the checklist of questions to guide research. Point out that if they can satisfactorily answer the first of these questions—that is, if they truly understand the value and purpose of their presentation—they will have a better idea which of the subsequent questions will be relevant to their inquiries. **L2**

Visual Instruction

Answer Student responses may include that an effective researcher is open minded, thorough, and hard working.

COOPERATIVE LEARNING ACTIVITY

The heart of an effective presentation is accurate, appropriate, and interesting information. Point out that finding information about a topic is generally not difficult. The art lies in identifying which information is truly valuable.

Assign the class a specific but easily researched topic such as the World Series, America's National Parks, or Ronald Reagan's presidency. For homework, have each student research the topic for ten facts—five that they consider essential information and five that they find interesting or unusual. Have them form groups of four or five and ask them to pool their research to create a single list of twenty facts that they feel would be included in an effective presentation. Ask groups to share their master lists with the class, explaining their criteria for selecting or rejecting information.

Secondary Sources

Ask students to list the advantages of using secondary sources. What might be the disadvantages? *(Advantages: convenience; the author has done the primary research for you; he or she may be an expert in the subject and has had more time for research. Disadvantages: the secondary material may not be exactly what you need; people learn more effectively firsthand.)*

Going Online

Have students study the graph in Figure 14–5. Ask what they notice about the general trend. How do they believe this will affect society? *(The graph shows a steady increase in online households. This might make the postal service obsolete, create more at-home workers, change the way we shop, study, and so on.)* What do students notice about the rate of increase, and what might this suggest? *(The curve is beginning to level off. This might suggest that the market has reached saturation point, that the economy is no longer so buoyant, or that some people don't need or want PCs.)*

Communication Tip

Your reference librarian can be the single most important research asset at your disposal. Trained not just to locate but to assess information, librarians do what Internet search engines cannot: They distinguish valuable information from the dubious or worthless.

Secondary Sources

A **secondary source** is an information source such as a book, periodical, radio or television program, or an Internet article that has been written by someone else about a particular topic. In essence, you are obtaining information on your topic secondhand. You are not speaking directly to the source or hearing his or her own words. You are not reading the source's autobiography. Instead, your information comes from someone else who is reporting on a subject he or she has researched.

Common Secondary Sources Books probably are the most commonly used secondary source. Books relating to your topic may not provide the most recent information, but they can provide you with extensive detail and often a historical perspective.

Most periodicals provide current information on a variety of subjects. Periodicals are publications such as magazines, newspapers, journals, or newsletters that are published at regular intervals. When researching issues related to the local community, local newspapers usually are available in the library and can provide valuable information. Many current and back issues of major newspapers published in large cities also are available in the library and on the Internet.

Secondary Sources at Work At work, you may be asked to research information for a report or presentation to be shared with a work group. Perhaps you need to use a summary of last year's sales figures found in your company's annual report. At work, informational reports and business documents, such as company handbooks or benefits information, are two other common types of secondary sources.

Secondary Sources Online The Internet can be thought of as the world's largest library. **Figure 14–5** shows the number of online households in the United States. Using the Internet, you can read electronic versions of newspapers and magazines, visit world-famous art museums, get up-to-the-minute broadcast news updates, check activity on the stock market, and find out what tomorrow's weather will be like at home or halfway around the world.

Unlike your local library, however, there is no research librarian to help you locate specific information or evaluate it for accuracy and validity. Unfortunately, some of the information on the Internet comes from unreliable sources. In fact, one of the issues facing the Internet is the unregulated availability of information that may be inaccurate or harmful. As a competent communicator, it is your responsibility to verify any information you find online.

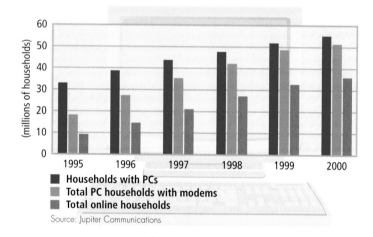

■ **Figure 14–5 Going Online in the United States**

Households with PCs
Total PC households with modems
Total online households

Source: Jupiter Communications

CRITICAL THINKING ACTIVITY

Point out that although the Internet is a rich source of information, it is also a source of opinion and misinformation. Remind students that sources officially associated with libraries or educational institutions will generally be more accurate than commercial sites.

Select four or five topics of general interest, such as sports or entertainment celebrities, famous places, and historical events or disasters. Assign students one topic each and direct them to conduct an Internet search. Ask them to bring to class material from one source that they consider accurate and authoritative and from another that they feel may not be reliable. Have them form topic-related groups to share and discuss their findings. Invite each group to present to the class examples of reliable and unreliable sources.

The World Wide Web The World Wide Web makes it much easier to locate information on the Internet. The World Wide Web, also known as WWW or the Web, is an easy-to-use interface to the Internet. Using the Web requires a personal computer with a modem and a software program called a "Web browser." Web browsers provide you with access to computerized indices called search engines. Search engines allow people to use keywords to locate information available from individual Internet sources called Web sites.

Some Web sites allow you to communicate with the originator of the Web site, the Webmaster, through e-mail. A Web site with linked e-mail can allow you to send and receive information on a topic, ask questions of experts on the subject, survey or poll selected populations for their opinions, and contact others to brainstorm new ideas.

Other Secondary Sources In addition to providing access to books, periodicals, and the Internet, libraries and media centers offer other secondary information sources. Many libraries also maintain vertical files of information about topics. Vertical files usually contain pamphlets and brochures about a topic, magazine or newspaper articles from little-known or non-indexed publications, and any other information that may relate to a topic. The information in these files generally is not listed in an index.

Documentary films and videos also can provide valuable information for projects and presentations. A librarian can be a valuable source for trying to locate much of the information in a library or media center. Often, a librarian can lead you to sources on your topic that you may not have realized were available. Your school library or media center may maintain various media resources for research purposes.

RECORDING INFORMATION ACCURATELY

Procedure	Description
Copy the information exactly as it is written.	To do this, photocopy, print, or carefully recopy the information. It is important to reread each item as you write it down. This will help you avoid errors. Accidentally misquoting information is sloppy research and can mislead you and your audience. Intentionally misquoting a source is unethical. As you conduct your research, make sure you get all the facts and write them down precisely. It is your responsibility to accurately quote every source you use.
Include a complete source citation with each piece of information.	It is unethical to claim someone else's work or ideas as your own, so it is important to credit your sources. Include the name of the sources. Include the name of the author or other originator, the title of the quoted material, the title of the publication, the publisher, the city and date of publication, and the page number.
	For Internet sources, include the full Internet address, such as *www.communicationapplications.glencoe.com*. Write down the date you found the information, what search engine you used, the author and title of the information, and what keywords you used to locate these sources. This will help you and others verify your information. You also should note the date the Web site was last updated and who maintains the site. You might also want to print the information to save as a reference.
Note the author's qualifications.	This can help establish the source's credibility. You also can help establish the context of quoted material by citing the specific audience and occasion, such as: Quoted from a speech given by President Harry S. Truman to a joint session of the U.S. Congress, Washington, D.C., March 12, 1947.

Preparing for Professional Presentations **461**

Recording Information Accurately

Have students read the guidelines in the table on this page and consider supplementing them with the following pointers:

- Information taken down verbatim from an original source should be highlighted or otherwise clearly marked to indicate that the words are not the student's own.

- If a student takes summary notes from a source, these should be in abbreviated form and phrased so as to avoid any combination of words that appear in the original.

- All notes should include a precise reference to the sources from which they came. It is easy to lose track of a source if it is not noted when the information is initially recorded.

- Ideas, as well as words, are the property of an author and must receive proper acknowledgment, whether in written or in oral presentations.

DID YOU KNOW?

The World Wide Web was developed in 1989 by Timothy Berners-Lee, an English computer scientist, whose aim was to facilitate communication between international researchers working with the European Laboratory for Particle Physics in Switzerland. Its speed and convenience soon attracted a much wider audience. Berners-Lee still oversees the Web's development as head of The WWW Consortium, based at the Massachusetts Institute of Technology, where he is a professor.

MEETING INDIVIDUAL NEEDS

MULTIPLE LEARNING STYLES

Linguistic Plagiarism, the unacknowledged use of other people's words or ideas, often occurs when students are tempted to take notes verbatim instead of summarizing material in their own words. Point out that taking written notes from source material should involve the same process as taking notes from a lecture, when there is little opportunity to copy exact words and phrases.

Activity Read to the class an informative article from a newspaper or magazine, directing students to take notes while you do so. Have them form groups to pool their information, then give them five to ten minutes to write a summary of the article using their notes, but without further consultation. Invite volunteers to read their summaries. Compare information and phrasing with the original and discuss whether the summaries were accurate, unplagiarized versions of the original.

Organizing Secondary Information

Students should realize that research does not stop with collecting information; thoughtful selection and editing is also involved. Large numbers of photocopied pages, for example, are not in a usable state until the material most relevant to the researcher has been highlighted for easy reference or transferred to cards or computer files.

Primary Sources

Point out that we are receiving primary source material all the time. It only becomes research, however, when it has been recorded and identified. Ask students to jot down three remarks that were made to them in the last twenty-four hours. For each quotation, have them record the speaker's name, the place, and the time the remark was made. Invite students to share their "research" with the class. **L1**

▪ Visual Instruction

Answer Student responses may include that other primary sources are surveys, questionnaires, and personal experiences.

Communication Tip

No matter how well you have planned your presentation, it is advisable to collect more information than you think you need. Presentations sometimes change their direction in the writing stage. If you have done extra research, you can accommodate new ideas without going back to the library.

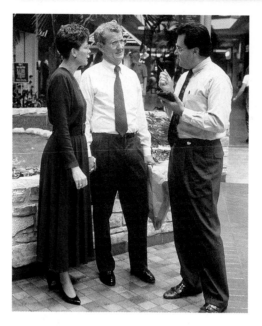

▪ Interviews, such as this one in a mall, can be a form of primary research. Besides interviews, what other primary sources allow the researcher to gather information personally?

Organizing Secondary Information

As a researcher, it is important to develop a systematic method of organizing the information you find. Some researchers record their information on computer. Others use index cards or notebooks with different sections for the different types of information they find. Still others use file folders for each category of information. Regardless of which system you use, it is a good idea to follow these guidelines for accurately recording your information.

Following these guidelines will help you record your researched information so that it can be used in an ethical and responsible manner. It also will allow you to find the information again at a later date, if necessary.

462   *Glencoe Communication Applications*

Primary Sources

After searching secondary sources on your topic, you may discover that you can't locate some of the information you need or want for your presentation. You may need to talk to experts on your topic or ask people firsthand how they feel about a specific issue. This type of information comes from a primary source. A primary source is someone, including yourself, who has firsthand knowledge or experience regarding a topic. A quote from one of your favorite musical performers is a primary source. So is information a person tells you directly. However, once you read the musician's words in a magazine or hear a news story about the performer's musical style, this becomes secondary-source information.

Obtaining information from primary sources is referred to as primary research. Primary research also includes any personal experiences and insights that you may have with a topic. Primary research can provide important information for many different types of presentations. If you have knowledge of a topic, your audience's perception of your credibility is likely to increase. Information in books and magazines can easily become outdated. However, primary research provides the most up-to-date information available.

Some primary sources can be found in libraries or on the Internet. Diaries, journals, autobiographies, and film and video footage of actual events as they occurred provide a firsthand perspective of an event. Other primary sources, such as interviews, allow the researcher to personally gather information.

Interviews Interviews are an excellent way to gather information on a topic. In addition, interviewing a primary source—such as an expert—can help you better understand the information and the people involved.

MEETING INDIVIDUAL NEEDS   MULTIPLE LEARNING STYLES

Interpersonal Point out that there is nothing mysterious or difficult about primary research. We are in a position to research material and record our findings at any moment during the day.

Activity Have students form pairs and interview each other on a subject they can both talk about without preparation: my favorite sport, family vacations, what I did last night, and so on. Direct them to take notes during the interview, including in their notes at least one direct quotation. After the interviews, have students write a paragraph or two summarizing their interviews, making sure that they include a passage directly quoting their subject. Invite volunteers to present their summaries to the class.

■ **Figure 14–6 Sample Questionnaire**

CAFETERIA QUESTIONNAIRE

In an effort to better meet your menu preferences, the cafeteria staff would like your responses to the following questions. Your input will be considered when next semester's menus are being planned. Please place your completed questionnaire in the box at the end of your serving line. Thank you!

1. How many times each week do you eat in the cafeteria?
   ___ 0   ___ 1   ___ 2   ___ 3   ___ 4   ___ 5

2. What type of meal do you usually purchase?
   ___Full meal   ___Sandwich   ___À la carte

3. What is your favorite food served in the cafeteria?
   _____

4. What is your least favorite food served in the cafeteria?
   _____

5. What food would you like to have served that currently is not offered?
   _____

6. Would you prefer more fast food to be served in the cafeteria?
   ___ Yes   ___ No   ___ No opinion

7. Would you be willing to pay more for fast food than for a standard cafeteria meal?
   ___ Yes   ___ No   ___ No opinion

8. How would you rate the quality of the food served in the cafeteria?
   ___ Excellent   ___ Good   ___ Average   ___ Poor

9. What is your grade level?
   ___ Freshman   ___ Sophomore   ___ Junior   ___ Senior

So, when is an interview an appropriate source for your research? Consider your topic. Would direct statements or opinions from a primary source add clarity, interest, or credibility? If so, what information do you need, and who can provide it?

Once you have determined who is the best available resource, you can begin planning the actual interview. For information on conducting interviews for primary research, refer to Chapter 9, Communicating in Interviews.

Survey Research Groups and organizations often conduct surveys to determine the public's understanding, opinion, or knowledge of an issue. They may survey individuals by asking them questions one-on-one, or they may administer a written survey, known as a questionnaire.

Oral surveys and written questionnaires are good tools for obtaining local and regional information that may not be available anywhere else. Careful planning can help you design a survey or questionnaire to obtain the exact information you need. Just as with interviews, first determine the purpose of the survey or questionnaire and the type of information you are seeking before you get to work. Do you want to know what presidential candidate people support? How your coworkers feel about your company's new vacation policy? What team most of your classmates want to win the Super Bowl? Each of these questions can be answered through a survey or questionnaire.

Survey Questions Once you have determined the purpose of your survey or questionnaire, ask yourself what types of questions will result in the information you need. Most questions used on surveys and questionnaires are formulated to generate a specific type of response. Look at the variety of questions in **Figure 14–6**. Some of the questions ask the respondents for a specific response, while others ask them to respond freely. Notice that respondents have been given the choice of answering "No opinion" when asked to indicate their feelings. It is important to offer a neutral response choice to keep results accurate.

Preparing for Professional Presentations **463**

Interviews

Work with the class to list topics that would benefit from interviews as part of the research process. *(Examples might include sporting events, current news stories, or policy changes.)* Ask whom students would interview if researching a presentation on the football team, plans for the senior prom, or teenage drug abuse. Discuss the reasons for their choices. **L1**

Survey Questions

Have students review the Cafeteria Questionnaire shown in Figure 14–6. Point out that the information collected from a survey of this sort can be used for a number of purposes. To illustrate this, ask students to respond to the questions on a separate piece of paper, giving their opinions about their own cafeteria. On the chalkboard, compile a list of their answers, breaking these down into percentages where relevant. Ask students what conclusions they would draw from the results of individual questions and from the survey as a whole. If they were administering the cafeteria, what action would they consider taking as a result of this class's response? **L2**

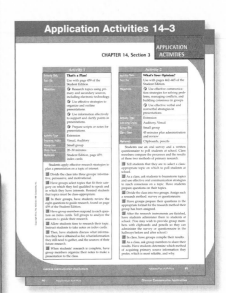

COOPERATIVE LEARNING ACTIVITY

What makes a good questionnaire? What makes people fill one out? Remind students that many of us have thrown away lengthy, apparently irrelevant survey forms. Point out that creating questionnaires requires careful planning as to the purpose of the survey and the nature of the individual questions.

As a class, list four or five topics on which all students will have an opinion. Divide students into groups and assign each group a topic. Ask each group to create a questionnaire of no more than ten questions related to their topic. Have groups read their questionnaires to the class, explaining the purpose of their surveys and reasons for their choice of questions.

Format of Questions

Have students share experiences they have had as participants in polls. Do they take the time to fill out questionnaires? If so, what determines their decision? Under what circumstances would they stop if solicited on the street by a pollster? How would they respond to e-mail polls, and why? Discuss with the class problems involved in surveying the public for information. Is there an ideal method of conducting surveys or are they all subject to problems and inaccuracies? **L2**

Practice for the Workplace

Market Research Have each group administer their survey to another group. Then, have each group critique the survey they took. Point out that respondents may not wish to answer questions that they consider too personal. Have students point out survey questions that might be too personal or are objectionable for another reason, such as vagueness or irrelevance. **L2**

Grammar Tip

The word *whom* has nearly disappeared from speech, but it should still be observed in writing. Use *whom* as the direct or indirect object of a verb or verbal or as the object of a preposition. The heading *Determining Whom to Poll* on this page correctly employs *whom* as the object of the participle *determining*.

As a rule, people do not want to spend a lot of time responding to surveys or questionnaires. For this reason, limit questions to those absolutely necessary to get the desired information. Questions also should be phrased as objectively as possible to avoid leading respondents to answer a certain way.

Format of Questions Once you have determined the questions to ask, you must determine the format you wish to use. Will you use a person-on-the-street approach in which you ask the questions directly? If so, a survey may be the best format to use.

Prior to administering your survey, create a master list of questions, leaving space to record the responses you will receive. When administering the survey, be sure to ask the questions in the same sequence to each respondent. This will help you obtain consistent results. This is particularly important if more than one person will be administering the surveys.

Do you need more responses than are possible through a limited one-to-one survey? Perhaps a questionnaire is your best choice. Questionnaires can be distributed to many respondents at once, collected in an orderly manner, then tabulated at your convenience.

To begin, write down your questions in a logical sequence, make photocopies, and distribute the questionnaire to the number of people you want to poll. As an alternative, you may wish to create the questionnaire electronically and then e-mail it to respondents or allow them to answer it online. Be sure to tell respondents how much time they will have to answer. Then, at the end of that time, collect the completed questionnaires. As with a face-to-face survey, you will need a master list of questions or a master response form on which to tabulate the results.

Determining Whom to Poll How do you determine who will be the sample for your poll? Because it would be extremely expensive and time-consuming to survey everyone who has an opinion about a particular topic, researchers only poll specific samples. A sample is the set of people you select to respond to a survey or questionnaire. They represent a smaller segment of the larger population the researchers are unable to poll.

Demographics After they determine which segment of the population will provide the most useful information, researchers study demographics that identify where that group exists. Researchers then select a representative percentage of that population as the sample for their survey or questionnaire. Usually the larger the sample, the more accurate the results of a survey.

Practice for the Workplace

Market Research Manufacturers and advertisers often conduct market research to determine market needs and learn customer reactions to new products.

BUSINESS PRACTICE *Activity*

Assume that you want to introduce a new product to students in your school. In groups of four or five, brainstorm a fictitious product, then develop a market survey to determine whether this product would sell to students in your school. For the market survey, list the number of people you would sample and provide ten questions to poll your sample population. Share your group's survey with the remainder of the class. As a class, evaluate the relevance of each group's survey.

REAL-WORLD CONNECTION

Political Polls Polling has long been used in establishing voter preferences, predicting elections, and influencing policy. Point out that the Internet is increasingly influential in the American political system as a means of understanding the opinions of the electorate.

Activity Have students type in the phrase *political poll* on an Internet search engine. Ask them to choose a site that interests them and to participate in a poll. Have them bring a printout of their questions to class and share their experiences with other students in groups. Invite individuals to discuss their online polling activities with the class. What do they feel was the purpose of the poll in which they participated? How would they evaluate the questions asked?

Figure 14–7 Demographic Representations

Percentage of Tall, Blond Boys in this Class (represents 1 boy)	Percentage of Tall, Blond Boys in this School (represents 50 boys)

Percentages The relationship between the size of a sample and the size of a total chosen population indicates how accurate your conclusions may be. Look at the two representations in **Figure 14–7.** If eight of the sixteen boys in your class are tall with blond hair, would it be safe to assume that one-half of all boys in your high school are tall and blond? Probably not, because your sample is too small to reflect reality. However, if you sampled 20 percent of the student body of your school, you could probably make a credible prediction.

Analyzing Results Once you have administered your surveys or questionnaires, you will need to tally the results. Was the information what you expected? Was one response given more than the others? Could anything about the survey or questionnaire or the way it was administered have affected the results?

EVALUATING SOURCE MATERIAL

When you research a project or presentation, you owe it to your audience to use the most ethical information available. Even the best-prepared presentation or project can be a disaster if the information is outdated, misleading, or incorrect. How do you sort through primary and secondary sources to find out what information is accurate and what is not? How do you determine whether the books, periodicals, tapes, films, and memos you've found are credible? Can you confirm that the conclusions of the writer are his or her own and aren't plagiarized from other sources?

Source Qualifications

Just because a person writes and publishes a book or article on a topic does not mean he or she is a qualified source. Following a sensational

Preparing for Professional Presentations **465**

Demographics

Have students consider what makes researchers choose certain segments of the population for their polls. Ask them whom they would poll if they wanted to discover preferences in brands of lipstick, allergy medication, political candidates, or tomato seeds. Lead students to understand that the nature of the poll often determines the population selected to participate in the survey. **L1**

Percentages

Have students review Figure 14–7. How many students were polled in each sample? *(Left sample: 16; right sample: 800.)* What are the actual percentages of tall, blond boys represented in each sample? *(Left sample: 50%; right sample: 20%)* Ask students why accurate poll figures might be important to business people or politicians. *(Students may respond that the results of survey polls may be used to determine the quantity of a product to manufacture or the amount of money to spend on a promotional campaign.)* **L2**

INCLUSION STRATEGIES

MEETING INDIVIDUAL NEEDS

Less-Proficient Readers Students who have difficulty understanding the significance of sample size in random polling may find the concept clearer with this exercise in classroom modeling. **Activity** Have students form groups and assign to each a topic about which everyone will have an opinion: sports, music, school, pets, food, and so on. Ask groups to create a two- or three-question poll on their subjects, with yes/no answers, and to administer it to the other groups. Have students tally the scores as percentages and write them on the chalkboard. Then, calculate with them the total class percentages for the same questions. Compare this figure to the group percentages. Discuss the differences between the group results and the actual result, as represented by the full class.

COMMUNICATION Strategies

DETERMINING RELIABLE SOURCES

Point out that it may sometimes be impractical or even impossible to double-check the accuracy of all sources. Students should qualify information they cannot fully support with phrases such as "According to _____" or "One source claims that . . ." As with all sources, these must be properly documented.

BECOMING A RELIABLE SOURCE

Practice documenting sources with the class by creating a Works Cited list. Use the guidelines on page 461 for recording accurate and complete information. Distribute to the students a variety of newspapers, books, and periodicals. Ask them to choose three sources, such as a book, a periodical article, and a newspaper article, including at least two different types, as models. Then, have them organize the appropriate information correctly for each source and arrange the sources alphabetically in a Works Cited list. Have students check their lists with a partner. Invite volunteers to write model lists on the chalkboard. **L2**

COMMUNICATION Strategies

DETERMINING RELIABLE SOURCES

- Check the qualifications of your sources.
- Verify that your sources—the writers, the publications, and the details—are trustworthy.
- Confirm the accuracy of the information in through another source. Discard research you can't support.

BECOMING A RELIABLE SOURCE

- In your notes, accurately quote and cite all statements that are not your own.
- Reread your research and restate the information in your own words. Make sure you don't misquote, plagiarize, or twist facts to draw false conclusions.
- Check to make sure that you clearly state your point, document your information with reliable research, and summarize your conclusions. Revise your presentation as necessary.

trial, a natural disaster, or some other dramatic news event, publishers, broadcasters, and the Internet often are flooded with information from would-be experts. Many of these individuals have no firsthand knowledge of the event, but instead rely on newscasts, unreliable sources, or their own opinions for information.

On the other hand, some sources actually conduct interviews, investigate the event, and communicate with law enforcement and other agencies to acquire as much knowledge as possible. Of these two types of sources, who is qualified and who isn't? These are questions you need to ask whenever you want to include an item of information in your presentation.

Internet sources may be especially unreliable. With the proper equipment, anyone can publish a Web site and have his or her information—accurate or not—read by any Internet surfer. As with printed materials, it is important to check the credentials of any source you use. An easy way to check any print or Internet source is to conduct a Web search using the person's name. This can help you see with what publications and organizations the person is associated. As a general rule of thumb, if you can't find the qualifications of a source, don't use the information. However, to help guide you in evaluating the qualifications of a source, ask the following questions about the source:

- What is the author's education or training related to this topic?
- What is the author's experience with this subject?

Source Credibility

The credibility of a source is a reflection of how others perceive his or her honesty and reliability. Some sources may be very well qualified to speak or write on a subject but may not be credible because of their public perception. No matter how accurate they may be, an audience will not believe what they are saying. For example, a legislator who has consistently voted against conservation legislation may know a great deal about the environment. However, he or she probably will have little credibility with an environmental action group.

Credible sources take care not to mislead their audience. They acknowledge their bias and try to document their ideas as objectively

INTERDISCIPLINARY CONNECTION

Social Studies A limited number of news outlets supply us with much of what we know about current events. News writers and reporters are subject to the same guidelines for substantiating sources as students are when preparing presentations or papers for classes. How well reporters evaluate their sources directly affects the accuracy of the information they are presenting.
Activity Have students bring to class a major news story from a newspaper or national newsmagazine. Ask them to list the sources that the writer identifies. Beside each source, have students identify his or her qualifications. Then, ask students to evaluate the sources. Why did the writer use them? Are they likely to be supplying the writer with accurate information? Invite students to present their findings to the class and to discuss their evaluations.

as possible. They also may have firsthand experiences that elevate their credibility. They may be known for their attention to detail and for conducting in-depth research. Tabloid publications often are criticized for doing weak research and printing unconfirmed rumors as fact. Many other publications, however, enjoy good reputations for checking facts and confirming their sources.

As you evaluate your sources, keep in mind that some people who communicate on specific issues do so to promote a particular viewpoint. This does not make what that person says right or wrong; it simply means that you, as an ethical communicator, must recognize that the information reflects someone else's bias. Everyone is entitled to an opinion on a topic. In fact, including a variety of viewpoints can lead to interesting interaction and discussion.

However, some sources are so biased that they discount or completely disregard facts or opinions that disagree with their point of view. These sources lose credibility. Remember, opinions are not facts, no matter how well they are presented. To evaluate the credibility of a source, consider the answers to these questions.

- What is the professional reputation of this source?

- What is the personal reputation of this source?

- What is the known bias of this source? Does that bias affect the source's information?

Source Competence

When you assess the competence of a source, you are assessing the ability of the source to make a qualified observation or judgment about the topic. A lawyer may attack the competence of witnesses in a court case by asking a series of questions: Were the witnesses in a position to actually see the crime? Did they really see what they think they saw? Did the witnesses have any conditions that impaired their ability to make accurate observations? When you are reading research materials, ask the same kinds of questions to evaluate the competence of each source.

Relevance of Information

When developing presentations, communicators need to structure their ideas carefully so that it is clear how each idea relates to the others. It also is important for supporting information to relate to the claims or conclusions you make in your presentation.

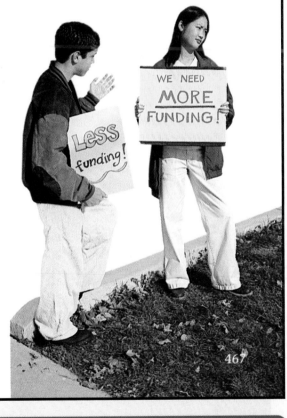

Someone who is biased and unwilling to listen to another's point of view is not a credible source. **Describe a credible source.**

CRITICAL THINKING ACTIVITY

In an age when misinformation is often represented as fact, it is important to bring a critical intelligence to all sources of news. Point out that while cynicism is never a virtue, a reader must always be alert to the possibility of deception.

Provide students with stories from tabloid-style newspapers. In groups, have them list the reasons they find these reports unreliable or unbelievable. Ask the groups to present their stories to the class and to discuss each other's analyses. Discuss with the class the importance of thorough, accurate reporting.

COMMUNICATION
PRACTICE LAB

Evaluating Sources

Have students follow the seven steps to gathering and analyzing sources outlined on this page. Discuss any problems that may have arisen in identifying the qualifications of the author. Ask students what options they think are open to a researcher when accurately assessing a source is difficult. *(Students may suggest that researchers should discard or qualify unverifiable material.)* Lead the class to understand that without the reader's or listener's confidence in the accuracy of their material, the information they wish to present will have little authority.

L2

3 ASSESS

Assign Section 3 Assessment as a homework or in-class activity.

🔵 Use *Interactive Tutor Self-Assessment Software* to review Section 3.

Section 14–3 Quiz

Irrelevant ideas distract from the purpose of a presentation and can keep you from achieving your presentation goals. Sometimes, audience members may introduce irrelevant issues on purpose to throw a presentation off course. However, if a presenter is well prepared and focused, he or she usually can stop such interruptions and bring the presentation back to the topic at hand.

The best question to ask yourself to determine the relevancy of the information is "How does this idea really relate or apply to my topic?" If you have trouble determining a link, then the information probably is irrelevant to the topic and you don't need to include it in your presentation.

Timeliness of Information

Because the accuracy and completeness of information can change over time, you should use the most recent information available to research your topic. In addition to sources in libraries, many presenters find the Internet to be a good source for recent information because it can be continually updated.

When determining the timeliness of your information, ask yourself, "Have I located the most recent information available on this topic?" If you have, then your information is as timely as possible and can be used to support your presentation.

Evaluating Your Research

Once you have located and evaluated the information for your presentation, it is time to revisit some of the decisions you have already made. Using what you have discovered in your research, step back and look at everything you have gathered. Have you located sufficient information to support your initial thoughts or choices for your presentation? Have you verified your initial

COMMUNICATION
PRACTICE LAB

Evaluating Sources

To practice gathering and analyzing sources, follow these steps:

Step 1 With a partner, choose a recent historical event to research.

Step 2 Have one person gather information on your topic using resources in your library. Have the other partner search the Internet for information on the same topic.

Step 3 Collect at least five sources per person, using the guidelines for recording accurate and complete information in the chart on page 461.

Step 4 Evaluate each source for accuracy and completeness. Identify the author, his or her related training or experience,

and the quality of the information. Is the source outdated, misleading, or inaccurate?

Step 5 Exchange sources. Confirm each other's evaluations.

Step 6 On a separate sheet of paper, list the facts that appear in two or more of the sources.

Step 7 Present your findings to the remainder of the class. Why is it important to use accurate and complete information when making communication decisions?

MEETING INDIVIDUAL NEEDS

GIFTED AND TALENTED

Changing Information In some fields, particularly the sciences, the state of knowledge is constantly changing. New developments or discoveries can render old theories obsolete overnight. Encourage students with a talent for research to demonstrate the importance of up-to-date information. Remind them that today's state-of-the-art knowledge may be outdated tomorrow.

Activity Have students choose an area of science, technology, mathematics, or medicine that is of interest to them. Ask them to research the history of learning in their chosen topic and to create a time line indicating when new theories or findings appeared, displacing earlier ideas. Students should present their time lines to the class, explaining the reason for the changes in information and assessing the current state of knowledge in the field.

choices or discovered new information that requires you to rethink things? If so, now is the time to change the focus of your topic or the purpose of your presentation. You will want to do this before you have a great deal of time invested in the preparation of the presentation itself. However, remember that the changes you make still must fit the needs of your audience, occasion, and task as well as your own needs.

Researching a presentation is a task that lasts throughout the preparation process. As you complete each step, you need to reevaluate the communication choices you have already made. When you make additional choices about other steps in the process, you will need to conduct research to support those choices. Your time will be well spent, however, leading to a well-thought-out presentation supported by accurate and complete research.

Reteaching Activity 14–3

Section 3 Assessment

4. What should you consider when determining what information sources are appropriate for a presentation?

5. **Compare and Contrast** What is the difference between a source's qualifications and its credibility? Why are both important?

Review Key Terms

1. Define the following terms and write each in a sentence: secondary source, primary source, sample.

Check Understanding

2. Why is it important to gather and use complete information when researching a presentation?

3. Compare the advantages of spoken surveys to written surveys, or questionnaires.

APPLICATION *Activity*

Comparing Primary and Secondary Sources Using secondary sources in your school or local libraries, find at least two references to teenagers' use of the Internet. Read the sources. On a sheet of paper make a list of the criteria evaluating the information you read. Assess your sources against the criteria.

Next, work with your classmates to create a questionnaire about the Internet to distribute in your school. Find out who uses the Internet, how often, and why. Collect and tabulate your data.

As a class, compare the information you gathered from your secondary sources to what you learned through primary research. What conclusions can you draw?

Preparing for Professional Presentations **469**

Enrichment Activity 14–3

4 CLOSE

Have students reread the opening paragraph of the section on page 458 and recall their answers to the Bellringer. Based upon their reading in this section, would they assess the presenter as a qualified and credible source? Ask them to explain their answers.

Extra-Credit Project

Ask students to analyze and evaluate the quality of information used in an investigative television news feature. Have them present their evaluations to the class, suggesting that they employ videotaped portions of the program to illustrate their presentations.

Section 3 Assessment Answers

1. Accept all reasonable sentences.
2. Gathering and using complete information allows the researcher to avoid bias and to discover new aspects of his or her topic.
3. Answers will vary, but a possible answer is that the pollster can observe and interpret the respondent's body language.
4. A researcher should use sources that are accurate and qualified. An appropriate source should also be credible.

5. A qualified source possesses accurate information. A credible source uses information ethically and objectively and is perceived to be presenting the truth. Qualified sources will not be credible if they conceal information or otherwise use their knowledge to mislead the public.

Application Activity In designing their questionnaires, students should follow the guidelines described on page 464.

Technology Skill

RESEARCHING ON THE WORLD WIDE WEB

The amazing growth of the World Wide Web has led to an explosion of information. To research the Web most effectively, it is important to learn how to use a search engine.

Learning the Skill

To begin researching on the Web, first select a search engine. On the search engine's home page, you will find a query box into which you can type words. In this box, type one or more words or a question that describes the type of information you are seeking. These are known as the keywords for your search.

When typing keywords, make them as specific to your research topic as possible. For example, to find information on becoming a biologist, you might use keywords such as *biologist, biology careers,* or *How do I become a biologist?* To further narrow your search, you can sometimes add more specific words or put quotation marks around your entry.

Once you have entered your keywords, click on the search button beside the query box. The results of your search appear, listed in order from the most accurate to the least accurate match. To investigate a search result, simply click on its title or Web address. This takes you directly to that Web site and instantly connects you to the world of information available on the Web.

Practicing the Skill

Imagine that you need to give a presentation on how to start a small business. Follow these steps to research your topic.

Step 1 Log on to the Internet.

Step 2 Choose a search engine by typing its address in the **Address, Location,** or **Go To** box. Press **Enter.**

Step 3 Search by typing the keywords *small business.* Press **Enter.**

Step 4 Look at the number of results. Were there hundreds? Thousands? Scroll down the list to view some of the results.

Step 5 Narrow your search by changing your keywords to *"starting a small business"* or by typing the query *"How do I start a small business?"*

Step 6 Look at the number of results now. Did you narrow your results? Click on a selection to begin your research!

APPLICATION Activity

Use a search engine to learn about finding a job in a field that interests you. Write a one-page essay describing the information you found in your research. Deliver your essay orally to the class.

EXTENDING THE CONTENT

Types of Searches Students overwhelmed by the enormous number of Web sites resulting from their keyword searches should know that search engines do not all locate information in the same manner. While many produce lists based on keywords, some of the best known engines, including *Encyclopaedia Britannica* and *Yahoo,* search by subject. Because the Web sites in subject-based lists are reviewed before inclusion, these engines generally provide shorter, more reliable lists. These same factors, however, tend to make them less varied and up-to-date.

Activity Have students compare finding information using three or four different search engines. Have them summarize their results and conclude which type of search engine they found most satisfactory.

Analyzing Your Presentation Preparation Skills

How Do You Rate?

On a separate sheet of paper, respond to the following statements. Put a check mark beside each skill you would like to improve.

KEY: A Always   **R** Rarely
       U Usually   **N** Never
       S Sometimes

1. I consider the amount of information available before I choose a professional presentation topic.

2. I try to speak only about topics that I know best.

3. Even if I know a topic well, I still research it thoroughly to find the latest information and to validate what I already know.

4. I analyze the information I gather and discard any that is not factual, credible, and verifiable.

5. I try to ask objective questions when conducting a survey.

6. Whenever possible, I conduct primary research to gather information.

7. I choose samples that accurately represent an overall population.

8. I work at all four aspects of being a good presenter: knowledge, character, good intentions, and genuineness.

9. I try to develop basic speaking skills so that I will be considered a competent presenter.

10. I choose effective language appropriate for the presentation topic, occasion, and audience.

How Do You Score?

Review your responses. Give yourself 5 points for every A, 4 for every U, 3 for every S, 2 for every R, and 1 for every N. Total your points and evaluate your score.

41–50 Excellent You may be surprised to find out how much you can improve your skills.

31–40 Good In this course, you can learn ways to make your skills better.

21–30 Fair Practice applying the skills taught in this course.

1–20 Needs Improvement Carefully monitor your improvement as you work through this course.

Setting Communication Goals

If you scored Excellent or Good, complete Part A. If your score was Fair or Needs Improvement, complete Part B.

Part A   1. I plan to put the following ideas into practice:

        2. I plan to share the following information about communication with the following people:

Part B   1. The behaviors I need to change most are:

        2. To bring about these changes, I will take these steps:

Have students respond to the ten statements using the key, then evaluate their presentation preparation strengths. Based on their scores, assign either Part A or Part B of the goal-setting activity. On an index card or sheet of paper, have students concretely define their communication goals to improve their current level of skill.

Communication Journal Activity

Point out that professional presentations are not restricted to the boardroom or auditorium. Students experience presentations every day in school. Ask students to describe in their journals a classroom presentation that they considered informative and interesting. Encourage them to analyze what made it successful.

Communication Tip

Since it is not always possible for students to choose presentation topics with which they are extremely familiar, encourage them to seek outside evaluation of their research while it is in preparation. Point out that scientists routinely submit their original papers for peer review. By sharing their research at an early stage with an interested adult or an informed peer, students might forestall problems that could occur if the work proceeded unchecked.

ENGLISH LANGUAGE LEARNERS

Overcoming Stage Fright Many students have apprehensions that even the best research will prove worthless in front of an audience. Fears of inadequate basic speaking skills compound the problem for students who are gaining fluency in the language. Rehearsing can defuse some of the anxiety. **Activity** Have students write on a piece of paper a number from 1 to 10, indicating how anxious they feel about speaking in front of an audience for an upcoming presentation—with 1 signifying no problem and 10, potential stage fright. Divide the students into random groups and ask them to compare their numbers. Invite the student with the highest number in each group to rehearse his or her presentation in front of the other group members. Have the next highest follow, as time permits. Encourage students to offer constructive criticism. **ELL**

Communication Through Writing

Writing an Inquiry

Writing an Inquiry

Objective: To learn how to write a letter of inquiry

Teaching Suggestions and Strategies

Tailoring an Inquiry for Your Needs

Students should understand that there are different varieties of inquiry. If you are asking for information from an organization whose business it is to dispense such information, the task is simple: state your purpose and objectives in as straightforward a manner as possible. A tourist bureau or public service organization will employ staff precisely for the purpose of sending out material.

Inquiries that are more complex than a simple request for information may require careful thought. Point out that requests for interviews or for services that are not routinely granted may be turned down if you do not make your purpose seem important or interesting. This can sometimes be accomplished by including as part of your objectives enough information about yourself and your needs to catch the reader's attention.

Making the reader feel important is another way to strengthen an inquiry. Although most people will see through an attempt at flattery, suggest to students that genuine admiration, simply expressed, is always welcome.

Whatever additions a student makes to a simple letter of inquiry, point out that brevity is essential. Few readers have the patience to turn to page 2!

Have you ever written an inquiry? An inquiry simply is a request for information. If you have sent a letter, e-mail, fax, or memo requesting information from someone, you have written an inquiry.

Because inquiries help you learn more about a subject, they are an important part of day-to-day research. You might use an inquiry to gather information for a project or presentation, to find out about a product or service, or to test the marketability of a product.

Determine Your Objectives and Purpose. Before writing an inquiry, it is important to understand exactly what you need to know and why. One way to clarify this is to write a purpose statement and objectives. A purpose statement concisely states what information you need. Objectives are the goals you hope to achieve with that information. A purpose statement and objectives provide direction for your inquiry.

Write Your Letter of Inquiry. Sometimes, it is difficult to find a source for the information you need. Other times, however, the amount of available information can be overwhelming. In these instances, it is important to narrow your research to only those sources that will be most helpful.

Begin your communication with a brief paragraph stating the purpose of the inquiry. Base this paragraph on your purpose statement.

In the second paragraph, address your objectives. It is important to make your request as clear as possible. Never assume that the reader will infer what you need to know.

Use a proper business-letter format for your inquiry. Be courteous, brief, and reasonable in your request. Remember, you are asking the reader for a favor: to provide you with information. If you are asking to meet with the person for a personal interview, suggest some possible dates, but remain flexible.

Finally, be sure to include your phone number and e-mail address, if applicable. Also, if you need the information by a certain date, politely mention this in your closing paragraph.

By following these few basic rules, you will be more likely to receive a positive response to your inquiry. Then you will have mastered another important skill for communicating in social and business contexts.

For additional information about business writing, see the *Guide to Business Communication* section of the Communication Survival Kit in the Appendix.

MEETING INDIVIDUAL NEEDS

MULTIPLE LEARNING STYLES

Linguistic "You won't get anything unless you ask" is a well-worn phrase, but, like many clichés, it is very true. Sometimes, the wildest request, if worded well, meets with success. Encourage students to have a little fun with their written inquiries while practicing the technique.

Activity Invite students to think of some extremely improbable proposals that they would like to see initiated at their school. *(Examples: allow students to bring pets to school; start a mud-wrestling team; purchase laptop computers for all students.)* Have students form groups and ask them to discuss how they would seriously request these initiatives. Then, ask them each to write a letter inquiring about the possibility of initiating one of the proposals. Invite volunteers to read their letters. Vote on the letter that seems most likely to succeed.

Communication Through Writing

The following letter is an example of an effective inquiry.

1351 High Street
Hometown, USA 76543

March 26, 2003

Ms. Jonna Butler
Butler Research Associates
1395 Central Road
Corpus Christi, Texas 78350

Dear Ms. Butler:

I am writing to inquire whether your research company does marketing research studies for small insurance firms. Star Financial Group is a market leader in insurance sales, ready to expand its business even further.

The research we are seeking would help us increase our sales of life insurance to more customers in the 35–50 age group. Although sales are strong in that area, we want to pinpoint new geographic areas in which to expand our efforts. We also would like to explore the demand for college savings plans. Would your firm be able to supply us with research in these areas?

I am anxious to hear how Butler Research Associates might be able to meet our needs. Please contact me at your earliest convenience. My phone number is 817-555-3232. Thank you for your time and attention.

Sincerely,

Reuben Garza

Reuben Garza
Marketing Director
Star Financial Group

WRITING *Activity*

Use the following steps to write an effective letter of inquiry.

- Think of a U.S. city that you might like to visit. Use the Internet or another source to research the address of that city's travel and tourism bureau or chamber of commerce.

- You will write an inquiry to this organization requesting information about hotel accommodations for an upcoming vacation. Determine a date for your trip and decide on a preferred price range for your accommodations: budget, mid-range, or luxury.

- Use this information to write a purpose statement and objectives for your letter.

- Write your letter. Begin by explaining the purpose of your inquiry.

- Request the exact information you need to meet your objectives. Provide any details the reader will need to know.

- Provide your own phone number, and e-mail address, if applicable.

- Suggest a possible response time.

- Thank the reader for his or her help.

- Write a business-style closing. Print and sign your letter.

Discuss all letters as a class. Did you discover ways to make your request clearer? Edit your letter to make it as reader-friendly as possible.

Preparing for Professional Presentations 473

Communication Through Writing

Teaching Activity

Have students read the sample letter of inquiry on this page. Point out that the statement of purpose in the first paragraph is relatively straightforward. The objectives, however, may take careful wording, especially if a request is out of the ordinary.

Give students practice writing objectives by asking them to form pairs and to read the following statements of purpose:

You are writing to ask whether

- there is handicapped access at a local building.
- fishing is permitted in a particular lake or stream.
- pets are allowed to stay in a guest house.
- you can spend a night at a college or university.
- you can have a personal tour backstage at a theater.

Have them discuss what the objectives might be for each of these purposes. Ask them to choose three of the above options and to write a paragraph of two or three sentences for each, stating the objectives. Invite students to read their paragraphs to the class.

WRITING *Activity*

Students' letters should be written in correct business form. They should be neat, centered on the page, and carefully proofread.

Grammar Tip

When a pronoun serves as the object of a verb or preposition, it must be in the objective case.

Additional Resources

Appendix, "Guide to Business Communication"

Glencoe Writer's Assistant CD-ROM

Glencoe Interactive Grammar Software

Grade 9 Writer's Choice, Lesson 2.4

GRAMMAR PRACTICE

Case of Pronouns

Have students write the correct pronoun from the choice in parentheses.

1. Address the letter to Mr. Sanchez and (her, she). *(her)*

2. (Her, She) and I will deliver it by hand. *(She)*

3. The message struck our boss and (we, us) as very funny. *(us)*

4. She read it with him and (me, I). *(me)*

5. Mr. Williams wrote a reply to (they, them) and us. *(them)*

GLENCOE
TECHNOLOGY

 MindJogger Videoquiz

Use *MindJogger* to review the Chapter 14 content.

Reviewing Key Terms

1. i

2. j

3. f

4. h

5. g

6. b

7. a

8. e

9. d

10. c

Visit the *Glencoe Communication Applications* Web site at **communicationapplications. glencoe.com** and click on **Chapter 14 Activity** for additional practice in preparing to make presentations.

Reviewing Key Terms

Number a sheet of paper from 1 to 10. Beside each number, write the letter of the vocabulary term that best fits that example.

1. a demonstration of how to use a printer

2. a group of shoppers responding to a mall survey

3. a review of a new best-seller

4. a pep talk to a company's sales force

5. a brief explanation of budget concerns to a small group of coworkers

6. an interview with a war veteran

7. the image projected by a respected newscaster

8. female college graduates, age 25–45, who are registered democrats

9. a campaign speech

10. a multimedia presentation to a group of computer professionals

a. ethos	**f.** informative presentation
b. primary source	**g.** professional presentation
c. formal presentation	**h.** motivational presentation
d. persuasive presentation	**i.** informal presentation
e. demographics	**j.** sample

Reviewing Key Concepts

On a separate sheet of paper, answer the following questions in complete sentences.

1. Describe the characteristics of a presenter who has a positive ethos.

2. How does a presenter decide on the style of language to use in a presentation?

3. What type of information is conveyed in a successful informative presentation?

4. Why might a presenter skip the steps of selecting and limiting a topic?

5. Name three types of secondary resources. Name three types of primary resources.

Reviewing Key Concepts

1. A presenter with positive ethos displays knowledge, character, good intent, and genuineness.

2. A presenter decides the style of language to use based on the specific context of his or her presentation. This includes knowledge of the speaker's own abilities, the audience, the occasion, and the task or purpose of the presentation.

3. Informative presentations include information that is easy to understand, accurate, interesting, relevant, and objective.

4. Speakers might skip the steps of selecting and limiting a topic when it is chosen for them in advance.

5. Secondary sources include books, periodicals, and the Internet. Primary sources include interviews, surveys, and autobiographies. (Accept other reasonable responses.)

Assessment and Activities

Reading and Critical Thinking Skill

1. **Inferring** Imagine you are presenting information on current fashion trends to a group of teens. How might you vary your presentation for the teens' parents?

2. **Evaluating** What are three questions you might use to evaluate whether someone has met his or her responsibilities as a presenter?

3. **Predicting** If a presenter appears to be very knowledgeable about his or her topic, how might it affect the audience at an informational presentation? A persuasive presentation? A motivational presentation?

Skill Practice Activity

Writing an Inquiry Imagine that you are in charge of reserving a meeting place for your company's annual awards banquet. This formal dinner meeting will take place on December 12 from 7 to 10 P.M., and sixty people will attend. Write a letter to a local hotel or convention center seeking information about appropriate meeting accommodations. Address your letter to the group sales manager or event planner. Create a purpose statement and objectives based on the questions you will need to ask. Then, use your purpose and objectives as a guideline for your letter.

Cooperative Learning Activity

Choosing a Sample Working in a group of three or four students, determine a survey topic related to teens and automobiles. What group of teens is represented by your topic? All teens everywhere? Only U.S. teens? Only males or females of a specific age? With this in mind, work with your group to choose a representative sample for your survey. Give a three-minute presentation explaining the accuracy of your survey sample and a realistic plan for surveying these individuals.

Chapter Project

Planning Using library resources and the Internet, locate secondary information on the topic of school uniforms. Evaluate the information in at least five of the sources you find. Take careful notes on the information that you decide is credible.

Create a class list of questions to ask your principal about a school-uniform policy. Create another list of questions to survey students, teachers, and parents about your topic. In groups of five or six, administer the surveys.

Presenting After compiling the survey results, each group should present its information to the class and answer these questions: What did your group learn from its survey? What did your group enjoy most about the research process? What would your group do differently next time?

Preparing for Professional Presentations **475**

Reading and Critical Thinking Skill

1. **Inferring** Students' answers will vary. Possible answers include displaying the fashions in more conservative ways and explaining specific trends in greater detail.

2. **Evaluating** Questions might include the following: Has the presenter exhibited basic speaking skills? Has he or she conveyed a knowledgeable, genuine image? Has he or she considered the audience?

3. **Predicting** The audience at an informational presentation would trust the presenter's information; at a persuasive presentation, be convinced of the presenter's viewpoint and/or act on it; at a motivational presentation, be emotionally affected and change their behaviors accordingly.

Skill Practice Activity

Writing an Inquiry

Urge students to consider their purpose and objectives as they write their letters. How will these affect the tone, wording, and organization of their letters? *(Tone and wording should be simple and businesslike. The details about the meeting should appear early in the letter.)*

Cooperative Learning Activity

Choosing a Sample

Have the class brainstorm some sample survey topics, such as how often teens drive cars, how many 16-year-olds have a car for their exclusive use, or how many teens have been involved in an automobile accident.

Chapter Project

Have students review judging the credibility of information in the library and on the Internet. Point out that on the subject of school uniforms, a variety of authorities, including school administrators, teachers, parents, and students, may be equally useful and credible.

Chapter 15 Planning Guide

SECTION RESOURCES

Daily Objectives

Section 1

1. Identify the four purposes of an introduction
2. Apply effective methods for getting an audience's attention
3. Develop clear thesis statements
4. Explain three reasons for audience orientation
5. Identify and explain the three purposes of a conclusion

Reproducible Resources

 Reproducible Lesson Plan 15-1
 Application Activities 15-1
 Guided Reading Workbook Activity 15-1
 Vocabulary Activity 15*
 Reteaching Activity 15-1*
 Enrichment Activity 15-1*
 Graphic Organizer Transparency Strategies and Activities 15-1

Multimedia Resources

 Graphic Organizer Transparency 15-1
 Chapter 15 Teaching Transparency
Interactive Tutor Self-Assessment
PuzzleMaker
 ExamView® Pro Testmaker
 Interactive Lesson Planner
 Communication in Action Video Chapter 15
MindJogger
 communicationapplications.glencoe.com
 Presentation Plus!

Section 2

1. Select appropriate strategies to organize a presentation
2. Explain Monroe's Motivated Sequence
3. Use effective strategies to outline a presentation

Reproducible Resources

 Reproducible Lesson Plan 15-2
 Application Activities 15-2
 Guided Reading Workbook Activity 15-2
 Vocabulary Activity 15*
Reteaching Activity 15-2*
 Enrichment Activity 15-2*
Graphic Organizer Transparency Strategies and Activities 15-2

Multimedia Resources

 Graphic Organizer Transparency 15-2
Chapter 15 Teaching Transparency
Interactive Tutor Self-Assessment
 PuzzleMaker
ExamView® Pro Testmaker
 Interactive Lesson Planner
 Communication in Action Video Chapter 15
 MindJogger
communicationapplications.glencoe.com
Presentation Plus!

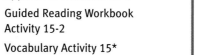 Use Glencoe's *Presentation Plus!* multimedia teacher tool to easily present dynamic lessons that engage and motivate your students. Using Microsoft PowerPoint®, you can customize the presentations to create your own personalized lessons.

* Also available in Spanish

 Blackline Master   CD-ROM   Software

 Transparency   Videodisc   Videocassette   Web site

Chapter 15 Planning Guide

FOR THE TEACHER

Getting Audience Attention

Have each student select a topic for a speech about something that is important to him or her—a cause, sport, hobby, type of music. Ask students to brainstorm a list of startling facts, humorous anecdotes, personal experiences, and memorable quotations that relate to this topic, writing each on a separate 3" x 5" card. Through the next few days, they should listen closely to people whose speaking ability they admire, noting ways they choose to introduce their topics into conversations, meetings, or formal speeches. Remind them to add to their lists and their cards as new ideas occur to them.

Students should then select the three ideas they think are best and use them in writing three different introductions to a speech on their topics. Ask them to deliver each of their introductions to a group of students in class and ask for their feedback on which most effectively captures their attention. Direct the students to create a file in which to keep their cards with introduction ideas and feedback.

CHAPTER RESOURCES

Resources for the Teacher

- *Do Not Go Naked into Your Next Presentation: Nifty Little Nuggets to Quiet the Nerves and Please the Crowd* by Ron Hoff, Andrews McMeel Publishing, 1997
- *How to Speak, How to Listen* by Mortimer Jerome Adler, Collier Books, 1997
- *Knockout Presentations: How to Deliver Your Message with Power, Punch, and Pizzazz* by Diane Diresta, Chandler House Press, 1998

Resources for the Student

- *How to Be the Life of the Podium: Openers, Closers and Everything in Between to Keep Them Listening* by Sylvia Simmons, AMACOM, 1993
- *The Big Book of Presentation Games: Wake-Em-Up Tricks, Icebreakers, & Other Fun Stuff* by John W. Newstrom and Edward Scannell (Contributor), McGraw-Hill, 1998

Block Scheduling

Block scheduling differs from traditional class scheduling in the amount of time allotted to each period. The extended time frame provided by block scheduling affords you the opportunity to implement a greater number of research-oriented and activity-intense projects to motivate and involve your students. Activities that are particularly suited to use within the block-scheduling framework are identified throughout this chapter by the following designation:

KEY TO ABILITY LEVELS

Teaching Strategies have been coded for varying learning styles and abilities.

L1 **BASIC** activities for all students

L2 **AVERAGE** activities for average to above-average students

L3 **CHALLENGING** activities for above-average students

ELL **English Language Learner** activities

Chapter 15 Resource Manager

The following materials may be used when teaching the chapter. Materials for specific lessons are also shown at point-of-use in the margins of the Teacher's Wraparound Edition.

TEACHING TRANSPARENCIES

Chapter 15 Teaching Transparency

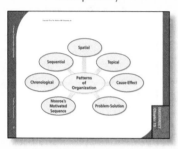

Graphic Organizer Transparency 15-1

Graphic Organizer Transparency 15-2

APPLICATION ACTIVITIES

Chapter 15, Section 1

Chapter 15, Section 2

Chapter 15, Cumulative

REINFORCEMENT AND REVIEW ACTIVITIES

Vocabulary Activity 15

Guided Reading Activity Workbook 15-1, 15-2

Reteaching Activities 15-1, 15-2

Chapter 15 Resource Manager

GLENCOE'S
ASSESSMENT
ADVANTAGE

Section Quizzes 15–1, 15–2

Chapter 15 Test, Forms A & B

Performance Assessment Activity 15

ENRICHMENT AND EXTENSION

Technology Application Activity 15

Enrichment Activities 15–1, 15–2

ORAL PRESENTATION ACTIVITIES

Activity 4

SPANISH RESOURCES

- Spanish Chapter and Unit Tests
- Spanish Vocabulary Activities
- Spanish Section Quizzes
- Spanish Reteaching Activities
- Spanish Enrichment Activities

MULTIMEDIA

- Interactive Tutor Self-Assessment
- ExamView® Pro Testmaker
- PuzzleMaker
- Communication in Action Videodisc and Videocassette
- MindJogger
- Interactive Lesson Planner
- Presentation Plus!
- Writer's Assistant
- Glencoe Interactive Grammar
- **communicationapplications.glencoe.com**

TEACHER PLANNING AND SUPPORT

- Reproducible Lesson Plans
- Interactive Lesson Planner
- Presentation Plus!

Organizing Presentations

WHY IT'S IMPORTANT

The key to delivering a well-organized presentation lies in taking the time to understand the parts of your presentation and putting them together in the most effective way.

 To better understand how to organize an effective presentation, view the **Communication in Action** Chapter 15 video lesson.

"Begin at the beginning and go on till you come to the end; then stop."
—The King, Lewis Carroll's *Alice in Wonderland*

WHY IT'S IMPORTANT

Ask students to read the quotation; then have them explain what is important about the beginning and ending of a communication. Ask: **Why does it matter how you organize the points in a presentation? How do you decide what goes first, second, and so on?** *(Students may suggest that the brain needs logic to join ideas into a meaningful whole or may mention the human convention of storytelling, which relies on a beginning, middle, and end. Also, well-organized points are easier for a presenter to remember and for listeners to understand. They are more convincing and more likely to be recalled.)*

Section 1

Parts of a Presentation

GUIDE TO READING

Objectives

1. Identify the five purposes of an introduction.
2. Apply effective methods for getting an audience's attention.
3. Develop clear thesis statements.
4. Explain three reasons for audience orientation.
5. Identify and explain the three purposes of a conclusion.

Terms to Learn

attention device
thesis statement
audience orientation

Have you ever sat through a presentation wondering when the speaker would get to the point? Have you left a presentation confused—not knowing what the speaker was trying to say? You may have even questioned whether or not the speaker really knew what he or she was talking about.

In all of these cases, it probably was the lack of organization that left you confused and questioning the credibility of the speaker. Disorganized presentations are usually ineffective. Once a presenter has determined the specific topic and purpose for a presentation and has gathered sufficient information, he or she should consider how to organize and outline it, or put it together effectively—the fifth step in the presentation preparation process, as shown in **Figure 15–1** on the next page.

Competent communicators want to give presentations that their audiences can follow, understand, and remember. A well-organized presentation, therefore, is clear and simple to understand; has a limited number of main ideas; and flows logically from point to point.

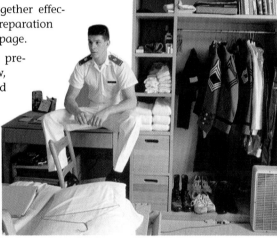

■ **An effective presenter must exhibit organization in a presentation much like military personnel must organize their belongings in a small space. Describe a well-organized presentation.**

Organizing Presentations **477**

1 FOCUS

Bellringer
Ask students into what main parts they organize their essays *(introduction, body, conclusion).* Then read the opening paragraph aloud and ask students to give one-sentence reasons such presentations did not make sense or hold their attention. Have students read the remainder of the page silently and brainstorm analogous situations in which organizing material beforehand leads to success in the activity that follows. *(Examples might include organizing study materials before studying for a test or ingredients before making a recipe.)*

You may use Graphic Organizer Transparency 15–1 to introduce this section.

Visual Instruction

Answer A well-organized presentation should be clear and simple to understand, with a limited number of main ideas that flow logically from point to point.

RESOURCE MANAGER

Teaching Tools

- Interactive Lesson Planner
- Reproducible Lesson Plan 15–1
- Application Activities 15–1

Reproducible Masters

- Guided Reading Activity Workbook 15–1
- Enrichment Activity 15–1
- Reteaching Activity 15–1
- Section Quiz 15–1
- Transparency Strategies and Activities Booklet 15–1

Transparencies

- Graphic Organizer Transparency 15–1
- Chapter 15 Teaching Transparency

Technology Resources

- Interactive Tutor Self-Assessment Software
- Presentation Plus! Software
- ExamView® Pro Testmaker
- PuzzleMaker Software
- communicationapplications.glencoe.com

2 TEACH

First Impressions

Ask students to list ways they try to make a good first impression on someone. *(Students may mention making the person feel at ease, using friendly body language, being well groomed, using good manners, and saying or doing something amusing or original.)* Point out that an introduction also creates a first impression. Have the class read the bulleted list of purposes for the introduction on this page. Ask them which one they think is most important. **L2**

Visual Instruction

Answer Students might suggest that a speaker needs to grab the audience's attention in the first few moments of a presentation before getting to the important information of the topic.

Figure 15–1 Steps of the Presentation Preparation Process

1. Determine a topic.
2. Limit the topic.
3. Determine the purpose.
4. Research the topic.
5. Organize and outline the presentation.
6. Select supporting information.
7. Prepare notes and manuscript for delivery.
8. Rehearse the presentation.

Most presentations consist of three main elements:

- introduction
- body
- conclusion

By carefully structuring these elements, the speaker makes it easier for the audience to understand the ideas.

Simply knowing the parts of a presentation, however, doesn't necessarily result in an effective presentation. A presenter also needs to understand the purpose of each part of a presentation, the strategies to use in preparing each part, and how to relate it to the other parts of the presentation.

THE INTRODUCTION

It is often said that first impressions are the most important. This is especially true for presentations. Therefore, you should devote the first 5 to 10 percent of your presentation time to the introduction.

During this brief period, you can play an important role in determining how your audience will receive your presentation. An audience who is turned off will be hard to win back. In the same way, an audience that has been grabbed by an interesting beginning, knows what to expect, is in the right frame of mind, and believes in your credibility will be attentive throughout your presentation.

The introduction of a presentation has five purposes. It serves to

- get the audience's attention
- state the thesis
- establish your ethos as a speaker
- orient the audience
- preview the main points

Get the Audience's Attention

By introducing your presentation, you have an opportunity to grab your audience's attention before getting to the important information of your topic. Audience members tend

This audience member has just lost interest in the presentation and is now considering what is on the menu. How can you prevent loss of attention during your own presentation?

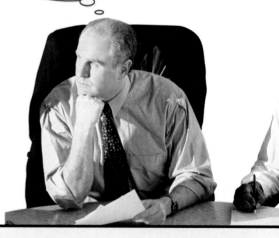

"I wonder what they are serving during the break. . . ."

ENGLISH LANGUAGE LEARNERS

MEETING INDIVIDUAL NEEDS

Cultural Views of Presentation Style American culture favors a direct approach to communication, in which ideas are fully explained and logically tied together. However, some cultures permit or encourage a more indirect style of sharing ideas, in which communicators suggest rather than spell out.

Activity Have students choose a custom or celebration from their native cultures to explain to the class. Ask them to make notes about the event, putting each detail on a separate 3" x 5" card. Then have students write down categories of information they need to tell the audience (such as steps in the activity, why it is important, and how it began) and organize the cards into these categories. If a card does not fit, they should omit it. **ELL**

AUDIENCE ATTENTION DEVICES

Attention Device	Sample Main Topic
Humor	Commitment to this month's sales goal
	Many people enjoy steak and eggs for breakfast, but have you ever thought about the roles of the steer and the chicken in that breakfast? Yes, the chicken was involved, but the steer was definitely committed to feeding us!
Quotations	United States space program
	Space—the final frontier. These are the voyages of the *Starship Enterprise*. Its five-year mission: To explore new worlds. To seek out life and new civilizations. To boldly go where no man has gone before.
Personal Experiences	Importance of extracurricular activities
	As a member of my high school drum corp, I developed some of my closest relationships. In fact, two of the guys who were in corp with me later became groomsmen in my wedding.
References to the Occasion, Audience, or Topic	Need for additional funds for science equipment at your school
	I would like to thank the members of the school board for allowing me to be with you this evening.
Rhetorical Questions	Internet addiction
	Do you surf the Web for hours on end? Do you spend more time scanning bulletin boards in cyberspace than reading books for your classes? Are you more connected emotionally with people in your chat groups than with friends or family members?—If so, you may be part of that growing portion of the population whom psychologists identify as Internet addicts.
Startling Statements	Importance of arts programs in public schools
	Ricardo seems like an average six-year-old boy. He loves to play soccer and ride his bike with his brother. He is also a gifted pianist and was recently invited to play at Carnegie Hall.
Stories	Need for handicap-accessible playground equipment at a neighborhood park
	Picture a warm spring day. Young children are enjoying the playground at Prestonwood Park. The laughter is contagious; the smiles on their faces beam. Elizabeth is a four-year-old who comes to the park nearly every day. She loves to swing. She sees other children who are running and playing. Elizabeth can't run. She is physically challenged and is in a wheelchair. There is no equipment in the park for Elizabeth.

to have little mental patience. If you fail to gain their attention within the first few moments of your speech, their minds will quickly wander.

Attention Device How do you compete with whatever is already on their minds—sports practice, family issues, lunch? You can easily and appropriately demand their attention by using attention devices. An attention device is a

tool used by speakers to grab the interest of an audience. Seven popular attention devices are

- humor
- quotations
- stories
- references to the occasion, audience, or topic
- rhetorical questions
- startling statements
- personal experiences

Organizing Presentations **479**

BUSINESS BRIEF

Pete Peterson, Wall Street financier who is in demand as a speaker all over the world, has found people recall points from his speeches months or years later, not because of their seriousness but because of his use of humor. He has developed what he calls the Peterson Principle: "If you want anything to stick to the bone, use some humor that is relevant to your message."

Getting Attention

Use the table on this page to guide students through various options for winning audience attention. For each example listed, have students suggest another topic and sample introductory comment. **L1**

MULTIPLE LEARNING STYLES

MEETING INDIVIDUAL NEEDS

Linguistic Students who excel in communicating with others can help demonstrate the importance of delivery style when using attention-getting devices.

Activity Provide or have students list presentation topics. Allow students to choose one for which they have an idea for a humorous anecdote, quotation, personal experience, or story. Have each student incorporate his or her attention-getting device into a presentation opening and practice delivering it in various styles. Invite students to deliver their introductions to the class two ways. The audience should listen to evaluate and choose the style they found most engaging.

Communication Tip

Wait to plan your introduction until you have selected the main points of your presentation and organized and outlined the body. Ideas for linking your introduction to your content come easier then.

Communication Tip

In a presentation, use quotations correctly and credit them to the right people. Verify exact wording of quotations against reliable sources. The following general dictionaries of quotations are available in most libraries:

- *Oxford Dictionary of Quotations*
- John Bartlett's *Familiar Quotations*
- Burton Stevenson's *Home Book of Quotations*

Making Connections

Point out that an attention-getting device will not help if it does not relate (and lead) directly to the main point of the talk. A joke should not be told just for the sake of telling a joke. Also explain that the length of the introduction should be proportional to the length of presentation. A story may be too long to introduce a short talk. Ask students to watch introductions used by newscasters. Have them evaluate the length of each and then share their findings with the class. **L3**

DID YOU KNOW?

A speaker can command the attention of listeners for about 20 minutes. In deciding the scope, content, and organization of a speech, keep this limitation in mind.

Choosing an Attention Device The attention device you choose will depend largely on your topic, your audience, and on the mood you want to set for your presentation. You probably would not want to begin a speech about an American war with a joke. Choosing an appropriate attention device will engage your audience and get it ready for the presentation you have prepared.

You may choose to follow the example of the following speaker. By asking audience members to picture a specific scene, this speaker places them directly in the action.

> *I want you to imagine this scene: It's a damp morning during the Christmas season in London. The city awakes to see streets swirling in a thick gray mist. But this is no ordinary London fog. As the clouds roll through the streets and seep into the houses, men, women, and children are gasping for breath. Within hours, hospital emergency rooms are crammed with people complaining of stinging lungs. When the fog finally lifts five days later, thousands are dead.*

By using a story, you can immediately get the audience involved in a topic that otherwise might have seemed abstract to them. If you use a true story, you can achieve further startling impact by pointing out that the scene actually occurred. This specific story also establishes a serious tone for the presentation.

Getting the audience's attention is just the first step in the introduction of a presentation. However, if you fail to grab the audience's interest, the rest of your introduction might just as well be your conclusion.

State Your Thesis

A thesis statement is a clearly written, simple sentence or question that states the point you expect to make in your presentation. The thesis

An audience member may have pictured this scene of London on a foggy morning as a result of the presenter's attention device. **What factors must one consider when choosing an attention device?**

statement lets an audience know from the beginning the one thing you expect them to get from your presentation. So, how do you determine your thesis? If you only had the time to say one sentence to your audience, what would it be? The answer is your thesis statement. Examples of clear thesis statements include the following:

- Employees will be able to select new health plan options next month.
- How can the band raise money to participate in the upcoming music festival?
- A new photocopy machine would be a wise investment.

This single statement or question will guide your entire presentation.

Establish Your Ethos as a Speaker

An introduction also provides the opportunity for the presenter to introduce him- or

INTERDISCIPLINARY CONNECTION

Social Studies Organizing skills learned in this chapter will help students use information effectively to support and clarify points in presentations for social studies classes.

Activity Have students confer with their social studies teachers to select a topic for a presentation. (Students may be able to arrange for credit in both classes for this activity.) After writing a thesis statement for a presentation on the topic and listing three or four major supporting points, have students choose an attention device suitable for the presentation, locate needed materials, and write their introductions.

herself to the audience. During the introduction, the presenter begins to establish credibility and genuineness as well as a common bond with the audience.

In establishing your ethos, you may wish to provide information about yourself, your specific expertise, or the research you have done on the topic. For example, if you are reporting the results of a recent walkathon to your local school board, it would be important to state that you were the chairperson of the fund-raiser. If you were a doctor speaking on the future of medical research, you could establish a positive ethos by mentioning your years of work in that field. Whatever your experience or expertise, be sure to share it with your audience. Be careful, however, not to brag. Simply state what you have done to gain the knowledge to be able to speak on your chosen topic.

Not all speakers need to share their expertise or background. Well-known speakers, for example, often are introduced to the audience by another person. However, these speakers may still have to build an ethos or convince the audience of their sincerity. Showing the audience that you are not only qualified to speak on a subject but also excited to do so will help you create a positive image as a speaker.

Orient the Audience

After hearing your thesis statement and establishing your ethos, you may need to include an audience orientation. An audience orientation provides audience members with information they likely do not already have but will need in order to understand a presentation. Not all presentations require this sort of audience preparation. A quick analysis of your audience will help you determine whether or not to provide an orientation. For more on audience analysis, you may wish to refer to Chapter 14.

In determining if an orientation is necessary, there are several different audience needs to consider. The three main types of audience orientations are

- definition
- background information
- motivation

Definition As an audience member, there are very few things as frustrating as listening to a presentation during which the presenter uses terms you don't understand. You may accept a single unfamiliar term that a presenter uses only once or twice; however, if several unfamiliar terms are used throughout a presentation, you may become confused or completely lose interest. This is particularly true if the unfamiliar term is used in the thesis statement. In addition, you may see the presenter as showing off an impressive vocabulary at the expense of the audience.

To avoid this confusion in your own presentations, consider the answers to the questions on the following page as you prepare.

Betty Ford has a well-known reputation as a speaker. How can an effective presenter establish ethos?

Organizing Presentations **481**

Audience Readiness

Explain to students that it is wise to know something about the way an audience thinks as well as its physical characteristics. For example, what prejudices do they bring to the topic? Do they lack a historical context for the topic? The introduction is the place to address these concerns. Ask students to brainstorm a list of communication techniques that motivate them to listen more attentively. Have students compare lists with a partner and add techniques they like. Encourage students to keep their lists and refer to them as they prepare presentations. **L2**

*inter*NET
A C T I V I T Y

Jargon Remind students that they likely use a jargon related to a sport, hobby, or area of study with which the "average" listener is not familiar. Sensitivity to audience background is a basic courtesy when preparing and making a presentation. Suggest to students that they explore a field that interests them and whose jargon they may find useful someday. Have students jot down meanings for each term they locate. Students may also find links to sites that discuss current topics in the field and "Ask-an-Expert" pages which may provide raw material for future presentations. **L1**

- Are there any terms I have used in my thesis statement that may be unfamiliar to my audience?
- Do I want my audience to consider a term from my thesis statement in light of my personal definition rather than the dictionary definition?

If the answer to either of these questions is "yes," you will need to make some adjustments to your speech. Include adequate definitions during an audience orientation or provide a handout that lists and explains each term.

Background Information What information does the audience need in order to understand your presentation? Background information can include the history of the topic, the current status of the topic, or the criteria by which you want the audience to evaluate your presentation. Frequently, the background information is a main point that does not fit in the organizational plan for a presentation. Remember that to the majority of the audience you are the expert on the topic. Provide listeners with enough information to understand your topic as well as you do.

Motivation If, after analyzing your audience, you feel audience members may be negative or apathetic to your topic, it is important to take action. You will need to include some additional or more in-depth information to motivate them to listen to and embrace your presentation.

Refer again to your analysis. What concerns or interests do your audience members have in common? How can your topic be related to those concerns or interests? What do these individuals have to gain by listening to your presentation? Stating the audience's motivation for attending your presentation often can help you "win over" those reluctant listeners. You might say, "Today, I am going to ask you to set aside the opinions and

*inter*NET
A C T I V I T Y

Jargon Sometimes, speakers who are very knowledgeable about a topic forget that audience members may not be familiar with the jargon being used. Log on to a reliable Internet search engine to access a site that provides information on jargon. Go to one of the sites and make a list of words associated with a particular field, such as medicine, law, finance, sports, or computer technology. Share your lists as a class.

impressions you have about the problem of the homeless. I am going to ask you to look at the issue from a new perspective."

Many of the attention devices explained earlier can be used to motivate an audience and build its interest in a topic. In fact, an interesting story, joke, or quote that also is tied closely to your topic can serve two purposes. It can both grab your audience's attention and motivate people to focus on your topic. You also might wish to point out how you are like your audience and why you are concerned about the topic. This can motivate listeners to feel it is important for them as well.

Evaluating Orientation Needs It is up to you to determine which of these audience orientation steps will be necessary for your individual presentation. If you are speaking to a group of professional peers, it may not be necessary to define any of the terms in your thesis statement. If you are speaking to people who already are aware of the background of your topic, you may find that they already are motivated to listen. In other words, there may be times when you

MULTIPLE LEARNING STYLES

Visual-Spatial Creating a visual representation of the principal purposes of the introduction of a presentation will help students recall them longer. In addition, it will help students focus on the various ways they might begin a presentation.

Activity Divide the class into groups of four or five students. Have them design and make posters that illustrate graphically the four purposes of an introduction and show their relationship to the overall presentation. Suggest that as part of their posters, students list some simple examples or brief tips. Have each group display its poster and explain why they organized it as they did.

need to use these steps and other times when you don't; the analysis you have made of your audience should be your guide.

Preview Your Main Points

Along with the thesis statement, the introduction should include a preview of your main points. This is a courtesy that you provide for your audience to let them know what to listen for in your presentation. This preview can be a single sentence, such as "Employees will be asked to select from three benefit plans next week." Or, it can actually list the main points separately: "Next week employees will be asked to select either the employee-only benefit package, the full-family benefit package, or the partial-family benefit package." Either way, the audience is alerted to listen for three main points to be covered in your presentation.

Put It All Together

At the end of your introduction, the audience should have no doubt about what it will gain by listening to your presentation. Audience members also should have a good idea of your relationship to the topic. With a well-planned and complete introduction you should gain the momentum you need to get through the longest part of your presentation: the main body.

THE BODY

In a presentation, you will rarely be able to share everything you know about a topic. To determine what information to include, focus on exactly what the audience needs to know to meet both your objective and theirs. The body of a presentation is made up of only two to five main points, each with supporting details and each connected with smooth transitions.

The general rule for deciding how many main points to develop in a presentation is that less is better. The time you are allowed for your presentation will be an important factor in determining how many main points to include. The body of a presentation usually makes up 75 to 85 percent of the presentation time. Obviously, this is the part of the presentation which will require the most preparation time and effort. Some suggestions to determine main points and make smooth transitions follow. Section 2 of this chapter will explain in more detail how to organize the main body of a presentation.

Determine the Main Points

The first step in determining the main points of a presentation is to consider the purpose of the presentation. What ideas do you need to communicate to the audience to accomplish this purpose? If you are asked to

 GLOBAL COMMUNICATION

Cultural Diversity

As a speaker, you can address, minimize, and demonstrate appreciation for cultural differences in your audience. First, research cultural practices so you can avoid offending audience members with inappropriate nonverbal gestures, attire, or language. Assume that you have been asked to give a brief presentation at a seminar in another country. The purpose of your presentation will be to describe your school traditions to your audience. Choose a country that you would like to visit. Research that country's greetings, customs, and any other cultural traditions that you would need to be aware of to make a presentation there.

Organizing Presentations **483**

Tailoring the Message to the Audience

Discuss with students how the type of audience could affect their way of presenting material. *(Students may point out the need to adjust difficulty level; to change the focus to interest different genders, ages, or professions; to change techniques to reach different sizes of audience; or to give background material for audiences not familiar with the topic.)* Invite volunteers to suggest techniques or statements they would use to introduce a presentation on social concerns of teenagers to the following audiences:

- classmates
- parents
- sixth graders
- teachers and administrators **L3**

 GLOBAL COMMUNICATION

Cultural Diversity

Students may find the Internet the best resource for this activity. Instruct them to read the advanced search instructions for the search engine they will use. For example, in a Boolean search, they can enter multiple phrases joined by AND to limit the sites they will access. Useful entries might include the name of the country as well as the search phrases *cultural differences, greetings,* and *customs.* Have students make posters showing things they would need to be sensitive to as they make their presentation. Remind students to include the name of the countries on their posters. **L2**

MEETING INDIVIDUAL NEEDS

INCLUSION STRATEGIES

Less-Proficient Readers Students who lag behind in reading and related language arts skills may need more time to gather and organize presentation material. You may want to suggest that they select a topic (and vocabulary) with which they are already familiar as they prepare their first presentations.

Activity Have students write an introduction for a presentation they would like to give on a favorite hobby, special interest, or other topic. Suggest that students begin by writing the theses for their presentations and descriptions of their audiences. After their introductions are written, ask students to evaluate them using these questions: Have I given all the background information the audience needs? Will this introduction appeal to and interest my audience? Have I told the audience my expectations?

Less Is More

train someone to change the bottle on the water cooler in the employee break room, your main points will be the steps necessary to change the bottle.

The second step in determining the main points of a presentation is to refer to your thesis statement. Each main point in a presentation must support the thesis statement and relate to the other main points. If you are making a presentation to the soccer team with the thesis statement "How can we raise money to participate in the state tournament?" each main point will be a way for the team to raise money. A main point about whether to drive individual cars or charter a bus to the tournament would not be appropriate.

The third factor in determining the main points for a presentation is the availability of information. No matter how important an idea may seem, if you do not have the information to support it, it should not be a main idea. Main ideas should be those that you can effectively back up with evidence.

Make Smooth Transitions

Transitions not only join the main points together but also link the introduction and

the conclusion to the main body. Weak transitions can leave your audience feeling lost or wondering where you are heading for your next point. On the other hand, smooth transitions allow you to move effortlessly from one point to another. This smooth flow of ideas is important because it allows the audience to remain focused on the issues of your presentation, not the organization of it.

Transitions may be a word, a phrase, or even one or more sentences. Expressions like "first of all," "next," and "on the other hand" all are commonly used transitions. A smooth

COMMUNICATION
Creating Smooth Transitions
PRACTICE LAB

To practice creating smooth transitions in a presentation, follow these steps:

Step 1 In small groups, look at the list of the purposes transitions can serve in a presentation.

Step 2 Brainstorm words and phrases that apply to each of these purposes. For example, a phrase that relates points

through time might be "later that week."

Step 3 Use each word or phrase to create a complete transition sentence for a presentation on computer technology.

Step 4 Discuss your transitions as a class. Was it more difficult to form transitions for some purposes than others?

INCLUSION STRATEGIES

Learning Disabled Some students may profit from a graphic presentation of chapter material. **Activity** Have students listen to a pre-recorded audiotape of the section. Working in groups, students could prepare simplified versions of the section, using diagrams with no more than two or three points. For example, one graphic could show overall organization—beginning, body, and ending; another could show goals to accomplish in the introduction—get attention and explain your topic. Each diagram could be accompanied by an example. Let groups exchange and discuss materials. If possible, photocopy the materials for students to use as they work through the chapter. Encourage them to add information to the graphics as the chapter progresses.

transition is one that clearly shows the relationship between the two points being linked. Using transitions can help you

- put ideas together
- illustrate a point
- compare or contrast points
- emphasize a point
- arrange points in order
- repeat or provide a summary of the important points
- relate points through location or time

By including a variety of transitions in your presentations, you can keep an audience on the right track.

■ **It is not always necessary to define technical terms in the thesis when presenting to professional peers.** What is the purpose of the conclusion in a presentation?

THE CONCLUSION

The conclusion of a presentation is the ending that pulls the presentation together and makes it memorable for the audience. While it is often overlooked by presenters, the conclusion is no less important to an effective presentation than any one of the main points. The conclusion leaves the audience with something to think about and remember. It also should be brief—no more than approximately 10 percent of your total presentation time.

A conclusion serves three purposes. It should

- summarize the main points of the presentation
- restate the thesis
- provide a clear ending to the presentation

Summarize the Presentation's Main Points

The summary of the presentation wraps up the main ideas of your presentation. It can be a simple restatement of your main points, such as "As you can see, we can raise money for the upcoming music festival by selling candy bars at football games, having a community citrus fruit sale, and sponsoring an Autumn Festival." The summary also can be a strong appeal that reinforces the central theme or value of your presentation. You might say, "No matter what methods of fund-raising we decide on, all band members must contribute their time and effort or no one will be able to attend the festival." Whatever form it takes, the summary leaves no doubt in the minds of the listeners about what they just heard.

Restate the Thesis

During the conclusion, you should restate the thesis of your presentation. This final statement of your topic or purpose serves as a vehicle to pull the entire presentation together.

This second thesis statement does not have to be identical to the first, but it must be clearly related. For instance, if your initial

Organizing Presentations **485**

DID YOU KNOW?

Listeners best recall the first and last things they hear in a presentation. This primacy–recency effect means it is important to state your main points in the introduction and conclusion.

■ **Visual Instruction**

Answer The conclusion should summarize the main points of the presentation, restate the thesis, and provide a clear ending.

GLENCOE
Online

For an additional Practice Lab for this section, have students visit the *Glencoe Communication Applications* Web site at **communicationapplications.glencoe.com.** Click on Communication Practice Lab 15.1. **L1**

INTERDISCIPLINARY CONNECTION

Language Arts Remind students that in written expression it is important to clearly and logically link sentences. Synonyms, repeated words, and transitions can be thought of as mortar used to link supporting ideas and to hold a paragraph together. In spoken communication, such connections are even more important.

Activity Reproduce a famous historic speech, such as Lincoln's "Gettysburg Address" or King's "I Have a Dream" speech, and distribute it to the class. Have students analyze it to highlight repetitions, synonyms, and transitions. Students should be ready to explain how each highlighted word or phrase helps listeners follow the main points and gives the speech coherence.

The End

The conclusion should take up 5 percent or less of your presentation's time. However, a good conclusion helps your audience remember your message and deserves more than 5 percent of your preparation time. Ask students to work with a partner to make a list of interesting ways to conclude a presentation. Let pairs share there list and create a class list students can copy into a writing journal for future reference. **L1**

3 ASSESS

Assign Section 1 Assessment as a homework or in-class activity.

🕐 Use *Interactive Tutor Self-Assessment Software* to review Section 1.

Peanuts reprinted by permission of United Features Syndicate, Inc.

thesis statement was phrased as a question, the second thesis statement might provide the answer. Imagine that your first thesis statement was "What is the biggest problem facing today's college students?" In this case, your second statement might be "The biggest problem facing today's college students is academic apathy." The second thesis also may serve to focus, provide a twist to, offer a solution for, or add specifics to the first thesis.

If you already have reviewed the main points of your presentation, you may be wondering why you need to restate the thesis. Shouldn't it be obvious? The truth is that, even after reviewing all the main points, your summary may fail to impress your purpose into the minds of audience members. Restating the thesis helps ensure that your audience will be fully informed before leaving your presentation. Don't leave your message to chance! Make it clear to your audience what you were trying to accomplish.

Provide a Clear Ending to the Presentation

Before ending the presentation, it is important to involve the audience in your topic one last time. This is your final chance to make a lasting impression. Many of the attention devices explained earlier can be used to end your presentation. As a presenter, it is up to you to decide how you will organize the conclusion and what special strategies you will employ.

Order of Elements Some presenters state their second thesis before their summary of main ideas. Other presenters prefer to switch this order. Deciding on which elements to put first and last should be based on what you feel will best suit your presentation and have the most impact on your audience.

Special Strategies There are as many special ways to conclude presentations as there are ways to begin them. Many effective speakers refer back to their introductions as a way of providing closure to their message. If they use a story as a narrative introduction, they may give it a different ending in the conclusion. If a presenter began with a quotation, he or she may refer to the same quotation or use another related quote in the conclusion.

A speaker might also use humor. For example, if you are presenting around lunchtime, you might follow the suggestion of one seasoned presenter. She recommends acknowledging in the introduction that the presentation is right before the lunch break. Then, you might end your conclusion by asking "What's for lunch?" In addition to interjecting a bit of humor into your

486   *Glencoe Communication Applications*

presentation, this strategy builds your rapport with audience members because they know that you too are ready for a break.

Finally, some presentations end by issuing a challenge to the audience. This focuses the content of the presentation back on the individual audience members by asking them to do something with what they have just heard. Asking them to take some action regarding the topic of your presentation is a great way to keep them thinking about your speech long after it has ended.

Competent communicators organize their presentations carefully so that their audiences will understand and follow the main message. Effective presenters know that the better an audience understands their message, the more likely they are to be influenced by that message.

Section 1 Assessment

Visit the *Glencoe Communication Applications* Web site at **communicationapplications. glencoe.com** and click on **Self-Check and Study Guide 15.1** to review your understanding of the parts of a presentation.

Review Key Terms

1. Define each term and write it in a sentence: attention device, thesis statement, audience orientation.

Check Understanding

2. Name the five purposes of an introduction.

3. Imagine that you are giving a presentation about year-round school. Use one of the seven devices you read about to get the attention of your audience. Explain your decision.

4. Write a thesis statement for each of the following presentations:

   • an informative presentation to a group of new students explaining the extracurricular activities at your school.

   • a persuasive presentation to a group of parents convincing them to volunteer to chaperone school activities.

5. Why might a presenter need to orient his or her audience?

6. **Analyze** What purpose does the following conclusion sentence serve? Explain your answer.

   To reduce the budget for this project, I suggest we use cheaper paper, switch overnight delivery companies, and train our staff to research effectively online.

APPLICATION *Activity*

Analyzing a Presentation Select one of the presentations found in the Appendix on pages 649–658. Work together in small groups according to the presentation chosen. Analyze the introduction and conclusion of your chosen presentation according to what you have read in this section. As a class, discuss your analyses.

Organizing Presentations **487**

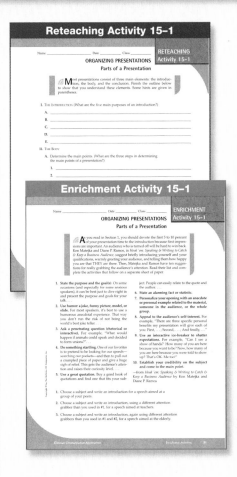

4 CLOSE

Ask students to summarize the main points they learned from studying this section. Then have students reread the objectives on page 477 and add to their summaries.

Extra-Credit Project

Have students choose a topic for a presentation they would like to make, write a thesis statement, then create three different introductions for the presentation. Ask students to evaluate which is best and explain why.

Section 1 Assessment Answers

1. Accept all reasonable sentences.

2. To get the audience's attention, to preview the presentation, to apply the presentation to the audience, to establish the speaker's ethos

3. Answers should reflect understanding of the seven attention devices.

4. Accept any reasonable theses.

5. To provide definitions of unfamiliar terms or background information and to motivate the audience

6. It summarizes the presentation's main points.

Application Activity Students' analyses will vary but should assess the introduction's effectiveness in grabbing attention, previewing the presentation's main points, applying it to listeners, and establishing the speaker's credibility. Students should evaluate how well the conclusion summed up main points, established a sense of completion, and led to a natural course of action.

Critical Thinking Skill

Synthesizing Information

Point out to students that synthesis is a skill one must use throughout life to evaluate information and make decisions. Much of the data available to us is not organized, nor are relationships between ideas and facts clear. Finding logical ways to link related data and reach conclusions is a skill learned through practice and trial and error. Learning the general patterns of logical organization (chronological, sequential, spatial, topical, cause-effect, problem-solution, Monroe's Motivated Sequence) will help students gain confidence in their ability to synthesize information. **L2**

Practicing the Skill

1. Logical headings might include "Average Productivity Figures" and "Introduction of New Software." Facts related to the selected headings should appear under them.

2. Students may select cause-effect as the first pattern of organization, with this change in the text order of data: 3, 4, 1, 2, 5.

3. Another logical pattern is chronological, for which the headings might be: Pre-Software Introduction and Post-Software Introduction.

Application Activity

Students' paragraphs will vary but should suggest software training for all workers as they are hired and periodic updates to software.

SYNTHESIZING INFORMATION

After you have researched your presentation, you may have a great deal of information about your topic. To organize the information, you will first want to synthesize it, or combine it, into logical groups.

◾ Learning the Skill

Use the steps listed below to synthesize information:

Step 1 Make a Random List Write your facts on a list as you gather them.

Step 2 Combine Information into Groups or Headings Mark the items on your list in some way, for example with a star or a dot. On separate paper, write headings and then transfer your items to the new list. Cross these items off your first list. Continue until you have transferred all items.

Step 3 Order the Headings Choose one of the patterns of organization discussed in Section 2. Make sure that you settle on a pattern of organization that makes sense and works to prove or disprove your thesis.

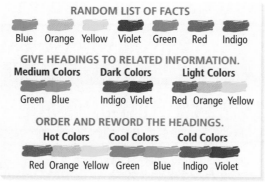

RANDOM LIST OF FACTS

Blue Orange Yellow Violet Green Red Indigo

GIVE HEADINGS TO RELATED INFORMATION.

Medium Colors	Dark Colors	Light Colors
Green Blue	Indigo Violet	Red Orange Yellow

ORDER AND REWORD THE HEADINGS.

Hot Colors	Cool Colors	Cold Colors
Red Orange Yellow	Green Blue	Indigo Violet

◾ Practicing the Skill

Synthesize the information about productivity in the online order division of a clothing company by following the steps below the list.

- Average productivity for January and February was 40 orders.
- Average productivity for March, April, May, and June was 100 orders.
- The company bought new order entry software in March.
- All workers have been trained on the new software system.
- Average productivity per worker after software training is 10 orders.

1. Combine the facts from the random list into related groups. Give each group a heading.

2. Order the headings according to one of the patterns of organization.

3. Put the information into a different pattern of organization. Reword your headings so they make sense within the new organization model.

APPLICATION *Activity*

Imagine you have a summer job working as an intern for a clothing company. Your supervisor asks you to gather information on the number of Internet orders filled in the six-month period from January through June. Using the information you just synthesized, write a one-paragraph summary of recommendations that you could present to your supervisor.

EXTENDING THE CONTENT

Synthesizing in the Classroom Synthesizing can be done informally by mentally making a list of tasks that have to be done during the day and organizing when and in what order they will be done; or synthesizing can be done formally by organizing information, such as class notes, under headings and using the synthesized information as a study tool.

Activity Suggest that students take a set of class notes in a subject such as history and synthesize the information. Review the steps to use, including making up headings, placing the information under the headings, and putting the headings in order. Suggest that students put their final product on note cards. Ask them to keep the cards and use them to help study for a quiz or test. Have them report back on whether synthesizing class notes in this way was helpful. 🔲

Patterns of Organization

GUIDE TO READING

Objectives

1. Select appropriate strategies to organize a presentation.
2. Explain Monroe's Motivated Sequence.
3. Use effective strategies to outline a presentation.

Terms to Learn

chronological order
sequential order
spatial order
topical order
Monroe's Motivated Sequence

*I*magine that you are listening to a presentation on how to set up your new computer. The presenter grabs your attention with a great joke. She then begins explaining how to load software, moves to connecting the power cables, and ends with attaching the mouse to the keyboard. Because the instructions are not in order, you are completely confused by the end of the presentation.

In the previous section, you learned that determining the main points included in the body is primarily based on providing adequate support for your thesis statement. Equally important to the successful presentation is a clear and logical organization of those main points.

As you determine the main points for your presentation, you probably will notice that they are connected to each other in various ways. By considering how your ideas relate to each other, you can decide how to arrange them in your presentation. The purpose of your presentation and the thesis statement will determine which pattern of organization will be most appropriate and effective. As **Figure 15–2** shows, there are several patterns from which to choose.

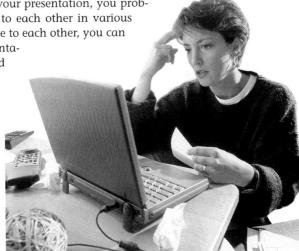

■ As in the example of installing a new computer, disorganized presentation of information can leave audience members confused. What determines which pattern of organization will be most effective?

Organizing Presentations **489**

1 FOCUS

Bellringer
Have students suggest what is confusing about presentations that are not in a logical order.
(Answers may include that receivers depend upon perceiving the relationships of ideas to each other to make sense of oral communications.)

You may use Graphic Organizer Transparency 15–2 to introduce this section.

Graphic Organizer Transparency 15–2

Communication Tip

Because it requires organization of ideas into principal concepts and related supporting details, an outline helps to determine the most effective way to organize a presentation. A presentation based on a prepared outline almost always is superior to one that is not.

Visual Instruction

Answer The purpose of presentation and the thesis statement determine the most effective pattern of organization.

RESOURCE MANAGER

Teaching Tools
- Interactive Lesson Planner
- Reproducible Lesson Plan 15–2
- Application Activities 15–2

Reproducible Masters
- Guided Reading Activity Workbook 15–2
- Enrichment Activity 15–2
- Reteaching Activity 15–2
- Section Quiz 15–2
- Transparency Strategies and Activities Booklet 15–2

Transparencies
- Graphic Organizer Transparency 15–2
- Chapter 15 Teaching Transparency

Technology Resources
- Interactive Tutor Self-Assessment Software
- Presentation Plus! Software
- ExamView® Pro Testmaker
- PuzzleMaker Software
- communicationapplications.glencoe.com

2 TEACH

Guided Reading Activity 15-2

GUIDED READING Activity 15-2

Name _____ Date _____ Class _____

ORGANIZING PRESENTATIONS

Patterns of Organization

As you read Section 2, answer the following items.

1. Define *chronological order* and state the two kinds of presentations in which it is used.

2. Discuss how sequential order differs from chronological order.

3. What are four types of spatial arrangement?

4. How are the points in a topical presentation arranged?

5. For which types of presentations is the cause-effect organizational pattern most useful?

6. Explain the two steps involved in the problem-solution organizational plan.

7. Why would a speaker want to use the advantage-disadvantage strategy?

8. List the five steps of Monroe's Motivated Sequence.

9. Why is Monroe's pattern for organizing persuasive messages effective?

10. What three things can an outline show you about your topic?

Organizing Ideas by Different Patterns

Refer students to Figure 15–2 and have them read the categories and the introductory text. Ask them to identify the four patterns used for informative presentations and then to choose a pattern for organizing each of the following topics logically:

- description of a historic monument *(spatial)*
- explanation of how to order books online *(sequential)*
- history of the development of the computer *(chronological)*
- key reasons for buying a cell phone *(topical)*

Ask students to explain their choices.

L2

■ **Figure 15–2 Patterns of Organization for Presentations**

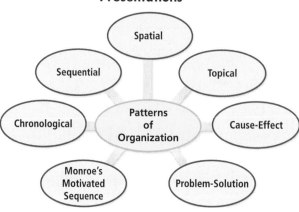

PATTERNS OF ORGANIZATION FOR INFORMATIVE PRESENTATIONS

An informative presentation is designed to provide an audience with new ideas and new information about a topic. It is important to present that information in such a way that the audience can easily understand and relate to what you have to say. As **Figures 15–3 through 15–6** show, there are four major patterns of organization used mainly in informative presentations. These patterns are:

- Chronological
- Spatial
- Sequential
- Topical

Chronological Order

Chronological order is an arrangement according to the time in which something occurs. When used in presentations, this pattern categorizes the main points as past, present, or future.

Chronological Order in Formal Presentations In presentations, chronological order is particularly useful if the purpose is informative, such as to explain the history of something. In a presentation on the history of a company, for example, you might begin by explaining how and when the company was formed, move on to the company's expansion over the years, describe its current status, and finish with what it plans for future development.

Chronological Order in Informal Presentations Chronological order also is appropriate for some informal presentations. Imagine that your supervisor has asked you for an update on a project to which you've been assigned. You will want to provide him or her with a summary of what you have accomplished up to that point in time. It will

■ **Figure 15–3 Chronological Order**

December 1963

Thesis Statement:	Our corporation has come a long way in the last forty years.
Main Point #1:	The company was organized in 1963.
Main Point #2:	The company expanded into two divisions in 1975.
Main Point #3:	The company merged with a smaller competitor in 1997.
Main Point #4:	The company has grown to meet the challenges of the new millennium.

MEETING INDIVIDUAL NEEDS
INCLUSION STRATEGIES

Less-Proficient Readers Some students who have difficulty processing the information they read may have trouble synthesizing it. Topics which lend themselves to organization by time (chronological and sequential patterns) can always be put into one, two, three order.

Activity Have students brainstorm a list of main points for a presentation on one of the following topics: a short history of the school, the events that transpired during a daring rescue, an account of a busy person's daily routine, a description of the key events in a person's life, or other topics of the students' choosing. Have students write each point on a separate 3" x 5" card and place the cards in chronological order. If any items cannot be placed, have students rewrite the items or delete them. Invite students to share their results.

COMMUNICATION PRACTICE LAB

Using Sequential Order

To practice using sequential order to organize a presentation, follow these steps:

Step 1 Choose an object that you use on a regular basis, such as a pencil sharpener or a hair dryer.

Step 2 Without actually using the object, explain to the class how to operate it. Be sure to include every necessary step and arrange the steps correctly.

Step 3 Ask for a volunteer to use the object exactly as you explained.

Step 4 Discuss your explanation with your classmates. Were your instructions clear and complete? Were they in the correct order? Could you have added any steps to make your classmate's task easier?

---

be much easier for your supervisor to understand your presentation if you can explain the project's progress chronologically.

Sequential Order

Sequential order is an arrangement according to the steps of a process. Sequential order is closely related to chronological order. However, instead of arranging information by time, information is arranged according to a particular succession. Any presentation that instructs someone how to do something from beginning to end might be structured sequentially. The number of main points will depend on the number of steps necessary to accomplish the object of the presentation. Other informative presentations may also be placed in sequential order.

Imagine that you have asked a friend for directions to his or her house. What if your friend were to list all the right turns you should take and then the left turns and then how many traffic lights you will pass on the total journey to his or her house? You might not be able to get there. Instead, you need the different turns and stoplights listed in the order that you will reach them. This allows you to know what step to take next.

It is also important to use sequential order when giving instructions for a task. If you omit a step or explain things out of order when explaining a task at work, the person you instruct may not be able to do his or her job.

■ **Figure 15–4 Sequential Order**

Thesis Statement:	It is easy to change the bottle on the water cooler.
Main Point #1:	Remove the empty bottle.
Main Point #2:	Open the full bottle of water.
Main Point #3:	Carefully lift the full bottle above the reservoir.
Main Point #4:	Quickly place the bottle opening into the reservoir opening.
Main Point #5:	Clean up any water spilled during step #4.

Organizing Presentations **491**

MEETING INDIVIDUAL NEEDS

MULTIPLE LEARNING STYLES

Bodily-Kinesthetic Students who communicate best through body language and demonstration may find it easiest to organize presentations by acting out the sequence of steps. Be sure students know that this is an acceptable, and even desirable, practice.

Activity Have students develop notes for a short how-to talk on an activity they know well. Brainstorm with the class a list of possible ideas in order to help students get started. After students have written the sequence of steps, suggest that as part of their revision process they act out each step exactly as written and in the order written. Are any additions or changes needed? If so, remind students to add them to their final product. Have students tell how doing the activity itself triggered additional ideas for the presentation.

COMMUNICATION PRACTICE LAB

Using Sequential Order

Have students follow the four steps in the Communication Practice Lab on this page to practice explaining what steps to follow to perform a certain task. Guide the class to see the importance of exact language, explicit details, and sometimes pictures or simultaneous demonstration to communicate directions successfully. **L2**

GLENCOE Online

For an additional Practice Lab for this section, have students visit the *Glencoe Communication Applications* Web site at communicationapplications.glencoe.com Click on Communication Practice Lab 15–2. **L1**

Step by Step

Describing things in sequential order is a common occurrence although it may not be apparent. Parents may tell their children their schedule for the day, or you may give students directions on steps to follow to complete a class assignment. Have students listen for a day for examples of directions being given in sequential order. Have them list each occurrence. Then have students share their lists with the class. **L2**

Grammar Tip

Adverbs That Show Time

Adverbs are useful as transitional expressions to show time relationships. Some typical transitions are *after, as soon as, before, currently, earlier, immediately, once, now, presently, since, soon, until,* and *whenever.*

Where in the World?

Explain that use of spatial order is especially helpful in organizing presentations that rely on visualization of physical parts of a whole—such as a specific place, for example. Ask students to visualize the following topics and assign near to far, top to bottom, left to right, side to side, or north to south (east to west) categories of spatial organization to each:

- an accident report (left to right)
- a road trip (north to south/east to west)
- a landscape painting (near to far)
- a person (top to bottom)
- a description of your home (side to side)

Students should explain their reasonings. Also invite them to mention any visual aids they would use in such a presentation. **L3**

Visual Instruction

Answer Students may identify top to bottom, side to side, north to south, east to west, left to right, or near to far as types of spatial arrangements.

Instead, he or she may have to find someone else who can explain the task better. This wastes valuable work time and can ultimately reflect poorly on you as a communicator.

Spatial Order

Spatial order is an arrangement according to how a topic is put together or by the physical location of its elements. Types of spatial arrangement include describing something from top to bottom, side to side, north to south, or east to west. A presentation that analyzes a company's quarterly sales might provide information sales district by sales district. Also, most television weather forecasters present the weather in a spatial pattern.

Topical Order

Sometimes, the main points for a presentation are related only by the fact that each is a part of the general topic. Topical order groups ideas by some logical theme or division. For example, imagine that you were asked to speak about deteriorating facilities at your high school. You might decide to limit your presentation to a discussion of the gymnasium, the cafeteria, and the science classrooms. Each is a

Television weather forecasters, like the one above, present the weather in spatial order. **List different types of spatial arrangements.**

valid point that fits your topic and thesis, but the only thing that connects them is the topic of deterioration. This presentation would definitely be suited to topical arrangement.

Arranging a Topical Presentation When using topical order, how do you know what point to present first, second, and last? Points in a topically arranged presentation usually are presented in order of their importance. Some will begin with the least important point and build to the most important. Others may place the most important information at the beginning and end of the presentation. This type of arrangement is based on the idea that an audience remembers the first and last things it hears better than the information in between.

The topical method of organizing an informative presentation provides a presenter with a lot of flexibility. In fact, the topical pattern of organization is sometimes used to persuade audiences to accept facts, values, or ideas. As such, you might choose it for a persuasive presentation, or you might want to choose one of the other patterns normally used for persuasive presentations.

Figure 15–5 Spatial Order

Thesis Statement:	Tri-Core's processor sales are up in every region of the country.
Main Point #1:	Sales are strongest in the Western Region.
Main Point #2:	Sales are growing at a rate of 20 percent in the Mountain Region.
Main Point #3:	Sales are up 9 percent in the Central Region.
Main Point #4:	Sales increases in the Eastern Region are behind those in the other regions.

INTERDISCIPLINARY CONNECTION

Art Artists use perspective techniques to give different elements in their paintings the illusion of distance. Students can learn to appreciate these techniques and articulate their understanding of works of art using spatial organizational techniques for descriptions.

Activity Have students search the Internet, art books from the library, or publications from an art museum for reproductions of artworks that are accompanied by interpretative paragraphs. Have students select a painting that is accompanied by explanatory material describing the painting in terms of spatial relations. Ask students to copy the material and have them highlight words that show the pattern of organization in the writing. Pair students and let them describe techniques used by their artists to each other, using spatial organization in their presentations.

Figure 15–6 **Topical Order**

Thesis Statement:	There are four primary categories of fireworks.
Main Point #1:	Skyrockets explode high in the air.
Main Point #2:	Roman candles shoot out separate bursts of colored flames.
Main Point #3:	Pinwheels throw sparks and flames as they whirl on a stick.
Main Point #4:	Lances are thin, colorful fireworks used in ground displays.

PATTERNS OF ORGANIZATION FOR PERSUASIVE AND MOTIVATIONAL PRESENTATIONS

As you've read, topical organization helps you put your thoughts in a logical order. However, a topical organization may not always be the most effective choice. Some persuasive presentations may need to be organized differently. Other patterns of persuasive presentations, as shown in Figures 15–7 through 15–9, are:

- Cause-effect
- Problem-solution
- Monroe's Motivated Sequence

Cause-Effect Organization

Cause-effect organization in a presentation consists of two parts. The first part—the cause—brings about some action, event, or situation. The second part—the effect—is the consequence of that action, event, or situation. This organizational pattern may be used for informative or persuasive presentations. It is also very effective for creating concern for a problem.

For example, in a presentation about a lack of employee parking at a work site, the first main point might be that local construction around the area has caused the situation. The second main point would then focus on the effects of the lack of parking, such as employee tardiness and morale problems. At this point, you have creative concern for the problem. Another persuasive use of cause-effect organization is found in Figure 15–7.

Problem-Solution Organization

Like the cause-effect pattern, the problem-solution pattern of organization is a two-step logical plan describing first a problem and then

Figure 15–7 **Cause-Effect**

Thesis Statement:	Students should have three weeks off for winter break.
Main Point #1:	Many families today are spread out throughout the country.
Main Point #2:	Travel to family gatherings is more time-consuming, giving students and their families less time to spend with loved ones.

Organizing Presentations **493**

Establishing Order of Importance

Point out that transitional phrases can be used to clarify order of importance and build interest in topical presentations. Phrases such as *first of all, of greater concern,* and *most important of all* establish that a speaker is building a case, with the most important reasons last. Working in pairs, have students create a 30-second radio commercial that lists reasons for buying a product in order of importance. **L3**

Communication Tip

Explain that two events may occur in sequence but may not be causally related. Have students test the cause-effect relationship of two events or facts by inserting the word *because*. If the word shows a true relationship, then the relation is causal, not just sequential.

CRITICAL THINKING ACTIVITY

Cause-effect relationships are often complex. A cause may have numerous effects, a number of factors may combine to cause something to happen, or one effect may become a cause of another event in a chain response. Cause-effect organization is often used in science to explain concepts such as plate tectonics, species extinction, or generation of electric current.

Have students scan a chapter in a science textbook and choose a process to explain to the class. Ask them to create a graphic organizer that shows the cause-effect relationship(s) of events in the process and uses a visual approach to enhance the presentation. When students have completed the work, ask them to present their graphic organizers. Have classmates tell whether they were able to understand the concept better and if the cause-effect-approach was helpful and why.

Comparing Uses of Cause-Effect and Problem-Solution Patterns

Have students review the sections on cause-effect and problem-solution organization patterns. Ask volunteers to define each pattern, referring to Figures 15–7 and 15–8 for help. Divide the class into two sections and assign each section one of the patterns to use to organize a topic (such as whether the school should allow advertising on campus). Have individuals make notes and then confer with others in their section to organize them. Bring groups together to compare the differences in emphasis between the two patterns. **L3**

■ **Visual Instruction**

Answer A presentation to persuade an audience to solve a problem requires problem-solving organization.

Monroe's Motivated Sequence Compared to Problem-Solution

Discuss similarities between problem-solution and this model of organizing. *(Both are based on identifying a problem and deriving a useful solution.)* Have students create side-by-side graphic organizers that illustrate the steps in both patterns and use the visuals to explain to a partner how each pattern might be used. **L3**

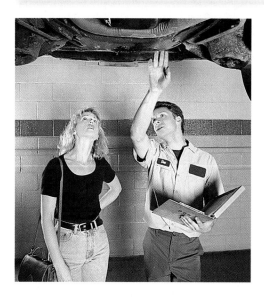

■ An auto mechanic explaining a problem to a customer, then offering a solution is similar to problem-solving organization. **What type of presentation tends to require problem-solving organization?**

a solution to this problem. It is usually used for presentations that persuade an audience to solve a problem or improve a situation. In a presentation in which you want the audience to sign a petition for more employee parking, for example, the first point would be the explanation of the problem. The second point would be the explanation of how increasing the number of parking spaces would solve the problem and benefit the audience.

When a presenter tries to show why one solution to a problem is better than another one, he or she will often describe the advantages and disadvantages. To convince the audience that the advantages outweigh the disadvantages, he or she probably would explain the disadvantages briefly and then spend the rest of the presentation describing the advantages. The presenter also may want to consider a visual depiction of how the advantages outnumber or outweigh the disadvantages.

The advantage-disadvantage strategy is effective if you believe the audience to be unlikely to accept your proposal. You will be better able to overcome audience members' resistance if you show that you have considered their point of view. Share that your proposition will affect them in a positive way and will be more beneficial than the action they had previously considered.

Monroe's Motivated Sequence

Monroe's Motivated Sequence, named after communication expert A. H. Monroe, is a five-part organizational strategy designed for speeches that seek to persuade or motivate an audience to take immediate action. It is based on two assumptions: all people have needs, and people can be persuaded by claims that satisfy those needs. The steps of Monroe's Motivated Sequence are

- attention
- visualization
- need
- action
- satisfaction

■ **Figure 15–8 Problem-Solution**

Thesis Statement:	We should purchase new computers for all of our customer service representatives.
Main Point #1:	Customers have to wait an average of 15 minutes before an employee can pull up the information and begin discussing a specific account.
Main Point #2:	Updated computers with faster processors would cut down on customer delays.

MEETING INDIVIDUAL NEEDS

MULTIPLE LEARNING STYLES

Intrapersonal Keeping a journal can help students to identify their thoughts and feelings and to assess the changes that occur over time in those thoughts and feelings.

Activity Have students write a personal goal they would like to achieve, such as improving a letter grade in a class or establishing a daily exercise routine. Have them devote one page in the journal to list cause-effect relationships (for example, Because I want to raise my grade, I must study longer). Ask them to devote another page in the journal to problem-solution issues (for example, How can I raise my letter grade?). This can then be followed by a list of solutions. Ask students who keep journals to evaluate the effectiveness for helping them reach their goals and to explain to the class why it has or has not been helpful.

Attention The attention step is very much like the introduction section of a standard presentation. According to Monroe, you cannot possibly hope to convince anyone of anything if you do not have his or her attention. The first step of the sequence is to create audience interest in learning or knowing more.

Need Once you have the interest of your audience, move into the "need" stage of the presentation. At this point, you make the audience aware that a problem or need exists. The problem is then related directly to audience members so they personally identify with it or perceive personal need. By the conclusion of this step, your audience should be ready to hear what is necessary to satisfy this need.

Satisfaction This is where you present the solution for the problem you just explained. As you show how this solution will work, you should include enough details for the audience to completely understand what you are talking about.

Visualization In this step, you help your audience visualize the benefits of your solution. This will help listeners "buy into" your plan. The key to developing an effective visualization step is the use of vivid imagery that makes your audience a part of the solution. Audience members should know how they will profit from your solution and how much better things will be once the solution is enacted.

Action Once the audience members are convinced your solution is beneficial, you are ready to ask them to do whatever is necessary. Tell people *exactly* what you want them to do and how to do it. For example, give them the address to write, the schedule for volunteers, or a pen they'll need to write a check. Make it as easy as possible for audience members to do what you want them to do. Complete the action step by reinforcing people's decision to do what you want. Remind them of how they will benefit by contributing their time, energy, or money. Make them feel good about their decision. Monroe's pattern for organizing persuasive messages is effective because it follows the natural process of human thinking and leads the audience step-by-step to the desired action. It is widely used in marketing. Think about the following commercial.

- Scene One—Attention: A young woman is running through the park. She is wearing jogging gear and is perspiring.
- Scene Two—Need: The jogger pauses, feeling as if she cannot continue another step. She is extremely thirsty.
- Scene Three—Satisfaction: She sees a vendor selling ice-cold bottled water.
- Scene Four—Visualization: She imagines how refreshing a bottle of water would be.
- Scene Five—Action: The commercial ends with the jogger heading toward the water stand. The logo for the brand of bottled water appears over the final scene, urging viewers to take the same action the young jogger did.

■ **Figure 15–9** **Monroe's Motivated Sequence**

Thesis Statement

Attention → Need → Satisfaction → Visualization → Action

Organizing Presentations **495**

Moving the Audience to Action

Have students work in pairs using Figure 15–9 to review the steps in Monroe's Motivated Sequence. Then have partners invent a product and create an advertisement using the five steps to convince consumers to buy it. After practicing, students can present their ads. After each ad has been presented, ask the audience to identify where each step occurred in the presentation. **L2**

Grammar Tip

Conjunctive Adverbs Conjunctive adverbs clarify the relationship between ideas of equal weight in a sentence. To compare advantages and disadvantages, a speaker might use conjunctive adverbs such as *however, nevertheless,* and *still*; or to emphasize advantages or disadvantages the speaker might use *furthermore, equally,* or *likewise*.

COOPERATIVE LEARNING ACTIVITY

Members of Congress often speak in order to persuade their colleagues to support a certain bill or motion. Sometimes a formal presentation is made and an organizational pattern is presented. This is often the case when an issue is introduced for discussion. Some patterns of organization work better for persuasive presentations than others.

Divide students into groups of four or five and assign them the task of watching C-Span to observe a presentation by a congressperson. If possible, a group member should record the presentation so the group can analyze its pattern of organization. Have groups play the presentations for the class, stopping them to identify parts of the organizational pattern and offering their analysis of why the speaker chose this pattern.

Practice for the Workplace

Organizational Patterns Review the organizational patterns covered in this section with the class, writing each on the board as a heading. Ask volunteers to describe workplace applications for each type of organization and write these beneath the appropriate heading. (Begin by giving an example: Sequential order might be used to teach new telemarketing employees the procedure for handling calls.) Then have students complete the activity. *(Answers may include sequential, spatial, and cause-effect.)* **L1**

BUSINESS BRIEF

James Lukaszewski, chairman of The Lukaszewski Group Inc. and a presenter for professionals and executives, points out the importance of using verbal contrasts in presentations. In analyzing a problem, issue, or opportunity, top-notch presenters "are able to verbally draw a dramatic contrast between good and bad, between bland and colorful, between emotional and factual." This technique simplifies concepts and enhances audience understanding.

Organization in Informal Presentations

Most of the presentations that have been discussed in this chapter are formal presentations, consciously prepared over a period of time. However, organization is just as important for informal presentations. When you are asked to show a new student around your school, you need to think about the most logical tour so that it will be easy for him or her to remember. A mechanic needs to explain what is wrong with the engine of a car in clear, logical sequence so that the owner will understand what repairs are needed and why. A medical office assistant needs to be able to explain to a patient how to take a prescribed medication so that the patient will get well. The success or failure of all these tasks will likely depend on how well organized and thought-out they are. Remember that the purpose of organizing your ideas is to present a message that is easy for your audience to follow, understand, and remember.

Workers attend a trade union presentation on improving facilities and salaries. What is the main purpose of preparing a presentation outline?

Practice for the Workplace

Organizational Patterns In the workplace, you may be asked to give presentations on a variety of topics. For each presentation, you will want to select the best organizational pattern for your topic.

BUSINESS PRACTICE *Activity*

Identify the type of organizational pattern you would use to develop a presentation on each of the following topics:

- seven steps to developing successful advertising on the Internet

- national sales quotas in retail sales reflect weather patterns across the United States

- Employee Assistance Programs: a positive response to employee stress and psychological wellness

PREPARING YOUR PRESENTATION OUTLINE

Now that you have decided on the organizational pattern you will use, you are ready to outline your presentation. An outline serves as the road map of your presentation. Once you have prepared your outline, you may need to revisit one or more of the first four steps of the preparation process. Your outline may even show you the limitations, flaws, or difficulties in your topic, taking you back to step number one. A good outline, however, provides your presentation with a direction, supporting information, and logical sections.

An outline for a presentation follows the structure of your presentation. Notice how the organization of the presentation is incorporated into the following outline.

I. Introduction
   A. Introductory Device
   B. Thesis Statement
   C. Establish Speaker Ethos
   D. Audience Orientation
      1. Definitions
      2. Background
      3. Motivation
   E. Preview Main Points
II. Body
   A. Main Point 1
   B. Main Point 2
   C. Main Point 3
III. Conclusion
   A. Summary
   B. Second Thesis Statement
   C. Concluding Device

When sharing with your audience, you fill in this basic structure with added support, humor, audio-visual aids, and more.

Preparing an Outline

There are many ways to begin preparing an outline for your presentation. One way is to begin by writing the names for the three main divisions of your speech—introduction, body, and conclusion—at the top of separate sheets of paper or note cards. Then, you can list the main points and any information from your research on the corresponding sheet of paper. If a piece of information supports more than one main idea, you can include it with each idea to which it applies.

Traditional outlines follow a specific format. Begin your outline with either the title or the thesis statement of your speech. Then, list each of the sections, indicated by Roman numerals. For example, for a presentation to inform your audience about the three top job opportunities for teenagers in your town, your main ideas in the body of the presentation might read:

II. Body
   A. Burger Town
   B. Kit 'n' Kapoodle
   C. Ed's Locker Room

Supporting Information Under each main idea, list your supporting information. This is where you should begin to include the results of your research. Each piece of supporting information will be indicated by a capital letter. The supporting material about Burger Town might look like this.

   A. Burger Town
      1. Flexible hours
      2. Good benefits
      3. Fun atmosphere

An outline may be made up of phrases, like the ones above, or of complete sentences. A sentence outline of the section on Burger Town might look like this.

   A. Burger Town is a restaurant that is a great place for teenagers to work.
      1. Employees are able to work flexible hours.
      2. Burger Town provides employees with good benefits.
      3. The working atmosphere at Burger Town is fun.

Details Details provide each of your supporting points with the content and interest you will need to keep an audience's attention. The detail part of your outline should include names, numbers, dates, events, and other specifics necessary to make your point to audience members.

You may include many levels of details in your presentation, depending upon how intricate or extensive your research is. The first level of details is indicated in an outline by numerals; the second level is marked by lower case letters. Following is a partial outline with details included.

Organizing Presentations **497**

Proper Form
Using the correct style of letters and numerals and understanding the order or level at which each is introduced can be confusing. Ask one group of volunteers to create a skeleton outline that can be photocopied and distributed to the class. Ask another group of volunteers to make an overhead transparency for you. Use it during the class discussion of outlining to clarify problems or to clear up confusion about proper outline form. **L3**

3 ASSESS

Assign Section 2 Assessment as a homework or in-class activity.

Use *Interactive Tutor Self-Assessment Software* to review Section 2.

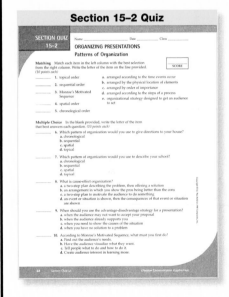

ENGLISH LANGUAGE LEARNERS

MEETING INDIVIDUAL NEEDS

Identifying Organizational Patterns Remind students that organizational patterns we readily use may or may not exist in other cultures and languages. English language learners may be particularly sensitive to the difficulties of attempting to identify organizational patterns that may be strange to them.

Activity As homework, have students choose a newspaper feature article or a television news program to analyze for organization. Provide students with questions similar to these to answer as they read or view the material: What pattern of organization was used? How can you tell? Why do you think the writer or producer chose this pattern? Was the organizational method effective? Why? Discuss the results with the students on an individual basis. **ELL**

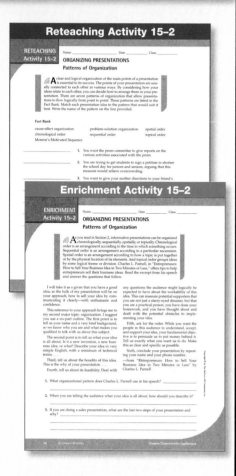

4 CLOSE

Have students read again the opening paragraph on page 489. Ask students what advice they would give the presenter on how to make the presentation more effective.

Extra-Credit Project

Ask students to diagram and show how they would use one or more of the organization patterns to persuade a parent or guardian to give them more freedom—for example, later curfew, larger allowance, or more online time.

498

A. Burger Town
  1. Flexible hours
      a. Open weeknight evenings until 10 P.M.
      b. Open Saturdays and Sundays from 9 A.M. until 11 P.M.
  2. Good benefits
      a. Up to two free meals per day per employee
      b. Health insurance available for around $50 per month
      c. Discounts at other Burger Town-owned companies
          (1) 25 percent off at Pizza Village
          (2) 15 percent off at Steak City

Proper Outline Form Besides the use of Roman numerals, letters, and numbers, you may have noticed other details about the outlines you have seen. Each level of detail, for example, is indented further. These indentions give you visual clues as to the general nature of each piece of information in your outline. The more broad or general the idea, the less indented it is.

It also is important to note that each section of your outline must have at least two parts. That is, you must begin with at least two main ideas. If a main idea has one supporting idea, it must have another. For every A, you need a B, for every 1 you need a 2, and so on.

Section 2 Assessment

Visit the *Glencoe Communication Applications* Web site at **communicationapplications. glencoe.com** and click on **Self-Check and Study Guide 15.2** to review your understanding of patterns of organization.

Review Key Terms

1. Define each term and write it in a sentence: chronological order, sequential order, spatial order, topical order, Monroe's Motivated Sequence.

Check Understanding

2. Using one of the following organization methods—chronological, sequential,

spatial, topical, cause-effect, problem-solution, advantage-disadvantage—organize a short presentation on developing good study skills.

3. Explain how Monroe's Motivated Sequence could be used for a speech asking your classmates to help solve the problem of litter on campus.

4. **Apply** Using what you have read, prepare an outline for a presentation on the importance of developing good study skills.

APPLICATION *Activity*

Analyzing Advertisements Select an advertisement from a newspaper or magazine and diagram it step by step using Monroe's Motivated Sequence. Next, develop a one- to three-minute presentation for that product using the diagram as a guide. Be sure to include all the steps of the sequence in your presentation. Share your presentations as a class or in small groups.

498 *Glencoe Communication Applications*

Section 2 Assessment Answers

1. Accept all reasonable sentences.
2. Answers should reflect students' choices but should demonstrate logical organization.
3. A sample response: (1) Focus attention—Suppose your parents or another person of importance arrived unannounced. (2) Establish need—See how shamefully shabby and ugly our campus looks. (3) Show solution—We can all help, and we will feel good about doing so. (4) Visualize benefits of solution—Appearance and pride lead to

improved performance; excellence is rewarded. (5) Call to action—Put all trash in receptacles; pick up litter as you leave today; be a part of excellence.

4. Outlines will vary but should follow correct outline form and should present content and ideas in a logical way.

Application Activity Students' diagrams should pinpoint each of the five steps. Students' presentations should illustrate each step.

Communication Self-Assessment

Evaluating How You Organize Presentations

How Do You Rate?

On a separate sheet of paper, use the key to respond to the following statements. Put a check mark at the end of each skill you would like to improve.

Key: A Always R Rarely
   U Usually N Never
   S Sometimes

1. I organize my presentations well.
2. When I work on the introduction to presentations, my first concern is involving the audience.
3. I preview the main points of my presentation to encourage the audience to listen for these points.
4. When I give a speech or a demonstration, I know how to give a concise statement of my thesis.
5. I am able to build interest in a topic by using definitions, background information, and motivation.
6. As I prepare a presentation, I choose the main points according to my thesis and what the audience needs to know.
7. When I give a presentation, I know how to use attention cycles and memory aids.
8. I use audience reaction to modify my presentation.
9. As I conclude a speech, I summarize the main points.
10. As I end a speech, I use an appropriate attention catcher.

How Do You Score?

Review your responses. Give yourself 5 points for every A, 4 for every U, 3 for every S, 2 for every R, and 1 for every N. Total your points and evaluate your score.

41–50 Excellent You may be surprised to find out how much you can improve your skills.

31–40 Good In this course, you can learn ways to make your skills better.

21–30 Fair Practice applying the skills taught in this course.

1–20 Needs Improvement Carefully monitor your improvement as you work through this course.

Setting Communication Goals

If you scored Excellent or Good, complete Part A. If your score was Fair or Needs Improvement, complete Part B.

Part A 1. I plan to put the following ideas into practice:

    2. I plan to share the following information about communication with the following people:

Part B 1. The behaviors I need to change most are:

    2. To bring about these changes I will take these steps:

Organizing Presentations   **499**

Communication Self-Assessment

Have students respond to the survey statements using the key provided. Then ask them to evaluate their presentation-organization skills using the scoring rubric. Based on their scores, have students complete either Part A or B of the goal-setting activity.

Communication Journal Activity

Point out to students that to accomplish goals, one must make them specific and concrete and review them often to assess progress. Have students write specific goals in their Communication Journals.

Communication Tip

Remind the class that progress toward accomplishing their goals will come only with practice. Encourage students to analyze presentations when they are a member of the audience. Have them make a mental note of what did or did not make the presentation interesting and effective.

Communication Tip

A cardinal rule in communicating is that you must convince the audience that what you are saying will make a difference in their lives. Visualization—helping the audience picture the benefits of your solutions—can accomplish this objective.

INTERDISCIPLINARY CONNECTION

Science Most students will have opportunities in science classes to create written or spoken presentations about the scientific concepts they are studying. Point out that logical organization is essential in experiment design, proofs, and explanation of theories.

Activity Have students analyze an experiment they have performed or observed in science class, showing which patterns were used to organize it. Require students to explain the reasons for use of these patterns.

Communication Through Writing

Designing a Checklist

Objectives: To understand the importance of completeness and sequence in designing a checklist; to create a checklist for a familiar activity.

Teaching Suggestions and Strategies

Connection to the Workplace

A checklist is a fundamental organizational tool for the workplace. It not only forces one to list all the steps involved in completing a task, but also asks one to break down the overall process into its major and supporting parts and to prioritize each of them.

Some on-the-job procedures are so commonplace and important that employers may print checklists for use by employees—examples include order forms for a sales force and claim-report forms for an insurance company. Such forms function as both checklists and the means of gathering data. However, far more often, workers make their own checklists. Some are as casual as prioritized lists of tasks in a daily planner or reminders of the steps in some essential work procedure, such as refilling the copy machine. Some are as complex as instructions for balancing a corporation's books at year-end or completing an inventory.

As the business world has become computerized, so have checklists. A worker might enter a checklist into the computer, keep it updated by inputting new data daily, and ask it for daily progress reports and reminders.

Designing a Checklist

To plan, prepare, and deliver an effective presentation, you'll need to keep track of many details. One of the best ways to make sure you don't forget something is to make a checklist. A checklist acts like a schedule to organize your preparation. By looking at a checklist, you can quickly see what you have done and what still needs to be completed. Criteria for a useful checklist is found in the list below.

> **Checklist Format Options**
>
> ☐ Check that the information is not outdated.
> ☐ Is the information outdated or current?
> ☐ Info current

Useful Checklists

- are easy to read
- include all important elements
- have all steps listed in order
- have room to add new items or notes

Making a Checklist The first step in making a checklist is to write down each step in your preparation. Mark off the steps as you complete them. If possible, keep your checklist under one page. If you have several different categories of information, classify the steps under subheads so that there are only a few steps in each group. You may choose to write each item as just a word or two, or you may want to make each item a statement or even a question. Which of the styles above might you use to remind yourself to check whether your information is current?

Using Your Checklist One of the most useful functions of your checklist is its ability to help you manage your time. Listing each individual task that you need to complete keeps you from being overwhelmed by the work that needs to be done. Listing the steps in the order they should be completed allows you to proceed down your checklist as you work. This prevents you from having to skip steps and come back to them later. It also means you can tell by glancing at your checklist approximately how well you are progressing. If you have four weeks to prepare a presentation, but you are only a tenth of the way through your checklist after three weeks, you will see that you need to work harder over the next week.

 For additional information about business writing, see the *Guide to Business Communication* section of the Communication Survival Kit in the Appendix.

CRITICAL THINKING ACTIVITY

A process that is completed by following a series of steps in a specific order illustrates a chain of consequences. Following the steps in the correct sequence has desirable consequences; completing them out of order has undesirable consequences. For example, failing to follow the steps in a bread recipe in order might result in an inedible product. Logic helps you to predict the consequences of various sequences. Organize the steps in the order that gives the best results.
Have students analyze the checklists they write for the Writing Activity on page 501 and determine what would happen if specific steps were completed out of order. Have students write the steps in their lists on 3" x 5" cards and shuffle them. Ask them to write a description of the consequences when steps are completed in this topsy-turvy order.

Communication Through Writing

Building Your Own Checklist Many of the steps listed in this text can serve as checklist items for you. For example, the list of the Steps of the Presentation Preparation Process, which appears on page 478 in this chapter, is a good start for a checklist. You can expand each step as necessary for your particular presentation. The sample checklist that follows expands on the step of recording your research.

If you are just learning to cite sources, you may want to expand that checklist item to include each element of the source citation. Personalize your checklist so it fits your own needs.

Recording Research

☑ Is each quotation perfectly accurate?

☑ Is each source cited completely?

☑ What are the author's qualifications?

☑ Is the source reliable?

☑ Is each source confirmed by another source?

☑ Is the information relevant to my presentation?

☑ Is the information presented objectively?

WRITING *Activity*

Use the following steps to make a checklist for something you know how to do that involves several steps.

- Brainstorm things you know how to do. For instance, you probably know how to pack a suitcase or set up a tent.

- Choose one of the things on your list and draw up a checklist for it. Assume that someone who has never performed the task before will be using your checklist to perform the task for the first time.

- What are the essential steps?

- In what order should the steps be performed?

- How might the steps be classified into subheads?

- Look over your work. Revise your writing so that each step is clear, in the right order, and complete.

Teaching Activity

Help students see the importance of exact description and sequence of steps in giving directions by asking volunteers to instruct you in how to write a cursive capital "B" on the chalkboard. Explain to students that you will move exactly as ordered but will pretend you do not know anything about the alphabet. Have students discuss what was difficult about the task. Did they at first omit steps? Did they have to add substeps?

WRITING *Activity*

Remind students to leave space after each essential step for sub-steps and descriptive details. You may want to have students write the final version of their checklists in outline form. Checklists should include all steps clearly spelled out and in distinct order.

Additional Resources

Appendix, "Guide to Business Communication"

Glencoe Writer's Assistant CD-ROM

Glencoe Interactive Grammar Software

Grade 9 Writer's Choice, Lesson 5.3

GRAMMAR PRACTICE

Parallel Structure

Revise the following partial outline to make its structure parallel. *(Possible corrections are shown.)*
How to Water Ski

I. Getting ready in the water
  A. Feet in ski boots
  B. Take a firm overhand grip on the handle of the tow bar. *(Grip tow bar)*

II. Signal boat to begin moving forward slowly. *(Preparing for the boat to move)*
  A. Take up slack in tow rope *(Tow rope tautness)*
  B. Rope between ski tips
  C. Tips parallel with points up

CHAPTER 15 Assessment and Activities

Visit the *Glencoe Communication Applications* Web site at **communicationapplications. glencoe.com** and click on **Chapter 15 Activity** for additional practice in organizing presentations.

Reviewing Key Terms

1. Sequential order
2. Monroe's Motivated Sequence
3. Topical order
4. Thesis statement
5. Audience orientation
6. Spatial order
7. Attention device
8. Chronological order

Reviewing Key Terms

On a separate sheet of paper, write the communication term that completes each statement.

1. Presentations arranged as a series of actions that lead to a specific result are in _____ .

2. _____ is a five-part strategy designed for speeches that seek immediate action.

3. _____ groups ideas by some logical theme or division.

4. A simple sentence that states the point of your presentation is called a(n) _____ .

5. Listeners get the information they need to understand a presentation from the _____ .

6. Presentations arranged by the physical location of the topic are organized in _____ .

7. A rhetorical question is an example of a(n) _____ with which to begin a presentation.

8. Presentations arranged by the time in which the points occur are organized in _____ .

Reviewing Key Concepts

1. A disorganized presentation usually fails to reach the audience; a well-organized one increases the speaker's credibility with the audience.

2. Gain audience attention and outline the main points to be covered

3. Introduction, body, conclusion

4. To establish ethos, presenters provide information about themselves and their expertise.

5. No more than 10 percent of the total presentation

6. 1) Their support for the thesis statement and relationship to each other, 2) the availability of information to support them, 3) their value in accomplishing the purpose

7. In order of their importance

Reviewing Key Concepts

1. Why should a presenter carefully organize a presentation?

2. What must a presenter do in the first few minutes of his or her speech?

3. Which are the three main elements of a presentation?

4. How do presenters establish their ethos with an audience?

5. How long should a presenter make his or her conclusion?

6. What three factors determine the main points of a presentation?

7. In a topically arranged presentation, how are points usually ordered?

8. Imagine your job is selling memberships to a health club. How might you use cause-effect organization in your sales presentation?

9. Give examples of informal presentations that need to be organized.

8. Answers may include that activities at the club lead to physical fitness.

9. Possible answers are medical assistants advising patients about how to use medication and a passerby giving a motorist directions.

Assessment and Activities

Reading and Critical Thinking Skill

1. **Synthesis** Imagine you are speaking to a group of people about preserving wildlife in their region of the country. Create an attention device to use in the introduction.

2. **Cause-Effect** How do many effective speakers provide closure to their message?

3. **Classifying Information** Which pattern of organization should you use to report the progress of a cross-country bike race?

4. **Applying Information** When is the advantage-disadvantage strategy an effective way to order a persuasive presentation?

Skill Practice Activity

Synthesizing Information In groups of four or five, brainstorm why it is or is not important to buy American-made goods. Supplement the discussion with information found in recent magazine or newspaper articles about the United States' role in world trade. Synthesize the information into logical segments. Prepare a thesis statement and an outline as if you were going to give a two-minute persuasive presentation on the topic.

Cooperative Learning Activity

Creating Concern for a Problem With a partner, brainstorm an environmental problem, such as the disappearance of the rain forests, that you believe poses a threat to humans. Use the following as a model to develop three main points for your chosen topic:

- Fewer forests means less habitat for endangered animal species
- Reduced forestland means fewer oxygen-producing plants
- Fewer rainforest plants can reduce medical research possibilities

Chapter Project

Planning Use the thesis statement your group developed in the Skill Practice Activity to prepare a two-minute persuasive presentation on the topic. Decide which organizational strategy best fits the topic, your thesis statement, and your audience of high school students. Have each member of the group try to develop an attention-grabbing introduction and a memorable conclusion. Vote for the most effective ones.

Presenting As a class, compare the thesis statements and organizational strategies of the different groups. How are they alike and how are they different? After the class has completed the comparison, listen to the groups' introductions and conclusions and evaluate how effective they are in getting audience attention and making the audience remember the group's message.

Organizing Presentations **503**

Reading and Critical Thinking Skill

1. **Synthesis** Sample answer: "I'm so happy to see so many people concerned about wildlife. If you had been in the Everglades in the early 1900s, the wood stork might not be endangered today. In the 1800s, visitors to the Everglades reported seeing clouds of storks flying overhead. Today, the wood stork is almost extinct."

2. **Cause–Effect** Speakers refer to their introduction in their conclusion.

3. **Classifying Information** spatial order

4. **Applying Information** If the audience appears disinclined to accept the presentation proposal, an advantage-disadvantage strategy may be effective.

Skill Practice Activity

Synthesizing Information

One possible thesis statement might be *It is important to buy American-made goods to help the American economy and its workers prosper.* Students might research the percentage of Americans unemployed or underemployed due to the close of factories whose goods could not compete with foreign goods.

Cooperative Learning Activity

Creating Concern for a Problem

Answers will vary but should state the problem, describe the value underlying the speakers' concern, and relate the negative effects to the audience.

Chapter Project

Check that students follow the chapter guidelines in developing their main points and that they correctly organize their information according to their chosen strategy.

On the chalkboard, copy the following headings: *Thesis Statements, Alike, and Different.* Record students' responses under the appropriate headings. Ask several students to explain why they thought one introduction or conclusion was better than another.

Chapter 16 Planning Guide

SECTION RESOURCES

Daily Objectives

Section 1

1. List and provide examples for the three types of proof
2. Select information to support and clarify main points
3. Develop effective audiovisual aids to enhance presentations

Reproducible Resources

 Reproducible Lesson Plan 16-1
 Application Activities 16-1
 Guided Reading Workbook Activity 16-1
 Vocabulary Activity 16*
 Reteaching Activity 16-1*
 Enrichment Activity 16-1*
Graphic Organizer Transparency Strategies and Activities 16-1

Multimedia Resources

 Graphic Organizer Transparency 16-1
 Chapter 16 Teaching Transparency
 Interactive Tutor Self-Assessment
 PuzzleMaker
 ExamView® Pro Testmaker
 Interactive Lesson Planner
 Communication in Action Video Chapter 16
 MindJogger
 communicationapplications.glencoe.com
Presentation Plus!

Section 2

1. Identify the three elements of oral style
2. Use language devices to enhance presentations
3. Explain the relationship between oral style and presentation effectiveness

Reproducible Resources

 Reproducible Lesson Plan 16-2
 Application Activities 16-2
 Guided Reading Workbook Activity 16-2
 Vocabulary Activity 16*
 Reteaching Activity 16-2*
 Enrichment Activity 16-2*
 Graphic Organizer Transparency Strategies and Activities 16-2

Multimedia Resources

 Graphic Organizer Transparency 16-2
 Chapter 16 Teaching Transparency
 Interactive Tutor Self-Assessment
 PuzzleMaker
ExamView® Pro Testmaker
 Interactive Lesson Planner
 Communication in Action Video Chapter 16
 MindJogger
 communicationapplications.glencoe.com
Presentation Plus!

Use Glencoe's *Presentation Plus!* multimedia teacher tool to easily present dynamic lessons that engage and motivate your students. Using Microsoft PowerPoint®, you can customize the presentations to create your own personalized lessons.

* Also available in Spanish

 Blackline Master   CD-ROM   Software

 Transparency   Videodisc   Videocassette   Web site

Chapter 16 Planning Guide

Convincing Presentations

Explain to the students that an effective presentation is convincing because the speaker supports his or her facts adequately and has an effective command of oral language. Tell the class that they will play a game of "Two Lies and a Truth" to bring this point home.

Have each student get together with two other students and plan their strategy. Each of them will prepare a brief talk, supposedly about something unusual that he or she has experienced. In fact, however, only one of these reminiscences is going to be true. The students' job will be to make the lies so realistic that the audience will believe them. They should work with their teammates to invent persuasive supporting details. Ask students to see if they can include phony statistics or quotes to strengthen their case.

Each team should get a turn in front of the class. After a performance, the audience must guess which of the three stories was true. When a lie fools the audience, have students discuss what it was about that particular presentation and presenter that made it succeed.

Resources for the Teacher

- *The Anatomy of Persuasion* by Norbert Aubuchon, Amacom, 1997
- *Effective Presentations: How to Present Facts, Figures, and Ideas Successfully* by Edward Hodnett, Parker Publishing Co. 1967
- *On Writing Well: An Informal Guide to Writing Non-Fiction* by William Zinsser, Harper Perennial, 1994

Resources for the Student

- *How to Debate* by Robert E. Dunbar, Watts, 1994
- *How to Lie with Statistics* by Darrell Huff, Norton, 1954
- *The Writer's Handbook* by John B. Karls and Roland Szymanski, Nat. Textbook, 1990

Block Scheduling

Block scheduling differs from traditional class scheduling in the amount of time allotted to each period. The extended time frame provided by block scheduling affords you the opportunity to implement a greater number of research-oriented and activity-intense projects to motivate and involve your students. Activities that are particularly suited to use within the block-scheduling framework are identified throughout this chapter by the following designation:

Teaching Strategies have been coded for varying learning styles and abilities.

- **L1** **BASIC** activities for all students
- **L2** **AVERAGE** activities for average to above-average students
- **L3** **CHALLENGING** activities for above-average students
- **ELL** **English Language Learner** activities

Chapter 16 Resource Manager

The following materials may be used when teaching the chapter. Materials for specific lessons are also shown at point-of-use in the margins of the Teacher's Wraparound Edition.

TEACHING TRANSPARENCIES

Chapter 16 Teaching Transparency

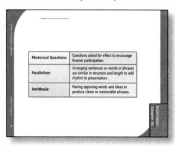

Graphic Organizer Transparency 16-1

Graphic Organizer Transparency 16-2

APPLICATION ACTIVITIES

Chapter 16, Section 1

Chapter 16, Section 2

Chapter 16, Cumulative

REINFORCEMENT AND REVIEW ACTIVITIES

Vocabulary Activity 16

Guided Reading Activity Workbook 16-1, 16-2

Reteaching Activities 16-1, 16-2

Chapter 16 Resource Manager

ASSESSMENT AND EVALUATION

Glencoe's ASSESSMENT ADVANTAGE

Section Quizzes 16-1, 16-2

Chapter 16 Test, Forms A & B

Performance Assessment Activity 16

ENRICHMENT AND EXTENSION

Technology Application Activity 16

Enrichment Activities 16-1, 16-2

ORAL PRESENTATION ACTIVITIES

Activities 5, 7, 11

SPANISH RESOURCES

- Spanish Chapter and Unit Tests
- Spanish Vocabulary Activities
- Spanish Section Quizzes
- Spanish Reteaching Activities
- Spanish Enrichment Activities

MULTIMEDIA

-   Interactive Tutor Self-Assessment
-   ExamView® Pro Testmaker
- PuzzleMaker
-   Communication in Action Videodisc and Videocassette
- MindJogger
- Interactive Lesson Planner
- Presentation Plus!
- Writer's Assistant
- Glencoe Interactive Grammar
- communicationapplications.glencoe.com

TEACHER PLANNING AND SUPPORT

- Reproducible Lesson Plans
- Interactive Lesson Planner
- Presentation Plus!

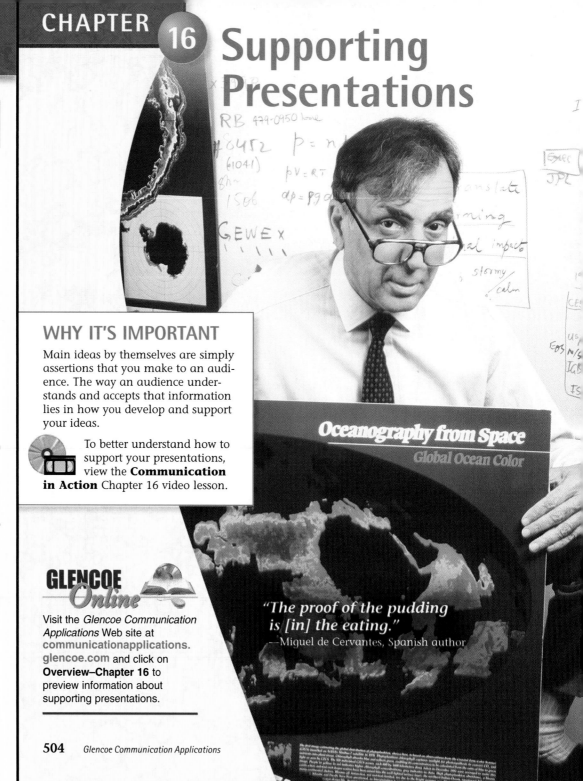

CHAPTER **16**

Supporting Presentations

WHY IT'S IMPORTANT

Main ideas by themselves are simply assertions that you make to an audience. The way an audience understands and accepts that information lies in how you develop and support your ideas.

To better understand how to support your presentations, view the **Communication in Action** Chapter 16 video lesson.

Oceanography from Space
Global Ocean Color

"The proof of the pudding is [in] the eating."
—Miguel de Cervantes, Spanish author

504 *Glencoe Communication Applications*

WHY IT'S IMPORTANT

Have students read the quotation on this page and ask them what they think Cervantes meant by these words. If necessary, lead them through a literal interpretation to a figurative one *(Literal: You don't know if a pudding is good until you've tasted it. Figurative: You will only discover the true quality of something by investigating it thoroughly.)* Ask: **How might this remark apply to preparing for a presentation?** *(Students may respond that a presentation without substance will not be a success.)*

Section 1

Using Support Materials

GUIDE TO READING

Objectives

1. List and provide examples for the three types of proof.
2. Select information to support and clarify main points.
3. Develop effective audiovisual aids to enhance presentations.

Terms to Learn

logical proof
statistic
specific instance
testimony

ethical proof
pathetic proof
amplification device

*W*hat structures give the Golden Gate Bridge the support it needs to keep from collapsing? How do the foundation and construction of a skyscraper support its many floors? How does a cast provide support for a broken bone? How do family members, friends, and teachers help support you?*

Just as bridges need support to function, so do ideas. An idea has little meaning if there is no supporting information to help prove it. When sharing your thoughts and ideas with an audience, the amount and quality of support that you provide will largely determine your success.

At this point in your presentation preparation, you have determined your main points, know what pattern of organization you will use, and probably have a very basic outline. You now need to think about how you will develop each of those main points.

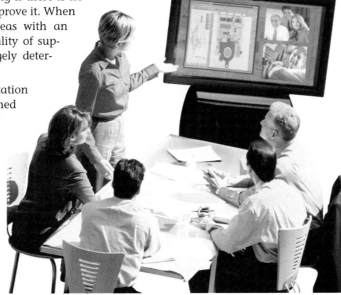

This presenter uses the support of a visual aid during her presentation. How do support materials affect a presentation?

Supporting Presentations **505**

1 FOCUS

Bellringer
Have students read the first paragraph of this section. Then, ask them to shut their books and to predict why the text has stressed the importance of support. Elicit from them the need to have supporting ideas in a presentation. Ask each student to jot down one statement that is generally considered to be true. (Example: Babe Ruth was a great baseball player.) Have them read the statement aloud and ask for supporting evidence from other students. (Example: He hit more than 700 home runs.) Lead students to understand the power that supporting evidence lends a generalization.

You may use Graphic Organizer Transparency 16–1 to introduce this section.

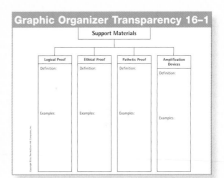

Graphic Organizer Transparency 16–1

Grammar Tip

A long prepositional phrase at the opening of the sentence—or a string of prepositional phrases—is generally followed by a comma. The first sentence of the third paragraph ("At this point . . .") opens with two prepositional phrases set apart by a comma.

Visual Instruction

Answer Support materials can reinforce the main ideas, making them more meaningful and persuasive.

RESOURCE MANAGER

Teaching Tools

 Interactive Lesson Planner
Reproducible Lesson Plan 16–1
Application Activities 16–1

Reproducible Masters

Guided Reading Activity Workbook 16–1
Enrichment Activity 16–1
Reteaching Activity 16–1
Section Quiz 16–1
Transparency Strategies and Activities Booklet 16–1

Transparencies

Graphic Organizer Transparency 16–1
Chapter 16 Teaching Transparency

Technology Resources

 Interactive Tutor Self-Assessment Software
Presentation Plus! Software
ExamView® Pro Testmaker
PuzzleMaker Software
communicationapplications.glencoe.com

2 TEACH

Supporting Information

Lead students to understand that it is better to start with too much information and to discard some of it than to struggle to find the perfect supporting information when starting their research. Divide the class into groups of three or four and assign each group a month of the year. Tell them that they have two minutes to brainstorm for as many reasons as they can as to why their month is better than all the others. Have them write their lists on the board. Discuss what information they might choose to retain if they actually were to develop their theses.
L1

Guided Reading Activity 16–1

Name _____ Date _____ Class _____

GUIDED READING Activity 16-1

SUPPORTING PRESENTATIONS
Using Support Materials

As you read Section 1, answer the following items.

1. What are the three basic steps to developing a point in a presentation? _____
2. What are the three types of proof that support information? _____
3. List the three types of logical proofs. _____
4. How are statistics useful? _____
5. How do specific instances relate information to an audience differently than statistics do? _____
6. What is a testimony and how is it used effectively? _____
7. A piece of supporting information that builds a speaker's credibility on a topic is called what? _____
8. List the six emotions to which a pathetic proof might appeal. _____
9. List four amplification devices. _____
10. Give the five benefits of audiovisual aids. _____
11. Into what three categories do most visual aids fall? _____
12. Give six examples of pictorial reproductions. _____
13. List three types of graphs. _____
14. List the six ways you can present your visual aids. _____

STEPS FOR DEVELOPING MAIN POINTS

There are three basic steps to developing a point in a presentation. First you state the point, then you support and amplify the point, and finally you restate and relate the point.

When you introduce a point to your audience, you can state it as either a simple declarative statement or a question. Then, you support your point with whatever information your audience needs to accept that your point is accurate. If you have stated your point as a question, your supporting information should answer it. Finally, after going through the first two steps, you will restate your original point with a brief summary and relate it to your thesis statement and the other points in your presentation.

These procedures have little meaning unless each of your points is supported. Meaningless statements waste an audience's time and energy. An extension of this idea is that a point is no more valid than the information that

Figure 16–1 Steps of the Presentation Preparation Process

1. Determine a topic.
2. Limit the topic.
3. Determine the purpose.
4. Research the topic.
5. Organize the presentation.
6. Select supporting information.
7. Prepare notes and manuscript for delivery.
8. Rehearse the presentation.

supports it—and a support element is no better than its source. With the skeleton, or outline, of your presentation prepared, you are ready to examine your research and ensure that each of your points is fully and accurately supported. Thus, as shown in **Figure 16–1**, you are ready for the sixth step of the presentation preparation process: selecting supporting information.

SELECTING SUPPORTING INFORMATION

The way you develop and support your main points can make or break your credibility with an audience. In any presentation, you are educating your audience. Well-developed main points that are adequately supported will help you to achieve this goal. The support materials you select can help you overcome barriers between you and your audience for a successful presentation.

Supporting a Point

The support materials that you select should reinforce your main points, making them more meaningful and persuasive. In other words, your support information should prove your points. Three types of proof that support information can provide are as follows:

- logical proofs
- ethical proofs
- pathetic proofs

Logical Proofs A *logical proof* is a specific piece of verifiable information that supports a statement. This type of information adds the strongest support to a point. There are three types of logical proofs. These are:

- statistics
- specific instances
- testimonies

Statistics A statistic is an item of information that represents numerical data. Statistics can be used effectively to reduce large amounts of information into general categories, as with average test scores or education levels. Statistics also can emphasize the size or amount of something. In addition, statistics are useful for indicating trends. For example, "From 1995 to today, spending has increased by $2 million."

Sometimes, statistics are the result of a thorough, scientific study or poll. Other times, statistics can be flawed or incomplete. Even if a statistic comes from a respected source, it may be open to question. For instance, two different sources may make conflicting claims. Imagine that one source claims the cheetah is the fastest animal in the world, while another source gives that distinction to the pronghorn antelope. The truth is that the cheetah runs faster, but it does so for only very short distances. In other words, the cheetah would win the 100-yard dash, but the antelope would win the marathon.

Variations in statistics also may be due to the demographics of the group polled, the specific wording of the questions, or the influence of the pollster on the respondent. Each of these factors can have an impact on a poll's results. Remember, the statistics you use to add interest or support to a presentation need to be thoroughly verified, but still may not provide absolute proof.

Specific Instances A specific instance is an account of an actual event or occurrence. Specific instances tend to relate information more directly and more personally to an audience than do statistics.

If you were making a presentation to a group of fellow students to convince them of the importance of learning the Heimlich maneuver, you might include the specific instance of the second-grade student who saved his principal from choking in the school cafeteria. The example provides dramatic proof to support your point.

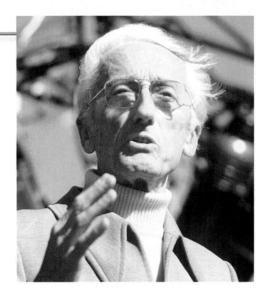

A testimony from Jacques Cousteau would be useful in a presentation on undersea exploration. **How is an expert testimony effective in creating credibility?**

Testimonies A testimony is a direct quotation or a summary of a quotation. When you think of testimony, you may think of quotations from people who are experts or authorities in their fields. This expert testimony is particularly effective for establishing credibility on topics you don't know much about. Quoting authorities whom your audience recognizes and respects also can be helpful when your topic is controversial or when the audience is skeptical of your personal motives or involvement.

The challenge to using testimony effectively in a presentation lies in determining exactly whom you should quote. Refer to the analysis of your audience when selecting quotations. When possible, select quotations from well-known authorities on your topic or from sources whom you know your audience admires and believes. Testimonies from well-recognized and respected sources will help you to be accepted by the audience.

Remember this, however: Just about any time you support your ideas with a quotation

Supporting Presentations **507**

Ethical Proofs

Ask students what type of speakers they would consider to be uniquely qualified to deliver a presentation on the following subjects:

Courage

The value of education

The dangers of drugs

The importance of exercise

(Answers might include a firefighter who had rescued three colleagues; a prominent judge who had fought his or her way up from poverty; a reformed addict; a former heart patient who had become a marathon runner.) **L2**

Pathetic Proofs

Point out to students that "negative campaigning," the technique of concentrating upon one's opponent's flaws instead of one's own positive attributes, is not always easy to control. Ask why it sometimes is effective and sometimes backfires. *(Students may respond that voters might be persuaded by one candidate's negative stories; they might also perceive that candidate as being mean and lacking substance.)* **L1**

COMMUNICATION PRACTICE LAB

Supporting a Presentation

Students should be encouraged to include all three kinds of supporting proof in their presentations. One of their presenters, for instance, might be a participant in the activity they are recommending (ethical proof). They might also find an emotional reason for supporting their activity—pride in a team, generosity in a community service project, for example—to provide pathetic proof. Statistics, specific stories about satisfied members, and videotaped testimony might all provide logical proof. **L2**

---

from one authority, someone probably will be able to find a contradictory quotation by another authority. You may decide to acknowledge the existence of contradictory information in order to illustrate to your audience that you have considered all aspects of your topic and that you are not trying to mislead your listeners. In general, however, select information that supports your ideas.

Ethical Proofs An *ethical proof* is a piece of supporting information that builds a speaker's credibility on a topic. Ethical proof demonstrates that you are uniquely qualified to speak on the topic. The most common ethical proof is personal experience. If a speaker making a presentation on overcoming learning disabilities reveals that he or she has dyslexia, that person may have more credibility than a speaker who has no learning disability.

A speaker does not have to personally experience some aspect of a topic to be credible, however. There are other ways to build ethos in a presentation. The speaker can explain his or her own personal concerns or interests in the topic, how he or she became interested in the topic, or what motivates his or her presentation.

Pathetic Proofs A *pathetic proof* is support material that gives emotional appeal to a presentation. A pathetic proof may appeal to an audience's sense of compassion, dignity, justice, pride, love, or generosity, as well as to other emotions. It asks audience members to react with their hearts as well as with their minds.

The number and type of pathetic proofs you use should be determined by how you want your audience to feel about your topic after your presentation. Be careful not to overuse emotional appeals, however. Listeners tend to be skeptical of speakers who rely heavily on pathetic proofs instead of logical ones. In addition, appeals to negative emotions, such as fear, hate, or prejudice, can create negative reactions in your audience. Audiences usually have a more immediate response to emotion, but eventually their logic prevails.

COMMUNICATION PRACTICE LAB

Supporting a Presentation

To practice supporting a presentation, follow these steps:

Step 1 In groups of four or five, discuss extracurricular activities at your school.

Step 2 Use the information from your discussion to choose three activities.

Step 3 Imagine that you will make a presentation to classmates persuading them to participate in the activities you have chosen. What skills can they learn from these activities? What types of people will they meet? Include these types of details in your presentation. Be sure to provide enough information to convince your classmates.

Step 4 Use proper form to create an outline with at least three main points for your presentation. Are there any points that need more information?

Step 5 Determine the type of proofs you will use to support each main point. Place these into your outline.

Step 6 Share your outlines as a class. Discuss whether each provides enough detail to create a convincing presentation.

MULTIPLE LEARNING STYLES

Linguistic Point out that if you are looking for a quotation to support your views, you will almost always find one. Students should understand that supporting quotations are a powerful tool but are not always to be believed.

Activity Have each student choose two themes or key words about which much has been said and written. (Examples: love, work, women, politics, war, or death) Ask them to search in a dictionary of quotations or on the Internet for noteworthy statements that people have made on their topics. Have them bring to class two contradicting quotations for each of their themes. Allow students to share their statements with a partner. Invite each pair to write two contradictory quotations on the board. Discuss with the class the use of quotations as supporting evidence.

Amplification Devices In addition to using logical, ethical, and pathetic proofs to support the main ideas in your presentation, you can add interest and depth to your ideas by amplifying them. To do this, you can use amplification devices. An amplification device is information that extends or clarifies an idea for an audience or does both. There are numerous amplification devices from which you can choose. Four of them are as follows:

- descriptions
- contrasts
- comparisons
- examples

Descriptions A description can help a listener better relate to the ideas you are presenting. It can also clarify an idea for your audience by providing details that other proofs may not have supplied.

For example, if you want to convince an audience that skiing is an exciting sport, you might help the listener feel the excitement through a vivid description. What details make the sport enjoyable for you? Create a description that helps your audience imagine the experience. Help the audience feel the chill of the wind, see the sparkling snow, experience the anticipation while riding the lift over the trees to the top of the slope, and feel the thrill of speeding down a winding, steep trail.

Comparisons A comparison can clarify information and ideas for your audience. If you want your audience to understand an aspect of your topic that may be unfamiliar to them, compare it to something you know your audience is familiar with. Explaining how one thing is like another can give the audience insight into what you mean.

Contrasts Just as comparisons can help an audience understand an idea by showing how two things are alike, contrasts can sharpen a listener's understanding by pointing out differences. Sometimes, it is just as important to tell the audience what something is not as it is to

Practice for the Workplace

Picture This Although visual aids are key elements of effective presentations, sometimes the most influential picture you can provide in a presentation is the one you create with your own words. By using the amplification devices described in this chapter, you can create a powerful mental image for your audience.

BUSINESS PRACTICE *Activity*

Assume that your school administrators have suggested that a local restaurant chain should replace your school cafeteria's lunch service. Your class has been assigned the task of debating the positive and negative effects of this proposal. Decide whether you would be for or against this proposal, then compose a statement that defends your position. Develop vivid descriptions of the current cafeteria's food and that of the proposed food service. Draw comparisons between the cafeteria's food and the restaurant's food. Show contrasts between the two services. Give examples of why your current cafeteria's service should or should not be replaced.

tell them what it is. Be careful, however, not to base all your descriptions on contrasts. Overusing contrasts can give your presentation a negative tone and can leave the audience confused.

Examples Not all examples are as factual as the statistics, specific instances, or testimonies in a logical proof. You also may choose to use hypothetical or fictional examples to clarify an idea in a presentation.

As you are preparing your presentation, you may realize that a scene from a movie could explain your ideas perfectly. Maybe a character in a book you have read faced a

Supporting Presentations **509**

Descriptions

Divide the class into groups and assign each group a subject with which students are familiar. (Examples: a school football game or dance, a camping holiday, summer in the city) Give each group a piece of paper and one writing implement. At the signal to start, groups should pass the paper around from person to person with each member quickly jotting down a memorable detail or image relating to the group's assigned topic. After a timed period, ask students to stop writing. Have groups read their lists to their fellow students. Give students a few minutes to individually write a descriptive paragraph on their theme, using ideas generated by the group. Invite volunteers to share their descriptions with the class. **L2**

Practice for the Workplace

Picture This Encourage students to strengthen their word pictures with firsthand research. Suggest that they make careful observations (ideally writing them in a notebook) at both the school cafeteria and the rival restaurant. Students' writing will be strengthened if it includes precise, sensory descriptions of what is offered at both establishments. **L2**

Comparisons

Lead students to understand that with a little imagination, just about any two things can be compared. Have them come up with a number of common objects—a shoe box, scissors, a car, and a laptop computer, for example. List these on the chalkboard. Then, ask students to complete the following statement: A good presentation is like a shoe box because . . . *(Possible answer: A good presentation is like a shoe box because it contains something that is truly useful.)* Go through all the items on the list and vote for the comparisons that are really effective. **L2**

EXTENDING THE CONTENT

Descriptive Writing Description is the stock in trade of the writer's craft. Point out to students that all serious writers strive to use a strong, precise vocabulary and to create memorable images. Lead students to understand that the same attention to words can strengthen the art of the presenter.

Activity Have students bring to school passages of vivid descriptive writing that they feel bring scenes to life. The sources might include periodicals, newspapers, novels, or ballads. Ask students to write paragraphs summarizing the reasons for their choices, referring to specific words or phrases that they feel heighten the descriptions. Invite volunteers to read their passages and explanations to the class.

CHAPTER 16, Section 1

COMMUNICATION *Strategies*

TESTING SUPPORT MATERIALS

Have students read the checklist for testing support materials. Ask them why it is important to take such care in establishing the accuracy of evidence. Which of the items on the checklist do students think would be most difficult to confirm, and why? *(Answers will vary, although some students may have difficulty identifying the reliability of the source.)* Point out that if you feel it is important to keep untested evidence, you must be careful to explain its possible unreliability. (Example: Although results were not completely recorded, evidence suggests that . . .)**L3**

Visual Instruction

Answer The visual aid can help make the information more concrete.

---

situation similar to the one you are describing. Hypothetical and fictional examples can be interesting ways to relate and expand your ideas for your audience. Examples can come from movies, plays, sports, music, history, or any other area that will help you relate to your audience and reflect their interests.

When choosing proofs to support the details of your presentation, take care to test their reliability. The Communication Strategies checklist provides some important questions to help you test your support materials.

DEVELOPING AUDIOVISUAL AIDS

It is often said that a picture is worth a thousand words. Most audiences will find a presenter's message more interesting, understand it more easily, and remember it longer if that message is presented visually as well as verbally.

This presenter is using a visual aid to explain a process. What effect does using audiovisual aids have on the audience?

COMMUNICATION *Strategies*

TESTING SUPPORT MATERIALS

✓ Were enough people sampled for the statistic to be worth citing?

✓ Were the results completely reported and recorded?

✓ Is the source biased? Does the bias affect the accuracy of the information?

✓ Is this information consistent with information from other sources? If not, what could account for the differences?

✓ Is the information the most recent you can find on the subject?

✓ Is the source reliable?

✓ How is the source qualified to make this observation or conclusion?

✓ Are the cases and examples typical? Were negative examples allowed or explained?

Reasons for Using Audiovisual Aids

Of course, presentations come in all shapes and sizes. Some may last only for a minute or two, while others can be quite lengthy. However, no matter what length a presentation is, it might benefit from the use of audiovisual aids. Following are a few reasons for using these effective tools:

- clarity
- interest
- retention
- professionalism
- presenter support

COOPERATIVE LEARNING ACTIVITY

Point out that examples from books or films are often just as powerful as examples from real life to the presenter looking for supporting evidence. In some cases, fictional examples will be even more effective than real-life ones because more people will be familiar with them. On index cards, write a number of themes that students might have encountered in books or movies. (Examples: Crime doesn't pay; nature can be merciless; money can't make you happy; love can soften the hardest heart) Divide students into teams of four or five and ask them to take turns choosing a theme card from a hat. Each team will have to match its theme with a suitable example from a movie, television program, or piece of fiction. A team that fails to think of an example passes its theme to the next group to try.

Clarity Audiovisual aids are used in presentations for a variety of reasons. The primary reason is for clarity. If you are discussing an object, you can make your message clearer by showing the object itself or a representation of the object. If you are citing statistics, showing how something works, or demonstrating a technique, a visual aid can make your information more concrete for your audience. Television and movies have conditioned us to expect a visual image. A visual aid can often clarify an idea for an audience when words are not completely effective.

Interest Audiovisual aids also add interest to your presentation. Which book would you rather read: one with page after page filled with nothing but writing or one that includes pictures throughout? Over five hundred pages of text or a condensed version read by a celebrity on audiocassette? If you are like most people, you often prefer the versions that include interesting sights and sounds. Audiovisual aids have the same effect in a presentation.

Retention A third reason for including audiovisual aids in a presentation is retention. A visual image tends to remain with an audience longer than a verbal image. This is why advertisers often use vivid color and unusual images in advertisements. Consumers may not remember everything that a product claims to do, but they are very likely to remember the images conveyed by its advertisements.

Professionalism A fourth benefit to using audiovisual aids is that they can give your presentation a professional image. High-quality visuals give an audience the impression that you have approached this presentation with a professional attitude. Sometimes, that alone can increase your ethos. Of course, poorly produced, messy, or illegible visual aids can have the opposite effect.

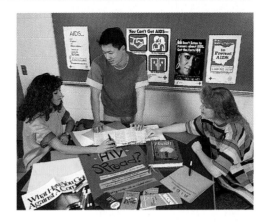

These three individuals are developing visual support to use in a presentation on AIDS. **How does the use of an audiovisual aid add clarity to a presentation?**

Presenter Support A fifth benefit to using audiovisual aids is that they are an excellent way to combat apprehension or stage fright. Visual aids heighten an audience's interest in your topic and shift the attention away from you as the presenter. Visuals also can serve as a prompt to jog your memory or as a visual representation of your notes. You might even create an organizational visual (a list of your main points, for example) that can add to the information in your notes.

Finally, preparing your visual aids gives you more opportunity to become familiar with the ideas of your presentation. The more familiar you are with what you plan to say, the less anxiety you are likely to feel about presenting it.

Types of Visual Aids

Most visual aids fall into one of three categories. These are as follows:

- objects and models
- pictorial reproductions
- pictorial symbols

Supporting Presentations **511**

Benefits of Audiovisual Aids

Ask students to respond to the five benefits of audiovisual aids listed here. Ask them to jot down on a piece of paper how they would rank these items in terms of importance. Poll the class for their ratings and make a master list on the chalkboard. Invite volunteers to share experiences of presentations they have attended or given when audiovisual aids were an important feature.

> **DID YOU KNOW?**
>
> Retention rates for new information vary considerably with the medium employed. According to some researchers, students retain only about 10 percent of what they read, 20 percent of what they hear, 30 percent of what they see, and 50 percent of what they see and hear simultaneously.

Interest

Point out that even 50 years ago audiovisual aids were not a standard supplement to presentations. Ask students their response to the increasing demand for variety and technical assistance. Do they believe audiences are less able to attend to lectures than they once were? *(Students might suggest that the great variety of media has changed the way people expect to be informed.)* **L2**

Visual Instruction

Answer The benefits of visual aids are they add clarity, create interest, positively affect retention, add a professional look, and help combat apprehension.

MEETING INDIVIDUAL NEEDS

ENGLISH LANGUAGE LEARNERS

A Presentation Without Words Point out that sometimes words simply get in the way of a presentation. This is especially true when the audience cannot understand your language! English language learners will be particularly able to appreciate the importance of visual instruction. **Activity** Have students form teams and ask them to create and produce an instructional video, giving a wordless lesson in some elementary aspect of life. (Examples: bicycle safety, installing a video monitor, cooking an instant dinner, brushing one's teeth) Students should aim for simple images and a step-by-step lesson plan. Encourage them to use a musical soundtrack if it seems appropriate. View the productions with the class and discuss the strengths and problems of instructions without words. **ELL**

Objects and Models

Students might need reminding that they were using objects as visual aids during grade school "show and tell" sessions. Give them an opportunity to refresh this skill by asking them to form pairs and to brainstorm for five situations in which a speaker might usefully employ an object as an aid in a presentation. Compile a list of their best suggestions on the chalkboard. Discuss with the class circumstances when aids are useful and others when they might distract from a presentation. **L1**

Animals as Visual Aids

Point out that most of us have witnessed guest appearances by pets or exotic animals used as visual aids during a presentation. (Remind students that examples of animals misbehaving on air are often featured on programs of comic television clips.) Invite students to share an instance they can recall when a presenter used an animal to illustrate a presentation. Did they find this to be a successful means of capturing the audience's interest? **L1**

Visual Instruction

Answer Passing the picture around diverts the audience's attention from the spoken presentation.

This presenter is projecting information on an overhead screen. Why is it a good idea to use an overhead projection for a pictorial reproduction instead of passing it around the room?

Your decision to use a particular type of visual aid depends on a number of factors. Most importantly, each aid should be based on the content of your presentation, the audience, and the occasion.

Objects and Models Objects and models add substance and precision to your presentation. Objects can be either live, like a tarantula, or inanimate, like a rock. Showing the actual subject of your presentation to audience members can clarify any descriptions you make of the object and help listeners to understand your explanations more fully. Allowing an audience to see, feel, and smell the object can reveal information that will often save a presenter time. It also actively engages an audience in the presentation.

Sometimes it is impractical to bring the actual subject of your presentation to the presentation itself. It may be too large or small, too dangerous, too rare, or too delicate to be handled. In these instances, you might want to consider using a model or representation of the object.

A model usually refers to a three-dimensional, scale-sized representation of an object. A model can give your audience a sense of depth and proportion that pictures

might not provide. Architects frequently use models of buildings to illustrate to an audience how a building will look before construction begins. Auto mechanics may use a model of an engine or transmission to explain to a client what needs to be repaired.

Models often enhance and clarify information for your audience. Sometimes, however, they can be a distraction, taking the audience's attention away from your message. This is particularly true for live objects. Even the slightest movement from a snake in a cage can distract a front-row audience member. He or she instantly focuses on the thought of the snake getting out of the cage and stops hearing what you are saying.

Audiences can also become so absorbed in a model of an object that they lose track of what you're saying. After a presentation, they may be able to describe the model in detail but not remember a word of your message. It usually is wise to keep the object or model out of sight any time you are not actively using it in your presentation. This keeps it from becoming an unnecessary distraction.

Pictorial Reproductions Photographs, slides, sketches, videotapes, cartoons, and drawings are all pictorial reproductions. In the absence of an object or a model, a picture can help the audience visualize some aspect of your topic.

The drawing in **Figure 16–2** was used by a student to illustrate the types of problems

---

> **Figure 16–2 An Illustration of Dyslexia**
>
> This si wrlat a qerson with dyslexia mihgt se wrlem reding this sentnce.

INTERDISCIPLINARY CONNECTION

Art Students should realize that architects frequently construct models of proposed buildings. These are used as visual aids in presentations at competitions or for clients who want to see a design before commissioning a project.

Activity Inform students that they have the responsibility of designing a rural school. They have enough material to create a single-story structure of 10,000 square feet with room partitions as necessary. Have them work in small groups to construct a model of this school for the local community's approval. Their models can be made out of cardboard and must clearly reveal the allocation of space necessary for approximately 100 elementary school students. Have students display their models in a presentation that simulates a community meeting.

TECHNOLOGY *Activity*

Making a Graph Graphs can be used to show trends, illustrate relationships, or compare data. Many computer programs can convert numerical data into a visual aid, such as a circle graph, bar graph, or line graph. You, however, have to choose the type of graph that best illustrates your data. Find out the number of freshmen, sophomores, juniors, and seniors at your school. Create a line graph, a circle graph, or a bar graph to illustrate the data. Which type of graph did you choose? Why? Which graph would work best if you displayed the data in percentage form? Why? Which type of graph would work best if you were to compare enrollment information over the last ten years?

faced by people with dyslexia. This was particularly effective because it allowed the presenter to translate complex ideas into visual terms that the audience could easily grasp.

Unless you are presenting to only one or two people, pictorial reproductions will probably need to be enlarged for easier viewing. Many photographs and drawings are not large enough to be seen unless they are enlarged or passed around a room. Passing the picture around diverts the attention of the audience away from what you are saying during your presentation. Many copy centers have equipment for making enlargements. As an alternative, you might make a transparency of your visual and use an overhead projector to enlarge it during your presentation.

Pictorial Symbols Abstract concepts and statistics are frequently presented through pictorial symbols. Pictorial symbols most commonly are used in graphs, charts, and diagrams.

Graphs Graphs are a good tool for simplifying and clarifying statistics. Audiences frequently have trouble understanding complex series of numbers. You can increase their understanding by using graphs to represent numerical data in visual form. Graphs are useful tools in a presentation because they can illustrate relationships among individual units and show statistical trends and patterns.

A line graph, such as the one shown in **Figure 16–3,** uses one or more lines to show change over a period of time or space. A single line graph can indicate an upward or downward trend in sales, production, profits, or employee productivity. A multiple line graph can show a relationship between two or more trends.

A bar graph is a good way to show comparisons between two or more items. It is also very easy to understand—even if your audience has no experience in reading graphs. A circle graph is a depiction of the various individual components of a whole. A circle graph looks like a pie. It is then divided into proportional segments—like pieces of pie—representing different parts of your information. A pie graph is a good way to show how all the parts of your topic fit together or what portion of a group or population is affected by your topic.

■ **Figure 16–3 Line Graph**

STUDENT LUNCH TRENDS:
McARTHUR HIGH SCHOOL

Supporting Presentations **513**

Ask students to imagine that they are conducting picture research for people who are giving the following presentations:

An Introduction to [name of your school]
Sports in America
Welcome to [name of your city or town]
Guarding Against Crime
Pollution: Problem of the Future

Their assignment is to choose five suitable photographs or other illustrations to be enlarged or projected during these presentations. Have students form groups and ask them to describe what they consider to be appropriate images to illustrate these topics. Discuss their choices with the class and choose five images that seem best suited to each presentation. **L2**

TECHNOLOGY *Activity*

Making a Graph Students should choose the bar graph to indicate the numbers of students per class. This is easy to read and gives them the opportunity to correlate the height of their bars with a precise number on a scale. The circle graph is the best choice for showing percentages. Its divisions give a visual representation of the proportion of the school each class occupies. A line graph, which shows changes over time, is the correct choice for comparing enrollment over the last ten years. **L2**

MULTIPLE LEARNING STYLES

Logical-Mathematical Point out that statistics by themselves often fail to interest an audience. When represented on a graph, however, the same figures may be clear and enlightening.
Activity Ask students to choose aspects of their school that are suitable for representation on graphs. (Topics might include numbers of students driving to school, prom attendance over the years, hours students spend doing homework.) Ask each student to research his or her topic and to produce two graphs of different types based on the findings. Have students present their graphs to the class.

Graphs
As a quick exercise in graphing, have students create bar graphs based on demographic statistics existing within the classroom. (Height and shoe size are appropriate subjects.) Have volunteers re-create their graphs on the chalkboard. Discuss how else the information might have been represented graphically. **L2**

Charts

Point out that publishers often use flowcharts or "book maps" when preparing a book for publication. This permits them to plan the location of text, illustrations, and headings. On the chalkboard, have students create a sequence of equal-sized rectangles, each divided in half by a vertical line. Inform them that these rectangles represent a book spread open (known as a spread), with each half-rectangle depicting a separate page. Have students form pairs and assign each a spread from this chapter. Students should find their appropriate rectangle on the board, keeping their pages in sequence. Instruct them to draw a miniature version of their assigned pages, including numbers and important text such as titles and headings. The completed exercise will represent a flowchart of Chapter 16. **L2**

COMMUNICATION *Strategies*

CREATING EFFECTIVE AUDIOVISUAL AIDS

Have students read the items on the checklist and ask them to create one rule that they feel sums up the essence of all these points. *(One possible answer: Visual aids must be easy to use and understand.)* Point out that technical wizardry is no substitute for careful preparation and clear thinking. **L1**

■ Visual Instruction

Answer Visual aids can also be presented on flip charts and posters, transparencies, slides, handouts, and computerized displays.

Charts While graphs are visual depictions of statistics, charts illustrate complex information that is not numerical. A flowchart, for example, may be very effective for a presenter who is explaining how something is done. A flowchart is a step-by-step diagram of the process that shows how each step leads to the next. This type of visual aid can help simplify even the most complex task.

The most common chart you will use is a table of information. A table groups information into columns and rows. Although tables may not always be particularly pretty to look at, they can help an audience grasp what you are talking about fairly quickly. They are also good for information that you may want your audience to write down, such as telephone numbers or addresses.

Computer-Generated Visual Aids

If you have access to a computer and printer, you may be able to create professional-looking visuals for your presentations. Depending on the software you have, you may be able to create anything from simple diagrams and tables to extremely sophisticated, full-color charts and graphs. Most of the graphics software that is available includes ready-made drawings, symbols, and other art elements to add color and emphasis to your main points. Some presentation-software packages will even allow you to add

One of the ways to present a visual aid is through the use of a VCR. Identify other ways to present a visual aid.

COMMUNICATION *Strategies*

CREATING EFFECTIVE AUDIOVISUAL AIDS

- Prepare audiovisual aids in advance of your presentation.
- Create audiovisual aids that can easily be seen or heard by your entire audience.
- Make visual aids easy to read. Use a limited number of fonts and designs. Choose a font that is easy to read. Use color to make your visuals clearer.
- Create visuals that are easy to use and understand.
- Practice using your visual aids before the presentation.

sound effects to your ideas. Using these tools effectively can help you make the most of your presentations.

Presenting Visual Aids

There are many ways to present visual aids. You can be as creative as you want, as long as your support materials enhance your presentation rather than replace it. As **Figure 16–4** shows, you may wish to present your visual aids using any of the following:

- flip charts/poster boards
- transparencies
- slides
- handouts
- video/audio cassettes
- computerized displays

■ MEETING INDIVIDUAL NEEDS ■ GIFTED AND TALENTED

Presenting with Visual Aids Point out that the selection of visual aids is an essential part of the research process in preparing for a presentation.

Activity Have students select topics that would interest them to research for presentations. Ask each to write a paragraph explaining his or her choice, do the research, prepare a presentation, and select five visual aids that he or she feels would enhance the audience's understanding and enjoyment. Instruct students that their visual aids must include at least one example from each of the three types of aids mentioned in the text: objects and models, pictorial reproductions, and pictorial symbols. Provide time for students to make their presentations.

Figure 16–4 Visual Aids

Choosing how to share your visuals with your audience will depend on a number of things. The style and tone of your presentation, as well as the occasion, audience, and purpose, all play a part in your decisions. In addition, you should try to take full advantage of your own artistic talents and the equipment you have available to you.

Using Computerized Displays

When using computerized displays, keep in mind some important cautions. First, it is very

Different presentations call for different types of visual aids. **Identify** the two types of visual aids utilized in this presentation.

COMMUNICATION
Strategies

PRESENTING AUDIOVISUAL AIDS

✓ Make sure any equipment you need (projector, easel, and so on) is available and operating correctly.

✓ Show visual aids at the time they are being discussed.

✓ Place audiovisual aids where your entire audience can clearly see or hear them.

✓ Avoid turning your back to your audience. Speak to your audience, not to your audiovisual aid.

✓ Do not hide behind your visual aids.

✓ Do not fidget with your audiovisual aids.

✓ Thoroughly explain all of your audiovisual aids.

✓ Do not pass visual aids around to the audience.

---

easy to get carried away with these technological wonders. The result can be a presentation that audience members remember for its special effects rather than for what you said.

You also need to think about what facilities you will need to allow your audience to properly view your display. Most computer monitors are too small for an audience larger than one or two people. Therefore, make sure a projection system is readily available before developing computerized graphics for a larger audience. If you do not have access to this type of equipment, you may

Supporting Presentations **515**

MEETING INDIVIDUAL NEEDS

MULTIPLE LEARNING STYLES

Bodily-Kinesthetic Remind students that for many people an introductory presentation is their first exposure to an organization or institution. Carefully chosen audiovisual aids can assist in making sure that a newcomer's first impression is a good one.

Activity Ask students to imagine that they are serving on a committee to introduce a group of exchange students to their school. Their job is to create the audiovisual aids for a presentation that will cover the school's academic and extracurricular activities, as well as give a general overview of the building itself and the student body. Students should produce materials such as a videotape or presentation slides that show their school in action.

Reteaching Activity 16–1

SUPPORTING PRESENTATIONS
Using Support Materials

RETEACHING
Activity 16–1

Enrichment Activity 16–1

SUPPORTING PRESENTATIONS
Using Support Materials

ENRICHMENT
Activity 16–1

4 CLOSE

Ask students to repeat the Bellringer exercise on page 505 with which they started this section, jotting down a statement generally considered to be true, such as Babe Ruth was a great baseball player. Again, have them read their statements aloud, but this time ask other students to suggest ways in which a presenter might effectively support these assertions.

Extra-Credit Project

Have students create a questionnaire, and ask them to poll ten teachers concerning their use of visual aids in the classroom. Students should make a chart of their findings and present their research to the class.

wish to print the graphics you design onto transparencies and use an overhead projector to display them during your presentation.

Regardless of what types of audiovisual aids you use, be sure to present them in a professional manner. Make sure text and images are easy to see and sound is easy to hear. Also, pay attention to feedback from your audience. Feedback from your audience is one of the best ways to judge the effectiveness of your audiovisual aids. Make mental notes about which types of aids are most effective. Then, use this knowledge in the future to become an even more effective presenter.

Placing Support Materials into Your Presentation

Now that you know the types of materials available to support the main points of your presentation, you will need to place the materials into the presentation. You might want to go back to your original outline and use it or pull the main points out of the outline and list them on a separate sheet of paper. In either case, review the information you have up to this time and list the support materials under the appropriate point. Be sure to include any ideas that you have for audiovisual aids as well.

Section 1 Assessment

Visit the *Glencoe Communication Applications* Web site at **communicationapplications. glencoe.com** and click on **Self-Check and Study Guide 16.1** to review your understanding of using support materials.

Review Key Terms

1. Define the following terms and write each in a sentence: logical proof, statistic, specific instance, testimony, ethical proof, pathetic proof, amplification device.

Check Understanding

2. How might you use each of the three types of proof to persuade your local school board to make

improvements to your school's cafeteria? Give one example of each.

3. Use an amplification device to support, clarify, and extend the main point "Swimming is a great way to get in shape."

4. **Apply** Imagine that you have been asked to share with one hundred teenagers your experience volunteering at a children's camp. What audiovisual aids might you use to enhance your presentation? List at least three and describe the reasons for your choices.

APPLICATION *Activity*

Using Audiovisual Aids Using markers and posterboard, craft materials, or the computer, create one of the audiovisual aids from your answer to Question 4 above. Practice your audiovisual aid with a classmate. Was it easy to use? Did your partner easily understand it? As a class, discuss any difficulties you encountered and brainstorm possible solutions. Make any improvements that might be needed.

516   *Glencoe Communication Applications*

Section 1 Assessment Answers

1. Accept all reasonable sentences.
2. Answers may include logical: Use statistics; ethical: Tell of your own personal experience waiting in long lines at lunch; pathetic: Appeal to the school board members' memories of eating in their own school cafeterias.
3. Answers may include a description of how refreshing diving into a pool is; a comparison between another low-impact exercise and swimming; a contrast between a sport with a high rate

of injury and swimming; or an example of a local woman who improved her heart rate and blood pressure by swimming laps every day for a year.

4. Answers should reflect an understanding of choosing audiovisual aids based on the topic and audience for a presentation.

Application Activity Students' work should reflect an understanding of creating and using effective audiovisual aids.

CREATING COMPUTER GRAPHICS

This chapter describes some of the numerous techniques that you can use to support a presentation. Many speakers generate computer graphics as visual aids for presentations.

Learning the Skill

Before you create any computer graphics, you will have to make some decisions about how they will work with your presentation. Review an outline of your presentation, then decide where visual aids will support an important or difficult point. Next, decide what kind of graphic is best suited to illustrate this point. Make a rough sketch of it so you have an idea of how it should look. Add a title and necessary labels now.

When your sketch is complete, go to the *Insert* menu on your graphics program and select the option that allows you to add pictures or art to your document. Many programs will allow you to either choose from a selection of images or create your own. Select or design the image you want to use, then follow the directions on the screen to insert it into the document.

After inserting the graphic, you can change its size by clicking on and dragging one of the corners of the image. To move the graphic, click on it and drag it to the desired location.

Once you have completed your graphic, ask yourself the following questions: Is the information accurate? Does it add to the clarity of a concept? Are the labels in the right places? Is the graphic in the right place within your presentation?

Practicing the Skill

Assume you are conducting a training seminar for new employees of a chain of pizza shops. Decide what kind of graphic will work best to describe how to make a pepperoni pizza, then make a sketch of it. Perform the following steps to make your sketch into a computer graphic.

Step 1 Go to the *Insert* menu.

Step 2 Choose *Add Pictures* or *Add Art*.

Step 3 Select or create the image that you want to use.

Step 4 Insert the graphic into your presentation document by following the directions on the screen.

Step 5 If necessary, change the size or position of the graphic.

Step 1
Go to
Insert menu

Step 2
Select
Add Art or
Add Picture

Step 3
Choose
an image

Step 4
Insert
image

Step 5
Adjust
size or
position

APPLICATION *Activity*

Choose *Add Table* from your *Insert* menu. Some programs have a separate *Table* menu. Create a table that shows your school classes and after-school activities for next week. Provide the days of the week, the name of each course or activity, and the time that you will be spending on each. Use your name in the title.

Supporting Presentations **517**

Creating Computer Graphics

Point out that computer graphics can be used both for designing handouts as part of a presentation and for the preparation of one's own manuscript or notes. Presenters find that graphics serve as eye-catching cues for employing visual aids or as reminders of what to emphasize and where to pause. As well as having students use ready-made clip art, suggest that they experiment with the following graphic techniques: text boxes—which isolate and frame quotes from the main text, drawing attention to key points in the document; drop caps—elongated capital letters at the beginning of paragraphs, which add a formal elegance to a document's appearance; predesigned art for words—another attention-getter available under pictures or art in most programs.

Practicing the Skill

When positioning their graphics, students should be aware that text and images can be integrated in a number of ways. Normally, the text "wraps" around the picture, but this can be altered so that one side is open to the margin or even so that the text runs right through the image. Point out that an effective presentation will reflect a thoughtful balance between the visual and the text.

Application Activity

Before students create their tables, organize a troubleshooting seminar in which a panel of student experts gives advice on problems newcomers to computer graphics may encounter.

MEETING INDIVIDUAL NEEDS — MULTIPLE LEARNING STYLES

Intrapersonal Computer graphics can transform an ordinary page of print into an individual statement. Encourage students who respond personally to the written word to collaborate with their computer's artistic ability!

Activity Have each student choose a poem or the lyrics to a classroom-appropriate song that he or she knows and enjoys. Ask them to type out the text and to set it in two distinct ways, using computer graphics to reflect the meaning of the words. Point out that page layout, font, images, color, and borders can all contribute to the total effect. Invite students to present their personalized poems to the class. Ask them to explain which version they prefer and why.

1 FOCUS

Bellringer

Have students jot down the following incomplete sentence: _____ has real style. Give them a minute to fill in the blank with as many names as they feel fit the description. Encourage them to think of entertainers, athletes, politicians, or other well-known figures. Have students share their lists with the class. Discuss reasons why they thought of certain names. Ask how they would define style.

You may use Graphic Organizer Transparency 16–2 to introduce this section.

Visual Instruction

Answer Oral style is the way a presenter uses language to express ideas.

Communication Tip

"Clarity, clarity, clarity," wrote William Strunk Jr. and E. B. White in *The Elements of Style*. "When you become hopelessly mired in a sentence, it is best to start fresh." When a sentence gets too long and complicated, try breaking it up into two shorter ones.

Section 2

Developing Your Oral Presentation Style

GUIDE TO READING

Objectives
1. Identify the three elements of oral style.
2. Use language devices to enhance presentations.
3. Explain the relationship between oral style and presentation effectiveness.

Terms to Learn
oral style
parallelism
antithesis

*D*o you know someone who is described as "having style"? What does that mean? It probably refers to the way he or she dresses, walks, styles his or her hair, or even the way that person acts. What do you consider to be the elements of style? How can you determine and develop your own style?

Believe it or not, everyone has style. Style is simply a way of doing things. However, whether someone's style is good or bad, updated or old-fashioned, exciting or boring is up to interpretation. Everyone who comes into contact with you—as you work, play, or even give a presentation—personally evaluates your style.

ELEMENTS OF ORAL STYLE

The idea of what is stylish is determined by individual preferences. For instance, you may find a speaker terribly dull while your best friend finds the same person interesting. There are some style basics, however, that can help ensure a positive reaction. This is especially true for oral style.

Maya Angelou is well known for her oral style. What is oral style?

RESOURCE MANAGER

Teaching Tools
- Interactive Lesson Planner
- Reproducible Lesson Plan 16–2
- Application Activities 16–2

Reproducible Masters
- Guided Reading Activity Workbook 16–2
- Enrichment Activity 16–2
- Reteaching Activity 16–2
- Section Quiz 16–2
- Transparency Strategies and Activities Booklet 16–2

Transparencies
- Graphic Organizer Transparency 16–2
- Chapter 16 Teaching Transparency

Technology Resources
- Interactive Tutor Self-Assessment Software
- Presentation Plus! Software
- ExamView® Pro Testmaker
- PuzzleMaker Software
- communicationapplications.glencoe.com

Oral style is the way a presenter uses language to express ideas. All of the effort you have put into planning your presentation can be lost if the language you use is too vague or is inappropriate for your audience and task. To begin developing oral style, consider the following three elements of style:

- clarity
- force
- beauty

Clarity

Clarity is essential to effective communication. If an audience gets confused and does not understand what you are trying to say to them, your presentation is likely to be a failure. Clear word choice and clear organization are essential for presenters and audiences alike.

Word Choice The necessity of clear, easy-to-understand language can be illustrated in a true story. A plumber wrote to a government agency to ask whether there was anything wrong with using hydrochloric acid to clean out drainpipes. The agency responded, "The efficacy of hydrochloric acid is indisputable, but the corrosive effect is incompatible with metallic permanence."

The plumber thanked the agency for approving his idea. Alarmed that the plumber had misunderstood their response, the agency replied, "We cannot assume responsibility for the production of toxic and noxious residue with hydrochloric acid and suggest you use an alternate procedure."

Again, the plumber thanked the agency for its approval. Appalled by the prospect of a plumber ruining hundreds of drainpipes, the agency sent a third reply: "Don't use hydrochloric acid. It eats holes in metal pipes!"

In a presentation, you do not have the luxury of repeating a message until you are sure the audience understands. You have one chance to communicate your idea. Therefore, the language you use must be as clear and easy to understand as possible.

Word Meanings You also need to consider the meanings of the words and phrases you plan to use. Many words carry connotations that go beyond their definitions. In general, presenters tend to use dictionary definitions when their task is to inform an audience and connotations when they want to get the audience emotionally involved in a topic.

Word Order Ideas should be phrased as simply as possible. This typically means using standard subject-verb-object order so that listeners can easily understand and follow your message. Misplaced modifiers often make a message confusing for your audience. Consider this example from a newspaper headline: "Lost Sisters Reunited After Eighteen Years at Grocery Checkout Counter." In this case, word order implied

Supporting Presentations **519**

COMMUNICATION Strategies
MAKING CLEAR PRESENTATIONS

- Choose words that are not too technical or difficult for your audience to understand.
- Consider the connotations of the words you use.
- Use standard subject-verb-object sentence order as much as possible, and be sure all modifying words and phrases are as close as possible to the words they modify.
- Use perception checks to confirm audience understanding.

---

2 TEACH

COMMUNICATION Strategies
MAKING CLEAR PRESENTATIONS

Students should understand that big words and complicated sentences do not necessarily lead to more effective communication. What is important is finding the right words and using them precisely to get your point across.

Word Choice

Ask students if they can define the word *gobbledygook*. *(Meaning: "unclear, wordy language.")* Where might they typically find examples of gobbledygook? *(Students may suggest that government officials, lawyers, or people in the medical profession are prone to such language.)* Point out that most professions have their own specialized vocabulary, which is often necessary in order to communicate precisely. When communicating with the public, however, it is everyone's obligation to speak or write clearly and simply. **L1**

Guided Reading Activity 16–2

GUIDED READING Activity 16–2

Name _____ Date _____ Class _____

SUPPORTING PRESENTATIONS
Developing Your Oral Presentation Style

As you read Section 2, complete the sentences below.

The way a presenter uses language to express ideas is called 1 _____ style. To begin developing this style, you should consider 2 _____, 3 _____, and 4 _____. Clear word choice and clear 5 _____ are essential for both presenters and audiences. Word 6 _____ and word 7 _____ should also be considered so that listeners can easily understand and follow your message.

8 _____ refers to the intensity or energy of your message. A presentation may be intense or relaxed, depending upon your 9 _____ 10 _____ structure also has an effect on the force of a 11 _____ presentation.

In the context of a presentation, beauty refers to 12 _____. In order to create an image, 13 _____ element, and 14 _____. Using vivid imagery in your language makes a presentation not only more 15 _____ but also more persuasive and 16 _____.

17 _____ language can make your speech more artistic, visual, and memorable. A device used to compare two things that are essentially different but have something in common is called a 18 _____. This device usually includes the words 19 _____ or as. A 20 _____ also shows what two things have in common without using like or as, creating a vivid image in the audience's mind. Another way to add style to language is to use 21 _____, which means to personify an inanimate, or 22 _____, object by giving it human characteristics.

Your presentations can be made even more interesting through the use of two 23 _____ language devices. Rhythm helps words fit together with an almost 24 _____ style. 25 _____ is the repetition of beginning consonant sounds in a series of close or adjoining 26 _____.

Speakers often use 27 _____ questions, asked simply to achieve an 28 _____; the purpose of these questions is to state main ideas in an effort to draw the audience into the presentation. Speakers also use 29 _____, which refers to arranging sentences so that words and phrases are similar in length and structure. This is effective because it adds 30 _____ to your presentation. Finally, speakers use 31 _____, which involves pairing opposing words or ideas together.

In order to link all the ideas together in a presentation you can use 32 _____, 33 _____, previews, and summaries. These strategies are essential to you and your listeners as they attempt to follow and understand your presentation.

34 Guided Reading Activity   Glencoe Communication Applications

---

MEETING INDIVIDUAL NEEDS

MULTIPLE LEARNING STYLES

Linguistic Unclear English can be a lot of fun! Encourage students to learn about clarity and sentence structure while exercising their talents as humorous writers.

Activity Write the following statements on the chalkboard: He saw a moose standing in the pond with his binoculars. After driving a taxi all day, the dog was waiting eagerly for him at home. She jumped out of bed and chased the dog wearing her pajamas. Ask students to explain what these sentences seem to mean and what they really mean. What is wrong with them? *(In each case there is a misplaced modifier.)* Have students rewrite the sentences so that their meaning is clear. Ask them to compose five similarly amusing, but misleading, sentences. Encourage students to copy or print out their favorite sentence for display, creating a picture to illustrate its literal meaning.

Force

Students should realize that while word choice and sentence structure can contribute to the force of a presentation, the tone and volume in which one speaks can be equally important. Write the following sentence on the board: I want to see you now. Invite volunteers to read this remark in two ways, imagining first that they are talking on the telephone to a friend and second that they are parents addressing a rebellious twelve-year-old. Point out that purpose and context help establish the tone of a remark.

COMMUNICATION PRACTICE LAB

Creating Visual Images

Students may find it easier to describe their perfect day if they picture a specific place that they know well and imagine it as it would appear under ideal conditions: the front porch, my backyard in springtime, the golf course in the summer. **L2**

GLENCOE Online

For an additional Practice Lab for this section, students can visit the *Glencoe Communication Applications* Web site at **communicationapplications.glencoe.com**. Click on Communication Practice Lab 16–2. **L1**

Beauty

Point out that the word *imagery* applies to senses other than sight. While vision certainly is an important sense, there are other significant forms of imagery, all of which contribute to the beauty of language: aural (hearing), olfactory (smell), tactile (touch), and taste. **L2**

---

that the people who discovered that they were related had spent years standing in line together.

Of course, incorrect word order sometimes can have a humorous effect in a presentation. More often, however, the result of unclear phrasing is confusion and embarrassment for both you and your audience.

Force

When considering the clarity of your presentation, there really is only one goal: the clearer, the better. However, in the area of force, you have a number of choices.

Force refers to the intensity or energy of your message. A presentation may be intense or relaxed, depending upon your purpose. If you plan to make an impassioned appeal for a worthy cause, your language needs to reflect intense emotion. You might choose words like *urgent* or *struggle* to engage your listeners. On the other hand, a presentation about using yoga to relieve stress might employ words like *tranquil* and *calming* to help set the tone.

Sentence structure also can have an effect on the force of a presentation. Short, choppy sentences tend to give an audience a sense of intensity or urgency. Long, fluid sentences tend to have the opposite effect, adding a relaxed tone to a presentation.

Beauty

It is important to consider the language of your presentation as carefully as an artist considers the colors for a painting. Like an artist's colors, the language you choose can add beauty and life to your message. In the context of a presentation, beauty usually refers to the following:

- visual image
- emotion element
- sound

COMMUNICATION PRACTICE LAB

Creating Visual Images

To practice creating visual images with words, follow these steps:

Step 1 Think of your favorite season. Imagine how a perfect day at that time of year might look.

Step 2 Brainstorm a list of words or phrases to describe that day.

Step 3 Using the words from your list, write one or two paragraphs to create a visual image of that day. Imagine that your audience has never experienced this type of day before.

Step 4 Trade descriptions with a classmate. Using your partner's description, sketch a picture of what he or she described.

Step 5 Look at your classmate's drawing of your perfect day. How complete was your description? Was your language precise enough to convey the right visual image?

Step 6 As a class, discuss what kinds of words tend to create the most vivid images. Create a class list of descriptive words to use as a reference when giving presentations.

MEETING INDIVIDUAL NEEDS — MULTIPLE LEARNING STYLES

Musical Asking students to read a passage in the "wrong" tone of voice is a favorite technique of directors at auditions. For students it serves to demonstrate the power of a speaker or singer to alter the emotional effect of a presentation.

Activity Give student volunteers song lyrics or a passage to read. Then, instruct them to read the selection aloud to the class in a number of ways: a mother to her baby, a drill sergeant to a new recruit, themselves to a policeman. Advise student actors to listen to the sound of their voices rather than to the meaning of what they read. Discuss with the class which versions did most to change the effect of the original passages.

GLOBAL COMMUNICATION

Translations

If you go to work for a multinational corporation, you may be involved in manufacturing or selling products in other countries. This means that you will have to pay close attention to word meanings when you are developing product instructions, logos, or advertisements. For example, if you ask for directions to a library in France or Spain, you will probably be shown to a bookstore. Ask the foreign language teachers at your school about other translation errors that occur in international communications.

Visual Image Competent communicators work to paint pictures with their words. The visual image a presenter creates in the minds of audience members can have a tremendous impact on a presentation's effectiveness.

Think, for example, about a presentation on preserving old-growth forests. Which paints a more effective image in your mind— a description of "mighty giants, towering over the forest floor" or "really big trees"? Using vivid and descriptive imagery in your language makes a presentation not only more interesting but also more persuasive and memorable.

Emotional Element Language also has an emotional impact on an audience. For example, the word *house* tends to elicit a fairly neutral response from an audience, but the word *home* can evoke much more positive emotions. Short, rapidly spoken sentences may convey a feeling of impatience or

urgency, while longer, more leisurely spoken sentences can have a relaxing effect on an audience. As a presenter, try to choose and arrange your words to elicit an appropriate emotional response from members of your audience.

Sound Poets, in particular, know how to master the specific sound of language. Since language is based on sound, it makes sense that the acoustic appeal of language is an important element in writing and speaking. Harsh, guttural words, such as *dark* and *growling*, tend to evoke negative responses from an audience. Soft, tender words, such as *lush* and *purring*, tend to bring more positive responses. Again, choose language sounds that will add to the overall impact of your message.

Improving Your Oral Style

One way to improve your oral style for a presentation is to write parts of the presentation in manuscript form. Because writing takes longer than speaking, you will have more time to make conscious decisions about the words and phrasing you will use in your presentation. This is particularly helpful if you have some communication apprehension about what you plan to say in the introduction or the conclusion of your presentation.

USING LANGUAGE DEVICES

Now that you have read about the basic elements of oral style, what can you do to develop a style of your own? You can begin to develop your own style by incorporating figurative language and stylistic devices into your presentations.

Supporting Presentations **521**

GLOBAL COMMUNICATION

Translations

Add to the list of words that students collect from their language teachers the following: *boot, bonnet, lift, braces, pavement, purse, chips, first floor, engaged.* Inform students that they are all words also used in British English but have different meanings across the Atlantic. See how many of these meanings students can guess. *(Answers are trunk of car, hood of car, elevator, suspenders, sidewalk, handbag, French fries, second floor, busy.)*

Language Tip

Appropriately, the word used to describe ugly sounds does not have a very pretty sound itself. *Cacophony* derives from the Greek *kakos* (bad) and *phone* (sound).

Emotional Element

Point out that words are rarely interchangeable; they have shades of meaning which make them uniquely suited to certain purposes. Awaken students to this fact by writing on the board the following sentence: I was surprised when Andre [or the name of any student] suddenly walked into the room. Ask students to think of a verb to substitute for *walked* and to use it in the sentence. Remind them that there are dozens of English verbs referring to forward motion on two feet. *(A few of them are mosey, wander, stroll, strut, stagger, saunter, amble, stride, shuffle, march, hobble, limp, promenade, barge, blunder, run, race, dash, skulk, sprint, dance, sidle, and skip.)* Experiment with different verbs in this sentence. How does Andre change as his manner of walking changes? **L2**

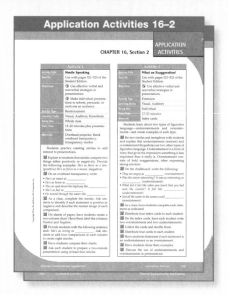

Metaphors and Analogies

Lead students to understand how metaphor can extend into analogy by writing on the chalkboard the following phrases: The ship of state; The world is a stage; This school is a zoo! Explain that each of these is a metaphor and that each can be extended into further metaphors to become analogies. Ask students to describe what the people represent in each of the metaphors. *(Answer: The people are, respectively, sailors, actors, and animals.)* Choose one of the metaphors on the board and ask the class to extend the analogy as far as they can. (Students might say that the ship's officers represent elected officials; the ordinary sailors are the voters; the ship's sails are the structures of government; the changing ocean represents the historical times through which the country passes.)
L3

■ **Visual Instruction**

Answer Analogies are effective to use when explaining a concept or process that is new to the audience.

Figurative Language

Figurative language can make your speech more artistic, visual, and memorable. Similes, metaphors, and personification are three effective ways to add interest to presentations.

Similes A simile is a device used to compare two things that are essentially different but that have something in common. A simile usually includes the word *like* or *as*, for example, "ran like the wind" or "white as snow." This type of comparison is very effective for helping an audience relate something it knows little about to something with which it is more familiar.

Be careful, however, when you use similes in your presentation. Some similes have been overused and sometimes can make a presentation seem somewhat stale. These include similes such as "fresh as a daisy," "fit as a fiddle," "busy as a bee," and "happy as a lark."

Metaphors A metaphor is a different kind of device for showing what two things have in common. Unlike a simile, however, a metaphor does not use the word *like* or *as*. Rather, a metaphor literally substitutes one kind of object or idea for another to suggest similarity. For example, "Her hands were ice cubes" and "a pillow of air" are metaphors. Metaphors tend to be subtler than similes, and, therefore, may not always be universally understood. However, a well-phrased metaphor can create a vivid image in the mind of your audience.

Sometimes, a single metaphor can be expanded and developed throughout an entire section of a presentation. These extended metaphors are called analogies. Analogies are effective tools to use when you are explaining a concept or process that is completely new to your audience. By comparing the entire idea or process to something that the audience already knows, you will increase their understanding of your message.

Personification Another way to add style to your language is to use personification. You personify an inanimate, or nonliving, object by giving it human characteristics. Shown in **Figure 16–5**, "The wind whispered through the trees" assigns the human characteristic of whispering to an inanimate object, the wind. Ronald Reagan personified the government when he said, "Government growing beyond our consent had become a lumbering giant, slamming shut the gates of opportunity, threatening to crush the very roots of our freedom."

Personification is useful for adding interest and intensity to your language. It also can help you relate even the most abstract concept to audience members by giving that concept familiar human traits.

Learning about language devices helps a speaker develop oral style.
When is an analogy effective in a presentation?

INCLUSION STRATEGIES

MEETING INDIVIDUAL NEEDS

Learning Disabilities Music is a stimulating means of learning for many students. Point out that songs are full of the rich, figurative language that contributes to effective communication. For example, Paul Simon's lyric "Like a bridge over troubled water, I will lay me down" is a simile that students can visualize.

Activity Have students bring to school recordings of classroom-appropriate songs that contain figurative language. Ask them to play their examples and to identify one or more figures of speech in the songs. Discuss with students what the phrases mean and how else the songwriters might have expressed themselves. Encourage them to illustrate one of the figures of speech as a reinforcement activity.

■ **Figure 16–5 Personification of Wind**

Stylistic Devices

Your presentations can be made even more interesting through the use of stylistic language devices. Stylistic devices add appeal to your ideas through the use of sound. Two of the most effective stylistic devices are rhythm and alliteration.

Rhythm Rhythm doesn't necessarily add to the meaning of a message. However, it can add appeal to your presentation. Rhythm helps words fit together with an almost musical style. Jesse Jackson, an American activist, minister, and gifted speaker, is well known for his use of rhythm, as well as other stylistic devices, in his speech. One of Jackson's most popular quotes is, "If [today's students] can conceive it and believe it, they can achieve it. They must know it is not their aptitude but their attitude that will determine their altitude." By carefully sequencing words to develop an interesting

string of sounds, Jackson enhances the impact and memorability of his words and ideas. You can do the same through the use of rhythm in your presentations.

Of course, a presentation is not a poem and, therefore, should not emphasize sound and rhythm at the expense of meaning. The meaning of your message should always take priority over style, but rhythm can add great acoustic appeal when used sparingly.

Alliteration A good way to make your ideas easy for your audience to remember is to use alliteration. Alliteration is the repetition of beginning consonant sounds in a series of close or adjoining words.

"The serpent slithered silently" is a particularly effective use of alliteration. Not only does the repeated *s* sound make an impact, but it also mimics the hissing sound classically associated with snakes. You probably remember many of the tongue twisters you learned as a child because of the alliteration they use.

Used sparingly, alliteration can add interest to your presentation and make it more appealing to your audience. Too much alliteration, on the other hand, can have an unintentionally humorous effect. It may draw so much attention to itself that the meaning of your message gets lost.

Rhetorical Devices

Rhetoric is a skilled, effective use of speech. A rhetorical device, then, is a tool for making speech more effective. These special tools,

Supporting Presentations **523**

REAL-WORLD CONNECTION

Language Devices on the Air Students should be aware that effective communicators all employ language devices to strengthen their presentations. Point out that a sports broadcast or situation comedy is as likely to provide examples as is a political speech.

Activity Have students take note of presentations on TV or radio over the course of a few days. Ask them to copy down five examples of language devices used by the presenters or actors. Beside each entry, make sure that students identify the speaker, date, and time. Have students share their findings with the class.

Grammar Tip

Parallelism is important within the syntax of a sentence as well as in a presentation. When comparing two activities, for instance, keep them grammatically parallel: Faulty: To swim is more fun than playing baseball. Correct: Swimming is more fun than playing baseball.

Communication Tip

Creating an effective summary requires careful thought. The presenter's aim should be to review the contents of the presentation without repeating words and phrases contained in the preview. Don't use all your best ideas in the opening paragraph. Save a powerful statement for the conclusion.

Transitions

Have students copy down the following terms: *meanwhile, next, below, opposite, second, more importantly, as a result, for that reason, similarly, in the same way, for example, namely.* Point out that these are all words and phrases that can be used as transitions. Have students find partners and give them ten minutes to write pairs of sentences, linking the second sentence to the first with an appropriate transition from their list. When time is up, ask students to copy on the chalkboard their best pair of sentences. Discuss their examples and the role of transitions in effective communication. **L2**

■ **Figure 16–6 Rhetorical Devices**

Rhetorical Questions:	Questions asked for effect to encourage listener participation.
Parallelism:	Arranging sentences so words or phrases are similar in structure and length to add rhythm to presentation.
Antithesis:	Pairing opposing words and ideas to produce clever or memorable phrases.

shown in **Figure 16–6**, not only can help you make your ideas clearer, but they also can help make your speech more memorable to your audience.

Rhetorical Questions As you read in Chapter 15, a rhetorical question is a question asked simply to achieve an effect. It is not intended to be answered aloud. Speakers often use rhetorical questions to state their main ideas in an effort to draw the audience into a presentation. Even though audience members don't answer a rhetorical question aloud, they are likely to form a mental response. In this way, a rhetorical question encourages listeners' participation in a topic.

Parallelism Presenters use parallelism to add structure and rhythm to a presentation. Parallelism is arranging sentences so that words and phrases are similar in length and structure. For example, two or more sentences may begin with the same noun, each may begin with a gerund, or each may contain the same prepositional phrase.

In some cases, parallelism is as simple as repeating a key word or statement throughout a topic point or an entire presentation. In his "I Have a Dream" speech, Martin Luther King Jr. used the phrases "I have a dream" and "Let freedom ring" as parallel elements. So effective were these devices that they have

become icons for the civil rights movement in the United States.

Parallel structure is effective because it adds rhythm to your presentation. As you read earlier, rhythm helps make your ideas more memorable. It also can make your presentation clearer and more enjoyable for an audience.

Antithesis A third type of rhetorical device is antithesis. Antithesis involves pairing opposing words or ideas together. It has long been a favorite of accomplished presenters because it tends to produce clever, memorable phrases. "Sink or swim" is a famous example of antithesis.

You may be thinking that oral style is great for famous speakers who make many presentations. However, even an everyday presentation can be livened up with a little creative style. Whatever you can do to help your audience enjoy and remember your words will bring you closer to achieving the overall goal of your presentation.

Developing Continuity

Once you have developed your main ideas and have experimented with the language you want to use in your presentation, you need to decide how to link your ideas together for your audience. You can do this by using the following tools:

- transitions
- signposts
- previews and summaries

Transitions As you learned earlier in Chapter 15, smooth transitions help you and your audience move effortlessly through your presentation. A clear transition (1) clarifies the relationship between the two thoughts it bridges, (2) brings closure to

INCLUSION STRATEGIES

Less-Proficient Readers Lead students to understand that transitional words and phrases are used in all forms of writing and speech. They are what make words and ideas flow smoothly. **Activity** Have students bring to class copies of magazines or newspapers that they enjoy reading. On the chalkboard, write a list of commonly used transitional words and phrases, such as *then, in addition, as a result*. Ask students to read their material silently, noting any of the words listed on the board that they believe are used to indicate a transition. (Encourage them to note any other transitional words they discover.) Ask volunteers to read their examples.

the previous point before beginning the next, and (3) alerts the listener that you are changing points.

The language of transitions includes transitional adverbs and conjunctions. "Having just seen . . . let's proceed," "On the other hand," "In addition," and "Finally," are all transitional phrases that are used to begin statements that bridge ideas together. Rhetorical questions can also be used to link one idea to another. "If this is really true, then what about . . . ?"

A transition may relate to what has just been said and may serve as a summary before going on to the next idea. For example, Raymond Smith, in his presentation on Cyberhate, uses this summary type of transition when he says, "Internet access alone, however, won't build bridges of understanding between people—or level the playing field between cyberhaters and the targets of their hate." He summarizes one idea, Internet access, but lets the audience know that more about creating understanding between people is to follow.

You can think of more transition strategies as you write your presentation and encounter the shifts and ideas that need linking. If you develop your statements and restatements carefully, clear transitions usually emerge naturally.

Signposts Signposts label main ideas as main ideas. In some cases this is as simple as saying, "My first point is . . . ," "My second point is . . . ," and so forth. Katherine Clark in her presentation *The Great Equalizers* simply numbers her main points 1, 2, 3, and so on and uses the numbers in her presentation as signposts.

Some transitional adverbs also stand alone as signposts. "Next," "Second," and "Finally," each can stand alone to signal a new idea. If all your main ideas (and nothing else) are stated as rhetorical questions, your audience should catch on fairly quickly that every time you ask a rhetorical question, you are beginning a new idea.

Previews and Summaries Previews and summaries can also be used to provide listening cues or memory hooks for your audience. If you follow the tradition of "tell them what you're going to tell them, tell them, and then tell them what you've told them," then you already know the importance of previews (tell them what you're going to tell them) and summaries (tell them what you've told them). Previews and summaries help an audience to follow your presentation and prevent them from getting lost in the information.

Internal previews can provide listening cues for your audience. If, for example, you have divided a main point explaining a problem into two sub-points, you may want to preview the sub-points to let the audience know what to listen for. "As I discuss this problem, I will focus on the conditions that underlie the problem and their causes." As a different preview, you could say, "I want you

interNET
ACTIVITY

I Have a Dream Dr. Martin Luther King Jr.'s equal rights speech presented in Washington, D.C., in 1963 is one of the most compelling and eloquent speeches of the twentieth century. You can access the text of this speech on the Internet by entering the phrase *I Have a Dream* into a search engine. Read the speech and identify examples of figurative language, stylistic devices, and rhetorical devices.

Supporting Presentations **525**

Reteaching Activity 16–2

RETEACHING
Activity 16-2

SUPPORTING PRESENTATIONS
Developing Your Oral Presentation Style

Enrichment Activity 16–2

ENRICHMENT
Activity 16-2

SUPPORTING PRESENTATIONS
Developing Your Oral Presentation Style

4 CLOSE

Have students review their responses to the Bellringer on page 518. Based on their reading in this section, students should explain whether they would now modify their definition of style.

Extra-Credit Project

Remind students that they are listening to presentations from teachers, administrators, and fellow students all day long. Have them make a record of ten language devices or other elements of oral style included in this chapter that they identify over the course of a week in school, noting the speaker's exact words, the subject, date, and time. Have students share their observations.

526

---

to consider three causes for this problem." In either instance, you are giving the audience a clue as to what you want them to get from the point.

Internal summaries keep the audience from getting lost during your presentation. It gives the audience a chance to catch up with you and refreshes their memory about what you just said that was important. Internal summaries are often used just before the last point of a presentation to summarize the content to that point. It keeps the audience

focused on what you want them to take as important from your presentation.

Effective transitions, signposts, and internal previews and summaries are evidence of clarity in speaking. These are strategies that can prove to be useful in your writing, but they are essential to you and your listeners as they attempt to follow and understand your presentation. The skillful use of these strategies indicates that you fully appreciate the value of a clear, polished presentation style and that you recognize your audience's hard work.

Section 2 Assessment

GLENCOE
Online

Visit the *Glencoe Communication Applications* Web site at **communicationapplications. glencoe.com** and click on **Self-Check and Study Guide 16.2** to review your understanding of oral presentation style.

Review Key Terms

1. Define the following terms and write each in a sentence: oral style, parallelism, antithesis.

Check Understanding

2. Identify and describe the three elements of oral style.

3. Choose a language device and use it to enhance a presentation on roller coasters.

4. **Predict** How might oral style make a difference in the effectiveness of a presentation?

APPLICATION *Activity*

Developing Oral Style As a class, brainstorm a list of presentation topics. Choose one of the topics and create an example of each type of language device for that topic. Share your examples as a class. Discuss which language devices were the most difficult to use and which were the easiest. Work together to develop helpful tips for creating language devices.

Section 2 Assessment Answers

1. Accept all reasonable sentences.
2. Clarity can be achieved by careful word choice and word order; force refers to the intensity or energy of a message; beauty refers to the visual images, emotions, and sounds that words can create.
3. Accept all reasonable answers that reflect students' understanding of simile, metaphor, personification, rhythm and rhyme, alliteration, rhetorical questions, parallelism, or antithesis.

4. Oral style makes presentations more enjoyable and memorable for an audience, helping a speaker achieve his or her overall presentation goal.

Application Activity Some students may find metaphors more difficult than similes and some may have difficulty using parallelism. Tips should reflect the proper use of language devices.

Supporting Presentations

How Do You Rate?

On a separate sheet of paper, use the key to respond to the following statements. Put a check mark at the end of each skill you would like to improve.

KEY: A Always   **R** Rarely
       U Usually   **N** Never
       S Sometimes

1. When I develop ideas, I introduce, amplify and support, and then restate them.

2. I try to balance evidence that supports my ideas by using logic, personal experiences, and emotional appeals.

3. When I amplify an idea, I use vivid descriptions and examples.

4. I use visual aids to give my presentation clarity, interest, and appeal.

5. I know when a model, videotape, graph, or pictorial image is the best means of supporting an idea.

6. My presentation skills include knowing where to put audiovisual materials and using audience feedback to assess their effectiveness.

7. My presentation style is clear because I use words my audience can understand and sentences that are concise and clearly constructed.

8. To involve the audience, I pair opposing words or ideas, ask rhetorical questions, and use sentences of similar length and structure.

How Do You Score?

Review your responses. Give yourself 5 points for every A, 4 for every U, 3 for every S, 2 for every R, and 1 for every N. Total your points and evaluate your score.

31–40 Excellent You may be surprised to find out how much you can improve your skills.

21–30 Good In this course, you can learn ways to make your skills better.

11–20 Fair Practice applying the skills taught in this course.

1–10 Needs Improvement Carefully monitor your improvement as you work through this course.

Setting Communication Goals

If you scored Excellent or Good, complete Part A. If your score was Fair or Needs Improvement, complete Part B.

Part A 1. I plan to put the following ideas into practice:

       2. I plan to share the following information about communication with the following people:

Part B 1. The behaviors I need to change most are:

       2. To bring about these changes, I will take these steps:

Supporting Presentations **527**

Have students respond to the ten statements using the key, then evaluate their listening strengths. Based on their scores, assign either Part A or Part B of the goal-setting activity. On an index card or sheet of paper, students should concretely define their communication goals to improve their current level of skill.

Communication Journal Activity

Many skills are required to support an effective presentation. Students need speaking and writing skills, experience with research procedures and technical equipment, and the good judgment to predict how an audience will respond to their efforts. Suggest that in their Communication Journals students describe one area in which they feel they need the most work and another in which they feel comfortable. Have them write a paragraph explaining each of their choices.

Communication Tip

Students should understand that the most important element of their presentation is themselves. They must never lose sight of who they are and what they believe. Audiences will forgive technical imperfections if a presenter comes across as a real person: genuine, informed, and committed to the task.

MEETING INDIVIDUAL NEEDS

INCLUSION STRATEGIES

Special Needs Point out that creating visual aids is an important skill in preparing for a presentation. Students with limited mobility can use a computer to help them create visual aids.

Activity Have students review their understanding of the skills described in this chapter as well as the results of the self-assessment activity printed on this page. Based on this information, ask them to use a computer to design a graph or chart profiling their own abilities in key areas. This should give a visual indication of their strengths and weaknesses in supporting presentations. Students' profiles should be visually arresting and easy to understand.

Writing a Thank-You Letter

Objective: To create a thank-you letter

Teaching Suggestions and Strategies

Connection to the Workplace

Students wondering why thank-you letters still exist in a world of telephones and e-mails should understand that the letter represents physical evidence of the writer's gratitude. It takes time to carefully compose a letter, to type it, fold it, put it in an envelope, and mail it. These simple actions combined represent a gift of time and thought from the writer to the recipient. In an age where time is increasingly money, this is no small sacrifice.

Lead students to understand that the thank-you letter also serves another purpose, making it as valuable to the writer as to the recipient. Writing a letter to a possible employer after an interview, for instance, puts your name back on the interviewer's desk. Likewise, thanking donors or volunteers for their support is crucial to their continued involvement. There are many generous people in the world, willing to work for no money. Very few of them will work for no thanks!

Grammar Tip

Two or more separate adjectives before a noun are separated by commas, except when the last adjective seems almost part of the noun itself. (Examples: sudden, surprising news; sudden bad news) If the two adjectives work together to modify the noun, they are often hyphenated. (Example: late-breaking news)

Communication Through Writing

Writing a Thank-You Letter

A thank-you letter is a way of expressing gratitude for a gift or an opportunity. It serves as a way to strengthen a professional relationship. For example, a recent high school or college graduate might write a thank-you letter to a possible employer after an interview. A supervisor might write a thank-you letter to an employee to show appreciation for a job done well. The procedure for writing a thank-you letter follows.

Use a Business Letter Format. The format for a thank-you letter is the same as that of a business letter, which was presented in Chapter 5. Start the note with a heading that includes your address and the date. The inside address, which consists of the name and address of the recipient, follows the heading. The salutation, or greeting, comes after the inside address and is followed by a colon. The next segment of the thank-you letter is the body, which contains the main part of your message. The closing comes after the body and may contain words like *Sincerely*, *Respectfully*, or *With warm regard*. Capitalize the first letter and place a comma after the closing. Follow this with your signature and typed name.

Organize Your Ideas. Use the principles of outlining presented in Chapter 15. Cluster your thoughts and brainstorm about what you want to say. Begin by stating your reason for writing. Explain the details, facts, and ideas you want to cover in the body of the letter. In the last paragraph of the letter, mention something that will help to build and develop your professional relationship with the other person.

Personalize the Letter. Sometimes, it is necessary to write to several people at the same time. When you do this, it is important to personalize each thank-you letter. You can do this by acknowledging your last contact with the person. You can also personalize each thank-you letter by passing along a greeting to the person's family or co-workers, if you have met them.

Be Sincere. Reinforce the notion that you are honest and your reader can trust you. If you are insincere or deceitful, you may offend your audience.

Create a Good Impression. Check your letter for mistakes. Use correct grammar, and do not misspell any words, especially names. It is worth the extra time and effort to proofread all parts of your letter. This extra step shows that you care about what you do.

For additional information about business writing, see the *Guide to Business Communication* section of the Communication Survival Kit in the Appendix.

REAL-WORLD CONNECTION

Writing Skills in the Business World Business leaders frequently comment about the need for better communication skills in young people, but students do not often have the opportunity to hear firsthand the basis for their remarks and complaints.

Activity Invite a local businessperson to speak to your class on the various forms of writing that his or her activities involve. Prepare transparencies of typical examples beforehand and have students come up with questions about the writing skills most employers look for in job applicants. Encourage a question and answer session about the importance of communication skills in the business world.

Ms. Audrey Whitstone
Sunnyside Hospital
5514 Alameda Street
Los Angeles, CA 90036

October 30, 2002

Mrs. Walter Maier
3515 Welcome Street
Huntington Beach, CA 92647

Dear Mrs. Maier:

I am writing to thank you for your support of our fall fund-raiser. Your attendance and financial contribution will surely help with our efforts to build a new children's wing.

As you know, we are committed to providing quality health care for children in a pleasant, home-like environment. Your attendance at our fund-raiser will go a long way toward making this dream possible. With revenues from the fund-raiser, we are now three-fourths of the way toward our goal. The care and concern shown by people like you have made a considerable difference in funding this project.

Mrs. Maier, we are grateful for your ten years of faithful service to Sunnyside Hospital and hope to see you at our December luncheon to honor patrons like you.

Sincerely,
Audrey Whitstone
Audrey Whitstone
Director of Development

 WRITING *Activity*

Assume that you are a member of a professional teaching organization. The organization has asked you to write a thank-you letter to a recent guest speaker. Write a thank-you letter using the following information. Use today's date and your own name and address. Make your letter as positive and personalized as possible.

- Your organization is called the National Teaching Association.

- Your group held its annual meeting last month in Washington, D.C.

- The name of the speaker was Wylie Butler. His address is 284 Connecticut Avenue, Washington, D.C. 20028.

- The topic of the speech was "Computers in the Classroom."

- The speaker appeared at a previous convention.

- A handbook summarizing the speaker's information was given to all of the teachers at the convention.

- Many teachers you have spoken to have already had great success using the speaker's suggestions.

GRAMMAR PRACTICE

Adjectives Before a Noun
Have students write the adjectives, inserting commas or hyphens as needed. If no comma is necessary, write N.

We received a five page letter yesterday. *(five-page; N)*

What a nasty young man! *(nasty young; N)*

Why don't you sell that rusty dilapidated car? *(rusty, dilapidated)*

Your brilliant emotional argument changed the jury's mind. *(brilliant emotional; N)*

He's taking a well-deserved vacation. *(well-deserved; N)*

Communication Through Writing

Teaching Activity
Ask students how many of them have ever received acknowledgment for their services in a thank-you letter. How did it make them feel? Have them read the letter printed on this page and ask them to put themselves in the position of Mrs. Maier, the donor who is thanked for her contribution to Sunnyside Hospital. Inform them that Mrs. Maier replied with a letter of her own. Have them compose the response they believe she would have sent.

WRITING *Activity*

Students' responses to this activity should be in business letter format. The body of the letter may be similar to the one provided here:

I am writing to thank you for your contribution to the National Teaching Association's annual convention, held in Washington, D.C., last month. The information you presented in your "Computers in the Classroom" seminar has been extremely useful. After the presentation you delivered to last year's convention, we were very pleased to have you return.

Your speech was informative and inspirational. It pleases our organization to know that there are people throughout the nation who are dedicated to bringing technology to our schools. Your handbooks were a wonderful gift. We have already seen great results using your methods.

It has been our pleasure to have you as our guest at these past two conventions. I hope you will consider speaking at one of our conferences again in the future.

Additional Resources
Appendix, "Guide to Business Communication"

Glencoe Writer's Assistant CD-ROM

Glencoe Interactive Grammar Software

Grade 9 Writer's Choice, Unit 1 Case Study

GLENCOE TECHNOLOGY

MindJogger Videoquiz

Use *MindJogger* to review the Chapter 16 content.

Visit the *Glencoe Communication Applications* Web site at **communicationapplications. glencoe.com** and click on **Chapter 16 Activity** for additional practice in developing and supporting your ideas.

Oceanography from Space
Global Ocean Color

Reviewing Key Terms

1. **False;** A <u>logical</u> proof adds the strongest support to a point.

2. **False;** A <u>statistic</u> is proof presented as a number.

3. **True**

4. **False;** A direct quote or summary of a quote is called a <u>testimony</u>.

5. **True**

6. **False;** A <u>pathetic</u> proof gives emotional appeal to a presentation.

7. **False;** A <u>description</u> is a kind of <u>amplification device</u>.

8. **False;** Oral style is the way a presenter uses <u>language to express ideas</u>.

9. **True**

10. **False;** <u>Antithesis</u> involves pairing opposing words.

Reviewing Key Concepts

1. Well-developed and supported main ideas can convince an audience of a presenter's credibility. They will also help a presenter educate his or her audience and overcome any barriers that may exist between presenter and audience.

2. To reduce large amounts of information into general categories; to emphasize the size or amount of something; to indicate trends.

Reviewing Key Terms

On a separate sheet of paper, write whether each statement below is true or false. Rewrite each false statement, deleting the term that makes it false and underlining the term that you substitute.

1. A pathetic proof adds the strongest support to a point.

2. A testimony is a type of proof presented as a number.

3. Specific instances tend to relate information more personally than statistics.

4. A direct quote or summary of a quote is called a specific instance.

5. The most common ethical proof is personal experience.

6. A logical proof gives emotional appeal to a presentation.

7. A verbal description is a kind of audiovisual aid.

8. Oral style is the way a presenter uses objects.

9. Arranging sentences so phrases are similar in length and structure is called parallelism.

10. Alliteration involves pairing opposing words.

Reviewing Key Concepts

1. Why is the way a presenter develops and supports his or her main points important?

2. For what three purposes can statistics be used in a presentation?

3. When is expert testimony particularly effective for establishing credibility?

4. Why should a presenter avoid overusing pathetic proofs?

5. Name four kinds of amplification devices.

6. In what five ways do audiovisual aids enhance a presentation?

7. How can a presenter keep a model or live object from distracting the audience's attention from his or her message?

8. What kind of graph best illustrates the relationship between two or more trends?

3. When a presenter knows little about a topic.

4. Listeners may be skeptical of presenters who use emotional arguments instead of logical ones. They may not appreciate appeals to negative emotions.

5. Descriptions, comparisons, contrasts, examples

6. Audiovisual aids enhance clarity, interest, retention, professionalism, and presenter support.

7. By keeping them out of sight when not in use.

8. A bar graph

Assessment and Activities

Reading and Critical Thinking Skill

1. **Making Comparisons** Compare the use of comparisons and contrasts as amplification devices.

2. **Classifying Information** In what category of audiovisual aids does a videotape belong?

3. **Summarization** Sum up the three ways to give your oral style clarity.

4. **Applying Information** Write a sentence that will give an audience a sense of urgency about preserving the environment.

5. **Synthesis** Create a passage for a presentation on how to preserve the environment by using two of the three rhetorical devices—rhetorical questions, parallelism, and antithesis.

Skill Practice Activity

Writing an Outline At the top of a separate sheet of paper, write the thesis statement "How can our environment be preserved?" Then, make an outline using phrases rather than sentences. List your main ideas six lines apart and number them with Roman numerals. Add supporting ideas, beginning with capital letters. Then, add details with numbers and more specific details with lowercase letters. Remember to indent each level of the outline.

Cooperative Learning Activity

Presenting Visual Aids As a class, organize into pairs. With your partner, pool the information in your outlines from the Skill Practice Activity. Next, brainstorm a list of the kinds of visuals that would support points in the outlines. Then, you and your partner each choose a way to present the visual aids from the following list: flip charts/poster boards, transparencies, slides, handouts, video/audio cassettes, and computerized displays. Create your visual aid and display it in the classroom beside your partner's work.

Chapter Project

Planning Find the words to a memorable speech, such as Abraham Lincoln's Gettysburg Address, Martin Luther King Jr.'s "I Have a Dream" Speech, or any other powerful speech. As you read the speech, look for the following language devices: similes, metaphors, personification, rhythm and rhyme, alliteration, rhetorical questions, parallelism, and antithesis.

Presenting On a poster, glue an enlarged copy of the speech you chose. Mark the examples of different language devices with different colored highlighters. Make a key at the bottom of the poster to show which color represents which device. Present your poster to the class, pointing out the various language devices. Display the poster in the classroom.

Supporting Presentations **531**

Reading and Critical Thinking Skill

1. **Making Comparisons** Comparisons and contrasts are both amplification devices, which a presenter uses in order to explain an idea by drawing attention to how it is alike or unlike another idea.

2. **Classifying Information** Videotapes are pictorial reproductions.

3. **Summarization** Students should summarize the importance of word choice, word meanings, and word order.

4. **Applying Information** Encourage students to review Section 2 for elements of oral style or for language devices that would give urgency to their statement.

5. **Synthesis** Accept reasonable responses. For example, rhetorical question: Are we willing to allow global warming to change our weather patterns?; antithesis: Life or death—that's what many species of primates are facing.

Skill Practice Activity

Writing an Outline

Students should use the traditional outline format—roman numerals for major divisions, capital letters for subcategories, Arabic numerals for subheads, and lowercase letters for minor heads. Each secondary head category should be indented under the primary head it follows.

Cooperative Learning Activity

Presenting Visual Aids

Students' choice of visual aids must be related to the subject of their outline and be the economical, space-related, and context-appropriate choice for their presentation. For example, a small-group presentation about endangered species might include magazine pictures of the species on a poster.

Chapter Project

Point out that the art of speech making is nothing new. The Greek philosopher Aristotle (384–322 B.C.) wrote extensively on the subject of oral presentation. Many of his instructions are still considered good practice. Students should realize that libraries have anthologies of famous speeches going back to ancient days. They may be interested to discover that the same devices they have studied in this chapter have been used for millennia by the world's greatest orators. If a speech is too long to be mounted conveniently on posterboard, have students enlarge an excerpt from it that includes the principal language devices they found. Encourage students to practice delivering their speeches in the style they feel the original orator might have used. Invite volunteers to perform their speeches for the class.

Chapter 17 Planning Guide

SECTION RESOURCES

Daily Objectives	Reproducible Resources	Multimedia Resources
Section 1 1. Describe when manuscript delivery is the best choice for a presentation 2. Summarize the advantages and disadvantages of extemporaneous and impromptu deliveries 3. Choose the best delivery method for a given situation	Reproducible Lesson Plan 17-1 Application Activities 17-1 Guided Reading Workbook Activity 17-1 Vocabulary Activity 17* Reteaching Activity 17-1* Enrichment Activity 17-1* Graphic Organizer Transparency Strategies and Activities 17-1	Graphic Organizer Transparency 17-1 Chapter 17 Teaching Transparency Interactive Tutor Self-Assessment PuzzleMaker ExamView® Pro Testmaker Interactive Lesson Planner Communication in Action Video Chapter 17 MindJogger communicationapplications.glencoe.com Presentation Plus!
Section 2 1. Identify and describe the four special types of group presentations 2. Analyze the appropriateness of each type of group presentation in a given context 3. Prepare, organize, and participate in a group presentation for an audience	Reproducible Lesson Plan 17-2 Application Activities 17-2 Guided Reading Workbook Activity 17-2 Vocabulary Activity 17* Reteaching Activity 17-2* Enrichment Activity 17-2* Graphic Organizer Transparency Strategies and Activities 17-2	Graphic Organizer Transparency 17-2 Chapter 17 Teaching Transparency Interactive Tutor Self-Assessment PuzzleMaker ExamView® Pro Testmaker Interactive Lesson Planner Communication in Action Video Chapter 17 MindJogger communicationapplications.glencoe.com Presentation Plus!
Section 3 1. Identify the factors that can contribute to communication apprehension 2. Utilize strategies to manage communication apprehension, build self-confidence, and gain command of information 3. Develop strategies to rehearse presentations	Reproducible Lesson Plan 17-3 Application Activities 17-3 Guided Reading Workbook Activity 17-3 Vocabulary Activity 17* Reteaching Activity 17-3* Enrichment Activity 17-3* Graphic Organizer Transparency Strategies and Activities 17-3	Graphic Organizer Transparency 17-3 Chapter 17 Teaching Transparency Interactive Tutor Self-Assessment PuzzleMaker ExamView® Pro Testmaker Interactive Lesson Planner Communication in Action Video Chapter 17 MindJogger communicationapplications.glencoe.com Presentation Plus!

* Also available in Spanish

Chapter 17 Planning Guide

Chapter 17 Resource Manager

The following materials may be used when teaching the chapter. Materials for specific lessons are also shown at point-of-use in the margins of the Teacher's Wraparound Edition.

TEACHING TRANSPARENCIES

Chapter 17 Teaching Transparency

Graphic Organizer Transparency 17-1

Graphic Organizer Transparency 17-2

Graphic Organizer Transparency 17-3

APPLICATION ACTIVITIES

Chapter 17, Section 1

Chapter 17, Section 2

Chapter 17, Section 3

Chapter 17, Cumulative

REINFORCEMENT AND REVIEW ACTIVITIES

Vocabulary Activity 17

Guided Reading Activity Workbook 17-1, 17-2, 17-3

Reteaching Activities 17-1, 17-2, 17-3

Chapter 17 Resource Manager

ASSESSMENT AND EVALUATION

Section Quizzes 17-1, 17-2, 17-3

Chapter 17 Test, Forms A & B

Performance Assessment Activity 17

ENRICHMENT AND EXTENSION

Technology Application Activity 17

Enrichment Activities 17-1, 17-2, 17-3

ORAL PRESENTATION ACTIVITIES

Activities 6, 8–10, 13, 14

SPANISH RESOURCES

- Spanish Chapter and Unit Tests
- Spanish Vocabulary Activities
- Spanish Section Quizzes
- Spanish Reteaching Activities
- Spanish Enrichment Activities

MULTIMEDIA

- Interactive Tutor Self-Assessment
- ExamView® Pro Testmaker
- PuzzleMaker
- Communication in Action Videodisc and Videocassette
- MindJogger
- Interactive Lesson Planner
- Presentation Plus!
- Writer's Assistant
- Glencoe Interactive Grammar
- **communicationapplications.glencoe.com**

TEACHER PLANNING AND SUPPORT

- Reproducible Lesson Plans
- Interactive Lesson Planner
- Presentation Plus!

CHAPTER **17** Preparing for Presentations

"There are no secrets to success. It is the result of preparation, hard work, and learning from failure."
—Colin Powell, retired U.S. Army General

WHY IT'S IMPORTANT

Preparation is important for success in many arenas, including presentations. Working to plan your speeches before you make them will help you meet your presentation goals.

To better understand the final steps in preparing a presentation, view the **Communication in Action** Chapter 17 video lesson.

WHY IT'S IMPORTANT

Have students read the quotation on this page. Ask: **Why might General Powell have included "learning from failure" as one of the three elements in his analysis of success?** *(Students may respond that few people succeed in their endeavors the first time or that failure points out the areas in which one needs to prepare more carefully.)* Lead students to understand that careful preparation will reduce the necessity of learning from failure.

Section 1

Preparing for Individual Presentations

GUIDE TO READING

Objectives

1. Describe when manuscript delivery is the best choice for a presentation.
2. Summarize the advantages and disadvantages of extemporaneous and impromptu deliveries.
3. Choose the best delivery method for a given situation.
4. Prepare notes and manuscripts for presentations.

Terms to Learn

method of delivery
manuscript presentation
extemporaneous presentation
impromptu presentation

Have you ever tried to repeat a funny story to some friends, only to discover that they failed to see the humor in it? That kind of thing can disappoint and bewilder you. The story was so funny when you first heard it. What happened?

Why didn't your friends laugh? The chances are good that the problem was the way you told the story. Much of the meaning of a message is in the way it is presented to an audience. If you want the audience to react in a certain way to a message, it's important to select the right way to present it.

SELECTING A METHOD OF DELIVERY

So far, you have worked to develop the message of your presentation. Now you need to select the best possible way of getting your idea across to your audience. In other words, it's time to select a method of

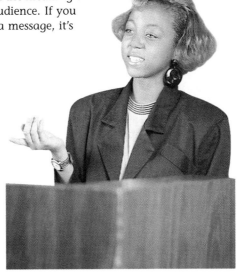

The success of a presentation can be determined by the preparation. What determines how an audience receives a message?

Preparing for Presentations **533**

Bellringer
Discuss with students the questions in the opening paragraph. Ask them whether they think the ability to tell a story well is a gift or a skill. How would they rate their own storytelling ability on a scale of one to ten? Invite volunteers who rated themselves highly to tell a short anecdote. Discuss their presentations with the class.

You may use Graphic Organizer Transparency 17–1 to introduce this section.

Visual Instruction

Answer The method of delivery as well as the message itself help determine how an audience receives a message.

RESOURCE MANAGER

Teaching Tools

- Interactive Lesson Planner
- Reproducible Lesson Plan 17–1
- Application Activities 17–1

Reproducible Masters

- Guided Reading Activity Workbook 17–1
- Enrichment Activity 17–1
- Reteaching Activity 17–1
- Section Quiz 17–1
- Transparency Strategies and Activities Booklet 17–1

Transparencies

- Graphic Organizer Transparency 17–1
- Chapter 17 Teaching Transparency

Technology Resources

- Interactive Tutor Self-Assessment Software
- Presentation Plus! Software
- ExamView® Pro Testmaker
- PuzzleMaker Software
- **communicationapplications.glencoe.com**

2 TEACH

Memorized Presentations

Some students may claim that a memorized presentation is impossible for them because they are not good at memorizing. Suggest that they have memorized more than they realize. Give students a minute to recall passages they know by heart. Remind them that poems, pledges, nursery or skipping rhymes, words to songs or advertisements, and the dialogue of movies all qualify. Have them write down any of their memorized passages for two minutes and then share them with a partner. Invite volunteers to recite passages for the class. Ask students how they memorized these lines. *(Answers will vary.)* Lead students to understand that much of what we memorize is accomplished without even trying. Memorizing a speech requires effort but is easier than most students might expect. **L1**

DID YOU KNOW?

According to the *Guinness Book of World Records*, Dominic O'Brien holds the record for memorizing the order of a single deck of shuffled cards. His time: 38.29 seconds.

Communication Tip

Don't start telling a joke unless you can remember the punch line and how to reach it. If you are unsure of your story, practice it carefully in your mind; otherwise, "I know a great joke" may be your famous last words.

---

delivery for your presentation. The **method of delivery** is the way you orally send your message to your audience. You can use any of four different methods of delivery for a presentation:

- memorized
- manuscript
- extemporaneous
- impromptu

Memorized Presentations

When you memorize something, you learn it word for word. If you are apprehensive about your presentation, you may reasonably think your best plan is to memorize it.

Disadvantages Be cautious about using memorization as a delivery method. It can end up in disaster! If you forget even one word, you can lose your place and then lose the message of the entire presentation.

Another disadvantage to memorized presentations is that, very often, they sound memorized. The presenter forgets to think about the meaning of his or her presentation when it is in progress. The presenter concentrates on the words of the presentation instead of the message the words should relay to the audience. The result is a formal, boring recitation, rather than a lively interaction with an audience. When you deliver a memorized presentation, you must remember that, although the message is quite familiar to you, each audience member is hearing it for the first time. Adapt to audience feedback to bring a memorized presentation to life.

Advantages Despite the drawbacks of memorizing an entire presentation, there are times when a presenter may wish to memorize parts of a presentation. For example, when making a sales pitch to a client, a salesperson should have memorized the main

features of his or her product or service. Having to flip through notes or ask someone else at a critical point in the presentation could damage the salesperson's credibility with his or her customer.

In addition, many presenters find it helpful to memorize just the introduction and conclusion of a presentation. This allows them to establish eye contact with audience members and be perceived with a positive image. Many presenters who use manuscript delivery, which you will learn about next, memorize the first and last sentence of each page so that they can maintain eye contact when turning the page. This helps the presenter keep the audience's attention focused on the message of the presentation instead of on the distraction of turning the page.

Manuscript Presentations

A **manuscript presentation** is delivered with the full text in front of the presenter. The presenter refers to the manuscript to be sure of his or her exact language during the presentation.

Advantages There are occasions when you may be asked to make a presentation on a very sensitive topic or when you will be held accountable for your exact words. Other times, the text of your presentation may be printed in a company newsletter or sent to local media. Perhaps the audiovisual aids in your presentation will make it necessary to use exact words to cue a technical assistant. In these cases, you will probably want to make a manuscript presentation.

Disadvantages Many beginning presenters are tempted to give manuscript presentations because they think it is the easiest type of presentation to give. Actually, unless you are very expressive when reading aloud, it can be difficult to keep an audience

---

INCLUSION STRATEGIES

Learning Disabled Some students may think that memorization is a difficult skill to learn. Help them memorize a poem by using simple strategies, such as memorizing manageable chunks at a time by memorizing one line at a time or memorizing rhyming couplets together. Suggest that they use rhythm and rhyme to recall lines.

Activity Allow time for students to memorize the poem and then give each student a turn to recite a single line of the poem. Continue until the poem is complete. Go around the room a second and third time, making sure everyone has an opportunity to recall a line. Finally, ask for volunteers to recite the whole poem for the class.

involved in a manuscript presentation. When you are tied to a manuscript, you do not have the flexibility to adapt your message to your audience. Audience members who do not understand your message will be left behind. Moreover, constantly looking down at the manuscript can keep you from developing eye contact and interacting well with your audience members. This can cause them to feel left out or, worse, to think that you don't know what you are talking about. Either impression damages your credibility.

Extemporaneous Presentations

An extemporaneous presentation is a presentation that is thoroughly prepared and rehearsed in advance and given with the use of notes. This is the type of presentation you might be asked to make to a group of new employees to explain your company's policies. Medical personnel sometimes make extemporaneous presentations to various support groups and special health-care interest groups. You may have a special cause or concern that motivates you to solicit funds or support. In any of these situations, an extemporaneous speech probably would be the best choice. In fact, *most* presentations you make are likely to be extemporaneous.

Advantages The first advantage is that you typically have plenty of time to prepare extemporaneous presentations. This preparation time allows you to adapt your presentation so that you can fully meet the needs of your specific audience, occasion,

Presidential candidate Bob Dole uses a TelePrompTer® to deliver a manuscript presentation. *What is a manuscript presentation?*

and task. An extemporaneous speech also encourages you to be more conversational in your presentation than you might be with a memorized or manuscript presentation.

Another advantage of an extemporaneous presentation is that it changes each time you give it. It is always fresh.

Disadvantages In some situations, being extemporaneous can be a disadvantage. For example, if you are required to say something in a specific way each time you present it, or if a record of your words is necessary, you probably would be better off using a manuscript. Another disadvantage of giving an effective extemporaneous presentation

Preparing for Presentations **535**

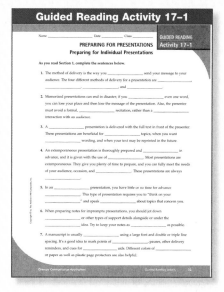

Guided Reading Activity 17-1

Manuscript Presentations

Ask students to think of circumstances in which a speaker might have to be accountable for his or her exact words. *(Students may suggest an economist dealing with precise statistics, a politician discussing racially sensitive issues, or a diplomat presenting a country's position before an international body.)* Lead them to understand that there are occasions when "off the cuff" remarks are inappropriate and even dangerous. Circumstances such as these call for manuscript presentations. **L2**

Communication Tip

When reading from a manuscript, you should look up periodically to establish eye contact with the audience. Highlight the passage that you will continue reading so that when you look down again you can find your place and continue speaking without hesitation.

Visual Instruction

Answer A manuscript presentation is one delivered with the full text in front of the presenter so that the presenter can be sure of his or her exact words.

REAL-WORLD CONNECTION

Assessing Impromptu Presentations Whenever people give information or opinions without time for preparation, they are making impromptu presentations. Lead students to understand that they are witnessing such performances all day long and encourage them to become critical listeners with the following exercise.

Activity Have students tape a brief, impromptu response that they encounter on radio or television. (Suggest that news or call-in programs are a good source of these informal presentations.) Ask them to present their recordings, encouraging the class to evaluate the effectiveness of the featured responses. Is the speaker informed, fluent, and believable? Discuss what makes some impromptu presentations more successful than others.

Impromptu Presentations

Point out that while everyone has to make impromptu presentations, not everyone feels that he or she is skilled at them. Ask students to evaluate themselves as impromptu speakers, ranking themselves from one to ten, with ten signifying excellent and one tongue-tied. Ask students to find a partner whose ranking is at least two numbers different from their own and have them explain their self-evaluations to each other. Then, invite volunteers to present their partner's strengths and weaknesses to the class. Discuss with students the skills necessary for successful impromptu speaking. **L2**

COMMUNICATION *Strategies*

MAKING AN EFFECTIVE IMPROMPTU PRESENTATION

Have students read the bulleted strategies for impromptu speakers. Ask them to choose the two steps that they consider most important and invite them to explain their choices. Under what circumstances would they not be able to observe all of these steps? *(Students may answer that being called on in class does not permit note taking or rehearsal.)* **L2**

▪ Visual Instruction

Answer An impromptu presentation requires speakers to "think on their feet" and speak accurately without formal preparation.

The person called upon to answer the question Wolf Blitzer asked during a White House briefing gave an **impromptu presentation. What is required of speakers in an impromptu presentation?**

is that it usually takes more rehearsal time than other types of presentations. That's because you need to be sure of what you plan to say and how you plan to say it.

Impromptu Presentations

For many people, the most intimidating type of presentation is the impromptu presentation. An impromptu presentation is a presentation for which there is little or no time for advance preparation. Many of the informal presentations you will be required to make at work will be impromptu. For instance, your supervisor may stop by your desk and ask for a brief update on your project. A client may inquire about a charge on an invoice, and you will need to give a brief presentation on the spot. Even if you're not aware of it, you probably make a number of impromptu presentations at school each day. When a teacher calls on you in class, your answer is an impromptu presentation. You may use this type of presentation to voice your opinions during committee or club meetings.

An impromptu presentation requires you to "think on your feet" and speak accurately about something with no formal preparation. This can be unnerving to even the most experienced presenter. However, you can take comfort in the fact that most impromptu presentations are on topics you already know something about or that affect you personally. If you are asked to make an impromptu statement on a topic that you know very little about, it is best to decline politely or delay until you have time to learn more.

However, there are many times when declining would be impossible or unwise. If you must make an impromptu presentation, remember the Communication Strategies below.

Advantages The biggest advantage of learning how to make an effective impromptu

COMMUNICATION *Strategies*

MAKING AN EFFECTIVE IMPROMPTU PRESENTATION

✓ Take a moment to gather your thoughts on the topic.

✓ Run through the parts of a presentation and the presentation process in your mind.

✓ Make notes on a small piece of paper.

✓ State a point, support it, restate it, and relate it to the next point.

✓ Remember to include a brief conclusion.

MEETING INDIVIDUAL NEEDS

INCLUSION STRATEGIES

Less-Proficient Readers Many students prepare notes that are more like manuscripts than ideas on which to expand. They have difficulty identifying main ideas for their notes.

Activity Ask students to use the headings in this chapter as a clue to main ideas. Suggest that they pay particular attention to the first and last sentences of each paragraph under a heading; often, the main idea is expressed in these sentences. Have students write notes for Extemporaneous Presentations by listing the heading and then giving the main idea of each paragraph under the heading.

presentation is that it gives you confidence to speak out on topics that concern you. Also, someone who makes good impromptu presentations at work often will be regarded as a leader or role model.

Disadvantages An obvious disadvantage of impromptu presentations is the lack of time to thoroughly prepare. Also, these presentations require you to think quickly and formulate ideas as you present them.

Memorized, manuscript, extemporaneous, and impromptu presentations make different demands on the presenter. However, no matter which method of delivery you use, your goal remains the same: to make the audience see your ideas and remember them.

PREPARING NOTES AND MANUSCRIPTS

With the exception of impromptu speeches, most of your presentations will allow you to follow the seventh step in the

■ **Figure 17–1 Steps of the Presentation Preparation Process**

| 1. Determine a topic. |
| 2. Limit the topic. |
| 3. Determine the purpose. |
| 4. Research the topic. |
| 5. Organize and outline the presentation. |
| 6. Select supporting information. |
| 7. Prepare notes and manuscript for delivery. |
| 8. Rehearse the presentation. |

■ **Figure 17–2 Impromptu Presentation Notes**

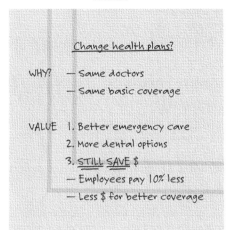

Presentation Preparation Process, as shown in **Figure 17–1**: Prepare your manuscript or notes or both for delivery. Once you have decided upon a method of delivery, you can then design the notes that will help you make a smooth presentation.

Notes for Impromptu Presentations

There really are no special techniques for developing notes for an impromptu presentation. You usually only have enough time to jot down the main ideas you want to cover in your talk. These notes can be written on any small piece of paper that you may have lying around—even if it is the back of an agenda or a napkin, such as the one in **Figure 17–2**.

As you think through what you want to say in your impromptu presentation, note the main ideas. If you know statistics or other types of support details, write them alongside or under the main idea. Try to keep your notes as brief as possible. You probably won't have time to rehearse, and

Preparing for Presentations **537**

Impromptu Speaking in Class

Many students will have experience with teachers who "cold call" on them in class, requiring an instant impromptu response. Discuss their reactions to this practice. Does it keep students more alert, or does it merely reward those who find impromptu speaking easy, while embarrassing those with less confidence? *(Answers will vary.)* **L1**

Practicing Impromptu Presentations

Point out that our ability to make impromptu presentations is largely governed by our knowledge of the topic. Have students spend a few moments jotting down subjects on which they feel that they could deliver an unrehearsed and informative one-minute speech. Then, ask them to write another list of topics that they could present with only an hour or two of preparation time. Invite students to read their lists to the class and to explain their reasons for choosing the topics. Encourage volunteers to present one of their "instant" topics to the class. **L3**

Communication Tip

The tendency of many inexperienced presenters is to speak too quickly, without sufficient moments of silence. Build pauses into your manuscript. Sometimes, the silence says as much as the words.

GIFTED AND TALENTED

Teaching a Mini-Lesson Point out that few professions depend more on impromptu speaking skills than that of a teacher. Suggest to students that teachers formally outline their lessons, but their effectiveness often depends on their ability to think quickly and to speak informatively and articulately.

Activity Invite students to practice their impromptu presentation skills (and to experience the classroom from the other side) by teaching a mini-lesson in a subject other than English or communication. Ask them to review notes or texts for any of their other courses and prepare and rehearse their presentations. Encourage volunteers to present their lessons to the class. Invite students to evaluate the presentations.

COMMUNICATION PRACTICE LAB

Preparing Notes for an Impromptu Presentation

Before students begin to review a chapter, make sure they understand the technique of skimming for information. Rapidly retrieving the most important facts should not require much reading. Instead, students should look at titles, topic sentences, and concluding paragraphs. Point out that this book is laid out in a format that makes it particularly easy to skim: The numerous headings and subheadings themselves constitute a chapter outline. By reviewing the print, students should be able to recall their previous reading and to piece together sufficient information to make adequate notes for an impromptu presentation. **L2**

For an additional Practice Lab for this section, students can visit the *Glencoe Communication Applications* Web site at communicationapplications.glencoe.com. Click on Communication Practice Lab 17–1. **L1**

---

you don't want to waste time during your presentation searching your notes for what to say next.

Notes for Extemporaneous Presentations

The notes for an extemporaneous presentation should evolve as you rehearse your presentation so that your actual presentation is made using the fewest notes possible. Your notes should be as unnoticeable as possible so they won't be a distraction during your presentation. Many experienced extemporaneous presenters like to use one or two index cards like the ones in **Figure 17–3.** Some prepare their notes on these cards vertically rather than horizontally so that they will be easier to handle.

Most effective extemporaneous presenters also will memorize their introductions and conclusions in order to establish eye contact with the audience right from the beginning of

Figure 17–3 **Notes for Extemporaneous Presentations**

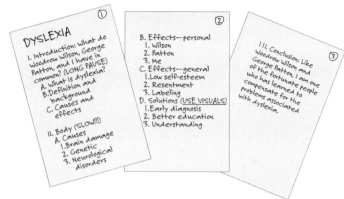

COMMUNICATION PRACTICE LAB

Preparing Notes for an Impromptu Presentation

To practice preparing notes for an impromptu presentation, follow these steps:

Step 1 Imagine that you have been asked to give an impromptu presentation on a chapter from this book.

Step 2 Choose a chapter on which you want to speak. Skim that chapter for several minutes.

Step 3 On a small piece of paper, take another minute to write brief notes for your presentation. Be sure to include the main ideas from the chapter.

Step 4 Discuss your notes as a class. What was most difficult about having to work within such a limited time frame? What strategies did you use to skim the chapter? How did you decide what to include in your notes?

CRITICAL THINKING ACTIVITY

Point out that writing notes for a presentation is a process of elimination. The presenter needs just enough key words and phrases to make connections between ideas and to remind him or her of the unwritten body of the speech. Copy and distribute to students an editorial or op-ed piece of general interest from a newspaper or weekly news magazine. Give them ten minutes to read the article and make notes on it. Inform them that with their notes alone they should be able to present the article as a speech. After the allotted time, have students put away the original article and form groups to compare notes and rehearse their speeches. Invite volunteers to deliver the editorial as an oral presentation. Ask an effective presenter to copy his or her notes on the board. Discuss with the class the process of note taking for extemporaneous presentations.

a presentation. They will begin their notes with their thesis statement and then list the main ideas, leaving room to include the support materials.

It is a good idea to include in your notes a reminder about any visual aids you plan to use during your presentation. Also, it can be a good idea to write delivery reminders in your notes, even simple ones like "smile" or "slow down." Include whatever you feel will help you present your ideas effectively.

Manuscripts for Manuscript Presentations

Most presentation manuscripts are typed using a large font and double or triple line spacing. Words and ideas that are intended to be emphasized may be formatted in bold or in a larger font so that they will stand out on the page. In some cases, a presenter may remind himself or herself to stress a specific idea or statement by positioning that information by itself on a page of the manuscript. This can be

GLOBAL COMMUNICATION
What Do You Mean?

Have you ever heard the phrase, "That car is a lemon?" This statement doesn't mean that the car is a piece of sour fruit, it means that the car is poorly made. Translated literally, however, this statement could confuse audience members who are unfamiliar with it. Slang, or informal language, is commonly used in conversation between friends. In a speech presented to an audience from another culture, however, slang is not appropriate. List ten examples of slang words or phrases that should be avoided in formal language. Define each word or phrase. What are some ways that these words and phrases could confuse an audience from another culture?

GLOBAL COMMUNICATION
What Do You Mean?

The language recommended for presentations is Standard English, the form of communication favored by the news media and public figures interested in making themselves understood to a broad spectrum of the population. (The use of slang in a presentation can be highly confusing to an audience from another region or culture. Some examples of slang or idiomatic phrases are *once in a blue moon*, which means "very rarely"; *raise the roof*, "become noisy and raucous"; and *bail out*, "leave a place.") **L2**

■ Visual Instruction

Answer Notes might include highlighting words and ideas to be emphasized, marking pauses and other delivery reminders, and cueing for visual aids.

3 ASSESS

Assign Section 1 Assessment as a homework or in-class activity.

🟊 Use *Interactive Tutor Self-Assessment Software* to review Section 1.

Former President Ronald Reagan studies his notes for a manuscript presentation. What kind of delivery reminders might presenters include in their notes?

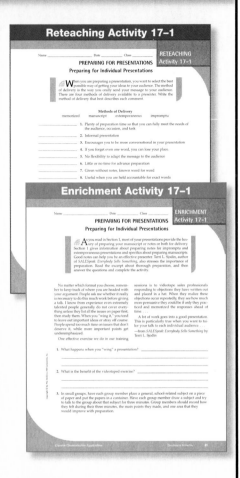

Reteaching Activity 17-1

Enrichment Activity 17-1

4 CLOSE

Ask students to reread the opening paragraph of this section on page 533. Ask whether what they have learned about preparing for presentations might improve their ability to tell effective stories.

Extra-Credit Project

Have each student interview two adults who regularly make presentations as part of their jobs. Ask them to include questions on preparation based on their reading of this section. What types of presentations do the interviewees make? How do they prepare for these presentations? Have their preparation methods changed over time? Have students summarize their interviews and present their summaries to the class.

---

a very effective method, but it can cause a simple three-page manuscript to stretch into fifteen or twenty pages.

In addition to marking points of emphasis, you can also mark pauses, other delivery reminders, and cues for visual aids on the manuscript. The key to preparing your manuscript lies in making notations or markings that allow you to easily get back into your presentation if you lose your place. You may wish to use different colors of ink, different fonts or formatting, or even different types and colors of paper.

One way to make the pages of a presentation manuscript easier to handle is to put them into plastic page protectors. If you put the pages back-to-back in the protectors, you will have fewer pages to turn, which will be less distracting for your audience. The plastic covers will also keep the pages from getting ragged and torn as you rehearse your presentation.

Good notes can help you be an effective presenter, no matter what type of delivery you are using. Your notes will help you remember not only important content points but also important points about your delivery.

Section 1 Assessment

Visit the *Glencoe Communication Applications* Web site at **communicationapplications. glencoe.com** and click on **Self-Check and Study Guide 17.1** to review your understanding of preparing for individual presentations.

Review Key Terms

1. Define each term and write it in a sentence: method of delivery, manuscript presentation, extemporaneous presentation, impromptu presentation.

Check Understanding

2. Under what circumstances might a manuscript delivery be the best choice for a presentation?

3. Compare and contrast the advantages and disadvantages of extemporaneous delivery and impromptu delivery.

4. **Synthesize** Imagine that you are the public-relations representative of your company who must present to the media an official statement about a product recall. What type of delivery method will you use? Why?

APPLICATION *Activity*

Preparing Notes and Manuscripts As a class, brainstorm the main points for a persuasive presentation on the topic of e-mail security. Choose one of these main points and use it to develop notes for part of an extemporaneous presentation. Then, use your notes to write a manuscript for your chosen main idea. Compare your notes and manuscript with classmates who chose the same main point. What similarities and differences do you notice?

Section 1 Assessment Answers

1. Accept all reasonable sentences.
2. If your topic is very sensitive, if you will be held accountable for your exact words, if your text will be printed later, or if you will be cueing an assistant
3. Extemporaneous: advantages are plenty of preparation time, more conversational, presentation changes each time you give it; disadvantages are presentation changes each time you give it, more rehearsal time required than with other delivery

types; impromptu: advantage is that it builds confidence; disadvantage is that it allows little time to thoroughly prepare.
4. Manuscript delivery: Your exact wording may be repeated word for word by the media.

Application Activity Students' work should reflect an understanding of effective notes and manuscripts for presentations.

Technology Skill

DEVELOPING A MULTIMEDIA PRESENTATION

Multimedia presentations use interactive CD-ROMs, computer-generated graphics, the Internet, slides, photographs, or video recordings. The following information explains how to develop a multimedia presentation.

Learning the Skill

When you're developing a multimedia presentation, there are several aspects to consider. First, consider how you will present your information in words. Think of the verbal portion of your presentation as the script. Your task is to choose visual media that will enhance the words. You can use any multimedia enhancement or any combination of enhancements to support your verbal information.

The next factor to consider is the setting of the presentation. The size and layout of the room should help you determine what multimedia enhancements you will be able to use effectively. If your presentation will be in a small room, for example, you may decide to show a videotape on a television monitor. This same strategy would not work as well in a large auditorium, however.

Another factor to consider is the cost in both time and money. For instance, overhead transparencies or slides will cost less and take less time to produce than video recordings or CD-ROMs. Make sure your schedule and budget will allow you to create the materials you want.

Before deciding on one or more multimedia enhancements, make sure the resources you will need are available to you. Don't decide to create an online presentation, for example, if you do not have access to the Internet for research, rehearsal, and performance.

Practicing the Skill

Follow the steps below to select multimedia enhancements that would strengthen a presentation on "How to Prepare and Use Notes and Text for Extemporaneous and Manuscript Deliveries." Describe how each enhancement would be used.

Step 1 Decide which multimedia enhancements will best support the verbal presentation of your subject.

Step 2 Decide whether the enhancements you have chosen are appropriate for the setting of the presentation.

Step 3 Consider the cost of the presentation in terms of both time and money.

Step 4 Make sure that the multimedia resources you need are available to you.

Step 5 Design your presentation.

Step 6 Review the results. Make any necessary improvements.

APPLICATION *Activity*

Develop a multimedia presentation using the theme "Safe Driving Habits." Address the topics of courtesy, defensive driving, traffic laws, and basic automobile maintenance. Choose the multimedia equipment that you will use in your presentation. Plan how each medium will be used, then produce your material after it has been approved by your teacher.

REAL-WORLD CONNECTION

Assessing Presentations Libraries, school districts, municipal governments, and civic organizations often have multimedia presentations open to the public. Encourage students to attend one of these presentations.

Activity Organize a calendar of presentations being made in your community in the next several weeks. Allow students to choose one of the presentations to attend. Ask students to assess the use of media in the presentations. Was the equipment needed for the presentation set up beforehand? Were the media used appropriate for the size of the room? Did they reinforce, rather than overshadow, the spoken presentation? Suggest that students summarize their assessments in brief paragraphs and share their summaries with the class.

Developing a Multimedia Presentation

Point out that the great variety of media available to students may make choosing the appropriate ones for their presentations more difficult. Suggest that students consider combining various media to help create interest. Emphasize the necessity to rehearse with the media so that they can coordinate the timing of visual and audio media to best enhance their presentations. Explain that presenters using more than one enhancement sequence the multimedia materials according to when they will be used in the presentation. Some also have assistants to change transparencies and start videotapes and audiotapes at appropriate times during the presentation. Remind students that the media materials they use should reinforce their verbal presentation, not overwhelm it.

Practicing the Skill

1. If possible, have media available for students' use.

2. Group students with varying learning styles and skills for the activity. Students can then assign roles within the groups based on each student's skills, strengths, and interests.

3. Descriptions of how each enhancement will be used in the presentation should include why the particular media choice was made.

4. As they assess the results of their media-enhanced presentations, students should determine what worked and what didn't work and why. They can use this information when making choices for other presentations.

Application Activity

The Secretary of State's office or driver's license facilities can be contacted by telephone or online to request materials on the topic "Safe Driving Habits." Encourage students to identify which considerations for choosing media for their presentations were most important.

1 FOCUS

Bellringer

Ask if they have ever attended or listened to a group presentation. (Remind them that radio and television provide many examples.) How much work do they imagine goes into such presentations? Could the same information have been presented by a single speaker?

✎ You may use Graphic Organizer Transparency 17–2 to introduce this section.

Graphic Organizer Transparency 17–2

Panel Discussion | Symposium

1. Individual speakers give prepared presentations on a specific topic.
2. The format is highly organized.
3. This type of presentation is better for small audiences.
4. There is little or no interaction among the presenters.
5. Participants are selected because they have special knowledge or expertise on the topic.
6. The format is informal.
7. Presenters discuss a topic as a group.
8. A leader keeps the discussion focused and flowing smoothly.
9. Presenters may interact or rehearse before the presentation.
10. This type of presentation is better for large audiences.

▪ Visual Instruction

Answer Group presentations offer a variety of speakers for a greater possibility of audience connection and for less likelihood that a presentation will become boring or tedious.

Grammar Tip

The plurals of most nouns are formed by adding *-s* or *-es* to the words. Some words, such as *symposium* have irregularly formed plurals—*symposia*. These plurals must be memorized.

Preparing for Group Presentations

GUIDE TO READING

Objectives

1. Identify and describe the four special types of group presentations.
2. Analyze the appropriateness of each type of group presentation in a given context.
3. Prepare, organize, and participate in a group presentation for an audience.

Terms to Learn

panel discussion
panel discussion-forum
symposium
symposium-forum

---

*I*magine seeing banners around your school with the following advertisements: "Join us for our 15th annual Women's Symposium!" or "Today's Panel Discussion—The Virtual Classroom," or "The French Club Presents Studying Abroad in Paris." What might a listener find interesting about any of these events?

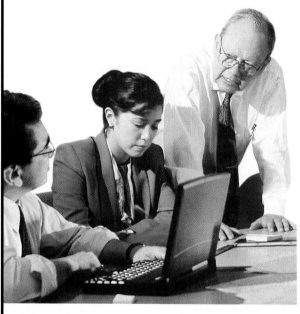

Even if you weren't interested in the subject matter of any of these presentations, you still might be intrigued by their group formats. Group presentations allow a variety of speakers to connect with an audience. That variety can add a spark to a topic.

GROUP PRESENTATIONS

Not all of the presentations that you make will be individual. The time may come when you are asked to participate with a group of coworkers, classmates, or community members in a formal group presentation. Formal group discussions often are the means by which companies share information—about new products and designs, trends, and innovations—or concerns about industry developments.

A group prepares for a formal presentation. What do group presentations offer?

542 *Glencoe Communication Applications*

RESOURCE MANAGER

Teaching Tools

- Interactive Lesson Planner
- Reproducible Lesson Plan 17–2
- Application Activities 17–2

Reproducible Masters

- Guided Reading Activity Workbook 17–2
- Enrichment Activity 17–2
- Reteaching Activity 17–2
- Section Quiz 17–2
- Transparency Strategies and Activities Booklet 17–2

Transparencies

- Graphic Organizer Transparency 17–2
- Chapter 17 Teaching Transparency

Technology Resources

- Interactive Tutor Self-Assessment Software
- Presentation Plus! Software
- ExamView® Pro Testmaker
- PuzzleMaker Software
- communicationapplications.glencoe.com

A group project at school may be delivered as an internal group presentation to your teacher or your classmates. In the workplace, group presentations may be given to an internal audience, such as a team of employees making proposals or status reports to others in their company. Other times, the audience for a group presentation may be external. Examples of external audiences include public officials explaining their plan to citizens or school officials informing parents of new policies.

Benefits of Group Presentations

Group presentations have a number of advantages over individual presentations. Because there is a variety of speakers, audience members have a greater opportunity to connect with at least one of them. This variety also helps keep the presentation from becoming boring or tedious for audience members.

Preparing a Group Presentation

It is important to remember that the people involved in a group presentation are all distinctive individuals. Therefore, when planning a presentation, group members should work together to determine a consistent overall approach and style. You don't want audience members to feel as if they are listening to several different speeches but rather to one cohesive speech presented by several speakers.

As a group, you might want to choose a leader or moderator. Alternatively, your group may instead choose to have a single spokesperson present the bulk of the information on each main idea. Other group members would then provide examples and extensions of each main idea.

> ### COMMUNICATION Strategies
>
> **STAGING AN EFFECTIVE GROUP PRESENTATION**
>
> ✓ **Feel free to move around the room during your presentation.**
>
> ✓ **Remove any physical barriers (such as a podium or a table) between group members and the audience.**
>
> ✓ **Place group members around the room to increase interest and to involve as many audience members as possible.**

Finally, determine the timing and set the pace of your presentation. Since variety is the major advantage of a group presentation, try to balance everyone's speaking time equally.

Rehearsing together can be important to the success of your presentation. You will learn more about rehearsing presentations later in this chapter. However, it is important to remember that when working with a group, rehearsing cues and transitions will help you make the smoothest presentation possible.

SPECIAL TYPES OF GROUP PRESENTATIONS

Throughout your school and work career, you may participate in many group presentations. In professional and social contexts, there are four special types of group presentations. They are

- panel discussion
- panel discussion-forum
- symposium
- symposium-forum

Preparing for Presentations **543**

Panel Discussion

Celebrity panel games and sports panel shows are popular fare on radio and television. Invite each student to assess one of these programs that he or she knows well. What is its purpose? Does it successfully provide information or entertainment? Do the panelists appear to be experts or otherwise prepared for their tasks? Does it follow a carefully organized format? How could it be improved? **L1**

▪ Visual Instruction

Answer The function of a panel discussion is to provide expert analysis of a problem.

Application Activities 17–2

Jesse Jackson is shown participating in a panel discussion. **What is the function of a panel discussion?**

Panel Discussion

A panel discussion is a formal presentation in which a group of people discusses an announced topic in front of an audience. The function of a panel usually is to provide expert analysis of a problem. The participants of the panel usually are selected because they have some special knowledge about the topic. Panel discussions provide the opportunity to present a variety of views to an audience in a short time frame.

If a panel group is made up of experts or celebrities from diverse locations, there is little likelihood that they will gather to rehearse before the panel. However, if you are involved in a local panel discussion group, you may wish to meet with other panel members prior to the discussion in order to prepare. This helps participants get to know each other, refine their topic, develop a plan for the presentation, agree to gather any additional information they need, and develop procedures for the discussion.

For maximum effectiveness, each panel member should be as prepared and informed as possible. Even one unprepared panel member can negatively influence the outcome of the presentation. The credibility of the overall group depends on the credibility of each individual group member. In addition, all members of the panel need to contribute on all aspects of the topic. This is because most of the information will be shared conversationally rather than as a formal presentation. Just as you wouldn't want one or two people to monopolize a conversation, audiences don't like to hear one or two speakers monopolize a panel discussion.

Format of a Panel Discussion

Even though the body of a panel discussion itself is informal, the format is highly organized, usually following the same organizational plan as an individual presentation. A predetermined leader or chairperson opens the discussion by introducing the members of the panel. The leader then goes on to introduce

544 *Glencoe Communication Applications*

MEETING INDIVIDUAL NEEDS

MULTIPLE LEARNING STYLES

Visual-Spatial Sometimes, panel discussion and entertainment shows are hilarious; sometimes, they are provocative or infuriating. Whatever one's response, panel discussion and entertainment shows are a staple of broadcasting.

Activity Have students examine radio or television programs that feature a panel. Ask them to write a critique of the program, including the purpose of the panel, the expertise and contributions of its members, and ways in which the panel could be improved. Remind students that even a panel show intended for comedy can be critiqued seriously. Have students present their critiques in presentations featuring brief audio or video clips of the panels they studied.

the topic and provide any audience orientation that may be needed. As you read in Chapter 15, an audience orientation may be necessary to give background information or to define unfamiliar terms.

The procedures that the group has decided upon also may be explained at this time. This may include how the discussion will flow from one topic to another or any other process the group will follow. The leader then may begin the discussion by previewing the main areas on which the discussion will focus. In other words, he or she will provide the introduction of the group presentation.

After the introduction, the entire group discusses the main ideas of the topic just as a presenter would cover the main points of a presentation. Some polite interruptions are allowed in order to keep a spirited discussion going. However, panel members should be courteous and respectful when other panel members are speaking.

The leader of the panel may enter the discussion and present information just like any other group member. However, his or her primary responsibility during this part of the discussion is to keep the panel focused on one topic at a time. It also is the leader's responsibility to provide helpful transitions from one main idea to the next.

At the end of the allotted time period, the leader should briefly summarize what the group has stated and conclude the discussion. If the audience will be allowed to comment or ask questions, the leader should establish the rules at this time. He or she will then act as the moderator of the audience interaction period.

Panel Discussion-Forum When post-discussion interaction with the audience is included as part of the presentation, it is called a *panel discussion-forum*. The audience and the panel members interact and continue the discussion following the panel's presentation.

COMMUNICATION PRACTICE LAB

Participating in a Panel Discussion

To prepare, organize, and participate in a panel discussion, follow these steps:

Step 1 As a class, brainstorm the five most important topics of interest to the students in your school.

Step 2 Divide into five groups according to topic. Choose a leader for your group.

Step 3 As a group, discuss your topic. Share or research enough information for a twenty- to thirty-minute panel discussion.

Step 4 Decide whether your presentation will be informative or persuasive.

Step 5 Prepare an introduction for your group leader to present.

Step 6 Hold your panel discussion with the other groups serving as your audience. Allow time for a question-and-answer session following your presentation.

Step 7 Discuss as a class the effectiveness of each presentation. Did group members all participate equally? Was enough information shared with audience members to adequately inform or persuade them?

Preparing for Presentations **545**

MULTIPLE LEARNING STYLES

Interpersonal Point out that panelists and audience members alike need to be sensitive listeners to get the most out of panel discussions.

Activity Brainstorm with students for a list of topics that are of general interest to the class. Ask for five or six volunteers to form a panel. Assign the panel one of the chosen topics and allow each member up to a minute to express his or her views on the subject. After each panelist has spoken, invite members of the audience to paraphrase as exactly as possible what the panelists said. Continue with a new panel and a new subject. Encourage all students to serve as panelists or audience responders.

Keeping Panel Discussions Civil

Point out that panel discussions aired on television and radio sometimes become heated and even out of control. Ask students whether they believe it is always possible for a leader to rein in emotional members of a panel. Is there an argument for allowing panelists to become loud and disrespectful? *(Some students may suggest that rowdy discussions transform a panel discussion into entertainment.)* **L1**

COMMUNICATION PRACTICE LAB

Participating in a Panel Discussion

Emphasize to students that whether their panel presentations are persuasive or informative, they will need substantial information to support a twenty- to thirty-minute discussion. Audiences are quick to detect when panelists run out of supporting material. *(Class answers to questions posed in Step 7 should reflect that students actively listened to each panel discussion and noted effective methods for informing and persuading an audience.)* **L2**

GLENCOE Online

For an additional Practice Lab for this section, students can visit the *Glencoe Communication Applications* Web site at communicationapplications.glencoe.com. Click on Communication Practice Lab 17–2. **L1**

3 ASSESS

Assign Section 2 Assessment as a homework or in-class activity.

❶ Use *Interactive Tutor Self-Assessment Software* to review Section 2.

Symposium

A symposium is a group presentation in which individual speakers give prepared presentations on aspects of a topic and have little or no interaction with the other presenters. Most often presenters for a symposium are selected because of their expertise on one specific aspect of a topic or for their differing points of view on a topic. Symposia usually are very formal events that do not include active audience participation.

During the actual presentation of a symposium, the leader or moderator has specific duties to perform to keep things flowing smoothly. He or she introduces the speakers and states the topic or topics of the symposium, once again shouldering the responsibility for the introduction. The leader or moderator then introduces each individual presentation, including summaries and transitions from one presentation to the next. Each of these individual presentations is a main point for the body of the group presentation.

These presenters are taking part in a symposium. What is a symposium?

One of the main duties of the leader or moderator is to keep the symposium moving and to prevent individual presentations from taking too long or getting off track. After all the presenters have spoken, the moderator also summarizes and concludes the total presentation.

Symposium-Forum When the audience is invited to ask questions or make comments after the individual presentations, the presentation is called a symposium-forum. As in a panel discussion-forum, in a symposium-forum the moderator is expected to control the forum part of the presentation. He or she should explain the rules for audience participation and then make sure the rules are followed. The moderator is usually the one who calls for each question and decides when a question has been sufficiently answered. When it is time to conclude the presentation, the moderator should thank the participants, summarize the presentation, and dismiss the audience and participants.

Group Presentation Choices

Each of these types of group presentations can be effective when it is presented with the audience and occasion in mind. Panel discussions are better for small audiences in comfortable surroundings. A symposium, with the speakers presenting from a podium or platform, can be overpowering for a small, casual group. On the other hand, it can be difficult for large audiences to understand a panel when each of the members is actively contributing to the discussion. A symposium is the better choice for a large audience and formal occasion.

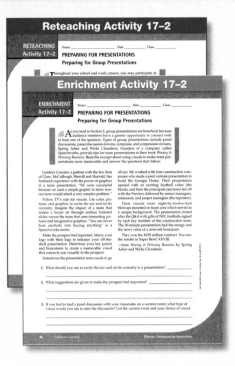

Section 2 Assessment

Visit the *Glencoe Communication Applications* Web site at **communicationapplications. glencoe.com** and click on **Self-Check and Study Guide 17.2** to review your understanding of preparing for group presentations.

Review Key Terms

1. Define each term and write it in a sentence: panel discussion, panel discussion-forum, symposium, symposium-forum.

Check Understanding

2. Identify and describe the four special types of group presentations.

3. Imagine that a college audience is interested in hearing different professors' opinions on a controversial political issue. Which type of group presentation might be most appropriate? Why?

4. **Analyze** What do you think would be the most difficult part of preparing a group presentation?

APPLICATION *Activity*

Making a Group Presentation Use your notes from the Application Activity in Section 1 to prepare a group presentation. Form groups large enough to cover each main point in your presentation. Then, decide which type of presentation your group will give. Use what you have read in this section to prepare your presentation, and then present it to classmates. Finally, discuss the three formats. Which type was most effective for this topic? Which was easiest to prepare? Which was the most difficult?

Preparing for Presentations **547**

---

4 CLOSE

Have students review their responses to the opening paragraph of this section on page 542. What have they learned about group presentations that has surprised or interested them? What do they feel is the most valuable aspect of presenting information as a team? *(Students may respond that a group adds variety to a presentation, permits members to share the workload, and allows individuals to talk about the areas they know best.)*

Extra-Credit Project

Ask students to attend a public panel discussion or symposium and to write a summary of the presentation. Have them pay special attention to the organization of the event and the role played by group members. Invite students to present their summaries to the class.

Section 2 Assessment Answers

1. Accept all reasonable sentences.
2. Panel discussion: formal presentation in which a group of people discusses an announced topic in front of an audience; panel discussion-forum: a panel discussion followed by questions and comments from the audience; symposium: group presentation in which individual speakers give prepared presentations; symposium-forum: a symposium in which audience members are invited to ask questions and make comments after each individual presentation.
3. A panel discussion-forum; accept reasons that reflect understanding of group presentations.
4. Answers should reflect an understanding of the steps in preparing a group presentation.

Application Activity Students' presentations should reflect an understanding of the three types of group presentations and a willingness on the part of each group member to participate in the preparation and performance of the presentation.

1 FOCUS

Bellringer

Have students read the opening paragraph of this section and ask them to think of a skill that they possess. How much work have they had to put into that activity in order to achieve their current level of ability? How much extra preparation would be necessary for them to achieve excellence in that field?

You may use Graphic Organizer Transparency 17–3 to introduce this section.

Graphic Organizer Transparency 17–3

Visual Instruction

Answer Rehearsal is important because it can help manage anxiety about making a presentation, can help the presenter gain command of information, and can provide an opportunity to develop language and presentation skills, thereby building confidence.

Rehearsing Presentations

GUIDE TO READING

Objectives

1. Identify the factors that can contribute to communication apprehension.
2. Utilize strategies to manage communication apprehension, build self-confidence, and gain command of information.
3. Develop strategies to rehearse presentations.

Terms to Learn

communication apprehension
visualization
internalization

*C*an you imagine Tiger Woods playing in a championship match without ever having swung a golf club? What about a pilot landing a plane without ever having rehearsed landings in a simulator? Imagine a chef creating a seven-layer cake for someone's wedding without ever having baked even a batch of cupcakes.

Rehearsal is important in the development of most skills. Athletes, actors, musicians, surgeons, and many other professionals spend much of their time not in actual performances but behind the scenes, practicing and refining their skills. They realize the importance of practicing so that when they actually perform, they can do so competently.

To improve your presentation skills, it is important to rehearse effectively. In fact, the eighth and final step of the Presentation Preparation Process, shown in **Figure 17–4**, is to rehearse.

Rehearsal is an important step in the process for three reasons. First, it can help you manage any anxiety you are

Rehearsing is important to the development of an effective presentation. Why is rehearsing important?

RESOURCE MANAGER

Teaching Tools

- Interactive Lesson Planner
- Reproducible Lesson Plan 17–3
- Application Activities 17–3

Reproducible Masters

- Guided Reading Activity Workbook 17–3
- Enrichment Activity 17–3
- Reteaching Activity 17–3
- Section Quiz 17–3
- Transparency Strategies and Activities Booklet 17–3

Transparencies

- Graphic Organizer Transparency 17–3
- Chapter 17 Teaching Transparency

Technology Resources

- Interactive Tutor Self-Assessment Software
- Presentation Plus! Software
- ExamView® Pro Testmaker
- PuzzleMaker Software
- communicationapplications.glencoe.com

■ Figure 17-4 Steps of the Presentation Preparation Process

| 1. Determine a topic. |
| 2. Limit the topic. |
| 3. Determine the purpose. |
| 4. Research the topic. |
| 5. Organize and outline the presentation. |
| 6. Select supporting information. |
| 7. Prepare notes and manuscript for delivery. |
| 8. Rehearse the presentation. |

feeling about your presentation. Second, it helps you gain command of your information. Third, it gives you an opportunity to develop your language and presentation skills, building the confidence you need for a successful presentation.

MANAGING COMMUNICATION APPREHENSION

Your hands are sweaty. You feel perspiration on your brow. Your cheeks are flushed. Your heart is racing. You may even feel faint or sick to your stomach. No, you're not coming down with the flu! You're about to make a presentation. Communication apprehension, sometimes known as "stage fright," is fear or nervousness associated with making a presentation.

The physical symptoms described above are the body's way of responding to the surge of adrenaline that is released when you face a challenge. It is only natural to feel some apprehension; you have invested time and energy in preparing your presentation, and you care about the audience's acceptance of it. When you feel panicked, however, remember this: You are not alone. Many surveys show that people fear speaking in public more than anything else.

Causes of Communication Apprehension

There are many reasons for presenters to feel some anxiety before making a presentation. One reason is that doing so may be a new experience for you, and most of us have some fear of things we have not done before. Also, making a presentation focuses audience members' attention directly on you, which may make you uncomfortable. Some people thrive on being the center of attention, while others dread it. No matter which type of person you are, it is impossible to avoid the spotlight when you make a presentation. In fact, being the center of attention is really what you want. You want audience members to understand your message, and the only way for that to happen is for them to focus on you and what you are saying.

Previous bad experiences also can increase your anxiety level. If you have ever had a negative experience giving a presentation, the thought of giving another one may make your stomach feel as if it is full of fluttering butterflies. Remember, though, making a presentation is like falling off a bike. Learning from your mistakes can help you make better decisions next time.

The possible consequences of a presentation are another cause of apprehension for some people. Perhaps the presentation will influence your chances for a raise or promotion at work. Maybe it will affect your standing in

Preparing for Presentations **549**

2 TEACH

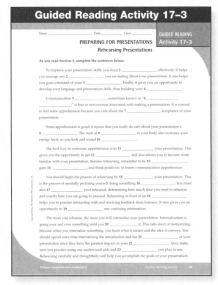

Communication Apprehension

Invite students to describe moments when they have been paralyzed with stage fright. How did they respond to the situation? How did their nerves affect the job they had to do? Encourage their anecdotes by sharing one of your own! **L1**

> ### DID YOU KNOW?
>
> Adrenaline, sometimes called the "emergency hormone," is released by the adrenal glands near the kidneys when the body believes that it is under threat. Among its effects is raising the levels of blood sugars and fatty acids. Drenched with adrenaline, the body is prepared for action—ready for "fight or flight."

EXTENDING THE CONTENT

Fear of Public Speaking According to Tad Simons, managing editor of *Presentations* magazine, "The truth about fear of public speaking—and the reason it is many people's No. 1 fear—is that it embodies so many of our most formidable and pervasive fears." Among the anxieties embodied by public speaking, Simons includes fear of the following: (1) failure, (2) not being perfect, (3) disappointing our superiors, (4) exposing our ignorance, (5) being laughed at, (6) losing control, (7) being judged, and (8) going "blank."

Activity On the chalkboard, list these eight fears and have students rank them according to how they respond to communication apprehension. Give them five minutes to write paragraphs explaining the fears that ranked at the top and bottom of their lists.

BUSINESS BRIEF

"There are two types of speakers," wrote the humorist Mark Twain, "those that are nervous and those that are liars." Ask students to interpret this witticism. *(Public speaking makes everyone nervous.)* How do they respond to Twain's generalization?

Benefits of Communication Apprehension

Point out that the body's "fight or flight" response to a rush of adrenaline prepares it to meet a challenge. The resulting nervousness indicates that your body is taking the job ahead seriously. By harnessing the "fight" reaction, one can become an assertive, powerful presenter. Feeling absolutely calm about an upcoming presentation is, in fact, something to worry about! **L1**

ACTIVITY

Stage Fright! Students will find a great number of sites on their Internet searches. Ask what they would infer from this fact. *(Some students will infer that stage fright is a problem affecting many people.)* Point out that the various courses offered on anxiety management are aimed largely at adults in the business world. Lead students to understand that one can learn to control communication apprehension, but one does not always outgrow it.

(Stage fright is frequently the result of the fear of being judged by others or the fear of making a mistake in front of others. Some performers fear what audience members will say about them. Some people are just shy. Ways to ease performance anxiety include using eye contact, moving during a performance, using gestures, and practicing.)

your community. A large portion of your final grade in a course may be determined by a single presentation. Any of these situations is enough to make a presenter nervous. In cases such as these, it may be best to remember that the calmer you are, the smoother your presentation will be. Work at calming yourself down, just as you work on being prepared and speaking clearly.

Benefits of Communication Apprehension

Believe it or not, some apprehension is good. It means that you really do care about the outcome of your presentation. Also, the rush of adrenaline in your body increases your energy level so that you can look and sound enthusiastic. Finally, a little apprehension may help you to remain focused on the task of your presentation.

It may help to know that audiences rarely realize how nervous you are during a presentation unless you tell them. Many of the symptoms of nervousness are not visible to others. Even if your jitters are detectable, they probably won't detract from a good presentation. Most audiences want a presenter to succeed.

Communication Apprehension Strategies

There are a number of ways to manage your communication apprehension. Possibly the best way to overcome whatever apprehension you experience before making a professional presentation is to rehearse it. When you rehearse a presentation, you try to simulate the presentation. Rehearsing gives you an opportunity to get feedback about your presentation from someone whose opinion you trust. The more you rehearse a presentation, the more familiar you are with what you

want to say and accomplish in the presentation. The more familiar you are with what you want to say and accomplish, the more confidence you have in the presentation and your ability to present it. Rehearsal strategies will be discussed later in this section.

In addition to rehearsing your presentation, there are three specific ways to effectively manage your stage fright. Remember to

- be prepared
- gain experience
- think positively

Be Prepared. One way to control communication apprehension is to be well prepared for your presentation. The better you know the information you want to deliver to the audience, the more confident you can be in presenting it. By following each of the steps in the presentation-preparation process, you can rest assured that your presentation will be well prepared.

Gain Experience. Another way to control communication apprehension is to give more presentations. This is a good way

ACTIVITY

Stage Fright! One of the most important things to remember about stage fright is that most people have it to some degree. For tips on how to prepare yourself mentally and physically for a presentation, search the Internet using the phrases *stage fright* and *performance anxiety*. What are some things that cause stage fright? What can be done to eliminate performance anxiety?

INTERDISCIPLINARY CONNECTION

Neurobiology Students may understand that our bodies create delicately balanced cocktails of chemicals to control our responses. Point out that nowhere are the effects of chemical secretions more dramatic than in the workings of the adrenal glands.

Activity Have students research the effects of communication apprehension on the human system. Ask them to feature the key areas of their findings on a poster and suggest that they illustrate their research with original drawings or photographs from magazines. Have students present their posters to the class. Discuss with students what they have learned about the importance of neurobiology in the presentation process.

By permission of Mell Lazarus and Creators Syndicate.

to control the fear of the unknown. If you have a job that requires you to make occasional presentations with significant consequences, volunteer to make some smaller, less critical presentations to gain experience. Experience is vital for producing confidence, and confidence helps build credibility.

Think Positively. If you think that you can do something, you usually can. Presenters who face their presentations with a positive outlook tend to develop the confidence necessary to overcome apprehension. On the other hand, speakers who think that their presentations will fail are much more likely to be victims of communication apprehension.

The idea of each of these strategies is to learn to control communication apprehension and make it work for you instead of against you. An experienced presenter may have summed it up best by stating, "The butterflies never really go away; it's just that after a while you teach them to fly in formation."

DEVELOPING REHEARSAL STRATEGIES

There are a number of strategies to make your rehearsal time as effective as it can be. For maximum benefit from your rehearsals,

- visualize
- plan your rehearsals
- rehearse with an audience
- internalize
- rehearse with your audiovisual aids and notes

Visualize

Begin the process of rehearsing your presentation by visualizing it. Look at the picture in **Figure 17–5** on page 552. **Visualization** is the process of mentally picturing yourself doing something successfully. Imagine making a successful presentation. Hear your name being announced and picture yourself walking confidently to the front of the room. Picture yourself making eye contact with the audience and starting the introduction with poise and self-assurance. Feel the sense of accomplishment you will have as you conclude your presentation knowing that you have done your very best.

Visualization is your mental rehearsal. It should focus only on the positive aspects of your presentation. Either ignore negative images or, better, turn them into positive images. For example, if a certain part of your presentation has been giving you problems, visualize getting through it without any trouble.

Preparing for Presentations **551**

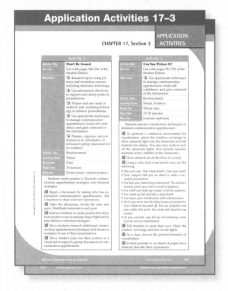

Be Prepared
Point out that the preparation for a spoken presentation is little different from preparations necessary for any performance, including sports, music, dance, driving tests, or academic exams. Invite students to share their experiences in preparing for an exhibition of any sort. How did they prepare for the occasion? What were the results of their preparation? **L1**

Gain Experience
While command of the subject is key to an effective presentation, sometimes, the only people completely free from stage fright are those with no sense of what the occasion involves. Point out that the complete beginner is sometimes unaffected by the nerves that beset people with more experience. Write the phrase "Ignorance is bliss" on the chalkboard and ask students to apply it to the subject of stage fright in any endeavor. **L1**

MULTIPLE LEARNING STYLES

Musical Students may realize that music is frequently employed as a means of mood enhancement at shopping malls, doctors' offices, or sporting events. It can also be effective in settling the mind or strengthening the resolve of someone preparing for a presentation.

Activity Ask students to find classroom-appropriate music that they might play to relax, inspire, or strengthen them in preparing for a presentation. Have them bring a recording of their choice to class and present an excerpt from it, together with a brief explanation of what it is the music "says" to them and why they believe it has that effect. Have students vote on selections that they believe would be effective for them.

Plan Your Rehearsals

Students should understand that knowledge of the physical space where they will make their presentation may influence how they rehearse. Ask them to jot down answers to the following question: What three things would you want to know in advance about the place where you are going to make a presentation? Have them pool their responses with a partner and ask each pair to write a question on the chalkboard. *(Questions may include How big is the room? Is there a sound system? Is there a stage? Do I have to bring my own audiovisual equipment? Are there distractions coming from outside?)* Discuss with students the importance of knowing about the venue of a presentation. **L2**

Ask students to read to themselves the paragraphs under the head Plan Your Rehearsals. As they read, have them consider when they would normally want to establish eye contact with their audience. Invite a volunteer to read this passage to the class as if he or she were making a presentation. Discuss the importance of rehearsal in the presentation process. **L2**

■ **Figure 17–5 Visualization**

Many athletes use visualization. It not only helps them improve the quality of their performance but actually can help them heal from injuries. Many athletes, like golfer Greg Norman and Olympian Picabo Street, visualize the positive outcome of an ideal round, game, or run. This mental preparation has helped a number of athletes overcome great odds due to an injury or a formidable opponent.

As valuable as this mental rehearsal is, athletes, entertainers, surgeons, and experienced presenters know that they must also physically prepare for their competition or performance. For your presentation to succeed, you also need to take time to physically rehearse.

Plan Your Rehearsals

A rehearsal should be planned almost as carefully as the presentation itself. Try to rehearse in a place that is similar to where the actual presentation will occur. The more authentic the rehearsal surroundings, the more at ease you will be during the actual speech.

Determine Rehearsal Time. How much time do you need to rehearse? This all depends on the presentation style and method of delivery you have chosen.

In general, extemporaneous presentations require the least amount of rehearsal time. You probably will just need to review your notes aloud, getting used to the way your ideas sound. Your ideas always sound different when you speak them aloud for the first time. You will need to make adjustments in your notes as you familiarize yourself with the physical presentation of your ideas. Then, rehearse again to make sure that you have included enough information in your notes to get you through your presentation. Practice using your audiovisual aids at least three or four times before making the presentation. Remember that an extemporaneous presentation will be different each time you present it. You will need to spend enough time rehearsing so that you are sure you'll say what you want to communicate with your audience each time you make the presentation.

MEETING INDIVIDUAL NEEDS

INCLUSION STRATEGIES

Special Needs Students should understand that a television news anchor who looks away from the camera is not engaging the viewer. Point out that news anchors read the news from TelePrompTers.

Activity Give small groups of students copies of a news story to rehearse for presentation. Explain that they should prepare poster-size cue cards, which will be used by the news anchor. Encourage students to be creative in trying to meet the needs of all viewers. For example, they may wish to have one student use sign language to report the story for the hearing impaired as another reads it and still another holds the cue cards. Give groups time to rehearse and invite volunteers to deliver their presentation to the class. If possible, videotape the performances.

Manuscript presentations, on the other hand, require more rehearsal time for you to thoroughly internalize the information. You need enough practice time for you to master the information in your presentation without having to read it to the audience. This will help you develop enough confidence with your presentation so that during the real performance you can look away from your manuscript to develop eye contact with your audience.

Memorized presentations generally require the most rehearsal time of all. The exact amount of rehearsal time needed for a memorized presentation depends on how quickly you can memorize. Just as actors on a stage must memorize their lines and moves, you will have to spend a great deal of time memorizing a presentation.

The rehearsal of any type of presentation can be accomplished in bits and pieces at first. Then, as you develop longer concentration skills and get the individual parts of the presentation ironed out, you can rehearse larger portions of the presentation at one time. Always plan enough rehearsal time to practice your entire presentation several times from start to finish. This helps you develop a sense of the complete presentation.

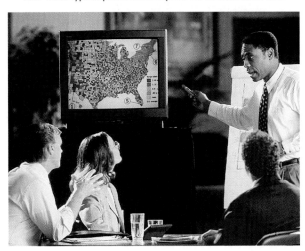
A professional group rehearses together in preparation for a presentation. **Which type of presentation requires the most rehearsal time?**

COMMUNICATION PRACTICE LAB

Visualizing

To practice visualizing a difficult activity, follow these steps:

Step 1 Brainstorm as a class a list of difficult activities. These might include physical activities, such as climbing a mountain or running a marathon, or mental ones, such as taking a final exam.

Step 2 Choose one activity from the list. Think about the steps involved in completing the activity. In running a marathon, for example, you might imagine everything from lacing up your running shoes, to warming up, to walking up to the starting point, running, pacing yourself, and finally crossing the finish line.

Step 3 Close your eyes and visualize yourself completing the activity successfully.

Step 4 Discuss your visualizations as a class. Was positive visualization difficult for you? Did negative images come to mind often? How did you address these negative ones?

Preparing for Presentations **553**

GLENCOE *Online*

For an additional Practice Lab for this section, students can visit the *Glencoe Communication Applications* Web site at **communicationapplications.glencoe.com.** Click on Communication Practice Lab 17–3. **L1**

BUSINESS BRIEF

Even the ancient Romans had useful advice for the modern presenter. According to the Latin playwright Seneca, "If a man does not know to what port he is steering, no wind is favorable to him." Write this statement on the board and ask students how it applies to the process of preparing for a presentation, particularly to visualization. *(Students may suggest that without a clearly envisioned goal, one will lack a sense of direction.)*

MEETING INDIVIDUAL NEEDS
MULTIPLE LEARNING STYLES

Logical-Mathematical Many students will find the process of visualization enhanced by actual images or steps representing the task ahead.

Activity Have each student create a sequence chart of the visualizing process. Ask them to think of challenging activities that they engage in or might like to attempt and to develop a series of images or steps that they would visualize in preparing for these activities. Suggest that students display their sequence of visualizations on poster board and present the series to the class. Discuss their choices and the function of visualization in preparing for a presentation.

Visual Instruction

Answer Manuscript requires more rehearsal time for the presenter to internalize and master the information.

Rehearse with an Audience

Suggest to students that running through a presentation in front of a younger brother or sister or even the family pet will help simulate the conditions of the real event. Point out that getting used to eyes on you while you talk is an important step in overcoming communication apprehension. **L1**

Communication Tip

Many presenters like to focus on one or two friendly members of an audience and to check on their responses from time to time during a presentation. This helps to personalize a large audience and to keep the presenter from worrying about everyone's response.

Visual Instruction

Answer Rehearsing with an audience helps the presenter interact with and receive feedback from listeners.

Decide How to Rehearse. There is no best way to rehearse a presentation. Select the rehearsal method that works best for you. Some presenters like to have a live audience to provide feedback during a rehearsal. Others prefer to rehearse facing a wall or corner so that they hear only their own voices with no distractions. Some like to watch themselves in a mirror or videotape their rehearsals in order to evaluate and make changes. Occasionally, a presenter will walk around a room, exaggerating his or her nonverbal strategies to get a feel for which ones work best. Experiment with each of these rehearsal methods or develop your own until you find the method that works for you.

Rehearse with an Audience

Try to rehearse with an audience, even if it is made up of only one or two people. An audience will help you practice interacting with and receiving feedback from listeners. During the

It is a good idea to rehearse with an audience when possible. **Why?**

TECHNOLOGY *Activity*

Variety is the Spice of Life The same is true in your presentations. One good way to hold your audience's attention is to use several media in presenting your information. With a group, brainstorm a list of ten speech topics that would be of interest to you. Identify how you could use music, slides, computer graphics, an overhead projector, a video recording, handouts, and posters in two of these presentations. Try to find a use for every medium with both speech topics.

rehearsal, try to develop eye contact with the audience as you present your ideas. Watch how listeners react to your presentation. Are there places where they seem confused or lost? If so, find a way to clarify the confusing information.

Following the rehearsed presentation, ask your listeners if they could understand your ideas, if they needed more details or description, and if your audiovisual aids could be clearly perceived and understood. That way, you have the time to make necessary changes or adjustments before your actual presentation.

Internalize

Internalization is going over and over something until you absorb it. In communication, internalization falls just short of memorizing. When you internalize something, you learn what it means and the idea it conveys. The words may be different each time you relay it to an audience, but the message is the same.

MULTIPLE LEARNING STYLES
MEETING INDIVIDUAL NEEDS

Interpersonal Point out that few methods of rehearsal are more effective than presenting in front of a trial audience.

Activity Brainstorm with students for a list of topics upon which they could give three- to five-minute extemporaneous presentations without extra research. Topics might include Highlights of My Educational Career, How to Survive Family Vacations, Advice to the New Driver. Give them time to write notes and rehearse their presentations. Encourage class members to listen critically and to offer constructive advice.

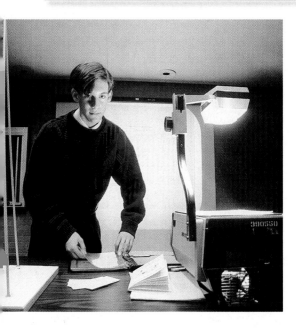

This young man prepares his visual aid equipment before a presentation. Why is it important to internalize an introduction and conclusion in rehearsal?

makes eye contact with only his or her notes or manuscript. Even if you are using a manuscript delivery, you need to rehearse several times with the manuscript so that you don't have to read to the audience and communicate solely with the paper in front of you. It is helpful to internalize at least the introduction, the conclusion, and the beginning and ending of each page of the manuscript so that you can turn pages without looking down. Internalizing any type of presentation will free you from your notes so you can develop eye contact with your audience.

Rehearse with Audiovisual Aids and Notes

Rehearse using your audiovisual aids and notes as you practice your presentation. Flip charts need to be flipped; projectors need to

Since the introduction and the conclusion of a presentation make the greatest impact on an audience, spend extra time internalizing those parts of your presentation. If you internalize your introduction and conclusion in rehearsal, you won't need to look at your notes during the first or last parts of your presentation. Your introduction, then, can fully accomplish its tasks—getting your audience's attention, previewing your presentation, applying your presentation to the audience, and establishing your ethos. Your conclusion can leave your audience with a positive image of you and your presentation.

As you rehearse, you also internalize the other information in your presentation so that you won't need to constantly rely on your notes or your manuscript. Audiences generally do not respond well to a presenter who

COMMUNICATION Strategies

HANDLING NOTES OR MANUSCRIPT

✓ Arrange your note cards or manuscript pages in a logical order.

✓ Practice turning pages or cards smoothly, with a minimum of shuffling and noise.

✓ If no table or podium is available, rehearse with your cards held in either hand but not in both hands. This gives you a free hand for gesturing and using your audio-visual aids.

✓ If you must hold your notes, write on only one side of the note card. Audiences may be distracted by any writing they can see on the backs of your cards.

Preparing for Presentations **555**

COMMUNICATION Strategies

HANDLING NOTES OR MANUSCRIPT

Have students form pairs and take notes on their partner's biographical information. Ask them to transfer their notes to one side of an index card and invite volunteers to present a brief oral biography of their partner, using their notes unobtrusively. **L2**

3 ASSESS

Assign Section 3 Assessment as a homework or in-class activity.

🕐 Use *Interactive Tutor Self-Assessment Software* to review Section 3.

Section 17–3 Quiz

Name _____ Date _____ Class _____ SECTION QUIZ 17-3

PREPARING FOR PRESENTATIONS
Rehearsing Presentations

SCORE

Matching Match each item in the left column with the best selection from the right column. Write the letter of the item on the line provided. Answers may be used more than once. *(10 points each)*

_____ 1. having "butterflies" in your stomach
_____ 2. learning the main ideas and points of a presentation
_____ 3. a quarterback picturing in his mind a touchdown pass
_____ 4. turning negative images into positive ones
_____ 5. similar to memorizing

a. visualization
b. communication apprehension
c. internalization

Multiple Choice In the blank provided, write the letter of the item that best answers each question. *(10 points each)*

_____ 6. Which of the following is *not* a likely cause of communication apprehension?
a. previous bad experiences while speaking
b. a presentation being a large part of your final grade
c. how well you do affecting your yearly bonus
d. having spoken to this group numerous times

_____ 7. What is a specific way to manage communication apprehension?
a. Believe in yourself and that you will do a great job.
b. Look at the negatives in order to be able to eliminate them next time.
c. Spend little time preparing to keep your mind from getting nervous.
d. Don't do many presentations.

_____ 8. Which presentation requires the most rehearsal time?
a. symposium
b. extemporaneous
c. manuscript
d. memorized

_____ 9. Why should you practice with an audience?
a. to get feedback from them
b. to make sure the room has enough space for everyone
c. to ensure that your audiovisual equipment works
d. to have time to practice pronunciations of unfamiliar words

_____ 10. Which of the following strategies for handling notes is *not* correct?
a. Arrange note cards in logical order.
b. Write on both sides of the note cards to avoid having too many.
c. Rehearse with your note cards held in only one hand.
d. Practice turning cards smoothly.

Visual Instruction

Answer Technical difficulties in handling visual aids and the unavailability of equipment needed for presenting the aids can destroy a presentation.

MEETING INDIVIDUAL NEEDS — MULTIPLE LEARNING STYLES

Bodily-Kinesthetic Point out that while technology has made presentations more enjoyable for the audience, it has not made the presenter's task any simpler. Making a smooth transition between notes and audiovisual aids is a skill that requires dexterity.

Activity Have students choose subjects of interest to them in any field. Ask them to prepare extemporaneous presentations of approximately five minutes using any two of the audiovisual aids mentioned in the Technology Activity on page 554. In their presentations, students should unobtrusively handle notes and aim for a seamless integration of words and aids.

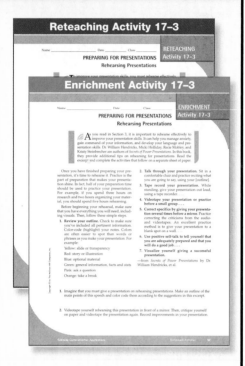

Reteaching Activity 17-3

Name _____ Date _____ Class _____ RETEACHING Activity 17-3
PREPARING FOR PRESENTATIONS
Rehearsing Presentations

Enrichment Activity 17-3

Name _____ Date _____ Class _____ ENRICHMENT Activity 17-3
PREPARING FOR PRESENTATIONS
Rehearsing Presentations

4 CLOSE

Have students review their responses to the Bellringer on page 548. Ask them to set a goal for themselves in the skill they considered when answering those questions. Suggest that they create a practice/preparation time line that they might follow to achieve that goal. Invite volunteers to share their time lines with the class.

Extra-Credit Project

Ask students to interview five individuals in different fields on the subject of preparation for a performance or presentation. Suggest that they ask their interviewees the same key questions about managing anxiety and effective rehearsing. Have them present their findings as a poster or a report.

be aimed and focused. These actions take time during a presentation and can present problems if you're not well prepared. Unfortunately, technical difficulties can destroy a presentation. Imagine, for example, that you have planned to use a number of overhead transparencies. However, at the last moment you discover that the only available overhead projector has a burned-out bulb. Audiences may lose interest while a presenter tries to fix an audiovisual aid that is not operating correctly. Rehearsal minimizes these inconveniences.

Also, make sure that your notes or manuscript will not detract from your message in the presentation. The rehearsal notes shown in the Communication Strategies checklist on the previous page can help you learn to handle your notes so they will not distract your audience members.

It is often said that the way to practice something is the way you will perform it. Making your rehearsal time as realistic as possible can help relieve your fears when the real presentation time rolls around. Moreover, the more fun you have rehearsing, the more lively and enthusiastic your presentation is likely to be. The more lively and enthusiastic your presentation is, the more interested your audience will be. The more interested your audience is, the more likely you are to accomplish the goals of your presentation.

Section 3 Assessment

Visit the *Glencoe Communication Applications* Web site at **communicationapplications. glencoe.com** and click on **Self-Check and Study Guide 17.3** to review your understanding of rehearsing presentations.

Review Key Terms

1. Define each term and write it in a sentence: communication apprehension, visualization, internalization.

Check Understanding

2. Name some of the causes of communication apprehension.

3. What is the most important strategy for managing communication apprehension? Name and describe three other management strategies.

4. **Hypothesize** How would you prepare thoroughly for a short extemporaneous presentation to your school board? Describe an ideal rehearsal session.

APPLICATION *Activity*

Managing Communication Apprehension What worries you most about giving a presentation? Write your main fears or concerns on the left side of a sheet of paper. Then, form groups of four to six students. As a group, discuss effective strategies for overcoming the most common presentation fears. Write any helpful pointers to the right of each fear you listed. Finally, discuss these tips as a class. Were you able to add pointers to your list? Write a brief plan for working these apprehension-management techniques into your rehearsals.

Section 3 Assessment Answers

1. Accept all reasonable sentences.
2. Fear of a new experience, being the center of attention, previous bad experiences, fear of possible unfavorable consequences.
3. Rehearsing; being prepared by following all of the steps in the presentation-preparation process; gaining experience by giving many small presentations before having to give a large one; thinking positively about your abilities and preparation.
4. Possible answer: First, I would visualize myself giving an effective presentation. I also would invite a few of my friends to serve as my practice audience. I would work to internalize my presentation by giving my presentation at full volume with gestures and movement. As my presentation developed and as my friends gave me feedback, I would make changes or mark reminders on my notes.

Application Activity Answers will differ from student to student but should reflect an understanding of managing communication apprehension.

Communication Self-Assessment

Preparing for Presentations

How Do You Rate?

On a separate sheet of paper, respond to the following statements. Put a check mark at the end of each skill you would like to improve.

KEY: A Always   **R** Rarely
      U Usually   **N** Never
      S Sometimes

1. I have no difficulty remembering the ideas for presentations.
2. I use extemporaneous speaking as often as possible.
3. When asked to give an impromptu speech, I organize my ideas quickly and present them without difficulty.
4. To avoid being misunderstood, I present with a manuscript.
5. I work with other group members to develop a consistent approach and style for a group presentation.
6. I practice for a group presentation by paying attention to consistency, cues, and transitions.
7. When I am the leader of a panel discussion, I keep the panel focused on one topic at a time.
8. I choose a symposium to present several different points of view.
9. When worried about a presentation, I remind myself that a little apprehension may improve delivery.
10. I try to rehearse presentations with one or two people as an audience.

How Do You Score?

Review your responses. Give yourself 5 points for every A, 4 for every U, 3 for every S, 2 for every R, and 1 for every N. Total your points and evaluate your score.

41–50 Excellent You may be surprised to find out how much you can improve your skills.

31–40 Good In this course, you can learn ways to make your skills better.

21–30 Fair Practice applying the skills taught in this course.

1–20 Needs Improvement Carefully monitor your improvement as you work through this course.

Setting Communication Goals

If you scored Excellent or Good, complete Part A. If your score was Fair or Needs Improvement, complete Part B.

Part A 1. I plan to put the following ideas into practice:
         2. I plan to share the following information about communication with the following people:

Part B 1. The behaviors I need to change most are:
         2. To bring about these changes, I will take these steps:

Communication Self-Assessment

Have students respond to the statements using the key, then evaluate their strengths. Based on their scores, assign either Part A or Part B of the goal-setting activity. Survey the class for the item on the self-assessment survey that scored the highest and lowest points. Discuss with students the possible reasons for the results and ways in which they could improve their skills.

Communication Journal Activity

Students should understand that under normal circumstances, they are exposed to presentations every day. In their Communication Journals, have them report briefly on five presentations they have heard over the course of a week. Ask them to classify the presentations as manuscript, memorized, extemporaneous, or impromptu. Each entry should include the reason for the presentation and whether or not the student felt it was well prepared.

Communication Tip

Encourage students to select someone whom they consider to be a model communicator. By asking what it is about this person's style of presentation that is so effective, students may discover communication skills of their own that they would like to develop.

MEETING INDIVIDUAL NEEDS — MULTIPLE LEARNING STYLES

Linguistic Students should understand that it is often the title of a presentation that draws an audience in the first place. According to Sam Deep and Lyle Sussman in *Smart Moves*, a book of business advice, appealing titles may ask a question, use subtitles, create intrigue, explain the main benefit of the presentation, or employ attention-getting words such as *you, new, amazing, power, secret, magic,* and *challenge*.

Activity Brainstorm with the class for a number of appealing presentation topics. Have them choose five of these topics and create catchy titles for each one. Write their suggestions on the chalkboard and vote on those that students find the most effective.

Writing an Executive Summary

Objective: To create an executive summary of a report

Teaching Suggestions and Strategies

Connection to the Workplace

Students should understand that an executive summary serves two purposes: (1) to give a thumbnail sketch of a report's findings or recommendations and (2) to direct the reader to an area of particular interest. Some readers will want no more than a very simple overview of the issues. Others will seek specific sections of the report to read in depth. To accomplish these tasks, the executive report must be laid out in a manner that is instantly intelligible to the scanning eye. The topic must be concisely presented and the principal points clearly differentiated from supporting details. This is accomplished through the use of different font styles, indentations, and spacing on the page. Point out that in a summary of this sort, design is almost as important as content. Longer reports sometimes have two executive reports: one to be taken in at a glance, the other a more detailed account. The latter will often include a formal conclusion.

Grammar Tip

When making comparisons using words ending in *-er* or *-est*, do not also use *more* or *most*. These words serve the same purpose and result in an unnecessary double comparison.

Writing an Executive Summary

Busy managers don't always have time to read an entire report. For this reason, writers often include an executive summary at the beginning of a report. An executive summary is an abbreviated version of a long report. Use the following tips to write a useful executive summary.

- Introduce the Subject of the Report.
- Provide Background Information.
- Include Reference Points.
- Organize the Information.
- Highlight Key Information.

Introduce the Subject of the Report. Briefly describe the topic of the report at the beginning of your executive summary. If the report is written in a problem-solution format, explain this in your summary. If it is an investigative report, discuss the goal of the investigation. Prepare the reader for the information that comes next.

Provide Background Information. Give your reader enough information so that he or she can understand the main points of the report. You can use statistics or other data to clarify your ideas.

Include Reference Points. Provide page references in your executive summary. These features make it easy for readers to quickly locate more detailed information within the original report.

Organize the Information. Executive summaries are easier to read if they are organized. Although there are no specific rules for organizing an executive summary, the document should be designed in a way that makes it easy to read and understand. You can organize facts, ideas, and recommendations by separating them into paragraphs, numbering them, or using headings. Organization is an important consideration because most of the people who receive your report will read the summary.

Highlight Key Information. Headings and subheads are tools that aid readers. The main headings should appear in bold or italic type. Subheads can also be in bold or italic type. If so, they should be indented or underlined. Important recommendations and findings should also be clearly marked.

A model of an executive summary is shown on the next page. Notice how the main ideas and key points are set off by the use of numbers, italics, and boldface type.

 For additional information about business writing, see the *Guide to Business Communication* section of the Communication Survival Kit in the Appendix.

REAL-WORLD CONNECTION

State of the School Address One of the most important presentations in the world, delivered annually in Washington, D.C., is the president's State of the Union address. Students should realize that this weighty speech starts off, as all speeches do, with a series of notes on a piece of paper. **Activity** Have students form groups and ask them to imagine that they have been commissioned to present a fifteen-minute State of the School address, which will describe the high and low points of the last school year and suggest a plan for the future. Give groups a few minutes to write down items that they feel should be covered in this speech. Then, ask them to write a possible schedule for the preparation and rehearsal of their State of the School presentation. Ask groups to present their agendas and schedules to the class.

Communication Through Writing

EXECUTIVE SUMMARY

Subject: Steps that Flexible Steel Products can take to meet pollution regulations

Recommendations are listed in order of importance

1. **By following all of these recommendations, Flexible Steel Products will exceed current industry pollution standards.**

2. **Upgrade Computer Systems:** Newer computers increase efficiency.
   Test Laboratory: A newer computer system can compute test results faster. This will help production run more smoothly (page 24).
   Steel Production: A digital thermostat system can maintain an accurate constant temperature in the blast furnace. Avoiding temperature changes within the furnace will help conserve fuel (page 26).
   Painted Products: Using computer programs that can calculate exact measurements of paint needed for each product will significantly reduce waste.

3. **Reuse Materials:**
   Chemicals: Flexible Steel can clean and reuse the chemical blend used to treat steel.
   Filters: Exhaust filters in the smokestacks are currently recycled after one use. A new process will allow them to be reused instead.

4. **Replace Heating System:** Flexible Steel Products can install a more efficient heating system for the building. A new natural gas system could cut pollution by up to 20 percent. For more information, see page 11 of the report.

WRITING Activity

Imagine that you are an advertising consultant. Stock Logic, a small investment firm, has hired you to determine the best way to spend its advertising budget. Write an executive summary for your report using the following information.

- 50 percent of the people who invest with large firms learn about those companies from national ads. The data is on page 7 of this report.

- Advertising nationally is extremely expensive. The rates appear on page 14 of the report.

- 30 percent of the people who invest learn about companies from local commercials. This information can be found on page 35 of the report.

- On page 40, the report shows that ads for television are the most expensive.

- The report states on page 45 that radio advertising is very beneficial for small firms.

- Stock Logic has lower fees than its competitors. 80 percent of the people who invest using the World Wide Web do so because the low fees. This is discussed on page 48.

Teaching Activity

Have students form groups and ask them to create an executive summary of Chapter 17. Remind them that the main subject areas are already indicated by the numerous headings and subheadings. Encourage students to stick to the main points. With students' assistance, create a master summary of the chapter on the chalkboard.

WRITING Activity

Students' responses to this activity may be similar to the example provided here:

Executive Summary
Subject: *Findings and recommendations for the advertising budget of Stock Logic Study done by Silver Star Research*

Recommendation One
Radio advertising offers the most.
We recommend that Stock Logic Investors put the bulk of its money into radio ads. (See page 35 of this report.) This idea stems from the data on page 45 of this report. Small companies have the best results with radio advertising.

Recommendation Two
National ads are too expensive.
Large companies have good success advertising in nationwide magazines and newspapers. However, the costs of these ads is far beyond the budgets of small firms. (See page 14.)

GRAMMAR PRACTICE

Double Comparisons
Have students rewrite each of the following sentences, correcting the double comparisons.

1. My executive summary turned out to be more longer than I'd wanted. *(. . . turned out to be longer . . .)*

2. He is working for one of the most richest companies in the world. *(. . . one of the richest companies . . .)*

3. Her employer was the most earliest to get involved in micro circuitry. *(. . . the earliest . . .)*

4. They are expected to work more harder and longer than workers at rival companies. *(. . . work harder and longer . . .)*

5. At the moment, AdTel is the most fastest growing company in the country. *(. . . AdTel is the fastest growing . . .)*

Additional Resources
Appendix, "Guide to Business Communication"

Glencoe Writer's Assistant CD-ROM

Glencoe Interactive Grammar Software

Grade 9 Writer's Choice, Lesson 5.1

Reviewing Key Terms

1. c
2. d
3. g
4. a
5. e
6. f
7. b

Reviewing Key Concepts

1. (1) memorized, (2) manuscript, (3) extemporaneous, and (4) impromptu

2. If you forget one word, you can lose your place in the presentation. Memorized presentations often sound formal and boring.

3. A manuscript presentation

4. They want to use the fewest notes possible so the notes won't be a distraction during the presentation.

5. By writing reminders such as "smile" or "slow down" in the notes

6. Group members develop a consistent overall approach and style for a presentation when they work together.

Reviewing Key Terms

Read each definition. On a separate sheet of paper, write the number of the definition and the letter of the term that fits the definition best.

1. Is given with little advance preparation
2. A group discussion in front of an audience where information is shared conversationally
3. Going over something until you absorb it
4. Is written out and read aloud to an audience
5. Individuals speak on aspects of the same topic but interact little with other speakers
6. Mentally picturing doing something well
7. Is rehearsed and given with the use of notes

---

a. manuscript presentation   **e.** symposium

b. extemporaneous presentation   **f.** visualization

c. impromptu presentation   **g.** internalization

d. panel discussion

Reviewing Key Concepts

1. What are four different methods of delivery for a presentation?
2. Explain two drawbacks of using memorization as a method of delivery.
3. Which method of delivery is best for a sensitive topic or for a presentation that will appear in print?
4. Why do many extemporaneous speakers use only one or two index cards for their notes?
5. How can a presenter use notes to help his or her delivery?
6. Why is preparing together important when group members plan a group presentation?
7. List three tips for staging an effective group presentation.
8. Why does each member of a panel need to contribute on all aspects of the topic?

---

7. (1) Move around the room during the presentation. (2) Remove barriers such as podiums or tables between group members and the audience. (3) Place group members around the room to increase audience interest.

8. Audiences do not like to hear one or two speakers monopolize a panel discussion.

Assessment and Activities

Reading and Critical Thinking Skill

1. **Compare and Contrast** How are extemporaneous and impromptu presentations alike and different?

2. **Summary** Summarize the methods for preparing a presentation manuscript.

3. **Classifying Information** You and three classmates are giving a presentation to the rest of the class. Is your audience internal or external?

4. **Synthesis** Make a list of a panel discussion leader's responsibilities.

5. **Predict** As a representative for a conservation organization, Jamar has given one presentation per week for the last six weeks. This experience has given him confidence. How will Jamar's confidence affect the next audience he addresses?

Skill Practice Activity

Writing an Executive Summary Recall the last time you felt communication apprehension. In an executive summary, describe the physical and emotional symptoms you felt. Then explain how you plan to apply the strategies in Section 3 of this chapter to effectively manage these stage fright symptoms during your next presentation. Include communication terms such as visualization and internalization in your summary.

Cooperative Learning Activity

Multimedia Presentation As a class, form groups of three. As a group, choose a historical period such as the Middle Ages or the Roaring Twenties. Have one member prepare a panel discussion-forum on the period. The other two members are responsible for collecting music and visuals—either slides or transparencies—that complement the presentation. Limit the presentation to five minutes. Include a question-and-answer session after the presentation.

Chapter Project

Planning Think of a career at which you would like to excel. What are some things that you can do in your everyday life that will contribute to your success in that field? If you would like to be a writer, for example, keeping a daily journal will help improve your language skills. Prepare a presentation that explains how regular daily activities can help you succeed professionally.

Presenting Conduct a symposium with the other students in your class. Choose another classmate to act as the moderator. Supply the moderator with a list of the group members' topics.

Chapter Project

Point out how various activities contribute to success in life. For instance, tutoring younger students might help students succeed later in careers that involve working with children. Remind students that a symposium is a formal affair that includes little or no audience participation. Ask the moderator to reread Section 2 to refresh his or her memory on the responsibilities of a moderator at a symposium.

Reading and Critical Thinking Skill

1. **Compare and Contrast** They are alike in that they are not completely written out but use notes instead. They are different in that an extemporaneous presentation is thoroughly rehearsed while an impromptu one is not.

2. **Summary** Double- or triple-space in a large font. Type words and ideas to be emphasized in bold print, a larger font, or on a separate page. Mark pages with delivery reminders and notes on audiovisual aids. Place pages back to back in plastic protectors.

3. **Classifying Information** Internal

4. **Synthesis** Students' answers should be similar to the following: A panel leader should introduce the members of the panel, introduce the topic, provide audience orientation, explain how the panel will proceed, preview the main ideas, keep the panel focused, provide helpful transitions, summarize what the group has said, establish rules for audience questions, and act as moderator.

5. **Predict** Answers will vary but students might suggest that an audience responds positively to a confident delivery.

Skill Practice Activity

Writing an Executive Summary

Students' summaries should mention the main strategies for managing communication apprehension.

Cooperative Learning Activity

Multimedia Presentation

You might show a few minutes from Ken Burns's *Civil War* series on video and point out how Burns uses words, pictures, and music to evoke an era. Remind students to use the rehearsal strategies described in Section 3. Allow time for presentations.

Chapter 18 Planning Guide

SECTION RESOURCES

Daily Objectives

Section 1

1. Explain the importance of an effective delivery
2. Explain how to achieve a positive stage presence
3. Distinguish between emphatic and descriptive gestures
4. Use effective verbal and nonverbal strategies in presentations
5. Make individual presentations to inform, persuade, or motivate an audience

Section 2

1. Interpret audience feedback
2. Respond empathically to audience interruptions
3. Participate effectively in a question-and-answer session following a presentation
4. Apply critical-listening strategies to evaluate a presentation
5. Evaluate the effectiveness of one's own presentation

Reproducible Resources

 Reproducible Lesson Plan 18-1
 Application Activities 18-1
 Guided Reading Workbook Activity 18-1
 Vocabulary Activity 18*
 Reteaching Activity 18-1*
 Enrichment Activity 18-1*
 Graphic Organizer Transparency Strategies and Activities 18-1

 Reproducible Lesson Plan 18-2
 Application Activities 18-2
 Guided Reading Workbook Activity 18-2
 Vocabulary Activity 18*
 Reteaching Activity 18-2*
 Enrichment Activity 18-2*
Graphic Organizer Transparency Strategies and Activities 18-2a, 18-2b, and 18-2c

Multimedia Resources

 Graphic Organizer Transparency 18-1
 Chapter 18 Teaching Transparency
 Interactive Tutor Self-Assessment
 PuzzleMaker
 ExamView® Pro Testmaker
Interactive Lesson Planner
 Communication in Action Video Chapter 18
 MindJogger
 communicationapplications.glencoe.com
 Presentation Plus!

 Graphic Organizer Transparency 18-2
 Chapter 18 Teaching Transparency
 Interactive Tutor Self-Assessment
 PuzzleMaker
 ExamView® Pro Testmaker
Interactive Lesson Planner
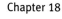 Communication in Action Video Chapter 18
 MindJogger
 communicationapplications.glencoe.com
 Presentation Plus!

Use Glencoe's *Presentation Plus!* multimedia teacher tool to easily present dynamic lessons that engage and motivate your students. Using Microsoft PowerPoint®, you can customize the presentations to create your own personalized lessons.

* Also available in Spanish

 Blackline Master   CD-ROM   Software
 Transparency   Videodisc   Videocassette   Web site

Chapter 18 Planning Guide

FOR THE TEACHER

Presentations

Explain to students that a presentation is something like a performance in which a person presents information to an audience. In most cases this is a speech, sometimes accompanied by exhibits or displayed material. Ask students to observe various presentations over a period of several days, perhaps in school, on television, or in other aspects of their lives. Have them try to judge each presentation in several ways: Does the speaker get his or her points across to the audience well? What kind of gestures, facial expressions, and other nonverbal communication does the speaker use? How involved is the audience with the speaker? How does the speaker respond to the audience?

Ask the class as a whole to discuss presentations they observed, sharing their answers to the questions and analyzing the presentations in other ways. Gather a consensus from the class of qualities of a good presentation—what works, what causes audiences to respond positively, what makes a speaker interesting, and so on.

CHAPTER RESOURCES

Resources for the Teacher

- *The McGraw-Hill 36-Hour Course: Business Presentations* by Lani Arrendondo, McGraw-Hill, 1994
- *A Practical Guide for Business Speaking* by Edward P. Bailey Jr., Oxford University Press, 1992
- *Winning 'em Over: A New Model for Managing in the Age of Persuasion* by Jay A. Conger, Simon & Schuster, 1998

Resources for the Student

- *Make Your Point!* by Cheryl Currid, Prima Publications, 1995
- *Making Successful Presentations: A Self-Teaching Guide* by Terry C. Smith, Wiley, 1991
- *The Presentations Kit: 10 Steps for Selling Your Ideas* by Claudyne Wilder, Wiley, 1994

Block Scheduling

Block scheduling differs from traditional class scheduling in the amount of time allotted to each period. The extended time frame provided by block scheduling affords you the opportunity to implement a greater number of research-oriented and activity-intense projects to motivate and involve your students. Activities that are particularly suited to use within the block-scheduling framework are identified throughout this chapter by the following designation:

KEY TO ABILITY LEVELS

Teaching Strategies have been coded for varying learning styles and abilities.

L1 **BASIC** activities for all students

L2 **AVERAGE** activities for average to above-average students

L3 **CHALLENGING** activities for above-average students

ELL **English Language Learner** activities

Chapter 18 Resource Manager

The following materials may be used when teaching the chapter. Materials for specific lessons are also shown at point-of-use in the margins of the Teacher's Wraparound Edition.

TEACHING TRANSPARENCIES

Chapter 18 Teaching Transparency

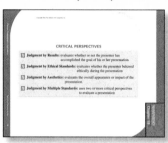

Graphic Organizer Transparency 18-1

Graphic Organizer Transparency 18-2

APPLICATION ACTIVITIES

Chapter 18, Section 1

Chapter 18, Section 2

Chapter 18, Cumulative

REINFORCEMENT AND REVIEW ACTIVITIES

Vocabulary Activity 18

Guided Reading Activity Workbook 18-1, 18-2

Reteaching Activities 18-1, 18-2

Chapter 18 Resource Manager

ASSESSMENT AND EVALUATION

Glencoe's **ASSESSMENT** ADVANTAGE

Section Quizzes 18–1, 18–2

Chapter 18 Test, Forms A & B

Performance Assessment Activity 18

ENRICHMENT AND EXTENSION

Technology Application Activity 18

Enrichment Activities 18–1, 18–2

ORAL PRESENTATION ACTIVITIES

Activities 12, 15–20

SPANISH RESOURCES

- Spanish Chapter and Unit Tests
- Spanish Vocabulary Activities
- Spanish Section Quizzes
- Spanish Reteaching Activities
- Spanish Enrichment Activities

MULTIMEDIA

- Interactive Tutor Self-Assessment
- ExamView® Pro Testmaker
- PuzzleMaker
- Communication in Action Videodisc and Videocassette
- MindJogger
- Interactive Lesson Planner
- Presentation Plus!
- Writer's Assistant
- Glencoe Interactive Grammar
- **communicationapplications.glencoe.com**

TEACHER PLANNING AND SUPPORT

- Reproducible Lesson Plans
- Interactive Lesson Planner
- Presentation Plus!

Making and Evaluating Presentations

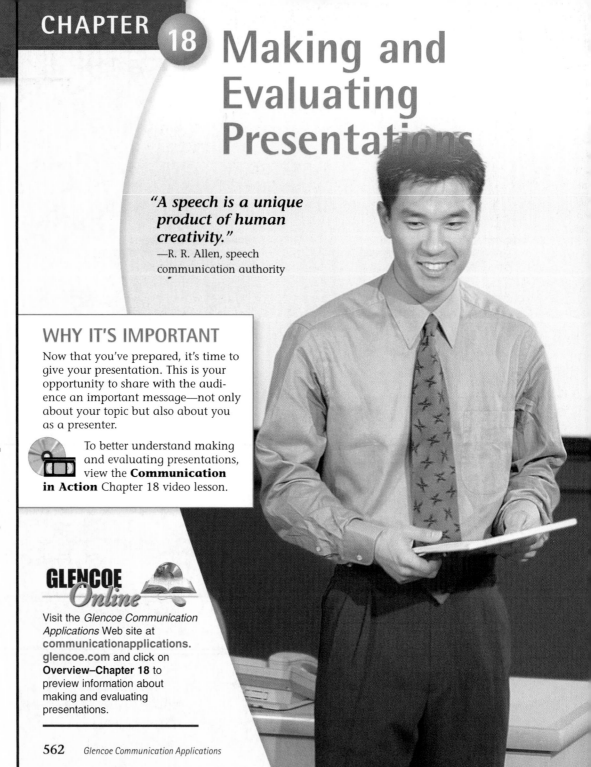

> *"A speech is a unique product of human creativity."*
> —R. R. Allen, speech communication authority

GLENCOE TECHNOLOGY

 MindJogger Videoquiz

Use *MindJogger* to preview the Chapter 18 content.

 VIDEODISC

Communication in Action

Have students view the Chapter 18 video and complete the Chapter 18 video lesson in the *Glencoe Communication in Action Strategies and Activities* booklet.

 Also available in VHS.

WHY IT'S IMPORTANT

Now that you've prepared, it's time to give your presentation. This is your opportunity to share with the audience an important message—not only about your topic but also about you as a presenter.

To better understand making and evaluating presentations, view the **Communication in Action** Chapter 18 video lesson.

GLENCOE Online

Direct students to **communication applications.glencoe.com**. Have them read the **Overview–Chapter 18** to identify the concepts they will study in the chapter. Ask a volunteer to list on the chalkboard or an overhead projector all concepts as they are offered.

GLENCOE Online

Visit the *Glencoe Communication Applications* Web site at **communicationapplications. glencoe.com** and click on **Overview–Chapter 18** to preview information about making and evaluating presentations.

562 *Glencoe Communication Applications*

WHY IT'S IMPORTANT

Ask a student to read aloud the quotation from R. R. Allen. Ask: **What is the connection between the speech Allen refers to and making presentations?** *(Answers should reflect the idea that a speech is one kind of presentation.)* Invite discussion. Then, have students preview the chapter by reading the headings and subheadings and looking at the photographs and captions.

Making a Presentation

GUIDE TO READING

Objectives

1. Explain the importance of an effective delivery.
2. Explain how to achieve a positive stage presence.
3. Distinguish between emphatic and descriptive gestures.
4. Use effective verbal and nonverbal strategies in presentations.
5. Make individual presentations to inform, persuade, or motivate an audience.

Terms to Learn

delivery

projecting

stage presence

emphatic gesture

descriptive gesture

*I*magine you arrive at school one morning and all your teachers are missing. Overnight, they were replaced with detailed guidebooks for each class. Your first reaction might be "All right! No teachers!" After a while, though, what do you think would happen to your interest level in class? Would a book meet all your communication needs? Do you think you would learn as much in class?

At one time or another, you probably have heard someone say, "It's not what you say but how you say it that counts." In the example above, certainly the basic information in the book would be similar to what your teacher might convey during the class. However, the book would be lacking that all-important human touch.

A guidebook cannot use facial expressions or body talk to help make messages clear. It cannot change its vocal characteristics to fit the situation and keep interest levels high. Most importantly, a book cannot check for understanding or adapt to feedback from its audience.

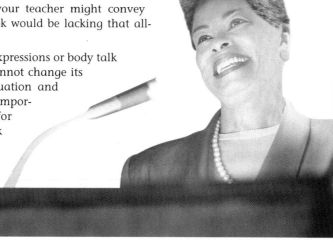

A speaker can offer information in a way that books can't. How does a speaker convey information differently from a book?

Making and Evaluating Presentations **563**

---

1 FOCUS

Bellringer

Have students read the scenario identified in the first paragraph on this page and respond to the questions. *(Most students will feel that their interest would eventually wane and a book could not really replace a teacher.)* Extend the discussion to include reasons students feel as they do.

You may use Graphic Organizer Transparency 18–1 to introduce this section.

Visual Instruction

Answer A speaker can use facial expressions and body talk to help make the message clear. Also, a speaker can check for understanding from his or her audience.

RESOURCE MANAGER

Teaching Tools

- Interactive Lesson Planner
- Reproducible Lesson Plan 18–1
- Application Activities 18–1

Reproducible Masters

- Guided Reading Activity Workbook 18–1
- Enrichment Activity 18–1
- Reteaching Activity 18–1
- Section Quiz 18–1
- Transparency Strategies and Activities Booklet 18–1

Transparencies

- Graphic Organizer Transparency 18–1
- Chapter 18 Teaching Transparency

Technology Resources

- Interactive Tutor Self-Assessment Software
- Presentation Plus! Software
- ExamView® Pro Testmaker
- PuzzleMaker Software
- communicationapplications.glencoe.com

2 TEACH

Effective Delivery of a Presentation

As students react to the example of the poor presentation, ask them to consider examples of both poor and good presentations they have experienced. Tell them to think about presentations they have seen on television as well as in "real life." Have them discuss the role they think practice and forethought had in the good presentations. **L2**

TECHNOLOGY *Activity*

Using an Overhead Projector You might want to mention that a speaker who has prepared transparencies for use with an overhead projector needs to make sure that a suitable projector will be available when needed. Ask students to extend the example: Even when a projector is available, what else could go wrong? *(Answers might include that it doesn't have a working light, it needs an extension cord to reach the nearest plug, there is no suitable screen to project the image onto, and so on.)* **L1**

In your teacherless classroom, you soon would discover that the way a message is presented greatly affects the way it is received. Without an effective delivery method, the information in the guidebook probably would not have as much of an impact on you, the audience. **Delivery** is how a presenter uses his or her body and voice to communicate a message to an audience. In the pages that follow, you will examine the most effective strategies for delivering the message of your presentation.

IMPORTANCE OF DELIVERY

Just like most worthwhile efforts, developing a polished delivery takes practice. The payoff, however, is well worth it. A polished delivery not only gives you confidence for making presentations, but it also causes audiences to perceive you as more credible. With these two important factors on your side, it is much easier to accomplish the goals of your presentations. Without them, it can be very difficult to make a positive impact on your audience.

Consider, for example, that you have spent hours helping a friend prepare a presentation to the new-products division of her company. She wants to describe a new use for one of the company's existing products that is no longer selling well. The friend has thoroughly researched the marketing background of the product, has consulted with sales representatives, and even has developed a prototype for a modification of the product. In all, she has spent a great deal of time researching and developing her presentation.

Unfortunately, the morning of the presentation, your friend got soaked in the rain while running from her car to the building. Because she was running late, she didn't have time for her hair and clothes to fully dry

before the meeting. She also was chatting when she was introduced to the group and did not hear until she was called a second time. To make matters worse, a minute or two into your friend's presentation, someone in the back asked her to speak up because she couldn't be heard. She mumbled that she was sorry, lost her place in her presentation, and ended up repeating herself.

When your friend finally unveiled her prototype, it was positioned poorly, causing her to speak with her back to the audience much of the time. In addition, she mispronounced several of the technical terms from her research.

Glad to finally finish with the presentation, your friend immediately bolted out of the room and went back to her office. She was notified that afternoon that the board had dismissed her idea and someone else would be researching other uses for the product. Of course, your friend was extremely disappointed. What went wrong?

Even though your friend put a lot of time and effort into preparing her presentation, she did not consider that the way she looked and sounded during her presentation would affect her credibility. In short, your friend forgot about the importance of an effective delivery.

TECHNOLOGY *Activity*

Using an Overhead Projector The best-prepared speakers consider all potential problems while getting ready for an upcoming presentation. Develop a list of problems you might encounter on the day you are to deliver a presentation. Next, provide a list of actions you might take to resolve or avoid these problems. Put your list of potential problems and solutions on a transparency and present them to the class using an overhead projector.

MEETING INDIVIDUAL NEEDS — ENGLISH LANGUAGE LEARNERS

Delivering Presentations Students may have little confidence in their ability to make smooth presentations because they may be self-conscious about accents and limited English proficiency. **Activity** Encourage students to use notes during their presentations. Suggest that on the notes they use phonetic spellings for English words they find difficult to pronounce. Encourage them to practice their speeches in front of someone more proficient in the language. This person can serve as a coach or mentor who helps students pronounce words or choose more precise words for their presentations. Remind students to provide constructive criticism as they help one another prepare for a presentation. **ELL**

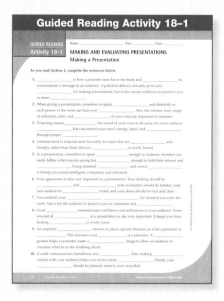

Some members of this audience appear to be having a hard time understanding the information. Identify ways to utilize your voice effectively.

Using Appropriate Vocal Characteristics

Two of the most important aspects of delivery are the quality and characteristics of your voice. Even a well-prepared presentation will be a failure if the audience cannot hear and understand your message. Remember to speak clearly and distinctly so that each person in the room can hear you. Also, remember what you read in Chapter 5 about developing a speaking voice that has a desirable, medium pitch and a broad enough range of inflection to convey emotion and interest.

Finally, pay special attention to the volume, tone, and rate of your voice. The following paragraphs provide some important tips for using these three characteristics effectively in your presentation.

Volume As you learned in Chapter 5, speaking too loudly or too softly can influence the way an audience perceives you and your message. In a presentation, the key to volume is to speak loudly enough so that the person farthest away can hear you clearly. This does not mean that you should shout if you are presenting to a large group. That can make the people closest to you very uncomfortable. Rather, you should be able to whisper and still be heard by the people in the back row. This is accomplished by projecting. Projecting means sending the sound of your voice to all areas of a room without shouting.

Projecting is a lot like throwing a ball to the person on the back row of your presentation. It takes only a certain amount of energy—no more, no less. You also must control the force or intensity of the throw. Finally, you have to consider the effects of outside factors, such as the other people in the room.

Your voice is very much like the ball in this example. You control its energy, force, and intensity through proper breathing. You also need to consider other existing factors. If some

Making and Evaluating Presentations **565**

Checking Voice Characteristics

In trying to analyze their own voice characteristics, students will have to hear themselves speak. Use a tape recorder to record from the back of the room a few minutes of each student reading aloud while standing at the front. This will give students a preliminary sense of how their voices sound when they make a presentation. **L1**

Visual Instruction

Answer Speak clearly and distinctly; use a speaking voice with a medium pitch and broad range of inflection; and pay attention to volume, rate, and tone.

INTERDISCIPLINARY CONNECTION

Drama Actors and professional speakers are very aware of using vocal characteristics such as tone, volume, and tempo to communicate well.

Activity Invite your school's drama instructor or a local actor or college drama teacher to talk to your class about the use of one's voice in getting a message across. Such a person will be able to demonstrate these vocal techniques, which will make them much more concrete to students. He or she may also give students vocal exercises that actors and or singers use to improve their vocal techniques.

VOICING YOUR PRESENTATION EFFECTIVELY

Have students read the list and brainstorm possible additions. Ask volunteers to demonstrate each point. Students may want to copy the list for their own future reference. You might also encourage students to demonstrate effective and less effective use of vocal qualities. **L2**

Grammar Tip

Pronouns such as *everyone*, *no one*, or *someone* are singular in form. Pronouns that refer to these pronouns should also be singular. For example, you would say, "Everyone gave his or her speech," not "Everyone gave their speech."

Fast and Slow

Demonstrate for students that the rate at which you speak can affect comprehensibility and ability to hold an audience's attention. Read a passage at a very rapid rate and ask students comprehension questions afterward. Then read another passage very slowly and ask students questions about the passage afterward. Finally, read a passage at a normal rate. Discuss with students how the rate of your reading affected their ability to listen to and understand you. Relate this listening experience to the need for speakers to speak at a rate that holds attention and is comfortable for listeners.

outside noise or the audience itself is creating a disturbance, you'll have to "toss" your voice a little harder to get it to that back row.

Tone Most presentations call for a relaxed, responsive, conversational tone of voice. Listeners tend to respond more favorably to voices that are conversational and friendly than to those that are harsh or overly formal. In general, audiences like to be talked "to" or "with" instead of "at." During your presentation, strive for a tone that reflects openness and friendliness. Think of how you would like to be talked to and imitate that tone.

Rate and Tempo In a presentation, remember to speak slowly enough so audience members can easily follow what you are saying but rapidly enough to hold their interest and attention. The rate and tempo of your presentation should reflect the mood and intensity of your message. It can be easily adapted for emphasis or clarity. For instance, you can emphasize an important statement by using a slow, deliberate rate of delivery. Increasing your rate can help you build emotion for a certain point in your presentation.

Your voice is an important tool of expression during a presentation. Volume, force, pitch, inflection, tone, and rate can all be adapted to provide emphasis and variety. However, any vocal techniques you use should be motivated by the content of your message and your sincere desire to communicate with your audience. When used appropriately, they can help you clearly convey meanings and feelings to make your presentation as effective as possible.

Improving Verbal Messages

An audience will judge how prepared you are as a presenter by the style of presentation you use during your presentation. If you want to convey an image to your audience that you

are intelligent and competent, you will need to sound intelligent and informed. You do this in a presentation by using standard diction and correct grammar.

Diction In a presentation to a large group of people, you will want everyone in the room to understand what you are saying. You will want to use standard diction that is commonly understood by all members of your audience. You will want to use language that is clear and distinctly articulated and enunciated. You should also verify that you are pronouncing words correctly so that you don't confuse your audience. Many of the standards about clear and articulate speech that you learned in Chapter 4 will also apply to the way you use language in a formal presentation.

VOICING YOUR PRESENTATION EFFECTIVELY

- Speak at a medium pitch with higher- and lower-pitched inflections.
- Use a broad range of inflection to convey emotion and make your presentation interesting.
- Choose a volume that is appropriate for the room size and audience size.
- Project your voice so that everyone in the room can hear you clearly.
- Use a friendly, conversational tone.
- Speak slowly enough to be understood but not so slowly that you're boring.
- Use standard diction and correct grammar.

MULTIPLE LEARNING STYLES

MEETING INDIVIDUAL NEEDS

Linguistic Students will benefit from paying close attention to television news broadcasters, whose use of language and good diction allow them to serve as models.

Activity Have students choose one or two television news anchors to watch regularly for several weeks. Ask students to identify techniques used by the anchors and to adopt the techniques for a short news presentation of their own. Students might read aloud a short newspaper article as though they were a news anchor.

Grammar In many of your daily communication interactions, a few grammatical slips will probably have no impact. However, when you are making a presentation, a grammatical error can greatly reduce your credibility with an audience. Even in an informal presentation, you may be able to get by with a grammatical violation here and there. In formal presentations, the rules for correct grammar apply. Subjects should agree with verbs, pronoun references should be clear, and modifiers should be correctly placed. If your language is a measure of the way an audience will perceive your preparedness, then you should use the most correct language you know how to use.

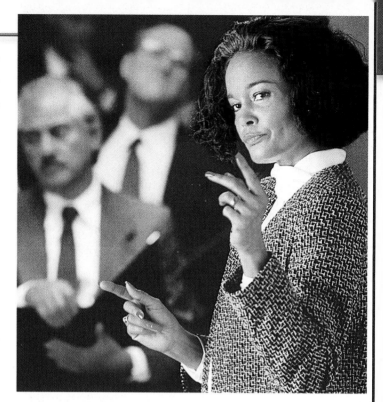

A professional appearance will send a message of competence to the audience. *What type of clothing is appropriate when making a presentation?*

Using Other Nonverbal Cues Appropriately

In the earlier example of the friend's presentation to her company, more consideration should have been given to her nonverbal messages. Your friend's hair and clothing were damp and probably a bit disheveled. She had to be introduced twice because she was talking instead of listening at the start of the meeting. These cues sent a message of unprofessionalism to her audience even before she began her presentation. They probably also planted seeds of doubt about her credibility.

Appearance What do you want your audience to perceive as you enter the room and approach the presentation area? Part of

the presentation process is to consider clothing and grooming as valuable visual aids to your presentation.

As you read in Chapter 5, you typically will want to wear simple, tailored clothes that are appropriate for yourself, the audience, the occasion, and the task. Any accessories should be simple and tasteful, and neither clothing nor accessories should distract the audience from your presentation.

Remember, too, that your hair and shoes are part of your appearance. Hair should be neatly and conservatively styled so that it does not hang down in your eyes or hide much of your face. You may consider combing it quickly before your presentation. Shoes should be neat, clean, and comfortable.

Making and Evaluating Presentations **567**

CRITICAL THINKING ACTIVITY

Work with another teacher or a sophisticated volunteer from your class to present two different versions of the same speech to your group. One of the presenters should "follow all the rules," using good verbal and nonverbal cues. The other should break several of the rules by dressing sloppily, speaking too slowly and mumbling, and so on. Begin by telling the class that they will hear the same presentation from two different people. Students should note which presentation is most successful and why. After the presentations, encourage students to discuss how they reacted to the two presentations.

Nonverbal Communication

If possible, show videotapes of effective and ineffective speakers. Turn off the sound for a graphic lesson to students in the importance of some of the points mentioned on pages 567–572. Encourage students to analyze the speakers' nonverbal communication in their presentations. Politicians are good examples to show, as are talk show hosts, news anchors, and sports announcers. **L2**

■ Visual Instruction

Answer An illusion created by the quality of the energy, poise, confidence, and control that a presenter conveys to an audience

Too Enthusiastic?

Can a speaker project an image that is too enthusiastic for the topic or the audience? Would it be appropriate for a businessperson to have a cheery bounciness when announcing labor cutbacks, for example? Discuss these questions with students. Ask them to identify well-known individuals or situations in which the speaker's enthusiasm seemed overwhelming or too frivolous. *(Students might suggest that many presenters in infomercials seem overly enthusiastic.)* Remind students that every occasion and audience is different and a presenter should adjust his or her presentation style to accommodate the differences. **L2**

It naturally follows that grooming and personal hygiene are important. You do not want any part of your appearance to distract your audience. If you want an audience to accept you as professional and well organized, make sure you project that visual image.

You may have heard the saying, "When you look good, you feel good." This simply means that taking a little extra effort with your appearance can help increase your confidence as a presenter. The more confident you are, the more you can concentrate on giving an effective presentation.

Your Entrance The way you approach the area where your presentation will be given is extremely important. Not only does it set the tone for your presentation, but it also can affect your own confidence. You begin to communicate a nonverbal message to the audience the moment you enter the room. From that point on, you establish what is known as "stage presence." **Stage presence** is an illusion created by the quality of the energy, poise, confidence, and control that a presenter conveys to an audience.

You will want the audience to perceive you as competent and sincere. Therefore, your gait and posture should convey confidence and enthusiasm. Ahead of time, watch yourself in a mirror as you practice entering the presentation area. Walk to the podium briskly, turn, and smile at your audience before you begin speaking. This gives the audience time to focus on you and what you are about to say. Don't rush the beginning of your presentation. Give yourself a minute to size up your audience and get settled before you begin.

A confident entrance not only projects a positive image to others, but it also is an effective strategy for battling communication apprehension. The more confident

and informed you appear, the more self-assured you will be. Self-assurance can make it easier to remember all the information you wish to convey in your message.

Posture Good posture also communicates confidence and enthusiasm to your audience. It begins with well-balanced, firm footing. If you begin to speak with your body off balance, you may begin to sway or shuffle during your presentation. These actions can tell an audience that you are nervous or uncertain about what you are saying and can damage your credibility.

Remember from Chapter 5 the image of a string through your spine. Your head should be held up, your shoulders back, and your arms relaxed. This is considered good posture for speaking. A tense body communicates tension and anxiety that can create a negative audience perception.

■ This speaker projects a positive stage presence. **What is stage presence?**

MULTIPLE LEARNING STYLES

Bodily-Kinesthetic Students who use body language effectively will be able to demonstrate for the class negative and positive nonverbal techniques.

Activity Ask one or two volunteers to pantomime positive and negative examples of speakers' entrances, posture, movement, gestures, facial expressions, and so on. The class can identify each negative and positive technique as they are role-played. Encourage them to discuss how each technique affects the way they view the performer.

When you use good posture during your presentation, you not only look more confident and credible, but you also sound better. When you stand up straight, you are better able to project your voice. This ultimately helps you communicate more effectively with everyone in your audience.

Movement Some amount of movement in a presentation is good. It keeps you from looking emotionless or overly tense. However, when you move from one position to another during your presentation, have a good reason. For instance, you may occasionally want to take a step to the left or to the right to emphasize a point or an idea. You may need to move closer to an audiovisual aid or field a question from a particular side of the audience. In a small or fairly informal presentation, you may wish to move out into your audience to make audience members feel more included.

Additionally, movement can be used to maintain control of an audience. If an audience is getting restless or unruly, simply stepping toward them or walking out into the room can bring their attention back to you and what you are saying. Try to be casual and conversational when you approach an audience. Walk at a slow or normal gait. A forceful or quick approach can be perceived as threatening and confrontational and can make an audience defensive. Becoming defensive will usually cause an audience to turn off what you have to say.

You will, however, want to watch carefully how much you move during a presentation. Constant movement can be distracting to an audience, because people may start watching you instead of listening to what you're saying. Therefore, have a reason for each movement.

Gestures Many presenters worry about what to do with their hands during a presentation. These people probably use their

Speakers use movement and gestures as nonverbal cues during a presentation. What is the problem with constant movement?

hands to reinforce their messages when talking with friends, but when they get in front of a group of people, their hands feel larger than life. Remember that the more natural you are as a presenter, the better you will be. Allow your hands to rest naturally at your side or on the podium when you are not using them for specific gestures.

Effectively using gestures in a presentation involves more than knowing what to do with your hands, however. When you communicate with an audience, you gesture with all parts of your body: You nod your head, you shrug your shoulders, or you lean toward your audience. In general, presenters use two types of gestures: emphatic gestures and descriptive gestures.

Emphatic Gestures An *emphatic gesture* stresses or places special attention on what a presenter is saying. It adds emphasis. Many popular presenters use emphatic gestures. They may slap their foreheads in disbelief or even bang their fists on the table. They may raise their eyebrows, roll their eyes, or gesture

Making and Evaluating Presentations **569**

Communication Tip

Think about a speaker or presenter you have seen whose presentations you liked very much. Analyze that speaker's nonverbal cues to decide what was especially appealing.

Dɪᴅ Yᴏᴜ Kɴᴏᴡ?

It takes many more muscles and energy to frown than to smile.

Visual Instruction

Answer Constant movement can be distracting.

Picture What I'm Saying

Magazines and newspapers often publish pictures of people speaking in informal and formal presentations. Ask students to cut out some of these pictures and bring them to class. Working as a class, devise captions—serious and humorous—of what individuals in the pictures might be saying. All captions should be based on the posture, movement, gestures, and facial expressions conveyed in the pictures. **L1**

INCLUSION STRATEGIES

Special Needs Students who use American sign language to communicate are often very expressive as they communicate a message.

Activity Have groups of students prepare a two-minute presentations on topics of their choice. Have each group share its speech with a student who uses American sign language. Ask the student to interpret the speech as it is given. Encourage students to discuss how the interpretation added to the spoken word.

Facial Expressions

Invite volunteers to act out various kinds of emotions silently with just their facial expressions. Let audience members decide what the actor is expressing in each case. **L1**

To Read or Not to Read

Explain to students that they should have notes in front of them as they make a presentation to ensure that they stay on track and don't forget something important. However, they should not attempt to write out every word of a speech and then read it aloud as their presentation. This would make their presentation sound unnatural and make them appear unapproachable. It also would prevent them from being comfortable making eye contact. They should use natural spoken language as much as possible as they talk through their speech, referring to their notes only as necessary. **L2**

broadly to include the audience. This type of gesture shows that the presenter is excited about his or her topic and wants the audience to be as involved as he or she is. This type of gesture, when motivated, sincere, and done in moderation, can greatly increase your credibility as a presenter.

Descriptive Gestures A *descriptive gesture* allows a presenter to create a mental image to help his or her audience visualize what he or she is talking about. In a way, descriptive gestures are a form of visual aid. They can help a presenter convey the size or shape of an object, the position of two or more objects in relation to each other, or other spatial information.

You can make your presentations more effective if you learn how to use gestures to your advantage. First, gestures should be motivated by the text of your message. They also should enhance what you are saying without distracting your audience. Finally, gestures should be sincere and spontaneous, not overly planned or rehearsed.

Facial Communication As you can see in **Figure 18–1**, facial expressions communicate a great deal to an audience. Have you ever watched the action on a television

Figure 18–1 **Facial Communication**

570 *Glencoe Communication Applications*

show when you couldn't hear the sound? If so, you probably were able to figure out the mood and attitude the actors were portraying without having to hear their words. Now, look around your classroom. You probably can tell who's interested and who's bored or daydreaming just by looking at your classmates' faces. Your facial expressions give an audience the same types of information when you make a presentation.

For the most part, use your facial expressions to tell audience members that you are interested in them and in the topic you are presenting. Try to look alert and focused. Also, allow yourself to convey emotions through your face. Remember, an important part of every message is its emotional content.

Smile! Finally, remember to smile whenever possible. When you smile at an audience, you communicate friendliness and sincerity. You also project an image of being comfortable with your subject and at ease with your audience. Such impressions increase your credibility and your personal appeal with the audience.

COOPERATIVE LEARNING ACTIVITY

Students can work in teams or pairs to do some additional research on the Internet. Suggest that they use a dependable search engine to find what they can about making presentations. Let them brainstorm possible keywords to use, such as *business presentations*, *making speeches*, and so on. Ask them to report to the whole class what types of information they discovered.

Eye Contact In many parts of the United States, we often think a person is more trustworthy if he or she looks us directly in the eye. A presenter who does not look at his or her audience loses its belief and trust as well as its attention. Therefore, the ability to develop eye contact with your audience is an important skill for an effective presenter to master.

The key to good eye contact is knowing your material. The better you know your material, the less you will have to rely on your notes, and the more you can look at your audience. The more you look at your audience, the more feedback you can receive. This allows you to adjust your message to make sure that everyone in your audience understands.

Eye contact also is an effective way to keep the audience involved in your presentation. By making eye contact with different members of your audience, you make people feel included and valued. Failure to make eye contact can have the opposite effect. For this reason, try to make eye contact with as many different audience members as possible. Not only will this make each person you look at feel special, but the farther away you are, the more people will think you have looked directly at them. With enough practice, you may be able to make an entire audience feel it has been personally included in your presentation.

Your Exit Once the spoken part of a presentation is over, some presenters are tempted to make the fastest getaway possible. However, just as you planned your entrance, you also should plan an orderly and controlled exit.

First, remain in position. Make sure that you smile and maintain eye contact with the audience for a few seconds after concluding your presentation. Sometimes, audience members will have questions about elements of your presentation. In other instances, they may want to come up and meet you. In any case, remember that you still are being evaluated by your audience—and your last impression may be almost as important as your first.

COMMUNICATION PRACTICE LAB

Using Nonverbal Cues Effectively

To practice using effective nonverbal cues in a presentation, follow these steps:

Step 1 Working in groups of four or five, choose a type of presentation: informative, persuasive, or motivational.

Step 2 Each member of the group should then create his or her own two-minute presentation of that type.

Step 3 Take turns making your presentations in front of the other group members. Use effective verbal strategies you learned in previous chapters and the effective nonverbal strategies you have just learned in this chapter.

Step 4 Have other group members take notes on your nonverbal behaviors in particular, pointing out which were effective, which were not, and why.

Step 5 Share your notes as a group. What conclusions can you draw about different types of nonverbal cues? Which were most or least effective for your specific type of presentation?

Step 6 After your group has discussed the notes, share your conclusions as a class.

COMMUNICATION PRACTICE LAB

Using Nonverbal Cues Effectively

Ask students to carry out the six steps in the Communication Practice Lab to assess their own use of nonverbal communication skills. You may want to invite each group to nominate one member whose presentation was especially effective to give her or his presentation to the whole class. **L2**

GLENCOE Online

For an additional Practice Lab for this section, students can visit the *Glencoe Communication Applications* Web site at **communicationapplications.glencoe.com**. Click on Communication Practice Lab 18–1. **L1**

3 ASSESS

Assign Section 1 Assessment as a homework or in-class activity.

Use *Interactive Tutor Self-Assessment Software* to review Section 1.

Section 18–1 Quiz

Reteaching Activity 18-1

RETEACHING Activity 18-1
MAKING AND EVALUATING PRESENTATIONS
Making a Presentation

Enrichment Activity 18-1

ENRICHMENT Activity 18-1
MAKING AND EVALUATING PRESENTATIONS
Making a Presentation

4 CLOSE

Have students reread the opening paragraph on page 563. Considering what they have learned in this section, students should explain the ways in which a person can communicate that a book cannot. *(People can communicate through language and nonverbal methods. A book relies on language and sometimes visual aids such as pictures and graphs.)* **L1**

Extra-Credit Project

Ask students to videotape examples of people on television, including actors in commercials, they think make effective presentations. Small groups of students can work together to choose those that appear to be the most effective. They can show their choices to the class and point out the characteristics that they believe make the presentations effective. **L2**

Your actions at this point will influence the way people remember you as a presenter. You want to make sure that the audience focuses on what you have just presented to them, not on watching you make your exit.

Above all, don't damage the credibility that you have worked so hard to build. Hurrying back to your chair or rushing out of the room could make you seem insincere or unprofessional. Audience members may get the idea that you didn't really want to be there at all. Instead, take this opportunity to convey warmth and approachability. Allow your movements, gestures, and facial expressions to reflect the same confidence and enthusiasm you had at the beginning and throughout your presentation.

Finally, congratulate yourself mentally for a job well done. You have carefully prepared and presented your presentation. By delivering a successful presentation, you've taken another giant step toward becoming a competent and professional communicator.

Section 1 Assessment

GLENCOE Online

Visit the *Glencoe Communication Applications* Web site at **communicationapplications. glencoe.com** and click on **Self-Check and Study Guide 18.1** to review your understanding of making a presentation.

Review Key Terms

1. Define each term and write it in a sentence: delivery, projecting, stage presence, emphatic gesture, descriptive gesture.

Check Understanding

2. Why is delivery an important aspect of a presentation?

3. Describe an entrance that projects a positive stage presence.

4. **Compare and Contrast** Give one example of an emphatic gesture and one example of a descriptive gesture. Explain how they are alike and how they are different.

APPLICATION *Activity*

Creating a Presentation Checklist Working with a partner, create a list of tips for using effective verbal and nonverbal strategies in presentations. Using your checklist, take turns giving a two-minute informative, persuasive, or motivational presentation. Check off each tip as you use it. Share your checklists with classmates and work together as a class to create a master presentation checklist.

Section 1 Assessment Answers

1. Accept all reasonable sentences.

2. It causes audiences to perceive the speaker as credible.

3. Gait and posture convey confidence, enthusiasm, and self-assurance.

4. Answers may include an emphatic gesture such as banging a fist on the table and a descriptive gesture such as showing with the hands the size of something. Both kinds of gestures reinforce the messages in the speech. An emphatic gesture puts special stress on something being said. A descriptive gesture helps the speaker create a mental image in the minds of the audience.

Application Activity Students' checklists should reflect what they have learned in this chapter as well as their own experience with both giving presentations and observing them.

DISTINGUISHING BETWEEN FACT AND OPINION

A fact is any piece of information that can be determined to be true without question. An opinion is a belief that cannot be supported by positive knowledge. Knowing the difference between the two will help you make decisions that are based on information rather than emotion.

Learning the Skill

When you are trying to tell the difference between a fact and an opinion, ask yourself if the statement is something that can be proved with your own senses. In other words, can you see, hear, taste, smell, or feel it for yourself? If someone says that ice is cold, you know it's true because you have touched ice before and it was cold. This is an observable fact. Next, check the statement for words that show comparison—words like *greatest*, *everyone*, *no one*, *better*, *worst*, *always*, or *never*. If you find any such words, the statement is probably based on opinion.

Some claims can be proved through research. These statements may involve past events or scientific claims. If you state that Neptune is farther away from the sun than Mars, you can prove it by finding information that supports your claim.

Finally, some claims are based on statistics. People tend to use only those statistics that are favorable to their position. The statistical information that is revealed is probably true, but it may not be entirely true. Therefore, claims that are based on statistical information should be carefully examined.

Practicing the Skill

Each statement below is based on fact or opinion. Decide which statements are facts and which are opinions and why.

1. Temperature is measured with a thermometer.

2. Dogs are the smartest animals.

3. Oranges are the best kind of fruit.

4. All spiders have eight legs.

5. Everyone supports the current tax laws.

APPLICATION *Activity*

Joseph Bruchac is a Native American storyteller. Is this statement a fact or an opinion? From the photo, find three statements about Joseph Bruchac that are facts. Explain why each claim is true. Now find or develop three statements about Bruchac that are opinions. What makes these statements opinions?

Distinguishing Between Fact and Opinion

Point out to students that learning how to distinguish between fact and opinion is a necessary skill in many aspects of daily life. For example, it is important to judge what you read in a newspaper editorial or hear from a candidate for political office in terms of fact and opinion. Invite discussion in which students volunteer other examples. **L1**

Practicing the Skill

1. Fact; you can prove and observe that a thermometer measures temperature.

2. Opinion; there is no way to prove what *smartest* means in terms of animals.

3. Opinion; people's ideas about which is "best" will vary and cannot be proved.

4. Fact; this is observable and provable by finding scientific information to support the statement.

5. Opinion; it is unlikely that every person shares the same opinion, and this could never be proved.

Application Activity

Students may also use the Internet or other sources for information about Joseph Bruchac. Make sure their facts are provable through research and their opinions cannot be similarly proved. **L2**

CRITICAL THINKING ACTIVITY

Bring in copies of a major newspaper for a period of a week. Have students find a news story that is covered for at least several days in different ways and about which at least one editorial or column has been written. Ask them to analyze the differences between the news stories and the editorial or column. Tell them to identify examples of fact and opinion.

Section 2

Evaluating Presentations

GUIDE TO READING

Objectives

1. Interpret audience feedback.
2. Respond empathically to audience interruptions.
3. Participate effectively in a question-and-answer session following a presentation.
4. Apply critical-listening strategies to evaluate a presentation.
5. Evaluate the effectiveness of one's own presentation.

Terms to Learn

critic
critical perspective
judgment by results
judgment by ethical standards
judgment by aesthetics
judgment by multiple standards

*I*t's the big day—time to give your presentation in front of the whole class. You've practiced so much that you feel as though you could give this presentation in your sleep. As you begin your presentation, however, you notice that not everyone is behaving like a perfect audience member. Two students are whispering, while another keeps interrupting to ask you questions. How do you handle the unexpected?

Giving a presentation in front of an audience can be very different from practicing in front of a mirror. When real, live people are involved, you never know quite what to expect. Speaking to an audience doesn't have to be unpleasant or distracting, however. In fact, one of the most rewarding aspects of public speaking is interacting with your listeners. By evaluating their reactions—and listening closely to their evaluations of you—you will quickly learn which methods work, which don't, and which can help you build a reputation as an interesting and talented presenter.

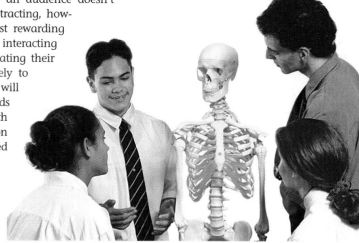

Listening to other's evaluations of your presentation will make you a better speaker. **What can you learn from an evaluation?**

---

1 FOCUS

Bellringer

Have students brainstorm possible answers to the question in the first paragraph on this page about how a speaker might handle the unexpected distractions. *(Students might suggest that the presenter ask people to hold their questions until the end of the presentation when time will be made to answer them. If several people do not seem to be paying attention, the presenter might change a vocal characteristic, show a visual, or make a gesture or movement that will draw attention back to him or her.)* **L1**

You may use Graphic Organizer Transparency 18–2 to introduce this section.

Graphic Organizer Transparency 18–2

CAUSE	EFFECT
1. Audience agrees with your message.	1. _____
2. Humor was used inappropriately.	2. _____
3. You have tapped audience emotion.	3. _____
4. Audience understands your message.	4. _____
5. Audience disagrees with your message.	5. _____
6. Audience is bored.	6. _____
7. Audience is confused.	7. _____
8. Q & A protocol is missing.	8. _____

Communication Tip

Speakers must remember that it is they who should be the center of attention and provider of their message, not their handouts or displays. Handouts and displays should reinforce and enhance what is being said. They should not be substituted for the spoken presentation.

Visual Instruction

Answer Which methods work and which don't

RESOURCE MANAGER

Teaching Tools

- Interactive Lesson Planner
- Reproducible Lesson Plan 18–2
- Application Activities 18–2

Reproducible Masters

- Guided Reading Activity Workbook 18–2
- Enrichment Activity 18–2
- Reteaching Activity 18–2
- Section Quiz 18–2
- Transparency Strategies and Activities Booklet 18–2

Transparencies

- Graphic Organizer Transparency 18–2
- Chapter 18 Teaching Transparency

Technology Resources

- Interactive Tutor Self-Assessment Software
- Presentation Plus! Software
- ExamView® Pro Testmaker
- PuzzleMaker Software
- communicationapplications.glencoe.com

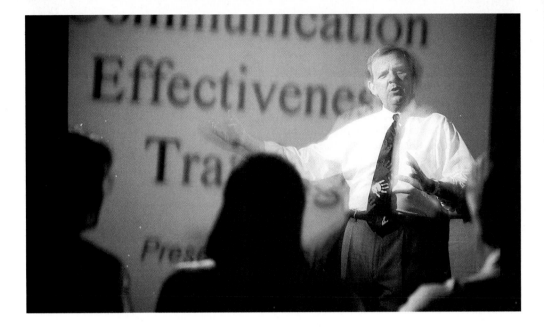

A presenter must always be aware of audience feedback. **Why?**

INTERACTING WITH THE AUDIENCE

Audience members do not typically carry on conversations with the presenter during a presentation, but they always provide feedback. This feedback can range from facial expressions and other types of body talk to verbal outbursts. It is important to evaluate audience feedback carefully, regardless of its form. It most often is positive, sometimes is negative, and always is educational.

Sometimes, audiences will cheer, encourage, heckle, boo, or even hold up signs relating to highly controversial topics or presenters. On rare occasions, audience members who feel very emotional about an issue may interrupt a presenter and shout some comment or question during the middle of a presentation. Fortunately, however, these interactions do not occur in most presentations. Instead, most audience feedback is limited to nonverbal responses. As a presenter, you will want to watch for these responses so you can be sure your message is having the intended effect.

Adapting Messages to Audience Feedback

When you make a presentation, you have a lot of responsibility. Not only do you have to research, prepare, and present your information effectively, but you also are responsible for how it is received. Sometimes, a presenter will need to adjust his or her nonverbal behaviors to eliminate distractions and make the message easier to hear and understand. Other times, however, it is the message itself that needs adjusting.

Of course, the fact that someone doesn't agree with a message doesn't mean the message content automatically should be changed. Many times, presenters are

Making and Evaluating Presentations **575**

2 TEACH

Appreciating an Audience

Students are familiar with being members of an audience—within the classroom and elsewhere. The idea of considering themselves as the presenter to an audience may be novel to them. Invite them to brainstorm what a presenter probably wants from an audience and how members of an audience can communicate with a presenter. **L1**

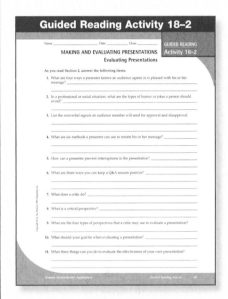

Grammar Tip

Dashes are used to indicate a pause in a thought that is stronger than that indicated by a comma or semicolon and not as strong as that indicated by a period. They are often used to set off parenthetical, or unessential, phrases in a sentence.

Visual Instruction

Answer So they can be sure the message has the intended effect

COOPERATIVE LEARNING ACTIVITY

Ask students to analyze how the hints in the following acronym can help them with their own presentations.
Audience—Who are the people in the audience? How many are there?
Understanding—What do they already know about the topic?
Demographics—What are their ages? Education? Background?
Interest—Why are they here to listen to your presentation?
Environment—Where will I stand when I speak? Will everyone be able to see me?
Needs—What are the needs of the listeners? What are my needs as speaker?
Customized—How can I custom fit my message to this audience?
Expectations—What do the listeners expect to learn from me?

RESPONDING EMPATHICALLY TO INTERRUPTIONS

If necessary, remind students that *empathically* means "with empathy, or with sensitivity and understanding of another's feelings." Ask students to add to the list any other responses they can think of. This list may be an especially important one for students to copy and to keep with them as they make presentations. Often an interruption can "rattle" a speaker so he or she is unable to think logically, and having this list handy may be extremely useful at such a time. **L1**

Language Tip

Point out to students that the words *empathic* and *emphatic* are easily confused and they must read them carefully to make sure which word is which. Explain that *empathic* has as its base the word *empathy*, which means "the capacity to share another person's feelings or thoughts." The word *emphatic* is the adjective form of the verb *emphasize*, so it means "done with emphasis, special significance, or stress." Students can help themselves distinguish between these two words by thinking of the related words.

---

responsible for delivering unpopular messages to listeners. However, if you anticipate a neutral or supportive response from your audience but get a negative reaction instead, you may need to adjust your message. Many times, this will mean adjusting your wording or the verbal style of your message rather than the actual content.

As a presenter, you can assess people's reaction to a message by monitoring their feedback. Do audience members look interested? Do they look puzzled? Are people actually leaving the room? Signals like these tell you whether or not it is necessary to adapt your message. For the most part, these signals take the form of audible feedback and body talk.

Audible Feedback Audible feedback is feedback you can hear. This may take the form of applause, vocalizations, and other nonverbal sounds. If not, it may be expressed as different types of verbal responses.

Nonverbal Sounds For instance, if audience members agree with what a presenter is saying or are pleased with a certain message, they may whistle or cheer. They may respond to a good joke by laughing or even applauding. These types of feedback help a presenter know that a message is coming through loud and clear and is generating the desired response.

If, on the other hand, a joke is followed by complete silence from the audience, the presenter may draw some different conclusions. Perhaps his or her attempt at humor seemed inappropriate or offensive to some audience members. Maybe the audience just didn't understand it. The presenter should note that the humor attempt failed and adapt his or her message to omit similar types of humor later on.

Some comedians have become enormously popular using outrageous or offensive humor. However, off-color humor and jokes that

---

RESPONDING EMPATHICALLY TO INTERRUPTIONS

- Never respond rudely to an interruption, no matter how rude it is.
- Rephrase a rude or hostile comment in a neutral, non-insulting way.
- Look for the person's real, underlying concern and address that—not the inappropriateness of the interruption itself.
- Offer to field questions and comments at the end of the presentation.

---

make fun of people generally are poor ethical choices for presenters in professional and social contexts. This includes humor about people of different ethnic groups, cultures, religions, ages, or gender. Also avoid making fun of people's choices of schools or clothing. You should also avoid other topics that may be related to socioeconomic status. This type of humor is sure to offend someone in your audience and generate negative—or even hostile—feedback.

In most public-speaking situations, the only person you can make fun of without any repercussions is yourself. In the right context, pointing out something funny about yourself can let others know you are approachable and not overly serious. Since everyone makes mistakes and has his or her own silly quirks, this type of humor often can help you bond with an audience. Be careful that you don't overdo it, though. Pointing out too many weaknesses may leave the impression that you really are weak.

MEETING INDIVIDUAL NEEDS

MULTIPLE LEARNING STYLES

Musical Musical performances virtually always get nonverbal audience feedback in the form of applause. Sometimes, audiences add other responses such as cheering (or booing).

Activity Have students view a videotaped concert performance and ask them to list ways that the audience reacted to the musical performances. Ask for their analyses of why audiences react in those ways and what each way communicates to the performer(s). Margaret Hillis, guest conductor of the Chicago Symphony Orchestra, once mentioned to an interviewer that after the orchestra did its work of performing, it was the audience's turn to do its work of being involved with the performance—by applauding. Ask students whether they agree with Ms. Hillis and why or why not.

Verbal Responses From time to time, audiences also use words to provide audible feedback. They may shout their agreement or disagreement with a presenter's comments. In some cases, they might offer a word or phrase to encourage a presenter or support or refute a point.

Verbal feedback typically does not happen as often as other forms of feedback. Seldom do audience members feel free to make verbal comments to the presenter while he or she is speaking. Still, it does happen. Verbal feedback is most likely to occur when either the message or the presenter taps into listeners' emotions.

For example, if a message is strongly opposed or supported by an audience, or if the presenters themselves are debating a topic, listeners may respond verbally. Sometimes, if a presenter has a great deal of notoriety, some audience members may attend a presentation for the sole purpose of protesting or otherwise getting the presenter's attention. These efforts often take the form of verbal interruptions of the message.

Nonverbal Feedback A presenter has only the time he or she is at the podium to provide information, motivate, or make a persuasive appeal to an audience. That is why it is important to make sure the audience understands the message. Audible feedback such as applause or verbal comments makes it fairly easy to assess listeners' perceptions. However, feedback is not always this obvious. Most of the time, audience feedback will be nonverbal.

Approval and Disapproval If audience members are smiling, nodding, taking notes, and maintaining eye contact with the presenter, they probably are understanding the message and responding positively. They may express disagreement or disapproval by refusing to make eye contact, murmuring comments to their neighbors, sitting rigidly or shifting uncomfortably in their seats, frowning, or shaking their heads "no."

■ **Feedback from an audience can be verbal and nonverbal.** What nonverbal signals generally indicate audience approval?

Making and Evaluating Presentations **577**

MULTIPLE LEARNING STYLES

Interpersonal Mention to students that a speaker or presenter does not have to simply wait to observe the reaction of his or her audience. It is appropriate for a speaker to ask the audience questions and even to ask whether they have understood a point the speaker has made.

Activity Have small groups of students brainstorm situations in which a speaker might—or perhaps should—interrupt his or her presentation to address the audience. What are some clues from the audience that might make a speaker's question appropriate? How can a speaker judge when to ask the audience a question? Groups should prepare and present a short oral report summarizing their brainstorming session.

Nonverbal Audience Feedback

Ask students for examples from their own experience of the ways audiences behave in response to presenters or speakers. What do such behaviors communicate to a speaker? How do audience members exhibiting these behaviors want the presenter to respond? **L3**

Communication Tip

In conversations, people communicate a great deal nonverbally with gestures, tone of voice, facial expressions, and so on. Even on the telephone, communication is often enhanced by tone of voice and voiced noises that are not words.

■ **Visual Instruction**

Answer Audience members are smiling, nodding, taking notes, and maintaining eye contact with the presenter.

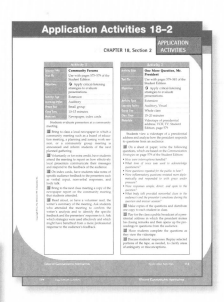

BUSINESS BRIEF

Professional presenters warn that handouts can sometimes be a problem. If passed around at the start of a presentation, they may distract the audience who spends time reading them instead of listening. On the other hand, well-prepared handouts are the best place for people to take notes that amplify a speaker's points. Many speakers provide their handouts before their speeches only if they think most audience members will be taking notes on them.

Visual Instruction

Answer Listen critically, deliberately, and empathically; make responses empathic and clearly stated.

Boredom If audience members feel a presenter is being ineffective and wasting their time, their nonverbal signals may be very similar to those for disapproval. They may begin side conversations, frown, shift in their chairs, or shake their heads "no." Restless or bored audience members also may tap their fingers or feet, yawn, check their watches repeatedly, or start looking around the room for something else to hold their interest. These audience members may just need the presenter to speed up the pace of the presentation or move on to new information or both.

Confusion When audience members are confused, they may send more subtle clues. They may look at one another in a questioning way, whisper questions back and forth, start searching through notes or handouts, or look around to see if others also are lost. It is especially important to pick up on this type of feedback because it signals that the message isn't coming through. Once the presenter is aware of audience confusion, he or she needs to take action and clarify his or her message.

Clarifying Information Once you notice signs of confusion in your audience, you can respond a number of ways. In a small, informal presentation, you might actually know the audience member or members who seem to be lost. If this is the case, you simply may wish to ask them where they stopped understanding. You can then go back to that point and explain your message more clearly.

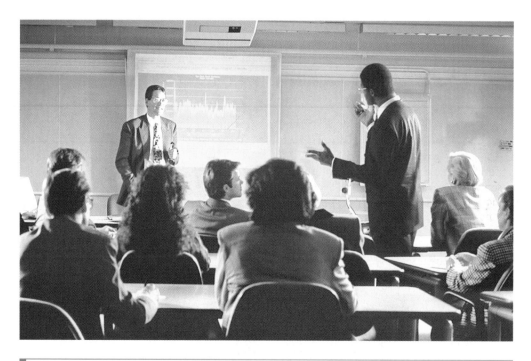

■ **A speaker responds to questions from an audience member.** Identify factors to keep in mind when responding to questions from the audience.

CRITICAL THINKING ACTIVITY

Have students consider the point of view of the audience in a presentation. How should an audience behave? What should a person who is part of an audience do during or after a presentation? Why? Suggest that students develop a list of audience dos and don'ts that reflect the best interests of members of an audience as well as those of a presenter.

Many times, however, you will not know the members of your audience. Even if you do, the potential for embarrassing someone may keep you from calling on him or her during the presentation. In these instances, it usually is better to stop, remark that some audience members look a little lost, and emphasize that you want everyone to understand the points you are making. Then, take the time to clarify your point before going on.

Restating the Message One effective method for clarifying information is to state it in a different way. Provide a brief summary of information up to that point, clarifying any areas that audience members might find particularly confusing. This may include stressing a specific order of events, grouping information into categories, pointing out important similarities or differences, or using visual aids. You also may wish to define additional terms or provide new examples to help your listeners understand.

Once the people who were looking puzzled begin nodding their heads or giving other non-verbal signals that they understand, you may move on with your presentation. In the meantime, be patient. Avoid looking frustrated with audience members who become confused. You might even put them at ease by commenting that this is a difficult concept or that it took you some time to understand it well yourself. This not only makes the audience feel better about not keeping up, but it also can help you build a bond with your listeners.

Responding to Questions

Many times, audience members will have questions about the information you are presenting. Although some presenters allow questions during a presentation, you may find it most effective to reserve questions until the end when they can be answered all at once. This prevents interruptions of your train of thought and keeps the audience from getting sidetracked by questions that have little to do with the content at hand. You cannot control what others will introduce into your presentation in

---

COMMUNICATION Strategies

HANDLING AUDIENCE QUESTIONS

✓ Ask for questions in a polite, inviting tone that indicates you genuinely want to help.

✓ Repeat each question before answering. This allows everyone to hear it and may eliminate duplicate questions later on.

✓ If a question is overly complicated or phrased in an insulting or accusatory manner, restate it more appropriately.

✓ Think through the question and respond simply and directly. Don't ramble or get sidetracked.

✓ Don't bluff—if you do not know the answer, say so. Offer to research the information and provide it later, if necessary.

✓ Keep your cool when faced with hostile questions. Resist the impulse to fight back.

✓ If someone tries to turn a question into a presentation, politely, but firmly, stop him or her. Interrupt the person and state his or her question as you understand it.

✓ Make a short statement to conclude the Q&A session, repeating key information and thanking audience members for their questions and interest.

Making and Evaluating Presentations **579**

COMMUNICATION Strategies

HANDLING AUDIENCE QUESTIONS

Point out that the list of strategies for handling audience questions is directed toward those asked in response to a presenter's call for questions at the end of a presentation. Review the list with students and ask them to brainstorm additions to it. **L2**

Being an Audience Member
Discuss with students how their points of view as audience members changes as they realize what they want from an audience when they are a presenter. How has thinking from a presenter's point of view helped them consider how to behave as an audience member? What will they do differently? Why? **L1**

MEETING INDIVIDUAL NEEDS

INCLUSION STRATEGIES

Less-Proficient Readers Students may find the communication strategies more helpful in an abbreviated form.

Activity Have small groups of students rewrite in an abbreviated form each strategy for handling audience questions. For example, they might rewrite the first strategy as "Be polite." After the groups have completed their lists, have them identify as a class the best abbreviated strategy. Compile the best ones and ask a volunteer to type a master list to be photocopied so that all class members can have a copy.

GLENCOE
Online

For an additional Practice Lab for this section, students can visit the *Glencoe Communication Applications* Web site at **communicationapplications.glencoe.com**. Click on Communication Practice Lab 18–2. **L1**

Listen and Respond

After giving a short content presentation or leading a class discussion, invite students to ask questions. Demonstrate strategies for listening to the questions and for answering them. For example, you might demonstrate how to restate or rephrase the question before answering it to ensure you understood what was being asked. After you have responded to all questions, discuss the strategies you used. **L2**

the form of questions or comments. Therefore, you may wish to reserve them until your message is complete.

One way to prevent interruptions of this kind is to announce at the beginning of your presentation that there will be a question-and-answer period directly following your presentation. Even if you had not planned such a "Q&A" period, you may determine during the course of your presentation that one is necessary. In this case, you might make a statement such as "I see that some of you are going to want to discuss specific details or related issues. I'll be happy to address your questions at the conclusion of my presentation."

As audience members voice their questions, listen critically, deliberatively, and empathically. Make your responses as empathic and as clearly stated as possible. If someone asks a question about something you already said in your presentation, try to find a different way to state the answer. If the person didn't understand the first time, hearing your exact words again probably won't help. On the other hand, if a question has already been answered during the Q&A session, it's all right to say, "I believe

that's already been covered." The checklist on page 579 provides additional tips for conducting Q&A sessions.

Setting Protocol for Q&A When beginning a Q&A session, it is important to set the protocol. Establishing a specific tone and expectations can keep discussions focused and productive.

Begin by setting a time limit. For example, you might say, "I'd like to open the floor to questions for the next fifteen minutes." Then, politely ask all participants to limit their questions to the topic of your presentation. This keeps participants on track and can help you avoid being stumped by an off-topic question.

For a Q&A session after a large presentation, you may wish to position a microphone in an aisle. Then, have audience members take turns asking their questions into the microphone. Explain that questioners should ask only one question at a time and remain standing at the microphone until that question has been answered. That way, if the presenter needs clarification or additional information, the person still has access to the microphone.

COMMUNICATION
Participating in a Q&A Session
PRACTICE LAB

To practice conducting a question-and-answer session after a presentation, follow these steps:

Step 1 Read a short, informative article from a magazine, newspaper, or other resource available to you.

Step 2 When you have finished reading your article, choose a partner.

Step 3 Present a one-minute summary of the article to your partner.

Step 4 Conduct a question-and-answer session with your partner. Use the strategies you have learned in this chapter.

Step 5 Switch roles with your partner. Listen critically to his or her summary and then ask questions. Practice stating questions clearly and appropriately.

Step 6 As a class, discuss what you learned about fielding questions from an audience. Work together to solve any problems you experienced.

580 *Glencoe Communication Applications*

After a smaller presentation, a microphone probably will not be necessary. Simply ask audience members to stand while their questions are asked and answered. This helps others hear the question clearly and helps the presenter locate the person to whom he or she is directing the answer.

Finally, try to establish a positive tone for the Q&A session. Project an attitude of willingness to answer questions. Rephrase harsh or inappropriate questions to eliminate as much negativity as possible. Maintain open, nonjudgmental facial expressions and body language. Staying positive shows your listeners you are willing to do anything you can to help them understand your message. This not only puts the audience at ease but also may establish you as a trusted resource for future information.

EVALUATING PRESENTATIONS

In previous chapters, you have read that the listener ultimately determines the meaning of a message. This means that we all continually evaluate what we hear and apply it to ourselves. In other words, we all are amateur evaluators, to a certain extent.

Sometimes, however, a presenter needs a more in-depth evaluation of his or her presentation. Perhaps he or she isn't sure about the effectiveness of a certain rhetorical strategy. Perhaps you have noticed something about your own presentation style that you think needs further analysis. In these cases, it is important to know how to effectively evaluate a professional presentation.

Acting as a Critic

When you evaluate your own or someone else's presentation, you do more than simply express personal opinions. You take on the role of a critic. A critic is someone who, through training and experience, is qualified to analyze and make judgments about something. Critics use their critical listening skills to determine the strengths and weaknesses of a presentation or other performance.

Listening Critically Think about the listening skills that you learned in Chapter 6. To properly evaluate a presentation, it is crucial to make full use of your critical, deliberative, and empathic listening skills.

You use your critical listening skills to comprehend the ideas and information presented in the presentation. Critical listening is used to determine if the presentation is reasonable and understandable. Is the information given during the presentation appropriate to the purpose and the occasion?

You use your deliberative listening skills to analyze and evaluate the presenter's information as a basis for making immediate or future decisions. Deliberative listening is used by the critic for a persuasive presentation to determine if the presenter uses logic well, seems to have the listener's best interests at heart, and makes sense.

You use empathic listening to try to understand why the presenter has approached the topic in this way. What is the presenter's motivation for making this presentation? You also use empathic listening to determine if the presenter selected the best way for the topic to be presented to a particular audience.

As a critic, you will need to develop a specific set of criteria by which you can evaluate a presentation. Go back to the Communication Strategies for Critical, Deliberative, and Empathic Listening in Chapter 6. These tips should help you to develop appropriate criteria for evaluating a presentation. In addition to these criteria for evaluating a presentation, you will want to consider the perspective from which the presentation will be evaluated.

Making and Evaluating Presentations **581**

Evaluating Presentations
Ask students to consider the possible circumstances in which they would want or need to evaluate the presentation of someone outside of the classroom. *(Answers may include presentations to them by a salesperson, by a political candidate, by someone who asks them to sign a petition, and so on.)* You may want to provide a list of the Communication Strategies for Critical, Deliberative, and Empathic Listening from Chapter 6 for students to review as they proceed through these pages. **L2**

Language Tip
The word *judgment* is spelled without an *e* in American usage and with an *e* (*judgement*) in British spelling. Some students whose training in the English language was influenced by British English (such as those from India) may have difficulties reconciling variations between the two versions of English.

Evaluating Printed Speeches
Review listening skills and then encourage students to listen to or read a speech that is presently in print. They might choose the text of such speeches as a president's inaugural speech, the Gettysburg Address, Sojourner Truth's "And Ain't I a Woman" speech, a governor's state of the state address, or the president's State of the Union address. Have students make a chart to analyze the speech critically, deliberately, and empathically. Suggest that students use their charts as the starting point for writing an analysis of the speech. **L3**

MEETING INDIVIDUAL NEEDS

MULTIPLE LEARNING STYLES

Intrapersonal As students read books and study literature, they are exposed to the idea of literary criticism and often read examples.

Activity Ask students to find examples of critiques, such as newspaper or magazine reviews of theatrical performances or books written by professional critics. Ask students to read the reviews and then to write a report identifying what the critics seem to look for and what information they provide their readers. Suggest that students also give their opinions about the purpose of a professional critic's review.

Critical Perspectives

Discuss with students the four types of critical perspectives listed in Figure 18–2 on this page. Explain that these perspectives are ways students can "look at" a presentation as they try to determine its value for themselves. You may want to point out that the perspective used for each presentation is likely to vary with the purposes both of the presenters and of the listeners, although students are likely to judge most presentations by the first three perspectives listed. **L3**

GLOBAL COMMUNICATION

Cultural Appreciation

Encourage students to work together to brainstorm the five guidelines mentioned to help themselves evaluate a presentation made by someone from another culture. You may want to involve students in your class or school whose background is another culture. Invite these students to provide their own insights into making and evaluating presentations. **L2**

Figure 18–2 Critical Perspectives

☑ **Judgment by Results:** evaluates whether or not the presenter has accomplished the goal of his or her presentation

☑ **Judgment by Ethical Standards:** evaluates whether the presenter behaved ethically during the presentation

☑ **Judgment by Aesthetics:** evaluates the overall appearance or impact of the presentation

☑ **Judgment by Multiple Standards:** uses two or more critical perspectives to evaluate a presentation

Using Critical Perspectives

Critics use one or more critical perspectives when they evaluate a presentation. A **critical perspective** is a standard by which a presentation is judged to be successful or unsuccessful. Not all presentations are judged by the same standards. In fact, these perspectives may be combined or used alone to determine the success of any particular presentation. As **Figure 18–2** shows, critics may evaluate a presentation based on any of the following perspectives:

- judgment by results
- judgment by ethical standards
- judgment by aesthetics
- judgment by multiple standards

Judgment by Results A **judgment by results** evaluates whether or not a presenter accomplished the goal of his or her presentation. If it was an informative presentation, did the audience gain new insight into the topic? If it was a persuasive presentation, was the audience persuaded to believe or do what was asked? If it was a motivational presentation, did audience members leave feeling inspired and more optimistic about themselves or their abilities?

Judgment by results can be very straightforward. For instance, if a presenter is giving a persuasive sales presentation, he or she will probably be judged by how many products are sold as a result of that presentation.

Sometimes, however, this perspective can be more complicated. If you fail to be motivated by a motivational presentation, the presentation is not automatically a failure. Rather, you should judge how it affected the audience as a whole. If everyone else seemed to be motivated to some degree, it was probably effective.

Judgment by Ethical Standards A second critical perspective is **judgment by ethical standards,** which determines whether a presenter behaved ethically in a presentation. With this perspective, it doesn't matter whether the goals of the presentation were accomplished. The most important point is whether the presenter violated any ethical standards during the presentation.

GLOBAL COMMUNICATION

Cultural Appreciation

As you have learned, people from other places in the world may have had experiences that are quite different from yours. Many examples of regional and cultural differences have been examined in this course. Using what you have learned, develop five guidelines that would be important to keep in mind when you are evaluating a presentation made by someone from another region or culture.

INTERDISCIPLINARY CONNECTION

Social Studies As students consider other cultures and guidelines for evaluating presenters from other cultures, draw their attention also to audience behavior. Point out that cultural differences exist in the ways audiences behave and are expected to behave in other cultures. For example, in China, audiences do not applaud for musical performances.

Activity Invite students from other cultures to describe performances and audience reactions in their native culture. To extend the concept of cultural similarities and differences, have students choose a culture and investigate ways in which the culture is similar to and different from their own.

When you use this perspective, you might say, "I told the truth about my company's product, used sound research to back up my main point, and used logical arguments." According to this perspective, it does not matter whether or not anyone bought the product as a result of your presentation. It only matters that you planned and presented an ethical persuasive presentation.

Judgment by ethical standards sometimes can be tricky for presenters because different standards may be set by any individual critic. Therefore, if a critic agrees to some degree with your point of view, he or she probably will declare the presentation effective. If the critic disagrees, he or she is likely to judge the presentation ineffective.

Judgment by Aesthetics Sometimes, the aesthetic, or artistic, form of a presentation is evaluated separately from its content. A *judgment by aesthetics* evaluates the overall appearance or impact of a presentation. A presentation is aesthetically effective if the presenter planned a proper introduction, body, and conclusion; used effective transitions, internal summaries, and audiovisual aids; dressed appropriately; and used other appropriate forms of nonverbal communication. Again, it doesn't matter whether the presenter actually accomplished the presentation's purpose. It is more important that he or she looked and sounded professional and well prepared.

Judgment by Multiple Standards
Most often, presentations are subject to a *judgment by multiple standards*, which uses two or more critical perspectives to determine the success of a presentation. For instance, a critic may decide that it is important that a presenter accomplishes his or her goal (judgment by results) by giving a professional-looking presentation (judgment by aesthetics). Sometimes, all three critical

COMMUNICATION Strategies

GUIDELINES FOR EVALUATING A PRESENTATION

✓ Establish a set of criteria based on what you have learned about effective speaking and listening and the critical perspective you have chosen.

✓ Begin by pointing out the presenter's strengths.

✓ Keep an open mind.

✓ Be specific about both positive and negative points.

✓ Don't just point out a weakness. Suggest a specific way to fix it.

✓ Don't get personal. Remember, you're evaluating the presentation, not the person.

✓ If something is just your opinion, say so.

✓ Be reasonable. If something was out of the presenter's control or beyond his or her experience, take that into consideration.

✓ Show empathy for the presenter. Make your comments tactful and understanding.

✓ Phrase your criticism in a way that you would find helpful if you were the presenter.

✓ Realize that the presenter may not agree with you. Don't argue or try to force your ideas.

✓ Focus on the future. Help the presenter envision making a perfect presentation next time.

✓ Be brief.

Making and Evaluating Presentations **583**

COMMUNICATION Strategies

GUIDELINES FOR EVALUATING A PRESENTATION

Review with students the Communication Strategies list, encouraging students to provide reasons they think each strategy is a good one to remember. Point out that the items on this list are things to remember when evaluating a person's presentation directly for that person. Ask: How might the points change when you are evaluating the presentation of a politician, a salesperson, or someone you see on TV? *(Students are likely to suggest that the evaluations would differ in their focus on the message, styles, presentation skills, and so on.)* **L2**

Cultural Differences in Evaluating

People in some cultures, including many Native American cultures, are taught not to draw attention to themselves or to judge others. Students from cultures with this viewpoint may have great difficulty bringing themselves to make presentations in public or to evaluate others.

MEETING INDIVIDUAL NEEDS — MULTIPLE LEARNING STYLES

Musical Students may appreciate a talented speaker for aesthetic reasons having to do with the way a speaker sounds—his or her voice modulation, rhythm, poetic choice of words and phrasing, and so on.

Activity Ask students to find examples of several speeches that they enjoy just for the "sound of them." As one example, you might mention that Martin Luther King Jr. was famous for his speaking ability and the way he delivered a speech. You might be able to help students find a recording of his famous "I Have a Dream" speech, which demonstrates many of these aesthetics.

Evaluating the Presentations of Others

You may want to review the evaluation form on this page with students, making sure they understand each question. Point out that for each presentation they evaluate, they may want to edit the form to make it more presentation-specific. For example, they may want to add a question about whether the presenter wandered from the topic, kept to the purpose of the presentation, and so on. **L2**

Language Tip

In devising an evaluation form, phrase questions so that they can be answered "yes" or "no." Such phrasing leads the reader to be able to judge on a graded scale as well.

Comparing Evaluations

Make a copy for each student of the evaluation form on this page. Show a videotaped speech presentation. You might choose one given by a student or a speech given at a seminar or convention. Ask students to use the form to evaluate the presentation. When students have completed the evaluation, divide the class into groups and have group members compare and contrast their evaluations. Encourage them to discuss similarities and differences in their evaluations and possible reasons for the differences. **L2**

■ **Figure 18–3 Evaluation of Others**

Evaluation Form
for Judgment by Multiple Standards

Presenter _____ Evaluator _____

Score each element on a scale from 1 to 5 in which 1 = needs improvement, 2 = fair, 3 = average, 4 = good, and 5 = excellent. Write your comments in the extra space beside each question.

Presentation Elements

Introduction
_____ Did the introduction capture listeners' attention?
_____ Did the presenter state the thesis and preview the main points of the presentation?
_____ Did the presenter apply the presentation to the audience?
_____ Did the presenter establish his or her ethos?

Main Body
_____ Was the information presented in a clear pattern of organization?
_____ Did the presenter support the main points with details?
_____ Did the presenter provide smooth transitions?
_____ Did the presenter keep the audience interested while covering the main points?

Conclusion
_____ Did the presenter summarize the main points and repeat the thesis?
_____ Was there a clear, organized end to the presentation?

Performance Elements

Oral Style
_____ Did the presenter make clear, effective word choices?
_____ Did the presenter seem to follow ethical standards?
_____ Was he or she interesting and/or creative?
_____ Did the presenter effectively adapt to audience feedback?

Nonverbal Cues
_____ Was the presenter's overall appearance professional and appropriate?
_____ Did the presenter seem confident and well prepared?
_____ Did he or she use appropriate vocal characteristics?
_____ Did he or she use appropriate nonverbal strategies?

Audiovisual Aids
_____ Was the presentation enhanced by the use of audiovisual aids?
_____ If so, were the audiovisual aids professional and easy to see and understand?

Total Score: _____ **of 100 possible points**

584   *Glencoe Communication Applications*

MEETING INDIVIDUAL NEEDS   MULTIPLE LEARNING STYLES

Logical-Mathematical Students can use the evaluation form as a model for developing their own.

Activity Ask students to develop their own evaluation form modeled after this one. Encourage them to design a rating scale for their form and then use their form to assess a presentation on television or videotape or one that they attend in person. Ask students to create a graphic—graph or chart—using the data from their rating scale.

perspectives may be required for the presentation to be judged effective. That is, the presenter must accomplish his or her goals, speak ethically, and give a polished performance for the presentation to be judged successful. As a critic, you probably will evaluate most presentations by all three perspectives.

Forming Your Evaluation

Whether you are evaluating your own presentation or someone else's, the goal is to help the presenter build on his or her strengths as well as eliminate weaknesses. Focusing only on the negative aspects of a presentation does little to help a presenter. Instead, it may make that person feel like a failure or as if he or she is being picked on.

Therefore, it is important to be as positive as possible in your evaluation. Focus on what the presenter did right, as well as what needs improvement. Once you have prepared yourself with a positive attitude, follow the guidelines in the Communication Strategies checklist on page 583 for being an effective critic.

Providing Written Evaluations

Most of the time when you listen to a presentation in a professional or social context, you will not be asked to evaluate the presentation in writing. In this class, however, you may be asked to complete a form for every presentation you evaluate. The type of form you will complete depends on whether you are assessing someone else's or your own work.

Evaluating Others' Presentations

Sometimes, it can be difficult to evaluate the presentation skills of a friend or classmate. You may feel awkward about pointing out

Practice for the Workplace

Listen Carefully Some professional presenters have a way of finding out how each audience member feels about a presentation: They ask. By offering a simple evaluation form to your audience, you can gain valuable feedback. In some instances, you may be expected to provide evaluation forms, so it's a good idea to have them available.

BUSINESS PRACTICE *Activity*

Create an evaluation form that an audience could use to assess a presentation that you give. Develop five questions for the form. Your questions should determine whether the audience's needs were met by your performance. The form should also give audience members an opportunity to provide you with constructive criticism.

flaws in a friend's performance, and you may feel embarrassed about pointing out a classmate's strengths.

To make criticism easier, consider this: The person you are evaluating probably wants to be the best presenter possible. You are helping him or her achieve this goal. In addition, being a critic helps you learn to listen critically—a skill that will prove valuable throughout your life. Finally, evaluating others' presentations helps you know what to watch for in your own presentations. It also may give you ideas for adding special touches to your own presentations.

Another way to make evaluations easier is to use an evaluation form such as the sample form in **Figure 18–3.** Most evaluation forms provide a list of criteria for a successful presentation. These criteria often are listed as objective questions that help you focus on

Making and Evaluating Presentations **585**

Practice for the Workplace

Listen Carefully Explain to students that as presenters, they have the opportunity to tailor their own evaluation form to the speech or presentation they will give. They can ask specific questions that let the audience members evaluate how they explained a complicated issue or inspired the audience to action, for example. You may want to allow students to work in pairs or small groups to develop an evaluation form suitable for an oral presentation they may be presenting. **L2**

DID **Y**OU **K**NOW?

By definition, communication takes place only when a message is both given and received. The role of the audience is not only to receive the message but to communicate to the speaker that the message has been received. This is why feedback, often in the form of evaluation, is so important to a presenter.

Learning by Evaluating

Encourage students to consider the evaluation process as a learning situation for both the evaluator and the person being evaluated. List ways that students can learn about how to improve their own presentation skills by assessing the presentations of others. For example, they might adapt strategies used by a presenter that they thought were particularly effective, or they might remember to project their voices after straining to listen to a speaker who did not project. **L1**

REAL-WORLD CONNECTION

Managing Audiences Professional speakers make a point of tailoring their presentations to their audiences. Professionals also know that it is their responsibility to maintain control of the presentation. If audience questions and comments seem to lead away from the topic, it is the presenter who must bring everyone back to the topic at hand.

Activity Ask students to watch for a presenter's ability to maintain control as they observe presentations in and out of school. Suggest that they also evaluate such presentations on the basis of suitability for the audience. Have each student prepare a written summary of his or her evaluation of one presentation.

Evaluating the Evaluation

Invite students to evaluate the form on this page, suggesting changes they think might make the form more suitable for specific presentation tasks that they are familiar with. **L2**

BUSINESS BRIEF

"Humor is a welcome addition to a speech," according to Eileen Kugler of Kugler Communications, a consulting firm. However, she counsels speakers to make sure that whatever humorous story or joke they tell has a connection to the content of their speech.

Preparation Elements

Read through the Preparation Elements on the Self-Evaluation Form with students. Suggest scenarios that might present problems for a presenter and ask students to suggest possible ways to avoid the problems or to solve them. For example, ask students what a presenter might do to avoid or solve this scenario: The presentation site does not have an overhead projector for viewing the transparencies he or she had prepared for the presentation. *(Students might suggest that he or she could call ahead of time to make sure the site had a projector and, if not, rent or borrow one. If that is not possible, he or she might ask for an easel and chart paper and hand-drawn graphics.)* **L2**

■ **Figure 18–4 Self-Evaluation**

Self-Evaluation Form

Score each element on a scale from 1 to 4 in which 1 = needs improvement, 2 = fair, 3 = good, and 4 = excellent. Write your comments in the extra space beside each question.

Preparation Elements
Information
_____ Did I choose an appropriate topic for self, listener, occasion, and task?
_____ Did I limit the topic enough to cover it thoroughly in _____ minutes?
_____ Did I conduct adequate research?
_____ Is my outline well organized and complete?
Tools
_____ Are my notes well organized, complete, and easy for me to use?
_____ Is all necessary audiovisual equipment available and operating correctly?
_____ Have I prepared interesting, easy-to-see, useful audiovisual aids?
_____ Have I practiced using and explaining my audiovisual aids?
Self
_____ Is the clothing for my presentation clean, pressed, and ready to wear?
_____ Am I confident that I have full command of the information I'm presenting?
_____ Have I practiced ways to manage performance apprehension and stage fright?

Content Elements
_____ Did my introduction state the thesis and main points?
_____ In the main body, did I support the main points with adequate information?
_____ Did I conclude by summarizing the main points and repeating the thesis?
_____ Did I provide a clear, organized end to the presentation?
_____ Did I make the overall content relevant to my audience?

Performance Elements
Oral Style
_____ Did I make my wording clear and my transitions smooth?
_____ Did I make my presentation interesting and creative?
Nonverbal Cues
_____ Was my overall appearance neat and professional?
_____ Did I pay attention to vocal characteristics such as pitch, volume, and rate?
_____ Did I stand up straight and use appropriate movements and gestures?
_____ Did I use friendly and appropriate facial expressions?
_____ Did I maintain eye contact with my audience and avoid staring at my notes?
Use of Audiovisual Aids
_____ Did I face the audience as I used my audiovisual aids?
_____ Were all my audiovisual aids easy for the audience to see and understand?

Total Score: _____ **of 100 possible points**

COOPERATIVE LEARNING ACTIVITY

Videotape students giving presentations in order to help them do their self-evaluations because it is difficult for them to concentrate on making the presentation and evaluating it at the same time. Let small groups of students work together to view each other's videotapes and brainstorm evaluations after each student has had an opportunity to do his or her own individually.

what is most important. To answer these questions effectively, you will need to use your best critical listening skills.

Evaluating Your Presentations

Sometimes, you can be the most effective critic of your own presentations. After all, you know exactly how you want to appear to your audience, what your most important point or goal is, and what your main strengths and weaknesses are. Finally, you have unlimited opportunities to evaluate your own work and make improvements before the actual performance.

To evaluate the effectiveness of your own presentation, you will need to see or hear yourself in action. Videotape yourself giving the presentation, as shown in **Figure 18–5,** record your presentation using an audiocassette recorder, or watch in a mirror. Again, as you observe your performance, watch closely and use your critical listening skills to analyze what is most important.

One of the most important things to remember in self-evaluation is to remain objective. That is, try to judge yourself by the same standards someone else would use. Don't make excuses by saying, "I can't do any better than that," or "That's just my personality or style." An outside critic would point out any weak areas and suggest ways to improve them. Do the same for yourself.

To help you focus on the most important aspects of your presentation—and to help you stay objective—you may wish to use a self-evaluation form such as the one in **Figure 18–4.** This type of form is similar to the one you read previously, except it goes into a bit more detail and explores the preparation process.

Learning from Evaluations

Often, it can be difficult to accept others' evaluations of our efforts. After all, nobody enjoys having a weakness pointed out. However, constructive criticism is vital to becoming a competent and effective presenter. In fact, when it comes to making professional presentations, the more you can be evaluated, the better.

Try to think of evaluations as a team effort to help you reach your full potential as a presenter. No one expects you to be an expert presenter at first, but everyone wants to help you reach that goal eventually. With this in mind, ask others for tips and suggestions for improvement. Then, try these ideas out to see if they work for you.

Dealing with Errors From time to time, a critic's comment or suggestion may be off base. If you think this is the case, don't get defensive. Just weigh the advice against what you've learned and what other evaluators have said about your work. If the idea seems inconsistent or unjustified, check it with an objective party. Then, decide whether you think the comment has merit. If it doesn't, shrug it off and move on. Don't waste time getting angry over a difference of opinion.

■ **Figure 18–5 Evaluating Your Presentation**

Making and Evaluating Presentations **587**

INCLUSION STRATEGIES

MEETING INDIVIDUAL NEEDS

Learning Disability Students may have difficulty making self-evaluations. As students consider learning from the evaluations of their presentations, invite them to think of other instances in which they must learn from evaluations of their own performances.

Activity Have students work with partners to make their evaluations and to consider methods students can use to improve presentation skills. Suggest that the partners focus on one technique and work to improve that skill and then address other techniques after they have mastered the first.

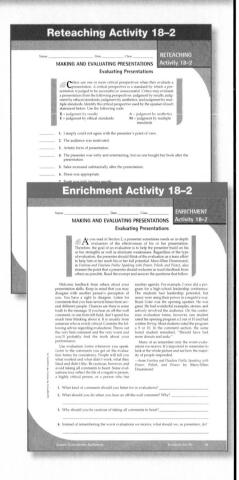

4 CLOSE

Have students reread the opening paragraph on page 574. Considering what they have learned in Section 2, how would their answers to the question at the end of the paragraph now be different? **L2**

Extra-Credit Project

Have students use the form on page 584 to evaluate a presentation they attend or observe. Ask them to adjust the form to include at least one question that is specific to the presentation. **L3**

588

Focusing on the Positive Finally, concentrate on the positive feedback you receive just as much as the negative. If you examine your evaluations carefully, you'll probably see that you have many of the valuable skills needed by professional presenters. By building on these skills and continuing to develop new ones, you'll quickly change your negatives to positives as you successfully achieve your presentation goals.

Section 2 Assessment

Visit the *Glencoe Communication Applications* Web site at **communicationapplications. glencoe.com** and click on **Self-Check and Study Guide 18.2** to review your understanding of evaluating presentations.

Review Key Terms

1. Define each term and write it in a sentence: critic, critical perspective, judgment by results, judgment by ethical standards, judgment by aesthetics, judgment by multiple standards.

Check Understanding

2. How might a bored audience member's nonverbal feedback differ from that of a confused audience member?

3. Imagine that while you are giving a motivational presentation, an audience member interrupts to ask if you will speak at his company meeting. Give an example of an empathic response.

4. **Hypothesize** Imagine that, during a question-and-answer session, someone asks you, "How can you possibly say this is the best plan for our group?" Give an appropriate response.

APPLICATION *Activity*

Evaluating a Presentation Choose one of the evaluation forms provided in this section and copy it onto a sheet of paper. Then, prepare a one- to two-minute presentation on a topic with which you are familiar. Use the form to evaluate your own presentation or the presentation of a partner (who, in turn, will evaluate your presentation). Discuss your evaluations as a class. Work together to devise a list of helpful hints for giving effective evaluations.

Section 2 Assessment Answers

1. Accept all reasonable sentences.
2. Answers may vary, but students may point out that someone who is bored may simply appear to want to do something else. A confused audience member may be more likely to look questioningly at someone else or search through notes or handouts.
3. Answers will vary, but students should demonstrate an understanding that as presenters they should not interrupt the flow of their speech to answer such an interruption.
4. Answers will vary, but students should demonstrate an understanding that such a hostile challenge should be answered politely.

Application Activity As pairs give and evaluate their presentations, ask them to jot down the helpful hints that they want to remember the next time they give or evaluate a presentation. The class as a whole can develop a master list of hints that they can add to the evaluation forms provided in this chapter.

Appraising Your Presentation and Evaluation Skills

How Do You Rate?

On a separate sheet of paper, use the key to respond to the following statements. Put a check mark at the end of each skill you would like to improve.

KEY: A Always   **R** Rarely
       U Usually   **N** Never
       S Sometimes

1. I practice my presentations to gain polish and confidence.

2. I project and pace my voice, using a conversational style of presentation.

3. I have mastered how to use nonverbal presentation strategies.

4. During a presentation, I make direct eye contact with my audience.

5. I use audience feedback to determine if I need to modify my presentation or repeat main ideas.

6. I answer questions and remain approachable to audience members.

7. I practice question-and-answer sessions.

8. When I evaluate presentations, I listen to find the main message and decide if it is worthwhile.

9. I include both strengths and needed improvements when I evaluate a presentation.

10. When I evaluate my own presentation skills, I try to be as objective as possible.

How Do You Score?

Review your responses. Give yourself 5 points for every A, 4 for every U, 3 for every S, 2 for every R, and 1 for every N. Total your points and evaluate your score.

41–50 Excellent You may be surprised to find out how much you can improve your skills.

31–40 Good In this course, you can learn ways to make your skills better.

21–30 Fair Practice applying the skills taught in this course.

1–20 Needs Improvement Carefully monitor your improvement as you work through this course.

Setting Communication Goals

If you scored Excellent or Good, complete Part A. If your score was Fair or Needs Improvement, complete Part B.

Part A   1. I plan to put the following ideas into practice:

         2. I plan to share the following information about communication with the following people:

Part B   1. The behaviors I need to change most are:

         2. To bring about these changes, I will take these steps:

Making and Evaluating Presentations   **589**

Communication Self-Assessment

Have students respond to the ten statements, using the key on this page. Then, have them evaluate their presentation skills. Based on their scores, assign either Part A or Part B of the goal-setting activity. On an index card or sheet of paper, students should concretely define their communication goals to improve their current level of skill. **L2**

Communication Journal Activity

Point out to students that people who write down their goals and review them regularly are more likely to accomplish their objectives than are people who merely think of areas of improvement. Have students list their goals in their Communication Journals. **L1**

Communication Tip

Suggest that students keep a list of the questions and their answers to review whenever they are going to give or evaluate a presentation. They can add their own goals to the list. You may want to recommend that students review these lists and update them as they attain some of those goals.

CRITICAL THINKING ACTIVITY

Lenny Laskowski, a professional speaker and author, says that a "speaker's ideas are accepted as believable only to the degree that the speaker is perceived to be credible." Credibility depends on the audience's perception of a speaker's "trustworthiness, competence, and good will." However, he also maintains that "the most fundamental factor" speakers project is the attitude they have toward themselves. In other words, their self-confidence demonstrates to the audience that they know what they are talking about and are to be believed. Ask students to react to these ideas and to discuss why they think such ideas can be helpful to them as they make and evaluate their own presentations.

Communication Through Writing

Communication Through Writing

Writing a Persuasive Sales Letter

Objective: To create a persuasive sales letter

Teaching Suggestions and Strategies

Connection to the Workplace

Point out that many businesses send some type of sales letter to clients or customers, both current and potential. Some companies, such as publishers of magazines or suppliers of some consumer goods, send such letters to thousands of people as potential customers. Often, this is the kind of letter that most people receive very frequently and is described by its recipients as "junk mail." However, many businesses send more specific persuasive sales letters to certain clients or potential clients.

Writing a Persuasive Sales Letter

Persuasive sales letters motivate people to buy goods and services. They are, very simply, product advertisements. These letters can be used to introduce or promote products, describe a product's advantages, convince consumers to take action, or make a sale. The basic format for a sales letter is the same as that of a standard business letter.

Spark Interest. To captivate your reader's attention, you will want to create interest in what you are selling. This can be accomplished by asking questions or making positive, factual statements about the quality of your product or service. You can also generate interest by appealing to emotion, comfort, or status.

Promote a Need. People do not question their need for food and water. However, a person might wonder why he or she would need an unfamiliar product or service. A good sales letter anticipates this response and explains how a product will meet the consumer's needs. For example, a sports magazine may be more appealing if it offers discounts on sports equipment to subscribers.

Why Buy Now? Give the reader a good reason to buy when he or she receives your letter. Some popular reasons are grand openings, free gifts, lower prices, or other incentives for buying before a given date. If a person is undecided about a product, the right promotion may convince him or her to take action.

State Your Product's Advantages. Part of creating demand for a product or service is describing it in some detail. Describe all of the positive points of your product or service in your sales letter. If your product has any unique features or capabilities, make them known to your readers. These points will attract the most attention if you mark them with arrows or bullets, as in the example on the next page.

Close the Sale. Give the reader an opportunity to purchase your product. Provide as many options as possible for consumers to take advantage of your product or service. Offer to set up a sales meeting, provide a telephone number, or encourage the reader to purchase the product by mail or on the Internet. If you make it easy for consumers to reach you, they will be more likely to accept your offer.

 For additional information about business writing, see the *Guide to Business Communication* section of the Communication Survival Kit in the Appendix.

MULTIPLE LEARNING STYLES

Visual-Spatial Visually oriented students will be interested in the way their letters look on the page.

Activity Encourage those who have access to word-processing computer programs to set up their letters with appropriate changes in type fonts and size as well as such features as bullets, boxes, and so on. If possible, have your school's art or graphic arts instructor or a local graphic designer critique students' work.

Communication Through Writing

e Cable Connection
13 West Connecticut Boulevard
errville, Texas 78029
ugust 26, 2002

Mrs. William Holland
450 Grand Avenue
Huntley, Illinois 60142

Dear Mrs. Holland:

Are you familiar with The Cable Connection? We supply *affordable* cable television services to residents of the Huntley Community. For just pennies a day, we will install 20 new channels of entertainment, just for you.

Yes! Twenty channels of

- arts
- entertainment
- sports
- movies
- documentary films
- nature programming

all for only $19.95 per month!

For a limited time, we are installing The Cable Connection in your area FREE OF CHARGE. At the time of installation, you pay only $19.95 for your first month's service.

Please act soon by calling the telephone number on the enclosed brochure. The call is free. We hope to hear from you soon.

Sincerely,
Ravi Patel
Mr. Ravi Patel
President, The Cable Connection

WRITING *Activity*

Assume that you work for a store that sells electronic equipment and appliances. Your store holds a clearance sale each spring. You have been asked to write a persuasive sales letter that will be sent to the customers on the store's mailing list. The purpose of the letter is to make the customers aware of the sale. Use your address for the business, today's date, and your own name. Use the information that follows to compose the rest of your sales letter.

- Address the letter to "A Valued Customer." Use any street address for the recipient.
- The name of the store is The Arc Appliance Store.
- During the sale, your store will offer brand-name merchandise for one-fourth to one-third off.
- You will give customers a free, two-year warranty on all purchases.
- Customers may finance appliances with no interest for one year.
- You carry products that conserve energy and require minimal service.
- You offer convenient products, such as lightweight vacuum cleaners.
- All entertainment devices come with programmable remote controls.

Teaching Activity

Have students assess the sample sales letter on this page. How does it meet the criteria established on page 590? Would they be tempted by this letter to buy the product? Why or why not? *(Students might suggest that because the cable service will be connected at no charge and the monthly fee is relatively low, they would consider buying the package. Some may want to compare this service to other services such as satellite disks.)*

Ask students to bring in examples of sales letters their family receives as direct mail and supply some yourself. Let students look over the samples and decide how each one sparks interest, promotes a need, explains why to buy now, states the advantages, and closes the sale. **L1**

WRITING *Activity*

Students' persuasive sales letters should follow the general format shown in the model and include the items listed in the assignment. Let students share and discuss their letters. **L2**

Grammar Tip

Proper nouns are capitalized in order to show that they refer to a specific person or thing. This includes brand names of products and names of companies and other organizations, as well as names of people and places.

Additional Resources

Appendix, "Guide to Business Communication"

Glencoe Writer's Assistant CD-ROM

Glencoe Interactive Grammar Software

Grade 9 Writer's Choice, Lessons 6.2 and 6.3

GRAMMAR PRACTICE

Capitalizing Proper Nouns

Have students capitalize the proper nouns and adjectives in the following sentences.

1. My brother gene got a job at central hardware. *(Gene, Central Hardware)*
2. Fred's uncle works for the federal bureau of investigation in chicago. *(Federal Bureau of Investigation, Chicago)*
3. The headquarters of rotary international is in evanston, illinois. *(Rotary International, Evanston, Illinois)*
4. The navajo reservation is in new mexico and arizona. *(Navajo, New Mexico, Arizona)*
5. The grand canyon and yellowstone park are on our vacation route next summer. *(Grand Canyon, Yellowstone Park)*

CHAPTER 18 Assessment and Activities

Visit the *Glencoe Communication Applications* Web site at **communicationapplications. glencoe.com** and click on **Chapter 18 Activity** for additional practice in making and evaluating presentations.

Reviewing Key Terms

1. stage presence
2. descriptive gesture
3. projecting
4. critic
5. delivery
6. emphatic gesture
7. critical perspective
8. judgment by results

Reviewing Key Terms

On a separate sheet of paper, write the communication term that completes each statement.

1. The image a presenter projects to an audience is called _____ .

2. A(n) _____ helps a presenter create a mental image for his or her audience.

3. _____ means sending your voice to all areas of a room without shouting.

4. Someone who is qualified to analyze and make judgments about something is a(n) _____ .

5. How a presenter uses his or her body and voice to communicate is called _____ .

6. Raising one's eyebrows or rolling one's eyes is an example of a(n) _____ .

7. A standard by which a presentation is judged successful or unsuccessful is called a(n) _____ .

8. A(n) _____ evaluates whether or not a speaker accomplished the goal of his or her presentation.

Reviewing Key Concepts

1. Name two ways a polished delivery helps a presenter when making a presentation.

2. Why do most presentations call for a relaxed, responsive, and conversational tone of voice?

3. How would a presenter use the rate of his or her delivery to emphasize an important statement?

4. List three guidelines for using gestures in presentations.

5. What should a presenter do immediately after his or her presentation?

6. When is an audience most likely to offer verbal feedback?

7. What message do audience members send by tapping their feet and checking their watches?

8. How should a presenter answer a question about something that he or she already covered in the presentation?

Reviewing Key Concepts

1. Gives the presenter confidence and causes the audience to perceive the presenter as more credible

2. Because listeners respond more favorably to voices that are conversational and friendly

3. Using a slow, deliberate rate of delivery can emphasize an important statement.

4. Allow your hands to rest naturally when not gesturing, use emphatic gestures to stress something you are saying, and use descriptive gestures to create a mental image for the audience.

5. Remain in position, smile, and maintain eye contact.

6. When the message or the presenter taps into the listeners' emotions

7. That they are bored

8. Restate it in a different way.

Assessment and Activities

Reading and Critical Thinking Skill

1. **Applying Information** Describe the hair and clothing of a successful presenter.

2. **Cause–Effect** How can a presenter make audience members feel included and valued during a presentation?

3. **Classifying Information** Which kind of audience feedback—body talk, non-verbal sound, or verbal response—is applause?

4. **Synthesis** Imagine you are speaking to an audience and commit a spoonerism, saying *ate of the start* instead of *state of the art*. Come up with a quip that will make fun of yourself and help you bond with the audience.

5. **Summary** Sum up strategies for presenters when responding empathically to interruptions.

Skill Practice Activity

Distinguishing Fact from Opinion Rewrite each of the following opinions as a fact.

Opinion: The salesperson's presentation was a complete failure.

Fact: No one ordered the salesperson's product.

1. The presentation was an artistic success.
2. The speaker's delivery was monotonous.
3. The conclusion to the presentation was excellent.
4. The presentation was boring.

Cooperative Learning Activity

Writing a Persuasive Sales Letter Imagine trying to persuade your principal to order this communication applications textbook. Write a sales letter and then exchange letters with a classmate. Use these questions to evaluate your partner's letter. Does the letter's introduction capture your attention? Will the letter appeal to the principal? Is the information clearly organized? Does the writer support the main points with details? Does the writer provide smooth transitions? Does the writer cover the main points in an interesting way? Does the letter end in a clear, organized manner?

Chapter Project

Planning Find a video that features a persuasive presentation. Watch the presenter and use the Evaluation Form for Judgments by Multiple Standards to evaluate him or her. Write a parody of the presentation from the video. Address a topic to which your classmates might relate. Practice using gestures and other techniques that the actor in the video used. Have someone tape the final version of your presentation. Watch yourself on video and evaluate yourself.

Presenting Give your presentation to the class and have the students evaluate you. Compare your scores to the score you gave the actor in the video.

Making and Evaluating Presentations **593**

Chapter Project

It may be helpful for several students to share the same video featuring a persuasive presentation. You may even want to allow members of each group to share their evaluations. However, each student should prepare his or her own parody of the presentation.

Reading and Critical Thinking Skill

1. **Applying Information** Specific answers will vary, but students should point out that the hair and clothing were neat, clean, and simple.

2. **Cause-Effect** By making eye contact with people in the audience

3. **Classifying Information** Nonverbal sound

4. **Synthesis** Answers will vary but should reflect students' respect for the audience and friendly manner.

5. **Summary** Answers may vary but should include those listed in the Communication Strategies checklist on page 576.

Skill Practice Activity

Distinguishing Fact from Opinion

Wording may vary but should be similar to the following:

1. The presentation's audiovisual aids clarified some important points.

2. The speaker's voice was a flat monotone without emotion.

3. The conclusion to the presentation summarized the main points.

4. Most members of the audience were looking at their watches and shifting in their seats by the end of the presentation.

Cooperative Learning Activity

Writing a Persuasive Sales Letter

You may want to invite students whose letters are particularly persuasive to share them with the rest of the class by posting them on the bulletin board. **L2**

Standardized Test Practice

Reading Comprehension
Multiple-Choice
Theme: Group Communication

Teaching Strategy

On any standardized reading test, students should read actively and check their understanding of the passage as they read.

However, they should not try to memorize the details of the passage. Students should always check back to the passage to find each answer.

In order to make it easier to find the relevant part of the passage when they need an answer, students can label paragraphs. To have students try this technique here, have them write on a separate sheet of paper. They should jot down a few words to summarize each paragraph after they read it.

For many tests, students will be able to write directly on the test booklet, next to each paragraph.

Sample Paragraph Labels:

1. influential musician—founded modern jazz

2. early trumpet playing success

3. great trumpet solos

4. great singer—emotional

5. recorded scat singing

6. trumpet players imitated him

7. singers imitated him

8. made jazz popular

9. founded jazz

Louis Armstrong—Father of Jazz

Singer and trumpeter Louis Armstrong was one of the most beloved performers of his time. A true jazz pioneer, he was able to captivate an audience with a combination of his sheer talent and endearing, larger-than-life persona. People who had the opportunity to hear him perform knew that they were in the presence of greatness. Armstrong's listeners were captivated by the emotion that he put into his playing and his genuine passion for music. Today, Louis Armstrong is remembered as one of the most influential musicians of the twentieth century. He has been widely imitated by almost everyone who has come after him, and his style formed the foundation for modern jazz music.

A Brilliant Soloist

Armstrong grew up in turn-of-the-century New Orleans, a musical city where he heard and absorbed a wide variety of musical styles. He learned to play the trumpet when he was still a teenager and developed his skill by playing in some of the city's brass bands and jazz outfits. Eventually, he was hired by King Oliver. Oliver's band, the Creole Jazz Band, was New Orleans' most popular jazz orchestra. At that time, jazz was mainly ensemble music. This meant that all musicians played at the same time and no one performer was featured over the others. However, Armstrong's playing was so skillful, so loud, and so energetic that it stood out from everyone else's. Soon, everyone in New Orleans had heard about King Oliver's new trumpeter. As Armstrong's fame grew, he started playing with other bands.

Armstrong's solos are among the greatest ever recorded. In many cases, he would play intricate passages created on the spot while the rest of the band supported him with simple chords. Just like a good public speaker knows how to improvise, Armstrong was able to develop a wide range of melodies and apply them as the music demanded it. Musical improvisation of that complexity

had never been heard before. Sometimes with just a few notes, Armstrong was able to enhance the mood of a piece, deepen its emotion, or inject it with a newfound energy.

A Great Singer

Armstrong was also a great singer. His voice was not beautiful or smooth, but it was perfect for expressing his playful, rhythmic style. Armstrong had an ability to add texture and warmth to familiar songs, often improving upon the original recordings. His talent for conveying emotion through the intonation of his voice was itself a unique form of communication. Only a performer with a personality as joyous as Armstrong's could have succeeded. His singing style inspired many imitators.

Armstrong was also one of the first artists to record "scat" singing. When a singer "scats," he stops singing the lyrics to the song and instead makes up nonsense words to imitate the sound of a particular instrument. Singers had been "scatting" in New Orleans for years, but Armstrong was among the first to put it on record with a song called "Heebie Jeebies." He later said that when he was recording "Heebie Jeebies" the sheet music that he was reading fell off the stand, so he had to make up something quickly. Most people who bought the record were amazed because they had never heard anything like it before. This innovation was just another way Armstrong was able to mesmerize his audience.

A Musical Innovator

When Louis Armstrong's records started selling, jazz musicians all around the country began to mimic his style. His influence was so <u>pervasive</u> that most trumpet players who recorded between 1927 and 1940 sound like him. The great jazz musician Miles Davis recognized Armstrong's importance when he said, "There's nothing you can play on the horn that Louis didn't play first."

Armstrong's records also opened the door for a whole new type of singing, influencing

 Test-Taking Tip

Paragraph labels should be short and to the point. Help students fine-tune their paragraph labeling skills. It will help them on many standardized tests to come!

 Test-Taking Tip

Students can sometimes use key words in the stem of the question to search though a passage for an answer. For example, for item number 3, students could search for *popularize* to find the right area. Of course, if the words are in the students' paragraph labels, their search is made easier.

vocalists as diverse as Bing Crosby, Ella Fitzgerald, Frank Sinatra, and Billie Holiday. Today, jazz singers still scat and improvise, following Armstrong's lead.

In addition to influencing his fellow musicians, Armstrong played a huge role in popularizing the music he had helped to create. He spent his life playing concerts throughout the world, bringing jazz to millions of people who had never heard it before. His sound was so vibrant and uplifting that it appealed to audiences of nearly every social, economic, and cultural background. Relying on music instead of words to deliver his message, Armstrong created deep emotional responses in his listeners. His recordings remain inspiring to this day.

When Louis Armstrong started playing jazz, he brought a whole new style to the genre. This style was so popular that it eventually replaced what came before it. Armstrong reinvented jazz. Everything that makes up jazz today—improvisation, inventive melodies and rhythm, "scat" singing—can be traced back to him. For this reason, many people call him the "father of jazz."

1 Louis Armstrong is compared to a good public speaker because he —

A had a voice that was perfect for expressing his playful, rhythmic style

B was very skilled at complex musical improvisation

C played solos that are among the greatest ever recorded

D relied on music instead of words to deliver his message

2 The main idea of this passage is that Louis Armstrong —

F filled his music with emotion

G grew up in the musically rich city of New Orleans

H created a style that influenced all jazz music

J recorded a song called "Heebie Jeebies"

3 Louis Armstrong helped to popularize jazz music by —

A opening the door to a whole new type of singing

B appealing to people of many different backgrounds

C being hired by King Oliver to play in his band

D influencing his fellow musicians

4 Information in this passage implies that Armstrong's trumpet playing was —

F powerful

G lazy

H incoherent

J relaxed

5 Which of these is a FACT in the passage?

A Louis Armstrong invented "scat" singing.

B Louis Armstrong never played the piano.

C Louis Armstrong played concerts all over the world.

D King Oliver's band was better than any other band.

6 In this passage, _pervasive_ means —

F limited

G subtle

H widespread

J destructive

Answers and Analyses

1. B Students need to find the section that makes this comparison. It is in paragraph 3.

2. H Students can look over all their paragraph labels to get a feel for the main idea of the passage. Choices F, G, and J are all just details dealt with in one part of the passage. Choice H describes the main idea of the entire passage.

3. B Students must look for the section of text that mentions how Armstrong made jazz popular. This can be found in paragraph 8. The other three choices are all details found in the passage, but they are not explicitly connected to the popularization of jazz.

4. F Paragraph 2 says that Armstrong's playing was skillful, loud, and energetic. Only "powerful" is a good generalization of the description given in the passage.

5. C A fact must be
1. in the passage and
2. not an opinion.
Choice A is contradicted in paragraph 5. Choice B is not mentioned at all. Choice C is mentioned in paragraph 8, and it is stated as a fact, not an opinion. Choice D is an opinion that is not mentioned in the passage, although students may be misled because it does say that the band was the "most popular" in New Orleans.

6. H Students should go back to the underlined word in the passage and read the context carefully. Even if they do not know what the word _pervasive_ means, they can still get the item correct. Most trumpet players were influenced, so his

Test-Taking Tip

Students should _always_ refer back to the passage and look for the specific section dealing with an item's topic.

influence was not _limited_ or _subtle_, but _widespread_. Students can also eliminate choice J, _destructive_, because it is far too negative for such an upbeat passage.

Communication Survival Kit

● Language Handbook

● Guide to Business Communication

Troubleshooter

The Troubleshooter will help you recognize and correct errors that you might make in your writing.

Sentence Fragment

Problem: A fragment that lacks a subject

This new computer is fantastic. (Is much faster than the old one.) *frag*

Solution: Add a subject to the fragment to make it a complete sentence.

This new computer is fantastic. It is much faster than the old one.

Problem: A fragment that lacks a complete verb

The patrons poured from the theater. (Theatergoers in excited groups.) *frag*

The jet suddenly plunged. (Passengers tumbling in the aisles.) *frag*

Solution A: Add a complete verb or an auxiliary verb to make the sentence complete.

The patrons poured from the theater. The theatergoers chattered in excited groups.

The jet suddenly plunged. Passengers were tumbling in the aisles.

Solution B: Combine the fragment with another sentence. Add commas to set off a nonessential phrase, or add a comma and a conjunction to separate two main clauses in a compound sentence.

The theatergoers, chattering in excited groups, poured from the theater.

The jet suddenly plunged, and passengers were tumbling in the aisles.

Problem: A fragment that is a subordinate clause

Tim scored the goal. (Although he was injured in the attempt.) *frag*

My term paper is about Robert Frost. (Who is my favorite poet.) *frag*

Solution A: Combine the fragment with another sentence. Add a comma to set off nonessential clauses.

Tim scored the goal, although he was injured in the attempt.

My term paper is about Robert Frost, who is my favorite poet.

Solution B: Rewrite the fragment as a complete sentence, eliminating the subordinating conjunction or the relative pronoun and adding a subject or other words necessary to make a complete thought.

Tim scored the goal. He was, however, injured in the attempt.

My term paper is about Robert Frost. He is my favorite poet.

Problem: A fragment that lacks both a subject and a verb

Keisha recited the poem. (From memory.) *frag*

Solution: Combine the fragment with another sentence.

Keisha recited the poem from memory.

> **Rule of Thumb:** Sentence fragments can make your writing hard to understand. Make sure that every sentence has a subject and a verb.

Run-on Sentence

Problem: Comma splice—two main clauses separated by only a comma

(We went canoeing last weekend, my shoulders still ache.) *run-on*

Solution A: Replace the comma with an end mark of punctuation, such as a period or a question mark, and begin the new sentence with a capital letter.

We went canoeing last weekend. My shoulders still ache.

Solution B: Place a semicolon between the two main clauses.

We went canoeing last weekend; my shoulders still ache.

Solution C: Add a coordinating conjunction after the comma.

We went canoeing last weekend, and my shoulders still ache.

Problem: Two main clauses with no punctuation between them

The museum has a new exhibit of modern art we haven't seen it yet. *run-on*

Solution A: Separate the main clauses with an end mark of punctuation, such as a period or a question mark, and begin the second sentence with a capital letter.

The museum has a new exhibit of modern art. We haven't seen it yet.

Solution B: Separate the main clauses with a semicolon.

The museum has a new exhibit of modern art; we haven't seen it yet.

Solution C: Add a comma and a coordinating conjunction between the main clauses.

The museum has a new exhibit of modern art, but we haven't seen it yet.

Problem: Two main clauses with no comma before the coordinating conjunction

We washed cars all day and then we went out for Chinese food. *run-on*

Solution: Add a comma before the coordinating conjunction to separate the two main clauses.

We washed cars all day, and then we went out for Chinese food.

> **Rule of Thumb:** It often helps to have someone else read your writing to see if it is clear. Since you know what the sentences are supposed to mean, you might sometimes miss the need for punctuation.

Lack of Subject-Verb Agreement

Problem: A subject that is separated from the verb by an intervening prepositional phrase

The bus with the band members leave at noon. *agr*

The peaks of the mountain range glistens with snow. *agr*

Solution: Ignore a prepositional phrase that comes between a subject and a verb. Make the verb agree with the subject, which is never the object of a preposition.

The bus with the band members leaves at noon.

The peaks of the mountain range glisten with snow.

Problem: A predicate nominative that differs in number from the subject

Raisins (is) a delicious snack. *agr*

Solution: Ignore the predicate nominative and make the verb agree with the subject of the sentence.

Raisins are a delicious snack.

Problem: A subject that follows the verb

Outside the mall (stands) six men. *agr*

Over there (is) several more. *agr*

Solution: In an inverted sentence, look for the subject *after* the verb. Then make sure the verb agrees with the subject.

Outside the mall stand six men.

Over there are several more.

> **Rule of Thumb:** Reversing the order of an inverted sentence may help you decide on the correct verb form: "Several more are over there."

Problem: A collective noun as the subject

The committee (meet) at 3:30 every Wednesday afternoon. *agr*

The committee (casts) their votes for chairperson. *agr*

Solution A: If the collective noun refers to a group as a whole, use a singular verb.

The committee meets at 3:30 every Wednesday afternoon.

Solution B: If the collective noun refers to each member of a group individually, use a plural verb.

The committee cast their votes for chairperson.

Problem: A noun of amount as the subject

Thirty-five years (are) the average lifespan of a hippopotamus. *agr*

Fifty pennies (fits) into a coin roll. *agr*

Solution: Determine whether the noun of amount refers to one unit (and is therefore singular) or whether it refers to a number of individual units (and is therefore plural).

Thirty-five years is the average lifespan of a hippopotamus.

Fifty pennies fit into a coin roll.

Problem: A compound subject that is joined by *and*

Speakers and a joystick (is) plugged into my computer. *agr*

Cookies and cream (are) my favorite kind of ice cream. *agr*

Solution A: If the parts of the compound subject do not belong to one unit or if they refer to different people or things, use a plural verb.

Speakers and a joystick are plugged into my computer.

Solution B: If the parts of the compound subject belong to one unit or if both parts refer to the same person or thing, use a singular verb.

Cookies and cream is my favorite kind of ice cream.

Problem: A compound subject that is joined by *or* or *nor*

Neither the dictionaries nor the thesaurus (are) on the shelves. *agr*

Solution: Make the verb agree with the subject that is closer to it.

Neither the dictionaries nor the thesaurus is on the shelves.

Neither the thesaurus nor the dictionaries are on the shelves.

Problem: A compound subject that is preceded by *many a, every,* or *each*

Every student and teacher (have passed) through these halls. *agr*

Solution: Use a singular verb when *many a, each,* or *every* precedes a compound subject.

Every student and teacher has passed through these halls.

Problem: A subject that is separated from the verb by an intervening expression

My mother, as well as her brothers, were born in Sweden. *agr*

Solution: Certain expressions, such as *as well as, in addition to,* and *together with,* do not change the number of the subject. Ignore these expressions between a subject and its verb. Make the verb agree with the subject.

My mother, as well as her brothers, was born in Sweden.

Problem: An indefinite pronoun as the subject

Everyone enjoy mysteries. *agr*

Several of the top-seeded players is in the finals. *agr*

Solution: Determine whether the indefinite pronoun is singular or plural, and make the verb agree. Some indefinite pronouns are singular—*another, anyone, everyone, one, each, either, neither, anything, everything, something,* and *somebody.* Some are plural—*both, many, few, several,* and *others.* Some can be singular or plural—*some, all, any, more, most,* and *none*—depending on the noun to which they refer.

Everyone enjoys mysteries.

Several of the top-seeded players are in the finals.

Lack of Pronoun-Antecedent Agreement

Problem: A singular antecedent that can be either male or female

A lawyer often settles his clients' cases out of court. *ant*

Solution A: Traditionally, a masculine pronoun was used to refer to an antecedent that might be either male or female. This usage ignores or excludes females and is not acceptable in contemporary writing. Reword the sentence to use *he or she, him or her,* and so on.

A lawyer often settles his or her clients' cases out of court.

Solution B: Reword the sentence so that both the antecedent and the pronoun are plural.

Lawyers often settle their clients' cases out of court.

Solution C: Reword the sentence to eliminate the pronoun.

A lawyer often settles clients' cases out of court.

Problem: A second-person pronoun that refers to a third-person antecedent

Ms. Rivelli likes to travel to cities where (you) can get around by bus. *ant*

Solution A: Use the appropriate third-person pronoun.

Ms. Rivelli likes to travel to cities where she can get around by bus.

Solution B: Use an appropriate noun instead of a pronoun.

Ms. Rivelli likes to travel to cities where people can get around by bus.

Problem: A singular indefinite pronoun as an antecedent

Neither of the girls remembered to bring (their) gym clothes. *ant*

Solution: *Another, any, every, each, one, either, neither, anything, everything, something,* and *somebody* are singular and therefore require singular personal pronouns, even when followed by a prepositional phrase that contains a plural noun.

Neither of the girls remembered to bring her gym clothes.

> **Rule of Thumb:** To help you remember that pronouns such as *each, either,* and *neither* are singular, think *each one, either one,* and *neither one.*

Lack of Clear Pronoun Reference

Problem: A pronoun reference that is weak or vague

The players were elated, (which) was long overdue. *ref*

The fire was nearing our camp, and (that) made us nervous. *ref*

Solution A: Rewrite the sentence, adding a clear antecedent for the pronoun.

The players were elated by their victory, which was long overdue.

Solution B: Rewrite the sentence, substituting a noun for the pronoun.

The fire was nearing our camp, and the situation made us nervous.

Problem: A pronoun that could refer to more than one antecedent

Dad and Uncle Mark started a company, and (he) is the president. *ref*

Now that the actors have agents, (they) are getting more work. *ref*

Solution A: Rewrite the sentence, substituting a noun for the pronoun.

Dad and Uncle Mark started a company, and Dad is the president.

Solution B: Rewrite the sentence, making the antecedent of the pronoun clear.

The actors are getting more work now that they have agents.

Problem: The indefinite use of *you* or *they*

When a loon utters its eerie cry, (you) get goosebumps. *ref*

In Boston (they) call a submarine sandwich a grinder. *ref*

Solution A: Rewrite the sentence, substituting a noun for the pronoun.

When a loon utters its eerie cry, listeners get goosebumps.

Solution B: Rewrite the sentence, eliminating the pronoun entirely.

In Boston a submarine sandwich is called a grinder.

Shift in Pronoun

Problem: An incorrect shift in person between two pronouns

They enjoy gliding, a sport in which (you) try to catch thermals to stay aloft. *pro*

I believe in telling the truth, even when (you) will be punished for it. *pro*

Once you have tasted this salsa, (everyone) will be amazed. *pro*

Solution A: Replace the incorrect pronoun with a pronoun that agrees with its antecedent.

They enjoy gliding, a sport in which they try to catch thermals to stay aloft.

I believe in telling the truth, even when I will be punished for it.

Once you have tasted this salsa, you will be amazed.

Solution B: Replace the incorrect pronoun with an appropriate noun.

They enjoy gliding, a sport in which pilots try to catch thermals to stay aloft.

Shift in Verb Tense

Problem: An unnecessary shift in tense

The astronomers focus on the comet and (compared) observations. *shift t*

Justine glided onto the ice as the audience (bursts) into applause. *shift t*

Solution: When two or more events occur at the same time, be sure to use the same verb tense to describe each event.

The astronomers focus on the comet and compare observations.

Justine glided onto the ice as the audience burst into applause.

Problem: A lack of correct shift in tenses to show that one event precedes or follows another

By the time help arrived, we (were stranded) on the ledge for hours. *shift t*

Solution: When two events have occurred at different times in the past, shift from the past tense to the past perfect tense to indicate that one action began and ended before another past action began.

By the time help arrived, we had been stranded on the ledge for hours.

> **Rule of Thumb:** When you need to use more than one verb tense in a sentence, it may help to first jot down the sequence of events you're writing about. Be clear in your mind which action happened first.

Incorrect Verb Tense or Form

Problem: An incorrect or missing verb ending

Last year my sister (work) on a ranch for the summer. *tense*

Has she (decide) what she would like to do this year? *tense*

Solution: Add *-ed* to a regular verb to form the past tense and the past participle.

Last year my sister worked on a ranch for the summer.

Has she decided what she would like to do this year?

Problem: An improperly formed irregular verb

We think our cat (runned) away last night. *tense*

I (have teared) an ad out of the "Lost Pets" section of the newspaper. *tense*

Solution: Irregular verbs form their past and past participle forms in some way other than by adding *-ed.* Memorize these forms, or look them up in a dictionary.

We think our cat ran away last night.

I have torn an ad out of the "Lost Pets" section of the newspaper.

Problem: Confusion between the past form and the past participle

We have occasionally (beat) their team. *tense*

Solution: Use the past participle form of an irregular verb, not the past form, when you use a form of the auxiliary verb *have.*

We have occasionally beaten their team.

Problem: Improper use of the past participle

Our glee club (sung) the national anthem at many games. *tense*

The thirsty picnickers (drunk) three cases of soda. *tense*

Solution A: The past participle of an irregular verb cannot stand alone as a verb. Add a form of the auxiliary verb *have* to the past participle to form a complete verb.

Our glee club has sung the national anthem at many games.

The thirsty picnickers have drunk three cases of soda.

Solution B: Replace the past participle with the past form of the verb.

Our glee club sang the national anthem at many games.

The thirsty picnickers drank three cases of soda.

Misplaced or Dangling Modifier

Problem: A misplaced modifier

Jenita got many compliments from her friends (in her new outfit.) *mod*

(Dazed and terrified,) we found the raccoon by the side of the road. *mod*

The birdwatchers spotted a yellow wagtail (who had binoculars.) *mod*

Solution: Modifiers that modify the wrong word or seem to modify more than one word in a sentence are called misplaced modifiers. Move the misplaced phrase as close as possible to the word or words it modifies.

In her new outfit, Jenita got many compliments from her friends.

We found the dazed and terrified raccoon by the side of the road.

The birdwatchers who had binoculars spotted a yellow wagtail.

Problem: Incorrect placement of the adverb *only*

Mustafa (only) collects stamps from island nations. *mod*

Solution: Place the adverb *only* immediately before the word or group of words it modifies.

Only Mustafa collects stamps from island nations.

Mustafa collects only stamps from island nations.

Mustafa collects stamps only from island nations.

> **Rule of Thumb:** Note that each time *only* is moved, the meaning of the sentence changes. Check to be sure your sentence says what you mean.

Problem: A dangling modifier

(After sandbagging for hours,) the floodwaters finally began to recede. *mod*

(Cutting the grass,) a bee stung my arm. *mod*

Solution: Rewrite the sentence, adding a noun to which the dangling phrase clearly refers. Often you will have to add other words or change the form of the verb to complete the meaning of the sentence.

After sandbagging for hours, the residents watched the floodwaters finally begin to recede.

Cutting the grass, I was startled when a bee stung my arm.

Missing or Misplaced Possessive Apostrophe

Problem: Singular nouns

The (duchess) jewels were stolen by that (airlines) luggage handler. *poss*

Solution: Use an apostrophe and -*s* to form the possessive of a singular noun, even one that ends in *s*.

The duchess's jewels were stolen by that airline's luggage handler.

Problem: Plural nouns ending in -*s*

The (veterans) parade will be held next Monday. *poss*

Solution: Use an apostrophe alone to form the possessive of a plural noun that ends in -*s*.

The veterans' parade will be held next Monday.

Problem: Plural nouns not ending in -*s*

The (womens) department is located on the third floor. *poss*

Solution: Use an apostrophe and -*s* to form the possessive of a plural noun that does not end in -*s*.

The women's department is located on the third floor.

Problem: Pronouns

Please put (everybodys) potluck dishes on the table. *poss*

(Their's) is the biggest yacht I have ever seen. *poss*

Solution A: Use an apostrophe and -*s* to form the possessive of a singular indefinite pronoun.

Please put everybody's potluck dishes on the table.

Solution B: Do not use an apostrophe with any of the possessive personal pronouns.

Theirs is the biggest yacht I have ever seen.

Problem: Confusion between *its* and *it's*

One of the buffalo calves has wandered away from (it's) mother. *poss*

(Its) about time that someone spoke up about this problem. *cont*

Solution: Do not use an apostrophe to form the possessive of *it*. Use an apostrophe to form the contraction of *it is*.

One of the buffalo calves has wandered away from its mother.

It's about time that someone spoke up about this problem.

Missing Commas with Nonessential Elements

Problem: Missing commas with nonessential participles or participial phrases

The author ˄ smiling graciously ˄ signed copies of her books. *com*

Putting it bluntly ˄ I will not allow a potbellied pig in the house. *com*

Solution: Determine whether the participle or participial phrase is essential to the meaning of the sentence. If it is not essential, set off the element with commas.

The author, smiling graciously, signed copies of her books.

Putting it bluntly, I will not allow a potbellied pig in the house.

Problem: Missing commas with nonessential adjective clauses

Oklahoma ˄ which is rich in oil ˄ suffered a bad drought in the 1930s. *com*

Solution: Determine whether the clause is essential to the meaning of the sentence. If it is not essential, set off the clause with commas.

Oklahoma, which is rich in oil, suffered a bad drought in the 1930s.

Problem: Missing commas with nonessential appositives

Minstrels ˄ medieval singers ˄ entertained at royal banquets. *com*

Solution: Determine whether the appositive is essential to the meaning of the sentence. If it is not essential, set off the appositive with commas.

Minstrels, medieval singers, entertained at royal banquets.

> **Rule of Thumb:** To determine whether a word, phrase, or clause is essential, try reading the sentence without it.

Problem: Missing commas with interjections and parenthetical expressions

Gee that was a beautiful ceremony. *com*

Your brother by the way has been waiting for you for an hour. *com*

Solution: Set off the interjection or parenthetical expression with commas.

Gee, that was a beautiful ceremony.

Your brother, by the way, has been waiting for you for an hour.

Missing Commas in a Series

Problem: Missing commas in a series of words, phrases, or clauses

The zoo's primate collection includes lemurs baboons and chimpanzees. *✓ com*

Juan scowled turned on his heel and stomped off. *✓ com*

The cat bounded out the window across the yard and over the fence. *✓ com*

We videotaped the newlyweds walking down the aisle cutting the wedding cake and dancing. *✓ com*

My sister is athletic my brother is musical and I am artistic. *✓ com*

Solution: When there are three or more items in a series, use a comma after each item that precedes the conjunction.

The zoo's primate collection includes lemurs, baboons, and chimpanzees.

Juan scowled, turned on his heel, and stomped off.

The cat bounded out the window, across the yard, and over the fence.

We videotaped the newlyweds walking down the aisle, cutting the wedding cake, and dancing.

My sister is athletic, my brother is musical, and I am artistic.

> **Rule of Thumb:** When you're having difficulty with a rule of usage, try rewriting the rule in your own words. Then check with your teacher to be sure you have grasped the concept.

Troublesome Words

This section will help you choose between words that are often confusing. It will also alert you to avoid certain words and expressions in school or business writing.

---

a, an

Use the article *an* when the word that follows begins with a vowel sound. Use *a* when the word that follows begins with a consonant sound. Therefore, use *a* when the word that follows begins with a long *u* sound ("yew").

Use the article *a* when the word that follows begins with a sounded *h*. Use *an* when the word that follows begins with an unsounded *h*.

An elephant stomped through **a** field.

An aunt of mine has **a** unique house.

A helmet from an ancient Roman soldier is quite **an** heirloom!

---

a lot, alot

This expression is always written as two words and means "a large amount." Some authorities discourage its use in formal English.

When the truck swerved, **a lot** of sand spilled from it.

When the truck swerved, **a large amount** of sand spilled from it.

---

accept, except

Accept is a verb meaning "to receive" or "to agree to." *Except* is occasionally used as a verb, but more often it is used as a preposition meaning "but."

Please **accept** my apologies.

All of the officers, **except** one, attended the meeting.

---

affect, effect

Affect is a verb meaning "to cause a change in; to influence." *Effect* may be a noun or a verb. As a noun it means "result." As a verb it means "to bring about or accomplish."

Exercise will **affect** your fitness level.

Exercise will have a beneficial **effect** on your fitness level.

Exercise will **effect** an improvement in your fitness level.

---

ain't

Ain't is never used in formal speaking and writing unless you are quoting the exact words of a character or real person. Instead of using *ain't,* use *am not, is not,* or a contraction such as *he isn't* or *I'm not.*

Muriel **isn't** coming to the party.

all ready, already

All ready is an adjective phrase that means "completely ready." *Already* is an adverb that means "before" or "by this time."

The climbers were **all ready** for their final ascent, but the storm was **already** upon them.

all right, alright

The expression *all right* should be written as two words.

Were the children **all right** after their frightening experience?

> **Rule of Thumb:** Dictionaries are good guides to the usage of a word. Even though some dictionaries do list the single word *alright,* they indicate that it is not a preferred spelling.

all together, altogether

Use *all together* to mean "in a group." Use the adverb *altogether* to mean "completely" or "on the whole."

The scholarship winners stood **all together** on the stage.

They seemed **altogether** thrilled with their awards.

amount, number

Use *amount* to refer to things that cannot be counted. Use *number* to refer to things that can be counted.

This recipe calls for a large **amount** of pepper.

This recipe calls for a large **number** of eggs.

anxious, eager

Anxious means "uneasy or worried about some event or situation." *Eager* means "having a keen interest" or "feeling impatient for something expected."

I am **anxious** about my dog's reaction to her shots.

The children are **eager** to go to the amusement park.

a while, awhile

A while is made up of an article and a noun. *In* and *for* often come before *a while,* forming a prepositional phrase. *Awhile* is an adverb.

I'll practice in **a while.** I'll practice for **a while.**

I'll rest **awhile** before practicing.

being as, being that

The expressions *being as* and *being that* are sometimes used instead of *because* or *since* in informal conversation. In formal speaking and writing, always use *because* or *since.*

Because Kendra has the flu, we'll need to find another debater.

Since it's already three o'clock, we'd better get ready to leave.

beside, besides

Beside means "at the side of." *Besides* usually means "in addition to."

The prime minister sat **beside** the president on the plane.

Besides playing hockey, the boys compete on the track team.

between, among

Use *between* to compare one person or thing with one other person or thing or with an entire group. Use *among* to show a relationship in which more than two persons or things are considered as a group.

When the twins dress alike, I can't see any difference **between** them.

There is quite a difference **between** Monet's painting and the others in the exhibit.

The members will settle the issue **among** themselves.

bring, take

Use *bring* to mean "to carry from a distant place to a closer one." Use *take* to mean the opposite: "to carry from a nearby place to a more distant one."

Please **bring** those videotapes over here.

When you go to the store, don't forget to **take** money with you.

can, may

Can indicates the ability to do something. *May* indicates permission to do something or the possibility of doing it.

May I wear your sweater if I **can** fix the button?

> **Rule of Thumb:** Although *can* is sometimes used in place of *may* in informal speech, you should distinguish between them when speaking and writing formally.

can't hardly, can't scarcely

These terms are considered double negatives because *hardly* and *scarcely* by themselves have a negative meaning. Therefore, avoid using *hardly* and *scarcely* with *not* or *-n't*.

Our entire class **can hardly** fit into the new classroom.

Without my glasses, I **can scarcely** see the movie screen.

capital, capitol

Use *capital* to refer to the city that is the center of government of a state or country, to money or other assets, or to a capital letter. Use *capitol* to refer to the building or group of buildings in which a state legislature meets.

Sacramento is the **capital** of California.

The **capitol** in Boston, Massachusetts, has a gold dome.

complement, compliment

A *complement* is something that fills up, completes, or makes perfect. A *compliment* is an expression of praise or admiration.

This sauce is a great **complement** for the fish.

He blushes whenever anyone pays him a **compliment.**

compose, comprise

Compose often means "to form by putting together." *Comprise* means "to contain; embrace."

The sauce was **composed** of tomatoes, fresh garlic, and chopped onions.

Our state **comprises** twelve counties.

continual, continuous

Continual describes repetitive action with pauses between occurrences. *Continuous* describes an action that continues with no interruption in space or time.

The jackhammer's **continual** bursts of noise were irritating.

The development of language is a **continuous** process.

could of, might of, must of, should of, would of

After the words *could, might, must, should,* or *would,* use the helping verb *have,* not the preposition *of.*

I don't know what **could have** gone wrong with that dishwasher.

We **must have** looked pretty silly covered with all those soapsuds!

different from, different than

The expression *different from* is generally preferred to *different than.*

John Coltrane's jazz is quite **different from** Charlie Parker's.

emigrate, immigrate

Use *emigrate* to mean "to leave one country to settle in another." Use *immigrate* to mean "to come to a country to live there permanently." Use *from* with *emigrate,* and *to* or *into* with *immigrate.*

My friend Zhu **emigrated** from China five years ago.

In the 1800s, many Irish **immigrated** to the United States.

> **Rule of Thumb:** Remember that the *e-* in *emigrate* comes from *-ex* ("out of"); the *im-* in *immigrate* comes from *in-* ("into").

ensure, assure, insure

Ensure means "to make sure of something or to guarantee it." *Assure* means "to reassure someone or to remove doubt." *Insure* means "to cover something with insurance or to secure it."

Excellent grades should **ensure** your acceptance by a college.

I **assure** you that I will be there to meet you at 4:30.

Mortgage contracts require home buyers to **insure** the property.

farther, further

Farther refers to physical distance. *Further* refers to degree or time.

I think the monument is **farther** north.

Maybe we should stop to ask for **further** directions.

fewer, less

Use *fewer* when referring to nouns that can be counted. Use *less* when referring to nouns that cannot be counted. *Less* may also be used with figures that are seen as single amounts or single quantities.

There were **fewer** snowstorms this winter than last.

Could we have a bit **less** noise, please?

I paid **less** than $10.00 for these jeans. [The amount of money is treated as a single sum, not as individual dollars.]

good, well

Use *good* as an adjective. *Well* may be used as an adverb of manner telling how ably or adequately something is done. *Well* also may be used as an adjective meaning "in good health."

Your hair looks **good** that way. [adjective after a linking verb]

Josie did **well** on her final exam. [adverb of manner]

Grandpa says he doesn't feel **well** enough to travel. [adjective meaning "in good health."]

had of

Do not use *of* between *had* and a past participle.

I wish I **had ordered** the shrimp instead of the salmon.

hanged, hung

Use *hanged* as the past tense when you mean "put to death by hanging." Use *hung* in all other instances.

In many countries, people were once **hanged** for minor offenses.

We **hung** a flag outside our house on Flag Day.

in, into

Use *in* to mean "inside" or "within." Use *into* to indicate movement or direction from outside to a point within.

After work, Mom soaks her feet **in** warm water.

I stepped backward and fell **into** the pool.

irregardless, regardless

Use *regardless.* The prefix *ir-* and the suffix *-less* both have negative meanings. When used together, they produce a double negative, which is incorrect.

We'll go camping this weekend **regardless** of the weather.

lay, lie

Lay means "to put" or "to place"; it takes a direct object. *Lie* means "to recline" or "to be positioned"; it never takes an object.

Lay your towel under that beach umbrella.

The dog likes to **lie** on the sunny deck.

learn, teach

Learn means "to gain knowledge." *Teach* means "to give knowledge."

I was twelve before I **learned** how to swim.

Mrs. Murata **teaches** algebra at our high school.

leave, let

Leave means "to go away." *Let* means "to allow" or "to permit."

Do you think she will **leave** before the holidays?

Will you **let** me borrow your notes?

like, as

Like is a preposition and introduces a prepositional phrase. *As* is a subordinating conjunction and introduces a subordinate clause. (*As* can be a preposition in some cases, as in *He served as ambassador to Ireland.*) Many authorities say that it is incorrect to use *like* before a clause.

My two-year-old sister can swim **like** a fish.

The doctor is certain, **as** we all are, that you will recover.

loose, lose

The adjective *loose* (lo͞os) means "free," "not firmly attached," or "not fitting tightly." The verb *lose* (lo͞oz) means "to have no longer," "to misplace," or "to fail to win."

You're likely to **lose** your **loose** change if you have a hole in your pocket.

Remember, it's not who wins or **loses** that matters.

passed, past

Passed is the past form and the past participle of the verb *pass*. *Past* may be an adjective, a preposition, an adverb, or a noun.

A truck **passed** us at a high rate of speed. [verb]

Learn from your **past** mistakes. [adjective]

Turn left just after you have gone **past** the church. [preposition]

As we were walking **past,** we saw smoke coming from the roof. [adverb]

The man's **past** was a mystery. [noun]

precede, proceed

Precede means "to go before" or "to come before." *Proceed* means "to continue" or "to move along."

Kennedy's and Johnson's terms in office **preceded** Nixon's.

Graduates will please **proceed** directly to the auditorium.

principal, principle

As an adjective, *principal* means "most important." *Principal* can also be a noun that refers to the head of a school. The noun *principle* often refers to a fundamental truth or a rule.

Dad has been chosen to be the **principal** speaker at the convention.

That **principle** is stated in the Bill of Rights.

raise, rise

The verb *raise* means "to cause to move upward"; it always takes an object. The verb *rise* means "to go up"; it is intransitive and does not take an object.

I always **raise** the shades immediately after I wake up.

The price of swimsuits will **rise** just before summer begins.

reason . . . is that, because

Because means "for the reason that." Therefore, do not use *because* after *reason . . . is.* Use either *reason . . . is that* or *because* alone.

The **reason** I am not going **is that** I wasn't invited.

I am not going **because** I wasn't invited.

respectfully, respectively

Use *respectfully* to mean "with respect."
Use *respectively* to mean "in the order named."

Always speak **respectfully** to the principal.

Pines and maples are evergreen and deciduous, **respectively.**

says, said

Says is the present-tense, third-person singular form of the verb *say*. *Said* is the past tense of *say*. Be careful not to use *says* when you are referring to the past.

Marina now **says** her family is moving to Alaska.

Last week, she **said** her family was moving to Hawaii.

sit, set

Sit means "to place oneself in a sitting position." It rarely takes an object. *Set* means "to place" or "to put," and it usually takes an object. When *set* is used to mean "the sun is going down," it does not take an object.

Please **sit** in that chair.

Please **set** down that remote control.

What time will the sun **set** tonight?

than, then

Than is a conjunction. Use it in comparisons or to show exception. The adverb *then* usually refers to time and can mean "at that time," "soon afterward," "the time mentioned," "at another time," "for that reason," or "in that case."

I know that Rachel is a better swimmer **than** I am.

I would rather be anywhere else **than** here.

My parents didn't even know one another **then.**

I went home and **then** stopped by Dad's office.

I had almost finished my errands by **then.**

If you can solve the puzzle, **then** please speak up.

their, they're, there

Their is the possessive form of *they*. *They're* is the contraction of *they are*. *There* is an adverb that often means "in that place." *There* is also sometimes used as an interjection, expressing a sense of completion.

There! The packages are finally on **their** way!

Did the Jacksons say when **they're** going to China?

You'll find the book you want over **there** on that shelf.

toward, towards

These words are interchangeable. Both prepositions mean "in the direction of."

A meteor is heading **toward** the moon.

A meteor is heading **towards** the moon.

where . . . at

Do not use *at* after a question with *where*.

Can you tell me **where** the post office is?

whereas, while

Both *whereas* and *while* can be used as conjunctions meaning "although." *Whereas* can also mean "in view of the fact that." *While* can be used as a conjunction or noun indicating time.

Gil's favorite sport is rowing, **whereas** Dwyla's is tennis.

While I can read German well, I still can't speak it fluently.

Whereas all the tests are in, class is dismissed.

Mom worked nights **while** she went to school.

Rule of Thumb: The conjunction *whereas* is usually reserved for very formal occasions.

who, whom

Use the nominative pronoun *who* for subjects.

Who caught that line drive? [subject of the verb]

Did he mention **who** won first prize? [subject of the noun clause *who won first prize*]

Who did you say will be working at the refreshment stand? [subject of the verb *will be working*]

Rule of Thumb: When a question contains an interrupting expression such as *did you say* or *do you think,* it helps to omit the interrupting phrase to determine whether to use *who* or *whom.*

Use the objective pronoun *whom* for the direct or indirect object of a verb or verbal or for the object of a preposition.

Whom are you choosing as a partner? [direct object of the verb *are choosing*]

Whom did you hear Geoff tutored in math? [direct object of the verb *tutored*]

Naomi told **whom** my secret? [indirect object]

From **whom** did you borrow this book? [object of the preposition *from*]

Rule of Thumb: When speaking informally, people often use *who* instead of *whom* as the direct object in sentences like *Who should we call?* In writing and in formal speech, however, distinguish between *who* and *whom.*

Mechanics

Capitalization

This section will help you recognize and use correct capitalization.

Rule	Example
Capitalize the first word in any sentence, including the first word of a direct quotation that is a complete sentence. Capitalize a sentence in parentheses unless it is contained within another sentence.	The sign in the diner said, "Servers who are tipped don't spill." The answer (all answers were read aloud) surprised him. (He blushed.)

> **Rule of Thumb:** Since people do not always speak in complete sentences, written dialogue may contain sentence fragments. In dialogue, capitalize the first word of each fragment, as well as of each complete sentence. For example: "Time to go home," Mom called.

Rule	Example
Always capitalize the pronoun no matter where it appears in a sentence.	I don't know if I can ever repay them for the kindnesses I've received.
Capitalize proper nouns, including **a.** names of individuals, titles used before a proper name, and titles used in direct address	King Hussein; Governor Jeanne Shaheen Thank you, General. [direct address]
b. names of ethnic groups, national groups, political parties and their members, and languages	Chinese Americans; Iraqis; the Republican Party; Democrats; Spanish
c. names of organizations, institutions, firms, monuments, bridges, buildings, and other structures	American Cancer Society; Field Museum; Hewlett-Packard Company; Statue of Liberty; Verrazano-Narrows Bridge; Chrysler Building; Wrigley Field
d. trade names and names of documents, awards, and laws	Levi's; Treaty of Versailles; Nobel Prize; Freedom of Information Act
e. geographical terms and regions or localities	Kenya; Tennessee; Lake Champlain; Fifth Avenue; Far East
f. names of planets and other heavenly bodies	Venus; Andromeda; Sirius; Io; Crab Nebula
g. names of ships, planes, trains, and spacecraft	HMS *Queen Elizabeth II*; the *Spruce Goose*; *Twentieth Century Limited*; *Challenger*

Rule	Example
h. names of most historical events, eras, calendar terms, and religious terms	Civil War; Great Depression; Age of Reason; Tuesday; March; Thanksgiving Day; Allah; Mormon; Hinduism; Christmas; Talmud
i. titles of literary works and publications, works of art, and musical compositions	*Beloved*; *Seventeen*; *The Thinker*; *American Gothic*; *Schindler's List*; "Kiss from a Rose"
j. specific names of school courses	Philosophy II
Capitalize proper adjectives (adjectives formed from proper nouns).	Central American governments; Elizabethan collar; Indian spices; Jewish synagogue

Punctuation

This section will help you use punctuation marks correctly.

Rule	Example
Use a **period** at the end of a declarative sentence or an imperative sentence (a polite command or request).	These prices are higher than I expected. Please hand me that spatula.
Use an **exclamation point** to show strong feeling or after a forceful command.	Wow! What a fantastic play that was!
Use a **question mark** to indicate a direct question.	What kind of computer do you have?
Use a **colon:** **a.** to introduce a list (especially after a statement that uses such words as *these, the following,* or *as follows*) and to introduce material that explains, illustrates, or restates preceding material	Noted American aviators include these: Wiley Post, Charles Lindbergh, and Amelia Earhart. Nathan must be feeling better: he asked to borrow my tennis racket.

> **Rule of Thumb:** Do not use a colon between a verb and its complement. To be used correctly, a colon must follow a complete sentence.

Rule	Example
b. to introduce a long or formal quotation	Winston Churchill said this about public speaking: "If you have an important point to make, don't try to be subtle or clever. Use a pile driver. . . ."

Rule	Example
c. in statements of precise time, in biblical chapter and verse references, and after business-letter salutations	2:34 A.M. 2 Kings 11:12 Dear Mr. Fleming: Ladies and Gentlemen:
Use a semicolon: a. to separate main clauses that are not joined by a coordinating conjunction	Hawaii's climate is mild all year round; many travelers choose to visit the islands in summer.
b. to separate main clauses joined by a conjunctive adverb or by an expression such as *for example* or *that is*	There are 132 Hawaiian islands; however, nearly all residents live on seven of the islands. Hawaiian muumuus and aloha shirts are often colorful; that is, they are brightly patterned.
c. to separate the items in a series when these items contain commas	Hawaiian words familiar to many mainlanders include *luau*, which means "feast"; *aloha*, which can mean "love," "welcome," or "farewell"; and *hula*, which means "dance."
d. to separate two main clauses joined by a coordinating conjunction when such clauses already contain several commas	Travel ads often focus on Oahu's attractions, such as Waikiki Beach, Pearl Harbor, and Diamond Head; but the state has many other interesting sites.
Use a comma: a. between the main clauses of a compound sentence	I recognize her, but I can't think of her name.
b. to separate three or more words, phrases, or clauses in a series	Ayala is a member of the Debaters' Club, the Glee Club, and the swimming team.
c. between coordinate modifiers	She is a smart, athletic student.
d. to set off interjections, parenthetical expressions, and conjunctive adverbs	Max is, in fact, a sports fanatic.
e. to set off long introductory prepositional phrases	After several days of constant exposure to the sun, your skin will be dry and leathery.

> **Rule of Thumb:** Use a comma after a short introductory prepositional phrase only if the sentence would be misread without it.

Rule	Example
f. to set off nonessential words, clauses, and phrases —introductory adverb clauses	Although Petra can read English well, her spoken English is not very fluent.
—internal adverb clauses that interrupt a sentence's flow	Those orange and black birds, unless I am mistaken, are Baltimore orioles.
—adjective clauses	Some of Frank Stella's paintings, which hang in many museums, have oddly shaped canvases.
—participles and participial phrases	The prize winners, beaming, rushed to the stage.
	Chasing after squirrels, the dog injured her foot.
—infinitive phrases	To speak frankly, I don't care for that design.
—appositives and appositive phrases	Dolphins and bats, both mammals, can hear much higher frequencies than humans can hear.

> **Rule of Thumb:** Nonessential elements can be removed without changing the meaning of the sentence.

Rule	Example
g. to set off quotations in dialogue	"Yesterday," announced Kayla, "I won the debate."
h. to set off an antithetical phrase	Dawna, unlike Theresa, enjoys playing chess.
i. to set off a title after a person's name	Michael Todesca, M.S.W.; Delyna Smith, chair of the committee
j. to separate the various parts of an address, a geographical term, or a date	St. Louis, Missouri Saturday, July 4 December 7, 1941 Cambridge, MA 02138
k. after the salutation of an informal letter and after the closing of all letters	Dear Mom and Dad, Sincerely,
l. to set off parts of a reference that direct the reader to the exact source	This rule is found in *The Chicago Manual of Style*, chapter 10, paragraph 83.
m. to set off words or names used in direct address and in tag questions	Keon, could you tutor me in algebra? You've never had chicken pox, have you?

Rule	Example
Use a **dash** to signal a change in thought or to set off and emphasize supplemental information or parenthetical comments.	Mammoth Cave—its name is appropriate—has about 300 miles of tunnels. Hiroko went to college here—in the United States, I mean.

> **Rule of Thumb:** A good test of the correct use of dashes is to delete the information that the dashes set off. If the remaining sentence retains its basic meaning, then the dashes were properly used. If the remaining sentence has lost crucial information, then the dashes were improperly used.

Rule	Example
Use **parentheses** to set off supplemental material. A complete parenthetical sentence contained within another sentence is not capitalized and needs no period. If a parenthetical expression contained within another sentence requires a question mark or exclamation point, put the punctuation mark *inside* the parentheses.	Plain popcorn (lightly salted if desired) is a healthful and filling snack. Locusts form swarms (these insects are usually solitary) when their food supply is exhausted. I felt an incredible sense of relief (just think what might have happened!) when the plane landed.
Use **quotation marks:** **a.** to enclose a direct quotation, as follows:	Speaking of another writer's novel, Gore Vidal remarked, "This is not at all bad, except as prose."
When a quotation is interrupted, use two sets of quotation marks.	"All the really good ideas I ever had," said artist Grant Wood, "came to me while I was milking a cow."
Use single quotation marks around a quotation within a quotation.	Joe Namath, the legendary quarterback, said, "Till I was 13, I thought my name was 'Shut Up.'"
In writing dialogue, begin a new paragraph and use a new set of quotation marks every time the speaker changes.	"Dad, may I borrow five dollars?" I asked. "What for?" Dad replied. "Um, actually, it's for your Father's Day present," I answered sheepishly.
b. to enclose titles of short works, such as stories, poems, essays, articles, chapters, and songs	"Barometer Soup" is a song on that Jimmy Buffett CD.

Rule	Example
c. to enclose unfamiliar slang terms and unusual expressions	What does the slang word "dis" mean? Tom Wolfe coined the expression "radical chic."

> **Rule of Thumb:** To tell whether question marks and exclamation points go inside or outside quotation marks, see how the quotation would be punctuated if it stood alone. If the quotation is a question or an exclamation, then the punctuation mark should go inside the quotation marks. If the quotation would end with a period, then the question mark or exclamation point should go outside the quotation marks.

Rule	Example
Use **italics**:	
a. for titles of books, lengthy poems, plays, films, television series, paintings and sculptures, long musical compositions, court cases, names of newspapers and magazines, ships, trains, airplanes, and spacecraft. Italicize and capitalize articles *(a, an, the)* at the beginning of a title only when they are part of the title.	*Beowulf* [long poem]; *Biography* [television series] *The Potato Eaters* [painting] *Appalachian Spring* [long musical composition] *Ebony* [magazine] *Eagle* [spacecraft] *Spirit of St. Louis* [airplane] *The Old Man and the Sea* [book] the *Boston Globe* [newspaper]
b. for foreign words and expressions that are not used frequently in English	The rider enjoyed the attention he got when he wore his *charro* costume.
c. for words, letters, and numerals used to represent themselves	The word *stationery*, with an *e*, refers to writing paper. I mistook your *3* for an *8*.
Use an **apostrophe**:	
a. to create a possessive form, as follows: Add an apostrophe and *-s* to all singular indefinite pronouns, singular nouns, plural nouns not ending in *-s,* and compound nouns. Add only an apostrophe to a plural noun that ends in *-s.*	nobody's fault New Mexico's climate children's welfare mass's density baby-sitter's duties seat belt's buckle flowers' petals Wongs' party
If two or more entities possess something jointly, use the possessive form for the last entity named. If they possess it individually, use the possessive form for each entity's name.	Aunt Ellie and Uncle Ed's house Newton's and Einstein's discoveries

Rule	Example
b. to express amounts of money or time that modify a noun	a twelve dollars' savings a two weeks' delay [You can use a hyphenated adjective instead: *a two-week delay*.]
c. in place of omitted letters or numerals	can't [cannot] the crash of '29
d. with *-s* to form the plural of letters, numerals, symbols, and words used as words.	7's *p*'s and *q*'s +'s Your speech contains too many *whosoever*'s and *nevertheless*'s.
Use a **hyphen:** **a.** after any prefix joined to a proper noun or proper adjective	mid-July pre-Raphaelite
b. after the prefixes *all-, ex-,* and *self-* joined to any noun or adjective; after the prefix *anti-* when it joins a word beginning with *i;* after the prefix *vice-* (except in *vice president*); and to avoid confusion between words that begin with *re-* and look like another word	ex-husband self-conscious anti-inflammatory vice-regent re-mark the sale tags make a snide remark re-sign the document resign from her job

Rule of Thumb: Remember that the prefix *anti-* requires a hyphen when followed by a word that begins with *i* in order to prevent spelling words with two successive *i*'s. Otherwise, *anti-* does not require a hyphen except before a capitalized word.

Rule	Example
c. in a compound adjective that precedes a noun	a thirty-year career his tear-stained face
d. in any spelled-out cardinal or ordinal numbers up to *ninety-nine* or *ninety-ninth* and with a fraction used as an adjective	forty-nine twenty-third two-thirds cup
e. to divide a word at the end of a line between syllables or pronounceable parts	sur-face en-hanced

Abbreviations

Abbreviations are shortened forms of words. This section will help you learn
how to use abbreviations correctly.

Rule	Example
Use only one period if an abbreviation occurs at the end of a sentence. If the sentence ends with a question mark or an exclamation point, use the period *and* the second mark of punctuation.	I addressed the letter to Jane Parsons, R.N. Do your friends live in the U.K.? It's already 11:00 P.M.!
Capitalize abbreviations of proper nouns and abbreviations related to dates and times.	George W. Bush Morrissey Blvd. 767 B.C. A.D. 1910 6:15 A.M.
Use all capital letters and no periods for abbreviations of organization names that are pronounced letter by letter or as words.	IBM SPCA NOAA AMA DOT NYPD NFL FBI GSA
When addressing mail, use the official ZIP-code abbreviations of state names (two capital letters, no periods).	AZ (Arizona) CA (California) IL (Illinois) OK (Oklahoma) SC (South Carolina) DC (District of Columbia)

> **Rule of Thumb:** In a letter it is appropriate to use a state abbreviation in the address. In other forms of writing, such as expository writing, spell out the name of a state.

Rule	Example
Use abbreviations for some personal titles.	Arthur Ashe Jr. Dr. Caitlin Connor Maj. Jacob Stern Olivia DiMario, A.R.N.P. Mrs. Anita Brown Rev. Billy Graham
Abbreviate units of measure used with numerals in technical or scientific writing, but not in ordinary prose.	mi. (mile) oz. (ounce) tsp. (teaspoon) l (liter) kg (kilogram) cm (centimeter)

Numbers and Numerals

This section will help you understand when to use numerals and when to spell
out numbers.

Rule	Example
In general, spell out cardinal and ordinal numbers that can be written in one or two words.	I am one of twenty-nine students in Ms. Chung's algebra class. For the hundredth time, please turn the radio off.
Spell out any number that occurs at the beginning of a sentence.	Six thousand five hundred tickets were sold for the festival on Saturday.
In general, use numerals (numbers expressed in figures) to express numbers that would be written in more than two words. Extremely high numbers are often expressed as a numeral followed by the word *million* or *billion*.	There are 767 students in our high school. In 1977 a Soviet woman parachuted to the earth from an altitude of 48,556 feet. The federal deficit was about $350 billion that year.
If related numbers appear in the same sentence, use all numerals.	There are over 25,000 seats in the arena, but only about 1,000 have been reserved to date.
Use numerals to express amounts of money, decimals, and percentages.	$1.1 trillion 2.2 children per family 99.99 percent
Use numerals to express the year and day in a date and to express the precise time with the abbreviations *A.M.* and *P.M.*	Martin Luther King Jr. died on April 4, 1968. The carpenter said he'd be here by 8:30 A.M.
Spell out a number to express a century or when the word *century* is used, or to express a decade when the century is clear from the context. When a century and a decade are expressed as a single unit, use numerals followed by -*s*.	The United Kingdom of Great Britain—including England, Scotland, and Wales—was formed early in the eighteenth century. In the forties, however, England and Scotland were still fighting. American involvement in the Vietnam War in the 1960s and early 1970s became very controversial.
Use numerals for streets and avenues numbered above ten and for all house, apartment, and room numbers.	1422 West 31st Street 623 Third Avenue Room 273 Apartment 3B
Use numerals to express page and line numbers.	You'll find that reference on page 952, line 23.

Spelling

The following basic rules, examples, and exceptions will help you master the spellings of many words.

ie and ei

Many writers find the rules for certain combinations of letters, like *ie* and *ei*, difficult to remember. One helpful learning strategy is to develop a rhyme to remember a rule. Look at the following rhyme for the *ie* and *ei* rule.

Rule	Example
Put *i* before *e*,	pier, grief, shriek, yield
except after *c*,	deceive, conceit, conceive
or when sounded like *a*,	heiress, weight, skein
as in *neighbor* and *weigh*.	feint, unveiled, eighty

SOME EXCEPTIONS: seize, leisure, weird, height, either, forfeit, protein, efficient.

-cede, -ceed, and -sede

Because different combinations of letters in English are sometimes pronounced the same way, it is often easy to make slight spelling errors. Except for the exceptions below, spell the *sēd* sound at the end of a word as *cede:*

    recede   intercede   secede

EXCEPTION: One word uses *-sede* to spell the final *sēd* sound: supersede.

EXCEPTION: Three words use *-ceed* to spell the final *sēd* sound: proceed, exceed, succeed.

Unstressed vowels

Notice the vowel sound in the second syllable of the word *or-i-gin.* This is the unstressed vowel sound; dictionary respellings use the *schwa* symbol (ə) to indicate it. Because any of several vowels can be used to spell this sound, writers are often uncertain about which vowel to use. To help spell words with unstressed vowels correctly, try thinking of a related word in which the syllable containing the vowel sound is stressed.

Unknown Spelling	Related Word	Correct Spelling
pos_tive	po**si**tion	po**si**tive
ess_nce	es**se**ntial	es**se**nce
insp_ration	in**spi**re	in**spi**ration
emph_sis	em**pha**tic	em**pha**sis

Adding prefixes

When adding a prefix to a word, keep the original spelling of the word. If the prefix forms a double letter, keep both letters.

> dis + obey = disobey
> ir + rational = irrational
> mis + laid = mislaid

Suffixes and the silent e

Many English words end in a silent letter *e*. Sometimes the *e* is dropped when a suffix is added. When adding a suffix that begins with a consonant to a word that ends in silent *e*, keep the *e*.

> idle + ness = idleness
> live + ly = lively

COMMON EXCEPTIONS: awe + ful = awful; judge + ment = judgment

When adding the suffix -*y* or a suffix that begins with a vowel to a word that ends in silent *e*, usually drop the *e*.

> grime + y = grimy
> sense + ible = sensible

COMMON EXCEPTION: mile + age = mileage

When adding a suffix that begins with *a* or *o* to a word that ends in *ce* or *ge*, keep the *e* so the word will retain the soft *c* or *g* sound.

> outrage + ous = outrageous
> notice + able = noticeable
> salvage + able = salvageable

When adding a suffix that begins with a vowel to a word that ends in *ee* or *oe*, keep the *e*.

> free + ing = freeing
> canoe + able = canoeable
> decree + ing = decreeing

Suffixes and the final y

When adding a suffix to a word that ends in a consonant + *y*, change the *y* to *i* unless the suffix begins with *i*. Keep the *y* in a word that ends in a vowel + *y*.

> pry + ed = pried
> betray + ed = betrayed
> essay + ist = essayist

> defy + ing = defying
> annoy + ing = annoying
> gray + ish = grayish

Doubling the final consonant

When adding a suffix to a word that ends in a consonant, double the final consonant if it is preceded by a single vowel and the word is one syllable, if the accent is on the last syllable and remains there even after the suffix is added, or if the word is made up of a prefix and a one-syllable word.

plug + ing = plugging   map + ed = mapped
propel + or = propellor   deter + ent = deterrent
recap + ing = recapping   disbar + ed = disbarred

Do not double the final consonant if the accent is not on the last syllable or if the accent shifts when the suffix is added. Also do not double the final consonant if it is preceded by two vowels or by another consonant. If the word ends in a consonant and the suffix begins with a consonant, do not double the final consonant.

alter + ed = altered   confer + ence = conference
contain + er = container   descend + ant = descendant
assess + ment = assessment   pain + ful = painful

Adding *-ly* and *-ness*

When adding *-ly* to a word that ends in a single *l*, keep the *l*. If the word ends in a double *l*, drop one *l*. When the word ends in a consonant + *le*, drop the *le*. When adding *-ness* to a word that ends in *n*, keep the *n*.

usual + ly = usually   shrill + ly = shrilly
crumble + ly = crumbly   plain + ness = plainness

Forming compound words

When joining a word that ends in a consonant to a word that begins with a consonant, keep both consonants.

class + mate = classmate   keep + sake = keepsake
book + store = bookstore   fiber + glass = fiberglass

Forming plurals

English words form plurals in many ways. Most nouns simply add -s. The following chart shows other ways of forming plural nouns and some common exceptions to the pattern.

GENERAL RULES FOR FORMING PLURALS		
If a noun ends in	**Rule**	**Example**
ch, s, sh, x, z	add -es	lynx, lynxes
a consonant + *y*	change *y* to *i* and add -es	calamity, calamities
o or a vowel + *y*	add -s	barrio, barrios; array, arrays
a consonant + *o* common exceptions	generally add -es but sometimes add only -s	tomato, tomatoes silo, silos; halo, halos
f or *ff* common exceptions	add -s change *f* to *v* and add -es	chef, chefs; cuff, cuffs leaf, leaves; loaf, loaves
lf	change *f* to *v* and add -es	calf, calves
fe	change *f* to *v* and add -s	wife, wives

A few plurals are exceptions to the rules in the previous chart, but they are easy to remember. The following chart lists these plurals and some examples.

SPECIAL RULES FOR FORMING PLURALS	
Rule	**Example**
To form the plural of proper names and one-word compound nouns, follow the general rules for plurals.	Shabazz, Shabazzes Friedman, Friedmans overleaf, overleaves
To form the plural of hyphenated compound nouns or compound nouns of more than one word, make the most important word plural.	mother-in-law, mothers-in-law chief of staff, chiefs of staff solicitor general, solicitors general
Some nouns have unusual plural forms.	foot, feet goose, geese louse, lice
Some nouns have the same singular and plural forms.	moose deer series

Commonly Misspelled Words

When you exchange written communication with someone, spelling matters. To have your business communications taken seriously, you have to present your ideas professionally, which means logically, clearly, and conventionally. If words are misspelled in your writing, readers may fear that there are also other, even more important, mistakes in it.

Whenever you prepare a written communication, check all spellings of which you are not certain. You might also want to keep handy a list of vocabulary words often used in your business that you have trouble remembering how to spell. Some of the words on this list might appear there.

absence	brought	dilemma	height	occurrence	requirement
abundant	budget	disappoint	illegal	offered	resistance
accessible	bulletin	efficient	immediately	omission	responsibility
accidentally	business	either	implement	opinion	restaurant
accommodate	calendar	eligible	importance	original	resume
achievement	campaign	embarrass	initial	paid	résumé
acknowledgment	canceled	emphasize	irrelevant	pamphlet	schedule
acquaintance	cannot	employee	itinerary	parallel	separate
acquisition	cashier	environment	judgment	particularly	sergeant
administrative	catalog	equipment	knowledge	permanent	similar
advantageous	ceiling	equipped	laboratory	persistent	sincerely
advertise	column	especially	leisure	persuade	strength
advisable	commission	essential	liability	pertinent	subpoena
aggressive	committee	exaggerate	library	physician	succeed
analysis	competitive	excellent	license	possession	successive
analyze	conceive	executive	lieutenant	precede	sufficient
apologize	confidential	existence	likelihood	precedent	superintendent
applicable	conscientious	extraordinary	maintenance	preferred	supersede
appropriate	conscious	facsimile (fax)	manageable	preliminary	supervisor
approximate	continuous	familiar	material	privilege	survey
argument	convenience	feasible	mileage	procedure	technique
assessment	coordinator	financial	miscellaneous	proceed	technology
assistance	correspondence	fiscal	mortgage	professor	tenant
attendance	courteous	foreign	necessary	programmed	thorough
attorney	deceive	forfeit	neighbor	quantity	through
average	decision	forty	neither	questionnaire	transferred
bankruptcy	defendant	fourth	nineteen	receipt	truly
beginner	defense	freight	ninety	receiving	usable
believe	definite	government	ninth	recipient	vendor
beneficiary	dependent	grammar	noticeable	recognize	volume
benefited	describe	grateful	objective	recommend	yield
bought	desirable	guarantee	occasion	reference	
boundary	development	handicapped	occasionally	relevant	
brochure	difference	harass	occur	representative	

Guide to Nonsexist Language

When you are writing about people and their professions in general, you know that the people may be either male or female. Traditionally, many professions had nouns for both males and females, such as *poet* and *poetess*. *Poetess* is no longer used, and *poet* can refer to both males and females. For other gender-neutral terms, refer to the following list.

Do Use	Don't Use
actor	actress
Briton	Englishman, Englishwoman
businessperson, businesspeople	businessman, businesswoman
chairperson, chair, moderator	chairman, chairwoman
a member of the clergy	clergyman, clergywoman
crafter, craftspeople	craftsmen
crewed space flight	manned space flight
fire fighter	fireman
fisher	fisherman
flight attendant	steward, stewardess
Framers, Founders	Founding Fathers
handmade, synthetic, manufactured	manmade
homemaker	housewife
humanity, human beings, people	mankind
it, its (in reference to ships, countries)	she, her, hers, he, his
land of origin, homeland	mother country, fatherland
letter carrier, mail carrier	mailman
police officer	policeman
representative	congressman, congresswoman
server	waiter, waitress
supervisor	foreman
watch, guard	watchman
worker	workman
workforce	manpower

Traditionally, masculine pronouns (*he, him, his*) were used to refer to mixed groups of people. It was understood that females were included. That is, a sentence such as *A surgeon must watch his patient's pulse* was understood to apply to both male and female surgeons. Now everyone is encouraged to use gender-neutral wording. Some possibilities for the sample sentence are *A surgeon must watch the patient's pulse*, *Surgeons must watch their patients' pulses*, and *A surgeon must watch his or her patient's pulse*.

Guide to Business Communication

Performance Appraisal Form

Annual Appraisal for Hourly Employees

Date _____

Employee _____   Job Assignment _____

Supervisor _____   Department _____

Date Hired _____   Previous Appraisal Date _____

PERFORMANCE AREAS	Outstanding	Above Average	Average	Below Average	Unsatisfactory	Not Applicable
JOB KNOWLEDGE						
Comment:						
QUALITY OF WORK Ability to effectively use time and materials Ability to meet deadlines/production schedules						
Comment:						
SAFETY Result of work under safe/unsafe practices						
Comment:						
ATTENDANCE ____ Days not at work since previous appraisal: Personal: ____ Illness: ____ ____ Days late to work since previous appraisal						
Comment:						
PERSONAL QUALITIES						
INITIATIVE/LEADERSHIP Takes on new tools, skills, or projects						
Comment:						
FLEXIBILITY Adjusts to new situations						
Comment:						
COOPERATION Works well with assigned teams and supervisors						
Comment:						
DEPENDABILITY Completes the job reliably						
Comment:						

EMPLOYEE'S PRESENT JOB DESCRIPTION (Attach current job description and note any changes in job assignments here.)

_____
_____
_____

EMPLOYEE'S STRENGTHS (What should the employee be commended for?)
1. _____
2. _____
3. _____

AREAS TO IMPROVE (What should the employee improve?)
1. _____
2. _____
3. _____

NOTE: What has been accomplished toward areas to improve set by the previous appraisal? If the employee has not taken any action, indicate why.

_____
_____
_____

SUMMARY RATING:
_____ Performance always exceeds job requirements.
_____ Performance is above average in meeting job requirements.
_____ Performance consistently meets job requirements.
_____ Performance does not always meet job requirements.
_____ Performance frequently does not meet job requirements.

SUMMARY COMMENTS ON RATING:

_____
_____
_____

EMPLOYEE'S COMMENTS:

_____
_____
_____

_____   _____
Employee's signature/date   Supervisor's signature/date

COMMENTS by next level of supervision:

_____
_____

_____
Manager's signature/date

Writing a Business Letter

You will often write business letters to people you don't know. A business letter is a formal communication tool that you can adapt for many specific purposes. Your writing makes a first impression for you. A neat, brief, well-organized letter will encourage a prompt and positive response.

Here is an example of an application letter typed in the block style. Notice that the writer follows the tips suggested in the chart on the next page.

BLOCK STYLE

The letter is addressed to a specific person.

The writer names the job she wants.

She lists her qualifications.

She tells why she would be a good person to hire.

She asks for an application form.

23 Sagebrush Avenue
Las Cruces, New Mexico 88005
January 10, 2002

Ms. Sarah Grimes, Director
Camp Piney Woods
2630 Nature Trail Road
Piney Woods, Maine 04737

Dear Ms. Grimes:

I would like to apply for a job as a junior counselor at Camp Piney Woods for the coming summer.

I will be sixteen in May and have completed my lifeguard training. In addition, I have worked with children eight to ten years old for the past two summers in the Parks and Recreation Department here in Las Cruces. My duties included conducting nature hikes and teaching craft classes.

Because I am a responsible and enthusiastic person who loves children and the outdoor life, I believe I would be an asset to Camp Piney Woods. I will be happy to send you references of people who know me and my interests and abilities.

Please send me an application form and let me know if there is any other information you need from me.

Yours truly,

Rosalia Diaz

Rosalia Diaz

Types of Business Letters

A business letter is a formal letter written either to communicate information or to request action. Business letters provide a direct and effective means of communicating on a wide variety of topics. Knowing how to write a good business letter is a skill you'll find useful throughout your life.

Use the business letter format whenever you want to inquire, make a request, order a product, complain, express your views on a subject, or apply for a job, a scholarship, or a special academic or recreational program.

TYPES OF BUSINESS LETTERS

Request Letter	Complaint Letter	Opinion Letter	Application Letter
• Be brief. • State your request clearly. • Include all necessary information. • Make your request specific and reasonable. • Include your phone number or a self-addressed, stamped envelope.	• Identify the product or service clearly. • Describe the problem accurately. • Request a specific solution. • Be polite. • Keep a copy of your letter until your complaint has been resolved.	• Identify and summarize the issue. • State your opinion and support it with reasons, facts, and examples. • Summarize your main points and offer a solution, if possible.	• Write to a specific person. • Describe the job or program for which you're applying. • List your qualifications. • Tell why you're the best person for the position or award. • Request an application form or an interview.

When you write a business letter, keep your specific goal or purpose clearly in mind. Business letters are not necessarily about business, but they do mean business, so don't let them wander off the subject. Be brief. Include only what is essential. Confine your letter to a single page. The people you are writing are busy. The shorter and more attractive your letter looks, the more likely it is that someone will read it.

Because the tone of a business letter should be formal, don't use slang or worn-out expressions. Don't be wordy. "Thank you" is better than "I wish to express my gratitude." Remember to be courteous, regardless of your purpose.

Most business letters require some kind of persuasive writing. When you write a letter of inquiry, you want to persuade someone to fill your request or send you a product. When you write a letter of complaint, you want to persuade someone to do something to correct a problem. In an opinion letter, you want to persuade someone to agree with you or to take action. In a letter of application, your goal is to persuade someone to hire you or to accept your qualifications for a particular program or award.

Editing Tip

Always edit business letters carefully. Errors in spelling, grammar, or typing will seriously reduce the effectiveness of your message.

Style

Business letters are usually written in one of two forms: the block style or the modified block style.

Block Style

In the block style, all lines begin at the left margin. Paragraphs are not indented. The letter on page 637 is typed in the block style.

Modified Block Style

In the modified block style, the heading, the closing, your signature, and your typed name begin at the center of the paper. The paragraphs may be indented—five spaces on a typewriter or half an inch on a computer—or not indented. The letter below is in the modified block style with paragraphs indented.

> **Presenting Tip**
>
> If you use a word processor to prepare your letter, keep it simple by using just one style of type. Too many different type styles will make your letter look casual and informal. Choose a type that looks serious.

MODIFIED BLOCK STYLE

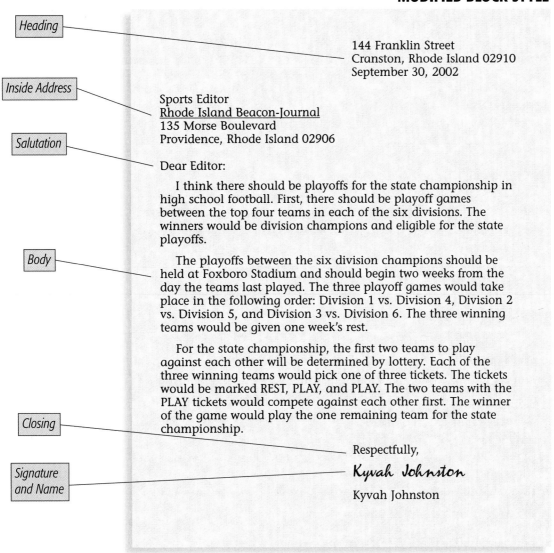

Heading

144 Franklin Street
Cranston, Rhode Island 02910
September 30, 2002

Inside Address

Sports Editor
Rhode Island Beacon-Journal
135 Morse Boulevard
Providence, Rhode Island 02906

Salutation

Dear Editor:

Body

I think there should be playoffs for the state championship in high school football. First, there should be playoff games between the top four teams in each of the six divisions. The winners would be division champions and eligible for the state playoffs.

The playoffs between the six division champions should be held at Foxboro Stadium and should begin two weeks from the day the teams last played. The three playoff games would take place in the following order: Division 1 vs. Division 4, Division 2 vs. Division 5, and Division 3 vs. Division 6. The three winning teams would be given one week's rest.

For the state championship, the first two teams to play against each other will be determined by lottery. Each of the three winning teams would pick one of three tickets. The tickets would be marked REST, PLAY, and PLAY. The two teams with the PLAY tickets would compete against each other first. The winner of the game would play the one remaining team for the state championship.

Closing

Respectfully,

Signature and Name

Kyvah Johnston

Kyvah Johnston

The Parts of a Business Letter

A business letter has six parts.

The Heading

There are three lines in the heading:
- your street address
- your city, state, and ZIP code
- the date

The Inside Address

The inside address has three or more lines:
- the name of the person to whom you're writing (with or without a courtesy title such as *Ms.*, *Mr.*, or *Dr.*)
- the title of the person to whom you're writing (A short title may be placed on the same line with the person's name. A long title requires a separate line.)
- the name of the business or organization
- the street address of the business or organization
- the city, state, and ZIP code

The Salutation, or Greeting

When you know the name of the person to whom you're writing, the salutation should include a courtesy title: *Dear Senator Gonzales* or *Dear Ms. Uchida.* If you don't know the name of the person, you can begin with *Dear* and the person's title: *Dear Editor* or *Dear Manager.* The salutation of a business letter is followed by a colon.

The Body

The body contains the message you want to communicate.

The Closing

The closing is a final word or phrase, such as *Respectfully* or *Yours truly.* The closing is followed by a comma.

Name and Signature

Type your name four lines below the closing. Then, sign your name in the space between the closing and your typed name.

Neatness Counts

Your letter is more likely to get a serious reading if you follow closely the formal rules for business letters.
- Type your letter or use a computer.
- Use unlined white 8 1/2" by 11" paper.
- Leave a two-inch margin at the top and at least a one-inch margin at the left, right, and bottom.
- Single-space the heading. Allow four to six blank lines between the heading and the inside address, depending on the length of your letter.
- Single-space the remaining parts of the letter, leaving an extra line between the parts and between the paragraphs in the body.

Presenting Tip

If your letter is very short, you can increase the left and right margins and center the letter vertically on the page. Your word-processing software may have a feature that will automatically center the letter for you.

Address Abbreviations

United States (U.S.)

In most cases, state names and street addresses should be spelled out. The postal abbreviations in the following lists should be used with ZIP codes in addressing envelopes. They may also be used with ZIP codes for return addresses and inside addresses in business letters. The traditional state abbreviations are seldom used nowadays, but occasionally it's helpful to know them.

State	Traditional	Postal
Alabama	Ala.	AL
Alaska	(none)	AK
Arizona	Ariz.	AZ
Arkansas	Ark.	AR
California	Calif.	CA
Colorado	Colo.	CO
Connecticut	Conn.	CT
Delaware	Del.	DE
District of Columbia	D.C.	DC
Florida	Fla.	FL
Georgia	Ga.	GA
Hawaii	(none)	HI
Idaho	(none)	ID
Illinois	Ill.	IL
Indiana	Ind.	IN
Iowa	(none)	IA
Kansas	Kans.	KS
Kentucky	Ky.	KY
Louisiana	La.	LA
Maine	(none)	ME
Maryland	Md.	MD
Massachusetts	Mass.	MA
Michigan	Mich.	MI
Minnesota	Minn.	MN
Mississippi	Miss.	MS
Missouri	Mo.	MO
Montana	Mont.	MT
Nebraska	Nebr.	NE
Nevada	Nev.	NV
New Hampshire	N.H.	NH
New Jersey	N.J.	NJ
New Mexico	N. Mex.	NM
New York	N.Y.	NY
North Carolina	N.C.	NC
North Dakota	N. Dak.	ND
Ohio	(none)	OH
Oklahoma	Okla.	OK
Oregon	Oreg.	OR
Pennsylvania	Pa.	PA
Rhode Island	R.I.	RI
South Carolina	S.C.	SC
South Dakota	S. Dak.	SD
Tennessee	Tenn.	TN
Texas	Tex.	TX
Utah	(none)	UT
Vermont	Vt.	VT
Virginia	Va.	VA
Washington	Wash.	WA
West Virginia	W. Va.	WV
Wisconsin	Wis.	WI
Wyoming	Wyo.	WY

Postal Address Abbreviations

The following address abbreviations are recommended by the U.S. Postal Service for use on envelopes to speed mailing. In most other writing, these words should be spelled out.

Alley	ALY	Estates	EST	North	N	Street	ST
Annex	ANX	Expressway	EXPY	Parkway	PKY	Terrace	TER
Avenue	AVE	Heights	HTS	Place	PL	Trace	TRCE
Boulevard	BLVD	Highway	HWY	Plaza	PLZ	Trail	TRL
Center	CTR	Island	IS	River	RIV	Turnpike	TPKE
Circle	CIR	Lake	LK	Road	RD	Viaduct	VIA
Court	CT	Lane	LN	South	S	Village	VLG
Drive	DR	Lodge	LDG	Square	SQ	West	W
East	E	Mount	MT	Station	STA		

Forms of Address

This chart shows the proper forms of address for writing letters to public officials, members of the armed services, and professional people. (To communicate with public officials by e-mail, see the feature on pages 645–646.) Shown here are the envelope's address, which is also the inside address, and an appropriate salutation. Where more than one salutation is supplied, the most formal is first.

The Person	The Address	The Salutation(s)
Public Officials		
President of the United States	The President The White House Washington, DC 20500	Mr./Madam President Dear Mr./Madam President

Vice President of the United States	The Vice President
	United States Senate
	Washington, DC 20510
	  or
	The Honorable *(full name)*
	Vice President of the United States
	Washington, DC 20501
		Sir/Madam
		Dear Mr./Madam Vice
		    President

Chief Justice of the United States	The Chief Justice of the United States Washington, DC 20543 *or* The Chief Justice The Supreme Court Washington, DC 20543	Sir/Madam Dear Mr./Madam Chief Justice
Cabinet Member	The Honorable *(full name)* Secretary *(department name)* Washington, DC *(ZIP code)* *or* The Secretary of *(department)* Washington, DC *(ZIP code)*	Sir/Madam Dear Mr./Madam Secretary
United States Senator	The Honorable *(full name)* United States Senator Washington, DC 20510 *or* The Honorable *(full name)* *(local address and ZIP code)*	Sir/Madam Dear Senator *(last name)*

The Person	The Address	The Salutation(s)

United States Representative	The Honorable *(full name)*
	House of Representatives
	Washington, DC 20515
	   or
	The Honorable *(full name)*
	Representative in Congress
	(local address and ZIP code)
		Sir/Madam
		Dear Mr./Ms./Mrs./Miss
		   (last name)

Governor	The Honorable *(full name)* Governor of *(name of state)* *(State Capital, State ZIP code)*	Sir/Madam Dear Governor *(last name)*
State Senator	The Honorable *(full name)* The *(name of state)* Senate *(State Capital, State ZIP code)*	Sir/Madam Dear Senator *(last name)*

State Representative or Assembly Member	The Honorable *(full name)*
	House of Representatives
	   or
	The *(name of state)* State Assembly
	(State Capital, State ZIP code)
		Sir/Madam
		Dear Mr./Ms./Mrs./Miss
		   (last name)

Mayor	The Honorable *(full name)* Mayor of *(city)* *(City, State ZIP code)* *or* The Mayor of the City of *(city)* *(City, State ZIP code)*	Sir/Madam Dear Mr./Madam Mayor Dear Mayor *(last name)*
Members of the Armed Services		
Rank	*(full rank)* *(full name)* U.S. Coast Guard, U.S. Air Force, U.S. Army, U.S. Marine Corps, or U.S. Navy *(local address)*	Dear *(full rank)* *(full name)*
Professional People		
President of a College or University	*(full name, followed by comma and abbreviation for highest degree earned)* President, *(name of college)* *(address)* *or* Dr. *(full name)* President, *(name of college)* *(address)*	Dear President *(last name)* Dear Dr. *(last name)*

The Person	The Address	The Salutation(s)
Dean of a College or University	*(full name, followed by comma and abbreviation for highest degree earned)* Dean, *(name of college)* *(address)* *or* Dr. *(full name)* Dean, *(name of college)* *(address)*	Dear Dean *(last name)* Dear Dr. *(last name)*

Professor	Professor *(full name)*
	Department of *(subject)*
	(name of college)
	(address)
	   or
	(full name, followed by comma and abbreviation for highest degree earned)
	Department of *(subject)*
	(name of college)
	(address)
	   or
	Dr. *(full name)*
	Professor of *(subject)*
	(name of college)
	(address)
		Dear Professor *(last name)*
		Dear Dr. *(last name)*

Member of Board of Education	Mr./Ms./Mrs./Miss *(full name)* Member, *(name of school district)* Board of Education *(address)*	Dear Mr./Ms./Mrs./Miss/Dr.
Principal	Mr./Ms./Mrs./Miss/Dr. *(full name)* Principal, *(name of school)* *(address of school)*	Dear Mr./Ms./Mrs./Miss/Dr.
Teacher	Mr./Ms./Mrs./Miss/Dr. *(full name)* *(name of school)* *(address of school)*	Dear Mr./Ms./Mrs./Miss/Dr.

Attorney	Mr./Ms./Mrs./Miss *(full name)*,
	Attorney at Law
	   or
	(full name), Esq.
	(address)
		Dear Mr./Ms./Mrs./Miss
		   (last name)

Dentist	*(full name)*, D.D.S. *(address)*	Dear Dr. *(last name)*
Physician	*(full name)*, M.D./D.O. *(address)*	Dear Dr. *(last name)*
Veterinarian	*(full name)*, D.V.M. *(address)*	Dear Dr. *(last name)*

Sending E-Mail to Public Officials

E-mail provides a quick and easy way for you to get in touch with public officials, such as your city mayor, state governor, United States senator or representative, or the president. You can also contact a specific government task force or committee. You might use e-mail to ask for information or to express your opinions on an issue.

You can find the names and e-mail addresses of government officials, departments, and committees at a number of Web sites. For example, you might try sites such as www.senate.gov, www.vote-smart.org, or www.info.gov. Alternatively, do a search using the name of your state, followed by *AND government*. A menu of choices will lead you to the names and e-mail addresses you seek. After you click on the e-mail address of an official, some sites will take you directly to your own e-mail screen and enter the address of that official in the *To* field.

Then, it's time to compose your message. Keep in mind that some elected officials read e-mail from only the people they represent. Often, officials do not read e-mail themselves. Instead, a staff member will read your message and, perhaps, send you a form e-mail response.

The following tips will help ensure that your request or message is taken seriously. (Note that many of these tips apply to all e-mail.)

- Make sure that your request is reasonable and that you are sending it to the appropriate person.

- Be aware that your e-mail address may influence whether your message is given a careful reading. Compare dude@net.com with tthompson@net.com.

- In the subject field, clearly and briefly identify the main idea of your message.

Many e-mail messages omit the salutation or greeting because the intended reader's name is already listed in the heading. However, it would be a sign of respect to use the traditional forms of address for government officials. You can find them listed on pages 642–644 in this Guide to Business Communication.

- Begin your message by briefly identifying yourself. If appropriate, point out that you live in the area that the reader represents.

- State your concern or request at the beginning of your message, where it is most likely to be read. If you do not grab the reader's attention immediately, your e-mail might be deleted without being read completely. After explaining why you are writing, go into the reasons for your concern or your request.

- If you are asking for information that cannot be e-mailed to you, include your street address or a fax number or both.

- You cannot sign your message, but do type your name at the end of it, especially if your name is not clear from your e-mail address.

- Be respectful, even if you feel that the official is misguided or misinformed about an issue.

- Don't ever threaten a government official, even as a joke. You can say you will not vote for this person again, but do not say you would like to cause injury or harm to him or her. Depending on your reader, you could end up being investigated.

- Do not type your whole message in capital letters. This looks like shouting to most readers. It may make them feel defensive or annoyed.

- Do not write when you are angry. You will be more likely to insult your reader and less likely to get the response you want.

- Avoid emoticons, such as these: ;-) :-(. You can use these little symbols in informal e-mails to your friends but not in messages to government officials.

- Break your message into paragraphs, just as you would in a letter. Discuss only one main idea in each paragraph.

- Find and correct misspellings, grammatical errors, and typographical errors. If you do not, your message may not be read at all. This might not seem fair, but it is a serious issue.

- Proofread your message to make sure the ideas flow smoothly and are expressed clearly.

Let public officials know what you are thinking with well-thought-out and carefully organized e-mail messages.

Personal Style Profile

INSTRUCTIONS: Make a copy of this page and the next page. For each of the following groups of three adjectives, write **3** by the term that **best** describes you, **1** by the term that **least** describes you, and **2** by the remaining term.

1. a. _____ Adventurous
    b. _____ Polished
    c. _____ Stable

2. a. _____ Receptive
    b. _____ Determined
    c. _____ Enthusiastic

3. a. _____ Steady
    b. _____ Exacting
    c. _____ Original

4. a. _____ Poised
    b. _____ Patient
    c. _____ Orderly

5. a. _____ Forceful
    b. _____ Persuasive
    c. _____ Settled

6. a. _____ Cautious
    b. _____ Bold
    c. _____ Outgoing

7. a. _____ Persistent
    b. _____ Cooperative
    c. _____ Brave

8. a. _____ Attractive
    b. _____ Controlled
    c. _____ Correct

9. a. _____ Competitive
    b. _____ Diplomatic
    c. _____ Accommodating

10. a. _____ Careful
    b. _____ Decisive
    c. _____ Popular

11. a. _____ Dependable
    b. _____ Accurate
    c. _____ Inventive

12. a. _____ Convincing
    b. _____ Consistent
    c. _____ Open-minded

13. a. _____ Positive
    b. _____ Cordial
    c. _____ Even-tempered

14. a. _____ Conservative
    b. _____ Eager
    c. _____ Entertaining

15. a. _____ Amiable
    b. _____ Systematic
    c. _____ Self-reliant

16. a. _____ Sociable
    b. _____ Unhurried
    c. _____ Precise

Scoring Sheet

INSTRUCTIONS: Write your scores in the spaces below. Then, add the scores in each column and enter the total for each column in the space provided.

DOMINANCE	INTERACTION	STABILITY	CONTROL
1a _____	1b _____	1c _____	2a _____
2b _____	2c _____	3a _____	3b _____
3c _____	4a _____	4b _____	4c _____
5a _____	5b _____	5c _____	6a _____
6b _____	6c _____	7a _____	7b _____
7c _____	8a _____	8b _____	8c _____
9a _____	9b _____	9c _____	10a _____
10b _____	10c _____	11a _____	11b _____
11c _____	12a _____	12b _____	12c _____
13a _____	13b _____	13c _____	14a _____
14b _____	14c _____	15a _____	15b _____
15c _____	16a _____	16b _____	16c _____

Total _____   *Total* _____   *Total* _____   *Total* _____

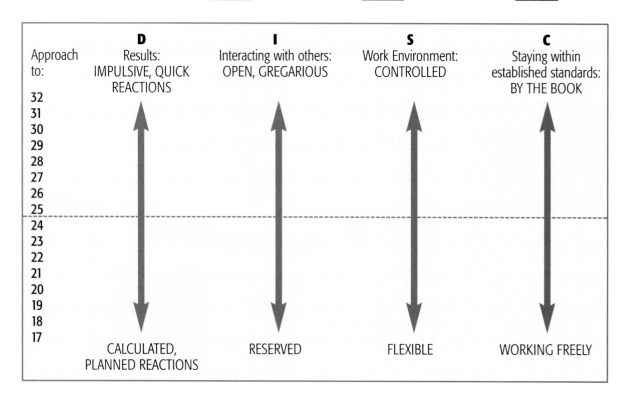

	D	**I**	**S**	**C**
Approach to:	Results: IMPULSIVE, QUICK REACTIONS	Interacting with others: OPEN, GREGARIOUS	Work Environment: CONTROLLED	Staying within established standards: BY THE BOOK

32
31
30
29
28
27
26
25
- - - - - - - - - - - -
24
23
22
21
20
19
18
17

| CALCULATED, PLANNED REACTIONS | RESERVED | FLEXIBLE | WORKING FREELY |

Informational Presentation

Mending the Body by Lending an Ear
THE HEALING POWER OF LISTENING; Address by CAROL
KOEHLER, Ph.D., *Assistant Professor of Communication and Medicine;*
Delivered to the International Listening Association Business Conference,
at the Ritz-Carlton Hotel, Kansas City, Missouri, March 19, 1998

I would like to start this morning by telling you two different stories. Each story has the same two characters and happens in the same location. Both stories occur within a twenty-four hour period.

Over the Christmas holidays, my husband and I were invited to a formal black-tie wedding. This was to be an elegant event, so we put on our best evening clothes. Adding to that, I wore my mother's diamond jewelry and this fabulous mink coat that I inherited. Just before we left the house, I telephoned my 86-year-old mother-in-law for her daily check-up. When she answered, her voice sounded a little strange, so my husband and I decided to stop at her apartment to make sure she was all right before we went to the wedding.

When we arrived, she seemed slightly disoriented (she was 86 years old but wonderfully healthy, sharp-witted, and self-sufficient). We called her physician to ask his advice, and he said to bring her to the local Emergency Room and have her checked out. We did that. This was a Saturday night, so the Emergency Room was pretty active. When we arrived, I in my mink and my husband in his tux, we looked noticeably different from the general population in the waiting room. While my husband filled out forms, the doctors took my mother-in-law into a makeshift curtained room. When I noticed that the staff had removed both her glasses and her hearing aid, I realized she would experience some anxiety, so at that point I decided to stay with her to keep her from being frightened. As I went into the room, a young doctor said, "Ma'am, you can't go in there." Without missing a beat, I

said, "Don't be ridiculous." With that, I went and found a chair in the waiting room, brought it into the examination room, and sat down. I remember thinking the staff looked a little bewildered, but no one challenged me at any time. When my mother-in-law's hands felt a little cool, I asked for a heated blanket, and one was brought immediately. So it went for the entire evening. We missed the wedding but finally got my mother-in-law in a permanent room about 2 a.m.

The next morning I went to the hospital about 10 o'clock in the morning, dressed in tennis shoes, a sweat suit, and no makeup. As I arrived at my mother-in-law's room, an unfamiliar doctor was just entering. I introduced myself and asked him to speak up so my mother-in-law would be aware of why he was there and what he was doing. I told him that she tends to be frightened by the unexpected, and without her glasses or hearing aid, she was already frightened enough. This thirty-something male doctor proceeded to examine my mother-in-law without raising his voice so that she could hear and without acknowledging me or my request in any way. Actually, he never really looked at either one of us.

In both these scenarios, I was listened to, not by ears alone, but by eyes, by gender, by age judgments, and by social status assessments. That started me thinking. . . .

Why did a recent article in the *Journal of the American Medical Association* indicate high dissatisfaction in traditional doctor-patient appointments? Why is it the *Wall Street*

Journal claims that perception of physician concern and not physician expertise is the deciding factor in the rising number of malpractice suits? Why did *The New England Journal of Medicine* report that the care and attention quotient is causing "alternative" medical practices to grow by leaps and bounds? Given this litany of events, what does it really mean to listen? And why, in the name of science, don't we produce better listeners in the medical profession?

The reasons are so obvious that they are sometimes overlooked. First, listening is mistakenly equated with hearing, and since most of us can hear, no academic priority is given to this subject in either college or med school. (This, by the way, flies in the face of those who measure daily time usage. Time experts say we spend 9 percent of our day writing, 16 percent reading, 30 percent speaking and 45 percent listening—just the opposite of our academic pursuits.) Second, we perceive power in speech. We put a value on those who have the gift of gab. How often have you heard the compliment, "He/she can talk to anyone?" Additionally, we equate speaking with controlling both the conversation and the situation. The third and last reason we don't listen is that we are in an era of information overload. We are bombarded with the relevant and the irrelevant, and it is easy to confuse them. Often, it's all just so much noise.

How can we address this depressing situation? Dan Callahan, a physician and teacher, argues that primacy in health care needs to be given to the notion of care over cure. Caring as well as curing humanizes our doctor-patient relationships.

Let's talk about what that might mean for health care. What comes to mind when someone is caring? (The audience responded with the words "warm," "giving," "interested," "genuine," and "sincere"). Now, what comes to mind when you think of the opposite of care? (The audience volunteered "cold," "uninterested," "egotistical," "busy," "distracted," and "selfish").

What might a caring doctor be like? If we take the word **CARE** and break it down, we find the qualities that are reflective of a therapeutic communicator—in other words, someone who listens not with ears alone.

C stands for concentrate. Physicians should hear with their eyes and ears. They should avoid the verbal and visual barriers that prevent real listening. It may be as simple as eye contact. (Some young doctors have told me they have a difficult time with looking people in the eye, and my advice is, "When you are uncomfortable, focus on the patient's mouth, and as the comfort level increases, move to the eyes.") In the placement of office furniture, try to keep the desk from being a barrier between you and the patient. Offer an alternative chair for consultations—one to the side of your desk and one in front of the desk. Let the patients have some control and power to decide their own comfort level.

A stands for acknowledge. Show them that you are listening by using facial expressions, giving vocal prompts, and listening between the lines for intent as well as content. Listen for their vocal intonation when responding to things like prescribed medication. If you hear some hesitation in their voice, say to them, "I hear you agreeing, but I'm getting the sound of some reservation in your voice. Can you tell me why?" And then acknowledge their response. Trust them and they will trust you.

R stands for response. Clarify issues by asking, "I'm not sure what you mean." Encourage continuing statements by saying "And then what?" or "Tell me more." The recurrent headache may mask other problems. Provide periodic recaps to focus information. Learn to take cryptic notes, and then return your attention to the patient. (Note taking is sometimes used as an avoidance tactic, and patients sense this.) Use body language by leaning toward the patient. Effective listening requires attention, patience, and the ability to resist the urge to control the conversation.

E stands for exercise emotional control. This means if your "hot buttons" are pushed by people who whine, and in walks someone who does that very thing, you are likely to fake interest in that patient. With your mind elsewhere, you will never really "hear" that person. Emotional blocks are based on previous experiences. They are sometimes activated by words, by tone of voice, by style of clothes or hair, or by ethnicity. It is not possible for us to be free of those emotional reactions, but the first step in controlling them is to recognize when you are losing control. One of the most useful techniques to combat emotional responses is to take a long deep breath when confronted with the urge to interrupt. Deep breathing redirects your response and, as a bonus, it is impossible to talk when you are deep breathing. Who of us would not choose the attentive, caring physician?

As it nears time for me to take that deep breath, I would just like to reiterate that listening is a learned skill, and learning to listen with CARE has valuable benefits for health care professionals and patients. As a wise man named J. Isham once said, "Listening is an attitude of the heart, a genuine desire to be with another, which both attracts and heals."

Thank you very much.

Persuasive Presentation

Managing the Privacy Revolution:
E-COMMERCE IS A GLOBAL ISSUE; Address by HAROLD McGRAW III, *President and Chief Executive Officer, The McGraw-Hill Companies; Delivered to the Privacy and American Business Conference, Arlington, Virginia, December 1, 1998*

I want to thank Privacy and American Business for hosting this conference—and for bringing together in one room so many key members of the business community, representatives of the U.S. Government, the European Union, and the government of Taiwan, as well as privacy advocates from academia and the think tanks—all of whom understand the challenges that accompany the many advantages of Electronic Commerce.

The international representation we see here today underscores the fact that E-Commerce is a global issue—one that transcends borders and barriers in a way few other issues have—and therefore presents challenges in terms of legislation and regulation that are qualitatively different than any we have faced in the past.

Without a doubt, E-Commerce is the kind of blink-of-an-electron event that has the potential to transform our economy, here at home and around the world—to the point that phrases like "here at home" and "around the world" are rendered electronically meaningless in terms of our old understanding of commerce, competition, and markets.

We're already seeing the impact of E-Commerce in the valuation of so-called "Internet stocks."

Case in point: EarthWeb, Inc., a provider of Internet-based IT services, went public last month. In its first week of trading, EarthWeb's shares soared from an offering price of $14 to more than $85 per share—a 600-percent increase in value!

And that's in spite of the fact that EarthWeb has yet to earn its first dollar in profit. Clearly, E-Commerce is a means of providing access to new markets on an unprecedented scale, a tool to reduce costs and to introduce efficiencies into the distribution process.

But in addition to that commercial promise, there's the promise of E-Commerce in expanding human potential: By erasing borders and making old barriers obsolete, E-Commerce provides people with a powerful tool in the ongoing effort to reach their full potential.

For all those reasons, understanding, utilizing, and embracing the electronic frontier may be the central issue challenging business today.

We at The McGraw-Hill Companies recognized early on that our future growth would be tied in significant ways to the growth of E-Commerce. Like other companies in this room, we have confidence in our products, and we naturally want to extend our reach to markets and consumers worldwide who—thanks to the marriage of modem, mouse, and Internet—now have even easier access to the products and services we offer.

All of that makes E-Commerce sound as if it's all "upside"—an easy way for companies to augment their revenues by connecting with consumers in markets they haven't been able to reach before.

But the fact is, E-Commerce remains a great unknown. It's possible to be website-rich and cash-poor—just as it's possible for undisciplined, unfocused investment in E-Commerce to become a black hole. Some of the "electronic unknowns" are tied to privacy issues, while others are entirely unrelated to it. At this point, neither customers nor companies fully understand what we're going to do with this technology—where the Internet will ultimately take us. That said, it's equally true we can't sit on the sidelines until things sort themselves out. Being ready to compete in the online world isn't optional—it is imperative.

Estimates about the potential for growth in E-Commerce are as easy to collect as they are hard to keep current. Here are a few of my own favorite "Leading Electronic Indicators":

In 1994, about 3 million people worldwide were connected to the Internet.
By 1996, the number had grown to 28 million.
By the end of 1998, Internet users will top 82 million.
In 1993—just 5 years ago—26,000 domain names were registered.
By the end of 1997, that number was 1.5 million.

Right now, the number of new websites is growing by 65,000 per day. At that rate, there will be more than 3,000 new websites between now and the time we're done eating lunch.

As for E-Commerce, total business-to-business sales will reach about $8 billion for 1998.

By 2002, estimates project total business-to-business sales at $327 billion for the U.S. and as much as $1.3 trillion globally.

It's hard for us to conceive of growth that rapid in a meaningful way. So look at it this way: What would be a good month for E-Commerce in 1998 will be a slow day in 2002.

Clearly, this is a medium—a virtual market—that is moving, as they say out in Silicon Valley, "at the speed of mind." But with all the well-deserved hype, it's easy to forget that the E-Commerce explosion is by no means inevitable.

Because there's one thing that can stop E-Commerce dead in its tracks. And any one of us has the power—literally—at our fingertips. All you need to do is sit down at your PC, use your mouse to slide the cursor over to the "Exit" icon—and click.

After all, that's how E-Commerce happens: One person at a time, one decision at a time, one click at a time—to the tune of $8 billion today, and as much as $327 billion in 2002.

As I see it, it's critical that we remember—as impressive as the prospects for E-Commerce are—this market is nothing more than the individual decision to purchase online, multiplied by millions of Internet users.

Consider this question: Why is it that some people will read their newspapers online, go online to do research for everything from the work they do to the vacation they take—but still won't buy something online?

It's a matter of trust.

That's one fact that technology doesn't change: Trust is the most precious asset any business has. It's the bedrock that business is built on—and in this era of new media, especially, trust becomes more critical than ever.

If people come to have trust that the system is secure, that private information remains private—they'll flock to E-Commerce in droves—and the predictions I cited a few minutes ago will be realized. Without trust, they won't. They'll move the cursor to Exit, and click, we're out of the game. That makes privacy policy imperative.

We know from surveys that two out of every three Internet users said that privacy matters so much that they'd leave a website if they were asked to provide private information.

Almost all consumers surveyed in the December 1998 Privacy and American Business/Harris Poll say it's important for them to know what information business are collecting about them.

Internet users understand better than most people that information is power. Information can be packaged and repackaged, assessed and analyzed, and used to individually tailor goods and services to a "market of one."

Now, none of that is nefarious—as long as the information has been obtained with the knowledge of the consumer.

Industry has made real progress in creating an awareness of the need for private-sector privacy policies—and many of the individuals and organizations who deserve the credit are represented this morning right here in this room.

Start with the Clinton Administration: Led by Vice President Gore, with his interest in all things Internet—and assisted by Ira Magaziner and Ambassador David Aaron, the "Virtual Secretaries of E-Commerce," this Administration has shown a real understanding of the private-sector potential to create a privacy protocol that gives consumers confidence.

The same can be said for the Department of Commerce's National Telecommunications and Information Administration and International Trade Administration, the FTC, and other agencies at work on this issue—each of which has given the private sector running room to craft a privacy policy that works for us all.

That's an effort that we at The McGraw-Hill Companies believe in. That's why we started work on our privacy policy in 1996. That's why we co-sponsored the first-ever multi-industry privacy conference back in March, with the American Business Press, the Association of American Publishers, the Information Industry Association, and the Magazine Publishers of America.

It's why we went to Cambridge, England, last July, to take part in the European Privacy Laws and Business Conference—to illustrate our understanding that privacy isn't just a U.S. issue, or an EU issue, but a global issue, just as the Internet is a global network. Privacy is an issue that spans countries and continents and cultures.

My aim today isn't to read a roll call and pass out the accolades, because for all the effort thus far, for all the progress the private sector has made, that would be premature.

Instead, my mission today is to underscore the sense of urgency that we must act. Because the fact of the matter is, our window of opportunity is closing. The chance for us to prove that the private sector can regulate itself is passing. And if the private sector does not act, government surely will.

A few minutes ago, I mentioned numbers like 65,000 per day and $327 billion dollars per year—numbers that float in the stratosphere of cyberspace. But the number that concerns me most today is far more modest by E-Commerce standards. The number is 80: the number of bills regulating privacy that were pending as the 105th Congress came to a close in October. In the 106th Congress, I have no doubt we'll see most if not all of those 80 bills reintroduced—and new bills added.

The message for us in the private sector is clear: The time has come for leadership. If we do not address the privacy issue—if we fail to do an effective job of regulating ourselves in terms of privacy protections—then the U.S. Government will do it for us. Or do it to us, as the case may be. And in a global network, so will the European Union, and any number of nations from Asia to Africa to Australia and Latin America, and everywhere else that the Internet can reach. And if that happens, not only will E-Commerce never be the same . . . E-Commerce may never be.

Now, I've heard that some companies are holding off on adopting a privacy policy because they think that if they don't have a stated policy, government entities that oversee the intersection of commerce and consumer interests won't be able to cite their policy against them. And in the early days of E-Commerce, I suspect it's been tempting to take that route. But I submit to you this morning that this "no-policy" policy's days are numbered.

We see signs that governments are beginning to act already. Case in point: the European Union, with its strict new Data Protection Directive, effective October 25. The clock is ticking. If we do not find a way to effectively regulate ourselves, government, and not just one government, but any number of governments, will do it for us.

And, despite the high level of mistrust among Internet users, the December poll results indicate that 69 percent would still prefer voluntary measures over government intervention.

This is our leadership moment—our time to take decisive action.

That's why I've come prepared today to share with all of you what works for us at The McGraw-Hill Companies.

It's a policy we post on our more than 80 company websites, built on four principles—expressed not in legalese that makes Internet users worry about loopholes, but in plain language people can understand. Together, they're the fruits of our extensive and intensive effort to create a privacy policy that's simple enough to understand and comprehensive enough to work.

The first principle is Notice: Tell prospective customers what information you're collecting—and what you're planning to do with it. When it comes to collecting information, uncertainty is the enemy: If you keep people in the dark about what's happening to their private information, they'll imagine the worst. Building Notice into your privacy policy builds confidence in customers.

The second principle is Choice: Adopt a policy with a procedure by which customers can choose not to have their information shared outside your company. It's a way of saying you recognize the information they've shared with you is—in important ways—still theirs.

The third principle is Security: Give the customers confidence that their information is safe from tampering, safe from theft, and safe from misappropriation and misuse.

The fourth and final principle is Review and Correction: Give customers a way to see what information has been collected from them—and a means to correct any errors in that data.

These four basics make a solid privacy policy—one that's understandable, defensible, and ultimately acceptable to most consumers. At least, that's what we're finding at The McGraw-Hill Companies.

There are Sensitive Data—such as specific financial data, certain medical data, and most information about children—that we believe merit additional protection. Having referred to children's privacy—and an important part of my organization focuses on the children's educational market—we have appointed what we call Personally-Identifiable Information Guardians, to help ensure that prior consent is obtained before data is collected from children under the age of 16, and to oversee the collection and security of children's data across all of our companies.

The fact of the matter is that smart privacy policy is smart business. We all profess to care about maintaining good customer relations—well, there's no better way to let customers know you take their concerns to heart than to respect and protect their privacy.

Certainly that's been our experience. Once people understand what we're doing—or more to the point, what we're not doing—with their personal information, their comfort level goes up. In fact, what we and other companies that have adopted privacy policies are finding is that once you inform the average consumer of your privacy policy, the opt-out rate is less than 5 percent.

But make no mistake: Privacy policy is only as good as the compliance component that gives it bite. To that end, I'm pleased to announce today our Compliance Mechanisms—procedures we've designed to be compatible and consistent with the "safe harbor" standards being negotiated this month by the U.S. Government and European Union.

Our compliance policy comprises five key components:

(One) Oversight: The McGraw-Hill Companies has established a Customer Privacy Steering Committee, comprising senior business and corporate executives, to make certain that privacy policy and privacy concerns are matters that merit the high-level attention they deserve and customers demand.

(Two) Review: Our corporate audit department in conjunction with our outside auditing firm and corporate staff have begun periodic random reviews of privacy policy compliance. Again, any evidence of failure to comply is pushed up to senior management, to ensure that changes are made to bring the business unit in question into compliance.

(Three) Ethics: At The McGraw-Hill Companies, integrity is the cornerstone of everything we do. That's why we have expanded our Code of Business Ethics to include a commitment to comply with our Privacy Policy—and to trigger disciplinary actions in cases where compliance is lacking.

(Four) A privacy point of contact: In each business unit, we have designated a Privacy Official—a person any customer can contact directly, by phone, fax, or e-mail, to raise their privacy concerns and make resolving their concerns our business.

(Five) Reporting: Beginning in 1999, after a full year's experience with our policy, we will post on our website and make available in print to our customers a business privacy report. It will tell customers about our commitment to our policy, our progress in implementing it across our corporation, and any changes in policy that we have made over the year.

We believe that this is an essential component of "self-certification"—letting stakeholders know you are doing in practice what your policy promises you'll do.

In essence, we have integrated our privacy policy and compliance mechanism into our business processes, and we as business leaders need to recognize that assuring internal compliance is critical but not easy. People get promoted, links get broken, accidents can happen. The key to success is having a process in place to quickly fix a problem and right the wrong.

If there's one thread that runs through all of this, it's that we've worked hard to instill a sense at The McGraw-Hill Companies that privacy is one area where we don't see a proprietary interest—although we do see a marketing advantage. And the fact of the matter is that no matter how much we or any other single company does to promote consumer privacy, if the rest of the Internet remains a kind of electronic version of the Old Wild West—where no one is safe and anything goes—we will suffer right along with everyone else.

Trust lost in the system is trust lost for everyone. That's one fundamental fact that technology doesn't change.

Of course, I don't pretend for a moment that our privacy policy constitutes the last word on this issue. There are ambitious, ongoing efforts in industry right now—efforts like:

the Direct Marketing Association's Privacy Promise,
the Information Industry Association's Fair Information Practices Principles,
and the work of the Online Privacy Alliance—
all efforts that we support and encourage.

These are great examples of the kind of benefits that flexibility brings when the private sector is given the freedom to take the initiative and innovate:

to adapt to changing circumstances,
to take advantage of next-generation technologies,
and to raise the bar, instead of settling for a "Floor's-the-Limit" approach.

There will be improvements in the future that will add to the level of protection afforded consumers—improvements we not only welcome but may well want to adopt, whether those changes are driven by the new EU Directive or by U.S. law or by new technology or changing consumer expectations.

Internet privacy is a "work in progress." As business leaders, we need to have the seriousness of purpose—and the steadiness of focus—to define a privacy policy that consumers find credible and that governments find adequate.

But the true test is whether our policy passes muster with the ultimate regulator of Internet use: the individual consumer.

And that really brings me full circle today.

Conferences like this one are enormously important—but only to the extent they recognize that the time to talk is over—and that the time to act is now.

I look forward to working with everyone in this room to take the lead—to put in place a privacy policy not only that we as citizens of the world's first Information Society can live with—but that we can grow and prosper with as the Information Economy unfolds. Thank you.

Motivational Presentation

Five Ways in Which Thinking Is Dangerous: Rebellion, Risks, and Outrageous Behavior; by Stephen Joel Trachtenberg; *Dr. Stephen Joel Trachtenberg, President of the University of Hartford, delivered his speech, "Five Ways in Which Thinking Is Dangerous: Rebellion, Risks, and Outrageous Behavior" at Newington High School Scholars' Breakfast, Newington, Connecticut, on June 3, 1986.*

It's an honor and a pleasure for me to be here today, and to have this opportunity to address this year's Newington High School Scholar's Breakfast.

I've been giving a lot of thought in recent weeks to what I ought to be saying to you this morning. The obvious thing would be to praise you for your hard work and your accomplishments and encourage you to continue achieving at this very high level.

But the more I thought about it, the less inclined I felt to do that. And when I asked myself why, a little voice inside my head replied as follows:

"Look, Steve, these kids are *teenagers*. And one thing we know about teenagers is that they are given to questioning the values handed them by adults. Sometimes they rebel in *not*-so-obvious ways. But if you go in there and praise them outright for their accomplishments, maybe one or two of them will reason that anything an adult tells them is good is probably bad."

Let me tell you, that voice inside my head really gave me pause. Basically it seemed to be suggesting that I use some reverse psychology. Instead of doing the obvious, I should do the *opposite* of the obvious.

In turn, that seemed to leave me only one course of action. I could come here today and *criticize* you for working so hard and accomplishing so much. I could urge you to relax a little, to lower your standards, and to try out the pleasures of poorer grades and a generally lower academic status. Then I imagined what the local newspapers would make of my remarks, and what the chances were that I would ever again be invited to address a group of students in any high school in Connecticut.

So I found myself back at Square One. Now I *really* had to get back to basics inside my head, and, drawing on all of the studying I did at Columbia, Yale, and Harvard, I reasoned as follows:

Those of us who have studied Western history of the 19th and 20th centuries know that the Romantic movement left us with a permanent bias in favor of rebellion, risk, and generally outrageous behavior. In other words, if you can pin an *"Establishment"* label on any particular set of behaviors . . . if you can make it sound as if everybody behaving in that particular way has a potbelly that is also bright yellow . . . then most folks in our culture will shy away from it, in favor of someone or something that is closer to Burt Reynolds or Humphrey Bogart.

Now I asked myself: Why is it that no one has considered the hypothesis that academic high achievement is actually as romantic, risky, and generally outrageous as being a pirate, or flying experimental jets, or doing any of the other things that most people are *afraid* to do? Maybe those who get high honors in a place like Newington High School are not just *smarter* than most of their contemporaries but braver too?

The more I considered this hypothesis the better I liked it, and I decided to entitle my talk today "The Five Major Risks of Academic High Achievement." An alternative and slightly broader title might be "Five Ways in Which Thinking is Dangerous."

Way Number One, it seems to me, is that thinking—analysis—the habit of probing deeply into things—can lead to depression.

Remember that people who are regarded as not being clever aren't necessarily lacking in brain-power. They just don't make use of the brain-power that they have available. And one of the reasons for that may be that when you inquire carefully into a lot of things that go on in our world, you find that many of them fall short of perfection. In fact, quite a few of them are positively lousy.

So you can't altogether blame folks who, rather than get upsetting answers, simply don't ask questions! They stay reasonably happy by not doing too much reasoning!

A second risk of academic high achievement is that there are those who will actually hold it against you—in other words, that it can sometimes lead to a lack of popularity where particular individuals are concerned. They're the ones who will label you a—quote—"brain," and imagine that this is a deadly blow, sort of like calling you a rat or a fink.

Though I imagine that some of you have had experiences like that, I wonder if you've considered the possibility that people like that are motivated by a good deal of fear and anxiety? Once you've established your reputation as having a lot of analytic capacity, *they* become nervous that you might turn that capacity in *their* direction. In other words, the person who fears your brain-power is probably a person with something to hide.

The third risk of academic high achievement lies, believe it or not, in your relationship to the adult world. I hope it won't come as a tremendous surprise when I tell you that many adults feel quite ambivalent where talented and high-achieving teenagers are concerned. On the one hand, they can't help but admire the energy and initiative teenagers like that are showing. At the same time, they can't altogether avoid the awareness that the young people they are admiring are also the—quote—"next generation" that is going to—quote—"take over the world."

In other words, a typical fear that adults have is that they are on the way to becoming obsolete. That's why dedicated teachers don't necessarily leap to their feet with enthusiasm when one of their students proves beyond a shadow of a doubt that they just made a mistake. *First* they wince. *Then* they manage to eke out a small smile. And *then*, having thought the whole thing over—then and *only* then—they leap enthusiastically to their feet!

A fourth risk of academic high achievement, in my opinion, is despair. Once you've set a high standard for yourself, there *have* to come moments when you ask yourself: "Can I keep this up?" At the age of 13 or 14 or 15, you ask whether you can keep going at this pace until you're *really old*—until you're 25, say, or 32. Then, when you've been doing it for 30 or 40 years, you wonder whether you can keep going at this pace until retirement. And after retirement, you look at the other vigorous senior citizens—every one of them playing championship gold or giving guest lectures at a nearby college—and you wonder whether you'll *ever* be able to take it easy! . . .

Finally, there is another risk of academic high achievement that bears some thinking about, which is that it often leads people to transform the world in which they are living, which in turn can cause a good deal of personal upset.

Let's say that you are in your teens or early twenties and you work really hard to develop a brand new concept and a brand new range of intellectual or scientific possibilities. Now the world begins to change because *you* dreamt up the microchip . . . or genetic engineering . . . or some altogether new way of looking at the human past. Well, by the time the revolution is peaking, you'll probably be 35 or 40 years of age—ready to settle down and be a little comfortable and complacent. At that point everything around you will get shaken up, and you'll find that your teenage son or daughter is criticizing you for being so completely out of it!

Now let me tote up the risks that I've set before you in the last few minutes:

Risk number one: You may find that you sometimes get depressed.
Risk number two: Some people won't like you.
Risk number three: Grown-ups may get a little nervous when they're near you.
Risk number four: You may feel an occasional twinge of despair over "keeping up the pace."
Risk number five: You may begin to have an impact on the world around you—and you will have to live with the changes you've helped to bring about.

Looking over those five risks of academic high achievement, I realize that they look very much like the risks of maturity. When you criticize someone for being too much of a kid, you usually mean that he or she is giggly even when that's not appropriate, that he or she tries to be universally popular, . . . that he or she expects life to be a nonending party, and that he or she can't imagine things being different from the way they are right now.

What that suggests to me is that academic high achievement—the kind represented here at Newington High School today—may also be a synonym for maturity. It carries some risks—which is *always* true of maturity. It means that life gets a little more complicated—which is what true adults take for granted as they try to get through an average day. It means that life is only *sometimes* a party, and that it is full of the unexpected.

Yes, there are some risks . . . but they are risks well taken. The benefits are worth the dangers. The eagle flying high always risks being shot at by some hare-brained human with a rifle. But eagles—and young eagles like *you*—still prefer the view from that risky height to what is available flying with the turkeys far, far below.

Personally, I admire eagles. That's because I am an unreconstructed romantic. And I admire *you* for what you've accomplished. Keep up the good work! My congratulations to you all!

Follow-up Letter After Job Interview

After a job interview, write a follow-up letter to the person who interviewed you. Your follow-up letter should be courteous and should show appreciation for the opportunity to interview for the job. You may also use the letter to mention highlights from your interview and show your interest in getting the job.

The following is an example of a follow-up letter typed in the block style. Notice that the writer follows the business letter format shown on pages 637–640.

Amanda Watson
1948 Durango Drive
Laramie, WY 82073

Ansellum Nasher
Nasher Food Service Staffing
717 South Third Street
Laramie, WY 82070

Dear Mr. Nasher:

Thank you for the opportunity to discuss the banquet coordinator position at The Ranch Restaurant. I appreciate the time you spent discussing the restaurant industry with me. Your company has an impressive reputation, and I would enjoy representing you and your staff.

I am still very interested in being The Ranch's banquet coordinator. I feel that my experience as a dining room manager, which we discussed during my interview, will help me excel at this job. I look forward to hearing from you soon.

Sincerely,

Amanda Watson

Amanda Watson

Glossary

This glossary lists the vocabulary words found in the selections in this book. The definition given is for the word as it is used in the selection; you may wish to consult a dictionary for other meanings of these words.

A

accommodation   maintaining harmony with others by giving in to their wishes; p. 398

acquiring   the physical process receiver-senders use to take in the sender's message; p. 49

action group   a group appointed to plan and implement a specific course of action; p. 322

active listening   participating fully in the communication process; p. 189

advocacy group   a group set up specifically to support, protect, defend, or lobby for a cause or group; p. 315

agitator   someone who injects negative energy into the group process; p. 350

ambiguous   open to interpretation; confusing; p. 140

amplification device   information that extends and/or clarifies an idea for an audience; p. 509

antithesis   a rhetorical device that involves pairing opposing words or ideas; p. 524

appointed leader   someone who is given his or her leadership position by a person in authority; p. 413

appreciative listening   listening to enjoy a speaker's message or a performance on an artistic level; p. 194

appropriateness   what is suitable for a specific situation; p. 4

articulation   clearly and distinctly uttering the consonant sounds of a word; p. 108

artifacts   articles of adornment used to decorate self or surroundings; p. 162

attending   the act of choosing, consciously or subconsciously, to focus your attention on verbal or nonverbal stimuli; p. 177

attention device   a tool used by speakers to grab the interest of an audience; p. 479

audience orientation   providing audience members with information they likely do not already have but will need in order to understand a presentation; p. 481

authoritarian leader   a leader who uses power to force followers to do what he or she wants them to do; p. 415

avoidance   keeping away from or withdrawing from something; p. 397

B

balanced leader   a leader who strives for an equal focus on both tasks and relationships; p. 416

barrier   any obstacle that blocks communication; p. 45

body language   the way people nonverbally express their feelings; p. 299

brainstorming   the process of quickly listing all ideas that come to mind regarding a specific topic; p. 335

C

channel   the space in which a message is transmitted; p. 44

chronological order   arrangement according to the time in which events occur; p. 490

closed question   a question that requires a very specific answer, often just one word; p. 239

coercion   trying to force others to go along with your wishes; p. 399

coercive power   the ability to force others to do something by punishing them if they do not comply; p. 424

collaboration working together to achieve a result; p. 401

colloquialism a term associated with a specific regional culture; p. 120

committee a group with a specialized task which is a part of the basic structure of an organization; p. 314

communication the process of creating and exchanging meaning through symbolic interaction; p. 3

communication apprehension fear or nervousness associated with making a presentation; p. 549

competent communicator someone who incorporates knowledge, attitude, and skills into his or her communication to communicate effectively and appropriately; p. 9

compromise settling differences by having each party give up something; p. 399

conflict a struggle between two or more parties who sense interference in achieving goals; p. 24

conflict over facts a disagreement over something that can be proven to be true or false; p. 388

conflict over policies a disagreement that deals with differences over how to best complete a task; p. 389

conflict over values a disagreement over priorities; p. 388

connotation emotions or feelings associated with a word; p. 125

conscientious style a style of communication that tends to be slow-paced and task-oriented; p. 226

constructive criticism a negative evaluation that brings about positive change; p. 259

context the situation in which communication occurs; p. 4

counseling interview an interview during which the interviewer helps the interviewee decide on a course of action; p. 279

criteria the standards or conditions that any solution must meet in order to be acceptable; p. 334

critic someone who, through training and experience, is qualified to analyze and make judgments about something; p. 581

critical listening listening to comprehend ideas and information in order to achieve a specific purpose or goal; p. 192

critical perspective the standard by which a speech is judged to be successful or unsuccessful; p. 582

culture the set of life patterns passed down from one generation to the next in a group of people; p. 16

culture shock confusion or anxiety that sometimes results when people come into contact with a culture different from their own; p. 17

D

data things that catch a communicator's attention, such as objects, people, sounds, thoughts, memories, and the messages sent by others; p. 48

decision making examining a set of alternatives and using reason and logic to select the best one; p. 336

decoding the mental process receiver-senders use to create meaning from language; p. 49

deliberative listening listening to understand, analyze, and evaluate messages to accept or reject a point of view, make a decision, or take action; p. 192

delivery the way a presenter uses his or her body and voice to communicate a message to an audience; p. 564

demeanor outward behavior; p. 298

democratic leader a leader who invites followers to participate in decision making in an effort to get the majority to agree with and commit to decisions; p. 416

demographics information about a group's age, gender, education, group affiliations, ethnicity, and sociocultural background; p. 445

denotation a word's objective description or meaning; p. 125

descriptive communication talk that paints a picture of the facts of a situation; p. 259

descriptive gesture a gesture used to create a mental image to help an audience visualize a message; p. 570

dialect a unique combination of speech sounds that identifies speech with a particular group of people; p. 110

diction the degree of clarity and distinctness in a person's speech; p. 107

direct question a question that is straightforward; asks exactly what the interviewer wants to know and leaves no room for ambiguity; p. 293

discriminate to treat differently based on reasons other than individual merit, or quality; p. 301

dominant style a style of communication that is fast-paced and more task-oriented than people-oriented; p. 224

E

emergent goal   a goal set by the group itself; p. 316

emergent leader   someone who is chosen by peers or members of a group because of his or her personality, power in the group, or the special circumstances of the group task; p. 414

emergent norm   any group norm that develops from the group interaction and the mix of the group members' personalities; p. 347

empathic listening   listening to understand, participate in, and enhance a relationship; p. 193

emphatic gesture   a gesture used to stress or place special attention on what a presenter is saying; p. 569

employment interview   a process for judging whether a job candidate is qualified and well-suited for a position; p. 280

encoding   the mental process of assigning meaning and language to data; p. 49

enunciation   clearly and distinctly uttering the vowel sounds of a word; p. 109

ethical proof   the supporting information that builds a speaker's credibility on a topic; p. 508

ethos   the image a presenter displays to an audience; p. 443

etiquette   an established code of behavior or courtesy; p. 254

evaluative communication   talk that tells how you interpret a behavior and how you feel about a situation; p. 259

exit interview   an interview used to determine why a person has decided to leave an organization; p. 278

expert power   the power held by the person who knows the most about the work that must be done; p. 425

extemporaneous presentation   a presentation thoroughly prepared and rehearsed in advance and presented with the use of notes; p. 535

F

facilitator   a group member who adds positive task energy to the group by helping group members follow through on tasks; p. 349

factual question   a question that seeks information that can be proven; p. 293

feed-forward   to offer an explanation that you want to make or a reason or explanation for a question, request, or offer; p. 80

feedback   one person's observable response to another's message; p. 46

filler   a word or phrase used to cover up a hesitancy in speech; p. 127

formal language   language that conforms to a highly structured set of rules; p. 118

formal presentation   a presentation scheduled in advance and usually involving individual or team research and audiovisual support; p. 442

formal social group   a group whose members are chosen by an organization to participate in community activities; p. 323

functional approach   the idea that leaders should both recognize and actively perform needed tasks; p. 417

G

grammar   the basic understandings and rules that regulate the use of a language; p. 106

group   a small number of people who identify and interact with one another because of a common interest, bond, or goal; p. 313

group discussion   three or more people exchanging ideas on a specific topic for a specific purpose; p. 354

group dynamics   the energy created as group members communicate and interact with each other in committees, teams, and other groups; p. 353

group goal   the specific tasks and expected outcome of a group; p. 315

group norms   informal, often unstated rules about what behavior is appropriate in a group; p. 345

groupthink   poor decision-making in a group caused by members having a stronger desire to agree with one another than to solve the problem; p. 352

H

hearing   the physical process of receiving sound; p. 176

highly closed question   a question that not only seeks a specific answer but may even provide answers from which to choose; p. 293

hypothetical question   a question that asks how a respondent might react in a given situation; p. 293

I

impatient listening   short bursts of active listening that are interrupted by noise and other distractions; p. 190

impromptu presentation   a presentation for which there is little or no time for advance preparation; p. 536

indirect question   a question that seeks specific information without directly asking for it; p. 293

inflection   the rising and falling of pitch that adds variety to speaking; p. 148

influencing style   a style of communication that is fast-paced and more people-oriented than task-oriented; p. 225

informal language   the language most often used in casual situations and with close interpersonal relationships; p. 120

informal presentation   a presentation that may occur on a daily or ongoing basis, is usually shorter and more spontaneous than a formal presentation, and may involve a smaller audience; p. 442

informal social group   a group in which membership may be encouraged, but not required, by an organization; p. 323

information-gathering group   a group designed specifically to gather data; p. 320

information-gathering interview   an interview in which an interviewer obtains information from an interviewee; p. 278

information-giving interview   an interview in which an interviewer gives information to an interviewee; p. 279

informational power   the power held by individuals who have access to needed information; p. 425

informative presentation   a presentation that conveys ideas and information in a clear, accurate, and objective manner to gain the audience's interest; p. 454

initiator   a group member who works to get the group started toward achieving the group goal; p. 348

integrating   blending things so that they function together as a whole; p. 220

internalization   going over and over something until you absorb it; p. 554

interpersonal communication   communication between two people; p. 54

interpreting   the process in which the receiver personalizes the sender's message to determine the meaning; p. 178

interview   a formal two-party communication in which at least one of the participants has a set purpose; p. 274

interview process   the sequence of actions that result in an effective interview; p. 283

interviewee   someone who provides information to an interviewer; p. 274

interviewer   someone who determines the purpose of an interview and ensures that the discussion remains focused on the purpose; p. 274

intrapersonal communication   communication that occurs in one's own mind; p. 54

investigative interview   an interview in which the interviewer uses questions to find out unknown information; p. 278

J

jargon   technical language; p. 119

judgment by aesthetics   evaluating the overall appearance or impact of a presentation; p. 583

judgment by ethical standards   evaluating whether a speaker behaved ethically in a presentation; p. 582

judgment by multiple standards   an evaluation using two or more critical perspectives to determine the success of a speech; p. 583

judgment by results   evaluating whether or not a speaker accomplished the goal of his or her presentation; p. 582

K

kinesics   the use of the body in communication; p. 153

L

laissez-faire leader   a leader who gives up his or her power to the members of the group; p. 416

leader   someone who influences or inspires others to act in specific ways to accomplish a common goal; p. 413

leading question   a question that suggests the desired answer; p. 293

legitimate power   power assigned to anyone who holds a particular position, office, or title; p. 424

listening   a physical and psychological process that involves acquiring, assigning meaning, and responding to symbolic messages from others; p. 172

logical proof   a specific piece of verifiable information that supports a statement; p. 506

M

maintenance need   a need that relates to the feelings of group members and their relationships to one another; p. 361

manuscript presentation   a presentation that is delivered with its full text in front of the presenter; p. 534

mass communication   electronic or print transmission of messages to the general public; p. 56

mass media   outlets of communication, such as radio, television, film, and print, that are designed to reach large audiences; p. 56

message   information that is exchanged between communicators; p. 40

method of delivery   a specific way of sending your message orally to your audience; p. 534

Monroe's Motivated Sequence   a five-part organizational strategy designed for speeches that seek to persuade or motivate an audience to take immediate action; named after communication expert A. H. Monroe; p. 494

motivational presentation   presentation that inspires or encourages an audience; p. 456

N

negotiation   bargaining with others to gain what you want; p. 400

neutral question   a question that implies no specific "right" or "wrong" answer; p. 293

noise   anything that interferes with a message; usually temporary; p. 44

nonverbal communication   a system of symbolic behaviors that includes all forms of communication except words; p. 136

norm   a stated or implied expectation; p. 5

O

one-to-group communication   communication that involves a speaker who seeks to inform, persuade, or motivate an audience; p. 55

open-ended question   a question that is broad in scope, requiring more than a single-word answer such as "Yes" or "No"; p. 239

opinion question   a question that asks for the respondent's judgment about something; p. 293

oral language   language that is spoken and heard rather than written and read; p. 102

oral style   the way a presenter uses language to express ideas; p. 519

organization   a number of people with specific responsibilities who are united for some purpose; p. 15

organizational culture   how an organization thinks, what it finds important, and how it conducts business; p. 17

P

panel discussion   a formal presentation in which a group of people discusses an announced topic in front of an audience; p. 544

panel discussion-forum   a panel discussion that includes post-discussion interaction with the audience; p. 545

parallelism   arranging sentences so that words and phrases are similar in length and structure; p. 524

paraphrase   repeating a message in your own words; p. 251

passive listening   not actively participating in interactions; p. 190

pathetic proof   support material that gives emotional appeal to a presentation; p. 508

perception check   a question that helps you determine the accuracy and validity of your perceptions; p. 78

perception   the process of assigning meaning to data about oneself or the surrounding world; p. 71

performance appraisal   an evaluation of how well a person has achieved goals and objectives over a set period of time; p. 279

personal perception   one's own understanding of reality; p. 75

personal style   a pattern of clear and consistent communication choices that reflect a person's individuality and distinguish him or her from other individuals; p. 222

persuasive presentation   a presentation that attempts to get an audience to voluntarily change its thoughts, beliefs, or actions on a topic; p. 454

pitch   highness or lowness of sound on a musical scale; p. 147

policy-making group   a group that has the task of creating procedural rules for all organizational members to follow; p. 321

power   the ability to get others to behave in a particular way or to carry out certain actions; p. 423

prescribed goal a goal that is assigned by a person in authority; p. 315

prescribed norm a rule for appropriate behavior that is routinely taught to new group members; p. 346

primary question a question that begins a new topic; p. 293

primary source someone, including oneself, who has firsthand knowledge or experience regarding a topic; p. 462

problem difficulty or uncertainty—a difference between the way something should be and the way it is; p. 331

problem solving the act of understanding the nature of a dilemma, creating alternative solutions, determining which solution is best, and implementing that solution; p. 331

professional presentation an informed, organized oral statement made to a group of professional or social peers, supervisors, clients, or members of the general public; p. 442

projecting sending the sound of your voice to all areas of a room without shouting; p. 565

pronunciation the correct way to say a word; p. 108

protocol a code of etiquette that is written and prescribed by an organization; p. 254

R

range the span from the highest to the lowest pitch possible for a speaker to reach; p. 148

rate how fast or how slowly an individual speaks; p. 149

receiver-sender a person who receives, or believes he or she has received, a message; p. 39

referent power influence held by someone who is respected, liked, or otherwise admired by his or her followers; p. 427

relationship skill a communication skill needed to nurture and maintain goodwill with people; p. 11

resistance the force generated within a person that keeps him or her from accepting another's use of power; p. 423

responding reacting internally, emotionally, and intellectually to a message; p. 179

reward power the ability to repay others in exchange for complying with a given direction; p. 424

role a part played in a specific setting or situation; p. 5

S

sample the set of people one selects to respond to a survey or questionnaire; p. 464

secondary question a question that helps the interviewer better understand the answer to a primary question; p. 293

secondary source an information source such as a book, periodical, radio or television program, or Internet article that has been written by someone else about a particular topic; p. 460

selective perception the mental process of choosing which data or stimuli to focus on from all that are available to you at any given time; p. 72

self-concept the view one has of oneself; p. 83

self-disclosure the deliberate revelation of significant personal information that is not readily apparent to others; p. 90

self-fulfilling prophecy a prediction or expectation that shapes your behavior, making the outcome more likely to occur; p. 88

self-talk the inner speech or mental conversations that one carries on with oneself; p. 54

sender-receiver a person who sends a message to someone; p. 39

sensory perception the complex physical process of taking in data through the five senses; p. 48

sequential order arrangement according to the steps of a process; p. 491

slang a type of informal language that is typically used for only a brief period of time by a limited group of people; p. 121

small-group communication communication within formal or informal groups or teams; p. 55

social group a group that someone joins for purely personal reasons; p. 322

social responsibility an obligation or willingness to work toward the well-being of others; p. 20

social ritual a communication situation that is frequently repeated in daily social interaction; p. 123

spatial order arrangement according to how a topic is put together or by the physical location of its elements; p. 492

specific instance an account of an actual event or occurrence; p. 507

stage presence an illusion created by the quality of the energy, poise, confidence, and control that a presenter conveys to an audience; p. 568

standard   an established level of requirement or excellence; p. 6

standard language   language used by the majority of knowledgeable communicators within a specific language; p. 120

statistic   an item of information that is presented as a number; p. 507

steady style   a style of communication that tends to be slow-paced and both people- and task-oriented; p. 226

structure   the way the different parts of a language are arranged; p. 105

style approach   the idea that a leader's communication method and use of power determines his or her success; p. 415

survey interview   an interview that gathers information from a number of people; p. 278

symposium   a group presentation in which individual speakers give prepared presentations on aspects of a topic with little or no interaction with the other presenters; p. 546

symposium-forum   a symposium that includes interaction with the audience; p. 546

T

tag   a statement or question added to the end of a statement to invite approval or cooperation from others; p. 127

task group   a group that is given a specific job, or a task, to complete; p. 318

task need   a need that relates directly to the business and goals of the group; p. 361

task skill   a communication skill needed to do a job, complete a task, or reach a goal effectively; p. 11

team   a small group that usually is given the power to make and implement decisions; p. 314

technical language   language associated with a particular profession, activity, or field of study; p. 119

tempo   the rhythmic quality of a person's speech; p. 149

testimony   a direct quote or summary of a quote; p. 507

thesis statement   a clearly written, simple sentence or question that states the point you expect to make in your presentation; p. 480

tone   a specific vocal quality; p. 149

topical order   arrangement that groups ideas by some logical theme or division; p. 492

trait approach   the idea that leaders share certain personality traits that help them lead successfully; p. 414

transactional   involving an exchange; p. 35

transmitting   the physical process of sending verbal and nonverbal messages; p. 49

U

understanding   a complex mental process that involves decoding the symbolic message received from others and then interpreting and assigning a personal meaning to that message; p. 178

ungrammatical language   language that does not use expected standards of grammar or mechanics; p. 122

V

visualization   the process of mentally picturing yourself doing something successfully; p. 551

vocabulary   all the word symbols that make up a particular code or language; p. 103

Spanish Glossary

A

acomodación (accommodation)   mantener la armonía con los demás cediendo a sus deseos; p. 398

acuerdo de grupo (groupthink)   decisiones ineficaces que toma un grupo debido a que sus miembros se preocupan más en lograr consenso que en solucionar el problema; p. 352

adornos (artifacts)   artículos para decoración ambiental o arreglo personal; p. 162

adquisición (acquiring)   proceso físico mediante el cual el receptor-emisor asimila el mensaje del emisor; p. 49

alcance de la voz (projecting)   transmitir el sonido de la voz a todos los rincones de un recinto sin necesidad de elevarla demasiado; p. 565

ambiguo (ambiguous)   que tiene más de una interpretación; causa confusión; p. 140

ansiedad comunicativa (communication apprehension)   temor o nerviosismo que se siente al hacer una exposición; p. 549

antítesis (antithesis)   recurso retórico que relaciona palabras o ideas opuestas; p. 524

apreciación estética (judgment by aesthetics)   evaluación de la apariencia general o del impacto de una exposición; p. 583

apreciación por normas éticas (judgment by ethical standards)   evaluación del comportamiento ético de un orador durante una exposición; p. 582

apreciación por normas múltiples (judgment by multiple standards)   evaluación para determinar la eficacia de una exposición en la que se usan dos o más perspectivas críticas; p. 583

apreciación por resultados (judgement by results)   evaluación para determinar si el orador cumplió con el objetivo de su exposición; p. 582

articulación (articulation)   pronunciación clara de las consonantes de una palabra; p. 108

autoridad de experto (expert power)   autoridad que ejerce una persona por ser la más calificada para realizar un trabajo; p. 425

B

barrera (barrier)   todo obstáculo que dificulta la comunicación; p. 45

C

cadencia (tempo)   manera proporcionada y grata de hablar que tiene una persona; p. 149

canal (channel)   medio por el que se transmite un mensaje; p. 44

capacidad de relación (relationship skill)   habilidad comunicativa requerida para cultivar y mantener buenas relaciones con los demás; p. 11

choque cultural (culture shock)   confusión o ansiedad que ocasionalmente resulta del contacto que tiene una persona con una cultura diferente a la propia; p. 17

cinésica (kinesics)   uso del cuerpo en relación con la comunicación; p. 153

circunstancia específica (specific instance)   hecho o suceso verdadero; p. 507

clasificación temática (topical order)   agrupación de ideas según una división o tema lógicos; p. 492

cláusula final interrogativa (tag)   declaración o pregunta que se usa al terminar un enunciado para obtener la aprobación o cooperación de los demás; p. 127

codificar (encoding)   proceso mental mediante el cual se asigna significado y lenguaje a la información; p. 49

coerción (coercion)   someter a otros a la voluntad o los deseos de uno; p. 399

colaboración (collaboration)   trabajo que se realiza en conjunto para alcanzar un objetivo; p. 401

comité (committee)   grupo que forma parte de la estructura básica de una organización al cual se le encomienda una tarea especializada; p. 314

comprensión (understanding)   proceso mental complejo mediante el cual se descifra e interpreta un mensaje simbólico, al que luego se da un significado personal; p. 178

comunicación (communication)   proceso mediante el cual se establece e intercambia significado a través de una interacción simbólica; p. 3

comunicación de individuo a grupo (one-to-group communication)   comunicación en la que participa un orador con el fin de informar, persuadir o motivar al público; p. 55

comunicación de masas (mass communication)   difusión electrónica o impresa de mensajes entre el público general; p. 56

comunicación en pequeños grupos (small-group communication)   comunicación que se da dentro de grupos formales o informales, o equipos; p. 55

comunicación evaluadora (evaluative communication)   conversación que ayuda a interpretar un comportamiento y lo que uno piensa sobre una situación; p. 259

comunicación expositiva (descriptive communication)   exposición de los hechos de una situación; p. 259

comunicación interpersonal (interpersonal communication)   comunicación entre dos personas; p. 54

comunicación intrapersonal (intrapersonal communication)   comunicación que tiene lugar en la mente de una persona; p. 54

comunicación no verbal (nonverbal communication)   sistema de comportamientos simbólicos que incluye todo tipo de comunicación, con excepción de palabras; p. 136

comunicador competente (competent communicator)   persona que integra conocimientos, actitud y habilidades para comunicarse eficaz y adecuamente; p. 9

concepto personal (self-concept)   opinión que uno tiene de sí mismo; p. 83

concesión mutua (compromise)   cesiones recíprocas que hacen las partes para conciliar diferencias; p. 399

conducta (demeanor)   comportamiento externo que exhibe una persona; p. 298

conflicto (conflict)   problema entre dos o más partes cuando piensan que el otro obstaculiza el logro de sus metas; p. 24

conflicto sobre hechos (conflict over facts)   desacuerdo sobre algo que al comprobarse podría resultar verdadero o falso; p. 388

conflicto sobre políticas (conflict over policies)   desacuerdo o diferencias en cuanto a la mejor manera de llevar a cabo una tarea; p. 389

conflicto sobre valores (conflict over values)   desacuerdo en cuanto a prioridades; p. 388

connotación (connotation)   emociones o sentimientos relacionados con una palabra; p. 125

contexto (context)   situación en la que se da la comunicación; p. 4

conveniencia (appropriateness)   calidad de adecuado para una situación específica; p. 4

conversación interna (self-talk)   conversaciones mentales que una persona sostiene con sí misma; p. 54

criterios (criteria)   requisitos o condiciones que deben satisfacerse para que una solución sea aceptada; p. 334

crítica constructiva (constructive criticism)   opinión negativa que genera un cambio positivo; p. 259

crítico (critic)   persona que como resultado de su formación y experiencia está capacitada para analizar y emitir opiniones; p. 581

cultura (culture)   conjunto de actividades humanas de un pueblo que se transmite de generación a eneración; p. 16

cultura de organización (organizational culture)   manera de pensar, prioridades y operaciones de una organización; p. 17

D

dato estadístico (statistic)   información representada en cifras; p. 507

datos (data)   elementos que captan la atención del comunicador como objetos, personas, sonidos, ideas, recuerdos y mensajes transmitidos por otros; p. 48

datos demográficos (demographics)   información referente a la edad, sexo, educación, afiliaciones, etnicidad y antecedentes socioculturales de un grupo; p. 445

denotación (denotation)   significado o definición objetiva de una palabra; p. 125

descodificar (decoding)   proceso mental mediante el cual el receptor y el emisor determinan el significado del lenguaje; p. 49

dialecto (dialect)   conjunto de sonidos y expresiones que forman la lengua de un determinado grupo; p. 110

dicción (diction)   grado de claridad y precisión con el que habla una persona; p. 107

dinámica de grupo (group dynamics)   energía generada por la comunicación o interacción de los miembros de comités, equipos y otros grupos; p. 353

discriminar (discriminate)   dar trato diferente a una persona por motivos no relacionados con su mérito o calidad personal; p. 301

discusión en grupo (group discussion)   tres o más personas que intercambian ideas sobre un tema específico con un propósito determinado; p. 354

E

elocuencia (delivery)   manera en que un presentador usa sus ademanes y voz para transmitir su mensaje al público; p. 564

emisor-receptor (sender-receiver)   persona que envía un mensaje a otra; p. 39

entrevista (interview)   comunicación formal entre dos partes en la cual uno de los participantes, por lo menos, tiene un propósito definido; p. 274

entrevista de asesoría (counseling interview)   entrevista durante la cual el entrevistador ayuda al entrevistado a tomar una decisión sobre la línea de acción que seguirá; p. 279

entrevista de encuesta (survey interview)   entrevista para recoger información de un grupo de personas; p. 278

entrevista de trabajo (employment interview)   proceso mediante el cual se determina si un postulante está calificado y es apto para un cargo; p. 280

entrevista final (exit interview)   entrevista para determinar la razón por la cual una persona deja una organización; p. 278

entrevista informativa (information-giving interview)   entrevista durante la cual el entrevistador proporciona información al entrevistado; p. 279

entrevista investigadora (investigative interview)   entrevista durante la cual el entrevistador formula preguntas para averiguar la información que necesita; p. 278

entrevista para obtener información (information-gathering interview)   entrevista durante la cual el entrevistado proporciona información al entrevistador; p. 278

entrevistado (interviewee)   persona que brinda información al entrevistador; p. 274

entrevistador (interviewer)   persona que determina el propósito de la entrevista y mantiene la conversación centrada en dicho propósito; p. 274

enunciación (enunciation)   pronunciación clara de las vocales de una palabra; p. 109

enunciación de tesis (thesis statement)   oración o pregunta sencilla escrita con claridad, que establece la idea u opinión que uno desea transmitir; p. 480

equipo (team)   pequeño grupo que cuenta generalmente con autoridad para adoptar e implementar decisiones; p. 314

escala (range)   tiempo que le toma a un orador modular la voz desde el tono más elevado al más atenuado; p. 148

escucha (listening)   proceso físico y psicológico mediante el cual uno adquiere, da significado y responde a los mensajes simbólicos de otros; p. 172

escucha activa (active listening)   participación plena en el proceso de comunicación; p. 189

escucha con empatía (empathic listening)   acción de escuchar para comprender, participar en una relación y fortalecer la misma; p. 193

escucha con sentido crítico (critical listening)   acción de esuchar para captar ideas e información a fin de lograr un objetivo o meta; p. 192

escucha de apreciación (appreciative listening)   acción de escuchar en la cual se disfruta del mensaje de un orador o una interpretación artística; p. 194

escucha deliberante (deliberative listening)   acción de escuchar para comprender, analizar y evaluar mensajes a fin de aceptar o rechazar un punto de vista, tomar una decisión o hacer una acción; p. 192

escucha impaciente (impatient listening)   intervalos cortos de escucha activa interrumpidos por ruidos y otras distracciones; p. 190

escucha pasiva (passive listening)   participación no activa en el proceso de comunicación; p. 190

estándar (standard)   norma o nivel de excelencia establecido; p. 6

estilo de influencia (influencing style)   modo de comunicación acelerada que se concentra más en las relaciones humanas que en la tarea; p. 225

estilo dominante (dominant style)   modo de comunicación acelerada que se concentra más en la meta que en las relaciones humanas; p. 224

estilo intencional (conscientious style)   modo de comunicación pausado y orientado hacia una tarea específica; p. 226

estilo oral (oral style)   manera en que el presentador usa el lenguaje para expresar sus ideas; p. 519

estilo personal (personal style)   patrón de modelos de comunicación definidos y constantes que reflejan la individualidad de una persona distinguiéndola de los demás; p. 222

estilo uniforme (steady style)   modo de comunicación pausado que se orienta tanto hacia una tarea específica como a las relaciones humanas; p. 226

estructura (structure)   orden que siguen las diferentes partes del lenguaje; p. 105

ética (ethos)   imagen que proyecta un presentador ante un público; p. 443

etiqueta (etiquette)   código de conducta o cortesía establecido; p. 254

evaluación del rendimiento (performance appraisal)   evaluación para determinar si una persona ha logrado eficazmente sus metas y objetivos en el transcurso de un tiempo dado; p. 279

evidencia conmovedora (pathetic proof)   material complementario que da un toque emotivo a una exposición; p. 508

evidencia ética (ethical proof)   información complementaria que ratifica el conocimiento que tiene el orador sobre un tema; p. 508

evidencia lógica (logical proof)   pieza específica de información comprobable que apoya una declaración; p. 506

evitar (avoidance)   manterse alejado o retirado de algo; p. 397

exposición con texto (manuscript presentation)   exposición durante la cual el presentador sigue un texto en su totalidad; p. 534

exposición formal (formal presentation)   exposición programada por anticipado que incluye investigación individual o colectiva y se complementa con material audiovisual; p. 442

exposición improvisada (impromptu presentation)   exposición que no ha sido preparada anticipadamente por falta de tiempo; p. 536

exposición informal (informal presentation)   exposición que puede darse a diario o en forma continua, que es generalmente breve y más espontánea que una exposición formal, y tiene un público menor; p. 442

exposición informativa (informative presentation)   exposición durante la cual las ideas e información son transmitidas de manera clara, precisa y objetiva para capturar la atención del público; p. 454

exposición motivadora (motivational presentation)   exposición para inspirar o animar al público; p. 456

exposición organizada extemporánea (extemporaneous presentation)   exposición debidamente preparada y ensayada, y presentada mediante el uso de notas; p. 535

exposición persuasiva (persuasive presentation) exposición cuyo objetivo es convencer al público para que cambie sus conceptos, opiniones o tendencias sobre un tema; p. 454

exposición profesional (professional presentation) exposición oral informada y organizada hecha ante un grupo de colegas o relaciones sociales, supervisores, clientes o público en general; p. 442

F

facilitador (facilitator) miembro de un grupo que imparte energía positiva ayudando a sus miembros en la conclusión de las tareas; p. 349

fuente primaria (primary source) persona, incluido uno mismo, que tiene conocimientos o experiencia directa sobre un tema; p. 462

fuente secundaria (secondary source) fuente informativa, por ejemplo un libro, publicación periódica, programa de radio o televisión o artículo en Internet, sobre un tema específico escrito por otra persona; p. 460

G

gesto descriptivo (descriptive gesture) ademán que se usa para crear una imagen mental y ayudar a la concurrencia a visualizar un mensaje; p. 570

gesto enfático (emphatic gesture) ademán que se usa para destacar el mensaje del presentador o darle más énfasis; p. 569

gramática (grammar) conceptos y normas básicas que regulan el uso de un idioma; p. 106

grupo (group) número reducido de personas que se identifican e interactúan unidas por un interés, lazo u objetivo común; p. 313

grupo de acción (action group) grupo nombrado para planificar e implementar un plan de acción específico; p. 322

grupo de trabajo (task group) grupo al que se le asigna la realización de una tarea específica; p. 318

grupo defensor (advocacy group) grupo establecido con el objeto de respaldar, proteger, velar o cabildear por una determinada causa o sector; p. 315

grupo normativo (policy-making group) grupo cuya función es establecer las normas que deben seguir los miembros de una organización; p. 321

grupo para obtener información (information-gathering group) grupo constituido específicamente para recopilar datos; p. 320

grupo social (social group) grupo al que uno pertenece por razones meramente personales; p. 322

grupo social formal (formal social group) grupo cuyos miembros son elegidos por una organización para participar en actividades de la comunidad; p. 323

grupo social informal (informal social group) grupo dentro del cual se promueve la afiliación pero no es requerida por una organización; p. 323

H

habilidad funcional (task skill) habilidad de comunicación que se requiere para hacer un trabajo, completar una tarea o lograr una meta con eficacia; p. 11

I

incorporación (internalization) la acción de repetir o repasar algo hasta ser absorbido; p. 554

inflexión (inflection) elevación o atenuación de la voz que da variedad al discurso; p. 148

información voluntaria (feed-forward) la acción de dar una razón o explicación para una pregunta, petición u oferta; p. 80

iniciador (initiator) miembro de un grupo que motiva al resto para tomar el camino hacia la meta fijada; p. 348

instigador (agitator) persona que infunde energía negativa en el proceso de grupo; p. 350

integrar (integrating) unificar las partes para que funcionen como un todo; p. 220

interpretación (interpreting)   proceso mediante el cual el receptor analiza el mensaje del emisor para determinar el sentido; p. 178

J

jerga (slang)   tipo de lenguaje informal usado generalmente por un determinado grupo durante un período limitado; p. 121

jerga profesional (jargon)   lenguaje técnico; p. 119

L

lenguaje corporal (body language)   manera de transmitir sentimientos sin recurrir a la expresión verbal; p. 299

lenguaje estándar (standard language)   lenguaje que usan la mayoría de los comunicadores experimentados dentro de un determinado idioma; p. 120

lenguaje formal (formal language)   lenguaje regido por un conjunto de reglas sumamente estructuradas; p. 118

lenguaje informal (informal language)   lenguaje que se usa generalmente en situaciones diarias y entre conocidos que mantienen una relación interpersonal; p. 120

lenguaje no gramatical (ungrammatical language)   lenguaje que no aplica normas ni conceptos gramaticales establecidos; p. 122

lenguaje oral (oral language)   lenguaje que se habla y escucha en vez de escribirse y leerse; p. 102

lenguaje técnico (technical language)   lenguaje propio de una profesión, actividad o campo de estudio determinados; p. 119

líder (leader)   persona que ejerce influencia en otros o los inspira a actuar de cierta manera para lograr una meta colectiva; p. 413

líder autoritario (authoritarian leader)   líder que ejerce poder entre sus seguidores a fin de imponer su voluntad; p. 415

líder democrático (democratic leader)   líder que incluye a sus partidarios en el proceso de toma de decisiones para lograr el acuerdo de la mayoría y la adopción de decisiones; p. 416

líder emergente (emergent leader)   persona elegida por sus compañeros o miembros de un grupo debido a su personalidad, autoridad dentro del grupo o circunstancias especiales de la meta; p. 414

líder equilibrado (balanced leader)   líder que da importancia tanto a las tareas como a las relaciones humanas; p. 416

líder laissez-faire (laissez-faire leader)   líder que cede su autoridad a los miembros del grupo; p. 416

líder nombrado (appointed leader)   persona escogida por una autoridad competente para ocupar un cargo de liderazgo; p. 413

lluvia de ideas (brainstorming)   actividad mediante la cual se generan rápidamente ideas sobre un tema específico; p. 335

M

mecanismo de atención (attention device)   recurso empleado por los oradores para capturar el interés del público; p. 479

mecanismo de explicación (amplification device)   información que amplía o clarifica una idea al público; p. 509

medios masivos de difusión (mass media)   fuentes de comunicación, por ejemplo la radio, la televisión, el cine y materiales impresos, diseñados para llegar a un público extenso; p. 56

mensaje (message)   información que intercambian dos comunicadores; p. 40

mesa redonda (panel discussion)   exposición formal frente a un público, en la que participan varias personas que exponen e intercambian opiniones sobre un tema; p. 544

mesa redonda-foro (panel discussion-forum)   mesa redonda que al finalizar incluye una sesión de preguntas y respuestas con participación del público; p. 545

meta colectiva (group goal)   tareas específicas de un grupo y los resultados que espera obtener; p. 315

meta emergente (emergent goal)   meta establecida por el grupo mismo; p. 316

meta establecida (prescribed goal)   meta fijada por una autoridad competente; p. 315

método de elocuencia (method of delivery)   manera personal de transmitir el mensaje al público; p. 534

método de estilo (style approach)   opinión de que el método de comunicación y la autoridad que ejerce un líder determinan su éxito; p. 415

método funcional (functional approach)   opinión de que los líderes deberían participar activamente en las tareas necesarias además de identificarlas; p. 417

muestra (sample)   grupo específico de personas elegidas para participar en una encuesta o cuestionario; p. 464

N

necesidad de apoyo (maintenance need)   necesidad asociada con los sentimientos de los miembros de un grupo y sus relaciones mutuas; p. 361

necesidad funcional (task need)   necesidad que se relaciona directamente con las actividades y metas del grupo; p. 361

negociación (negotiation)   la acción de transar con otros para conseguir lo que se desea; p. 400

norma (norm)   expectativa establecida o implicada; p. 5

norma emergente (emergent norm)   toda norma que surge de la interacción del grupo y la combinación de las personalidades de sus miembros; p. 347

norma establecida (prescribed norm)   norma de comportamiento que se imparte a los nuevos miembros de un grupo; p. 346

O

oír (hearing)   proceso físico de percibir los sonidos; p. 176

orden cronológico (chronological order)   secuencia de eventos según la fecha en que ocurrieron; p. 490

orden espacial (spatial order)   orden que se sigue en el desarrollo de un tema o según la ubicación física de sus elementos; p. 492

orden secuencial (sequential order)   disposición de algo según los pasos de un proceso; p. 491

organización (organization)   conjunto de personas que comparten un fin y cumplen responsabilidades específicas; p. 15

orientación para el público (audience orientation)   información suministrada con la cual posiblemente no cuenta la concurrencia pero que necesitará para comprender una exposición; p. 481

P

parafrasear (paraphrase)   repetir un mensaje usando palabras propias; p. 251

paralelismo (parallelism)   la acción de colocar las oraciones de manera que las palabras y frases sean de tamaño y estructura similares; p. 524

percepción (perception)   proceso mediante el cual se asigna significado a la información sobre uno mismo o el ambiente que lo rodea; p. 71

percepción personal (personal perception)   interpretación que tiene una persona de la realidad; p. 75

percepción selectiva (selective perception)   proceso mental que permite elegir la información o los estímulos deseados que están disponibles en un momento dado; p. 72

percepción sensorial (sensory perception)   proceso físico y complejo de adquisición de conocimientos o información a través de los cinco sentidos; p. 48

perspectiva crítica (critical perspective)   norma según la cual se evalúa la eficacia o ineficacia de un discurso; p. 582

poder (power)   autoridad que ejerce una persona sobre otras para hacer que se comporten de cierta manera o lleven a cabo determinadas actividades; p. 423

poder coercitivo (coercive power)   capacidad de forzar a otros a hacer algo, tomando represalias si sus órdenes no son cumplidas; p. 424

poder de retribución (reward power)   capacidad de recompensar a alquien que sigue las instrucciones dadas; p. 424

poder informador (referent power)   influencia que ejerce una persona que es respetada, considerada y admirada por sus seguidores; p. 427

poder informativo (informational power)   autoridad que ejerce una persona que tiene acceso a información importante; p. 425

poder legítimo (legitimate power)   poder otorgado a una persona que ocupa un puesto, función o cargo específicos; p. 424

postura característica (trait approach)   opinión de que los líderes poseen ciertos rasgos comunes que los ayudan a ejercer su posición de liderazgo; p. 414

pregunta básica (primary question)   pregunta que da inicio a un nuevo tema; p. 293

pregunta cerrada (closed question)   pregunta que requiere una respuesta específica, a menudo de una palabra; p. 239

pregunta concreta (factual question)   pregunta que requiere información que pueda comprobarse; p. 293

pregunta de interpretación abierta (open-ended question)   pregunta de amplio alcance que no puede contestarse con una sola palabra como "Sí" o "No"; p. 239

pregunta de opinión (opinion question)   pregunta para averiguar el punto de vista que tiene el entrevistado sobre un tema; p. 293

pregunta directa (direct question)   pregunta clara y sencilla; pregunta que permite al entrevistador averiguar exactamente lo que desea saber sin dar lugar a dudas o confusión; p. 293

pregunta hipotética (hypothetical question)   pregunta sobre cómo reaccionaría una persona en una situación determinada; p. 293

pregunta indirecta (indirect question)   pregunta que busca información específica sin preguntar directamente por ella; p. 293

pregunta neutral (neutral question)   pregunta que no implica específicamente una respuesta "correcta" o "equivocada"; p. 293

pregunta que sugiere la respuesta (leading question)   pregunta que propone la contestación o reacción esperada; p. 293

pregunta secundaria (secondary question)   pregunta que facilita al entrevistador la comprensión de una pregunta básica; p. 293

pregunta sumamente cerrada (highly closed question)   pregunta que no solamente busca una respuesta específica sino que incluso podría ofrecer varias opciones de respuesta; p. 293

presencia de escena (stage presence)   ilusión creada por la calidad de la energía, aplono, confidencia y control que proyecta un presentador ante un público; p. 568

prestar atención (attending)   acción de concentrar la atención, consciente o subconscientemente, en un estímulo verbal o no verbal; p. 177

problema (problem)   dificultad o incertidumbre; situación que se presenta de manera diferente a la esperada; p. 331

proceso de la entrevista (interview process)   sucesión de pasos que se dan durante una entrevista eficaz; p. 283

profecía de realización personal (self-fulfilling prophecy)   predicción o expectativa que modela el comportamiento, aumentando las posibilidades de obtener los resultados esperados; p. 88

pronunciación (pronunciation)   manera correcta de decir una palabra; p. 108

protocolo (protocol)   código de comportamiento establecido y prescripto por una organización; p. 254

R

receptor-emisor (receiver-sender)   persona que recibe, o cree haber recibido, un mensaje; p. 39

regionalismo (colloquialism)   término propio de una cultura regional específica; p. 120

reglas del grupo (group norms)   normas de carácter informal, generalmente tácitas, sobre el comportamiento que debe observarse dentro de un grupo; p. 345

relleno (filler)   palabra o frase que se usa para disimular algún titubeo al hablar; p. 127

resistencia (resistance)   fuerza interna que impide a una persona aceptar la autoridad de otra; p. 423

resolución de problemas (problem solving)   acción de entender la naturaleza de un dilema estableciendo alternativas de solución, identificando la mejor solución e implementándola; p. 331

responsabilidad social (social responsibility)   obligación o interés en trabajar en beneficio de los demás; p. 20

respuesta (responding)   reacción interna, emocional e intelectual a un mensaje; p. 179

retroinformación (feedback)   manera cómo responde una persona ante el mensaje de otra; p. 46

revelación personal (self-disclosure)   revelación deliberada de importante información personal que no es aparente a los demás; p. 90

ritmo (rate)   rapidez o lentitud con la que habla una persona; p. 149

rito social (social ritual)   situación comunicativa que se repite frecuentemente en la interacción social diaria; p. 123

rol (role)   papel que asume una persona en una situación o circunstancia específica; p. 5

ruido (noise)   todo lo que interfiere con un mensaje; generalmente de manera temporal; p. 44

S

Secuencia motivadora de Monroe (Monroe's Motivated Sequence)   estrategia organizativa de cinco partes que se usa en discursos con el propósito de persuadir o motivar al público para que adopte una línea de acción inmediata; lleva el nombre del especialista en comunicaciones A.H. Monroe; p. 494

simposio (symposium)   serie de exposiciones preparadas sobre un mismo tema y presentadas por diversos oradores con poca o ninguna interacción entre ellos; p. 546

simposio-foro (symposium-forum)   simposio con la participación del público; p. 546

T

testimonio (testimony)   cita directa o resumen de una cita; p. 507

tomar de decisiones (decision making)   analizar en forma lógica y racional un conjunto de alternativas para elegir la más eficaz; p. 336

tono (pitch)   elevación o atenuación de los sonidos en una escala musical; p. 147; (tone)   cualidad vocal específica; p. 149

transaccional (transactional)   que tiene que ver con un intercambio de algo; p. 35

transmisión (transmitting)   proceso físico de transmitir mensajes verbales y no verbales; p. 49

V

verificación de la percepción (perception check)   pregunta que ayuda a determinar la validez y precisión de las percepciones que tiene una persona; p. 78

visualización (visualization)   representación mental que una persona hace de sí misma, en la cual realiza una tarea con éxito; p. 551

vocabulario (vocabulary)   conjunto de palabras que forman parte de un código o lenguaje específico; p. 103

Index

Page numbers in *italics* indicate definitions.

A

Absentee agitators, 351
Absenteeism, 332
Absolute language, 125
Accessibility in communication, 61–62
Accommodation as conflict resolution style, 398–399
Accuracy
　of directions, 246–247
　in recording information, 461
Accusatory language, strategies for avoiding, 125
Achievement, celebrating, 430
Acquiring, *49*
　in listening process, 176–177
　message, 49
Action, in Monroe's Motivated Sequence, 495–496
Action groups, *332*
Action verbs, 96
Active listening, *189*, 190
Actual message, 43
Addition in articulation, 108
Adjectives, using colorful, 96
Adjustment in feedback, 50
Advantage-disadvantage organization, 494
Adverbs, 96
　transitional, 525
Advertising, word-of-mouth, 212
Aesthetics, judgment by, 583
Age
　appropriate strategies for dealing with, 265
　of audience, 445
Agendas, 369, 376–377
Agitators, *350–352*
　chairperson as, 370
　dealing with, 350–351
　negative behavior of, 350
　positive behavior of, 351–352
　types of, 351
Alliteration, 523–524
Ambiguous communication, *140–141*
Amplification devices, 509–510
Analogies, 484, 522–523
Anticipatory listening, 190
Antithesis, *524*
Appearance, 152–153, 297

dress in, 152, 297–298, 364–365
grooming in, 152–153, 298, 364–365
in presentation, 567–568
Appreciative listening, *194–195*
Appropriateness, *4*
　of answers in interviews, 276
　in communication choices, 6, 8
　and context, 6–8
　in conversations, 241
　in dealing with diversity, 263–265
　of demeanor in interviews, 298
　of feedback, 183
　of image in presentation, 443–444
　for listener, 7
　in making choices, 7
　for the occasion, 7
　of questions in interviews, 247–249, 289–291
　of requests, 244–246
　in responding to criticism, 262
　in responding to directions of others, 250–251
　in responding to requests and questions, 248–249
　for self, 7
　standards for, in vocabulary, 104
　for task, 8
　in use of power, 424–428
　of verbal strategies, in groups, 361–364
　of vocal characteristics, 567–568
　of volume, 148–149
Approval, showing, 577
Aroma therapy, 163
Articulation, *108–109*
Artifacts, *162–163*
Assertiveness
　demonstrating, in conversation, 241
　professional image projecting, 146
Assumptions
　avoiding, in directions, 247
　making, 75
Assumptive language, 125
Assurance in feedback, 47
Attendance
　consideration of, in presentation, 447
Attending, in listening process, *177*
Attention, in Monroe's Motivated

Sequence, 496
Attention devices, *479–480*, 482
Attitudes, 10–11
　of audience, 446
　changing, 11
　conveying, in oral language, 112
　impact of, 10–11
　managing, 11
　in personal perception, 76
　rating scale for, 10
Audible feedback, 576–577
Audience
　adapting messages to feedback from, 575–578
　attitude of, 446
　consideration of, in message context, 444–447
　demographics of, 445–446
　gathering information on, 446–447
　getting attention of, 478–480
　handling questions from, 579–580
　interacting with, 575–576
　in limiting the topic, 452
　orientation of, for presentation, *481–483*
　previewing presentation for, 483
　rehearsing presentation with, 554
　targeting writing to, 64
Audiovisual aids
　creating effective, 514
　reasons for using, 510–511
　rehearsing with, 556–558
Authoritarian leadership, *415*
Avoidance
　advantages of, 398
　as conflict resolution strategy, 397–398
　physical, 397–398
　problems with, 398
　psychological, 398

B

Bar graph, 513
Barriers, *45*
　in communication, 45–46
　to hearing, 176–177
　to listening, 184–185
Beauty, 520–521

Index

Delivery, 564
  importance of, in presentation, 564
  method of, *534–536*
  responsibility of presenter in, 442–443
  selecting method for, 533–537
Demeanor, appropriate, for interviews, 298–300
Demographics, *445*
  of audience, 444–446
  in survey research, 464
Denotation, *125–126*
Descriptions, 509
Details
  in directions, 247
  finding supporting, 393
Dialect, *110–111*
  cultural, 110–111
  ethnic, 110–111
  regional, 110, 120
Diction, *107–109*, 568
Differences, appropriate strategies for dealing with, 263–267
Directions
  giving clear and accurate, 246–247
  responding appropriately to, 247–251
Disapproval, showing, 577
Discriminate, *301*
Discussion, group, 354–358, 369–371
Distance, 157–159
  intimate, 157–158
  in nonverbal communication, 365
  personal, 158
  public, 158–159
  social, 158
  violating norms of, 159
Distracted listening, 190
Distractor agitators, 351
Diversity, 114
  appropriate strategies for dealing with, 263–266
  cultural, 483
  dealing with, 24
  effects of, 23–24
  in organizations, 22–27
Dominant style, *224*
Drafting, 28–29
Dress
  appropriate for interviews, 297
  in group communication, 364–365
  in nonverbal communication, 153
Duration, vocal, 149

E

Editing, 28–29, 97
Education of audience, 446
Electronic research and reporting, 21
E-mail
  emoticons in, 155
  format of message in, 121, 130–131
  sending copies of, 219
Emoticons, 155
Emotional element, 521
Empathy
  in interpersonal relationships, 216–217
  in listening, 193–194, 243, 368
  in responding to interruptions, 576
Emphasis, listening for, 187
Employees
  absenteeism by, 332
  communication with and between, 210–213
  desired skills in potential, 10–12
Employment interview, 280–281
  laws governing questions in, 301–302
  preparing for, 284–292
  purpose of, 277
  questions in, 289, 290
  requesting, in cover letter, 304–305
  research for, 287–289
  structure of, 285–287
  videotaping mock, 291
Employment questions, laws governing, 301–302
Encoding, *49*, 102
Enrichment, 23–24
Entrance in presentation, 570
Enunciation, *109*
Environment, 20–21
  and climate, 37–39
Environmental conflict, 386–387
Environmental cues, as nonverbal communication, 157–164
Equality in interpersonal communication, 217
Errors, dealing with, in presentation, 587
Ethical proofs, 508
Ethical standards, judgment by, 582–583

Ethics

Ethics
  in communication, 58–59, 242
  in interviewing, 302
Ethnic background of audience, 446
Ethnic dialect, 110–111
Ethnicity, appropriate strategies for dealing with, 264–265
Ethos, *443*
  establishing, as a speaker, 480–481
Etiquette, *254*
  cultural, 256
  in giving criticism, 259–260
  in making introductions, 255–256
  in receiving criticism, 260–262
  in using telephone, 256–259
Etymology, 119
Evaluation
  of audience, 443–447
  of effectiveness of communication, 253–265
  of group effectiveness, 371–374
  of personal interaction with others, 92–93
  of personal style, 223–229
  of presentations, 581–588
Event-planning committees, 327–331
Examples, 512
Exit in presentation, 573
Expectations
  fulfilling others', 89–90
  fulfilling your own, 89
  in personal perception, 76–77
Explanation, asking speaker for, 250–251
External barriers, 46
External noise, 45
External stress, as cause of conflict, 390
Eye communication, 156–157
Eye contact, 217, 365, 571

F

Face-to-face meetings, 316–317
  benefits of, 316–317
Facial communication, 156–157, 217, 570–571
Facial grooming, 153
Facilitator, *349–350*
  chairperson as, 370
  negative behavior of, 350
  positive behavior of, 349–350

Index

I

Ideas, stating, 362–363
Identity, 16
Image
  projecting, through oral language, 111
  and sound, 106–107
Imagining, 124
Immediacy
  demonstrating, 241–242
  professional image projecting, 146
Immediate memory, 184, 185
Impatient listening, *190*
Impromptu presentations, *536–538*
  notes for, 537–538
Inappropriate questions, 249
Inference, making, 326
Inflection of voice, *148*
Influencing style, *225*
Informal presentations, *442, 444*
  chronological order in, 490–491
  organization in, 496
Informal social groups, *324*
Information
  analyzing, 13
  clarifying, in presentation, 578–579
  gaining command of, 551–558
  gathering, 276–277
  in global communication, 288
  giving and seeking, 123
  locating, 459–461
  recalling, 187
  recording accurately, 461
  relevance of, 467–468
  requesting, 244–245
  selecting supporting, 506–510
  skimming for, 282
  surveying availability of, 453–454
  synthesizing, 488
  timeliness of, 468
Information-gathering interviews, *278*
  questions in, 289, 290
  research for, 286
Information-giving interviews, *279*
  questions in, 290, 291
  research for, 287
Informative presentation, *454*
Initiative, taking, in conflict-resolution meeting, 403
Initiator, *348–349*
  chairperson as, 370

negative behavior of, 349
  positive behavior of, 348–349
Inquiry, writing, 472–473
Insight in feedback, 47
Integrating, *219*
Intensity in selective perception, 73
Intentional message, 42
Intent of presenter, 444
Interaction
  analyzing style of, 91–92
  with audience, 575–581
  evaluating style of, 92–94
Interactor, self as, 90–94
Interdependence, determining level of, in conflict, 387–388
Interdependent communication, practicing, 209
Interest, as reason for using audiovisual aids, 511
Internal barriers, 45
Internalization, *554–555*
Internal noise, 44
Internal previews, 525–526
Internal summaries, 525–526
Interpersonal communication, 54–55, 237–251
  characteristics of productive, 215–219
  empathy in, 216–217
  equality in, 217
  openness in, 216
  positiveness in, 219
  role of, 208
  supportiveness in, 217–218
Interpersonal conflict, 384–385
  analyzing personal style to prevent, 229–230
Interpersonal perception checks, 79–81
Interpersonal relationships, 206–230
  appropriate listening skills in, 215–217, 219
  appropriate nonverbal skills in, 215–219
  appropriate verbal skills in, 215–219
  importance of, 208–209
  personal style in, 222–230
  in professional and social contexts, 208–215
  understanding, 207–220
Interpersonal skills, 236–266
  in asking appropriate questions, 247

in conversations, 238–251
in giving directions, 246–247
integrating, with task skills, 219–220
in responding appropriately to directions, 250–251
Interpretations, checking, 179
Interpreting, *178–179*
Interruptions, responding empathically to, 576
Interviewee, *274*
  goal of, 284
  questions for, 300
  role of, 275–277
Interviewers, *274*
  goal of, 284
  questions for, 300
  roles of, 274–275
Interviews, *272–274, 275–302*
  actual, 292–294
  appropriate questions in, 300–302
  body in, 293
  body language in, 299–300
  building skills for, 280
  closing, 294
  counseling, *279*
  demeanor in, 298–300
  dress for, 297
  employment, *280–305*
    interviewer questions for, 290–291
    laws governing questions in, 301–302
    preparing for, 284–292
    purpose of, 279–281
    requesting, in cover letter, 304–305
    research for, 287–289
    videotaping mock, 291
  ethics in, 302
  exit, *278*
  information-gathering, *278*
    questions in, 289, 290
    research for, 286
  information-giving, *279*
    questions in, 289–290, 291
    research for, 287
  interpersonal skills in, 208
  investigative, *278–279*
  moderately scheduled, 286
  nonscheduled, 286
  opening, 292
  personal appearance for, 298

R

S

Index

Testimonies, 507–508
Thank-you letter
  sending, following interview, 294
  writing, 528–529
Thesis statement, in presentation, 480, 485
Time
  arranging, in planning meeting, 369
  consideration of, in presentation, 447–448
  in nonverbal communication, 365
Time communication, 161–162
Timeliness of information, 468
Time management, 161
Tone, *149*
  muscular, 154
  setting, in interview, 292
  of thank-you note, 294
  vocal, 149, 366, 566
Topical order, *492*
Topics
  choosing appropriate, in conversation, 240
  determining, for presentation, 451–452
  limiting, for presentation, 452–454
Touch, 160–161
Traditions, 21
Trait approach, *414*
Traits, leadership, 414–415
Transactional process, *35*
Transitions, 525
  in presentations, 484
Translations, 521
Transmitting, 49
Troublesome language, strategies for avoiding, 125

U

Unclear guidelines, conflict over, 389
Understanding, in listening process, *178–179*
Ungrammatical language, *122*
Unintentional message, 42–43
Uniqueness, in selective perception, 73
Unity, 16

V

Values, 19–20
  conflict over, 388
  organizational, 19–20
  personal, 19
  in personal perception, 76
Verbal communication, relation to nonverbal communication, 136–138
Verbal messages, improving, 566–567
Verbal responses, 577
Verbal skills for interviews, 299
Verbal strategies, effective, in groups, 361–364
Verbs, using action, 96–97
Videoconferencing, 359
Vision, promoting, 428
Visual aids
  presenting, 514–516
  types of, 511–514
Visual images, 521
  creating, 520
Visualization, *551*
Visualizing
  in Monroe's Motivated Sequence, 496
  as rehearsal strategy, 553
  success, 90
Vocabulary, *103*. *See also* Words
  in adding interest, 104–105
  appropriateness of, 104
  importance in building, 105
Vocal characteristics, using appropriate, in presentation, 565–567
Vocalizations, 150–151
Voice
  duration of, 149
  improving, 151
  inflection of, 148
  pitch of, 147–148
  production of, 151
  range of, 148
  tempo of, 149
  tone of, 149, 366, 566
  volume of, 148–149, 366, 565
Voice mail, 252
Volume, vocal, 148–149, 366, 565

W

Word-of-mouth advertising, 212
Word-processing programs, 143
Words. *See also* Vocabulary
  choice of, 519
  connotations of, 125–126
  defined by context, 221
  denotations of, 125–126
  etymology of, 119
  meaning of, 519
  order of, 519–520
Workers, focusing, on task, 429
Workplace
  listening in, 173–174
  prescribed norms in, 346
Work team, self-managed, 322
World Wide Web, research on, 461, 470
Writing
  business letter, 166–167
  clarity and conciseness in, 96–97
  complaint letter, 232–233
  cover letter, 304–305
  defining purpose of, 64–65
  formatting business messages in, 130–131
  inquiry, 472–473
  meeting agenda, 376–377
  meeting summary, 432–433
  memo, 340–341
  notes, 198–199
  persuasive sales letter, 590–591
  response to complaint letter, 408–409
  résumés, 268–269
  thank-you letter, 528–529
  using correctness in, 64–65
Writing process
  drafting, 28–29
  editing/proofreading, 28–29
  prewriting, 28–29
  publishing/presenting, 28–29
  revising, 28–29
Written evaluations, 585–587
Written language, differences between oral language and, 102–103

Y

"You" messages, 123

Acknowledgments

Ballpoint pen design element for Communication Through Writing pages: PhotoEssentials.

Collage of business memos design element for Communication Through Writing pages: First Image.

Cover (tl)Jon Feingersh/The Stock Market, (tr)Bryan Peterson/FPG, (c)Telegraph Colour Library/Masterfile, (bl)Graham French/Masterfile, (br)First Image; **v** Joe Sohm/Stock Boston; **vi** Jose L. Pelaez/The Stock Market; **viii** Bruce Ayres/Tony Stone Images; **xi** Fisher & Thatcher/Tony Stone Images; **2** Daryl Benson/Masterfile; **3** Aaron Haupt; **4** Doug Martin; **5** Michael Newman/PhotoEdit; **14** CORBIS; **17** ©The New Yorker Collection 1994, Mick Stevens from cartoonbank.com. All rights reserved; **19** Steve Woit/Stock Boston; **20** Courtesy City Year; **21** Melanie Carr/Uniphoto Picture Agency; **22** (l)©1998 DUOMO NBA/F. Medina, (c)Courtesy Mary Kay Inc., (r)Brooks Kraft/Corbis Sygma; **25** (t)Brent Turner/BLT Productions, (b)©The New Yorker Collection 1981, Mischa Richter from cartoonbank.com. All rights reserved; **32** Tony Freeman/PhotoEdit; **33** ©1998 DUOMO/Chris Trotman; **38** William Hart/PhotoEdit; **39** SuperStock; **41 43** Doug Martin; **44** Robin L. Sachs/PhotoEdit; **46** Steve Raymer/CORBIS; **53** Index Stock Photography; **55** Aaron Haupt; **56** David Young-Wolff/PhotoEdit; **59** Jeff Zaruba/The Stock Market; **61** Mary Kate Denny/PhotoEdit; **66** Tony Freeman/PhotoEdit; **68** Tom Able-Green/Allsport; **69** Ken Chernus/FPG; **70** Tim Defrisco/Allsport; **71** Reprinted with permission from *Modern Maturity.* Copyright, American Association of Retired Persons; **72** Aaron Haupt; **80** Reprinted by permission of John Jonik from *Psychology Today;* **83** David Young-Wolff/PhotoEdit; **87** Bruce Forster/Tony Stone Images; **88** Tony Freeman/PhotoEdit; **90** Ariel Skelley/The Stock Market; **98** Tom Able-Green/Allsport; **100** Joe Marquette/AP/Wide World Photos; **101** Dick Hemingway: Photographs; **103** Rafael Macia/Photo Researchers; **104** Robbie Jack/CORBIS; **106** Reprinted by permission of Sidney Harris; **109** Ron Chapple/FPG; **110** CORBIS; **111** Aaron Haupt; **113** North Wind Picture Archives; **116** The Gorilla Foundation/koko.org/Ronald H. Cohn; **118** Bob Daemmrich/Tony Stone Images; **119** Llewellyn/Uniphoto; **120** Richard Hamilton Smith/CORBIS; **123** Bonnie Kamin/PhotoEdit; **124** Timothy Shonnard/Tony Stone Images; **126** Steve Chenn/CORBIS; **132** Joe Marquette/AP/Wide World Photos; **134** James Goodwin/Tony Stone Images; **135** Walter Hodges/Tony Stone Images; **136** David Young-Wolff/PhotoEdit; **138** Sandy Felsenthal/CORBIS; **140** Tom McCarthy/The Stock Market; **144** Mark Peterson/Saba Press Photos; **145** Pablo Corral V/CORBIS; **148** Sergio Dorantes/CORBIS; **150** Fisher & Thatcher/Tony Stone Images; **151** Danny Lehman/CORBIS; **154** Dave Bartruff/CORBIS; **156** PhotoDisc, Inc.; **159** Mark Richards/PhotoEdit; **168** James Goodwin/Tony Stone Images; **170** Don Smetzer/Tony Stone Images; **171** Owen Franken/CORBIS; **174** Steve Chenn/CORBIS; **175** PhotoEdit; **179** Jim Cummins/FPG; **182** Anne Rippy/The Image Bank; **188** Ted Spiegel/CORBIS; **189** (b)PEANUTS reprinted by permission of United Feature Syndicate, Inc., (t)Jose L. Pelaez/The Stock Market; **190** W.B. Spunbarg/PhotoEdit; **191** Ronnen Eshel/CORBIS; **194** Myrleen Cate/PhotoEdit; **200** Don Smetzer/Tony Stone Images; **204–205** Jose L. Pelaez/The Stock Market; **206** R.W. Jones/CORBIS; **207** Jose L. Pelaez/The Stock Market; **208** Walter Hodges/Tony Stone Images; **210** DILBERT reprinted by permission of United Feature Syndicate, Inc.; **211** Jon Riley/Tony Stone Images; **212** Paul Barton/The Stock Market; **213** Roger Ressmeyer/CORBIS; **214** Lawrence Manning/CORBIS; **216** Jon Feingersh/The Stock Market; **217** Annie Griffiths Belt/CORBIS; **222** Chris Brown/Saba Press Photos; **223** Ariel Skelley/The Stock Market; **224** Robert Daly/Tony Stone Images; **228** Bill Luster/CORBIS; **234** R.W. Jones/CORBIS; **236** William Taufic/The Stock Market; **237** Zigy Kaluzny/Tony Stone Images; **238** Stewart Cohen/Tony Stone Images; **241** Bob Daemmrich/Stock Boston; **243** Bruce Ayres/Tony Stone Images; **245** Marc Romanelli/The Image Bank; **249** Gabe Palmer/The Stock Market; **250** Will Hart/PhotoEdit; **253** Michael Newman/PhotoEdit; **260** Jose L. Pelaez/The Stock Market; **261** Aaron Haupt; **263** Walter Hodges/Tony

Stone Images; **264** Erik Lesser/Liaison Agency; **270** William Taufic/The Stock Market; **272** Michael A. Keller/The Stock Market; **273** Robert Maass/CORBIS; **274** David Young-Wolff/PhotoEdit; **276** Doug Martin; **278** Robert Brenner/PhotoEdit; **280** By permission of Mell Lazarus and Creators Syndicate; **283** Etena Rooraid/PhotoEdit; **285** Martin Simon/Saba Press Photos; **286** Paul Redman/Tony Stone Images; **287** Tony Freeman/PhotoEdit; **288** Jon Riley/Tony Stone Images; **291** Zigy Kaluzny/Tony Stone Images; **296** Michael Newman/PhotoEdit; **306** Michael A. Keller/The Stock Market; **310–311** Bruce Ayres/Tony Stone Images; **312** Sylvain Coffie/Tony Stone Images; **313** SuperStock; **316** Geoff Butler; **321** Aaron Haupt/Stock Boston; **322** Steve Hansen Photography/Stock Boston; **323** Tony Stone Images; **324** A. Ramey/PhotoEdit; **327** Geoff Butler; **328** Loren Santow/Tony Stone Images; **330** Icon Images; **331** Mark Richards/PhotoEdit; **333** Aaron Haupt; **335** Geoff Butler; **342** Sylvain Coffie/Tony Stone Images; **344** AFP/CORBIS; **345** Aaron Haupt; **346** Douglas Peebles/CORBIS; **349** Bob Daemmrich/Tony Stone Images; **354** The Far Side ©1993 FARWORKS, INC. Used by permission. All rights reserved; **356** Ron Chapple/FPG; **360** David Roth/Tony Stone Images; **361** Aaron Haupt; **362** First Image; **363 through 371** Aaron Haupt; **378** AFP/CORBIS; **380** NW Owen/Black Star; **381** David Young-Wolff/PhotoEdit; **382** Mug Shots/The Stock Market; **384** Jon Feingersh/The Stock Market; **386** THE BORN LOSER reprinted by permission of Newspaper Enterprise Association, Inc.; **388** Telegraph Colour Library/FPG; **390** GARFIELD ©1999 Paws, Inc. Reprinted with permission of UNIVERSAL PRESS SYNDICATE. All rights reserved; **394** Lonnie Duke/Tony Stone Images; **395** Michael Newman/PhotoEdit; **398** Bob Daemmrich/Stock Boston; **400** Richard Bloom/Saba Press Photos; **402** Tom & DeeAnn McCarthy/The Stock Market; **404** Fisher & Thatcher/Tony Stone Images; **410** NW Owen/Black Star; **412** Dirck Halstead/Liaison Agency; **413** Robert Kusel/Tony Stone Images; **414** Pablo Corral V/CORBIS; **419** Sam Sargent/Liaison Agency; **421** Michael Rosenfeld/Tony Stone Images; **423** Michael Rosenfeld/Tony Stone Images; **425** Andy Sacks/Tony Stone Images; **426** Darleen Rubin/Corbis Outline; **429** Walter Hodges/Tony Stone Images; **434** Dirck Halstead/Liaison Agency; **438–439** Fisher & Thatcher/Tony Stone Images; **440** Steve Niedorf/The Image Bank; **441** Ron Chapple/FPG; **443** John S. Stewart/AP/Wide World Photos; **448** Michael Newman/PhotoEdit; **450** Arthur Grace/Corbis Sygma; **452** Walter Hodges/Tony Stone Images; **454** Spencer Grant/Stock Boston; **456** Bruce Ayres/Tony Stone Images; **458** Benelux Press/The Stock Market; **462** Bob Daemmrich/Tony Stone Images; **467** Aaron Haupt; **474** Steve Niedorf/The Image Bank; **476** Bob Daemmrich/Stock Boston; **477** Tim Wright/CORBIS; **478** Kaluzny/Thatcher/Tony Stone Images; **480** Shaun Egan/Tony Stone Images; **481** Reuters/Mike Theiler/Archive Photos; **485** Tony Stone Images; **486** PEANUTS reprinted by permission of United Feature Syndicate, Inc.; **489** Walter Hodges/Tony Stone Images; **492** Bob Daemmrich/Stock Boston; **494** Jonathan Kirn/Liaison Agency; **496** Caroline Penn/CORBIS; **502** Bob Daemmrich/Stock Boston; **504** Jim Sugar Photography/CORBIS; **505** Fisher & Thatcher/Tony Stone Images; **507** Craig Lovell/CORBIS; **510** Andy Sacks/Tony Stone Images; **511** file photo; **512** Lonnie Duka/Tony Stone Images; **514** Doug Martin; **515** David Rubinger/CORBIS; **518** Thomas J. Croke/Liaison Agency; **522** Mark Lewis/Tony Stone Images; **532** Roger Ressmeyer/CORBIS; **533** Tim Cairns; **534** Joseph Sohm, Chromo Sohm Inc./CORBIS; **535** Simon Martin/Saba Press Photos; **539** CORBIS; **542** Kaluzny/Thatcher/Tony Stone Images; **544** Jacques M. Chenet/CORBIS; **546** file photo; **548** Layne Kennedy/CORBIS; **550** By permission of Mell Lazarus and Creators Syndicate; **553** Daniel Bosler/Tony Stone Images; **554** Gregg Mancuso/Stock Boston; **555** Layne Kennedy/CORBIS; **560** Roger Ressmeyer/CORBIS; **562** Ron Chapple/FPG; **563** Fisher & Thatcher/Tony Stone Images; **565** Nathan Benn/CORBIS; **567** Bruce Ayres/Tony Stone Images; **568** Fisher & Thatcher/Tony Stone Images; **569** Bruce Ayres/Tony Stone Images; **569** Rene Sheret/Tony Stone Images; **573** John Pflug; **574** Mug Shots/The Stock Market; **575** Stewart Cohen/Tony Stone Images; **577** Tim Brown/Tony Stone Images; **578** Tim Brown/Tony Stone Images; **592** Ron Chapple/FPG.